LITERATURE
Second Edition

A Collection of Mythology and Folklore,
Short Stories, Poetry, and Drama,

James Burl Hogins
San Diego Mesa College

 SCIENCE RESEARCH ASSOCIATES, INC.
Chicago, Palo Alto, Toronto, Henley-on-Thames, Sydney, Paris
A Subsidiary of IBM

Acknowledgments

We would like to thank the following for their help in reviewing the first edition of *Literature;* many of their suggestions have been incorporated into this edition:

Katrina Hench Averill, Daytona Beach Community College; Diana Culbertson, Kent State University; Kirby L. Duncan, Stephen F. Austin State University; George F. LaVaque, Thornton Community College; Mary Elizabeth Lincks, Manatee Junior College; Dorothy McIntyre, Cleveland County Technical Institute; James O'Malley, Triton College; R. Scott Oury, Triton College; Frank Sexton, Pensacola Junior College; Joyce O'Shea, Greensville Technical College; Sean Shesgreen, Northern Illinois University; Wallace Judd; and Ernest Boston, Department of English, South Carolina State College.

Editor: James C. Budd
Sponsoring Editors: Gerald Richardson, Robert D. Bovenschulte
Artists: Bonnie Brown, Patty Dwyer, Nancy Freeman, Nancy Golub, Katsumi Omura, Barbara Ravizza, Jack Tom, Dennis Ziemienski; color photo by Hans Hinz

The text of *Literature, Second Edition* is set in Palatino, a modern typeface designed by Herman Zapf. (Palatino, strongly calligraphic in style, was named for a famous sixteenth-century penman.) Display type is Americana. Composition: Black Dot, Inc., with special attention from Richard Haefele and Paula Johnson

Library of Congress Cataloging in Publication Data
Hogins, James Burl, comp.
Literature.

Includes index.
1. Literature—Collections. I. Title.
PN6014.H518 1978 808.8 77-2623
ISBN 0-574-22040-2

Table of Contents

General Introduction   xxv

Mythology, Folklore, and Religious Motifs

Introduction   2

PRELITERATE TALES

The Indians and Death   7
The Numbakulla and the First Aborigines *(Australian)*   11
The Perverted Message *(African)*   12
The Leftover Eye *(African)*   13

RELIGION AND MYTHOLOGY

Daniel, Bel, and the Snake   14
Northern Mythology   16
The Gods, the Creation, and the Earliest Heroes, *Edith Hamilton*   19
King Midas and the Golden Touch, *Bulfinch*   28

FABLES

One-Way Traffic, *Aesop*   29
Why Some Men Are Loutish Brutes, *Aesop*   29

AMERICAN LEGENDS AND TALL TALES

Sunrise in His Pocket, *Davy Crockett*   30
They Have Yarns (from "The People Yes"), *Carl Sandburg*   31
A Fable, *Samuel Clemens*   35
This Is the Way I Was Raised Up, *Mrs. Marvin Watts*   37
de Witch'ooman an' de Spinnin' Wheel   39

FAIRY TALES

The Three Wishes, *Joseph Jacobs*   41
The Field of Boliauns, *Joseph Jacobs*   43
The Husband Who Was to Mind the House,
    Sir George W. Dasent   45

MOTIFS

The Pact with the Devil
    Jonathan Moulton and the Devil   47

The Hero Against All Odds
    Gilgamesh 52
    David 57
    Beowulf 60
    Robin Hood and the Butcher 66
    Brer Rabbit's Cool Air Swing 68
    Jack and the King's Girl 70

Fiction

Introduction 74

CLASSIC

The Minister's Black Veil, *Nathaniel Hawthorne* 93
The Death of Ivan Ilych, *Leo Tolstoy* 104
The Revolt of Mother, *Mary E. Wilkins Freeman* 149
The Pins, *Guy de Maupassant* 162
The Luck of Roaring Camp, *Bret Harte* 167

MODERN

The Judgment, *Franz Kafka* 177
The Rocking-Horse Winner, *D. H. Lawrence* 187
A Painful Case, *James Joyce* 200
A Dill Pickle, *Katherine Mansfield* 208
Hills Like White Elephants, *Ernest Hemingway* 214
The Use of Force, *William Carlos Williams* 218
A Rose for Emily, *William Faulkner* 222
The Other Wife, *Colette* 231
Flight, *John Steinbeck* 234
The Circular Ruins, *Jorge Luis Borges* 250
Chee's Daughter, *Juanita Platero and Siyowin Miller* 256

CONTEMPORARY

Girls in Their Summer Dresses, *Irwin Shaw* 267
The Condor and the Guests, *Evan S. Connell, Jr.* 275
A Worn Path, *Eudora Welty* 282
A Summer's Reading, *Bernard Malamud* 289
Confessions of a Burglar, *Woody Allen* 296
A Summer Tragedy, *Arna Bontemps* 300
The Hobbyist, *Frederick Brown* 309
Neighbors, *Ray Carver* 312
Winter Rug, *Richard Brautigan* 317
Dotson Gerber Resurrected, *Hal Bennett* 320

Poetry

Introduction 334

Arise, My Love, and Come Away, *Song of Solomon* 352
Edward, *Anonymous* 354
The Twa Corbies, *Anonymous* 356
Sir Patrick Spens, *Anonymous* 357
They Flee from Me, *Sir Thomas Wyatt* 359
Crabbed Age and Youth, *Anonymous* 360
Since There's No Help, *Michael Drayton* 360
The Passionate Shepherd to His Love, *Christopher Marlowe* 361
The Nymph's Reply to the Shepherd, *Sir Walter Raleigh* 362
Sonnet 18 (Shall I compare thee to a summer's day?),
    William Shakespeare 363
Sonnet 29 (When, in disgrace with fortune and men's eyes),
    William Shakespeare 364
Sonnet 30 (When to the sessions of sweet silent thought),
    William Shakespeare 365
Sonnet 97 (How like a winter hath my absence been),
    William Shakespeare 365
Sonnet 98 (From you have I been absent in the spring),
    William Shakespeare 366
Sonnet 130 (My mistress's eyes are nothing like the sun),
    William Shakespeare 366
Song from Love's Labours Lost, *William Shakespeare* 367
Hymn to Diana, *Ben Jonson* 368
Song: To Celia, *Ben Jonson* 369
The Good-Morrow, *John Donne* 370
The Bait, *John Donne* 372
A Valediction: Forbidding Mourning, *John Donne* 373
Holy Sonnet XIX, *John Donne* 375
Delight in Disorder, *Robert Herrick* 376
To the Virgins, to Make Much of Time, *Robert Herrick* 376
Upon Julia's Clothes, *Robert Herrick* 377
To Julia, Under Lock and Key, *Owen Seaman* 377
Song, *Oliver Herford* 378
Song, *Thomas Carew* 379
On a Girdle, *Edmund Waller* 380
On the Late Massacre in Piedmont, *John Milton* 380
On His Blindness, *John Milton* 381
The Constant Lover, *Sir John Suckling* 382
Say, But Did You Love So Long?, *Sir Toby Matthews* 382
To His Coy Mistress, *Andrew Marvell* 383

Song for Saint Cecelia's Day, *John Dryden*   385
Describes Rationally the Irrational Effects of Love,
    Juana de Asbaje   387
Little Black Boy, *William Blake*   389
The Chimney Sweep, *William Blake*   390
The Tiger, *William Blake*   392
The Indian Burying Ground, *Philip Freneau*   393
A Red, Red Rose, *Robert Burns*   395
Lines Written in Early Spring, *William Wordsworth*   396
Composed upon Westminster Bridge, *William Wordsworth*   397
The Solitary Reaper, *William Wordsworth*   397
Kubla Khan, *Samuel Taylor Coleridge*   398
Work without Hope, *Samuel Taylor Coleridge*   401
When We Two Parted, *George Gordon, Lord Byron*   402
Ozymandias, *Percy Bysshe Shelley*   403
Song to the Men of England, *Percy Bysshe Shelley*   403
Ode to a Nightingale, *John Keats*   405
La Belle Dame sans Merci, *John Keats*   407
O Lovely Fishermaiden, *Heinrich Heine*   409
Sonnet 14 *from* Sonnets from the Portuguese, *Elizabeth*
    Barrett Browning   410
Ulysses, *Alfred, Lord Tennyson*   410
The Eagle, *Alfred, Lord Tennyson*   413
My Last Duchess, *Robert Browning*   413
Rabbi Ben Ezra, *Robert Browning*   415
The Latest Decalogue, *Arthur Hugh Clough*   422
Battle Hymn of the Republic, *Julia Ward Howe*   422
When Lilacs Last in the Dooryard Bloom'd, *Walt Whitman*   424
Cavalry Crossing a Ford, *Walt Whitman*   423
To a Common Prostitute, *Walt Whitman*   433
When I Heard the Learn'd Astronomer, *Walt Whitman*   433
To the Reader, *Charles Baudelaire*   434
Spleen, *Charles Baudelaire*   436
Dover Beach, *Matthew Arnold*   437
The Blessed Damozel, *Dante Gabriel Rossetti*   438
Modern Love, *George Meredith*   443
#61 (Papa above!), *Emily Dickinson*   444
#324 (Some keep the Sabbath going to Church), *Emily*
    Dickinson   445
#328, (A Bird came down the Walk), *Emily Dickinson*   446
#441 (This is my letter to the World), *Emily Dickinson*   447
#465, (I heard a Fly buzz—when I died), *Emily Dickinson*   447
#712 (Because I could not stop for Death), *Emily Dickinson*   448
#986 (A narrow Fellow in the Grass), *Emily Dickinson*   449

#1207 (He preached upon "Breadth" till it argued him narrow),
    Emily Dickinson — 450
#1463 (A Route of Evanescence), *Emily Dickinson* — 451
#1755 (To make a prairie it takes a clover and one bee),
    Emily Dickinson — 451
The Man He Killed, *Thomas Hardy* — 452
Spring and Fall, *Gerard Manley Hopkins* — 453
Pied Beauty, *Gerard Manley Hopkins* — 454
Terence, This Is Stupid Stuff, *A. E. Housman* — 454
from A Shropshire Lad (On Moonlight Heath and Lonesome
    Bank), *A. E. Housman* — 457
The Second Coming, *William Butler Yeats* — 458
The Wild Swans at Coole, *William Butler Yeats* — 460
Leda and the Swan, *William Butler Yeats* — 461
Non Sum Qualis Eram Bonae Sub Regno Cynarae, *Ernest
    Dowson* — 462
The Village Atheist, *Edgar Lee Masters* — 464
Mr. Flood's Party, *Edwin Arlington Robinson* — 465
Richard Cory, *Edwin Arlington Robinson* — 468
Karma, *Edwin Arlington Robinson* — 469
from War Is Kind, III, *Stephen Crane* — 470
from War Is Kind, XXI, *Stephen Crane* — 470
from The Black Riders, III, *Stephen Crane* — 471
from The Black Riders, XXIV, *Stephen Crane* — 471
from The Black Riders, XLVII, *Stephen Crane* — 472
from The Black Riders, XLVIII, *Stephen Crane* — 472
When It Is Given You to Find a Smile, *Enrique Gonzalez
    Martinez* — 473
Sympathy, *Paul Laurence Dunbar* — 474
Patterns, *Amy Lowell* — 475
The Taxi, *Amy Lowell* — 478
Dust of Snow, *Robert Frost* — 479
After Apple-Picking, *Robert Frost* — 479
Fire and Ice, *Robert Frost* — 480
Birches, *Robert Frost* — 481
The Panther, *Rainer Maria Rilke* — 483
Prayers of Steel, *Carl Sandburg* — 484
Grass, *Carl Sandburg* — 484
The West Wind, *John Masefield* — 485
The Emperor of Ice-Cream, *Wallace Stevens* — 486
Domination of Black, *Wallace Stevens* — 487
Peter Quince at the Clavier, *Wallace Stevens* — 489
Study of Two Pears, *Wallace Stevens* — 491
Of Modern Poetry, *Wallace Stevens* — 493

Gulls, *William Carlos Williams*   494
This Is Just to Say, *William Carlos Williams*   495
The Red Wheelbarrow, *William Carlos Williams*   495
Snake, *D. H. Lawrence*   496
Portrait d'une Femme, *Ezra Pound*   499
A Virginal, *Ezra Pound*   501
Roses Only, *Marianne Moore*   501
The Monkeys, *Marianne Moore*   502
The Mind Is an Enchanting Thing, *Marianne Moore*   503
Poetry, *Marianne Moore*   505
Shine, Republic, *Robinson Jeffers*   507
Shine, Perishing Republic, *Robinson Jeffers*   508
The Love Song of J. Alfred Prufrock, *T. S. Eliot*   509
Journey of the Magi, *T. S. Eliot*   514
The Hollow Men, *T. S. Eliot*   516
Blue Girls, *John Crowe Ransom*   520
Bells for John Whiteside's Daughter, *John Crowe Ransom*   521
God's World, *Edna St. Vincent Millay*   522
A Poet Speaks from the Visitor's Gallery, *Archibald
    MacLeish*   523
"Dover Beach": A Note to That Poem, *Archibald MacLeish*   525
Dr. Sigmund Freud Discovers the Sea Shell, *Archibald
    MacLeish*   526
Indian Summer, *Dorothy Parker*   527
Résumé, *Dorothy Parker*   528
Dulce et Decorum Est, *Wilfred Owen*   528
Arms and the Boy, *Wilfred Owen*   529
American Farm, 1934, *Genevieve Taggard*   530
Lady Love, *Paul Eluard*   532
The Naked and the Nude, *Robert Graves*   533
Litany for Dictatorships, *Stephen Vincent Benét*   534
The Rehearsal, *Horace Gregory*   538
Ode to the Confederate Dead, *Allen Tate*   540
Frankie and Johnny, *Anonymous*   543
Truth, *James Hearst*   545
Southern Mansion, *Arna Bontemps*   546
Reflections on Ice Breaking, *Ogden Nash*   547
Inter-Office Memorandum, *Ogden Nash*   547
Dream Deferred, *Langston Hughes*   548
I, Too, Sing America, *Langston Hughes*   549
John Doe, Jr., *Bonaro W. Overstreet*   550
Incident, *Countee Cullen*   551
from Machu Picchu, III, IV, V, *Pablo Neruda*   552
Come Live with Me and Be My Love, *C. Day Lewis*   554

If I Could Only Live at the Pitch That Is Near Madness, *Richard Eberhart*   555

The Day After Sunday, *Phyllis McGinley*   556

Twelve Songs, VIII, *W. H. Auden*   557

The Unknown Citizen, *W. H. Auden*   558

Museums, *Louis MacNeice*   560

Elegy for Jane, *Theodore Roethke*   561

I Knew a Woman, *Theodore Roethke*   562

Snake, *Theodore Roethke*   563

The Bad Children, *Carl Bode*   564

Nice Day for a Lynching, *Kenneth Patchen*   565

The Heavy Bear, *Delmore Schwartz*   566

For Rhoda, *Delmore Schwartz*   567

Auto Wreck, *Karl Shapiro*   568

Buick, *Karl Shapiro*   570

The Conscientious Objector, *Karl Shapiro*   571

Reading Time: 1 Minute 26 Seconds, *Muriel Rukeyser*   572

Love Poem, *John Frederick Nims*   573

Lessons of the War: Naming of Parts, *Henry Reed*   575

Lessons of the War: Judging Distances, *Henry Reed*   576

Life, Friends, Is Boring, *John Berryman*   578

Fern Hill, *Dylan Thomas*   579

Do Not Go Gentle into That Good Night, *Dylan Thomas*   582

Poem in October, *Dylan Thomas*   583

Dilemma, *David Ignatow*   585

The Death of the Ball Turret Gunner, *Randall Jarrell*   585

Eighth Air Force, *Randall Jarrell*   586

May All Earth Be Clothed in Light, *George Hitchcock*   587

Award, *Ray Durem*   588

Survival in Missouri, *John Ciardi*   589

Suburban Homecoming, *John Ciardi*   590

English A, *John Ciardi*   590

Game Called on Account of Darkness, *Peter Viereck*   592

After the Convention, *Robert Lowell*   593

We Real Cool, *Gwendolyn Brooks*   594

from The Children of the Poor, *Gwendolyn Brooks*   594

Underwear, *Lawrence Ferlinghetti*   595

A Coney Island of the Mind, *Lawrence Ferlinghetti*   598

To David, about His Education, *Howard Nemerov*   599

Life Cycle of the Common Man, *Howard Nemerov*   600

Santa Claus, *Howard Nemerov*   601

A Simile for Her Smile, *Richard Wilbur*   603

Mind, *Richard Wilbur*   603

Formal Application, *Donald W. Baker*   604

Deer among Cattle, *James Dickey*   606
April Inventory, *W. D. Snodgrass*   607
Curiosity, *Alastair Reid*   609
A Wicker Basket, *Robert Creeley*   611
Joy, *Robert Creeley*   612
For No Clear Reason, *Robert Creeley*   612
A Blessing, *James Wright*   613
Abraham's Madness, *Bink Noll*   614
As by Water, *W. S. Merwin*   615
In the Night Fields, *W. S. Merwin*   616
Black Jackets, *Thom Gunn*   617
Secretary, *Ted Hughes*   619
Onan, *Paris Leary*   619
Daddy, *Sylvia Plath*   621
The Disquieting Muses, *Sylvia Plath*   623
Mad Girl's Love Song, *Sylvia Plath*   625
The Rebel, *Mari Evans*   626
When in Rome, *Mari Evans*   626
Lies, *Yevgeny Yevtushenko*   628
Corner, *Ralph Pomeroy*   629
A Poem for Black Hearts, *LeRoi Jones*   630
The Pill versus the Springhill Mine Disaster, *Richard Brautigan*   631
A Hell of a Day, *Tim Reynolds*   632
The European Shoe, *Michael Benedikt*   633
Dancing in the Street, *Al Young*   634
Death Was a Trick, *Jerome Mazzaro*   636
I, the Fake Mad Bomber and Walking It Home Again,
    Byron Black   636
Photograph of My Father in His Twenty-Second Year,
    Raymond Carver   638
Bankruptcy, *Raymond Carver*   639
Goodbye and Hello, *Tim Buckley*   639
I Would Not Be Here, *John Hartford*   642
Sisterhood, *Marilyn Hacker*   644
In a Prominent Bar in Secaucus One Day, *X. J. Kennedy*   646
Dress Rehearsal Rag, *Leonard Cohen*   647
The Geni in the Jar, *Nicki Giovanni*   649
Filling Station, *Elizabeth Bishop*   650
from Blue Meridian, *Jean Toomer*   652
If We Must Die, *Claude McKay*   652
Ten Haiku   653
Death in a Plane, *de Andrade*   654
The Hissing of Summer Lawns, *John Guerin and Joni Mitchell*   658
Today Is a Day of Great Joy, *Victor Hernandez Cruz*   659

Drama

Introduction 662

Oedipus Rex, *Sophocles* 670
Othello, *Shakespeare* 717
Miss Julie, *August Strindberg* 812
Ile, *Eugene O'Neill* 843
The Man with the Flower in His Mouth, *Luigi Pirandello* 858
The Jewels of the Shrine, *James E. Henshaw* 866
Picnic on the Battlefield, *Fernando Arrabal* 882
A View from the Bridge, *Arthur Miller* 896

Glossary

952

Index

970

Thematic Table of Contents

Human Values: Expectations, the Vision of Humankind, People and Their Dreams, Their Philosophies

Poetry:

The Tiger
The Indian Burying Ground
Work without Hope
Ozymandias
Ulysses
The Eagle
Battle Hymn of the Republic
When I Heard the Learn'd Astronomer
Spleen
Terence, This Is Stupid Stuff
The Second Coming
from The Black Riders XXIV, XLVII, and XLVIII
Patterns
Fire and Ice
Birches
The Panther
Prayers of Steel
Roses Only
The Monkeys
American Farm, 1934
Dream Deferred
If I Could Only Live at the Pitch That Is Near Madness

The Unknown Citizen
Snake (Roethke)
The Conscientious Objector
Dilemma
Survival in Missouri
We Real Cool
April Inventory
Curiosity
Joy
For No Clear Reason

Short Stories:

The Revolt of Mother
The Rocking-Horse Winner
A Dill Pickle
The Circular Ruins
Chee's Daughter
The Condor and the Guests

Drama:

A View from the Bridge
Picnic on the Battlefield

People Create

Poetry:

Study of Two Pears
Of Modern Poetry
The Red Wheelbarrow
Poetry
A Poet Speaks from the Visitor's Gallery
Reading Time: 1 Minute 26 Seconds

A Coney Island of the Mind
Today Is a Day of Great Joy

Short Stories:

The Circular Ruins
The Hobbyist

Illuminating People's Foibles: Irony, Comedy, Satire

Poetry:

The Nymph's Reply to the Shepherd
To Julia, Under Lock and Key
Song (Herford)
Ozymandias
The Latest Decalogue
#1207 (He preached upon "Breadth")
The Man He Killed
from A Shropshire Lad (On Moonlight Heath)
Mr. Flood's Party
Richard Cory
The Naked and the Nude
Litany for Dictatorships
The Rehearsal
Reflections on Ice Breaking
Inter-Office Memorandum
I, Too, Sing America
The Day after Sunday
Twelve Songs, VIII
Museums
Lessons of the War: Naming of Parts
Lessons of the War: Judging Distances

Life, Friends, Is Boring
Award
Suburban Homecoming
To David, about His Education
Life Cycle of the Common Man
Santa Claus
Mind
Formal Application
April Inventory
The Hissing of Summer Lawns

Short Stories:

The Pins
The Other Wife
The Hobbyist
The Condor and the Guests
Confessions of a Burglar
Dotson Gerber Resurrected
Winter Rug

Drama:

Picnic on the Battlefield

Persons in Conflict with Nature (Persons versus a Hostile Environment)

Poetry:

Lines Written in Early Spring
Work without Hope
Dover Beach
from War Is Kind, III and XXI
Patterns

Secretary
Death in a Plane

Drama:

The Man with the Flower in His Mouth
Oedipus

People in Harmony with Nature and Their Environment

Poetry:

Sonnet 18 (Shall I compare thee)
Sonnet 97 (How like a winter)
Sonnet 98 (From you have I been absent)

Composed upon Westminster Bridge
The Solitary Reaper
When Lilacs Last in the Dooryard Bloom'd
#328 (A Bird came down the Walk)

#441 (This is my letter to the World)
#986 (A narrow Fellow in the Grass)
Dust of Snow
Birches
The West Wind
God's World
May All Earth Be Clothed in Light

Short Stories:

The Revolt of Mother
Flight
The Circular Ruins
Chee's Daughter
A Worn Path

PEOPLE AND THEIR MYTHS

Poetry:

Hymn to Diana
Ulysses
The Wild Swans at Coole
The Second Coming
Leda and the Swan
Peter Quince at the Clavier
Santa Claus
Onan

Short Stories:

The Minister's Black Veil
The Hobbyist

Drama:

Oedipus
A View from the Bridge

YOUTH AND AGE

Poetry:

Crabbed Age and Youth
To the Virgins, to Make Much of Time
Ulysses
Rabbi Ben Ezra
Spring and Fall
The Wild Swans at Coole
Mr. Flood's Party
Blue Girls
Fern Hill

To David, about His Education
April Inventory

Short Stories:

Chee's Daughter
The Use of Force

Drama:

The Jewels of the Shrine
A View from the Bridge

PEOPLE AND LAWS: MORALITY

Poetry:

Sir Patrick Spens
Song: To Celia
On the Late Massacre in Piedmont
The Chimney Sweep
Song to the Men of England
The Man He Killed
from A Shropshire Lad (On Moonlight
   Heath)

Patterns
Grass
Shine, Perishing Republic
Dulce et Decorum Est
Arms and the Boy
Litany for Dictatorships
The Rehearsal

Ode to the Confederate Dead
Inter-Office Memorandum
I, Too, Sing America
John Doe, Jr.
Nice Day for a Lynching
Eighth Air Force
Award
Underwear
Santa Claus
Formal Application
Curiosity
Lies

Short Stories:

Flight
A Rose for Emily
Dotson Gerber Resurrected

Drama:

Oedipus
Othello
Miss Julie
A View from the Bridge
Picnic on the Battlefield

Man and Woman

Poetry:

They Flee from Me
Since There's No Help
Sonnet 130 (My mistress's eyes)
Upon Julia's Clothes
On a Girdle
O Lovely Fishermaiden
My Last Duchess
To a Common Prostitute
Modern Love
Patterns
A Virginal
Lady Love
Frankie and Johnny
Reflections on Ice Breaking
I Knew a Woman
English A

Short Stories:

The Death of Ivan Ilych
The Revolt of Mother
The Pins
A Painful Case
A Dill Pickle
Hills Like White Elephants
A Rose for Emily
The Other Wife
Girls in Their Summer Dresses
The Condor and the Guests
Neighbors

Drama:

Othello
Miss Julie
A View from the Bridge

People and Spirit: God, Spiritual Values, and the Mystical Experience

Poetry:

Holy Sonnet XIX
On His Blindness
Describes Rationally the Irrational Effects of Love
Praise for the Fountain Opened
The Tiger

Kubla Khan
Ode to a Nightingale
Battle Hymn of the Republic
When Lilacs Last in the Dooryard Bloom'd
The Blessed Damozel

#61 (Papa above!)
#324 (Some keep the Sabbath going to Church)
#986 (A narrow Fellow in the Grass)
Pied Beauty
The Second Coming
The Village Atheist
Gulls
Journey of the Magi
Dr. Sigmund Freud Discovers the Sea Shell

The Bad Children
Game Called on Account of Darkness
Santa Claus
Daddy

Drama:

Oedipus

Short Stories:

The Minister's Black Veil
A Worn Path

DEFINING THE SELF: PERSONS DISCOVER THEMSELVES

Poetry:

Edward
Sonnet 29 (When in disgrace)
On His Blindness
To the Reader
Terence, This Is Stupid Stuff
The Wild Swans at Coole
Richard Cory
from The Black Riders, III
When It Is Given You to Find a Smile
Sympathy
Patterns
After Apple-Picking
Birches
Snake (Lawrence)
The Mind Is an Enchanting Thing
The Love Song of J. Alfred Prufrock
The Hollow Men
"Dover Beach": A Note to That Poem
Indian Summer
from Machu Picchu, III, IV, V
If I Could Only Live at the Pitch That Is Near Madness

The Heavy Bear
For Rhoda
Reading Time: 1 Minute 26 Seconds
A Coney Island of the Mind
Life Cycle of the Common Man
Curiosity
A Wicker Basket
Black Jackets
The Disquieting Muses
Bankruptcy

Short Stories:

A Painful Case
The Use of Force
A Summer's Reading
Dotson Gerber Resurrected

Drama:

Oedipus

PERSONS AMONG PEOPLE: PEOPLE OF MANY COLORS—BLACK, BROWN, RED, WHITE

Poetry:

I, Too, Sing America
Incident
Nice Day for a Lynching

Award
When in Rome
A Poem for Black Hearts

Short Stories:

Flight
Chee's Daughter
A Summer Tragedy
Dotson Gerber Resurrected

Drama:

A View from the Bridge

THE FAMILY: SISTERS, PARENTS, MOTHERS AND DAUGHTERS, FATHERS AND SONS, AND SO ON

Poetry:

Edward
The Bad Children
Do Not Go Gentle into That Good
   Night
The Children of the Poor
Abraham's Madness
Daddy
The Disquieting Muses
Photograph of My Father in His Twen-
   ty-Second Year

The Revolt of Mother
The Judgment
The Rocking-Horse Winner
The Use of Force
Flight
Chee's Daughter

Short Stories:

The Death of Ivan Ilych

Drama:

Oedipus
The Jewels of the Shrine
A View from the Bridge
Picnic on the Battlefield

INITIATION, COMING OF AGE

Poetry:

Indian Summer
Poem in October
Black Jackets

Short Stories:

The Judgment
Flight
A Summer's Reading

THE SOCIAL CONTRACT: PERSONS VERSUS INSTITUTIONS, TRADITIONS, CUSTOMS

Poetry:

The Passionate Shepherd
The Constant Lover
Say, But Did You Love So Long
The Chimney Sweep
Richard Cory
Sympathy
Prayers of Steel
Grass
Shine, Republic

Shine, Perishing Republic
The Love Song of J. Alfred Prufrock
The Hollow Men
Dulce et Decorum Est
Arms and the Boy
Southern Mansion
John Doe, Jr.
Come Live with Me and Be My Love
The Unknown Citizen

Museums
The Conscientious Objector
The Death of the Ball Turret Gunner
Suburban Homecoming
After the Convention
Onan
Corner
Dancing in the Street
I, the Fake Mad Bomber and Walking It
   Home Again
Goodbye and Hello

Short Stories:

The Minister's Black Veil
The Revolt of Mother
Flight
Chee's Daughter
Dotson Gerber Resurrected

Drama:

Oedipus
A View from the Bridge
Picnic on the Battlefield

VARIATIONS UPON LOVE

Poetry:

Since There's No Help
The Passionate Shepherd
The Nymph's Reply to the Shepherd
Sonnet 18 (Shall I compare thee)
Sonnet 29 (When in disgrace)
Song: To Celia
The Good-Morrow
A Valediction: Forbidding Mourning
Delight in Disorder
Song (Carew)
To His Coy Mistress
A Red, Red Rose
When We Two Parted
La Belle Dame sans Merci
O Lovely Fishermaiden
Sonnet 14 from Sonnets from the Por-
   tugese
The Blessed Damozel
Leda and the Swan
Non Sum Qualis Eram Bonae Sub
   Regno Cynarae
The Taxi

Elegy for Jane
Buick
Love Poem
English A
A Simile for Her Smile
A Blessing
Mad Girl's Love Song

Short Stories:

The Revolt of Mother
A Dill Pickle
A Rose for Emily
Hills Like White Elephants
The Use of Force

Drama:

Othello
A View from the Bridge
Miss Julie

PEOPLE'S MORTALITY: LIFE AND DEATH, BIRTH AND DYING, HOPE AND
REBIRTH

Poetry:

Edward
The Twa Corbies

Sir Patrick Spens
Sonnet 30 (When to the sessions of
   sweet silent thought)

The Indian Burying Ground
Ode to a Nightingale
La Belle Dame sans Merci
Ulysses
Rabbi Ben Ezra
When Lilacs Last in the Dooryard
  Bloom'd
#465 (I heard a Fly buzz—when I died)
#712 (Because I could not stop for
  Death)
Spring and Fall
The Wild Swans at Coole
After Apple-Picking
Fire and Ice
The West Wind
The Emperor of Ice-Cream
Domination of Black
Journey of the Magi
Bells for John Whiteside's Daughter
Résumé
American Farm, 1934
from Machu Picchu, III, IV, V
Elegy for Jane

Auto Wreck
Do Not Go Gentle into That Good
  Night

Short Stories:

The Death of Ivan Ilych
The Luck of Roaring Camp
The Judgment
A Painful Case
Hills Like White Elephants
Flight
The Circular Ruins
A Worn Path
Chee's Daughter
Winter Rug
A Summer Tragedy

Drama:

Oedipus
Miss Julie
A View from the Bridge
Picnic on the Battlefield

Structure and Shaping Elements of Poetry, Short Stories, and Drama

SATIRE, IRONY

Poetry:

They Flee from Me
Since There's No Help
The Nymph's Reply to the Shepherd
The Constant Lover
When I Heard the Learn'd Astronomer
#1207 (He preached upon "Breadth")
The Man He Killed
Richard Cory
Arms and the Boy
Incident
The Unknown Citizen
Life, Friends, Is Boring
Dilemma
To David, about His Education

COMEDY, HUMOR

Poetry:

To Julia, Under Lock and Key
Song (Herford)
#61 (Papa above!)
#324 (Some keep the Sabbath going to Church)
Indian Summer
Resumé
Inter-Office Memorandum

IMAGERY, METAPHOR, SIMILE

Poetry:

Sonnet 18 (Shall I compare thee to a summer's day?)

Santa Claus
Death in a Plane
The Hissing of Summer Lawns

Short Stories:

The Luck of Roaring Camp
The Pins
A Dill Pickle
A Rose for Emily
Confessions of a Burglar
The Hobbyist

Drama:

Othello
Ile
Miss Julie
Picnic on the Battlefield

Short Stories:

The Pins
Confessions of a Burglar
The Hobbyist
Winter Rug

Drama:

Picnic on the Battlefield
The Jewels of the Shrine

Sonnet 97 (How like a winter hath my absence been)
The Good Morrow

A Red, Red Rose
The Solitary Reaper
O Lovely Fishermaiden
To the Reader
Dover Beach
When It Is Given You to Find a Smile
The Taxi
Birches
The Red Wheelbarrow
The Mind Is an Enchanting Thing
The Love Song of J. Alfred Prufrock
Lady Love
Ode to the Confederate Dead
Elegy for Jane
Auto Wreck
Buick
Reading Time: 1 Minute 26 Seconds
Love Poem
Do Not Go Gentle into That Good
   Night

Mind
Joy
Mad Girl's Love Song
The Pill versus the Springhill Mine
   Disaster
Ten Haiku
Today Is a Day of Great Joy

Short Stories:

The Minister's Black Veil
The Rocking-Horse Winner
Hills Like White Elephants
Flight
The Condor and the Guests

Drama:

Othello
Ile

RHYTHM AND METER

Poetry:

Edward
Lines Written in Early Spring
Battle Hymn of the Republic
Spring and Fall
After Apple-Picking
Prayers of Steel
Domination of Black
Snake (Roethke)
Fern Hill
Poem in October
A Poem for Black Hearts

Goodbye and Hello
I Would Not Be Here

Short Stories:

The Judgment
The Other Wife
Flight
Winter Rug

Drama:

Oedipus
Othello

SOUND—RHYME, LYRICISM, ALLITERATION, AND ASSONANCE

Poetry:

Sir Patrick Spens
Sonnet 30 (When to the sessions of
   sweet silent thought)
Upon Julia's Clothes
On the Late Massacre in Piedmont
Song to the Men of England
Cavalry Crossing a Ford
#1463 (A Route of Evanescence)

Pied Beauty
The West Wind
Study of Two Pears
Snake (Lawrence)
"Dover Beach": A Note to That Poem
A Simile for Her Smile
In a Prominent Bar in Secaucus One
   Day

DICTION

Poetry:

To His Coy Mistress
Kubla Khan
When Lilacs Last in the Dooryard
    Bloom'd
#328 (A Bird came down the Walk)
from War Is Kind, III and XXI
This Is Just to Say
Roses Only
Poetry
Bells for John Whiteside's Daughter

Lessons of the War: Naming of Parts
Lessons of the War: Judging Distances
The Children of the Poor
Dancing in the Street
Sisterhood

Short Stories:

The Judgment
A Rose for Emily
The Condor and the Guests
A Summer Tragedy

PLOT

Poetry:

The Twa Corbies

Short Stories:

The Pins
The Luck of Roaring Camp
The Rocking-Horse Winner

A Rose for Emily
A Summer Tragedy

Drama:

Oedipus
Othello
Miss Julie

CHARACTER

Poetry:

To a Common Prostitute
Curiosity
Black Jackets

Short Stories:

The Minister's Black Veil
The Revolt of Mother
A Rose for Emily

The Girls in Their Summer Dresses
A Worn Path

Drama:

Othello
Miss Julie
The Jewels of the Shrine
A View from the Bridge

SENSE AND MEANING

Poetry:

#1755 (To make a prairie it takes a
    clover and one bee)
Study of Two Pears
A Virginal
Underwear
As by Water

Short Stories:

The Minister's Black Veil
The Judgment
The Rocking-Horse Winner
Hills Like White Elephants
The Use of Force

Drama:

Picnic on the Battlefield

DESCRIPTION

Poetry:

Arise, My Love, and Come Away
Describes Rationally the Irrational Effects of Love
Composed upon Westminster Bridge
The Eagle
May All Earth Be Clothed in Light
A Blessing
Secretary
Corner
Photograph of My Father in His Twenty-Second Year

Short Stories:

The Use of Force
A Rose for Emily
Flight

Drama:

Ile
The Man with the Flower in His Mouth

POINT OF VIEW

Poetry:

My Last Duchess
#465 (I heard a Fly buzz—when I died)
#712 (Because I could not stop for Death)
The Death of the Ball Turret Gunner
Formal Application
When in Rome
Death in a Plane

Short Stories:

The Minister's Black Veil
The Revolt of Mother
The Rocking-Horse Winner
Hills Like White Elephants

Drama:

Miss Julie
The Jewels of the Shrine
Picnic on the Battlefield

TONE

Poetry:

When We Two Parted
The Latest Decalogue
Terence, This Is Stupid Stuff
Mr. Flood's Party
Patterns
The Emperor of Ice-Cream
Dulce et Decorum Est
Come Live with Me and Be My Love
Award
Suburban Homecoming

April Inventory
The Disquieting Muses

Short Stories:

Hills Like White Elephants
The Other Wife
Confessions of a Burglar
Winter Rug
Dotson Gerber Resurrected

Drama:

Miss Julie

THEME

Poetry:

The Passionate Shepherd to His Love
To the Virgins, to Make Much of Time

La Belle Dame sans Merci
Sonnet 14 *from* Sonnets from the Portuguese

Ulysses
Sympathy
Peter Quince at the Clavier
Blue Girls
Dr. Sigmund Freud Discovers the Sea
   Shell
from Machu Picchu, III, IV, V
English A
Lies

A Painful Case
Flight
Chee's Daughter

Drama:

Othello
The Man with the Flower in His Mouth
A View from the Bridge

Short Stories:

The Minister's Black Veil
The Death of Ivan Ilych

Symbolism, Allegory

Poetry:

Arise, My Love, and Come Away
The Chimney Sweep
The Tiger
Ozymandias
Ode to a Nightingale
The Second Coming
The Wild Swans at Coole
Leda and the Swan
from The Black Riders II, XXIV, XLVII
Journey of the Magi
The Hollow Men
Truth
Dream Deferred
Nice Day for a Lynching
The Heavy Bear
Game Called on Account of Darkness

In the Night Fields
Daddy
A Hell of a Day
The Geni in the Jar

Short Stories:

The Minister's Black Veil
The Luck of Roaring Camp
The Judgment
The Rocking-Horse Winner
A Rose for Emily
The Condor and the Guests

Drama:

The Man with the Flower in His Mouth
Picnic on the Battlefield
A View from the Bridge

General
Introduction

The impulse to tell stories, sing songs, and act out events seems to be spontaneous in people. "Tell me a story about when you were little," begs the child, delighted to hear how different—and yet how similar—life was before he or she came along. "In the beginning God created Heaven and Earth," intones the churchman, and he explains to his congregation how their problems can be solved in the light of what happened long ago in Israel. A parable or story can be more palatable and powerful than almost any plain speech.

The roots of the oral tradition are primitive and obscure, but it was that tradition which carried civilization well past the time after writing became established. Part of it remains viable to this day, having been preserved in literary creations such as Mother Goose rhymes, fairy tales, the Norse legends, the Greek myths, the *Iliad,* and the *Odyssey.* In most countries at most times in history a relatively small percentage of the populace has been literate. This does not mean, however, that most people have been unable to appreciate or contribute to the culture in other ways, such as continuing the oral tradition. The fact that our knowledge of Greek drama came to us through fragments of written versions does not mean that writing was the only (or even the major) way in which contemporaries of the classic dramatists knew these works.

First, then, came the stories, poems, plays, and songs that were valued enough to be passed along through memorization and repetition. Some of these and some new works were put into writing by the few scribes (in Egyptian, Greek, and Roman times) and scholars (in the Middle Ages) of Western civilization. With the invention of printing and the introduction of mass education, suddenly anyone could create a work of literature, and it could become almost instantly known and judged by countless people throughout the world.

It is hard to say why people have always been drawn to such imaginative creations. Perhaps it began as a way of finding answers to apparently unanswerable questions about the universe and humankind—or perhaps it began as one way of alleviating boredom. Whatever the reason, the attraction has lasted over a long period of time. And on it goes today.

The possible benefits are obvious. Individually, we can talk or listen to only a few people at a time. Our interaction with them is limited by a thousand factors. But in college we want to know more and experience more, and the printed word makes this easy. We can, when we wish, share the emotions of a person who lived in the time of Elizabeth I; we can be stimulated by the arguments that provoked the French Revolution. We may be locked in one place and one kind of life, but through literature we can approach the perspective of a lumberjack, an eighteenth-century sailor, a Russian peasant woman, a Japanese samurai.

Of course, the appreciation of literature does require one thing of the reader: the willing suspension of disbelief. Unlike the economist, the historian, the politician, or the newspaper reporter, the author does not pretend that what he or she is presenting is always factually true. Literature does not merely offer facts. Let's look at what it does offer.

WHAT CAN BE FOUND THROUGH LITERATURE

Literature offers a form of escape. Through literature you are released from the bounds of self. You are able to experience what it is to be a poor Italian artisan, to endure the Napoleonic war, or to be an unwanted child. Your passport is simply your own imagination.

Literature offers you affiliation. We are all really alone. Perhaps no man is an island in John Donne's sense, but in another sense each of us is made up of our own particular experiences. We used to feel closer to others through affiliations with family, institutions, and the traditions of our particular culture; slowly, however, these bonds have been eroded.

But if you have had an experience, it sometimes makes you feel less lonely and strange to know that others—in other times and other places—have had a similar one. Maybe you feel that your relatives, your neighbors, and your friends do not understand you; but somewhere, someplace, there is an author who can put into words what you feel—and perhaps even justify those feelings. Our response on such occasions— regardless of the work's merit by some abstract method of measurement—is to feel warm and relieved. We may even say to someone else, "Read this and you will see what I mean."

Literature offers truth and order. Many nonfiction books and articles claim to be more factual and more complete than they really are. If their authors were honest, they would all have to say, "We really don't know everything that went into these events; we really don't know all the reasons; we really don't know all of the consequences." Their air of authority and dogmatism is often assumed because the authors know that people like to believe that they have found out "what really happened" at the Kennedy assassination, in the last election, in the unhappy life and death of a movie star.

But science and art have this in common: given the exact dimensions of the laboratory experiment or the mathematical world, what happens is exact, describable, and accurate. Given the world of a particular book, story, play, set of poems, picture, or piece of music, what happens to those particular characters or in that particular setting is exact, describable, and accurate. The artist, of course, has the additional burden of making what happens seem believable and realistic, because it is hard for the reader to resist comparing the reality of the work with the reality he lives in. The reader may say, "But I don't believe there are any people like that." However, if authors have done their work well, they will have laid foundations that make the characters and their actions credible. (Of course, our tendency to compare the artist's universe to our own may work in an author's favor. He or she can add verisimilitude to an otherwise unconvincing narrative merely by including details that we are familiar with in one way or another.)

Literature offers you insight. Literature, perhaps more than any other art form, offers an opportunity for enlightenment and enjoyment. Sometimes it describes, organizes, and helps us understand feelings and situations. Literature helps us discover ourselves and identify who we are. When we read how characters work out problems or conflicts, it says something to us about the way *we* approach life's complexities. And yet, after all is said and done, a piece of literature has an existence in and of itself; it can offer us *ways* in which to search, but we must do the searching for ourselves.

Literature is relatively inexpensive, it encompasses so much, and you can pick it up and put it down at will. Most of all, perhaps it taps the wealth of your own imagination as no other medium can. It would seem that only fools would allow themselves to be cut off from something that has so many advantages and almost no drawbacks. So while you no doubt have probably already come in contact with literature—if not in your private life, then in textbooks at school—this book is intended to make the introduction formal.

DEFINITION OF LITERATURE

In all of our extolling of literature thus far, we have not actually defined it. The fact is that there are very few good definitions. Literature has been equated with "imaginative or creative writing," but good nonfiction would fit the same description. If this book were being written long ago, it would be easier to establish fairly definite boundaries in respect to the scope of our concern. We could restrict the term to the traditional three genres and consider fiction, drama, and poetry, and we would know what we meant by these terms. But over the years the lines of distinction have become more and more vague. As authors experiment in form and subject, definitions of literature change.

If we define fiction as "prose literary work whose content is produced by the imagination and is not necessarily based on fact," does this mean that the works of Tom Wolfe are not fiction? If we define poetry as "composition designed to convey a vivid and imaginative sense of experience, characterized by the use of condensed language chosen for its sound and suggestive power, as well as its meaning, and by the use of literary techniques, such as structured meter, natural cadences, rhyme, and metaphor," can we include Mari Evans' "When in Rome"? If drama is defined as "prose or verse written to be performed by actors on a stage," does it include O'Neill's extended stage directions? And do any of these descriptions fit light verse or the worst stories in slick magazines? (In the introductions to the genres, you will find more extensive discussions of the merits of these definitions.)

Literature is writing that is regarded as having an intrinsic worth beyond its immediate appeal. Literature is the creative expression of individual experiences that nevertheless have universal appeal. Literature has form, beauty of expression, and intellectual as well as emotional appeal. Further, we can look at the substance of literature and find a number of characteristics that are common to all works:

- Each work uses or builds on certain conventions of the particular genre it represents. These conventions are somewhat artificial, but custom has made them acceptable. (Examples include an operatic star singing two arias after having been fatally stabbed, a poem describing a state of mind in perfect iambic pentameter, and the division of a story into chapters or a play into acts.) Even character types, themes, or motifs can become a matter of convention.

- All works use conflict, either overt or implicit, as an organizing principle. The conflict may be between one's view of oneself and one's view of others, between what is and what was, between tradition and change, between what is and what is not said, between innocence and maturity, or between any of the countless other contrasts that make the human condition both happy and sad.

- Literature usually moves from the specific to the general, though the generalization may only be implied. One character or incident often represents all such people or incidents.

- All works offer a certain richness of ambiguity that encourages enjoyment and interpretation at different levels of complexity. If the work is a classic, it has become one because its ambiguities may be reinterpreted with application to each succeeding generation of readers.

- Literature usually deals with experience. Philosophical ideas may be discussed, but they are most often presented in terms of personal experience.

- Literary works of high quality offer a story, a situation, an image, or a metaphor, rather than a direct statement of what the author wishes to communicate. Instead of simply describing an emotion or an experience, an author endeavors to recreate it for the reader.

- Literature is usually the product of a mysterious inner compulsion combined with a fully conscious discipline. While a student essay on the feeling of loneliness after the death of one's mother or on the social stigma attached to an unwanted pregnancy may carry conviction, it is not necessarily (or usually) art. Art is also form. On the other hand, an artist may modify a deeply felt personal experience—frequently in order to make it more universal—but unless we can sense the feeling behind it, it seems artificial. When both form and feeling are present, the reader is likely to experience the work in terms of Emily Dickinson's definition of poetry—as something that makes one feel as though the top of his head had been blown off.

- All well-written works have unity. After reading a work, the reader should feel that each part contributed to the whole, that things were there for a reason, and that the ending or outcome was an inevitable outgrowth of what came before.

- All works take advantage of literary elements such as plot, characterization, imagery, diction, tone, style, and pace that are appropriate to that particular piece.

Why Study Literature?

Most of these characteristics will become apparent in anything more than a superficial reading of a literary work. Admittedly, studying a work in order to find theme elements is not a prerequisite to enjoying the piece itself. In fact, people who have learned to enjoy literature often resist analyzing it. To them paraphrasing is deadly and analyzing a poem is analogous to dissecting it. Why not then just offer an anthology of prose, poetry, and drama, and let students make what they will of it?

Analysis asks readers to interact with a work and thereby helps them get more out of it. Analysis not only contributes to a better understanding of individual works, but it also enables one to develop some procedures for approaching new pieces and some criteria for judging them. In analyzing a particular piece, however, it is impossible to make absolute judgments. Fashions and emphasis change in literature as they do in life. But overall trends can be pointed out, and comparisons between works can be made.

This book deals with a few of the mechanics of literature. In a sense, to say that students have to understand the mechanics before they can enjoy literature is like saying that they must know the technical aspects of anatomy before they can appreciate the beauty of the human body—or that they must understand all of the mechanical operations of a car in order to drive it well. However, the more interested one gets in a subject, the more details one wants to know about it. Since the mechanics contribute to the overall effect of the work, understanding them will facilitate a better understanding of the work as a whole. As long as the mechanics do not get in the way of the substance, studying them can make for a more meaningful and pleasurable experience.

About This Book

The selections in this book begin with the area of mythology, because this is where literature began. The other genre are arranged in the time-honored order—fiction, poetry, and plays—from the most to the least familiar to the reader.

The selections in this book are meant to present a variety of works, themes, viewpoints, stances, and techniques. Most of them are pieces written in the twentieth century, because these are more obviously enjoyable in our times; they require less historical background on the part of the reader, and they will be the basis for new works that will be written in the twenty-first century. The selections are arranged chronologically within the genre so that you can see how the passage of time has changed both what is considered appropriate subject matter and how a subject is handled. Of course, there are always some mavericks—writers who demonstrate that genius recognizes no restrictions as to subject or technique.

Some observers have been surprised at the revived interest in folklore and mythology among today's youth and scoffingly pass it off by saying, "They're searching for something." Since the day man crawled in out of the cold, he has been searching for something, for answers, and his search has been catalogued in the long pages of philosophy and literature. When we read literature, we are being given the opportunity to learn the history—the successes and the failures—of that search.

This anthology does not purport to be a definitive collection of the best, or most representative, or most useful works of Western civilization. These works are, however, ones that have survived the years—or centuries—of changing standards of literary excellence, and they will give you an account of what good literature is.

MYTHS, FOLKLORE, AND RELIGIOUS MOTIFS

Introduction to Folklore

In humankind's thirst for progress—the eagerness to adopt the new and discard the old, the worship of the contrived and contempt for the plain—an entire body of knowledge and art form that was once familiar to everyone has come to be known and appreciated only by a few. Stories that used to be part of every childhood have been supplanted by modern "relevant" tales, such as accounts of trips to the dentist and narratives of life in the ghetto. If it had not been for several factors—among them the academicians who demanded that candidates for degrees know something about Greek and Roman mythology, the devoted folklorists who painstakingly tracked aged backwoodsmen to their hilltop cabins in search of a new folk tale, and the public's sporadic interest in ethnic histories—folk literature might well have become an extinct genre.

That we have allowed this rich heritage almost to slip away from us is more than a shame. Folk tales, legends, myths, and fables transmitted orally are part of the earliest and most delightful evidence of the human creative genius. Later writers may have turned out more sophisticated pieces, but many of their stories and dramas are merely some type of folk tale parading in modern dress and are often considerably weaker than the original version.

Who then are the unsung creators of the first detective story, the first love poem, the first domestic tragedy? It is impossible to know, since true folklore admits no authorship. These tales have been developed over the centuries by the common people themselves, by their entertainers, and by their religious leaders in answer to such basic questions as: Where did we come from? What determines our fate? What happens to us after death? Who or what controls the weather? We are still asking some of these questions—but now we look to science or formal religion or philosophy for the answers. But the old answers have merit, and they shouldn't be discarded.

It must be emphasized that folklore is not merely the product of a society without writing. For example, although the brothers Grimm collected fairy tales from an illiterate peasantry, at the same time in the same area lived very well-educated individuals who were certainly literate. In general, then, we may define folklore as *special stories and information transmitted orally from generation to generation without reliable ascription as to author.* Thus in the widest sense, folklore includes gestures, songs, and beliefs, as well as sayings, riddles, and the like. And it can arise in modern times much as it did long ago.

The stories here are only one version of a particular folk tale. When the tale was still alive orally, it was changed and embroidered in each new telling. The tellers might add to a story they had heard or subtract details from it; they might act out parts or sing them. They would do whatever they felt was necessary to hold the audience's interest. Each of these stories, then, is an individualized account that has passed from the oral tradition into the written one and thus has become permanently fixed.

Since these tales grew out of the typical experiences of our ancestors, their specific content varies from one culture group to another. For instance, there have been a number of different names given to mischievous or evil supernatural creatures—witches, goblins, trolls. Certain issues have concerned all groups everywhere: the conflict between parents and children, the interest in the origin of the world, the establishment of an ethic, and the fear of death.

DEFINITIONS AND CATEGORIES

For purposes of comparison, folk tales have been classified in a number of ways: according to the characters, the plot, the subject matter, the motifs, the style of treatment, and so on. Specialists in this area differentiate, for example, between myth, legend, fairy tales, fables, epics, and tall tales, although—depending on how the theme is treated—a story may qualify under more than one heading.

Myth, it seems, is the earliest and most basic form of these stories. Whether myths have any basis in events that were once known to be facts is at this distance impossible to tell. It appears that a myth was at one time considered by the group that fostered it to be a true story of their past. Present-day anthropologists and folklorists have variously defined myth as: a narrative associated with a rite or ritual, usually untrue historically; a story about the gods and their actions, a religious tale from prehistory that deals with the creating and ordering of the universe and the problems that continue to confront mankind; or a story that a particular group believes in as an explanation for an event or practice.

The familiar European *fairy tales* appear to be a more recent version of older folk literature: the supernatural heroes of the myths have in the fairy tales become virtuous, good-hearted humans. In myths, the outcome is only occasionally satisfactory from the human standpoint, since the gods play by different rules. In fairy tales, the good characters are always rewarded, and the evil ones are always punished. While myths are perhaps true stories set in the dawn of history, fairy tales are usually outright fiction set in a never-never land.

Another group of tales falls under the heading of *allegory.* These stories may be considered almost extended analogies. They express abstract meanings in terms of concrete illustrations, each element in the allegory standing for some idea or characteristic. When the purpose of the tale is to exemplify a moral (whether stated or implicit), it may be called a *parable* or a *fable.* If the characters in such a tale are animals, it is called a *beast fable* or *beast epic.* These stories point out human foibles, teach a lesson without preaching, or convey messages in a way that will escape the attention of disapproving authorities.

The *dilemma tale* is one in which a problem is presented to the reader, and several alternatives are described without a solution being stated.

Although stories in the foregoing classifications are almost wholly the product of the imagination, another group of folk tales has more factual basis. These are semihistorical accounts, or *legends,* connected with historical persons. For example, both Charlemagne and Johnny Appleseed did exist and did perform at least some of the deeds attributed to them. There is even a suspicion that King Arthur and his round table were not completely fictitious creations.

Somewhat related to the legend is the *epic,* a long narrative poem that mixes adventure, morality, and tragedy. It is characterized by definite structural elements, including the epic catalog and epic battle. The few true epics that date from preliterate times are thought to be based on actual events.

Perhaps the most American type of folk tale is the *tall tale,* in which the hero accomplished almost superhuman feats. The German Baron Munchhausen is almost the only foreign rival of Paul Bunyan, John Henry, Stormalong, Pecos Bill (and the countless other inventions of the frontier mind, who are palely shadowed in some of the works of Mark Twain and the Liar's Clubs today). The tall tale was never intended to be believed. It is frankly fictitious and spoofs the listeners.

THE FUNCTION OF FOLKTALES

Why have humans over the centuries diverted their energies from the business of life—such as finding food, maintaining shelter, and raising a family—to tell these stories? Folk tales (especially myths) may well be the end product of a process in which people have tried to resolve the tensions resulting from conflicts in their inner lives—first by means of ritual, then through art. Art, like ritual, provided a way for the individual to deal on another plane with those matters he or she found frustrating in real life. The person could then identify priests, heroes, or kings with power and could then feel exalted through their victories and become absolved through their sufferings.

These tales can entertain, explain, reinforce, transmit values, warn, create a sense of group identity, sanction customs, institutions, and rituals, attempt to pierce the veil of destiny, and act as a psychological safety valve—an outlet for dreams and desires. In any event, many of these plots and themes have been reworked successfully by generations of tellers and writers, and interest in them never seems to diminish.

THEMES THROUGH THE AGES

Some of the most frequently repeated motifs include: the devil or genie in a bottle, lamp, knapsack, or other container; the pact with the devil; the sacrifice of a human victim; the cruel stepmother; the trials of a hero; objects and people that are not what they seem (old women are in reality fairy godmothers, toads are princes, deer are fair maidens); and sex as a trap (sirens lure ships to destruction, Vivien shuts the wizard Merlin up in a tree, Circe turns Odysseus' shipmates into swine).

For a while during the eighteenth and nineteenth centuries, interest in these tales revived, and the link between the oral and literary tradition was strengthened. Collecting folk tales and rewording them in literary form became the vogue. The brothers Grimm performed a heroic task of gathering European stories (most of which are much too gory in their original form to be suitable for young children), and Andrew Lang did the same for the English-speaking peoples. At the same time, Sir James Frazer tried to correlate many of the myths and rituals found throughout the known world. Gothic satires became popular; Bram Stoker gave us the immortal Dracula (the culmination of other vampire tales), and Mary Shelley wrote of Frankenstein's monster.

Modern writers have returned to the same sources to find them still profitable. There have been James Joyce's *Ulysses,* the many works of Thomas Mann, John Barth's *Chimera,* and Albert Camus' *The Myth of Sisyphus,* to name only a few. And in our day the use of mythology and legend has not stopped in scholarly or literary circles. Far from Broadway, audiences have applauded *Fiddler on the Roof,* from Sholom Aleichem's adaptation of folk tales about Chelm and other Yiddish places; *Camelot,* which was based on the Arthurian legends; and *Jesus Christ, Superstar,* which was based on the Bible.

WHY STUDY FOLKLORE?

What rewards does studying these early stories offer? Some people view them as a guide to prehistoric events. (The treasures of Troy were unearthed because one man took Homer seriously.) Others study myths as a metaphor for human beings' unconscious but predictable behavior.

It is tempting to get sidetracked into all the connections that *can* be made between this folk art and our own lives, but there is really no need to look so far afield for significance. For a student of English, the study of this subject is especially important, since folklore is the source of themes, motifs, metaphors, and allusions that are encountered throughout literature—from the plays of Shakespeare to the poetry of Shelley to the short stories of your favorite author. In reading these stories, we can reclaim our inheritance, see where we've come from, add richness to our own ideas, and just have fun.

The Indians and Death

In those days long ago neither the Indians nor the animals were subject to Death. They all lived for ever, and there was yet enough room for everyone. Only the coyote, discontented grumbler that he was, went about grousing: "Why do we have to be squashed here like this? If only the old were to die, we'd be far better off." And he ran all over the prairie, shouting so loudly that he could be heard in both forest and desert. But no one paid any heed to his talk, for it was well-known that the coyote was a scoundrel who always tried to make trouble for everything and everybody.

This time, however, it soon became apparent that he would not so easily give up the idea that had lodged firmly in his crooked, dishevelled head. And when the snow remained lying on the ground especially long that year and famine threatened, he again started to shout:

"There, you see? I told you! There are too many of us, and that's why we are hungry. If only the old were to die, there would be plenty to eat for all of us."

In the end the Great Shaman heard of the coyote's suggestions. The wise old man became very angry and wanted to punish the evil-minded ruf-fian, but then he thought better of it and decided to call a meeting, which he hoped would prove to the coyote how repugnant his suggestion really was to one and all. Perhaps, thought the Great Shaman, the coyote may yet mend his ways.

And thus the Indians and the animals assembled at the foot of the Sacred Rock, with the Great Shaman sitting on a tree-stump on top of the cliff; his head-dress touched the sky when he raised his head to address them in the following words:

"My children! I could no longer bear to listen to the yelping of your brother coyote, who keeps proposing that we bring Death into the world. That is why I have now called you together. Tell the coyote what you think of his idea, so that he may be taught a lesson."

The animals conferred together quietly, while the coyote sat alone, scratching behind his ears with his paw and getting up every now and again to trot from one to the other, pricking up his ears to hear what they were saying.

All of a sudden he called out:

"O Great Shaman, I never intended to harm anyone! But there isn't enough food to go round, and we can't all survive." His cunning

THE INDIANS AND DEATH Reproduced by the Permission of The Hamlyn Publishing Group Limited from AMERICAN INDIAN TALES AND LEGENDS eyes were narrowed into mere slits. "It was never my intention that those who die should not return to this world."

"What is it you suggest, then?" asked the squirrel.

"I would tell you, only . . . I don't know, nobody trusts me, that's the trouble."

"Go on, tell us!" the Indians urged him, and the Great Shaman leaned forward in order to hear him better.

"Very well, then," said the coyote. "I suggest we make a hole in heaven, and all the dead can move there for a time. Then, when there is again enough food for all, we'll simply call them back."

"But there isn't a tree so high," murmured the bear.

"I have thought it all out," replied the coyote smugly. "An Indian arrow will reach the sky. Then a second arrow can be shot to join up with the first, then a third and a fourth, until they link heaven and earth. Anyone can climb up then, and it will be even easier to get down again."

The coyote's proposal seemed sensible enough. A little too pat, the Great Shaman said to himself; but think as he might, he could find no objection. Even the most sceptical among them approved of the idea. The coyote was smiling benevolently. If only they knew!

In the meantime the Indians had run off to fetch their bows and arrows, bringing as many as they could carry. Then the best marksmen prepared to shoot.

Whizz! the first arrow whistled over their heads and pierced a low cloud. It was immediately followed by another, which split the first arrow all the way up to its feather ornament and stuck fast.

The animals looked on in admiration as the Indians displayed their marksmanship. Not a single arrow went astray. The coyote ran about under the bowmen's legs, getting in the way and giving advice as if it had been he who had taught them to shoot.

Now the long line of arrows reached down as far as the Sacred Rock. The Great Shaman rose from his tree-stump, and he pulled at the arrows to test their strength. They held firm, strong enough to take even a bear's weight.

By this time dusk had set in, and the Great Shaman motioned with his hand for the crowd to disperse and go home.

"Go to sleep now, but as from this day, Death will be here with us; it is you who have decided so. I shall now open a door in the Sacred Rock for Death to come through, and those whom it chooses will climb up to heaven to stay there for a certain time. . . . "

Night settled over the country-side—the first night in which Death walked the Indian country, the first night during which an old badger died in his den, a lonely hunter in his cabin, and an eagle in his eyrie high up among the rocks.

The dead walked in the dark to the Sacred Rock, and before dawn the last of them had vanished inside the hole in the star-filled sky.

Time passed. Soon the weeping of the bereaved could be heard everywhere, and many went to the Great Shaman for advice. But even he was powerless to help for the time being.

"We must wait for the stars to sink a little lower," he told all comers. "As they are now, they cannot hear us calling."

Night after night, therefore, people as well as animals fixed their eyes on the sky, waiting for the return of those who had left them.

Only the coyote was nowhere to be seen. He had taken to his lair, and those who passed by it heard strange grating noises coming from inside. They wondered what the old rascal might be doing, but mostly they were convinced that he was afraid to come out in case they wanted to punish him for his little prank that had caused all the trouble.

However, a new and even more dastardly plan had taken shape in that crooked skull of his. The coyote had brought sharp-edged stones to his lair and now spent long days sharpening his teeth on them, making his fangs sharper than the Indian tomahawk. It was this that produced those strange sounds that could be heard coming from his lair.

When at last he all but cut his own tongue on his teeth, the coyote decided he had done all he could to prepare himself for the task in hand, and he went out quietly into the night.

It was the last hour before dawn, and everything was absolutely still. The coyote crept stealthily up to the Sacred Rock, putting his paws down cautiously so as not to give himself away by as much as a disturbed blade of grass.

He stopped at the foot of the cliff and listened. There was complete silence everywhere, only the night wind could be heard whistling in the rock crevices. There was thus nothing to prevent him from carrying out his evil intent. Standing up on his hind legs, he caught hold of the last arrow with his teeth and began to gnaw at it. The soft wood soon gave way, but the remaining arrows were still firmly attached to the sky. This infuriated the coyote—in his rage he shook the line of arrows furiously, hoping to pry the first one loose from the cloud above.

He succeeded only too well; with a resounding crash, the arrows came tumbling down about his ears. Some landed on his back with a thump, and the coyote squealed with pain: "Wowww! Wowww!"

Bruised and battered, he crept back to his lair. Pandemonium broke out. The noise had awakened the bear and he, discovering what had happened, quickly roused the others, as well as the Great Shaman.

But there was nothing to be done—the dead could now never return to the land of the living again.

The Great Shaman was very angry. Without a moment's hesitation he pronounced judgment over the culprit:

"You must leave our midst as punishment. We were long patient with you, hoping that you might mend your ways, but all to no avail. Now go out into the prairie, where you will henceforth live alone, so that you should not do any more mischief."

The coyote heard the verdict and, seeing that there was no other way, trotted off humbly, his tail between his legs.

He wandered a whole day long and perhaps even longer, finally settling down in a lonely spot where there was no other living creature for miles around—so afraid was he of the wise magician.

Now at last he began to regret his evil ways, and ever since then he has been wailing and begging to be allowed to return. But though his pleas are often to be heard, no one takes pity on him and calls him back, just as Death, whom he so carelessly brought into the world, will never go back to its abode in the Sacred Rock.

Considerations

1. In such a pictorial tale it seems odd that the figure of Death is not clearly defined, not fully personified. Why do you suppose this the case?
2. Are the motives of the coyote explained in the legend? What are his motives? Why is the coyote, instead of another animal, chosen to depict the bringer of Death?
3. What relationships between the Indians and animals are depicted in this tale?
4. Is the character of the Great Shaman clearly presented? How does he differ from god figures in other myths?

The Numbakulla and the First Aborigines

The myths of the central Australian Aranda tribe describing the creation of the first aborigines differ markedly from those of other Australian peoples.

The Aranda myth tells how, at one time in the dim and ghostly past, two great beings called the Numbakulla brothers, who lived in the western sky, saw a number of embryonic creatures, the Inapatua, whom it was the duty of those two creators to make into aboriginal men and women.

These Inapatua were crouched under low boulders on the shores of the salt lakes; the outlines of the different parts of their bodies could be vaguely seen in the rounded masses of which their forms consisted. They had no powers of sight or hearing, or even of movement.

Coming to earth with their stone knives, the Numbakulla took the incomplete bodies of the Inapatua, and began to make them into human beings. Using their knives, they first released the arms and legs of each body; then, by making four cuts at the end of the extremities, made the fingers and toes. The newly created people could now stand upright. With knives, the Numbakulla opened the eyes and the mouth of each one, and with their fingers formed the nose and the ears. The Inapatua then became fully developed men and women.

Gradually these newly formed people increased in numbers and spread over the land, gathering their food and obeying the complex laws of tribal behaviour that belong only to the men and women of the Aranda tribe.

Considerations

1. Why might the Aranda tribesmen attribute plurality to their creators, the Numbakulla brothers?
2. In what way could the sea location of the Aranda tribe have influenced their interpretation of the creation of mankind? In comparison to widely accepted theories of evolution, does this interpretation seem more or less sophisticated than Christianity's?

Reprinted from The Dreamtime: *Australian Aboriginal Myths,* Charles P. Mountford, Adelaide: Rigby Limited. Copyright 1965 Rigby Limited.

The Perverted Message

The Moon, it is said, once sent an insect to men, saying, "Go to men and tell them, 'As I die, and dying live; so you shall also die, and dying live.'"

The insect started with the message but while on his way was overtaken by the hare, who asked, "On what errand are you bound?" The insect answered, "I am sent by the Moon to men, to tell them that as she dies and dying lives, so shall they also die and dying live."

The hare said, "As you are an awkward runner, let me go." With these words he ran off, and when he reached men, he said, "I am sent by the Moon to tell you, 'As I die and dying perish, in the same manner you also shall die and come wholly to an end.'"

The hare then returned to the Moon and told her what he had said to men. The Moon reproached him angrily, saying, "Do you dare tell the people a thing which I have not said?"

With these words the Moon took up a piece of wood and struck the hare on the nose. Since that day the hare's nose has been slit, but men believe what Hare had told them.

Considerations

1. Why is the Moon a good spokesman for a theory of life in death?
2. What is the impact of the perverted version of the Moon's message?

African Folktales and Sculpture, ed. Paul Radin and James Johnson Sweeney. Bollingen Series XXXII. © 1952, 1964 by Bollingen Foundation. Folktale 13, "The Origin of Death," reprinted by permission of Princeton University Press, publisher of the Bollingen Series.

The Leftover Eye

Pay heed to this tale. This is a tale of things that have never happened. But we will suppose these things did happen for certainly there are such things possible.

This is a tale of a man who was blind. His mother, too, was blind. His wife and his wife's mother were also blind. They dwelt together in a wretched condition; their farm was poor and their house was badly built. They consulted together and decided to go away. They would journey until they came to some place where their lot would be better.

They set out and traveled along the road. As they walked, the man stumbled over something. He picked it up and felt it, and then knew he had come upon seven eyes. He immediately gave two eyes to his wife, and then took two for himself. Of the three eyes remaining to him, he gave one to his mother and another to his wife's mother. He was left with one eye in his hand. Kai, this was a startling thing. Here was his mother with her one eye looking at him hopefully. There was his wife's mother with her one eye looking at him hopefully. To whom should he give the leftover eye?

If he gives the eye to his mother he will forever be ashamed before his wife and her mother. If he gives it to his wife's mother, he will fear the angry and disappointed heart of his own mother. A mother, know you, is not something to be played with.

This is difficult indeed. Here is the sweetness of his wife. She is good and loving. How can he hurt her? Yet his mother, too, is a good mother and loving. Can he thus injure her? Which would be easier, and which would be the right way to do this thing?

If this thing would come to you, which would you choose?

Considerations

1. What are the ironies of this tale?
2. What might give impetus for such a tale to be written?
3. Is this a perfect dilemma? Is it solvable?
4. Are the eyes symbolic?

Reprinted by permission of Horizon Press, New York. From YES AND NO. THE INTIMATE FOLKLORE OF AFRICA © 1961.

Daniel, Bel, and the Snake

A Detective Story

When King Astyages was gathered to his fathers he was succeeded on the throne by Cyrus the Persian. Daniel was a confidant of the king, the most honoured of all the King's Friends.

Now the Babylonians had an idol called Bel, for which they provided every day twelve bushels of fine flour, forty sheep, and fifty gallons of wine. The king held it to be divine and went daily to worship it, but Daniel worshipped his God. So the king said to him, "Why do you not worship Bel?" He replied, "Because I do not believe in man-made idols, but in the living God who created heaven and earth and is sovereign over all mankind." The king said, "Do you think that Bel is not a living god? Do you not see how much he eats and drinks each day?" Daniel laughed and said, "Do not be deceived, your majesty; this Bel of yours is only clay inside and bronze outside, and has never eaten anything."

Then the king was angry, and summoned the priests of Bel and said to them, "If you cannot tell me who it is that eats up all these provisions, you shall die; but if you can show that it is Bel that eats them, then Daniel shall die for blasphemy against Bel."

Daniel said to the king, "Let it be as you command." (There were seventy priests of Bel, not counting their wives and children.) Then the king went with Daniel into the temple of Bel. The priests said, "We are now going outside; set out the food yourself, your majesty, and mix the wine; then shut the door and seal it with your signet. When you come back in the morning, if you do not find that Bel has eaten it all, let us be put to death; but if Daniel's charges against us turn out to be false, then he shall die." They treated the whole affair with contempt, because they had made a hidden entrance under the table, and they regularly went in by it and ate everything up.

So when the priests had gone, the king set out the food for Bel; and Daniel ordered his servants to bring ashes and sift them over the whole temple in the presence of the king alone. Then they left the temple, closed the door, sealed it with the king's signet, and went away. During the night the priests, with their wives and children, came as usual and ate and drank everything. Early in the morning the king came, and Daniel with him. The king said, "Are the

From *The New English Bible.* © The Delegates of the Oxford University Press and the Syndics of the Cambridge University Press 1961, 1970. Reprinted by permission.

seals intact, Daniel?" He answered, "They are intact, your majesty." As soon as he opened the door, the king looked at the table and cried aloud, "Great art thou, O Bel! In thee there is no deceit at all." But Daniel laughed and held back the king from going in. "Just look at the floor," he said, "and judge whose footprints these are." The king said, "I see the footprints of men, women, and children." In a rage he put the priests under arrest, with their wives and children. Then they showed him the secret doors through which they used to go in and consume what was on the table. So the king put them to death, and handed Bel over to Daniel, who destroyed the idol and its temple.

Considerations

1. What attributes in Daniel's character are particularly striking? Why is he a fit hero for this tale?
2. From this account of Daniel can you make inferences about the "living God" he worshipped? What is the relation of that God to mankind?

Northern Mythology

The stories which have engaged our attention thus far relate to the mythology of southern regions. But there is another branch of ancient superstitions which ought not to be entirely overlooked. It belongs to the nations from which some of us, through our English ancestors, derive our origin. It is that of the northern nations, called Scandinavians, who inhabited the countries now known as Sweden, Denmark, Norway, and Iceland. These mythological records are contained in two collections called the Eddas, of which the oldest is in poetry and dates back to the year 1056, the more modern or prose Edda being of the date of 1640.

According to the Eddas there was once no heaven above nor earth beneath, but only a bottomless deep, and a world of mist in which flowed a fountain. Twelve rivers issued from this fountain, and when they had flowed far from their source, they froze into ice, and one layer accumulating over another, the great deep was filled up.

Southward from the world of mist was the world of light. From this flowed a warm wind upon the ice and melted it. The vapours rose in the air and formed clouds, from which sprang Ymir, the Frost giant and his progeny, and the cow Audhumbla, whose milk afforded nourishment and food to the giant. The cow got nourishment by licking the hoar frost and salt from the ice. While she was one day licking the salt stones there appeared at first the hair of a man, on the second day the whole head, and on the third the entire form endowed with beauty, agility, and power. This new being was a god, from whom and his wife, a daughter of the giant race, sprang the three brothers Odin, Vili, and Ve. They slew the giant Ymir, and out of his body formed the earth, of his blood the seas, of his bones the mountains, of his hair the trees, of his skull the heavens, and of his brain clouds, charged with hail and snow. Of Ymir's eyebrows the gods formed Midgard (mid earth), destined to become the abode of man.

Odin then regulated the periods of day and night and the seasons by placing in the heavens the sun and moon, and appointing to them their respective courses. As soon as the sun began to shed its rays upon the earth, it caused the vegetable world to bud and sprout. Shortly after the gods had created the world they walked by the side of the sea, pleased with their new work, but found that it was still incomplete, for it was without human beings. They therefore took an ash tree and made a man out of it, and they made a woman out of an alder, and called the man Aske and the woman Embla. Odin then gave them life and soul, Vili reason and motion, and Ve bestowed upon them the senses, expressive features, and speech. Midgard was then given them as their residence, and they became the progenitors of the human race.

The mighty ash tree Ygdrasill was supposed to support the whole universe. It sprang from the body of Ymir, and had three immense roots, extending one into Asgard (the dwelling of the gods), the other into Jotunheim (the abode of the giants), and the third to Niffleheim (the regions of darkness and cold). By the side of each of these roots is a spring, from which it is watered. The root that extends into Asgard is carefully tended by the three Norns, goddesses, who are regarded as the dispensers of fate. They are Urdur (the past), Verdandi (the present), Skuld (the future). The spring at the Jotunheim side is Ymir's well, in which wisdom and wit lie hidden, but that of Niffleheim feeds the adder Nidhogge (darkness), which perpetually gnaws at the root. Four harts run across the branches of the tree and bite the buds; they represent the four winds. Under the tree lies Ymir, and when he tries to shake off its weight the earth quakes.

Asgard is the name of the abode of the gods, access to which is only gained by crossing the bridge Bifrost (the rainbow). Asgard consists of golden and silver palaces, the dwellings of the gods, but the most beautiful of these is Valhalla, the residence of Odin. When seated on his throne he overlooks all heaven and earth. Upon his shoulders are the ravens Hugin and Munin, who fly every day over the whole world, and on their return report to him all they have seen and heard. At his feet lie his two wolves, Geri and Freki, to whom Odin gives all the meat that is set before him, for he himself stands in no need of food. Mead is for him both

food and drink. He invented the Runic characters, and it is the business of the Norns to engrave the runes of fate upon a metal shield. From Odin's name, spelt Woden, as it sometimes is, came Wednesday, the name of the fourth day of the week.

Odin is frequently called Alfdaur (All-father), but this name is sometimes used in a way that shows that the Scandinavians had an idea of a deity superior to Odin, uncreated and eternal.

OF THE JOYS OF VALHALLA

Valhalla is the great hall of Odin, wherein he feasts with his chosen heroes, all those who have fallen bravely in battle, for all who die a peaceful death are excluded. The flesh of the boar Schrimnir is served up to them, and is abundant for all. For although this boar is cooked every morning, he becomes whole again every night. For drink the heroes are supplied abundantly with mead from the she-goat Heidrum. When the heroes are not feasting they amuse themselves with fighting. Every day they ride out into the court or field and fight until they cut each other in pieces. This is their pastime; but when meal time comes they recover from their wounds and return to feast in Valhalla.

THE VALKYRIOR

The Valkyrior are warlike virgins, mounted upon horses and armed with helmets and spears. Odin, who is desirous to collect a great many heroes in Valhalla, to be able to meet the giants in a day when the final contest must come, sends down to every battlefield to make choice of those who shall be slain. The Valkyrior are his messengers, and their name means "Choosers of the slain." When they ride forth on their errand, their armour sheds a strange flickering light, which flashes up over the northern skies, making what men call the "Aurora Borealis," or "Northern Lights."[1]

OF THOR AND THE OTHER GODS

Thor, the thunderer, Odin's eldest son, is the strongest of gods and men, and possesses three very precious things. The first is a hammer, which both the Frost and the Mountain giants know to their cost, when they see it hurled against them in the air, for it has split many a skull of their fathers and kindred. When thrown, it returns to his hand of its own accord. The second rare thing he possesses is called the belt of strength. When he girds it about him his divine might is doubled. The third, also very precious, is his iron gloves, which he puts on whenever he would use his mallet efficiently.

From Thor's name is derived our word Thursday.

Frey is one of the most celebrated of the gods. He presides over rain and sunshine and all the fruits of the earth. His sister Freya is the most propitious of the goddesses. She loves music, spring, and flowers, and is particularly fond of the Elves (fairies). She is very fond of love ditties, and all lovers would do well to invoke her.

Bragi is the god of poetry, and his song records the deeds of warriors. His wife, Iduna, keeps in a box the apples which the gods, when they feel old age approaching, have only to taste of to become young again.

Heimdall is the watchman of the gods, and is therefore placed on the borders of heaven to prevent the giants from forcing their way over the bridge Bifrost (the rainbow). He requires less sleep than a bird, and sees by night as well as by day a hundred miles around him. So acute is his ear that no sound escapes him, for he can even hear the grass grow and the wool on a sheep's back.

Considerations

1. In what ways is Odin similar to or different from creative gods of other mythologies?
2. In Valhalla the heroes cut each other into pieces but are made whole again at the end of the day; the boar Schrimnir is reborn each day. What are the implications of and possible reasons for these phenomena?
3. Does Norse mythology seem to cover all fields of man's activities? Why do you suppose there is a heavy emphasis on the warlike endeavors of man?

1. Gray's ode, "The Fatal Sisters," is founded on this superstition.

The Gods, the Creation, and the Earliest Heroes

EDITH HAMILTON

1 THE GODS

*Strange clouded fragments of an ancient
    glory,
Late lingerers of the company divine,
They breathe of that far world where from
    they come,
Lost halls of heaven and Olympian air.*

The Greeks did not believe that gods created the universe. It was the other way about: the universe created the gods. Before there were gods heaven and earth had been formed. They were the first parents. The Titans were their children, and the gods were their grandchildren.

THE TITANS AND THE TWELVE GREAT OLYMPIANS

The Titans, often called the Elder Gods, were for untold ages supreme in the universe. They were of enormous size and of incredible strength. There were many of them, but only a few appear in the stories of mythology. The most important was CRONUS, in Latin SATURN. He ruled over the other Titans until his son Zeus dethroned him and seized the power for himself. The Romans said that when Jupiter, their name for Zeus, ascended the throne, Saturn fled to Italy and brought in the Golden Age, a time of perfect peace and happiness, which lasted as long as he reigned.

The other notable Titans were OCEAN, the river that was supposed to encircle the earth; his wife TETHYS; HYPERION, the father of the sun, the moon and the dawn; MNEMOSYNE, which means Memory; THEMIS, usually translated by Justice; and LAPETUS, important because of his sons, ATLAS, who bore the world on his shoulders, and PROMETHEUS, who was the savior of mankind. These alone among the older gods were not banished with the coming of Zeus, but they took a lower place.

The twelve great Olympians were supreme among the gods who succeeded to the Titans. They were called the Olympians because Olympus was their home. What Olympus was, however, is not easy to say. There is no doubt that at first it was held to be a mountain top, and generally identified with Greece's highest mountain, Mt. Olympus in Thessaly, in the northeast of Greece. But even in the earliest Greek poem the *Iliad,* this idea is beginning to give way to the idea of an Olympus in some mysterious region far above all the mountains of the earth. In one passage of the *Iliad* Zeus talks to the gods from "the topmost peak of many-ridged

Olympus," clearly a mountain. But only a little further on he says that if he willed he could hang earth and sea from a pinnacle of Olympus, clearly no longer a mountain. Even so, it is not heaven. Homer makes Poseidon say that he rules the sea, Hades the dead, Zeus the heavens, but Olympus is common to all three.

Wherever it was, the entrance to it was a great gate of clouds kept by the Seasons. Within were the gods' dwellings, where they lived and slept and feasted on ambrosia and nectar and listened to Apollo's lyre. It was an abode of perfect blessedness. No wind, Homer says, ever shakes the untroubled peace of Olympus; no rain ever falls there or snow; but the cloudless firmament stretches around it on all sides and the white glory of sunshine is diffused upon its walls.

The twelve Olympians made up a divine family:—

(1) Zeus (Jupiter), the chief; his two brothers next, (2) Poseidon (Neptune), and (3) Hades, also called Pluto: (4) Hestia (Vesta), their sister; (5) Hera (Juno), Zeus's wife, and (6) Ares (Mars), their son; Zeus's children: (7) Athena (Minerva), (8) Apollo, (9) Aphrodite (Venus), (10) Hermes (Mercury), and (11) Artemis (Diana); and Hera's son (12) Hephaestus (Vulcan), sometimes said to be the son of Zeus too.

Zeus (Jupiter)

Zeus and his brothers drew lots for their share of the universe. The sea fell to Poseidon, and the underworld to Hades. Zeus became the supreme ruler. He was Lord of the Sky, the Rain-god and the Cloud-gatherer, who wielded the awful thunderbolt. His power was greater than that of all the other divinities together. In the *Iliad* he tells his family, "I am mightiest of all. Make trial that you may know. Fasten a rope of gold to heaven and lay hold, every god and goddess. You could not drag down Zeus. But if I wished to drag you down, then I would. The rope I would bind to a pinnacle of Olympus and all would hang in air, yes, the very earth and the sea too."

Nevertheless he was not omnipotent or omniscient, either. He could be opposed and deceived. Poseidon dupes him in the *Iliad* and so does Hera. Sometimes, too, the mysterious power, Fate, is spoken of as stronger than he. Homer makes Hera ask him scornfully if he proposes to deliver from death a man Fate has doomed.

He is represented as falling in love with one woman after another and descending to all manner of tricks to hide his infidelity from his wife. The explanation why such actions were ascribed to the most majestic of the gods is, the scholars say, that the Zeus of song and story has been made by combining many gods. When his worship spread to a town where there was already a divine ruler the two were slowly fused into one. The wife of the early god was then transferred to Zeus. The result, however, was unfortunate and the later Greeks did not like these endless love affairs.

Still, even in the earliest records Zeus had grandeur. In the *Iliad* Agamemnon prays: "Zeus, most glorious, most great, God of the storm-cloud, thou that dwellest in the heavens." He demanded, too, not only sacrifices from men, but right action. The Greek Army at Troy is told "Father Zeus never helps liars or those who break their oaths." The two ideas of him, the low and the high, persisted side by side for a long time.

His breastplate was the aegis, awful to behold; his bird was the eagle, his tree the oak. His oracle was Dodona in the land of oak trees. The god's will was revealed by the rustling of the oak leaves which the priests interpreted.

HERA (JUNO)

She was Zeus's wife and sister. The Titans Ocean and Tethys brought her up. She was the protector of marriage, and married women were her peculiar care. There is very little that is attractive in the portrait the poets draw of her. She is called, indeed, in an early poem,

Golden-throned Hera, among immortals
  the queen.
Chief among them in beauty, the glorious
  lady
All the blessed in high Olympus revere,
Honor even as Zeus, the lord of the thunder.

But when any account of her gets down to details, it shows her chiefly engaged in punishing the many women Zeus fell in love with, even when they yielded only because he coerced or tricked them. It made no difference to Hera how reluctant any of them were or how innocent; the goddess treated them all alike. Her implacable anger followed them and their children too. She never forgot an injury. The Trojan War would have ended in an honorable peace, leaving both sides unconquered, if it had not been for her hatred of a Trojan who had judged another goddess lovelier than she. The wrong of her slighted beauty remained with her until Troy fell in ruins.

In one important story, the Quest of the Golden Fleece, she is the gracious protector of heroes and the inspirer of heroic deeds, but not in any other. Nevertheless she was venerated in every home. She was the goddess married women turned to for help. Ilithyia (or Eileithyia), who helped women in childbirth, was her daughter.

The cow and the peacock were sacred to her. Argos was her favorite city.

POSEIDON (NEPTUNE)

He was the ruler of the sea, Zeus's brother and second only to him in eminence. The Greeks on both sides of the Aegean were seamen and the God of the Sea was all-important to them. His wife was Amphitrite, a granddaughter of the Titan, Ocean. Poseidon had a splendid palace beneath the sea, but he was oftener to be found in Olympus.

Besides being Lord of the Sea he gave the first horse to man, and he was honored as much for the one as for the other.

Lord Poseidon, from you this pride is ours,
The strong horses, the young horses, and
  also the rule of the deep.

Storm and calm were under his control:—

*He commanded and the storm wind rose
And the surges of the sea.*

But when he drove in his golden car over the waters, the thunder of the waves sank into stillness, and tranquil peace followed his smooth-rolling wheels.

He was commonly called "Earthshaker" and was always shown carrying his trident, a three-pronged spear, with which he would shake and shatter whatever he pleased.

He had some connection with bulls as well as with horses, but the bull was connected with many other gods too.

HADES (PLUTO)

He was the third brother among the Olympians, who drew for his share the underworld and the rule over the dead. He was also called Pluto, the God of Wealth, of the precious metals hidden in the earth. The Romans as well as the Greeks called him by this name, but often they translated it into *Dis,* the Latin word for rich. He had a far-famed cap or helmet which made whoever wore it invisible. It was rare that he left his dark realm to visit Olympus or the earth, nor was he urged to do so. He was not a welcome visitor. He was unpitying, inexorable, but just; a terrible, not an evil god.

His wife was Persephone (Proserpine) whom he carried away from the earth and made Queen of the Lower World.

He was King of the Dead—not Death himself, whom the Greeks called Thanatos and the Romans, Orcus.

PALLAS ATHENA (MINERVA)

She was the daughter of Zeus alone. No mother bore her. Full-grown and in full armor, she sprang from his head. In the earliest account of her, the *Iliad,* she is a fierce and ruthless battle-goddess, but elsewhere she is warlike only to defend the State and the home from outside enemies. She was pre-eminently the Goddess of the City, the protector of civilized life, of handicrafts and agriculture; the inventor of the bridle, who first tamed horses for men to use.

She was Zeus's favorite child. He trusted her to carry the awful aegis, his buckler, and his devastating weapon, the thunderbolt.

The word oftenest used to describe her is "gray-eyed," or, as it is sometimes translated, "flashing-eyed." Of the three virgin goddesses she was the chief and was called the Maiden, Parthenos, and her temple the Parthenon. In later poetry she is the embodiment of wisdom, reason, purity.

Athens was her special city; the olive created by her was her tree; the owl her bird.

PHOEBUS APOLLO

The son of Zeus and Leto (Latona), born in the little island of Delos. He has been called "the most Greek of all the gods." He is a beautiful figure in Greek poetry, the master musician who delights Olympus as he plays on his golden lyre; the lord too of the silver bow, the Archer-god, far-shooting; the Healer, as well, who first taught men the healing art. Even more than of these good and lovely endowments, he is the God of Light, in whom is no darkness at all, and so he is the God of Truth. No false word ever falls from his lips.

O Phoebus, from your throne of truth,
From your dwelling-place at the heart of
the world,
You speak to men.
By Zeus's decree no lie comes there.
No shadow to darken the word of truth.
Zeus sealed by an everlasting right
Apollo's honour, that all may trust
With unshaken faith when he speaks.

Delphi under towering Parnassus, where Apollo's oracle was, plays an important part in mythology. Castalia was its sacred spring; Cephissus its river. It was held to be the center of the world, so many pilgrims came to

it, from foreign countries as well as Greece. No other shrine rivaled it. The answers to the questions asked by the anxious seekers for Truth were delivered by a priestess who went into a trance before she spoke. The trance was supposed to be caused by a vapor rising from a deep cleft in the rock over which her seat was placed, a three-legged stool, the tripod.

Apollo was called Delian from Delos, the island of his birth, and Pythian from his killing of a serpent, Python, which once lived in the caves of Parnassus. It was a frightful monster and the contest was severe, but in the end the god's unerring arrows won the victory. Another name often given him was "the Lycian," variously explained as meaning Wolf-god, God of Light, and God of Lycia. In the *Iliad* he is called "the Sminthian," the Mouse-god, but whether because he protected mice or destroyed them no one knows. Often he was the Sun-god too. His name Phoebus means "brilliant" or "shining." Accurately, however, the Sun-god was Helios, child of the Titan Hyperion.

Apollo at Delphi was a purely beneficent power, a direct link between gods and men, guiding men to know the divine will, showing them how to make peace with the gods; the purifier, too, able to cleanse even those stained with the blood of their kindred. Nevertheless, there are a few tales told of him which show him pitiless and cruel. Two ideas were fighting in him as in all the gods: a primitive, crude idea and one that was beautiful and poetic. In him only a little of the primitive is left.

The laurel was his tree. Many creatures were sacred to him, chief among them the dolphin and the crow.

ARTEMIS (DIANA)

Also called Cynthis, from her birthplace, Mount Cynthus in Delos.

Apollo's twin sister, daughter of Zeus and Leto. She was one of the three maiden goddesses of Olympus:—

Golden Aphrodite who stirs with love all creation,
Cannot bend nor ensnare three hearts: the pure maiden Vesta,
Gray-eyed Athena who cares but for war and the arts of the craftsmen,
Artemis, lover of woods and the wild chase over the mountain.

She was the Lady of Wild Things, Huntsman-in-chief to the gods, an odd office for a woman. Like a good hunstman, she was careful to preserve the young; she was "the protectress of dewy youth" everywhere. Nevertheless, with one of those startling contradictions so common in mythology, she kept the Greek Fleet from sailing to Troy until they sacrificed a maiden to her. In many another story, too, she is fierce and revengeful. On the other hand, when women died a swift and painless death, they were held to have been slain by her silver arrows.

As Phoebus was the Sun, she was the Moon, called Phoebe and Selene (Luna in Latin). Neither name originally belonged to her. Phoebe was a Titan, one of the older gods. So too was Selene—a moon-goddess, indeed, but not connected with Apollo. She was the sister of Helios, the sun-god with whom Apollo was confused.

In the later poets, Artemis is identified with Hecate. She is "the goddess with three forms," Selene in the sky, Artemis on earth, Hecate in the lower world and in the world above when it is wrapped in darkness. Hecate was the Goddess of the Dark of the Moon, the black nights when the moon is hidden. She was associated with deeds of darkness, the Goddess of the Crossways, which were held to be ghostly places of evil magic. An awful divinity,

> *Hecate of hell,*
> *Mighty to shatter every stubborn thing.*
> *Hark! Hark! her hounds are baying through the town.*
> *Where three roads meet, there she is standing.*

It is a strange transformation from the lovely Huntress flashing through the forest, from the Moon making all beautiful with her light, from the pure Maiden-Goddess for whom

Whoso is chaste of spirit utterly
May gather leaves and fruits and flowers.
The unchaste never.

In her is shown most vividly the uncertainty between good and evil which is apparent in every one of the divinities.

The cypress was sacred to her; and all wild animals, but especially the deer.

APHRODITE (VENUS)

The Goddess of Love and Beauty, who beguiled all, gods and men alike; the laughter-loving goddess, who laughed sweetly or mockingly at those her wiles had conquered; the irresistible goddess who stole away even the wits of the wise.

She is the daughter of Zeus and Dione in the *Iliad,* but in the later poems she is said to have sprung from the foam of the sea, and her name was explained as meaning "the foam-risen." *Aphros* is foam in Greek. This sea-birth took place near Cythera, from where she was wafted to Cyprus. Both islands were ever after sacred to her, and she was called Cytherea or the Cyprian as often as by her proper name.

One of the Homeric Hymns, calling her "Beautiful, golden goddess," says of her:—

The breath of the west wind bore her
Over the sounding sea,
Up from the delicate foam,
To wave-ringed Cyprus, her isle.
And the Hours golden-wreathed
Welcomed her joyously.
They clad her in raiment immortal,
And brought her to the gods.
Wonder seized them all as they saw
Violet-crowned Cytherea.

The Romans wrote of her in the same way. With her, beauty comes. The winds flee before her and the storm clouds; sweet flowers embroider the earth; the waves of the sea laugh; she moves in radiant light. Without her there is no joy nor loveliness anywhere. This is the picture the poets like best to paint of her.

But she had another side too. It was natural that she should cut a poor figure in the *Iliad,* where the battle of heroes is the theme. She is a soft, weak creature there, whom a mortal need not fear to attack. In later poems she is usually shown as treacherous and malicious, exerting a deadly and destructive power over men.

In most of the stories she is the wife of Hephaestus (Vulcan), the lame and ugly god of the forge.

The myrtle was her tree; the dove her bird—sometimes, too, the sparrow and the swan.

HERMES (MERCURY)

Zeus was his father and Maia, daughter of Atlas, his mother. Because of a very popular statue his appearance is more familiar to us than that of any other god. He was graceful and swift of motion. On his feet were winged sandals; wings were on his low-crowned hat, too, and on his magic wand, the Caduceus. He was Zeus's Messenger, who "flies as fleet as thought to do his bidding."

Of all the gods he was the shrewdest and most cunning; in fact he was the Master Thief, who started upon his career before he was a day old.

The babe was born at the break of day,
And ere the night fell he had stolen away
Apollo's herds.

Zeus made him give them back, and he won Apollo's forgiveness by presenting him with the lyre which he had just invented, making it out of a tortoise's shell. Perhaps there was some connection between that very early story of him and the fact that he was God of Commerce and the Market, protector of traders.

In odd contrast to this idea of him, he was also the solemn guide of the dead, the Divine Herald who led the souls down to their last home.

He appears oftener in the tales of mythology than any other god.

ARES (MARS)

The God of War, son of Zeus and Hera, both of whom, Homer says, detested him. Indeed, he is hateful throughout the *Iliad,* poem of war though it is. Occasionally the heroes "rejoice in the delight of Ares' battle," but far oftener in having escaped "the fury of the ruthless god." Homer calls him murderous, bloodstained, the incarnate curse of mortals; and, strangely, a coward, too, who bellows with pain and runs away when he is wounded. Yet he has a train of attendants on the battlefield which should inspire anyone with confidence. His sister is there, Eris, which means Discord, and Strife, her son. The Goddess of War, Enyo,—in Latin Bellona,—walks beside him, and with her are Terror and Trembling and Panic. As they move, the voice of groaning arises behind them and the earth streams with blood.

The Romans liked Mars better than the Greeks liked Ares. He never was to them the mean whining deity of the *Iliad,* but magnificent in shining armor, redoubtable, invincible. The warriors of the great Latin heroic poem, the *Aeneid,* far from rejoicing to escape from him, rejoice when they see that they are to fall "on Mars' field of renown." They "rush on glorious death" and find it "sweet to die in battle."

Ares figures little in mythology. In one story he is the lover of Aphrodite and held up to the contempt of the Olympians by Aphrodite's husband, Hephaestus: but for the most part he is little more than a symbol of war. He is not a distinct personality, like Hermes or Hera or Apollo.

He had no cities where he was worshiped. The Greeks said vaguely that he came from Thrace, home of a rude, fierce people in the northeast of Greece.

Appropriately, his bird was the vulture. The dog was wronged by being chosen as his animal.

HEPHAESTUS
(VULCAN AND MULCIBER)

The God of Fire, sometimes said to be the son of Zeus and Hera, sometimes of Hera alone, who bore him in retaliation for Zeus's having brought forth Athena. Among the perfectly beautiful immortals he only was ugly. He was lame as well. In one place in the *Iliad* he says that his shameless mother, when she saw that he was born deformed, cast him out of heaven; in another place he declares that Zeus did this, angry with him for trying to defend Hera. This second story is the better known, because of Milton's familiar lines: Mulciber was

> *Thrown by angry Jove*
> *Sheer o'er the crystal battlements: from morn*
> *To noon he fell, from noon to dewy eve,*
> *A summer's day, and with the setting sun*
> *Dropt from the zenith like a falling star,*
> *On Lemnos, the Aegean isle.*

These events, however, were supposed to have taken place in the far-distant past. In Homer he is in no danger of being driven from Olym-

popular on earth as in heaven. With Athena, he was important in the life of the city. The two were the patrons of handicrafts, the arts which along with agriculture are the support of civilization; he the protector of the smiths as she of the weavers. When children were formally admitted to the city organization, the god of the ceremony was Hephaestus.

Hestia (Vesta)

She was Zeus's sister, and like Athena and Artemis a virgin goddess. She has no distinct personality and she plays no part in the myths. She was the Goddess of the Hearth, the symbol of the home, around which the newborn child must be carried before it could be received into the family. Every meal began and ended with an offering to her.

Hestia, in all dwellings of men and immortals
Yours is the highest honor, the sweet wine offered
First and last at the feast, poured out to you duly.
Never without you can gods or mortals hold banquet.

pus; he is highly honored there, the workman of the immortals, their armorer and smith, who makes their dwellings and their furnishings as well as their weapons. In his workshop he has handmaidens he has forged out of gold who can move and who help him in his work.

In the later poets his forge is often said to be under this or that volcano, and to cause eruptions.

His wife is one of the three Graces in the *Iliad,* called Aglaia in Hesiod; in the *Odyssey* she is Aphrodite.

He was a kindly, peace-loving god,

Each city too had a public hearth sacred to Hestia, where the fire was never allowed to go out. If a colony was to be founded, the colonists carried with them coals from the hearth of the mother-city with which to kindle the fire on the new city's hearth.

In Rome her fire was cared for by six virgin priestesses, called Vestals.

King Midas and the Golden Touch

BULFINCH

Bacchus, on a certain occasion, found his old schoolmaster and foster-father, Silenus, missing. The old man had been drinking, and in that state wandered away, and was found by some peasants, who carried him to their king, Midas. Midas recognized him, and treated him hospitably, entertaining him for ten days and nights with an unceasing round of jollity. On the eleventh day he brought Silenus back, and restored him in safety to his pupil. Whereupon Bacchus offered Midas his choice of a reward, whatever he might wish. He asked that whatever he might touch should be changed into *gold.* Bacchus consented, though sorry that he had not made a better choice. Midas went his way, rejoicing in his new-acquired power, which he hastened to put to the test. He could scarce believe his eyes when he found a twig of an oak, which he plucked from the branch, become gold in his hand. He took up a stone; it changed to gold. He touched a sod; it did the same. He took an apple from the tree; you would have thought he had robbed the garden of the Hesperides. His joy knew no bounds, and as soon as he got home, he ordered the servants to set a splendid repast on the table. Then he found to his dismay that whether he touched bread, it hardened in his hand; or put a morsel to his lip, it defied his teeth. He took a glass of wine, but it flowed down his throat like melted gold.

In consternation at the unprecedented affliction, he strove to divest himself of his power; he hated the gift he had lately coveted. But all in vain; starvation seemed to await him. He raised his arms, all shining with gold, in prayer to Bacchus, begging to be delivered from his glittering destruction. Bacchus, merciful deity, heard and consented. "Go," said he, "to the River Pactolus, trace the stream to its fountain-head, there plunge your head and body in, and wash away your fault and its punishment." He did so, and scarce had he touched the waters before the gold-creating power passed into them, and the river sands became changed into *gold,* as they remain to this day.

One-Way Traffic

Why Some Men Are Loutish Brutes

AESOP

ONE-WAY TRAFFIC

An old lion, who was too weak to hunt or fight for his food, decided that he must get it by his wits. He lay down in a cave, pretending to be ill, and whenever any animals came to visit him, he seized them and ate them. When many had perished in this way, a fox who had seen through the trick came and stood at a distance from the cave, and inquired how he was. "Bad," the lion answered, and asked why he did not come in. "I would have come in," said the fox, "but I saw a lot of tracks going in and none coming out."

A wise man recognizes danger signals in time to avoid injury.

WHY SOME MEN ARE LOUTISH BRUTES

On the orders of Zeus, Prometheus fashioned men and beasts. Seeing that the beasts were much more numerous, Zeus commanded him to unmake some of them and turn them into men, and he did as he was told. But those who had not originally been fashioned as men, even though they now had a human form, still had the minds of beasts.

Considerations

1. What elements of style are common to the two fables? Why are they appropriate?
2. What are the advantages of using imaginary people or animals instead of realistic characters in fables?
3. Is the fable an appropriate medium for moralizing? Is that its primary purpose?

From FABLES OF AESOP trans. by S. A. Handford (1954), pp. 163, 13. Copyright © 1954 by S. A. Handford. Reprinted by permission of Penguin Books Ltd.

Sunrise in His Pocket

DAVY CROCKETT

One January morning it was so all-screwen-up cold that the forest trees war so stiff that they couldn't shake, and the very day-break froze fast as it war tryin' to dawn. The tinder-box in my cabin would no more ketch fire than a sunk raft at the bottom o' the sea. Seein' that daylight war so far behind time, I thought creation war in a fair way for freezin' fast.

"So," thinks I, "I must strike a leetle fire from my fingers, light my pipe, travel out a few leagues, and see about it."

Then I brought my knuckles together like two thunder clouds, but the sparks froze up afore I could begin to collect 'em—so out I walked, and endeavored to keep myself unfriz by goin' at a hop, step and jump gait, and whistlin' the tune of "fire in the mountains!" as I went along in three double quick time. Well, arter I had walked about twenty-five miles up the peak o' Daybreak Hill, I soon discovered what war the matter. The airth had actually friz fast in her axis, and couldn't turn round; the sun had got jammed between two cakes o' ice under the wheels, an' thar he had bin shinin' and workin' to get loose, till he friz fast in his cold sweat.

"C-r-e-a-t-i-o-n!" thought I, "this are the toughest sort o' suspension, and it mustn't be endured—somethin' must be done, or human creation is done for."

It war then so antedeluvian and premature cold that my upper and lower teeth an' tongue war all collapsed together as tight as a friz oyster. I took a fresh twenty pound bear off o' my back that I'd picked up on the road, an' beat the animal agin the ice till the hot ile began to walk out on him at all sides. I then took an' held him over the airth's axes, an' squeezed him till I thaw'd 'em loose, poured about a ton on it over the sun's face, give the airth's cog-wheel one kick backward, till I got the sun loose—whistled "Push along, keep movin'!" an' in about fifteen seconds the airth gin a grunt, and begun movin'—the sun walked up beautiful, salutin' me with sich a wind o' gratitude that it made me sneeze. I lit my pipe by the blaze o' his top-knot, shouldered my bear, an' walked home, introducin' the people to fresh daylight with a piece of sunrise in my pocket, with which I cooked my bear steaks, an' enjoyed one o' the best breakfasts I had tasted for some time. If I didn't, jist wake some mornin' and go with me to the office o' sunrise!

"Sunrise in His Pocket" by Davy Crockett in FOLKLORE IN AMERICAN LITERATURE edited by John T. Flanagan and Arthur Palmer Hudson (Harper & Row, 1958)

They Have Yarns

FROM *The People Yes*

CARL SANDBURG

They have yarns
Of a skyscraper so tall they had to put
hinges
On the two top stories so to let the
moon go by,
Of one corn crop in Missouri when
the roots
Went so deep and drew off so much
water
The Mississippi riverbed that year
was dry,
Of pancakes so thin they only had
one side,
Of "a fog so thick we shingled the
barn and six feet out on the fog,"
Of Pecos Pete straddling a cyclone in
Texas and riding it to the west coast
where "it rained out under him,"
Of the man who drove a swarm of
bees across the Rocky Mountains
and the Desert "and didn't lose a
bee,"   10

Of a mountain railroad curve where
the engineer in his cab can touch
the caboose and spit in the conductor's eye,
Of the boy who climbed a cornstalk
growing so fast he would have
starved to death if they hadn't shot
biscuits up to him,
Of the old man's whiskers: "When
the wind was with him his whiskers arrived a day before he did,"
Of the hen laying a square egg and
cackling "Ouch!" and of hens laying eggs with the dates printed on
them,
Of the ship captain's shadow: it froze
to the deck one cold winter night,
Of mutineers on that same ship put to
chipping rust with rubber hammers,
Of the sheep counter who was fast
and accurate: "I just count their

---

2 **skyscraper so tall.** The structure so tall that hinges are needed to protect the sun and the moon turns up frequently in American folklore. Captain Stormalong, hero of New England tall tales, built a mast with such an arrangement, according to Charles Edward Brown's *Old Stormalong Yarns.* Paul Bunyan built an oil rig with a similar arrangement, according to John Lee Brooks' "Paul Bunyan, Oil Man" in *Follow de Drinkin' Gourd* 9 **Pecos Pete,** or Pecos Bill (the name usually given him in Texas windies), thus busted a cyclone. See Edward O'Reilly, "The Saga of Pecos Bill," *Century,* October 1923 10 **swarm of bees.** The boast about herding the swarm of bees occurs in the play *Lightnin'* (1918) by Winchell Smith and Frank Bacon 12 **the boy . . . cornstalk.** This story is told of Paul Bunyan's handyman, Swede Charlie, in Ida Turney's "The Scissorbills" in *Paul Bunyan Marches on* 15 **ship captain's shadow.** In Mark Twain's *Following the Equator,* Ch. XXVI, the ship's mate had this difficulty on an arctic voyage

feet and divide by four,"
Of the man so tall he must climb a
ladder to shave himself,
Of the runt so teeny-weeny it takes
two men and a boy to see him,
Of mosquitoes: one can kill a dog,
two of them a man,   20
Of a cyclone that sucked cookstoves
out of the kitchen, up the chimney
flue, and on to the next town,
Of the same cyclone picking up
wagon-tracks in Nebraska and
dropping them over in the Dako-
tas,
Of the hook-and-eye snake unlock-
ing itself into forty pieces, each
piece two inches long, then in nine
seconds flat snapping itself together again,
Of the watch swallowed by the
cow—when they butchered her a
year later the watch was running
and had the correct time,
Of horned snakes, hoop snakes that
roll themselves where they want to
go, and rattlesnakes carrying bells
instead of rattles on their tails,
Of the herd of cattle in California
getting lost in a giant redwood tree
that had hollowed out,
Of the man who killed a snake by

putting its tail in its mouth so it
swallowed itself,
Of railroad trains whizzing along so
fast they reach the station before
the whistle,
Of pigs so thin the farmer had to tie
knots in their tails to keep them
from crawling through the cracks
in their pens,
Of Paul Bunyan's big blue ox, Babe,
measuring between the eyes forty-
two axhandles and a plug of Star
tobacco exactly,   30
Of John Henry's hammer and the
curve of its swing and his singing of
it as "a rainbow round my
shoulder."
   "Do tell!"
   "I want to know!"
   "You don't say so!"
   "For the land's sake!"
   "Gosh all fish-hooks!"
   "Tell me some more.
   I don't believe a word you say
   but I love to listen
   to your sweet harmonica   40
   to your chin-music.
   Your fish stories hang to-
      gether
   when they're just a pack of
      lies:

---

20 **mosquitoes.** Sandburg may be recalling the mosquitoes described by a steamboat mate, Mr. H., in Ch. XXXIV of Mark Twain's *Life on the Mississippi.* If so he errs in his statistics. Says Twain of Mr. H.: "He said that two of them could whip a dog, and that four of them could hold a man down. . . 'butcher' him." Mr. Sandburg appears to be exaggerating somewhat   25 **horned snakes.** Sandburg may have confused these with "horn-snakes," which are described in H. E. Taliaferro's *Fisher River Scenes and Characters.* This snake, as described by Uncle Davy, an eyewitness, was ten feet long, had a head as big as a saucer, and had a stinger in his tail which was "six inches long and sharp as a needle." "This snake," said Uncle Davy, "he cotched the eend uv his tail in his mouth, he did, and come rollin' down the mounting . . . jist like a hoop." The snake landed, by chance, so that his stinger caught in a tree, and soon the tree was "dead as a herrin'; all the leaves was wilted like a fire had gone through its branches." This happened in North Carolina   30 **blue ox,** Babe, a wonderful animal, very helpful in logging operations. Babe could pull great sleds of logs, could pile lumber with his tail, and make himself useful in many other ways   31 **John Henry,** folk hero of the Negroes, was a great steel-driver who died in a contest with a steel-driving machine. See "John Henry of the Cape Fear" in *Bundles of Troubles and Other Tarheel Tales*

you ought to have a leather
  medal:
you ought to have a statue
  carved of butter: you deserve
  a large bouquet of turnips."

"Yessir," the traveler drawled,
"Away out there in the petrified
  forest
everything goes on the same as usual.   50
The petrified birds sit in their petrified nests
and hatch their petrified young from
  petrified eggs."

A high pressure salesman jumped off
  the Brooklyn Bridge and was saved
  by a policeman. But it didn't take
  him long to sell the idea to the
  policeman. So together they
  jumped off the bridge.

One of the oil men in heaven started
  a rumor of a gusher down in hell.
  All the other oil men left in a hurry
  for hell. As he gets to thinking
  about the rumor he had started he
  says to himself there might be
  something in it after all. So he
  leaves for hell in a hurry.

"The number 42 will win this raffle,
  that's my number" And when he
  won they asked him whether he
  guessed the number or had a system. He said he had a system, "I
  took up the old family album and
  there on page 7 was my grandfather and grandmother both on
  page 7. I said to myself this is easy
  for 7 times 7 is the number that will

win and 7 times 7 is 42."

Once a shipwrecked sailor caught
  hold of a stateroom door and
  floated for hours till friendly hands
  from out of the darkness threw him
  a rope. And he called across the
  night, "What country is this?" and
  hearing voices answer, "New Jersey," he took a fresh hold of the
  floating stateroom door and called
  back half-wearily, "I guess I'll float
  a little farther."

An Ohio man bundled up the tin roof
  of a summer kitchen and sent it to a
  motorcar maker with a complaint
  of his car not giving service. In
  three weeks a new car arrived for
  him and a letter: "We regret delay
  in shipment but your car was received in a very bad order."
A Dakota cousin of this Ohio man
  sent six years of tin can accumula-
  tions to the same works, asking
  them to overhaul his car. Two
  weeks later came a rebuilt car, five
  old tin cans, and a letter: "We are
  also forwarding you five parts not
  necessary in our new model."
Thus fantasies heard at filling stations in the midwest. Another relates to a Missouri mule who took
  aim with his heels at an automobile
  rattling by. The car turned a somer-
  sault, lit next a fence, ran right
  along through a cornfield till it
  came to a gate, moved onto the
  road and went on its way as though
  nothing had happened. The mule
  heehawed with desolation, "What's
  the use?"

---

49 **the petrified forest,** a forest in Yellowstone Park apparently discovered by the guide Jim
Bridger. See biographies by J. C. Alter (1925; rev. ed., 1962) and Stanley Vestal (1946). One of the
most remarkable facts about this forest was that there the law of gravity was petrified

Another tells of a farmer and his family stalled on a railroad crossing, how they jumped out in time to see a limited express knock it into flinders, the farmer calling, "Well, I always did say that car was no shucks in a real pinch."   60

When the Masonic Temple in Chicago was the tallest building in the United States west of New York, two men who would cheat the eyes out of you if you gave 'em a chance, took an Iowa farmer to the top of the building and asked him, "How is this for high?" They told him that for $25 they would go down in the basement and turn the building around on its turntable for him while he stood on the roof and saw how this seventh wonder of the world worked. He handed them $25. They went. He waited. They never came back.

This is told in Chicago as a folk tale, the same as the legend of Mrs. O'Leary's cow kicking over the barn lamp that started the Chicago fire, when the Georgia visitor, Robert Toombs, telegraphed an Atlanta crony, "Chicago is on fire, the whole city burning down, God be praised!"

Nor is the prize sleeper Rip Van Winkle and his scolding wife forgotten, nor the headless horseman scooting through Sleepy Hollow

Nor the sunken treasure-ships in coves and harbors, the hideouts of gold and silver sought by Coronado, nor the Flying Dutchman rounding the Cape doomed to nevermore pound his ear nor ever again take a snooze for himself

Nor the sailor's caretaker Mother Carey seeing to it that every seafaring man in the afterworld has a seabird to bring him news of ships and women, an albatross for the admiral, a gull for the deckhand

Nor the sailor with a sweetheart in every port of the world, nor the ships that set out with flying colors and all the promises you could ask, the ships never heard of again,

Nor Jim Liverpool, the riverman who could jump across any river and back without touching land he was that quick on his feet,

Nor Mike Fink along the Ohio and the Mississippi, half wild horse and half cock-eyed alligator, the rest of him snags and snapping turtle. "I can out-run, out-jump, out-shoot, out-brag, out-drink, and out-fight, rough and tumble, no holds barred, any man on both sides of the river from Pittsburgh to New Orleans and back again to St. Louis. My trigger finger itches and I want to go redhot. War, famine and bloodshed puts flesh on my bones, and hardship's my daily bread."

Nor the man so lean he threw no shadow: six rattlesnakes struck at him at one time and every one missed him.

A Fable

Samuel Clemens

Once upon a time an artist who had painted a small and very beautiful picture placed it so that he could see it in the mirror. He said, "This doubles the distance and softens it, and it is twice as lovely as it was before."

The animals out in the woods heard of this through the housecat, who was greatly admired by them because he was so learned, and so refined and civilized, and so polite and high-bred, and could tell them so much which they didn't know before, and were not certain about afterward. They were much excited about this new piece of gossip, and they asked questions, so as to get at a full understanding of it. They asked what a picture was, and the cat explained.

"It is a flat thing," he said; "wonderfully flat, marvelously flat, enchantingly flat and elegant. And, oh, so beautiful!"

That excited them almost to a frenzy, and they said they would give the world to see it. Then the bear asked:

"What is it that makes it so beautiful?"

"It is the looks of it," said the cat.

This filled them with admiration and uncertainty, and they were more excited than ever. Then the cow asked:

"What is a mirror?"

"It is a hole in the wall," said the cat. "You look in it, and there you see the picture, and it is so dainty and charming and ethereal and inspiring in its unimaginable beauty that your head turns round and round, and you almost swoon with ecstasy."

The ass had not said anything as yet; he now began to throw doubts. He said there had never been anything as beautiful as this before, and probably wasn't now. He said that when it took a whole basketful of sesquipedalian adjectives to whoop up a thing of beauty, it was time for suspicion.

It was easy to see that these doubts were having an effect upon the animals, so the cat went off offended. The subject was dropped for a couple of days, but in the meantime curiosity was taking a fresh start, and there was a revival of interest perceptible. Then the animals assailed the ass for spoiling what could possibly have been a pleasure to them, on a mere suspicion that the picture was not beautiful, without any evidence that such was the case. The ass was not troubled; he was calm, and said there was one way to find out who was in the right, himself or the cat: he would go and look in that hole, and come back and tell what he found there. The animals felt relieved and grateful, and asked him to go at once—which he did.

But he did not know where he ought to stand; and, so, through error, he stood between the picture and the mirror. The result was that the picture had no chance, and didn't show up. He returned home and said:

"The cat lied. There was nothing in that hole but an ass. There wasn't a sign of a flat thing visible. It was a handsome ass, and friendly, but just an ass, and nothing more."

The elephant asked:

"Did you see it good and clear? Were you close to it?"

"I saw it good and clear, O Hathi, King of Beasts. I was so close that I touched noses with it."

"This is very strange," said the elephant; "the cat was always truthful before—as far as we could make out. Let another witness try. Go, Baloo, look in the hole, and come and report."

So the bear went. When he came back, he said:

"Both the cat and the ass have lied; there was nothing in the hole but a bear."

Great was the surprise and puzzlement of the animals. Each was now anxious to make the test himself and get at the straight truth. The elephant sent them one at a time.

First, the cow. She found nothing in the hole but a cow.

The tiger found nothing in it but a tiger.

The lion found nothing in it but a lion.

The leopard found nothing in it but a leopard.

The camel found a camel, and nothing more.

The Hathi was wroth, and said he would have the truth, if he had to go and fetch it himself. When he returned, he abused his whole subjectry for liars, and was in an unappeasable fury with the moral and mental blindness of the cat. He said anybody but a near-sighted fool could see that there was nothing in the hole but an elephant.

MORAL, BY THE CAT

You can find in a text whatever you bring, if you will stand between it and the mirror of your imagination. You may not see your ears, but they will be there.

1909

This Is the Way I Was Raised Up

MRS. MARVIN WATTS

The following article was given to us by its author, Mrs. Watts, during a recent visit to her home. It was painstakingly written out in pencil on notebook paper that had been folded and refolded many times. It is presented here exactly as it was given to us.—Editor

my dadie raised the stuff we lived one   he groed the corn to make our bread   he groed they cane to make our syrup allso groed they Beans and Peas to make the soup beans out of and dried leather Britches beans and dried fruit enough to last all winter he Killed enough meat to last all winter

he Killed a beaf and a Sheep and two or three hogs for the winter   he diden have mutch money for anything   we just had our biskets for sunday morning and when mother ran out of coffie she parched chustnuts and ground them one her coffie mill to make coffie out of   and when it rained and the mills coulden grind our bread we ate potatoes for bread my dad usto make our shoes   I can remember waring them   my mother usto weaved woal cloth to make blankets and cloths out of   I have worn woal dresses and my dad has worn home made Britches out of woven woal to   my mother also knit our Stockings and socks to   I have hope my dad Shear Sheep a lot of times to get that wool my mother would wash it and Spen it make it into thread and then weave it one her loom to make her blankets and cloth out of   we usto have corn Shukings to get our corn all shucked

we had our crib full   that lasted till the next fall every body in the neighborhood come and my mother cooked a big dinner for the crowd seames as every body was happie to   I rember when my mother had to cook one the fire place   she cooked her dried fruit and every thing one the fire place   it sure was good back in them dayes to   I usto help my brothers Saw wood to make fires out of to keep warm   we lived in a log house   it was pretty hard to keep warm by an open fire place but we never was Sick back then   we played out the bigest Snow ever com   we had a Spring to cary our watter from and my dad had to take his Shovel and ditch out a way through the Snow for us to get to the Spring   the snow was waist deep we usto make our play houses out in the woods   make our rag dolls to play with   my brothers Sawed pine wagon wheels and made there wagons to play with   I have sent to the mountains and hope my dad and brothers Snake out tan bark to get a little money to buy things with   One Xmas Santa Clause gave us three or four sticks of candie and a ornge   he put it in our Stocking and we was as pleased as if he had give us a box full of candy   we lived one a hill out of site of the road and we was toaled the was a car coming through that day   it was a teamotel ford tom mitchel was driving it and we sit one the hill all day to get to see it   we haden never saw a car   that was our firston

De Witch'-ooman
an' de Spinnin'-Wheel

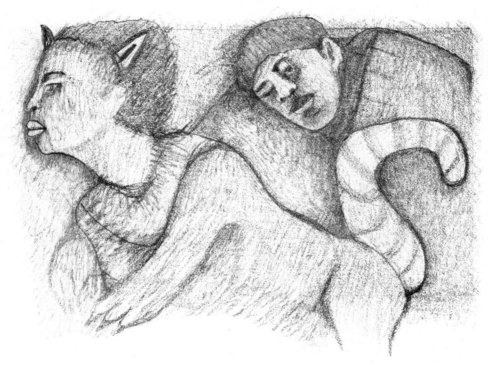

THE WITCH PREVENTED FROM REENTERING HER SKIN:
A TALE FROM LOUISIANA.

One time dey wuz a man whar rid up at night ter a cabin in de eedge o' de swamp. He wuz dat hongry an' ti'd dat he say ter hissef: "Ef I kin git a hunk o' co'n-pone and a slice o' bakin', I doan kur what I pays!" On dat here come a yaller-'ooman spankin' out'n de cabin. She wuz spry on her foot ez a catbird, an' her eyes wuz sof' an' shiny. She ax de man fer ter light an' come in de cabin, an' git some supper. An' Lawd! how he mouf do water when he cotch a glimpst er de skillet on de coals! He

Reprinted from JOURNAL OF AMERICAN FOLKLORE XVIII. By permission of Houghton Mifflin Company.

luk it so well dat he stay; an' he sot eroun' in dat cabin ontwel he git so fat dat de grease fa'r run out'n he jaws when he look up at de sun. De yaller-'ooman she spen' her time cookin' fer him, an' waitin' on him wi' so much oberly, dat at las' de man, he up an' marry dat yaller-'ooman.

At fus' dey git erlong tollable well, but a'ter erwhile he gin ter notice dat sump'n curus 'bout dat yaller-'ooman. She ain' never in de cabin when he wake up in de night time! So, he mek up his min' fer ter spy on her. He lay down one night on de fo' pos' bed in de cornder, 'ten luk he sleep. De yaller-'ooman watch him out'n de een o' her eye, an' when she hear him gin a sno' (caze *cose* he 'ten luk he sno') she jump up an' pat a juba in de middle o' de flo'. Den she reach down a big gridi'on fum de wall, an' take out some coals, an' haul de big spinnin'-wheel close ter de ha'th. Den, she sot herself down on dat gridi'on, an' soon ez it wuz red-hot she 'gin ter spin her skin off'n her body on de spinnin'-wheel. "Tu'n an' spin, come off skin, tu'n an' spin,

come off skin." An' fo' de Lawd, de skin come off'n dat witch-'ooman's body, berginning at de top o' her head, ez slick es de shush come off de ear o' corn. An' when it wuz fa'r off, dan she wuz a gret big yaller cat. Den, she tuk her skin an' chuck it onder de bed. "Lay dar, skin," she say, "wi' dat fool nigger sno'in' in de bed, ontwel I come back. I gwine ter ha' some fum, I is."

Wi' dat she jump out'n de winder an' lope off. Soon ez she wuz gone de man, he jump out'n de bed an' tuk out skin an' fill it plum full o' salt an' pepper, un' th'ow it back onder de bed. Den he crope out an' watch thro' de key-hole ontwel de witch-'ooman come home. She laugh whilse she wuz rakin' out de skin fum onder de bed, an' shakin' herse'f inter it. But when she feel de salt an' pepper, she laugh on de yether side her mouf. She moan an' groan so you kin hear her a mile! But she ain' able ter git out'n dat skin, an' de man watch her thoo de key-hole twel she fall down an' die on de flo'.

Well-Loved Fairy Tales

We have heard many of these stories from childhood, perhaps not realizing that we share them with other countries. Not only do they delight the child's ear but they also intrigue the scholar's mind. They are indeed fairy tales, full of make-believe, exaggeration, coincidence, and truth.

The Three Wishes

JOSEPH JACOBS

Once upon a time, and be sure 'twas a long time ago, there lived a poor woodman in a great forest, and every day of his life he went out to fell timber. So one day he started out, and the goodwife filled his wallet and slung his bottle on his back, that he might have meat and drink in the forest. He had marked out a huge old oak, which, thought he, would furnish many and many a good plank. And when he was come to it, he took his ax in his hand and swung it round his head as though he were minded to fell the tree at one stroke. But he hadn't given one blow, when what should he hear but the pitifullest entreating, and there stood before him a fairy who prayed and beseeched him to spare the tree. He was dazed, as you may fancy, with wonderment and affright, and he couldn't open his mouth to utter a word. But he found his tongue at last, and, "Well," said he, "I'll e'en do as thou wishest."

"You've done better for yourself than you know," answered the fairy, "and to show I'm not ungrateful, I'll grant you your next three wishes, be they what they may." And therewith the fairy was no more to be seen, and the woodman slung his wallet over his shoulder and his bottle at his side, and off he started home.

But the way was long, and the poor man was regularly dazed with the wonderful thing that had befallen him, and when he got home there was nothing in his noddle but the wish to sit down and rest. Maybe, too, 'twas a trick of the fairy's. Who can tell? Anyhow down he sat by the blazing fire, and as he sat he waxed hungry, though it was a long way off supper-time yet.

"Hasn't thou naught for supper, dame?" said he to his wife.

"Nay, not for a couple of hours yet," said she.

"Ah!" groaned the woodman, "I

wish I'd a good link of black pudding [sausage] here before me."

No sooner had he said the word, when clatter, clatter, rustle, rustle, what should come down the chimney but a link of the finest black pudding the heart of man could wish for.

If the woodman stared, the good-wife stared three times as much. "What's all this?" says she.

Then all the morning's work came back to the woodman, and he told his tale right out, from beginning to end, and as he told it the goodwife glowered and glowered, and when he had made an end of it she burst out,

"Thou bee'st but a fool, Jan, thou bee'st but a fool; and I wish the pudding were at thy nose, I do indeed."

And before you could say Jack Robinson, there the goodman sat and his nose was the longer for a noble link of black pudding.

He gave a pull but it stuck, and she gave a pull but it stuck, and they both pulled till they had nigh pulled the nose off, but it stuck and stuck.

"What's to be done now?" said he.

" 'T isn't so very unsightly," said she, looking hard at him.

Then the woodman saw that if he wished, he must need wish in a hurry; and wish he did, that the black pudding might come off his nose. Well! there it lay in a dish on the table, and if the goodman and goodwife didn't ride in a golden coach, or dress in silk and satin, why they had at least as fine a black pudding for their supper as the heart of man could desire.

The Field of Boliauns

Joseph Jacobs

One fine day in harvest—it was indeed Lady-day in harvest, that everybody knows to be one of the greatest holidays in the year—Tom Fitzpatrick was taking a ramble through the ground, and went along the sunny side of a hedge; when all of a sudden he heard a clacking sort of noise a little before him in the hedge. "Dear me," said Tom, "but isn't it surprising to hear the stonechatters singing so late in the season?" So Tom stole on, going on the tops of his toes to try if he could get a sight of what was making the noise, to see if he was right in his guess. The noise stopped; but as Tom looked sharply through the bushes, what should he see in a nook of the hedge but a brown pitcher, that might hold about a gallon and a half of liquor; and by and by a little wee teeny tiny bit of an old man, with a little *motty* of a cocket hat stuck upon the top of his head, a deeshy daushy leather apron hanging before him, pulled out a little wooden stool, and stood up upon it, and dipped a little piggin into the pitcher, and took out the full of it, and put it beside the stool, and then sat down under the pitcher, and began to work at putting a heelpiece on a bit of a broque just fit for himself.

"Well, by the powers," said Tom to himself, "I often heard tell of the Leprechauns, and to tell God's truth, I never rightly believed in them—but here's one of them in real earnest. If I go knowingly to work, I'm a made man. They say a body must never take their eyes off them, or they'll escape."

Tom now stole on a little farther, with his eye fixed on the little man just as a cat does with a mouse. So when he got up quite close to him, "God bless your work, neighbor," said Tom.

The little man raised up his head, and "Thank you kindly," said he.

"I wonder you'd be working on the holiday!" said Tom.

"That's my own business, not yours," was the reply.

"Well, maybe you'd be civil enough to tell *us* what you've got in the pitcher there?" said Tom.

"That I will, with pleasure," said he; "it's good beer."

"Beer!" said Tom. "Thunder and fire! where did you get it?"

"Where did I get it, is it? Why, I made it. And what do you think I made it of?"

"Devil a one of me knows," said Tom; "but of malt, I suppose, what else?"

"There you're out. I made it of heath."

"Of heath!" said Tom bursting out laughing; "sure you don't think me such a fool as to believe that?"

"Do as you please," said he, "but what I tell you is the truth. Did you never hear tell of the Danes?"

"Well, what about *them?*" said Tom.

"Why, all the about them there is, is that when they were here they taught us to make beer out of the heath, and the secret's in my family ever since."

"Will you give a body a taste of your beer?" said Tom.

"I'll tell you what it is, young man, it would be fitter for you to be looking after your father's property than to be bothering decent quiet people with your foolish questions. There now, while you're idling away your time here, there's the cows have broke into the oats, and are knocking the corn all about."

Tom was taken so by surprise with this that he was just on the very point of turning round when he recollected himself; so, afraid that the like might happen again, he made a grab at the Leprechaun, and caught him up in his hand; but in his hurry he overset the pitcher, and spilt all the beer, so that he could not get a taste of it to tell what sort it was. He then swore that he would kill him if he did not show him where his money was. Tom looked so wicked and so bloody-minded that the little man was quite frightened; so, says he, "Come along with me a couple of fields off, and I will show you a crock of gold."

So they went, and Tom held the Leprechaun fast in his hand, and never took his eyes from off him, though they had to cross hedges and ditches, and a crooked bit of bog, till at last they came to a great field all full of boliauns, and the Leprechaun pointed to a big boliaun, and says he:

"Dig under that boliaun, and you'll get the great crock all full of guineas."

Tom in his hurry had never thought of bringing a spade with him, so he made up his mind to run home and fetch one; and that he might know the place again he took off one of his red garters, and tied it round the boliaun.

Then he said to the Leprechaun: "Swear ye'll not take that garter away from that boliaun." And the Leprechaun swore right away not to touch it.

"I suppose," said the Leprechaun, very civilly, "you have no further occasion for me?"

"No," says Tom; "you may go away now, if you please, and God speed you, and may good luck attend you wherever you go."

"Well, good-bye to you, Tom Fitzpatrick," said the Leprechaun; "and much good may it do you when you get it."

So Tom ran for dear life, till he came home and got a spade, and then away with him, as hard as he could go, back to the field of boliauns; but when he got there, lo and behold! not a boliaun in the field but had a red garter, the very model of his own, tied about it; and as to digging up the whole field, that was all nonsense, for there were more than forty good Irish acres in it. So Tom came home again with the spade on his shoulder, a little cooler than he went, and many's the hearty curse he gave the Leprechaun every time he thought of the neat turn he had served him.

The Husband Who Was to Mind the House

SIR GEORGE W. DASENT

Once upon a time there was a man so surly and cross, he never thought his wife did anything right in the house. So, one evening in hay-making time, he came home, scolding and swearing, and showing his teeth and making a dust.

"Dear love, don't be so angry; there's a good man," said his goody; "tomorrow let's change our work. I'll go out with the mowers and mow, and you shall mind the house at home."

Yes, the husband thought that would do very well. He was quite willing, he said.

So early next morning his goody took a scythe over her neck, and went out into the hayfield with the mowers and began to mow; but the man was to mind the house, and do the work at home.

First of all he wanted to churn the butter; but when he had churned a while, he got thirsty, and went down to the cellar to tap a barrel of ale. So, just when he had knocked in the bung, and was putting the tap into the cask, he heard overhead the pig come into the kitchen. Then off he ran up the cellar steps, with the tap in his hand, as fast as he could, to look after the pig, lest it should upset the churn; but when he got up, and saw that the pig had already knocked the churn over, and stood there, routing and grunting amid the cream which was running all over the floor, he got so wild with rage that he quite forgot his ale barrel and ran at the pig as hard as he could. He caught it, too, just as it ran out of doors, and gave it such a kick that piggy lay for dead on the spot. Then all at once he remembered he had the tap in his hand; but when he got down to the cellar, every drop of ale had run out of the cask.

Then he went into the dairy and found enough cream left to fill the churn again, and so he began to churn, for butter they must have for dinner. When he had churned a bit, he remembered that their milking cow was still shut up in the byre, and hadn't had a bit to eat or a drop to drink all the morning, though the sun was high. Then all at once he thought 'twas too far to take her down to the meadow, so he'd just get her up on the housetop—for the house, you must know, was thatched with sods, and a fine crop of grass was growing there. Now their house lay close up against a steep down, and he thought if he laid a plank across to the thatch at the back he'd easily get the cow up.

But still he couldn't leave the churn, for there was his little babe crawling about the floor, and "if I leave it," he thought, "the child is sure to upset it!" So he took the churn on his back and went out with it; but then he thought he'd better first water the cow before he turned her out on the thatch; so he took up a bucket to draw water out of the well; but, as he stooped down at the well's brink, all the cream ran out of the churn over his shoulders, down the well.

Now it was near dinner time, and he hadn't even got the butter yet; so he thought he'd best boil the porridge, and filled the pot with water, and hung it over the fire. When he had done that, he thought the cow might perhaps fall off the thatch and break her legs or her neck. So he got up on the house to tie her up. One end of the rope he made fast to the cow's neck, and the other he slipped down the chimney and tied round his own thigh; and he had to make haste, for the water now began to boil in the pot, and he had still to grind the oatmeal.

So he began to grind away; but while he was hard at it, down fell the cow off the housetop after all, and as she fell, she dragged the man up the chimney by the rope. There he stuck fast; and as for the cow, she hung halfway down the wall. . . .

And now the goody had waited seven lengths and seven breadths for her husband to come and call them home to dinner; but never a call they had. At last she thought she'd waited long enough, and went home. But when she got there and saw the cow hanging in such an ugly place, she ran up and cut the rope in two with her scythe. But as she did this, down came her husband out of the chimney; and so when his old dame came inside the kitchen, there she found him standing on his head in the porridge pot.

The Pact with the Devil

Feelings that somebody else has all the luck all the time may account for one of the oldest beliefs to appear in all cultures. We would all like to believe that, whether it takes spells, sacrifices, or prayers, if you know how to go about it, you can gain some special advantage over the people around you. The favored method in Judeo-Christian countries has been a pact with the devil. What do you want: money, success, popularity, power? It's all available at the same low price—a human soul.

As might be expected when one party to such a contract is the personification of evil and the other party is a human who is trying to use unfair means to reach his goals, the terms of the agreement are rarely carried out in good faith. The devil has been known to give his client fool's gold. Many of the variations on the theme also include some attempt by the human to evade the final payment. However, few escape paying, perhaps most notably the characters in Stephen Vincent Benet's "The Devil and Daniel Webster." As the old saying goes, he who sups with the Devil needs a long spoon.

Jonathan Moulton and the Devil

No one in the town of Hampton, in colonial New Hampshire, was as rich as Jonathan Moulton. And no one ever had so great a passion for money. He spent the evenings sitting at his fireplace gloating over his wealth and devising schemes of how to become still richer.

"I would sell my soul to be the wealthiest man in the province," he muttered one evening. The fire was dying down in the fireplace, but Moulton didn't notice it. "Yes, I would sell my soul for it," he repeated dreamily.

A sudden explosion made Moulton sit up with a start. With astonishment he saw a shower of sparks come down the chimney, and from its midst a man elegantly dressed in black velvet stepped out. Even more astonishing was the condition of his clothes. Although the chimney was narrow, they were not in the least disheveled or smudged.

"I am at your service, Moulton,"

Reprinted by permission of Lothrop, Lee and Shepard Co., Inc. from TALES OUR SETTLERS TOLD, by Joseph and Edith Raskin. Copyright © 1971 by Joseph and Edith Raskin.

the man said with a low bow. As Moulton just stared at him, he went on, "Let us get on with our business. I am expected at the governor's in ten minutes." To show that he meant what he said, he picked up a red-hot coal and used it as a light to look at his watch.

This was the strangest thing Moulton had ever heard. Portsmouth, where the governor lived, was a long distance away from Hampton. No human being, not even the fastest bird, could possibly cover that distance in such a short time. Gradually the truth began to dawn upon Moulton.

"You are the Devil, aren't you?" he stammered.

"What's in a name?" The man in black laughed. "I heard your offer. Now, is it to be a bargain or not?"

Moulton pricked up his ears. He had always claimed that neither man nor the Devil himself could get the better of him in a trade.

"How can I be sure that you will keep your part of the bargain?" he asked suspiciously.

Giving him a scornful glance, the Devil touched his wig. At once a shower of gold guineas fell to the floor and rolled all over the room.

Greedily Moulton got on his hands and knees to pick them up. But no sooner did he touch them than he had to drop them. The coins were red hot.

Seeing Moulton peevishly getting back to his feet, the Devil chuckled. "Try again," he said. As Moulton shook his head, the Devil urged him on. "Don't be afraid."

Moulton hesitated, but the glitter of the coins made him overcome his caution, and he touched one. To his surprise, the coin was now cool. He weighed it in his hand, then tossed it on the table to hear its ring. There was no doubt—it was a real gold coin.

With a satanic smile, the Devil waited as Moulton crawled over the floor feverishly gathering the coins.

"Are you satisfied?" he demanded when Moulton had finished.

"Yes, indeed," Moulton gasped, still panting from his exertion.

"Now that you are convinced that I can make you the richest man in the province, let us conclude our agreement," the Devil prompted, extracting a paper from his breast pocket. "Now listen: 'I, the Devil, on the first day of every month shall fill your boots in payment for your soul. It shall become the Devil's property forthwith upon the signing of this paper.' Agreed?" Shaking his finger, which glittered with diamonds, he added, "Don't try to play tricks on me. I know you, Moulton, and I shall keep an eye on you."

Still dazed by what was happening, Moulton did not reply.

Not in the least perturbed, the Devil dipped a pen in the inkhorn at his belt and offered it to Moulton.

"Sign," he demanded, pointing to a blank space on the paper already crowded with a variety of flourishing signatures.

Moulton stepped back, wavering.

"If you are afraid, return the money you have pocketed and we will call off the deal."

A hopeful thought that somehow he would manage to get the better of the deal occurred to Moulton. He seized the pen, but before signing stole a glance at the long list of names on the paper. He was amazed to notice how many of the names he knew. "I shall at least be in good company," he mused. Thus encouraged, he finally signed his name.

"Excellent," the Devil said. Taking the paper out of Moulton's hands, he folded it and put it back in his breast pocket. "Now, my friend, be sure you keep faith with me." Then, bowing grandly and flinging his cape about him, he vanished up the chimney.

That night Moulton stayed awake thinking of all kinds of schemes. However, hard as he racked his brain, he could think of no trick clever enough to outwit the Devil. Then he remembered the boots. He examined his own boots and tossed them aside. Even filled to the brim they would not hold enough coins to satisfy him.

The sun hardly began to send out rays to announce its rising when Moulton knocked at the shoemaker's door.

"What can I do for you?" the shoemaker asked, pleased to have such a prominent visitor.

"I need a pair of boots, much larger than the ones I have on, such that would reach up to my thighs," Moulton said.

The shoemaker raised his brows. "Sorry, I don't have such boots," he said. "But maybe I could make you a pair."

Moulton thought it over. He could have boots made that would hold many more coins than his. But then, the Devil might notice that the boots were new and suspect his scheme.

"No, thanks," he said and, cutting the visit short, headed for the blacksmith's shop.

The blacksmith was an enormous fellow. Moulton had seen him at the town fairs towering over the heads of others. Surely his boots would be enormous. The door of the blacksmith shop was open, but he did not enter. He did not have to. From where he stood he could see the boots of the blacksmith, who was busy working at his anvil. They were disappointingly short, hardly reaching halfway to his knees.

Moulton walked off wondering who in town could possibly have the size of boots he wanted. He could think of no one worth the trouble of approaching. Suddenly, seeing a soldier a distance away, he quickened his pace. At closer range the soldier appeared at least as tall as the blacksmith. His boots were long, reaching almost to his thighs.

"Are you a stranger here?" Moulton asked, catching up with him.

"So I am," the soldier replied.

"Could you do me a favor and sell me your boots? I'll pay handsomely for them," Moulton dangled a pouchful of coins before him.

"Now, now," the soldier chided, taken aback. Then, reconsidering, he said, "For so much money I don't mind if I do go barefoot for a while." He took off his boots and handed them over to Moulton in exchange for the pouch of money.

Although the boots were heavy and clumsy, Moulton carried them away with the speed of a young mare. "Ho, there! These are only copper coins you gave me!" he heard the soldier shouting after him. But before the soldier could collect his wits, Moulton had disappeared into his house, secure behind the locked doors.

The Devil kept his promise. On the first day of every month Moulton hung the boots on the crane in the fireplace, and the Devil stuffed them full of guineas.

Moulton became the most prosperous man in the province. Some people envied him, but most of them feared him. "That man would outwit the Devil himself," they grumbled. Hearing it, Moulton smiled to himself—that was precisely what he was planning to do.

One morning the Devil came as usual to fill the boots. But no matter how many coins he poured into them, they remained empty. It was like pouring the money into a bottomless pit.

Puzzled, the Devil decided to come down the chimney to see what was wrong. The chimney was choked up with coins. Enraged, he tore the boots from the crane and examined them. What he saw made him grind his teeth. That conniving Moulton had cut off the soles! And the coins that he had poured into the bottomless boots covered the entire room knee deep!

The Devil uttered a horrible curse and disappeared. That night Moulton's house was burned to the ground. All the precious money Moulton had hidden in the wooden panels of the walls and ceiling disappeared in the fire. Moulton himself escaped with nothing but his nightshirt on.

Watching his house turning into ashes, Moulton wept and tore his hair. Vanishing before his eyes was not only all the gold the Devil had given him, but his own money that he had hoarded for so many years. What would his life be without his wealth? Suddenly it dawned upon him that not all was really lost. His gold coins might have melted, but they could not possibly have turned to ashes. Spurred by his overwhelming desire to rescue his gold, he dashed madly into the burning debris.

Afterward, there was a rumor that someone had seen Moulton coming out of the burning ruins in the company of a man in black, then both disappearing into thin air. One thing was certain—Jonathan Moulton was never seen again.

The Hero
Against All Odds

Examine the folktales of any group and you are sure to find stories about at least one legendary or mythical hero. The glory of some of the heroes of pre-literature was so great that we still know their names: the Aztec Quetzalcoatl, the Sumerian Gilgamesh, the Greek Hercules, the Celtic King Arthur, the Germanic Siegfried. Admiration of the hero figure of course was not a human characteristic that mysteriously disappeared with the development of the printing press. The media have created cult heroes out of living individuals, and a few fictional characters, such as the Lone Ranger and James Bond, have gained wide popularity chiefly because of their mythic qualities.

Just what qualities are admired in a hero vary from age to age and place to place. Primitive Germanic heroes were valued for their strength and loyalty; Christian heroes were praised for gentleness, humility, and spirituality. Others were admired for personal beauty and charm or for daring and persistence. According to many theorists, the life stories of most of the early mythic heroes progress through a well-defined, predictable series of at least eight stages: miraculous birth, initiation, preparation and withdrawal, trial and quest, death (as a scapegoat), descent into the underworld, resurrection, and ascension/atonement.

Whatever the underlying cultural needs that this process satisfies, each stage has its own special significance. Sometimes the message (the moral, if you will, of one stage) expresses so well the temper of a particular time that its theme crops up again and again as a component of popular stories. For example, for some time now the appeal for our age seems to lie in those occasions where the hero, often with little on his side, manages to make it successfully through a series of tests. Sometimes it is courage that carries him through, sometimes skill, sometimes luck; occasionally it is his wits. The message conveyed is encouraging: you too can win. After a period of anti-heroes, likeable but bewildered souls waffling about battered by the winds of ill fortune, the popularity of a sort of true hero is once again on the rise—the heroes of Kung Fu, the James Bonds, and what have you. In the following section you will meet heroes of many countries, all overcoming a variety of obstacles.

Gilgamesh

And even as he cried he saw that his companion no longer stirred nor opened his eyes; and when he felt Enkidu's heart it was beating no more.

Then Gilgamesh took a cloth and veiled the face of Enkidu, even as men veil a bride on the day of her espousal. And he paced to and fro and cried aloud, and his voice was the voice of a lioness robbed of her whelps. And he stripped off his garments and tore his hair and gave himself up to mourning.

All night long he gazed upon the prostrate form of his companion and saw him grow stiff and wizened, and all the beauty was departed from him. "Now," said Gilgamesh, "I have seen the face of death and am sore afraid. One day I too shall be like Enkidu."

When morning came he had made a bold resolve.

On an island at the far ends of the earth, so rumor had it, lived the only mortal in the world who had ever escaped death—an old, old man, whose name was Utnapishtim. Gilgamesh decided to seek him out and learn from him the secret of eternal life.

As soon as the sun was up he set out on his journey, and at last, after traveling long and far, he came to the end of the world and saw before him a huge mountain whose twin peaks touched the sky and whose roots reached down to nethermost hell. In front of the mountain there was a massive gate, and the gate was guarded by fearsome and terrible creatures, half man and half scorpion.

Gilgamesh flinched for a moment and screened his eyes from their hideous gaze. Then he recovered himself and strode boldly to meet them.

When the monsters saw that he was unafraid, and when they looked on the beauty of his body, they knew at once that no ordinary mortal was before them. Nevertheless they challenged his passage and asked the purpose of his coming.

Gilgamesh told them that he was on his way to Utnapishtim, to learn the secret of eternal life.

"That," replied their captain, "is a thing which none has ever learned, nor was there ever a mortal who succeeded in reaching that ageless sage. For the path which we guard is the path of the sun, a gloomy tunnel twelve leagues long, a road where the foot of man may not tread."

"Be it never so long," rejoined the hero, "and never so dark, be the pains and the perils never so great, be the heat never so searing and the cold never so sharp, I am resolved to tread it!"

At the sound of these words the

sentinels knew for certain that one who was more than a mortal was standing before them, and at once they threw open the gate.

Boldly and fearlessly Gilgamesh entered the tunnel, but with every step he took the path became darker and darker, until at last he could see neither before nor behind. Yet still he strode forward, and just when it seemed that the road would never end, a gust of wind fanned his face and a thin streak of light pierced the gloom.

When he came out into the sunlight a wondrous sight met his eyes, for he found himself in the midst of a faery garden, the trees of which were hung with jewels. And even as he stood rapt in wonder the voice of the sun-god came to him from heaven.

"Gilgamesh," it said, "go no farther. This is the garden of delights. Stay awhile and enjoy it. Never before have the gods granted such a boon to a mortal, and for more you must not hope. The eternal life which you seek you will never find."

But even these words could not divert the hero from his course and, leaving the earthly paradise behind him, he proceeded on his way.

Presently, footsore and weary, he saw before him a large house which had all the appearance of being a hospice. Trudging slowly toward it, he sought admission.

But the alewife, whose name was Siduri, had seen his approach from afar and, judging by his grimy appearance that he was simply a tramp, she had ordered the postern barred in his face.

Gilgamesh was at first outraged and threatened to break down the door, but when the lady called from the window and explained to him the cause of her alarm his anger cooled, and he reassured her, telling her who he was and the nature of his journey and the reason he was so disheveled. Thereupon she raised the latch and bade him welcome.

Later in the evening they fell to talking, and the alewife attempted to dissuade him from his quest. "Gilgamesh," she said, "that which you seek you will never find. For when the gods created man they gave him death for his portion; life they kept for themselves. Therefore enjoy your lot. Eat, drink, and be merry; for *that* were you born!"

But still the hero would not be swerved, and at once he proceeded to inquire of the alewife the way to Utnapishtim.

"He lives," she replied, "on a far-away isle, and to reach it you must cross an ocean. But the ocean is the ocean of death, and no man living has sailed it. Howbeit, there is at present in this hospice a man named Ur-shanabi. He is the boatman of that aged sage, and he has come hither on an errand. Maybe you can persuade him to ferry you across."

So the alewife presented Gilgamesh to the boatman, and he agreed to ferry him across.

"But there is one condition," he said. "You must never allow your hands to touch the waters of death, and when once your pole has been dipped in them you must straightway discard it and use another, lest any of the drops fall upon your fingers. Therefore take your ax and hew down six-score poles; for it is a long voyage, and you will need them all."

Gilgamesh did as he was bidden, and in a short while they had boarded the boat and put out to sea.

But after they had sailed a number of days the poles gave out, and they had well nigh drifted and foundered, had not Gilgamesh torn off his shirt and held it aloft for a sail.

Meanwhile, there was Utnapishtim, sitting on the shore of the island, looking out upon the main, when suddenly his eyes descried the familiar craft bobbing precariously on the waters.

"Something is amiss," he murmured. "The gear seems to have been broken."

And as the ship drew closer he saw the bizarre figure of Gilgamesh holding up his shirt against the breeze.

"That is not my boatman," he muttered. "Something is surely amiss."

When they touched land Urshanabi at once brought his passenger into the presence of Utnapishtim, and Gilgamesh told him why he had come and what he sought.

"Young man," said the sage, "that which you seek you will never find. For there is nothing eternal on earth. When men draw up a contract they set a term. What they acquire today, tomorrow they must leave to others. Age-long feuds in time die out. Rivers which rise and swell, in the end subside. When the butterfly leaves the cocoon it lives but a day. Times and seasons are appointed for all."

"True," replied the hero. "But you yourself are a mortal, no whit different from me; yet you live forever. Tell me how you found the secret of life, to make yourself like the gods."

A faraway look came into the eyes of the old man. It seemed as though all the days of all the years were passing in procession before him. Then, after a long pause, he lifted his head and smiled.

"Gilgamesh," he said slowly, "I will tell you the secret—a secret high and holy, which no one knows save the gods and myself." And he told him the story of the great flood which the gods had sent upon the earth in the days of old, and how Ea, the kindly lord of wisdom, had sent him warning of it in the whistle of the wind which soughed through the wattles of his hut. At Ea's command he had built an ark, and sealed it with pitch and asphalt, and loaded his kin and his cattle within it, and sailed for seven days and seven nights while the waters rose and the storms raged and the lightnings flashed. And on the seventh day the ark had grounded on a mountain at the end of the world, and he had opened a window in the ark and sent out a dove, to see if the waters had subsided. But the dove had returned, for want of place to rest. Then he had sent out a swallow, and the swallow too had come back. And at last he had sent out a raven, and the raven had not returned. Then he had led forth his kinsmen and his cattle and offered thanksgiving to the gods. But suddenly the god of the winds had come down from heaven and led him back into the ark, along with his wife, and set it afloat upon the waters once more, until it came to the island on the far horizon, and there the gods had set him to dwell forever.

When Gilgamesh heard the tale he knew at once that his quest had been vain, for now it was clear that the old man had no secret formula to give him. He had become immortal, as he now revealed, by special grace of the gods and not, as Gilgamesh had imagined, by possession of some hidden knowledge. The sun-god had been right, and the scorpion-men had been right, and the alewife had been right: that which he had sought he would never find—at least on this side of the grave.

When the old man had finished his story he looked steadily into the drawn face and tired eyes of the hero. "Gilgamesh," he said kindly, "you must rest awhile. Lie down and sleep for six days and seven nights." And no sooner had he said these words than, lo and behold, Gilgamesh was fast asleep.

Then Utnapishtim turned to his wife. "You see," said he, "this man who seeks to live forever cannot even go without sleep. When he awakes he will, of course, deny it—men were liars ever—so I want you to give him proof. Every day that he sleeps bake a loaf of bread and place it beside him. Day by day those loaves will grow staler and moldier, and after seven nights, as they lie in a row beside him, he will be able to see from the state of each how long he has slept."

So every morning Utnapishtim's wife baked a loaf, and she made a mark on the wall to show that another day had passed; and naturally, at the end of six days, the first loaf was dried out, and the second was like leather, and the third was soggy, and the fourth had white specks on it, and the fifth was filled with mold, and only the sixth looked fresh.

When Gilgamesh awoke, sure enough, he tried to pretend that he had never slept. "Why," said he to Utnapishtim, "the moment I take a nap you go jogging my elbow and waking me up!" But Utnapishtim showed him the loaves, and then Gilgamesh knew that he had indeed been sleeping for six days and seven nights.

Thereupon Utnapishtim ordered him to wash and cleanse himself and make ready for the journey home. But even as the hero stepped into his boat to depart Utnapishtim's wife drew near.

"Utnapishtim," said she, "you cannot send him away empty-handed. He has journeyed hither with great effort and pain, and you must give him a parting gift."

The old man raised his eyes and gazed earnestly at the hero. "Gilgamesh," he said, "I will tell you a secret. In the depths of the sea lies a plant. It looks like a buckthorn and pricks like a rose. If any man come into possession of it, he can, by tasting it, regain his youth!"

When Gilgamesh heard these words he tied heavy stones to his feet and let himself down into the depths of the sea; and there, on the bed of the ocean, he espied the plant. Caring little that it pricked him, he grasped it between his fingers, cut the stones from his feet, and waited for the tide to wash him ashore.

Then he showed the plant to Urshanabi the boatman. "Look," he cried, "it's the famous plant called Graybeard-grow-young! Whoever tastes it, gets a new lease on life! I will carry it back to Erech and give it to the people to eat. So will I at least have some reward for my pains!"

After they had crossed the perilous waters and reached land, Gilgamesh and his companion began the long journey on foot to the city of Erech. When they had traveled fifty leagues the sun was already beginning to set, and they looked for a place to pass the night. Suddenly they came upon a cool spring.

"Here let us rest," said the hero, "and I will go bathe."

So he stripped off his clothes and placed the plant on the ground and went to bathe in the cool spring. But as soon as his back was turned a serpent came out of the waters and, sniffing the fragrance of the plant, carried it away. And no sooner had it tasted of it than at once it sloughed off its skin and regained its youth.

When Gilgamesh saw that the precious plant had now passed from his hands forever he sat down and wept. But soon he stood up and, resigned at least to the fate of all mankind, he returned to the city of Erech, back to the land whence he had come.

David

Now the Philistines gathered together their armies to battle, and were gathered together at Shochoh, which belongeth to Judah, and pitched between Shochoh and Azekah, in Ephes-dammim. And Saul and the men of Israel were gathered together, and pitched by the valley of Elah, and set the battle in array against the Philistines. And the Philistines stood on a mountain on the one side, and Israel stood on a mountain on the other side: and there was a valley between them. And there went out a champion out of the camp of the Philistines, named Goliath, of Gath, whose height was six cubits and a span. And he had a helmet of brass upon his head, and he was armed with a coat of mail; and the weight of the coat was five thousand shekels of brass. And he had greaves of brass upon his legs, and a target of brass between his shoulders. And the staff of his spear was like a weaver's beam; and his spear's head weighed six hundred shekels of iron: and one bearing a shield went before him. And he stood and cried unto the armies of Israel, and said unto them, Why are ye come out to set your battle in array? am not I a Philistine, and ye servants to Saul? choose you a man for you, and let him come down to me. If he be able to fight with me, and to kill me, then will we be your servants: but if I prevail against him, and kill him, then shall ye be our servants, and serve us. And the Philistine said, I defy the armies of Israel this day; give me a man, that we may fight together. When Saul and all Israel heard those words of the Philistine, they were dismayed, and greatly afraid.

Now David was the son of that Ephrathite of Bethlehem—Judah, whose name was Jesse; and he had eight sons: and the man went among men for an old man in the days of Saul. And the three eldest sons of Jesse went and followed Saul to the battle: and the names of his three sons that went to the battle were Eliab the firstborn, and next unto him Abinadab, and the third Shammah. And David was the youngest: and the three eldest followed Saul. But David went and returned from Saul to feed his father's sheep at Bethlehem. And the Philistine drew near morning and evening, and presented himself forty days.

And Jesse said unto David his son, Take now for thy brethren an ephah of this parched corn, and these ten loaves, and run to the camp to thy brethren; and carry these ten cheeses unto the captain of their thousand, and look how thy brethren fare, and take their pledge.

Now Saul, and they, and all the men of Israel, were in the valley of Elah, fighting with the Philistines. And David rose up early in the morning, and left the sheep with a keeper, and took, and went, as Jesse had commanded him; and he came to the trench, as the host was going forth to the fight, and shouted for the battle. For Israel and the Philistines had put the battle in array, army against army. And David left his carriage in the hand of the keeper of the carriage, and ran into the army, and came and saluted his brethren. And as he talked with them, behold, there came up the champion, the Philistine of Gath, Goliath by name, out of the armies of the Philistines, and spake according to the same words: and David heard them.

And all the men of Israel, when they saw the man, fled from him, and were sore afraid. And the men of Israel said, Have ye seen this man that is come up? surely to defy Israel is he come up: and it shall be, that the man who killeth him, the king will enrich him with great riches, and will give him his daughter, and make his father's house free in Israel. And David spake to the men that stood by him, saying, What shall be done to the man that killeth this Philistine, and taketh away the reproach from Israel? for who is this uncircumcised Philistine, that he should defy the armies of the living God? And the people answered him after this manner, saying, So shall it be done to the man that killeth him.

And Eliab his eldest brother heard when he spake unto the men; and Eliab's anger was kindled against David, and he said, Why camest thou down hither? and with whom has thou left those few sheep in the wilderness? I know thy pride, and the naughtiness of thine heart; for thou art come down that thou mightest see the battle. And David said, What have I now done? Is there not a cause? And he turned from him toward another, and spake after the same manner: and the people answered him again after the former manner.

And when the words were heard which David spake, they rehearsed them before Saul: and he sent for him. And David said to Saul, Let no man's heart fail because of him; thy servant will go and fight with this Philistine. And Saul said to David, Thou art not able to go against this Philistine to fight with him: for thou art but a youth, and he a man of war from his youth. And David said unto Saul, Thy servant kept his father's sheep, and there came a lion, and a bear, and took a lamb out of the flock: and I went out after him, and smote him, and delivered it out of his mouth: and when he arose against me, I caught him by his beard, and smote him, and slew him. Thy servant slew both the lion and the bear: and this uncircumcised Philistine shall be as one of them, seeing he hath defied the armies of the living God. David said moreover, The Lord that delivered me out of the paw of the lion, and out of the paw of the bear, he will deliver me out of the hand of this Philistine. And Saul said unto David, Go, and the Lord be with thee. And Saul armed David with his armor, and he put a helmet of brass upon his head; also he armed him with a coat of mail. And David girded his sword upon his armor, and he assayed to go; for he had not proved it. And David said unto Saul, I cannot go with these; for I have not proved them. And David put them off him.

And he took his staff in his hand, and chose him five smooth stones out of the brook, and put them in a shepherd's bag which he had, even in a scrip; and his sling was in his hand: and he drew near to the Philistine.

And the Philistine came on and drew near unto David; and the man that bore the shield went before him. And when the Philistine looked about, and saw David, he disdained him: for he was but a youth, and ruddy, and of a fair countenance. And the Philistine said unto David, Am I a dog, that thou comest to me with staves? And the Philistine cursed David by his gods. And the Philistine said to David, Come to me, and I will give thy flesh unto the fowls of the air, and to the beasts of the field. Then said David to the Philistine, Thou comest to me with a sword, and with a spear, and with a shield: but I come to thee in the name of the Lord of hosts, the God of the armies of Israel, whom thou hast defied. This day will the Lord deliver thee into mine hand; and I will smite thee, and take thine head from thee; and I will give the carcasses of the host of the Philistines this day unto the fowls of the air, and to the wild beasts of the earth; that all the earth may know that there is a God in Israel. And all this assembly shall know that the Lord saveth not with sword and spear: for the battle is the Lord's, and he will give you into our hands.

And it came to pass, when the Philistine arose, and came and drew nigh to meet David, that David hasted, and ran toward the army to meet the Philistine. And David put his hand in his bag, and took thence a stone, and slang it, and smote the Philistine in his forehead, that the stone sunk into his forehead; and he fell upon his face to the earth.

So David prevailed over the Philistine with a sling and with a stone, and smote the Philistine, and slew him; but there was no sword in the hand of David. Therefore David ran, and stood upon the Philistine, and took his sword, and drew it out of the sheath thereof, and slew him, and cut off his head therewith. And when the Philistines saw their champion was dead, they fled. And the men of Israel and of Judah arose, and shouted, and pursued the Philistines, until thou come to the valley, and to the gates of Ekron. And the wounded of the Philistines fell down by the way to Shaaraim, even unto Gath, and unto Ekron. And the children of Israel returned from chasing after the Philistines, and they spoiled their tents. And David took the head of the Philistine, and brought it to Jerusalem; but he put his armor in his tent.

And when Saul saw David go forth against the Philistine, he said unto Abner, the captain of the host, Abner, whose son is this youth? And Abner said, As thy soul liveth, O king, I cannot tell. And the king said, Inquire thou whose son the stripling is. And as David returned from the slaughter of the Philistine, Abner took him, and brought him before Saul with the head of the Philistine in his hand. And Saul said to him, Whose son art thou, thou young man? And David answered, I am the son of thy servant Jesse the Bethlehemite.

Beowulf

BEOWULF *is an Old English epic (long narrative poem) that is believed to have been composed or developed sometime during the first half of the eighth century. In subject matter it is similar to Norse sagas and to the later Arthurian legends; its tone is somber and powerful. The tale heralds the valor of the hero Beowulf, noble descendant of the Geats (a vanished northern tribe). The epic is divided into two parts: the first (which is in two sections) concerns the hero's defense of the kingdom of the Danish King Hrothgar; the second tells of his defense of his own kingdom. The following episode takes place after the hero has joined Hrothgar's court and* has proved his prowess as a wrestler and swimmer of great strength and courage.

The mead-hall (Heorot), which was the central gathering place of the court of Hrothgar, had for the previous twelve years been menaced by the monster Grendel who crept in at night to slaughter the sleeping courtiers. Not only was Grendel terrifying to behold, but his very existence was a reminder of the supernatural and all the forces that still held out against civilization in that period. Who better then to put an end to his depredations than Beowulf, champion of early civilization, hero without fear?

The fires were burnt out on the hearths when the last of Hrothgar's train had departed. Then Beowulf and his companions set themselves to fastening tightly the door of the hall. They secured it with wooden bolts and tied it with leathern thongs, and so strong was it that no mortal could have passed through.

Then the warriors of Geatsland unfolded their cloaks upon the benches and laid themselves down to slumber, and Beowulf stretched his great length upon the dais of the king, and resolved that through the long night he would never once close his eyes. Near the door lay the young Hondscio, Beowulf's favorite earl, who swore that if any one broke through the door of Heorot he would be the first to give the intruder battle.

Silence crept over the shrouded forms where they lay upon the floor and benches, and there was no sound save their steady breathing and the faint sighing of the night-wind in the trees about the hall.

Beowulf, upon his couch, lay still as death, but his eyes moved here and there in the deepening gloom of the hall, and his breast rose and fell evenly with his breathing.

Outside, a fog was creeping up from the sea, obscuring the moon in milky eclipse, and at last there was not even the sound of the wind in the trees. To Beowulf the deep silence seemed full of moving things invisible to human eyes.

Gradually there came over him a kind of drowsiness that he fought to ward off. His eyelids fluttered against his eyes, and then he swooned with a sleep that lay upon his weary limbs like a heavy garment.

And the fog thickened and wound itself about the vast mead-hall in thick veils of damp gloom. The moon faded in the fog's depth, and the trees dripped with moisture, and the sound of this dripping was the only sound that came through the night.

But suddenly there was a rustling among the wet trees, and a noise like the deep grunt of a pig, but soft and low, startled the fog-bound night, and the drops of mist-water on the trees fell sharply to the ground like heavy rain. Then the fog parted evenly, and in the wide path it made through the night a Shadow loomed gigantic in all that was left of moonlight.

Slowly, slowly it neared the great hall of Heorot, and the night shuddered at its coming, and behind it, as it moved, the fog closed again with a sucking sound. And the Shadow stood before the great door of the hall, and swayed hideously in the ghastly light.

Within Heorot there was a deep stillness, and Beowulf and the Geatish earls slept soundly, with no knowledge of what stood so evilly beyond the door. For the monstrous Shadow was the fiend Grendel, and standing there in the fog-strewn night he placed a spell upon those who slept in Heorot, and the spell he wove was a spell to make sleep more soundly those who already slept.

But Beowulf hung between sleeping and waking, and while the spell did not completely deaden his senses, it so ensnared his waking dream that he fought desperately against it in his half-sleep and was not quite over-powered. This Grendel did not know as he placed his great shoulder to the door of Heorot, while Beowulf on his couch tossed in the nightmare that possessed him.

Little by little the thongs that se-cured the door gave way, and the huge wooden bolts yielded under the pressure that was strained against them, but no sound broke upon the silent struggle that went on between Grendel and the door.

Beowulf tossed and turned in wak-ing, but the other earls of Geatsland fell deeper and deeper into the swooning sleep.

Then with a rush, the door flew wide, and the fog and salt-smelling night swept in and filled Heorot with strange odors. And in the doorway, swaying this way and that, stood Grendel, huge and dark against the dark night, the fog weaving about him in white veils, and the door of the hall limp on its hinges.

And Beowulf came out of his dream-spell and saw what stood so vast and evil in the doorway. But his eyes were heavy with the spell that clung to him as the wisps of fog clung about the body of Grendel, and only slowly was he able to distinguish the monster. Through his nightmare, now, there came the sense of what had befallen him, and he strove to cast the last remnant of the magic from him as he saw the great form of Grendel swoop down upon the in-nocent form of young Hondscio, catch him up in enormous hands, and tear him limb from sleeping limb.

And Beowulf struggled, and on the earthen floor of Heorot Grendel swayed with his prey.

And now at last Beowulf saw what manner of thing this Grendel was. His legs were like the trunks of trees and they were covered with a kind of gray dry scale that made a noise like paper as the fiend moved this way and that. The body of the beast was shaped like that of a man, but such a man as no mortal eyes had ever be-fore beheld, and the size and shape of it were something to be marveled at.

The head was the head neither of beast or man, yet had something of the features of both, and the great jaw was filled with blunt fangs that ground the bones of the unhappy Hondscio to pulp. Shaggy matted hair hung over the low forehead, and the eyes in the face of Grendel were the color of milk.

Horror-struck upon his couch, Be-owulf felt his limbs in thrall and could move neither leg nor arm to raise himself as Grendel devoured the body of the young Hondscio.

And when Grendel had finished his horrid meal, the beast straightened a little his vast form and looked now to the left, now to the right, until his gaze fell upon the length of Beowulf. Then the milk-white eyes burned with a dull light that was like the light of the moon, and slowly, slowly Grendel moved toward the dais.

But Beowulf, stung with loathing, leaped from his bed.

Silently they fought in the fog-strewn hall of Heorot. Silently their bodies twisted and bent, this way and that, and Beowulf kept Grendel's huge hands with their long claws of sharp bone from him, and Grendel in turn sought to tear apart the quick body that slipped so easily through his arms and legs.

All about them lay the sleeping earls, and not one moved in the deep magic of his slumber as the two fought that silent fight.

Their bodies wove in and out among the sleepers, and Beowulf felt the hot reek of Grendel's breath upon his cheek, and the sweat stood out on Beowulf's broad brow and ran down into his eyes and blinded him. And Grendel's huge hands sought over and over again to clasp his opponent's head, to crush it in their iron grip.

Then the fight became a deadly struggle in one far corner of the hall, and neither one gained any advantage over the other. Then Beowulf slipped. On the earthen floor of Heorot they fell together and the force of their fall made the earth tremble, as when two giants fight in mortal combat.

But Grendel's hold lessened, and fear smote the heart of the fiend. He strove only to free himself from Beowulf's grasp and flee into the night, away from this white youth whose strength was the strength of thirty men.

And now Beowulf had the upper hand, and flew at the giant's throat. But here his hands clutched at thick scales upon which he could get no grip. Grendel nearly took the advantage, but before he could seize Beowulf, the lord of Geatsland had fastened both mighty hands upon the monster's arm, and with a sudden twist that forced a groan of agony from Grendel's lips, leaped behind him, forcing the imprisoned arm high up Grendel's back, and the beast fell prone on the floor.

Now came the final struggle, and sweat poured from Beowulf, while from Grendel there oozed a slimy sap that smelled like vinegar, and sickened Beowulf. But he clung to the monster's arm, and slowly, slowly he felt its great muscles and sinews give way, and as his foot found Grendel's neck, he prayed to all the gods for help, and called upon his father Ecgtheow for strength to sustain him in this desperate effort.

And the mighty arm of Grendel gave way in the terrible hands of Beowulf, and, with a piercing shriek that shook the gilded rafters of Heorot, Grendel stumbled forward, leaving in Beowulf's hands the gory arm.

At that very moment the spell that lay upon the sleeping warriors of Geatsland was broken, and the thirteen remaining earls struggled, as Beowulf had lately struggled, with the nightmare that was in their eyes, and swam out of sleep into waking.

Beowulf fell back upon the dais, the bleeding arm of Grendel in his hands. And Grendel, with a prolonged and ghastly wail, his blunt fangs gnashing together in dumb fury, stumbled toward the door, and before Beowulf could recover, the fiend was away into the fog which swallowed him as surely and completely as though he had plunged into the everlasting sea.

And Beowulf, his magic-dazed companions crowding and babbling behind him in the doorway of Heorot, looked out into the fog-wet night, and the only sound that came to their dulled ears was the steady drip, drip, drip of the mist from the black trees.

When dawn crept clear and untroubled across the woodland and touched the gold-bright hall of Heorot, there came from all quarters the subjects and servants of Hrothgar the king. In twos and threes they came at first, then in a great crowd, for the sleep of the world had been troubled the previous night, and now, half eager, half in consuming fear, the lords and peasantry of Daneland hurried to great Heorot.

At the wide doorway they rushed, and then, in amaze and wonder, they stopped: for within the hall there was a sight which for a moment made them afraid to enter, and those in front were held spellbound by what they saw, and those behind pushed eagerly forward in order to see.

For high toward the roof-tree of Heorot the brawny men of Geatsland were hoisting the mangled arm and torn shoulder of Grendel, and the people marveled at the sight of this arm, the largest and most terrible arm in all the world, the torn sinews hanging dead, the red ooze of the beast's blood clotted and caked on the cruel curved fingers with their hooked talons of bone.

Upon the dais of the king stood Beowulf, wrapped close in his scarlet mantle, his yellow hair about his head like a golden cloud, and his sea-blue eyes flashing with the pride of a conqueror.

Then the crowding people flocked into the hall, and a shout went up from a hundred throats as the arm swung high from the roof. And men hastened away to the bower of Hrothgar, and summoned the king and his lady Wealhtheow to view this token of the stricken Grendel.

And the king and queen entered Heorot speedily, and hastened to Beowulf. They grasped his two hands in theirs, and Hrothgar spoke in a loud voice, praising him:

"Beowulf, son of strong Ecgtheow, hail! This is truly an end to Grendel. Thrice blessed are you, my son, and upon.you may all the rewards of the gods be showered. You have delivered Daneland from a curse that has been the undoing of our people and of our power during twelve long years. Again and yet again, hail to you, Beowulf, great hero of Geatsland!"

Then the lady Wealhtheow the Beautiful praised him also, and hung upon his arm, and called her servants to prepare a great feast for all the people. And the feasting and drinking lasted all that day and well into the night.

Considerations

1. Although it is not apparent in this excerpt, the epic as a whole has both pagan and Christian aspects. In fact, there is a continuing scholarly debate as to whether *Beowulf* is an epic told by a Christian borrowing heavily from ancient material or is a rather complete tale of antiquity with some Christian notions added later. What is apparent, however, is the contrast between the growing code of civilization represented by Beowulf and the barbaric world that spawned Grendel. How are these opposing forces depicted?
2. In addition to loyalty and courage, what other personal qualities does Beowulf demonstrate?
3. The mood of the piece is heavy and somber. Does the intensity this builds up add to or detract from the story's power?

Robin Hood and the Butcher

Walking in the forest as was his daily custom, Robin Hood one day observed a butcher riding along the way, carrying good store of meat on his mare's back, which he was to sell in the market.

"Good morrow, good fellow," said Robin to the butcher.

"Good fellow," replied the butcher, "heavens keep me from Robin Hood fellow, for if I meet with him, I may chance to fall short of my journey, and my meat of the market."

"I like thy company well. What hast thou to sell?" said Robin Hood.

"Flesh, master," said the butcher, "with which I am going to Nottingham market."

"What is the price of thy flesh," said Robin Hood, "and of thy mare that bears it? Tell me, for if thou wilt use me well, I will buy both."

"Four mark," said the butcher. "I cannot bate anything of it."

"Sit down then and tell thy money," said Robin Hood. "I will try for once if I can thrive by being a butcher."

The money being told, Robin Hood gets up on the mare, and away he rides with the meat to Nottingham market, where he made such good penniworths that he had sold all his meat by ten of the clock in the morn.

He sold more meat for one penny than others could do for five. The butchers in the market, that had their stands near him, said one to another, "Certainly this man's meat is nought and putrefied, or else he hath stolen it. From whence comes he?"

Saith another, "I never did see him before."

"That will I tell you by and by," said a third butcher, and, stepping to Robin Hood, said unto him, "Brother, thou art the freest butcher that ever came to this market; we be all of one trade; come, let us dine together."

"Accurst be he that will deny a butcher so fair an invitation," said Robin Hood, and, going with him to the inn, the table was suddenly covered and furnished, and the best man in the company being to say grace, Robin Hood at the upper end of the table did put off his bonnet. He was no sooner sat, but he called for a cup of sack and drank to them all, desiring them to be merry, for if there were five pounds to pay, he would pay every farthing.

"Thou art the bravest blade," said the butchers, "that ever came to Nottingham market." Robin Hood still called for more wine, and the cups trouled up and down the table, insomuch that the sheriff, who had newly alighted and taken his chamber in the inn, hearing of it, said that he must be some prodigal that had sold his land and would now spend it all at once. This coming to Robin Hood's ear, he after dinner took the opportunity to speak with the sheriff.

Said the sheriff, "Good fellow, thou hast made a good market today; hast thou any more horned beasts to sell?"

"Yes, that I have," said Robin Hood to master sheriff. "I have two or three hundred, and a hundred acres of good land to keep them on as ever the crow flew over, which if you will buy of me, I will make you as good assurance of it as ever my father made me."

The sheriff, being a covetous man and persuading himself that he would make him Robin Hood's penniworths, commanded his horse to be brought forth, and, taking some money with him for the purchase, he rode with Robin Hood, who led him into the forest for a mile or two. The sheriff being laden with good store of gold, and surprised with the melancholy of the place, said he did wish himself at Nottingham again.

"And why so?" said Robin Hood.

"I tell thee plainly," said the sheriff, "I do not like thy company."

"No?" said Robin Hood. "Then I will provide you better."

"God keep me from Robin Hood," said the sheriff, "for this is the haunt he useth."

Robin Hood, smiling, observed a herd of three hundred gallant deer feeding in the forest close by him and demanded of the sheriff how he liked those horned beasts, assuring him that they were the best that he could show him. With that he blew his horn, whereupon Little John with fifty more of his associates came presently in, to whom Robin Hood imparted that he had brought with him the sheriff of Nottingham to dine with him.

"He is welcome," said Little John. "I know he hath store of gold and will honestly pay for his dinner."

"Ay, ay," said Robin Hood, "never doubt it." And taking off the sheriff's portmantle, he took to himself the three hundred pounds that was in it. Then leading the sheriff back through the forest, he desired him to remember him kindly to his wife, and so went laughing away.

Brer Rabbit's Cool Air Swing

Mr. Man he have a fine garden.

Brer Rabbit he visit Mr. Man's garden every day and destroy the lastest thing in it, twell Mr. Man plum wore out with old Brer Rabbit.

Mr. Man he set a trap for old Brer Rabbit down 'longside the big road.

One day when Mr. Man going down to the crossroads, he look in his trap, and sure 'nough, there old Brer Rabbit.

Mr. Man he say, "Oh, so old man, here you is. Now I'll have you for my dinner."

Mr. Man he take a cord from his pocket, and tie Brer Rabbit high on a limb of a sweet gum tree, and he leave Brer Rabbit swinging there twell he come back from the crossroads, when he aim to fotch Brer Rabbit home and cook him for his dinner.

Brer Rabbit he swing thisaway in the wind and thataway in the wind, and he swing thisaway in the wind and thataway in the wind, and he think he time done come. Poor old Brer Rabbit don't know where he's at.

Presently here come Brer Wolf loping down the big road. When Brer Wolf see old Brer Rabbit swinging thisaway and thataway in the wind, Brer Wolf he stop short and he say, "God a'mighty, man! what you doing up there?" Brer Rabbit he say, "This just my cool air swing. I just taking a swing this morning."

But Brer Rabbit he just know Brer Wolf going to make way with him. Brer Rabbit he just turn it over in his mind which way he going to get to. The wind it swing poor Brer Rabbit way out thisaway and way out thataway. While Brer Rabbit swinging, he work his brain, too.

Brer Wolf he say, "Brer Rabbit, I got you fast; now I going to eat you up." Brer Rabbit he say, "Brer Wolf, open your mouth and shut your eyes, and I'll jump plum in your mouth." So Brer Wolf turns his head up and shut his eyes. Brer Rabbit he feel in his pocket and take out some pepper, and Brer Rabbit he throw it plum down Brer Wolf's throat. Brer Wolf he nigh 'bout 'stracted with the misery. He cough and he roll in the dirt, and he get up and he strike out for home, coughing to beat all. And Brer Rabbit he swing thisaway and thataway in the wind.

Presently here come Brer Squirrel. When Brer Squirrel he see the wind swing Brer Rabbit way out thisaway and way out thataway, Brer Squirrel he that 'stonished, he stop short. Brer Squirrel he say, "Fore the Lord, Brer Rabbit, what you done done to yourself this yer time?"

Brer Rabbit he say, "This yer my

cool air swing, Brer Squirrel. I taking a fine swing this morning." And the wind it swing Brer Rabbit way out thisaway and way back thataway.

Brer Rabbit he fold his hands, and look mighty restful and happy, like he settin' back fanning hisself on his front porch.

Brer Squirrel he say, "Please sir, Brer Rabbit, let me try your swing one time."

Brer Rabbit he say, "Certainly, Brer Squirrel, you do me proud," and Brer Rabbit he make like he make haste to turn hisself loose.

Presently Brer Rabbit he say, "Come up here, Brer Squirrel, and give me a hand with this knot," and Brer Squirrel he make haste to go up and turn Brer Rabbit loose, and Brer Rabbit he make Brer Squirrel fast to the cord. The wind it swing Brer Squirrel way out thisaway and way out thataway, and Brer Squirrel he think it fine.

Brer Rabbit he say, "I go down to the spring to get a fresh drink. You can swing twell I come back."

Brer Squirrel he say, "Take your time, Brer Rabbit, take your time." Brer Rabbit he take his time, and scratch out for home fast as he can go, and he ain't caring how long Brer Squirrel swing.

Brer Squirrel he swing thisaway and he swing thataway, and he think it fine.

Presently here come Mr. Man. When Mr. Man he see Brer Squirrel, he plum 'stonished. He say, "Oh, so old man, I done hear of many and many your fine tricks, but I never done hear you turn yourself into a squirrel before. Powerful kind of you, Brer Rabbit, to give me fine squirrel dinner."

Mr. Man he take Brer Squirrel home and cook him for dinner.

Considerations

1. This tale, though not from the Joel Chandler Harris "Uncle Remus" series, has many of the characteristics of those Southern Black folk tales. These featured a common trickster of African tales (the rabbit), but in an adaptation that some critics see as a clever satire of the ways of white plantation owners. How might this tale fit such an interpretation?
2. What facets of human nature are illustrated in this tale?

Jack and the King's Girl

Jack had an uncle lived a right smart distance from where he and his mother lived at, and he decided one time he'd like to go up and see his uncle.

Jack had done got so he wasn't lazy no more—not so much as he used to be. So he worked hard all week, gettin' in wood and fixin' ever'thing up around the place, then he pulled out.

Had to go right by the King's house on the way to his uncle's. The King had a awful pretty girl, but all her life she never had laughed, and the King had put out a adver-tize-ment that anybody that would make her laugh could marry her.

Jack got down close to where the King lived and that girl was out on the porch, she saw Jack, says, "Where ye started, Jack?"

Jack told her and she says to him, "I hope ye have a good time."

So Jack went on. His uncle was awful pleased to see him. They'd work a little and ever' night some-body'd come there to play and make music. Jack had such a good time he plumb forgot about goin' back home.

So fin'ly his uncle says to him, "Jack, your mother'll be gettin' un-easy about you. She'll be needin' ye about gettin' up wood, too. Don't you reckon you better go on back home?"

Jack says, "Yes. I guess I had better go, pretty soon."

"You fix up and go back today, Jack, and I'll give ye a present. I'm goin' to give you a big darnin' needle. You can take that and learn how to sew your own overhalls when they get tore."

So he went and hunted up a big darnin' needle he had, put a long thread in it and gave it to Jack.

Jack pulled out, put the thread over his shoulder and let the needle swing down behind him.

Got down to the King's house; that girl was there, says, "You gettin' back, are ye, Jack?"

"Yes," says Jack. "Had a awful good time."

"What's that you got over your shoulder?"

"Hit's a big darnin' needle uncle gave me, to hire me to go back home."

"Needle?" she says. "Law me! I never did see a man tote a needle that-a-way. You ought to stick that in your shirt bosom."

"Well'm," says Jack.

Jack got in home, told his mother all about what a good time he'd had. Started in to workin' about the place, and he kept studyin' about gettin' back to his uncle's again.

So fin'ly Jack's mother says to him,

says, "You've worked right good this week, Jack. You fix up your wood and all, and I'll let you go back to your uncle's again. But you mustn't stay so long this time."

Jack got ever'thing fixed up and pulled out.

Got to the King's house; that girl was there, says, "Hello, Jack. Where ye started this time?"

Jack told her. She says, "Hope ye have a good time, and get another good present."

Well, Jack and his uncle went several places that week, and Jack had such a good time a-hearin' fiddle music and banjo pickin' he never studied about goin' back home.

So one day his uncle says, "You better go on back home now, Jack. I'm goin' to give ye another premium. Hit's a swoard my grandpa gave me. Hit was used in the Revolutionary War."

He went and got the swoard and gave it to Jack. Jack started on home. He took that swoard and stuck it right through his shirt bosom and out the other side.

The King's girl was out in the yard, saw Jack comin', says, "Hello, Jack."

Then she saw that swoard stickin' out of Jack's shirt, says, "Law me, Jack! You've plumb ruined your shirt. Why, you ought to have carried that on your shoulder."

"Well'm," says Jack, "next time I will."

Jack got back home, played around with that swoard till fin'ly he got a little tired of it. So he worked right on all week, got ever'thing shaped up, says to his mother, "How about me goin' back to uncle's again?"

His mother let him go. Jack saw the King's girl out at the gate and stopped and talked to her awhile. Got back to his uncle's and had a big time. A gang of young folks 'uld come up there to Jack's uncle's place and they'd get to makin' music and singin' old songs, stay till nearly daylight. Then him and his uncle 'uld go some other place the next night, till fin'ly his uncle says, "Hit's about time you went back home, Jack."

"Yes, I reckon it is," says Jack.

"I'm goin' to give ye a nice present today. Maybe hit'll keep you home a month this time. I got a young colt here. You can take it home with ye and break it to ride. Hit'll take ye some time to get it broke good."

So he got a halter and brought Jack the colt. Jack thanked him and started on home. Got down close to the King's place, Jack got right down under the colt and got it up on his shoulder.

The King's girl saw him comin' a-totin' that colt, she ran out to the fence, says, "Law me, Jack. You the awfulest fool man I ever did see. You ought to ride that."

"Well'm," says Jack, "I'll try to think of that next time."

When Jack got home, he went to foolin' around with his colt, never thought a thing about goin' back to his uncle's till nearly about a month. Then his colt began to get sort of old to him, and he com-menced to talk about goin' back to see his uncle.

"Why, Jack," says his mother, "I 'lowed you wouldn't never leave your colt."

"Well," says Jack, "you can take care of it while I'm gone."

So Jack got all his work done up and pulled out again.

That girl was out in the yard and her and Jack talked awhile, then Jack went on to his uncle's.

They worked around the place a little, went huntin' a time or two, and ever' night some young folks 'uld come up there and Jack 'uld get to frolickin' with 'em. They made music and got to playin' Weevily Wheat and Skip to My Lou and runnin' eight-handed reels and all. Jack never did have such a good time and his uncle was an awful good hand to call figures. Jack plumb forgot all about that colt and his mother bein' likely to run out of firewood, till pretty soon his uncle said he reckoned Jack better be gettin' on back.

"Yes," says Jack, "I guess I ought to have went 'fore this time."

"I got a nice little heifer up here, Jack, and I'm goin' to give it to you so you can have a good milk cow to go with your horse. You keep it fed up real well, and your mother can milk it for ye."

Got him a line and tied that heifer by the horns, gave it to Jack. Jack thanked him and started leadin' his heifer on back home.

Jack got down close to the King's house, he saw that girl was out at the washin' place where they were all a-workin' with the clothes. So Jack remembered and he went to jump on that heifer's back; somehow or other he landed on it hind side to, grabbed hold on its tail and started in hollerin'. That young heifer started bawlin' and jumpin' from one side the road to the other, and went a-gallopin' on down to where the King's folks was a-washin' at. The King's girl looked up and saw Jack gettin' shook up and down and a-slippin' first one side, then the other'n, on the heifer's back and him a-hold of its tail and a-hollerin' for help, and she raised up and laughed so loud they heard her all over town. She stood there and laughed and slapped her hands till the King came out. And when he saw Jack and that calf, he started in to laughin' too, laughed till he had to sit down.

Fin'ly some of 'em caught the heifer and holp Jack off.

The old King took Jack over in town and bought him a new suit of clothes. Then he hitched up two fine horses to a buggy and rode Jack and his girl over to a big church and had 'em married.

The girl she went on home with Jack, and the last time I was down there they were all gettin' on right well.

Considerations

1. This American Southern mountain folk tale combines elements of the hero tale, the African trickster tale, and the European numbskull tale, yet its style is as obviously American as the works of Mark Twain. What elements—other than setting—does "Jack and the King's Girl" have in common with other American stories in this book?
2. What is the effect of having a king be approachable even by Jack?
3. Does this story have a moral?

FICTION

Classic
Modern
Contemporary

Introduction to Fiction

Here is a story from a newspaper:

Miss Jennifer Thompson, 63, of 1712 Brundage Road, was listed in fair condition at St. Francis Hospital here today as a result of last night's fire that caused an estimated $7500 damage in her small apartment. According to firemen, a cigarette that had been smoldering in a wastebasket apparently burst into flames when Miss Thompson opened the door to her living room.

Miss Thompson managed to call the fire department but was then overcome by smoke inhalation.

Here is another way in which you might read about the same event:

Jenny slowly brushed her hair back with one hand while she tried sleepily to find the doorknob with the other. She thought, "How odd that I dozed off so early. Where is that smell of smoke coming from? Where's that wretched knob?"

The door was always hard to open. How often she had reached the living room too late to answer the phone just because she had had to fight a stupid door.

Finally it gave, and suddenly the smoke-filled gray of the room was shot through with the red of flames. Jenny stumbled to the phone. As she grabbed up the receiver, she watched her beautiful sofa and white fur rug become part of the blaze.

The purpose of the first piece is to inform. Theoretically, most of the information could be checked for accuracy. Its tone is objective and impersonal. The second version, on the other hand, is a personal recreation of an experience.

Although the story, or narrative, is basically an old form, fiction as we know it today is considered to be a relatively new genre compared to poetry and drama. The tradition of fiction started with myth and legend and allegory. But the fictional characters in these imaginary worlds were mostly one-dimensional abstractions, personified as Love, Greed, War, or even Sir Valiant in Faith. The evolution from allegory to novel (and short story), from the sermon about an abstraction in human guise to the story of the individual whose personal experience might have universal application, took a long time. Perhaps the first step toward a new mode was taken in 1382 when Geoffrey Chaucer translated Boccacio's phrase "E con gli occulti ferri i Tradimenti" (literally meaning "And treachery with hidden weapons") as "The smyler with the knyf under the cloke." Suddenly this character is a person rather than an abstraction.

For a long time, writing fiction was considered undignified; Sir Walter Scott and Jane Austen published their first works under pseudonyms. Reading fiction was considered even more vulgar, and the romances that filled the lending libraries of Regency England were thought to be suitable only for chambermaids. Perhaps part of the problem lay in the use of the word *fiction,* which implies falseness. This usage was avoided for a while by calling stories histories, thus giving an air of respectability to them. (The idea that fiction is false can be argued against in the sense that whatever man creates is real.) Even the most fantastic science-fiction story exists in its own reality. A story is a living thing, filled with experiences that are real—in the sense that we can relate to them. We draw on our own lives' experiences to respond to and understand the meanings that writers extract from human experience. The characters in a good story have feelings, personalities, desires, conflicts, motivations—in fact all the human elements of so-called "real" people. Very likely a writer's characters are drawn from characteristics of people he or she knows. In any event, the experience of reading good fiction is very real; we are simply taken for a period of time into a different level of reality.

Just what is fiction? The task of definition is difficult because a wide variety of prose writing has borne this label. Most of the fiction—as most of the literature—of Western civilization tends toward invention rather than transcription, toward creation rather than observation. Yet, as you can see, creation is born out of transcription and observation. That is why fiction does more than entertain and give pleasure: it gives us new insights into various aspects of human existence. It helps us perceive things in new ways, makes us think and wonder about—and evaluate—life and experience on a personal level.

Writers of fiction may base their stories on situations taken from real life. They then must add other details in order to make the scene real—information about how the people in the situation felt and what they thought that couldn't possibly be known. Yet this is not pure invention: characters must work within a framework of personality and must be consistent in their actions and reactions. The author gets this knowledge of people from closer observation of "reality." He or she is likely to have the characters act in ways that reveal something about human nature, the details of their backgrounds, and the relation of each to the other characters or to the setting. But unless the characters operate within a human framework, they will not be believable, and the story will not be effective. In this process, the author will probably, consciously or unconsciously, reveal something about his or her own attitudes as well, which gives the work a further dimension of reality.

There are certain basic elements that operate in a work of fiction. An understanding of these elements will heighten your pleasure in reading and provide additional levels of meaning and appreciation.

PLOT

Let us consider a scene (as Brooks and Warren suggest) in a railroad car that is passing slowly through a town. Two people, a man and a woman, are seated in the car, looking out the same window. It is late at night, and the streets of the town are lit up; the coach is in darkness. The man and woman are spectators of a drama that is taking place outside their window. Under a street light stand another man and woman. The woman's back is to the tracks, but in the few moments it takes the train to pass, the spectators can see her shake her head at the man. He appears to hit her; she bends over and supports herself against the side of the building. The train passes on.

Such are the basic ingredients. The natural question the witnesses ask themselves is, "Why did he do that?" They begin to speculate. The woman will tend to interpret the scene by projecting her own feelings and assumptions, and the man will do the same. Now, what happened on the street can be interpreted in any number of ways. The interpretation each witness makes reveals something of his or her own personality.

Even in this short sketch you can see the possibilities for expansion into a short story through the development of some of the basic elements of fiction. There is opportunity for the description of characters and setting, the development of atmosphere, and the use of the key moment (seeing the scene). There could be a plot involving conflict—either between the characters or within the minds of each of them. The way the events unfold could easily be linked to the outcome or resolution of the story.

A story has a beginning, a middle, and an end; or, to put it differently: an introduction, conflict, tension or some kind of rising action, a key moment that is a turning point or climax, and a resolution or denouement (the point at which elements are tied together for some conclusion).

Let's examine the structure of the plot in "Flight," by John Steinbeck. The story opens with a couple of paragraphs on the setting and the family background. We are introduced to the characters—Mama, Pepe, Emilio, and Rosy—and see Pepe throwing his knife, foreshadowing the later use of this knife. Words like *huddled, rotting,* and *crouched* prepare the reader for the defensive position the Torres family has taken—poor, uneducated, the father dead, the ways of officialdom against them. Mama's words "a boy gets to be a man when a man is needed" prepare the way for later events.

The action rises as a result of Mama's need for medicine, Pepe's ride to town (dressed in his father's things), and an action—a killing—that takes place offstage. The conflict comes when Pepe must deal with the consequences of his action. Mama sends him to the hills to die.

Pepe's departure is the turning point. Suspense is built on whether he will escape, or when, where, and how he will meet death. As Pepe goes up through the canyon, his identification with his father, marked at first, is slowly stripped away. He's not only a man now; he's his own man. He loses the knife, the hat, the horse, the gun.

There now is a falling action, the closing of the story (or the denouement). The climax of the story is very near the end as Pepe comes to terms with himself and his destiny—the end he has chosen. He stands up against the sky and allows himself to be shot. With the unravelling of the story is a reminder that Pepe is taken back to the earth from which he came.

The action in a plot is usually progressive, because one force acts upon another. However, even when events are not ordered chronologically, one can find these basic elements of plot at work. Plot, then, is the arrangement of events in a story, or the structure of the action.

POINT OF VIEW

A critical issue in any story is its point of view. The importance of point of view may easily be overlooked, but the choice of the narrator influences the total structure of the story. The reader knows only as much as the person acting as narrator, because everything is seen through the narrator's eyes. If one character acts as the narrator, the point of view is said to be limited to that character. A character who tells his own story will, of course, know only what goes on inside his own head. The observer who is a participant in the story is less directly and emotionally involved. The omniscient point of view (in which the author acts as an all-knowing narrator, free to comment on the action) would seem most appropriate for retelling the railway vignette outlined earlier, because all of the thoughts and experiences of people inside and outside the railroad car could become part of the story. The author may, however, choose to use a self-effacing, or objective, point of view, in which case actions and conversations are presented objectively, in detail, without authorial comment.

Point of view also dictates distance. Anything written in the first person will seem immediate and personal; the reader will almost feel himself part of the action. To illustrate this, consider a familiar story written in the third person:

Again he said: "There was once a man who had two sons; and the younger said to his father, 'Father, give me my share of the property.' So he divided his estate between them. A few days later the younger son turned the whole of his share into cash and left home for a distant country, where he squandered it in reckless living. He had spent it all when a severe famine fell upon that country and he began to feel the pinch. So he went and attached himself to one of the local landowners, who sent him on to his farm to mind the pigs. He would have been glad to fill his belly with the pods that the pigs were eating, but no one gave him anything. Then he came to his senses and said, 'How many of my father's paid servants have more food than they can eat, and here am I, starving to death! I will set off and go to my father, and say to him, "Father, I have sinned, against God and against you; I am no longer fit to be called your son; treat me as one of your paid servants.' So he set out for his father's house. But while he was still a long way off his father saw him, and his heart went out to him. He ran to meet him, flung his arms around him, and kissed him. The son said, 'Father, I have sinned, against God and against you; I am no longer fit to be called your son.' But the father said to his servants, 'Quick! fetch a robe, my best one, and put it on him; put a ring on his finger and shoes on his feet. Bring the fatted calf and kill it, and let us have a feast to celebrate the day. For this son of mine was dead and has come back to life; he was lost and is found.' And the festivities began.

"Now the elder son was out on the farm; and on his way back, as he approached the house, he heard music and dancing. He called one of the servants and asked what it meant. The servant told him, 'Your brother has come home, and your father has killed the fatted calf because he has him back safe and sound.' But he was angry and refused to go in. His father came out and pleaded with him; but he retorted, 'You know how I have slaved for you all these years; I never once disobeyed your orders; and you never gave me so much as a kid for a feast with my friends. But now that this son of yours turns up, after running through your money with his women, you kill the fatted calf for him!' 'My boy,' said the father, 'you are always with me, and everything I have is yours. How could we help celebrating this happy day? Your brother here was dead and has come back to life, was lost and is found.'"

Now imagine how the victim would begin the tale if it were told in the first person:

When the famine struck the countryside, I was penniless and was forced to work for a landowner tending his pigs. At that point, I was not beyond eating some of their food if I could have gotten it, but the owner watched the whole operation too closely. I felt that if someone did not offer me something to eat soon, I would not know what to do.

I found myself in this horrible situation due to my having spent my share of my Father's estate. . . .

An equally valid but different point of view would be that of a worker on the father's estate who was an observer yet almost a participant.

An author must decide what point of view best suits his or her material and purpose. In some stories several points of view may be used. When this is done, it is usually for a particular purpose, and paying attention to such a shift will usually tell you something about how the author wants you to feel toward the characters or the theme.

The narrator is not necessarily the character upon whom the story is focused. A story told in the first person by a bystander may focus on a character who particularly intrigues or annoys the storyteller. Only if the teller's character and actions are the major elements in the story's development is he the focus of the story. Often it is clear whose story a particular piece is. There is no question that "A Worn Path" is Phoenix Jackson's story. But in "Hills Like White Elephants" is it the man's story, the woman's story, or both? Here the author has used the objective point of view and has not focused on one character more than the other.

There are basically four points of view:

1. The narrator presents the story in the first person, directly through a character. He tells his own story or one in which he has participated as a minor character. The story sounds "real" because of the personal pronoun *I*. This type of narrator describes characters' thoughts and feelings through his own personal perspective and observation. Often he offers opinions, interpretations, and conclusions and reveals prejudices.

For example, in "The Use of Force," by William Carlos Williams (p. 218), the story is told totally in the first person. The narrator is also the main character, and all the other characters, action, and significance of events are perceived through him alone. Any conclusions or interpretations given are purely subjective. The story is of a doctor who is called to examine a little girl who may have diphtheria. The child is hostile and uncooperative; her parents are ineffectual. The doctor's attitudes, emotions, and opinions of his patient and her parents are transmitted to us through his experience alone. For example:

> The child was fully dressed and sitting on her father's lap near the kitchen table. He tried to get up, but I motioned for him not to bother, took off my overcoat, and started to look things over. I could see that they were all very nervous, eyeing me up and down distrustfully. As often, in such cases, they weren't telling me more than they had to, it was up to me to tell them: that's why they were spending three dollars on me.

From this we get the mood and tone of the work and the story from the perspective of one individual. He makes subjective assumptions about the actions of people.

2. The third-person, or dramatic, point of view involves a narrator who is a detached observer. He generally makes no judgments; he relates the story as though he were merely a spectator watching events and telling us about them. This type of narrator usually becomes aware of the event and action along with the reader and is probably more objective than the first-person narrator.

Guy de Maupassant uses this point of view in "The Pins" (p. 162). The story merely unfolds through an anonymous observer. He does not participate in the action in any way. He reveals no attitudes, takes no sides, and does not react to the people, events, or situations. With the exception of the opening scene, the story is entirely in dialogue, as though the narrator were simply relating an overheard conversation.

3. In the totally omniscient point of view, the narrator is godlike; he or she knows everything about the characters and events of the story—the thoughts, feelings, desires, and motives of the people in the narrative, as well as their pasts, presents, and futures. The perspective is not limited to one character; the narrator gets into the consciousness of all. The omniscient narrator often intrudes with comments, judgments, and opinions.

An example of this category can be seen in Malamud's "A Summer's Reading." The narrator does not participate in the story but is aware of the lives of everyone in it.

> One night, unable to stand the heat anymore, he burst into the street at one A.M., a shadow of himself. He hoped to sneak to the park without being seen, but there were people all over the block, wilted and listless, waiting for a breeze. George lowered his eyes and walked, in disgrace, away from them, but before long he discovered they were still friendly to him. He figured Mr. Cattanzara hadn't told on him.

Not only does the speaker know the reasons behind George's actions, he knows why the neighborhood people behave as they do.

4. On the other hand, the narrator in a story may be only partially omniscient; that is, he may know everything about only one character and tell the story through that character's eyes, thoughts, observations, emotions, and perspective. He perceives the other characters as being outside the main one; all action, reaction, events, and situations are interpreted by one individual alone.

James Joyce's "A Painful Case" (p. 200), is such a story. The narrator knows all about Mr. Duffy:

> Mr. James Duffy lived in Chapelizod because he wished to live as far as possible from the city of which he was a citizen and because he found all the other suburbs of Dublin mean, modern, and pretentious.

> Mr. Duffy abhorred anything which betokened physical or mental disorder. A medieval doctor would have called him saturnine.

> He had an odd autobiographical habit which led him to compose in his mind from time to time a short sentence about himself containing a subject in the third person and a predicate in the past tense.

This narrator knows all the personal idiosyncrasies, private thoughts, emotions, desires, habits, and motivations that make up this particular character, and the plot and events unfold within his perspective. This type of point of view is not necessarily objective.

THEME

In our discussion of plot there was a brief paraphrase of "Flight." This is useful in analyzing the specific structure of the plot, but what is missing in that paraphrase? Is this simply a story about a tragic occurrence in the life of a family? What else is the story about? What is its theme or dominant idea?

There are generally three different themes in literature: man against society; man against nature (including God); and man against himself. One theme in "Flight" is man against society—shown in the unhappy effect of the encounter between two cultures and their values. The minority culture represented by Mama, Pepe, Emilio, and Rosy has a code of behavior which differs from that of the society at large. The society at large—white American—emphasizes law and order, impersonal justice; under its rules one should not kill to repay an insult, and a killer should give himself up and stand trial. Mama and Pepe believe his initial action to have been valid, and that then it is correct to run away, even though this may lead to death.

A second theme in this story is man against himself—the initiation rite, the struggle of a boy becoming a man. Pepe's span as a man is very brief, measured in hours, but he does rise to the challenge and become one.

> "When did Pepe come to be a man?" Emilio asked. "Last night," said Rosy. "Last night in Monterey."

As he encounters and overcomes each new obstacle in his journey upward (note the direction), the losses, the animals, the danger, the fear, the weakness of his own body and mind, Pepe confirms his new status as a man. Being a man means putting aside games and enduring hardship; this Pepe has done.

> He leaned back on his elbow and gnawed at the tough strong meat. His face was blank, but it was a man's face.

And Pepe faces death as tradition says a man should.

> He crawled slowly and mechanically to the top of a big rock on the ridge peak. Once there, he rose slowly, swaying to his feet, and stood erect. Far below he

could see the dark brush where he had slept. He braced his feet and stood there black against the morning sky.

Plot and theme interact; each plays a part in shaping and defining the other. Often there is a theme that the author himself is not aware of, but which the reader perceives. The work itself has a life of its own, and in this sense the theme is dynamic and relevant to time, place, and change in attitudes—both personal and cultural. (Critics are constantly discovering new themes in the literature of all ages. Fine literature lives because it has a universal appeal.)

The theme is the author's statement of some human experience: it is the point of the story. We can say that the plot is what happens, and that the theme is what those happenings mean. The theme of a story may be any subject the author feels strongly about. (It should not be confused with a moral.) Usually it is suggested rather than stated. Ideally it will have universality, which makes it meaningful in a large context. In other words, a story may, on the surface, be nothing more than the description of what happened to a particular group of people in a particular set of circumstances. If that is all there is to the story, readers will probably feel at most a passing interest in it.

The stories that are read again and again by generations of readers are those that contain something more, something deeper, than superficial description. They contain something—a message, idea, or attitude—that is applicable to all readers in all times. Tolstoy's "The Death of Ivan Ilych" is an excellent example. Although it was written in the nineteenth century about a member of the Russian middle class, the underlying feelings expressed in it are very similar to those many people have today. Tolstoy's ideas are still relevant for modern readers.

CHARACTER

Just as plot reveals theme, characters build into plot and theme. These three elements work together to create a cohesive story. In "A Summer Tragedy," it is essential for the success of the story that we believe in the Pattons, sympathize with them, and experience their dilemma with them. From the beginning, the cost they are willing to pay for their dignity and sense of self-respect is established.

Old Jeff Patton, the black share farmer, fumbled with his bow tie. His fingers trembled and the high stiff collar pinched his throat. A fellow loses his hand for such vanities after thirty or forty years of simple life.

Jennie sat on the side of the bed and old Jeff Patton got down on one knee while she tied the bow knot. It was a slow and painful ordeal for each of them in this position. Jeff's bones cracked, his knee ached, and it was only after a half dozen attempts that Jennie worked a semblance of a bow into the tie.

Throughout their persistence in the face of pain, weakness, and misfortune is emphasized.

Jennie disappeared again through the dim passage into the shed room. Being blind was no handicap to her in the black hole. Jeff heard the cane placed against the wall beside the door and knew that his wife was on easy ground.

. . . He felt dazed and weak. He swung the car out into the yard, made a half turn and drove around to the front door. When he took his hands off the wheel, he noticed that he was trembling violently. He cut off the motor and climbed to the ground to wait for Jennie.

Jeff's industrious nature is also a matter of record.

He could not help reflecting that the crops were good. He knew what that meant, too; he had made forty-five of them with his own hands.

His is a code of strength, of not complaining, of not giving in.

Jeff thought it killed a good many share farmers as well as mules, but he had no sympathy for them. He had always been strong, and he had been taught to have no patience with weakness in men. Women or children might be tolerated if they were puny, but a weak man was a curse. . . .

The characters are developed through the explanation of their views given by the third-person narrator:

Jeff felt a familiar excitement, a thrill, as they came down the first slope to the immense levels on which the cotton was growing. He could not help reflecting that the crops were good.

their actions:

She cried aloud in a dry cracked voice that suggested the rattle of fodder on dead stalks. She cried aloud like a child, for she had never learned to suppress a genuine sob.

and their dialogue:

"You ain't really scairt, is you, Jeff?"
"Nah, baby, I ain't scairt."
"You know how we agreed—we gotta keep on goin'."
"I don't know," he said with a shiver.
"I reckon it's the only thing to do."

Having established that Jeff and Jennie Patton can't be complained about on any score, that life has treated them harshly, but they have done the best anyone could, the author presents an insoluble dilemma. Given the circumstances, given these individuals with their self-sufficient, proud, dignified natures, how could the resolution be other than what they elected? In principle we may disapprove of suicide and think it's a sign of weakness. In principle, we might hate to see these two end their lives, but such is the strength of the characterization that we would be hard put to argue for any other outcome. They persuade us and cause us to question ourselves, rather than leave us questioning them.

As you can see, the characters cannot be divorced from the plot and theme, which are to a great degree developed through them. Characterization presents human beings, their thoughts, attitudes, prejudices, mental states—indeed all of the aspects that make up a person. The character must be consistent to be believable. Once the author has established a basic personality, all of the action in the story must be congruent to it.

SYMBOLISM

As discussed, theme is the meaning of the subject or story, and there are elements working within the theme to broaden the meaning even further. To put it differently, certain elements set up more than one level of meaning. The author may want to call forth associations in you that will make a statement without explicitly spelling it out. For example, he or she may wish you to perceive an abstract idea in a concrete object (or person). In this case, the object or person represents more than just itself. There are many levels of meaning in Kafka's "The Judgment" (p. 177). The story seems rather simple: a young man sits down to write to an old friend and tells him of his engagement to be married. He is successful in business but carries a sense of guilt for neglecting his father, for being happy in his situation while his friend is alone and far from home, for planning to marry while his friend is still single, and possibly even for marrying without love, as it seems to be a match of convenience. Fearing a bizarre confrontation with his father, he is sentenced to death by the old man and then becomes his own executioner by jumping off a bridge.

Now let's examine this story on a different level. In a political context, the father could represent power and authority as inevitable and irrevocable as the courts that pass judgments on individuals. The father is presented as whimsical; he changes position from moment to moment: the friend does exist; the friend does not exist. This echoes a kind of exploitation common to power structures. There is no truth involved; only the (father) power counts.

The state of bachelorhood could represent the state outside the institution of marriage and family, a state unequal to the traditional institutions. Georg, a materialist, is about to relinquish his freedom and bachelorhood to become a part of one of society's strongest institutions. He is passive and conforming.

The friend could represent the rebel or activist—the one who refuses to conform and comply with society's order, and who therefore removes himself from it. (The friend's activities in Russia, in fact, *are* political.) Georg's father's suggestion that he has been keeping the friend informed puts Georg in a subordinate position. Even though the friend and the father may represent two political extremes, the two powers respect each other, whereas the underdog (Georg) earns no respect at all.

In this interpretation, then, Georg, his father, his friend, and the state of bachelorhood symbolize much more than their concrete existences.

Now let us consider a Freudian interpretation. Georg is a passive individual, his friend an active one. Perhaps the friend represents Georg's alter ego, the qualities he lacks. The absence of the friend could represent an alienation from these qualities, or the divorce within the self. Georg knows something is lacking, but doesn't know how to bring meaning into his life through action. He therefore feels guilty and judges himself.

He attempts to supplant his father in their business, as in the Freudian view a son seeks to replace the father.

> "Am I well covered up?" asked the father once more, seeming to be strangely intent upon the answer.
> "Don't worry, you're well covered up." "No!" cried his father, cutting short the answer, threw the blankets off with a strength that sent them all flying in a moment and sprang erect in bed. Only one hand lightly touched the ceiling to steady him.
> "You wanted to cover me up, I know, my young sprig, but I'm far from being covered up yet. And even if this is the last strength I have, it's enough for you, too much for you."

In this scene the father realizes the son's ambitions and accuses him of wanting to "cover him up." This could symbolize replacement. The father asserts himself and his position with a surprising strength to reclaim his position of authority.

The classic conflict between father and son for woman can be seen in the father's statement:

> "Just take your bride on your arm and try getting in my way! I'll sweep her from your very side, you don't know how."

The father here asserts his sexuality, suggesting that he is still far more vital than his son. This sexual symbolism is strengthened in the previous quote, when the father "sprang erect in bed." The sexual suggestion here is plain.

Even the strange scene with the charwoman can be seen in the symbolic sense. She restores a sort of superficial order to the room, as it was before the confrontation. She might symbolize the epitome of illusion: ignore the real meaning or cause and sweep it all under the carpet; clean up the mess for a superficial and illusory cleanliness.

Thus Kafka uses concrete realities to communicate ideas and situations that are not part of the external reality of the story.

Basically there are four types of symbols:

1. The literary symbol, such as in "The Judgment," in which Kafka uses certain images to evoke certain ideas—for example, in the scene where Georg carries his father to bed as one would a child.

> He carried his father to bed in his arms. It gave him a dreadful feeling to notice that while he took the few steps toward the bed the old man on his breast was playing with his watch chain. He could not lay him down on the bed for a moment, so firmly did he hang on to the watch chain.

The watch chain can symbolize Georg's manhood—the father is playing with it—or it could symbolize his own, which he is still hanging on to. This in turn could also symbolize a reversal of roles: again, the son becomes the father, thus reinforcing the idea of the struggle between father and son for authority.

2. A natural symbol is one that represents a quality naturally associated with it, such as spring represents rebirth or new life. In the beginning of "The Judgment," Georg is sitting in a sunny room "in the very height of spring" writing to his friend about his engagement and his plan to begin a "new life."

3. Conventional symbols are those that have become familiar to everyone, such as a lamb as the symbol of Christ, the flag as the symbol of a country, and so forth.

4. Private symbols are those that are significant to the author in a private way, and, unless he explains them, their meanings are anyone's guess. Kafka undoubtedly used many private symbols, which in part accounts for the difficult and sometimes baffling (but engrossing) quality of most of his work.

Symbolism, as you have seen, adds a richness of suggestion and provides different levels of meaning by expressing abstract concepts through the use of concrete objects.

IRONY

Frequently an author creates a situation or statement that is surprisingly incongruous or even the opposite of what it seems to (or should) be. The use of irony occurs in various types of stories for various effects.

For example, two types of irony are used in Katherine Mansfield's "A Dill Pickle," (p. 208) which is the story of a chance meeting between former lovers. Many negative memories (and some positive ones) are evoked in the mind of the woman as she listens, or half listens, to the man tell her about his life since they parted. While she flits from memory to memory of her past with this man, he talks on, and finally says, "What a marvellous listener you are." The statement is ironic under the circumstances.

There is an ironic situation as well. She thinks,

Ah, God! What had she done! How had she dared to throw away her happiness like this. This was the only man who had ever understood her. Was it too late? Could it be too late? She was that glove that he held in his fingers. . . .

Although she was the one to end the relationship, her present receptiveness to him constitutes an irony of situation. He seems to have matured somewhat, become a bit more independent, and has found a full life without her; he speaks of their relationship only in terms of the past. They seem to have switched positions.

Other examples of irony can be found in Hemingway's "Hills Like White Elephants" (p. 214). This story is essentially a dialogue between a man and a woman involved in an emotional relationship. They are passing the time in a bar in Spain, waiting for a train. Apparently the woman is pregnant, and the man wishes her to have an abortion, obviously against her desire. At one point, in answer to her question, "And you think then we'll be all right and be happy?" he replies, "I know we will. You don't have to be afraid. I've known lots of people that have done it." She then responds, "So have I. . . . And afterward they were all so happy." One detects a shade of sarcasm here; she seems to mean the opposite of what she says. Her closing statement is yet another example of verbal irony. The man asks her if she is feeling better, and she answers: "I feel fine," she said. "There's nothing wrong with me. I feel fine." We feel that perhaps she is protesting too much. In the context of the story, she again seems to mean the opposite of what she is saying.

This kind of ironic contrast is often used to reinforce the theme, expand characterization, lend a humorous or sarcastic element to the work, and generally give it additional interest, variety, or surprise.

FIGURATIVE LANGUAGE

An important element in all of literature is the use of figurative language. In "Flight" (p. 234), John Steinbeck writes:

> The farm buildings huddled like little clinging aphids on the mountain skirts, crouched low to the ground as though the wind might blow them into the sea.

This description of the buildings evokes a stronger mental image than if he had simply said, "The farm buildings were at the foot of a mountain." The type of figure of speech Steinbeck uses is called a *simile,* a direct comparison of two things basically unalike. Generally a simile will use words such as *like* and *as* (see above quote) to set up the comparison.

Another figure of speech is used by Steinbeck on p. 244:

> In the mountains the sun is high in its arc before it penetrates the gorges. The hot face looked over the hill and brought instant heat with it.

The use of "the hot face" gives human qualities to the sun; it becomes more than just the sun. Another example of this:

> On the other side the hill rose up sharply, and at the top the jagged rotten teeth of the mountain showed against the sky.

Again, the mountain is given human characteristics. This is called *personification,* which is a device that gives human qualities or characteristics to inanimate objects, animals, or abstractions.

In "A Painful Case" (p. 200), Joyce writes, "He gnawed the rectitude of his life; he felt that he had been outcast from life's feast." Joyce uses the images of food and eating to describe Mr. Duffy's emotional state. This device is a *metaphor;* it implies a likeness between unlike things. Unlike the simile, which uses connectives such as *like* or *as,* the metaphor simply asserts the image.

The use of figurative language takes us beyond the literal and gives the writing a colorful and imaginative quality. It also evokes various emotions and associations in us and is therefore linked to imagery, which is a sensory impression created by special uses of language. Figurative language connects the abstract with a particular or universal experience, thus allowing us to see ordinary things in a fresh, new light.

ATMOSPHERE AND SETTING

In the first few sentences of "Girls in Their Summer Dresses," Shaw establishes the atmosphere for his story.

Fifth Avenue was shining in the sun when they left the Brevoort and started walking toward Washington Square. The sun was warm, even though it was November and everything looked like Sunday morning—the buses, and the well-dressed people walking slowly in couples and the quiet buildings with the windows closed.

This creates a certain mood or feeling in us, which is important in developing action and theme. It also informs us of the time, season, and environment, and gives the story the quality of a "real" experience.

Changing the setting and atmosphere can suggest a change of psychological environment or mood as in "The Judgment." When Georg is sitting in a sunny room, we feel the pleasant laziness of a springtime Sunday morning. But when he enters his father's room, not only do the setting and atmosphere change but the mood and situation as well. The reader feels this change with Georg:

It surprised Georg how dark his father's room was even on this sunny morning. So it was overshadowed as much as that by the high wall on the other side of the narrow courtyard. His father was sitting by the window in a corner hung with various mementoes of Georg's dead mother, reading a newspaper which he held to one side before his eyes in an attempt to overcome a defect of vision. On the table stood the remains of his breakfast, not much of which seemed to have been eaten.

A setting can also be symbolic, as Georg's room is in light, his father's in darkness. Light and dark can symbolize knowledge and ignorance, respectively, or in the context of this particular story, youth and age or vitality and infirmity.

As we have seen, authors can make many subtle statements by manipulating mood through setting and atmosphere. Through this device they create a world for their characters and a background against which we perceive the action.

TECHNIQUE AND STYLE

Style is that special quality that makes a writer's work unmistakably his own. The particular way a writer uses the various elements of fiction makes for his or her own unique trademark. Just as the theme is very personal to each author, so are the style, the tone, and the use of rhetorical devices like symbolism and figurative language. The tone of a work reflects both the author's attitude toward the subject and toward the reader. An author's *style* is a particularly characteristic way of writing, and it involves all of the elements of writing, such as sentence structure, diction, tone, and use of figurative language. He may write long involved sentences or very short clipped sentences; he may use a lot of description or none at all; his statements may be vague and general or very precise. (In the stories in this collection, those by Hemingway and Faulkner are good examples of their authors' very noticeable styles).

One characteristic of an author's style is the extent to which he uses or doesn't use figurative language and symbolism. In the writings of authors such as Hawthorne, many objects and events are laden with symbolic significance. A light is not merely a light—it is hope, a new beginning, or even life itself. Occasionally dialogue is used to express the author's ideas more personally and directly through one character who acts as his spokesman. For example, Hemingway's male characters are often Hemingway in thin disguise. When this occurs, the author is said to be using a *persona.* Different authors use dialogue in different ways to reveal something about characters or to advance action.

In addition to the various elements already discussed, there are other techniques a writer can employ to create special effects. For example, Hemingway mainly used *dialogue* in his story, "Hills Like White Elephants." The dialogue is an integral part of the action, plot, theme, and characterization. In this story it is vivid and realistic; we feel as though we are eavesdropping on a private conversation. The effect is dramatic—very much like a movie or play. The information necessary for us to understand the characters and situation comes directly from the dialogue. The author does not comment or explain. Characterization is established through dialogue alone, and it remains consistent to each character throughout. Dialogue also plays an important part in creating the atmosphere and mood.

The order in which action and events occur can be chronological, or the author can deliberately move us to events of another place and time. These *flashbacks* often reveal special insights into characters by giving the reader additional information about a particular character and his motivations. For example, a flashback occurs in the story "A Dill Pickle," by Katherine Mansfield (p. 208.)

> . . . Yet, what had remained in her mind of that particular afternoon was an absurd scene over the tea table. A great many people taking tea in a Chinese pagoda, and he behaving like a maniac about the wasps—waving them away, flapping at them with his straw hat, serious and infuriated out of all proportion to the occasion. How delighted the sniggering tea drinkers had been. And how she had suffered.

This flashback tells us something about the earlier relation between this man and woman, who he thought was important, how she regarded this. This scene of the past, contrasted to the present, gives us a broader insight into the characters. The flashback is used as an organizational device in that it rearranges time and causes us to focus our attention on a particular aspect of plot or character.

Another technique authors use is *suspense*. Often the author will provide a hint about events that are to come. This tends to build up tension and suspense. For example, in "The Revolt of Mother," by Mary E. Wilkins Freeman, the technique called *foreshadowing* is used. This is a story of a hard-working farm woman who, when she learns that her husband is building a new barn instead of a much-needed and long-promised new home, revolts against his domination and stubbornness and moves the family into the barn. She makes her point, and her husband ultimately agrees to construct a new home for his family. Her "revolt" comes at a time when her daughter is about to be married and both she and her daughter are embarrassed at the shabbiness of their tiny home where the wedding is to be held.

> "I've been thinking—I don't see how we're goin' to have any—wedding in this room. I'd be ashamed to have his folks come if we didn't have anybody else.
>
> "Mebee we can have some new paper before then; I can put it on. I guess you won't have no call to be ashamed of your belongin's."
>
> "We might have the wedding in the new barn," said Nanny, with gentle pettishness. "Why, mother, what makes you look so?"
>
> Mrs. Penn had started, and was staring at her with a curious expression. She turned again to her work, and spread out a pattern carefully on the cloth. "Nothin'," said she.

This scene gives a hint of events to come. We may not know exactly what sort of action is to take place, but we recognize a signal of a significant coming event. When we begin to relate this scene to the other events in the story, it becomes particularly meaningful. Foreshadowing can be so subtle that at times we must read the story a second time to appreciate the skillful use of this technique. Foreshadowing links various elements within a story and is therefore an important unifying device.

An author's style, then, is the unique way in which he says what he has to say through the use of various rhetorical techniques and the skillful use of the various elements of fiction.

The selections that follow are for the most part short stories. Short stories differ from the novel or novella chiefly in matters of complexity, development, number of episodes, and number of loose ends (material that is introduced without being an essential part of the story's development, or denouement). The process of selectivity is so keen in a short story and the scope is so brief (usually 3000–5000 words) that there isn't space for the leisurely establishment of mood and setting that there is in a novel. In a well-written short story, each word helps establish the overall impression.

Within these limits, short stories touch on almost as wide a variety of themes as novels. Many of the first short stories written are stories in which adventure is more important than characterization. These stories are highly plotted; there is a quick introduction to the characters, a complication (or complications) of some kind, conflict, a climax, and then a resolution.

Many modern short stories lack an obvious plot or theme. Many of the nebulous, "what's-the-point?" type baffle readers who try to come up with a single definitive statement about what the author was trying to say. A judgment as to when a description of "a slice of life" is merely that and when it becomes a short story involves criteria outside the province of this text. You will find that the stories that have been included here are not of that variety.

An attempt has been made in this collection to balance themes and settings and yet to include representative pieces by some of the most important writers of our times. You will find a preponderant number of stories about relatively well-to-do urban men and women who are alienated, unhappy, aimless, and unmotivated, aspiring to little and doing less, and yet the sampling is representative. For a number of years during the middle of the twentieth century it seems as though the majority of good writers dealt with this subject at least tangentially.

The struggle against malevolent authority may have preoccupied many novelists and several dramatists, but short-story writers seem to have remained more concerned with the human condition as reflected in personal relationships.

The Minister's Black Veil

NATHANIEL HAWTHORNE

The sexton stood in the porch of Milford meeting-house, pulling busily at the bell-rope. The old people of the village came stooping along the street. Children, with bright faces, tripped merrily beside their parents, or mimicked a graver gait, in the conscious dignity of their Sunday clothes. Spruce bachelors looked sidelong at the pretty maidens, and fancied that the Sabbath sunshine made them prettier than on week days. When the throng had mostly streamed into the porch, the sexton began to toll the bell, keeping his eye on the Reverend Mr. Hooper's door. The first glimpse of the clergyman's figure was the signal for the bell to cease its summons.

"But what has good Parson Hooper got upon his face?" cried the sexton in astonishment.

All within hearing immediately turned about, and beheld the semblance of Mr. Hooper, pacing slowly his meditative way towards the meeting-house. With one accord they started, expressing more wonder than if some strange minister were coming to dust the cushions of Mr. Hooper's pulpit.

"Are you sure it is our parson?" inquired Goodman Gray of the sexton.

"Of a certainty it is good Mr. Hooper," replied the sexton. "He was to have exchanged pulpits with Parson Shute, of Westbury; but Parson Shute sent to excuse himself yesterday, being to preach a funeral sermon."

The cause of so much amazement may appear sufficiently slight. Mr. Hooper, a gentlemanly person, of about thirty, though still a bachelor, was dressed with due clerical neatness, as if a careful wife had starched his band, and brushed the weekly dust from his Sunday's garb. There was but one thing remarkable in his appearance. Swathed about his forehead, and hanging down over his face, so low as to be shaken by his breath, Mr. Hooper had on a black veil. On a nearer view it seemed to consist of two folds of crape, which entirely concealed his features, except the mouth and chin, but probably did not intercept his sight, further than to give a darkened aspect to all living and inanimate things. With this gloomy shade before him, good Mr. Hooper walked onward, at a slow and quiet pace, stooping somewhat, and looking on the ground, as is customary with abstracted men, yet nodding kindly to those of his parishioners who still waited on the meeting-house steps. But so wonder-struck were they that his greeting hardly met with a return.

"I can't really feel as if good Mr. Hooper's face was behind that piece of crape," said the sexton.

"I don't like it," muttered an old woman, as she hobbled into the meeting-house. "He has changed himself into something awful, only by hiding his face."

"Our parson has gone mad!" cried Goodman Gray, following him across the threshold.

A rumor of some unaccountable phenomenon had preceded Mr. Hooper into the meeting-house, and set all the congregation astir. Few could refrain from twisting their heads towards the door; many stood upright, and turned directly about; while several little boys clambered upon the seats, and came down again with a terrible racket. There was a general bustle, a rustling of the women's gowns and shuffling of the men's feet, greatly at variance with that hushed response which should attend the entrance of the minister. But Mr. Hooper appeared not to notice the perturbation of his people. He entered with an almost noiseless step, bent his head mildly to the pews on each side, and bowed as he passed his oldest parishioner, a white-haired great-grandsire, who occupied an arm-chair in the centre of the aisle. It was strange to observe how slowly this venerable man became conscious of something singular in the appearance of his pastor. He seemed not fully to partake of the prevailing wonder, till Mr. Hooper had ascended the stairs, and showed himself in the pulpit, face to face with his congregation, except for the black veil. That mysterious emblem was never once withdrawn. It shook with his measured breath, as he gave out the psalm; it threw its obscurity between him and the holy page, as he read the Scriptures; and while he prayed, the veil lay heavily on his uplifted countenance. Did he seek to hide it from the dread Being whom he was addressing?

Such was the effect of this simple piece of crape, that more than one woman of delicate nerves was forced to leave the meeting-house. Yet perhaps the pale-faced congregation was almost as fearful a sight to the minister, as his black veil to them.

Mr. Hooper had the reputation of a good preacher, but not an energetic one: he strove to win his people heavenward by mild, persuasive influences, rather than to drive them thither by the thunders of the Word. The sermon which he now delivered was marked by the same characteristics of style and manner as the general series of his pulpit oratory. But there was something, either in the sentiment of the discourse itself, or in the imagination of the auditors, which made it greatly the most powerful effort that they had ever heard from their pastor's lips. It was tinged, rather more darkly than usual, with the gentle gloom of Mr. Hooper's temperament. The subject had reference to secret sin, and those sad mysteries which we hide from our nearest and dearest, and would fain conceal from our own consciousness, even forgetting that the Omniscient can detect them. A subtle power was breathed into his words. Each member of the congregation, the most innocent girl, and the man of hardened breast, felt as if the preacher had crept upon them, behind his awful veil, and discovered their hoarded iniquity of deed or thought. Many spread their clasped hands on their bosoms. There was nothing terrible in what Mr. Hooper said, at least, no violence; and yet, with every tremor of his melancholy voice, the hearers quaked. An unsought pathos came hand in hand with awe. So sensible were the audience of some unwonted attribute in their minister, that they longed for a breath of wind to blow aside the veil, almost believing that a stranger's visage would be discovered, though the form, gesture, and voice were those of Mr. Hooper.

At the close of the services, the people hurried out with indecorous confusion, eager to communicate their pent-up amazement, and conscious of lighter spirits the moment they lost sight of the black veil. Some gathered in little circles, huddled closely together, with their mouths all whispering in the centre; some went homeward alone, wrapt in silent meditation; some talked loudly, and profaned the Sabbath day with ostentatious laughter. A few shook their sagacious heads, intimating that they could penetrate the mystery; while one or two affirmed that there was no mystery at all, but only that Mr. Hooper's eyes were so weakened by the midnight lamp, as to require a shade. After a brief interval, forth came good Mr. Hooper also, in the rear of his flock. Turning his veiled face from one group to another, he

paid due reverence to the hoary heads, saluted the middle aged with kind dignity as their friend and spiritual guide, greeted the young with mingled authority and love, and laid his hands on the little children's heads to bless them. Such was always his custom on the Sabbath day. Strange and bewildered looks repaid him for his courtesy. None, as on former occasions, aspired to the honor of walking by their pastor's side. Old Squire Saunders, doubtless by an accidental lapse of memory, neglected to invite Mr. Hooper to his table, where the good clergyman had been wont to bless the food, almost every Sunday since his settlement. He returned, therefore, to the parsonage, and, at the moment of closing the door, was observed to look back upon the people, all of whom had their eyes fixed upon the minister. A sad smile gleamed faintly from beneath the black veil, and flickered about his mouth, glimmering as he disappeared.

"How strange," said a lady, "that a simple black veil, such as any woman might wear on her bonnet should become such a terrible thing on Mr. Hooper's face!"

"Something must surely be amiss with Mr. Hooper's intellects," observed her husband, the physician of the village. "But the strangest part of the affair is the effect of this vagary, even on a sober-minded man like myself. The black veil, though it covers only our pastor's face, throws its influence over his whole person, and makes him ghostlike from head to foot. Do you not feel it so?"

"Truly do I," replied the lady; "and

I would not be alone with him for the world. I wonder he is not afraid to be alone with himself!"

"Men sometimes are so," said her husband.

The afternoon service was attended with similar circumstances. At its conclusion, the bell tolled for the funeral of a young lady. The relatives and friends were assembled in the house, and the more distant acquaintances stood about the door, speaking of the good qualities of the deceased, when their talk was interrupted by the appearance of Mr. Hooper, still covered with his black veil. It was now an appropriate emblem. The clergyman stepped into the room where the corpse was laid, and bent over the coffin, to take a last farewell of his deceased parishioner. As he stooped, the veil hung straight down from his forehead, so that, if her eyelids had not been closed forever, the dead maiden might have seen his face. Could Mr. Hooper be fearful of her glance, that he so hastily caught back the black veil? A person who watched the interview between the dead and living, scrupled not to affirm, that, at the instant when the clergyman's features were disclosed, the corpse had slightly shuddered, rustling the shroud and muslin cap, though the countenance retained the composure of death. A superstitious old woman was the only witness of this prodigy. From the coffin Mr. Hooper passed into the chamber of the mourners, and thence to the head of the staircase, to make the funeral prayer. It was a tender and heart-dissolving prayer, full of sorrow, yet so imbued with celestial hopes, that the music of a heavenly harp, swept by the fingers of the dead, seemed faintly to be heard among the saddest accents of the minister. The people trembled, though they but darkly understood him when he prayed that they, and himself, and all of mortal race, might be ready, as he trusted this young maiden had been, for the dreadful hour that should snatch the veil from their faces. The bearers went heavily forth, and the mourners followed, saddening all the street, with the dead before them, and Mr. Hooper in his black veil behind.

"Why do you look back?" said one in the procession to his partner.

"I had a fancy," replied she, "that the minister and the maiden's spirit were walking hand in hand."

"And so had I, at the same moment," said the other.

That night, the handsomest couple in Milford village were to be joined in wedlock. Though reckoned a melancholy man, Mr. Hooper had a placid cheerfulness for such occasions, which often excited a sympathetic smile where livelier merriment would have been thrown away. There was no quality of his disposition which made him more beloved than this. The company at the wedding awaited his arrival with impatience, trusting that the strange awe, which had gathered over him throughout the day, would now be dispelled. But such was not the result. When Mr. Hooper came, the first thing that their eyes rested on was the same horrible black veil, which had added deeper gloom to the funeral, and could portend nothing but evil to the wedding. Such was its immediate effect on the guests that a cloud seemed to have rolled duskily from beneath the black crape, and dimmed the light of the candles. The bridal pair stood up before the minister. But the bride's cold fingers quivered in the tremulous hand of the bridegroom, and her deathlike paleness caused a whisper that the maiden who had been buried a few hours before was come from her grave to be married. If ever another wedding was so dismal, it was that famous one where they tolled the wedding knell. After performing the ceremony, Mr. Hooper raised a glass of wine to his lips, wishing happiness to the new-married couple in a strain of mild pleasantry that ought to have brightened the features of the guests, like a cheerful gleam from the hearth. At that instant, catching a glimpse of his figure in the looking-glass, the black veil involved his own spirit in the horror with which it overwhelmed all others. His frame shuddered, his lips grew white, he spilt the untasted wine upon the carpet, and rushed forth into the darkness. For the Earth, too, had on her Black Veil.

The next day, the whole village of Milford talked of little else than Parson Hooper's black veil. That, and the mystery concealed behind it, supplied a topic for discussion between acquaintances meeting in the street, and good women gossiping at their open windows. It was the first item of news that the tavern-keeper told to his guests. The children babbled of it on their way to school. One imitative little imp covered his face with an old black handkerchief, thereby so affrighting his playmates that the panic seized himself, and he well-nigh lost his wits by his own waggery.

It was remarkable that of all the busybodies and impertinent people in the parish, not one ventured to put the plain question to Mr. Hooper, wherefore he did this thing. Hitherto, whenever there appeared the slightest call for such interference, he had never lacked advisers, nor shown himself averse to be guided by their judgment. If he erred at all, it was by so painful a degree of self-distrust, that even the mildest censure would lead him to consider an indifferent action as a crime. Yet, though so well acquainted with this amiable weakness, no individual among his parishioners chose to make the black veil a subject of friendly remonstrance. There was a feeling of dread, neither plainly confessed nor carefully concealed, which caused each to shift the responsibility upon another, till at length it was found expedient to send a deputation of the church, in order to deal with Mr. Hooper about the mystery, before it should grow into a scandal. Never did an embassy so ill discharge its duties. The minister received them with friendly courtesy, but became silent, after they were seated, leaving to his visitors the whole burden of introducing their important business. The topic, it might be supposed, was obvious enough. There was the black veil swathed round Mr. Hooper's forehead, and concealing every feature above his placid mouth, on which, at times, they could perceive the glimmering of a melancholy smile. But that piece of crape, to their imagination, seemed to hang down before his heart, the symbol of a fearful secret between him and them. Were the veil but cast aside, they might speak freely of it, but not till then. Thus they sat a considerable time, speechless, confused, and shrinking uneasily from Mr. Hooper's eye, which they felt to be fixed upon them with an invisible glance. Finally, the deputies returned abashed to their constituents, pronouncing the matter too weighty to be handled, except by a council of the churches, if, indeed, it might not require a general synod.

But there was one person in the village unappalled by the awe with which the black veil had impressed all beside herself. When the deputies returned without an explanation, or even venturing to demand one, she, with the calm energy of her character, determined to chase away the strange cloud that appeared to be settling round Mr. Hooper, every moment more darkly than before. As his plighted wife, it should be her privilege to know what the black veil concealed. At the minister's first visit, therefore, she entered upon the subject with a direct simplicity, which made the task easier both for him and her. After he had seated himself, she fixed her eyes steadfastly upon the veil, but could discern nothing of the dreadful gloom that had so overawed the multitude: it was but a double fold of crape, hanging down from his forehead to his mouth, and slightly stirring with his breath.

"No," said she aloud, and smiling, "there is nothing terrible in this piece of crape, except that it hides a face which I am always glad to look upon. Come, good sir, let the sun shine from behind the cloud. First lay aside your black veil: then tell me why you put it on."

Mr. Hooper's smile glimmered faintly.

"There is an hour to come," said he, "when all of us shall cast aside our veils. Take it not amiss, beloved friend, if I wear this piece of crape till then."

"Your words are a mystery, too," returned the young lady. "Take away the veil from them, at least."

"Elizabeth, I will," said he, "so far as my vow may suffer me. Know, then, this veil is a type and a symbol, and I am bound to wear it ever, both in light and darkness, in solitude and before the gaze of multitudes, and as with strangers, so with my familiar friends. No mortal eye will see it withdrawn. This dismal shade must separate me from the world: even you, Elizabeth, can never come behind it!"

"What grievous affliction hath befallen you," she earnestly inquired, "that you should thus darken your eyes forever?"

"If it be a sign of mourning," replied Mr. Hooper, "I, perhaps, like most other mortals, have sorrows dark enough to be typified by a black veil."

"But what if the world will not believe that it is the type of an innocent sorrow?" urged Elizabeth. "Beloved and respected as you are, there may be whispers that you hide your face under the consciousness of secret sin. For the sake of your holy office, do away this scandal!"

The color rose into her cheeks as she intimated the nature of the rumors that were already abroad in the village. But Mr. Hooper's mildness did not forsake him. He even smiled again—that same sad smile, which always appeared like a faint glimmering of light, proceeding from the obscurity beneath the veil.

"If I hide my face for sorrow, there is cause enough," he merely replied; "and if I cover it for secret sin, what mortal might not do the same?"

And with this gentle, but unconquerable obstinacy did he resist all her entreaties. At length Elizabeth sat silent. For a few moments she appeared lost in thought, considering, probably, what new methods might be tried to withdraw her lover from so dark a fantasy, which, if it had no other meaning, was perhaps a symptom of mental disease. Though of a firmer character than his own, the tears rolled down her cheeks. But, in an instant, as it were, a new feeling took the place of sorrow: her eyes were fixed insensibly on the black veil, when, like a sudden twilight in the air, its terrors fell around her. She arose, and stood trembling before him.

"And do you feel it then, at last?" said he mournfully.

She made no reply, but covered her eyes with her hand, and turned to leave the room. He rushed forward and caught her arm.

"Have patience with me, Elizabeth!" cried he passionately. "Do not desert me, though this veil must be between us here on earth. Be mine, and hereafter there shall be no veil over my face, no darkness between our souls! It is but a mortal veil—it is not for eternity! O! you know not how lonely I am, and how frightened, to be alone behind my black veil. Do not leave me in this miserable obscurity forever!"

"Lift the veil but once, and look me in the face," said she.

"Never! It cannot be!" replied Mr. Hooper.

"Then farewell!" said Elizabeth.

She withdrew her arm from his grasp, and slowly departed, pausing at the door, to give one long shuddering gaze, that seemed almost to penetrate the mystery of the black veil. But, even amid his grief, Mr. Hooper smiled to think that only a material emblem had separated him from happiness, though the horrors, which it shadowed forth, must be drawn darkly between the fondest of lovers.

From that time no attempts were made to remove Mr. Hooper's black veil, or, by a direct appeal, to discover the secret which it was supposed to hide. By persons who claimed a superiority to popular prejudice, it was reckoned merely an eccentric whim, such as often mingles with the sober actions of men otherwise rational, and tinges them all with its own semblance of insanity. But with the multitude, good Mr. Hooper was irreparably a bugbear. He could not walk the street with any peace of mind, so conscious was he that the gentle and timid would turn aside to avoid him, and that others would make it a point of hardihood to throw themselves in his way. The impertinence of the latter class compelled him to give up his customary walk at sunset to the burial ground; for when he leaned pensively over the gate, there would always be faces behind the gravestones, peeping at his black veil. A fable went the rounds that the stare of the dead people drove him thence. It grieved him, to the very depth of his kind heart, to observe how the children fled from his approach, breaking up their merriest sports, while his melancholy figure was yet afar off. Their instinctive dread caused him to feel more strongly than aught else, that a preternatural horror was interwoven with the threads of the black crape. In truth, his own antipathy to the veil was known to be so great, that he never willingly passed before a mirror, nor stooped to drink at a still fountain, lest, in its peaceful bosom, he should be affrighted by himself. This was what gave plausibility to the whispers, that Mr. Hooper's conscience tortured him for some great crime too horrible to be entirely concealed, or otherwise than so obscurely intimated. Thus, from beneath the black veil, there rolled a cloud into the sunshine, and ambiguity of sin or sorrow, which enveloped the poor minister, so that love or sympathy could never reach him. It was said that ghost and fiend consorted with him there. With self-shudderings and outward terrors, he walked continually in its shadow, groping darkly within his own soul, or gazing through a medium that saddened the whole world. Even the lawless wind, it was believed, respected his dreadful secret, and never blew aside the veil. But still good Mr. Hooper sadly smiled at the pale visages of the worldly throng as he passed by.

Among all its bad influences, the black veil had the one desirable effect, of making its wearer a very efficient clergyman. By the aid of his mysterious emblem—for there was no other apparent cause—he became a man of awful power over souls that were in agony for sin. His converts always regarded him with a dread peculiar to themselves, affirming, though but figuratively, that, before he brought them to celestial light, they had been with him behind the black veil. Its gloom, indeed, enabled him to sympathize with all dark affections. Dying sinners cried aloud for Mr. Hooper, and would not yield their breath till he appeared; though ever, as he stooped to whisper consolation, they shuddered at the veiled face so near their own. Such were the terrors of the black veil, even when Death had bared his visage! Strangers came long distances to attend service at his church, with the mere idle purpose of gazing at his figure, because it was forbidden them to behold his face. But many were made to quake ere they departed! Once, during Governor Belcher's administration, Mr. Hooper was appointed to preach the election sermon. Covered with his black veil, he stood before the chief magistrate, the council, and the representatives, and wrought so deep an impression, that the legislative measures of that year were characterized by all the gloom and piety of our earliest ancestral sway.

In this manner Mr. Hooper spent a long life, irreproachable in outward act, yet shrouded in dismal suspicions; kind and loving, though unloved, and dimly feared; a man apart from men, shunned in their health and joy, but ever summoned to their aid in mortal anguish. As years wore on, shedding their snows above his sable veil, he acquired a name throughout the New England churches, and they called him Father Hooper. Nearly all his parishioners, who were of mature age when he was settled, had been borne away by many a funeral: he had one congregation in the church, and a more crowded one in the church-yard; and having wrought so late into the evening, and done his work so well, it was now good Father Hooper's turn to rest.

Several persons were visible by the shaded candlelight, in the death chamber of the old clergyman. Natural connections he had none. But there was the decorously grave, though unmoved physician, seeking only to mitigate the last pangs of the patient whom he could not save. There were the deacons, and other eminently pious members of his church. There, also, was the Reverend Mr. Clark, of Westbury, a young and zealous divine, who had ridden in haste to pray by the bedside of the expiring minister. There was the nurse, no hired handmaiden of death, but one whose calm affection had endured thus long in secrecy, in solitude, amid the chill of age, and would not perish, even at the dying hour. Who, but Elizabeth! And there lay the hoary head of good Father Hooper upon the death pillow, with the black veil still swathed about his brow, and reaching down over his face, so that each more difficult gasp of his faint breath caused it to stir. All through life that piece of crape had hung between him and the world: it had separated him from cheerful brotherhood and woman's love, and kept him in that saddest of all prisons, his own heart; and still it lay upon his face, as if to deepen the gloom of his darksome chamber, and shade him from the sunshine of eternity.

For some time previous, his mind had been confused, wavering doubtfully between the past and the present, and hovering forward, as it were, at intervals, into the indistinctness of the world to come. There had been feverish turns, which tossed him from side to side, and wore away what little strength he had. But in his most convulsive struggles, and in the wildest vagaries of his intellect, when no other thought retained its sober influence, he still showed an awful solicitude lest the black veil should slip aside. Even if his bewildered soul could have forgotten, there was a faithful woman at his pillow, who, with averted eyes, would have covered that aged face, which she had last beheld in the comeliness of manhood. At length the death-stricken old man lay quietly in the torpor of mental and bodily exhaustion, with an imperceptible pulse, and breath that grew fainter and fainter, except when a long, deep, and irregular inspiration seemed to prelude the flight of his spirit.

The minister of Westbury approached the bedside.

"Venerable Father Hooper," said he, "the moment of your release is at hand. Are you ready for the lifting of the veil that shuts in time from eternity?"

Father Hooper at first replied merely by a feeble motion of his head; then, apprehensive, perhaps, that his meaning might be doubtful, he exerted himself to speak.

"Yea," said he, in faint accents, "my soul hath a patient weariness until that veil be lifted."

"And is it fitting," resumed the Reverend Mr. Clark, "that a man so given to prayer, of such a blameless example, holy in deed and thought, so far as mortal judgment may pronounce; is it fitting that a father in the church should leave a shadow on his memory, that may seem to blacken a life so pure? I pray you, you venerable brother, let not this thing be! Suffer us to be gladdened by your triumphant aspect as you go to your reward. Before the veil of eternity be lifted, let me cast aside this black veil from your face!"

And thus speaking, the Reverend Mr. Clark bent forward to reveal the mystery of so many years. But, exerting a sudden energy, that made all the beholders stand aghast, Father Hooper snatched both his hands from beneath the bedclothes, and pressed them strongly on the black veil, resolute to struggle, if the minister of Westbury would contend with a dying man.

"Never!" cried the veiled clergyman. "On earth, never!"

"Dark old man!" exclaimed the affrighted minister, "with what horrible crime upon your soul are you now passing to the judgment?"

Father Hooper's breath heaved; it rattled in his throat; but, with a mighty effort, grasping forward with his hands, he caught hold of life, and held it back till he should speak. He even raised himself in bed; and there he sat, shivering with the arms of death around him, while the black veil hung down, awful, at that last moment, in the gathered terrors of a lifetime. And yet the faint, sad smile, so often there, now seemed to glimmer from its obscurity, and linger on Father Hooper's lips.

"Why do you tremble at me alone?" cried he, turning his veiled face round the circle of pale spectators. "Tremble also at each other! Have men avoided me, and women shown no pity, and children screamed and fled, only for my black veil? What, but the mystery which it obscurely typifies, has made this piece of crape so awful? When the friend shows his inmost heart to his friend; the lover to his best beloved; when man does not vainly shrink from the eye of his Creator, loathsomely treasuring up the secret of his sins, then deem me a monster, for the symbol beneath which I have lived, and die! I look around me, and, lo! on every visage a Black Veil!"

While his auditors shrank from one another, in mutual affright, Father Hooper fell back upon his pillow, a veiled corpse, with a faint smile lingering on the lips. Still veiled, they laid him in his coffin, and a veiled corpse they bore him to the grave. The grass of many years has sprung up and withered on that grave, the burial stone is moss-grown, and good Mr. Hooper's face is dust; but awful is still the thought that it mouldered beneath the Black Veil!

Considerations

Virtually any reading of Nathaniel Hawthorne, America's first great short-story writer, must make note of his preoccupation with sin, guilt, evil, and the way these problems of moral existence were dealt with in New England. Superficially this story may be seen as a study of the effect of one person's guilt—whatever that guilt may be—on all the people around him; in this case, the effects of a minister's guilt on his parishioners. On one hand, children run away from him, the guilty feel the urge to stay away, and even the woman who feels some personal interest in him refuses to stay with him as long as he wears the black veil.

On the other hand, among all of its bad influences, the black veil had the one desirable effect of making its wearer a very efficient clergyman. "Dying sinners cried aloud for him, strangers came long distances to attend services . . . the governor asked him to speak. . . ."

But beyond all of that is a question of what the work conveys in moral terms. The author labels his story a parable, which is sometimes defined as "an earthly story with a heavenly meaning." Hawthorne makes it obvious he wants the reader to look beneath the surface.

Our closest loved ones we cannot know exactly for they too are veiled.

The clue lies not in what the veil is covering or why the minister decided to wear it. What is important is the fact that he was wearing it—a veil, a mask, something which separated him from everyone else. Thus his veil is probably a symbol of the mask everyone wears.

Perhaps our masks do hide iniquities. "Each member of the congregation, the most innocent girl, and the man of hardened breast, felt as if the preacher had crept upon them, behind his awful veil, and discovered their hoarded iniquity of deed or thought." In fact, given Hawthorne's emphasis on guilt or sin, this is the most likely point of connection.

Yet our twentieth-century minds may add to this the fact that we learn to wear masks for protection as well as because of guilt. Eliot says in "Prufrock" that there will be time to prepare a face to meet the faces that you meet. Psychologists the world over deal with how we cover up—how we wear our masks or our veils. "The earth too had on her black veil," meaning that even in nature nothing is absolutely clear. We are no longer overly troubled by the moral guilt that is suggested, but we do not see the mysteries, and we cannot see into another's psyche.

Regardless of the reason, however, the effect is the same. The minister's veil separated him—even in the midst of the most favorable circumstances—from cheerful brotherhood and another's love. So too are we isolated. He was kept in that saddest of all prisons, his own mind—and perhaps we're all destined for that.

They buried him with it; he was unknown ever afterwards.

The Death of Ivan Ilych

Leo Tolstoy

I

During an interval in the Melvinski trial in the large building of the Law Courts, the members and public prosecutor met in Ivan Egorovich Shebek's private room, where the conversation turned on the celebrated Krasovski case. Fëdor Vasilievich warmly maintained that it was not subject to their jurisdiction, Ivan Egorovich maintained the contrary, while Peter Ivanovich, not having entered into the discussion at the start, took no part in it but looked through the *Gazette* which had just been handed in.

"Gentlemen," he said, "Ivan Ilych has died!"

"You don't say so!"

"Here, read it yourself," replied Peter Ivanovich, handing Fëdor Vasilievich the paper still damp from the press. Surrounded by a black border were the words: "Praskovya Fëdorovna Golovina, with profound sorrow, informs relatives and friends of the demise of her beloved husband Ivan Ilych Golovin, Member of the Court of Justice, which occurred on February the 4th of this year 1882. The funeral will take place on Friday at one o'clock in the afternoon."

Ivan Ilych had been a colleague of the gentlemen present and was liked by them all. He had been ill for some weeks with an illness said to be incurable. His post had been kept open for him, but there had been conjectures that in case of his death Alexeev might receive his appointment, and that either Vinnikov or Shtabel would succeed Alexeev. So on receiving the news of Ivan Ilych's death the first thought of each of the gentlemen in that private room was of the changes and promotions it might occasion among themselves or their acquaintances.

"I shall be sure to get Shtabel's place or Vinnikov's," thought Fëdor Vasilievich. "I was promised that long ago, and the promotion means an extra eight hundred rubles a year for me beside the allowance."

"Now I must apply for my brother-in-law's transfer from Kaluga," thought Peter Ivanovich. "My wife will be very glad, and then she won't be able to say that I never do anything for her relations."

"I thought he would never leave his bed again," said Peter Ivanovich aloud. "It's very sad."

"But what really was the matter with him?"

From THE DEATH OF IVAN ILYCH AND OTHER STORIES by Leo Tolstoy, translated by Louise and Aylmer Maude and published by Oxford University Press.

"The doctors couldn't say—at least they could, but each of them said something different. When last I saw him I thought he was getting better."

"And I haven't been to see him since the holidays. I always meant to go."

"Had he any property?"

"I think his wife had a little—but something quite trifling."

"We shall have to go to see her, but they live so terribly far away."

"Far away from you, you mean. Everything's far away from your place."

"You see, he never can forgive my living on the other side of the river," said Peter Ivanovich, smiling at Shebek. Then, still talking of the distances between different parts of the city, they returned to the Court.

Besides considerations as to the possible transfers and promotions likely to result from Ivan Ilych's death, the mere fact of the death of a near acquaintance aroused, as usual, in all who heard of it the complacent feeling that, "it is he who is dead and not I."

Each one thought or felt, "Well, he's dead but I'm alive!" But the more intimate of Ivan Ilych's acquaintances, his so-called friends, could not help thinking also that they would now have to fulfil the very tiresome demands of propriety by attending the funeral service and paying a visit of condolence to the widow.

Fëdor Vasilievich and Peter Ivanovich had been his nearest acquaintances. Peter Ivanovich had studied law with Ivan Ilych and had considered himself to be under obligations to him.

Having told his wife at dinner-time of Ivan Ilych's death and of his conjecture that it might be possible to get her brother transferred to their circuit, Peter Ivanovich sacrificed his usual nap, put on his evening clothes, and drove to Ivan Ilych's house.

At the entrance stood a carriage and two cabs. Leaning against the wall in the hall downstairs near the cloak-stand was a coffin-lid covered with cloth of gold, ornamented with gold cord and tassels, that had been polished up with metal powder. Two ladies in black were taking off their fur cloaks. Peter Ivanovich recognized one of them as Ivan Ilych's sister, but the other was a stranger to him. His colleague Schwartz was just coming downstairs, but on seeing Peter Ivanovich enter he stopped and winked at him, as if to say: "Ivan Ilych has made a mess of things—not like you and me."

Schwartz's face with his Piccadilly whiskers and his slim figure in evening dress, had as usual an air of elegant solemnity which contrasted with the playfulness of his character and had a special piquancy here, or so it seemed to Peter Ivanovich.

Peter Ivanovich allowed the ladies to precede him and slowly followed them upstairs. Schwartz did not come down but remained where he was, and Peter Ivanovich understood that he wanted to arrange where they should play bridge that evening. The ladies went upstairs to the widow's room, and Schwartz with seriously compressed lips but a playful look in his eyes, indicated by a twist of his eyebrows the room to the right where the body lay.

Peter Ivanovich, like everyone else on such occasions, entered feeling uncertain what he would have to do. All he knew was that at such times it is always safe to cross oneself. But he was not quite sure whether one should make obeisances while doing so. He therefore adopted a middle course. On entering the room he began crossing himself and made a slight movement resembling a bow. At the same time, as far as the motion of his head and arm allowed, he surveyed the room. Two young men— apparently nephews, one of whom was a high-school pupil—were leaving the room, crossing themselves as they did so. An old woman was standing motionless, and a lady with strangely arched eyebrows was saying something to her in a whisper. A vigorous, resolute Church Reader, in a frock-coat, was reading something in a loud voice with an expression that precluded any contradiction. The butler's assistant, Gerasim, stepping lightly in front of Peter Ivanovich, was strewing something on the floor. Noticing this, Peter Ivanovich was immediately aware of a faint odour of a decomposing body.

The last time he had called on Ivan Ilych, Peter Ivanovich had seen Gerasim in the study. Ivan Ilych had been particularly fond of him and he was performing the duty of a sick nurse.

Peter Ivanovich continued to make the sign of the cross slightly inclining his head in an intermediate direction between the coffin, the Reader, and the icons on the table in a corner of the room. Afterwards, when it seemed to him that this movement of his arm in crossing himself had gone on too long, he stopped and began to look at the corpse.

The dead man lay, as dead men always lie, in a specially heavy way, his rigid limbs sunk in the soft cushions of the coffin, with the head forever bowed on the pillow. His yellow waxen brow with bald patches over his sunken temples was thrust up in the way peculiar to the dead, the protruding nose seeming to press on the upper lip. He was much changed and had grown even thinner since Peter Ivanovich had last seen him, but, as is always the case with the dead, his face was handsomer and above all more dignified than when he was alive. The expression on the face said that what was necessary had been accomplished, and accomplished rightly. Besides this there was in that expression a reproach and a warning to the living. This warning seemed to Peter Ivanovich out of place, or at least not applicable to him. He felt a certain discomfort and so he hurriedly crossed himself once more and turned and went out of the door—too hurriedly and too regardless of propriety, as he himself was aware.

Schwartz was waiting for him in the adjoining room with legs spread wide apart and both hands toying with his top-hat behind his back. The mere sight of that playful, well-groomed, and elegant figure refreshed Peter Ivanovich. He felt that Schwartz was above all these happenings and would not surrender to any depressing influences. His very look said that this incident of a church service for Ivan Ilych could not be a sufficient reason for infringing the order of the session—in other words, that it would certainly not prevent his unwrapping a new pack of cards and shuffling them that evening while a footman placed four fresh candles on the table: in fact, that there was no reason for supposing that this incident would hinder their spending the evening agreeably. Indeed he said this in a whisper as Peter Ivanovich passed him, proposing that they should meet for a game at Fëdor Vasilievich's. But apparently Peter Ivanovich was not destined to play bridge that evening. Praskovya Fëdorovna (a short, fat woman who despite all efforts to the contrary had continued to broaden steadily from her shoulders downwards and who had the same extraordinarily arched eyebrows as the lady who had been standing by the coffin), dressed all in black, her head covered with lace, came out of her own room with some other ladies, conducted them to the room where the dead body lay, and said: "The service will begin immediately. Please go in."

Schwartz, making an indefinite bow, stood still, evidently neither accepting nor declining this invitation. Praskovya Fëdorovna, recognizing Peter Ivanovich, sighed, went close up to him, took his hand, and said: "I know you were a true friend to Ivan Ilych . . ." and looked at him awaiting some suitable response. And Peter Ivanovich knew that, just as it had been the right thing to cross himself in that room, so what he had to do here was to press her hand, sigh, and say, "Believe me. . . ." So he did all this and as he did it felt that the desired result had been achieved: that both he and she were touched.

"Come with me. I want to speak to you before it begins," said the widow. "Give me your arm."

Peter Ivanovich gave her his arm and they went to the inner rooms, passing Schwartz, who winked at Peter Ivanovich compassionately.

"That does for our bridge! Don't object if we find another player. Perhaps you can cut in when you do escape," said his playful look.

Peter Ivanovich sighed still more deeply and despondently, and Praskovya Fëdorovna pressed his arm gratefully. When they reached the drawing-room, upholstered in pink cretonne and lighted by a dim lamp, they sat down at the table—she on a sofa and Peter Ivanovich on a low pouffe, the springs of which yielded spasmodically under his weight. Praskovya Fëdorovna had been on the point of warning him to take another seat, but felt that such a warning was out of keeping with her present condition and so changed her mind. As he sat down on the pouffe Peter Ivanovich recalled how Ivan Ilych had arranged this room and had consulted him regarding this pink cretonne with green leaves. The whole room was full of furniture and knick-knacks, and on her way to the sofa the lace of the widow's black shawl caught on the carved edge of the table. Peter Ivanovich rose to detach it, and the springs of the pouffe, relieved of his weight, rose also and gave him a push. The widow began detaching her shawl herself, and Peter Ivanovich again sat down, suppressing the rebellious springs of the pouffe under him. But the widow had not quite freed herself and Peter Ivanovich got up again, and again the pouffe rebelled and even creaked. When this was all over she took out a clean cambric handkerchief and began to weep. The episode with the shawl and the struggle with the pouffe had cooled Peter Ivanovich's emotions and he sat there with a sullen look on his face. This awkward situation was interrupted by Sokolov, Ivan Ilych's butler, who came to report that the plot in the cemetery that Praskovya Fëdorovna had chosen would cost two hundred rubles. She stopped weeping and, looking at Peter Ivanovich with the air of a victim, remarked in French that it was very hard for her. Peter Ivanovich made a silent gesture signifying his full conviction that it must indeed be so.

"Please smoke," she said in a magnanimous yet crushed voice, and turned to discuss with Sokolov the price of the plot for the grave.

Peter Ivanovich while lighting his cigarette heard her inquiring very circumstantially into the prices of different plots in the cemetery and finally decide which she would take. When that was done she gave instructions about engaging the choir. Sokolov then left the room.

"I look after everything myself," she told Peter Ivanovich, shifting the albums that lay on the table; and noticing that the table was endangered by his cigarette-ash, she immediately passed him an ash-tray, saying as she did so: "I consider it an affectation to say that my grief prevents my attending to practical affairs. On the contrary, if anything can—I won't say console me, but—distract me, it is seeing to everything concerning him." She again took out her handkerchief as if preparing to cry, but suddenly, as if mastering her feeling, she shook herself and began to speak calmly. "But there is something I want to talk to you about."

Peter Ivanovich bowed, keeping control of the springs of the pouffe, which immediately began quivering under him.

"He suffered terribly the last few days."

"Did he?" said Peter Ivanovich.

"Oh, terribly! He screamed unceasingly, not for minutes but for hours. For the last three days he screamed incessantly. It was unendurable. I cannot understand how I bore it; you could hear him three rooms off. Oh, what I have suffered!"

"Is it possible that he was conscious all that time?" asked Peter Ivanovich.

"Yes," she whispered. "To the last moment. He took leave of us a quarter of an hour before he died, and asked us to take Volodya away."

The thought of the sufferings of this man he had known so intimately, first as a merry little boy, then as a school-mate, and later as a grown-up colleague, suddenly struck Peter Ivanovich with horror, despite an unpleasant consciousness of his own and this woman's dissimulation. He again saw that brow, and that nose pressing down on the lip, and felt afraid for himself.

"Three days of frightful suffering and then death! Why, that might suddenly, at any time, happen to me," he thought, and for a moment felt terrified. But—he did not himself know how—the customary reflection at once occurred to him that this had happened to Ivan Ilych and not to him, and that it should not and could not happen to him, and to think that it could would be yielding to depression which he ought not to do, as Schwartz's expression plainly showed. After which reflection Peter Ivanovich felt reassured, and began to ask with interest about the details of Ivan Ilych's death, as though death was an accident natural to Ivan Ilych but certainly not to himself.

After many details of the really dreadful physical sufferings Ivan Ilych had endured (which details he learnt only from the effect those sufferings had produced on Praskovya Fëdorovna's nerves) the widow apparently found it necessary to get to business.

"Oh, Peter Ivanovich, how hard it is! How terribly, terribly hard!" and she again began to weep.

Peter Ivanovich sighed and waited for her to finish blowing her nose. When she had done so he said, "Believe me . . ." and she again began talking and brought out what was evidently her chief concern with him—namely, to question him as to how she could obtain a grant of money from the government on the occasion of her husband's death. She made it appear that she was asking Peter Ivanovich's advice about her pension, but he soon saw that she already knew about that to the minutest detail, more even than he did himself. She knew how much could be got out of the government in consequence of her husband's death, but wanted to find out whether she could not possibly extract something more. Peter Ivanovich tried to think of some means of doing so, but after reflecting for a while and, out of propriety, condemning the government for its niggardliness, he said he thought that nothing more could be

got. Then she sighed and evidently began to devise means of getting rid of her visitor. Noticing this, he put out his cigarette, rose, pressed her hand, and went out into the ante-room.

In the dining-room where the clock stood that Ivan Ilych had liked so much and had bought at an antique shop, Peter Ivanovich met a priest and a few acquaintances who had come to attend the service, and he recognized Ivan Ilych's daughter, a handsome young woman. She was in black and her slim figure appeared slimmer than ever. She had a gloomy, determined, almost angry expression, and bowed to Peter Ivanovich as though he were in some way to blame. Behind her, with the same offended look, stood a wealthy young man, an examining magistrate, whom Peter Ivanovich also knew and who was her fiancé, as he had heard. He bowed mournfully to them and was about to pass into the death-chamber, when from under the stairs appeared the figure of Ivan Ilych's schoolboy son, who was extremely like his father. He seemed a little Ivan Ilych, such as Peter Ivanovich remembered when they studied law together. His tear-stained eyes had in them the look that is seen in the eyes of boys of thirteen or fourteen who are not pure-minded. When he saw Peter Ivanovich he scowled morosely and shamefacedly. Peter Ivanovich nodded to him and entered the death-chamber. The service began: candles, groans, incense, tears, and sobs. Peter Ivanovich stood looking gloomily down at his feet. He did not look once at the dead man, did not yield to any depressing influence, and was one of the first to leave the room. There was no one in the anteroom, but Gerasim darted out of the dead man's room, rummaged with his strong hands among the fur coats to find Peter Ivanovich's and helped him on with it.

"Well, friend Gerasim," said Peter Ivanovich, so as to say something. "It's a sad affair, isn't it?"

"It's God's will. We shall all come to it some day," said Gerasim, displaying his teeth—the even, white teeth of a healthy peasant—and, like a man in the thick of urgent work, he briskly opened the front door, called the coachman, helped Peter Ivanovich into the sledge, and sprang back to the porch as if in readiness for what he had to do next.

Peter Ivanovich found the fresh air particularly pleasant after the smell of incense, the dead body, and carbolic acid.

"Where to, sir?" asked the coachman.

"It's not too late even now. . . . I'll call round on Fëdor Vasilievich."

He accordingly drove there and found them just finishing the first rubber, so that it was quite convenient for him to cut it.

II

Ivan Ilych's life had been most simple and most ordinary and therefore most terrible.

He had been a member of the Court of Justice, and died at the age of forty-five. His father had been an official who after serving in various ministries and departments in Petersburg had made the sort of career which brings men to positions from which by reason of their long service they cannot be dismissed, though they are obviously unfit to hold any responsible position, and for whom therefore posts are especially created, which though fictitious carry salaries of from six to ten thousand rubles that are not fictitious, and in receipt of which they live on to a great age.

Such was the Privy Councillor and superfluous member of various superfluous institutions, Ilya Epimovich Golovin.

He had three sons, of whom Ivan Ilych was the second. The eldest son was following in his father's footsteps only in another department, and was already approaching that stage in the service at which a similar sinecure would be reached. The third son was a failure. He had ruined his prospects in a number of positions and was now serving in the railway department. His father and brothers, and still more their wives, not merely disliked meeting him, but avoided remembering his existence unless compelled to do so. His sister had married Baron Greff, a Petersburg official of her father's type. Ivan Ilych was *le phénix de la famille* as people said. He was neither as cold and formal as his elder brother nor as wild as the younger, but was a happy mean between them—an intelligent, polished, lively and agreeable man. He had studied with his younger brother at the School of Law, but the latter had failed to complete the course and was expelled when he was in the fifth class. Ivan Ilych finished the course well. Even when he was at the School of Law he was just what he remained for the rest of his life: a capable, cheerful, good-natured, and sociable man, though strict in the fulfilment of what he considered to be his duty: and he considered his duty to be what was so considered by those in authority. Neither as a boy nor as a man was he a toady, but from early youth was by nature attracted to people of high station as a fly is drawn to the light, assimilating their ways and views of life and establishing friendly relations with them. All the enthusiasms of childhood and youth passed without leaving much trace on him; he succumbed to sensuality, to vanity, and latterly among the highest classes to liberalism, but always within limits which his instinct unfailingly indicated to him as correct.

At school he had done things which had formerly seemed to him very horrid and made him feel disgusted with himself when he did them; but when later on he saw that such actions were done by people of good position and that they did not regard them as wrong, he was able not exactly to regard them as right, but to forget about them entirely or not be at all troubled at remembering them.

Having graduated from the School of Law and qualified for the tenth rank of the civil service, and having received money from his father for his equipment, Ivan Ilych ordered himself clothes at Scharmer's, the fashionable tailor, hung a medallion inscribed *respice finem** on his watch-chain, took leave of his professor and the prince who was patron of the school, had a farewell dinner with his comrades at Donon's first-class restaurant, and with his new and fashionable portmanteau, linen, clothes, shaving and other toilet appliances, and a travelling rug, all purchased at the best shops, he set off for one of the provinces where, through his father's influence, he had been attached to the Governor as an official for special service.

In the province Ivan Ilych soon arranged as easy and agreeable a position for himself as he had had at the School of Law. He performed his official tasks, made his career, and at the same time amused himself pleasantly and decorously. Occasionally he paid official visits to country districts, where he behaved with dignity both to his superiors and inferiors, and performed the duties entrusted to him, which related chiefly to the sectarians, with an exactness and incorruptible honesty of which he could not but feel proud.

In official matters, despite his youth and taste for frivolous gaiety, he was exceedingly reserved, punctilious, and even severe; but in society he was often amusing and witty, and always good-natured, correct in his manner, and *bon enfant*,† as the governor and his wife—with whom he was like one of the family—used to say of him.

In the province he had an affair with a lady who made advances to the elegant young lawyer, and there was also a milliner; and there were carousals with aides-de-camp who visited the district, and after-supper visits to a certain outlying street of doubtful reputation; and there was too some obsequiousness to his chief and even

---

respice finem: look to the end.   †*bon enfant:* a good child.

to his chief's wife, but all this was done with such a tone of good breeding that no hard names could be applied to it. It all came under the heading of the French saying: *"Il faut que jeunesse se passe."** It was all done with clean hands, in clean linen, with French phrases, and above all among people of the best society and consequently with the approval of people of rank.

So Ivan Ilych served for five years and then came a change in his official life. The new and reformed judicial institutions were introduced, and new men were needed. Ivan Ilych became such a new man. He was offered the post of examining magistrate, and he accepted it though the post was in another province and obliged him to give up the connexions he had formed and to make new ones. His friends met to give him a send-off; they had a group-photograph taken and presented him with a silver cigarette-case, and he set off to his new post.

As examining magistrate Ivan Ilych was just as *comme il faut* and decorous a man, inspiring general respect and capable of separating his official duties from his private life, as he had been when acting as an official on special service. His duties now as examining magistrate were far more interesting and attractive than before. In his former position it had been pleasant to wear an undress uniform made by Scharmer, and to pass through the crowd of petitioners and officials who were timorously awaiting an audience with the governor, and who envied him as with free and easy gait he went straight into his chief's private room to have a cup of tea and a cigarette with him. But not many people had then been directly dependent on him—only police officials and the sectarians when he went on special missions—and he liked to treat them politely, almost as comrades, as if he were letting them feel that he who had the power to crush them was treating them in this simple, friendly way. There were then but few such people. But now, as an examining magistrate, Ivan Ilych felt that everyone without exception, even the most important and self-satisfied, was in his power, and that he need only write a few words on a sheet of paper with a certain heading, and this or that important, self-satisfied person would be brought before him in the role of an accused person or a witness, and if he did not choose to allow him to sit down, would have to stand before him and answer his questions. Ivan Ilych never abused his power; he tried on the contrary to soften its expression, but the consciousness of it and of the possibility of softening its effect, supplied the chief interest and attraction of his office. In his work itself, especially in his examinations, he very soon acquired a method of eliminating all considerations irrelevant to the legal aspect of the case, and reducing even the most complicated case to a form in which it would be presented on paper only in its externals, completely excluding his personal opinion of the matter, while above all observ-

Il faut . . . passe: You're only young once.

ing every prescribed formality. The work was new and Ivan Ilych was one of the first men to apply the new Code of 1864.

On taking up the post of examining magistrate in a new town, he made new acquaintances and connexions, placed himself on a new footing, and assumed a somewhat different tone. He took up an attitude of rather dignified aloofness towards the provincial authorities, but picked out the best circle of legal gentlemen and wealthy gentry living in the town and assumed a tone of slight dissatisfaction with the government, of moderate liberalism, and of enlightened citizenship. At the same time, without at all altering the elegance of his toilet, he ceased shaving his chin and allowed his beard to grow as it pleased.

Ivan Ilych settled down very pleasantly in this new town. The society there, which inclined towards opposition to the Governor, was friendly, his salary was larger, and he began to play *vint*, which he found added not a little to the pleasure of life, for he had a capacity for cards, played good-humouredly, and calculated rapidly and astutely, so that he usually won.

After living there for two years he met his future wife, Praskovya Fëdorovna Mikhel, who was the most attractive, clever, and brilliant girl of the set in which he moved, and among other amusements and relaxations from his labours as examining magistrate, Ivan Ilych established light and playful relations with her.

While he had been an official on special service he had been accustomed to dance, but now as an ex-amining magistrate it was exceptional for him to do so. If he danced now, he did it as if to show that though he served under the reformed order of things, and had reached the fifth official rank, yet when it came to dancing he could do it better than most people. So at the end of an evening he sometimes danced with Praskovya Fëdorovna, and it was chiefly during these dances that he captivated her. She fell in love with him. Ivan Ilych had at first no definite intention of marrying, but when the girl fell in love with him he said to himself: "Really, why shouldn't I marry?"

Praskovya Fëdorovna came of a good family, was not bad looking, and had some little property. Ivan Ilych might have aspired to a more brilliant match, but even this was good. He had his salary, and she, he hoped, would have an equal income. She was well connected, and was a sweet, pretty, and thoroughly correct young woman. To say that Ivan Ilych married because he fell in love with Praskovya Fëdorovna and found that she sympathized with his views of life would be as incorrect as to say that he married because his social circle approved of the match. He was swayed by both these considerations: the marriage gave him personal satisfaction, and at the same time it was considered the right thing by the most highly placed of his associates.

So Ivan Ilych got married.

The preparations for marriage and the beginning of married life, with its conjugal caresses, the new furniture, new crockery, and new linen, were very pleasant until his wife became pregnant—so that Ivan Ilych had begun to think that marriage would not impair the easy, agreeable, gay and always decorous character of his life, approved of by society and regarded by himself as natural, but would even improve it. But from the first months of his wife's pregnancy, something new, unpleasant, depressing, and unseemly, and from which there was no way of escape, unexpectedly showed itself.

His wife, without any reason—*de gaieté de coeur** as Ivan Ilych expressed it to himself—began to disturb the pleasure and propriety of their life. She began to be jealous without any cause, expected him to devote his whole attention to her, found fault with everything, and made coarse and ill-mannered scenes.

At first Ivan Ilych hoped to escape from the unpleasantness of this state of affairs by the same easy and decorous relation to life that had served him heretofore: he tried to ignore his wife's disagreeable moods, continued to live in his usual easy and pleasant way, invited friends to his house for a game of cards, and also tried going out to his club or spending his evenings with friends. But one day his wife began upbraiding him so vigorously, using such coarse words, and continued to abuse him every time he did not fulfil her demands, so resolutely and with such evident determination not to give way till he submitted—that is, till he stayed at home and was bored just as she was—that he became alarmed. He now realized that matrimony—at any rate with Praskovya Fëdorovna—was not always conducive to the pleasures and amenities of life, but on the contrary often infringed both comfort and propriety, and that he must therefore entrench himself against such infringement. And Ivan Ilych began to seek for means of doing so. His official duties were the one thing that imposed upon Praskovya Fëdorovna, and by means of his official work and the duties attached to it he began struggling with his wife to secure his own independence.

With the birth of their child, the attempts to feed it and the various failures in doing so, and with the real and imaginary illnesses of mother and child, in which Ivan Ilych's sympathy was demanded but about which he understood nothing, the need of securing for himself an existence outside his family life became still more imperative.

As his wife grew more irritable and exacting and Ivan Ilych transferred the centre of gravity of his life more and more to his official work, so did he grow to like his work better and became more ambitious than before.

Very soon, within a year of his wedding, Ivan Ilych had realized that marriage, though it may add some comforts to life, is in fact a very intricate and difficult affair towards which in order to perform one's duty, that is, to lead a decorous life approved of by society, one must adopt a definite attitude just as towards one's official duties.

And Ivan Ilych evolved such an attitude towards married life. He only

---

**de gaieté de coeur*: out of sheer wantonness.

required of it those conveniences—dinner at home, housewife, and bed—which it could give him, and above all that propriety of external forms required by public opinion. For the rest he looked for light-hearted pleasure and propriety, and was very thankful when he found them, but if he met with antagonism and querulousness he at once retired into his separate fenced-off world of official duties, where he found satisfaction.

Ivan Ilych was esteemed a good official, and after three years was made Assistant Public Prosecutor. His new duties, their importance, the possibility of indicting and imprisoning anyone he chose, the publicity his speeches received, and the success he had in all these things, made his work still more attractive.

More children came. His wife became more and more querulous and ill-tempered, but the attitude Ivan Ilych had adopted towards his home life rendered him almost impervious to her grumbling.

After seven years' service in that town he was transferred to another province as Public Prosecutor. They moved, but were short of money and his wife did not like the place they moved to. Though the salary was higher the cost of living was greater, besides which two of their children died and family life became still more unpleasant for him.

Praskovya Fëdorovna blamed her husband for every inconvenience they encountered in their new home. Most of the conversations between husband and wife, especially as to the children's education, led to topics which recalled former disputes, and those disputes were apt to flare up again at any moment. There remained only those rare periods of amorousness which still came to them at times but did not last long. These were islets at which they anchored for a while and then again set out upon that ocean of veiled hostility which showed itself in their aloofness from one another. This aloofness might have grieved Ivan Ilych had he considered that it ought not to exist, but he now regarded the position as normal, and even made it the goal at which he aimed in family life. His aim was to free himself more and more from those unpleasantnesses and to give them a semblance of harmlessness and propriety. He attained this by spending less and less time with his family, and when obliged to be at home he tried to safeguard his position by the presence of outsiders. The chief thing however was that he had his official duties. The whole interest of his life now centred in the official world and that interest absorbed him. The consciousness of his power, being able to ruin anybody he wished to ruin, the importance, even the external dignity of his entry into court, or meetings with his subordinates, his success with superiors and inferiors, and above all his masterly handling of cases, of which he was conscious—all this gave him pleasure and filled his life, together with chats with his colleagues, dinners, and bridge. So that on the whole Ivan Ilych's life continued to flow as he considered it should do—pleasantly and properly.

So things continued for another seven years. His eldest daughter was already sixteen, another child had died, and only one son was left, a schoolboy and a subject of dissension. Ivan Ilych wanted to put him in the School of Law, but to spite him Praskovya Fëdorovna entered him at the High School. The daughter had been educated at home and had turned out well: the boy did not learn badly either.

III

So Ivan Ilych lived for seventeen years after his marriage. He was already a Public Prosecutor of long standing, and had declined several proposed transfers while awaiting a more desirable post, when an unanticipated and unpleasant occurrence quite upset the peaceful course of his life. He was expecting to be offered the post of presiding judge in a University town, but Happe somehow came to the front and obtained the appointment instead. Ivan Ilych became irritable, reproached Happe, and quarrelled both with him and with his immediate superiors—who became colder to him and again passed him over when other appointments were made.

This was in 1880, the hardest year of Ivan Ilych's life. It was then that it became evident on the one hand that his salary was insufficient for them to live on, and on the other that he had been forgotten, and not only this, but that what was for him the greatest and most cruel injustice appeared to others a quite ordinary occurrence. Even his father did not consider it his duty to help him. Ivan Ilych felt himself abandoned by everyone, and that they regarded his position with a salary of 3,500 rubles as quite normal and even fortunate. He alone knew that with the consciousness of the injustices done him, with his wife's incessant nagging, and with the debts he had contracted by living beyond his means, his position was far from normal.

In order to save money that summer he obtained leave of absence and went with his wife to live in the country at her brother's place.

In the country, without his work, he experienced *ennui* for the first time in his life, and not only *ennui* but intolerable depression, and he decided that it was impossible to go on living like that, and that it was necessary to take energetic measures.

Having passed a sleepless night pacing up and down the veranda, he decided to go to Petersburg and bestir himself, in order to punish those who had failed to appreciate him and to get transferred to another ministry.

Next day, despite many protests from his wife and her brother, he started for Petersburg with the sole object of obtaining a post with a salary of five thousand rubles a year. He was no longer bent on any particular department, or tendency, or kind of activity. All he now wanted was an appointment to another post with a salary of five thousand rubles, either in the administration, in the banks, with the railways, in one of the Empress Marya's Institutions, or even in the customs—but it had to carry with it a salary of five thousand rubles and be in a ministry other than that in which they had failed to appreciate him.

And this quest of Ivan Ilych's was crowned with remarkable and unexpected success. At Kursk an acquaintance of his, F. I. Ilyin, got into the first-class carriage, sat down beside Ivan Ilych, and told him of a telegram just received by the Governor of Kursk announcing that a change was about to take place in the ministry: Peter Ivanovich was to be superseded by Ivan Semënovich.

The proposed change, apart from its significance for Russia, had a special significance for Ivan Ilych, because by bringing forward a new man, Peter Petrovich, and consequently his friend Zachar Ivanovich, it was highly favourable for Ivan Ilych, since Zachar Ivanovich was a friend and colleague of his.

In Moscow this news was confirmed, and on reaching Petersburg Ivan Ilych found Zachar Ivanovich and received a definite promise of an appointment in his former department of Justice.

A week later he telegraphed to his wife: "Zachar in Miller's place. I shall receive appointment on presentation of report."

Thanks to this change of personnel, Ivan Ilych had unexpectedly obtained an appointment in his former ministry which placed him two stages above his former colleagues besides giving him five thousand rubles salary and three thousand five hundred rubles for expenses connected with his removal. All his ill humour towards his former enemies and the whole department vanished, and Ivan Ilych was completely happy.

He returned to the country more cheerful and contented than he had been for a long time. Praskovya Fëdorovna also cheered up and a truce was arranged between them. Ivan Ilych told of how he had been fêted by everybody in Petersburg, how all those who had been his enemies were put to shame and now fawned on him, how envious they were of his appointment, and how much everybody in Petersburg had liked him.

Praskovya Fëdorovna listened to all this and appeared to believe it. She did not contradict anything, but only made plans for their life in the town to which they were going. Ivan Ilych saw with delight that these plans were his plans, that he and his wife agreed, and that, after a stumble, his life was regaining its due and natural character of pleasant lightheartedness and decorum.

Ivan Ilych had come back for a short time only, for he had to take up his new duties on the 10th of September. Moreover, he needed time to settle into the new place, to move all his belongings from the province, and to buy and order many additional things: in a word, to make such arrangements as he had resolved on, which were almost exactly what Praskovya Fëdorovna too had decided on.

Now that everything had happened so fortunately, and that he and his wife were at one in their aims and moreover saw so little of one another, they got on together better than they had done since the first years of marriage. Ivan Ilych had thought of taking his family away with him at once, but the insistence of his wife's brother and her sister-in-law, who had suddenly become particularly amiable and friendly to him and his family, induced him to depart alone.

So he departed, and the cheerful state of mind induced by his success and by the harmony between his wife and himself, the one intensifying the other, did not leave him. He found a delightful house, just the thing both he and his wife had dreamt of—spacious, lofty reception rooms in the old style, a convenient and dignified study, rooms for his wife and daughter, a study for his son—it might have been specially built for them. Ivan Ilych himself superintended the arrangements, chose the wallpapers, supplemented the furniture (preferably with antiques which he considered particularly *comme il faut*), and supervised the upholstering. Everything progressed and progressed and approached the ideal he had set himself: even when things were only half completed they exceeded his expectations. He saw what a refined and elegant character, free from vulgarity, it would all have when it was ready. On falling asleep he pictured to himself how the reception-room would look. Looking at the yet unfinished drawing-room he could see the fireplace, the screen, the what-not, the little chairs dotted here and there, the dishes and plates on the walls, and the bronzes, as they would be when everything was in place. He was pleased by the thought of how his wife and daughter, who shared his taste in this matter, would be impressed by it. They were certainly not expecting as much. He had been particularly successful in finding, and buying cheaply, antiques which gave a particularly aristocratic character to the whole place. But in his letters he intentionally understated everything in order to be able to surprise them. All this so absorbed him that his new duties—though he liked his official work—interested him less than he had expected. Sometimes he even had moments of absentmindedness during the Court Sessions, and would consider whether he should have straight or curved cornices for his curtains. He was so interested in it all that he often did things himself, rearranging the furniture, or rehanging the curtains. Once when mounting a step-ladder to show the upholsterer, who did not understand, how he wanted the hangings draped, he made a false step and slipped, but being a strong and agile man he clung on and only knocked his side against the knob of the window frame. The bruised place was painful but the pain soon passed, and he felt particularly bright and well just then. He wrote: "I feel fifteen years younger." He thought he would have everything ready by September, but it dragged on till mid-October. But the result was charming not only in his eyes but to everyone who saw it.

In reality it was just what is usually seen in the houses of people of moderate means who want to appear rich, and therefore succeed only in resembling others like themselves: there were damasks, dark wood, plants, rugs, and dull and polished bronzes—all the things people of a certain class have in order to resemble other people of that class. His house was so like the others that it would never have been noticed, but to him it all seemed to be quite exceptional. He was very happy when he met his family at the station and brought them to the newly furnished house all lit up, where a footman in a white tie opened the door into the hall decorated with plants, and when they went on into the drawing-room and the study uttering exclamations of delight. He conducted them everywhere, drank in their praises eagerly, and beamed with pleasure. At tea that evening, when Praskovya Fëdorovna among other things asked him about his fall, he laughed and showed them how he had gone flying and had frightened the upholsterer.

"It's a good thing I'm a bit of an athlete. Another man might have been killed, but I merely knocked myself, just here; it hurts when it's touched, but it's passing off already—it's only a bruise."

So they began living in their new home—in which, as always happens, when they got thoroughly settled in they found they were just one room short—and with the increased income, which as always was just a little (some five hundred rubles) too little, but it was all very nice.

Things went particularly well at first, before everything was finally arranged and while something had still to be done: this thing bought, that thing ordered, another thing moved, and something else adjusted. Though there were some disputes between husband and wife, they were both so well satisfied and had so much to do that it all passed off without any serious quarrels. When nothing was left to arrange it became rather dull and something seemed to be lacking, but they were then mak-

ing acquaintances, forming habits, and life was growing fuller.

Ivan Ilych spent his mornings at the law court and came home to dinner, and at first he was generally in a good humour, though he occasionally became irritable just on account of his house. (Every spot on the tablecloth or the upholstery, and every broken window-blind string, irritated him. He had devoted so much trouble to arranging it all that every disturbance of it distressed him.) But on the whole his life ran its course as he believed life should do: easily, pleasantly, and decorously.

He got up at nine, drank his coffee, read the paper, and then put on his undress uniform and went to the law courts. There the harness in which he worked had already been stretched to fit him and he donned it without a hitch: petitioners, inquiries at the chancery, the chancery itself, and the sittings public and administrative. In all this the thing was to exclude everything fresh and vital, which always disturbs the regular course of official business, and to admit only official relations with people, and then only on official grounds. A man would come, for instance, wanting some information. Ivan Ilych, as one in whose sphere the matter did not lie, would have nothing to do with him: but if the man had some business with him in his official capacity, something that could be expressed on officially stamped paper, he would do everything, positively everything he could within the limits of such relations, and in doing so would maintain the semblance of friendly human relations, that is, would observe the courtesies of life. As soon as the official relations ended, so did everything else. Ivan Ilych possessed this capacity to separate his real life from the official side of affairs and not mix the two, in the highest degree, and by long practice and natural aptitude had brought it to such a pitch that sometimes, in the manner of a virtuoso, he would even allow himself to let the human and official relations mingle. He let himself do this just because he felt that he could at any time he chose resume the strictly official attitude again and drop the human relation. And he did it all easily, pleasantly, correctly, and even artistically. In the intervals between the sessions he smoked, drank tea, chatted a little about politics, a little about general topics, a little about cards, but most of all about official appointments. Tired, but with the feelings of a virtuoso— one of the first violins who has played his part in an orchestra with precision—he would return home to find that his wife and daughter had been out paying calls, or had a visitor, and that his son had been to school, had done his homework with his tutor, and was duly learning what is taught at High Schools. Everything was as it should be. After dinner, if they had no visitors, Ivan Ilych sometimes read a book that was being much discussed at the time, and in the evening settled down to work, that is, read official papers, compared the depositions of witnesses, and noted paragraphs of the Code applying to them. This was neither dull nor amusing. It was dull when he might have been playing bridge, but if no bridge was available it was at any rate

better than doing nothing or sitting with his wife. Ivan Ilych's chief pleasure was giving little dinners to which he invited men and women of good social position, and just as his drawing-room resembled all other drawing-rooms so did his enjoyable little parties resemble all other such parties.

Once they even gave a dance. Ivan Ilych enjoyed it and everything went off well, except that it led to a violent quarrel with his wife about the cakes and sweets. Praskovya Fёdorovna had made her own plans, but Ivan Ilych insisted on getting everything from an expensive confectioner and ordered too many cakes, and the quarrel occurred because some of those cakes were left over and the confectioner's bill came to forty-five rubles. It was a great and disagreeable quarrel. Praskovya Fёdorovna called him "a fool and an imbecile," and he clutched at his head and made angry allusions to divorce.

But the dance itself had been enjoyable. The best people were there, and Ivan Ilych had danced with Princess Trufonova, a sister of the distinguished founder of the Society "Bear my Burden."

The pleasures connected with his work were pleasures of ambition; his social pleasures were those of vanity; but Ivan Ilych's greatest pleasure was playing bridge. He acknowledged that whatever disagreeable incident happened in his life, the pleasure that beamed like a ray of light above everything else was to sit down to bridge with good players, not noisy partners, and of course to four-handed bridge (with five players it was annoying to have to stand out, though one pretended not to mind), to play a clever and serious game (when the cards allowed it) and then to have supper and drink a glass of wine. After a game of bridge, especially if he had won a little (to win a large sum was unpleasant), Ivan Ilych went to bed in specially good humour.

So they lived. They formed a circle of acquaintances among the best people and were visited by people of importance and by young folk. In their views as to their acquaintances, husband, wife and daughter were entirely agreed, and tacitly and unanimously kept at arm's length and shook off the shabby friends and relations who, with much show of affection, gushed into the drawing-room with its Japanese plates on the walls. Soon these shabby friends ceased to obtrude themselves and only the best people remained in the Golovins' set.

Young men made up to Lisa, and Petrishchev, an examining magistrate and Dmitri Ivanovich Petrishchev's son and sole heir, began to be so attentive to her that Ivan Ilych had already spoken to Praskovya Fëdorovna about it, and considered whether they should not arrange a party for them, or get up some private theatricals.

So they lived, and all went well, without change, and life flowed pleasantly.

IV

They were all in good health. It could not be called ill health if Ivan Ilych sometimes said that he had a queer taste in his mouth and felt some discomfort in his left side.

But this discomfort increased and, though not exactly painful, grew into a sense of pressure in his side accompanied by ill humour. And his irritability became worse and worse and began to mar the agreeable, easy, and correct life that had established itself in the Golovin family. Quarrels between husband and wife became more and more frequent, and soon the ease and amenity disappeared and even the decorum was barely maintained. Scenes again became frequent, and very few of those islets remained on which husband and wife could meet without an explosion. Praskovya Fëdorovna now had good reason to say that her husband's temper was trying. With characteristic exaggeration she said he had always had a dreadful temper, and that it had needed all her good nature to put up with it for twenty years. It was true that now the quarrels were started by him. His bursts of temper always came just before dinner, often just as he began to eat his soup. Sometimes he noticed that a plate or dish was chipped, or the food was not right, or his son put his elbow on the table, or his daughter's hair was not done as he liked it, and for all this he blamed Praskovya Fëdorovna. At first she retorted and said disagreeable things to him, but once or twice he fell into such a rage at the beginning of dinner that she realized it was due to some physical derangement brought on by taking food, and so she restrained herself and did not answer, but only hurried to get the dinner over. She regarded this self-restraint as highly praiseworthy. Having come to the conclusion that her husband had a dreadful temper and made her life miserable, she began to feel sorry for herself, and the more she pitied herself the more she hated her husband. She began to wish he would die; yet she did not want him to die because then his salary would cease. And this irritated her against him still more. She considered herself dreadfully unhappy just because not even his death could save her, and though she concealed her exasperation, that hidden exasperation of hers increased his irritation also.

After one scene in which Ivan Ilych had been particularly unfair and after which he had said in explanation that he certainly was irritable but that it was due to his not being well, she said that if he was ill it should be attended to, and insisted on his going to see a celebrated doctor.

He went. Everything took place as he had expected and as it always does. There was the usual waiting and the important air assumed by the doctor, with which he was so familiar (resembling that which he himself assumed in court), and the sounding and listening, and the questions which called for answers that were foregone conclusions and were evidently unnecessary, and the look of importance which implied that "if only you put yourself in our hands we will arrange everything—we know indubitably how it has to be done, always in the same way for everybody alike." It was all just as it was in the law courts. The doctor put on just the same air towards him as he himself put on towards an accused person.

The doctor said that so-and-so indicated that there was so-and-so inside the patient, but if the investi-gation of so-and-so did not confirm this, then he must assume that and that. If he assumed that and that, then . . . and so on. To Ivan Ilych only one question was important: was his case serious or not? But the doctor ignored that inappropriate question. From his point of view it was not the one under consideration, the real question was to decide between a floating kidney, chronic catarrh, or appendicitis. It was not a question of Ivan Ilych's life or death, but one between a floating kidney and appendicitis. And that question the doctor solved brilliantly, as it seemed to Ivan Ilych, in favour of the appendix, with the reservation that should an examination of the urine give fresh indications the matter would be reconsidered. All this was just what Ivan Ilych had himself brilliantly accomplished a thousand times in dealing with men on trial. The doctor summed up just as brilliantly, looking over his spectacles triumphantly and even gaily at the accused. From the doctor's summing up Ivan Ilych concluded that things were bad, but that for the doctor, and perhaps for everybody else, it was a matter of indifference, though for him it was bad. And this conclusion struck him painfully, arousing in him a great feeling of pity for himself and of bitterness towards the doctor's indifference to a matter of such importance.

He said nothing of this, but rose, placed the doctor's fee on the table, and remarked with a sigh: "We sick people probably often put inappropriate questions. But tell me, in general, is this complaint dangerous, or not? . . ."

The doctor looked at him sternly over his spectacles with one eye, as if to say: "Prisoner, if you will not keep to the questions put to you, I shall be obliged to have you removed from the court."

"I have already told you what I consider necessary and proper. The analysis may show something more." And the doctor bowed.

Ivan Ilych went out slowly, seated himself disconsolately in his sledge, and drove home. All the way home he was going over what the doctor had said, trying to translate those complicated, obscure, scientific phrases into plain language and find in them an answer to the question: "Is my condition bad? Is it very bad? or is there as yet nothing much wrong?" And it seemed to him that the meaning of what the doctor had said was that it was very bad. Everything in the streets seemed depressing. The cabmen, the houses, the passers-by, and the shops, were dismal. His ache, this dull gnawing ache that never ceased for a moment, seemed to have acquired a new and more serious significance from the doctor's dubious remarks. Ivan Ilych now watched it with a new and oppressive feeling.

He reached home and began to tell his wife about it. She listened, but in the middle of his account his daughter came in with her hat on, ready to go out with her mother. She sat down reluctantly to listen to this tedious story, but could not stand it long, and her mother too did not hear him to the end.

"Well, I am very glad," she said. "Mind now to take your medicine regularly. Give me the prescription and I'll send Gerasim to the chemist's." And she went to get ready to go out.

While she was in the room Ivan Ilych had hardly taken time to breathe, but he sighed deeply when she left it.

"Well," he thought, "perhaps it isn't so bad after all."

He began taking his medicine and following the doctor's directions, which had been altered after the examination of the urine. But then it happened that there was a contradiction between the indications drawn from the examination of the urine and the symptoms that showed themselves. It turned out that what was happening differed from what the doctor had told him, and that he had either forgotten, or blundered, or hidden something from him. He could not, however, be blamed for that, and Ivan Ilych still obeyed his orders implicitly and at first derived some comfort from doing so.

From the time of his visit to the doctor, Ivan Ilych's chief occupation was the exact fulfilment of the doctor's instructions regarding hygiene and the taking of medicine, and the observation of his pain and his excretions. His chief interests came to be people's ailments and people's health. When sickness, deaths, or recoveries were mentioned in his presence, especially when the illness resembled his own, he listened with agitation which he tried to hide, asked questions, and applied what he heard to his own case.

The pain did not grow less, but Ivan Ilych made efforts to force himself to think that he was better. And he could do this so long as nothing agitated him. But as soon as he had any unpleasantness with his wife, or a lack of success in his official work, or held bad cards at bridge, he was at once acutely sensible of his disease. He had formerly borne such mischances, hoping soon to adjust what was wrong, to master it and attain success, or make a grand slam. But now every mischance upset him and plunged him into despair. He would say to himself: "There now, just as I was beginning to get better and the medicine had begun to take effect, comes this accursed misfortune, or unpleasantness . . ." And he was furious with the mishap, or with the people who were causing the unpleasantness and killing him, for he felt that this fury was killing him but could not restrain it. One would have thought that it should have been clear to him that this exasperation with circumstances and people aggravated his illness, and that he ought therefore to ignore unpleasant occurrences. But he drew the very opposite conclusion: he said that he needed peace, and he watched for everything that might disturb it and became irritable at the slightest infringement of it. His condition was rendered worse by the fact that he read medical books and consulted doctors. The progress of his disease was so gradual that he could deceive himself when comparing one day with another—the difference was so slight. But when he consulted the doctors it seemed to him that he was getting worse, and even very rapidly. Yet despite this he was continually consulting them.

That month he went to see another celebrity, who told him almost the same as the first had done but put his questions rather differently, and the interview with this celebrity only increased Ivan Ilych's doubts and fears. A friend of a friend of his, a very good doctor, diagnosed his illness again quite differently from the others, and though he predicted recovery, his questions and suppositions bewildered Ivan Ilych still more and increased his doubts. A homoeopathist diagnosed the disease in yet another way, and prescribed medicine which Ivan Ilych took secretly for a week. But after a week, not feeling any improvement and having lost confidence both in the former doctor's treatment and in this one's, he became still more despondent. One day a lady acquaintance mentioned a cure effected by a wonder-working icon. Ivan Ilych caught himself listening attentively and beginning to believe that it had occurred. This incident alarmed him. "Has my mind really weakened to such an extent?" he asked himself. "Nonsense! It's all rubbish. I mustn't give way to nervous fears but having chosen a doctor must keep strictly to his treatment. That is what I will do. Now it's all settled. I won't think about it, but will follow the treatment seriously till summer, and then we shall see. From now there must be no more of this wavering!" This was easy to say but impossible to carry out. The pain in his side oppressed him and seemed to grow worse and more incessant, while the taste in his mouth grew stranger and stranger. It seemed to him that his breath had a disgusting smell, and he was conscious of a loss of appetite and strength. There was no deceiving himself: something terrible, new, and more important than anything before in his life, was taking place within him of which he alone was aware. Those about him did not understand or would not understand it, but thought everything in the world was going on as usual. That tormented Ivan Ilych more than anything. He saw that his household, especially his wife and daughter who were in a perfect whirl of visiting, did not understand anything of it and were annoyed that he was so depressed and so exacting, as if he were to blame for it. Though they tried to disguise it he saw that he was an obstacle in their path, and that his wife had adopted a definite line in regard to his illness and kept to it regardless of anything he said or did. Her attitude was this: "You know," she would say to her friends, "Ivan Ilych can't do as other people do, and keep to the treatment prescribed for him. One day he'll take his drops and keep strictly to his diet and go to bed in good time, but the next day unless I watch him he'll suddenly forget his medicine, eat sturgeon—which is forbidden—and sit up playing cards till one o'clock in the morning."

"Oh, come, when was that?" Ivan Ilych would ask in vexation. "Only once at Peter Ivanovich's."

"And yesterday with Shebek."

"Well, even if I hadn't stayed up, this pain would have kept me awake."

"Be that as it may you'll never get well like that, but will always make us wretched."

Praskovya Fëdorovna's attitude to Ivan Ilych's illness, as she expressed it both to others and to him, was that it was his own fault and was another of the annoyances he caused her. Ivan Ilych felt that this opinion escaped her involuntarily—but that did not make it easier for him.

At the law courts too, Ivan Ilych noticed, or thought he noticed, a strange attitude towards himself. It sometimes seemed to him that people were watching him inquisitively as a man whose place might soon be vacant. Then again, his friends would suddenly begin to chaff him in a friendly way about his low spirits, as if the awful, horrible, and unheard-of thing that was going on within him, incessantly gnawing at him and irresistibly drawing him away, was a very agreeable subject for jests. Schwartz in particular irritated him by his jocularity, vivacity, and *savoir-faire,* which reminded him of what he himself had been ten years ago.

Friends came to make up a set and they sat down to cards. They dealt, bending the new cards to soften them, and he sorted the diamonds in his hand and found he had seven. His partner said "No trumps" and supported him with two diamonds. What more could be wished for? It ought to be jolly and lively. They would make a grand slam. But suddenly Ivan Ilych was conscious of that gnawing pain, that taste in his mouth, and it seemed ridiculous that in such circumstances he should be pleased to make a grand slam.

He looked at his partner Mikhail Mikhaylovich, who rapped the table with his strong hand and instead of snatching up the tricks pushed the cards courteously and indulgently towards Ivan Ilych that he might have the pleasure of gathering them up without the trouble of stretching out his hand for them. "Does he think I am too weak to stretch out my arm?" thought Ivan Ilych, and forgetting what he was doing he over-trumped his partner, missing the grand slam by three tricks. And what was most awful of all was that he saw how upset Mikhail Mikhaylovich was about it but did not himself care. And it was dreadful to realize why he did not care.

They all saw that he was suffering, and said: "We can stop if you are tired. Take a rest." Lie down? No, he was not at all tired, and he finished the rubber. All were gloomy and silent. Ivan Ilych felt that he had diffused this gloom over them and could not dispel it. They had supper and went away, and Ivan Ilych was left alone with the consciousness that his life was poisoned and was poisoning the lives of others, and that this poison did not weaken but penetrated more and more deeply into his whole being.

With this consciousness, and with physical pain besides that terror, he must go to bed, often to lie awake the greater part of the night. Next morning he had to get up again, dress, go to the law courts, speak, and write; or if he did not go out, spend at home those twenty-four hours a day each of which was a torture. And he had to live thus all alone on the brink of an abyss, with no one who understood or pitied him.

v

So one month passed and then another. Just before the New Year his brother-in-law came to town and stayed at their house. Ivan Ilych was at the law courts and Praskovya Fëdorovna had gone shopping. When Ivan Ilych came home and entered his study he found his brother-in-law there—a healthy, florid man—unpacking his portmanteau himself. He raised his head on hearing Ivan Ilych's footsteps and looked up at him for a moment without a word. That stare told Ivan Ilych everything. His brother-in-law opened his mouth to utter an exclamation of surprise but checked himself, and that action confirmed it all.

"I have changed, eh?"

"Yes, there is a change."

And after that, try as he would to get his brother-in-law to return to the subject of his looks, the latter would say nothing about it. Praskovya Fëdorovna came home and her brother went out to her. Ivan Ilych locked the door and began to examine himself in the glass, first full face, then in profile. He took up a portrait of himself taken with his wife, and compared it with what he saw in the glass. The change in him was immense. Then he bared his arms to the elbow, looked at them, drew the sleeves down again, sat down on an ottoman, and grew blacker than night.

"No, no, this won't do!" he said to himself, and jumped up, went to the table, took up some law papers and began to read them, but could not continue. He unlocked the door and went into the reception-room. The door leading to the drawing-room was shut. He approached it on tiptoe and listened.

"No, you are exaggerating!" Praskovya Fëdorovna was saying.

"Exaggerating! Don't you see it? Why, he's a dead man! Look at his eyes—there's no light in them. But what is it that is wrong with him?"

"No one knows. Nikolaevich [that was another doctor] said something, but I don't know what. And Leshchetitsky [this was the celebrated specialist] said quite the contrary . . ."

Ivan Ilych walked away, went to his own room, lay down, and began musing: "The kidney, a floating kidney." He recalled all the doctors had told him of how it detached itself and swayed about. And by an effort of imagination he tried to catch that kidney and arrest it and support it. So little was needed for this, it seemed to him. "No, I'll go to see Peter Ivanovich again." [That was the friend whose friend was a doctor.] He rang, ordered the carriage, and got ready to go.

"Where are you going, Jean?" asked his wife, with a specially sad and exceptionally kind look.

This exceptionally kind look irritated him. He looked morosely at her.

"I must go to Peter Ivanovich."

He went to see Peter Ivanovich, and together they went to see his friend, the doctor. He was in, and Ivan Ilych had a long talk with him.

Reviewing the anatomical and physiological details of what in the doctor's opinion was going on inside him, he understood it all.

There was something, a small thing, in the vermiform appendix. It might all come right. Only stimulate the energy of one organ and check the activity of another, then absorption would take place and everything would come right. He got home rather late for dinner, ate his dinner, conversed cheerfully, but could not for a long time bring himself to go back to work in his room. At last, however, he went to his study and did what was necessary, but the consciousness that he had put something aside—an important, intimate matter which he would revert to when his work was done—never left him. When he had finished his work he remembered that this intimate matter was the thought of his vermiform appendix. But he did not give himself up to it, and went to the drawing-room for tea. There were callers there, including the examining magistrate who was a desirable match for his daughter, and they were conversing, playing the piano, and singing. Ivan Ilych, as Praskovya Fëdorovna remarked, spent that evening more cheerfully than usual, but he never for a moment forgot that he had postponed the important matter of the appendix. At eleven o'clock he said good-night and went to his bedroom. Since his illness he had slept alone in a small room next to his study. He undressed and took up a novel by Zola, but instead of reading it fell into thought, and in his imagination that desired improvement in the vermiform appendix occurred. There was the absorption and evacuation and the re-establishment of normal activity. "Yes, that's it!" he said to himself. "One need only assist nature, that's all." He remembered his medicine, rose, took it, and lay down on his back watching for the beneficent action of the medicine and for it to lessen the pain. "I need only take it regularly and avoid all injurious influences. I am already feeling better, much better." He began touching his side: it was not painful to the touch. "There, I really don't feel it. It's much better already." He put out the light and turned on his side . . . "The appendix is getting better, absorption is occurring." Suddenly he felt the old, familiar, dull gnawing pain, stubborn and serious. There was the same familiar loathsome taste in his mouth. His heart sank and he felt dazed. "My God! My God!" he muttered. "Again, again! and it will never cease." And suddenly the matter presented itself in a quite different aspect. "Vermiform appendix! Kidney!" he said to himself. "It's not a question of appendix or kidney, but of life and . . . death. Yes, life was there and now it is going, going and I cannot stop it. Yes. Why deceive myself? Isn't it obvious to everyone but me that I'm dying, and that it's only a question of weeks, days . . . it may happen this moment. There was light and now there is darkness. I was here and now I'm going there! Where?" A chill came over him, his breathing ceased, and he felt only the throbbing of his heart.

"When I am not, what will there be? There will be nothing. Then where shall I be when I am no more? Can this be dying? No, I don't want to!" He jumped up and tried to light the candle, felt for it with trembling hands, dropped candle and candlestick on the floor, and fell back on his pillow.

"What's the use? It makes no difference," he said to himself, staring with wide-open eyes into the darkness. "Death. Yes, death. And none of them know or wish to know it, and they have no pity for me. Now they are playing." (He heard through the door the distant sound of a song and its accompaniment.) "It's all the same to them, but they will die too! Fools! I first, and they later, but it will be the same for them. And now they are merry . . . the beasts!"

Anger choked him and he was agonizingly, unbearably, miserable. "It is impossible that all men have been doomed to suffer this awful horror!" He raised himself.

"Something must be wrong. I must calm myself—must think it all over from the beginning." And he again began thinking. "Yes, the beginning of my illness: I knocked my side, but I was quite well that day and the next. It hurt a little, then rather more. I saw the doctor, then followed despondency and anguish, more doctors, and I drew nearer to the abyss. My strength grew less and I kept coming nearer and nearer, and now I have wasted away and there is no light in my eyes. I think of the appendix—but this is death! I think of mending the appendix, and all the while here is death! Can it really be death?" Again terror seized him and he gasped for breath. He leant down and began feeling for the matches, pressing with his elbow on the stand beside the bed. It was in the way and hurt him, he grew furious with it, pressed on it still harder, and upset it. Breathless and in despair he fell on his back, expecting death to come immediately.

Meanwhile the visitors were leaving. Praskovya Fëdorovna was seeing them off. She heard something fall and came in.

"What has happened?"

"Nothing. I knocked it over accidentally."

She went out and returned with a candle. He lay there panting heavily, like a man who has run a thousand yards, and stared upwards at her with a fixed look.

"What is it, Jean?"

"No . . . o . . . thing. I upset it." ("Why speak of it? She won't understand," he thought.)

And in truth she did not understand. She picked up the stand, lit his candle, and hurried away to see another visitor off. When she came back he still lay on his back, looking upwards.

"What is it? Do you feel worse?"

"Yes."

She shook her head and sat down.

"Do you know, Jean, I think we must ask Leshchetitsky to come and see you here."

This meant calling in the famous specialist, regardless of expense. He smiled malignantly and said "No." She remained a little longer and then went up to him and kissed his forehead.

While she was kissing him he hated her from the bottom of his soul and with difficulty refrained from pushing her away.

"Good-night. Please God you'll sleep."

"Yes."

VI

Ivan Ilych saw that he was dying, and he was in continual despair.

In the depth of his heart he knew he was dying, but not only was he not accustomed to the thought, he simply did not and could not grasp it.

The syllogism he had learnt from Kiezewetter's Logic: "Caius is a man, men are mortal, therefore Caius is mortal," had always seemed to him correct as applied to Caius, but certainly not as applied to himself. That Caius—man in the abstract—was mortal, was perfectly correct, but he was not Caius, not an abstract man, but a creature quite, quite separate from all others. He had been little Vanya, with a mamma and a papa, with Mitya and Volodya, with the toys, a coachman and a nurse, afterwards with Katenka and with all the joys, griefs, and delights of childhood, boyhood, and youth. What did Caius know of the smell of that striped leather ball Vanya had been so fond of? Had Caius kissed his mother's hand like that, and did the silk of her dress rustle so for Caius? Had he rioted like that at school when the pastry was bad? Had Caius been in love like that? Could Caius preside at a session as he did? "Caius really was mortal, and it was right for him to die; but for me, little Vanya, Ivan Ilych, with all my thoughts and emotions, it's altogether a different matter. It cannot be that I ought to die. That would be too terrible."

Such was his feeling.

"If I had to die like Caius, I should have known it was so. An inner voice would have told me so, but there was nothing of the sort in me and I and all my friends felt that our case was quite different from that of Caius. And now here it is!" he said to himself. "It can't be. It's impossible! But here it is. How is this? How is one to understand it?"

He could not understand it, and tried to drive this false, incorrect, morbid thought away and to replace it by other proper and healthy thoughts. But that thought, and not the thought only but the reality itself, seemed to come and confront him.

And to replace that thought he called up a succession of others, hoping to find in them some support. He tried to get back into the former current of thoughts that had once screened the thought of death from him. But strange to say, all that had formerly shut off, hidden, and destroyed, his consciousness of death, no longer had that effect. Ivan Ilych now spent most of his time in attempting to re-establish that old current. He would say to himself: "I will take up my duties again—after all I used to live by them." And banishing all doubts he would go to the law courts, enter into conversation with his colleagues, and sit carelessly as was his wont, scanning the crowd with a thoughtful look and leaning both his emaciated arms on the arms of his oak chair; bending over as usual to a colleague and drawing his papers nearer he would interchange whispers with him, and then suddenly raising his eyes and sitting erect would pronounce certain words and open the proceedings. But suddenly in the midst of those proceedings the pain in his side, regardless of the stage the proceedings had reached, would begin its own gnawing work. Ivan Ilych would turn his attention to it and try to drive the thought of it away, but without success. *It* would come and stand before him and look at him, and he would be petrified and the light would die out of his eyes, and he would again begin asking himself whether *It* alone was true. And his colleagues and subordinates would see with surprise and distress that he, the brilliant and subtle judge, was becoming confused and making mistakes. He would shake himself, try to pull himself together, manage somehow to bring the sitting to a close, and return home with the sorrowful consciousness that his judicial labours could not as formerly hide from him what he wanted them to hide, and could not deliver him from *It*. And what was worst of all was that *It* drew his attention to itself not in order to make him take some action but only that he should look at *It*, look it straight in the face: look at it and without doing anything, suffer inexpressibly.

And to save himself from this condition Ivan Ilych looked for consolations—new screens—and new screens were found and for a while seemed to save him, but then immediately fell to pieces or rather became transparent, as if *It* penetrated them and nothing could veil *It*.

In these latter days he would go into the drawing-room he had arranged—that drawing-room where he had fallen and for the sake of which (how bitterly ridiculous it seemed) he had sacrificed his life—for he knew that his illness originated with that knock. He would enter and see that something had scratched the polished table. He would look for the cause of this and find that it was the bronze ornamentation of an album, that had got bent. He would take up the expensive album which he had lovingly arranged, and feel vexed with his daughter and her friends for their untidiness—for the album was torn here and there and some of the photographs turned upside down. He would put it carefully in order and bend the ornamentation back into position. Then it would occur to him to place all those things in another corner of the room, near the plants. He would call the footman, but his daughter or wife would come to help him. They would not agree, and his wife would contradict him, and he would dispute and grow angry. But that was all right, for then he did not think about *It*. *It* was invisible.

But then, when he was moving something himself, his wife would say: "Let the servants do it. You will hurt yourself again." And suddenly *It* would flash through the screen and he would see it. It was just a flash, and he hoped it would disappear, but he would involuntarily pay attention to his side. "It sits there as before, gnawing just the same!" And he could no longer forget *It*, but could distinctly see it looking at him from behind the flowers. "What is it all for?"

"It really is so! I lost my life over that curtain as I might have done when storming a fort. Is that possible? How terrible and how stupid. It can't be true! It can't, but it is."

He would go to his study, lie down, and again be alone with *It*: face to face with *It*. And nothing could be done with *It* except to look at it and shudder.

VII

How it happened it is impossible to say because it came about step by step, unnoticed, but in the third month of Ivan Ilych's illness, his wife, his daughter, his son, his acquaintances, the doctors, the servants, and above all he himself, were aware that the whole interest he had for other people was whether he would soon vacate his place, and at last release the living from the discomfort caused by his presence and be himself released from his sufferings.

He slept less and less. He was given opium and hypodermic injections of morphine, but this did not relieve him. The dull depression he experienced in a somnolent condition at first gave him a little relief, but only as something new, afterwards it became as distressing as the pain itself or even more so.

Special foods were prepared for him by the doctors' orders, but all those foods became increasingly distasteful and disgusting to him.

For his excretions also special arrangements had to be made, and this was a torment to him every time—a torment from the uncleanliness, the unseemliness, and the smell, and from knowing that another person had to take part in it.

But just through this most unpleasant matter, Ivan Ilych obtained comfort. Gerasim, the butler's young assistant, always came in to carry the things out. Gerasim was a clean, fresh peasant lad, grown stout on town food and always cheerful and bright. At first the sight of him, in his clean Russian peasant costume, engaged in that disgusting task embarrassed Ivan Ilych.

Once when he got up from the commode too weak to draw up his trousers, he dropped into a soft armchair and looked with horror at his bare, enfeebled thighs with the muscles so sharply marked on them.

Gerasim with a firm light tread, his heavy boots emitting a pleasant smell of tar and fresh winter air, came in wearing a clean Hessian apron, the sleeves of his print shirt tucked up over his strong bare young arms; and refraining from looking at his sick master out of consideration for his feelings, and restraining the joy of life that beamed from his face, he went up to the commode.

"Gerasim!" said Ivan Ilych in a weak voice.

Gerasim started, evidently afraid he might have committed some blunder, and with a rapid movement turned his fresh, kind, simple young face which just showed the first downy signs of a beard.

"Yes, sir?"

"That must be very unpleasant for you. You must forgive me. I am helpless."

"Oh, why, sir," and Gerasim's eyes beamed and he showed his glistening white teeth, "what's a little trouble? It's a case of illness with you, sir."

And his deft strong hands did their accustomed task, and he went out of the room stepping lightly. Five minutes later he as lightly returned.

Ivan Ilych was still sitting in the same position in the armchair.

"Gerasim," he said when the latter had replaced the freshly-washed utensil. "Please come here and help me." Gerasim went up to him. "Lift me up. It is hard for me to get up, and I have sent Dmitri away."

Gerasim went up to him, grasped his master with his strong arms deftly but gently, in the same way that he stepped—lifted him, supported him with one hand, and with the other drew up his trousers and would have set him down again, but Ivan Ilych asked to be led to the sofa. Gerasim, without an effort and without apparent pressure, led him, almost lifting him, to the sofa and placed him on it.

"Thank you. How easily and well you do it all!"

Gerasim smiled again and turned to leave the room. But Ivan Ilych felt his presence such a comfort that he did not want to let him go.

"One thing more, please move up that chair. No, the other one—under my feet. It is easier for me when my feet are raised."

Gerasim brought the chair, set it down gently in place, and raised Ivan Ilych's legs on to it. It seemed to Ivan Ilych that he felt better while Gerasim was holding up his legs.

"It's better when my legs are higher," he said. "Place that cushion under them."

Gerasim did so. He again lifted the legs and placed them, and again Ivan Ilych felt better while Gerasim held his legs. When he set them down Ivan Ilych fancied he felt worse.

"Gerasim," he said. "Are you busy now?"

"Not at all, sir," said Gerasim, who had learnt from the townfolk how to speak to gentlefolk.

"What have you still to do?"

"What have I to do? I've done everything except chopping the logs for tomorrow."

"Then hold my legs up a bit higher, can you?"

"Of course I can. Why not?" And

Gerasim raised his master's legs higher and Ivan Ilych thought that in that position he did not feel any pain at all.

"And how about the logs?"

"Don't trouble about that, sir. There's plenty of time."

Ivan Ilych told Gerasim to sit down and hold his legs, and began to talk to him. And strange to say it seemed to him that he felt better while Gerasim held his legs up.

After that Ivan Ilych would sometimes call Gerasim and get him to hold his legs on his shoulders, and he liked talking to him. Gerasim did it all easily, willingly, simply, and with a good nature that touched Ivan Ilych. Health, strength, and vitality in other people were offensive to him, but Gerasim's strength and vitality did not mortify but soothed him.

What tormented Ivan Ilych most was the deception, the lie, which for some reason they all accepted, that he was not dying but was simply ill, and that he only need keep quiet and undergo a treatment and then something very good would result. He however knew that do what they would nothing would come of it, only still more agonizing suffering and death. This deception tortured him—their not wishing to admit what they all knew and what he knew, but wanting to lie to him concerning his terrible condition, and wishing and forcing him to participate in that lie. Those lies—lies enacted over him on the eve of his death and destined to degrade this awful, solemn act to the level of their visitings, their curtains, their sturgeon for dinner—were a terrible agony for Ivan Ilych. And strangely enough, many times when they were going through their antics over him he had been within a hairbreadth of calling out to them: "Stop lying! You know and I know that I am dying. Then at least stop lying about it!" But he had never had the spirit to do it. The awful, terrible act of his dying was, he could see, reduced by those about him to the level of a casual, unpleasant, and almost indecorous incident (as if someone entered a drawing-room diffusing an unpleasant odour) and this was done by the very decorum which he had served all his life long. He saw that no one felt for him, because no one even wished to grasp his position. Only Gerasim recognized it and pitied him. And so Ivan Ilych felt at ease only with him. He felt comforted when Gerasim supported his legs (sometimes all night long) and refused to go to bed, saying: "Don't you worry, Ivan Ilych. I'll get sleep enough later on," or when he suddenly became familiar and exclaimed: "If you weren't sick it would be another matter, but as it is, why should I grudge a little trouble?" Gerasim alone did not lie; everything showed that he alone understood the facts of the case and did not consider it necessary to disguise them, but simply felt sorry for his emaciated and enfeebled master. Once when Ivan Ilych was sending him away he even said straight out: "We shall all of us die, so why should I grudge a little trouble?"—expressing the fact that he did not think his work burdensome, because he was doing it for a dying man and hoped someone would do the same for him when his time came.

Apart from this lying, or because of it, what most tormented Ivan Ilych was that no one pitied him as he wished to be pitied. At certain moments after prolonged suffering he wished most of all (though he would have been ashamed to confess it) for someone to pity him as a sick child is pitied. He longed to be petted and comforted. He knew he was an important functionary, that he had a beard turning grey, and that therefore what he longed for was impossible, but still he longed for it. And in Gerasim's attitude towards him there was something akin to what he wished for, and so that attitude comforted him. Ivan Ilych wanted to weep, wanted to be petted and cried over, and then his colleague Shebek would come, and instead of weeping and being petted, Ivan Ilych would assume a serious, severe, and profound air, and by force of habit would express his opinion on a decision of the Court of Cassation and would stubbornly insist on that view. This falsity around him and within him did more than anything else to poison his last days.

VIII

It was morning. He knew it was morning because Gerasim had gone, and Peter the footman had come and put out the candles, drawn back one of the curtains, and begun quietly to tidy up. Whether it was morning or evening, Friday or Sunday, made no difference, it was all just the same: the gnawing, unmitigated, agonizing pain, never ceasing for an instant, the consciousness of life inexorably waning but not yet extinguished, the approach of that ever dreaded and hateful Death which was the only reality, and always the same falsity. What were days, weeks, hours, in such a case?

"Will you have some tea, sir?"

"He wants things to be regular, and wishes the gentlefolk to drink tea in the morning," thought Ivan Ilych, and only said "No."

"Wouldn't you like to move onto the sofa, sir?"

"He wants to tidy up the room, and I'm in the way. I am uncleanliness and disorder," he thought, and said only:

"No, leave me alone."

The man went on bustling about. Ivan Ilych stretched out his hand. Peter came up, ready to help.

"What is it, sir?"

"My watch."

Peter took the watch which was close at hand and gave it to his master.

"Half-past eight. Are they up?"

"No, sir, except Vladimir Ivanich" (the son) "who has gone to school. Preskovya Fëdorovna ordered me to wake her if you asked for her. Shall I do so?"

"No, there's no need to." "Perhaps I'd better have some tea," he thought, and added aloud: "Yes, bring me some tea."

Peter went to the door, but Ivan Ilych dreaded being left alone. "How can I keep him here? Oh yes, my medicine." "Peter, give me my medicine." "Why not? Perhaps it may still do me some good." He took a spoonful and swallowed it. "No, it won't help. It's all tomfoolery, all decep-tion," he decided as soon as he became aware of the familiar, sickly, hopeless taste. "No, I can't believe in it any longer. But the pain, why this pain? If it would only cease just for a moment!" And he moaned. Peter turned towards him. "It's all right. Go and fetch me some tea."

Peter went out. Left alone Ivan Ilych groaned not so much with pain, terrible though that was, as from mental anguish. Always and for ever the same, always these endless days and nights. If only it would come quicker! If only *what* would come quicker? Death, darkness? . . . No, no! Anything rather than death!

When Peter returned with the tea on a tray, Ivan Ilych stared at him for a time in perplexity, not realizing who and what he was. Peter was disconcerted by that look and his embarrassment brought Ivan Ilych to himself.

"Oh, tea! All right, put it down. Only help me to wash and put on a clean shirt."

And Ivan Ilych began to wash. With pauses for rest, he washed his hands and then his face, cleaned his teeth, brushed his hair, and looked in the glass. He was terrified by what he saw, especially by the limp way in which his hair clung to his pallid forehead.

While his shirt was being changed he knew that he would be still more frightened at the sight of his body, so he avoided looking at it. Finally he was ready. He drew on a dressing-gown, wrapped himself in a plaid, and sat down in the armchair to take his tea. For a moment he felt refreshed, but as soon as he began to drink the tea he was again aware of the same taste, and the pain also returned. He finished it with an effort, and then lay down stretching out his legs, and dismissed Peter.

Always the same. Now a spark of hope flashes up, then a sea of despair rages, and always pain; always pain, always despair, and always the same. When alone he had a dreadful and distressing desire to call someone, but he knew beforehand that with others present it would be still worse. "Another dose of morphine—to lose consciousness. I will tell him, the doctor, that he must think of something else. It's impossible, impossible, to go on like this."

An hour and another pass like that. But now there is a ring at the door bell. Perhaps it's the doctor? It is. He comes in fresh, hearty, plump, and cheerful, with that look on his face that seems to say: "There now, you're in a panic about something, but we'll arrange it all for you directly!" The doctor knows this expression is out of place here, but he has put it on once for all and can't take it off—like a man who has put on a frock-coat in the morning to pay a round of calls.

The doctor rubs his hands vigorously and reassuringly.

"Brr! How cold it is! There's such a sharp frost; just let me warm myself!" he says, as if it were only a matter of waiting till he was warm, and then he would put everything right.

"Well now, how are you?"

Ivan Ilych feels that the doctor would like to say: "Well, how are your affairs?" but that even he feels that this would not do, and says instead: "What sort of a night have you had?"

Ivan Ilych looks at him as much as to say: "Are you really never ashamed of lying?" But the doctor does not wish to understand this question, and Ivan Ilych says: "Just as terrible as ever. The pain never leaves me and never subsides. If only something . . ."

"Yes, you sick people are always like that . . . There, now I think I am warm enough. Even Praskovya Fëdorovna, who is so particular, could find no fault with my temperature. Well, now I can say good-morning," and the doctor presses his patient's hand.

Then, dropping his former playfulness, he begins with a most serious face to examine the patient, feeling his pulse and taking his temperature, and then begins the sounding and auscultation.

Ivan Ilych knows quite well and definitely that all this is nonsense and pure deception, but when the doctor, getting down on his knee, leans over him, putting the ear first higher than lower, and performs various gymnastic movements over him with a significant expression on his face, Ivan Ilych submits to it all as he used to submit to the speeches of the lawyers, though he knew very well that they were all lying and why they were lying.

The doctor, kneeling on the sofa, is still sounding him when Praskovya Fëdorovna's silk dress rustles at the door and she is heard scolding Peter for not having let her know of the doctor's arrival.

She comes in, kisses her husband, and at once proceeds to prove that she has been up a long time already, and only owing to a misunderstanding failed to be there when the doctor arrived.

Ivan Ilych looks at her, scans her all over, sets against her the whiteness and plumpness and cleanness of her hands and neck, the gloss of her hair, and the sparkle of her vivacious eyes. He hates her with his whole soul. And the thrill of hatred he feels for her makes him suffer from her touch.

Her attitude towards him and his disease is still the same. Just as the doctor had adopted a certain relation to his patient which he could not abandon, so had she formed one towards him—that he was not doing something he ought to do and was himself to blame, and that she reproached him lovingly for this—and she could not now change that attitude.

"You see he doesn't listen to me and doesn't take his medicine at the proper time. And above all he lies in a position that is no doubt bad for him—with his legs up."

She described how he made Gerasim hold his legs up.

The doctor smiled with a contemptuous affability that said: "What's to be done? These sick people do have foolish fancies of that kind, but we must forgive them."

When the examination was over the doctor looked at his watch, and then Praskovya Fëdorovna announced to Ivan Ilych that it was of course as he pleased, but she had sent today for a celebrated specialist who would examine him and have a consultation with Michael Danilovich (their regular doctor).

"Please don't raise any objections. I am doing this for my own sake," she said ironically, letting it be felt that she was doing it all for his sake and only said this to leave him no right to refuse. He remained silent, knitting his brows. He felt that he was so surrounded and involved in a mesh of falsity that it was hard to unravel anything.

Everything she did for him was entirely for her own sake, and she told him she was doing for herself what she actually was doing for herself, as if that was so incredible that he must understand the opposite.

At half-past eleven the celebrated specialist arrived. Again the sounding began and the significant conversations in his presence and in another room, about the kidneys and the appendix, and the questions and answers, with such an air of importance that again, instead of the real question of life and death which now alone confronted him, the question arose of the kidney and appendix which were not behaving as they ought to and would now be attacked by Michael Danilovich and the specialist and forced to mend their ways.

The celebrated specialist took leave of him with a serious though not hopeless look, and in reply to the timid question Ivan Ilych, with eyes glistening with fear and hope, put to him as to whether there was a chance of recovery, said that he could not vouch for it but there was a possibility. The look of hope with which Ivan

Ilych watched the doctor out was so pathetic that Praskovya Fëdorovna, seeing it, even wept as she left the room to hand the doctor his fee.

The gleam of hope kindled by the doctor's encouragement did not last long. The same room, the same pictures, curtains, wall-paper, medicine bottles, were all there, and the same aching suffering body, and Ivan Ilych began to moan. They gave him a subcutaneous injection and he sank into oblivion.

It was twilight when he came to. They brought him his dinner and he swallowed some beef tea with difficulty, and then everything was the same again and night was coming on.

After dinner, at seven o'clock, Praskovya Fëdorovna came into the room in evening dress, her full bosom pushed up by her corset, and with traces of powder on her face. She had reminded him in the morning that they were going to the theatre. Sarah Bernhardt was visiting the town and they had a box, which he had insisted on their taking. Now he had forgotten about it and her toilet offended him, but he concealed his vexation when he remembered that he had himself insisted on their securing a box and going because it would be an instructive and aesthetic pleasure for the children.

Praskovya Fëdorovna came in, self-satisfied but yet with a rather guilty air. She sat down and asked how he was, but, as he saw, only for the sake of asking and not in order to learn about it, knowing that there was nothing to learn—and then went on to what she really wanted to say: that she would not on any account have gone but that the box had been taken and Helen and their daughter were going, as well as Petrishchev (the examining magistrate, their daughter's fiancé) and that it was out of the question to let them go alone; but that she would have much preferred to sit with him for a while; and he must be sure to follow the doctor's orders while she was away.

"Oh, and Fëdor Petrovich" (the fiancé) "would like to come in. May he? And Lisa?"

"All right."

Their daughter came in in full evening dress, her fresh young flesh exposed (making a show of that very flesh which in his own case caused so much suffering), strong, healthy, evidently in love, and impatient with illness, suffering, and death, because they interfered with her happiness.

Fëdor Petrovich came in too, in evening dress, his hair curled à la Capoul, a tight stiff collar round his long sinewy neck, an enormous white shirt-front and narrow black trousers tightly stretched over his strong thighs. He had one white glove tightly drawn on, and was holding his opera hat in his hand.

Following him the schoolboy crept in unnoticed, in a new uniform, poor little fellow, and wearing gloves. Terribly dark shadows showed under his eyes, the meaning of which Ivan Ilych knew well.

His son had always seemed pathetic to him, and now it was dreadful to see the boy's frightened look of pity. It seemed to Ivan Ilych that Vasya was the only one besides Gerasim who understood and pitied him.

They all sat down and again asked how he was. A silence followed. Lisa asked her mother about the opera-glasses, and there was an altercation between mother and daughter as to who had taken them and where they had been put. This occasioned some unpleasantness.

Fëdor Petrovich inquired of Ivan Ilych whether he had ever seen Sarah Bernhardt. Ivan Ilych did not at first catch the question, but then replied: "No, have you seen her before?"

"Yes, in *Adrienne Lecouvreur*."

Praskovya Fëdorovna mentioned some rôles in which Sarah Bernhardt was particularly good. Her daughter disagreed. Conversation sprang up as to the elegance and realism of her acting—the sort of conversation that is always repeated and is always the same.

In the midst of the conversation Fëdor Petrovich glanced at Ivan Ilych and became silent. Ivan Ilych was staring with glittering eyes straight before him, evidently indignant with them. This had to be rectified, but it was impossible to do so. The silence had to be broken, but for a time no one dared to break it and they all became afraid that the conventional deception would suddenly become obvious and the truth become plain to all. Lisa was the first to pluck up courage and break that silence, but by trying to hide what everybody was feeling, she betrayed it.

"Well, if we are going it's time to start," she said, looking at her watch, a present from her father, and with a faint and significant smile at Fëdor Petrovich relating to something known only to them. She got up with a rustle of her dress.

They all rose, said good-night, and went away.

When they had gone it seemed to Ivan Ilych that he felt better; the falsity had gone with them. But the pain remained—that same pain and that same fear that made everything monotonously alike, nothing harder and nothing easier. Everything was worse.

Again minute followed minute and hour followed hour. Everything remained the same and there was no cessation. And the inevitable end of it all became more and more terrible.

"Yes, send Gerasim here," he replied to a question Peter asked.

IX

His wife returned late at night. She came in on tiptoe, but he heard her, opened his eyes, and made haste to close them again. She wished to send Gerasim away and to sit with him herself, but he opened his eyes and said: "No, go away."

"Are you in great pain?"

"Always the same."

"Take some opium."

He agreed and took some. She went away.

Till about three in the morning he was in a state of stupefied misery. It seemed to him that he and his pain were being thrust into a narrow, deep black sack, but though they were pushed further and further in they could not be pushed to the bottom. And this, terrible enough in itself, was accompanied by suffering. He struggled but yet cooperated. And suddenly he broke through, fell, and regained consciousness. Gerasim was sitting at the foot of the bed dozing quietly, while he himself lay with his emaciated stockinged legs resting on Gerasim's shoulders; the same shaded candle was there and the same unceasing pain.

"Go away, Gerasim," he whispered.

"It's all right, sir. I'll stay a while."

"No. Go away."

He removed his legs from Gerasim's shoulders, turned sideways onto his arm, and felt sorry for himself. He only waited till Gerasim had gone into the next room and then restrained himself no longer but wept like a child. He wept on account of his helplessness, his terrible loneliness, the cruelty of man, the cruelty of God, and the absence of God.

"Why has Thou done all this? Why hast Thou brought me here? Why, why dost Thou torment me so terribly?"

He did not expect an answer and yet wept because there was no answer and could be none. The pain again grew more acute, but he did not stir and did not call. He said to himself: "Go on! Strike me! But what is it for? What have I done to Thee? What is it for?"

Then he grew quiet and not only ceased weeping but even held his breath and became all attention. It was as though he were listening not to an audible voice but to the voice of his soul, to the current of thoughts arising within him.

"What is it you want?" was the first clear conception capable of expression in words, that he heard.

"What do you want? What do you want?" he repeated to himself.

"What do I want? To live and not to suffer," he answered.

And again he listened with such concentrated attention that even his pain did not distract him.

"To live? How?" asked his inner voice.

"Why, to live as I used to—well and pleasantly."

"As you lived before, well and pleasantly?" the voice repeated.

And in imagination he began to recall the best moments of his pleasant life. But strange to say none of those best moments of his pleasant life now seemed at all what they had then seemed—none of them except the first recollections of childhood. There, in childhood, there had been something really pleasant with which it would be possible to live if it could return. But the child who had experienced that happiness existed no longer, it was like a reminiscence of somebody else.

As soon as the period began which had produced the present Ivan Ilych, all that had then seemed joys now melted before his sight and turned into something trivial and often nasty.

And the further he departed from childhood and the nearer he came to the present the more worthless and doubtful were the joys. This began with the School of Law. A little that was really good was still found there—there was light-heartedness, friendship, and hope. But in the upper classes there had already been fewer of such good moments. Then during the first years of his official career, when he was in the service of the Governor, some pleasant moments again occurred: they were the memories of love for a woman. Then all became confused and there was still less of what was good; later on again there was still less that was good, and the further he went the less there was. His marriage, a mere accident, then the disenchantment that followed it, his wife's bad breath and the sensuality and hypocrisy: then that deadly official life and those preoccupations about money, a year of it, and two, and ten, and twenty, and always the same thing. And the longer it lasted the more deadly it became. "It is as if I had been going downhill while I imagined I was going up. And that is really what it was. I was going up in public opinion, but to the same extent life was ebbing away from me. And now it is all done and there is only death."

"Then what does it mean? Why? It can't be that life is so senseless and horrible. But if it really has been so horrible and senseless, why must I die and die in agony? There is something wrong!"

"Maybe I did not live as I ought to have done," it suddenly occurred to him. "But how could that be, when I did everything properly?" he replied, and immediately dismissed from his mind this, the sole solution of all the riddles of life and death, as something quite impossible.

"Then what do you want now? To live? Live how? Live as you lived in the law courts when the usher proclaimed 'The judge is coming!' The judge is coming, the judge!" he repeated to himself. "Here he is, the judge. But I am not guilty!" he exclaimed angrily. "What is it for?" And he ceased crying, but turning his face to the wall continued to ponder on the same question: Why, and for what purpose, is there all this horror? But however much he pondered he found no answer. And whenever the thought occurred to him, as it often did, that it all resulted from his not having lived as he ought to have done, he at once recalled the correctness of his whole life and dismissed so strange an idea.

Another fortnight passed. Ivan Ilych now no longer left his sofa. He would not lie in bed but lay on the sofa, facing the wall nearly all the time. He suffered ever the same unceasing agonies and in his loneliness pondered always on the same insoluble question: "What is this? Can it be that it is Death?" And the inner voice answered: "Yes, it is Death."

"Why these sufferings?" And the voice answered, "For no reason—they just are so." Beyond and besides this there was nothing.

From the very beginning of his illness, ever since he had first been to see the doctor, Ivan Ilych's life had been divided between two contrary and alternating moods: now it was despair and the expectation of this uncomprehended and terrible death, and now hope and an intently interested observation of the functioning of his organs. Now before his eyes there was only a kidney or an intestine that temporarily evaded its duty, and now only that incomprehensible and dreadful death from which it was impossible to escape.

These two states of mind had alternated from the very beginning of his illness, but the further it progressed the more doubtful and fantastic became the conception of the kidney, and the more real the sense of impending death.

He had but to call to mind what he had been three months before and what he was now, to call to mind with what regularity he had been going downhill, for every possibility of hope to be shattered.

Latterly during that loneliness in which he found himself as he lay facing the back of the sofa, a loneliness in the midst of a populous town and surrounded by numerous acquaintances and relations but that yet could not have been more complete anywhere—either at the bottom of the sea or under the earth—during that terrible loneliness Ivan Ilych had lived only in memories of the past. Pictures of his past rose before him one after another. They always began with what was nearest in time and then went back to what was the most remote—to his childhood—and

rested there. If he thought of the stewed prunes that had been offered him that day, his mind went back to the raw shrivelled French plums of his childhood, their peculiar flavour and the flow of saliva when he sucked their stones, and along with the memory of that taste came a whole series of memories of those days: his nurse, his brother, and their toys. "No, I mustn't think of that . . . It is too painful," Ivan Ilych said to himself, and brought himself back to the present—to the button on the back of the sofa and the creases in its morocco. "Morocco is expensive, but it does not wear well: there had been a quarrel about it. It was a different kind of quarrel and a different kind of morocco that time when we tore father's portfolio and were punished, and Mamma brought us some tarts . . ." And again his thoughts dwelt on his childhood, and again it was painful and he tried to banish them and fix his mind on something else.

Then again together with that chain of memories another series passed through his mind—of how his illness had progressed and grown worse. There also the further back he looked the more life there had been. There had been more of what was good in life and more of life itself. The two merged together. "Just as the pain went on getting worse and worse, so my life grew worse and worse," he thought. "There is one bright spot there at the back, at the beginning of life, and afterwards all becomes blacker and blacker and proceeds more and more rapidly—in inverse ratio to the square of the distance from death," thought Ivan

Ilych. And the example of a stone falling downwards with increasing velocity entered his mind. Life, a series of increasing sufferings, flies further and further towards its end— the most terrible suffering. "I am flying . . ." He shuddered, shifted himself, and tried to resist, but was already aware that resistance was impossible, and again with eyes weary of gazing but unable to cease seeing what was before them, he stared at the back of the sofa and waited— awaiting that dreadful fall and shock and destruction.

"Resistance is impossible!" he said to himself. "If I could only understand what it is all for! But that too is impossible. An explanation would be possible if it could be said that I have not lived as I ought to. But it is impossible to say that," and he remembered all the legality, correctitude, and propriety of his life. "That at any rate can certainly not be admitted," he thought, and his lips smiled ironically as if someone could see that smile and be taken in by it. "There is no explanation! Agony, death . . . What for?"

XI

Another two weeks went by in this way and during that fortnight an event occurred that Ivan Ilych and his wife had desired. Petrishchev formally proposed. It happened in the evening. The next day Praskovya Fëdorovna came into her husband's room considering how best to inform him of it, but that very night there had been a fresh change for the worse in his condition. She found him still lying on the sofa but in a different position. He lay on his back, groaning and staring fixedly in front of him.

She began to remind him of his medicines, but he turned his eyes towards her with such a look that she did not finish what she was saying; so great an animosity, to her in particular, did that look express.

"For Christ's sake let me die in peace!" he said.

She would have gone away, but just then their daughter came in and went up to say good morning. He looked at her as he had done at his wife, and in reply to her inquiry about his health said dryly that he would soon free them all of himself. They were both silent and after sitting with him for a while went away.

"Is it our fault?" Lisa said to her mother. "It's as if we were to blame! I am sorry for papa, but why should we be tortured?"

The doctor came at his usual time. Ivan Ilych answered "Yes" and "No," never taking his angry eyes from him, and at last said: "You know you can do nothing for me, so leave me alone."

"We can ease your sufferings."

"You can't even do that. Let me be."

The doctor went into the drawing-room and told Praskovya Fëdorovna that the case was very serious and that the only resource left was opium to allay her husband's sufferings, which must be terrible.

It was true, as the doctor said, that Ivan Ilych's physical sufferings were terrible, but worse than the physical sufferings were his mental sufferings, which were his chief torture.

His mental sufferings were due to the fact that that night, as he looked at Gerasim's sleepy, good-natured face with its prominent cheek-bones, the question suddenly occurred to him: "What if my whole life has really been wrong?"

It occurred to him that what had appeared perfectly impossible before, namely that he had not spent his life as he should have done, might after all be true. It occurred to him that his scarcely perceptible attempts to struggle against what was considered good by the most highly placed people, those scarcely noticeable impulses which he had immediately suppressed, might have been the real thing, and all the rest false. And his professional duties and the whole arrangement of his life and of his family, and all his social and official interests, might all have been false. He tried to defend all those things to himself and suddenly felt the weakness of what he was defending. There was nothing to defend.

"But if that is so," he said to himself, "and I am leaving this life with the consciousness that I have lost all that was given me and it is impossible to rectify it—what then?"

He lay on his back and began to pass his life in review in quite a new way. In the morning when he saw first his footman, then his wife, then his daughter, and then the doctor, their every word and movement confirmed to him the awful truth that had been revealed to him during the night. In them he saw himself—all that for which he had lived—and saw clearly that it was not real at all, but a terrible and huge deception which had hidden both life and death. This consciousness intensified his physical suffering tenfold. He groaned and tossed about, and pulled at his clothing which choked and stifled him. And he hated them on that account.

He was given a large dose of opium and became unconscious, but at noon his sufferings began again. He drove everybody away and tossed from side to side.

His wife came to him and said:

"Jean, my dear, do this for me. It can't do any harm and often helps. Healthy people often do it."

He opened his eyes wide.

"What? Take communion? Why? It's unnecessary! However . . ."

She began to cry.

"Yes, do, my dear. I'll send for our priest. He is such a nice man."

"All right. Very well," he muttered.

When the priest came and heard his confession, Ivan Ilych was softened and seemed to feel a relief from his doubts and consequently from his sufferings, and for a moment there came a ray of hope. He again began to think of the vermiform appendix and the possibility of correcting it. He received the sacrament with tears in his eyes.

When they laid him down again afterwards he felt a moment's ease, and the hope that he might live awoke in him again. He began to think of the operation that had been suggested to him. "To live! I want to live!" he said to himself.

His wife came to congratulate him after his communion, and when uttering the usual conventional words she added:

"You feel better, don't you?"

Without looking at her he said "Yes."

Her dress, her figure, the expression of her face, the tone of her voice, all revealed the same thing. "This is wrong, it is not as it should be. All you have lived for and still live for is falsehood and deception, hiding life and death from you." And as soon as he admitted that thought, his hatred and his agonizing physical suffering again sprang up, and with that suffering a consciousness of the unavoidable, approaching end. And to this was added a new sensation of grinding shooting pain and a feeling of suffocation.

The expression of his face when he uttered that "yes" was dreadful. Having uttered it, he looked her straight in the eyes, turned on his face with a rapidity extraordinary in his weak state and shouted:

"Go away! Go away and leave me alone!"

XII

From that moment the screaming began that continued for three days, and was so terrible that one could not hear it through two closed doors without horror. At the moment he answered his wife he realized that he was lost, that there was no return, that the end had come, the very end, and his doubts were still unsolved and remained doubts.

"Oh! Oh! Oh!" he cried in various intonations. He had begun by

screaming "I won't!" and continued screaming on the letter *O*.

For three whole days, during which time did not exist for him, he struggled in that black sack into which he was being thrust by an invisible, resistless force. Struggled as a man condemned to death struggles in the hands of the executioner, knowing that he cannot save himself. And every moment he felt that despite all his efforts he was drawing nearer and nearer to what terrified him. He felt that his agony was due to his being thrust into that black hole and still more to his not begin able to get right into it. He was hindered from getting into it by his conviction that his life had been a good one. That very justification of his life held him fast and prevented his moving forward, and it caused him most torment of all.

Suddenly some force struck him in the chest and side, making it still harder to breathe, and he fell through the hole and there at the bottom was a light. What had happened to him was like the sensation one sometimes experiences in a railway carriage when one thinks one is going backwards while one is really going forwards and suddenly becomes aware of the real direction.

"Yes, it was all not the right thing," he said to himself, "but that's no matter. It can be done. But what *is* the right thing?" he asked himself, and suddenly grew quiet.

This occurred at the end of the third day, two hours before his death. Just then his schoolboy son had crept softly in and gone up to the bedside. The dying man was still screaming and waving his arms. His hand fell on the boy's head, and the boy caught it, pressed it to his lips, and began to cry.

At that very moment Ivan Ilych fell through and caught sight of the light, and it was revealed to him that though his life had not been what it should have been, this could still be rectified. He asked himself, "What *is* the right thing?" and grew still, listening. Then he felt that someone was kissing his hand. He opened his eyes, looked at his son, and felt sorry for him. His wife came up to him and he glanced at her. She was gazing at him openmouthed, with undried tears on her nose and cheek and a despairing look on her face. He felt sorry for her too.

"Yes, I am making them wretched," he thought. "They are sorry, but it will be better for them when I die." He wished to say this but had not the strength to utter it. "Besides, why speak? I must act," he thought. With a look at his wife he indicated his son and said: "Take him away . . . sorry for him . . . sorry for you too . . ." He tried to add, "forgive me," but said "forgo" and waved his hand, knowing that He whose understanding mattered would understand.

And suddenly it grew clear to him that what had been oppressing him and would not leave him was dropping away at once from two sides, from ten sides, and from all sides. He was sorry for them, he must act so as not to hurt them and free himself from these sufferings. "How good and how simple!" he thought. "And the pain?" he asked himself. "What has become of it? Where are you, pain?"

He turned his attention to it.

"Yes, here it is. Well, what of it? Let the pain be."

"And death . . . where is it?"

He sought his former accustomed fear of death and did not find it. "Where is it? What death?" There was no fear because there was no death.

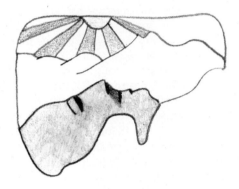

In place of death there was light.

"So that's what it is!" he suddenly exclaimed aloud. "What joy!"

To him all this happened in a single instant, and the meaning of that instant did not change. For those present his agony continued for another two hours. Something rattled in his throat, his emaciated body twitched, then the gasping and rattle became less and less frequent.

"It is finished!" said someone near him.

He heard these words and repeated them in his soul.

"Death is finished," he said to himself. "It is no more!"

He drew in a breath, stopped in the midst of a sigh, stretched out, and died.

Considerations

By beginning the story at the end—with Ivan's death—Tolstoy makes sure that wondering what is going to happen to Ivan does not distract our attention from the story. The point of view we are given is occasionally that of the impartial observer, but most often it is that of Ivan. We share his coping with life, his perception of his friends, relatives, and colleagues, his sickness, his obsessions, and his coming to terms with death.

In the span of one short novel Tolstoy catalogs the life of a man: he grows up, he marries for many of the same reasons that many men marry, his marriage becomes difficult, he enjoys somewhat superficial pleasures, and finally he comes face to face with his own mortality. This confrontation with the self is achieved in the most dramatic and ironic way possible—through a commonplace incident. Why is the use of such an incident so effective? Is it because it recalls to us the countless similar ironies that we have encountered in real life—the simple operation that went wrong, the childhood disease that permanently crippled and disfigured? Is it because it reflects the possible vast consequences of something normally considered insignificant? Is it because it shows the absurdity of life itself? Is it because in his almost ludicrous difficulties, Ivan is all too easily us?

While we can understand Ivan and pity him, we find ourselves also disliking him. As long as things are going well, when he has money and health, Ivan is pleasant and generous. He is no better but certainly no worse than the rest of us. Suddenly, however, something occurs to set him apart, and everything turns sour. He is sure that others—including his wife—are more interested in themselves than in him. (How do you suppose he would have acted had he been in his wife's place?) He becomes petulant and fretful. His physical suffering is nothing to the suffering of his mind—on one level because "no one pitied him as he wished to be pitied," and on another because he is unable to comfort himself with the certainty that his life has been worthwhile: "Maybe I did not live as I ought to have done. . . . But how could that be, when I did everything properly?" What comment could Tolstoy be making about the concept of living "properly"?

In a moment of light (which could symbolize afterlife, the infinite, or merely a sudden clear insight) he recognizes that what is done is done, that only a few duties remain to those he is leaving, and that then he will be finished with it all. How such a feeling should come to a man shown earlier as so insensitive and unimaginative is unexplained. Does the ending turn the story of Ivan's essentially tawdry life into something of beauty and hope? Are any of Ivan's (or our) questions about the meaning of life or death answered in this story?

The Revolt of Mother

MARY E. WILKINS FREEMAN

"Father!"

"What is it?"

"What are them men diggin' over there in the field for?"

There was a sudden dropping and enlarging of the lower part of the old man's face, as if some heavy weight had settled therein; he shut his mouth tight, and went on harnessing the great bay mare. He hustled the collar on to her neck with a jerk.

"Father!"

The old man slapped the saddle upon the mare's back.

"Look here, father, I want to know what them men are diggin' over in the field for, an' I'm goin' to know."

"I wish you'd go into the house, mother, an' 'tend to your own affairs," the old man said then. He ran his words together, and his speech was almost as inarticulate as a growl.

But the woman understood; it was her most native tongue. "I ain't goin' into the house till you tell me what them men are doin' over there in the field," said she.

Then she stood waiting. She was a small woman, short and straight-waisted like a child in her brown cotton gown. Her forehead was mild and benevolent between the smooth curves of gray hair; there were meek downward lines about her nose and mouth; but her eyes, fixed upon the old man, looked as if the meekness had been the result of her own will, never of the will of another.

They were in the barn, standing before the wide open doors. The spring air, full of the smell of growing grass and unseen blossoms, came in their faces. The deep yard in front was littered with farm wagons and piles of wood; on the edges, close to the fence and the house, the grass was a vivid green, and there were some dandelions.

The old man glanced doggedly at his wife as he tightened the last buckles on the harness. She looked as immovable to him as one of the rocks in his pastureland, bound to the earth with generations of blackberry vines. He slapped the reins over the horse, and started forth from the barn.

"Father!" said she.

The old man pulled up. "What is it?"

"I want to know what them men are diggin' over there in that field for."

"They're diggin' a cellar, I s'pose, if you've got to know."

"A cellar for what?"

"A barn."

"A barn? You ain't goin' to build a barn over there where we was goin' to have a house, father?"

The old man said not another

word. He hurried the horse into the farm wagon, and clattered out of the yard, jouncing as sturdily on his seat as a boy.

The woman stood a moment looking after him, then she went out of the barn across a corner of the yard to the house. The house, standing at right angles with the great barn and a long reach of sheds and outbuildings, was infinitesimal compared with them. It was scarcely as commodious for people as the little boxes under the barn eaves were for doves.

A pretty girl's face, pink and delicate as a flower, was looking out of one of the house windows. She was watching three men who were digging over in the field which bounded the yard near the road line. She turned quietly when the woman entered.

"What are they digging for, mother?" said she. "Did he tell you?"

"They're diggin' for—a cellar for a new barn."

"Oh, mother, he ain't going to build another barn?"

"That's what he says."

A boy stood before the kitchen glass combing his hair. He combed slowly and painstakingly, arranging his brown hair in a smooth hillock over his forehead. He did not seem to pay any attention to the conversation.

"Sammy, did you know father was going to build a new barn?" asked the girl.

The boy combed assiduously.

"Sammy!"

He turned, and showed a face like his father's under his smooth crest of hair. "Yes, I s'pose I did," he said, reluctantly.

"How long have you known it?" asked his mother.

"'Bout three months, I guess."

"Why didn't you tell of it?"

"Didn't think 'twould do no good."

"I don't see what father wants another barn for," said the girl, in her sweet, slow voice. She turned again to the window, and stared out at the digging men in the field. Her tender, sweet face was full of a gentle distress. Her forehead was as bald and innocent as a baby's with the light hair strained back from it in a row of curl papers. She was quite large, but her soft curves did not look as if they covered muscles.

Her mother looked sternly at the boy. "Is he goin' to buy more cows?"

The boy did not reply; he was tying his shoes.

"Sammy, I want you to tell me if he's goin' to buy more cows."

"I s'pose he is."

"How many?"

"Four, I guess."

His mother said nothing more. She went into the pantry, and there was a clatter of dishes. The boy got his cap from a nail behind the door, took an old arithmetic from the shelf, and started for school. He was lightly built, but clumsy. He went out of the yard with a curious spring in the hips, that made his loose homemade jacket tilt up in the rear.

The girl went to the sink, and began to wash the dishes that were piled up there. Her mother came promptly out of the pantry, and shoved her aside. "You wipe 'em," said she, "I'll wash. There's a good many this mornin'."

The mother plunged her hands vigorously into the water, the girl wiped the plates slowly and dreamily. "Mother," said she, "don't you think it's too bad father's going to build that new barn, much as we need a decent house to live in?"

Her mother scrubbed a dish fiercely. "You ain't found out yet we're women-folks, Nanny Penn," said she. "You ain't seen enough of men-folks yet to. One of these days you'll find it out, an' then you'll know that we know only what men-folks think we do, so far as any use of it goes, an' how we'd ought to reckon men-folks in with Providence, an' not complain of what they do any more than we do of the weather."

"I don't care; I don't believe George is anything like that, anyhow," said Nanny. Her delicate face flushed pink, her lips pouted softly, as if she were going to cry.

"You wait an' see. I guess George Eastman ain't no better than other men. You hadn't ought to judge father, though. He can't help it, 'cause he don't look at things jest the way we do. An' we've been pretty comfortable here, after all. The roof don't leak—ain't never but once—that's one thing. Father's kept it shingled right up."

"I do wish we had a parlor."

"I guess it won't hurt George Eastman any to come to see you in a nice clean kitchen. I guess a good many girls don't have as good a place as this. Nobody's ever heard me complain."

"I ain't complained either, mother."

"Well, I don't think you'd better, a good father an' a good home as you've got. S'pose your father made you go out an' work for your livin'? Lots of girls have to that ain't no stronger an' better able to than you be."

Sarah Penn washed the frying-pan with a conclusive air. She scrubbed the outside of it as faithfully as the inside. She was a masterly keeper of her box of a house. Her one living-room never seemed to have in it any of the dust which the friction of life with inanimate matter produces. She swept, and there seemed to be no dirt to go before the broom; she cleaned, and one could see no difference. She was like an artist so perfect that he has apparently no art. To-day she got out a mixing bowl and a board, and rolled some pies, and there was no more flour upon her than upon her daughter who was doing finer work. Nanny was to be married in the fall, and she was sewing on some white cambric and embroidery. She sewed industriously while her mother cooked; her soft milkwhite hands and wrists showed whiter than her delicate work.

"We must have the stove moved out in the shed before long," said Mrs. Penn. "Talk about not havin' things, it's been a real blessin' to be able to put a stove up in that shed in hot weather. Father did one good thing when he fixed that stove-pipe out there."

Sarah Penn's face as she rolled her pies had that expression of meek vigor which might have characterized one of the New Testament saints. She was making mince-pies. Her husband, Adoniram Penn, liked them better than any other kind. She baked twice a week. Adoniram often liked a piece of pie between meals. She hurried this morning. It had been later than usual when she began, and she wanted to have a pie baked for dinner. However deep a resentment she might be forced to hold against her husband, she would never fail in sedulous attention to his wants.

Nobility of character manifests itself at loopholes when it is not provided with large doors. Sarah Penn's showed itself to-day in flaky dishes of pastry. So she made the pies faithfully, while across the table she could see, when she glanced up from her work, the sight that rankled in her patient and steadfast soul—the digging of the cellar of the new barn in the place where Adoniram forty years ago had promised her their new house should stand.

The pies were done for dinner. Adoniram and Sammy were home a few minutes after twelve o'clock. The dinner was eaten with serious haste. There was never much conversation at the table in the Penn family. Adoniram asked a blessing, and they ate promptly, then rose up and went about their work.

Sammy went back to school, taking soft sly lopes out of the yard like a rabbit. He wanted a game of marbles before school, and feared his father would give him some chores to do. Adoniram hastened to the door and called after him, but he was out of sight.

"I don't see what you let him go for, mother," said he. "I wanted him to help me unload that wood."

Adoniram went to work out in the yard unloading wood from the wagon. Sarah put away the dinner dishes, while Nanny took down her curl papers and changed her dress. She was going down to the store to buy some more embroidery and thread.

When Nanny was gone, Mrs. Penn went to the door. "Father!" she called.

"Well, what is it!"

"I want to see you jest a minute, father."

"I can't leave this wood nohow. I've got to git it unloaded an' go for a load of gravel afore two o'clock. Sammy had ought to helped me. You hadn't ought to let him go to school so early."

"I want to see you jest a minute."

"I tell ye I can't, nohow, mother."

"Father, you come here." Sarah Penn stood in the door like a queen; she held her head as if it bore a crown; there was that patience which makes authority royal in her voice. Adoniram went.

Mrs. Penn led the way into the kitchen, and pointed to a chair. "Sit down, father," said she; "I've got somethin' I want to say to you."

He sat down heavily; his face was quite stolid, but he looked at her with restive eyes. "Well, what is it, mother?"

"I want to know what you're buildin' that new barn for, father?"

"I ain't got nothin' to say about it."

"It can't be you think you need another barn?"

"I tell ye I ain't got nothin' to say

about it, mother; an' I ain't goin' to say nothin'."

"Be you goin' to buy more cows?"

Adoniram did not reply; he shut his mouth tight.

"I know you be, as well as I want to. Now, father, look here"—Sarah Penn had not sat down; she stood before her husband in the humble fashion of a Scripture woman—"I'm goin' to talk real plain to you; I never have sence I married you, but I'm goin' to now. I ain't never complained, an' I ain't goin' to complain now, but I'm goin' to talk plain. You see this room here, father; you look at it well. You see there ain't no carpet on the floor, an' you see the paper is all dirty, an' droppin' off the wall. We ain't had no new paper on it for ten year, an' then I put it on myself, an' it didn't cost but ninepence a roll. You see this room, father; it's all the one I've had to work in an' eat in an' sit in sence we was married. There ain't another woman in the whole town whose husband ain't got half the means you have but what's got better. It's all the room Nanny's got to have her company in; an' there ain't one of her mates but what's got better, an' their fathers not so able as hers is. It's all the room she'll have to be married in. What would you have thought, father, if we had had our weddin' in a room no better than this? I was married in my mother's parlor, with a carpet on the floor, an' stuffed furniture, an' a mahogany card-table. An' this is all the room my daughter will have to be married in. Look here, father!"

Sarah Penn went across the room as though it were a tragic stage. She flung open a door and disclosed a tiny bedroom, only large enough for a bed and bureau, with a path between. "There father," said she—"there's all the room I've had to sleep in forty year. All my children were born there—the two that died, an' the two that's livin'. I was sick with a fever there."

She stepped to another door and opened it. It led into the small, ill-lighted pantry. "Here," said she, "is all the buttery I've got—every place I've got for my dishes, to set away my victuals in, an' to keep my milkpans in. Father, I've been takin' care of the milk of six cows in this place, an' now you're goin' to build a new barn, an' keep more cows, an' give me more to do in it."

She threw open another door. A narrow crooked flight of stairs wound upward from it. "There, father," said she, "I want you to look at the stairs that go up to them two unfinished chambers that are all the places our son an' daughter have had to sleep in all their lives. There ain't a prettier girl in town nor a more ladylike one than Nanny, an' that's the place she has to sleep in. It ain't so good as your horse's stall; it ain't so warm an' tight."

Sarah Penn went back and stood before her husband. "Now, father," said she, "I want to know if you think you're doin' right an' accordin' to what you profess. Here, when we was married, forty year ago, you promised me faithful that we should have a new house built in that lot over in the field before the year was out. You said you had money enough, an' you wouldn't ask me to live in no such place as this. It is forty year now, an' you've been makin' more money, an' I've been savin' of it for you ever since, an' you ain't built no house yet. You've built sheds an' cow-houses an' one new barn, an' now you're goin' to build another. Father, I want to know if you think it's right. You're lodgin' your dumb beasts better than you are your own flesh an' blood. I want to know if you think it's right."

"I ain't got nothin' to say."

"You can't say nothin' without ownin' it ain't right, father. An' there's another thing—I ain't complained; I've got along forty year, an' I s'pose I should forty more, if it wasn't for that—if we don't have another house, Nanny she can't live with us after she's married. She'll have to go somewhere else to live away from us, an' it don't seem as if I could have it so, noways, father. She wasn't ever strong. She's got considerable color, but there wasn't never any backbone to her. I've always took the heft of everything off her, an' she ain't fit to keep house an' do everything herself. She'll be all worn out inside of a year. Think of her doin' all the washin' an' ironin' an' bakin' with them soft white hands an' arms, an' sweepin'! I can't have it so, noways, father."

Mrs. Penn's face was burning; her mild eyes gleamed. She had pleaded her little cause like a Webster; she had ranged from severity to pathos; but her opponent employed that obstinate silence which makes eloquence futile with mocking echoes. Adoniram arose clumsily.

"Father, ain't you got nothin' to say?" said Mrs. Penn.

"I've got to go off after that load of gravel. I can't stan' here talkin' all day."

"Father, won't you think it over, an' have a house built there instead of a barn?"

"I ain't got nothin' to say."

Adoniram shuffled out. Mrs. Penn went into her bedroom. When she came out, her eyes were red. She had a roll of unbleached cotton cloth. She spread it out on the kitchen table, and began cutting out some shirts for her husband. The men over in the field had a team to help them this afternoon; she could hear their halloos. She had a scanty pattern for the shirts; she had to plan and piece the sleeves.

Nanny came home with her embroidery, and sat down with her needlework. She had taken down her curl papers, and there was a soft roll of fair hair like an aureole over her forehead; her face was as delicately fine and clear as porcelain. Suddenly she looked up, and the tender red flamed all over her face and neck. "Mother," said she.

"What say?"

"I've been thinking—I don't see how we're goin' to have any— wedding in this room. I'd be ashamed to have his folks come if we didn't have anybody else."

"Mebee we can have some new paper before then; I can put it on. I guess you won't have no call to be ashamed of your belongin's."

"We might have the wedding in the new barn," said Nanny, with gentle pettishness. "Why, mother, what makes you look so?"

Mrs. Penn had started, and was staring at her with a curious expression. She turned again to her work, and spread out a pattern carefully on the cloth. "Nothin'," said she.

Presently Adoniram clattered out of the yard in his two-wheeled dump cart, standing as proudly upright as a Roman charioteer. Mrs. Penn opened the door and stood there a minute looking out; the halloos of the men sounded louder.

It seemed to her all through the spring months that she heard nothing but the halloos and the noises of saws and hammers. The new barn grew fast. It was a fine edifice for this little village. Men came on pleasant Sundays, in their meeting suits and clean shirt bosoms, and stood around it admiringly. Mrs. Penn did not speak of it, and Adoniram did not mention it to her, although sometimes, upon a return from inspecting it, he bore himself with injured dignity.

"It's a strange thing how your mother feels about the new barn," he said, confidentially, to Sammy one day.

Sammy only grunted after an odd fashion for a boy; he had learned it from his father.

The barn was all completed ready for use by the third week in July. Adoniram had planned to move his stock in on Wednesday; on Tuesday he received a letter which changed his plans. He came in with it early in the morning, "Sammy's been to the post-office," said he, "an' I've got a letter from Hiram." Hiram was Mrs. Penn's brother, who lived in Vermont.

"Well," said Mrs. Penn, "what does he say about the folks?"

"I guess they're all right. He says he thinks if I come up country right off there's a chance to buy jest the kind of a horse I want." He stared reflectively out of the window at the new barn.

Mrs. Penn was making pies. She went on clapping the rolling-pin into the crust, although she was very pale, and her heart beat loudly.

"I dun' know but what I'd better go," said Adoniram. "I hate to go off jest now, right in the midst of hayin', but the ten-acre lot's cut, an' I guess Rufus an' the others can git along without me three or four days. I can't get a horse round here to suit me, nohow, an' I've got to have another for all that wood-haulin' in the fall. I told Hiram to watch out, an' if he got wind of a good horse to let me know. I guess I'd better go."

"I'll get out your clean shirt an' collar," said Mrs. Penn calmly.

She laid out Adoniram's Sunday suit and his clean clothes on the bed in the little bedroom. She got his shaving-water and razor ready. At last she buttoned on his collar and fastened his black cravat.

Adoniram never wore his collar and cravat except on extra occasions. He held his head high, with a rasped dignity. When he was all ready, with his coat and hat brushed, and a lunch of pie and cheese in a paper bag, he hesitated on the threshold of the door. He looked at his wife, and his manner was definitely apologetic. "If them cows come to-day, Sammy can drive 'em into the new barn," said he; "an' when they bring the hay up, they can pitch it in there."

"Well," replied Mrs. Penn.

Adoniram set his shaven face ahead and started. When he had

cleared the door-step, he turned and looked back with a kind of nervous solemnity. "I shall be back by Saturday if nothin' happens," said he.

"Do be careful, father," returned his wife.

She stood in the door with Nanny at her elbow and watched him out of sight. Her eyes had a strange, doubtful expression in them; her peaceful forehead was contracted. She went in, and about her baking again. Nanny sat sewing. Her wedding-day was drawing nearer, and she was getting pale and thin with her steady sewing. Her mother kept glancing at her.

"Have you got that pain in your side this mornin'?" she asked.

"A little."

Mrs. Penn's face, as she worked, changed, her perplexed forehead smoothed, her eyes were steady, her lips firmly set. She formed a maxim for herself, although incoherently with her unlettered thoughts. "Unsolicited opportunities are the guideposts of the Lord to the new roads of life," she repeated in effect, and she made up her mind to her course of action.

"S'posin' I *had* wrote to Hiram," she muttered once, when she was in the pantry—"s'posin' I had wrote, an' asked him if he knew of any horse? But I didn't, an' father's goin' wa'n't none of my doin'. It looks like a providence." Her voice rang out quite loud at the last.

"What you talkin' about, mother?" called Nanny.

"Nothin'."

Mrs. Penn hurried her baking; at eleven o'clock it was all done. The load of hay from the west field came slowly down the cart track, and drew up at the new barn. Mrs. Penn ran out. "Stop!" she screamed, "stop!"

The men stopped and looked; Sammy upreared from the top of the load, and stared at his mother.

"Stop!" she cried out again. "Don't you put the hay in that barn; put it in the old one."

"Why, he said to put it in here," returned one of the haymakers, wonderingly. He was a young man, a neighbor's son, whom Adoniram hired by the year to help on the farm.

"Don't you put the hay in the new barn; there's room enough in the old one, ain't there?" said Mrs. Penn.

"Room enough," returned the hired man, in his thick, rustic tones. "Didn't need the new barn, nohow, far as room's concerned. Well, I s'pose he changed his mind." He took hold of the horses' bridles.

Mrs. Penn went back to the house. Soon the kitchen windows were darkened, and a fragrance like warm honey came into the room.

Nanny laid down her work. "I thought father wanted them to put the hay into the new barn?" she said, wonderingly.

"It's all right," replied her mother.

Sammy slid down from the load of hay, and came in to see if dinner was ready.

"I ain't goin' to get a regular dinner to-day, as long as father's gone," said his mother. "I've let the fire go out. You can have some bread an' milk an' pie. I thought we could get along." She set out some bowls of milk, some bread, and a pie on the kitchen table. "You'd better eat your dinner now," said she. "You might jest as well get through with it. I want you to help me afterwards."

Nanny and Sammy stared at each other. There was something strange in their mother's manner. Mrs. Penn did not eat anything herself. She went into the pantry, and they heard her moving dishes while they ate. Presently she came out with a pile of plates. She got the clothes-basket out of the shed, and packed them in it. Nanny and Sammy watched. She brought out cups and saucers, and put them in with the plates.

"What you goin' to do, mother?" inquired Nanny, in a timid voice. A sense of something unusual made her tremble, as if it were a ghost. Sammy rolled his eyes over his pie.

"You'll see what I'm goin' to do," replied Mrs. Penn. "If you're through, Nanny, I want you to go up-stairs an' pack up your things; an' I want you, Sammy, to help me take down the bed in the bedroom."

"Oh, mother, what for?" gasped Nanny.

"You'll see."

During the next few hours a feat was performed by this simple, pious New England mother which was equal in its way to Wolfe's storming of the Heights of Abraham. It took no more genius and audacity of bravery for Wolfe to cheer his wondering soldiers up those steep precipices, under the sleeping eyes of the enemy, than for Sarah Penn, at the head of her children, to move all their little household goods into the new barn while her husband was away.

Nanny and Sammy followed their mother's instructions without a murmur; indeed, they were overawed. There is a certain uncanny and superhuman quality about all such purely original undertakings as their mother's was to them. Nanny went back and forth with her light load, and Sammy tugged with sober energy.

At five o'clock in the afternoon the little house in which the Penns had lived for forty years had emptied itself into the new barn.

Every builder builds somewhat for unknown purposes, and is in a measure a prophet. The architect of Adoniram Penn's barn, while he designed it for the comfort of four-footed animals, had planned better than he knew for the comfort of humans. Sarah Penn saw at a glance its possibilities. Those great box-stalls, with quilts hung before them, would make better bedrooms than the one she had occupied for forty years, and there was a tight carriage-room. The harness-room, with its chimney and shelves, would make a kitchen of her dreams. The great middle space would make a parlor, by-and-by, fit for a palace. Up-stairs there was as much room as down. With partitions and windows, what a house would there be! Sarah looked at the row of stanchions before the allotted space for cows, and reflected that she would have her front entry there.

At six o'clock the stove was up in the harness room, the kettle was boiling, and the table set for tea. It looked almost as home-like as the abandoned house across the yard had ever done. The young hired man milked, and Sarah directed him calmly to bring the milk to the new barn. He came gaping, dropping little blots of foam from the brimming pails on the grass. Before the next morning he had spread the story of Adoniram Penn's wife moving into the new barn all over the little village. Men assembled in the store and talked it over, women with shawls over their heads scuttled into each other's houses before their work was done. Any deviation from the ordinary course of life in this quiet town was enough to stop all progress in it. Everybody paused to look at the staid, independent figure on the side track. There was a difference of opinion with regard to her. Some held her to be insane; some, of a lawless and rebellious spirit.

Friday the minister went to see her. It was in the forenoon, and she was at the barn door shelling peas for dinner. She looked up and returned his salutation with dignity, then she went on with her work. She did not invite him in. The saintly expression of her face remained fixed, but there was an angry flush over it.

The minister stood awkwardly before her, and talked. She handled the peas as if they were bullets. At last she looked up, and her eyes showed the spirit that her meek front had covered for a lifetime.

"There ain't no use talkin', Mr. Hersey," said she. "I've thought it all over an' over, an' I believe I'm doin' what's right. I've made it the subject of prayer, an' it's betwixt me an' the Lord an' Adoniram. There ain't no call for nobody else to worry about it."

"Well, of course, if you have brought it to the Lord in prayer, and feel satisfied that you are doing right, Mrs. Penn," said the minister, helplessly. His thin gray-bearded face was pathetic. He was a sickly man; his youthful confidence had cooled; he had to scourge himself up to some of his pastoral duties as relentlessly as a Catholic ascetic, and then he was prostrated by the smart.

"I think it's right jest as much as I think it was right for our forefathers to come over here from the old country 'cause they didn't have what belonged to 'em," said Mrs. Penn. She arose. The barn threshold might have been Plymouth Rock from her bearing. "I don't doubt you mean well, Mr. Hersey," said she, "but there are things people hadn't ought to interfere with. I've been a member of the church for over forty years. I've got my own mind an' my own feet, an' I'm goin' to think my own thoughts an' go my own way, an' nobody but the Lord is goin' to dictate to me unless I've a mind to have him. Won't you come in an' set down? How is Mis' Hersey?"

"She is well, I thank you," replied the minister. He added some more perplexed apologetic remarks; then he retreated.

He could expound the intricacies of every character-study in the Scriptures, he was competent to grasp the Pilgrim Fathers and all historical innovators, but Sarah Penn was beyond him. He could deal with primal cases, but parallel ones worsted him. But, after all, although it was aside from his providence, he wondered more how Adoniram Penn would deal with his wife than how the Lord would. Everybody shared the wonder. When Adoniram's four new cows arrived,

Sarah ordered three to be put in the old barn, the other in the house shed where the cooking-stove had stood. That added to the excitement. It was whispered that all four cows were domiciled in the house.

Towards sunset on Saturday, when Adoniram was expected home, there was a knot of men in the road near the new barn. The hired man had milked, but he still hung around the premises. Sarah Penn had supper all ready. There were brown-bread and baked beans and a custard pie; it was the supper that Adoniram loved on a Saturday night. She had on a clean calico, and she bore herself imperturbably. Nanny and Sammy kept close at her heels. Their eyes were large, and Nanny was full of nervous tremors. Still there was to them more pleasant excitement than anything else. An inborn confidence in their mother over their father asserted itself.

Sammy looked out of the harness-room window. "There he is," he announced, in an awed whisper. He and Nanny peeped around the casing. Mrs. Penn kept on about her work. The children watched Adoniram leave the new horse standing in the drive while he went to the house door. It was fastened. Then he went around to the shed. That door was seldom locked, even when the family was away. The thought how her father would be confronted by the cow flashed upon Nanny. There was a hysterical sob in her throat. Adoniram emerged from the shed and stood looking about in a dazed fashion. His lips moved; he was saying something, but they could not hear what it was. The hired man was peeping around a corner of the old barn, but nobody saw him.

Adoniram took the new horse by the bridle and led him across the yard to the new barn. Nanny and Sammy slunk close to their mother. The barn doors rolled back, and there stood Adoniram, with the long mild face of the Great Canadian farm horse looking over his shoulder.

Nanny kept behind her mother, but Sammy stepped suddenly forward, and stood in front of her.

Adoniram stared at the group. "What on airth you all down here for?" said he. "What's the matter over to the house?"

"We've come here to live, father," said Sammy. His shrill voice quavered out bravely.

"What"—Adoniram sniffed—"what is it smells like cookin'?" said he. He stepped forward and looked in the open door of the harness-room. Then he turned to his wife. His old bristling face was pale and frightened. "What on airth does this mean, mother?" he gasped.

"You come in here, father," said Sarah. She led the way into the harness-room and shut the door. "Now, father," said she, "you needn't be scared. I ain't crazy. There ain't nothin' to be upset over. But we've come here to live, an' we're goin' to live here. We've got jest as good a right here as new horses an' cows. The house wasn't fit for us to live in any longer, an' I made up my mind I wa'n't goin' to stay there. I've done my duty by you forty year, an' I'm goin' to do it now; but I'm goin' to live here. You've got to put in some windows and partitions; an' you'll have to buy some furniture."

"Why, mother!" the old man gasped.

"You'd better take your coat off an' get washed—there's the wash basin—an' then we'll have supper."

"Why, mother!"

Sammy went past the window, leading the new horse to the old barn. The old man saw him, and shook his head speechlessly. He tried to take off his coat, but his arms seemed to lack the power. His wife helped him. She poured some water into the tin basin, and put in a piece of soap. She got the comb and brush, and smoothed his thin gray hair after he had washed. Then she put the beans, hot bread, and tea on the table. Sammy came in, and the family drew up. Adoniram sat looking dazedly at his plate, and they waited.

"Ain't you goin' to ask a blessin', father?" said Sarah.

And the old man bent his head and mumbled.

All through the meal he stopped eating at intervals, and stared furtively at his wife; but he ate well. The home food tasted good to him, and his old frame was too sturdily healthy to be affected by his mind. But after supper he went out, and sat down on the step of the smaller door at the right of the barn, through which he had meant his Jerseys to pass in stately file, but which Sarah designed for her front house door, and he leaned his head on his hands.

After the supper dishes were cleared away and the milk-pans washed, Sarah went out to him. The twilight was deepening. There was a clear green glow in the sky. Before them stretched the smooth level of field; in the distance was a cluster of hay-stacks like the huts of a village; the air was very cool and calm and sweet. The landscape might have been an ideal one of peace.

Sarah bent over and touched her husband on one of his thin, sinewy shoulders. "Father!"

The old man's shoulders heaved: he was weeping.

"Why, don't do so, father," said Sarah.

"I'll—put up the—partitions, an' —everything you—want, mother."

Sarah put her apron up to her face; she was overcome by her own triumph.

Adoniram was like a fortress whose walls had no active resistance, and went down the instant the right besieging tools were used. "Why, mother," he said, hoarsely, "I hadn't no idee you was so set on't as all this comes to."

Considerations

After the earliest pioneer hardships were past, a few capable female writers enlivened the scene of early American fiction: Sarah Orne Jewett (1849–1909), Kate Chopin (1851–1904), and Mary E. Wilkins Freeman (1852–1930). Mary Freeman was born of Puritan Salem parentage and lived less than half her life away from her birthplace. She probably read little compared to many authors, and her output was relatively small. However, her work offers a memorable commentary on early American rural life.

For such an early fiction writer, Mrs. Freeman is surprisingly competent at some of the most highly regarded modern techniques. The sharp clear details of her characters are shown more through their own actions and dialogue than through description. The story progresses along a single line toward the denouement and close, each new facet of the daughter's frailty or the father's insensitivity forging another link in the chain of events that makes the outcome seem inevitable. Neither of the main characters is overdrawn: the father is more unnoticing than cruel, the mother more dutiful than spineless.

The accent in this story is on human relationships—especially the feelings of a woman in that time and place and what she thought was expected of her. The Sarah of this story is a woman of integrity who works hard for her family, and keeps her word even if her husband does not. Is she in any sense an early proponent of women's liberation? Does she question the superiority of the male? When she does revolt, what does she revolt against or for? The motivating force behind her action seems to be the desire for a better life for her daughter. Is such motivation simply a cliché today? Do people continue to believe that no sacrifice is too great to make for their children?

Perhaps the heroine's name, Sarah, was selected for its overtones of the Biblical Sarah—a woman who emerged from her shell late in life to give birth to a child who would continue the lineage leading to Christ. Generally, as Robert Graves put it, "man does, woman is." Occasionally, however, woman acts as well.

Does Sarah feel that she has won a battle when she changes the housing arrangements? Does she exhibit a sense of triumph? What do you think her and her husband's relationship will be like in the future?

The Pins

GUY DE MAUPASSANT

"Ah, my friend, women are such vicious animals!"

"Why do you say that?"

"Because they've played an abominable trick on me."

"On you?"

"Yes."

"Women, or a woman?"

"Two women."

"Both at once?"

"Yes."

"What was the trick?"

The two young men were sitting at one of the outside tables of a big café on the boulevard, drinking liqueurs mixed with water, those apéritifs that look like infusions made with all the different hues of a box of water colors.

They were about the same age: between twenty-five and thirty. One was blond, the other dark. They had the semi-elegance of outside brokers, of men who go to the stock market and drawing rooms, are frequent visitors everywhere, live everywhere, love everywhere. The dark-haired one said:

"I believe I've told you about my affair with a woman I met on the beach at Dieppe, the wife of a head clerk in a government office."

"Yes."

"Well, you know how it is . . . I already had a mistress in Paris, and I loved her very much. She was an old friend, a good friend—a habit, in short, and I was attached to her."

"And to your habit too?"

"Yes, to both. And she has a very likable husband. I'm fond of him too. He's a good, warmhearted man, a real friend! My life was centered around their house. But . . ."

"But what?"

"But they can't leave Paris, so I found myself womanless in Dieppe."

"Why did you go there?"

"For a change of air. You can't stay on the boulevard all the time."

"Yes, and then?"

"And then one day on the beach I met the woman I told you about."

"The head clerk's wife?"

"Yes. She was terribly bored. Her husband came only on Sundays, and he's horrible. I understand her very well. So we laughed and danced together."

"And everything else?"

"Yes, later. Anyway, we met, we liked each other, I told her so, she made me repeat it so she could understand better, and she didn't put up any obstacles when I decided to make our friendship closer."

"Did you love her?"

"Yes, a little; she's very nice."

"And the other one?"

"She was in Paris! For six weeks things went very well, and we were still on the best of terms with each other when we came back here. Do you know how to break off with a woman when she's given you no reason at all to complain of her?"

"Of course."

"How do you do it?"

"I drop her."

"But how do you go about dropping her?"

"I stop going to her house."

"But what if she comes to yours?"

"I . . . I'm not at home."

"What if she comes back?"

"I tell her I'm indisposed."

"What if she takes care of you?"

"I . . . play some sort of dirty trick on her."

"What if she accepts it?"

"I write anonymous letters to her husband to make sure he keeps a close watch on her on days when she expects to see me."

"That's serious! I have no resistance. I don't know how to break off. I collect women. There are some I see no more than once a year, others every ten months, others every three, others whenever they feel like going out to dinner in a cabaret. Those I've already spaced out don't bother me, but I often have trouble when I try to space out a new one."

"Go on with your story."

"Well, the clerk's wife was still full of fiery passion, and she'd given me no cause for complaint, as I've already said. Since her husband is in his office all day, she began coming to see me unexpectedly. Twice she almost ran into my habit."

"Good God!"

"Yes. So I put them both on a fixed schedule, to avoid confusion. Monday and Saturday for the old one, Tuesday, Thursday and Sunday for the new one."

"Why the preference for the new one?"

"She's younger."

"That only gave you two days a week to rest."

"That's enough for me."

"Congratulations!"

"But then the most ridiculous and annoying thing in the world happened to me. Things had been going perfectly for four months; my mind was completely at rest and I was really very happy when suddenly, last Monday, everything fell apart.

"I was waiting for my habit at her usual time, a quarter past one, smoking a good cigar.

"I was daydreaming, thoroughly satisfied with myself, when I realized that she was late. I was surprised because she'd always been very punctual. But I thought she'd only been delayed. Half an hour went by, then an hour, then an hour and a half, and I finally decided she wasn't coming at all for some reason or other: a bad headache, perhaps, or an unwelcome visitor. It's annoying to go on waiting uselessly like that, and it makes me very nervous. When I was sure she wasn't coming, I went out. Not knowing what else to do, I went to her house.

"I found her reading a novel.

" 'Well?' I said to her.

"She answered calmly, 'I couldn't come. I was busy.'

" 'Busy with what?'

" 'With . . . various things.'

" 'What kind of things?'

" 'A boring visit.'

"I assumed she didn't want to tell me the real reason, and since she was still very calm I didn't worry about it. I expected to make up for lost time with the other one the next day.

"On Tuesday I was . . . excited, and very much in love, in anticipation, with the clerk's wife. I was surprised that she hadn't come earlier than the time we'd agreed on. I kept watching the clock, and following the minute hand impatiently.

"I saw it pass one-fifteen, then one-thirty, then two o'clock . . . I couldn't stay still, I walked back and forth in my bedroom. First I'd put my forehead against the window, then I'd put my ear to the door to listen for her coming up the stairs.

"Two-thirty, then three o'clock! I picked up my hat and hurried to her house. She was reading, my friend, reading a novel!

" 'Well?' I said to her anxiously.

"She answered, as calmly as my habit, 'I couldn't come. I was busy.'

" 'Busy with what?'

" 'With . . . various things.'

" 'What kind of things?'

" 'A boring visit.'

"Naturally I assumed immediately that they both knew everything; but she seemed so placid, so serene, that I finally rejected my suspicion and convinced myself it was only a strange coincidence, because I couldn't imagine she could be so deceptive. After an hour of friendly talk—with at least twenty interruptions when her little girl came into the room—I had to leave. I was very annoyed.

"And the next day . . ."

"It was the same thing?"

"Yes . . . and the day after that. And it went on for three weeks like that, with no explanation, no clue to the reason for their odd behavior, although I suspected the secret behind it."

"They knew everything?"

"Of course. But how? I suffered all sorts of torments before I knew."

"How did you finally find out?"

"By letters. They both wrote to me on the same day, in the same words, to tell me they were through with me forever."

"And what else did they say?"

"I'll tell you . . . As you know, women always have an army of pins on them. I'm familiar with hairpins and I'm careful about them, I keep an eye out for them, but the others are much more treacherous, those damned little black-headed pins. They all look alike to us, fools that we are, but women can distinguish them very easily, as easily as we can distinguish a horse from a dog.

"It turned out that one day the clerk's wife had left one of those revealing little pins stuck in the curtain beside my mirror. My habit immediately spotted its little black head, no bigger than a flea. She pulled it out without saying anything and stuck one of her own pins in the same place. It was black too, but differently shaped.

"The next day, when the clerk's wife reached out her hand to take back her pin, she noticed the substitution and became suspicious. She stuck two pins in the curtain, with one crossed over the other.

"My habit answered this telegraphic signal with three black pinheads in a row.

"Once they'd begun this exchange, they went on communicating, without saying anything, just to keep track of each other. Then my habit became bolder: she wrapped a pin in a little piece of thin paper on which she'd written: 'General Delivery, Boulevard Malesherbes. C.D.'

"Then they wrote to each other. I was lost. As you can imagine, they didn't tell each other everything from the start. They went about it cautiously, with all sorts of ruses, and all the prudence that's required in such cases. But finally my habit had the courage to make an appointment with the clerk's wife.

"I don't know what they said to each other. I only know that I was the subject of their conversation. And there you are!"

"That's all?"

"Yes."

"They've both stopped seeing you?"

"No, I still see them as a friend; we haven't broken off completely."

"And have they seen each other again?"

"Yes; they've become close friends."

"Well, well . . . Doesn't that give you an idea?"

"No, what idea?"

"Don't be thickheaded: the idea of having them both stick their pins in your curtain at the same time."

Considerations

This story opens with the hyperbolic statement of an injured man: "women are such vicious animals." And with a bit of prompting from his friend, he then proceeds to support his claim. Is he upset because his pride has been hurt or because the sweet rewards of his own little game are no longer available? Considering how neatly and self-indulgently he had arranged his life, is he merely angry at the thought of having to go through all of the annoying preliminaries and tedious working out of understandings with new women?

We would never expect de Maupassant to tell us the usual story of a tricked man. As in so many other of his tightly constructed pieces, he proves to be a polished O. Henry, capping his comment on human frailties with an ending that is both surprising and ironic. (An acknowledged master of the French short story, de Maupassant wrote in two distinctly different veins. Besides stories ending with a twist, he wrote dark, brooding, dramatic tales full of ambiguity and obscurity.)

The final sentence lingers in our minds: "Don't be thickheaded: the idea of having them both stick their pins in your curtain at the same time." In what sense is it ironic? Is it intended to suggest what might actually happen in the future, or does it simply resemble the punch-line to a joke?

Pins play such a large part in this story that it is natural to wonder if they represent something more than metal objects. They could be symbols of female tidiness or vanity, of sharpness, of teasing, of anticipation, or of that which holds things together. Did de Maupassant intend them to call forth these associations? Or are they meant to be no more than what in reality they are—pins?

What view of male-female relationships is presented in this story? What is the man's attitude toward women? How does the author characterize the women in the story?

The Luck of Roaring Camp

Bret Harte

There was commotion in Roaring Camp. It could not have been a fight, for in 1850 that was not novel enough to have called together the entire settlement. The ditches and claims were not only deserted, but "Tuttle's grocery" had contributed its gamblers, who, it will be remembered, calmly continued their game the day that French Pete and Kanaka Joe shot each other to death over the bar in the front room. The whole camp was collected before a rude cabin on the outer edge of the clearing. Conversation was carried on in a low tone, but the name of a woman was frequently repeated. It was a name familiar enough in the camp,—"Cherokee Sal."

Perhaps the less said of her the better. She was a coarse, and it is to be feared, a very sinful woman. But at that time she was the only woman in Roaring Camp, and was just then lying in sore extremity, when she most needed the ministration of her own sex. Dissolute, abandoned, and irreclaimable, she was yet suffering a martyrdom hard enough to bear even when veiled by sympathizing womanhood, but now terrible in her loneliness. The primal curse had come to her in that original isolation which must have made the punishment of the first transgression so dreadful. It was, perhaps, part of the expiation of her sin, that, at a moment when she most lacked her sex's intuitive tenderness and care, she met only the half-contemptuous faces of her masculine associates. Yet a few of the spectators were, I think, touched by her sufferings. Sandy Tipton thought it was "rough on Sal," and, in the contemplation of her condition, for a moment rose superior to the fact that he had an ace and two bowers in his sleeve.

It will be seen, also, that the situation was novel. Deaths were by no means uncommon in Roaring Camp, but a birth was a new thing. People had been dismissed from the camp effectively, finally, and with no possibility of return; but this was the first time that anybody had been introduced *ab initio*. Hence the excitement.

"You go in there, Stumpy," said a prominent citizen known as "Kentuck," addressing one of the loungers. "Go in there, and see what you kin do. You've had experience in them things."

Perhaps there was a fitness in the selection. Stumpy, in other climes, had been the putative head of two families; in fact, it was owing to some legal informality in these proceedings that Roaring Camp—a city of refuge—was indebted to his company. The crowd approved the choice, and Stumpy was wise enough to bow to the majority. The door closed upon the extempore surgeon and midwife, and Roaring Camp sat down outside, smoked its pipe, and awaited the issue.

The assemblage numbered about a hundred men. One or two of these were actual fugitives from justice, some were criminal, and all were reckless. Physically, they exhibited no indication of their past lives and character. The greatest scamp had a Raphael face, with a profusion of blond hair; Oakhurst, a gambler, had the melancholy air and intellectual abstraction of a Hamlet; the coolest and most courageous man was scarcely over five feet in height, with a soft voice and an embarrassed, timid manner. The term "roughs" applied to them was a distinction rather than a definition. Perhaps in the minor details of fingers, toes, ears, etc., the camp may have been deficient, but these slight omissions did not detract from their aggregate force. The strongest man had but three fingers on his right hand; the best shot had but one eye.

Such was the physical aspect of the men that were dispersed around the cabin. The camp lay in a triangular valley, between two hills and a river. The only outlet was a steep trail over the summit of a hill that faced the cabin, now illuminated by the rising moon. The suffering woman might have seen it from the rude bunk whereon she lay,—seen it winding like a silver thread until it was lost in the stars above.

A fire of withered pine boughs added sociability to the gathering. By degrees the natural levity of Roaring Camp returned. Bets were freely offered and taken regarding the result. Three to five that "Sal would get through with it"; even, that the child would survive; side bets as to the sex and complexion of the coming stranger. In the midst of an excited discussion an exclamation came from those nearest the door, and the camp stopped to listen. Above the swaying and moaning of the pines, the swift rush of the river, and the crackling of the fire rose a sharp, querulous cry—a cry unlike anything heard before in the camp. The pines stopped moaning, the river ceased to rush, and the fire to crackle. It seemed as if Nature had stopped to listen too.

The camp rose to its feet as one man! It was proposed to explode a barrel of gun-powder, but, in consideration of the situation of the mother, better counsels prevailed, and only a few revolvers were discharged; for, whether owing to the rude surgery of the camp, or some other reason, Cherokee Sal was sinking fast. Within an hour she had climbed, as it were, that rugged road that led to the stars, and so passed out of Roaring Camp, its sin and shame forever. I do not think that the announcement disturbed them much, except in speculation as to the fate of the child. "Can he live now?" was asked of Stumpy.

The answer was doubtful. The only other being of Cherokee Sal's sex and maternal condition in the settlement was an ass. There was some conjecture as to fitness, but the experiment was tried. It was less problematical than the ancient treatment of Romulus and Remus, and apparently as successful.

When these details were completed, which exhausted another hour, the door was opened, and the anxious crowd, who had already formed themselves into a queue, entered in single file. Beside the low bunk or shelf, on which the figure of the mother was starkly outlined below the blankets, stood a pine table. On this a candle-box was placed, and within it, swathed in staring red flannel, lay the last arrival at Roaring Camp. Beside the candle-box was placed a hat. Its use was soon indicated. "Gentlemen," said Stumpy, with a singular mixture of authority and *ex officio* complacency—"Gentlemen will please pass in at the front door, round the table, and out at the back door. Them as wishes to contribute anything toward the orphan will find a hat handy." The first man entered with his hat on; he uncovered, however, as he looked about him, and so, unconsciously, set an example to the next. In such communities good and bad actions are catching. As the procession filed in, comments were audible,—criticisms addressed, perhaps, rather to Stumpy, in the character of showman,—"Is that him?" "Mighty small specimen"; "Hasn't more'n got the color"; "Ain't bigger nor a derringer." The contributions were as characteristic: A silver tobacco box; a doubloon; a navy revolver, silver mounted; a gold specimen; a very beautifully embroidered lady's handkerchief (from Oakhurst the gambler); a diamond breastpin, a diamond ring (suggested by the pin, with the remark from the giver that he "saw that pin and went two diamonds better"); a slung shot; a Bible (contributor not detected); a golden spur; a silver teaspoon (the initials, I regret to say, were not the giver's); a pair of surgeon's shears; a lancet; a Bank of England note for £5; and about $200 in loose gold and silver coin. During these proceedings Stumpy maintained a silence as impassive as the dead on his left—a gravity as inscrutable as that of the newly-born on his right. Only one incident occurred to break the monotony of the curious procession. As Kentuck bent over the candle-box half curiously, the child turned, and, in a spasm of pain, caught at his groping finger, and held it fast for a moment. Kentuck looked foolish and embarrassed. Something like a blush tried to assert itself in his weather-beaten cheek. "The d—d little cuss!" he said, as he extricated his finger, with, perhaps, more tenderness and care than he might have been deemed capable of showing. He held that finger a little apart from its fellows as he went out, and examined it curiously. The examination provoked the same original remark in regard to the child. In fact, he seemed to enjoy repeating it. "He rastled with my finger," he remarked to Tipton, holding up the member, "the d—d little cuss!"

It was four o'clock before the camp sought repose. A light burnt in the cabin where the watchers sat, for Stumpy did not go to bed that night. Nor did Kentuck. He drank quite freely and related with great gusto his experience, invariably ending with his characteristic condemnation of the newcomer. It seemed to relieve him of any unjust implication of sentiment, and Kentuck had the weaknesses of the nobler sex. When everybody else had gone to bed, he walked down to the river, and whistled reflectingly. Then he walked up the gulch, past the cabin, still whistling with demonstrative unconcern. At a large redwood tree he paused and retraced his steps, and again passed the cabin. Halfway down to the river's bank he again paused, and then returned and knocked at the door. It was opened by Stumpy. "How goes it?" said Kentuck, looking past Stumpy toward the candle-box. "All serene," replied Stumpy. "Anything up?" "Nothing." There was a pause—an embarrassing one— Stumpy still holding the door. Then Kentuck had recourse to his finger, which he held up to Stumpy. "Rastled with it,—the d—d little cuss," he said, and retired.

The next day Cherokee Sal had such rude sepulture as Roaring Camp afforded. After her body had been committed to the hillside, there was a formal meeting of the camp to discuss what should be done with her infant. A resolution to adopt it was unanimous and enthusiastic. But an animated discussion in regard to the manner and feasibility of providing for its wants at once sprung up. It was remarkable that the argument partook of none of those fierce personalities with which discussions were usually conducted at Roaring Camp. Tipton proposed that they should send the child to Red Dog—a distance of forty miles—where female attention could be procured. But the unlucky suggestion met with fierce and unanimous opposition. It was evident that no plan which entailed parting from their new acquisition would for a moment be entertained. "Besides," said Tom Ryder, "them fellows at Red Dog would swap it, and ring in somebody else on us." A disbelief in the honesty of other camps prevailed at Roaring Camp as in other places.

The introduction of a female nurse in the camp also met with objection. It was argued that no decent woman could be prevailed to accept Roaring Camp as her home, and the speaker urged that "they didn't want any more of the other kind." This unkind allusion to the defunct mother, harsh as it may seem, was the first spasm of propriety—the first symptom of the camp's regeneration. Stumpy advanced nothing. Perhaps he felt a certain delicacy in interfering with the selection of a possible successor in office. But when questioned, he averred stoutly that he and "Jinny"—the mammal before alluded to—could manage to rear the child. There was something original, independent, and heroic about the plan that pleased the camp. Stumpy was retained. Certain articles were sent for to Sacramento. "Mind," said the treasurer, as he pressed a bag of gold-dust into the expressman's hand, "the best that can be got—lace, you know, and filigree-work and frills,—d—n the cost!"

Strange to say, the child thrived. Perhaps the invigorating climate of the mountain camp was compensation for material deficiencies. Nature took the foundling to her broader breast. In that rare atmosphere of the Sierra foothills—that air pungent with balsamic odor, that ethereal cordial, at once bracing and exhilarating, he may have found food and nourishment, or a subtle chemistry that transmuted asses' milk to lime and phosphorus. Stumpy inclined to the belief that it was the latter and good nursing. "Me and that ass," he would say, "has been father and mother to him! Don't you," he would add, apostrophizing the helpless bundle before him, "never go back on us."

By the time he was a month old, the necessity of giving him a name became apparent. He had generally been known as "the Kid," "Stumpy's boy," "the Cayote" (an allusion to his vocal powers) and even by Kentuck's endearing diminutive of "the d—d little cuss." But these were felt to be vague and unsatisfactory, and were at last dismissed under another influence. Gamblers and adventurers are generally superstitious, and Oakhurst one day declared that the baby had brought "the luck" to Roaring Camp. It was certain that of late they had been successful. "Luck" was the name agreed upon, with the prefix of Tommy for greater convenience. No allusion was made to the mother, and the father was unknown. "It's better," said the philosophical Oakhurst, "to take a fresh deal all round. Call him Luck, and start him fair." A day was accordingly set apart for the christening. What was meant by this ceremony the reader may imagine, who has already gathered some idea of the reckless irreverence of Roaring Camp. The master of ceremonies was one "Boston," a noted wag, and the occasion seemed to promise the greatest facetiousness. This ingenious satirist had spent two days in preparing a burlesque of the church service, with pointed local allusions. The choir was properly trained, and Sandy Tipton was to stand godfather. But after the procession had marched to the grove with music and banners, and the child had been deposited before a mock altar, Stumpy stepped before the expectant crowd. "It ain't my style to spoil fun, boys," said the little man, stoutly, eyeing the faces around him, "but it strikes me that this thing ain't exactly on the squar. It's playing it pretty low down on this yer baby to ring in fun on him that he ain't goin' to understand. And ef there's going to be any god-fathers round, I'd like to see who's got any better rights than me." A silence followed Stumpy's speech. To the credit of all humorists be it said that the first man to acknowledge its justice was the satirist, thus stopped of his fun. "But," said Stumpy, quickly, following up his advantage, "we're here for a christening, and we'll have it. I proclaim you Thomas Luck, according to the laws of the United States and the State of California, so help me God." It was the first time that the name of the Deity had been uttered otherwise but profanely in the camp. The form of christening was perhaps even more ludicrous than the satirist had conceived; but strangely enough, nobody saw it and nobody laughed. "Tommy" was christened as seriously as he would have been under a Christian roof, and cried and was comforted in as orthodox fashion.

And so the work of regeneration began in Roaring Camp. Almost imperceptibly a change came over the settlement. The cabin assigned to "Tommy Luck"—or "The Luck," as he was more frequently called—first showed signs of improvement. It was kept scrupulously clean and whitewashed. Then it was boarded, clothed and papered. The rosewood cradle—packed eighty miles by mule—had, in Stumpy's way of putting it, "sorter killed the rest of the furniture." So the rehabilitation of the cabin became a necessity. The men who were in the habit of lounging in at Stumpy's to see "how The Luck got on" seemed to appreciate the change, and, in self-defense, the rival establishment of "Tuttle's grocery" bestirred itself, and imported a carpet and mirrors. The reflections of the latter on the appearance of Roaring Camp tended to produce stricter habits of personal cleanliness. Again Stumpy imposed a kind of quarantine upon those who aspired to the honor and privilege of holding "The Luck." It was a cruel mortification to Kentuck—who, in the carelessness of a large nature and the habits of frontier life, had begun to regard all garments as a second cuticle, which, like a snake's, only sloughed off through decay—to be debarred this privilege from certain prudential reasons. Yet such was the subtle influence of innovation that he thereafter appeared regularly every afternoon in a clean shirt, and face still shining from his ablutions. Nor were moral and social sanitary laws neglected. "Tommy," who was supposed to spend his whole existence in a persistent attempt to repose, must not be disturbed by noise. The shouting and yelling which had gained the camp its infelicitous title were not permitted within hearing distance of Stumpy's. The men conversed in whispers, or smoked with Indian gravity. Profanity was tacitly given up in these sacred precincts, and throughout the camp a popular form of expletive, known as "D—n the luck!" and "Curse the luck!" was abandoned, as having a new personal bearing. Vocal music was not interdicted, being supposed to have a soothing, tranquilizing quality, and one song, sung by "Man-o'-War Jack," an English sailor from Her Majesty's Australian colonies, was quite popular as a lullaby. It was a lugubrious recital of the exploits of "the *Arethusa,* Seventy-four," in a muffled minor, ending with a prolonged dying fall at the burden of each verse, "On b-o-o-o-ard of the *Arethusa.*" It was a fine sight to see Jack holding The Luck, rocking from side to side as if with the motion of a ship, and crooning forth this naval ditty. Either through the peculiar rocking of Jack or the length of his song—it contained ninety stanzas, and was continued with conscientious deliberation to the bitter end—the lullaby generally had the desired effect. At such times the men would lie at full length under the trees, in the soft summer twilight, smoking their pipes and drinking in the melodious utterances. An indistinct idea that this was pastoral happiness pervaded the camp. "This 'ere kind o' think," said the Cockney Simmons, meditatively reclining on his elbow, "is 'evingly." It reminded him of Greenwich.

On the long summer days The Luck was usually carried to the gulch, from whence the golden store of Roaring Camp was taken. There, on a blanket spread over pine boughs, he would lie while the men were working in the ditches below. Latterly, there was a rude attempt to decorate this bower with flowers and sweet-smelling shrubs, and generally some one would bring him a cluster of wild honey-suckles, azaleas, or the painted blossoms of Las Mariposas. The men had suddenly awakened to the fact that there were beauty and significance in these trifles, which they had so long trodden carelessly beneath their feet. A flake of glittering mica, a fragment of variegated quartz, a bright pebble from the bed of the creek, became beautiful to eyes thus cleared and strengthened, and were invariably put aside for "The Luck." It was wonderful how many treasures the woods and hillsides yielded that "would do for Tommy." Surrounded by playthings such as never child out of fairyland had before, it is to be hoped that Tommy was content. He appeared to be serenely happy, albeit there was an infantine gravity about him, a contemplative light in his round gray eyes, that sometimes worried Stumpy. He was always tractable and quiet, and it is recorded that once, having crept beyond his "corral"—a hedge of tessellated pine boughs, which surrounded his bed—he dropped over the bank on his head in the soft earth, and remained with his mottled legs in the air in that position for at least five minutes with unflinching gravity. He was extricated without a murmur. I hesitate to record the many other instances of his sagacity, which rest, unfortunately, upon the statements of prejudiced friends. Some of them were not without a tinge of superstition. "I crep' up the bank just now," said Kentuck one day, in a breathless state of excitement, "and dern my skin if he wasn't a talking to a jaybird as was a-sittin on his lap. There they was, just as free and sociable as anything you please, a-jawin at each other just like two cherrybums." Howbeit, whether creeping over the pine boughs or lying lazily on his back, blinking at the leaves above him, to him the birds sang, the squirrels chattered, and the flowers bloomed. Nature was his nurse and playfellow. For him she would let slip between the leaves golden shafts of sunlight that fell just within his grasp; she would send wandering breezes to visit him with the balm of bay and resinous gums; to him the tall redwoods nodded familiarly and sleepily, the bumblebees buzzed, and the rooks cawed a slumbrous accompaniment.

Such was the golden summer of Roaring Camp. They were "flush times"—and the Luck was with them. The claims had yielded enormously. The camp was jealous of its privileges and looked suspiciously on strangers. No encouragement was given to immigration, and, to make their seclusion more perfect, the land on either side of the mountain wall that surrounded the camp they duly pre-empted. This, and a reputation for singular proficiency with the revolver, kept the reserve of Roaring Camp inviolate. The expressman—their only connecting link with the surrounding world—sometimes told wonderful stories of the camp. He would say, "They've a street up there in 'Roaring,' that would lay over any street up there in Red Dog. They've got vines and flowers round their houses, and they wash themselves twice a day. But they're mighty rough on strangers, and they worship an Ingin baby."

With the prosperity of the camp came a desire for further improvement. It was proposed to build a hotel in the following spring, and to invite one or two decent families to reside there for the sake of "The Luck," who might perhaps profit by female companionship. The sacrifice that this concession to the sex cost these men, who were fiercely skeptical in regard to its general virtue and usefulness, can only be accounted for by their affection for Tommy. A few still held out. But the resolve could not be carried into effect for three months, and the minority meekly yielded in the hope that something might turn up to prevent it. And it did.

The winter of '51 will long be remembered in the foothills. The snow lay deep on the sierras, and every mountain creek became a river, and every river a lake. Each gorge and gulch was transformed into a tumultuous watercourse that descended the hillsides, tearing down giant trees and scattering its drift and debris along the plain. Red Dog had been twice under water, and Roaring Camp had been forewarned. "Water put the gold into them gulches," said Stumpy; "it's been here once and will be here again!" And that night the North Fork suddenly leaped over its banks, and swept up the triangular valley of Roaring Camp.

In the confusion of rushing water, crashing trees, and crackling timber, and the darkness which seemed to flow with the water and blot out the fair valley, but little could be done to collect the scattered camp. When the morning broke, the cabin of Stumpy nearest the river-bank was gone. Higher up the gulch they found the body of its unlucky owner; but the pride—the hope—the joy—the Luck—of Roaring Camp had disappeared. They were returning with sad hearts, when a shout from the bank recalled them.

It was a relief-boat from down the river. They had picked up, they said, a man and an infant, nearly exhausted, about two miles below. Did anybody know them, and did they belong here?

It needed but a glance to show them Kentuck lying there, cruelly crushed and bruised, but still holding The Luck of Roaring Camp in his arms. As they bent over the strangely assorted pair, they saw that the child was cold and pulseless. "He is dead," said one. Kentuck opened his eyes. "Dead?" he repeated feebly. "Yes, my man, and you are dying too." A smile lit the eyes of the expiring Kentuck. "Dying!" he repeated, "he's ataking me with him—tell the boys I've got the Luck with me now"; and the strong man, clinging to the frail babe as a drowning man is said to cling to a straw, drifted away into the shadowy river that flows forever to the unknown sea.

Considerations

The setting is important here—a California frontier gold-mining town, just after the big gold rush. This is an example of local-color writing, and it is easy to see why it is called that. Local color is the forerunner of realism. Rather than just being a realistic depiction of events involving humans, local-color writing pictures nature as a malignant or benign force that also bears on the characters. As beautiful as nature can be and as beneficial as it is in some ways, look what happens at the end of this story—the river that was there before man and will be there afterwards, comes roaring down the valley.

When realism and romanticism come together in local color, we find powerful descriptive passages, such as this one:

> The camp lay in a triangular valley between two hills and a river. The only outlet was a steep trail over the summit of a hill that faced the cabin now illuminated by the rising moon. . . . The suffering woman might have seen it from the rude bank whereon she lay. . . .

Carried to extremes, even human emotions and actions may be attributed to nature:

> Above the swaying and moaning of the pines, the swift rush of the river, and the crackling of the fire rose a sharp, querulous cry—a cry unlike anything heard before in the camp. The pines stopped moaning, the river ceased to rush, and the fire to crackle. It seemed as if Nature had stopped to listen too.

The combination of realism and romanticism produces contrasts that result in a certain tension. "Luck" opens by stating that a killing wouldn't cause a group to gather here, thus establishing that this is truly rough country. However, in the hardest of circumstances, with the hardest kind of men—fugitives, liars, con artists—what should appear but the classic symbol of innocence and helplessness: a baby. There is a marked contrast between the former actions of the men and the tenderness deep in their hearts (displayed by their caring for the orphan).

And the diction is also mixed. The dialogue, if not dialect or slang, is at least colloquial; yet the descriptions include a rather high—level vocabulary: "the putative head of two families," "the expiation of her sin," "these slight omissions did not detract from their aggregate force."

"Luck" is a moral story—moral even in the Biblical sense. Just as we see the baby Moses changing an empire and the baby Jesus changing a civilization, now the baby Luck is changing a frontier camp. As in the mustard-seed parable, a tiny thing comes along, seemingly insignificant, but it has the greatest power in the world—the power to grow and make things bigger and better. As Luck grew and the men cared for him, their lives changed. They cleaned up, talked of building a hotel, and painted the house.

The hard facts of realism finally win out, however. Few people manage to live happily ever after, and Harte acknowledges that. As if not to let romanticism carry it away, the story comes to an abrupt and touching end.

The Judgment

Franz Kafka

It was a Sunday morning in the very height of spring. Georg Bendemann, a young merchant, was sitting in his own room on the first floor of one of a long row of small, ramshackle houses stretching beside the river which were scarcely distinguishable from each other except in height and coloring. He had just finished a letter to an old friend of his who was now living abroad, had put it into its envelope in a slow and dreamy fashion, and with his elbows propped on the writing table was gazing out of the window at the river, the bridge and the hills on the farther bank with their tender green.

He was thinking about his friend, who had actually run away to Russia some years before, being dissatisfied with his prospects at home. Now he was carrying on a business in St. Petersburg, which had flourished to begin with but had long been going downhill, as he always complained on his increasingly rare visits. So he was wearing himself out to no purpose in a foreign country, the unfamiliar full beard he wore did not quite conceal the face Georg had known so well since childhood, and his skin was growing so yellow as to indicate some latent disease. By his own account he had no regular connection with the colony of his fellow countrymen out there and almost no social intercourse with Russian families, so that he was resigning himself to becoming a permanent bachelor.

What could one write to such a man, who had obviously run off the rails, a man one could be sorry for but could not help. Should one advise him to come home, to transplant himself and take up his old friendships again—there was nothing to hinder him—and in general to rely on the help of his friends? But that was as good as telling him, and the more kindly the more offensively, that all his efforts hitherto had miscarried, that he should finally give up, come back home, be gaped at by everyone as a returned prodigal, that only his friends knew what was what and that he himself was just a big child who should do what his successful and home-keeping friends prescribed. And was it certain, besides, that all the pain one would have to inflict on him would achieve its object? Perhaps it would not even be possible to get him to come home at all—he said himself that he was now out of touch with commerce in his native country—and then he would still be left an alien in a foreign land embittered by his friends' advice and more than ever estranged from them. But if he did follow their advice and then didn't fit in at home—not out of malice, of course, but through force of circumstances—couldn't get on with his friends or without them, felt humiliated, couldn't be said to have either friends or a country of his own any longer, wouldn't it have been better for him to stay abroad just as he was? Taking all this into account, how could one be sure that he would make a success of life at home?

For such reasons, supposing one wanted to keep up correspondence with him, one could not send him any real news such as could frankly be told to the most distant acquaintance. It was more than three years since his last visit, and for this he offered the lame excuse that the political situation in Russia was too uncertain, which apparently would not permit even the briefest absence of a small business man while it allowed hundreds of thousands of Russians to travel peacefully abroad. But during these three years Georg's own position in life had changed a lot. Two years ago his mother had died, since when he and his father had shared the household together, and his friend had of course been informed of that and expressed his sympathy in a letter phrased so dryly that the grief caused by such an event, one had to conclude, could not be realized in a distant country. Since that time, however, Georg had applied himself with greater determination to the business as well as to everything else.

Perhaps during his mother's lifetime his father's insistence on having everything his own way in the business had hindered him from develop-

ing any real activity of his own, perhaps since her death his father had become less aggressive, although he was still active in the business, perhaps it was mostly due to an accidental run of good fortune—which was very probable indeed—but at any rate during those two years the business had developed in a most unexpected way, the staff had had to be doubled, the turnover was five times as great, no doubt about it, farther progress lay just ahead.

But Georg's friend had no inkling of this improvement. In earlier years, perhaps for the last time in that letter of condolence, he had tried to persuade Georg to emigrate to Russia and had enlarged upon the prospects of success for precisely Georg's branch of trade. The figures quoted were microscopic by comparison with the range of Georg's present operations. Yet he shrank from letting his friend know about his business success, and if he were to do it now retrospectively that certainly would look peculiar.

So Georg confined himself to giving his friend unimportant items of gossip such as rise at random in the memory when one is idly thinking things over on a quiet Sunday. All he desired was to leave undisturbed the idea of the home town which his friend must have built up to his own content during the long interval. And so it happened to Georg that three times in three fairly widely separated letters he had told his friend about the engagement of an unimportant man to an equally unimportant girl, until indeed, quite contrary to his intentions, his friend began to show some interest in this notable event.

Yet Georg preferred to write about things like these rather than to confess that he himself had got engaged a month ago to a Fräulein Frieda Brandenfeld, a girl from a well-to-do family. He often discussed this friend of his with his fiancée and the peculiar relationship that had developed between them in their correspondence. "So he won't be coming to our wedding," she said, "and yet I have a right to get to know all your friends." "I don't want to trouble him," answered Georg, "don't misunderstand me, he would probably come, at least I think so, but he would feel that his hand had been forced and he would be hurt, perhaps he would envy me and certainly he'd be discontented and without being able to do anything about his discontent he'd have to go away again alone. Alone—do you know what that means?" "Yes, but may he not hear about our wedding in some other fashion?" "I can't prevent that, of course, but it's unlikely, considering the way he lives." "Since your friends are like that, Georg, you shouldn't ever have got engaged at all." "Well, we're both to blame for that; but I wouldn't have it any other way now." And when, breathing quickly under his kisses, she still brought out: "All the same, I do feel upset," he thought it could not really involve him in trouble were he to send the news to his friend. "That's the kind of man I am and he'll just have to take me as I am," he said to himself, "I can't cut myself to another pattern that might make a more suitable friend for him."

And in fact he did inform his friend, in the long letter he had been writing that Sunday morning, about his engagement, with these words: "I have saved my best news to the end. I have got engaged to a Fräulein Frieda Brandenfeld, a girl from a well-to-do family, who only came to live here a long time after you went away, so that you're hardly likely to know her. There will be time to tell you more about her later, for today let me just say that I am very happy and as between you and me the only difference in our relationship is that instead of a quite ordinary kind of friend you will now have in me a happy friend. Besides that, you will acquire in my fiancée, who sends her warm greetings and will soon write you herself, a genuine friend of the opposite sex, which is not without importance to a bachelor. I know that there are many reasons why you can't come to see us, but would not my wedding be precisely the right occasion for giving all obstacles the go-by? Still, however that may be, do just as seems good to you without regarding any interests but your own."

With this letter in his hand Georg had been sitting a long time at the writing table, his face turned towards the window. He had barely acknowledged, with an absent smile, a greeting waved to him from the street by a passing acquaintance.

At last he put the letter in his pocket and went out of his room across a small lobby into his father's room, which he had not entered for months. There was in fact no need for him to enter it, since he saw his father daily at business and they took their midday meal together at an eating house; in the evening, it was true, each did as he pleased, yet even then, unless Georg—as mostly happened—went out with friends or, more recently, visited his fiancée, they always sat for a while, each with his newspaper, in their common sitting room.

It surprised Georg how dark his father's room was even on this sunny morning. So it was overshadowed as much as that by the high wall on the other side of the narrow courtyard. His father was sitting by the window in a corner hung with various mementoes of Georg's dead mother, reading a newspaper which he held to one side before his eyes in an attempt to overcome a defect of vision. On the table stood the remains of his breakfast, not much of which seemed to have been eaten.

"Ah, Georg," said his father, rising at once to meet him. His heavy dressing gown swung open as he walked and the skirts of it fluttered round him.—"My father is still a giant of a man," said Georg to himself.

"It's unbearably dark here," he said aloud.

"Yes, it's dark enough," answered his father.

"And you've shut the window, too?"

"I prefer it like that."

"Well, it's quite warm outside," said Georg, as if continuing his previous remark, and sat down.

His father cleared away the breakfast dishes and set them on a chest.

"I really only wanted to tell you," went on Georg, who had been vacantly following the old man's movements, "that I am now sending the news of my engagement to St. Pe-

tersburg." He drew the letter a little way from his pocket and let it drop back again.

"To St. Petersburg?" asked his father.

"To my friend there," said Georg, trying to meet his father's eye.—In business hours he's quite different, he was thinking, how solidly he sits here with his arms crossed.

"Oh yes. To your friend," said his father, with peculiar emphasis.

"Well, you know, Father, that I wanted not to tell him about my engagement at first. Out of consideration for him, that was the only reason. You know yourself he's a difficult man. I said to myself that someone else might tell him about my engagement, although he's such a solitary creature that that was hardly likely—I couldn't prevent that—but I wasn't ever going to tell him myself."

"And now you've changed your mind?" asked his father, laying his enormous newspaper on the window sill and on top of it his spectacles, which he covered with one hand.

"Yes, I've been thinking it over. If he's a good friend of mine, I said to myself, my being happily engaged should make him happy too. And so I wouldn't put off telling him any longer. But before I posted the letter I wanted to let you know."

"Georg," said his father, lengthening his toothless mouth, "listen to me! You've come to me about this business, to talk it over with me. No doubt that does you honor. But it's nothing, it's worse than nothing, if you don't tell me the whole truth. I don't want to stir up matters that shouldn't be mentioned here. Since the death of our dear mother certain things have been done that aren't right. Maybe the time will come for mentioning them, and maybe sooner than we think. There's many a thing in the business I'm not aware of, maybe it's not done behind my back—I'm not going to say that it's done behind my back—I'm not equal to things any longer, my memory's failing, I haven't an eye for so many things any longer. That's the course of nature in the first place, and in the second place the death of our dear mother hit me harder than it did you.—But since we're talking about it, about this letter, I beg you, Georg, don't deceive me. It's a trivial affair, it's hardly worth mentioning, so don't deceive me. Do you really have this friend in St. Petersburg?"

Georg rose in embarrassment., "Never mind my friends. A thousand friends wouldn't make up to me for my father. Do you know what I think? You're not taking enough care of yourself. But old age must be taken care of. I can't do without you in the business, you know that very well, but if the business is going to undermine your health, I'm ready to close it down tomorrow forever. And that won't do. We'll have to make a change in your way of living. But a radical change. You sit here in the dark, and in the sitting room you would have plenty of light. You just take a bit of breakfast instead of properly keeping up your strength. You sit by a closed window, and the air would be so good for you. No, Father! I'll get the doctor to come, and we'll follow his orders. We'll change your room, you can move into the

front room and I'll move in here. You won't notice the change, all your things will be moved with you. But there's time for all that later, I'll put you to bed now for a little, I'm sure you need to rest. Come, I'll help you to take off your things, you'll see I can do it. Or if you would rather go into the front room at once, you can lie down in my bed for the present. That would be the most sensible thing."

Georg stood close beside his father, who had let his head with its unkempt white hair sink on his chest.

"Georg," said his father in a low voice, without moving.

George knelt down at once beside his father, in the old man's weary face he saw the pupils, over-large, fixedly looking at him from the corners of the eyes.

"You have no friend in St. Petersburg. You've always been a leg-puller and you haven't even shrunk from pulling my leg. How could you have a friend out there! I can't believe it."

"Just think back a bit, Father," said Georg, lifting his father from the chair and slipping off his dressing gown as he stood feebly enough, "it'll soon be three years since my friend came to see us last. I remember that you used not to like him very much. At least twice I kept you from seeing him, although he was actually sitting with me in my room. I could quite well understand your dislike of him, my friend has his peculiarities. But then, later, you got on with him very well. I was proud because you listened to him and nodded and asked him questions. If you think back you're bound to remember. He used to tell us the most incredible stories of the Russian Revolution. For instance, when he was on a business trip to Kiev and ran into a riot, and saw a priest on a balcony who cut a broad cross in blood on the palm of his hand and held the hand up and appealed to the mob. You've told that story yourself once or twice since."

Meanwhile Georg had succeeded in lowering his father down again and carefully taking off the woolen drawers he wore over his linen underpants and his socks. The not particularly clean appearance of this underwear made him reproach himself for having been neglectful. It should have certainly been his duty to see that his father had clean changes of underwear. He had not yet explicitly discussed with his bride-to-be what arrangements should be made for his father in the future, for they had both of them silently taken it for granted that the old man would go on living alone in the old house. But now he made a quick, firm decision to take him into his own future establishment. It almost looked, on closer inspection, as if the care he meant to lavish there on his father might come too late.

He carried his father to bed in his arms. It gave him a dreadful feeling to notice that while he took the few steps towards the bed the old man on his breast was playing with his watch chain. He could not lay him down on the bed for a moment, so firmly did he hang on to the watch chain.

But as soon as he was laid in bed, all seemed well. He covered himself up and even drew the blankets farther than usual over his shoulders. He looked up at Georg with a not unfriendly eye.

"You begin to remember my friend, don't you?" asked Georg, giving him an encouraging nod.

"Am I well covered up now?" asked his father, as if he were not able to see whether his feet were properly tucked in or not.

"So you find it snug in bed already," said Georg, and tucked the blankets more closely round him.

"Am I well covered up?" asked the father once more, seeming to be strangely intent upon the answer.

"Don't worry, you're well covered up."

"No!" cried his father, cutting short the answer, threw the blankets off with a strength that sent them all flying in a moment and sprang erect in bed. Only one hand lightly touched the ceiling to steady him.

"You wanted to cover me up, I know, my young sprig, but I'm far from being covered up yet. And even if this is the last strength I have, it's enough for you, too much for you. Of course I know your friend. He would have been a son after my own heart. That's why you've been playing him false all these years. Why else? Do you think I haven't been sorry for him? And that's why you had to lock yourself up in your office—the Chief is busy, mustn't be disturbed—just so that you could write your lying little letters to Russia. But thank goodness a father doesn't need to be taught how to see through his son. And now that you thought you'd got him down, so far down that you could set your bottom on him and sit on him and he wouldn't move, then my fine son makes up his mind to get married!"

Georg stared at the bogey conjured up by his father. His friend in St. Petersburg, whom his father suddenly knew too well, touched his imagination as never before. Lost in the vastness of Russia he saw him. At the door of an empty, plundered warehouse he saw him. Among the wreckage of his showcases, the slashed remnants of his wares, the falling gas brackets, he was just standing up. Why did he have to go so far away!

"But attend to me!" cried his father, and Georg, almost distracted, ran toward the bed to take everything in, yet came to a stop halfway.

"Because she lifted up her skirts," his father began to flute, "because she lifted her skirts like this, the nasty creature," and mimicking her he lifted his shirt so high that one could see the scar on his thigh from his war wound, "because she lifted her skirts like this and this you made up to her, and in order to make free with her undisturbed you have disgraced your mother's memory, betrayed your friend and stuck your father into bed so that he can't move. But he can move, or can't he?"

And he stood up quite unsupported and kicked his legs out. His insight made him radiant.

Georg shrank into a corner, as far away from his father as possible. A long time ago he had firmly made up his mind to watch closely every least movement so that he should not be surprised by any indirect attack, a pounce from behind or above. At this moment he recalled this long-forgotten resolve and forgot it again, like a man drawing a short thread through the eye of a needle.

"But your friend hasn't been betrayed after all!" cried his father, emphasizing the point with stabs of his forefinger. "I've been representing him here on the spot."

"You comedian!" Georg could not resist the retort, realized at once the harm done and, his eyes starting in his head, bit his tongue back, only too late, till the pain made his knees give.

"Yes, of course I've been playing a comedy! A comedy! That's a good expression! What other comfort was left to a poor old widower? Tell me—and while you're answering me be you still my living son—what else was left to me, in my back room, plagued by a disloyal staff, old to the marrow of my bones? And my son strutting through the world, finishing off deals that I had prepared for him, bursting with triumphant glee and stalking away from his father with the closed face of a respectable business man! Do you think I didn't love you, I, from whom you are sprung?"

Now he'll lean forward, thought Georg, what if he topples and smashes himself! These words went hissing through his mind.

His father leaned forward but did not topple. Since Georg did not come any nearer, as he had expected, he straightened himself again.

"Stay where you are, I don't need you! You think you have strength enough to come over here and that you're only hanging back of your own accord. Don't be too sure! I am still much the stronger of us two. All by myself I might have had to give way, but your mother has given me so much of her strength that I've established a fine connection with your friend and I have your customers here in my pocket!"

"He has pockets even in his shirt!" said Georg to himself, and believed that with this remark he could make him an impossible figure for all the world. Only for a moment did he think so, since he kept on forgetting everything.

"Just take your bride on your arm and try getting in my way! I'll sweep her from your very side, you don't know how!"

Georg made a grimace of disbelief. His father only nodded, confirming the truth of his words, towards Georg's corner.

"How you amused me today, coming to ask me if you should tell your friend about your engagement. He knows it already, you stupid boy, he knows it all! I've been writing to him, for you forgot to take my writing things away from me. That's why he hasn't been here for years, he knows everything a hundred times better than you do yourself, in his left hand he crumples your letters unopened while in his right hand he holds up my letters to read through!"

In his enthusiasm he waved his arm over his head. "He knows everything a thousand times better!" he cried.

"Ten thousand times!" said Georg, to make fun of his father, but in his very mouth the words turned into deadly earnest.

"For years I've been waiting for you to come with some such ques-

tion! Do you think I concern myself with anything else? Do you think I read my newspapers? Look!" and he threw Georg a newspaper sheet which he had somehow taken to bed with him. An old newspaper, with a name entirely unknown to Georg.

"How long a time you've taken to grow up! Your mother had to die, she couldn't see the happy day, your friend is going to pieces in Russia, even three years ago he was yellow enough to be thrown away, and as for me, you see what condition I'm in. You have eyes in your head for that!"

"So you've been lying in wait for me!" cried Georg.

His father said pityingly, in an off-hand manner: "I suppose you wanted to say that sooner. But now it doesn't matter." And in a louder voice: "So now you know what else there was in the world besides yourself, till now you've known only about yourself! An innocent child, yes, that you were, truly, but still more truly have you been a devilish human being!— And therefore take note: I sentence you now to death by drowning!"

Georg felt himself urged from the room, the crash with which his father fell on the bed behind him was still in his ears as he fled. On the staircase, which he rushed down as if its steps were an inclined plane, he ran into his charwoman on her way up to do the morning cleaning of the room. "Jesus!" she cried, and covered her face with her apron, but he was already gone. Out of the front door he rushed, across the roadway, driven towards the water. Already he was grasping at the railings as a starving man clutches food. He swung himself over, like the distinguished gymnast he had once been in his youth, to his parents' pride. With weakening grip he was still holding on when he spied between the railings a motor-bus coming which would easily cover the noise of his fall, called in a low voice:

"Dear parents, I have always loved you, all the same," and let himself drop.

At this moment an unending stream of traffic was just going over the bridge.

Considerations

This is the literature of the nightmares of the interior state. Such writing is highly symbolic and probably easily interpreted only by a psychoanalyst, but it does have that vaguely demarcated, subtly shifting quality of the experiences that we all recognize from our own dreams.

So completely does Kafka capture the outlines of our common nightmares that we remember the feel of his stories long after the details have escaped us. And we continue to call baffling and disturbing experiences in our own lives Kafkaesque.

To try to approach a Kafka story through purely rational means is to try to catch quicksilver between your fingers. On the surface "The Judgment" is a simple enough story: Georg, while trying to adjust to the demands of the family business, keeps his ties with a longtime friend, plans to get married, and deals with his aging father. Then suddenly he bolts from the house after an interview with his father and commits suicide, crying "Dear parents, I have always loved you, all the same." But for each of the supposed facts that we find in the story we can find a contradiction. Does Georg in fact have a friend? Is he really planning to get married? Just how helpless is his father and how has Georg been dealing with him prior to the opening of the story?

One thing that remains unchanging, however—one thing that can be documented—is Georg's continual devastating feeling of guilt. He feels guilty about specific actions or inactions on his part; he feels guilty about the contrast between his flourishing business and the misfortunes of his friend; he feels guilty about having neglected his father. Georg feels guilty in anticipation and in retrospection. He seems to have been aware of an overwhelming guilt for most of his life, a guilt that was only waiting for the words "I sentence you now to death by drowning!" to be expunged. Are we given any clue as to why Georg is guilt-ridden? What might Kafka be saying about guilt?

The shifting quality of fact and perception is most apparent in Georg's interactions with his father. At the beginning of the story the old man seems well enough. Georg hasn't entered his father's room for months because his father comes out for meals and to meet over business matters: " 'My father is still a giant of a man,' said Georg to himself." Yet suddenly his father must be treated like a baby and put to bed: he can hardly move his legs. Then almost as quickly the father regains his strength and springs to the attack: "I'm far from being covered up yet." At that, in spite of his having supposedly organized his life well, acquired an acceptable fiancée, and dealt expertly with business matters, Georg is reduced to a little boy: "Georg shrank into a corner, as far away from his father as possible. A long time ago he had firmly made up his mind to watch closely every least movement so that he should not be surprised by any indirect attack, a pounce from behind or above." What, one wonders, is the father's physical and mental state? Why does he continue to hold such power over his son?

Georg makes feeble efforts to excuse his guilt to himself: " ' That's the kind of man I am and he'll just have to take me as I am,' he said to himself, 'I can't cut myself to another pattern that might make a more suitable friend for him.' " And he tries desperately to save his self-assurance: " 'He has pockets even in his shirt!' said Georg to himself, and believed that with this remark he could make him an impossible figure for all the world. Only for a moment did he think so. . ." But he knows—and we know—that this battle for freedom and peace of mind cannot be won. We know, though he seems not to, that his chief obstacle is not his father but the enemy within himself.

Even the most cursory efforts to decipher this story reveal its labyrinthine nature. The meaning of the symbols in this story are as vague and shifting as the story itself. For example, is the father a menacing individual, or does he represent the judgment of parents on children, or is he the superego in Georg's own mind condemning him for not living up to his own high goals? Is the friend real or is he Georg's alter ego, a self he had rejected but one about whom the father could say, "He would have been a son after my own heart"?

Rereading the story will probably not settle any of these questions. Each person must decide upon his own answers. However, it seems surprising that Kafka's renderings of the struggles in a father-son relationship have not been given more prominence in psychological discussions, since they provide such a strong and logical contrast to the Oedipal theme (while Oedipus remains ever victorious over his father, Kafka is ever the loser). Here the son is threatened by the father when he attempts to possess the female, who is a stand-in for his mother: "Just take your bride on your arm and try getting in my way! I'll sweep her from your very side, you don't know how!" Georg gives up all claims to manhood—and ultimately his life—in order to propitiate the overwhelming force.

The Rocking-Horse Winner

D. H. LAWRENCE

There was a woman who was beautiful, who started with all the advantages, yet she had no luck. She married for love, and the love turned to dust. She had bonny children, yet she felt they had been thrust upon her, and she could not love them. They looked at her coldly, as if they were finding fault with her. And hurriedly she felt she must cover up some fault in herself. Yet what it was that she must cover up she never knew. Nevertheless, when her children were present, she always felt the centre of her heart go hard. This troubled her, and in her manner she was all the more gentle and anxious for her children, as if she loved them very much. Only she herself knew that at the centre of her heart was a hard little place that could not feel love, no, not for anybody. Everybody else said of her: "She is such a good mother. She adores her children." Only she herself, and her children themselves, knew it was not so. They read it in each other's eyes.

There were a boy and two little girls. They lived in a pleasant house, with a garden, and they had discreet servants, and felt themselves superior to anyone in the neighbourhood.

Although they lived in style, they felt always an anxiety in the house. There was never enough money. The mother had a small income, and the father had a small income, but not nearly enough for the social position which they had to keep up. The father went into town to some office. But though he had good prospects, these prospects never materialized. There was always the grinding sense of the shortage of money, though the style was always kept up.

At last the mother said: "I will see if I can't make something." But she did not know where to begin. She racked her brains, and tried this thing and the other, but could not find anything successful. The failure made deep lines come into her face. Her children were growing up, they would have to go to school. There must be more money, there must be more money. The father, who was always very handsome and expensive in his tastes, seemed as if he never would be able to do anything worth doing. And the mother, who had a great belief in herself, did not succeed any better, and her tastes were just as expensive.

And so the house came to be haunted by the unspoken phrase: There must be more money! There must be more money! The children could hear it all the time, though nobody said it aloud. They heard it at Christmas, when the expensive and splendid toys filled the nursery. Behind the shining modern rocking horse, behind the smart doll's-house, a voice would start whispering: "There must be more money! There must be more money!" And the children would stop playing, to listen for a moment. They would look into each other's eyes, to see if they had all heard. And each one saw in the eyes of the other two that they too had heard. "There must be more money! There must be more money!"

It came whispering from the springs of the still-swaying rocking horse, and even the horse, bending his wooden, champing head, heard it. The big doll, sitting so pink and smirking in her new pram, could hear it quite plainly, and seemed to be smirking all the more self-consciously because of it. The foolish puppy, too, that took the place of the Teddy bear, he was looking so extraordinarily foolish for no other reason but that he heard the secret whisper all over the house: "There must be more money!"

Yet nobody ever said it aloud. The whisper was everywhere, and therefore no one spoke it. Just as no one ever says: "We are breathing!" in spite of the fact that breath is coming and going all the time.

"Mother," said the boy Paul one day, "why don't we keep a car of our own? Why do we always use uncle's, or else a taxi?"

"Because we're the poor members of the family," said the mother.

"But why are we, mother?"

"Well—I suppose," she said slowly and bitterly, "it's because your father has no luck."

The boy was silent for some time.

"Is luck money, mother?" he asked, rather timidly.

"No, Paul. Not quite. It's what causes you to have money."

"Oh!" said Paul vaguely. "I thought when Uncle Oscar said filthy lucker, it meant money."

"Filthy lucre does mean money," said the mother. "But it's lucre, not luck."

"Oh!" said the boy. "Then what is luck, mother?"

"It's what causes you to have money. If you're lucky you have money. That's why it's better to be born lucky than rich. If you're rich, you may lose your money. But if you're lucky, you will always get more money."

"Oh! Will you? And is father not lucky?"

"Very unlucky, I should say," she said bitterly.

The boy watched her with unsure eyes.

"Why?" he asked.

"I don't know. Nobody ever knows why one person is lucky and another unlucky."

"Don't they? Nobody at all? Does nobody know?"

"Perhaps God. But He never tells."

"He ought to, then. And aren't you lucky either, mother?"

"I can't be, if I married an unlucky husband."

"But by yourself, aren't you?"

"I used to think I was, before I married. Now I think I am very unlucky indeed."

"Why?"

"Well—never mind! Perhaps I'm not really," she said.

The child looked at her, to see if she meant it. But he saw, by the lines of her mouth, that she was only trying to hide something from him.

"Well, anyhow," he said stoutly, "I'm a lucky person."

"Why?" said his mother, with a sudden laugh.

He stared at her. He didn't even know why he had said it.

"God told me," he asserted, brazening it out.

"I hope He did, dear!" she said, again with a laugh, but rather bitter.

"He did, mother!"

"Excellent!" said the mother, using one of her husband's exclamations.

The boy saw she did not believe him; or, rather, that she paid no attention to his assertion. This angered him somewhat, and made him want to compel her attention.

He went off by himself, vaguely, in a childish way, seeking for the clue to "luck." Absorbed, taking no heed of other people, he went about with a sort of stealth, seeking inwardly for luck. He wanted luck, he wanted it, he wanted it. When the two girls were playing dolls in the nursery, he would sit on his big rocking horse, charging madly into space, with a frenzy that made the little girls peer at him uneasily. Wildly the horse careered, the waving dark hair of the boy tossed, his eyes had a strange glare in them. The little girls dared not speak to him.

When he had ridden to the end of his mad little journey, he climbed down and stood in front of his rocking horse, staring fixedly into its lowered face. Its red mouth was slightly open, its big eye was wide and glassy-bright.

"Now!" he would silently command the snorting steed. "Now, take me to where there is luck! Now take me!"

And he would slash the horse on the neck with the little whip he had asked Uncle Oscar for. He knew the horse could take him to where there was luck, if only he forced it. So he would mount again, and start on his furious ride, hoping at last to get there. He knew he could get there.

"You'll break your horse, Paul!" said the nurse.

"He's always riding like that! I wish he'd leave off!" said his elder sister Joan.

But he only glared down on them in silence. Nurse gave him up. She could make nothing of him. Anyhow he was growing beyond her.

One day his mother and his Uncle Oscar came in when he was on one of his furious rides. He did not speak to them.

"Hallo, you young jockey! Riding a winner?" said his uncle.

"Aren't you growing too big for a rocking horse? You're not a very little boy any longer, you know," said his mother.

But Paul only gave a blue glare from his big, rather close-set eyes. He would speak to nobody when he was in full tilt. His mother watched him with an anxious expression on her face.

At last he suddenly stopped forcing his horse into the mechanical gallop, and slid down.

"Well, I got there!" he announced

fiercely, his blue eyes still flaring, and his sturdy long legs straddling apart.

"Where did you get to?" asked his mother.

"Where I wanted to go," he flared back at her.

"That's right, son!" said Uncle Oscar. "Don't you stop till you get there. What's the horse's name?"

"He doesn't have a name," said the boy.

"Gets on without all right?" asked the uncle.

"Well, he has different names. He was called Sansovino last week."

"Sansovino, eh? Won the Ascot. How did you know his name?"

"He always talks about horse races with Bassett," said Joan.

The uncle was delighted to find that his small nephew was posted with all the racing news. Bassett, the young gardener, who had been wounded in the left foot in the war and had got his present job through Oscar Cresswell, whose batman he had been, was a perfect blade of the "turf." He lived in the racing events, and the small boy lived with him.

Oscar Cresswell got it all from Bassett.

"Master Paul comes and asks me, so I can't do more than tell him, sir," said Bassett, his face terribly serious, as if he were speaking of religious matters.

"And does he ever put anything on a horse he fancies?"

"Well—I don't want to give him away—he's a young sport, a fine sport, sir. Would you mind asking him yourself? He sort of takes a pleasure in it, and perhaps he'd feel I was giving him away, sir, if you don't mind."

Bassett was serious as a church.

The uncle went back to his nephew, and took him off for a ride in the car.

"Say, Paul, old man, do you ever put anything on a horse?" the uncle asked.

The boy watched the handsome man closely.

"Why, do you think I oughtn't to?" he parried.

"Not a bit of it! I thought perhaps you might give me a tip for the Lincoln."

The car sped on into the country, going down to Uncle Oscar's place in Hampshire.

"Honour bright?" said the nephew.

"Honour bright, son!" said the uncle.

"Well, then, Daffodil."

"Daffodil! I doubt it, sonny. What about Mirza?"

"I only know the winner," said the boy. "That's Daffodil."

"Daffodil, eh?"

There was a pause. Daffodil was an obscure horse comparatively.

"Uncle!"

"Yes, son?"

"You won't let it go any further, will you? I promised Bassett."

"Bassett be damned, old man! What's he got to do with it?"

"We're partners. We've been partners from the first. Uncle, he lent me my first five shillings, which I lost. I promised him, honour bright, it was only between me and him; only you gave me that ten-shilling note I started winning with, so I thought you were lucky. You won't let it go any further, will you?"

The boy gazed at his uncle from those big, hot, blue eyes, set rather close together. The uncle stirred and laughed uneasily.

"Right you are, son! I'll keep your tip private. Daffodil, eh? How much are you putting on him?"

"All except twenty pounds," said the boy. "I keep that in reserve."

The uncle thought it a good joke.

"You keep twenty pounds in reserve, do you, you young romancer? What are you betting, then?"

"I'm betting three hundred," said the boy gravely. "But it's between you and me, Uncle Oscar! Honour bright?"

The uncle burst into a roar of laughter.

"It's between you and me all right, you young Nat Gould," he said, laughing. "But where's your three hundred?"

"Bassett keeps it for me. We're partners."

"You are, are you! And what is Bassett putting on Daffodil?"

"He won't go quite as high as I do, I expect. Perhaps he'll go a hundred and fifty."

"What, pennies?" laughed the uncle.

"Pounds," said the child, with a surprised look at his uncle. "Bassett keeps a bigger reserve than I do."

Between wonder and amusement Uncle Oscar was silent. He pursued the matter no further, but he determined to take his nephew with him to the Lincoln races.

"Now, son," he said, "I'm putting twenty on Mirza, and I'll put five for you on any horse you fancy. What's your pick?"

"Daffodil, uncle."

"No, not the fiver on Daffodil!"

"I should if it was my own fiver," said the child.

"Good! Good! Right you are! A fiver for me and a fiver for you on Daffodil."

The child had never been to a race meeting before, and his eyes were blue fire. He pursed his mouth tight, and watched. A Frenchman just in front had put his money on Lancelot. Wild with excitement, he flayed his arms up and down, yelling "Lancelot! Lancelot!" in his French accent.

Daffodil came in first, Lancelot second, Mirza third. The child, flushed and with eyes blazing, was curiously serene. His uncle brought him four five-pound notes, four to one.

"What am I do to with these?" he cried, waving them before the boy's eyes.

"I suppose we'll talk to Bassett," said the boy. "I expect I have fifteen hundred now; and twenty in reserve; and this twenty."

His uncle studied him for some moments.

"Look here, son!" he said. "You're not serious about Bassett and that fifteen hundred, are you?"

"Yes, I am. But it's between you and me, uncle. Honour bright!"

"Honour bright all right, son! But I must talk to Bassett."

"If you'd like to be a partner, uncle, with Bassett and me, we could all be partners. Only, you'd have to promise, honour bright, uncle, not to let it be beyond us three. Bassett and I are lucky, and you must be lucky, because it was your ten shillings I started winning with . . ."

Uncle Oscar took both Bassett and Paul into Richmond Park for an afternoon, and there they talked.

"It's like this, you see, sir," Bassett said. "Master Paul would get me talking about racing events, spinning yarns, you know, sir. And he was always keen on knowing if I'd made or if I'd lost. It's about a year since, now, that I put five shillings on Blush of Dawn for him—and we lost. Then the luck turned, with that ten shillings he had from you, that we put on Singhalese. And since that time, it's been pretty steady, all things considered. What do you say, Master Paul?"

"We're all right when we're sure," said Paul. "It's when we're not quite sure that we go down."

"Oh, but we're careful then," said Bassett.

"But when are you sure?" smiled Uncle Oscar.

"It's Master Paul, sir," said Bassett, in a secret, religious voice. "It's as if he had it from heaven. Like Daffodil, now, for the Lincoln. That was as sure as eggs."

"Did you put anything on Daffodil?" asked Oscar Cresswell.

"Yes, sir, I made my bit."

"And my nephew?"

Bassett was obstinately silent, looking at Paul.

"I made twelve hundred, didn't I, Bassett? I told uncle I was putting three hundred on Daffodil."

"That's right," said Bassett, nodding.

"But where's the money?" asked the uncle.

"I keep it safe locked up, sir. Master Paul he can have it any minute he likes to ask for it."

"What, fifteen hundred pounds?"

"And twenty! and forty, that is, with the twenty he made on the course."

"It's amazing!" said the uncle.

"If Master Paul offers you to be partners, sir, I would, if I were you; if you'll excuse me," said Bassett.

Oscar Cresswell thought about it.

"I'll see the money," he said.

They drove home again, and sure enough, Bassett came round to the garden-house with fifteen hundred pounds in notes. The twenty pounds reserve was left with Joe Glee, in the Turf Commission deposit.

"You see, it's all right, uncle, when I'm sure! Then we go strong, for all we're worth. Don't we, Bassett?"

"We do that, Master Paul."

"And when are you sure?" said the uncle, laughing.

"Oh, well, sometimes I'm absolutely sure, like about Daffodil," said the boy; "and sometimes I have an idea; and sometimes I haven't even an idea, have I, Bassett? Then we're careful, because we mostly go down."

"You do, do you! And when you're sure, like about Daffodil, what makes you sure, sonny?"

"Oh, well, I don't know," said the boy uneasily. "I'm sure, you know, uncle; that's all."

"It's as if he had it from heaven, sir," Bassett reiterated.

"I should say so!" said the uncle.

But he became a partner. And when the Leger was coming on, Paul was "sure" about Lively Spark, which was a quite inconsiderable horse. The boy.insisted on putting a thousand on the horse, Bassett went for five hundred, and Oscar Cresswell two hundred. Lively Spark came in first, and the betting had been ten to one against him. Paul had made ten thousand.

"You see," he said, "I was absolutely sure of him."

Even Oscar Cresswell had cleared two thousand.

"Look here, son," he said, "this sort of thing makes me nervous."

"It needn't, uncle! Perhaps I shan't be sure again for a long time."

"But what are you going to do with your money?" asked the uncle.

"Of course," said the boy, "I started it for mother. She said she had no luck, because father is unlucky, so I thought if I was lucky, it might stop whispering."

"What might stop whispering?"

"Our house. I hate our house for whispering."

"What does it whisper?"

"Why—why"—the boy fidgeted—"why, I don't know. But it's always short of money, you know, uncle."

"I know it, son, I know it."

"You know people send mother writs, don't you, uncle?"

"I'm afraid I do," said the uncle.

"And then the house whispers, like people laughing at you behind your back. It's awful, that is! I thought if I was lucky . . ."

"You might stop it," added the uncle.

The boy watched him with big blue eyes that had an uncanny cold fire in them, and he said never a word.

"Well, then!" said the uncle. "What are we doing?"

"I shouldn't like mother to know I was lucky," said the boy.

"Why not, son?"

"She'd stop me."

"I don't think she would."

"Oh!"—and the boy writhed in an odd way—"I don't want her to know, uncle."

"All right, son! We'll manage it without her knowing."

They managed it very easily. Paul, at the other's suggestion, handed over five thousand pounds to his uncle, who deposited it with the family lawyer, who was then to inform Paul's mother that a relative had put five thousand pounds into his hands, which sum was to be paid out a thousand pounds at a time on the mother's birthday, for the next five years.

"So she'll have a birthday present of a thousand pounds for five successive years," said Uncle Oscar. "I hope it won't make it all the harder for her later."

Paul's mother had her birthday in November. The house had been "whispering" worse than ever lately, and, even in spite of his luck, Paul could not bear up against it. He was very anxious to see the effect of the birthday letter, telling his mother about the thousand pounds.

When there were no visitors, Paul now took his meals with his parents, as he was beyond the nursery control. His mother went into town nearly every day. She had discovered that she had an odd knack of sketching furs and dress materials, so she worked secretly in the studio of a friend who was the chief "artist" for the leading drapers. She drew the figures of ladies in furs and ladies in silk and sequins for the newspaper advertisements. This young woman artist earned several thousand pounds a year, but Paul's mother only made several hundreds, and she was again dissatisfied. She so wanted to be first in something, and she did not succeed, even in making sketches for drapery advertisements.

She was down to breakfast on the morning of her birthday. Paul watched her face as she read her letters. He knew the lawyer's letter. As his mother read it, her face hardened and became more expressionless. Then a cold, determined look came on her mouth. She hid the letter under the pile of others, and said not a word about it.

"Didn't you have anything nice in the post for your birthday, mother?" said Paul.

"Quite moderately nice," she said, her voice cold and absent.

She went away to town without saying more.

But in the afternoon Uncle Oscar appeared. He said Paul's mother had had a long interview with the lawyer, asking if the whole five thousand could be advanced at once, as she was in debt.

"What do you think, uncle?" said the boy.

"I leave it to you, son."

"Oh, let her have it, then! We can get some more with the other," said the boy.

"A bird in the hand is worth two in the bush, laddie!" said Uncle Oscar.

"But I'm sure to know for the Grand National; or the Lincolnshire; or else the Derby. I'm sure to know for one of them," said Paul.

So Uncle Oscar signed the agreement, and Paul's mother touched the whole five thousand. Then something very curious happened. The voices in the house suddenly went mad, like a chorus of frogs on a spring evening. There were certain new furnishings, and Paul had a tutor. He was really going to Eton, his father's school, in the following autumn. There were flowers in the winter, and a blossoming of the luxury Paul's mother had been used to. And yet the voices in the house, behind the sprays of mimosa and almond blossom, and from under the piles of iridescent cushions, simply trilled and screamed in a sort of ecstasy: "There must be more money! Oh-h-h, there must be more money. Oh, now, now-w! Now-w-w-w—there must be more money—more than ever! More than ever!"

It frightened Paul terribly. He studied away at his Latin and Greek with his tutors. But his intense hours were spent with Bassett. The Grand National had gone by: he had not "known," and had lost a hundred pounds. Summer was at hand. He was in agony for the Lincoln. But even for the Lincoln he didn't "know" and he lost fifty pounds. He became wild-eyed and strange, as if something were going to explode in him.

"Let it alone, son! Don't you bother about it!" urged Uncle Oscar. But it was as if the boy couldn't really hear what his uncle was saying.

"I've got to know for the Derby! I've got to know for the Derby!" the child reiterated, his big blue eyes blazing with a sort of madness.

His mother noticed how overwrought he was.

"You'd better go to the seaside. Wouldn't you like to go now to the seaside, instead of waiting? I think you'd better," she said, looking down at him anxiously, her heart curiously heavy because of him.

But the child lifted his uncanny blue eyes.

"I couldn't possibly go before the Derby, mother!" he said. "I couldn't possibly!"

"Why not?" she said, her voice becoming heavy when she was opposed. "Why not? You can still go from the seaside to see the Derby with your Uncle Oscar, if that's what you wish. No need for you to wait here. Besides, I think you care too much about these races. It's a bad sign. My family has been a gambling family, and you won't know till you grow up how much damage it has done. But it has done damage. I shall have to send Bassett away, and ask Uncle Oscar not to talk racing to you, unless you promise to be reasonable about it; go away to the seaside and forget it. You're all nerves!"

"I'll do what you like, mother, so long as you don't send me away till after the Derby," the boy said.

"Send you away from where? Just from this house?"

"Yes," he said, gazing at her.

"Why, you curious child, what makes you care about this house so much, suddenly? I never knew you loved it."

He gazed at her without speaking. He had a secret within a secret, something he had not divulged, even to Bassett or to his Uncle Oscar.

But his mother, after standing undecided and a little bit sullen for some moments, said:

"Very well, then! Don't go to the seaside till after the Derby, if you don't wish it. But promise me you won't let your nerves go to pieces. Promise you won't think so much about horse racing and events, as you call them!"

"Oh, no," said the boy casually. "I won't think much about them, mother. You needn't worry. I wouldn't worry, mother, if I were you."

"If you were me and I were you," said his mother, "I wonder what we should do!"

"But you know you needn't worry, don't you?" the boy repeated.

"I should be awfully glad to know it," she said wearily.

"Oh, well, you can, you know. I mean, you ought to know you needn't worry," he insisted.

"Ought I? Then I'll see about it," she said.

Paul's secret of secrets was his wooden horse, that which had no name. Since he was emancipated from a nurse and a nursery-governess, he had had his rocking horse removed to his own bedroom at the top of the house.

"Surely, you're too big for a rocking horse!" his mother had remonstrated.

"Well, you see, mother, till I can have a real horse, I like to have some sort of animal about," had been his quaint answer.

"Do you feel he keeps you company?" she laughed.

"Oh, yes! He's very good, he always keeps me company, when I'm there," said Paul.

So the horse, rather shabby, stood in an arrested prance in the boy's bedroom.

The Derby was drawing near, and the boy grew more and more tense. He hardly heard what was spoken to him, he was very frail, and his eyes were really uncanny. His mother had sudden seizures of uneasiness about him. Sometimes, for half-an-hour, she would feel a sudden anxiety about him that was almost anguish. She wanted to rush to him at once, and know he was safe.

Two nights before the Derby, she was at a big party in town, when one of her rushes of anxiety about her boy, her first-born, gripped her heart till she could hardly speak. She fought with the feeling, might and main, for she believed in common sense. But it was too strong. She had to leave the dance and go downstairs to telephone to the country. The children's nursery-governess was terribly surprised and startled at being rung up in the night.

"Are the children all right, Miss Wilmot?"

"Oh, yes, they are quite all right."

"Master Paul? Is he all right?"

"He went to bed as right as a trivet. Shall I run up and look at him?"

"No," said Paul's mother reluctantly. "No! Don't trouble. It's all right. Don't sit up. We shall be home fairly soon." She did not want her son's privacy intruded upon.

"Very good," said the governess.

It was about one o'clock when Paul's mother and father drove up to their house. All was still. Paul's mother went to her room and slipped off her white fur coat. She had told her maid not to wait up for her. She heard her husband downstairs, mixing a whisky-and-soda.

And then, because of the strange anxiety at her heart, she stole upstairs to her son's room. Noiselessly she went along the upper corridor. Was there a faint noise? What was it?

She stood, with arrested muscles, outside his door, listening. There was a strange, heavy, and yet not loud noise. Her heart stood still. It was a soundless noise, yet rushing and powerful. Something huge, in violent, hushed motion. What was it? What in God's name was it? She ought to know. She felt that she knew the noise. She knew what it was.

Yet she could not place it. She couldn't say what it was. And on and on it went, like a madness.

Softly, frozen with anxiety and fear, she turned the door handle.

The room was dark. Yet in the space near the window, she heard and saw something plunging to and fro. She gazed in fear and amazement.

Then suddenly she switched on the light, and saw her son, in his green pyjamas, madly surging on the rocking horse. The blaze of light suddenly lit him up, as he urged the wooden horse, and lit her up, as she stood, blonde, in her dress of pale green and crystal, in the doorway.

"Paul!" she cried. "Whatever are you doing?"

"It's Malabar!" he screamed, in a powerful, strange voice. "It's Malabar."

His eyes blazed at her for one strange and senseless second, as he ceased urging his wooden horse. Then he fell with a crash to the ground, and she, all her tormented motherhood flooding upon her, rushed to gather him up.

But he was unconscious, and unconscious he remained, with some brain-fever. He talked and tossed, and his mother sat stonily by his side.

"Malabar! It's Malabar! Bassett, Bassett, I know it! It's Malabar!"

So the child cried, trying to get up and urge the rocking horse that gave him his inspiration.

"What does he mean by Malabar?" asked the heart-frozen mother.

"I don't know," said the father stonily.

"What does he mean by Malabar?" she asked her brother Oscar.

"It's one of the horses running for the Derby," was the answer.

And, in spite of himself, Oscar Cresswell spoke to Bassett, and himself put a thousand on Malabar: at fourteen to one.

The third day of the illness was critical: they were waiting for a change. The boy, with his rather long, curly hair, was tossing ceaselessly on the pillow. He neither slept nor regained consciousness, and his eyes were like blue stones. His mother sat, feeling her heart had gone, turned actually into a stone.

In the evening, Oscar Cresswell did not come, but Bassett sent a message, saying could he come up for one moment, just one moment? Paul's mother was very angry at the intrusion, but on second thought she agreed. The boy was the same. Perhaps Bassett might bring him to consciousness.

The gardener, a shortish fellow with a little brown moustache, and sharp little brown eyes, tiptoed into the room, touched his imaginary cap to Paul's mother, and stole to the bedside, staring with glittering, smallish eyes, at the tossing, dying child.

"Master Paul!" he whispered. "Master Paul! Malabar come in first all right, a clean win. I did as you told me. You've made over seventy thousand pounds, you have; you've got over eighty thousand. Malabar came in all right, Master Paul."

"Malabar! Malabar! Did I say Malabar, mother? Did I say Malabar? Do you think I'm lucky, mother? I knew Malabar, didn't I? Over eighty thousand pounds! I call that lucky, don't you, mother? Over eighty thousand pounds! I knew, didn't I know I knew? Malabar came in all right. If I ride my horse till I'm sure, then I tell you, Bassett, you can go as high as you like. Did you go for all you were worth, Bassett?"

"I went a thousand on it, Master Paul."

"I never told you, mother, that if I can ride my horse, and get there, then I'm absolutely sure—oh, absolutely! Mother, did I ever tell you? I'm lucky."

"No, you never did," said the mother.

But the boy died in the night.

And even as he lay dead, his mother heard her brother's voice saying to her: "My God, Hester, you're eighty-odd thousand to the good and a poor devil of a son to the bad. But, poor devil, poor devil, he's best gone out of a life where he rides his rocking horse to find a winner."

Considerations

How should the events of this story be considered? Are they mystical? Are they a neurotic fantasy? Is the story science fiction? Is it an allegory? Is it symbolic, and if so, what are the symbols and what do they mean?

The story is obviously complicated, and it is impossible to pin down every conceivable interpretation. But a few can be isolated. (In addition, just simply reading it, enjoying it, and leaving it alone is one way of approaching it. We don't *have* to explain everything, just as we don't in our own lives.)

The relationship between the boy and his mother seems to be fairly strong and a central factor in the development of the story. How odd then that the story opens stating that the mother really doesn't love the children, as though that's perhaps the most important fact we should know.

Then we are told, "She felt that she must cover up some fault in herself." It's easy to identify with that complaint. How many individuals are there who don't have a fault they want to cover up?

What's being covered up here? One very pointed clue is: "At the center of herself there's a hard point." The mother can't love her children—she can't be what she expects herself to be, and consequently she doesn't love herself. She cannot be what society around her wishes her to be. That goes for her husband as well. Are there other reasons for the coverup?

The second major force is the obsessional phrase, "we need money." Why? Paul doesn't really understand. To keep up appearances? He doesn't know what appearances are. He knows only that the entire house whispers. He can feel the tension. Might he think that the tension is responsible for the lack of love? Or is he even aware of that lack?

The haunting phrase, "There must be more money," permeates not only the lives of the people in the house, it goes so far as to invade the actual world of matter as well—the rocking horse itself is penetrated by the comment, the doll sitting in its new pram, and the house begins to whisper. If it is such a part of your life, that kind of craving must make it seem like even the earth itself is whispering—that nature itself is demanding.

What are the reasons for this overwhelming desire for money in the story? For the parents it seems to be social (refer to the scene in the dress shop where one woman has thousands, but even with the fake inheritance Paul's mother has only hundreds). For Paul it seems to be something like silencing the whispers or living up to some standard. What are our reasons for wanting more money? Perhaps they include wanting to pay bills, to travel—but what else?

What was the whispering? There is no possible scientific definition, but psychologically speaking it could be a lot of things. Is it the desire to live up to parents' expectations—the whispering, nagging, urging on to do this? After all, we often still discuss how the Puritan ethic of 200 years ago still drives us on today. If the whispering refers to real walls making audible sounds, the story is unbelievable; but if it refers to what happens deep inside (as in "the center of herself"), it's very real.

Again the impetus can be traced back to the accent on the mother. "I shouldn't like mother to know I was lucky," said the boy. "Why not, son?" "She'd stop me." "I don't think she would." "Oh, I don't want her to know, uncle."

Mother especially (father is a shadow figure for several good reasons) defines all her problems in terms of money and luck. Here another difference in viewpoint can be seen. This was written at a time when the debate was still raging as to whether there's a scientific or a religious explanation for everything. In a way the story deals with that. She says that the reason they don't have social connections is that they don't have enough money, and the reason for that is they're down on their luck. Paul says, "God told me." His mother as much as scoffs at that. What's more believable in saying, "We're down on our luck" rather than "God wills this"? And can luck—or the lack of it—be contagious? The family supposedly got their bad luck from the father; the gardener and Uncle Oscar got their good luck from Paul.

Can the outlook in a situation like this ever be optimistic? The five thousand didn't seem to satisfy the whispers. Many things were bought with it, but the more money that was spent, the louder the voices became. Does Lawrence even suggest a solution, or does the fact of Paul's death just solidify the hopelessness of it all?

A Painful Case

James Joyce

Mr James Duffy lived in Chapelizod because he wished to live as far as possible from the city of which he was a citizen and because he found all the other suburbs of Dublin mean, modern and pretentious. He lived in an old sombre house and from his windows he could look into the disused distillery or upwards along the shallow river on which Dublin is built. The lofty walls of his uncarpeted room were free from pictures. He had himself bought every article of furniture in the room: a black iron bedstead, an iron washstand, four cane chairs, a clothesrack, a coal-scuttle, a fender and irons and a square table on which lay a double desk. A bookcase had been made in an alcove by means of shelves of white wood. The bed was clothed with white bed-clothes and a black and scarlet rug covered the foot. A little hand-mirror hung above the washstand and during the day a white-shaded lamp stood as the sole ornament of the mantelpiece. The books on the white wooden shelves were arranged from below upwards according to bulk. A complete Wordsworth stood at one end of the lowest shelf and a copy of the *Maynooth* *Catechism,* sewn into the cloth cover of a notebook, stood at one end of the top shelf. Writing materials were always on the desk. In the desk lay a manuscript translation of Hauptmann's *Michael Kramer,* the stage directions of which were written in purple ink, and a little sheaf of papers held together by a brass pin. In these sheets a sentence was inscribed from time to time and, in an ironical moment, the headline of an advertisement for *Bile Beans* had been pasted on to the first sheet. On lifting the lid of the desk a faint fragrance escaped—the fragrance of new cedarwood pencils or of a bottle of gum or of an over-ripe apple which might have been left there and forgotten.

Mr Duffy abhorred anything which betokened physical or mental disorder. A mediaeval doctor would have called him saturnine. His face, which carried the entire tale of his years, was of the brown tint of Dublin streets. On his long and rather large head grew dry black hair and a tawny moustache did not quite cover an unamiable mouth. His cheekbones also gave his face a harsh character; but there was no harshness in the eyes which, looking at the world from under their tawny eyebrows, gave the impression of a man ever alert to greet a redeeming instinct in others but often disappointed. He lived at a little distance from his body, regarding his own acts with doubtful sideglances. He had an odd autobiographical habit which led him to compose in his mind from time to time a short sentence about himself containing a subject in the third person and a predicate in the past tense. He never gave alms to beggars and walked firmly, carrying a stout hazel.

He had been for many years cashier of a private bank in Baggot Street. Every morning he came in from Chapelizod by tram. At midday he went to Dan Burke's and took his lunch—a bottle of lager beer and a small trayful of arrowroot biscuits. At four o'clock he was set free. He dined in an eating-house in George's Street where he felt himself safe from the society of Dublin's gilded youth and where there was a certain plain honesty in the bill of fare. His evenings were spent either before his landlady's piano or roaming about the outskirts of the city. His liking for Mozart's music brought him sometimes to an opera or a concert: these were the only dissipations of his life.

He had neither companions nor friends, church nor creed. He lived his spiritual life without any communion with others, visiting his relatives at Christmas and escorting them to the cemetery when they died. He performed these two social duties for old dignity's sake but conceded nothing further to the conventions which regulate the civic life. He allowed himself to think that in certain cir-

cumstances he would rob his bank but, as these circumstances never arose, his life rolled out evenly—an adventureless tale.

One evening he found himself sitting beside two ladies in the Rotunda. The house, thinly peopled and silent, gave distressing prophecy of failure. The lady who sat next him looked round at the deserted house once or twice and then said:

—What a pity there is such a poor house to-night! It's so hard on people to have to sing to empty benches.

He took the remark as an invitation to talk. He was surprised that she seemed so little awkward. While they talked he tried to fix her permanently in his memory. When he learned that the young girl beside her was her daughter he judged her to be a year or so younger than himself. Her face, which must have been handsome, had remained intelligent. It was an oval face with strongly marked features. The eyes were very dark blue and steady. Their gaze began with a defiant note but was confused by what seemed a deliberate swoon of the pupil into the iris, revealing for an instant a temperament of great sensibility. The pupil reasserted itself quickly, this half-disclosed nature fell again under the reign of prudence, and her astrakhan jacket, moulding a bosom of a certain fulness, struck the note of defiance more definitely.

He met her again a few weeks afterwards at a concert in Earlsfort Terrace and seized the moments when her daughter's attention was diverted to become intimate. She alluded once or twice to her husband but her tone was not such as to make the allusion a warning. Her name was Mrs Sinico. Her husband's great-great-grandfather had come from Leghorn. Her husband was captain of a mercantile boat plying between Dublin and Holland; and they had one child.

Meeting her a third time by accident he found courage to make an appointment. She came. This was the first of many meetings; they met always in the evening and chose the most quiet quarters for their walks together. Mr Duffy, however, had a distaste for underhand ways and, finding that they were compelled to meet stealthily, he forced her to ask him to her house. Captain Sinico encouraged his visits, thinking that his daughter's hand was in question. He had dismissed his wife so sincerely from his gallery of pleasures that he did not suspect that anyone else would take an interest in her. As the husband was often away and the daughter out giving music lessons Mr Duffy had many opportunities of enjoying the lady's society. Neither he nor she had had any such adventure before and neither was conscious of any incongruity. Little by little he entangled his thoughts with hers. He lent her books, provided her with ideas, shared his intellectual life with her. She listened to all.

Sometimes in return for his theories she gave out some fact of her own life. With almost maternal solicitude she urged him to let his nature open to the full; she became his confessor. He told her that for some time he had assisted at the meetings of an Irish Socialist Party where he had felt himself a unique figure amidst a score of sober workmen in a garret lit by an inefficient oil-lamp. When the party had divided into three sections, each under its own leader and in its own garret, he had discontinued his attendances. The workmen's discussions, he said, were too timorous; the interest they took in the question of wages was inordinate. He felt that they were hard-featured realists and that they resented an exactitude which was the product of a leisure not within their reach. No social revolution, he told her, would be likely to strike Dublin for some centuries.

She asked him why did he not write out his thoughts. For what, he asked her, with careful scorn. To compete with phrasemongers, incapable of thinking consecutively for sixty seconds? To submit himself to the criticisms of an obtuse middle class which entrusted its morality to policemen and its fine arts to impresarios?

He went often to her little cottage outside Dublin; often they spent their evenings alone. Little by little, as their thoughts entangled, they spoke of subjects less remote. Her companionship was like a warm soil about an exotic. Many times she allowed the dark to fall upon them, refraining from lighting the lamp. The dark discreet room, their isolation, the music that still vibrated in their ears united them. This union exalted him, wore away the rough edges of his character, emotionalised his mental life. Sometimes he caught himself listening to the sound of his own voice. He thought that in her eyes he would ascend to an angelical stature; and, as he attached the fervent nature of his companion more and more closely to him, he heard the strange impersonal voice which he recognised as his own, insisting on the soul's incurable loneliness. We cannot give ourselves, it said: we are our own. The end of these discourses was that one night during which she had shown every sign of unusual excitement, Mrs Sinico caught up his hand passionately and pressed it to her cheek.

Mr Duffy was very much surprised. Her interpretation of his words disillusioned him. He did not visit her for a week; then he wrote to her asking her to meet him. As he did not wish their last interview to be troubled by the influence of their ruined confessional they met in a little cakeshop near the Parkgate. It was cold autumn weather but in spite of the cold they wandered up and down the roads of the Park for nearly three hours. They agreed to break off their intercourse: every bond, he said, is a bond to sorrow. When they came out of the Park they walked in silence towards the tram; but here she began to tremble so violently that, fearing another collapse on her part, he bade her good-bye quickly and left her. A few days later he received a parcel containing his books and music.

Four years passed. Mr Duffy returned to his even way of life. His room still bore witness of the orderliness of his mind. Some new pieces of music encumbered the music-stand in the lower room and on his shelves stood two volumes by Nietzsche: *Thus Spake Zarathustra* and *The Gay Science.* He wrote seldom in the sheaf of papers which lay in his desk. One

of his sentences, written two months after his last interview with Mrs Sinico, read: Love between man and man is impossible because there must not be sexual intercourse and friendship between man and woman is impossible because there must be sexual intercourse. He kept away from concerts lest he should meet her. His father died; the junior partner of the bank retired. And still every morning he went into the city by tram and every evening walked home from the city after having dined moderately in George's Street and read the evening paper for dessert.

One evening as he was about to put a morsel of corned beef and cabbage into his mouth his hand stopped. His eyes fixed themselves on a paragraph in the evening paper which he had propped against the water-carafe. He replaced the morsel of food on his plate and read the paragraph attentively. Then he drank a glass of water, pushed his plate to one side, doubled the paper down before him between his elbows and read the paragraph over and over again. The cabbage began to deposit a cold white grease on his plate. The girl came over to him to ask was his dinner not properly cooked. He said it was very good and ate a few mouthfuls of it with difficulty. Then he paid his bill and went out.

He walked along quickly through the November twilight, his stout hazel stick striking the ground regularly, the fringe of the buff *Mail* peeping out of a side-pocket of his tight reefer over-coat. On the lonely road which leads from the Parkgate to Chapelizod he slackened his pace.

His stick struck the ground less emphatically and his breath, issuing irregularly, almost with a sighing sound, condensed in the wintry air. When he reached his house he went up at once to his bedroom and, taking the paper from his pocket, read the paragraph again by the failing light of the window. He read it not aloud, but moving his lips as a priest does when he reads the prayers *Secreto*. This was the paragraph:

DEATH OF A LADY AT SYDNEY PARADE

A PAINFUL CASE

To-day at the City of Dublin Hospital the Deputy Coroner (in the absence of Mr Leverett) held an inquest on the body of Mrs Emily Sinico, aged forty-three years, who was killed at Sydney Parade Station yesterday evening. The evidence showed that the deceased lady, while attempting to cross the line, was knocked down by the engine of the ten o'clock slow train from Kingstown, thereby sustaining injuries of the head and right side which led to her death.

James Lennon, driver of the engine, stated that he had been in the employment of the railway company for fifteen years. On hearing the guard's whistle he set the train in motion and a second or two afterwards brought it to rest in response to loud cries. The train was going slowly.

P. Dunne, railway porter, stated that as the train was about to start he observed a woman attempting to cross the lines. He ran towards her and shouted but, before he could reach her, she was caught by the buffer of the engine and fell to the ground.

A juror—You saw the lady fall?

Witness—Yes.

Police Sergeant Croly deposed that when he arrived he found the deceased lying on the platform apparently dead. He had the body taken to the waiting-room pending the arrival of the ambulance.

Constable 57E corroborated.

Dr Halpin, assistant house surgeon of the City of Dublin Hospital, stated that the deceased had two lower ribs fractured and had sustained severe contusions of the right shoulder. The right side of the head had been injured in the fall. The injuries were not sufficient to have caused death in a normal person. Death, in his opinion, had been probably due to shock and sudden failure of the heart's action.

Mr H. B. Patterson Finlay, on behalf of the railway company, expressed his deep regret at the accident. The company had always taken every precaution to prevent people crossing the lines except by the bridges, both by placing notices in every station and by the use of patent spring gates at level crossings. The deceased had been in the habit of crossing the lines late at night from platform to platform and, in view of certain other circumstances of the case, he did not think the railway officials were to blame.

Captain Sinico, of Leoville, Sydney Parade, husband of the deceased, also gave evidence. He stated that the deceased was his wife. He was not in Dublin at the time of the accident as he had arrived only that morning from Rotterdam. They had been married for twenty-two years and had lived happily until about two years ago when his wife began to be rather intemperate in her habits.

Miss Mary Sinico said that of late her mother had been in the habit of going out at night to buy spirits. She, witness, had often tried to reason with her mother and had induced her to join a league. She was not at home until an hour after the accident.

The jury returned a verdict in accordance with the medical evidence and exonerated Lennon from all blame.

The Deputy Coroner said it was a most painful case, and expressed great sympathy with Captain Sinico and his daughter. He urged on the railway company to take strong measures to prevent the possibility of similar accidents in the future. No blame attached to anyone.

Mr Duffy raised his eyes from the paper and gazed out of his window on the cheerless evening landscape. The river lay quiet beside the empty distillery and from time to time a light appeared in some house on the Lucan road. What an end! The whole narrative of her death revolted him and it revolted him to think that he had ever spoken to her of what he held sacred. The threadbare phrases, the inane expressions of sympathy, the cautious words of a reporter won over to conceal the details of a commonplace vulgar death attacked his stomach. Not merely had she degraded herself; she had degraded him. He saw the squalid tract of her vice, miserable and malodorous. His soul's companion! He thought of the hobbling wretches whom he had seen carrying cans and bottles to be filled by the barman. Just God, what an end! Evidently she had been unfit to live, without any strength of purpose, an easy prey to habits, one of the wrecks on which civilisation has been reared. But that she could have sunk so low! Was it possible he had deceived himself so utterly about her? He remembered her outburst of that night and interpreted it in a harsher sense than he had ever done. He had no difficulty now in approving of the course he had taken.

As the light failed and his memory began to wander he thought her hand touched his. The shock which had first attacked his stomach was now attacking his nerves. He put on his overcoat and hat quickly and went out. The cold air met him on the threshold; it crept into the sleeves of his coat. When he came to the public-house at Chapelizod Bridge he went in and ordered a hot punch.

The proprietor served him obsequiously but did not venture to talk. There were five or six working-men in the shop discussing the value of a gentleman's estate in County Kildare. They drank at intervals from their huge pint tumblers and smoked, spitting often on the floor and sometimes dragging the sawdust over their spits with their heavy boots. Mr Duffy sat on his stool and gazed at them, without seeing or hearing them. After a while they went out and he called for another punch. He sat a long time over it. The shop was very quiet. The proprietor sprawled on the counter reading the *Herald* and yawning. Now and again a tram was heard swishing along the lonely road outside.

As he sat there, living over his life with her and evoking alternately the two images in which he now conceived her, he realised that she was dead, that she had ceased to exist, that she had become a memory. He began to feel ill at ease. He asked himself what else could he have done. He could not have carried on a comedy of deception with her; he could not have lived with her openly. He had done what seemed to him best. How was he to blame? Now that she was gone he understood how lonely her life must have been, sitting night after night alone in that room. His life would be lonely too until he, too, died, ceased to exist, became a memory—if anyone remembered him.

It was after nine o'clock when he left the shop. The night was cold and gloomy. He entered the Park by the first gate and walked along under the gaunt trees. He walked through the bleak alleys where they had walked four years before. She seemed to be near him in the darkness. At moments he seemed to feel her voice touch his ear, her hand touch his. He stood still to listen. Why had he withheld life from her? Why had he sentenced her to death? He felt his moral nature falling to pieces.

When he gained the crest of the Magazine Hill he halted and looked along the river towards Dublin, the lights of which burned redly and hospitably in the cold night. He looked down the slope and, at the base, in the shadow of the wall of the Park, he saw some human figures lying. Those venal and furtive loves filled him with despair. He gnawed the rectitude of his life; he felt that he had been outcast from life's feast. One human being had seemed to love him and he had denied her life and happiness: he had sentenced her to ignominy, a death of shame. He knew that the prostrate creatures down by the wall were watching him and wished him gone. No one wanted him; he was outcast from life's feast. He turned his eyes to the grey gleaming river, winding along towards Dublin. Beyond the river he saw a goods train winding out of Kingsbridge Station, like a worm with a fiery head winding through the darkness, obstinately and laboriously. It passed slowly out of sight; but still he heard in his ears the laborious drone of the engine reiterating the syllables of her name.

He turned back the way he had come, the rhythm of the engine pounding in his ears. He began to doubt the reality of what memory told him. He halted under a tree and allowed the rhythm to die away. He could not feel her near him in the darkness nor her voice touch his ear. He waited for some minutes listening. He could hear nothing: the night was perfectly silent. He listened again: perfectly silent. He felt that he was alone.

Considerations

Joyce is regarded by many as a major craftsman of the short story and novel in the English language. He was economical with his words, picking each as a poet selects his for its many nuances. This particular story exemplifies well Joyce's concern with the craft of writing.

The focus of the story shifts several times as though there were completely divided scenes. At first the focus is on Duffy, on his keeping himself to himself, somewhat old-maidishly set in his ways and enjoying it. This section ends with the comment "his life rolled out evenly—an adventureless tale." Then he meets a particular individual one evening at the Rotunda. The relationship reaches a crisis point and Duffy makes a decision: "fearing another collapse on her part, he bade her good-bye quickly and left her. A few days later he received a parcel containing his books and music."

The transition to the next scene is dealt with swiftly: "Four years passed." A paragraph is sufficient to summarize the little there is to tell about the events that took place during those four years in the once-again adventureless tale of Duffy's existence. Part of the pattern of these years was to "read the evening paper for dessert," a habit which leads us to the closing section: "One evening as he was about to put a morsel of corned beef and cabbage into his mouth his hand stopped." The newspaper tells him how Mrs. Sinico's life ended. We have seen the lady only through Duffy's eyes, so we can only conjecture about what her life must have been like during those four years. According to Captain Sinico's testimony, he and his wife had lived happily until two years before when she began to be rather intemperate in her habits. Was there something else that happened to reduce her to such a state? This possibility is not really suggested by the author, since Duffy—through whose eyes we see the world—takes the death personally. His first reaction is to consider her end an insult directed at him: "not merely had she degraded herself, she had degraded him."

Had the story ended there we might be justified in thinking Duffy a consummate egotist and this scene the proof of it. But the story continues: "He gnawed the rectitude of his life; he felt that he had been outcast from life's feast. One human being had seemed to love him and he had denied her life and happiness: he had sentenced her to ignominy, a death of shame." What could account for this drastic change in his feelings?

After reading the story, we see that even the title is rich in ambiguity. The pronouncement of Mrs. Sinico's death as a painful case ostensibly gives rise to the title. In what sense is the whole story a painful case, and Mr. Duffy's life the most painful case of all?

Why is the ending of the story particularly effective? What is the impact of the last word?

A Dill Pickle

KATHERINE MANSFIELD

And then, after six years, she saw him again. He was seated at one of those little bamboo tables decorated with a Japanese vase of paper daffodils. There was a tall plate of fruit in front of him, and very carefully, in a way she recognized immediately as his "special" way, he was peeling an orange.

He must have felt that shock of recognition in her for he looked up and met her eyes. Incredible! He didn't know her! She smiled; he frowned. She came towards him. He closed his eyes an instant, but opening them his face lit up as though he had struck a match in a dark room. He laid down the orange and pushed back his chair, and she took her little warm hand out of her muff and gave it to him.

"Vera!" he exclaimed. "How strange. Really, for a moment I didn't know you. Won't you sit down? You've had lunch? Won't you have some coffee?"

She hesitated, but of course she meant to.

"Yes, I'd like some coffee." And she sat down opposite him.

"You've changed. You've changed very much," he said, staring at her with that eager, lighted look. "You look so well. I've never seen you look so well before."

"Really?" She raised her veil and unbuttoned her high fur collar. "I don't feel very well. I can't bear this weather, you know."

"Ah, no. You hate the cold. . . ."

"Loathe it." She shuddered. "And the worst of it is that the older one grows . . ."

He interrupted her. "Excuse me," and tapped on the table for the waitress. "Please bring some coffee and cream." To her: "You are sure you won't eat anything? Some fruit, perhaps. The fruit here is very good."

"No, thanks. Nothing."

"Then that's settled." And smiling just a hint too broadly he took up the orange again. "You were saying—the older one grows—"

"The colder," she laughed. But she was thinking how well she remembered that trick of his—the trick of interrupting her—and of how it used to exasperate her six years ago. She used to feel then as though he, quite suddenly, in the middle of what she was saying, put his hand over her lips, turned from her, attended to something different, and then took his hand away, and with just the same slightly too broad smile, gave her his attention again. . . . Now we are ready. That is settled.

"The colder!" He echoed her words, laughing too. "Ah, ah. You still say the same things. And there is another thing about you that is not changed at all—your beautiful voice—your beautiful way of speaking." Now he was very grave; he leaned towards her, and she smelled the warm, stinging scent of the orange peel. "You have only to say one word and I would know your voice among all other voices. I don't know what it is—I've often wondered—that makes your voice such a—haunting memory. . . . Do you remember that first afternoon we spent together at Kew Gardens? You were so surprised because I did not know the names of any flowers. I am still just as ignorant for all your telling me. But whenever it is very fine and warm, and I see some bright colours —it's awfully strange—I hear your voice saying: 'Geranium, marigold and verbena.' And I feel those three words are all I recall of some forgotten, heavenly language. . . . You remember that afternoon?"

"Oh, yes, very well." She drew a long, soft breath, as though the paper daffodils between them were almost too sweet to bear. Yet, what had remained in her mind of that particular afternoon was an absurd scene over the tea table. A great many people taking tea in a Chinese pagoda, and he behaving like a maniac about the wasps—waving them away, flapping at them with his straw hat, serious and infuriated out of all proportion to the occasion. How delighted the sniggering tea drinkers had been. And how she had suffered.

But now, as he spoke, that memory faded. His was the truer. Yes, it had been a wonderful afternoon, full of geranium and marigold and verbena, and—warm sunshine. Her thoughts lingered over the last two words as though she sang them.

In the warmth, as it were, another memory unfolded. She saw herself sitting on a lawn. He lay beside her, and suddenly, after a long silence, he rolled over and put his head in her lap.

"I wish," he said, in a low, troubled voice, "I wish that I had taken poison and were about to die—here now!"

At that moment a little girl in a white dress, holding a long, dripping water lily, dodged from behind a bush, stared at them, and dodged back again. But he did not see. She leaned over him.

"Ah, why do you say that? I could not say that."

But he gave a kind of soft moan, and taking her hand he held it to his cheek.

"Because I know I am going to love you too much—far too much. And I shall suffer so terribly, Vera, because you never, never will love me."

He was certainly far better looking now than he had been then. He had lost all that dreamy vagueness and indecision. Now he had the air of a man who has found his place in life, and fills it with a confidence and an assurance which was, to say the least, impressive. He must have made money, too. His clothes were admirable, and at that moment he pulled a Russian cigarette case out of his pocket.

"Won't you smoke?"

"Yes, I will." She hovered over them. "They look very good."

"I think they are. I get them made for me by a little man in St. James's Street. I don't smoke very much. I'm not like you—but when I do, they must be delicious, very fresh cigarettes. Smoking isn't a habit with me; it's a luxury—like perfume. Are you still so fond of perfumes? Ah, when I was in Russia . . ."

She broke in: "You've really been to Russia?"

"Oh, yes. I was there for over a year. Have you forgotten how we used to talk of going there?"

"No, I've not forgotten."

He gave a strange half laugh and leaned back in his chair. "Isn't it curious. I have really carried out all those journeys that we planned. Yes, I have been to all those places that we talked of, and stayed in them long enough to—as you used to say, 'air oneself' in them. In fact, I have spent the last three years of my life travelling all the time. Spain, Corsica, Siberia, Russia, Egypt. The only country left is China, and I mean to go there, too, when the war is over."

As he spoke, so lightly, tapping the end of his cigarette against the ashtray, she felt the strange beast that had slumbered so long within her bosom stir, stretch itself, yawn, prick up its ears, and suddenly bound to its feet, and fix its longing, hungry stare upon those far away places. But all she said was, smiling gently: "How I envy you."

He accepted that. "It has been," he said, "very wonderful—especially Russia. Russia was all that we had imagined, and far, far more. I even spent some days on a river boat on the Volga. Do you remember that boatman's song that you used to play?"

"Yes." It began to play in her mind as she spoke.

"Do you ever play it now?"

"No, I've no piano."

He was amazed at that. "But what has become of your beautiful piano?"

She made a little grimace. "Sold. Ages ago."

"But you were so fond of music," he wondered.

"I've no time for it now," said she.

He let it go at that. "That river life," he went on, "is something quite special. After a day or two you cannot realize that you have ever known another. And it is not necessary to know the language—the life of the boat creates a bond between you and the people that's more than sufficient. You eat with them, pass the day with them, and in the evening there is that endless singing."

She shivered, hearing the boatman's song break out again loud and tragic, and seeing the boat floating on the darkening river with melancholy trees on either side. . . . "Yes, I should like that," said she, stroking her muff.

"You'd like almost everything about Russian life," he said warmly. "It's so informal, so impulsive, so free without question. And then the peasants are so splendid. They are such human beings—yes, that is it. Even the man who drives your carriage has—has some real part in what is happening. I remember the evening a party of us, two friends of mine and the wife of one of them, went for a picnic by the Black Sea. We took supper and champagne and ate and drank on the grass. And while we were eating the coachman came up. 'Have a dill pickle,' he said. He wanted to share with us. That seemed to me so right, so—you know what I mean?"

And she seemed at that moment to be sitting on the grass beside the mysteriously Black Sea, black as vel-

sucked in her cheeks; the dill pickle was terribly sour. . . .

"Yes, I know perfectly what you mean," she said.

In the pause that followed they looked at each other. In the past when they had looked at each other like that they had felt such a boundless understanding between them that their souls had, as it were, put their arms round each other and

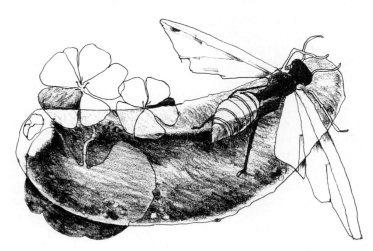

vet, and rippling against the banks in silent, velvet waves. She saw the carriage drawn up to one side of the road, and the little group on the grass, their faces and hands white in the moonlight. She saw the pale dress of the woman outspread and her folded parasol, lying on the grass like a huge pearl crochet hook. Apart from them, with his supper in a cloth on his knees, sat the coachman. "Have a dill pickle," said he, and although she was not certain what a dill pickle was, she saw the greenish glass jar with a red chili like a parrot's beak glimmering through. She

dropped into the same sea, content to be drowned, like mournful lovers. But now, the surprising thing was that it was he who held back. He who said:

"What a marvellous listener you are. When you look at me with those wild eyes I feel that I could tell you things that I would never breathe to another human being."

Was there just a hint of mockery in his voice or was it her fancy? She could not be sure.

"Before I met you," he said, "I had never spoken of myself to anybody. How well I remember one night, the night that I brought you the little

Christmas tree, telling you all about my childhood. And of how I was so miserable that I ran away and lived under a cart in our yard for two days without being discovered. And you listened, and your eyes shone, and I felt that you had even made the little Christmas tree listen too, as in a fairy story."

But of that evening she had remembered a little pot of caviare. It had cost seven and sixpence. He could not get over it. Think of it—a tiny jar like that costing seven and sixpence. While she ate it he watched her, delighted and shocked.

"No, really, that is eating money. You could not get seven shillings into a little pot that size. Only think of the profit they must make. . . ." And he had begun some immensely complicated calculations. . . . But now good-bye to the caviare. The Christmas tree was on the table, and the little boy lay under the cart with his head pillowed on the yard dog.

"The dog was called Bosun," she cried delightedly.

But he did not follow. "Which dog? Had you a dog? I don't remember a dog at all."

"No, no. I mean the yard dog when you were a little boy." He laughed and snapped the cigarette case to.

"Was he? Do you know I had forgotten that. It seems such ages ago. I cannot believe that it is only six years. After I had recognized you to-day—I had to take such a leap—I had to take a leap over my whole life to get back to that time. I was such a kid then." He drummed on the table. "I've often thought how I must have bored you.

And now I understand so perfectly why you wrote to me as you did—although at the time that letter nearly finished my life. I found it again the other day, and I couldn't help laughing as I read it. It was so clever—such a true picture of me." He glanced up. "You're not going?"

She had buttoned her collar again and drawn down her veil.

"Yes, I am afraid I must," she said, and managed a smile. Now she knew that he had been mocking.

"Ah, no, please," he pleaded. "Don't go just for a moment," and he caught up one of her gloves from the table and clutched at it as if that would hold her. "I see so few people to talk to nowadays, that I have turned into a sort of barbarian," he said. "Have I said something to hurt you?"

"Not a bit," she lied. But as she watched him draw her glove through his fingers, gently, gently, her anger really did die down, and besides, at the moment he looked more like himself of six years ago. . . .

"What I really wanted then," he said softly, "was to be a sort of carpet—to make myself into a sort of carpet for you to walk on so that you need not be hurt by the sharp stones and the mud that you hated so. It was nothing more positive than that—nothing more selfish. Only I did desire, eventually, to turn into a magic carpet and carry you away to all those lands you longed to see."

As he spoke she lifted her head as though she drank something; the strange beast in her bosom began to purr. . . .

"I felt that you were more lonely

than anybody else in the world," he went on, "and yet, perhaps, that you were the only person in the world who was really, truly alive. Born out of your time," he murmured, stroking the glove, "fated."

Ah, God! What had she done! How had she dared to throw away her happiness like this. This was the only man who had ever understood her. Was it too late? Could it be too late? *She* was that glove that he held in his fingers. . . .

"And then the fact that you had no friends and never had made friends with people. How I understood that, for neither had I. Is it just the same now?"

"Yes," she breathed. "Just the same. I am as alone as ever."

"So am I," he laughed gently, "just the same."

Suddenly with a quick gesture he handed her back the glove and scraped his chair on the floor. "But what seemed to me so mysterious then is perfectly plain to me now. And to you, too, of course. . . . It simply was that we were such egoists, so self-engrossed, so wrapped up in ourselves that we hadn't a corner in our hearts for anybody else. Do you know," he cried, naive and hearty, and dreadfully like another side of that old self again, "I began studying a Mind System when I was in Russia, and I found that we were not peculiar at all. It's quite a well known form of . . ."

She had gone. He sat there, thunder-struck, astounded beyond words. . . . And then he asked the waitress for his bill.

"But the cream has not been touched," he said. "Please do not charge me for it."

Considerations

This is almost a mystery story. We are given a number of clues, but we are left wondering what happened to this man and woman six years ago and what has happened to each of them in the intervening time. When the man tells her of a coachman offering him a dill pickle, it is as though he is pointing out the quaint customs of the people; she translates the story in her mind into a much more formal setting with the coachman sitting apart from the group "with his supper in a cloth on his knees." The incident with the dill pickle—an object so mundane, yet significant enough to give the story its title—holds the key to the difference between their perceptions.

What is the discrepancy between what he remembers of their relationship and the aspects of it upon which he chose to model his life? In what ways have they reversed roles? How is her receptiveness to him now ironic? What is the significance of the difference between the real flowers of their first meeting and the paper flowers on the table that separates them now? What does his final comment suggest about his ability to feel?

Hills Like White Elephants

ERNEST HEMINGWAY

The hills across the valley of the Ebro were long and white. On this side there was no shade and no trees and the station was between two lines of rails in the sun. Close against the side of the station there was the warm shadow of the building and a curtain, made of strings of bamboo beads, hung across the open door into the bar, to keep out flies. The American and the girl with him sat at a table in the shade, outside the building. It was very hot and the express from Barcelona would come in forty minutes. It stopped at this junction for two minutes and went on to Madrid.

"What should we drink?" the girl asked. She had taken off her hat and put it on the table.

"It's pretty hot," the man said.

"Let's drink beer."

"Dos cervezas," the man said into the curtain.

"Big ones?" a woman asked from the doorway.

"Yes. Two big ones."

The woman brought two glasses of beer and two felt pads. She put the felt pads and the beer glasses on the table and looked at the man and the girl. The girl was looking off at the line of hills. They were white in the sun and the country was brown and dry.

"They look like white elephants," she said.

"I've never seen one," the man drank his beer.

"No, you wouldn't have."

"I might have," the man said. "Just because you say I wouldn't have doesn't prove anything."

The girl looked at the bead curtain. "They've painted something on it," she said. "What does it say?"

"Anis del Toro. It's a drink."

"Could we try it?"

The man called "Listen" through the curtain. The woman came out from the bar.

"Four reales."

"We want two Anis del Toro."

"With water?"

"Do you want it with water?"

"I don't know," the girl said. "Is it good with water?"

"It's all right."

"You want them with water?" asked the woman.

"Yes, with water."

"It tastes like licorice," the girl said and put the glass down.

"That's the way with everything."

"Yes," said the girl. "Everything tastes of licorice. Especially all the things you've waited so long for, like absinthe."

"Oh, cut it out."

"You started it," the girl said. "I was being amused. I was having a fine time."

"Well, let's try and have a fine time."

"All right. I was trying. I said the mountains looked like white elephants. Wasn't that bright?"

"That was bright."

"I wanted to try this new drink. That's all we do, isn't it—look at things and try new drinks?"

"I guess so."

The girl looked across at the hills.

"They're lovely hills," she said. "They don't really look like white elephants. I just meant the coloring of their skin through the trees."

"Should we have another drink?"

"All right."

The warm wind blew the bead curtain against the table.

"The beer's nice and cool," the man said.

"It's lovely," the girl said.

"It's really an awfully simple operation, Jig," the man said. "It's not really an operation at all."

The girl looked at the ground the table legs rested on.

"I know you wouldn't mind it, Jig. It's really not anything. It's just to let the air in."

The girl did not say anything.

"I'll go with you and I'll stay with you all the time. They just let the air in and then it's all perfectly natural."

"Then what will we do afterward?"

"We'll be fine afterward. Just like we were before."

"What makes you think so?"

"That's the only thing that bothers us. It's the only thing that's made us unhappy."

The girl looked at the bead curtain, put her hand out and took hold of two of the strings of beads.

"And you think then we'll be all right and be happy."

"I know we will. You don't have to be afraid. I've known lots of people that have done it."

"So have I," said the girl. "And afterward they were all so happy."

"Well," the man said, "if you don't want to you don't have to. I wouldn't have you do it if you didn't want to. But I know it's perfectly simple."

"And you really want to?"

"I think it's the best thing to do. But I don't want you to do it if you don't really want to."

"And if I do it you'll be happy and things will be like they were and you'll love me?"

"I love you now. You know I love you."

"I know. But if I do it, then it will be nice again if I say things are like white elephants, and you'll like it?"

"I'll love it. I love it now but I just can't think about it. You know how I get when I worry."

"If I do it you won't ever worry?"

"I won't worry about that because it's perfectly simple."

"Then I'll do it. Because I don't care about me."

"What do you mean?"

"I don't care about me."

"Well, I care about you."

"Oh, yes. But I don't care about

me. And I'll do it and then everything will be fine."

"I don't want you to do it if you feel that way."

The girl stood up and walked to the end of the station. Across, on the other side, were fields of grain and trees along the banks of the Ebro. Far away, beyond the river, were mountains. The shadow of a cloud moved across the field of grain and she saw the river through the trees.

"And we could have all this," she said. "And we could have everything and every day we make it more impossible."

"What did you say?"

"I said we could have everything."

"We can have everything."

"No, we can't."

"We can have the whole world."

"No, we can't."

"We can go everywhere."

"No, we can't. It isn't ours any more."

"It's ours."

"No, it isn't. And once they take it away, you never get it back."

"But they haven't taken it away."

"We'll wait and see."

"Come on back in the shade," he said. "You mustn't feel that way."

"I don't feel any way," the girl said. "I just know things."

"I don't want you to do anything that you don't want to do—"

"Nor that isn't good for me," she said. "I know. Could we have another beer?"

"All right. But you've got to realize—"

"I realize," the girl said. "Can't we maybe stop talking?"

They sat down at the table and the girl looked across at the hills on the dry side of the valley and the man looked at her and at the table.

"You've got to realize," he said, "that I don't want you to do it if you don't want to. I'm perfectly willing to go through with it if it means anything to you."

"Doesn't it mean anything to you? We could get along."

"Of course it does. But I don't want anybody but you. I don't want any one else. And I know it's perfectly simple."

"Yes, you know it's perfectly simple."

"It's all right for you to say that, but I do know it."

"Would you do something for me now?"

"I'd do anything for you."

"Would you please please please please please please please stop talking?"

He did not say anything but looked at the bags against the wall of the station. There were labels on them from all the hotels where they had spent nights.

"But I don't want you to," he said, "I don't care anything about it."

"I'll scream," the girl said.

The woman came out through the curtains with two glasses of beer and put them down on the damp felt pads. "The train comes in five minutes," she said.

"What did she say?" asked the girl.

"That the train is coming in five minutes."

The girl smiled brightly at the woman, to thank her.

"I'd better take the bags over to the other side of the station," the man said. She smiled at him.

"All right. Then come back and we'll finish the beer."

He picked up the two heavy bags and carried them around the station to the other tracks. He looked up the tracks but could not see the train. Coming back, he walked through the barroom, where people waiting for the train were drinking. He drank an Anis at the bar and looked at the people. They were all waiting reasonably for the train. He went out through the bead curtain. She was sitting at the table and smiled at him.

"Do you feel better?" he asked.

"I feel fine," she said. "There's nothing wrong with me. I feel fine."

Considerations

In "Hills Like White Elephants" the main characters are again a man and a woman who have had some sort of emotional relationship before the story opens. The setting here is raw, as is the situation. The dialogue is Hemingway at his best—terse, clear, believable. The characters reveal themselves; the author makes no comment.

Much of our feeling about the couple comes from what the girl says. Her remarks are bitter, but we accept them as true. She sums up the sterility and pointlessness of their lives by noting, "That's all we do, isn't it—look at things and try new drinks." The relationship is dry and dying, but it may be too valuable to discard even though it seems useless. If the man has his way, the embryo will be aborted and the two adults will continue in the future as they did in the past.

The hills are "like white elephants." What might the two sides of the valley represent? In what way are they a metaphor for the decision about the unborn child?

At one point we read that the man sees people waiting "reasonably" for the train. Does this mean that in the author's opinion the woman is unreasonable? Or is the author simply stating things from the man's point of view? To his egocentric mind, is she not acting unreasonably? Why would she want to trade the known and relatively comfortable relationship they have had for an uncertain and complicated future?

After we read the last line of the story, a puzzling question remains. Do these young people go on to Madrid, the city they are headed for in the beginning? Or do they go in the other direction? At first we assume that they are going to go on; we believe that the girl has agreed to the abortion and that the man is going to get his way. But the story says that he carries the bags to the *other* side of the station and that when he comes back, "she was sitting at the table and smiled at him." He asks her if she feels better now. Does the question mean that he has changed his mind and that they will keep this child, or were the bags on the wrong side of the station to begin with?

The Use of Force

WILLIAM CARLOS WILLIAMS

They were new patients to me, all I had was the name Olson. Please come down as soon as you can, my daughter is very sick.

When I arrived I was met by the mother, a big startled looking woman, very clean and apologetic who merely said, Is this the doctor? and let me in. In the back, she added. You must excuse us, doctor, we have her in the kitchen where it is warm. It is very damp here sometimes.

The child was fully dressed and sitting on her father's lap near the kitchen table. He tried to get up, but I motioned for him not to bother, took off my overcoat and started to look things over. I could see that they were all very nervous, eyeing me up and down distrustfully. As often, in such cases, they weren't telling me more than they had to, it was up to me to tell them: that's why they were spending three dollars on me.

The child was fairly eating me up with her cold, steady eyes, and no expression to her face whatever. She did not move and seemed, inwardly, quiet; an unusually attractive little thing, and as strong as a heifer in appearance. But her face was flushed, she was breathing rapidly, and I realized that she had a high fever. She had magnificent blonde hair, in profusion. One of those picture children often reproduced in advertising leaflets and the photogravure sections of the Sunday papers.

She's had a fever for three days, began the father and we don't know what it comes from. My wife has given her things, you know, like people do, but it don't do no good. And there's been a lot of sickness around. So we tho't you'd better look her over and tell us what is the matter.

As doctors often do I took a trial shot at it as a point of departure. Has she had a sore throat?

Both parents answered me together. No . . . No, she says her throat don't hurt her.

Does your throat hurt you? added the mother to the child. But the little girl's expression didn't change nor did she move her eyes from my face.

Have you looked?

I tried to, said the mother, but I couldn't see.

As it happens we had been having a number of cases of diphtheria in the school to which this child went during that month and we were all, quite apparently, thinking of that, though no one had as yet spoken of the thing.

Well, I said, suppose we take a look at the throat first. I smiled in my best professional manner and asking for the child's first name I said, come on, Mathilda, open your mouth and let's take a look at your throat.

Nothing doing.

Aw, come on, I coaxed, just open your mouth wide and let me take a look. Look, I said opening both hands wide, I haven't anything in my hands. Just open up and let me see.

Such a nice man, put in the mother. Look how kind he is to you. Come on, do what he tells you to. He won't hurt you.

At that I ground my teeth in disgust. If only they wouldn't use the word "hurt" I might be able to get somewhere. But I did not allow myself to be hurried or disturbed but speaking quietly and slowly I approached the child again.

As I moved my chair a little nearer suddenly with one catlike movement both her hands clawed instinctively for my eyes and she almost reached them too. In fact she knocked my glasses flying and they fell, though unbroken, several feet away from me on the kitchen floor.

Both the mother and father almost turned themselves inside out in embarrassment and apology. You bad girl, said the mother, taking her and shaking her by one arm. Look what you've done. The nice man . . .

For heaven's sake, I broke in. Don't call me a nice man to her. I'm here to look at her throat on the chance that she might have diphtheria and possibly die of it. But that's nothing to her. Look here, I said to the child, we're going to look at your throat. You're old enough to understand what I'm saying. Will you open it now by yourself or shall we have to open it for you?

Not a move. Even her expression hadn't changed. Her breaths however were coming faster and faster. Then the battle began. I had to do it. I had to have a throat culture for her own protection. But first I told the parents that it was entirely up to them. I explained the danger but said that I would not insist on a throat examination so long as they would take the responsibility.

If you don't do what the doctor says you'll have to go to the hospital, the mother admonished her severely.

Oh yeah? I had to smile to myself. After all, I had already fallen in love with the savage brat, the parents were contemptible to me. In the ensuing struggle they grew more and more abject, crushed, exhausted while she surely rose to magnificent heights of insane fury of effort bred of her terror of me.

The father tried his best, and he was a big man but the fact that she was his daughter, his shame at her behavior and his dread of hurting her made him release her just at the critical times when I had almost achieved success, till I wanted to kill him. But his dread also that she might have diphtheria made him tell me to go on, go on though he himself was almost fainting, while the mother moved back and forth behind us raising and lowering her hands in an agony of apprehension.

Put her in front of you on your lap,

I ordered, and hold both her wrists.

But as soon as he did the child let out a scream. Don't, you're hurting me. Let go of my hands. Let them go I tell you. Then she shrieked terrifyingly, hysterically. Stop it! Stop it! You're killing me!

Do you think she can stand it, doctor! said the mother.

You get out, said the husband to his wife. Do you want her to die of diphtheria?

Come on now, hold her, I said.

Then I grasped the child's head with my left hand and tried to get the wooden tongue depressor between her teeth. She fought, with clenched teeth, desperately! But now I also had grown furious—at a child. I tried to hold myself down but I couldn't. I know how to expose a throat for inspection. And I did my best. When finally I got the wooden spatula behind the last teeth and just the point of it into the mouth cavity, she opened up for an instant but before I could see anything she came down again and gripping the wooden blade between her molars she reduced it to splinters before I could get it out again.

Aren't you ashamed, the mother yelled at her. Aren't you ashamed to act like that in front of the doctor?

Get me a smooth-handled spoon of some sort, I told the mother. We're going through with this. The child's mouth was already bleeding. Her tongue was cut and she was scream-

ing in wild hysterical shrieks. Perhaps I should have desisted and come back in an hour or more. No doubt it would have been better. But I have seen at least two children lying dead in bed of neglect in such cases, and feeling that I must get a diagnosis now or never I went at it again. But the worst of it was that I too had got beyond reason. I could have torn the child apart in my own fury and enjoyed it. It was a pleasure to attack her. My face was burning with it.

The damned little brat must be protected against her own idiocy, one says to one's self at such times. Others must be protected against her. It is a social necessity. And all these things are true. But a blind fury, a feeling of adult shame, bred of a longing for muscular release are the operatives. One goes on to the end.

In a final unreasoning assault I overpowered the child's neck and jaws. I forced the heavy silver spoon back of her teeth and down her throat till she gagged. And there it was— both tonsils covered with membrane. She had fought valiantly to keep me from knowing her secret. She had been hiding that sore throat for three days at least and lying to her parents in order to escape just such an outcome as this.

Now truly she was furious. She had been on the defensive before but now she attacked. Tried to get off her father's lap and fly at me while tears of defeat blinded her eyes.

Considerations

This story, written by a doctor, is more than a doctor's report of a house call.

The bare elements of the scene we are shown are not uncommon to the general physician; they may even be familiar to us. Few children (or adults, though they usually control themselves better) enjoy being examined by a doctor. Many people face a doctor reluctantly because they do not want their worst fears confirmed, regardless of how medically advisable it may be to settle the matter. Most parents are indecisive and inept when trying to choose between giving their children temporary mental or physical pain and helping carry out what they hope will be beneficial treatment. This kind of parental dithering (and often an irritated contempt of doctors) has been a major contributing factor in getting parents barred from being with their children in doctor's offices and hospitals.

Such mundane elements are, however, only the pretext for Williams to give us a more important description—the description of what is involved in the use of force. What began ordinarily enough in an attempt to follow the appropriate medical procedures ends in a battle of wills. The doctor actually admires the child's spirit in thwarting his efforts. But he knows he must conquer it, and like diphtheria, pleasure in the use of force can spread quickly: "I too had got beyond reason. I could have torn the child apart in my own fury and enjoyed it. It was a pleasure to attack her."

Suddenly we see that the problem is no longer medical—it is psychological and philosophical. Here in microcosm is the kind of impulse that has operated for centuries as incredible evil has been done in the name of good. It may begin with genuine concern, but soon determination to overcome resistance becomes the key to the situation. Finally, a dark and sinister impulse converts the whole encounter into an occasion for the sensual enjoyment of power. Primitive instincts now overpower reason. What a pleasant feeling it is to find such valid justification for giving reign to one's need to dominate.

Has the doctor won? He did get his throat culture and he did impose his will on the child. But is the story finished? Obviously the use of force was in the doctor's favor this time, but what will happen in future years? Is not the use of force always a risk, not only because the victory is likely to be only temporary, but because it may lead to cancer of the soul?

A Rose for Emily

WILLIAM FAULKNER

1

When Miss Emily Grierson died, our whole town went to her funeral: the men through a sort of respectful affection for a fallen monument, the women mostly out of curiosity to see the inside of her house, which no one save an old manservant—a combined gardener and cook—had seen in at least ten years.

It was a big, squarish frame house that had once been white, decorated with cupolas and spires and scrolled balconies in the heavily lightsome style of the seventies, set on what had once been our most select street. But garages and cotton gins had encroached and obliterated even the august names of that neighborhood; only Miss Emily's house was left, lifting its stubborn and coquettish decay above the cotton wagons and the gasoline pumps—an eyesore among eyesores. And now Miss Emily had gone to join the representatives of those august names where they lay in the cedar-bemused cemetery among the ranked and anonymous graves of Union and Confederate soldiers who fell at the battle of Jefferson.

Alive, Miss Emily had been a tradition, a duty, and a care; a sort of hereditary obligation upon the town, dating from that day in 1894 when Colonel Sartoris, the mayor—he who fathered the edict that no Negro woman should appear on the streets without an apron—remitted her taxes, the dispensation dating from the death of her father on into perpetuity. Not that Miss Emily would have accepted charity. Colonel Sartoris invented an involved tale to the effect that Miss Emily's father had loaned money to the town, which the town, as a matter of business, preferred this way of repaying. Only a man of Colonel Sartoris' generation and thought could have invented it, and only a woman could have believed it.

When the next generation, with its more modern ideas, became mayors and aldermen, this arrangement created some little dissatisfaction. On the first of the year they mailed her a tax notice. February came, and there was no reply. They wrote her a formal letter, asking her to call at the sheriff's office at her convenience. A week later the mayor wrote her himself, offering to call or send his car for her and received in reply a note on paper of an archaic shape, in a thin flowing calligraphy in faded ink, to the effect that she no longer went out at all. The tax notice was also enclosed, without comment.

They called a special meeting of the Board of Aldermen. A deputation waited upon her, knocked at the door through which no visitor had passed since she ceased giving china-painting lessons eight or ten years earlier. They were admitted by the old Negro into a dim hall from which a stairway mounted into still more shadow. It smelled of dust and disuse—a close, dank smell. The Negro led them into the parlor. It was furnished in heavy, leather-covered furniture. When the Negro opened the blinds of one window, they could see that the leather was cracked; and when they sat down, a faint dust rose sluggishly about their thighs, spinning with slow motes in the single sun-ray. On a tarnished gilt easel before the fireplace stood a crayon portrait of Miss Emily's father.

They rose when she entered—a small, fat woman in black, with a thin gold chain descending to her waist and vanishing into her belt, leaning on an ebony cane with tarnished gold head. Her skeleton was small and spare; perhaps that was why what would have been merely plumpness in another was obesity in her. She looked bloated, like a body long submerged in motionless water, and of that pallid hue. Her eyes, lost in the fatty ridges of her face, looked like two small pieces of coal pressed into a lump of dough as they moved from one face to another while the visitors stated their errand.

She did not ask them to sit. She just stood in the door and listened quietly until the spokesman came to a stumbling halt. Then they could hear the invisible watch ticking at the end of the gold chain.

Her voice was dry and cold. "I have no taxes in Jefferson. Colonel Sar-

toris explained it to me. Perhaps one of you can gain access to the city records and satisfy yourselves."

"But we have. We are the city authorities, Miss Emily. Didn't you get a notice from the sheriff, signed by him?"

"I received a paper, yes," Miss Emily said. "Perhaps he considers himself the sheriff . . . I have no taxes in Jefferson."

"But there is nothing on the books to show that, you see. We must go by the—"

"See Colonel Sartoris. I have no taxes in Jefferson."

"But, Miss Emily—"

"See Colonel Sartoris." (Colonel Sartoris had been dead almost ten years.) "I have no taxes in Jefferson. Tobe!" The Negro appeared. "Show these gentlemen out."

2

So she vanquished them, horse and foot, just as she had vanquished their fathers thirty years before about the smell. That was two years after her father's death and a short time after her sweetheart—the one we believed would marry her—had deserted her. After her father's death she went out very little; after her sweetheart went away, people hardly saw her at all. A few of the ladies had the temerity to call, but were not received, and the only sign of life about the place was the Negro man—a young man then—going in and out with a market basket.

"Just as if a man—any man—could keep a kitchen properly," the ladies said; so they were not surprised when the smell developed. It was another link between the gross, teeming world and the high and mighty Griersons.

A neighbor, a woman, complained to the major, Judge Stevens, eighty years old.

"But what will you have me do about it, madam?" he said.

"Why, send her word to stop it," the woman said. "Isn't there a law?"

"I'm sure that won't be necessary," Judge Stevens said. "It's probably just a snake or a rat that nigger of hers killed in the yard. I'll speak to him about it."

The next day he received two more complaints, one from a man who came in diffident deprecation. "We really must do something about it, Judge. I'd be the last one in the world to bother Miss Emily, but we've got to do something." That night the Board of Aldermen met—three graybeards and one younger man, a member of the rising generation.

"It's simple enough," he said. "Send her word to have her place cleaned up. Give her a certain time to do it in, and if she don't . . ."

"Dammit, sir," Judge Stevens said, "will you accuse a lady to her face of smelling bad?"

So the next night, after midnight, four men crossed Miss Emily's lawn and slunk about the house like burglars, sniffing along the base of the brickwork and at the cellar openings while one of them performed a regular sowing motion with his hand out of a sack slung from his shoulder. They broke open the cellar door and sprinkled lime there, and in all the outbuildings. As they recrossed the lawn, a window that had been dark was lighted and Miss Emily sat in it, the light behind her, and her upright torso motionless as that of an idol. They crept quietly across the lawn and into the shadow of the locusts that lined the street. After a week or two the smell went away.

That was when people had begun to feel really sorry for her. People in our town, remembering how old lady Wyatt, her great-aunt, had gone completely crazy at last, believed that the Griersons held themselves a little too high for what they really were. None of the young men were quite good enough for Miss Emily and such. We had long thought of them as a tableau, Miss Emily a slender figure in white in the background, her father a spraddled silhouette in the foreground, his back to her and clutching a horsewhip, the two of them framed by the back-flung front door. So when she got to be thirty and was still single, we were not pleased exactly, but vindicated; even with insanity in the family she wouldn't have turned down all of her chances if they had really materialized.

When her father died, it got about that the house was all that was left to her; and in a way, people were glad. At last they could pity Miss Emily. Being left alone, and a pauper, she had become humanized. Now she too would know the old thrill and the old despair of a penny more or less.

The day after his death all the ladies prepared to call at the house and offer condolence and aid, as is our custom. Miss Emily met them at the door, dressed as usual and with no trace of grief on her face. She told them that her father was not dead. She did that for three days, with the ministers calling on her, and the doctors, trying to persuade her to let them dispose of the body. Just as they were about to resort to law and force, she broke down, and they buried her father quickly.

We did not say she was crazy then. We believed she had to do that. We remembered all the young men her father had driven away, and we knew that with nothing left, she would have to cling to that which had robbed her, as people will.

3

She was sick for a long time. When we saw her again, her hair was cut short, making her look like a girl, with a vague resemblance to those angels in colored church windows— sort of tragic and serene.

The town had just let the contracts for paving the sidewalks, and in the summer after her father's death they began the work. The construction company came with niggers and mules and machinery, and a foreman named Homer Barron, a Yankee—a big, dark, ready man, with a big voice and eyes lighter than his face. The little boys would follow in groups to hear him cuss the niggers, and the niggers singing in time to the rise and fall of picks. Pretty soon he knew everybody in town. Whenever you heard a lot of laughing anywhere about the square, Homer Barron would be in the center of the group. Presently we began to see him and Miss Emily on Sunday afternoons driving in the yellow-wheeled buggy and the matched team of bays from the livery stable.

At first we were glad that Miss Emily would have an interest, because the ladies all said, "Of course a Grierson would not think seriously of a Northerner, a day laborer." But there were still others, older people, who said that even grief could not cause a real lady to forget *noblesse oblige*—without calling it *noblesse oblige*. They just said, "Poor Emily. Her kinsfolk should come to her." She had some kin in Alabama; but years ago her father had fallen out with them over the estate of old lady Wyatt, the crazy woman, and there was no communication between the two families. They had not even been represented at the funeral.

And as soon as the old people said, "Poor Emily," the whispering began. "Do you suppose it's really so?" they said to one another. "Of course it is. What else could . . ." This behind their hands; rustling of craned silk and satin behind jalousies closed upon the sun of Sunday afternoon as the thin, swift clop-clop-clop of the matched team passed: "Poor Emily."

She carried her head high enough —even when we believed that she was fallen. It was as if she demanded more than ever the recognition of her dignity as the last Grierson; as if it had wanted that touch of earthiness to reaffirm her imperviousness. Like when she bought the rat poison, the arsenic. That was over a year after they begun to say "Poor Emily," and while the two female cousins were visiting her.

"I want some poison," she said to

the druggist. She was over thirty then, still a slight woman, though thinner than usual, with cold, haughty black eyes in a face the flesh of which was strained across the temples and about the eyesockets as you imagine a lighthouse-keeper's face ought to look. "I want some poison," she said.

"Yes, Miss Emily. What kind? For rats and such? I'd recom—"

"I want the best you have. I don't care what kind."

The druggist named several. "They'll kill anything up to an elephant. But what you want is—"

"Arsenic," Miss Emily said. "Is that a good one?"

"Is . . . arsenic? Yes, ma'am. But what you want—"

"I want arsenic."

The druggist looked down at her. She looked back at him, erect, her face like a strained flag. "Why, of course," the druggist said. "If that's what you want. But the law requires you to tell what you are going to use it for."

Miss Emily just stared at him, her head tilted back in order to look him eye for eye, until he looked away and went and got the arsenic and wrapped it up. The Negro delivery boy brought her the package; the druggist didn't come back. When she opened the package at home there was written on the box, under the skull and bones: "For rats."

4

So the next day we all said, "She will kill herself"; and we said it would be the best thing. When she had first begun to be seen with Homer Barron, we had said, "She will marry him." Then we said, "She will persuade him yet," because Homer himself had remarked—he liked men, and it was known that he drank with the younger men in the Elk's Club—that he was not a marrying man. Later we said, "Poor Emily," behind the jalousies as they passed on Sunday afternoon in the glittering buggy, Miss Emily with her head high and Homer Barron with his hat cocked and a cigar in his teeth, reins and whip in a yellow glove.

Then some of the ladies began to say that it was a disgrace to the town, and a bad example to the young people. The men did not want to interfere, but at last the ladies forced the Baptist minister—Miss Emily's people were Episcopal—to call upon her. He would never divulge what happened during that interview, but he refused to go back again. The next Sunday they again drove about the streets, and the following day the minister's wife wrote to Miss Emily's relations in Alabama.

So she had blood-kin under her roof again and we sat back to watch developments. At first nothing happened. Then we were sure that they were to be married. We learned that Miss Emily had been to the jeweler's and ordered a man's toilet set in silver, with the letters H. B. on each piece. Two days later we learned that she had bought a complete outfit of men's clothing, including a nightshirt, and we said, "They are married." We were really glad. We were glad because the two female cousins were even more Grierson than Miss Emily had ever been.

So we were not surprised when

Homer Barron—the streets had been finished some time since—was gone. We were a little disappointed that there was not a public blowing-off, but we believed that he had gone on to prepare for Miss Emily's coming, or to give her a chance to get rid of the cousins. (By that time it was a cabal, and we were all Miss Emily's allies to help circumvent the cousins.) Sure enough, after another week they departed. And, as we had expected all along, within three days Homer Barron was back in town. A neighbor saw the Negro man admit him at the kitchen door at dusk one evening.

And that was the last we saw of Homer Barron. And of Miss Emily for some time. The Negro man went in and out with the market basket, but the front door remained closed. Now and then we would see her at a window for a moment, as the men did that night when they sprinkled the lime, but for almost six months she did not appear on the streets. Then we knew that this was to be expected too; as if the quality of her father which had thwarted her woman's life so many times had been too virulent and too furious to die.

When we next saw Miss Emily, she had grown fat and her hair was turning gray. During the next few years it grew grayer and grayer until it attained an even pepper-and-salt iron-gray, when it ceased turning. Up to the day of her death at seventy-four it was still that vigorous iron-gray, like the hair of an active man.

From that time on her front door remained closed, save for a period of six or seven years, when she was about forty, during which she gave lessons in china-painting. She fitted up a studio in one of the downstairs rooms, where the daughters and grand-daughters of Colonel Sartoris' contemporaries were sent to her with the same regularity and in the same spirit that they were sent to church on Sundays with a twenty-five cent piece for the collection plate. Meanwhile her taxes had been remitted.

The newer generation became the backbone and the spirit of the town, and the painting pupils grew up and fell away and did not send their children to her with boxes of color and tedious brushes and pictures cut from the ladies' magazines. The front door closed upon the last one and remained closed for good. When the town got free postal delivery, Miss Emily alone refused to let them fasten the metal numbers above her door and attach a mailbox to it. She would not listen to them.

Daily, monthly, yearly we watched the Negro grow grayer and more stooped, going in and out with the market basket. Each December we sent her a tax notice, which would be returned by the post office a week later, unclaimed. Now and then we would see her in one of the downstairs windows—she had evidently shut up the top floor of the house—like the carven torso of an idol in a niche, looking or not looking at us, we could never tell which. Thus she passed from generation to generation—dear, inescapable, impervious, tranquil, and perverse.

And so she died. Fell ill in the house filled with dust and shadows, with only a doddering Negro man to wait on her. We did not even know she was sick; we had long since given up trying to get any information from the Negro. He talked to no one, probably not even to her, for his voice had grown harsh and rusty, as if from disuse.

She died in one of the downstairs rooms, in a heavy walnut bed with a curtain, her gray head propped on a pillow yellow and moldy with age and lack of sunlight.

5

The Negro met the first of the ladies at the front door and let them in, with their hushed, sibilant voices and their quick, curious glances, and then he disappeared. He walked right through the house and out the back and was not seen again.

The two female cousins came at once. They held the funeral on the second day, with the town coming to look at Miss Emily beneath a mass of bought flowers, with the crayon face of her father musing profoundly above the bier and the ladies sibilant and macabre; and the very old men—some in their brushed Confederate uniforms—on the porch and the lawn, talking of Miss Emily as if she had been a contemporary of theirs, believing that they had danced with her and courted her perhaps, confusing time with its mathematical progression, as the old do, to whom all the past is not a diminishing road but, instead, a huge meadow which no winter ever quite touches, divided from them now by the narrow bottleneck of the most recent decade of years.

Already we knew that there was one room in that region above stairs which no one had been in forty years,

and which would have to be forced. They waited until Miss Emily was decently in the ground before they opened it.

The violence of breaking down the door seemed to fill this room with pervading dust. A thin, acrid pall as of the tomb seemed to lie everywhere upon this room decked and furnished as for a bridal; upon the valance curtains of faded rose color, upon the roseshaded lights, upon the dressing table, upon the delicate array of crystal and the man's toilet things backed with tarnished silver, silver so tarnished that the monogram was obscured. Among them lay a collar and tie, as if they had just been removed, which, lifted, left upon the surface a pale crescent in the dust. Upon a chair hung the suit, carefully folded; beneath it the two mute shoes and the discarded socks.

The man himself lay in the bed.

For a long while we just stood there, looking down at the profound and fleshless grin. The body had apparently once lain in the attitude of an embrace, but now the long sleep that outlasts love, that conquers even the grimace of love, had cuckolded him. What was left of him, rotted beneath what was left of the nightshirt, had become inextricable from the bed in which he lay; and upon him and upon the pillow beside him lay that even coating of the patient and biding dust.

Then we noticed that in the second pillow was the indentation of a head. One of us lifted something from it, and leaning forward, that faint and invisible dust dry and acrid in the nostrils, we saw a long strand of iron-gray hair.

Considerations

Haunting is the term that best describes this story. Long after you forget the plots and characters of most other works of literature, you'll remember this one. How is such a deep impression created? Not by explicit gory details, certainly.

Faulkner invites the reader to be part of his small town—"our most select street." "We were not pleased exactly, but vindicated." The tale might be told by a boy who was growing up there and curious enough to note it all down. It might be one of the older ladies—but it is definitely an outsider. The actions of the upper class are seen "through a glass darkly" and known only by hearsay. There's gossip and speculation enough, but not much fuel for the fire. For example, what happened while Miss Emily was sick? The reader and (apparently) the writer don't know—just that: "She was sick for a long time. When we saw her again. . . ." It's easy to imagine each new bit of information being seized on, and, going the rounds, being wrung dry. But how much can one ever really expect to know about one's neighbors?

The foundations for behavior on all sides are firmly laid. Miss Emily's irascible and domineering father, the disappearing sweetheart, the fact of the strange smell when Miss Emily was in her thirties, the purchase of the arsenic, the fact that no stranger (a category which included almost everyone) ever made it past Miss Emily's front parlor.

Still, what is the purpose of all this? Is it merely a piece of Gothic writing or a study of madness? Basically what we are presented with is, to most of us, a seemingly odd method of dealing with a relatively common problem. What seems odd to us in the final quarter of the twentieth century, however, may not be mad but merely the outcome of a different set of standards and rules for behavior. In fact, a recurring motif in Faulkner's work is the contrast between cultures—the old South and the new. Miss Emily could not more obviously be part of the old. "From that time on her front door remained closed, save for a period of six or seven years, when she was about forty, during which she gave lessons in china-painting." "When the town got free postal delivery, Miss Emily alone refused to let them fasten the metal numbers above her door and attach a mailbox to it. She would not listen to them." "Thus she passed from generation to generation—dear, inescapable, impervious, tranquil, and perverse."

How else would a woman of her background, certain of possessing special rights, proud, secretive, disdainful of dependence but without relatives to defend her—especially male—handle an insult or threat from a presumptuous newcomer? Colonel Sartoris, a man of her own background, followed the same set of rules: "He who fathered the edict that no Negro woman should appear on the streets without an apron—

remitted her taxes, the dispensation dating from the death of her father on into perpetuity." Judge Stevens and his peers on the Board of Aldermen operated similarly; they would give Miss Emily no order to clean her place up. "Dammit, sir," Judge Stevens said, "Will you accuse a lady to her face of smelling bad?"

Even the succeeding generations carried some memory of the old distinctions. They tried to tax Miss Emily but accepted her rebuffs. Their curiosity was not allowed to violate the spirit of her right to privacy: "Already we knew that there was one room in that region above the stairs which no one had been in in forty years, and which would have to be forced. They waited until Miss Emily was decently in the ground before they opened it."

Throughout the story there is the feeling of a small town. We would like to believe it could happen only there. The story fits in with some longstanding preconceptions about the way the South handled certain things, but clannishness is not unknown in New England and Western communities as well. However, again according to current beliefs, such clannishness is more a thing of the past. Who knows whether its going may be more to be mourned than applauded? Surely the creeping awareness of a secret madness and the activities hinted at by the closing view of a long gray hair can be handled better than on the front page of the evening tabloids.

The Other Wife

COLETTE

'For two? This way, Monsieur and Madame, there's still a table by the bay window, if Madame and Monsieur would like to enjoy the view.'

Alice followed the *maître d'hôtel*.

'Oh, yes, come on Marc, we'll feel we're having lunch on a boat at sea . . .'

Her husband restrained her, passing his arm through hers.

'We'll be more comfortable there.'

'There? In the middle of all those people? I'd much prefer . . .'

'Please, Alice.'

He tightened his grip in so emphatic a way that she turned round.

'What's the matter with you?'

He said 'sh' very quietly, looking at her intently, and drew her towards the table in the middle.

'What is it, Marc?'

'I'll tell you darling. Let me order lunch. Would you like shrimps? Or eggs in aspic?'

'Whatever *you* like, as you know.'

They smiled at each other, wasting the precious moments of an overworked, perspiring *maître d'hôtel* who stood near to them, suffering from a kind of St. Vitus's dance.

'Shrimps,' ordered Marc. 'And then eggs and bacon. And cold chicken with cos lettuce salad. Cream cheese? *Spécialité de la maison*? We'll settle for the *spécialité*. Two very strong coffees. Please give lunch to my chauffeur, we'll be leaving again at two o'clock. Cider? I don't trust it. . . . Dry champagne.'

He sighed as though he had been moving a wardrobe, gazed at the pale noonday sea, the nearly white sky, then at his wife, finding her pretty in her little Mercury-type hat with its long hanging veil.

'You're looking well, darling. And all this sea-blue colour gives you green eyes, just imagine! And you put on weight when you travel. . . . It's nice, up to a point, but only up to a point!'

Her rounded bosom swelled proudly as she leant over the table.

'Why did you stop me taking that place by the bay window?'

It did not occur to Marc Séguy to tell a lie.

'Because you'd have sat next to someone I know.'

'And whom I don't know?'

'My ex-wife.'

She could not find a word to say and opened her blue eyes wider.

'What of it, darling? It'll happen again. It's not important.'

Alice found her tongue again and asked the inevitable questions in their logical sequence.

"The Other Wife" from THE OTHER WOMAN by Colette, translated by Margaret Crosland. Published in the U.S. by Bobbs-Merrill and the British Commonwealth, including Canada, by Peter Owen, London.

'Did she see you? Did she know that you'd seen her? Point her out to me.'

'Don't turn round at once, I beg you, she must be looking at us. A lady with dark hair, without a hat, she must be staying at this hotel . . . On her own, behind those children in red . . .'

'Yes, I see.'

Sheltered behind broad-brimmed seaside hats, Alice was able to look at the woman who fifteen months earlier had still been her husband's wife. 'Incompatibility,' Marc told her. 'Oh, it was total incompatibility! We divorced like well-brought-up people, almost like friends, quietly and quickly. And I began to love you, and you were able to be happy with me. How lucky we are that in our happiness there haven't been any guilty parties or victims!'

The woman in white, with her smooth, lustrous hair over which the seaside light played in blue patches, was smoking a cigarette, her eyes half closed. Alice turned back to her husband, took some shrimps and butter and ate composedly.

'Why didn't you ever tell me,' she said after a moment's silence, 'that she had blue eyes too?'

'But I'd never thought about it!'

He kissed the hand that she stretched out to the bread basket and she blushed with pleasure. Dark-skinned and plump, she might have seemed slightly earthy, but the changing blue of her eyes, and her wavy golden hair, disguised her as a fragile and soulful blonde. She showed overwhelming gratitude to her husband. She was immodest without knowing it and her entire person revealed overconspicuous signs of extreme happiness.

They ate and drank with good appetite and each thought that the other had forgotten the woman in white. However, Alice sometimes laughed too loudly and Marc was careful of his posture, putting his shoulders back and holding his head up. They waited some time for coffee, in silence. An incandescent stream, a narrow reflection of the high and invisible sun, moved slowly over the sea and shone with unbearable brilliance.

'She's still there, you know,' Alice whispered suddenly.

'Does she embarrass you? Would you like to have coffee somewhere else?'

'Not at all! It's she who ought to be embarrassed! And she doesn't look as though she's having a madly gay time, if you could see her . . .'

'It's not necessary. I know that look of hers.'

'Oh, was she like that?'

He breathed smoke through his nostrils and wrinkled his brows.

'Was she like that? No. To be frank, she wasn't happy with me.'

'Well, my goodness!'

'You're delightfully generous, darling, madly generous. . . . You're an angel, you're. . . . You love me . . . I'm so proud, when I see that look in your eyes . . . yes, the look you have now. . . . She. . . . No doubt I didn't succeed in making her happy. That's all there is to it, I didn't succeed.'

'She's hard to please!'

Alice fanned herself irritably, and cast brief glances at the woman in white who was smoking, her head leaning against the back of the cane chair, her eyes closed with an expression of satisfied lassitude.

Marc shrugged his shoulders modestly.

'That's it,' he admitted. 'What can one do? We have to be sorry for people who are never happy. As for us, we're so happy. . . . Aren't we, darling?'

She didn't reply. She was looking with furtive attention at her husband's face, with its good colour and regular shape, at his thick hair, with its occasional thread of white silk, at his small, well-cared-for hands. She felt dubious for the first time, and asked herself: 'What more did she want, then?'

And until they left, while Marc was paying the bill, asking about the chauffeur and the route, she continued to watch, with envious curiosity, the lady in white, that discontented, hard-to-please, superior woman. . . .

Considerations

This story carries the hallmarks of Colette's usual excellent style: brief, concise, swift descriptive sketches that leave an aftertaste (which makes you wonder if you've quite caught it all), a gentle commentary—if you care to notice it—on the peculiar quirks of human psychology.

This time the focus is on a little-mentioned aspect of the dog-in-the-manger situation. We all like to have the affirmation that what we have chosen is valid, good, and desirable. We want to hear from others not only, "I like your car, I like your house," and so on, but we crave the signs of upset that confirm that we have, so to speak, "acquired" someone that our peers would have wanted. To know that they have rejected our "find" as inferior makes us pause and reassess our choice— have we perhaps become a junk collector, an unwitting treasurer of old unconsidered trifles? Why we should be so uncertain of our own judgment is hard to say, but the trait seems to be rather common.

The cast here is small. We can judge two members by their actions: the pompous husband, self-righteous, directive, not really accustomed to rejection in his well-cushioned world but at this moment at least grateful for the possession (since a possession it so obviously is) of a properly adoring and appreciative woman. The wife, romantic, sensual, voluptuous, from a somewhat lower background, at least initially getting satisfaction out of bending to his wishes—out of the way he physically, and evidently financially fulfills every woman's dreams.

Flight

JOHN STEINBECK

About fifteen miles below Monterey, on the wild coast, the Torres family had their farm, a few sloping acres above a cliff that dropped to the brown reefs and to the hissing white waters of the ocean. Behind the farm the stone mountains stood up against the sky. The farm buildings huddled like little clinging aphids on the mountain skirts, crouched low to the ground as though the wind might blow them into the sea. The little shack, the rattling, rotting barn were gray-bitten with sea salt, beaten by the damp wind until they had taken on the color of the granite hills. Two horses, a red cow and a red calf, half a dozen pigs and a flock of lean, multi-colored chickens stocked the place. A little corn was raised on the sterile slope, and it grew short and thick under the wind, and all the cobs formed on the landward sides of the stalks.

Mama Torres, a lean, dry woman with ancient eyes, had ruled the farm for ten years, ever since her husband tripped over a stone in the field one day and fell full length on a rattlesnake. When one is bitten on the chest there is not much that can be done.

Mama Torres had three children, two undersized black ones of twelve and fourteen, Emilio and Rosy, whom Mama kept fishing on the rocks below the farm when the sea was kind and when the truant officer was in some distant part of Monterey County. And there was Pepé, the tall smiling son of nineteen, a gentle, affectionate boy, but very lazy. Pepé had a tall head, pointed at the top, and from its peak, coarse black hair grew down like a thatch all around. Over his smiling little eyes Mama cut a straight bang so he could see. Pepé had sharp Indian cheekbones and an eagle nose, but his mouth was as sweet and shapely as a girl's mouth, and his chin was fragile and chiseled. He was loose and gangling, all legs and feet and wrists, and he was very lazy. Mama thought him fine and brave, but she never told him so. She said, "Some lazy cow must have got into thy father's family, else how could I have a son like thee." And she said, "When I carried thee, a sneaking lazy coyote came out of the brush and looked at me one day. That must have made thee so."

Pepé smiled sheepishly and stabbed at the ground with his knife to keep the blade sharp and free from rust. It was his inheritance, that knife, his father's knife. The long heavy blade folded back into the black handle. There was a button on the handle. When Pepé pressed the button, the blade leaped out ready for use. The knife was with Pepé always, for it had been his father's knife.

One sunny morning when the sea below the cliff was glinting and blue and the white surf creamed on the reef, when even the stone mountains looked kindly, Mama Torres called out the door of the shack, "Pepé, I have a labor for thee."

There was no answer. Mama listened. From behind the barn she heard a burst of laughter. She lifted her full long skirt and walked in the direction of the noise.

Pepé was sitting on the ground with his back against a box. His white teeth glistened. On either side of him stood the two black ones, tense and expectant. Fifteen feet away a redwood post was set in the ground. Pepé's right hand lay limply in his lap, and in the palm the big black knife rested. The blade was closed back into the handle. Pepé looked smiling at the sky.

Suddenly Emilio cried, "Ya!"

Pepé's wrist flicked like the head of a snake. The blade seemed to fly open in mid-air, and with a thump the point dug into the redwood post, and the black handle quivered. The three burst into excited laughter. Rosy ran to the post and pulled out the knife and brought it back to Pepé. He closed the blade and settled the knife carefully in his listless palm again. He grinned self-consciously at the sky.

"Ya!"

The heavy knife lanced out and sunk into the post again. Mama moved forward like a ship and scattered the play.

"All day you do foolish things with

the knife, like a toy-baby," she stormed. "Get up on thy huge feet that eat up shoes. Get up!" She took him by one loose shoulder and hoisted at him. Pepé grinned sheepishly and came half-heartedly to his feet.

"Look!" Mama cried. "Big lazy, you must catch the horse and put on him thy father's saddle. You must ride to Monterey. The medicine bottle is empty. There is no salt. Go thou now, Peanut! Catch the horse."

A revolution took place in the relaxed figure of Pepé. "To Monterey, me? Alone? *Si,* Mama."

She scowled at him. "Do not think,

big sheep, that you will buy candy. No, I will give you only enough for the medicine and the salt."

Pepé smiled. "Mama, you will put the hatband on the hat?"

She relented then. "Yes, Pepé. You may wear the hatband."

His voice grew insinuating, "And the green handkerchief, Mama?"

"Yes, if you go quickly and return with no trouble, the silk green handkerchief will go. If you make sure to take off the handkerchief when you eat so no spot may fall on it. . . ."

"*Si,* Mama. I will be careful. I am a man."

"Thou? A man? Thou art a peanut."

He went into the rickety barn and brought out a rope, and he walked agilely enough up the hill to catch the horse.

When he was ready and mounted before the door, mounted on his father's saddle that was so old that the oaken frame showed through torn leather in many places, then Mama brought out the round black hat with the tooled leather band, and she reached up and knotted the green silk handkerchief about his neck. Pepé's blue denim coat was much darker than his jeans, for it had been washed much less often.

Mama handed up the big medicine bottle and the silver coins. "That for the medicine," she said, "and that for the salt. That for a candle to burn for the papa. That for *dulces*[1] for the little ones. Our friend Mrs. Rodriguez will give you dinner and maybe a bed for the night. When you go to the church say only ten Paternosters[2] and only twenty-five Ave Marias.[3] Oh! I know, big coyote. You would sit there flapping your mouth over Aves all day while you looked at the candles and the holy pictures. That is not good devotion to stare at the pretty things."

The black hat, covering the high pointed head and black thatched hair of Pepé, gave him dignity and age. He sat the rangy horse well. Mama thought how handsome he was, dark and lean and tall. "I would not send thee now alone, thou little one, except for the medicine," she said softly. "It is not good to have no medicine, for who knows when the toothache will come, or the sadness of the stomach. These things are."

"Adios, Mama," Pepé cried. "I will come back soon. You may send me often alone. I am a man."

"Thou art a foolish chicken."

He straightened his shoulders, flipped the reins against the horse's shoulder and rode away. He turned once and saw that they still watched him, Emilio and Rosy and Mama. Pepé grinned with pride and gladness and lifted the tough buckskin horse to a trot.

When he had dropped out of sight over a little dip in the road, Mama turned to the black ones, but she spoke to herself. "He is nearly a man now," she said. "It will be a nice thing to have a man in the house again." Her eyes sharpened on the children. "Go to the rocks now. The tide is going out. There will be abalones to be found." She put the iron

---

1. Sweets, candy.   2. Literal Latin for our father; The Lord's Prayer or a word formula used as a prayer.   3. Literally, hail, Mary; salutation to the Virgin Mary.

hooks into their hands and saw them down the steep trail to the reefs. She brought the smooth stone *metate* to the doorway and sat grinding her corn to flour and looking occasionally at the road over which Pepé had gone. The noonday came and then the afternoon, when the little ones beat the abalones on a rock to make them tender and Mama patted the tortillas to make them thin. They ate their dinner as the red sun was plunging down toward the ocean. They sat on the doorsteps and watched the big white moon come over the mountain tops.

Mama said, "He is now at the house of our friend Mrs. Rodriguez. She will give him nice things to eat and maybe a present."

Emilio said, "Some day I too will ride to Monterey for medicine. Did Pepé come to be a man today?"

Mama said wisely, "A boy gets to be a man when a man is needed. Remember this thing. I have known boys forty years old because there was no need for a man."

Soon afterwards they retired, Mama in her big oak bed on one side of the room, Emilio and Rosy in their boxes full of straw and sheepskins on the other side of the room.

The moon went over the sky and the surf roared on the rocks. The roosters crowed the first call. The surf subsided to a whispering surge a-gainst the reef. The moon dropped toward the sea. The roosters crowed again.

The moon was near down to the water when Pepé rode on a winded horse to his home flat. His dog bounced out and circled the horse yelping with pleasure. Pepé slid off

the saddle to the ground. The weath-ered little shack was silver in the moonlight and the square shadow of it was black to the north and east. Against the east the piling mountains were misty with light; their tops melted into the sky.

Pepé walked wearily up the three steps and into the house. It was dark inside. There was a rustle in the cor-ner.

Mama cried out from her bed. "Who comes? Pepé, is it thou?"

"*Si*, Mamma."

"Did you get the medicine?"

"*Si*, Mama."

"Well, go to sleep, then. I thought you would be sleeping at the house of Mrs. Rodriguez." Pepé stood silently in the dark room. "Why do you stand there, Pepé? Did you drink wine?"

"*Si*, Mama."

"Well, go to bed then and sleep out the wine."

His voice was tired and patient, but very firm. "Light the candle, Mama. I must go away into the mountains."

"What is this, Pepé? You are crazy." Mama struck a sulphur match and held the little blue burr until the flame spread up the stick. She set light to the candle on the floor beside her bed. "Now, Pepé, what is this you say?" She looked anxiously into his face.

He was changed. The fragile quali-ty seemed to have gone from his chin. His mouth was less full than it had been, the lines of the lips were straighter, but in his eyes the greatest change had taken place. There was no laughter in them any more nor any bashfulness. They were sharp and bright and purposeful.

He told her in a tired monotone,

told her everything just as it had happened. A few people came into the kitchen of Mrs. Rodriguez. There was wine to drink. Pepé drank wine. The little quarrel—the man started toward Pepé and then the knife—it went almost by itself. It flew, it darted before Pepé knew it. As he talked, Mama's face grew stern, and it seemed to grow more lean. Pepé finished. "I am a man now, Mama. The man said names to me I could not allow."

Mama nodded. "Yes, thou art a man, my poor little Pepé. Thou art a man. I have seen it coming on thee. I have watched you throwing the knife into the post, and I have been afraid." For a moment her face had softened, but now it grew stern again. "Come! We must get you ready. Go. Awaken Emilio and Rosy. Go quickly."

Pepé stepped over to the corner where his brother and sister slept among the sheepskins. He leaned down and shook them gently. "Come, Rosy! Come, Emilio! The mama says you must arise."

The little black ones sat up and rubbed their eyes in the candlelight. Mama was out of bed now, her long black skirt over her nightgown. "Emilio," she cried. "Go up and catch the other horse for Pepé. Quickly, now! Quickly." Emilio put his legs in his overalls and stumbled sleepily out the door.

"You heard no one behind you on the road?" Mama demanded.

"No, Mama. I listened carefully. No one was on the road."

Mama darted like a bird about the room. From a nail on the wall she took a canvas water bag and threw it on the floor. She stripped a blanket from her bed and rolled it into a tight tube and tied the ends with string. From a box beside the stove she lifted a flour sack half full of black stringy jerky. "Your father's black coat, Pepé. Here, put it on."

Pepé stood in the middle of the floor watching her activity. She reached behind the door and brought out the rifle, a long 38-56, worn shiny the whole length of the barrel. Pepé took it from her and held it in the crook of his elbow. Mama brought a little leather bag and counted the cartridges into his hand. "Only ten left," she warned. "You must not waste them."

Emilio put his head in the door. " 'Qui 'st 'l caballo,[4] Mama."

"Put on the saddle from the other horse. Tie on the blanket. Here, tie the jerky to the saddle horn."

Still Pepé stood silently watching his mother's frantic activity. His chin looked hard, and his sweet mouth was drawn and thin. His little eyes followed Mama about the room almost suspiciously.

Rosy asked softly, "Where goes Pepé?"

Mama's eyes were fierce. "Pepé goes on a journey. Pepé is a man now. He has a man's thing to do."

Pepé straightened his shoulders. His mouth changed until he looked very much like Mama.

At last the preparation was finished. The loaded horse stood outside the door. The water bag dripped a

---

4. Here is the horse.

line of moisture down the bay shoulder.

The moonlight was being thinned by the dawn and the big white moon was near down to the sea. The family stood by the shack. Mama confronted Pepé. "Look, my son! Do not stop until it is dark again. Do not sleep even though you are tired. Take care of the horse in order that he may not stop of weariness. Remember to be careful with the bullets—there are only ten. Do not fill thy stomach with jerky or it will make thee sick. Eat a little jerky and fill thy stomach with grass. When thou comest to the high mountains, if thou seest any of the dark watching men, go not near to them nor try to speak to them. And forget not thy prayers." She put her lean hands on Pepé's shoulders, stood on her toes and kissed him formally on both cheeks, and Pepé kissed her on both cheeks. Then he went to Emilio and Rosy and kissed both of their cheeks.

Pepé turned back to Mama. He seemed to look for a little softness, a little weakness in her. His eyes were searching, but Mama's face remained fierce. "Go now," she said. "Do not wait to be caught like a chicken."

Pepé pulled himself into the saddle. "I am a man," he said.

It was the first dawn when he rode up the hill toward the little canyon which let a trail into the mountains. Moonlight and daylight fought with each other, and the two warring qualities made it difficult to see. Before Pepé had gone a hundred yards, the outlines of his figure were misty; and long before he entered the canyon, he had become a gray, indefinite shadow.

Mama stood stiffly in front of her doorstep, and on either side of her stood Emilio and Rosy. They cast furtive glances at Mama now and then.

When the gray shape of Pepé melted into the hillside and disappeared, Mama relaxed. She began the high, whining keen of the death wail. "Our beautiful—our brave," she cried. "Our protector, our son is gone." Emilio and Rosy moaned beside her. "Our beautiful—our brave, he is gone." It was the formal wail. It rose to a high piercing whine and subsided to a moan. Mama raised it three times and then she turned and went into the house and shut the door.

Emilio and Rosy stood wondering in the dawn. They heard Mama whimpering in the house. They went out to sit on the cliff above the ocean. They touched shoulders. "When did Pepé come to be a man?" Emilio asked.

"Last night," said Rosy. "Last night in Monterey." The ocean clouds turned red with the sun that was behind the mountains.

"We will have no breakfast," said Emilio. "Mama will not want to cook." Rosy did not answer him. "Where is Pepé gone?" he asked.

Rosy looked around at him. She drew her knowledge from the quiet air. "He has gone on a journey. He will never come back."

"Is he dead? Do you think he is dead?"

Rosy looked back at the ocean again. A little steamer, drawing a line of smoke sat on the edge of the horizon. "He is not dead," Rosy explained. "Not yet."

Pepé rested the big rifle across the

saddle in front of him. He let the horse walk up the hill and he didn't look back. The stony slope took on a coat of short brush so that Pepé found the entrance to a trail and entered it.

When he came to the canyon opening, he swung once in his saddle and looked back, but the houses were swallowed in the misty light. Pepé jerked forward again. The high shoulder of the canyon closed in on him. His horse stretched out its neck and sighed and settled to the trail.

It was a well-worn path, dark soft leaf-mold earth strewn with broken pieces of sandstone. The trail rounded the shoulder of the canyon and dropped steeply into the bed of the stream. In the shallows the water ran smoothly, glinting in the first morning sun. Small round stones on the bottom were as brown as rust with sun moss. In the sand along the edges of the stream the tall, rich wild mint grew, while in the water itself the cress, old and tough, had gone to heavy seed.

The path went into the stream and emerged on the other side. The horse sloshed into the water and stopped. Pepé dropped his bridle and let the beast drink of the running water.

Soon the canyon sides became steep and the first giant sentinel redwoods guarded the trail, great round red trunks bearing foliage as green and lacy as ferns. Once Pepé was among the trees, the sun was lost. A perfumed and purple light lay in the pale green of the underbrush. Gooseberry bushes and blackberries and tall ferns lined the stream, and overhead the branches of the redwoods met and cut off the sky.

Pepé drank from the water bag, and he reached into the flour sack and brought out a black string of jerky. His white teeth gnawed at the string until the tough meat parted. He chewed slowly and drank occasionally from the water bag. His little eyes were slumberous and tired, but the muscles of his face were hard set. The earth of the trail was black now. It gave up a hollow sound under the walking hoofbeats.

The stream fell more sharply. Little waterfalls splashed on the stone. Five-fingered ferns hung over the water and dripped spray from their fingertips. Pepé rode half over in his saddle, dangling one leg loosely. He picked a bay leaf from a tree beside the way and put it into his mouth for a moment to flavor the dry jerky. He held the gun loosely across the pommel.

Suddenly he squared in his saddle, swung the horse from the trail and kicked it hurriedly up behind a big redwood tree. He pulled up the reins tight against the bit to keep the horse from whinnying. His face was intent and his nostrils quivered a little.

A hollow pounding came down the trail, and a horseman rode by, a fat man with red cheeks and a white stubble beard. His horse put down its head and blubbered at the trail when it came to the place where Pepé had turned off. "Hold up!" said the man and he pulled up his horse's head.

When the last sound of the hoofs died away, Pepé came back into the trail again. He did not relax in the saddle any more. He lifted the big rifle and swung the lever to throw a shell into the chamber, and then he let down the hammer to half cock.

The trail grew very steep. Now the

redwood trees were smaller and their tops were dead, bitten dead where the wind reached them. The horse plodded on; the sun went slowly overhead and started down toward the afternoon.

Where the stream came out of a side canyon, the trail left it. Pepé dismounted and watered his horse and filled up his water bag. As soon as the trail had parted from the stream, the trees were gone and only the thick brittle sage and manzanita and chaparral edged the trail. And the soft black earth was gone, too, leaving only the light tan broken rock for the trail bed. Lizards scampered away into the brush as the horse rattled over the little stones.

Pepé turned in his saddle and looked back. He was in the open now: he could be seen from a distance. As he ascended the trail the country grew more rough and terrible and dry. The way wound about the bases of great square rocks. Little gray rabbits skittered in the brush. A bird made a monotonous high creaking. Eastward the bare rock mountaintops were pale and powder-dry under the dropping sun. The horse plodded up and up the trail toward a little V in the ridge which was the pass.

Pepé looked suspiciously back every minute or so, and his eyes sought the tops of the ridges ahead. Once, on a white barren spur, he saw a black figure for a moment, but he looked quickly away, for it was one of the dark watchers. No one knew who the watchers were, nor where they lived, but it was better to ignore them and never to show interest in them. They did not bother one who stayed on the trail and minded his own business.

The air was parched and full of light dust blown by the breeze from the eroding mountains. Pepé drank sparingly from his bag and corked it tightly and hung it on the horn again. The trail moved up the dry shale hillside, avoiding rocks, dropping under clefts, climbing in and out of old water scars. When he arrived at the little pass he stopped and looked back for a long time. No dark watchers were to be seen now. The trail behind was empty. Only the high tops of the redwoods indicated where the stream flowed.

Pepé rode on through the pass. His little eyes were nearly closed with weariness, but his face was stern, relentless and manly. The high mountain wind coasted sighing through the pass and whistled on the edges of the big blocks of broken granite. In the air, a red-tailed hawk sailed over close to the ridge and screamed angrily. Pepé went slowly through the broken jagged pass and looked down on the other side.

The trail dropped quickly, staggering among broken rock. At the bottom of the slope there was a dark crease, thick with brush, and on the other side of the crease a little flat, in which a grove of oak trees grew. A scar of green grass cut across the flat. And behind the flat another mountain rose, desolate with dead rocks and starving little black bushes. Pepé drank from the bag again for the air was so dry that it encrusted his nostrils and burned his lips. He put the horse down the trail. The hooves slipped and struggled on the steep way, starting little stones that rolled off into the brush. The sun was gone behind the westward mountain now, but still it glowed brilliantly on the oaks and on the grassy flat. The rocks and the hillsides still sent up waves of the heat they had gathered from the day's sun.

Pepé looked up to the top of the next dry withered ridge. He saw a dark form against the sky, a man's figure standing on top of a rock, and he glanced away quickly not to appear curious. When a moment later he looked up again, the figure was gone.

Downward the trail was quickly covered. Sometimes the horse floundered for footing, sometimes set his feet and slid a little way. They came at last to the bottom where the dark chaparral was higher than Pepé's head. He held up his rifle on one side and his arm on the other to shield his face from the sharp brittle fingers of the brush.

Up and out of the crease he rode, and up a little cliff. The grassy flat was before him, and the round comfortable oaks. For a moment he studied the trail down which he had come, but there was no movement and no sound from it. Finally he rode out over the flat, to the green streak, and at the upper end of the damp he found a little spring welling out of the earth and dropping into a dug basin before it seeped out over the flat.

Pepé filled his bag first, and then he let the thirsty horse drink out of the pool. He led the horse to the clump of oaks, and in the middle of the grove, fairly protected from sight on all sides, he took off the saddle and the bridle and laid them on the ground. The horse stretched his jaws sideways and yawned. Pepé knotted the lead rope about the horse's neck and tied him to a sapling among the oaks, where he could graze in a fairly large circle.

When the horse was gnawing hungrily at the dry grass, Pepé went to the saddle and took a black string of jerky from the sack and strolled to an oak tree on the edge of the grove, from under which he could watch the trail. He sat down in the crisp dry oak leaves and automatically felt for his big black knife to cut the jerky, but he had no knife. He leaned back on his elbow and gnawed at the tough strong meat. His face was blank, but it was a man's face.

The bright evening light washed the eastern ridge, but the valley was darkening. Doves flew down from the hills to the spring, and the quail came running out of the brush and joined them, calling clearly to one another.

Out of the corner of his eye Pepé saw a shadow grow out of the bushy crease. He turned his head slowly. A big spotted wildcat was creeping toward the spring, belly to the ground, moving like thought.

Pepé cocked his rifle and edged the muzzle slowly around. Then he looked apprehensively up the trail and dropped the hammer again. From the ground beside him he picked an oak twig and threw it toward the spring. The quail flew up with a roar and the doves whistled away. The big cat stood up: for a long moment he looked at Pepé with cold yellow eyes, and then fearlessly walked back into the gulch.

The dusk gathered quickly in the deep valley. Pepé muttered his prayers, put his head down on his arm and went instantly to sleep.

The moon came up and filled the valley with cold blue light, and the wind swept rustling down from the peaks. The owls worked up and down the slopes looking for rabbits. Down in the brush of the gulch a coyote gabbled. The oak trees whispered softly in the night breeze.

Pepé started up, listening. His horse had whinnied. The moon was just slipping behind the western ridge, leaving the valley in darkness behind it. Pepé sat tensely gripping his rifle. From far up the trail he heard an answering whinny and the crash of shod hooves on the broken rock. He jumped to his feet, ran to his horse and led it under the trees. He threw on the saddle and cinched it tight for the steep trail, caught the unwilling head and forced the bit into the mouth. He felt the saddle to make sure the water bag and the sack of jerky were there. Then he mounted and turned up the hill.

It was velvet dark. The horse found the entrance to the trail where it left the flat, and started up, stumbling and slipping on the rocks. Pepé's hand rose up to his head. His hat was gone. He had left it under the oak tree.

The horse had struggled far up the trail when the first change of dawn came into the air, a steel grayness as light mixed thoroughly with dark. Gradually the sharp snaggled edge of the ridge stood out above them, rotten granite tortured and eaten by the winds of time. Pepé had dropped his

reins on the horn, leaving direction to the horse. The brush grabbed at his legs in the dark until one knee of his jeans was ripped.

Gradually the light flowed down over the ridge. The starved brush and rocks stood out in the half light, strange and lonely in high perspective. Then there came warmth into the light. Pepé drew up and looked back, but he could see nothing in the darker valley below. The sky turned blue over the coming sun. In the waste of the mountainside, the poor dry brush grew only three feet high. Here and there, big outcroppings of unrotted granite stood up like moldering houses. Pepé relaxed a little. He drank from his water bag and bit off a piece of jerky. A single eagle flew over, high in the light.

Without warning Pepé's horse screamed and fell on its side. He was almost down before the rifle crash echoed up from the valley. From a hole behind the struggling shoulder, a stream of bright crimson blood pumped and stopped and pumped and stopped. The hooves threshed on the ground. Pepé lay half stunned beside the horse. He looked slowly down the hill. A piece of sage clipped off beside his head and another crash echoed up from side to side of the canyon. Pepé flung himself frantically behind a bush.

He crawled up the hill on his knees and on one hand. His right hand held the rifle up off the ground and pushed it ahead of him. He moved with the instinctive care of an animal. Rapidly he wormed his way toward one of the big outcroppings of granite on the hill above him. Where the brush was high he doubled up and ran, but where the cover was slight he wriggled forward on his stomach, pushing the rifle ahead of him. In the last little distance there was no cover at all. Pepé poised and then he darted across the space and flashed around the corner of the rock.

He leaned panting against the stone. When his breath came easier he moved along behind the big rock until he came to a narrow split that offered a thin section of vision down the hill. Pepé lay on his stomach and pushed the rifle barrel through the slit and waited.

The sun reddened the western ridges now. Already the buzzards were settling down toward the place where the horse lay. A small brown bird scratched in the dead sage leaves directly in front of the rifle muzzle. The coasting eagle flew back toward the rising sun.

Pepé saw a little movement in the brush far below. His grip tightened on the gun. A little brown doe stepped daintily out on the trail and crossed it and disappeared into the brush again. For a long time Pepé waited. Far below he could see the little flat and the oak trees and the slash of green. Suddenly his eyes flashed back at the trail again. A quarter of a mile down there had been a quick movement in the chaparral. The rifle swung over. The front sight nestled in the V of the rear sight. Pepé studied for a moment and then raised the rear sight a notch. The little movement in the brush came again. The sight settled on it. Pepé squeezed the trigger. The explosion crashed down the mountain and up

the other side, and came rattling back. The whole side of the slope grew still. No more movement. And then a white streak cut into the granite of the slit and a bullet whined away and a crash sounded up from below. Pepé felt a sharp pain in his right hand. A sliver of granite was sticking out from between his first and second knuckles and the point protruded from his palm. Carefully he pulled out the sliver of stone. The wound bled evenly and gently. No vein nor artery was cut.

Pepé looked into a little dusty cave in the rock and gathered a handful of spider web, and he pressed the mass into the cut, plastering the soft web into the blood. The flow stopped almost at once.

The rifle was on the ground. Pepé picked it up, levered a new shell into the chamber. And then he slid into the brush on his stomach. Far to the right he crawled, and then up the hill, moving slowly and carefully, crawling to cover and resting and then crawling again.

In the mountains the sun is high in its arc before it penetrates the gorges. The hot face looked over the hill and brought instant heat with it. The white light beat on the rocks and reflected from them and rose up quivering from the earth again, and the rocks and bushes seemed to quiver behind the air.

Pepé crawled in the general direction of the ridge peak, zig-zagging for cover. The deep cut between his knuckles began to throb. He crawled close to a rattlesnake before he saw it, and when it raised its dry head and made a soft beginning whirr, he backed up and took another way. The quick gray lizards flashed in front of him, raising a tiny line of dust. He found another mass of spider web and pressed it against his throbbing hand.

Pepé was pushing the rifle with his left hand now. Little drops of sweat ran to the ends of his coarse black hair and rolled down his cheeks. His lips and tongue were growing thick and heavy. His lips writhed to draw saliva into his mouth. His little dark eyes were uneasy and suspicious. Once when a gray lizard paused in front of him on the parched ground and turned its head sideways he crushed it flat with a stone.

When the sun slid past noon he had not gone a mile. He crawled exhaustedly a last hundred yards to a patch of high sharp manzanita, crawled desperately, and when the patch was reached he wriggled in among the tough gnarly trunks and dropped his head on his left arm. There was little shade in the meager brush, but there was cover and safety. Pepé went to sleep as he lay and the sun beat on his back. A few little birds hopped close to him and peered and hopped away. Pepé squirmed in his sleep and he raised and dropped his wounded hand again and again.

The sun went down behind the peaks and the cool evening came, and then the dark. A coyote yelled from the hillside, Pepé started awake and looked about with misty eyes. His hand was swollen and heavy; a little thread of pain ran up the inside of his arm and settled in a pocket in his armpit. He peered about and then stood up, for the mountains were

black and the moon had not yet risen. Pepé stood up in the dark. The coat of his father pressed on his arm. His tongue was swollen until it nearly filled his mouth. He wriggled out of the coat and dropped it in the brush, and then he struggled up the hill, falling over rocks and tearing his way through the brush. The rifle knocked against stones as he went. Little dry avalanches of gravel and shattered stone went whispering down the hill behind him.

After a while the old moon came up and showed the jagged ridge top ahead of him. By moonlight Pepé traveled more easily. He bent forward so that his throbbing arm hung away from his body. The journey uphill was made in dashes and rests, a frantic rush up a few yards and then a rest. The wind coasted down the slope rattling the dry stems of the bushes.

The moon was at meridian when Pepé came at last to the sharp backbone of the ridge top. On the last hundred yards of the rise no soil had clung under the wearing winds. The way was on solid rock. He clambered to the top and looked down on the other side. There was a draw like the last below him, misty with moonlight, brushed with dry struggling sage and chaparral. On the other side the hill rose up sharply and at the top the jagged rotten teeth of the mountain showed against the sky. At the bottom of the cut the brush was thick and dark.

Pepé stumbled down the hill. His throat was almost closed with thirst. At first he tried to run, but immediately he fell and rolled. After that he went more carefully. The moon was just disappearing behind the mountains when he came to the bottom. He crawled into the heavy brush feeling with his fingers for water. There was no water in the bed of the stream, only damp earth. Pepé laid his gun down and scooped up a handful of mud and put it in his mouth, and then he spluttered and scraped the earth from his tongue with his finger, for the mud drew at his mouth like a poultice. He dug a hole in the stream bed with his fingers, dug a little basin to catch water; but before it was very deep his head fell forward on the damp ground and he slept.

The dawn came and the heat of the day fell on the earth, and still Pepé slept. Late in the afternoon his head jerked up. He looked slowly around. His eyes were slits of wariness. Twenty feet away in the heavy brush a big tawny mountain lion stood looking at him. Its long thick tail waved gracefully, its ears erect with interest, not laid back dangerously. The lion squatted down on its stomach and watched him.

Pepé looked at the hole he had dug in the earth. A half inch of muddy water had collected in the bottom. He tore the sleeve from his hurt arm, with his teeth ripped out a little square, soaked it in the water and put it in his mouth. Over and over he filled the cloth and sucked it.

Still the lion sat and watched him. The evening came down but there was no movement on the hills. No birds visited the dry bottom of the cut. Pepé looked occasionally at the lion. The eyes of the yellow beast drooped as though he were about to sleep. He yawned and his long thin red tongue curled out. Suddenly his head jerked around and his nostrils quivered. His big tail lashed. He stood up and slunk like a tawny shadow into the thick brush.

A moment later Pepé heard the sound, the faint far crash of horses' hooves on gravel. And he heard something else, a high whining yelp of a dog.

Pepé took his rifle in his left hand and he glided into the brush almost as quietly as the lion had. In the darkening evening he crouched up the hill toward the next ridge. Only when the dark came did he stand up. His energy was short. Once it was dark he fell over the rocks and slipped to his knees on the steep slope, but he moved on and on up the hill, climbing and scrabbling over the broken hillside.

When he was far up toward the top, he lay down and slept for a little while. The withered moon, shining on his face awakened him. He stood up and moved up the hill. Fifty yards away he stopped and turned back, for he had forgotten his rifle. He walked heavily down and poked about in the brush, but he could not find his gun. At last he lay down to rest. The pocket of pain in his armpit had grown more sharp. His arm seemed to swell out and fall with every heartbeat. There was no position lying down where the heavy arm did not press against his armpit.

With the effort of a hurt beast, Pepé got up and moved again toward the top of the ridge. He held his swollen arm away from his body with his left hand. Up the steep hill he dragged himself, a few steps and a rest, and a few more steps. At last he was nearing the top. The moon showed the uneven sharp back of it against the sky.

Pepé's brain spun in a big spiral up and away from him. He slumped to the ground and lay still. The rock ridge top was only a hundred feet above him.

The moon moved over the sky. Pepé half turned on his back. His tongue tried to make words, but only a thick hissing came from between his lips.

When the dawn came, Pepé pulled himself up. His eyes were sane again. He drew his great puffed arm in front of him and looked at the angry wound. The black line ran up from his wrist to his armpit. Automatically he reached in his pocket for the big black knife, but it was not there. His eyes searched the ground. He picked up a sharp blade of stone and scraped at the wound, sawed at the proud flesh and then squeezed the green juice out in big drops. Instantly he threw back his head and whined like a dog. His whole right side shuddered at the pain, but the pain cleared his head.

In the gray light he struggled up the last slope to the ridge and crawled over and lay down behind a line of rocks. Below him lay a deep canyon exactly like the last, waterless and desolate. There was no flat, no oak trees, not even heavy brush in the bottom of it. And on the other side a sharp ridge stood up, thinly brushed with starving sage, littered with broken granite. Strewn over the hill

there were giant outcroppings, and on the top the granite teeth stood out against the sky.

The new day was light now. The flame of sun came over the ridge and fell on Pepé where he lay on the ground. His coarse black hair was littered with twigs and bits of spider web. His eyes had retreated back into his head. Between his lips the tip of his black tongue showed.

He sat up and dragged his great arm into his lap and nursed it, rocking his body and moaning in his throat. He threw back his head and looked up into the pale sky. A big black bird circled nearly out of sight, and far to the left another was sailing near.

He lifted his head to listen, for a familiar sound had come to him from the valley he had climbed out of; it was the crying yelp of hounds, excited and feverish, on a trail.

Pepé bowed his head quickly. He tried to speak rapid words but only a thick hiss came from his lips. He drew a shaky cross on his breast with his left hand. It was a long struggle to get to his feet. He crawled slowly and mechanically to the top of a big rock on the ridge peak. Once there, he rose slowly, swaying to his feet, and stood erect. Far below he could see the dark brush where he had slept. He braced his feet and stood there, black against the morning sky.

There came a ripping sound at his feet. A piece of stone flew up and a bullet droned off into the next gorge. The hollow crash echoed up from below. Pepé looked down for a moment and then pulled himself straight again.

His body jarred back. His left hand fluttered helplessly toward his breast. The second crash sounded from below. Pepé swung forward and toppled from the rock. His body struck and rolled over and over, starting a little avalanche. And when at last he stopped against a bush, the avalanche slid slowly down and covered up his head.

Considerations

There are several ways to read this story. On one level it can be seen as an excellent story of initiation, the tragic burden of maturity assumed with courage and a certain grandeur. At the beginning we see Pepé as the eldest boy of a small fatherless rural family. He is unsophisticated, and, we suspect, a bit slow-witted. His transition from boyhood to manhood occurs abruptly, literally overnight, and with little apparent preparation.

Says Mama, "A boy gets to be a man when a man is needed. . . . I have known boys forty years old because there was no need for a man." What, then, marks the transition from boyhood to manhood? When Pepé returns from town, prepared for flight, his mother does not condemn what he has done; she does not question or reproach him. Instead she accepts and supports him, helps him on his way, gives him all the advice she can, and then—again accepting—mourns him as dead. The pages of fact or fiction record few mothers who refrain so well from interfering in their children's lives.

The death that precipitates Pepé's flight is a critical event, yet it takes place offstage and we learn of it only through what Pepé says. One reason for this is that it is not a central concern of the story. It is a result: the cause in itself could be called the rules of the game, a code of conduct, or one definition of what it is to be a man. However, whether we agree that the characteristics Pepé admires and the actions he has taken are the hallmarks of a "man" is not important. Since Pepé and his family believe in this code, we must for the moment accept it.

Others—it is hard to tell just who they may be—disagree with Pepé about the correctness of his conduct. They represent a different culture, a different code. Pepé is aware of this and, like a man, he is prepared to take the consequences for breaking their rules. Here then seems to be another theme: what happens when the laws of one's subculture violate the laws of another, stronger group?

In Pepé's journey to his doom he is very much alone. Details are clear and sharply etched, making the scenes he passes as vivid to us as to the boy-man looking at them for the last time. The mysterious dark watchers appear but Pepé never meets them. The shots that wound and later kill him seem almost to come from a disembodied source, the very elements exacting retribution. Pepé does not protest his fate. He runs as best he can, then stands up to accept the deadly bullet. All of his life has been spent close to the soil; as he runs, he becomes more and more a part of the natural world. When finally the rocks fall down to cover his head, it seems as though the earth has reclaimed its own. Why does Pepé accept his death as he does? Why must he die? Who or what is responsible for his death?

The Circular Ruins

And if he left off dreaming about you . . . .
THROUGH THE LOOKING-GLASS, IV

JORGE LUIS BORGES

Nobody saw him come ashore in the encompassing night, nobody saw the bamboo craft run aground in the sacred mud, but within a few days everyone knew that the quiet man had come from the south and that his home was among the numberless villages upstream on the steep slopes of the mountain, where the Zend language is barely tainted by Greek and where lepers are rare. The fact is that the gray man pressed his lips to the mud, scrambled up the bank without parting (perhaps without feeling) the brushy thorns that tore his flesh, and dragged himself, faint and bleeding, to the circular opening watched over by a stone tiger, or horse, which once was the color of fire and is now the color of ash. This opening is a temple which was destroyed ages ago by flames, which the swampy wilderness later desecrated, and whose god no longer receives the reverence of men. The stranger laid himself down at the foot of the image.

Wakened by the sun high overhead, he noticed—somehow without amazement—that his wounds had healed. He shut his pale eyes and slept again, not because of weariness but because he willed it. He knew that this temple was the place he needed for his unswerving purpose; he knew that downstream the encroaching trees had also failed to choke the ruins of another auspicious temple with its own fire-ravaged, dead gods; he knew that his first duty was to sleep. Along about midnight, he was awakened by the forlorn call of a bird. Footprints, some figs, and a water jug told him that men who lived nearby had looked on his sleep with a kind of awe and either sought his protection or else were in dread of his witchcraft. He felt the chill of fear and searched the crumbling walls for a burial niche, where he covered himself over with leaves he had never seen before.

His guiding purpose, though it was supernatural, was not impossible. He wanted to dream a man; he wanted to dream him down to the last detail and project him into the world of reality. This mystical aim had taxed the whole range of his mind. Had anyone asked him his own name or anything about his life before then, he would not have known what to answer. This forsaken, broken temple suited him because it held few visible things, and also because the neighboring villagers would look after his frugal needs. The rice and fruit of their offerings were nourishment enough for his body, whose one task was to sleep and to dream.

At the outset, his dreams were chaotic; later on, they were of a dialectic nature. The stranger dreamed himself at the center of a circular amphitheater which in some way was also the burnt-out temple. Crowds of silent disciples exhausted the tiers of seats; the faces of the farthest of them hung centuries away from him and at a height of the stars, but their features were clear and exact. The man lectured on anatomy, cosmography, and witchcraft. The faces listened, bright and eager, and did their best to answer sensibly, as if they felt the importance of his questions, which would raise one of them out of an existence as a shadow and place him in the real world. Whether asleep or awake, the man pondered the answers of his phantoms and, not letting himself be misled by impostors, divined in certain of their quandaries a growing intelligence. He was in search of a soul worthy of taking a place in the world.

After nine or ten nights he realized, feeling bitter over it, that nothing could be expected from those pupils who passively accepted his teaching but that he might, however, hold hopes for those who from time to time hazarded reasonable doubts about what he taught. The former, although they deserved love and affection, could never become real; the latter, in their dim way, were already real. One evening (now his evenings were also given over to sleeping, now he was only awake for an hour or two at dawn) he dismissed his vast dream-school forever and kept a single disciple. He was a quiet, sallow, and at times rebellious young man with sharp features akin to those of his dreamer. The sudden disappearance of his fellow pupils did not disturb him for very long, and his progress, at the end of a few private lessons, amazed his teacher. Nonetheless, a catastrophe intervened. One morning, the man emerged from his sleep as from a sticky wasteland, glanced up at the faint evening light, which at first he confused with the dawn, and realized that he had not been dreaming. All that night and the next day, the hideous lucidity of insomnia weighed down on him. To tire himself out he tried to explore the surrounding forest, but all he managed, there in a thicket of hemlocks, were some snatches of broken sleep, fleetingly tinged with visions of a crude and worthless nature. He tried to reassemble his school, and barely had he uttered a few brief words of counsel when the whole class went awry and vanished. In his almost endless wakefulness, tears of anger stung his old eyes.

He realized that, though he may penetrate all the riddles of the higher and lower orders, the task of shaping the senseless and dizzying stuff of dreams is the hardest that a man can attempt—much harder than weaving a rope of sand or of coining the faceless wind. He realized that an initial failure was to be expected. He then swore he would forget the populous vision which in the beginning had led him astray, and he sought another method. Before attempting it, he spent a month rebuilding the strength his fever had consumed. He gave up all thoughts of dreaming and almost at once managed to sleep a reasonable part of the day. The few times he dreamed during this period he did not dwell on his dreams. Before taking up his task again, he waited until the moon was a perfect circle. Then, in the evening, he cleansed himself in the waters of the river, worshiped the gods of the planets, uttered the prescribed syllables of an all-powerful name, and slept. Almost at once, he had a dream of a beating heart.

He dreamed it throbbing, warm, secret. It was the size of a closed fist, a darkish red in the dimness of a human body still without a face or sex. With anxious love he dreamed it for fourteen lucid nights. Each night he perceived it more clearly. He did not touch it, but limited himself to witnessing it, to observing it, to correcting it now and then with a look. He felt it, he lived it from different distances and from many angles. On the fourteenth night he touched the pulmonary artery with a finger and then the whole heart, inside and out. The examination satisfied him. For one night he deliberately did not dream; after that he went back to the heart again, invoked the name of a planet, and set out to envision another of the principal organs. Before a year was over he came to the skeleton, the eyelids. The countless strands of hair were perhaps the hardest task of all. He dreamed a whole man, a young man, but the young man could not stand up or speak, nor could he open his eyes. Night after night, the man dreamed him asleep.

In the cosmogonies of the Gnostics, the demiurges mold a red Adam who is unable to stand on his feet; as clumsy and crude and elementary as that Adam of dust was the Adam of dreams wrought by the nights of the magician. One evening the man was at the point of destroying all his handiwork (it would have been better for him had he done so), but in the end he restrained himself. Having exhausted his prayers to the gods of the earth and river, he threw himself down at the feet of the stone image that may have been a tiger or a stallion, and asked for its blind aid. That same evening he dreamed of the image. He dreamed it alive, quivering; it was no unnatural cross between tiger and stallion but at one and the same time both these violent creatures and also a bull, a rose, a thunderstorm. This manifold god revealed to him that its earthly name was Fire, that there in the circular temple (and in others like it) sacrifices had once been made to it, that it had been worshiped, and that through its magic the phantom of the man's dreams would be wakened to life in such a way that—except for Fire itself and the dreamer—every being in the world would accept him as a man of flesh and blood. The god ordered that, once instructed in the rites, the disciple should be sent downstream to the other ruined temple, whose pyramids still survived, so that in that abandoned place some human voice might exalt him. In the dreamer's dream, the dreamed one awoke.

The magician carried out these orders. He devoted a period of time (which finally spanned two years) to initiating his disciple into the riddles of the universe and the worship of Fire. Deep inside, it pained him to say good-bye to his creature. Under the pretext of teaching him more fully, each day he drew out the hours set aside for sleep. Also, he reshaped the somewhat faulty right shoulder. From time to time, he was troubled by the feeling that all this had already happened, but for the most part his days were happy. On closing his eyes he would think, "Now I will be with my son." Or, less frequently, "The son I have begotten awaits me and he will not exist if I do not go to him."

Little by little, he was training the young man for reality. On one occasion he commanded him to set up a flag on a distant peak. The next day, there on the peak, a fiery pennant shone. He tried other, similar exercises, each bolder than the one before. He realized with a certain bitterness that his son was ready—and perhaps impatient—to be born. That night he kissed him for the first time and sent him down the river to the other temple, whose whitened ruins were still to be glimpsed over miles and miles of impenetrable forest and swamp. At the very end (so that the boy would never know he was a phantom, so that he would think himself a man like all men), the magician imbued with total oblivion his disciple's long years of apprenticeship.

His triumph and his peace were blemished by a touch of weariness. In the morning and evening dusk, he prostrated himself before the stone idol, perhaps imagining that his unreal son was performing the same rites farther down the river in other circular ruins. At night he no longer dreamed, or else he dreamed the way all men dream. He now perceived with a certain vagueness the sounds and shapes of the world, for his absent son was taking nourishment from the magician's decreasing consciousness. His life's purpose was fulfilled; the man lived on in a kind of ecstasy. After a length of time that certain tellers of the story count in years and others in half-decades, he was awakened one midnight by two rowers. He could not see their faces, but they spoke to him about a magic man in a temple up north who walked on fire without being burned. The magician suddenly remembered the god's words. He remembered that of all the creatures in the world, Fire was the only one who knew his son was a phantom. This recollection, comforting at first, ended by tormenting him. He feared that his son might wonder at this strange privilege and in some way discover his condition as a mere appearance. Not to be a man but to be the projection of another man's dreams—what an unparalleled humiliation, how bewildering! Every father cares for the child he has begotten—he has allowed—in some moment of confusion or happiness. It is understandable, then, that the magician should fear for the future of a son thought out organ by organ and feature by feature over the course of a thousand and one secret nights.

The end of these anxieties came suddenly, but certain signs foretold it. First (after a long drought), a far-off cloud on a hilltop, as light as a bird;

next, toward the south, the sky, which took on the rosy hue of a leopard's gums; then, the pillars of smoke that turned the metal of the nights to rust; finally, the headlong panic of the forest animals. For what had happened many centuries ago was happening again. The ruins of the fire god's shrine were destroyed by fire. In a birdless dawn the magician saw the circling sheets of flame closing in on him. For a moment, he thought of taking refuge in the river, but then he realized that death was coming to crown his years and to release him from his labors. He walked into the leaping pennants of flame. They did not bite into his flesh, but caressed him and flooded him without heat or burning. In relief, in humiliation, in terror, he understood that he, too, was an appearance, that someone else was dreaming him.

Considerations

Borges' piece seems almost out of place when set alongside other stories of the period. However, Borges lived in South America, out of the mainstream of literary circles. Also, he was interested in philosophical matters and much of his writing seems dreamlike or part of a fantasy or science-fiction genre. His literary progenitors could be H. G. Wells, H. P. Lovecraft, Lord Dunsany, or even Edgar Allan Poe.

The epigraph for the Circular Ruins is taken from a scene in Lewis Carroll's *Through the Looking Glass* in which Alice and the Red Queen discuss what might be called the nature of one's own reality. Descartes may have regarded his ability to think as proof positive of his own existence, but the Red Queen proclaimed otherwise. According to her, Alice only *thought* she thought and existed; in reality, she was part of a dream the sleeping White King was having. "And," said the Red Queen, "if he left off dreaming about you . . .". Though the epigraph remains unfinished, the prediction is obvious. Alice would cease to exist.

Speculation on such mysteries is not new, but age does little to dim our fascination with the subject. Try transferring the idea of an infinite series of worlds to the visual medium. What if the television picture of the people looking at a television set on which there is a picture of people looking at a television set stretches on into infinity? And what if that infinity stretches both ways, so that you—who believe yourself to be the viewer—are in fact appearing on someone else's television screen for his amusement? Science has made this kind of puzzle even more attractive; having seen the worlds of microbes living out their small (and perhaps to them interesting) lives in a drop of water, aren't we encouraged to wonder whose drop of water we inhabit?   While the puzzle of the story would seem to offer chiefly an intellectual involvement, something about it remains to haunt us. Perhaps the story taps some hidden archetypal fears. Or perhaps it is just vague enough to remind us of our own shadowy dreams.

Why did Borges choose to tell the story from this point of view? What kinds of details does he give to make it seem more real? How does he set up the possibility of the ending he gives it? It takes place in a dim Eastern—perhaps African—place. Would a different setting have been more effective?

Certainly the story's ambiguity invites other interpretations. What kinds of insights might a psychological or a sociological approach add? Could what is recorded in the story be the hallucinations of a schizophrenic or the fantasies of an alienated individual who feels himself a victim of his society?

Chee's Daughter

Juanita Platero and Siyowin Miller

The hat told the story, the big, black, drooping Stetson. It was not at the proper angle, the proper rakish angle for so young a Navaho. There was no song, and that was not in keeping either. There should have been at least a humming, a faint, all-to-himself "he he he heya," for it was a good horse he was riding, a slender-legged, high-stepping buckskin that would race the wind with light knee-urging. This was a day for singing, a warm winter day, when the touch of the sun upon the back belied the snow high on distant mountains.

Wind warmed by the sun touched his high-boned cheeks like flicker feathers, and still he rode on silently, deeper into Little Canyon, until the red rock walls rose straight upward from the stream bed and only a narrow piece of blue sky hung above. Abruptly the sky widened where the canyon walls were pushed back to make a wide place, as though in ancient times an angry stream had tried to go all ways at once.

This was home—this wide place in the canyon—levels of jagged rock and levels of rich red earth. This was home to Chee, the rider of the buckskin, as it had been to many generations before him.

He stopped his horse at the stream and sat looking across the narrow ribbon of water to the bare-branched peach trees. He was seeing them each springtime with their age-gnarled limbs transfigured beneath veils of blossom pink; he was seeing them in autumn laden with their yellow fruit, small and sweet. Then his eyes searched out the indistinct furrows of the fields beside the stream, where each year the corn and beans and squash drank thirstily of the overflow from summer rains. Chee was trying to outweigh today's bitter betrayal of hope by gathering to himself these reminders of the integrity of the land. Land did not cheat! His mind lingered deliberately on all the days spent here in the sun caring for the young plants, his songs to the earth and to the life springing from it— ". . . In the middle of the wide field . . . Yellow Corn Boy . . . He has started both ways . . . ," then the harvest and repayment in full measure. Here was the old feeling of wholeness and of oneness with the sun and earth and growing things.

Chee urged the buckskin toward the family compound where, secure in a recess of overhanging rock, was his mother's dome-shaped hogan, red rock and red adobe like the ground on which it nestled. Not far

Reprinted from *Common Ground* with the permission of the American Council for Nationalities Service. © 1948 by American Council for Nationalities Service.

from the hogan was the half-circle of brush like a dark shadow against the canyon wall—corral for sheep and goats. Farther from the hogan, in full circle, stood the horse corral made of heavy cedar branches sternly interlocked. Chee's long thin lips curved into a smile as he passed his daughter's tiny hogan squatted like a round Pueblo oven beside the corral. He remembered the summer day when together they sat back on their heels and plastered wet adobe all about the circling wall of rock and the woven dome of piñon twigs. How his family laughed when the Little One herded the bewildered chickens into her tiny hogan as the first snow fell.

Then the smile faded from Chee's lips and his eyes darkened as he tied his horse to a corral post and turned to the strangely empty compound. "Someone has told them," he thought, "and they are inside weeping." He passed his mother's deserted loom on the south side of the hogan and pulled the rude wooden door toward him, bowing his head, hunching his shoulders to get inside.

His mother sat sideways by the center fire, her feet drawn up under her full skirts. Her hands were busy kneading dough in the chipped white basin. With her head down, her voice was muffled when she said, "The meal will soon be ready, son."

Chee passed his father sitting against the wall, hat over his eyes as though asleep. He passed his older sister who sat turning mutton ribs on a crude wire grill over the coals, noticed tears dropping on her hands. "She cared more for my wife than I realized," he thought.

Then because something must be said sometime, he tossed the black Stetson upon a bulging sack of wool and said, "You have heard, then." He could not shut from his mind how confidently he had set the handsome new hat on his head that very morning, slanting the wide brim over one eye: he was going to see his wife and today he would ask the doctors about bringing her home; last week she had looked so much better.

His sister nodded but did not speak. His mother sniffled and passed her velveteen sleeve beneath her nose. Chee sat down, leaning against the wall. "I suppose I was a fool for hoping all the time. I should have expected this. Few of our people get well from the coughing sickness. But *she* seemed to be getting better."

His mother was crying aloud now and blowing her nose noisily on her skirt. His father sat up, speaking gently to her.

Chee shifted his position and started a cigarette. His mind turned back to the Little One. At least she was too small to understand what had happened, the Little One who had been born three years before in the sanitarium where his wife was being treated for the coughing sickness, the Little One he had brought home to his mother's hogan to be nursed by his sister whose baby was a few months older. As she grew fat-cheeked and sturdy-legged, she followed him about like a shadow; somehow her baby mind had grasped that of all those at the hogan who cared for her and played with her, he—Chee—belonged most to her. She sat cross-legged at his elbow when he worked silver at the forge; she rode before him in the saddle when he drove the horses to water; often she lay wakeful on her sheep-pelts until he stretched out for the night in the darkened hogan and she could snuggle warm against him.

Chee blew smoke slowly and some of the sadness left his dark eyes as he said, "It is not as bad as it might be. It is not as though we are left with nothing."

Chee's sister arose, sobs catching in her throat, and rushed past him out the doorway. Chee sat upright, a terrible fear possessing him. For a moment his mouth could make no sound. Then: "The Little One! Mother, where is she?"

His mother turned her stricken face to him. "Your wife's people came after her this morning. They heard yesterday of their daughter's death through the trader at Red Sands."

Chee started to protest but his mother shook her head slowly. "I didn't expect they would want the Little One either. But there is nothing you can do. She is a girl child and belongs to her mother's people; it is custom."

Frowning, Chee got to his feet, grinding his cigarette into the dirt floor. "Custom! When did my wife's parents begin thinking about custom? Why, the hogan where they live doesn't even face the East!" He started toward the door. "Perhaps I can overtake them. Perhaps they don't realize how much we want her here with us. I'll ask them to give my daughter back to me. Surely, they won't refuse."

His mother stopped him gently with her outstretched hand. "You couldn't overtake them now. They were in the trader's car. Eat and rest, and think more about this."

"Have you forgotten how things have always been between you and your wife's people?" his father said.

That night, Chee's thoughts were troubled—half-forgotten incidents became disturbingly vivid—but early the next morning he saddled the buckskin and set out for the settlement of Red Sands. Even though his father-in-law, Old Man Fat, might laugh, Chee knew that he must talk to him. There were some things to which Old Man Fat might listen.

Chee rode the first part of the fifteen miles to Red Sands expectantly. The sight of sandstone buttes near Cottonwood Spring reddening in the morning sun brought a song almost to his lips. He twirled his reins in salute to the small boy herding sheep toward many-colored Butterfly Mountain, watched with pleasure the feathers of smoke rising against tree-darkened western mesas from the hogans sheltered there. But as he approached the familiar settlement sprawled in mushroom growth along the highway, he began to feel as though a scene from a bad dream was becoming real.

Several cars were parked around the trading store which was built like two log hogans side by side, with red gas pumps in front and a sign across the tarpaper roofs: *Red Sands Trading Post—Groceries Gasoline Cold Drinks Sandwiches Indian Curios.* Back of the trading post an unpainted frame house and outbuildings squatted on the drab, treeless land. Chee and the Little One's mother had lived there when they stayed with his wife's people. That was according to custom —living with one's wife's people—but Chee had never been convinced that it was custom alone which prompted Old Man Fat and his wife to insist that their daughter bring her husband to live at the trading post.

Beside the Post was a large hogan of logs, with brightly painted pseudo-Navaho designs on the roof—a hogan with smoke-smudged windows and a garish blue door which faced north to the highway. Old Man Fat had offered Chee a hogan like this one. The trader would build it if he and his wife would live there and Chee would work at his forge making silver jewelry where tourists could watch him. But Chee had asked instead for a piece of land for a cornfield and help in building a hogan far back from the highway and a corral for the sheep he had brought to this marriage.

A cold wind blowing down from the mountains began to whistle about Chee's ears. It flapped the gaudy Navaho rugs which were hung in one long bright line to attract tourists. It swayed the sign *Navaho Weaver at Work* beside the loom where Old Man Fat's wife sat hunched in her striped blanket, patting the colored thread of a design into place with a wooden comb. Tourists stood watching the weaver. More tourists stood in a knot before the hogan where the sign said: *See Inside a Real Navaho Home 25c.*

Then the knot seemed to unravel as a few people returned to their cars; some had cameras; and there against the blue door Chee saw the Little One standing uncertainly. The wind was plucking at her new purple blouse and

wide green skirt; it freed truant strands of soft dark hair from the meager queue into which it had been tied with white yarn.

"Isn't she cunning!" one of the women tourists was saying as she turned away.

Chee's lips tightened as he began to look around for Old Man Fat. Finally he saw him passing among the tourists collecting coins.

Then the Little One saw Chee. The uncertainty left her face and she darted through the crowd as her father swung down from his horse. Chee lifted her in his arms, hugging her tight. While he listened to her breathless chatter, he watched Old Man Fat bearing down on them, scowling.

As his father-in-law walked heavily across the gravelled lot, Chee was reminded of a statement his mother sometimes made: "When you see a fat Navaho, you see one who hasn't worked for what he has."

Old Man Fat was fattest in the middle. There was indolence in his walk even though he seemed to hurry, indolence in his cheeks so plump they made his eyes squint, eyes now smoldering with anger.

Some of the tourists were getting into their cars and driving away. The old man said belligerently to Chee, "Why do you come here? To spoil our business? To drive people away?"

"I came to talk with you," Chee answered, trying to keep his voice steady as he faced the old man.

"We have nothing to talk about," Old Man Fat blustered and did not offer to touch Chee's extended hand.

"It's about the Little One." Chee settled his daughter more comfortably against his hip as he weighed carefully all the words he had planned to say. "We are going to miss her very much. It wouldn't be so bad if we knew that *part* of each year she could be with us. That might help you too. You and your wife are no longer young people and you have no young ones here to depend upon." Chee chose his next words remembering the thriftlessness of his wife's parents, and their greed. "Perhaps we could share the care of this little one. Things are good with us. So much snow this year will make lots of grass for the sheep. We have good land for corn and melons."

Chee's words did not have the expected effect. Old Man Fat was enraged. "Farmers, all of you! Long-haired farmers! Do you think everyone must bend his back over the short-handled hoe in order to have food to eat?" His tone changed as he began to brag a little. "We not only have all the things from cans at the trader's, but when the Pueblos come past here on their way to town we buy their salty jerked mutton, young corn for roasting, dried sweet peaches."

Chee's dark eyes surveyed the land along the highway as the old man continued to brag about being "progressive." *He* no longer was tied to the land. He and his wife made money easily and could *buy* all the things they wanted. Chee realized too late that he had stumbled into the old argument between himself and his wife's parents. They had never understood his feeling about the land—that a man took care of his land and it in turn took care of him. Old Man Fat and his wife scoffed at him, called

him a Pueblo farmer, all during that summer when he planted and weeded and harvested. Yet they ate the green corn in their mutton stews, and the chili paste from the fresh ripe chilis, and the tortillas from the cornmeal his wife ground. None of this working and sweating in the sun for Old Man Fat, who talked proudly of his easy way of living—collecting money from the trader who rented this strip of land beside the highway, collecting money from the tourists.

Yet Chee had once won that argument. His wife had shared his belief in the integrity of the earth, that jobs and people might fail one but the earth never would. After that first year she had turned from her own people and gone with Chee to Little Canyon.

Old Man Fat was reaching for the Little One. "Don't be coming here with plans for my daughter's daughter," he warned. "If you try to make trouble, I'll take the case to the government man in town."

The impulse was strong in Chee to turn and ride off while he still had the Little One in his arms. But he knew his time of victory would be short. His own family would uphold the old custom of children, especially girl children, belonging to the mother's people. He would have to give his daughter up if the case were brought before the Headman of Little Canyon, and certainly he would have no better chance before a strange white man in town.

He handed the bewildered Little One to her grandfather who stood watching every movement suspiciously. Chee asked, "If I brought you a few things for the Little One, would that be making trouble? Some velvet for a blouse, or some of the jerky she likes so well . . . this summer's melon?"

Old Man Fat backed away from him. "Well," he hesitated, as some of the anger disappeared from his face and beads of greed shone in his eyes. "Well," he repeated. Then as the Little One began to squirm in his arms and cry, he said, "No! No! Stay away from here, you and all your family."

The sense of his failure deepened as Chee rode back to Little Canyon. But it was not until he sat with his family that evening in the hogan, while the familiar bustle of meal preparing went on about him, that he began to doubt the wisdom of the things he'd always believed. He smelled the coffee boiling and the oily fragrance of chili powder dusted into the bubbling pot of stew; he watched his mother turning round crusty fried bread in the small black skillet. All around him was plenty—a half of mutton hanging near the door, bright strings of chili drying, corn hanging by the braided husks, cloth bags of dried peaches. Yet in his heart was nothing.

He heard the familiar sounds of the sheep outside the hogan, the splash of water as his father filled the long drinking trough from the water barrel. When his father came in, Chee could not bring himself to tell a second time of the day's happenings. He watched his wiry, soft-spoken father while his mother told the story, saw his father's queue of graying hair quiver as he nodded his head with sympathetic exclamations.

Chee's doubting, acrid thoughts kept forming: Was it wisdom his father had passed on to him or was his inheritance only the stubbornness of a long-haired Navaho resisting change? Take care of the land and it will take care of you. True, the land had always given him food, but now food was not enough. Perhaps if he had gone to school he would have learned a different kind of wisdom, something to help him now. A schoolboy might even be able to speak convincingly to this government man whom Old Man Fat threatened to call, instead of sitting here like a clod of earth itself—Pueblo farmer indeed. What had the land to give that would restore his daughter?

In the days that followed, Chee herded sheep. He got up in the half-light, drank the hot coffee his mother had ready, then started the flock moving. It was necessary to drive the sheep a long way from the hogan to find good winter forage. Sometimes Chee met friends or relatives who were on their way to town or to the road camp where they hoped to get work; then there was friendly banter and an exchange of news. But most of the days seemed endless; he could not walk far enough or fast enough from his memories of the Little One or from his bitter thoughts. Sometimes it seemed his daughter trudged beside him, so real he could almost hear her footsteps—the muffled pad-pad of little feet clad in deerhide. In the glare of a snow bank he would see her vivid face, brown eyes sparkling. Mingling with the tinkle of sheep bells he heard her laughter.

When, weary of following the small sharp hoof marks that crossed and recrossed in the snow, he sat down in the shelter of a rock, it was only to be reminded that in his thoughts he had forsaken his brotherhood with the earth and sun and growing things. If he remembered times when he had flung himself against the earth to rest, to lie there in the sun until he could no longer feel where he left off and the earth began, it was to remember also that now he sat like an alien against the same earth; the belonging-together was gone. The earth was one thing and he was another.

It was during the days when he herded sheep that Chee decided he must leave Little Canyon. Perhaps he would take a job silversmithing for one of the traders in town. Perhaps, even though he spoke little English, he could get a job at the road camp with his cousins; he would ask them about it.

■ Springtime transformed the mesas. The peach trees in the canyon were shedding fragrance and pink blossoms on the gentled wind. The sheep no longer foraged for the yellow seeds of chamiso but ranged near the hogan with the long-legged new lambs, eating tender young grass.

Chee was near the hogan on the day his cousins rode up with the message for which he waited. He had been watching with mixed emotions while his father and his sister's husband cleared the fields beside the stream.

"The boss at the camp says he needs an extra hand, but he wants to know if you'll be willing to go with the camp when they move it to the other side of the town?" The tall cousin shifted his weight in the saddle.

The other cousin took up the explanation. "The work near here will last only until the new cut-off beyond Red Sands is finished. After that, the work will be too far away for you to get back here often."

That was what Chee had wanted—to get away from Little Canyon—yet he found himself not so interested in the job beyond town as in this new cut-off which was almost finished. He pulled a blade of grass, split it thoughtfully down the center as he asked questions of his cousins. Finally he said: "I need to think more about this. If I decide on this job I'll ride over."

Before his cousins were out of sight down the canyon Chee was walking toward the fields, a bold plan shaping in his mind. As the plan began to flourish, wild and hardy as young tumbleweed, Chee added his own voice softly to the song his father was singing: ". . . In the middle of the wide field . . . Yellow Corn Boy . . . I wish to put in."

Chee walked slowly around the field, the rich red earth yielding to his footsteps. His plan depended upon this land and upon the things he remembered most about his wife's people.

Through planting time Chee worked zealously and tirelessly. He spoke little of the large new field he was planting because he felt so strongly that just now this was something between himself and the land. The first days he was ever stooping, piercing the ground with the pointed stick, placing the corn kernels there, walking around the field and through it, singing, ". . . His track leads into the ground . . . Yellow Corn Boy . . . his track leads into the ground." After that, each day Chee walked through his field watching for the tips of green to break through; first a few spikes in the center and then more and more until the corn in all parts of the field was above ground. Surely, Chee thought, if he sang the proper songs, if he cared for this land faithfully, it would not forsake him now, even though through the lonely days of winter he had betrayed the goodness of the earth in his thoughts.

Through the summer Chee worked long days, the sun hot upon his back, pulling weeds from around young corn plants; he planted squash and pumpkin; he terraced a small piece of land near his mother's hogan and planted carrots and onions and the moisture-loving chili. He was increasingly restless. Finally he told his family what he hoped the harvest from this land would bring him. Then the whole family waited with him, watching the corn: the slender graceful plants that waved green arms and bent to embrace each other as young winds wandered through the field, the maturing plants flaunting their pollen-laden tassels in the sun, the tall and sturdy parent corn with new-formed ears and a froth of purple, red and yellow corn-beards against the dusty emerald of broad leaves.

Summer was almost over when Chee slung the bulging packs across two pack ponies. His mother helped him tie the heavy rolled pack behind the saddle of the buckskin. Chee knotted the new yellow kerchief

about his neck a little tighter, gave the broad black hat brim an extra tug, but these were only gestures of assurance and he knew it. The land had not failed him. That part was done. But this he was riding into? Who could tell?

When Chee arrived at Red Sands, it was as he had expected to find it—no cars on the highway. His cousins had told him that even the Pueblo farmers were using the new cut-off to town. The barren gravel around the Red Sands Trading Post was deserted. A sign banged against the dismantled gas pumps *Closed until further notice.*

Old Man Fat came from the crude summer shelter built beside the log hogan from a few branches of scrub cedar and the sides of wooden crates. He seemed almost friendly when he saw Chee.

"Get down, my son," he said, eyeing the bulging packs. There was no bluster in his voice today and his face sagged, looking somewhat saddened; perhaps because his cheeks were no longer quite full enough to push his eyes upward at the corners. "You are going on a journey?"

Chee shook his head. "Our fields gave us so much this year, I thought to sell or trade this to the trader. I didn't know he was no longer here."

Old Man Fat sighed, his voice dropping to an injured tone. "He says he and his wife are going to rest this winter; then after that he'll build a place up on the new highway."

Chee moved as though to be traveling on, then jerked his head toward the pack ponies. "Anything you need?"

"I'll ask my wife," Old Man Fat

said as he led the way to the shelter. "Maybe she has a little money. Things have not been too good with us since the trader closed. Only a few tourists come this way." He shrugged his shoulders. "And with the trader gone—no credit."

Chee was not deceived by his father-in-law's unexpected confidences. He recognized them as a hopeful bid for sympathy and, if possible, something for nothing. Chee made no answer. He was thinking that so far he had been right about his wife's parents: their thriftlessness had left them with no resources to last until Old Man Fat found another easy way of making a living.

Old Man Fat's Wife was in the shelter working at her loom. She turned rather wearily when her husband asked with noticeable deference if she would give him money to buy supplies. Chee surmised that the only income here was from his mother-in-law's weaving.

She peered around the corner of the shelter at the laden ponies, and then she looked at Chee. "What do you have there, my son?"

Chee smiled to himself as he turned to pull the pack from one of the ponies, dragged it to the shelter where he untied the ropes. Pumpkins and hardshelled squash tumbled out, and the ears of corn—pale yellow husks fitting firmly over plump ripe kernels, blue corn, red corn, yellow corn, many-colored corn, ears and ears of it—tumbled into every corner of the shelter.

"Yooooh," Old Man Fat's Wife exclaimed as she took some of the ears in her hands. Then she glanced up at her son-in-law. "But we have no money for all this. We have sold almost everything we own—even the brass bed that stood in the hogan."

Old Man Fat's brass bed. Chee concealed his amusement as he started back for another pack. That must have been a hard parting. Then he stopped, for, coming from the cool darkness of the hogan was the Little One, rubbing her eyes as though she had been asleep. She stood for a moment in the doorway and Chee saw that she was dirty, barefoot, her hair uncombed, her little blouse shorn of all its silver buttons. Then she ran toward Chee, her arms outstretched. Heedless of Old Man Fat and his wife, her father caught her in his arms, her hair falling in a dark cloud across his face, the sweetness of her laughter warm against his shoulder.

It was the haste within him to get this slow waiting game played through to the finish that made Chee speak unwisely. It was the desire to swing her before him in the saddle and ride fast to Little Canyon that prompted his words. "The money doesn't matter. You still have something. . . ."

Chee knew immediately that he had overspoken. The old woman looked from him to the corn spread before her. Unfriendliness began to harden in his father-in-law's face. All the old arguments between himself and his wife's people came pushing and crowding in between them now.

Old Man Fat began kicking the ears of corn back onto the canvas as he eyed Chee angrily. "And you rode all the way over here thinking that for a little food we would give up our daughter's daughter?"

Chee did not wait for the old man to reach for the Little One. He walked dazedly to the shelter, rubbing his cheek against her soft dark hair and put her gently into her grandmother's lap. Then he turned back to the horses. He had failed. By his own haste he had failed. He swung into the saddle, his hand touching the roll behind it. Should he ride on into town?

Then he dismounted, scarcely glancing at Old Man Fat, who stood uncertainly at the corner of the shelter, listening to his wife. "Give me a hand with this other pack of corn, Grandfather," Chee said, carefully keeping the small bit of hope from his voice.

Puzzled, but willing, Old Man Fat helped carry the other pack to the shelter, opening it to find more corn as well as carrots and round pale yellow onions. Chee went back for the roll behind the buckskin's saddle and carried it to the entrance of the shelter where he cut the ropes and gave the canvas a nudge with his toe. Tins of coffee rolled out, small plump cloth bags; jerked meat from several butcherings spilled from a flour sack, and bright red chilis splashed like flames against the dust.

"I will leave all this anyhow," Chee told them. "I would not want my daughter nor even you old people to go hungry."

Old Man Fat picked up a shiny tin of coffee, then put it down. With trembling hands he began to untie one of the cloth bags—dried sweet peaches.

The Little One had wriggled from her grandmother's lap, unheeded, and was on her knees, digging her hands into the jerked meat.

"There is almost enough food here to last all winter," Old Man Fat's Wife sought the eyes of her husband.

Chee said, "I meant it to be enough. But that was when I thought you might send the Little One back with me." He looked down at his daughter noisily sucking jerky. Her mouth, both fists were full of it. "I am sorry that you feel you cannot bear to part with her."

Old Man Fat's Wife brushed a straggly wisp of gray hair from her forehead as she turned to look at the Little One. Old Man Fat was looking too. And it was not a thing to see. For in that moment the Little One ceased to be their daughter's daughter and became just another mouth to feed.

"And why not?" the old woman asked wearily.

■ Chee was settled in the saddle, the barefooted Little One before him. He urged the buckskin faster, and his daughter clutched his shirtfront. The purpling mesas flung back the echo: ". . . My corn embrace each other. In the middle of the wide field . . . Yellow Corn Boy embrace each other."

Considerations

This story gives us some feeling of the overwhelming importance of Indian tradition. No matter what the individual's emotions, he must follow the laws. One law—*the daughter of a dead mother must be given to her mother's people*—causes the crisis in this story. Another law—*be good to the land*—seems to solve it.

Following these rules is hard for Chee. His upbringing battles constantly with his emotions, but tradition wins. Each new detail adds to the tension and makes the struggle harder. He remembers the way his daughter couldn't sleep at night until she snuggled up against him. He knows the grandparents who have taken his daughter haven't done so because they really believe the old teachings. How do we know that they are not upholders of tradition? Why do they want the child?

Chee does not use their shortcomings to justify his breaking the Indian law. He goes home to till the land; spring and summer come and go. We admire him and yet we wonder how he can stand it.

All at once it seems as though Chee will win. One tradition has brought him its reward. The fields grow and are green. It is as though God or nature were giving him hope. So he goes to get his child.

His chances are good. The old people need food; he wants his child. He is in a strong bargaining position. If her grandparents give her back, he won't have broken the custom. The threat was only a bluff after all. But his will power fails: his emotions take over. He can't bargain for his child; he won't let her be without the best possible food. He is ready to accept what he must. And with that he wins.

If Chee hadn't regained his daughter, would this have been a more dramatic, a more effective story? Have the authors tacked on a sentimental ending? Given the characters, is the ending justifiable? Why are the grandparents finally willing to give up the child? Is their doing so consistent with their characters as described earlier in the story?

The Girls in Their Summer Dresses

IRWIN SHAW

Fifth Avenue was shining in the sun when they left the Brevoort and started walking toward Washington Square. The sun was warm, even though it was November and everything looked like Sunday morning—the buses, and the well-dressed people walking slowly in couples and the quiet buildings with the windows closed.

Michael held Frances' arm tightly as they walked downtown in the sunlight. They walked lightly, almost smiling, because they had slept late and had a good breakfast and it was Sunday. Michael unbuttoned his coat and let it flap around him in the mild wind. They walked, without saying anything, among the young and pleasant-looking people who somehow seem to make up most of the population of that section of New York City.

"Look out," Frances said, as they crossed Eighth Street. "You'll break your neck."

Michael laughed and Frances laughed with him.

"She's not so pretty, anyway," Frances said. "Anyway, not pretty enough to take a chance breaking your neck looking at her."

Michael laughed again. He laughed louder this time, but not as solidly. "She wasn't a bad-looking girl. She had a nice complexion. Country-girl complexion. How did you know I was looking at her?"

Frances cocked her head to one side and smiled at her husband under the tip-tilted brim of her hat. "Mike, darling . . ." she said.

Michael laughed, just a little laugh this time. "O.K.," he said. "The evidence is in. Excuse me. It was the complexion. It's not the sort of complexion you see much in New York. Excuse me."

Frances patted his arm lightly and pulled him along a little faster toward Washington Square.

"This is a nice morning," she said. "This is a wonderful morning. When I have breakfast with you it makes me feel good all day."

"Tonic," Michael said. "Morning pick-up. Rolls and coffee with Mike and you're on the alkali side, guaranteed."

"That's the story. Also, I slept all night, wound around you like a rope."

"Saturday night," he said. "I permit such liberties only when the week's work is done."

"You're getting fat," she said.

"Isn't it the truth? The lean man from Ohio."

"I love it," she said, "an extra five pounds of husband."

"I love it, too," Michael said gravely.

"I have an idea," Frances said.

"My wife has an idea. That pretty girl."

"Let's not see anybody all day," Frances said. "Let's just hang around with each other. You and me. We're always up to our neck in people, drinking their Scotch, or drinking our Scotch, we only see each other in bed . . ."

"The Great Meeting Place," Michael said. "Stay in bed long enough and everybody you ever knew will show up there."

"Wise guy," Frances said. "I'm talking serious."

"O.K., I'm listening serious."

"I want to go out with my husband all day long. I want him to talk only to me and listen only to me."

"What's to stop us?" Michael asked. "What party intends to prevent me from seeing my wife alone on Sunday? What party?"

"The Stevensons. They want us to drop by around one o'clock and they'll drive us into the country."

"The lousy Stevensons," Mike said, "Transparent. They can whistle. They can go driving in the country by themselves. My wife and I have to stay in New York and bore each other tête-à-tête."

"Is it a date?"

"It's a date."

Frances leaned over and kissed him on the tip of the ear.

"Darling," Michael said. "This is Fifth Avenue."

"Let me arrange a program," Frances said. "A planned Sunday in New York for a young couple with money to throw away."

"Go easy."

"First let's go see a football game. A professional football game," Frances said, because she knew Michael loved to watch them. "The Giants are playing. And it'll be nice to be outside all day today and get hungry and later we'll go down to Cavanagh's and get a steak as big as a blacksmith's apron, with a bottle of wine, and after that, there's a new French picture at the Filmarte that everybody says . . . Say, are you listening to me?"

"Sure," he said. He took his eyes off the hatless girl with the dark hair, cut dancer-style, like a helmet, who was walking past him with the self-conscious strength and grace dancers have. She was walking without a coat and she looked very solid and strong and her belly was flat, like a boy's, under her skirt, and her hips swung boldly because she was a dancer and also because she knew Michael was looking at her. She smiled a little to herself as she went past and Michael noticed all these things before he looked back at his wife. "Sure," he said, "we're going to watch the Giants and we're going to eat steak and we're going to see a French picture. How do you like that?"

"That's it," Frances said flatly. "That's the program for the day. Or maybe you'd just rather walk up and down Fifth Avenue."

"No," Michael said carefully. "Not at all."

"You always look at other women," Frances said. "At every damn woman in the City of New York."

"Oh, come now," Michael said, pretending to joke. "Only pretty ones. And, after all, how many pretty women *are* there in New York? Seventeen?"

"More. At least you seem to think so. Wherever you go."

"Not the truth. Occasionally, maybe, I look at a woman as she passes. In the street. I admit, perhaps in the street I look at a woman once in a while . . ."

"Everywhere," Frances said, "Every damned place we go. Restaurants, subways, theaters, lectures, concerts."

"Now, darling," Michael said, "I look at everything. God gave me eyes and I look at women and men and subway excavations and moving pictures and the little flowers of the field. I casually inspect the universe."

"You ought to see the look in your eye," Frances said, "as you casually inspect the universe on Fifth Avenue."

"I'm a happily married man." Michael pressed her elbow tenderly, knowing what he was doing. "Example for the whole twentieth century, Mr. and Mrs. Mike Loomis."

"You mean it?"

"Frances, baby . . ."

"Are you *really* happily married?"

"Sure," Michael said, feeling the whole Sunday morning sinking like lead inside him. "Now what the hell is the sense in talking like that?"

"I would like to know." Frances walked faster now, looking straight ahead, her face showing nothing, which was the way she always managed it when she was arguing or feeling bad.

"I'm wonderfully happily married,"

Michael said patiently. "I am the envy of all men between the ages of fifteen and sixty in the State of New York."

"Stop kidding," Frances said.

"I have a fine home," Michael said. "I got nice books and a phonograph and nice friends. I live in a town I like the way I like and I do the work I like and I live with the woman I like. Whenever something good happens, don't I run to you? When something bad happens, don't I cry on your shoulder?"

"Yes," Frances said. "You look at every woman that passes."

"That's an exaggeration."

"Every woman." Frances took her hand off Michael's arm. "If she's not pretty you turn away fairly quickly. If she's halfway pretty you watch her for about seven steps . . ."

"My lord, Frances!"

"If she's pretty you practically break your neck . . ."

"Hey, let's have a drink," Michael said, stopping.

"We just had breakfast."

"Now, listen, darling," Mike said, choosing his words with care, "it's a nice day and we both feel good and there's no reason why we have to break it up. Let's have a nice Sunday."

"I could have a fine Sunday if you didn't look as though you were dying to run after every skirt on Fifth Avenue."

"Let's have a drink," Michael said.

"I don't want a drink."

"What do you want, a fight?"

"No," Frances said so unhappily that Michael felt terribly sorry for her. "I don't want a fight. I don't know why I started this. All right, let's drop it. Let's have a good time."

They joined hands consciously and walked without talking among the baby carriages and the old Italian men in their Sunday clothes and the young women with Scotties in Washington Square Park.

"I hope it's a good game today," Frances said after a while, her tone a good imitation of the tone she had used at breakfast and at the beginning of their walk. "I like professional football games. They hit each other as though they're made out of concrete. When they tackle each other," she said, trying to make Michael laugh, "they make divots. It's very exciting."

"I want to tell you something," Michael said very seriously. "I have not touched another woman. Not once. In all the five years."

"All right," Frances said.

"You believe that, don't you?"

"All right."

They walked between the crowded benches, under the scrubby city park trees.

"I try not to notice it," Frances said, as though she were talking to herself. "I try to make believe it doesn't mean anything. Some men're like that, I tell myself, they have to see what they're missing."

"Some women're like that, too," Michael said. "In my time I've seen a couple of ladies."

"I haven't even looked at another man," Frances said, walking straight ahead, "since the second time I went out with you."

"There's no law," Michael said.

"I feel rotten inside, in my stomach, when we pass a woman and you look at her and I see that look in your eye and that's the way you looked at me the first time, in Alice Maxwell's house. Standing there in the living room, next to the radio, with a green hat on and all those people."

"I remember the hat," Michael said.

"The same look," Frances said. "And it makes me feel bad. It makes me feel terrible."

"Sssh, please, darling, ssh . . ."

"I think I would like a drink now," Frances said.

They walked over to a bar on Eighth Street, not saying anything, Michael automatically helping her over curbstones, and guiding her past automobiles. He walked, buttoning his coat, looking thoughtfully at his neatly shined heavy brown shoes as they made the steps toward the bar. They sat near a window in the bar and the sun streamed in, and there was a small cheerful fire in the fireplace. A little Japanese waiter came over and put down some pretzels and smiled happily at them.

"What do you order after breakfast?" Michael asked.

"Brandy, I suppose," Frances said.

"Courvoisier," Michael told the waiter. "Two Courvoisier."

The waiter came with the glasses and they sat drinking the brandy, in the sunlight. Michael finished half his and drank a little water.

"I look at women," he said. "Correct. I don't say it's wrong or right, I look at them. If I pass them on the street and I don't look at them, I'm fooling you, I'm fooling myself."

"You look at them as though you

want them," Frances said, playing with her brandy glass. "Every one of them."

"In a way," Michael said, speaking softly and not to his wife, "in a way that's true. I don't do anything about it, but it's true."

"I know it. That's why I feel bad."

"Another brandy," Michael called. "Waiter, two more brandies."

"Why do you hurt me?" Frances asked. "What're you doing?"

Michael sighed and closed his eyes and rubbed them gently with his fingertips. "I love the way women look. One of the things I like best about New York is the battalions of women. When I first came to New York from Ohio that was the first thing I noticed, the million wonderful women, all over the city. I walked around with my heart in my throat."

"A kid," Frances said. "That's a kid's feeling."

"Guess again," Michael said. "Guess again. I'm older now, I'm a man getting near middle age, putting on a little fat and I still love to walk along Fifth Avenue at three o'clock on the east side of the street between Fiftieth and Fifty-seventh Streets, they're all out then, making believe they're shopping, in their furs and their crazy hats, everything all concentrated from all over the world into eight blocks, the best furs, the best clothes, the handsomest women, out to spend money and feeling good about it, looking coldly at you, making believe they're not looking at you as you go past."

The Japanese waiter put the two drinks down, smiling with great happiness.

"Everything is all right?" he asked.

"Everything is wonderful," Michael said.

"If it's just a couple of fur coats," Frances said, "and forty-five-dollar hats . . ."

"It's not the fur coats. Or the hats. That's just the scenery for that particular kind of woman. Understand," he said, "you don't have to listen to this."

"I want to listen."

"I like the girls in the offices. Neat, with their eyeglasses, smart, chipper, knowing what everything is about, taking care of themselves all the time." He kept his eye on the people going slowly past outside the window. "I like the girls on Forty-fourth Street at lunch time, the actresses, all dressed up on nothing a week, talking to the good-looking boys, wearing themselves out being young and vivacious outside Sardi's, waiting for producers to look at them. I like the salesgirls in Macy's, paying attention to you first because you're a man, leaving lady customers waiting, flirting with you over socks and books and phonograph needles. I got all this stuff accumulated in me because I've been thinking about it for ten years and now you've asked for it and here it is."

"Go ahead," Frances said.

"When I think of New York City, I think of all the girls, the Jewish girls, the Italians girls, the Irish, Polack, Chinese, German, Negro, Spanish, Russian girls, all on parade in the city. I don't know whether it's something special with me or whether every man in the city walks around with the same feeling inside him, but

I feel as though I'm at a picnic in this city. I like to sit near the women in the theaters, the famous beauties who've taken six hours to get ready and look it. And the young girls at the football games, with the red cheeks, and when the warm weather comes, the girls in their summer dresses . . ." He finished his drink. "That's the story. You asked for it, remember. I can't help but look at them. I can't help but want them."

"You want them," Frances repeated without expression. "You said that."

"Right," Michael said, being cruel now and not caring, because she had made him expose himself. "You brought this subject up for discussion, we will discuss it fully."

Frances finished her drink and swallowed two or three times extra. "You say you love me?"

"I love you, but I also want them. O.K."

"I'm pretty, too," Frances said. "As pretty as any of them."

"You're beautiful," Michael said, meaning it.

"I'm good for you," Frances said, pleading. "I've made a good wife, a good housekeeper, a good friend. I'd do any damn thing for you."

"I know," Michael said. He put his hand out and grasped hers.

"You'd like to be free to . . ." Frances said.

"Sssh."

"Tell the truth." She took her hand away from under his.

Michael flicked the edge of his glass with his finger. "O.K.," he said gently. "Sometimes I feel I would like to be free."

"Well," Frances said defiantly, drumming on the table, "anytime you say . . ."

"Don't be foolish." Michael swung his chair around to her side of the table and patted her thigh.

She began to cry, silently, into her handkerchief, bent over just enough so that nobody else in the bar would notice. "Some day," she said, crying, "you're going to make a move . . ."

Michael didn't say anything. He sat watching the bartender slowly peel a lemon.

"Aren't you?" Frances asked harshly. "Come on, tell me. Talk. Aren't you?"

"Maybe," Michael said. He moved his chair back again. "How the hell do I know?"

"You know," Frances persisted. "Don't you know?"

"Yes," Michael said after a while, "I know."

Frances stopped crying then. Two or three snuffles into the handkerchief and she put it away and her face didn't tell anything to anybody. "At least do me one favor," she said.

"Sure."

"Stop talking about how pretty this woman is, or that one. Nice eyes, nice breasts, a pretty figure, good voice," she mimicked his voice. "Keep it to yourself. I'm not interested."

"Excuse me." Michael waved to the waiter. "I'll keep it to myself."

Frances flicked the corner of her eyes. "Another brandy," she told the waiter.

"Two," Michael said.

"Yes, ma'am, yes, sir," said the waiter, backing away.

Frances regarded him coolly across the table. "Do you want me to call the Stevensons?" she asked. "It'll be nice in the country."

"Sure," Michael said. "Call them up."

She got up from the table and walked across the room toward the telephone. Michael watched her walk, thinking, what a pretty girl, what nice legs.

Considerations

It would seem that the writers of this particular time and this place have become almost obsessed with the peculiarities of the male-female relationship. They describe it in endless detail, documenting each nuance objectively or passionately, encouraging the reader to take one side or the other, but rarely offering a solution as to why it is so (if it is so).

Irwin Shaw has captured, like a fly trapped in amber, the classic mid-twentieth-century model of the relationship between two sophisticated young urban American adults. While Hemingway's couple came from the thirties and Colette's are French upper-middle-class, Frances and Michael are the New Yorkers of the day before yesterday. True, there is conflict here also. But it doesn't come from an awareness of empty lives; it isn't part of a search for meaning. It's simply a difference between the typical (or stereotypical) female idea of what a relationship should be and the male version of the same relationship. Whether these divergent ideas represent basic biological differences, the product of upbringing, an example of Riesman's inner-directed individual encountering an other-directed one, or a substantiation of the divinely predestined role differences observed long ago by Milton ("he for God only, she for God in him"), the author does not try to explain. He merely delineates the two focuses.

Frances' version of a happy weekend is intensely interpersonal—defined in terms of just the two of them. "Let's just hang around with each other . . . we only see each other in bed. I want to go out with my husband all day long. I want him to talk only to me and listen only to me." For Michael—and for most males of his era and background—the arrangement as it has been is quite satisfactory. Except in the heat of the chase, he apparently doesn't see too much point in such "mushy stuff."

Would we really be justified in calling Michael insensitive? Perhaps that is the conclusion the author intended. Certainly Michael seems unconcerned with the effect that his "casually inspecting the universe" has on Frances. But looking at Michael in conjunction with the male halves of the couples in other modern stories about such relationships raises some more basic questions. Usually the males have seemed content, the females unhappy—is it in the nature of women to find things to worry about or to want to change? Are they never satisfied? Is there, as claimed by Women's Liberation proponents, something inherent in all male-female relationships that conflicts with the woman's best interests? Are most men clods, whereas women are sensitive plants? Are men stable and accepting, whereas women are emotional and self-destructive? Or do most modern women (at least initially) allow the wishes of the men in their lives to dictate the rules of the game, then spend their remaining days regretting it? Were things really happier in those times when women were unliberated and unquestioning?

In this particular situation, the immediate provocation for the discord is the attention Michael pays to other women. This is that occasion. How that particular habit is viewed by each of them *should* say something about their personalities. Yet what it says is unclear. Why is Frances annoyed? Does she think that his view of her is as casual as his view of women he doesn't know? Why does she acquiesce, meekly go to call the Stevensons, if she objects so strongly?

It does seem that Michael may have a severe limitation in his ability to relate to a woman. The final sentence, "Michael watched her walk, thinking what a pretty gal, what nice legs," might be taken as an indication that he regards even a women who lives with him and loves him as just a pleasing arrangement of curves and lines designed for his entertainment. In that case he would stand revealed as a shallow, egocentric person.

But isn't a more charitable interpretation possible if we agree that it is natural to experience an abstract aesthetic pleasure in other people—as one would find in a painting or a car or a racehorse? After all, why shouldn't Michael enjoy the girls in their summer dresses as the embodiment of life and youth and spirit? Perhaps thinking of Frances in these terms does not preclude having warmer or more sentimental thoughts about her; these may merely be an additional accolade.

The Condor and the Guests

EVAN S. CONNELL, JR.

In Peru a female condor was staked inside a wooden cage. Every so often a male bird would get into this trap and would then be sold to a zoo or a museum. One of these captured condors, however, was sold to an American, J. D. Botkin of Parallel, Kansas.

It cost Mr. Botkin a great deal of money to get his bird into the United States, but he had traveled quite a bit and was proud of his ability to get anything accomplished that he set his mind to. At his home in Parallel he had a chain fastened about the bird's neck. The other end of the chain was padlocked to a magnolia tree which he had had transplanted to his back yard from the French Quarter of New Orleans on an earlier trip.

All the rest of that first day the condor sat in the magnolia tree and looked across the fields of wheat, but just before sundown it lifted its wings and spread them to the fullest extent as if testing the wind; then with a slow sweep of utter majesty it rose into the air. It took a second leisurely sweep with its wings, and a third. However, on the third stroke it came to the end of the chain. Then it made a sort of gasping noise and fell to the

earth while the magnolia swayed from the shock. After its fall the gigantic bird did not move until long after dark when it got to its feet and climbed into the tree. Next morning as the sun rose it was on the same branch, looking south like a gargoyle taken from the ramparts of some cathedral.

Day after day it sat in the magnolia tree without moving, but every sundown it tried to take off. A pan of meat left nearby was visited only by a swarm of flies.

Almost a week following the bird's arrival Mr. Botkin was eating lunch at the Jupiter Club when he met his friend, Harry Apple, and said to him, "You seen my bird yet?"

Harry Apple was a shrunken, bald-headed man who never had much to say. He answered Mr. Botkin's question by slowly shaking his head. Mr. Botkin then exclaimed that Harry hadn't lived, and clapping him on the shoulder said he was giving a dinner party on Wednesday—a sort of anniversary of the condor's first week in Kansas—and asked if Harry could make it.

After the invitation had been extended, Harry Apple sat silently for almost a minute and stared into space. He had married a tall, smoke-haired ex-show-girl of paralyzing beauty and he understood that she was the reason for the invitations he received.

At last he nodded, saying in his melancholy voice, "Sure. I'll bring Mildred, too."

Mr. Botkin clapped him on the shoulder and proposed a toast, "To the condor!"

Harry sipped his drink and murmured, "Sure."

Mr. Botkin also got the Newtons and the Huddlestuns for dinner. He was not too pleased about the Huddlestuns; Suzie Huddlestun's voice always set him on edge, and "Tiny" was a bore. He had asked the Bagleys, but Chuck Bagley was going to an insurance convention in Kansas City. He had also asked the Gerlachs, the Ridges, and the Zimmermans, but none of them could make it, so he settled for Suzie and Tiny. They were delighted with the invitation.

On the evening of the party "Fig" Newton and his wife had not arrived by seven o'clock, so Mr. Botkin said to the others—Mildred and Harry Apple, and Suzie and Tiny Huddlestun, "Well, by golly, this calls for a drink!"

With cocktails in their hands the guests wandered down to the magnolia tree and stood in a half-circle, shaking the ice in their glasses and looking critically upward. The men stood a bit closer to the tree than the ladies did in order to show that they were not afraid of the condor. The ladies did not think the somber bird would do anything at all and they would rather have sat on the porch and talked.

Tiny Huddlestun was an enormous top-heavy man who had been a wrestler when he was young. His larynx had been injured by a vicious Turk during a match in Joplin, so that now his voice was a sort of quavering falsetto. He bobbled the ice in his glass with an index finger as big as a sausage and said in his falsetto, "That a turkey you got there, Botkin?"

His wife laughed and squeezed his arm. Even in platform shoes she did not come up to his chin, and the difference in their sizes caused people to speculate. She never listened to what he said but every time she heard his voice she laughed and squeezed him.

Mildred Apple said a little sulkily, "J.D., I want it to do something exciting." The cocktail was making her feel dangerous.

Mr. Botkin snapped his fingers. "By golly!" He swallowed the rest of his drink, took Harry's empty glass, and went back to the house. In a few minutes he returned with fresh drinks and a green and yellow parrot riding on his shoulder. Solemnly he announced, "This here's Caldwell."

"Caldwell?" shrieked Suzie Huddlestun, and began to laugh so hard that she clutched Tiny's coat for support.

Mr. Botkin was laughing, too, although he did not want to because he disliked Suzie. His belt went under his belly like a girth under a horse, and as he laughed the belt creaked. It was several minutes before he could pat the perspiration from his strawberry face and gasp, "By golly!" He turned to the Apples who had stood by politely smiling, and explained, "Old Nowlin Caldwell at the Pioneer Trust."

"Caldwell," the parrot muttered, walking around on Mr. Botkin's shoulder.

Tiny Huddlestun had been hugging his wife. He released her and cleared his throat. "You going to eat that bird at Thanksgiving, Botkin?"

Mr. Botkin ignored him and said, leaning his head over next to the parrot, "Looky there, Caldwell, that condor don't even move. He's scared to death of you. You get on up there and tear him to pieces."

The parrot jumped to the ground and ran to the magnolia tree. The tree had not done well in the Kansas climate and was a stunted little thing with ragged bark and weak limbs which were turning their tips toward the ground. The parrot hooked its way up the trunk with no trouble, but at the lowest fork paused to watch the condor.

Mr. Botkin waved a hand as big as a spade.

The parrot went on up, more slowly, however, stopping every few seconds to consider. Finally it crept out on the same limb and in a burst of confidence clamped its bright little claws into the wood beside the condor's talons. Then it imitated the black giant's posture and blinked down at the guests, which caused all of them except Harry Apple to break into laughter. The chain clinked. This alarmed the parrot; it whipped its head around and found itself looking into one of the condor's flat eyes.

"Eat 'im up!" Tiny shouted.

But the parrot fell out of the tree and ran toward the house, flailing its brilliant wings in the grass and screaming.

While his guests were still chuckling Mr. Botkin pointed far to the south where thunderheads were building up and said, "That's what the Andes look like."

The guests were all studying the familiar clouds when Fig Newton's sedan squeaked into the driveway. Mr. Botkin waved to Fig and his wife and went into the kitchen to get more drinks. To the colored girl Mrs. Botkin had hired for the evening he said, "Ever see a bird like that?"

The colored girl looked out the window immediately and answered with enthusiasm, "No, sir, Mr. Botkin!" But this did not seem to satisfy him so she added, "No sir, I sure never have!"

"You bet your sweet bottom you haven't." He was chipping some ice. "Because that's a condor."

"What's he eat?" she asked, but since he did not answer she felt it had been a silly question and turned her head away in shame.

Mr. Botkin shook up the drinks, bumped open the screen door with his stomach, and carried the tray into the yard. After he had greeted Fig and Laura Newton he said, "That little darky in the kitchen is scared to death of this bird. She wouldn't come near it for the world."

Fig answered, "Generally speaking, colored people are like that." He had a nervous habit of twitching his nose each time he finished speaking, which was the reason that hundreds of high-school students spoke of him as "Rabbit" Newton.

"Make him fly, J.D.," Laura said. "I want to admire his strength!" She was dressed in imitation gypsy clothes with a purple bandanna tied around her hips and a beauty mole painted on her temple. She did a little gypsy step across the yard, shaking her head so the gold earrings bounced against her cheeks. She lifted her glass high in the air. "Oh, make him fly!"

"Yes, do," added Mildred Apple. She had finished her drink quickly when she saw Laura's costume and now she stood on one leg so that her hips curved violently.

Mrs. Botkin, an egg-shaped little woman with wispy white hair that lay on her forehead like valentine lace, looked at her husband and started to say something. Then she puckered her lips and stopped.

Fig had been waiting for a pause. Now he drew attention to himself and said in measured tones, "Ordinarily the Negro avoids things he does not understand."

There was a polite silence until his nose twitched.

Then Mr. Botkin, whose cheeks had been growing redder with each drink, said, "You know what its name is?"

"What?" cried Suzie.

"Sambo," put in Fig, imitating a drawl. A laugh trembled at his lips, but nobody else laughed so he tasted his drink.

"Sherlock Holmes?" guessed Laura. Only Suzie tittered at this, and Laura glanced at her sourly.

Mr. Botkin finally said, "Well, I'm going to tell you—it's Samson."

He waited until the guests' laughter had died away and then he told them that the name of the female in Peru was Delilah. He joined the laughter this time, his belt creaking and the perspiration standing out all over his face. When the guests had quieted down to head-wagging chuckles he said, "Well, by golly, I'll stir this Samson up!" He picked some sticks off the grass and began tossing them into the magnolia. At last one hit the condor's chest, but the huge bird seemed to be asleep.

"The damn thing won't eat, either!" he exclaimed in a gust of irritation.

"Won't *eat?*" shrilled Suzie Huddlestun, standing in the circle of Tiny's arms. "Gee, what's it live on if it don't eat?"

Mr. Botkin ignored her.

Fig cleared his throat. Pointing upward he said, "If you will look at that branch, you'll see it is bent almost like a strung bow."

Mrs. Botkin suddenly turned to her husband and laid a hand on his sleeve. "Dear—"

Everybody looked at her in mild surprise, as always happened when she decided to say anything. She pressed a wisp of hair back into place and breathed, "Why don't you let the bird go?"

There was an uncomfortable pause, which Laura Newton broke by dancing around the back yard again. The candystripe skirt sailed around her bony goose legs. "How many want the condor to fly?" she asked, and thrusting her glass high in the air she cried, "Vote!"

Tiny Huddlestun had been squeezing his wife, but now he held his glass as high as possible without spilling the liquor and looked around with pleasure, knowing that nobody was tall enough to match the height of his ballot. Suzie's glass, clutched in her childlike hand, came just above his ear.

Mildred Apple sulkily lifted hers and so did Fig. Mr. Botkin had been watching with a curious sort of interest. His glass had gone up as soon as Laura proposed the vote. He looked at his wife, and she quickly lifted hers.

"Harry?" Laura cried.

Harry Apple continued drinking.

Mrs. Botkin murmured, "I think dinner's ready." She fluttered her hands about in weak desperation, but nobody looked at her.

Laura asked in a different tone, "Harry?" She was still holding the glass above her head.

Harry stood flat-footed and glared at the ground. A little drunkenly he swirled the ice in his glass.

After a few seconds of silence Mrs. Botkin coughed and started toward the porch; the guests filed after her. Mildred Apple was wearing white jersey. She got directly ahead of Laura and walked as if she were about to start a hula. Suzie and Tiny swung hands. Mr. Botkin, scowling, brought up the rear.

During salad Laura Newton talked mostly to the people on either side of Harry. Burgundy wine from France was served with the steaks, and while they were beginning on that the sun went down. Then one by one the guests stopped cutting their meat and looked through the porch screen.

Fig Newton twisted the Phi Beta Kappa key on his chain as he watched the condor lift first one foot and then the other from its branch. Tiny Huddlestun leaned his hambone elbows on the table and raised himself partly out of his chair in order to see over Mrs. Botkin's fluffy white head. Of the guests, only Harry Apple did not look; he stared at his wine glass, turning it slowly with his fingers on the stem. Mr Botkin's eyes had narrowed in anticipation; he waited for the flight like an Occidental Buddha.

The condor's wings spread, brushing the leaves of other branches, and at the size of the bird Laura dropped her fork. Nobody picked it up, so it lay on the flagstones, its tines sending out a persistent hum.

The black condor lifted its feet again. This caused the chain which dangled from its neck to sway back and forth.

The dinner table was quiet. Only some June bugs fizzed angrily as they tried to get through the screens.

Mildred Apple said abruptly, "I'm cold." Nobody looked at her, so she went on in a sharp tone, "Why doesn't somebody switch off that fan? I tell you I'm cold. I won't sit here all night in a draft. I won't!"

Mr. Botkin did not turn his head, but growled, "Shut up."

Mildred was shocked, but she recovered quickly. "Don't you *dare* tell me to shut up! I won't stand for it! Do you hear?" Mr. Botkin paid no attention to her, so she turned petulantly to Harry, who was looking at his glass.

"Switch it off yourself," murmured Laura.

Mildred's eyes began to glitter. "I will not!"

"I'm sure nobody else is going to," Laura said in a dry voice.

Fig was getting ready to say some-

thing when Suzie Huddlestun gasped, "Oh!"

The condor took off so slowly that it did not seem real; it appeared only to be stretching, yet it was in the air. When its immense wings had spread and descended a second time, its talons rose above the top branches, curling into metalhard globes. For an instant the condor hung in the purple sky like an insignia of some great war plane, then its head was jerked down. It made its one sound, dropped to the warm ground, and lay without moving.

Laura Newton observed sourly, "What a simple bird." She looked across her tack-hammer nose at Harry.

Tiny grinned. "Now's the time to cook that turkey for Thanksgiving, Botkin." He looked all around the table, but nobody chuckled, and his eyes came back to Suzie. She laughed.

Fig took a sip of water and then cleared his throat. "Fowl," he said, after frowning in thought, "are not overly intelligent."

Twilight was ending. The guests could not see the condor distinctly, but only what looked like a gunny sack under the dying magnolia. Much later, while they were arguing bitterly over their bridge scores, they heard the condor's chain clinking and soon a branch creaked.

Considerations

Is there any person in this story who is worthy of respect? The host of the party, who callously uproots living things to add to his collection? The shallow, inane guests whose cocktail game at the expense of a bird seems appalling?

We feel for the plight of the bird as a bird. Can't we also see it as a symbol? The treatment it receives can be seen as commentary on how these people—whoever they represent—treat people as well. They are detached from the human race, viewing everyone outside their circle as specimens, bugs on the wall, or things put on earth for their entertainment. They are like the Sunday visitors who mob a disaster area and bring their children to gawk at the distress of others as though it were part of a planned sideshow.

How does the author reinforce our distaste for these characters? One way is by giving them silly names. The names serve a further purpose: they convert their owners into symbols. By using these names the author is not only making fun of the characters but also is making sure we don't regard them as real people in a real place. They clearly become representative of whoever in the world would behave this way. We are forced to ask, "Do I know someone like that?" Some of the names communicate their owner's personalities. We associate Botkin with *bodkin*, like *knife*; it makes us think of viciousness or of stabbing those who trust you in the back. Can you find any hidden meaning in the other names—Tiny, Fig Newton, or Harry Apple, for instance?

Why might Connell have used a condor here? Certainly a condor is unusual enough to be plausible as part of Botkin's collection. How does the condor's wildness contrast with the behavior of the party members?

Perhaps most significant of all is the idea that a bird is a symbol of freedom. A condor seems especially appropriate to communicate this idea. He lives high above the highest Peruvian mountains beyond the smallness of mankind. To chain such a creature in such surroundings is almost blasphemous.

When the condor takes off, there is one feeble attempt at a joke that doesn't work even among such hardened types. It is almost as if even the worst of them respond to something they can't quite understand. The condor will not give up—the last line indicates that. Deep inside the genes there is the will to freedom.

A Worn Path

EUDORA WELTY

It was December—a bright frozen day in the early morning. Far out in the country there was an old Negro woman with her head tied in a red rag, coming along a path through the pinewoods. Her name was Phoenix Jackson. She was very old and small and she walked slowly in the dark pine shadows, moving a little from side to side in her steps, with the balanced heaviness and lightness of a pendulum in a grandfather clock. She carried a thin, small cane made from an umbrella, and with this she kept tapping the frozen earth in front of her. This made a grave and persistent noise in the still air, that seemed meditative like the chirping of a solitary little bird.

She wore a dark striped dress reaching down to her shoe tops, and an equally long apron of bleached sugar sacks, with a full pocket: all neat and tidy, but every time she took a step she might have fallen over her shoelaces, which dragged from her unlaced shoes. She looked straight ahead. Her eyes were blue with age. Her skin had a pattern all its own of numberless branching wrinkles and as though a whole little tree stood in the middle of her forehead, but a golden color ran underneath, and the two knobs of her cheeks were illu-·mined by a yellow burning under the dark. Under the red rag her hair came down on her neck in the frailest of ringlets, still black, and with an odor like copper.

Now and then there was a quivering in the thicket. Old Phoenix said, "Out of my way, all you foxes, owls, beetles, jack rabbits, coons and wild animals! . . . Keep out from under these feet, little bob-whites. . . . Keep the big wild hogs out of my path. Don't let none of those come running my direction. I got a long way." Under her small black-freckled hand her cane, limber as a buggy whip, would switch at the brush as if to rouse up any hiding things.

On she went. The woods were deep and still. The sun made the pine needles almost too bright to look at, up where the wind rocked. The cones dropped as light as feathers. Down in the hollow was the mourning dove— it was not too late for him.

The path ran up a hill. "Seem like there is chains about my feet, time I get this far," she said, in the voice of argument old people keep to use with themselves. "Something always take a hold of me on this hill—pleads I should stay."

After she got to the top she turned and gave a full, severe look behind her where she had come. "Up through pines," she said at length. "Now down through oaks."

Her eyes opened their widest, and she started down gently. But before she got to the bottom of the hill a bush caught her dress.

Her fingers were busy and intent, but her skirts were full and long, so that before she could pull them free in one place they were caught in another. It was not possible to allow the dress to tear. "I in the thorny bush," she said. "Thorns, you doing your appointed work. Never want to let folks pass, no sir. Old eyes thought you was a pretty little *green* bush."

Finally, trembling all over, she stood free, and after a moment dared to stoop for her cane.

"Sun so high!" she cried, leaning back and looking, while the thick tears went over her eyes. "The time getting all gone here."

At the foot of this hill was a place where a log was laid across the creek.

"Now comes the trial," said Phoenix.

Putting her right foot out, she mounted the log and shut her eyes. Lifting her skirt, leveling her cane fiercely before her, like a festival figure in some parade, she began to march across. Then she opened her eyes and she was safe on the other side.

"I wasn't as old as I thought," she said.

But she sat down to rest. She spread her skirts on the bank around her and folded her hands over her knees. Up above her was a tree in a pearly cloud of mistletoe. She did not dare to close her eyes, and when a little boy brought her a plate with a slice of marble-cake on it she spoke to him. "That would be acceptable," she said. But when she went to take it there was just her own hand in the air.

So she left that tree, and had to go through a barbed-wire fence. There she had to creep and crawl, spreading her knees and stretching her fingers like a baby trying to climb the steps. But she talked loudly to herself: she could not let her dress be torn now, so late in the day, and she could not pay for having her arm or her leg sawed off if she got it caught fast where she was.

At last she was safe through the fence and risen up out in the clearing. Big dead trees, like black men with one arm, were standing in the purple stalks of the withered cotton field. There sat a buzzard.

"Who you watching?"

In the furrow she made her way along.

"Glad this not the season for bulls," she said, looking sideways, "and the good Lord made his snakes to curl up and sleep in the winter. A pleasure I don't see no two-headed snake coming around that tree, where it come once. It took a while to get by him, back in the summer."

She passed through the old cotton and went into a field of dead corn. It whispered and shook and was taller than her head. "Through the maze now," she said, for there was no path.

Then there was something tall, black, and skinny there, moving before her.

At first she took it for a man. It could have been a man dancing in the field. But she stood still and listened, and it did not make a sound. It was as silent as a ghost.

"Ghost," she said sharply, "who be you the ghost of? For I have heard of nary death close by."

But there was no answer—only the ragged dancing in the wind.

She shut her eyes, reached out her hand, and touched a sleeve. She found a coat and inside that an emptiness, cold as ice.

"You scarecrow," she said. Her face lighted. "I ought to be shut up for good," she said with laughter. "My senses is gone. I too old. I the oldest people I ever know. Dance, old scarecrow," she said, "while I dancing with you."

She kicked her foot over the furrow, and with mouth drawn down, shook her head once or twice in a little strutting way. Some husks blew down and whirled in streamers about her skirts.

Then she went on, parting her way from side to side with the cane, through the whispering field. At last she came to the end, to a wagon track where the silver grass blew between the red ruts. The quail were walking around like pullets, seeming all dainty and unseen.

"Walk pretty," she said. "This the easy place. This the easy going."

She followed the track, swaying through the quiet bare fields, through the little strings of trees silver in their dead leaves, past cabins silver from weather, with the doors and windows boarded shut, all like old women under a spell sitting there. "I walking in their sleep," she said, nodding her head vigorously.

In a ravine she went where a spring was silently flowing through a hollow log. Old Phoenix bent and drank. "Sweet-gum makes the water sweet," she said, and drank more. "Nobody know who made this well, for it was here when I was born."

The track crossed a swampy part where the moss hung as white as lace from every limb. "Sleep on, alligators, and blow your bubbles." Then the track went into the road.

Deep, deep the road went down between the high green-colored banks. Overhead the live-oaks met, and it was as dark as a cave.

A black dog with a lolling tongue came up out of the weeds by the ditch. She was meditating, and not ready, and when he came at her she only hit him a little with her cane. Over she went in the ditch, like a little puff of milkweed.

Down there, her senses drifted away. A dream visited her, and she reached her hand up, but nothing reached down and gave her a pull. So she lay there and presently went to talking. "Old woman," she said to herself, "that black dog come up out of the weeds to stall you off, and now there he sitting on his fine tail, smiling at you."

A white man finally came along and found her—a hunter, a young man, with his dog on a chain.

"Well, Granny!" he laughed. "What are you doing there?"

"Lying on my back like a June-bug waiting to be turned over, mister," she said, reaching up her hand.

He lifted her up, gave her a swing in the air, and set her down. "Anything broken, Granny?"

"No sir, them old dead weeds is springy enough," said Phoenix, when she had got her breath. "I thank you for your trouble."

"Where do you live, Granny?" he asked, while the two dogs were growling at each other.

"Away back yonder, sir, behind the ridge. You can't even see it from here."

"On your way home?"

"No sir, I going to town."

"Why, that's too far! That's as far as I walk when I come out myself, and I get something for my trouble." He patted the stuffed bag he carried, and there hung down a little closed claw. It was one of the bob-whites, with its beak hooked bitterly to show it was dead. "Now you go on home, Granny!"

"I bound to go to town, mister," said Phoenix. "The time come around."

He gave another laugh, filling the whole landscape. "I know you old colored people! Wouldn't miss going to town to see Santa Claus!"

But something held old Phoenix very still. The deep lines in her face went into a fierce and different radiation. Without warning, she had seen with her own eyes a flashing nickel fall out of the man's pocket onto the ground.

"How old are you, Granny?" he was saying.

"There is no telling, mister," she said, "no telling."

Then she gave a little cry and clapped her hands and said, "Git on away from here, dog! Look! Look at that dog!" She laughed as if in admiration. "He ain't scared of nobody. He a big black dog." She whispered, "Sic him!"

"Watch me get rid of that cur," said the man. "Sic him, Pete! Sic him!"

Phoenix heard the dogs fighting, and heard the man running and throwing sticks. She even heard a gunshot. But she was slowly bending forward by that time, further and further forward, the lids stretched down over her eyes, as if she were doing this in her sleep. Her chin was lowered almost to her knees. The yellow palm of her hand came out from the fold of her apron. Her fingers slid down and along the ground under the piece of money with the grace and care they would have in lifting an egg from under a setting hen. Then she slowly straightened up, she stood erect, and the nickel was in her apron pocket. A bird flew by. Her lips moved. "God watching me the whole time. I come to stealing."

The man came back, and his own dog panted about them. "Well, I scared him off that time," he said, and then he laughed and lifted his gun and pointed it at Phoenix.

She stood straight and faced him.

"Doesn't the gun scare you?" he said, still pointing it.

"No, sir, I seen plenty go off closer by, in my day, and for less than what I done," she said, holding utterly still.

He smiled, and shouldered the gun. "Well, Granny," he said, "you must be a hundred years old, and scared of nothing. I'd give you a dime if I had any money with me. But you take my advice and stay home, and nothing will happen to you."

"I bound to go on my way, mister," said Phoenix. She inclined her head in the red rag. Then they went in different directions, but she could hear the gun shooting again and again over the hill.

She walked on. The shadows hung from the oak trees to the road like curtains. Then she smelled wood-smoke, and smelled the river, and she saw a steeple and the cabins on their steep steps. Dozens of little black children whirled around her. There ahead was Natchez smiling. Bells were ringing. She walked on.

In the paved city it was Christmas time. There were red and green electric lights strung and crisscrossed everywhere, and all turned on in the daytime. Old Phoenix would have been lost if she had not distrusted her eyesight and depended on her feet to know where to take her.

She paused quietly on the sidewalk where people were passing by. A lady came along in the crowd, carrying an armful of red-, green- and silver-wrapped presents; she gave off perfume like the red roses in hot summer, and Phoenix stopped her.

"Please, missy, will you lace up my shoe?" She held up her foot.

"What do you want, Grandma?"

"See my shoe," said Phoenix. "Do all right for out in the country, but wouldn't look right to go in a big building."

"Stand still then, Grandma," said the lady. She put her packages down on the sidewalk beside her and laced and tied both shoes tightly.

"Can't lace 'em with a cane," said Phoenix. "Thank you, missy. I doesn't mind asking a nice lady to tie up my shoe, when I gets out on the street."

Moving slowly and from side to side, she went into the big building, and into a tower of steps, where she walked up and around and around until her feet knew to stop.

She entered a door, and there she saw nailed up on the wall the document that had been stamped with the gold seal and framed in the gold frame, which matched the dream that was hung up in her head.

"Here I be," she said. There was a fixed and ceremonial stiffness over her body.

"A charity case, I suppose," said an attendant who sat at the desk before her.

But Phoenix only looked above her head. There was sweat on her face, the wrinkles in her skin shone like a bright net.

"Speak up, Grandma," the woman said. "What's your name? We must have your history, you know. Have you been here before? What seems to be the trouble with you?"

Old Phoenix only gave a twitch to her face as if a fly were bothering her.

"Are you deaf?" cried the attendant.

But then the nurse came in.

"Oh, that's just old Aunt Phoenix," she said. "She doesn't come for herself—she has a little grandson. She makes these trips just as regular as clockwork. She lives away back off the Old Natchez Trace." She bent down. "Well, Aunt Phoenix, why don't you just take a seat? We won't keep you standing after your long trip." She pointed.

The old woman sat down, bolt upright in the chair.

"Now, how is the boy?" asked the nurse.

Old Phoenix did not speak.

"I said, how is the boy?"

But Phoenix only waited and stared straight ahead, her face very solemn and withdrawn into rigidity.

"Is his throat any better?" asked the nurse. "Aunt Phoenix, don't you hear me? Is your grandson's throat any better since the last time you came for the medicine?"

With her hands on her knees, the old woman waited, silent, erect and motionless, just as if she were in armor.

"You mustn't take up our time this way, Aunt Phoenix," the nurse said. "Tell us quickly about your grandson, and get it over. He isn't dead, is he?"

At last there came a flicker and then a flame of comprehension across her face, and she spoke.

"My grandson. It was my memory had left me. There I sat and forgot why I made my long trip."

"Forgot?" The nurse frowned. "After you came so far?"

Then Phoenix was like an old woman begging a dignified forgiveness for waking up frightened in the night. "I never did go to school, I was too old at the Surrender," she said in a soft voice. "I'm an old woman without an education. It was my memory fail me. My little grandson, he is just the same, and I forgot it in the coming."

"Throat never heals, does it?" said the nurse, speaking in a loud, sure voice to old Phoenix. By now she had a card with something written on it, a little list. "Yes. Swallowed lye. When was it?—January—two-three years ago—"

Phoenix spoke unasked now. "No, missy, he not dead, he just the same. Every little while his throat begin to close up again, and he not able to swallow. He not get his breath. He not able to help himself. So the time come around, and I go on another trip for the soothing medicine."

"All right. The doctor said as long as you came to get it, you could have it," said the nurse. "But it's an obstinate case."

"My little grandson, he sit up there in the house all wrapped up, waiting by himself," Phoenix went on. "We is the only two left in the world. He suffer and it don't seem to put him back at all. He got a sweet look. He going to last. He wear a little patch quilt and peep out holding his mouth open like a little bird. I remembers so plain now. I not going to forget him again, no, the whole enduring time. I could tell him from all the others in creation."

"All right." The nurse was trying to hush her now. She brought her a bottle of medicine. "Charity," she said, making a check mark in a book.

Old Phoenix held the bottle close to her eyes, and then carefully put it into her pocket.

"I thank you," she said.

"It's Christmas time, Grandma," said the attendant. "Could I give you a few pennies out of my purse?"

"Five pennies is a nickel," said Phoenix stiffly.

"Here's a nickel," said the attendant.

Phoenix rose carefully and held out her hand. She received the nickel and then fished the other nickel out of her pocket and laid it beside the new one. She stared at her palm closely, with her head on one side.

Then she gave a tap with her cane on the floor.

"This is what come to me to do," she said. "I going to the store and buy my child a little windmill they sells, made out of paper. He going to find it hard to believe there such a thing in the world. I'll march myself back where he waiting, holding it straight up in this hand."

She lifted her free hand, gave a little nod, turned around, and walked out of the doctor's office. Then her slow step began on the stairs, going down.

Considerations

It would be easy to exhaust one's vocabulary in describing the heroine of "The Worn Path" and the feeling that the story provokes. *Gallant, triumphant, victorious,* and *courageous* are inadequate words to express the effect of this tribute to the human spirit.

Phoenix Jackson hasn't had much in life. Her worldly significance is negligible. Yet watching her march herself along makes us feel with her, draws us into an incredible journey, and immerses us too in this obsession. This is a greater adventure than the moon landing.

The author hints from the beginning that she will win. The phoenix was a mythical bird that eternally arose ever new from the ashes of the fire that destroyed it. How appropriate is the name for this indomitable-willed old lady?

She starts out in December, the signs of dead nature all around. The details of the early paragraphs build a contrast between poverty and isolation and the fruits of indestructible courage. The cane Phoenix used may have been thin and small and put together from an old umbrella, but it was "limber as a buggy whip." Her dress and apron were neat and tidy even though her shoelaces dragged from her unlaced shoes.

In her journey, Phoenix faced as many obstacles as any Greek hero had to overcome. Patient, cautious, encouraging herself, the lady added success to success, never arrogant, never angry, able to appreciate even the part of nature that stood against her. These may be the most strikingly poignant moments of the story. "Keep out from under these feet, little bob-whites . . ." "I in the thorny bush . . . Thorns, you doing your appointed work." . . . "A pleasure I don't see no two-headed snake coming around that tree, where it come once. It took a while to get by him, back in the summer."

Another author in another story might rest content with the suspense resolved as Phoenix reaches her goal, gets the medicine, and turns to go. Surely anything further would be an anticlimax. But no, in the final two paragraphs, the celebration of the individual is not merely continued, but it rises to an almost unbearable pitch. Phoenix is not one who settles for just maintaining life; things will improve. This woman—whom even a fool could have told there was no hope for and at best, sorrow—will climb up out of the adequate today, no matter how slightly, with her old eyes firmly set on a brighter tomorrow.

A Summer's Reading

George Stoyonovich was a neighborhood boy who had quit high school on an impulse when he was sixteen, run out of patience, and though he was ashamed everytime he went looking for a job, when people asked him if he had finished and he had to say no, he never went back to school. This summer was a hard time for jobs and he had none. Having so much time on his hands, George thought of going to summer school, but the kids in his classes would be too young. He also considered registering in a night high school, only he didn't like the idea of the teachers always telling him what to do. He felt they had not respected him. The result was he stayed off the streets and in his room most of the day. He was close to twenty and had needs with the neighborhood girls, but no money to spend, and he couldn't get more than an occasional few cents because his father was poor, and his sister Sophie, who resembled George, (a tall bony girl of twenty-three), earned very little and what she had she kept for herself. Their mother was dead, and Sophie had to take care of the house.

Very early in the morning George's father got up to go to work in a fish market. Sophie left at about eight for her long ride in the subway to a cafeteria in the Bronx. George had his coffee by himself, then hung around in the house. When the house, a five-room railroad flat above a butcher store, got on his nerves he cleaned it up—mopped the floors with a wet mop and put things away. But most of the time he sat in his room. In the afternoons he listened to the ball game. Otherwise he had a couple of old copies of the *World Almanac* he had bought long ago, and he liked to read in them and also the magazines and newspapers that Sophie brought home, that had been left on the tables in the cafeteria. They were mostly picture magazines about movie stars and sports figures, also usually the *News* and *Mirror*. Sophie herself read whatever fell into her hands, although she sometimes read good books.

She once asked George what he did in his room all day and he said he read a lot too.

"Of what besides what I bring home? Do you ever read any worthwhile books?"

"Some," George answered, although he really didn't. He had tried to read a book or two that Sophie had in the house but found he was in no mood for them. Lately he couldn't stand made-up stories, they got on his nerves. He wished he had some hobby to work at—as a kid he was good in carpentry, but where could he work at it? Sometimes during the day he went for walks, but mostly he did

Reprinted with the permission of Farrar, Straus & Giroux, Inc. from THE MAGIC BARREL by Bernard Malamud, Copyright © 1956, 1958 by Bernard Malamud. "A Summer's Reading" originally appeared in *The New Yorker*.

his walking after the hot sun had gone down and it was cooler in the streets.

In the evening after supper George left the house and wandered in the neighborhood. During the sultry days some of the storekeepers and their wives sat in chairs on the thick, broken sidewalks in front of their shops, fanning themselves, and George walked past them and the guys hanging out on the candy store corner. A couple of them he had known his whole life, but nobody recognized each other. He had no place special to go, but generally, saving it till the last, he left the neighborhood and walked for blocks till he came to a darkly lit little park with benches and trees and an iron railing, giving it a feeling of privacy. He sat on a bench here, watching the leafy trees and the flowers blooming on the inside of the railing, thinking of a better life for himself. He thought of the jobs he had had since he had quit school—delivery boy, stock clerk, runner, lately working in a factory— and he was dissatisfied with all of them. He felt he would someday like to have a good job and live in a private house with a porch, on a street with trees. He wanted to have some dough in his pocket to buy things with, and a girl to go with, so as not to be so lonely, especially on Saturday nights. He wanted people to like and respect him. He thought about these things often but mostly when he was alone at night. Around midnight he got up and drifted back to his hot and stony neighborhood.

One time while on his walk George met Mr. Cattanzara coming home very late from work. He wondered if he was drunk but then could tell he wasn't. Mr. Cattanzara, a stocky, bald-headed man who worked in a change booth on an IRT station, lived on the next block after George's, above a shoe repair store. Nights, during the hot weather, he sat on his stoop in an undershirt, reading the *New York Times* in the light of the shoemaker's window. He read it from the first page to the last, then went up to sleep. And all the time he was reading the paper, his wife, a fat woman with a white face, leaned out of the window, gazing into the street, her thick white arms folded under her loose breast, on the window ledge.

Once in a while Mr. Cattanzara came home drunk, but it was a quiet drunk. He never made any trouble, only walked stiffly up the street and slowly climbed the stairs into the hall. Though drunk, he looked the same as always, except for his tight walk, the quietness, and that his eyes were wet. George liked Mr. Cattanzara because he remembered him giving him nickels to buy lemon ice with when he was a squirt. Mr. Cattanzara was a different type than those in the neighborhood. He asked different questions than the others when he met you, and he seemed to know what went on in all the newspapers. He read them, as his fat sick wife watched from the window.

"What are you doing with yourself this summer, George?" Mr. Cattanzara asked. "I see you walkin' around at nights."

George felt embarrassed. "I like to walk."

"What are you doin' in the day now?"

"Nothing much just right now. I'm

waiting for a job." Since it shamed him to admit he wasn't working, George said, "I'm staying home—but I'm reading a lot to pick up my education."

Mr. Cattanzara looked interested. He mopped his hot face with a red handkerchief.

"What are you readin'?"

George hesitated, then said, "I got a list of books in the library once, and now I'm gonna read them this summer." He felt strange and a little unhappy saying this, but he wanted Mr. Cattanzara to respect him.

"How many books are there on it?"

"I never counted them. Maybe around a hundred."

Mr. Cattanzara whistled through his teeth.

"I figure if I did that," George went on earnestly, "it would help me in my education. I don't mean the kind they give you in high school. I want to know different things than they learn there, if you know what I mean."

The change maker nodded. "Still and all, one hundred books is a pretty big load for one summer."

"It might take longer."

"After you're finished with some, maybe you and I can shoot the breeze about them?" said Mr. Cattanzara.

"When I'm finished," George answered.

Mr. Cattanzara went home and George continued on his walk. After that, though he had the urge to, George did nothing different from usual. He still took his walks at night, ending up in the little park. But one evening the shoemaker on the next block stopped George to say he was a good boy, and George figured that

Mr. Cattanzara had told him all about the books he was reading. From the shoemaker it must have gone down the street, because George saw a couple of people smiling kindly at him, though nobody spoke to him personally. He felt a little better around the neighborhood and liked it more, though not so much he would want to live in it forever. He had never exactly disliked the people in it, yet he had never liked them very much either. It was the fault of the neighborhood. To his surprise, George found out that his father and Sophie knew about his reading too. His father was too shy to say anything about it—he was never much of a talker in his whole life—but Sophie was softer to George, and she showed him in other ways she was proud of him.

As the summer went on George felt in a good mood about things. He cleaned the house every day, as a favor to Sophie, and he enjoyed the ball games more. Sophie gave him a buck a week allowance, and though it still wasn't enough and he had to use it carefully, it was a helluva lot better than just having two bits now and then. What he bought with the money—cigarettes mostly, an occasional beer or movie ticket—he got a big kick out of. Life wasn't so bad if you knew how to appreciate it. Occasionally he bought a paperback book from the newsstand, but he never got around to reading it, though he was glad to have a couple of books in his room. But he read thoroughly Sophie's magazines and newspapers. And at night was the most enjoyable time, because when he passed the storekeepers sitting outside their stores, he could tell they regarded him highly. He walked erect, and though he did not say much to them, or they to him, he could feel approval on all sides. A couple of nights he felt so good that he skipped the park at the end of the evening. He just wandered in the neighborhood, where people had known him from the time he was a kid playing punchball whenever there was a game of it going; he wandered there, then came home and got undressed for bed, feeling fine.

For a few weeks he had talked only once with Mr. Cattanzara, and though the change maker had said nothing more about the books, asked no questions, his silence made George a little uneasy. For a while George didn't pass in front of Mr. Cattanzara's house anymore, until one night, forgetting himself, he approached it from a different direction than he usually did when he did. It was already past midnight. The street, except for one or two people, was deserted, and George was surprised when he saw Mr. Cattanzara still reading his newspaper by the light of the street lamp overhead. His impulse was to stop at the stoop and talk to him. He wasn't sure what he wanted to say, though he felt the words would come when he began to talk; but the more he thought about it, the more the idea scared him, and he decided he'd better not. He even considered beating it home by another street, but he was too near Mr. Cattanzara, and the change maker might see him as he ran, and get annoyed. So George unobtrusively crossed the street, trying to make it seem as if he had to look in a store window on the other side, which he

did, and then went on, uncomfortable at what he was doing. He feared Mr. Cattanzara would glance up from his paper and call him a dirty rat for walking on the other side of the street, but all he did was sit there, sweating through his undershirt, his bald head shining in the dim light as he read his *Times,* and upstairs his fat wife leaned out of the window, seeming to read the paper along with him. George thought she would spy him and yell out to Mr. Cattanzara, but she never moved her eyes off her husband.

George made up his mind to stay away from the change maker until he had got some of his softback books read, but when he started them and saw they were mostly story books, he lost his interest and didn't bother to finish them. He lost his interest in reading other things too. Sophie's magazines and newspapers went unread. She saw them piling up on a chair in his room and asked why he was no longer looking at them, and George told her it was because of all the other reading he had to do. Sophie said she had guessed that was it. So for most of the day, George had the radio on, turning to music when he was sick of the human voice. He kept the house fairly neat, and Sophie said nothing on the days when he neglected it. She was still kind and gave him his extra buck, though things weren't so good for him as they had been before.

But they were good enough, considering. Also his night walks invariably picked him up, no matter how bad the day was. Then one night George saw Mr. Cattanzara coming down the street toward him. George was about to turn and run but he recognized from Mr. Cattanzara's walk that he was drunk, and if so, probably he would not even bother to notice him. So George kept on walking straight ahead until he came abreast of Mr. Cattanzara and though he felt wound up enough to pop into the sky, he was not surprised when Mr. Cattanzara passed him without a word, walking slowly, his face and body stiff. George drew a breath in relief at his narrow escape, when he heard his name called, and there stood Mr. Cattanzara at his elbow, smelling like the inside of a beer barrel. His eyes were sad as he gazed at George, and George felt so intensely uncomfortable he was tempted to shove the drunk aside and continue on his walk.

But he couldn't act that way to him, and, besides, Mr. Cattanzara took a nickel out of his pants pocket and handed it to him.

"Go buy yourself a lemon ice, Georgie."

"It's not that time anymore, Mr. Cattanzara," George said, "I am a big guy now."

"No, you ain't," said Mr. Cattanzara, to which George made no reply he could think of.

"How are all your books comin' along now?" Mr. Cattanzara asked. Though he tried to stand steady, he swayed a little.

"Fine, I guess," said George, feeling the red crawling up his face.

"You ain't sure?" The change maker smiled slyly, a way George had never seen him smile.

"Sure, I'm sure. They're fine."

Though his head swayed in little arcs, Mr. Cattanzara's eyes were steady. He had small blue eyes which could hurt if you looked at them too long.

"George," he said, "name me one book on that list that you read this summer, and I will drink to your health."

"I don't want anybody drinking to me."

"Name me one so I can ask you a question on it. Who can tell, if it's a good book maybe I might wanna read it myself."

George knew he looked passable on the outside, but inside he was crumbling apart.

Unable to reply, he shut his eyes, but when—years later—he opened them, he saw that Mr. Cattanzara had, out of pity, gone away, but in his ears he still heard the words he had said when he left: "George, don't do what I did."

The next night he was afraid to leave his room, and though Sophie argued with him he wouldn't open the door.

"What are you doing in there?" she asked.

"Nothing."

"Aren't you reading?"

"No."

She was silent a minute, then asked, "Where do you keep the books you read? I never see any in your room outside of a few cheap trashy ones."

He wouldn't tell her.

"In that case you're not worth a buck of my hard-earned money. Why should I break my back for you? Go on out, you bum, and get a job."

He stayed in his room for almost a week, except to sneak into the kitchen when nobody was home. Sophie railed at him, then begged him to come out, and his old father wept, but George wouldn't budge, though the weather was terrible and his small room stifling. He found it very hard to breathe, each breath was like drawing a flame into his lungs.

One night, unable to stand the heat anymore, he burst into the street at one A.M., a shadow of himself. He hoped to sneak to the park without being seen, but there were people all over the block, wilted and listless, waiting for a breeze. George lowered his eyes and walked, in disgrace, away from them, but before long he discovered they were still friendly to him. He figured Mr. Cattanzara hadn't told on him. Maybe when he woke up out of his drunk the next morning, he had forgotten all about meeting George. George felt his confidence slowly come back to him.

That same night a man on a street corner asked him if it was true that he had finished reading so many books, and George admitted he had. The man said it was a wonderful thing for a boy his age to read so much.

"Yeah," George said, but he felt relieved. He hoped nobody would mention the books anymore, and when, after a couple of days, he accidentally met Mr. Cattanzara again, *he* didn't, though George had the idea he was the one who had started the rumor that he had finished all the books.

One evening in the fall, George ran out of his house to the library, where he hadn't been in years. There were books all over the place, wherever he looked, and though he was struggling to control an inward trembling, he easily counted off a hundred, then sat down at a table to read.

Considerations

The key to "A Summer's Reading" seems to be ideas about the relationship between books and education and also about ambition—or the lack of it—and George's need for people to like and respect him.

From the first we see that the problem is not that George was basically lazy. He'd had several jobs since he quit school—"delivery boy, stock clerk, runner, lately working in a factory—and he was dissatisfied with all of them." He had thought of going back to school, but once again he was stopped by the fact that he thought the teachers didn't respect him. He was close to twenty. He'd quit when he was sixteen. He'd survived thus far without making any great efforts, what was different now?

Into this summer of difference, of a possible turning point, comes a strong figure. Mr. Cattanzara was not a *new* figure in George's life. But Mr. Cattanzara asked different questions from the other neighbors, he read *The New York Times* from the first page to the last, and he seemed to know what went on in all the newspapers.

What ends up being an important incident in George's summer—and maybe in his life—began in a spur-of-the-moment response to a question from Mr. Cattanzara. George didn't think much about the excuse he gave for the way he was spending his time, but then he started getting feedback from the shoemaker down the block and other people in the neighborhood. Then even his family seemed to know about his reading program and seemed to be impressed.

Have you ever been saddled with the results of an idle remark, a boast that you really didn't mean? Why did Mr. Cattanzara say George wasn't a big guy now? What did he mean by: "George, don't do what I did"?

It seems that George's life started going well all at once, and then just as suddenly it all fell apart. Not only had Mr. Cattanzara said what he said, George's sister Sophie started asking him where the books he read were. Peculiarly (or not?) the more pressure George felt to read, the less able he was to even look at the things he had been reading.

How or why had Mr. Cattanzara started the rumor that George had finished all the books? Why did George suddenly go to the library one evening in the fall? Why didn't he do that in the summer when it would have saved him some worry? What is the story about—self-respect? Pressure? The inability to move when trapped by anxiety? How difficult reading is for some people? Or what it's like to grow up?

Confessions of a Burglar

WOODY ALLEN

(Following are excerpts from the soon-to-be-published memoirs of Virgil Ives, who is currently serving the first of four consecutive ninety-nine-year sentences for various felonies. Mr. Ives plans on working with children when he gets out.)

Sure I stole. Why not? Where I grew up, you had to steal to eat. Then you had to steal to tip. Lots of guys stole fifteen per cent, but I always stole twenty, which made me a big favorite among the waiters. On the way home from a heist, I'd steal some pajamas to sleep in. Or if it was a hot night, I'd steal underwear. It was a way of life. I had a bad upbringing, you might say. My dad was always on the run from the cops and I never saw him out of disguise till I was twenty-two. For years, I thought he was a short, bearded man with dark glasses and a limp; actually, he was tall and blond and resembled Lindbergh. He was a professional bank robber, but sixty-five was the mandatory retirement age, so he had to get out. Spent his last few years in mail fraud, but the postal rates went up and he lost everything.

Mom was wanted, too. Of course in those days it wasn't the way it is now, with women demanding equal rights, and all. Back then, if a woman turned to crime the only opportunities open to her were blackmail and, once in a while, arson. Women were used in Chicago to drive getaway cars, but only during the drivers' strike, in 1926. Terrible strike. It lasted eight weeks, and whenever a gang pulled a job and ran out with the money they were forced to walk or take a cab.

I had a sister and two brothers. Jenny married money. Not an actual human being—it was a pile of singles. My brother Vic got in with a gang of plagiarists. He was in the middle of signing his name to "The Waste Land" when the feds surrounded the house. He got ten years. Some rich kid from a highfalutin family who signed Pound's "Cantos" got off on probation. That's the law for you. Charlie—that's my youngest brother—he's been a numbers runner, a fence, and a loan shark. Never could find himself. Eventually he was arrested for loitering. He loitered for seven years, till he realized it was not the kind of crime that brought in any money.

The first thing I ever stole was a loaf of bread. I was working for Rifkin's Bakery, where my job was to remove the jelly from doughnuts that had gone stale and transfer it to fresh goods. It was very exacting work, done with a rubber tube and a scalpel. If your hands shook, the jelly went on the floor and old man Rifkin would pull your hair. Arnold Rothstein, who we all looked up to, came in one day and said he wanted to get his hands on a loaf of bread but he absolutely refused to pay for it. He hinted that this was a chance for some smart kid to get into the rackets. I took that as a cue, and each day when I left I put one slice of rye under my coat, until after three weeks I had accumulated a whole loaf. On the way to Rothstein's office, I began to feel remorse, because even though I hated Rifkin his wife had once let me take home two seeds from a roll when my uncle was dying. I tried to return the bread, but I got caught while I was trying to figure out which loaf each slice belonged to. The next thing I knew, I was in Elmira Reformatory.

Elmira was a tough joint. I escaped five times. Once I tried to sneak out in the back of a laundry truck. The guards got suspicious, and one of them poked me with his stick and asked me what the hell I was doing lying around in a hamper. I looked him right in the eye and said, "I'm some shirts." I could tell he was dubious. He kept pacing back and forth and staring at me. I guess I got a little panicky. "I'm some *shirts,*" I told him. "Some denim work shirts—blue ones." Before I could say another word, my arms and legs were manacled and I was back in stir.

I learned everything I knew about crime at Elmira: how to pick pockets, how to crack a safe, how to cut glass—all the fine points of the trade. For instance, I learned (and not even all professional criminals know this) that in the event of a shootout with the cops, the cops are always allowed the first two shots. It's just the way it's done. Then you return fire. And if a cop says, "We have the house surrounded, come out with your hands up," you don't just shoot wildly. You say, "I'd prefer not to," or "I'd rather not at this particular time." There's a right way to do these things, but today . . . Well, why go into all that?

For the next few years of my life I was the best damn burglar you ever saw. People talk about Raffles, but Raffles had his style and I had mine. I had lunch with Raffles' son once. Nice guy. We ate at the old Lindy's. He stole the pepper mill. I stole the silverware and napkins. Then he took the ketchup bottle. I took his hat. He got my umbrella and tiepin. When we left we kidnapped a waiter. It was quite a haul. The original Raffles began as a cat burglar. (I couldn't do that, because the whiskers make me sneeze.) He'd dress up in this beat-up cat suit and dart over rooftops. In the end, he was caught by two guys from Scotland Yard dressed as dogs. I suppose you've heard of the Kissing Bandit? He'd break into a joint and rob the victim, and if it was a woman he'd kiss her. It was sad the way the law finally nailed him. He had two old dowagers tied up and he was prancing in front of them singing "Gimme a Little Kiss, Will Ya, Huh?" when he slipped on a footstool and fractured his pelvis.

Those boys made all the headlines, but I pulled off some capers that the police never did figure out. Once, I entered a mansion, blew the safe, and removed six thousand dollars while a couple slept in the same room. The husband woke up when the dynamite went off, but when I assured him that the entire proceeds would go to the Boys' Clubs of America he went back to sleep. Cleverly, I left behind some fingerprints of Franklin D. Roosevelt, who was President then. Another time, at a big diplomatic cocktail party, I stole a woman's diamond necklace while we were shaking hands. Used a vacuum cleaner on her—an old Hoover. Got her necklace and earrings. Later, when I opened the bag I found some false teeth there, which belonged to the Dutch Ambassador.

My most beautiful job, though, was when I broke into the British Museum. I knew that the entire floor of the Rare Gems Room was wired and the slightest pressure on it would set off an alarm. I was lowered in upside down by a rope from the skylight, so I wouldn't touch the ground. I came through neat as you please, and in a minute I was hovering over the famous Kittridge Diamonds in their display case. As I pulled out my glass cutter a little sparrow flew in through the skylight and landed on the floor. The alarm sounded and eight squad cars arrived. I got ten years. The sparrow got twenty to life. The bird was out in six months, on probation. A year later, he was picked up in Fort Worth for pecking Rabbi Morris Klugfein into a state of semiconsciousness.

What advice would I give the average homeowner to protect himself against burglars? Well, the first thing is to keep a light on in the house when you go out. It must be at least a sixty-watt bulb; anything less and the burglar will ransack the house, out of contempt for the wattage. Another good idea is to keep a dog, but this is not foolproof. Whenever I was about to rob a house with a dog in it, I threw in some dog food mixed with Seconal. If that didn't work, I'd grind up equal parts of chopped meat and a novel by Theodore Dreiser. If it happens that you are going out of town and must leave your house unguarded, it's a good idea to put a cardboard silhouette of yourself in the window. Any silhouette will do. A Bronx man once placed a cardboard silhouette of Montgomery Clift in his window and then went to Kutsher's for the weekend. Later, Montgomery Clift himself happened to walk by and saw the silhouette, which caused him great anxiety. He attempted to strike up a conversation, and when it failed to answer for seven hours Clift returned to California and told his friends that New Yorkers were snobbish.

If you surprise an intruder in the act of burglarizing your home, do not panic. Remember, he is as frightened as you are. One good device is to rob *him.* Seize the initiative and relieve the burglar of his watch and wallet. Then he can get into your bed while you make a getaway. Trapped by this defense, I once wound up living in Des Moines for six years with another man's wife and three children, and only left when I was fortunate enough to surprise another burglar, who took my place. The six years I lived with that family were happy ones, and I often look back on them with affection, although there is also much to be said for working on a chain gang.

Considerations

Like most humor and all parody, the success of this selection depends to a great degree on the reader's knowledge. If you don't know what is being referred to or what the true state of affairs is—either through lack of information or observation—you can't appreciate the twist Woody Allen, one of our great contemporary humorists, has put on it. Even the headnote of this piece, for example, contains a fleeting commentary on the current penal situation.

What kinds of things would it help to know? Who Raffles really was. How the rich were supposed to have regarded President Franklin D. Roosevelt. The way the theft was carried out in the movie *Topkapi.* The story of the Birdman of Alcatraz. The way that the writing of Theodore Dreiser affects some people.

The organization of the piece, short as it is, is autobiographical fiction, with the inevitable summary advice at the end. A more serious author could have (and indeed some have) taken this same pattern and made us cry for the speaker—his deprived childhood, his sweatshop youth, his early brush with the rackets. Woody Allen makes us laugh.

A Summer Tragedy

ARNA BONTEMPS

Old Jeff Patton, the black share farmer, fumbled with his bow tie. His fingers trembled and the high stiff collar pinched his throat. A fellow loses his hand for such vanities after thirty or forty years of simple life. Once a year, or maybe twice if there's a wedding among his kinfolks, he may spruce up; but generally fancy clothes do nothing but adorn the wall of the big room and feed the moths. That had been Jeff Patton's experience. He had not worn his stiff-bosomed shirt more than a dozen times in all his married life. His swallow-tailed coat lay on the bed beside him, freshly brushed and pressed, but it was as full of holes as the overalls in which he worked on weekdays. The moths had used it badly. Jeff twisted his mouth into a hideous toothless grimace as he contended with the obstinate bow. He stamped his good foot and decided to give up the struggle.

"Jennie," he called.

"What's that, Jeff?" His wife's shrunken voice came out of the adjoining room like an echo. It was hardly bigger than a whisper.

"I reckon you'll have to he'p me wid this heah bow tie, baby," he said meekly. "Dog if I can hitch it up."

Her answer was not strong enough to reach him, but presently the old woman came to the door, feeling her way with a stick. She had a wasted, dead-leaf appearance. Her body, as scrawny and gnarled as a string bean, seemed less than nothing in the ocean of frayed and faded petticoats that surrounded her. These hung an inch or two above the tops of her heavy unlaced shoes and showed little grotesque piles where the stockings had fallen down from her negligible legs.

"You oughta could do a heap mo' wid a thing like that'n me—beingst as you got yo' good sight."

"Looks like I oughta could," he admitted. "But ma fingers is gone democrat on me. I get all mixed up in the looking glass an' can't tell wicha way to twist the devilish thing."

Jennie sat on the side of the bed and old Jeff Patton got down on one knee while she tied the bow knot. It was a slow and painful ordeal for each of them in this position. Jeff's bones cracked, his knee ached, and it was only after a half dozen attempts that Jennie worked a semblance of a bow into the tie.

"I got to dress maself now," the old woman whispered. "These is ma old shoes an' stockings, and I ain't so much as unwrapped ma dress."

"Well, don't worry 'bout me no

mo', baby,' Jeff said. "That 'bout finishes me. All I gotta do now slip on that old coat 'n ves' and I'll be fixed to leave."

Jennie disappeared again through the dim passage into the shed room. Being blind was no handicap to her in that black hole. Jeff heard the cane placed against the wall beside the door and knew that his wife was on easy ground. He put on his coat, took a battered top hat from the bedposts and hobbled to the front door. He was ready to travel. As soon as Jennie could get on her Sunday shoes and her old black silk dress, they would start.

Outside the tiny log house, the day was warm and mellow with sunshine. A host of wasps were humming with busy excitement in the trunk of a dead sycamore. Gray squirrels were searching through the grass for hickory nuts and blue jays were in the trees, hopping from branch to branch. Pine woods stretched away to the left like a black sea. Among them were scattered scores of log houses like Jeff's, houses of black share farmers. Cows and pigs wandered freely among the trees. There was no danger of loss. Each farmer knew his own stock and knew his neighbor's as well as he knew his neighbor's children.

Down the slope to the right were the cultivated acres on which the colored folks worked. They extended to the river, more than two miles away, and they were today green with the unmade cotton crop. A tiny thread of a road, which passed direcly in front of Jeff's place, ran through these green fields like a pencil mark.

Jeff, standing outside the door, with his absurd hat in his left hand, surveyed the wide scene tenderly. He had been forty-five years on these acres. He loved them with the unexplained affection that others have for the countries to which they belong.

The sun was hot on his head, his collar still pinched his throat, and the Sunday clothes were intolerably hot. Jeff transferred the hat to his right hand and began fanning with it. Suddenly the whisper that was Jennie's voice came out of the shed room.

"You can bring the car round front whilst you's waitin'," it said feebly. There was a tired pause; then it added, "I'll soon be fixed to go."

"A'right, baby," Jeff answered. "I'll get it in a minute."

But he didn't move. A thought struck him that made his mouth fall open. The mention of the car brought to his mind, with new intensity, the trip he and Jennie were about to take. Fear came into his eyes; excitement took his breath. Lord, Jesus!

"Jeff . . . O Jeff," the old woman's whisper called.

He awakened with a jolt. "Hunh, baby?"

"What you doin'?"

"Nuthin. Jes studyin'. I jes been turnin' things round'n round in ma mind."

"You could be gettin' the car," she said.

"Oh yes, right away, baby."

He started round to the shed, limping heavily on his bad leg. There were three frizzly chickens in the yard. All his other chickens had been killed or stolen recently. But the frizzly chickens had been saved somehow. That was fortunate indeed, for these curious creatures had a way of devouring "Poison" from the yard and in that way protecting against conjure and black luck and spells. But even the frizzly chickens seemed now to be in a stupor. Jeff thought they had some ailment; he expected all three of them to die shortly.

The shed in which the old T-model Ford stood was only a grass roof held up by corner poles. It had been built by tremulous hands at a time when the little rattletrap car had been re- garded as a peculiar treasure. And, miraculously, despite wind and downpour it still stood.

Jeff adjusted the crank and put his weight upon it. The engine came to life with a splutter and bang that rattled the old car from radiator to taillight. Jeff hopped into the seat and put his foot on the accelerator. The sputtering and banging increased. The rattling became more violent. That was good. It was good banging, good sputtering and rattling, and it meant that the aged car was still in running condition. She could be de- pended on for this trip.

Again Jeff's thoughts halted as if paralyzed. The suggestion of the trip fell into the machinery of his mind like a wrench. He felt dazed and weak. He swung the car out into the yard, made a half turn and drove around to the front door. When he took his hands off the wheel, he noticed that he was trembling vi- olently. He cut off the motor and climbed to the ground to wait for Jennie.

A few minutes later she was at the window, her voice rattling against the pane like a broken shutter.

"I'm ready, Jeff."

He did not answer, but limped into the house and took her by the arm. He led her slowly through the big room, down the step and across the yard.

"You reckon I'd oughta lock the do'?" he asked softly.

They stopped and Jennie weighed the question. Finally she shook her head.

"Ne' mind the do'," she said. "I don't see no cause to lock up things."

"You right," Jeff agreed. "No cause to lock up."

Jeff opened the door and helped his wife into the car. A quick shudder passed over him. Jesus! Again he trembled.

"How come you shaking so?" Jen- nie whispered.

"I don't know," he said.

"You mus' be scairt, Jeff."

"No, baby, I ain't scairt."

He slammed the door after her and went around to crank up again. The motor started easily. Jeff wished that it had not been so responsive. He would have liked a few more minutes in which to turn things around in his head. As it was, with Jennie chiding him about being afraid, he had to keep going. He swung the car into the little pencil-mark road and started off toward the river, driving very slowly, very cautiously.

Chugging across the green coun- tryside, the small battered Ford seemed tiny indeed. Jeff felt a familiar excitement, a thrill, as they came down the first slope to the immense levels on which the cotton was grow- ing. He could not help reflecting that the crops were good. He knew what that meant, too; he had made forty-five of them with his own hands. It was true that he had worn out nearly a dozen mules, but that was the fault of old man Stevenson, the owner of the land. Major Stevenson had the odd notion that one mule was all a share farmer needed to work a thirty-acre plot. It was an expensive notion, the way it killed mules from overwork, but the old man held to it. Jeff thought it killed a good many share farmers as well as mules, but he had no sympathy for them. He had always been strong, and he had been taught to have no patience with weakness in men. Women or children might be tolerated if they were puny, but a weak man was a curse. Of course, his own children—

Jeff's thought halted there. He and Jennie never mentioned their dead children any more. And naturally he did not wish to dwell upon them in his mind. Before he knew it, some remark would slip out of his mouth and that would make Jennie feel blue. Perhaps she would cry. A woman like Jennie could not easily throw off the grief that comes from losing five grown children within two years. Even Jeff was still staggered by the blow. His memory had not been much good recently. He frequently talked to himself. And, although he had kept it a secret, he knew that his courage had left him. He was terrified by the least unfamiliar sound at night. He was reluctant to venture far from home in the daytime. And that habit of trembling when he felt fearful was now far beyond his control. Sometimes he became afraid and trembled without knowing what had frightened him. The feeling would just come over him like a chill.

The car rattled slowly over the dusty road. Jennie sat erect and silent, with a little absurd hat pinned to her hair. Her useless eyes seemed very large, very white in their deep sockets. Suddenly Jeff heard her voice, and he inclined his head to catch the words.

"Is we passed Delia Moore's house yet?" she asked.

"Not yet," he said.

"You must be drivin' might slow, Jeff."

"We might just as well take our time, baby."

There was a pause. A little puff of steam was coming out of the radiator of the car. Heat wavered above the hood. Delia Moore's house was nearly half a mile away. After a moment Jennie spoke again.

"You ain't really scairt, is you, Jeff?"

"Nah, baby, I ain't scairt."

"You know how we agreed—we gotta keep on goin'."

Jewels of perspiration appeared on Jeff's forehead. His eyes rounded, blinked, became fixed on the road.

"I don't know," he said with a shiver. "I reckon it's the only thing to do."

"Hm."

A flock of guinea fowls, pecking in the road, were scattered by the passing car. Some of them took to their wings; others hid under bushes. A blue jay, swaying on a leafy twig, was annoying a roadside squirrel. Jeff held an even speed till he came near Delia's place. Then he slowed down noticeably.

Delia's house was really no house at all, but an abandoned store building converted into a dwelling. It sat near a crossroads, beneath a single black cedar tree. There Delia, a cattish old creature of Jennie's age, lived alone. She had been there more years than anybody could remember, and long ago had won the disfavor of such women as Jennie. For in her young days Delia had been gayer, yellower and saucier than seemed proper in those parts. Her ways with menfolks had been dark and suspicious. And the fact that she had had as many husbands as children did not help her reputation.

"Yonder's old Delia," Jeff said as they passed.

"What she doin'?"

"Jes sittin' in the do'," he said.

"She see us?"

"Hm," Jeff said. "Musta did."

That relieved Jennie. It strengthened her to know that her old enemy had seen her pass in her best clothes. That would give the old she-devil something to chew her gums and fret about, Jennie thought. Wouldn't she have a fit if she didn't find out? Old evil Delia! This would be just the thing for her. It would pay her back for being so evil. It would also pay her, Jennie thought, for the way she used to grin at Jeff—long ago when her teeth were good.

The road became smooth and red, and Jeff could tell by the smell of the air that they were nearing the river. He could see the rise where the road turned and ran along parallel to the stream. The car chugged on monotonously. After a long silent spell, Jennie leaned against Jeff and spoke.

"How many bale o' cotton you think we got standin'?" she said.

Jeff wrinkled his forehead as he calculated.

" 'Bout twenty-five, I reckon."

"How many you make las' year?"

"Twenty-eight," he said. "How come you ask that?"

"I's jes thinkin'," Jennie said quietly.

"It don't make a speck o' difference though," Jeff reflected. "If we get much or if we get little, we still gonna be in debt to old man Stevenson when he gets through counting up agin us. It's took us a long time to learn that."

Jennie was not listening to these words. She had fallen into a trance-like meditation. Her lips twitched. She chewed her gums and rubbed her gnarled hands nervously. Suddenly she leaned forward, buried her face in the nervous hands and burst into tears. She cried aloud in a dry cracked voice that suggested the rattle of fodder on dead stalks. She cried aloud like a child, for she had never learned to suppress a genuine sob. Her slight old frame shook heavily and seemed hardly able to sustain such violent grief.

"What's the matter, baby?" Jeff asked awkwardly. "Why you cryin' like all that?"

"I's jes thinkin'," she said.

"So you the one what's scairt now, hunh?"

"I ain't scairt, Jeff, I's jes thinkin' 'bout leavin' eve'thing like this— eve'thing we been used to. It's right sad-like."

Jeff did not answer, and presently Jennie buried her face again and cried.

The sun was almost overhead. It beat down furiously on the dusty wagon-path road, on the parched roadside grass and the tiny battered car. Jeff's hands, gripping the wheel, became wet with perspiration; his forehead sparkled. Jeff's lips parted. His mouth shaped a hideous grimace. His face suggested the face of a man being burned. But the torture passed and his expression softened again.

"You mustn't cry, baby," he said to his wife. "We gotta be strong. We can't break down."

Jennie waited a few seconds, then said, "You reckon we oughta do it, Jeff? You reckon we oughta go 'head an' do it, really?"

Jeff's voice choked; his eyes blurred. He was terrified to hear Jennie say the thing that had been in his mind all morning. She had egged him on when he had wanted more than anything in the world to wait, to reconsider, to think things over a little longer. Now she was getting cold feet. Actually there was no need of thinking the questions through again. It would only end in making the same painful decision once more. Jeff knew that. There was no need of fooling around longer.

"We jes as well to do like we planned," he said. "They ain't nothin' else for us now—it's the bes' thing."

Jeff thought of the handicaps, the near impossibility, of making another crop with his leg bothering him more and more each week. Then there was always the chance that he would have another stroke, like the one that had made him lame. Another one might kill him. The least it could do would be to leave him helpless. Jeff gasped —Lord, Jesus! He could not bear to

think of being helpless, like a baby, on Jennie's hands. Frail, blind Jennie.

The little pounding motor of the car worked harder and harder. The puff of steam from the cracked radiator became larger. Jeff realized that they were climbing a little rise. A moment later the road turned abruptly and he looked down upon the face of the river.

"Jeff."

"Hunh?"

"Is that the water I hear?"

"Hm. Tha's it."

"Well, which way you goin' now?"

"Down this-a way," he said. "The road runs 'long 'side o' the water a lil piece."

She waited a while calmly. Then she said, "Drive faster."

"A'right, baby," Jeff said.

The water roared in the bed of the river. It was fifty or sixty feet below the level of the road. Between the road and the water there was a long smooth slope, sharply inclined. The slope was dry, the clay hardened by prolonged summer heat. The water below, roaring in a narrow channel, was noisy and wild.

"Jeff."

"Hunh?"

"How far you goin'?"

"Jes a lil piece down the road."

"You ain't scairt, is you, Jeff?"

"Nah, baby," he said trembling. "I ain't scairt."

"Remember how we planned it, Jeff. We gotta do it like we said. Brave-like."

"Hm."

Jeff's brain darkened. Things suddenly seemed unreal, like figures in a dream. Thoughts swam in his mind foolishly, hysterically, like little blind fish in a pool within a dense cave. They rushed, crossed one another, jostled, collided, retreated and rushed again. Jeff soon became dizzy. He shuddered violently and turned to his wife.

"Jennie, I can't do it. I can't." His voice broke pitifully.

She did not appear to be listening. All the grief had gone from her face. She sat erect, her unseeing eyes wide open, strained and frightful. Her glossy black skin had become dull. She seemed as thin, as sharp and bony, as a starved bird. Now, having suffered and endured the sadness of tearing herself away from beloved things, she showed no anguish. She was absorbed with her own thoughts, and she didn't even hear Jeff's voice shouting in her ear.

Jeff said nothing more. For an instant there was light in his cavernous brain. The great chamber was, for less than a second, peopled by characters he knew and loved. They were simple, healthy creatures, and they behaved in a manner that he could understand. They had quality. But since he had already taken leave of them long ago, the remembrance did not break his heart again. Young Jeff Patton was among them, the Jeff Patton of fifty years ago who went down to New Orleans with a crowd of country boys to the Mardi Gras doings. The gay young crowd, boys with candy-striped shirts and rouged-brown girls in noisy silks, was like a picture in his head. Yet it did not make him sad. On that very trip Slim Burns had killed Joe Beasley—the crowd had been broken up. Since then Jeff Patton's world had been the Greenbriar Plantation. If there had been other Mardi Gras carnivals, he had not heard of them. Since then there had been no time; the years had fallen on him like waves. Now he was old, worn out. Another paralytic stroke (like the one he had already suffered) would put him on his back for keeps. In that condition, with a frail blind woman to look after him, he would be worse off than if he were dead.

Suddenly Jeff's hands became steady. He actually felt brave. He slowed down the motor of the car and carefully pulled off the road. Below, the water of the stream boomed, a soft thunder in the deep channel. Jeff ran the car onto the clay slope, pointed it directly toward the stream and put his foot heavily on the accelerator. The little car leaped furiously down the steep incline toward the water. The movement was nearly as swift and direct as a fall. The two old black folks, sitting quietly side by side, showed no excitement. In another instant the car hit the water and dropped immediately out of sight.

A little later it lodged in the mud of a shallow place. One wheel of the crushed and upturned little Ford became visible above the rushing water.

Considerations

Maybe this story is not as glamorous as Hamlet's endlessly turning his fateful decision over and over in his mind, approaching and retreating from the final action, but it's equally dramatic and equally true to humankind.

The story opens with Jeff and Jennie dressing up, and for a while it seems like perhaps merely some important occasion has interrupted their routine. Only gradually is a sense of pressure introduced—but not with particularly tragic overtones. The age, the tiredness, the drained and dried-out quality of the two is mirrored in a thousand ways: her shrunken voice, her body less than nothing, negligible legs. Later, outside, there is the rattle of fodder on dead stalks.

If the immediate setting in which Jeff and Jennie appear is dusty and worn, in contrast there is also the happy outside—warm and mellow with sunshine, the busy excitement of the wasps, the green fields that Jeff knows and loves and takes pride in. Throughout most of the story, in counterpoint to the descriptions that are dark and heavy are the rays of light and life. Although it eventually becomes obvious what Jeff and Jennie are travelling toward—a negation and cessation of their painful situation—there are continual signs of how tied up the two still are with the world around them. Jeff surveys the growing crops tenderly—he "loved them with unexplained affection." Jennie is still tied to memories of past fights and losses: "It strengthened Jennie to know that her old enemy had seen her pass in her best clothes . . . wouldn't she have a fit if she didn't find out? Old evil Delia!" (How close to the sound of *devil*.) Jeff felt a familiar excitement, a thrill as they came to the cotton later on in their journey, reemphasizing his attachment to the land, his pride in himself.

Here we come to a point to consider: what is Jeff doing here? "He had been taught to have no patience with weakness in men." The reason, then, or apparent reason that brought him to this plight is Jenny. There is the chance of his having another stroke that would kill him or leave him helpless for frail, blind Jennie to take care of. If it had been just him, one wonders if this decision would have been made.

Even had Jeff, alone, made a decision for death, there are indications that he might not have carried it out, for in the final analysis it takes the strength of both to get the car over the edge. Jennie asks if Jeff is scared, he must deny it; she breaks down, he bucks *her* up, says "we gotta be strong." Each reinforces the resolve of the other.

Not only is the colloquial language appropriate to the contents of the story, but so is the form. There is the continual questioning of the decision, the rehearsal of the well-known reasons for reaching this decision, there is repetition in places, the kind of repetition characteristic of the barely contained, nearly hysteric state of bracing oneself to face death. There is the heightened awareness of the physical, of each loved and hated thing that one is saying goodbye to, including the person that one used to be long ago when times were good.

The end comes, as it should, suddenly and quickly—after the long preparation and inner debates, the finishing stroke, the old couple and their final treasure crushed and done with. The story ends. What else is there to say?

The Hobbyist

FREDRIC BROWN

"I heard a rumor," Sangstrom said, "to the effect that you"—he turned his head and looked about him to make absolutely sure that he and the druggist were alone in the tiny prescription pharmacy. The druggist was a gnomelike, gnarled little man who could have been any age from 50 to 100. They were alone, but Sangstrom dropped his voice just the same—"to the effect that you have a completely undetectable poison."

The druggist nodded. He came around the counter and locked the front door of the shop, then walked toward a doorway behind the counter. "I was about to take a coffee break," he said. "Come with me and have a cup."

Sangstrom followed him around the counter and through the doorway to a back room ringed by shelves of bottles from floor to ceiling. The druggist plugged in an electric percolator, found two cups and put them on a table that had a chair on either side of it. He motioned Sangstrom to one of the chairs and took the other himself. "Now," he said, "tell me. Whom do you want to kill and why?"

"Does it matter?" Sangstrom asked. "Isn't it enough that I pay for——"

The druggist interrupted him with an upraised hand. "Yes, it matters. I must be convinced that you deserve what I can give you. Otherwise . . . ." He shrugged.

"All right," Sangstrom said. "The *whom* is my wife. The *why*. . . ." He started the long story. Before he had quite finished, the percolator had completed its task and the druggist briefly interrupted to get the coffee for them. Sangstrom concluded his story.

The little druggist nodded. "Yes, I occasionally dispense an undetectable poison. I do so freely; I do not charge for it if I think the case is deserving. I have helped many murderers."

"Fine," Sangstrom said. "Please give it to me, then."

The druggist smiled at him. "I already have. By the time the coffee was ready, I had decided that you deserved it. It was, as I said, free. But there is a price for the antidote."

Sangstrom turned pale. But he had anticipated—not this, but the possibility of a double cross or some form of blackmail. He pulled a pistol from his pocket.

The little druggist chuckled. "You daren't use that. Can you find the antidote—" he waved at the

Reprinted by permission of Mrs. Elizabeth C. Brown and the Agents for the Estate of Fredric Brown, Scott Meredith Literary Agency, Inc., 845 Third Avenue, New York, N.Y. 10022.

shelves—"among those thousands of bottles? Or would you find a faster, more virulent poison? Or if you think I'm bluffing, that you are not really poisoned, go ahead and shoot. You'll know the answer within three hours, when the poison starts to work."

"How much for the antidote?" Sangstrom growled.

"Quite reasonable, a thousand dollars. After all, a man must live; even if his hobby is preventing murders, there's no reason why he shouldn't make money at it, is there?"

Sangstrom growled and put the pistol down, but within reach, and took out his wallet. Maybe after he had the antidote, he'd still use that pistol. He counted out $1000 in $100 bills and put them on the table.

The druggist made no immediate move to pick them up. He said, "And one other thing—for your wife's safety and mine. You will write a confession of your intention—your former intention, I trust—to murder your wife. Then you will wait till I go out and mail it to a friend of mine on the homicide detail. He'll keep it as evidence in case you ever *do* decide to kill your wife. Or me, for that matter.

"When that is in the mail, it will be safe for me to return here and give you the antidote. I'll get you paper and pen. Oh, one other thing— although I do not absolutely insist on it. Please help spread the word about my undetectable poison, will you? One never knows, Mr. Sangstrom. The life you save, if you have any enemies, just might be your own."

Considerations

It's always nice, so they say, to have a hobby. The hobby with which this little druggist enlivened his days, though, is unexpected. Or perhaps what's unexpected is the unconventional way in which he pursues it. After all, police detectives in fact and fiction are supposed to devote their lives to preventing crime, especially the crime of murder. Certainly a private citizen can be excused for having the same goal. And can't he even be excused for his odd tactics in following his hobby? After all, the police have *their* suspects brought to them: informants, possible victims, public-spirited bystanders report attempted murders and the police have their work scheduled for the day. The druggist hasn't this built-in resource. It says much for his ingenuity that he came up with such an economical way of filtering would-be murderers out of the general population.

And it says much for the craft of this particular author that the reader enters so thoroughly into the spirit of the thing. If art, especially fiction, calls for the "willing suspension of disbelief" on the part of the audience, we instinctively give it to this piece. On the face of it, the story is absurd. Yet something engages us. We begin by thinking perhaps we've started a mystery story: a who or how or why dunnit. Yet we survive happily the disappointment of finding it's not. We feel some kinship with Sangstrom initially. (Who has not at one time thought how much life would be improved with just one death, the death of somebody else, of course?)

But Brown doesn't encourage us to carry this identification closer—he doesn't, for example, let Sangstrom gain our sympathy by saying exactly what his wife has done. We aren't invited to speculate about the reasons behind the druggist's hobby, about the rest of his life, either. It is the scheme itself Brown wishes to keep our attention on, a variation on that ever-delightful situation, the biter has been bitten. Justice—poetic and apt—is dear to most civilized souls. This delight, plus the almost believable air of the whole story—as though a friend had told us this experience secondhand—combine to lure us into daydreaming a bit afterwards, half expecting that someday soon a rumor will reach us about an undetectable poison available from that nice little old man in the faded neighborhood drugstore just around the corner.

Neighbors

A cup of sugar, an egg, a stick of butter, and thou

RAYMOND CARVER

Bill and Arlene Miller were a happy couple. But now and then they felt they alone among their circle had been passed by somehow, leaving Bill to attend to his bookkeeping duties and Arlene occupied with secretarial chores. They talked about it sometimes, mostly in comparison with the lives of their neighbors, Harriet and Jim Stone. It seemed to the Millers that the Stones lived a fuller and brighter life, one very different from their own. The Stones were always going out for dinner, or entertaining at home, or traveling about the country somewhere in connection with Jim's work.

The Stones lived across the hall from the Millers. Jim was a salesman for a machine-parts firm and often managed to combine business with a pleasure trip, and on this occasion the Stones would be away for ten days, first to Cheyenne, then on to St. Louis to visit relatives. In their absence, the Millers would look after the Stones' apartment, feed Kitty, and water the plants.

Bill and Jim shook hands beside the car. Harriet and Arlene held each other by the elbows and kissed lightly on the lips.

"Have fun," Bill said to Harriet.

"We will," said Harriet. "You kids have fun too."

Arlene nodded.

Jim winked at her. "Bye, Arlene. Take good care of the old man."

"I will," Arlene said.

"Have fun," Bill said.

"You bet," Jim said, clipping Bill lightly on the arm. "And thanks again, you guys."

The Stones waved as they drove away, and the Millers waved too.

"Well, I wish it was us," Bill said.

"God knows, we could use a vacation," Arlene said. She took his arm and put it around her waist as they climbed the stairs to their apartment.

After dinner Arlene said, "Don't forget. Kitty gets liver flavoring the first night." She stood in the kitchen doorway folding the handmade tablecloth that Harriet had bought for her last year in Santa Fe.

Bill took a deep breath as he entered the Stones' apartment. The air was already heavy and it was always vaguely sweet. The sunburst clock over the television said half-past eight. He remembered when Harriet had come home with the clock, how she crossed the hall to show it to

Arlene, cradling the brass case in her arms and talking to it through the tissue paper as if it were an infant.

Kitty rubbed her face against his slippers and then turned onto her side, but jumped up quickly as Bill moved to the kitchen and selected one of the stacked cans from the gleaming drainboard. Leaving the cat to pick at her food, he headed for the bathroom. He looked at himself in the mirror and then closed his eyes and then opened them. He opened the medicine chest. He found a container of pills and read the label: *Harriet Stone. One each day as directed,* and slipped it into his pocket. He went back to the kitchen, drew a pitcher of water and returned to the living room. He finished watering, set the pitcher on the rug, and opened the liquor cabinet. He reached in back for the bottle of Chivas Regal. He took two drinks from the bottle, wiped his lips on his sleeve and replaced the bottle in the cabinet.

Kitty was on the couch sleeping. He flipped the lights, slowly closing and checking the door. He had the feeling he had left something.

"What kept you?" Arlene said. She sat with her legs turned under her, watching television.

"Nothing. Playing with Kitty," he said, and went over to her and touched her breasts.

"Let's go to bed, honey," he said.

The next day Bill took only ten of the twenty minutes' break allotted for the afternoon, and left at fifteen minutes before five.

He parked the car in the lot just as Arlene hopped down from the bus.

He waited until she entered the building, then ran up the stairs to catch her as she stepped out of the elevator.

"Bill! God, you scared me. You're early," she said.

He shrugged. "Nothing to do at work," he said.

She let him use her key to open the door. He looked at the door across the hall before following her inside.

"Let's go to bed," he said.

"Now?" She laughed. "What's gotten into you?"

"Nothing. Take your dress off." He grabbed for her awkwardly, and she said, "Good God, Bill."

He unfastened his belt.

Later they sent out for Chinese food, and when it arrived they ate hungrily, without speaking, and listened to records.

"Let's not forget to feed Kitty," she said.

"I was just thinking about that," he said. "I'll go right over."

He selected a can of fish for the cat, then filled the pitcher and went to water. When he returned to the kitchen the cat was scratching in her box. She looked at him steadily for a minute before she turned back to the litter. He opened all the cupboards and examined the canned goods, the cereals, the packaged foods, the cocktail and wine glasses, the china, the pots and pans. He opened the refrigerator. He sniffed some celery, took two bites of cheddar cheese, and chewed on an apple as he walked into the bedroom. The bed seemed enormous, with a fluffy white bedspread draped to the floor. He pulled out a nightstand drawer, found a half-empty package of cigarettes and stuffed them into his pocket. Then he stepped to the closet and was opening it when the knock sounded at the front door.

He stopped by the bathroom and flushed the toilet on his way.

"What's been keeping you?" Arlene said. "You've been over here more than an hour."

"Have I really?" he said.

"Yes, you have," she said.

"I had to go to the toilet," he said.

"You have your own toilet," she said.

"I couldn't wait," he said.

That night they made love again.

In the morning he had Arlene call in for him. He showered, dressed, and made a light breakfast. He tried to start a book. He went out for a walk and felt better, but after a while, hands still in his pockets, he returned to the apartment. He stopped at the Stones' door on the chance he might hear the cat moving about. Then he let himself in at his own door and went to the kitchen for the key.

Inside it seemed cooler than his apartment, and darker too. He wondered if the plants had something to do with the temperature of the air. He looked out the window, and then he moved slowly through each room considering everything that fell under his gaze, carefully, one object at a time. He saw ashtrays, items of furniture, kitchen utensils, the clock. He saw everything. At last he entered the bedroom, and the cat appeared at his feet. He stroked her once, carried her into the bathroom and shut the door.

He lay down on the bed and stared at the ceiling. He lay for a while with his eyes closed, and then he moved his hand into his pants. He tried to recall what day it was. He tried to remember when the Stones were due back, and then he wondered if they would ever return. He could not remember their faces or the way they talked and dressed. He sighed, and then with effort rolled off the bed to lean over the dresser and look at himself in the mirror.

He opened the closet and selected a Hawaiian shirt. He looked until he found Bermudas, neatly pressed and hanging over a pair of brown twill slacks. He shed his own clothes and slipped into the shorts and the shirt. He looked in the mirror again. He went to the living room and poured himself a drink and sipped it on his way back to the bedroom. He put on a dark suit, a blue shirt, a blue and white tie, black wing-tip shoes. The glass was empty and he went for another drink.

In the bedroom again he sat on a chair, crossed his legs, and smiled, observing himself in the mirror. The telephone rang twice and fell silent. He finished the drink and took off the suit. He rummaged the top drawers until he found a pair of panties and a brassiere. He stepped into the panties and fastened the brassiere, then looked through the closet for an outfit. He put on a black and white checkered skirt which was too snug and which he was afraid to zipper, and a burgundy blouse that buttoned up the front. He considered her shoes, but understood they would not fit. For a long time he looked out the living-room window from behind the curtain. Then he returned to the bedroom and put everything away.

He was not hungry. She did not eat much either, but they looked at each other shyly and smiled. She got up from the table and checked that the key was on the shelf, then quickly cleared the dishes.

He stood in the kitchen doorway and smoked a cigarette and watched her pick up the key.

"Make yourself comfortable while I go across the hall," she said. "Read the paper or something." She closed her fingers over the key. He was, she said, looking tired.

He tried to concentrate on the news. He read the paper and turned on the television. Finally he went across the hall. The door was locked.

"It's me. Are you still there, honey?" he called.

After a time the lock released and Arlene stepped outside and shut the door. "Was I gone so long?" she said.

"Well you were," he said.

"Was I?" she said. "I guess I must have been playing with Kitty."

He studied her, and she looked away, her hand still resting on the doorknob.

"It's funny," she said. "You know, to go in someone's place like that."

He nodded, took her hand from the knob, and guided her toward their own door. He let them into their apartment. "It is funny," he said. He noticed white lint clinging to the back of her sweater, and the color was high in her cheeks. He began kissing her on the neck and hair and she turned and kissed him back.

"Oh, damn," she said. "Damn,

damn," girlishly clapping her hands. "I just remembered. I really and truly forgot to do what I went over there for. I didn't feed Kitty or do any watering." She looked at him. "Isn't that stupid?"

"I don't think so," he said. "Just a minute, I'll get my cigarettes and go back with you."

She waited until he had closed and locked their door, and then she took his arm at the muscle and said, "I guess I should tell you. I found some pictures."

He stopped in the middle of the hall. "What kind of pictures?"

"You can see for yourself," she said, and watched him.

"No kidding." He grinned. "Where?"

"In a drawer," she said.

"No kidding," he said.

And then she said, "Maybe they won't come back," and was at once astonished at her words.

"It could happen," he said. "Anything could happen."

"Or maybe they'll come back and," but she did not finish.

They held hands for the short walk across the hall, and when he spoke she could barely hear his voice.

"The key," he said. "Give it to me."

"What?" she said. She gazed at the door.

"The key," he said, "you have the key."

"My God," she said, "I left the key inside."

He tried the knob. It remained locked. Then she tried the knob, but it would not turn. Her lips were parted, and her breathing was hard, expectant. He opened his arms and she moved into them.

"Don't worry," he said into her ear. "For God's sake, don't worry." They stayed there. They held each other. They leaned into the door as if against a wind, and braced themselves.

Considerations

Let's examine this story's details before considering how it achieves its effect. The first thing we learn about the Millers is that they think their life is drab compared to the Stones'. This notion is one important factor in what follows. Then there are the plants that need to be watered and the cat that needs to be fed. Without these, what excuse would the Millers have for entering the Stones' apartment? (One wonders how the Stones managed such problems on previous trips—or have the Millers played this game before?)

Bill's behavior during his trips to the Stones' apartment is described fairly specifically. Arlene's is not. Why might this be? What effect does each approach create? Do they find much support for their idea that the Stones lead a glamorous life?

So much is implied in this story and so little actually said that you can find yourself reading almost every section twice, trying to decide what ideas about these people came from the author's head and what were added from your own. Even the ending is ambiguous. On what basis can we justify drawing the worst possible conclusions about what is about to happen? Even if the Millers are locked out and the evidence of their snooping locked in, surely there must be a fairly easy solution, given enough time—a building superintendent, a locksmith, or whatever resources one usually calls on to help open locked doors. What explains the fright Arlene and Bill seem to feel, the fright that mysteriously communicates itself to us?

The story's fascination lies in part in its ambiguity, which encourages us to use our own imaginations. Another source of fascination is the tension the story creates. The actions take place furtively: we wait for someone to catch these two in the act, or even for them to surprise each other. There is an aura of sexual tension as well.

Isn't there a further dimension to the story? Aren't we fascinated because we are afraid our neighbors, given the same opportunities, would take the same steps to find out about us? Beyond that, aren't we fascinated because we can with equal ease imagine ourselves doing exactly the same thing?

Winter Rug

RICHARD BRAUTIGAN

My credentials? Of course. They are in my pocket. Here: I've had friends who have died in California and I mourn them in my own way. I've been to Forest Lawn and romped over the place like an eager child. I've read *The Loved One, The American Way of Death, Wallets in Shrouds* and my favorite, *After Many a Summer Dies the Swan.*

I have watched men standing beside hearses in front of mortuaries directing funerals with walky-talkies as if they were officers in a metaphysical war.

Oh, yes: I was once walking with a friend past a skid row hotel in San Francisco and they were carrying a corpse out of the hotel. The corpse was done tastefully in a white sheet with four or five Chinese extras looking on, and there was a very slow-moving ambulance parked out front that was prohibited by law from having a siren or to go any faster than thirty-seven miles an hour and from showing any aggressive action in traffic.

My friend looked at the lady or gentleman corpse as it went by and said, "Being dead is one step up from living in that hotel."

As you can see, I am an expert on death in California. My credentials stand up to the closest inspection. I am qualified to continue with another story told to me by my friend who also works as a gardener for a very wealthy old woman in Marin County. She had a nineteen-year-old dog that she loved deeply and the dog responded to this love by dying very slowly from senility.

Every day my friend went to work the dog would be a little more dead. It was long past the proper time for the dog to die, but the dog had been dying for so long that it had lost the way to death.

This happens to a lot of old people in this country. They get so old and live with death so long that they lose the way when it comes time to actually die.

Sometimes they stay lost for years. It is horrible to watch them linger on. Finally the weight of their own blood crushes them.

Anyway, at last the woman could not stand to watch the senile suffering of her dog any longer and called up a veterinarian to come and put the dog to sleep.

She instructed my friend to build a coffin for the dog, which he did, figuring it was one of the fringe clauses of gardening in California.

The death doctor drove out to her estate and was soon in the house carrying a little black bag. That was a mistake. It should have been a large pastel bag. When the old woman saw the little black bag, she paled visibly. The unnecessary reality of it scared her, so she sent the veterinarian away with a generous check in his pocket.

Alas, having the veterinarian go away did not solve the dog's basic problem: He was so senile that death had become a way of life and he was lost from the act of dying.

The next day the dog walked into the corner of a room and couldn't get out of it. The dog stood there for hours until it collapsed from exhaustion, which conveniently happened to be just when the old woman came into the room, looking for the keys to her Rolls-Royce.

She started crying when she saw the dog lying there like a mutt puddle in the corner. Its face was still pressed against the wall and its eyes were watering in some human kind of way that dogs get when they live with people too long and pick up their worst characteristics.

She had her maid carry the dog to his rug. The dog had a Chinese rug that he had slept on since he was a puppy in China before the fall of Chiang Kai-shek. The rug had been worth a thousand American dollars, then, having survived a dynasty or two.

The rug was worth a lot more now, being in rather excellent shape with actually no more wear and tear than it would get being stored in a castle for a couple of centuries.

The old woman called the veterinarian again and he arrived with his little black bag of tricks and how to find the way back to death after hav-

ing lost it for years, years that led oneself to being trapped in the corner of a room.

"Where is your pet?" he said.

"On his rug," she said.

The dog lay exhausted and sprawled across beautiful Chinese flowers and things from a different world. "Please do it on his rug," she said. "I think he would like that."

"Certainly," he said. "Don't worry. He won't feel a thing. It's painless. Just like falling asleep."

"Good-bye, Charlie," the old woman said. The dog of course didn't hear her. He had been deaf since 1959.

After bidding the dog farewell, the old woman took to bed. She left the room just as the veterinarian was opening his little black bag. The veterinarian needed PR help desperately.

Afterward my friend took the coffin in the house to pick up the dog. A maid had wrapped the body in the rug. The old woman insisted that the dog be buried with the rug and its head facing West in a grave near the rose garden, pointing toward China. My friend buried the dog with its head pointing toward Los Angeles.

As he carried the coffin outside he peeked in at the thousand-dollar rug. Beautiful design, he said to himself. All you would have to do would be to vacuum it a little and it would be as good as new.

My friend is not generally known as a sentimentalist. Stupid dead dog! he said to himself as he neared the grave, Damn dead dog!

"But I did it," he told me. "I buried that dog with the rug and I don't know why. It's a question that I'll ask myself forever. Sometimes when it rains at night in the winter, I think of that rug down there in the grave, wrapped around a dog."

Considerations

Much that may be said about this Brautigan story could be said about other fiction by this author. Brautigan, perhaps more than any of the other writers of current impressionist-absurdist works, writes fiction that borders on lyric poetry. There is great compression of language, intensity of feeling, and overwhelming use of imagery. The work speaks almost entirely to the unconscious. The ambiguity opens out wider vistas, invites the reader to make his own interpretations. Such plot as there is is usually not long or complex. The sentences too are generally deceptively simple and short. Tension of the "Will this character overcome these obstacles?" kind is almost entirely missing. In fact, the reader is shown only a few facets of the characters and only one or two points of feeling.

The descriptions and events unroll like a "pale marble movie" or a dream flickering past us. We see them vividly, yet their reality is at odd angles to normal existence. We can imagine the events of "Winter Rug" taking place—almost.

The incongruous metaphors and similes arrest our attention—men directing funerals talk into walkie-talkies as if they were "officers in a metaphysical war"; the dog lies in the corner "like a mutt puddle." We feel they apply better than anything we have noticed before—but we feel almost a little haunted by them. This feeling is another Brautigan characteristic: some sadness but a lot of zest and fun, or, in the often misapplied term, *bittersweet.*

Can one seriously question the choices that these people made? Isn't there a truth, a balance, other than the obvious materialism versus sentiment, that the whole story represents? Or does it represent anything?

Dotson Gerber Resurrected

HAL BENNETT

We saw the head of Mr. Dotson Gerber break ground at approximately nine o'clock on a bright Saturday morning in March out near our collard patch, where Poppa had started to dig a well and then filled it in. Of course, none of us knew then that the shock of red hair and part of a head sprouting from the abandoned well belonged to Mr. Dotson Gerber, who'd been missing from his farm since early last fall. We were black folk, and the fact that a white man like Mr. Dotson Gerber was missing from his home was of small importance to us. Unless that white man suddenly started growing from the ground near our collard patch like Mr. Dotson Gerber was doing now for Momma, my sister Millicent and me. We'd come running because of a commotion the chickens had made, thinking that a minx or a weasel might have got after them. And found Mr. Dotson Gerber's head instead.

"Good Jesus," Millicent said, "I do think I'm going to faint." Millicent had been prone to fainting ever since she'd seen two black men kissing behind some boxes in the factory where she worked. Now she was getting ready to faint again. But Momma snatched her roughly by the apron.

"Girl, you *always* fainting, you don't hardly give other people a chance." And Momma fainted dead away, which left Millicent conscious for the time being and looking very desperate. But she didn't faint and I was glad of that, because I certainly didn't want to be alone with Mr. Dotson Gerber sprouting from the ground. A dozen or so chickens were still raising a ruckus about the unexpected appearance of a white man's head where they were accustomed to pecking for grain. Screeching at the top of her voice, Millicent shooed the chickens away while I tugged Momma into the shade and propped her against the barn. Then we went back to looking at Mr. Dotson Gerber.

I have mentioned the well that Poppa started to dig because it was apparent that Mr. Dotson Gerber had been planted standing up in that hole. Which, of course, explained why his head was growing out first. Although, as I have said, neither Millicent nor I knew then that what we were looking at belonged to Mr. Dotson Gerber. It took Poppa to tell us that.

He came riding on Miss Tricia from the stable, where he'd been saddling her. "Why you children making all that noise out there?" he called from the road. When we didn't answer, he yanked the reins and rode Miss Tricia toward us. "Millicent, was that you I heard hollering? What you all doing out here?" Poppa asked again.

"There's a white man growing from the ground," I said.

Poppa nearly fell off Miss Tricia. "A *what*?"

"A white man. He's growing from that hole where you started to dig the well."

"I *know* I'm going to faint now," Millicent said. And she wrapped her hands around her throat as though to choke herself into unconsciousness. But Poppa and I both ignored her and she was too curious to faint right then. So she stopped choking herself and watched Poppa jump down from Miss Tricia to inspect the head. He walked all around it, poking it from time to time with his shoe.

"That'd be Mr. Dotson Gerber," he finally pronounced.

By this time, Momma had revived and was watching Poppa with the rest of us. "Poppa, how you know that's Mr. Dotson Gerber? Why, he could be any old white man! There's hardly enough of him above ground for anybody to recognize."

"I know it's Mr. Dotson Gerber because I planted him there," Poppa said. He told us how Mr. Gerber had come out to the farm last fall to inspect the well that he was digging, which had been part of Mr. Gerber's job here in Alcanthia County. "He kept calling me Uncle," Poppa said, with some bitterness. "I told him respectfully that my name is Walter Beaufort, or that he could even call me *Mr.* Beaufort, if he'd a mind to. After all, things have changed so much nowadays, I told him I certainly wouldn't think any less of him if he called me Mr. Beaufort. I told him that black people don't appreciate white folks' calling us Uncle any longer. But he just kept on calling me that, so I hit him in the head with my shovel." We all looked at Mr. Dotson Gerber's head; and it was true that there was a wide gash in his skull that could only have been caused by a shovel. "I didn't intend to kill him," Poppa said. "I just wanted to teach him some respect. After all, things *have* changed. But when I found out he was dead, I stood him up in that hole I was digging and covered him up. I never expected to see him growing out of the ground this way."

"Well, that's not the problem now," Millicent said. "The problem now is, what are we going to do with him?"

Momma moved a step closer to Mr. Gerber and cautiously poked him with her toe. "If it weren't for that red hair," she said, "somebody might mistake him for a cabbage."

"He don't look like no cabbage to me," Millicent said. It was clear that she was annoyed because Momma had fainted before she'd had a chance to.

"I didn't say he looked like a cabbage," Momma said. "I said somebody might mistake him for a cabbage."

"He too red to be a cabbage," Millicent said stubbornly. "Anyway, we still ought to do something· about him. It just don't look right, a white man growing like this on a colored person's farm. Suppose some white people see it?"

The 9:10 Greyhound to Richmond went by then. Momma and Poppa shaded their eyes to watch it speed down the far road; but Millicent and I were of today's generation and we hardly looked. Although there had been a time when the passing of the Richmond bus was the most exciting event of everybody's day in Burnside. But the years in between had brought many changes. There was electricity now, and television and telephones. Several factories and supermarkets had opened up on the highway, so that farming became far less profitable than working in the factories and spending weekly wages in the glittering markets, where everything that had formerly come from soil was sold now in tin cans and plastic wrappers. Because nobody in Burnside farmed anymore. Like almost everyone else, Momma and Poppa and Millicent all worked in the factories. And Momma bought at the supermarkets, like everyone else. The land around us, given over to weeds, was overgrown now like a graveyard in those first green days of spring.

Momma and Poppa watched the bus until it disappeared. "That Greyhound, she sure do go," Momma said. "It's Saturday now and I bet she's crowded with nigger men going to Richmond for them white hussies on Clay Street."

Millicent grunted. "Let them help themselves," she said bitterly. "After what I seen, a nigger man don't mean a thing to me no more."

"You're right there, sugar," Momma agreed. "A nigger man, he ain't worth a damn."

Millicent curled her lip and she and Momma looked at Poppa and me as though there were something dirty and pathetic about being a black man. I had seen this expression on their faces before—a wan kind of pity mixed with distaste and the sad realization that being a black man is next to being nothing at all. And the black woman is always telling the black man that with her eyes and lips and hips, telling him by the way she moves beside him on the road and underneath him in the bed, *Nigger, oh, I love you, but I know you ain't never going to be as good as a white man.* That's the way Momma and Millicent looked at Poppa and me while they cut us dead right there on the spot. They almost fell over each other, talking about how low and no-good nigger men are. And they weren't just joking; they really meant it. I saw it in their faces and it hurt me to my heart. I just didn't know what to do. I reached out and caught Poppa's arm, that's how hurt I was. He seemed to understand, because he wrapped his arm around me and I could feel some of his strength draining into me. So Momma and Millicent stood there ridiculing us on one side of Mr. Dotson Gerber's head, and Poppa and I stood there on the other.

Then, when Momma and Millicent

were all through with their tirade, Poppa said very quietly, "I'm riding in to Dillwyn now. I'm going to turn myself over to the sheriff for killing Mr. Gerber here."

There was a kind of joy in Poppa's voice that I suppose no black woman can ever understand, and Momma and Millicent looked at Poppa as though he had suddenly lost his mind. But I was 16 years old, which is old enough to be a man if you're black, and I understood why Poppa was so happy about killing that white man. Until now, he'd always had to bury his rich, black male rage in the far corner of some infertile field, lest it do harm to him and to the rest of us as well. But by telling that he'd killed that white man, he would undo all the indignities he had ever suffered in the name of love.

Now Momma looked afraid. "Turn yourself in to the sheriff? What you talking about, Walter Beaufort? What kind of foolishness you talking?" She tried humor to change Poppa's somber mood, laughing in a big hullabaloo. "I bet you been hitting the plum wine again," she said joyously.

But Poppa shook his head. "You always accuse me of that when you want to make light of what I'm saying. But I haven't been near that plum wine, not today. And what I'm saying is plain enough. I've killed a white man and I want somebody to know it."

"*We* know it," Momma said. "Ain't that good enough?"

"I want them to know it," Poppa said. "I want them to know he's dead and I want them to know why he's dead."

"Because he didn't call you Mr.?" Momma said. There wasn't a white man in Alcanthia County who didn't call her Auntie, and she started to rage scornfully at the idea of Poppa's rebelling at being called Uncle. "Now, I could see it if you said you were going to hide out for a while, killing that white man and all that——"

But Poppa stopped her with an angry jerk of his hand. "It's not that way at all, Hattie. I don't aim to hide no more. I been hiding too long already—if you understand what I mean. The time's come for me to stop hiding. I'm going to Dillwyn and tell the sheriff what I've done."

Momma jumped straight up in the air. "Walter Beaufort, you gone *crazy* or something? No, I don't understand what you mean. Why didn't you tell the sheriff last year? Why you got to tell him now? Nobody even knows you killed Mr. Gerber. And to give yourself up now, that don't make no sense at all."

"Some things don't never make no sense," Poppa said. He cocked his eye at me. "You coming with me to the sheriff, boy? Somebody's got to ride Miss Tricia back here to home."

I got up onto Miss Tricia with him and we rode off to find the sheriff.

"I think I'm going to faint," I heard Millicent say behind me. But when I looked around, she was still standing there with her mouth hanging open.

As Poppa and I went up the road, Momma's voice followed us like an angry wind. "You see what I mean about *niggers*, Millicent?" Moaning sadly, half happy and afraid at the same time, a kind of turbulent satisfaction marred her voice as she shrieked at Millicent. "You see what I mean about *niggers,* child?"

"That black bitch," Poppa muttered. I don't know whether he knew I heard him or not. He kicked Miss Tricia viciously in the ribs and the mule leaped into a surprised gallop, heading to Dillwyn for Poppa to give himself up to the sheriff. After the way Momma and Millicent had carried on, I didn't see what else he could do.

Even here in Burnside, we had heard that black is beautiful. But I don't think that many of us believed it, because black is ugly and desperate and degraded wherever the white man is sitting on your neck. Still, Millicent and I had worn Afros for a while to show our black pride; but they were too hard to keep clean here in the country, there is so much dust and dirt blowing about. And our kind of hair picks up everything that goes by. Besides, the white people who owned the factories took Afro hairdos as a sign of militancy and threatened to fire everybody who wore one. So everybody went back to getting their hair cut short or straightening it like before.

I was thinking about that as I rode with Poppa to the sheriff's office. I thought about Millicent, too, and the black men she'd seen kissing in the factory. She never would tell who they were, and sometimes I wondered whether it might not have been just a story that she made up to justify her saying that all black men are sissies. At any rate, she complained quite openly that no black man had

made love to her since last Halloween, which was almost five months ago and probably explained why she was so jumpy and threatening to faint all the time.

As for me, I thought I knew why no black men were interested in Millicent. For one thing, they could go to Richmond and Charlottesville and get white women, now that they had money to spend on the whores there. Also, the black men I'd talked to told me that they didn't find black women so desirable anymore, the way they were dressing and acting and perfuming themselves like white women on television, now that they had money to do so.

So the black men went to Richmond and paid white women, because their own women were trying to act white. And the black women were turning their backs on their own men, because—if Millicent was any example—they thought that black men were sissies. It was all very confusing.

I was old enough to have had myself a woman or two by then. But I was very hung up on Mrs. Palmer and her five daughters; I hope you know what I mean. There was a time when black people said that doing something like that to yourself would make you crazy. Now they said that it would make you turn white. Which was sufficient reason for some black boys to stop. But not me. I actually did it more. But all that happened was that sometimes I felt dizzy and depressed. Sometimes I felt weak. But I never did turn white.

Sheriff Dave Young's office was closed when we got to Dillwyn. Some white men sitting around told us that the sheriff was away to a Christian conference. "He's a deacon in the white Baptist church, you know. He'll be away for the rest of the week." There were some hounds lying around, sleeping in the dust, and one or two of them opened a drowsy eye and looked at Poppa and me without curiosity. The white men looked at us as though we were two hounds who had by some miracle managed to get up onto a mule. That's the way white men are in the South. As for Poppa and me, we looked right through those white men, which is really a very good way of rebelling by pretending that you're looking at nothing. There are other sly ways that we Southern black people have of rebelling—like grinning, or licking our tongue out behind the white man's back, spitting in his water when he's not looking, imitating his way of talking—which is why so many Northern black people think that Southern black people are such natural clowns, when what we're really doing is rebelling. Not as dramatic as a Molotov cocktail or a pipe bomb, but it certainly is satisfying, and a whole lot safer, too. Furthermore, it must be said that we do not hate whites here as black people apparently do in the North. Although we nearly always view them with pity and suspicion, for *they* think that we hate them, as they might very well do if the tables were reversed.

"Uncle, is there any particular reason why you want to see the sheriff?"

"No, sir, no, sir, none at all," Poppa said. He thanked them the way he was supposed to, grinning a little, and rode away.

"Where we going now, Poppa? Back to home?"

He shook his head. "We going to Mr. Dotson Gerber's house up the street yonder. I expect his wife is home. I expect she'd like to know what happened to her husband."

When we got to Mrs. Dotson Gerber's, there was a decrepit old white lady sitting in a rocking chair on her porch and waving a small Confederate flag over the banister, like a child does at a parade. She was the mother of Mr. Dotson Gerber's wife. And while colored people said quite openly that the old lady was touched in the head, white people claimed that she had *arthritis;* and they said that she waved the Confederate flag to exercise her arm, as though to conceal from black people the fact that any white had ever lost her mind.

She waved the flag and rocked every once in a while, pushing at the banister with spidery legs that ended in two fluffy slippers that had once been white. Her pale blue eyes were as sharp as a hawk's behind her wire-rimmed glasses; but it was hard to tell whether she was looking into the past or the future, waving and rocking, smiling from time to time.

Poppa got down from Miss Tricia and walked over to the fence. "Good morning, ma'am," he said respectfully. It was dangerous not to be respectful, just in case the old white woman wasn't crazy and really did have arthritis in her arm. She could raise a ruckus for Poppa's disrespecting her that could cause him to wind up on the end of a rope. "I came to see Mrs. Dotson Gerber, ma'am," Poppa said politely, while the old lady rocked and waved the flag outrageously. She might have been saluting Lee's army marching proudly on its way to Appomattox, which was only a few miles away. Her eyes grew large and happy. But she didn't pay any attention at all to Poppa, even when he asked a second and a third time for Mrs. Dotson Gerber. She had arthritis, all right, that old woman. She had arthritis in the brain, that's where she had it.

Just then, Mrs. Dotson Gerber came to the screen door. Drying her hands on a pink apron, she inspected Poppa for a minute, as though trying to figure out whether he was safe or not. "Is that you, Uncle Walter?" She squinted through the screen. "Did you want to talk to me?"

"Yes, ma'am, Mrs. Gerber. I did come to talk to you. I got something to tell you."

"I certainly don't see why you came to my front door," Mrs. Gerber said peevishly, coming out onto the porch. "I *never* receive colored people at my front door, and I'm sure you know that, Uncle Walter. Besides, it bothers my mother's arthritis, people talking all around her." She inspected the crazy old woman, who was waving the Confederate flag and rocking vigorously.

"Well, ma'am . . . I'm sorry I came to your front door. I certainly do know better than that. But I've come to tell you about your husband."

Mrs. Gerber seemed to stop breathing. "My husband?" She dashed from the porch and stood at the fence near Poppa. "You know where my husband is?"

"Yes, ma'am. He's out in my collard patch—where my collard patch used to be."

"What's he doing out there?"

Poppa looked embarrassed. "He came to inspect the well I was digging. We got in an argument and I hit him with my shovel."

Mrs. Gerber turned very white, indeed. "You killed him?"

"I'm afraid so, ma'am. I buried him there in the well."

Mrs. Gerber tapped her bottom teeth with her forefinger. She was a sort of pretty white woman and certainly a lot younger than Mr. Dotson Gerber had been. Behind her on the porch, the crazy old woman rocked on, waving the flag at Southern armies that only she could see. "Mom-

ma's arthritis isn't too good today,"
Mrs. Gerber said absently, patting
her hair. After a while, she said, "So
Dotson is dead. All of us wondered
what happened when he didn't come
home last year. Knowing him, I was
almost certain that he'd gone and got
himself killed." But she didn't seem
too upset. "Actually, Uncle Walter,
you've done me a big favor. Dotson
used to treat my poor mother something terrible, laughing at her arthritis all the time." She patted her
hair again, although every strand
seemed to be perfectly in place. "I
suppose you know that I'm to get
married again this summer, to a very
respectable man here in Alcanthia?"

"No, ma'am, I didn't know that."

"Well, I'm surprised," Mrs. Gerber
said. "I thought that colored people
knew everything. Anyway, he's a
very respectable man. Very decent
and very intelligent, too, I need not
say. We both figured that Dotson was
dead after all these months. That's
why we decided to get married." She
looked at Poppa almost gently. "But I
never supposed you'd be the one to
kill him, Uncle Walter. Why, you've
even been here and done a little work
for Dotson and me around the
house."

"Yes, ma'am."

"He really must've provoked you,
Uncle Walter. What did he do?"

"He kept calling me Uncle. I asked
him not to, but he kept on."

"Yes, that sounds like Dotson. He
could be mean that way. I suppose
you want me to stop calling you Uncle, too?"

"I'd appreciate it if you would,
ma'am. I mean, it's an actual fact that

I'm not your uncle, so I'd appreciate
your not calling me that."

Now Mrs. Gerber nibbled on her
thumb. Her mother rocked on and
on, waving the flag. "All right, I'll
stop calling you Uncle," Mrs. Gerber
said, "if you promise not to tell anybody about my husband being buried
out there in your collard patch. After
all, I'm planning on being married to
a very decent man. It would be a big
embarrassment to me—and to him,
too—if anybody found out about Dotson being buried in a collard patch.
As much as he hates collard greens."
It was clear from the tone of her voice
that the disgrace lay not in Mr. Dotson Gerber's being dead but in his
being buried in our collard patch.

"There ain't no collards there
now." Poppa said, trying to placate
Mrs. Gerber some. "Why, we haven't
done any farming for years."

"But collards were there," Mrs.
Gerber said, almost stomping her
foot. "And Dotson couldn't stand collards. I just hope you won't tell anybody else about this, Uncle Walter. I
don't know what my fiancé would say
if he knew about this. Considering
that he's willing to marry me and to
put up with Momma's arthritis in the
bargain, I certainly wouldn't want
him to know about Dotson. Why, I
don't know what he'd do if he ever
found out about Dotson. You haven't
told anybody else, have you?"

"I went to the sheriff, but he's out
of town until next week."

"You went to tell the sheriff?" She
seemed absolutely horrified. "Mr.
Beaufort, I know I have no right
asking you to think about me and my
feelings in all this. But you ought to at

least think about your own family. You know what they'll do to you if they find out about this?"

"I know," Poppa said.

"And you don't care?"

"I certainly do care. I don't want to die. I want to live. But I've killed me a white man. That's not something that somebody like me does every day. I think I want folks to know about it."

"But why now?" she cried. "Why didn't you say something before? Before I went out and got myself engaged?"

"It didn't seem important before. Besides, Mr. Gerber was still in the ground then. He ain't in the ground anymore, not exactly."

From time to time, white people had gone past and looked at Poppa and Mrs. Gerber as they talked. "I think you all ought to go around to the back door," Mrs. Gerber said. "My husband-to-be certainly wouldn't like it known that I stood on my own front porch and carried on a conversation with colored people. . . ." She turned very red then and took a step or two away, as though she was afraid that Poppa might hit her with a shovel. But Poppa started laughing very gently, the way a man does when he weighs the value of things and finds out that what is important to other people seems absurd to him. And he looked at Mrs. Gerber with a kind of amused pity darkening his eyes, as though he realized now that no white person could ever understand why he wanted him to know about Mr. Dotson Gerber.

"We're going on home," Poppa said. "And don't you worry none about Mr. Gerber, ma'am. We'll take care of him. Your husband-to-be won't ever find out."

"What do you intend to do?" Mrs. Gerber wanted to know.

Poppa's face lit up with a great big grin. Not the kind of tame, painful grin that a black man puts on when he's rebelling. But a large, beautiful grin that showed all of his teeth and gums. "I'm going to plant collard greens around him," Poppa said.

Mrs. Gerber wrinkled her nose in distaste. "Dotson certainly wouldn't like that, if he knew. And you mean *over* him, don't you?"

Now Poppa and I both laughed. We hadn't told her that Mr. Gerber was growing straight up from the ground. And she wouldn't have believed us if we had told her. That's how white people are. "Goodbye, ma'am," Poppa said to Mrs. Gerber. She nodded and went into her house. On the porch, her mother waved the Confederate flag triumphantly. The rocker squeaked like the tread of strident ghosts. We climbed up onto Miss Tricia and rode home.

And we were nearly halfway there before I finally figured out why that old crazy white woman was on Mrs. Gerber's porch. They kept her there instead of buying a doorbell and using electricity. That way, when people talked to her, Mrs. Gerber heard them and came outside to see who it was. Smart. Sometimes I had to give it to white people. They were very smart, indeed.

Momma and Millicent were waiting for us when we got home. "Did you tell the sheriff?" Momma said.

She looked haggard and very unhappy.

"The sheriff wasn't there," Poppa said. "He won't be home until next week." With Momma and Millicent following us, he rode Miss Tricia out to the collard patch and gave me the reins. "Take her to the stable, boy." But I watched while he knelt and worked the dirt into a mound around Mr. Gerber's head. "There, that ought to do it," Poppa said. "Tomorrow, I'm going to plant me some collard greens here." He stood up happily and wiped his hands on the seat of his overalls.

Momma's mouth dropped open. She ran to Mr. Dotson Gerber's head and tried to stomp it back into the ground. But Poppa stopped her firmly. "You've gone stark crazy!" Momma cried.

Poppa slapped her right in the mouth. She spun around like a top. He slapped her again and sent her spinning the other way. "I don't want no more trouble out of you," Poppa said.

Momma melted against him like warm cheese. "All right, sugar. You won't have no more trouble out of me, sugar."

I rode Miss Tricia down to the stable. Millicent had enough sense to keep her mouth shut for a change, and Momma and Poppa went on up to the house with their arms wrapped around each other. I hadn't seen them together like that for years.

And that is how Poppa started farming again. Helped on by sun and spring rain, Mr. Dotson Gerber and the collards grew rapidly together. It would not be an exaggeration to say that Mr. Gerber's body growing there seemed to fertilize the whole field. Although in no time at all, he was taller than the collards and still growing. Most of his chest and arms was out of the ground by the end of March. And by the middle of April, he had cleared the ground down to his ankles. In his tattered clothes, the wild red hair, his large blue eyes wide and staring, he seemed more some kind of monster than a resurrected man. The sun and wind had burned his skin nearly as black as ours. And while there was small chance of anybody seeing him—people in Burnside didn't visit anymore, now that most of them worked in the factories— Poppa still thought it might be a good idea to cover Mr. Gerber up. "You'd better put a sack over his head and some gloves on his hands," he said. Later on, Poppa put a coat and some sunglasses on Mr. Gerber, along with an old straw hat. He propped a stick behind Mr. Gerber and passed another one through the sleeves of Mr. Gerber's coat for him to rest his arms on. He really looked like a scarecrow then, and we stopped worrying about people finding out about him. In truth, however, it must be said that Mr. Gerber made a very poor scarecrow, indeed, because the birds hardly paid any attention to him. It was fortunate for us that birds don't especially like collard greens.

Poppa worked a few hours in the collard patch every night after he came home from the factory. Momma helped him sometimes. Sometimes Millicent and I helped him, too. Then one day, Poppa quit his job at the factory and hitched Miss Tricia to the plow. "You farming again?" Momma asked him. She had been very tame with Poppa since he'd slapped her.

"I'm farming again," Poppa said.

Momma just nodded. "That's very nice, sugar. That's really very nice."

In no time at all, Poppa had planted all the old crops that used to grow on our farm—all kinds of vegetables, wheat, corn. He went to Dillwyn and bought a couple of pigs and a cow. All the neighbors knew what he was doing. But they kept on working at the factories and spending their money at the supermarkets. Until one day, a neighbor woman showed up to buy some collard greens. Poppa sold her a large basketful for a dollar. "I'm just sick to death of storebought food," she said.

"I know what you mean," Poppa said. "You come back, you hear?" In a little while, other people came to buy tomatoes, string beans, white potatoes, golden corn from the tall green stalks.

Summer droned on. Poppa worked his crops. Word reached us that Mrs. Dotson Gerber had married her decent white man. After school had let out, I had begun to help Poppa full time. Momma finally quit her job at the factory and helped, too. But mostly, she took care of selling and of managing the money that we were making. As for Millicent, I spied her one day making love down in the pea patch. And that black man she was with, he certainly was no sissy. That was all Millicent needed and all a black man needed, too—someplace green and growing to make love in. I

never heard Millicent talk about fainting after that, although she did talk about getting married.

Around the end of summer, Sheriff Dave Young came to our farm. "Some of the fellows said you were looking for me," he told Poppa. "But I figured it wasn't really too important, since you never came back."

"It wasn't important, Sheriff."

He bought a watermelon that Poppa let him have very cheap. "You got a good business going here," Sheriff Young said. "Some of the white farmers been talking about doing the same thing."

"It'd be good if they did," Poppa said. The sheriff put his watermelon into his car and drove away.

When fall came and the leaves turned red and gold and brown, Mr. Dotson Gerber turned like all the other growing things and shriveled away to nothing. Poppa seemed very satisfied then, looking over his fields. And I knew how he must have felt, standing there looking at Mr. Dotson Gerber and all the other dead things that would live again next spring.

The Greyhound to Richmond went by and Poppa shielded his eyes to watch. I think that I understood everything about him then and it hurt me so much that I deliberately turned my back. The lesson of that summer seemed a particularly bitter one, because we had done everything and we had done nothing. Mr. Dotson Gerber would certainly be growing in my father's fields every spring forever. And my father, my poor father would always watch and admire the Greyhound to Richmond. The same way that in the deepest and sincerest and blackest part of himself he would always hate himself and believe that God is the greatest white man of all.

"That Greyhound, she sure do run," Poppa said. He sounded very satisfied, indeed. God knew he'd killed a white man. With God know-ing, that was knowledge enough. But I was thinking about how it feels to be black and forever afraid. And about the white man, god*damn* him, how he causes everything. Even when He is God. Even when he is dead.

Considerations

"Dotson Gerber Resurrected" is beautifully constructed. Consider that great opening line, "We saw the head of Mr. Dotson Gerber break ground at approximately nine o'clock on a bright Saturday morning in March out near our collard patch, where Poppa had started to dig a well and then filled it in." What does it do in the story? Among other things, it arouses our interest, it establishes the story's earthy tone quickly and clearly, and it prepares us to suspend our disbelief. Since "we" saw the unbelievable, there can be no debate over whether it happened. Indeed, with all the details of time and place furnished, who could doubt it? The entire middle section is made up of vignettes, little stories that have their own beginning, middle, and end. The final paragraph is firm, tying it all together, "But I was thinking about how it feels to be black and forever afraid. And about the white man, god*damn* him, how he causes everything. Even when he is God. Even when he is dead."

Again and again the believable seems to be balanced against the unbelievable. Compare the very realistic description of Poppa going to see the sheriff and Poppa going to see Mrs. Gerber with the surrealism of Mrs. Gerber's reaction, to say nothing of that of her arthritic old grandmother rocking on the front porch.

The irony, the humor, and the tempo of this story are major assets. Would we be able to appreciate them as much if the story were really written in dialect? Notice the way Bennett gives the impression of dialect by using middle-American speech and adding a few colloquialisms, a few double negatives, and a few "yes ma'ams."

The characters in this story are to some extent stereotypes. What kinds of people do they represent? What do we remember the story for? Is it basically the humorous product of a very rich imagination? Does it communicate a feeling that the white man causes everything, even when he is God, even when he is dead? Or is it a veiled salute to the ingenious black man who tells the truth, goes his own way, and somehow comes out on top?

POETRY

Introduction
to Poetry

In the moments of unusual high points or low points in our lives, even the most bitter, cynical, or average of us may turn to poetry for expression—if only in the form of a mass-produced card that conveys sympathy, birthday wishes, or greetings. You might argue that the reason for this is convention, pure and simple, or you might suggest that the poetry on the card gets at a sentiment we don't normally have words to express. On a more philosophical level, poetry gets at the "truth" of experiences somewhat differently from other ways of expression. The experiences available to humans don't change, although the form may.

We're all familiar with song lyrics also. For some of us, certain lyrics—one kind of poetry—can express something deep within us and immortalize treasured moments in our lives. Thus while formal poetry may not be an entirely familiar language, we do seek out some version of it on many occasions. Those who read it, both professionally and as entertainment, never accuse it of being hard or a riddle but view it simply as another way of using the language. Poetry is not written merely to tease you or cover up with layer on layer of language. But it's not unusual for an uninitiated person to protest, "Well, why don't you just say what you mean?" The poet *is* saying what he or she means.

ONE WAY TO LOOK AT A POEM

O Western wind, when wilt thou blow,
That the small rain down can rain?
Christ, that my love were in my arms
And I in my bed again!

You will probably agree that this sixteenth-century anonymous lyric poem appears to be a simple, straightforward expression of loneliness for one's love. Indeed, that is the poem's subject—but what other elements does it contain? This poem has survived until the twentieth century. Why? Why have hundreds of thousands of people responded to it? Why have you?

Let's take a closer look at it. Possibly the first level of response is emotional. Perhaps it evokes memories of a similar experience that you have had and to which you can relate. Second, you may respond to the poem's rhythm; read silently or aloud, a definite rhythm is obvious. At this point you understand the subject and have responded to the emotional aspect and the sound. What else is there? We might discover the answer to this question by asking more questions:

1. What do the wind and rain have to do with loneliness?
2. Why is the rain *small*?
3. Does the poem mean more than it says?
4. Why does the poet use so many words beginning with a *w* in the first line?

These questions are valid. Similar ones should be asked and answered about any poem if you want to experience poetry fully. In this introduction we will briefly point out various elements that operate in certain poems in order to give you a model for approaching poetry. Let us look at the elements of the first poem more closely.

1. The western wind brings the rain, and rain traditionally stands for life and fertility. Perhaps while the speaker in the poem is separated from his love his world is sterile and barren. He associates the life-giving rain with the person who gives him love.

2. Since the rain is used as a positive image in this poem, it would be inappropriate to have it pour down in torrents. The word *small* suggests a soft and gentle rain, caressing, not destructive. It may be a spring rain, brought by the western wind—a wind that is warm rather than cold, as a northern one would be. This suggestion further reinforces the idea of life and fertility connected with rain and spring.

3. The last two lines clearly state that the speaker longs to be in bed with his lover again, thus expressing sexual loneliness and desire. If we refer once again to the image of the rain and its connotations and see the entire poem in the context of this fertility symbol, the whole poem coheres in a beautiful way. If you missed the sensual aspects of this poem, the fault may be in the reading. The poem means what it says.

4. Four words begin with *w* in the first line: *Western, wind, when,* and *wilt.* In addition, the final word, *blow,* ends with a *w.* All of these *w* sounds, particularly when read aloud, create a sense impression of the sound of the wind. This device, called *alliteration,* also reinforces the image of the lover's loneliness, as the sound of the wind can be a lonely one.

There are other elements that might be discovered on a closer reading of this poem, and there are many more questions to be asked and answered. We offer a few to demonstrate how deceptively simple a poem can appear, and how the enjoyment of it can be multiplied by spending a little time to think about it, to try to analyze and understand it.

The following poem was written by William Carlos Williams, a twentieth-century poet. It was written in a different time and place and looks different from the first poem. Let's take a closer look.

> I have eaten
> the plums
> that were in
> the icebox
>
> and which
> you were probably
> saving
> for breakfast
>
> Forgive me
> they were delicious
> so sweet
> and so cold

The subject seems to be simple; someone has been unable to resist the temptation to eat some fruit that someone else was obviously saving. The speaker is feeling a bit guilty about it; in the second stanza he (or she?) confesses that he knew the plums did not belong to him; in the third he offers an apology and requests forgiveness, as well as rationalizes what he has done. (Restating the subject in different words this way is called *paraphrasing.*)

What are some of the elements that work in this poem? The senses are brought into play in the third stanza, when the plums are described in terms of taste and touch. You can readily make associations with past experiences of your own and imagine the fragrance of the fruit, its juiciness, and whatever other characteristics that memory may evoke. You can also respond on an emotional level, again associating your personal experience with the speaker's. He seems to feel the pleasure of eating the fruit, mingled with a touch of guilt. Perhaps you empathize with him because these feelings are familiar.

The lack of punctuation rather speeds up the reading and tends to create an almost breathless feeling, as though the speaker wanted to explain as quickly as he could—before he was scolded. The rhythm tends to slow down in the last stanza; one can't help but pause between *delicious* and *so* (lines 11 and 12), which stops the reader (as if to show how the tempting fruit had stopped the person in the poem).

The poet gives us little more to go on other than a strong sensory experience and a succinct verbal image of a situation. The language is simple and economical and does not seem to be heavily symbolic or ambiguous.

It is easy to get carried away and free your imagination to interpret poetry in the light of personal associations and experiences. For example, one can image a hen-pecked husband making this timid confession and apology before a shrew of a wife, or perhaps even more timidly leaving the poem taped to the door of the refrigerator. (Perhaps the wife is moved by it; or perhaps the whole thing ends in divorce.)

INTERPRETATIONS

As you can see, once you begin this line of approach, it becomes difficult to stop. Many overly enthusiastic students (and critics) get carried away with an interpretation. The point is to work with what the poet has given you—no more, no less. This is not to discourage your using your imagination, but to emphasize that in analyzing a poem, any conclusions and interpretations should really be supported by evidence within the poem itself. Otherwise you might have a fun flight of the imagination but be no nearer to understanding the meaning of the poem. In other words, don't read more into a poem than is actually there—but don't ignore anything it has to offer.

While prose usually delivers a straightforward statement, poetry is a much more subtle form of communication. Like prose, it communicates ideas, insights, emotions, stories, opinions, attitudes, and human experiences of all kinds. But poetry can distill these things down to their essences.

Many people, remembering their first brush with poetry in school, where it was dissected, analyzed, and categorized, may think of poetry as too artificial and alien. But is it? During the ordinary business of everyday life people must constantly try to interpret what other people mean. A significant proportion of anyone's time is spent on wondering: "What did she mean by that?" "I know he said that, but. . . ." The closer the relationship, the more time and energy we devote to interpreting the possible meanings of communications. Both our joys and our sorrows come out of that experience.

Now if we could all carry this attitude with us as we take the leap from daily life to creative language—in this case, poetry—we would find interpretation simpler and beneficial. Unfortunately, in the area of creative language, we want things to be simple, linear, and without shade—as one-to-one as mathematical language. We want a red apple in a poem to be only a red apple, whereas even in our commonest experiences it isn't that—it's an apple for the teacher, the fruit that drove Adam and Eve out of the Garden of Eden, something that is cool, crisp, crunchy and refreshing, and so on and on, linking with each of our personal memories.

Such a bias, acquired early, too often prevents people from discovering a potentially great experience. As you have seen in the two examples above, the basic material of poetry is that which is natural and familiar to us: images and experiences we all deal with, the rhythm of life captured with burning intensity and concentration. The poet takes this raw material, this common experience, and makes something new of it. He or she sees new relations between objects, ideas, and experiences and offers us new perceptions and perspectives. If we learn to read a poem well, like the poet, we learn to see things in a fresh way.

Sometimes the poet's intention is to provide some new insight, something philosophical and thought provoking. Sometimes the aim is to amuse or soothe us. Sometimes he or she desires merely to create a mood or sensory experience or to evoke a specific emotion and draw us into it. For the most part, this is what poetry is all about. If we choose to examine or discuss the technique used in a poem, it is only in order to increase our awareness and appreciation of the complexity and skill that is hidden within it. Understanding what the poet is saying brings enjoyment on one level. Understanding *how* it is being said intensifies and expands the pleasure into a full poetry experience. Any good poem has stood—and will continue to stand—up to analysis and dissection. Only a weak one will crumble under close scrutiny.

Definition

Certain people have long puzzled over exactly what poetry is, and they have come up with a number of definitions—none of which has suited everybody. According to Wordsworth, "All good poetry is the spontaneous overflow of powerful feelings. . . ." Coleridge said that prose is words in their best order, but poetry is the best words in their best order. Keats said, "Poetry . . . should strike the Reader as a wording of his own highest thoughts, and appear almost a Remembrance."

Frost agreed with part of Keats' statement: he said that for him the initial delight is in the surprise of remembering something he didn't know he knew. A poem, he added, is a legitimate way of saying one thing and meaning another. (Or, as you will see later, it is a way of saying one thing and meaning more.) Some people feel that poetry is that moment of flash inside a poem that cannot be long sustained. It may not even happen in every poem. (Emily Dickinson best expressed that point of view when she said that if she felt as though the top of her head was blown off, she knew it was poetry.)

As you can see from just the above comments, there are many approaches to defining poetry. Some critics define it in terms of form, some in terms of content. Some emphasize the process the poet goes through in writing a poem, while some describe a poem's effect on the reader. Along with this view, many people feel that if one likes a poem and responds to it on any level, it is poetry. To a certain extent this is true. A personal response is valid and important, because, after all, reading poetry is a subjective experience.

CHARACTERISTICS OF POETRY

Whichever view you subscribe to, you should recognize certain things that are inherent in all poetry. A poem is intensely personal. What the poet has written may be an opinion or it may be a scientific fact; poetry may tell a story, but the story will be presented in a much different way than in fiction. In poetry the emphasis is less on action and plot and more on the sensations, images, and thoughts that accompany an experience. When you feel that a poem is "right," it is not because you have been swayed by the poet's logic or the evidence marshalled to support his or her opinion. Rather you have been able to identify with the poet and find a common area between his view of experience and your own.

The language is intense and compressed. One word is used to stand for many things and evoke many images. Yet this too is not entirely foreign to our daily lives: the advertising commercial calls for a few connections in your mind. But poetry calls for even more. When we consider a single word in one of Keats' lyrics, we move through a network of connections. An entire book has been written on the types of ambiguities that enrich the meaning of a poem.

Who writes poems? All sorts of people have been (or have become) poets. Wallace Stevens was an insurance company executive, William Carlos Williams was a doctor, Geoffrey Chaucer was a government employee, and John Donne was a clergyman. There have been young poets (Dylan Thomas wrote at least a preliminary version of all of his most important works before he was seventeen), and there have been middle-aged poets (Robert Frost and Wallace Stevens were over forty before their work was published). There have been widely travelled poets (Robert Browning and Lord Byron) and recluses (Emily Dickinson).

FORM AND SUBJECT MATTER

The form and subject matter of poetry have changed, or at least have become more flexible, over a period of time. At one point, poetry had to have rhyme, meter, and specific form, and generally recognizable symbols had to be used. Now free verse and (often obscure) private symbolism are more in favor. Once poetry had to concern itself with exalted personal emotions and reflections. (Remember, Keats believed it should reflect high thoughts and ideals.) Poets of today use language more freely than ever before, and modern poems may deal with practically any subject. Neither of these extremes is per se the only possible view of poetry. Most of us, after we read poetry for a time, begin to have favorite poems in every period, on all subjects, and by various poets.

Admittedly, the techniques, forms, styles, and even themes of poetry seem to vary with time. But the temper of the times is usually less important than the poet's own temperament in deciding these matters. The subject—something that concerned the poet so deeply that he or she was moved to write about it—and the theme—what he tried to show about his subject—can be almost anything at any point in history.

"On His Blindness," written by the seventeenth-century poet John Milton, is an example of a subject that moved the poet to write a poem. Milton went blind at the age of forty-three. This poem deals with his experience of blindness, his attitude toward his condition, and his religious faith. There are poets whose poems are chiefly imagery, such as some of Keats' works ("Eve of St. Agnes" is a good example). There are those whose emphasis is on man's relation to nature, such as Wordsworth; there are those who emphasize private insights, such as Robert Frost in his "After Apple-Picking"; there are passionate writers of messages, such as Walt Whitman. Just look at the topics of the first twenty poems in this collection—morals and manners, good times and bad, happiness and death—to get some idea of the variety of topics poems can cover. (Although the first twenty poems come from early English writing, the same general topics concern poets of today.)

WAYS TO CLASSIFY POETRY

Poets and poems are often classified by school: pre-Raphaelite, imagist, vorticist, objectivist, romantic, symbolist, and so on. This means merely that the poets have subscribed to a certain philosophy and a set of self-imposed conditions in terms of conventions, attitudes, or appropriate subject matter. Occasionally, the classification has been made by scholars who have seen some similarities in thought or style. For the most part, learning such categories is not essential; however, it can be a useful way of approaching a poem, because it tells you what to look for and gives you some context in which to interpret the poem. But it can also lead to prejudgement and prejudice. If someone believes he doesn't like the romantic poets because their work is supposedly too flowery and lofty, he will never know the pleasure he could find in reading the satiric verse of Lord Byron, one of the romantic poets.

But talking about the school of poetry to which a poet belongs is only one way of classifying poetry. There are other categories that are frequently used for purposes of discussion. These categories refer to the poems themselves. First, poems may be classified according to subject matter. There are *odes,* which are lyric poems with varying line lengths and sudden shifts in mood on serious or perhaps dignified subjects (see Keats' "Ode to a Nightingale," p. 405). There are *elegies,* which are poems lamenting the death of someone loved or respected, or dealing with the subject of death in general (see Whitman's "When Lilacs Last in the Dooryard Bloomed," pp. 424–25). *Pastoral verse* refers to poems that extol the virtues of idealized country life (see Marlowe's "The Passionate Shepherd to His Love," p. 361). Sometimes this type of classification includes a reference to the approach used. There are *ballads,* which are impersonal, narrative, highly dramatic poems that usually deal with the subjects of physical courage or love (see "Sir Patrick Spens," p. 357). *Lyrics* are songlike, personal, individualistic poems that convey a state of mind or feeling (see Frost's "Dust of Snow," p. 479). *Epics* are long narrative poems written in an elevated style that tell the story of a hero of high rank or importance who performs great deeds (examples include the *Iliad,* the *Odyssey,* and "Paradise Lost"). *Dramatic monologues,* which are in some ways similar to soliloquies in plays, present the words of one individual, supposedly spoken to a silent listener, which reveal something about the speaker's personality, (see Browning's "My Last Duchess," p. 413 and Tennyson's "Ulysses," p. 410).

To increase your own enjoyment of poetry, you should be aware of the various elements that work in a poem, which together create a unity.

SOME BASIC ELEMENTS OF POETRY

1. Form: Meter and Rhyme

The form of poetry basically involves two things: sound and rhythm. Perhaps the thing about poetry that seems most artificial is the terminology that has been devised to talk about the conventions of sound and rhythm. Why are these matters important enough to warrant special attention? All of life is rhythmic. Nature is built on the rhythm of the seasons. Our most intimate language has the rhythm of breath and heartbeat. Poetry is based on such impulses. Some of the names of different types of poems *(ballad,* for instance, which comes from the French word for *to dance)* still denote this attention to sound and rhythm. Yeats indicated the necessity of these elements when he called sound "that subtle monotony of voice which runs through the nerves like fire" and said that the purpose of rhythm is "to keep us in that state of perhaps real trance, in which the mind liberated from the pressure of the will is unfolded in symbols."

Meter, then, is the rhythmic regularity or pattern in the lines of poetry. For example, *iambic pentameter* means that the line consists of five "feet" (the pattern of stressed and unstressed syllables), each of which has one unaccented syllable followed by an accented one. As an example, here are two lines from Shelley's "Ozymandias," which is written in iambic pentameter: (The sign ' indicates a stressed syllable; –indicates an unstressed one.)

Í mȳet | a trȧv|eller frōm | an ānt|ique land
Who said: | "Two vast | and trunk|less legs | of stone

You can see and hear that there are five stressed beats to every line. Counting accented syllables and indicating rhyme schemes with letters is called *scansion.* If the words at the ends of lines rhyme in some pattern, that pattern is called a rhyme *scheme.* Now let us scan the rhyme scheme of the same poem:

Look on my works, ye Mighty, and despair!. . . . . .A
Nothing beside remains. Round the decay . . . . . . .B
Of that colossal wreck, boundless and bare. . . . . . .A
The lone and level sands stretch far away." . . . . . .B

As you can see, each letter indicates a rhyme: A rhymes with A; B rhymes with B.

The combination of the meter and the rhyme scheme determines the form of a poem. A few special forms of poems have been used repeatedly in English verse. Best known are *sonnets* (fourteen-line poems written in iambic pentameter, rhymed either *abab cdcd, efef gg,* or *abbaabba cdecde,* or some variation thereof). The first rhyme scheme is characteristic of the English or Shakespearean sonnet, and the second is the *Italian* or *Petrarchan* form. The *villanelle* is another special form; it is a nineteen-line poem that consists of five three-line stanzas and a final four-line one, with a rhyme scheme of *aba aba aba aba aba abaa* (such as Dylan Thomas' "Do Not Go Gentle into That Good Night" on p. 582). There are also special stanza forms, such as the *couplet* (two end-rhymed lines, as used in Shakespeare's sonnets), *common meter* (a four-line stanza rhyming *abab,* in which the first and third lines are iambic *tetrameter,* and the second and fourth are iambic *trimeter*), and *rhyme royal* (a seven-line stanza in iambic pentameter, rhymed *ababbcc*).

Although not all poems can be classified in terms of a fixed poem or stanza form, every poem can be described in terms of line length, meter, and rhyme. For example, when we speak of Shakespeare or Milton using *blank verse,* we mean that the lines are unrhymed iambic pentameter. If we say that a poem is written in *free verse,* a form much admired today, we mean that the lines are unrhymed and also irregular in meter.

When we talk about *unrhymed verse,* though, we are only saying that the last word in a given line does not rhyme with the last word in another line. There are all sorts of internal rhymes and repeated similar sounds that add to the sound of the poem. Internal rhyme may consist of perfect rhyme (repetition of identical vowel and consonant sounds) and/or *alliteration* (repetition of initial consonant or vowel sounds in a sequence of words, such as "sweet silent spring" or "apt alliteration's artful aid"). A good example of internal rhyme and alliteration can be seen in Coleridge's "Kubla Khan," p. 398:

And from this chasm, with ceaseless turmoil seething (line 17)

The combination of the *s* sounds created by the *c's* and the *s's* both in the middle and at the end of the words echo the hissing sound of the chasm.

As if this earth in fast thick pants were breathing (line 18)

There is a whisper of the *s* sound now, but Coleridge uses a different device: *word choice.* We are forced to pause after the words *fast* and *thick* and *pants;* these pauses are akin to the sound of panting and again echo the panting of the earth.

Five miles meandering with a mazy motion (line 25)

This is a beautiful example of alliteration. All of the *m's* create a gentle, languid, liquid sound that strengthens the image of the river. The effect is a lazy "meandering" sound that is almost lulling and hypnotic. Again, we must slow down to pronounce those repeated *m's,* which in so doing has the tendency to simulate the sound and feeling of the sacred river.

Other types of rhyme are *consonance* (repetition of final consonant sounds with different preceding vowel sounds, such as *born-turn*); and *assonance* (repetition of similar stressed vowel sounds with different consonant sounds, such as *make-late*). When assonance or consonance is substituted for end rhyme, the poet is said to be using approximate or *near rhyme,* which is also called *slant* rhyme. Emily Dickinson often uses slant rhyme; for example, note the second- and fourth-line rhymes in this stanza from her #328, p. 446:

Like one in danger, Cautious,
I offered him a Crumb
And he unrolled his feathers
and rowed him softer home—

2. The Emotional Element

Often the first response to a poem is emotional. We respond because it conveys an emotion that is part of our personal experience. William Blake's "The Chimney Sweep" (p. 390), is a poem that has immediate emotional appeal. The very first line, "When my mother died I was very young," usually evokes sympathy in the reader. This poem is actually a social commentary, in which Blake speaks out against the exploitation of children as chimney sweeps. (This type of labor caused the deaths of many young children in England.) At the first reading, we are moved by the poem's emotional aspects; it is only after closer reading that we begin to recognize the harsh criticism and social implications of the work and to realize that it is much more than a pathetic and moving little poem.

3. Imagery: The Sensory Element

Another strong area of response to poetry is on the sensory level. In reading poetry, we actually become part of the experience when our senses are brought into play. Sense imagery makes us recall personal sensory experiences that we can bring into the poetic experience. For example, look at Keats' "Ode to a Nightingale" (p. 405). This poem appeals to all five senses:

Touch: The first stanza vividly creates strong physical feelings and sensations. The reader is brought into a dreamlike state, "as though of hemlock I had drunk. . . ." and experiences an atmosphere of somnolence. Frost's "Birches" is another example of strong tactile imagery (p. 481):

Where your face burns and tickles with the cobwebs
Broken across it, and one eye is weeping
From a twig's having lashed across it open.

One can almost feel the sensations these poets describe.

Taste: The entire second stanza of Keats' "Ode to a Nightingale" appeals to the sense of taste. Keats was a master of synaesthesia; that is, the blending of two or more senses into one. For example, the line, "O for a beaker of the warm South," combines the sense of taste with the sense of touch. A paraphrasing of this line might be, "I wish I had a glassful of warmth."

Sight: Keats' third stanza creates a strong visual image of age (lines 24 through 26):

> Here, where men sit and hear each other groan;
> Where palsy shakes a few, sad, last gray hairs,
> Where youth grows pale, and specter-thin, and dies;

We also respond to the physical sensations of line 23:

> The weariness, the fever, and the fret

These sensory images work together to create a vivid visual image.

Smell: The fifth stanza uses the sense of smell (and perhaps the sixth sense, instinct, as well) to "see" the environment, to identify each living thing by its fragrance or vibration:

> I cannot see what flowers are at my feet,
> Nor what soft incense hangs upon the boughs,
> But, in embalmed darkness, guess each sweet
> Wherewith the seasonable month endows.

Sound/hearing: Stanza eight creates the sound of a bell:

> Forlorn! the very word is like a bell
> To toll me back from thee to my sole self,

In the last two lines of stanza six, Keats uses music imagery to reinforce the sensory experience of sound:

> Still wouldst thou sing, and I have ears in vain—
> to thy high requiem become a sod.

As you can see, through the skillful use of sensory imagery, Keats creates an exquisite, sensual experience. Even if we experience the poem on the sensual level alone, it is highly pleasurable and beautiful. But responding to it in conjunction with its other elements—and with an understanding of them—completes the experience. Imagery, then, is figurative language that conveys sensory impressions.

4. Diction

We have discussed responding to poetry on the emotional and sensory levels. But what makes us respond? How does the poet create this experience for us? The emotional and sensory elements are working in the first stanza of "The Hollow Men," by T. S. Eliot (p. 516):

> We are the hollow men
> We are the stuffed men
> Leaning together
> Headpiece filled with straw. Alas!
> Our dried voices, when
> We whisper together
> Are quiet and meaningless
> As wind in dry grass
> Or rats' feet over broken glass
> In our dry cellar.

The futility and despair of men without purpose and hope come through vividly, as does the visual image of "hollow" and "stuffed" scarecrowlike men. But how does Eliot create this effect? Remember Coleridge's definition of poetry: the best words in their best order.

The word *hollow* sets up many associations: empty, meaningless, void, vacuum, desolation, and so on. "Headpiece filled with straw" rather than *head* reinforces the feeling of nonbeing or absence of humanness. These words create a certain emotional impact. The phrase, "Our dried voices," begins to create a sensory image that is strengthened by words like *whisper* and *quiet* in the last three lines of this stanza. These words again evoke the sounds and feelings of dryness, barrenness, and sterility. At this point you can probably provide your own definition of diction: the choice of certain words and the ways they are used to create a particular effect.

Poets must use words that contribute to the sound and rhythm of the poem. There are other factors, however, that they must also consider. For example, they may wish to use highly connotative words (words that carry nonliteral meanings because of suggested or implied meanings) in order to appeal to the reader's emotions. They may decide to use figurative language to make their writing more effective. If the poem uses images or symbols, they must carefully choose concrete words that will convey the image or suggest the multilevel meanings of the symbol.

5. Symbolism

A poet often uses certain myths of his society and culture—certain familiar images and objects that appear in literature, painting, and dreams—in order to enrich a poem and give it different meanings on different levels. These symbols can be used in a traditional way or in a new way that the poet creates to symbolize something else. Poets, particularly some of the modern ones, often use private symbols as well, and these are often difficult to comprehend. As we have mentioned, many symbols are traditional, such as the symbol of rain as life or fertility, and so forth. Symbolism is often used in poetry, since a great deal can be said or implied by using a single symbol. This is a valuable device in a genre in which brevity and word economy are essential.

An example of a private symbol might be William Blake's "The Tiger" (p. 392). Does the tiger symbolize evil, or is it a symbol of power and strength? Perhaps Delmore Schwartz's "The Heavy Bear" (p. 566) offers a more obvious private symbol, that of the "inescapable" animal side of man. Generally speaking, a symbol is an object or image that stands for something else.

6. Figurative Language

We have mentioned that poets see things in new ways, discover new relations, and convey them through the skillful use of words. In describing something, the poet searches for an imaginative, fresh, and original way of expression. In his Sonnet 18 (p. 363), Shakespeare uses figurative language to express certain ideas and create certain images. For example, in line 5, instead of saying "the sun," he writes "the eye of heaven." This form of expression allows the reader to see and think of the sun in a different way. It becomes more than just a sun: it takes on human qualities and characteristics (personification). The following line, "And often is his gold complexion dimmed," reinforces the image of a personified sun. This type of figure of speech is called a *metaphor*. In Sonnet 97 (p. 365), Shakespeare again uses a figure of speech. In the first line he states that his absence from his love has been like winter:

> How like a winter hath my absence been
> From thee, the pleasure of the fleeting year!

Throughout the poem he develops this image with appropriate diction, using phrases and words like "fleeting year," "what freezings," "dark days," and "December." He is saying that without his love, he is feeling lonely and cold. But look how he uses figurative language to create the sentiment in a unique and beautiful way. As stated before, generally when the word *like* is used ("How like a winter . . ."), the image is called a *simile,* which is a figure of speech in which two basically unlike objects, things, or ideas are directly compared.

Examples of *comparison and contrast* can be found in Shakespeare's Sonnet 130 (p. 366), in which he sets up extravagant ones to describe his mistress. There is humor working here, and his diction is at times rather harsh for a love poem. But you can see the obvious effectiveness of this use of figurative language.

Often a poet will refer indirectly to historical events, biblical works, mythology, or works of other poets. T. S. Eliot and Ezra Pound are particularly known for their heavy use of *allusion.* For example, in Eliot's "The Love Song of J. Alfred Prufrock" (p. 509), there are several such references:

Line 93: "To have squeezed the universe into a ball . . ." refers to Marvell's "To His Coy Mistress," in which Marvell writes:

> Let us roll all our strength and all
> Our sweetness up into one ball,
> And tear our pleasures with rough strife
> Through the iron gates of life:
> Thus, though we cannot make our sun
> Stand still, yet we will make him run (p. 384).

Lines 81–83 recall the biblical story of John the Baptist and Salome:

> But though I have wept and fasted, wept and prayed,
> Though I have seen my head (grown slightly bald) brought
>   in upon a platter. . . .

This type of reference—allusion—can work as a metaphor, a simile, or a symbol, relating past works, events, and ideas with the present ones dealt with in the poem. Often, particularly in difficult works such as Hart Crane's "The Bridge," Ezra Pound's "Hugh Selwyn Mauberley," or Eliot's "The Wasteland," allusions are so obscure and esoteric that it is necessary to try to look them up in order to understand the poems.

(There are other devices and figures of speech that are explained in the glossary. These are the basic tools a poet uses to give his work interest, beauty, variety, and uniqueness.)

7. Mood and Tone

The poet, by his choice of words, how he orders them, the figures of speech he uses, and the sound and rhythm of his work, creates an atmosphere and reveals an attitude—either his own or that of the speaker in the poem (they are not necessarily the same). Edwin Arlington Robinson creates a specific atmosphere in "Mr. Flood's Party" (p. 465): It is one of the quiet loneliness and weariness of age, of the sense of isolation and realization that death is near. The attitude is quietly cynical, sympathetic, and empathetic, but realistic in the sense that the person in the poem accepts the facts of loneliness and fear and the futility of a life of sorrow that ends in death. Yet the speaker keeps a sense of humor through it all, as we can see in stanza three, in which he describes the tender way in which Mr. Flood handles his jug of booze, ". . . as a mother lays her sleeping child. . . ." Yet even the humor is tinged with a sort of the bittersweet. The attitude expressed by the poet or speaker toward the subject is called *tone,* and the total effect or atmosphere of the work is called *mood.*

8. Subject and Theme (Ambiguity)

The poet has a particular theme or subject in mind when he or she composes a poem, and one of the basic steps in understanding poetry is discovering just what the subject and theme are. First we must consider the poem on two levels—the literal and the figurative. On the literal level, we analyze what facts are presented, what the poem says, and what its surface or obvious meaning is. For example, Emily Dickinson's poem #324 seems, on the surface, to be a personal statement about the way she chooses to "keep the Sabbath." Upon closer reading and analysis, we discover a deeper statement about religious attitudes. We find a subtle criticism of organized religion and long-winded clergymen,

> God preaches, a noted Clergyman—
> And the sermon is never long,

and the dogma that one has to work in order to get to heaven,

> So instead of getting to Heaven, at last—
> I'm going, all along,

while missing all of the rich experiences of the present because of a promise of a hereafter. This idea emerges only after careful reading. This is the poem's theme, or dominant idea.

Subject and theme relate to ambiguity. Shelley's "Ozymandias" offers us an example of this element. Its subject is the report of a world traveler who visited an "antique land." The theme deals with the effects of time on power and achievement—that nothing lasts. The statement of Ozymandias is a challenge to all to match his achievements, but ironically, nothing of him remains but the ruins of his statue. Line 8 (p. 403) carries a double or ambiguous meaning:

> "The hand that mocked them and the heart that fed;"

Mocked is used in the derisive sense—mocking a king who believed he could conquer time—as well as in the sense of copying or imitating a likeness as a sculptor "mocks" an image in clay. Both meanings are valid and important for understanding this poem. When skillfully used, ambiguity, or multiple meaning, adds additional dimensions to poetry.

9. Style and Technique

Poets, like painters, composers, architects, actors, and dancers—indeed artists of any kind—develop personal styles that are unique to each. In the case of writers, they are recognizable to the careful reader. In fact, many students enjoy reading one poet again and again because that quality—style—is both emotionally and intellectually satisfying. Anyone, for example, can recognize the mature work of Amy Lowell, because of the clear and memorable images she creates. Her poems have a very special human quality about them—the images are universal enough for us to relate to, regardless of our background or experiences with her works. For instance, "Patterns" (p. 475) is concerned with a woman receiving a letter saying that her future husband has been killed in a pattern called war. But the distinctive style of Lowell's poem comes not from harshness, as we might expect, but from a special gentleness, restrained anger, hushed outrage, controlled bitterness. To get at these feelings, the poet uses simple, clear mental pictures—flowers, water in a fountain, a stiff brocade dress, and a lover's game. Blended into a beautiful poem, "Patterns" has style.

Besides images (and often in addition to them), other poets use rhythm, and other techniques for achieving individuality in their poems. Robert Browning, for instance, in "My Last Duchess" (p. 413) uses the technique of dramatic monologue—a duke is instructing another man concerning a new duchess. Browning allows the duke to make a fool of himself by talking about his last wife. The result is a poem of memorable style.

Dorothy Parker's wit always comes through in her poems (pp. 527–28). She uses short lines, ironic twists, and unusual rhyming words to communicate her wit, and the result is a pleasing style.

Style, then, is a special quality of poetry that comes through to us in various ways, created by numerous methods and devices, but come through to us it does.

10. Judging Poetry

As you can see, poetry is composed of many elements. These elements do not necessarily operate all at once in every poem. In fact, this is rarely the case. Because of the emotional, personal appeal of poetry and the relative inexperience of most of us in judging such things, it might be helpful to consider a few of the ways poetry is ordinarily judged. Honesty, consistency, conciseness, suggestiveness, effectiveness of imagery, appropriateness of form and diction to subject matter, and completeness are all qualities that should be apparent in a good poem. The author should not become wrapped up in the use of language just for its own sake or include unjustified words or emotion in the poem. (A poet's reputation is no guarantee that he or she will adhere to these principles. Ella Wheeler Wilcox has written honest poems; William Wordsworth has written some laughable ones.)

A final word about reading poetry: Read slowly, carefully, and aloud, if possible. First, read to experience the feeling of the poem as a whole—its music, sound, and rhythm. Next, explore your own associations and experiences in responding to the subject, theme, and emotional elements. Then be objective and explore the different elements working in the poem and see how they operate together to produce the whole effect. Next, examine the possible levels of meaning and how they are conveyed. Remember—the elements must be seen in context with each other.

If you believe that poetry is read, published, and sold in lesser quantities these days than works of fiction or drama, you may be overlooking one major source of poetry. Appreciation of the poetry in the lyrics to popular music is reminiscent of past days when poetry was recited or sung rather than read. For example, here is an example of the lyrics of a popular rock group, Jethro Tull, written by Ian Anderson:

Slipstream

Well the lush separation enfolds you
and the products of wealth
push you along the bow wave
of their spiritless undying selves.
And you press on God's waiter your last dime
as He hands you the bill.
And you spin in the slipstream
tideless unreasoning
paddle right out of the mess.

Now that you are familiar with some of the basic elements of poetry, you might enjoy analyzing this poem. Several devices are apparent: alliteration, metaphor, ambiguity. Can you find more?

The question might be asked: Why the old stuff, why the old poetry? If you are the least interested in the history of ideas, then it makes sense, of course, to drop back in time and study the expression of the ideas that have come along. Second, if you are interested in the history of the form, of course it makes obvious sense. Third, many of us read it because the human feelings of love, hate, pain, suffering, oppression, and depression simply have not changed. We still love and we still hate. It's just a matter of human interest to see how they dealt with it and expressed it then.

Poetry can be enjoyed and appreciated by everyone. When it is good, the power and intensity of its language and imagery establish communication with even the unsophisticated. One need not know the technical aspects of poetry in order to appreciate it; yet those who have come to know poetry well often speak of it almost with love, claiming that the better and more detailed their knowledge, the more heightened the pleasure they experience.

In light of this, you should at least give poetry a chance. If it doesn't live up to what it is claimed to be, you will have lost little. But if it does turn out to be as great as it is said to be, it will be an experience you wouldn't want to miss.

Arise, My Love, and Come Away

Song of Solomon 2:8–3:5

The voice of my beloved!
  Behold, he comes,
leaping upon the mountains,
  bounding over the hills.
My beloved is like a gazelle,   5
  or a young stag.
Behold, there he stands
  behind our wall,
gazing in at the windows,
  looking through the lattice.   10
My beloved speaks and says to me:
"Arise, my love, my fair one,
  and come away;
for lo, the winter is past,
  the rain is over and gone.
The flowers appear on the earth,   15
  the time of singing has come,

and the voice of the turtledove
   is heard in our land.
The fig tree puts forth its figs,
   and the vines are in blossom;   20
   they give forth fragrance.
Arise, my love, my fair one,
   and come away.
O my dove, in the clefts of the rock,
   in the covert of the cliff,   25
let me see your face,
   let me hear your voice,
for your voice is sweet,
   and your face is comely.
Catch us the foxes,
   the little foxes,   30
that spoil the vineyards,
   for our vineyards are in blossom."

My beloved is mine and I am his,
   he pastures his flock among the lilies.   35
Until the day breathes
   and the shadows flee,
turn, my beloved, be like a gazelle,
   or a young stag upon rugged mountains.

Upon my bed by night   40
   I sought him whom my soul loves;
I sought him, but found him not;
   I called him, but he gave no answer.
"I will rise now and go about the city,
   in the streets and in the squares;   45
I will seek him whom my soul loves."
   I sought him, but found him not.
The watchmen found me,
   as they went about in the city.
"Have you seen him whom my soul loves?"   50
Scarcely had I passed them,
   when I found him whom my soul loves.
I held him, and would not let him go
until I had brought him into my mother's house,
   and into the chamber of her that conceived me.
I adjure you, O daughters of Jerusalem,
   by the gazelles or the hinds of the field,
that you stir not up nor awaken love until it please.

Edward

ANONYMOUS

"Why dois your brand sae drap wi bluid,
    Edward, Edward,
Why dois your brand sae drap wi bluid,
    And why sae sad gang yee O?"
"O I hae killed my hauke sae guid,
    Mither, mither,
O I hae killed my hauke sae guid,
    And I had nae mair bot hee O."

"Your haukis bluid was nevir sae reid,
    Edward, Edward,   10
Your haukis bluid was nevir sae reid,
    My deir son I tell thee O."
"O I hae killed my reid-roan steid,
    Mither, mither,
O I hae killed my reid-roan steid,
    That erst was sae fair and frie O."

"Your steid was auld, and ye hae gat mair,
    Edward, Edward,
Your steid was auld, and ye hae gat mair,
    Sum other dule ye drie O."   20

---

1 **gang,** walk, go   8 **mair,** more   9 **reid,** red   16 **erst,** once   20 **dule,** sorrow **drie,** suffer

"O I hae killed my fadir deir,
       Mither, mither,
O I hae killed my fadir deir,
   Alas, and wae is mee O!"

"And whatten penance wul ye drie for that,
       Edward, Edward?
And whatten penance will ye drie for that?
   My deir son, now tell me O."
"Ile set my feit in yonder boat,
       Mither, mither,   30
Ile set my feit in yonder boat,
   And Ile fare ovir the sea O."

"And what wul ye doe wi your towirs and your ha,
       Edward, Edward?
And what wul ye doe wi your towirs and your ha,
   That were sae fair to see O?"
"Ile let thame stand tul they doun fa,
       Mither, mither,
Ile let thame stand tul they doun fa,
   For here nevir mair maun I bee O."   40

"And what wul ye leive to your bairns and your wife,
       Edward, Edward?
And what wul ye leive to your bairns and your wife,
   Whan ye gang ovir the sea O?"
"The warldis room, late them beg thrae life,
       Mither, mither,
The warldis room, late them beg thrae life,
   For thame nevir mair wul I see O."

"And what wul ye leive to your ain mither deir,
       Edward, Edward?   50
And what wul ye leive to your ain mither deir?
   My deir son, now tell me O."
"The curse of hell frae me sall ye beir,
       Mither, mither,
The curse of hell frae me sall ye beir,
   Sic counseils ye gave to me O."

---

31 **feit,** feet 33 **ha,** hall. This so-called satirical legacy is a feature of popular literature
37 **fa,** fall

The Twa Corbies

ANONYMOUS

As I was walking all alane,
I herd twa corbies making a mane;
The tane unto the t' other say,
"Where sall we gang and dine to-day?"

"In behint yon auld fail dyke,
I wot there lies a new slain knight;
And naebody kens that he lies there,
But his hawk, his hound, and lady fair.

"His hound is to the hunting gane,
His hawk to fetch the wild-fowl hame,
His lady's ta'en another mate,
So we may mak our dinner sweet.

"Ye'll sit on his white hause-bane,
And I'll pike out his bonny blue een;
Wi ae lock o his gowden hair
We'll theek our nest when it grows bare.

"Mony a one for him makes mane,
But nane sall ken where he is gane;
Oer his white banes when they are bare,
The wind sall blaw for evermair."

Sir Patrick Spens

ANONYMOUS

The king sits in Dumferling toune,
  Drinking the blude-reid wine:
"O whar will I get a guid sailor,
  To sail this schip of mine?"

Up and spak an eldern knicht,
  Sat at the kings richt kne:
"Sir Patrick Spens is the best sailor
  That sails upon the se."

The king has written a braid letter,
  And signd it wi his hand,   10
And sent it to Sir Patrick Spens,
  Was walking on the sand.

The first line that Sir Patrick red,
  A loud lauch lauched he;
The next line that Sir Patrick red,
  The teir blinded his ee.

"O wha is this has don this deid,
  This ill deid don to me,
To send me out this time o' the yeir,
  To sail upon the se!   20

"Mak hast, mak haste, my mirry men all,
  Our guid schip sails the morne."
"Oh say na sae, my master deir,
  For I feir a deadlie storme.

"Late late yestreen I saw the new moone,
   Wi the auld moone in hir arme,
And I feir, I feir, my deir master,
   That we will cum to harme."

O our Scots nobles wer richt laith
   To weet their cork-heild schoone,   30
Bot lang owre a' the play wer playd,
   Thait hats they swam aboone.

O lang, lang may their ladies sit,
   Wi thair fans into their hand,
Or eir they se Sir Patrick Spens
   Cum sailing to the land.

O lang, lang may the ladies stand,
   Wi thair gold kems in their hair,
Waiting for thair ain deir lords,
   For they'll se thame na mair.   40

Haf owre, half owre to Aberdour,
   It's fiftie fadom deip,
And thair lies guid Sir Patrick Spens,
   Wi the Scots lords at his feit.

Considerations

"Edward," "The Twa Corbies," and "Sir Patrick Spens" all come from
the literature of the common people of England. These ballads were
originally sung or recited and were thus transmitted from one generation
to the next. Eventually they were written down. Each of them now bears
the clear mark of a skillful writer. Each tells a dramatic and tragic story.

1. The structure of "Edward" includes the use of incremental repetitions
   and refrains. What do the refrains "Edward, Edward" and "Mither,
   mither" add to the ballad?
2. "The Twa Corbies" (or "The Two Crows"), unlike most ballads,
   contains no action. What story is implied?
3. "Sir Patrick Spens" provides an excellent example of the way in which
   ballads skip over some details and present others with minute care.
   Does the poem give you a sufficiently vivid picture of the shipwreck,
   or do you think more information about it should have been included?
4. Why does "Sir Patrick Spens" end as it does? Would it be better if it
   stopped with the reactions of the ladies left behind to weep?

They Flee from Me

SIR THOMAS WYATT

They flee from me that sometime did me seek
With naked foot stalking in my chamber.
I have seen them gentle, tame, and meek
That now are wild, and do not remember
That sometime they put themselves in danger
To take bread at my hand; and now they range,
Busily seeking with a continual change.

Thanked be fortune, it hath been otherwise
Twenty times better; but once in special,
In thin array, after a pleasant guise,
When her loose gown from her shoulders did fall,
And she me caught in her arms long and small;
Therewithal sweetly did me kiss
And softly said, *Dear heart, how like you this?*

It was no dream: I lay broad waking.
But all is turned now thorough my gentleness
Into a strange fashion of forsaking;
And I have leave to go of her goodness;
And she also to use new-fangleness.
But since that I so kindly am served,
I would fain know what she hath deserved.

Considerations

1. How does Wyatt use an animal motif to reveal to us what he thinks about a woman who used to pay attention to him but now does not? Why does he use "they" in the first stanza and "she" in the second and third?

2. Although Wyatt introduced the Italian sonnet form into English verse, in this poem he uses rhyme royal—a seven line stanza in iambic pentameter rhyming *ababbcc*. Note, however, that the meter is not totally consistent. Do you think this is a mistake on the poet's part? Iambic meter is considered to be the fastest meter, so whenever the rhythm is broken it seems to halt the motion. Why might this be an advantage in the second line?

3. What kind of question is the poet asking in the final two lines? What is the tone of the poem?

Crabbed Age and Youth

ANONYMOUS

Crabbed Age and Youth
Cannot live together:
Youth is full of pleasance,
Age is full of care;
Youth like summer morn,   5
Age like winter weather;
Youth like summer brave,
Age like winter bare.
Youth is full of sport,
Age's breath is short;
Youth is nimble, Age is lame;
Youth is hot and bold,
Age is weak and cold;
Youth is wild, and Age is tame.
Age, I do abhor thee;   15
Youth, I do adore thee;
O my Love, my Love is young!
Age, I do defy thee.
O sweet shepherd, hie thee!
For methinks thou stay'st too long.

Since There's No Help

MICHAEL DRAYTON

Since there's no help, come, let us kiss and part.
Nay, I have done; you get no more of me.
And I am glad, yea, glad with all my heart
That thus so cleanly I myself can free.
Shake hands for ever; cancel all our vows;   5
And when we meet at any time again,
Be it not seen in either of our brows
That we one jot of former love retain.
Now at the last gasp of Love's latest breath,
When, his pulse failing, Passion speechless lies,   10
When Faith is kneeling by his bed of death,

And Innocence is closing up his eyes—
   Now, if thou wouldst, when all have given him over,
   From death to life thou might'st him yet recover.

Considerations

1. This poem is written in the English sonnet form. The English sonnet is also known as the Shakespearean sonnet—not because he was the only one to use it, but because he developed it and made it famous. In the poem Drayton begins with an assertion. Does he mean what he says? What evidence is there that he does or does not?
2. If the relationship is going to be saved, what is going to save it—love, passion, faith, innocence?
3. Why might Drayton have shifted from using "you" to "thou" at the end of the poem?
4. Does it seem to be love that motivates the speaker to suggest parting, or is it hurt pride?

The Passionate Shepherd to His Love

CHRISTOPHER MARLOWE

Come live with me and be my love,
And we will all the pleasures prove
That hills and valleys, dales and fields,
And all the craggy mountains yields.

There will we sit upon the rocks
And see the shepherds feed their flocks,
By shallow rivers, to whose falls
Melodious birds sing madrigals.

There will I make thee beds of roses
And a thousand fragrant posies,   10
A cap of flowers, and a kirtle
Embroider'd all with leaves of myrtle.

A gown made of the finest wool,
Which from our pretty lambs we pull,
Fair linèd slippers for the cold,
With buckles of the purest gold.

Considerations

1. The proposal made by Marlowe in this poem seems to be ageless. The next poem by Sir Walter Raleigh answers this one. C. Day Lewis decided to bring it up to date in his "Come Live With Me and Be My Love" (p. 554). Compare all of these poems in order to determine which seems the most realistic and which the most romantic.
2. The pastoral setting is obviously appropriate for a shepherd and his love. Can you, however, detect some exaggeration in the description?

The Nymph's Reply to the Shepherd

SIR WALTER RALEIGH

If all the world and love were young,
And truth in every shepherd's tongue,
These pretty pleasures might me move,
To live with thee and be thy love.

But time drives flocks from field to fold,
When rivers rage, and rocks grow cold;
And Philomel becometh dumb;
The rest complains of cares to come.

The flowers do fade, and wanton fields
To wayward Winter reckoning yields;   10
A honey tongue, a heart of gall,
Is fancy's spring, but sorrow's fall.

Thy gowns, thy shoes, thy bed of roses,
Thy cap, thy kirtle, and thy posies,
Soon break, soon wither, soon forgotten,
In folly ripe, in reason rotten.

Thy belt of straw and ivy buds,
Thy coral clasps and amber studs,
All these in me no means can move,
To come to thee and be thy love.   20

But could youth last, and love still breed,
Had joys no date, nor age no need,
Then these delights my mind might move,
To live with thee and be thy love.

Sonnet 18

WILLIAM SHAKESPEARE

Shall I compare thee to a summer's day?
Thou art more lovely and more temperate:
Rough winds do shake the darling buds of May,
And summer's lease hath all too short a date:
Sometime too hot the eye of heaven shines,   5
And often is his gold complexion dimmed;
And every fair from fair sometimes declines,
By chance or nature's changing course untrimmed;
But thy eternal summer shall not fade,
Nor lose possession of that fair thou owest;   10
Nor shall Death brag thou wander'st in his shade,
When in eternal lines to time thou growest:
  So long as men can breathe, or eyes can see,
  So long lives this, and this gives life to thee.

Considerations

1. The Shakespearean sonnet is arranged in three quatrains—usually indicated by the punctuation—and a final couplet. Generally, the first twelve lines state a question that is answered in the last two, or the first part conveys a lament or a sense of loneliness with the couplet providing comfort. Combine these requirements with the restrictions imposed by writing in iambic pentameter, and you will see that there are not many subjects a poet can treat adequately using this form—love, the transitoriness of life, the ravages of time, and death being the ones most favored. In this and the following sonnets, try to discover what problem is being stated and what answer is given.

2. In Sonnet 18 what reasons does the poet give for not using the summer's day metaphor in describing his loved one?

3. What is the effect of the final couplet?

Sonnet 29

WILLIAM SHAKESPEARE

When, in disgrace with fortune and men's eyes,
I all alone beweep my outcast state,
And trouble deaf heaven with my bootless cries,
And look upon myself, and curse my fate,
Wishing me like to one more rich in hope,   5
Featured like him, like him with friends possessed,
Desiring this man's art and that man's scope,
With what I most enjoy contented least;
Yet in these thoughts myself almost despising,
Haply I think on thee—and then my state,   10
Like to the lark at break of day arising
From sullen earth, sings hymns at heaven's gate;
   For thy sweet love remembered such wealth brings
   That then I scorn to change my state with kings.

Sonnet 30

WILLIAM SHAKESPEARE

When to the sessions of sweet silent thought
I summon up remembrance of things past,
I sigh the lack of many a thing I sought,
And with old woes new wail my dear time's waste.
Then can I drown an eye, unused to flow,   5
For precious friends hid in death's dateless night,
And weep afresh love's long since canceled woe,
And moan the expense of many a vanished sight.
Then can I grieve at grievances foregone,
And heavily from woe to woe tell o'er   10
The sad account of fore-bemoanéd moan,
Which I new pay as if not paid before.
   But if the while I think on thee, dear friend,
   All losses are restored and sorrows end.

Sonnet 97

WILLIAM SHAKESPEARE

How like a winter hath my absence been
From thee, the pleasure of the fleeting year!
What freezings have I felt, what dark days seen!
What old December's bareness everywhere!
And yet this time removed was summer's time;   5
The teeming autumn, big with rich increase,
Bearing the wanton burden of the prime,
Like widowed wombs after their lords' decease:
Yet this abundant issue seemed to me
But hope of orphans and unfathered fruit;   10
For summer and his pleasures wait on thee,
And, thou away, the very birds are mute;
   Or, if they sing, 'tis with so dull a cheer
   That leaves look pale, dreading the winter's near.

Sonnet 98

WILLIAM SHAKESPEARE

From you have I been absent in the spring,
When proud-pied April, dressed in all his trim,
Hath put a spirit of youth in everything,
That heavy Saturn laughed and leapt with him,
Yet nor the lays of birds, nor the sweet smell   5
Of different flowers in odor and in hue,
Could make me any summer's story tell,
Or from their proud lap pluck them where they grew;
Nor did I wonder at the lily's white,
Nor praise the deep vermilion in the rose: 10
They were but sweet, but figures of delight,
Drawn after you, you pattern of all those.
   Yet seemed it winter still, and, you away,
   As with your shadow I with these did play.

Sonnet 130

WILLIAM SHAKESPEARE

My mistress' eyes are nothing like the sun;
Coral is far more red than her lips' red;
If snow be white, why then her breasts are dun;
If hairs be wires, black wires grow on her head.
I have seen roses damasked, red and white,   5
But no such roses see I in her cheeks;
And in some perfumes is there more delight
Than in the breath that from my mistress reeks.
I love to hear her speak, yet well I know
That music hath a far more pleasing sound;   10
I grant I never saw a goddess go;
My mistress, when she walks, treads on the ground.
   And yet, by heaven, I think my love as rare
   As any she belied with false compare.

Considerations

1. Sonnet 130 is in sharp contrast to most of the poems men have written to women. It is almost as if the poet were answering that kind of poetry with something that gets at the humanity of the woman—and not totally uncomplimentarily. Would you say that this sonnet has anything in common with John Frederick Nims' "Love Poem" (p. 573)?

2. In Shakespeare's day, poets and lovers were given to making exaggerated comparisons in order to describe their loves' attributes. (See Thomas Carew's "Song" on p. 379 for an example.) What trite and false ways of detailing beauty does this sonnet list?

3. While most of this sonnet merely denies the traditional comparisons, there are two places where Shakespeare uses rather harsh terms in describing his mistress. Where are these places, and why might the poet have used such terms?

4. Explain the closing couplet. Should this make the woman feel better?

Song

from *Love's Labours Lost*

WILLIAM SHAKESPEARE

When icicles hang by the wall,
   And Dick the shepherd blows his nail,
And Tom bears logs into the hall,
   And milk comes frozen home in pail,
When blood is nipped and ways be foul,   5
Then nightly sings the staring owl,
"Tu-whit, tu-who!" A merry note,
While greasy Joan doth keel the pot.
When all aloud the wind doth blow,
   And coughing drowns the parson's saw,   10
And birds sit brooding in the snow,
   And Marian's nose looks red and raw,
When roasted crabs hiss in the bowl,
Then nightly sings the staring owl,
"Tu-whit, tu-who!" A merry note,
While greasy Joan doth keel the pot.

Considerations

1. For all those who believe that the noble and beautiful are the only fit subjects for poetry, Shakespeare must certainly come as a disappointment. The stark winter scene he paints here is nothing like a sentimental Currier-and-Ives Christmas card. Does he suggest anything at all pleasant about rural Elizabethan life in the winter?
2. Is the phrase "A merry note" meant seriously or ironically?
3. What elements of this poem qualify it to be a song?

Hymn to Diana

BEN JONSON

Queen and Huntress, chaste and fair,
  Now the sun is laid to sleep,
Seated in thy silver chair
  State in wonted manner keep:
    Hesperus entreats thy light,   5
    Goddess excellently bright.

Earth, let not thy envious shade
  Dare itself to interpose;
Cynthia's shining orb was made
  Heaven to clear when day did close: 10
    Bless us then with wishéd sight,
    Goddess excellently bright.

Lay thy bow of pearl apart
  And thy crystal-shining quiver;
Give unto the flying hart   15
  Space to breathe, how short soever:
    Thou that mak'st a day of night,
    Goddess excellently bright.

Song: To Celia

BEN JONSON

Come, my Celia, let us prove,
While we can, the sports of love.
Time will not be ours for ever;
He, at length, our good will sever;
Spend not then his gifts in vain. 5
Suns that set may rise again;
But if once we lose this light,
'T is with us perpetual night.
Why should we defer our joys?
Fame and rumor are but toys. 10
Cannot we delude the eyes
Of a few poor household spies?
Or his easier ears beguile,
Thus removéd by our wile?
'T is no sin love's fruits to steal; 15
But the sweet theft to reveal,
To be taken, to be seen,
These have crimes accounted been.

Song: to Celia, sung by Volpone in *Volpone,* III, vi. **10. toys,** trifles. **13. his.** The reference is to Celia's husband, Corvino.

The Good-Morrow

JOHN DONNE

I wonder, by my troth, what thou and I
Did till we loved? were we not weaned till then?
But sucked on country pleasures, childishly?
Or snorted we in the seven sleepers' den?
'Twas so; but this, all pleasures fancies be.
If ever any beauty I did see,
Which I desired, and got, 'twas but a dream of thee.

And now good-morrow to our waking souls,
Which watch not one another out of fear;
For love all love of other sights controls,   10
And makes one little room an everywhere.
Let sea-discoverers to new worlds have gone;
Let maps to other, worlds on worlds have shown;
Let us possess one world; each hath one, and is one.

My face in thine eye, thine in mine appears,
And true plain hearts do in the faces rest;
Where can we find two better hemispheres
Without sharp north, without declining west?
Whatever dies, was not mixed equally;
If our two loves be one, or thou and I   20
Love so alike that none do slacken, none can die.

Considerations

1. This poem contains an extended conceit of the kind found in the poetry of a number of seventeenth-century English poets. The conceits were originally striking concepts or ideas about a particular object which in poetry became extended, complex metaphors and similes. Ladies were no longer compared to roses but to something new and surprising—usually to an unpoetic or even scientific object. The effect created was frequently thought-provoking, novel, and witty. What conceit is Donne using here to describe their love? What images are used?
2. What actual physical situation is being described in line 15?
3. In the first four lines Donne refers to an event described in several myths and legends—the imprisonment for a number of years of some children in the early Christian era. For what purpose is this reference made?
4. The last three lines deal with the medieval concept of the perfect union of the four elements in nature. It was believed that a perfect mixture of these elements sustained life, whereas an unequal mixture caused death. What saves the ending from sentimentality?
5. Is the appeal of the poem intellectual or sensual?

The Bait

JOHN DONNE

Come live with me and be my love,
And we will some new pleasures prove,
Of golden sands and crystal brooks,
With silken lines and silver hooks.

There will the river whispering run,
Warmed by thine eyes more than the sun.
And there th' enamored fish will stay,
Begging themselves they may betray.

When thou wilt swim in that live bath,
Each fish, which every channel hath,
Will amorously to thee swim,
Gladder to catch thee, than thou him.

If thou, to be so seen, beest loath,
By sun or moon, thou darkenest both;
And if myself have leave to see,
I need not their light, having thee.

Let others freeze with angling reeds,
And cut their legs with shells and weeds,
Or treacherously poor fish beset
With strangling snare, or windowy net.

Let coarse bold hands from slimy nest
The bedded fish in banks out-wrest,
Or curious traitors, sleave-silk flies,
Bewitch poor fishes' wandering eyes.

For thee, thou needest no such deceit,
For thou thyself art thine own bait;
That fish that is not catched thereby,
Alas, is wiser far than I.

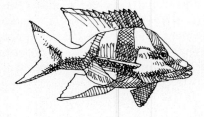

A Valediction:
Forbidding Mourning

JOHN DONNE

As virtuous men pass mildly away,
  And whisper to their souls to go,
Whilst some of their sad friends do say,
  "The breath goes now," and some say, "No":

So let us melt, and make no noise,   5
  No tear-floods nor sigh-tempests move;
'Twere profanation of our joys
  To tell the laity our love.

Moving of the earth brings harms and fears;
  Men reckon what it did, and meant;   10
But trepidation of the spheres,
  Though greater far, is innocent.

Dull sublunary lovers' love
  —Whose soul is sense—cannot admit
Absence, because it doth remove   15
  Those things which elemented it.

But we by a love so far refined
    That ourselves know not what it is,
Inter-assuréd of the mind,
    Care less eyes, lips, and hands to miss.   20

Our two souls therefore, which are one,
    Though I must go, endure not yet
A breach, but an expansiön,
    Like gold to airy thinness beat.

If they be two, they are two so   25
    As stiff twin compasses are two;
Thy soul, the fixed foot, makes no show
    To move, but doth if the other do.

And though it in the center sit,
    Yet, when the other far doth roam,   30
It leans, and hearkens after it,
    And grows erect as that comes home.

Such wilt thou be to me, who must;
    Like the other foot, obliquely run;
Thy firmness makes my circle just,   35
    And makes me end where I begun.

Considerations

1. In this poem Donne is talking about leaving his wife, presumably to go on a trip to the continent. What conceit does he use to describe their relationship and how closely they are tied together? Does the metaphor suggest that both of their roles are equally important?
2. To what natural phenomena does he compare their love?
3. In lines 7–8 he is describing a variation of the supposed task of churchmen—to tell the laymen about Christian love. In what sense is Donne's statement a variation? To whom does "laity" refer here? Is his emphasis then on the spiritual rather than the physical aspect of their love? What other evidence is there in the poem that it is or is not?

Holy Sonnet XIX

JOHN DONNE

Oh, to vex me, contraries meet in one;
Inconstancy unnaturally hath begot
A constant habit; that when I would not
I change in vows, and in devotion.
As humorous is my contrition
As my profane love, and as soon forgot:
As riddlingly distempered, cold and hot,
As praying, as mute; as infinite, as none.
I durst not view heaven yesterday; and today
In prayers, and flattering speeches I court God:
Tomorrow I quake with true fear of his rod.
So my devout fits come and go away
Like a fantastic ague: save that here
Those are my best days, when I shake with fear.

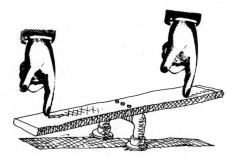

Considerations

Donne wrote many poems dealing with the male-female relationship, but he also wrote deeply religious poetry. The confusion expressed in this poem has been experienced by most of us at some time. St. Paul complained that when he tried to do one thing, he ended up doing another (Romans 7:14–25). In "West-running Brook" Frost expresses the same theme.

1. How is the word "humorous" meant in line 5?
2. Donne's syntax gets rather complicated in lines 5–8. What would a prose translation of these lines be?
3. Why are his best days those when he "shakes with fear"?

Delight in Disorder

ROBERT HERRICK

A sweet disorder in the dress
Kindles in clothes a wantonness;
A lawn about the shoulders thrown
Into a fine distraction,
An erring lace, which here and there
Enthralls the crimson stomacher,
A cuff neglectful, and thereby
Ribands to flow confusedly,
A winning wave, deserving note,
In the tempestuous petticoat,
A careless shoe-string, in whose tie
I see a wild civility,
Do more bewitch me than when art
Is too precise in every part.

To the Virgins,
to Make Much of Time

ROBERT HERRICK

Gather ye rose-buds while ye may,
    Old Time is still a-flying:
And this same flower that smiles today,
    Tomorrow will be dying.

The glorious lamp of heaven, the Sun,
    The higher he's a-getting
The sooner will his race be run,
    And nearer he's to setting.

That age is best which is the first,
    When youth and blood are warmer;
But being spent, the worse, and worst
    Times still succeed the former.

Then be not coy, but use your time,
And while ye may, go marry;
For having lost but once your prime,
You may for ever tarry.

Upon Julia's Clothes

ROBERT HERRICK

Whenas in silks my Julia goes,
Then, then (methinks) how sweetly flows
The liquefaction of her clothes.

Next, when I cast mine eyes and see
That brave vibration each way free,
O how that glittering taketh me!

Considerations

The parodies that follow should be read in conjunction with Robert Herrick's poems. Parodists usually try to capitalize on both the style and content of the work they parody. How well do these succeed?

To Julia, Under Lock and Key

OWEN SEAMAN

(A form of bethrothal gift in America is an anklet secured by a padlock, of which the other party keeps the key)

When like a bud my Julia blows
In lattice-work of silken hose,
Pleasant I deem it is to note

How, 'neath the nimble petticoat,
Above her fairy shoe is set
The circumvolving zonulet.
And soothly for the lover's ear
A perfect bliss it is to hear
About her limb so lithe and lank
My Julia's ankle-bangle clank.
Not rudely tight, for 't were a sin
To corrugate her dainty skin;
Nor yet so large that it might fare
Over her foot at unaware;
But fashioned nicely with a view
To let her airy stocking through:
So as, when Julia goes to bed,
Of all her gear disburdenèd,
This ring at least she shall not doff
Because she cannot take it off.
And since thereof I hold the key,
She may not taste of liberty,
Not though she suffer from the gout,
Unless I choose to let her out.

Song

OLIVER HERFORD

Gather Kittens while you may,
Time brings only Sorrow;
And the Kittens of To-day
Will be Old Cats To-morrow.

Song

THOMAS CAREW

Ask me no more where Jove bestows,
When June is past, the fading rose;
For in your beauty's orient deep
These flowers, as in their causes, sleep.

Ask me no more whither do stray   5
The golden atoms of the day;
For in pure love heaven did prepare
Those powders to enrich your hair.

Ask me no more whither doth haste
The nightingale when May is past;
For in your sweet, dividing throat
She winters and keeps warm her note.

Ask me no more where those stars 'light
That downwards fall in dead of night;
For in your eyes they sit, and there   15
Fixéd become as in their sphere.

Ask me no more if east or west
The phoenix builds her spicy nest;
For unto you at last she flies,
And in your fragrant bosom dies.

Considerations

Here is a mild version of the high-flown Elizabethan rhetoric Shakespeare was taking exception to in Sonnet 130. Flamboyant writing had its day and disappeared, but Carew is still remembered because of this poem.

1. In what sense is Carew flattering the woman addressed in this poem by comparing her beauty to fading roses?
2. The phoenix was a mythical bird that was supposed to have periodically cast itself into a fire and risen reborn from its own ashes. In light of this, what is the meaning of the final stanza?

On a Girdle

EDMUND WALLER

That which her slender waist confined
Shall now my joyful temples bind;
No monarch but would give his crown,
His arms might do what this has done.

It was my heaven's extremest sphere,   5
The pale which held that lovely deer;
My joy, my grief, my hope, my love,
Did all within this circle move.

A narrow compass, and yet there
Dwelt all that's good and all that's fair;   10
Give me but what this ribband bound,
Take all the rest the sun goes round!

On the Late Massacre in Piedmont

JOHN MILTON

Avenge, O Lord, Thy slaughtered saints, whose bones
Lie scattered on the Alpine mountains cold;
Even them who kept Thy truth so pure of old
When all our fathers worshiped stocks and stones,
Forget not; in Thy book record their groans   5
Who were Thy sheep, and in their ancient fold
Slain by the bloody Piedmontese, that rolled
Mother with infant down the rocks. Their moans
To vales redoubled to the hills, and they
To heaven. Their martyred blood and ashes sow   10
O'er all the Italian fields, where still doth sway
The triple Tyrant, that from these may grow
A hundredfold, who, having learnt Thy way,
Early may fly the Babylonian woe.

Considerations

Besides being one of the foremost English poets, John Milton was secretary to Cromwell, and in this capacity he registered a formal protest against the Duke of Savoy's massacre of some Alpine mountaineers whose forefathers had broken away from the Roman Catholic Church in the twelfth century.

1. The Lord is addressed in this sonnet. Is it a prayer?
2. "The triple Tyrant" and "the Babylonian woe" refer to the Pope and the Roman Catholic Church respectively. What is the general message of lines 10–14?

On His Blindness

JOHN MILTON

When I consider how my light is spent
   Ere half my days in this dark world and wide,
   And that one talent which is death to hide
   Lodged with me useless, though my soul more bent
To serve therewith my Maker, and present
   My true account, lest He returning chide,
   "Doth God exact day-labor, light denied?"
   I fondly ask. But Patience, to prevent
That murmur, soon replies, "God doth not need
   Either man's work or his own gifts. Who best
   Bear his mild yoke, they serve him best. His state
Is kingly: thousands at his bidding speed,
   And post o'er land and ocean without rest;
   They also serve who only stand and wait."

Considerations

1. Of the 23 sonnets Milton wrote (all in the Italian form) this is perhaps the most famous. It was written about his loss of his sight at age 43. In it he alludes to the parable of the talents (Matthew 25:14–30). The sonnet is structured in two parts. Where does the division occur?
2. In what sense could he "fondly ask" the question he proposes?
3. Is this appropriate language for talking about one's blindness?

The Constant Lover

SIR JOHN SUCKLING

Out upon it! I have loved
   Three whole days together;
And am like to love three more,
   If it prove fair weather.

Time shall moult away his wings,   5
   Ere he shall discover
In the whole wide world again
   Such a constant lover.

But the spite on't is, no praise
   Is due at all to me;   10
Love with me had made no stays,
   Had it any been but she.

Had it any been but she,
   And that very face,
There had been at least ere this   15
   A dozen dozen in her place.

Say, but Did You Love So Long?

SIR TOBY MATTHEWS

Say, but did you love so long?
   In troth, I needs must blame you;
Passion did your judgment wrong,
   Or want of reason shame you.

Truth, time's fair and witty daughter,   5
   Shortly shall discover
Y' are a subject fit for laughter,
   And more fool than lover.

But I grant you merit praise
  For your constant folly;   10
Since you doted three whole days,
  Were you not melancholy?

She to whom you proved so true,
  And that very, very face,
Puts each minute such as you   15
  A dozen dozen to disgrace.

To His Coy Mistress

ANDREW MARVELL

Had we but world enough, and time,
This coyness, lady, were no crime.
We would sit down, and think which way
To walk, and pass our long love's day.
Thou by the Indian Ganges' side   5
Shouldst rubies find: I by the tide
Of Humber would complain. I would
Love you ten years before the flood,
And you should, if you please, refuse
Till the conversion of the Jews;   10
My vegetable love should grow
Vaster than empires and more slow;
An hundred years should go to praise
Thine eyes, and on thy forehead gaze;
Two hundred to adore each breast,   15
But thirty thousand to the rest;
An age at least to every part,
And the last age should show your heart.
For, lady, you deserve this state;
Nor would I love at lower rate.   20

---

7. **Humber,** an estuary in the east coast of England. **complain,** i.e., utter love complaints.
8. **flood,** the Biblical deluge, *Genesis,* 6,7.

But at my back I always hear
Time's wingéd chariot hurrying near;
And yonder all before us lie
Deserts of vast eternity.
Thy beauty shall no more be found,   25
Nor in thy marble vault shall sound
My echoing song; then worms shall try
That long preserved virginity;
And your quaint honor turn to dust,
And into ashes all my lust: 30
The grave's a fine and private place,
But none, I think, do there embrace.

Now therefore, while the youthful hue
Sits on thy skin like morning dew,
And while thy willing soul transpires   35
At every pore with instant fires,
Now let us sport us while we may,
And now, like amorous birds of prey,
Rather at once our time devour
Than languish in his slow-chapped power,   40
Let us roll all our strength and all
Our sweetness up into one ball,
And tear our pleasures with rough strife
Thorough the iron gates of life:
Thus, though we cannot make our sun   45
Stand still, yet we will make him run.

29. **quaint,** proud.   40. **slow-chapped,** slowly crushing.

Considerations

1. Marvell is classed, along with Donne, as a metaphysical poet. Do you
   see any similarities between their styles?
2. What does the first line mean? What does "world enough" have to do
   with the consummation of their love?
3. This poem is written in the form of a syllogism: If A were true then B
   would follow: A is not true; therefore C follows. How does the
   structure of the poem reflect this form?
4. Marvell uses hyperbole freely, perhaps in mockery of the exaggera-
   tions of poets like Carew. Why measure time by the span between
   "ten years before the Flood" and "till the conversion of the Jews?"
   What other figures of speech are employed? Why are descriptions

such as "vegetable love," "deserts of vast eternity," and "amorous birds of prey" particularly effective?

5. What is the tone of the second stanza? Is it maintained or altered by lines 31–32?

6. The allusion at the end of the poem is to Joshua making the sun stand still in order to win a battle. How is this an appropriate allusion? How does the experience of the lovers differ from Joshua's?

7. Is this poem about love or time?

A Song for St. Cecelia's Day

JOHN DRYDEN

From harmony, from heavenly harmony,
    This universal frame began:
  When Nature underneath a heap
    Of jarring atoms lay,
  And could not heave her head,
The tuneful voice was heard from high:
    "Arise, ye more than dead."

Then cold and hot and moist and dry
  In order to their stations leap,
    And Music's power obey.   10
From harmony, from heavenly harmony,
    This universal frame began:
    From harmony to harmony
Through all the compass of the notes it ran,
The diapason closing full in Man.

What passion cannot Music raise and quell
   When Jubal struck the chorded shell,
  His listening brethren stood around,
   And wondering, on their faces fell
  To worship that celestial sound.   20
Less than a god they thought there could not dwell
   Within the hollow of that shell
   That spoke so sweetly and so well.
What passion cannot Music raise and quell!

   The trumpet's loud clangor
    Excites us to arms
  With shrill notes of anger
    And mortal alarms.
  The double, double, double beat
   Of the thundering drum   30
   Cries: "Hark! the foes come;
Charge, charge, 'tis too late to retreat!"

The soft complaining flute
   In dying notes discovers
   The woes of hopeless lovers,
Whose dirge is whispered by the warbling lute.
   Sharp violins proclaim

Their jealous pangs and desperation,
Fury, frantic indignation,
Depth of pains, and height of passion,   40
   For the fair, disdainful dame.

But oh! what art can teach,
What human voice can reach
   The sacred organ's praise?
  Notes inspiring holy love,
Notes that wing their heavenly ways
   To mend the choirs above.

Orpheus could lead the savage race;
And trees unrooted left their place,
   Sequacious of the lyre;   50
But bright Cecilia raised the wonder higher:
When to her organ vocal breath was given,
An angel heard, and straight appeared,
   Mistaking earth for heaven.

GRAND CHORUS

As from the power of sacred lays
   The spheres began to move,
And sung the great Creator's praise
   To all the blessed above;
So when the last and dreadful hour
This crumbling pageant shall devour,   60
The trumpet shall be heard on high,
The dead shall live, the living die,
And Music shall untune the sky.

Considerations

St. Cecelia was a third-century martyr. Since she was supposed to have invented the pipe organ, she became the patron saint of music. This poem was written by Dryden for an annual festival held in her honor. (Dryden, like Donne, wrote poetry in several veins. You can see his other side in such vicious satires as "Mac Flecknoe."

1. In a number of places, Dryden attempts to replicate the sense and sound of certain musical instruments. What devices does he use to do this? How successful is he?
2. What analogy is being made in this poem?
3. *Diapason* comes from a Greek word that means "concord through all the notes." What is the implication then of line 15?
4. What event is described in the Grand Chorus?

Describes Rationally
The Irrational Effects of Love

JUANA DE ASBAJE

This torment of love
that is in my heart,
I know I feel it
and know not why.

Reprinted from AN ANTHOLOGY OF MEXICAN POETRY compiled by Octavio Paz and translated by Samuel Beckett. By permission of Indiana University Press.

I feel the keen pangs
of a frenzy desired
whose beginning is longing
and end melancholy.

And when I my sorrow
more softly bewail,
I know I am sad
and know not why.

I feel for the juncture
I crave a fierce panting,
and when I come might it
withhold mine own hand.

For if haply it offers
after much weary vigil,
mistrust spoils its savour
and terror dispels it.

Now patient, now fretful,
by conflicting griefs torn,
who for him much shall suffer,
and with him suffer nought.

On scant foundations
my sad cares raise
with delusive conceits
a mountain of feeling.

And when that proud mass
falls asunder I find
that the arrogant fabric
was poised on a pin.

Beguiled perhaps by grief
I presume without reason
no fulfilment can ever
my passion assuage.

And though nigh disabused,
still the same grief assails me,
that I suffer so sore
for so little a cause.

Perhaps the wounded soul sweeping
to take its revenge
repents it and wreaks
other vengeance on me.

In my blindness and folly
I, gladly deceived,
beseech disenchantment
and desire it not.

Considerations

Juana de Asbaje (also known as Inez de la Cruz) is considered the most memorable figure in the colonial poetry of Spanish America. There were few creative outlets available for intelligent, artistically talented women in the Latin countries of her day. Fortunately, the order of nuns she joined gave her an unusual amount of freedom to write and study—even when the subject matter was not theological.

1. Is the suffering she describes engendered by the fact that she cannot account for her feelings rationally? Or do stanzas 4 and 5 suggest that the problem is her fear that fulfillment will not live up to her expectations?
2. This is, of course, a translation, and it is therefore hard to know the intent of the original. However, might the poet have meant "assume" rather than "presume" in stanza 9? How is "presume" appropriate?
3. Is this poem predominantly spiritual, psychological, or sensual?

The Little Black Boy

from *Songs of Innocence*

WILLIAM BLAKE

My mother bore me in the southern wild,
And I am black, but O! my soul is white;
White as an angel is the English child,
But I am black, as if bereaved of light.

My mother taught me underneath a tree,   5
And, sitting down before the heat of day,
She took me on her lap and kisséd me,
And, pointing to the east, began to say:

"Look on the rising sun—there God does live,
And gives His light, and gives His heat away;   10
And flowers and trees and beasts and men receive
Comfort in morning, joy in the noonday.

"And we are put on earth a little space,
That we may learn to bear the beams of love;
And these black bodies and this sunburnt fact   15
Is but a cloud, and like a shady grove.

"For when our souls have learned the heat to bear,
The cloud will vanish; we shall hear His voice,
Saying: "Come out from the grove, My love and care,
And round My golden tent like lambs rejoice.'"   20

Thus did my mother say, and kisséd me;
And thus I say to little English boy.
When I from black and he from white cloud free,
And round the tent of God like lambs we joy,

I'll shade him from the heat, till he can bear   25
To lean in joy upon our Father's knee;
And then I'll stand and stroke his silver hair,
And be like him, and he will then love me.

The Chimney Sweep

from *Songs of Innocence*

WILLIAM BLAKE

When my mother died I was very young,
And my father sold me while yet my tongue
Could scarcely cry " 'weep! 'weep! 'weep! 'weep!"
So your chimneys I sweep & in soot I sleep.

There's little Tom Dacre, who cried when his head
That curl'd like a lambs back, was shav'd, so I said,
"Hush, Tom! never mind it, for when your head's bare,
You know that the soot cannot spoil your white hair."

And so he was quiet, & that very night,
As Tom was a-sleeping he had such a sight!
That thousands of sweepers, Dick, Joe, Ned & Jack,
Were all of them lock'd up in coffins of black;

And by came an Angel who had a bright key,
And he open'd the coffins & set them all free;
Then down a green plain, leaping, laughing they run,
And wash in a river and shine in the Sun;

Then naked & white, all their bags left behind,
They rise upon clouds, and sport in the wind.
And the Angel told Tom, if he'd be a good boy,
He'd have God for his father & never want joy.

And so Tom awoke; and we rose in the dark
And got with our bags & our brushes to work.
Tho' the morning was cold, Tom was happy & warm;
So if all do their duty, they need not fear harm.

Considerations

In his two volumes of poems, *Songs of Innocence* and *Songs of Experience,* Blake examines two aspects of life. He believed that innocence and experience are part of the celestial plan, that both are necessary to a proper existence. Innocence must be shaped by experience to prove fruitful. To dramatize this philosophy, he wrote a series of poems in which two poems were devoted to each subject, the two poems conveying two differing viewpoints; he then divided the poems into two books. The first book considers problems of good and evil from a simple, direct, questioning perspective—from the outlook of a child. In the second book the same questions are raised—the nature of good and evil, man's place in the universe, and so on—but they are approached from the viewpoint of maturity. "The Chimney Sweep" is from *Songs of Innocence;* it has a parallel verse in *Songs of Experience.*

1. "The Chimney Sweep" is social commentary as well as poetry. The church (accused rather more directly in the companion piece by the voice of experience) had not spoken out against this form of child labor, which had caused the death of many young people in London. What is the irony in the small sweep's cry " 'weep! 'weep! 'weep! 'weep!"? What is meant by the "coffins of black"? Does the last line have the same tone as the rest of the sweep's story?

The Tiger

from *Songs of Experience*

WILLIAM BLAKE

Tiger! Tiger! burning bright
In the forests of the night,
What immortal hand or eye
Could frame thy fearful symmetry?

In what distant deeps or skies
Burnt the fire of thine eyes?
On what wings dare he aspire?
What the hand dare seize the fire?

And what shoulder, and what art,
Could twist the sinews of thy heart?   10
And when thy heart began to beat,
What dread hand? and what dread feet?

What the hammer? what the chain?
In what furnace was thy brain?
What the anvil? what dread grasp
Dare its deadly terrors clasp?

When the stars threw down their spears
And watered heaven with their tears,
Did he smile his work to see?
Did he who made the Lamb make thee?   20

Tiger! Tiger! burning bright
In the forests of the night,
What immortal hand or eye
Dare frame thy fearful symmetry?

Considerations

"The Tiger," which is from *Songs of Experience,* is the counterpart of "The Lamb." It is one of the most complex and highly symbolic poems in the series. Is the tiger simply a tiger, or, as the lamb stood for one quality of divinity, may the tiger not represent another? Or, could he represent man—a complex being with an awesome capacity for doing evil or good?

1. A number of questions are asked in the poem about the genesis of the tiger. What clue to the answer is given in the first question? The chief characteristic of the one who made the tiger appears to be power: not only *could* he do it, but he *dared* to do it. What image is implicit in lines 8–16?
2. How does the poet express the feeling he has about the tiger?
3. What answer is called for to the question in line 20? What philosophy is suggested?

The Indian Burying-Ground

PHILIP FRENEAU

In spite of all the learn'd have said,
I still my old opinion keep;
The *posture,* that *we* give the dead,
Points out the soul's eternal sleep.

Text: the 1795 edition

Not so the ancients of these lands—
The Indian, when from life releas'd,
Again is seated with his friends,
And shares again the joyous feast.

His imag'd birds, and painted bowl,
And ven'son, for a journey dress'd,   10
Bespeak the nature of the soul,
Activity, that knows no rest.

His bow, for action ready bent,
And arrows, with a head of stone,
Can only mean that life is spent,
And not the finer essence gone.

Thou, stranger, that shalt come this way,
No fraud upon the dead commit—
Observe the swelling turf, and say
They do not *lie,* but here they *sit.*   20

Here still a lofty rock remains,
On which the curious eye may trace
(Now wasted, half, by wearing rains)
The fancies of a ruder race.

Here still an aged elm aspires,
Beneath whose far-projecting shade
(And which the shepherd still admires)
The children of the forest play'd!

There oft a restless Indian queen
(Pale *Shebah,* with her braided hair)   30
And many a barbarous form is seen
To chide the man that lingers there.

By midnight moons, o'er moistening dews,
In habit for the chace array'd,
The hunter still the deer pursues,
The hunter and the deer, a shade!

---

8 joyous feast. "The North American Indians bury their dead in a sitting posture; decorating the corpse with wampum, the images of birds, quadrupeds, &c: And (if that of a warrior) with bows, arrows, tomahawks, and other military weapons."—Freneau

And long shall timorous fancy see
The painted chief, and pointed spear,
And Reason's self shall bow the knee
To shadows and delusions here.   40

Considerations

Philip Freneau has been called the father of American poetry. In style
and subject matter his poetry is representative of the transition from the
neo-classic to the romantic approach in early nineteenth-century American verse. At least on the surface, this poem proclaims the superiority of
the Indians over the white man. How is that premise established? Does
the last stanza contradict it?

A Red, Red Rose

ROBERT BURNS

O, my luve is like a red, red rose,
   That's newly sprung in June.
O, my luve is like the melodie,
   That's sweetly played in tune.

As fair art thou, my bonie lass,   5
   So deep in luve am I,
And I will luve thee still, my dear,
   Till a' the seas gang dry.

Till a' the seas gang dry, my dear,
   And the rocks melt wi' the sun!   10
And I will luve thee still, my dear,
   While the sands o' life shall run.

And fare thee weel, my only luve,
   And fare thee weel a while!
And I will come again, my luve,
   Tho' it were ten thousand mile!

Lines Written in Early Spring

WILLIAM WORDSWORTH

I heard a thousand blended notes,
While in a grove I sate reclined,
In that sweet mood when pleasant thoughts
Bring sad thoughts to the mind.

To her fair works did Nature link   5
The human soul that through me ran;
And much it grieved my heart to think
What man has made of man.

Through primrose tufts, in that green bower,
The periwinkle trailed its wreaths;   10
And 'tis my faith that every flower
Enjoys the air it breathes.

The birds around me hopped and played,
Their thoughts I cannot measure—
But the least motion which they made,   15
It seemed a thrill of pleasure.

The budding twigs spread out their fan,
To catch the breezy air;
And I must think, do all I can,
That there was pleasure there.   20

If this belief from heaven be sent,
If such be Nature's holy plan,
Have I not reason to lament
What man has made of man?

Considerations

1. Does Wordsworth express a realistic view of nature in this poem?
2. Do pleasant thoughts inevitably bring sad thoughts to mind?
3. The last two lines contain a question. The question is preceded by
   what two assumptions? Are the assumptions necessary for the
   question to be valid?

Composed upon Westminster Bridge

WILLIAM WORDSWORTH

Earth has not anything to show more fair:
Dull would he be of soul who could pass by
A sight so touching in its majesty:
This City now doth like a garment wear
The beauty of the morning; silent, bare,   5
Ships, towers, domes, theaters, and temples lie
Open unto the fields, and to the sky;
All bright and glittering in the smokeless air.
Never did sun more beautifully steep
In his first splendor valley, rock, or hill;   10
Ne'er saw I, never felt, a calm so deep!
The river glideth at his own sweet will:
Dear God! the very houses seem asleep;
And all that mighty heart is lying still!

Considerations

1. Considering the emphasis that the Romantic poets put on the merits of a return to nature and a sympathy for rural life, what elements could Wordsworth see in London that he approved of?
2. What figures of speech are used in this poem?
3. Can you find any of the usual divisions of thought in this sonnet?

The Solitary Reaper

WILLIAM WORDSWORTH

Behold her, single in the field,
Yon solitary Highland lass!
Reaping and singing by herself;
Stop here, or gently pass!
Alone she cuts and binds the grain,
And sings a melancholy strain;
O listen! for the vale profound
Is overflowing with the sound.

No nightingale did ever chaunt
More welcome notes to weary bands   10
Of travelers in some shady haunt,
Among Arabian sands:
A voice so thrilling ne'er was heard
In springtime from the cuckoo-bird,
Breaking the silence of the seas   15
Among the farthest Hebrides.

Will no one tell me what she sings?—
Perhaps the plaintive numbers flow
For old, unhappy, far-off things,
And battles long ago;   20
Or is it some more humble lay,
Familiar matter of today?
Some natural sorrow, loss, or pain,
That has been, and may be again

Whate'er the theme, the maiden sang   25
As if her song could have no ending;
I saw her singing at her work,
And o'er the sickle bending;—
I listened, motionless and still;
And, as I mounted up the hill,   30
The music in my heart I bore,
Long after it was heard no more.

Kubla Khan

SAMUEL TAYLOR COLERIDGE

In Xanadu did Kubla Khan
A stately pleasure dome decree:
Where Alph, the sacred river, ran
Through caverns measureless to man
   Down to a sunless sea.   5
So twice five miles of fertile ground
With walls and towers were girdled round:

And there were gardens bright with sinuous rills,
Where blossomed many an incense-bearing tree;
And here were forests ancient as the hills,   10
Enfolding sunny spots of greenery.

But oh! that deep romantic chasm which slanted
Down the green hill athwart a cedarn cover!
A savage place! as holy and enchanted
As e'er beneath a waning moon was haunted   15
By woman wailing for her demon lover!
And from this chasm, with ceaseless turmoil seething,
As if this earth in fast thick pants were breathing,
A mighty fountain momently was forced:
Amid whose swift half-intermitted burst   20
Huge fragments vaulted like rebounding hail,
Or chaffy grain beneath the thresher's flail:
And 'mid these dancing rocks at once and ever
It flung up momently the sacred river.
Five miles meandering with a mazy motion   25
Through wood and dale the sacred river ran,
Then reached the caverns measureless to man,
And sank in tumult to a lifeless ocean:
And 'mid this tumult Kubla heard from far
Ancestral voices prophesying war!   30
   The shadow of the dome of pleasure
   Floated midway on the waves:
   Where was heard the mingled measure
   From the fountain and the caves.
It was a miracle of rare device,   35
A sunny pleasure dome with caves of ice!

A damsel with a dulcimer
In a vision once I saw:
It was an Abyssinian maid,
And on her dulcimer she played,   40
Singing of Mount Abora.
Could I revive within me
Her symphony and song,
To such a deep delight 'twould win me,
That with music loud and long,   45
I would build that dome in air,
That sunny dome! those caves of ice!
And all who heard should see them there,
And all should cry, Beware! Beware!
His flashing eyes, his floating hair!   50
Weave a circle round him thrice,
And close your eyes with holy dread,
For he on honeydew hath fed,
And drunk the milk of Paradise.

Considerations

In his lengthy preface to "Kubla Khan," Coleridge gives this account of
how it was written:

In the summer of the year 1797, the author, then in ill health, had
retired to a lonely farmhouse between Porlock and Lynton, on the
Exmoor confines of Somerset and Devonshire. In consequence of a
slight indisposition, an anodyne had been prescribed, from the effects
of which he fell asleep in his chair at the moment he was reading the
following sentence, or words of the same substance, in Purchas's
Pilgrimage: "Here the Khan Kubla commanded a palace to be built,
and a stately garden thereunto. And thus ten miles of fertile ground
were inclosed with a wall." The author continued for about three hours
in a profound sleep, at least of the external senses, during which time
he has the most vivid confidence that he could not have composed less
than from two to three hundred lines; if that indeed can be called
composition in which all the images rose up before him as *things,* with
a parallel production of the correspondent expressions, without any
sensation or consciousness of effort. On awaking he appeared to
himself to have a distinct recollection of the whole, and taking his pen,
ink, and paper, instantly and eagerly wrote down the lines that are
here preserved. At this moment he was unfortunately called out by a
person on business from Porlock, and detained by him above an hour,
and on his return to his room, found, to his no small surprise and

mortification, that though he still retained some vague and dim recollection of the general purport of the vision, yet, with the exception of some eight or ten scattered lines and images, all the rest had passed away like the images on the surface of a stream into which a stone had been cast, but, alas! without the after restoration of the latter!

1. Should we treat this poem as a fragment or does it seem to be complete? If you hadn't read Coleridge's explanation, would your answer have been different? Why?
2. The complex construction and the symbolism in this poem have been discussed in a number of books. Almost everyone agrees that there are major contrasts between the first 36 lines and the last section. The pleasure dome in the first 36 lines is spoken of as a concrete fact—something that was successfully built. What is the attitude of the last section?
3. If the building of the pleasure dome is a metaphor, to what is it being compared? How then can the last section of the poem be read?
4. Who is the "he" referred to in lines 48–54? What is the meaning of these lines?

Work without Hope

SAMUEL TAYLOR COLERIDGE

All Nature seems at work. Slugs leave their lair—
The bees are stirring—birds are on the wing—
And Winter slumbering in the open air,
Wears on his smiling face a dream of Spring!

And I the while, the sole unbusy thing,   5
Nor honey make, nor pair, nor build, nor sing.
 Yet well I ken the banks where amaranths blow,
Have traced the fount whence streams of nectar flow.
Bloom, O ye amaranths! bloom for whom ye may,
For me ye bloom not! Glide, rich streams, away!   10
With lips unbrightened, wreathless brow, I stroll:
And would you learn the spells that drowse my soul?

Work without Hope draws nectar in a sieve,
And Hope without an object cannot live.

When We Two Parted

GEORGE GORDON, LORD BYRON

When we two parted
    In silence and tears
Half broken-hearted
    To sever for years,
Pale grew thy cheek and cold,   5
    Colder thy kiss;
Truly that hour foretold
    Sorrow to this.

The dew of the morning
    Sunk chill on my brow—   10
It felt like the warning
    Of what I feel now.
Thy vows are all broken,
    And light is thy fame;
I hear thy name spoken,   15
    And share in its shame.

They name thee before me,
    A knell to mine ear;
A shudder comes o'er me—
    Why wert thou so dear?   20
They know not I knew thee,
    Who knew thee too well—
Long, long shall I rue thee,
    Too deeply to tell.

In secret we met—   25
    In silence I grieve
That thy heart could forget,
    Thy spirit deceive.
If I should meet thee
    After long years,   30
How should I greet thee?—
    With silence and tears.

Ozymandias

PERCY BYSSHE SHELLEY

I met a traveller from an antique land
Who said: "Two vast and trunkless legs of stone
Stand in the desert. Near them, on the sand,
Half sunk, a shattered visage lies, whose frown,
And wrinkled lip, and sneer of cold command,
Tell that its sculptor well those passions read
Which yet survive, stamped on these lifeless things,
The hand that mocked them and the heart that fed;
And on the pedestal these words appear:
'My name is Ozymandias, king of kings;
Look on my works, ye Mighty, and despair!'
Nothing beside remains. Round the decay
Of that colossal wreck, boundless and bare
The lone and level sands stretch far away."

Considerations

1. "Ozymandias" is a sonnet, even though many readers feel that it is unlike the more traditional sonnets. Can you account for this?
2. The speaker in the poem is perhaps just the *persona* of the poet and the traveller simply reported what he saw. The characters of special interest to us are the sculptor and Ozymandias, the king who thought he could conquer time. We know the folly of such a dream; what lines indicate that the sculptor also knew it?
3. Why is the inscription on the pedestal ironic?

Song to the Men of England

PERCY BYSSHE SHELLEY

I

Men of England, wherefore plough
For the lords who lay ye low?
Wherefore weave with toil and care
The rich robes your tyrants wear?

II

Wherefore feed, and clothe, and save,
From the cradle to the grave,
Those ungrateful drones who would
Drain your sweat—nay, drink your blood?

III

Wherefore, Bees of England, forge
Many a weapon, chain, and scourge,
That these stingless drones may spoil
The forced produce of your toil?

IV

Have ye leisure, comfort, calm,
Shelter, food, love's gentle balm
Or what is it ye buy so dear
With your pain and with your fear?

V

The seed ye sow, another reaps;
The wealth ye find, another keeps;
The robes ye weave, another wears;
The arms ye forge, another bears.

VI

Sow seed,—but let no tyrant reap;
Find wealth,—let no impostor heap;
Weave robes,—let not the idle wear;
Forge arms,—in your defence to bear.

VII

Shrink to your cellars, holes, and cells;
In halls ye deck another dwells.
Why shake the chains ye wrought? Ye see
The steel ye tempered glance on ye.

VIII

With plough and spade, and hoe and loom,
Trace your grave, and build your tomb,
And weave your winding-sheet, till fair
England be your sepulchre.

Ode to a Nightingale

JOHN KEATS

My heart aches, and a drowsy numbness pains
  My sense, as though of hemlock I had drunk,
Or emptied some dull opiate to the drains
  One minute past, and Lethe-wards had sunk
'Tis not through envy of thy happy lot,
  But being too happy in thine happiness—
    That thou, light-wingèd Dryad of the Trees,
    In some melodious plot
Of beechen green, and shadows numberless,
  Singest of summer in full-throated ease.   10

O, for a draught of vintage! that hath been
  Cooled a long age in the deep-delvèd earth,
Tasting of Flora and the country green,
  Dance, and Provençal song, and sunburnt mirth!
O for a beaker full of the warm South,
  Full of the true, the blushful Hippocrene,
    With beaded bubbles winking at the brim,
    And purple-stainèd mouth;
  That I might drink, and leave the world unseen,
  And with thee fade away into the forest dim: 20

Fade far away, dissolve, and quite forget
  What thou among the leaves hast never known,
The weariness, the fever, and the fret
  Here, where men sit and hear each other groan;
Where palsy shakes a few, sad, last gray hairs,
  Where youth grows pale, and specter-thin, and dies;
    Where but to think is to be full of sorrow
    And leaden-eyed despairs,
  Where Beauty cannot keep her lustrous eyes,
  Or new Love pine at them beyond tomorrow.   30

Away! away! for I will fly to thee,
  Not charioted by Bacchus and his pards,
But on the viewless wings of Poesy,
  Though the dull brain perplexes and retards:
Already with thee! tender is the night,
  And haply the Queen-Moon is on her throne,

Clustered around by all her starry Fays;
　　But here there is no light,
Save what from heaven is with the breezes blown
　　Through verdurous glooms and winding mossy ways.　　40

I cannot see what flowers are at my feet,
　　Nor what soft incense hangs upon the boughs,
But, in embalmèd darkness, guess each sweet
　　Wherewith the seasonable month endows
The grass, the thicket, and the fruit-tree wild;
　　White hawthorn, and the pastoral eglantine;
　　　　Fast fading violets covered up in leaves;
　　　　And mid-May's eldest child,
The coming musk-rose, full of dewy wine,
　　The murmurous haunt of flies on summer eves.　　50

Darkling I listen; and, for many a time,
　　I have been half in love with easeful Death,
Called him soft names in many a musèd rime,
　　To take into the air my quiet breath;
Now more than ever seems it rich to die,
　　To cease upon the midnight with no pain,
　　　　While thou art pouring forth thy soul abroad
　　　　In such an ecstasy!
Still wouldst thou sing, and I have ears in vain—
　　To thy high requiem become a sod.　　60

Thou wast not born for death, immortal Bird!
　　No hungry generations tread thee down;
The voice I hear this passing night was heard
　　In ancient days by emperor and clown:
Perhaps the self-same song that found a path
　　Through the sad heart of Ruth, when, sick for home,
　　　　She stood in tears amid the alien corn;
　　　　The same that oft-times hath
Charmed magic casements, opening on the foam
　　Of perilous seas, in faery lands forlorn.　　70

Forlorn! the very word is like a bell
　　To toll me back from thee to my sole self,
Adieu! the fancy cannot cheat so well
　　As she is famed to do, deceiving elf.
Adieu! adieu! thy plaintive anthem fades

Past the near meadows, over the still stream,
Up the hillside; and now 'tis buried deep
In the next valley glades:
Was it a vision, or a waking dream?
Fled is that music—Do I wake or sleep?   80

Considerations

1. In this poem Keats uses a ten-line stanza divided by rhyme scheme into a quatrain and a sestet. What is established in the first four lines that is commented on in the last six? Is this pattern consistent throughout the poem?
2. This particular poem is famous for its exquisite imagery and lyric style. What sensual imagery not depending on eyesight is used in lines 41–50?
3. Inasmuch as this poem is based on fantasy and imagination, what is the answer to the question in the last line?

La Belle Dame sans Merci*

JOHN KEATS

Oh, what can ail thee, knight-at-arms,
    Alone and palely loitering?
The sedge has withered from the lake,
    And no birds sing.

Oh, what can ail thee, knight-at-arms,
    So haggard and so woe-begone?
The squirrel's granary is full,
    And the harvest's done.

I see a lily on thy brow,
    With anguish moist and fever dew;   10
And on thy cheeks a fading rose
    Fast withereth too.

_____
*The beautiful lady without pity (or compassion)

"I met a lady in the meads,
   Full beautiful—a faery's child;
Her hair was long, her foot was light,
   And her eyes were wild.

"I made a garland for her head,
   And bracelets too, and fragrant zone;
She looked at me as she did love,
   And made sweet moan.   20

"I set her on my pacing steed;
   And nothing else saw all day long;
For sideways would she lean, and sing
   A feary's song.

"She found me roots of relish sweet,
   And honey wild, and manna-dew,
And sure in language strange she said,
   'I love thee true.'

"She took me to her elfin grot,
   And there she wept, and sighed full sore,   30
And there I shut her wild, wild eyes,
   With kisses four.

"And there she lullèd me asleep,
   And there I dreamed—ah! woe betide!—
The latest dream I ever dreamed
   On the cold hill side.

"I saw pale kings and princes too,
   Pale warriors, death-pale were they all,
They cried—'La Belle Dame sans Merci
   Hath thee in thrall!'   40

"I saw their starved lips in the gloam,
   With horrid warning gapèd wide;
And I awoke, and found me here
   On the cold hill's side.

And this is why I sojourn here,
   Alone and palely loitering;
Though the sedge is withered from the lake
   And no birds sing."

Considerations

1. Here we see another facet of Keats' diverse poetic talents. This is a literary ballad (which means that it was written by an author whose name is known but it was patterned on the old popular ballad form). What kinship does it have to "The Twa Corbies" (p. 356) and "Sir Patrick Spens" (p. 357)?
2. Cite some of the lines or phrases Keats uses to convey a sense of loneliness and unearthliness.
3. There is more than one way to interpret line 35. What do you think happened to the knight during the course of this poem?
4. Can you find any justification for reading this poem as a story about unrequited love?

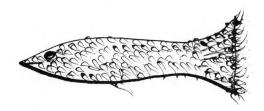

O Lovely Fishermaiden

A Translation by Louis Untermeyer

HEINRICH HEINE

O lovely fishermaiden,
  Come, bring your boat to land;
And we will sit together
  And whisper, hand in hand.

O rest upon my bosom,
  And fear no harm from me.
You give your body daily,
  Unfearing to the sea. . . .

My heart is like the ocean
  With storm and ebb and flow—
And many a pearly treasure
  Burns in the depths below.

from

Sonnets from the Portuguese

ELIZABETH BARRETT BROWNING

14

If thou must love me, let it be for naught
Except for love's sake only. Do not say
"I love her for her smile—her look—her way
Of speaking gently—for a trick of thought
That falls in well with mine, and certes brought   5
A sense of pleasant ease on such a day"—
For these things in themselves, Belovéd, may
Be changed, or change for thee—and love, so wrought,
May be unwrought so. Neither love me for
Thine own dear pity's wiping my cheeks dry—   10
A creature might forget to weep, who bore
Thy comfort long, and lose thy love thereby!
But love me for love's sake, that evermore
Thou mayst love on, through love's eternity.

Ulysses

ALFRED, LORD TENNYSON

It little profits that an idle king,
By this still hearth, among these barren crags,
Matched with an aged wife, I mete and dole
Unequal laws unto a savage race,
That hoard, and sleep, and feed, and know not me.   5

---

2. crags. On the bleak island of Ithaca, the home of Ulysses.   **3. aged wife**, Penelope.

I cannot rest from travel; I will drink
Life to the lees. All times I have enjoyed
Greatly, have suffered greatly, both with those
That loved me, and alone; on shore, and when
Through scudding drifts the rainy Hyades   10
Vexed the dim sea. I am become a name;
For always roaming with a hungry heart
Much have I seen and known—cities of men
And manners, climates, councils, governments,
Myself not least, but honored of them all—   15
And drunk delight of battle with my peers,
Far on the ringing plains of windy Troy.
I am a part of all that I have met;
Yet all experience is an arch wherethrough
Gleams that untraveled world whose margin fades   20
Forever and forever when I move.
How dull it is to pause, to make an end,
To rust unburnished, not to shine in use!
As though to breathe were life! Life piled on life
Were all too little, and of one to me   25
Little remains; but every hour is saved
From that eternal silence, something more,
A bringer of new things; and vile it were
For some three suns to store and hoard myself,
And this gray spirit yearning in desire   30
To follow knowledge like a sinking star,
Beyond the utmost bound of human thought
    This is my son, mine own Telemachus,
To whom I leave the scepter and the isle—
Well-loved of me, discerning to fulfill   35
This labor, by slow prudence to make mild
A rugged people, and through soft degrees
Subdue them to the useful and the good.
Most blameless is he, centered in the sphere
Of common duties, decent not to fail   40
In offices of tenderness, and pay
Meet adoration to my household gods,
When I am gone. He works his work, I mine.
    There lies the port; the vessel puffs her sail;
There gloom the dark, broad seas. My mariners,   45
Souls that have toiled, and wrought, and thought with me—

---

10. Hyades, a group of seven stars in the constellation Taurus. They were associated with the rainy season.   **27. eternal silence,** a pagan view of death.

That ever with a frolic welcome took
The thunder and the sunshine, and opposed
Free hearts, free foreheads—you and I are old;
Old age hath yet his honor and his toil.   50
Death closes all; but something ere the end,
Some work of noble note, may yet be done,
Not unbecoming men that strove with gods.
The lights begin to twinkle from the rocks;
The long day wanes; the slow moon climbs; the deep   55
Moans round with many voices. Come, my friends.
'Tis not too late to seek a newer world.
Push off, and sitting well in order smite
The sounding furrows; for my purpose holds
To sail beyond the sunset, and the baths   60
Of all the western stars, until I die.
It may be that the gulfs will wash us down;
It may be we shall touch the Happy Isles,
And see the great Achilles, whom we knew.
Though much is taken, much abides; and though   65
We are not now that strength which in old days
Moved earth and heaven, that which we are, we are—
One equal temper of heroic hearts,
Made weak by time and fate, but strong in will
To strive, to seek, to find, and not to yield.

---

49. you, Ulysses' companions. The attitude expressed here is modern. **63. Happy Isles,** the Islands of the Blest, identified with the Elysian Fields as the abode of just men after death. **64. Achilles,** the most famous of the Greek heroes in the Trojan War. After slaying Hector and dragging his body three times around the walls. Achilles was finally killed by Paris, wounded with a poisoned arrow in the heel, his only vulnerable spot. The arms of Achilles were awarded to Ulysses.
65. Though . . . yield. These lines express Tennyson's favorite doctrine of the unconquerable will. Cf. Henley's *Invictus.*

Considerations

1. This poem was written after the death of Tennyson's close personal friend Arthur Hallam. By using as his spokesman the aging Ulysses, restless after returning from his wanderings, the poet was able to give voice to his own need for going on. If the poem lacks appeal because it appears to be about old age, consider that there are moments when even the young feel that they can't go on. How is that dilemma stated and resolved in the poem?

The Eagle

Alfred, Lord Tennyson

Fragment

He clasps the crag with crooked hands;
Close to the sun in lonely lands,
Ringed with the azure world, he stands.

The wrinkled sea beneath him crawls;
He watches from his mountain walls,   5
And like a thunderbolt he falls.

Considerations

1. What does the subtitle "Fragment" indicate? Is this more or less of a
fragment than "Kubla Khan" (p. 398)?
2. How accurately do the images of what the eagle sees convey the
height at which he stands?

My Last Duchess

Robert Browning

Ferrara

That's my last Duchess painted on the wall,
Looking as if she were alive. I call
That piece a wonder, now: Frà Pandolf's hands
Worked busily a day, and there she stands.
Will't please you sit and look at her? I said
"Frà Pandolf" by design, for never read
Strangers like you that pictured countenance,
The depth and passion of its earnest glance
But to myself they turned (since none puts by
The curtain I have drawn for you, but I)   10
And seemed as they would ask me, if they durst,
How such a glance came there; so, not the first

Are you to turn and ask thus. Sir, 'twas not
'Her husband's presence only, called that spot
Of joy into the Duchess' cheek: perhaps
Frà Pandolph chanced to say, "Her mantle laps
Over my lady's wrist too much," or "Paint
Must never hope to reproduce the faint
Half-flush that dies along her throat": such stuff
Was courtesy, she thought, and cause enough   20
For calling up that spot of joy. She had
A heart—how shall I say?—too soon made glad,
Too easily impressed: she liked whate'er
She looked on, and her looks went everywhere.
Sir, 'twas all one! My favor at her breast,
The dropping of the daylight in the West,
The bough of cherries some officious fool
Broke in the orchard for her, the white mule
She rode with round the terrace—all and each
Would draw from her alike the approving speech,   30
Or blush, at least. She thanked men,—good! but thanked
Somehow—I know not how—as if she ranked
My gift of a nine-hundred-years-old name
With anybody's gift. Who'd stoop to blame
This sort of trifling? Even had you skill
In speech—(which I have not)—to make your will
Quite clear to such an one, and say, "Just this
Or that in you disgusts me; here you miss,
Or there exceed the mark"—and if she let
Herself be lessoned so, nor plainly set   40
Her wits to yours, forsooth, and made excuse,
—E'en then would be some stooping; and I choose
Never to stoop. Oh sir, she smiled, no doubt,
Whene'er I passed her; but who passed without
Much the same smile? This grew; I gave commands;
Then all smiles stopped together. There she stands
As if alive. Will't please you rise? We'll meet
The company below, then. I repeat,
The Count your master's known munificence
Is ample warrant that no just pretence   50
Of mine for dowry will be disallowed;
Though his fair daughter's self, as I avowed
At starting, is my object. Nay, we'll go
Together down, sir. Notice Neptune, though,
Taming a sea-horse, thought a rarity,
Which Claus of Innsbruck cast in bronze for me!

Considerations

This is generally considered to be the finest example of the dramatic monologue in English poetry. There are two characters, but only one of them, the Duke, speaks. He is addressing the emissary of a count whose daughter is scheduled to be the next duchess. The setting is the Duke's residence; they are looking at the Duke's art treasures—at one painting in particular.

1. What impression is given by the phrase "That's my last Duchess"? Does this mean he has had others before her?
2. In two places the Duke speaks of the painting as being so excellent that the Duchess looks as if she were alive. Is this merely a customary comment of praise or does it mean that the Duchess is dead? (In that time and place, highly connected men could dispose of their wives by having the marriage annulled and banishing the ladies to a convent.)
3. How do the Duke's statements reveal his character? How does he view his wife? According to his account, were the Duchess' actions malicious or unreasonable? Why did he object to them?
4. Do you think the poem could just as well have ended with the Duke's condescending offer to the emissary to go downstairs together? What purpose is served by the final sentence?

Rabbi Ben Ezra

ROBERT BROWNING

Grow old along with me!
The best is yet to be,
The last of life, for which the first was made.
Our times are in his hand
Who saith, "A whole I planned;   5
Youth shows but half. Trust God; see all, nor be afraid!"

Not that, amassing flowers,
Youth sighed, "Which rose make ours,
Which lily leave and then as best recall?"
Not that, admiring stars,   10
It yearned, "Nor Jove, nor Mars;
Mine be some figured flame which blends, transcends them all!"

---

7. Not that. *Not that* of ll. **7** and 10 and *Not for* of l.

Not for such hopes and fears
Annulling youth's brief years,
Do I remonstrate—folly wide the mark!   15
Rather I prize the doubt
Low kinds exist without,
Finished and finite clods, untroubled by a spark.

Poor vaunt of life indeed,
Were man but formed to feed   20
On joy, to solely seek and find and feast.
Such feasting ended, then
As sure an end to men;
Irks care the crop-full bird? Frets doubt the maw-crammed beast?

Rejoice we are allied   25
To that which doth provide
And not partake, effect and not receive!
A spark disturbs our clod;
Nearer we hold of God
Who gives, than of his tribes that take, I must believe. 30

Then, welcome each rebuff
That turns earth's smoothness rough,
Each sting that bids nor sit nor stand but go!
Be our joys three parts pain!
Strive, and hold cheap the strain;   35
Learn, nor account the pang; dare, never grudge the throe!

For thence—a paradox
Which comforts while it mocks—
Shall life succeed in that it seems to fail:
What I aspired to be,   40
And was not, comforts me;
A brute I might have been, but would not sink i' the scale.

13 go with *Do I remonstrate* of 15. 24. Irks . . . bird, does care irk the crop-full bird?
40. What . . . me. Cf. *A Grammarian's Funeral*, ll. 113–120, *Saul*, ll. 295–296, and *Andrea del Sarto*, ll. 97–98.

What is he but a brute
Whose flesh has soul to suit,
Whose spirit works lest arms and legs want play?   45
To man, propose this test—
Thy body at its best,
How far can that project thy soul on its lone way?

Yet gifts should prove their use:
I own the Past profuse   50
Of power each side, perfection every turn;
Eyes, ears took in their dole,
Brain treasured up the whole;
Should not the heart beat once, "How good to live and learn"?

Not once beat, "Praise be thine!   55
I see the whole design,
I, who saw power, see now Love perfect too;
Perfect I call thy plan.
Thanks that I was a man!
Maker, remake, complete—I trust what thou shalt do!"   60

For pleasant is this flesh;
Our soul, in its rose-mesh
Pulled ever to the earth, still yearns for rest.
Would we some prize might hold
To match those manifold   65
Possessions of the brute—gain most, as we did best!

Let us not always say,
"Spite" of this flesh today
I strove, made head, gained ground upon the whole!"
Asthe bird wings and sings,   70
Let us cry, "All good things
Are ours, nor soul helps flesh more, now, than flesh helps soul!"

Therefore I summon age
To grant youth's heritage,
Life's struggle having so far reached its term.   75
Thence shall I pass, approved
A man, for aye removed
From the developed brute—a god, though in the germ.

---

57. I . . . too. Cf. *Saul,* ll. 242, 305–306. **61–72.** Cf. *Fra Lippo Lippi,* ll. 205–214.

And I shall thereupon
Take rest, ere I be gone   80
Once more on my adventure brave and new;
Fearless and unperplexed,
When I wage battle next,
What weapons to select, what armor to indue.

Youth ended, I shall try   85
My gain or loss thereby;
Leave the fire ashes, what survives is gold.
And I shall weigh the same,
Give life its praise or blame.
Young, all lay in dispute; I shall know, being old.   90

For note, when evening shuts,
A certain moment cuts
The deed off, calls the glory from the gray;
A whisper from the west
Shoots—"Add this to the rest,   95
Take it and try its worth. Here dies another day."

So, still within this life,
Though lifted o'er its strife,
Let me discern, compare, pronounce at last,
"This rage was right i' the main,   100
That acquiescence vain;
The Future I may face, now I have proved the Past."

For more is not reserved
To man, with soul just nerved
To act tomorrow what he learns today;   105
Here, work enough to watch
The Master work, and catch
Hints of the proper craft, tricks of the tool's true play.

---

81. adventure . . . new, the life of an old person after the passions and problems of youth
are left behind.   **84. to indue,** to put on.   **87. Leave . . . ashes,** if the fire leaves ashes.

As it was better, youth
Should strive, through acts uncouth,   110
Toward making, than repose on aught found made;
So, better, age, exempt
From strife, should know, than tempt
Further. Thou waitedst age; wait death nor be afraid!

Enough now, if the Right   115
And Good and Infinite
Be named here, as thou callest thy hand thine own,
With knowledge absolute,
Subject to no dispute
From fools that crowded youth, nor let thee feel alone.   120

Be there, for once and all,
Severed great minds from small,
Announced to each his station in the Past!
Was I, the world arraigned,
Were they, my soul disdained,   125
Right? Let age speak the truth and give us peace at last!

Now, who shall arbitrate?
Ten men love what I hate,
Shun what I follow, slight what I receive;
Ten, who in ears and eyes   130
Match me. We all surmise,
They this thing, and I that; whom shall my soul believe?

Not on the vulgar mass
Called "work," must sentence pass—
Things done, that took the eye and had the price;   135
O'er which, from level stand,
The low world laid its hand,
Found straightway to its mind, could value in a trice:

But all, the world's coarse thumb
And finger failed to plumb,   140
So passed in making up the main account;
All instincts immature,
All purposes unsure,
That weighed not as his work, yet swelled the man's amount:

---

124. **Was I.** Supply *whom* after *I* and also after *they, l. 125.*

Thoughts hardly to be packed   145
Into a narrow act,
Fancies that broke through language and escaped;
All I could never be,
All, men ignored in me,
This, I was worth to God, whose wheel the pitcher shaped.   150

Aye, note that Potter's wheel,
That metaphor! and feel
Why time spins fast, why passive lies our clay—
Thou, to whom fools propound,
When the wine makes its round,   155
"Since life fleets, all is change; the Past gone, seize today!"

Fool! All that is, at all,
Lasts ever, past recall;
Earth changes, but thy soul and God stand sure.
What entered into thee,   160
That was, is, and shall be.
Time's wheel runs back or stops; Potter and clay endure.

He fixed thee 'mid this dance
Of plastic circumstance,
This Present, thou, forsooth, would fain arrest—   165
Machinery just meant
To give thy soul its bent,
Try thee and turn thee forth, sufficiently impressed.

What though the earlier grooves,
Which ran the laughing loves   170
Around thy base, no longer pause and press?
What though, about thy rim,
Skull-things in order grim
Grow out, in graver mood, obey the sterner stress?

Look not thou down but up!   175
To uses of a cup,
The festal board, lamp's flash, and trumpet's peal,
The new wine's foaming flow,
The Master's lips aglow!
Thou, heaven's consummate cup, what needst thou with earth's
    wheel?   180

---

151. Potter's wheel. Cf. *Isaiah,* 64:8: "But now, o lord, thou art our father; we are the clay, and thou our potter; and we all are the work of thy hand." Cf. also Fitzgerald's *Rubaiyat,* ll. 325–360.

But I need, now as then,
Thee, God, who moldest men;
And since, not even while the whirl was worst,
Did I—to the wheel of life
With shapes and colors rife,   185
Bound dizzily—mistake my end, to slake Thy thirst.

So, take and use Thy work;
Amend what flaws may lurk,
What strain o' the stuff, what warpings past the aim!
My times be in Thy hand!   190
Perfect the cup as planned!
Let age approve of youth, and death complete the same!

Considerations

Here Browning is using a character to express his own thoughts—in this case, his philosophy of life. Rabbi Ben Ezra was a twelfth century Jewish philosopher, astronomer, physician, and poet—a Renaissance man before the Renaissance. The poem mixes quotations from the Rabbi's writings with the ideas that Browning had already expressed in other poems.

1. Does Browning make you feel the reality of the Rabbi? Can you visualize him as well as tell something about his character?
2. Try to put in your own words the Rabbi's attitude toward the past, toward himself, and toward God.
3. Compare the view of death expressed here with the one found in Whitman's "When Lilacs Last in the Dooryard Bloom'd" (p. 424). Could any differences in viewpoint be accounted for by the fact that one poet was contemplating a natural death at the end of a long life, while the other was writing about death by violence?
4. It has been said that Browning's syntax occasionally obscured his thoughts. Can you explain line 24: "Irks care the crop-full bird? Frets doubt the maw-crammed beast?" How much of a problem do lines such as these pose to understanding the poem?

The Latest Decalogue

ARTHUR HUGH CLOUGH

Thou shalt have one God only; who
Would be at the expense of two?
No graven images may be
Worshipped, except the currency.
Swear not at all; for, for thy curse
Thine enemy is none the worse.
At church on Sunday to attend
Will serve to keep the world thy friend.
Honor thy parents; that is, all
From whom advancement may befall.   10
Thou shalt not kill; but need'st not strive
Officiously to keep alive.
Do not adultery commit;
Advantage rarely comes of it.
Thou shalt not steal; an empty feat,
When it's so lucrative to cheat.
Bear not false witness; let the lie
Have time on its own wings to fly.
Thou shalt not covet, but tradition
Approves all forms of competition.   20

Battle Hymn of the Republic

JULIA WARD HOWE

Mine eyes have seen the glory of the coming of the Lord:
He is trampling out the vintage where the grapes of wrath are
    stored;
He hath loosed the fateful lightning of his terrible swift sword;
    His truth is marching on.

Reprinted from *The Poems of Arthur Hugh Clough* edited by H. F. Lowery, A. L. P. Norrington, and F. L. Mulhauser, 1951, pp. 60–60, by permission of the Clarendon Press, Oxford.

Chorus
> Glory! glory! Hallelujah!
> Glory! glory! Hallelujah!
> Glory! glory! Hallelujah
>   His truth is marching on!

I have seen him in the watch-fires of a hundred circling camps;
They have builded him an altar in the evening dews and damps;   10
I can read his righteous sentence by the dim and flaring lamps:
  His day is marching on.

I have read a fiery gospel, writ in burnished rows of steel:
"As ye deal with my contemners, so with you my grace shall deal;
Let the Hero, born of woman, crush the serpent with his heel,
  Since God is marching on."

He has sounded forth the trumpet that shall never call retreat;
He is sifting out the hearts of men before his judgment-seat;
Oh, be swift, my soul, to answer him! be jubilant, my feet!
  Our God is marching on.   20

In the beauty of the lillies Christ was born across the sea,
With a glory in his bosom that transfigures you and me:
As he died to make men holy, let us die to make men free,
  While God is marching on.

Considerations

This poem, written to be sung to the tune of "John Brown's Body," was first published in 1862. Militancy and Christianity here share the same goals, with at least two passages from the Bible to sanctify the alliance. Lines 1–4 are based on Revelations 19:11, 14, 15. "Let the Hero, born of woman, crush the serpent with his heel" is taken from Genesis 3:15.

1. Are the abstractions discussed in this poem—religion, violence, and glory—appealingly presented? Would the poem be more effective if some of the adjectives were changed ("I have read an ancient gospel" instead of "I have read a fiery gospel" for example)?
2. If you have never heard this sung, would the archaic word choices ("mine eyes," "hath loosed," and so on) seem awkward? Would the impact of the refrain at each verse's end be lessened? How effective would you consider it as a poem?

When Lilacs Last
In the Dooryard Bloom'd

WALT WHITMAN

1

When lilacs last in the dooryard bloom'd,
And the great star early droop'd in the western sky in the night,
I mourn'd, and yet shall mourn with ever-returning spring.

Ever-returning spring, trinity sure to me you bring,
Lilac blooming perennial and drooping star in the west,
And thought of him I love.

2

O powerful western fallen star!
O shades of night—O moody, tearful night!
O great star disappear'd—O the black murk that hides the star!
O cruel hands that hold me powerless—O helpless soul of me!
O harsh surrounding cloud that will not free my soul.

3

In the dooryard fronting an old farm-house near the whitewash'd
    palings,
Stands the lilac-bush tall-growing with heart-shaped leaves of rich
    green,
With many a pointed blossom rising delicate, with the perfume strong
    I love,
With every leaf a miracle—and from this bush in the dooryard,
With delicate-color'd blossoms and heart-shaped leaves of rich green,
A sprig with its flower I break.

4

In the swamp in secluded recesses,
A shy and hidden bird is warbling a song.

Solitary the thrush,
The hermit withdrawn to himself, avoiding the settlements,
Sings by himself a song.

Song of the bleeding throat,
Death's outlet song of life, (for well dear brother I know,
If thou wast not granted to sing thou would'st surely die.)

5

Over the breast of the spring, the land, amid cities,
Amid lanes and through old woods, where lately the violets peep'd
   from the ground, spotting the gray debris,
Amid the grass in the fields each side of the lanes, passing the endless
   grass,
Passing the yellow-spear'd wheat, every grain from its shroud in the
   dark-brown fields uprisen,
Passing the apple-tree blows of white and pink in the orchards,
Carrying a corpse to where it shall rest in the grave,
Night and day journeys a coffin.

6

Coffin that passes through lanes and streets,
Through day and night with the great cloud darkening the land,
With the pomp of the inloop'd flags with the cities draped in black,
With the show of the States themselves as of crape-veil'd women
   standing,
With processions long and winding and the flambeaus of the night,
With the countless torches lit, with the silent sea of faces and the
   unbared heads,
With the waiting depot, the arriving coffin, and the sombre faces,
With dirges through the night, with the thousand voices rising strong
   and solemn,
With all the mournful voices of the dirges pour'd around the coffin,
The dim-lit churches and the shuddering organs—where amid these
   you journey,
With the tolling tolling bells' perpetual clang,
Here, coffin that slowly passes,
I give you my sprig of lilac.

7

(Nor for you, for one alone,
Blossoms and branches green to coffins all I bring,
For fresh as the morning, thus would I chant a song for you
O sane and sacred death.

All over bouquets of roses,
O death, I cover you over with roses and early lilies,
But mostly and now the lilac that blooms the first,
Copious I break, I break the sprigs from the bushes,
With loaded arms I come, pouring for you,
For you and the coffins all of you O death.)

8

O western orb sailing the heaven,
Now I know what you must have meant as a month since I walk'd,
As I walk'd in silence the transparent shadowy night,
As I saw you had something to tell as you bent to me night after night,
As you droop'd from the sky low down as if to my side, (while the
    other stars all look'd on,)
As we wander'd together the solemn night, (for something I know not
    what kept me from sleep,)
As the night advanced, and I saw on the rim of the west how full you
    were of woe,
As I stood on the rising ground in the breeze in the cool transparent
    night,
As I watch'd where you pass'd and was lost in the netherward black of
    the night,
As my soul in its trouble dissatisfied sank, as where you sad orb,
Concluded, dropt in the night, and was gone.

9

Sing on there in the swamp,
O singer bashful and tender, I hear your notes, I hear your call,
I hear, I come presently, I understand you,
But a moment I linger, for the lustrous star has detain'd me,
The star my departing comrade holds and detains me.

10

O how shall I warble myself for the dead one there I loved?
And how shall I deck my song for the large sweet soul that has
    gone?
And what shall my perfume be for the grave of him I love?

Sea-winds blown from east and west,
Blown from the Eastern sea and blown from the Western sea, till there
    on the prairies meeting,
These and with these and the breath of my chant,
I'll perfume the grave of him I love.

11

O what shall I hang on the chamber walls?
And what shall the pictures be that I hang on the walls,
To adorn the burial-house of him I love?

Pictures of growing spring and farms and homes,
With the Fourth-month eve at sundown, and the gray smoke lucid and
  bright,
With floods of the yellow gold of the gorgeous, indolent, sinking sun,
  burning, expanding the air,
With the fresh sweet herbage under foot, and the pale green leaves of
  the trees prolific,
In the distance the flowing glaze, the breast of the river, with a
  wind-dapple here and there,
With ranging hills on the banks, with many a line against the sky, and
  shadows,
And the city at hand with dwellings so dense, and stacks of chimneys,
And all the scenes of life and the workshops, and the workmen
  homeward returning.

12

Lo, body and soul—this land,
My own Manhattan with spires, and the sparkling and hurrying tides,
  and the ships,
The varied and ample land, the South and the North in the light,
  Ohio's shores and flashing Missouri,
And ever the far-spreading prairies cover'd with grass and corn.

Lo, the most excellent sun so calm and haughty,
The violet and purple morn with just-felt breezes,
The gentle soft-born measureless light,
The miracle spreading bathing all, the fulfill'd noon,
The coming eve delicious, the welcome night and the stars,
Over my cities shining all, enveloping man and land.

13

Sing on, sing on you gray-brown bird,
Sing from the swamps, the recesses, pour your chant from the bushes,
Limitless out of the dusk, out of the cedars and pines.

Sing on dearest brother, warble your reedy song,
Loud human song, with voice of uttermost woe.

O liquid and free and tender!
O wild and loose to my soul—O wondrous singer!

You only I hear—yet the star holds me, (but will soon depart,)
Yet the lilac with mastering odor holds me.

14

Now while I sat in the day and look'd forth,
In the close of the day with its light and the fields of spring, and the
  farmers preparing their crops,
In the large unconscious scenery of my land with its lakes and forests,
In the heavenly aerial beauty, (after the perturb'd winds and the
  storms,)
Under the arching heavens of the afternoon swift passing, and the
  voices of children and women,
The many-moving sea-tides, and I saw the ships how they sail'd,
And the summer approaching with richness, and the fields all busy
  with labor,
And the infinite separate houses, how they all went on, each with its
  meals and minutia of daily usages,
And the streets how their throbbings throbb'd, and the cities pent—lo,
  then and there,
Falling upon them all and among them all, enveloping me with the
  rest,
Appear'd the cloud, appear'd the long black trail,
And I knew death, its thought, and the sacred knowledge of death.

Then with the knowledge of death as walking one side of me,
And the thought of death close-walking the other side of me,
And I in the middle as with companions, and as holding the hands of
  companions,
I fled forth to the hiding receiving night that talks not,
Down to the shores of the water, the path by the swamp in the
  dimness,
To the solemn shadowy cedars and ghostly pines so still.

And the singer so shy to the rest receiv'd me,
The gray-brown bird I know receiv'd us comrades three,
And he sang the carol of death, and a verse for him I love.

From deep secluded recesses,
From the fragrant cedars and the ghostly pines so still,
Came the carol of the bird.

And the charm of the carol rapt me,
As I held as if by their hands my comrades in the night,
And the voice of my spirit tallied the song of the bird.

Come lovely and soothing death,
Undulate round the world, serenely arriving, arriving,
In the day, in the night, to all, to each,
Sooner or later delicate death.

Prais'd be the fathomless universe,
For life and joy, and for objects and knowledge curious,
And for love, sweet love—but praise! praise! praise!
For the sure-enwinding arms of cool-enfolding death.

Dark mother always gliding near with soft feet,
Have none chanted for thee a chant of fullest welcome?
Then I chant it for thee, I glorify thee above all,
I bring thee a song that when thou must indeed come, come
*   unfalteringly.*

Approach strong deliveress,
When it is so, when thou hast taken them I joyously sing the dead,
Lost in the loving floating ocean of thee,
Laved in the flood of thy bliss O death.

From me to thee glad serenades,
Dances for thee I propose saluting thee, adornments and feastings for
*   thee,*
And the sights of the open landscape and the high-spread sky are fitting,
And life and the fields, and the huge and thoughtful night.

The night in silence under many a star,
The ocean shore and the husky whispering wave whose voice I know,
And the soul turning to thee O vast and well-veil'd death,
And the body gratefully nestling close to thee.

Over the tree-tops I float thee a song,
Over the rising and sinking waves, over the myriad fields and the prairies
*   wide,*
Over the dense-pack'd cities all and the teeming wharves and ways,
I float this carol with joy, with joy to thee O death.

15

To the tally of my soul,
Loud and strong kept up the gray-brown bird,
With pure deliberate notes spreading filling the night.

Loud in the pines and cedars dim,
Clear in the freshness moist and the swamp-perfume,
And I with my comrades there in the night.

While my sight that was bound in my eyes unclosed,
As to long panoramas of visions.

And I saw askant the armies,
I saw as in noiseless dreams hundreds of battle-flags,
Borne through the smoke of the battles and pierc'd with missiles I saw
    them,
And carried hither and yon through the smoke, and torn and bloody,
And at last but a few shreds left on the staffs, (and all in silence,)
And the staffs all splinter'd and broken.
I saw battle-corpses, myriads of them,
And the white skeletons of young men, I saw them,
I saw the debris and debris of all the slain soldiers of the war,
But I saw they were not as was thought,
They themselves were fully at rest, they suffer'd not,
The living remain'd and suffer'd, the mother suffer'd,
And the wife and the child and the musing comrade, suffer'd,
And the armies that remain'd suffer'd.

16

Passing the visions, passing the night,
Passing, unloosing the hold of my comrades' hands,
Passing the song of the hermit bird and the tallying song of my soul,
Victorious song, death's outlet song, yet varying ever-altering song,
As low and wailing, yet clear the notes, rising and falling, flooding the
    night,
Sadly sinking and fainting, as warning and warning, and yet again
    bursting with joy,
Covering the earth and filling the spread of the heaven,
As that powerful psalm in the night I heard from recesses,
Passing, I leave thee lilac with heart-shaped leaves,
I leave thee there in the dooryard, blooming, returning with spring.

I cease from my song for thee,
From my gaze on thee in the west, fronting the west, communing with
    thee,
O comrade lustrous with silver face in the night.

Yet each to keep and all, retrievements out of the night,
The song, the wondrous chant of the gray-brown bird,
And the tallying chant, the echo arous'd in my soul,
With the lustrous and drooping star with the countenance full of woe,
With the holders holding my hand nearing the call of the bird,
Comrades mine and I in the midst, and their memory ever to keep, for
    the dead I loved so well,

For the sweetest, wisest soul of all my days and lands—and this for his
   dear sake,
Lilac and star and bird twined with the chant of my soul,
There in the fragrant pines and the cedars dusk and dim.

Considerations

Walt Whitman is one of those writers whose work causes a violent
reaction in most readers—they are either stimulated by it or they think it
is uncomfortably overwritten. Whitman himself once called his own
proclamations a barbaric yawp, and it is just this undisciplined power and
openness that offends some readers. His pantheistic beliefs led to a
celebration of all aspects of life. He glorified the physical body as well as
the soul at a time when such frank expressions were alien to proper
society. All of this enjoyment and wonder, coupled perhaps with an
affection for ritual chant, produced one of his most characteristic and
irritating habits—that of listing each small part of whatever whole he
might be describing. When one is attuned to the particular subject, the
words piling on each other create an exultation not unlike that deriving
from really driving music.

   Both in content and technique, Whitman's work had an extraordinary
influence on the poets who came after him. His poems can be divided
into several categories. The first, which this poem represents, deals with
the cosmic-philosophical. It is considered by many to be one of the finest
elegies ever written.

1. The subject of the poem is the death of Abraham Lincoln, although
   his name is never mentioned. The feeling is, in general, somber; it
   begins with mourning and only at the end does it express a hint of
   optimism and promise. How does Whitman manage the shift from
   sorrow to hope?
2. Three symbols are used throughout this poem—lilacs, a star, and a
   solitary thrush. What do they symbolize? Are they still effective

symbols today? How are they used to produce a mood of controlled gloom?

3. Whitman had seen Lincoln frequently and admired him greatly, so Lincoln's assassination and funeral were as personal for him as were John Kennedy's for most of us today. Is there any reason (such as changed word usage or topical references) why this poem would not fit a similar occurrence in our times?

Cavalry Crossing a Ford

WALT WHITMAN

A line in long array where they wind betwixt green islands,
They take a serpentine course, their arms flash in the sun—hark to the musical clank,
Behold the silvery river, in it the splashing horses loitering stop to drink,
Behold the brown-faced men, each group, each person a picture, the negligent rest on the saddles,
Some emerge on the opposite bank, others are just entering the ford—while,
Scarlet and blue and snowy white,
The guidon flags flutter gayly in the wind.

Considerations

The two preceding poems are from Whitman's *Drum Taps,* a collection of poems written about his experiences in the Union Army during the Civil War. He served for some time with the Union troops as a noncombatant, tending the sick, helping dress wounds, and writing letters for soldiers who were dying.

1. What feeling or attitude is Whitman trying to convey in these poems?
2. Compare these two poems to modern descriptions of military life, such as the one found in Jarrell's "Eighth Air Force" (p. 586).

To a Common Prostitute

WALT WHITMAN

Be composed—be at ease with me—I am Walt Whitman, liberal and
  lusty as Nature,
Not till the sun excludes you do I exclude you,
Not till the waters refuse to glisten for you and the leaves to rustle for
  you, do my words refuse to glisten and rustle for you.

My girl I appoint with you an appointment, and I charge you that you
  make preparations to be worthy to meet me,
And I charge you that you be patient and perfect till I come.
Till then I salute you with a significant look that you do not forget me.

When I Heard
The Learn'd Astronomer

WALT WHITMAN

When I heard the learn'd astronomer,
When the proofs, the figures, were ranged in columns before me,
When I was shown the charts and diagrams, to add, divide, and
  measure them,
When I sitting heard the astronomer where he lectured with much
  applause in the lecture-room,
How soon unaccountable I became tired and sick,
Till rising and gliding out I wander'd off by myself,
In the mystical moist night-air, and from time to time,
Look'd up in perfect silence at the stars.

To the Reader

A Translation by C. F. MacIntyre

Charles Baudelaire

By folly, error, stinginess, and vice
our flesh is worked, our souls inhabited,
and all our dear remorses are well fed,
as beggars nourish their own fleas and lice.

Our sins are stubborn, our repentance mean;
pretending to pay fatly what we vowed,
we run back gaily to the muddy road,
thinking with cheap tears to wash off the stain.

On the pillow of evil, Satan Trismegist
a long time cradles our enchanted souls,   10
and the all-precious metal of our will
is turned to fumes by this wise alchemist.

We find allurement in repugnant things;
unawed, each day another step we sink
toward Hell, across tenebrous depths that stink.
It is the Devil pulls the leading-strings!

Like a mean lecher kissing and sucking thin
the martyred breast of some poor ancient tart,
we steal in passing any furtive sport
and squeeze it, like an orange, to the skin.   20

Swarming and crowding, like a million worms,
the Demons in our brain are on a spree,
and when we breathe, in our lungs quietly
Death's unseen river flows and dully mourns.

If poison, dagger, arson, and the rough
assault of rape have not with droll designs
adorned the vulgar canvas doom assigns,
it is because our soul's not bold enough.

Originally published by the University of California Press; reprinted by permission of The Regents of the University of California.

But among jackals, panthers, and hound-bitches,
monkeys and vultures, scorpions and serpents,   30
the yelping, roaring, growling monsters, rampant
in the infamous menagerie of our vices,

is one more vicious, ugly, and perverse!
Though he makes no great gesture, no loud cry,
he would gladly turn our earth into debris
and in a yawn engulf the universe;

Ennui—his unwilling tears brim over
as, pulling at his hookah, he dreams of scaffolds.
You know him, reader, this fastidious scoundrel,
—hypocritical reader, my fellow, my brother!   40

Considerations

Baudelaire is often classified as belonging to a school of decadence that
flourished in the second half of the nineteenth century. Many writers of
this school took as their model the poems of Edgar Allan Poe. For them,
love was linked with death, as pleasure was with pain. Corpses, ghosts,
torture, and an almost erotic stimulation produced by filth were among
their subjects. The preceding poem comes from a book called *Flowers of
Evil*.

1. Compare the images in "To the Reader" with those used in "Spleen."
   What feeling does each kind produce?
2. Compare "Spleen" with poems like "The Twa Corbies" (p. 356), "La
   Belle Dame sans Merci" (p. 407), "The Hollow Men" (p. 516), and
   "Machu Picchu" (p. 552), which also have a somewhat morbid
   appeal. Can you make any generalizations about the power and
   attraction of such poems or the impetus—social, psychological, or
   historical—that caused them to be written? Can you think of any
   contemporary poetry that is similar in tone to "Spleen"?

Spleen

CHARLES BAUDELAIRE

When the low and heavy sky presses like a lid
On the groaning heart, a prey to slow cares,
And when from a horizon holding the whole orb
There is cast at us a sky more sad than night;

When earth is changed to a damp dungeon,
Where Hope, like a bat.
Flees beating the walls with its timorous wings,
And knocking its head on the rotting ceilings;

When the rain spreads out vast trails
Like the bars of a huge prison,
And when, like filthy spiders, silent people stretch
Threads to the depths of our brains,

Suddenly the bells jump furiously
And hurl to the sky a horrible shriek,
Like some wandering landless spirits
Starting an obstinate complaint.

—And long hearses, with no drums, no music,
File slowly through my soul: Hope,
Conquered, cries, and despotic atrocious Agony
Plants on my bent skull its flag of black.

Dover Beach

MATTHEW ARNOLD

The sea is calm tonight,
The tide is full, the moon lies fair
Upon the straits;—on the French coast the light
Gleams and is gone; the cliffs of England stand,
Glimmering and vast, out in the tranquil bay.
Come to the window, sweet is the night-air!
Only, from the long line of spray
Where the sea meets the moon-blanched land,
Listen! you hear the grating roar
Of pebbles which the waves draw back, and fling,   10
At their return, up the high strand,
Begin, and cease, and then again begin,
With tremulous cadence slow, and bring
The eternal note of sadness in.

Sophocles long ago
Heard it on the Ægaean, and it brought
Into his mind the turbid ebb and flow
Of human misery; we
Find also in the sound a thought,
Hearing it by this distant northern sea.   20

The Sea of Faith
Was once, too, at the full, and round earth's shore
Lay like the folds of a bright girdle furled.
But now I only hear
Its melancholy, long, withdrawing roar,
Retreating, to the breath
Of the night-wind, down the vast edges drear
And naked shingles of the world.

Ah, love, let us be true
To one another! for the world, which seems   30
To lie before us like a land of dreams,
So various, so beautiful, so new,
Hath really neither joy, nor love, nor light,
Nor certitude, nor peace, nor help for pain;
And we are here as on a darkling plain
Swept with confused alarms of struggle and flight,
Where ignorant armies clash by night.

Considerations

1. Compare this poem with Wordsworth's "Lines Written in Early Spring" (p. 396). Does looking at the peacefulness of nature inevitably lead one to contrast it to the human dilemma?
2. Does Arnold see any possibility of happiness or peace, and if so, where?
3. Is the change of locale from the sea to the darkling plain obtrusive? How are these images related?
4. Do the shorter lines have more impact than the longer ones? Why might Arnold have used shorter lines at certain points?
5. How applicable is the message of this poem to other times in history?

The Blessed Damozel

DANTE GABRIEL ROSSETTI

The blessed damozel leaned out
  From the gold bar of heaven;
Her eyes were deeper than the depth
  Of waters stilled at even;
She had three lilies in her hand,   5
  And the stars in her hair were seven.

Her robe, ungirt from clasp to hem,
  No wrought flowers did adorn,
But a white rose of Mary's gift,
  For service meetly worn;   10
Her hair that lay along her back
  Was yellow like ripe corn.

---

10. For . . . worn, fittingly worn in the service of the Virgin Mary.

Herseemed she scarce had been a day
  One of God's choristers;
The wonder was not yet quite gone   15
  From that still look of hers;
Albeit, to them she left, her day
  Had counted as ten years.

(To *one* it is ten years of years.
  . . . Yet now, and in this place,   20
Surely she leaned o'er me—her hair
  Fell all about my face. . . .
Nothing: the autumn fall of leaves.
  The whole year sets apace.)

It was the rampart of God's house   25
  That she was standing on;
By God built over the sheer depth
  The which is Space begun;
So high, that looking downward thence
  She scarce could see the sun.   30

It lies in heaven, across the flood
  Of ether, as a bridge.
Beneath, the tides of day and night
  With flame and darkness ridge
The void, as low as where this earth   35
  Spins like a fretful midge.

Around her, lovers, newly met
  'Mid deathless love's acclaims,
Spoke evermore among themselves
  Their heart-remembered names;   40
And the souls mounting up to God
  Went by her like thin flames.

And still she bowed herself and stooped
  Out of the circling charm;
Until her bosom must have made   45
  The bar she leaned on warm,
And the lilies lay as if asleep
  Along her bended arm.

---

13. Herseemed, it seemed to her. **36. midge,** a kind of small gnat.

From the fixed place of heaven she saw
   Time like a pulse shake fierce   50
Through all the worlds. Her gaze still strove
   Within the gulf to pierce
Its path; and now she spoke as when
   The stars sang in their spheres.

The sun was gone now; the curled moon   55
   Was like a little feather
Fluttering far down the gulf; and now
   She spoke through the still weather.
Her voice was like the voice the stars
   Had when they sang together.   60

(Ah, sweet! Even now, in that bird's song,
   Strove not her accents there,
Fain to be harkened? When those bells
   Possessed the midday air,
Strove not her steps to reach my side   65
   Down all the echoing stair?)

"I wish that he were come to me,
   For he will come," she said.
"Have I not prayed in heaven?—on earth,
   Lord, Lord, has he not prayed?   70
Are not two prayers a perfect strength?
   And shall I feel afraid?

"When round his head the aureole clings,
   And he is clothed in white,
I'll take his hand and go with him   75
   To the deep wells of light;
As unto a stream we will step down,
   And bathe there in God's sight.

"We two will stand beside that shrine,
   Occult, withheld, untrod,   80
Whose lamps are stirred continually
   With prayers sent up to God;
And see our old prayers, granted, melt
   Each like a little cloud.

"We two will lie i' the shadow of   85
   That living mystic tree
Within whose secret growth the Dove
   Is sometimes felt to be,
While every leaf that His plumes touch
   Saith His Name audibly.   90

"And I myself will teach to him,
   I myself, lying so,
The songs I sing here; which his voice
   Shall pause in, hushed and slow,
And find some knowledge at each pause,   95
   Or some new thing to know."

(Alas! We two, we two, thou say'st!
   Yea, one wast thou with me
That once of old. But shall God lift
   To endless unity   100
The soul whose likeness with thy soul
   Was but its love for thee?)

"We two," she said, "will seek the groves
   Where the lady Mary is,
With her five handmaidens, whose names   105
   Are five sweet symphonies,
Cecily, Gertrude, Magdalen,
   Margaret, and Rosalys.

"Circlewise sit they, with bound locks
   And foreheads garlanded;   110
Into the fine cloth white like flame
   Weaving the golden thread,
To fashion the birth-robes for them
   Who are just born, being dead.

---

86. **living . . . tree,** the tree of life (see *Revelation,* 22).   87. **Dove,** a symbol of the Holy Spirit, the third member of the Trinity; cf. *Luke,* 3:22.   107. **Cecily . . . Rosalys.** These are names of famous Christian saints. *St. Cecilia* (third century) is the patron saint of the blind and of musicians (see Dryden's *A Song for St. Cecilia's Day.* Vol. I); *St. Gertrude* (seventh century) is the patron saint of travelers; *St. Mary Magdalen* is the patron saint of penitents; *St. Margaret* is the chosen type of female innocence and meekness; *St. Rosalie* (twelfth century) is the patron saint of the city of Palermo, Sicily.

"He shall fear, haply, and be dumb;   115
    Then will I lay my cheek
To his, and tell about our love,
    Not once abashed or weak;
And the dear Mother will approve
    My pride, and let me speak.   120

"Herself shall bring us, hand in hand,
    To Him round whom all souls
Kneel, the clear-ranged unnumbered heads
    Bowed with their aureoles;   125
And angels meeting us shall sing
    To their citherns and citoles.

"There will I ask of Christ the Lord
    Thus much for him and me—
Only to live as once on earth   130
    With Love, only to be,
As then awhile, forever now,
    Together, I and he."

She gazed and listened and then said,
    Less sad of speech than mild—   135
"All this is when he comes." She ceased.
    The light thrilled toward her, filled
With angels in strong, level flight.
    Her eyes prayed, and she smiled.

(I saw her smile.) But soon their path   140
    Was vague in distant spheres;
And then she cast her arms along
    The golden barriers,
And laid her face between her hands,
    And wept. (I heard her tears.)

Considerations

In mid-nineteenth century England a number of poets and artists—
Rossetti among them—formed a group called the pre-Raphaelites. While
in some ways their principles were akin to those expressed by the
romantics—they were against industrialization, artistic artificiality, and

---

126. citherns and citoles, medieval stringed musical instruments.

state controlled art, and for self-expression and above all else truth—
their artistic tastes were different. It wasn't common man and unorna-
mented nature that interested them, but the richness of the Renaissance
and the courts of the Middle Ages. The images and settings of their
literature and paintings are characteristically sensuous, exotic, and
mystical.

1. In this poem Rossetti deliberately reverses the situation Poe dealt with
   in "The Raven." Instead of a lover pining hopelessly for a "sainted
   maiden whom the angels named Lenore," Rossetti pictures a blessed
   damosel leaning out of the window of heaven, yearning for the man
   she left on earth. Is the outcome of her plight clear? Why?
2. In "The Raven," the setting, the events, and the style combine to
   create a dark, haunting, hopeless mood. How effectively do you feel
   such elements are used in "The Blessed Damosel"?

Modern Love

GEORGE MEREDITH

48

Their sense is with their senses all mixed in,
Destroyed by subtleties these women are!
More brain, O Lord, more brain! or we shall mar
Utterly this fair garden we might win.
Behold! I looked for peace, and thought it near.   5
Our inmost hearts had opened, each to each
We drank the pure daylight of honest speech.
Alas! that was the fatal draft, I fear.
For when of my lost Lady came the word,
This woman, O this agony of flesh!   10
Jealous devotion bade her break the mesh,
That I might seek that other like a bird.
I do adore the nobleness! despise
The act! She has gone forth, I know not where.
Will the hard world my sentience of her share?   15
I feel the truth; so let the world surmise.

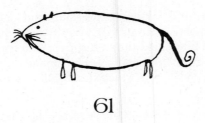

61

EMILY DICKINSON

Papa above!
Regard a Mouse
O'erpowered by the Cat!
Reserve within thy kingdom
A "Mansion" for the Rat!

Snug in seraphic Cupboards
To nibble all the day,
While unsuspecting Cycles
Wheel solemnly away!

Considerations

The genius of Emily Dickinson was discovered by the world only after she was dead; it continues to be rediscovered by succeeding generations. She is one of those rare artists whose work appeals to both children and graduate students. The surface simplicity of her poetry makes it immediately accessible to everyone; the complexities that lie beneath that surface have been the subject of endless debates.

Her life was both mysterious and utterly uneventful. She never travelled far from her New England home, but with access to her father's library, the Bible, and a few hymnbooks, her mind encompassed the world. She took subjects not often treated in poetry and made them important and exciting, creating really delightful poems about the most mundane topics. Yet she did not neglect the classic themes: religion, nature, love, and death.

1. What attitudes toward God, organized religion, and the minister are revealed in this and the following poem?
2. Do the level of diction and the familarities affect the acceptability of this poem?

324

EMILY DICKINSON

Some keep the Sabbath going to Church—
I keep it, staying at Home—
With a Bobolink for a Chorister—
And an Orchard, for a Dome—

Some keep the Sabbath in Surplice—
I just wear my Wings—
And instead of tolling the Bell, for Church,
Our little Sexton—sings.

God preaches, a noted Clergyman—
And the sermon is never long,   10
So instead of getting to Heaven, at last—
I'm going, all along.

328

EMILY DICKINSON

A Bird came down the Walk—
He did not know I saw—
He bit an Angleworm in halves
And ate the fellow, raw,

And then he drank a Dew
From a convenient Grass—
And then hopped sidewise to the Wall
To let a Beetle pass—

He glanced with rapid eyes
That hurried all around—   10
They looked like frightened Beads, I thought—
He stirred his Velvet Head

Like one in danger, Cautious,
I offered him a Crumb
And he unrolled his feathers
And rowed him softer home—

Than Oars divide the Ocean,
Too silver for a seam—
Or Butterflies, off Banks of Noon
Leap, plashless as they swim.   20

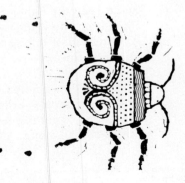

441

EMILY DICKINSON

This is my letter to the World
That never wrote to Me—
The simple News that Nature told—
With tender Majesty

Her Message is committed
To Hands I cannot see—
For love of Her—Sweet—countrymen—
Judge tenderly—of Me

465

EMILY DICKINSON

I heard a Fly buzz—when I died—
The Stillness in the Room
Was like the Stillness in the Air—
Between the Heaves of Storm—

The Eyes around—had wrung them dry—
And Breaths were gathering firm
For that last Onset—when the King
Be witnessed—in the Room—

I willed my Keepsakes—Signed away
What portion of me be   10
Assignable—and then it was
There interposed a Fly—

With Blue—uncertain stumbling Buzz—
Between the light—and me—
And then the Windows failed—and then
I could not see to see—

712

EMILY DICKINSON

Because I could not stop for Death,
He kindly stopped for me;
The carriage held but just ourselves
And Immortality.

We slowly drove; he knew no haste,   5
And I had put away
My labor and my leisure too,
For his civility.

We passed the school, where children strove,
At recess, in the ring,   10
We passed the fields of gazing grain,
We passed the setting sun.

Or rather, he passed us;
The dews drew quivering and chill;
For only gossamer, my gown;   15
My tippet, only tulle.

We paused before a house that seemed
A swelling of the ground;
The roof was scarcely visible.
The cornice, in the ground.   20

Since then, 'tis centuries, and yet
Feels shorter than the day
I first surmised the horses' heads
Were toward eternity.

Considerations

1. What sort of a character is Death in this poem? In what mood did she
   accompany him?
2. Is there irony in the poet's use of "kindly" and "civility"? Or does she
   mean that death brings a certain relief?
3. What is the implication of the description of school children at play in
   the third stanza? Or are they at play?

4. At what point do you realize that the speaker has passed from life to death?
5. Rhyme makes only a slight contribution to the poetic beauty of this poem. What other devices does Emily Dickinson use for poetic effect? In what way is the rhythm appropriate to the subject?
6. Compare this poem with Ransom's "Bells for John Whiteside's Daughter" (p. 521) and Roethke's "Elegy for Jane" (p. 561). Is Miss Dickinson's view of death more dated, more sentimental? How might she have responded to Dylan Thomas' "Do Not Go Gentle into That Good Night" (p. 582)?

986

EMILY DICKINSON

A narrow Fellow in the Grass
Occasionally rides—
You may have met Him—did you not
His notice sudden is—

The Grass divides as with a Comb—
A spotted shaft is seen—
And then it closes at your feet
And opens further on—

He likes a Boggy Acre
A Floor too cool for Corn—   10
Yet when a Boy, and Barefoot—
I more than once at Noon
Have passed, I thought, a Whip lash
Unbraiding in the Sun
When stooping to secure it
It wrinkled, and was gone—

Several of Nature's People
I know, and they know me—
I feel for them a transport
Of cordiality—   20

But never met this Fellow
Attended, or alone
Without a tighter breathing
And Zero at the Bone—

Considerations

1. If you compare this poem with "Sir Patrick Spens" (p. 357) you will
   discover that it is written in ballad-like stanzas called common meter
   (a stanza pattern also frequently found in old Protestant hymns). Do
   any of Miss Dickinson's other poems in this book have the same
   pattern? How do these poems differ from the traditional ballad?
2. As with almost all great artists, Emily Dickinson was not afraid to
   break the rules of tradition. For example, her meter is not always
   consistent. Her critics say this is a fault; her defenders believe it is a
   virtue. Often her rhymes are approximate rhymes rather than true
   rhymes. Do you think she deliberately avoided the true rhymes such
   as *abides, guides,* or *hides* that could have been used at the end of line
   4? If so, why might she have done so?
3. Compare this description of an encounter with a snake with that of
   Lawrence (p. 496) and Roethke (p. 563). Despite stylistic differences,
   do the three poems convey essentially the same message? Why would
   three such dissimilar poets find a snake a fit subject for poetry?

1207

EMILY DICKINSON

He preached upon "Breadth" till it argued him narrow—
The Broad are too broad to define
And of "Truth" until it proclaimed him a Liar—
The Truth never flaunted a Sign—

Simplicity fled from his counterfeit presence
As Gold the Pyrites would shun—
What confusion would cover the innocent Jesus
To meet so enabled a Man!

1463

EMILY DICKINSON

A Route of Evanescence
With a revolving Wheel—
A Resonance of Emerald—
A Rush of Cochineal—
And every Blossom on the Bush
Adjusts its tumbled Head—
The mail from Tunis, probably,
An easy Morning's Ride—

1755

EMILY DICKINSON

To make a prairie it takes a clover and one bee,
One clover, and a bee,
And revery.
The revery alone will do,
If bees are few.

The Man He Killed

THOMAS HARDY

"Had he and I but met
By some old ancient inn,
We should have sat us down to wet
Right many a nipperkin!

"But ranged as infantry,
And staring face to face,
I shot at him as he at me,
And killed him in his place.

"I shot him dead because—
Because he was my foe,
Just so—my foe of course he was;
That's clear enough; although

"He thought he'd 'list, perhaps,
Off-hand like—just as I—
Was out of work—had sold his traps—
No other reason why.

"Yes; quaint and curious war is!
You shoot a fellow down
You'd treat if met where any bar is,
Or help to half-a-crown."

Considerations

1. Hardy is best known as a novelist who wrote about life in the English midlands. His books express a pessimistic philosophy, a view of man as the pawn of fate. Does "The Man He Killed" convey this attitude?
2. Does it seem possible that the killer could ever have contemplated the solution that is the subject of Shapiro's "The Conscientious Objector" (p. 571)? Or would he have had more in common with the soldiers described in Jarrell's "Eighth Air Force" (p. 586)?

Spring and Fall

GERARD MANLEY HOPKINS

Márgarét, are you grieving
Over Goldengrove unleaving?
Leáves, líke the things of man, you
With your fresh thoughts care for, can you?
Ah! ás the heart grows older
It will come to such sights colder   5
By and by, nor spare a sigh
Though worlds of wanwood leafmeal lie;
And yet you wíll weep and know why.
Now no matter, child, the name:
Sórrow's spríngs áre the same,   10
Nor mouth had, no nor mind, expressed
What heart heard of, ghost guessed:
It ís the blight man was born for,
It is Margaret you mourn for.

Considerations

1. In "Spring and Fall" the speaker addresses Margaret as though she were younger and less knowledgeable. What universal experience is being discussed here? What do the last two lines mean?
2. Hopkins often included accents to make sure that the lines were properly read. Would you have accented the same words anyway, or do the accents influence the interpretation of the lines?
3. Since Hopkins was a Jesuit priest, his poetry usually involves some theological message. Is that true of this poem?

Reprinted from POEMS (1918). By permission of the Oxford University Press.

Pied Beauty

GERARD MANLEY HOPKINS

Glory be to God for dappled things—
  For skies of couple-color as a brinded cow;
    For rose-moles all in stipple upon trout that swim;
Fresh-firecoal chestnut-falls; finches' wings;
  Landscape plotted and pieced—fold, fallow, and plow;
    And áll trádes, their gear and tackle and trim.

All things counter, original, spare, strange;
  Whatever is fickle, freckled (who knows how?)
    With swift, slow; sweet, sour; adazzle, dim;
He fathers-forth whose beauty is past change:
    Praise him.

Considerations

The poetry of Gerard Manley Hopkins was published a number of years
after his death. The acceptance and influence it has had is due to the
techniques used, rather than the subject matter. Most remarkable was
his development of what he called *sprung rhythm,* a pattern adapted from
Anglo-Saxon poetry. Each line has a fixed number of stressed syllables
and an unspecified number of unstressed syllables. While his poetry may
appear as loose as free verse, it is actually highly formal. It is also rich in
symbols and ambiguities that Hopkins hoped would convey the color and
emotional impact of experience. What kind of religious outlook would
you associate with this poem? What purpose is served by the alliteration
and assonance?

Terence, This Is Stupid Stuff

A. E. HOUSMAN

"Terence, this is stupid stuff:
You eat your victuals fast enough;
There can't be much amiss, 'tis clear,

To see the rate you drink your beer.
But oh, good Lord, the verse you make,   5
It gives a chap the belly-ache.
The cow, the old cow, she is dead;
It sleeps well, the horned head:
We poor lads, 'tis our turn now
To hear such tunes as killed the cow.   10
Pretty friendship 'tis to rhyme
Your friends to death before their time
Moping melancholy mad:
Come, pipe a tune to dance to, lad.''

Why, if 'tis dancing you would be,   15
There's brisker pipes than poetry.
Say, for what were hop-yards meant,
Or why was Burton built on Trent?
Oh many a peer of England brews
Livelier liquor than the Muse,   20
And malt does more than Milton can
To justify God's ways to man.
Ale, man, ale's the stuff to drink
For fellows whom it hurts to think:
Look into the pewter pot   25
To see the world as the world's not.
And faith, 'tis pleasant till 'tis past:
The mischief is that 'twill not last.
Oh I have been to Ludlow fair
And left my necktie God knows where,   30
And carried half-way home, or near,
Pints and quarts of Ludlow beer:
Then the world seemed none so bad,
And I myself a sterling lad;
And down in lovely muck I've lain,   35
Happy till I woke again.
Then I saw the morning sky:
Heigho, the tale was all a lie;
The world, it was the old world yet,
I was I, my things were wet,   40
And nothing now remained to do
But begin the game anew.

Therefore, since the world has still
Much good, but much less good than ill,
And while the sun and moon endure   45

Luck's a chance, but trouble's sure,
I'd face it as a wise man would,
And train for ill and not for good.
'Tis true, the stuff I bring for sale
Is not so brisk a brew as ale: 50
Out of a stem that scored the hand
I wrung it in a weary land.
But take it: if the smack is sour,
The better for the embittered hour;
It should do good to heart and head   55
When your soul is in my soul's stead;
And I will friend you, if I may,
In the dark and cloudy day.

There was a king reigned in the East:
There, when kings will sit to feast,   60
They get their fill before they think
With poisoned meat and poisoned drink.
He gathered all that springs to birth
From the many-venomed earth;
First a little, thence to more,   65
He sampled all her killing store;
And easy, smiling, seasoned sound,
Sate the king when healths went round.
They put arsenic in his meat
And stared aghast to watch him eat;   70
They poured strychnine in his cup
And shook to see him drink it up:
They shook, they stared as white's their shirt:
Them it was their poison hurt.
—I tell the tale that I heard told.   75
Mithridates, he died old.

Considerations

In much of Housman's poetry there is a feeling of pessimism, an awareness that life is swiftly passing by. He does not, however, suggest that one seize the moment, perhaps because he felt nothing would be gained by doing so.

1. Does this poem indicate why he adopted such an attitude? With such a bleak outlook, why would one bother to write or read poetry?

2. How does the story of Mithridates, the king who built up an immunity to poisons by sampling them all, summarize Housman's approach to life?

from

A Shropshire Lad

A. E. HOUSMAN

9

On moonlit heath and lonesome bank
 The sheep beside me graze,
And yon the gallows used to clank
 Fast by the four cross ways.

A careless shepherd once would keep   5
 The flocks by moonlight there,
And high amongst the glimmering sheep
 The dead man stood on air.

They hang us now in Shrewsbury jail;
 The whistles blow forlorn,   10
And trains all night groan on the rail
 To men that die at morn.

There sleeps in Shrewsbury jail tonight,
 Or wakes, as may betide,
A better lad, if things went right,   15
 Than most that sleep outside.

---

9. Shrewsbury, the county seat of Shropshire; in its jail criminals sentenced to death were executed.

And naked to the hangman's noose
  The morning clocks will ring
A neck God made for other use
  Than strangling in a string.   20

And sharp the link of life will snap,
  And dead on air will stand
Heels that held up as straight a chap
  As treads upon the land.

So here I'll watch the night and wait   25
  To see the morning shine,
When he will hear the stroke of eight
  And not the stroke of nine;

And wish my friend as sound a sleep
  As lads' I did not know,
That shepherded the moonlit sheep
  A hundred years ago.

The Second Coming

WILLIAM BUTLER YEATS

Turning and turning in the widening gyre[1]
The falcon cannot hear the falconer;
Things fall apart; the centre cannot hold;
Mere anarchy is loosed upon the world,
The blood-dimmed tide is loosed, and every-   5
    where
The ceremony of innocence is drowned;
The best lack all conviction, while the worst
Are full of passionate intensity.

---

[1] Circular or spiral movement.

Reprinted with permission of The Macmillan Companies of New York, London, Canada, and M. B. Yeats from COLLECTED POEMS by William Butler Yeats. Copyright 1924 by The Macmillan Company, renewed 1952 by Bertha Georgie Yeats.

Surely some revelation is at hand;
Surely the Second Coming[2] is at hand.   10
The Second Coming! Hardly are those words out
When a vast image out of *Spiritus Mundi*[3]
Troubles my sight: somewhere in sands of the
       desert
A shape with lion body and the head of a man,
A gaze blank and pitiless as the sun,   15
Is moving its slow thighs, while all about it
Reel shadows of the indignant desert birds.
The darkness drops again; but now I know
That twenty centuries of stony sleep
Were vexed to nightmare by a rocking cradle,   20
And what rough beast, its hour come round at
       last,
Slouches towards Bethlehem to be born?

Considerations

1. The phrase "the center cannot hold" has been used by historian Kenneth Clarke to express the uneasy state of man in the rapidly changing world today. Does this poem offer any help in the search for stability or certainty?
2. The poem's title refers to that future time when Christ will return to earth for 1,000 years. Eschatologists of Christian belief think they have evidence that this event—and the end of time as we know it—is at hand because the restoration of the state of Israel has provided one of the expected signs. Even historians who do not give credence to such mystic predictions have noted a cyclical shape to human existence. Yeats believed in a cyclical theory of history in which one historical era dies and another opposite one is born every 2,000 years. Given such beliefs, could you make a case for this being a hopeful poem?
3. The symbols of the gyre, the falcon, and the falconer appear in many of Yeats' poems. What do they represent here? Does the "shape with lion body and the head of a man" seem to be a wholly private symbol or does it have some historical reference?
4. What are some of the connotations of the last two lines?

---

2 Related to the second coming of Christ is Yeats's conviction that the approaching end of an historical cycle of 2000 years would bring a new age.   3 Literally world spirit. For Yeats it means the "general mind," or our collective consciousness penetrating the future.

The Wild Swans at Coole

WILLIAM BUTLER YEATS

The trees are in their autumn beauty,
The woodland paths are dry,
Under the October twilight the water
Mirrors a still sky;
Upon the brimming water among the stones   5
Are nine-and-fifty swans.

The nineteenth autumn has come upon me
Since I first made my count;
I saw, before I had well finished,
All suddenly mount   10
And scatter wheeling in great broken rings
Upon their clamorous wings.

I have looked upon those brilliant creatures,
And now my heart is sore.
All's changed since I, hearing at twilight,   15
The first time on this shore,
The bell-beat of their wings above my head,
Trod with a lighter tread.

Unwearied still, lover by lover,
They paddle in the cold   20
Companionable streams or climb the air;
Their hearts have not grown old;
Passion or conquest, wander where they will,
Attend upon them still.

But now they drift on the still water   25
Mysterious, beautiful;
Among what rushes will they build,
By what lake's edge or pool
Delight men's eyes when I awake some day
To find they have flown away?   30

Considerations

1. What is the dominant tone of the poem? How does the poet create it?
2. Almost unconsciously man establishes points of reference against which he checks his place in time and space. Yeats' point of reference here is a flock of wild swans. How does he indicate that he has changed? Will he or the swans last the longest?
3. To which of our senses does the poet's imagery appeal? What are the implications of such descriptions as "cold companionable stream" and "climb the air"?
4. The number of swans Yeats mentions seems to be a symbol of some kind. A number such as fifty or sixty could be an approximation, the result of a guess, but "nine-and-fifty" is so precise that it must be significant. In addition, the swans are paired, lover and lover. Might the fact that one must have no mate be the reason for picking an uneven number? What are some other possible interpretations of the swans as a symbol?

Leda and the Swan

WILLIAM BUTLER YEATS

A sudden blow: the great wings beating still
Above the staggering girl, her thighs caressed
By the dark webs, her nape caught in his bill,
He holds her helpless breast upon his breast.

Reprinted with permission of the Macmillan Companies of New York, London, Canada, and M. B. Yeats from COLLECTED POEMS by William Butler Yeats. Copyright 1928 by The Macmillan Company, renewed 1956 by Bertha Georgie Yeats.

How can those terrified vague fingers push
The feathered glory from her loosening thighs?
And how can body, laid in that white rush,
But feel the strange heart beating where it lies?

A shudder in the loins engenders there
The broken wall, the burning roof and tower   10
And Agamemnon dead:
                Being so caught up,
So mastered by the brute blood of the air,
Did she put on his knowledge with his power
Before the indifferent beak could let her drop?

Considerations

The poem deals with a sexual union and the resulting offspring.
According to Greek legend, Zeus disguised himself as a swan and
seduced Leda, a very beautiful Greek maiden. Eventually, (on separate
occasions) Leda gave birth to four children: the twins, Castor and Pollux;
Helen, the central figure in the Trojan War; and Clytemnestra, the wife
and murderer of Agamemnon, a victor in the war.

1. This poem can be read in many ways. What do the end products of
   power combined with beauty seem to be?
2. Is there an implication by the use of the word "could" in the last line
   that man has seized something—knowledge and perhaps even immortality—that the gods did not intend to give?
3. Is this a sonnet?

Non Sum Qualis Eram Bonae
Sub Regno Cynarae

ERNEST DOWSON

Non sum qualis eram bonae
sub regno Cynarae

Last night, ah, yesternight, betwixt her lips and mine
  There fell thy shadow, Cynara! thy breath was shed
Upon my soul between the kisses and the wine;
And I was desolate and sick of an old passion,
  Yea, I was desolate and bow'd my head:
I have been faithful to thee, Cynara! in my fashion.

All night upon mine heart I felt her warm heart beat,
Night-long within mine arms in love and sleep she lay;
Surely the kisses of her bought red mouth were sweet;
But I was desolate and sick of an old passion,
    When I awoke and found the dawn was gray:
I have been faithful to Thee, Cynara! in my fashion.

I have forgot much, Cynara! gone with the wind,
Flung roses, roses, riotously with the throng,
Dancing, to put thy pale lost lilies out of mind;
But I was desolate and sick of an old passion,
    Yea, all the time, because the dance was long:
I have been faithful to thee, Cynara! in my fashion.

I cried for madder music and for stronger wine,
But when the feast is finish'd and the lamps expire,
Then falls thy shadow, Cynara! the night is thine;
And I am desolate and sick of an old passion,
    Yea, hungry for the lips of my desire:
I have been faithful to thee, Cynara! in my fashion.

Considerations

1. The title, which is an elaboration on a quotation from the Roman
   writer, Horace, suggests that the speaker has not been the same since
   Cynara left. Are there any clues as to when or where the poem is set?
   Are there several ways of interpreting the tone of the line "I have
   been faithful to thee, Cynara! in my fashion"? How do you think the
   poet meant the line?
2. Lines 4 and 6 in each verse are the same. Can you suggest a reason for
   this?
3. Compare this to Nims' "Love Poem" (p. 573). If you were a woman,
   which would you rather have written about you?

The Village Atheist

EDGAR LEE MASTERS

Ye young debaters over the doctrine
Of the soul's immortality,
I who lie here was the village atheist,
Talkative, contentious, versed in the arguments
Of the infidels.
But through a long sickness
Coughing myself to death
I read the *Upanishads* and the poetry of Jesus.
And they lighted a torch of hope and intuition
And desire which the Shadow,   10
Leading me swiftly through the caverns of darkness,
Could not extinguish.
Listen to me, ye who live in the senses
And think through the senses only:
Immortality is not a gift,
Immortality is an achievement;
And only those who strive mightily
Shall possess it.

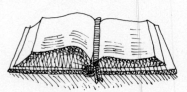

Considerations

1. This selection is from *Spoon River Anthology,* a collection of poems in which former inhabitants of Spoon River who are now dead recount their life stories. Who is speaking in this poem? Does the title suggest that his function or only source of recognition lay in his being an atheist?
2. What caused him to change from an atheist to a believer?
3. How does the figurative language in lines 9–12 present an image of what happened after the speaker died?
4. What does the speaker mean when he says, "Immortality is an achievement"?

Mr. Flood's Party

EDWIN ARLINGTON ROBINSON

Old Eben Flood,[1] climbing alone one night
Over the hill between the town below
And the forsaken upland hermitage
That held as much as he should ever know
On earth again of home, paused warily.   5
The road was his with not a native near;
And Eben, having leisure, said aloud,
For no man else in Tilbury Town[2] to hear:
"Well, Mr. Flood, we have the harvest moon
Again, and we may not have many more;   10
The bird is on the wing, the poet says,
And you and I have said it here before.
Drink to the bird." He raised up to the light
The jug that he had gone so far to fill,
And answered huskily: "Well, Mr. Flood,   15
Since you propose it, I believe I will."

Alone, as if enduring to the end
A valiant armor of scarred hopes outworn,
He stood there in the middle of the road

---

1 Ebb and flood, the passing of time.   2 Though this happens to be Robinson's name for
Gardiner, Maine, where he was reared, the name is of no consequence.

Like Roland's ghost winding a silent horn.[3]   20
Below him, in the town among the trees,
Where friends of other days had honored him,
A phantom salutation of the dead
Rang thinly till old Eben's eyes were dim.

Then, as a mother lays her sleeping child   25
Down tenderly, fearing it may awake,
He set the jug down slowly at his feet
With trembling care, knowing that most things break;
And only when assured that on firm earth
It stood, as the uncertain lives of men   30
Assuredly did not, he paced away,
And with his hand extended paused again:

"Well, Mr. Flood, we have not met like this
In a long time; and many a change has come
To both of us, I fear, since last it was   35
We had a drop together. Welcome home!"
Convivially returning with himself,
Again he raised the jug up to the light;
And with an acquiescent quaver said:
"Well, Mr. Flood, if you insist, I might.   40

"Only a very little, Mr. Flood—
For auld lang syne. No more sir; that will do."
So, for the time, apparently it did,
And Eben evidently thought so too;
For soon amid the silver loneliness   45
Of night he lifted up his voice and sang,
Secure, with only two moons listening,
Until the whole harmonious landscape rang—

"For auld lang syne." The weary throat gave out,
The last word wavered, and the song was done.   50
He raised again the jug regretfully
And shook his head, and was again alone.
There was not much that was ahead of him,
And there was nothing in the town below—
Where strangers would have shut the many doors   55
That many friends had opened long ago.

---

3 Hero of the tales in the Charlemagne cycle; the defender of the Christians against the
Saracens. The implication in ll. 19–20 is that Eben, like Roland, sounds his horn only to
find his friends dead.

Considerations

Much of Robinson's poetry is suffused with a quiet, understated cynicism. His characters seem to meet the worst that life has to offer; there is even a hint that that is all life has to offer. He writes of men who feel strangely out of step with the time and place in which they live, of individuals with an unexplained psychological weakness, of those who have outlived their friends. Each plays a role, living off illusions and fantasies as long as he can. Pretense is a burden, but isn't it better than admitting that life is basically lonely and bleak?

1. Who is Mr. Flood? Why does he live alone? What takes place in the poem?
2. How do you feel toward Mr. Flood? What determines your attitude?
3. Does the poem give you insight into old people's loneliness? Can you imagine yourself in Mr. Flood's situation?
4. Throughout the poem there is a strong sense of isolation and movement toward death. What images does the poet use to create this impression? What do the occasional touches of humor add to the tone of the poem?
5. Does it contribute anything to your understanding of the poem to know that the bird and the jug that appear in the opening stanza are allusions to "The Rubiayat of Omar Khayyam"?
6. In what way is the poem's title ironic?

Richard Cory

EDWIN ARLINGTON ROBINSON

Whenever Richard Cory went down town,
We people on the pavement looked at him:
He was a gentleman from sole to crown,
Clean favored, and imperially slim.

And he was always quietly arrayed,
And he was always human when he talked;
But still he fluttered pulses when he said,
"Good-morning," and he glittered when he walked.

And he was rich—yes, richer than a king—
And admirably schooled in every grace:
In fine, we thought that he was everything
To make us wish that we were in his place.

So on we worked, and waited for the light,
And went without the meat, and cursed the bread;
And Richard Cory, one calm summer night,
Went home and put a bullet through his head.

Richard Cory is reprinted by permission of Charles Scribner's Sons from THE CHILDREN OF THE NIGHT by Edwin Arlington Robinson (1897).

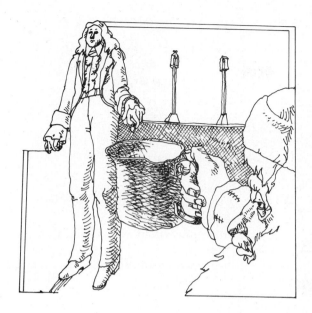

Karma

EDWIN ARLINGTON ROBINSON

Christmas was in the air and all was well
With him, but for a few confusing flaws
In divers of God's images. Because
A friend of his would neither buy nor sell
Was he to answer for the axe that fell?   5
He pondered; and the reason for it was,
Partly, a slowly freezing Santa Claus
Upon the corner, with his beard and bell.

Acknowledging an improvident surprise,
He magnified a fancy that he wished   10
The friend whom he had wrecked were here again.
Not sure of that, he found a compromise;
And from the fulness of his heart he fished
A dime for Jesus who died for men.

Reprinted with permission of Macmillan Publishing Co., Inc. from COLLECTED POEMS by Edwin Arlington Robinson.
Copyright 1925 by Edwin Arlington Robinson, renewed 1953 by Ruth Nivison and Barbara R. Holt.

from

War Is Kind

STEPHEN CRANE

III

To the maiden
The sea was blue meadow,
Alive with little froth-people
Singing.
To the sailor, wrecked,
The sea was dead grey walls
Superlative in vacancy,
Upon which nevertheless at fateful time
Was written
The grim hatred of nature.

from

War Is Kind:

STEPHEN CRANE

XXI

A man said to the universe:
"Sir, I exist!"
"However," replied the universe,
"The fact has not created in me
A sense of obligation."

Reprinted from THE COLLECTED POEMS OF STEPHEN CRANE. By permission of Alfred A. Knopf, Inc.

from

The Black Riders

STEPHEN CRANE

III

In the desert
I saw a creature, naked, bestial,
Who, squatting upon the ground,
Held his heart in his hands,
And ate of it.
I said, "Is it good, friend?"
"It is bitter—bitter," he answered.
"But I like it
Because it is bitter,
And because it is my heart."

from

The Black Riders

STEPHEN CRANE

XXIV

I saw a man pursuing the horizon;
Round and round they sped.
I was disturbed at this;
I accosted the man.
"It is futile," I said,
"You can never—"

"You lie," he cried,
And ran on.

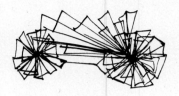

from

The Black Riders

STEPHEN CRANE

XLVII

"Think as I think," said a man,
"Or you are abominably wicked;
You are a toad."
And after I had thought of it,
I said, "I will, then, be a toad."

from

The Black Riders

STEPHEN CRANE

XLVIII

Once there was a man—
Oh, so wise!
In all drink
He detected the bitter,
And in all touch
He found the sting,
At last he cried thus:
"There is nothing—
No life,
No joy,
No pain—
There is nothing save opinion,
And opinion be damned."

When It Is Given You
To Find a Smile

ENRIQUE GONZALEZ MARTÍNEZ

When it is given you to find a smile
in the tenuous drop of moisture by
the porous stone distilled, in the mist,
in the sun, in the bird and in the wind;

when nothing to your eyes remains inert,
or formless, or colourless, or remote,
and when you penetrate the mystery
and the life of silence, dark and death;

when to the different courses of the cosmos
your gaze extends, and your own effort is
the effort of a powerful microscope
bringing into view invisible worlds;

then in the blazing conflagration of
an infinite and superhuman love,
with the Saint of Assisi you will say
brother to tree and cloud and savage beast.

You will feel in the unnumbered throng
of things and beings the being that is yours;
you will be all terror with the abyss
and with the summit you will be all pride.

The ignoble dust will stir your love
that maculates the whiteness of the lily,
your blessing will be on the sandy beaches,
your adoration for the insect's flight;

and you will kiss the talon of the thorn
and the dahlia's silken draperies. . . .
And you will piously put off your sandals
in order not to bruise the wayside stones.

Reprinted from AN ANTHOLOGY OF MEXICAN POETRY compiled by Octavio Paz and translated by Samuel Beckett.
By permission of Indiana University Press.

Sympathy

PAUL LAURENCE DUNBAR

I know what the caged bird feels, alas!
When the sun is bright on the upland slopes;
When the wind stirs soft through the springing grass
And the river flows like a stream of glass;
When the first bird sings and the first bud opes,
And the faint perfume from its chalice steals—
I know what the caged bird feels!

I know why he beats his wing!
Till its blood is red on the cruel bars;
For he must fly back to his perch and cling
When he fain would be on the bough a-swing;
And a pain still throbs in the old, old scars
And they pulse again with a keener sting—
I know why he beats his wing!

I know why the caged bird sings, ah me,
When his wing is bruised and his bosom sore,
When he beats his bars and would be free;
It is not a carol of joy or glee,
But a prayer that he sends from his heart's deep core,
But a plea, that upward to Heaven he flings—
I know why the caged bird sings!

Reprinted by permission of DODD, MEAD & COMPANY, INC. from THE COMPLETE POEMS OF PAUL LAURENCE
DUNBAR.

Patterns

AMY LOWELL

I walk down the garden-paths,
And all the daffodils
Are blowing; and the bright blue squills.
I walk down the patterned garden-paths
In my stiff, brocaded gown.   5
With my powdered hair and jewelled fan,
I too am a rare
Pattern. As I wander down
The garden-paths.

My dress is richly figured,   10
And the train
Makes a pink and silver stain
On the gravel, and the thrift
Of the borders.
Just a plate of current fashion,   15
Tripping by in high-heeled, ribboned shoes.
Not a softness anywhere about me,
Only whalebone and brocade.
And I sink on a seat in the shade
Of a lime-tree. For my passion   20
Wars against the stiff brocade.
The daffodils and squills
Flutter in the breeze
As they please.

And I weep;   25
For the lime-tree is in blossom
And one small flower has dropped upon my bosom.
And the plashing of waterdrops
In the marble fountain
Comes down the garden-paths.   30
The dripping never stops.
Underneath my stiffened gown
Is the softness of a woman bathing in a marble basin,
A basin in the midst of hedges grown
So thick, she cannot see her lover hiding,   35
But she guesses he is near,
And the sliding of the water
Seems the stroking of a dear
Hand upon her.
What is Summer in a fine brocaded gown!   40
I should like to see it lying in a heap upon the ground.
All the pink and silver crumpled up on the ground.

I would be the pink and silver as I ran along the paths,
And he would stumble after,
Bewildered by my laughter.   45
I should see the sun flashing from his sword-hilt and the buckles on
   his shoes.
I would choose
To lead him in a maze along the patterned paths,
A bright and laughing maze for my heavy-booted lover.
Till he caught me in the shade,   50
And the buttons of his waistcoat bruised my body as he clasped me
Aching, melting, unafraid.
With the shadows of the leaves and the sundrops,
And the plopping of the waterdrops,
All about us in the open afternoon—   55
I am very like to swoon
With the weight of this brocade,
For the sun sifts through the shade.

Underneath the fallen blossom
In my bosom,   60
Is a letter I have hid.
It was brought to me this morning by a rider from the Duke.
"Madam, we regret to inform you that Lord Hartwell
Died in action Thursday se'nnight."
As I read it in the white, morning sunlight,   65

The letters squirmed like snakes.
"Any answer, Madam?" said my footman.
"No," I told him.
"See that the messenger takes some refreshment.
No, no answer."   70
And I walked into the garden,
Up and down the patterned paths,
In my stiff, correct brocade.
The blue and yellow flowers stood up proudly in the sun,
Each one.   75
I stood upright too,
Held rigid to the pattern
By the stiffness of my gown.
Up and down I walked,
Up and down.   80

In a month he would have been my husband.
In a month, here underneath this lime,
We would have broke the pattern;
He for me, and I for him,   85
He as Colonel, I as Lady,
On this shady seat.
He had a whim
That sunlight carried blessing.
And I answered, "It shall be as you have said."   90
Now he is dead.

In Summer and in Winter I shall walk
Up and down
The patterned garden-paths
In my stiff, brocaded gown.   95
The squills and daffodils
Will give place to pillared roses, and to asters, and to snow.
I shall go
Up and down,
In my gown.   100
Gorgeously arrayed,
Boned and stayed.
And the softness of my body will be guarded from embrace
By each button, hook, and lace.
For the man who should loose me is dead,   105
Fighting with the Duke in Flanders,
In a pattern called a war.
Christ! What are patterns for?

The Taxi

AMY LOWELL

When I go away from you
The world beats dead
Like a slackened drum.
I call out for you against the jutted stars
And shout into the ridges of the wind.   5
Streets coming fast,
One after the other,
Wedge you away from me,
And the lamps of the city prick my eyes
So that I can no longer see your face.   10
Why should I leave you,
To wound myself upon the sharp edges of the night?

Considerations

1. What situation is being described in this poem? Where is the poet going?
2. What is the taxi's connection with what is happening? How does the poet use images to suggest the taxi ride?
3. Most of the images are built around the final metaphor. Which one is different? What is its contribution to the poem?
4. What is the emotional level of the poem? Does the speaker's crying out heighten the effect?
5. Despite the fact that the final lines are probably intended as a rhetorical question, they lead us to speculate on possible answers. Does the phrasing suggest that the poet's lover has wounded her feelings? Does it suggest that she intends to remain with him? Could these lines be merely an extravagant way of saying that she hates to leave when the evening ends?

Dust of Snow

ROBERT FROST

The way a crow
Shook down on me
The dust of snow
From a hemlock tree

Has given my heart   5
A change of mood
And saved some part
Of a day I had rued.

After Apple-Picking

ROBERT FROST

My long two-pointed ladder's sticking through a tree
Toward heaven still,
And there's a barrel that I didn't fill
Beside it, and there may be two or three
Apples I didn't pick upon some bough.   5
But I am done with apple-picking now.
Essence of winter sleep is on the night,
The scent of apples: I am drowsing off.
I cannot rub the strangeness from my sight
I got from looking through a pane of glass   10
I skimmed this morning from the drinking trough
And held against the world of hoary grass.
It melted, and I let it fall and break.
But I was well
Upon my way to sleep before it fell,   15
And I could tell
What form my dreaming was about to take.
Magnified apples appear and disappear,
Stem-end and blossom-end,
And every fleck of russet showing clear.   20

My instep arch not only keeps the ache,
It keeps the pressure of a ladder-round.
I feel the ladder sway as the boughs bend.
And I keep hearing from the cellar bin
The rumbling sound   25
Of load on load of apples coming in.
For I have had too much
Of apple-picking: I am overtired
Of the great harvest I myself desired.
There were ten thousand fruit to touch,   30
Cherish in hand, lift down, and not let fall.
For all
That struck the earth,
No matter if not bruised or spiked with stubble,
Went surely to the cider-apple heap   35
As of no worth.
One can see what will trouble
This sleep of mine, whatever sleep it is.
Were he not gone,
The woodchuck could say whether it's like his   40
Long sleep, as I describe its coming on,
Or just some human sleep.

Fire and Ice

ROBERT FROST

Some say the world will end in fire,
Some say in ice.
From what I've tasted of desire
I hold with those who favor fire.
But if it had to perish twice,   5
I think I know enough of hate
To say that for destruction ice
Is also great
And would suffice.

Considerations

This is a deceptively simple work by a master craftsman. It is as tightly written as a Bach fugue.

1. Who says "the world will end in fire" and who says it will end in ice? What is meant by these predictions?
2. What observation is Frost making about desire when he suggests that the world will end in fire? What does his personal experience of desire have to do with it?

Birches

ROBERT FROST

When I see birches bend to left and right
Across the lines of straighter darker trees,
I like to think some boy's been swinging them.
But swinging doesn't bend them down to stay.
Ice-storms do that. Often you must have seen them   5
Loaded with ice a sunny winter morning
After a rain. They click upon themselves
As the breeze rises, and turn many-colored
As the stir cracks and crazes their enamel.
Soon the sun's warmth makes them shed crystal shells   10
Shattering and avalanching on the snow-crust—
Such heaps of broken glass to sweep away

You'd think the inner dome of heaven had fallen.
They are dragged to the withered bracken by the load,
And they seem not to break; though once they are bowed   15
So low for long, they never right themselves:
You may see their trunks arching in the woods
Years afterwards, trailing their leaves on the ground
Like girls on hands and knees that throw their hair
Before them over their heads to dry in the sun.   20
But I was going to say when Truth broke in
With all her matter-of-fact about the ice-storm
I should prefer to have some boy bend them
As he went out and in to fetch the cows—
Some boy too far from town to learn baseball,   25
Whose only play was what he found himself,
Summer or winter, and could play alone.
One by one he subdued his father's trees
By riding them down over and over again
Until he took the stiffness out of them,   30
And not one but hung limp, not one was left
For him to conquer. He learned all there was
To learn about not launching out too soon
And so not carrying the tree away
Clear to the ground. He always kept his poise   35
To the top branches, climbing carefully
With the same pains you use to fill a cup
Up to the brim, and even above the brim.
Then he flung outward, feet first, with a swish,
Kicking his way down through the air to the ground.   40
So was I once myself a swinger of birches.
And so I dream of going back to be.
It's when I'm weary of considerations,
And life is too much like a pathless wood
Where your face burns and tickles with the cobwebs   45
Broken across it, and one eye is weeping
From a twig's having lashed across it open.
I'd like to get away from earth awhile
And then come back to it and begin over.
May no fate willfully misunderstand me   50
And half grant what I wish and snatch me away
Not to return. Earth's the right place for love:
I don't know where it's likely to go better.
I'd like to go by climbing a birch tree,
And climb black branches up a snow-white trunk   55

Toward heaven, till the tree could bear no more,
But dipped its top and set me down again.
That would be good both going and coming back.
One could do worse than be a swinger of birches.

Considerations

1. Compare this poem with Dylan Thomas' "Fern Hill" (p. 579). Is Frost celebrating the events of his boyhood (as Thomas does), or is he using the images of bent-over birches and youthful games to say something about the fatigue one feels as the result of life's struggle?
2. What is the relationship of lines 14–16 to lines 43–49?
3. Does Frost say in this poem why he wishes to continue living?

The Panther

A Translation by Jessie Lemont

RAINER MARIA RILKE

His weary glance, from passing by the bars,
Has grown into a dazed and vacant stare;
It seems to him there are a thousand bars
And out beyond those bars the empty air.

The pad of his strong feet, that ceaseless sound
Of supple tread behind the iron bands,
Is like a dance of strength circling around,
While in the circle, stunned, a great will stands.

But there are times the pupils of his eyes
Dilate, the strong limbs stand alert, apart,
Tense with the flood of visions that arise
Only to sink and die within his heart.

Reprinted from POEMS OF RAINER MARIA RILKE, copyright 1943. By permission of Columbia University Press.

Prayers of Steel

CARL SANDBURG

Lay me on an anvil, O God.
Beat me and hammer me into a crowbar.
Let me pry loose old walls.
Let me lift and loosen old foundations.

Lay me on an anvil, O God.   5
Beat me and hammer me into a steel spike.
Drive me into the girders that hold a skyscraper together.
Take red-hot rivets and fasten me into the central girders.
Let me be the great nail holding a skyscraper through blue nights into
    white stars.

Grass

CARL SANDBURG

Pile the bodies high at Austerlitz and Waterloo.
Shovel them under and let me work—
    I am the grass; I cover all.

And pile them high at Gettysburg
And pile them high at Ypres and Verdun.   5
Shovel them under and let me work.
Two years, ten years, and passengers ask the conductor:
    What place is this?
    Where are we now?

I am the grass.   10
Let me work.

Considerations

1. What do Austerlitz, Waterloo, Gettysburg, Ypres, and Verdun have in
   common? What names could we add to these?

2. Whose bodies are being talked about?
3. What is the attitude of the grass toward the dead? How does the poet convey this? Does the poet share this attitude?
4. There are two basic images used in the poem. Explain their relationship.
5. How do imagery and repetition help build the intensity of the poem?

The West Wind

JOHN MASEFIELD

It's a warm wind, the west wind, full of birds' cries;
I never hear the west wind but tears are in my eyes.
For it comes from the west lands, the old brown hills,
And April's in the west wind, and daffodils.
It's a fine land, the west land, for hearts as tired as mine,   5
Apple orchards blossom there, and the air's like wine.
There is cool green grass there, where men may lie at rest,
And the thrushes are in song there, fluting from the nest.

"Will you not come home, brother? you have been long away,
It's April, and blossom time, and white is the spray;   10
And bright is the sun, brother, and warm is the rain—
Will you not come home, brother, home to us again?

Reprinted with permission of The Macmillan Company from POEMS by John Masefield. Copyright 1912 by The Macmillan Company, renewed 1940 by John Masefield.

The young corn is green, brother, where the rabbits run,
It's blue sky, and white clouds, and warm rain and sun.
It's song to a man's soul, brother, fire to a man's brain,   15
To hear the wild bees and see the merry spring again.

Larks are singing in the west, brother, above the green wheat,
So will ye not come home, brother, and rest your tired feet?
I've a balm for bruised hearts, brother, sleep for aching eyes,"
Says the warm wind, the west wind, full of birds' cries.   20

It's the white road westwards is the road I must tread
To the green grass, the cool grass, and rest for heart and head,
To the violets and the brown brooks and the thrushes' song,
In the fine land, the west land, the land where I belong.

The Emperor of Ice-Cream

WALLACE STEVENS

Call the roller of big cigars,
The muscular one, and bid him whip
In kitchen cups concupiscent curds.
Let the wenches dawdle in such dress
As they are used to wear, and let the boys   5
Bring flowers in last month's newspapers.
Let be be finale of seem.[1]
The only emperor is the emperor of ice-cream.

Take from the dresser of deal,[2]
Lacking the three glass knobs, that sheet   10
On which she embroidered fantails once
And spread it so as to cover her face.
If her horny feet protrude, they come
To show how cold she is, and dumb.
Let the lamp affix its beam.[3]   15
The only emperor is the emperor of ice-cream.

---

[1] Let actuality (what is) be the end of seeming.   [2] Pine or fir wood.   [3] Let the truth assert itself.

Considerations

1. What experience is being communicated here?
2. Stevens once said, "The imagination loses vitality as it ceases to adhere to what is real. When it adheres to the unreal and intensifies what is unreal, while its effect may be extraordinary, that effect is the maximum effect that it will ever have." In this poem, which details seem most realistic? Which seem strictly symbolic?
3. Various interpretations have been made of lines 4–6, seeing in them either an indifference to the death or a following of ritual. What other meanings could they have?
4. In what ways do lines 7–8 and 15–16 connect the two stanzas of the poem?
5. Does knowing that Wallace Stevens was an insurance company executive shed any light on the images used in the poem?

Domination of Black

WALLACE STEVENS

At night, by the fire,
The colors of the bushes
And of the fallen leaves,
Repeating themselves,
Turned in the room,   5
Like the leaves themselves
Turning in the wind.
Yes: but the color of the heavy hemlocks
Came striding.
And I remembered the cry of the peacocks.   10

The colors of their tails
Were like the leaves themselves
Turning in the wind,
In the twilight wind.
They swept over the room,   15
Just as they flew from the boughs of the hemlocks
Down to the ground.
I heard them cry—the peacocks.
Was it a cry against the twilight
Or against the leaves themselves   20

Turning in the wind,
Turning as the flames
Turned in the fire,
Turning as the tails of the peacocks
Turned in the loud fire,   25
Loud as the hemlocks
Full of the cry of the peacocks?
Or was it a cry against the hemlocks?

Out of the window,
I saw how the planets gathered   30
Like the leaves themselves
Turning in the wind.
I saw how the night came,
Came striding like the color of the heavy hemlocks.
I felt afraid.   35
And I remembered the cry of the peacocks.

Considerations

1. The images in this poem include the fire, the leaves, the peacocks, the hemlocks, and the planets. Are these intended as pleasant or frightening images?
2. The cry of peacocks was once believed to be a bad omen. What is it linked with in this poem?
3. What are some of the techniques Stevens uses to create a turning, swirling, sweeping impression?

Peter Quince at the Clavier[1]

WALLACE STEVENS

I

Just as my fingers on these keys
Make music, so the selfsame sounds
On my spirit make a music, too.

Music is feeling, then, not sound;
And thus it is that what I feel,
Here in this room, desiring you,

Thinking of your blue-shadowed silk,
Is music. It is like the strain
Waked in the elders by Susanna.[2]

Of a green evening, clear and warm,   10
She bathed in her still garden, while
The red-eyed elders watching, felt

The bases of their beings throb
In witching chords, and their thin blood
Pulse pizzicati of Hosanna.

---

1 Peter Quince is the carpenter in Shakespeare's *A Midsummer Night's Dream* who directs the play of *Pyramus and Thisbe*.
2 According to an apocryphal Old Testament story, two elders spied on the young and beautiful Susanna in her bath. Susanna, faithful to her husband, spurned the advances of the elders, who then accused her of attempting to seduce them. The prophet Daniel saved Susanna from execution.

II

In the green water, clear and warm,
Susanna lay.
She searched
The touch of springs,
And found   20
Concealed imaginings.
She sighed,
For so much melody.
Upon the bank, she stood
In the cool
Of spent emotions.
She felt, among the leaves,
The dew
Of old devotions.

She walked upon the grass,   30
Still quavering.
The winds were like her maids,
On timid feet,
Fetching her woven scarves,
Yet wavering.

A breath upon her hand
Muted the night.
She turned—
A cymbal crashed,
And roaring horns.   40

III

Soon, with a noise like tambourines,
Came her attendant Byzantines.

They wondered why Susanna cried
Against the elders by her side;

And as they whispered, the refrain
Was like a willow swept by rain.

Anon, their lamps' uplifted flame
Revealed Susanna and her shame.

And then, the simpering Byzantines
Fled, with a noise like tambourines.   50

IV

Beauty is momentary in the mind—
The fitful tracing of a portal;
But in the flesh it is immortal.

The body dies; the body's beauty lives.
So evenings die, in their green going,
A wave, interminably flowing.
So gardens die, their meek breath scenting
The cowl of winter, done repenting.
So maidens die, to the auroral
Celebration of a maiden's choral.

60

Susanna's music touched the bawdy strings
Of those white elders; but, escaping,
Left only Death's ironic scraping.
Now, in its immortality, it plays
On the clear viol of her memory,
And makes a constant sacrament of praise.

Study of Two Pears

WALLACE STEVENS

I

Opusculum paedagogum.*
The pears are not viols,
Nudes or bottles.
They resemble nothing else.

II

They are yellow forms
Composed of curves
Bulging toward the base.
They are touched red.

5

---

*A small job of teaching.

III

They are not flat surfaces
Having curved outlines.   10
They are round
Tapering toward the top.

IV

In the way they are modelled
There are bits of blue.
A hard dry leaf hangs   15
From the stem.

V

The yellow glistens.
It glistens with various yellows,
Citrons, oranges and greens
Flowering over the skin.   20

VI

The shadows of the pears
Are blobs on the green cloth.
The pears are not seen
As the observer wills.

Considerations

1. When this poem is read silently, it is difficult to hear its musical
   quality. Read it aloud instead. Are you aware of assonance, consonance, alliteration, and rhythm?
2. Do you agree with Stevens' belief that imagination must begin with
   reality? Can you think of examples from literature or art that you
   consider imaginative but which did not originate in reality?
3. What is the difference between "flat surfaces/Having curved outlines"
   and "round/Tapering toward the top"?
4. What level of diction is used in the poem? Does the poet use any
   figurative language?
5. To which of our senses does the imagery appeal?
6. What is the meaning of the last two lines of the poem?

Of Modern Poetry

WALLACE STEVENS

The poem of the mind in the act of finding
What will suffice. It has not always had
To find: the scene was set; it repeated what
Was in the script.
           Then the theatre was changed   5
To something else. Its past was a souvenir.
It has to be living, to learn the speech of the place.
It has to face the men of the time and to meet
The women of the time. It has to think about war
And it has to find what will suffice. It has   10
To construct a new stage. It has to be on that stage
And, like an insatiable actor, slowly and
With meditation speak words that in the ear,
In the delicatest ear of the mind, repeat,
Exactly, that which it wants to hear, at the sound   15
Of which, an invisible audience listens,
Not to the play, but to itself, expressed
In an emotion as of two people, as of two
Emotions becoming one. The actor is
A metaphysician in the dark, twanging   20
An instrument, twanging a wiry string that gives
Sounds passing through sudden rightnesses, wholly
Containing the mind, below which it cannot descend,
Beyond which it has no will to rise.
                     It must   25
Be the finding of a satisfaction, and may
Be of a man skating, a woman dancing, a woman
Combing. The poem of the act of the mind.

Considerations

1. Compare this view of poetry with that stated by Marianne Moore (p. 501). What characteristics of poetry does Stevens emphasize?
2. There are paradoxical implications in the use of the phrase "what will suffice" in connection with poetry. How can poetry be evaluated in such terms?

Gulls

WILLIAM CARLOS WILLIAMS

My townspeople, beyond in the great world,
are many with whom it were far more
profitable for me to live than here with you.
These whirr about me calling, calling!
and for my own part I answer them, loud as I can,   5
but they, being free, pass!
I remain! Therefore, listen!
For you will not soon have another singer.

First I say this: You have seen
the strange birds, have you not, that sometimes   10
rest upon our river in winter?
Let them cause you to think well then of the storms
that drive many to shelter. These things
do not happen without reason.

And the next thing I say is this: 15
I saw an eagle once circling against the clouds
over one of our principal churches—
Easter, it was—a beautiful day!—.
three gulls came from above the river
and crossed slowly seaward!   20
Oh, I know you have your own hymns, I have heard them—
and because I knew they invoked some great protector
I could not be angry with you, no matter
how much they outraged true music—

You see, it is not necessary for us to leap at each other,   25
and, as I told you, in the end
the gulls moved seaward very quietly.

This Is Just to Say

WILLIAM CARLOS WILLIAMS

I have eaten
the plums
that were in
the icebox

and which   5
you were probably
saving for breakfast

Forgive me
they were delicious
so sweet   10
and so cold

The Red Wheelbarrow

WILLIAM CARLOS WILLIAMS

so much depends
upon

a red wheel
barrow

glazed with rain
water

beside the white
chickens

Considerations

1. This short poem describes a simple scene. What images does the poet use? Would the inclusion of more details have enabled you to visualize things more clearly?
2. Why does "glazed with rainwater" present a more vivid image than, for example, "covered with rainwater"?
3. Characterize the language of this poem. In what way is it appropriate to the subject and the statement being made about it?
4. What depends on the wheelbarrow?
5. Note the structure of the poem. What effect do you think the use of rhyme would have had?

Snake

D. H. LAWRENCE

A snake came to my water-trough
On a hot, hot day, and I in pyjamas for the heat,
To drink there.

In the deep, strange-scented shade of the great dark
    carob-tree
I came down the steps with my pitcher 5
And must wait, must stand and wait, for there he was
at the trough before me.

He reached down from a fissure in the earth-wall in
   the gloom
And trailed his yellow-brown slackness soft-bellied
   down, over the edge of the stone trough
And rested his throat upon the stone bottom,
And where the water had dripped from the tap, in a
   small clearness,   10
He sipped with his straight mouth,
Softly drank through his straight gums, into his slack
   long body,
Silently.
Someone was before me at my water-trough,
And I, like a second comer, waiting.   15

He lifted his head from his drinking, as cattle do,
And looked at me vaguely, as drinking cattle do,
And flickered his two-forked tongue from his lips, and
   mused a moment,
And stooped and drank a little more,
Being earth-brown, earth-golden from the burning
   bowels of the earth   20
On the day of Sicilian July, with Etna smoking.

The voice of my education said to me
He must be killed,
For in Sicily the black, black snakes are innocent, the
   gold are venomous.

And voices in me said, If you were a man   25
You would take a stick and break him now, and finish
   him off.

But must I confess how I liked him,
How glad I was he had come like a guest in quiet, to
   drink at my water-trough
And depart peaceful, pacified, and thankless,
Into the burning bowels of this earth?   30

Was it cowardice, that I dared not kill him?
Was it perversity, that I longed to talk to him?
Was it humility, to feel so honoured?
I felt so honoured.

And yet those voices: 35
If you were not afraid, you would kill him!

And truly I was afraid, I was most afraid,
But even so, honoured still more
That he should seek my hospitality
From out the dark door of the secret earth.   40

He drank enough
And lifted his head, dreamily, as one who has drunken,
And flickered his tongue like a forked night on the air,
    so black,
Seeming to lick his lips,
And looked around like a god, unseeing, into the air,   45
And slowly turned his head,
And slowly, very slowly, as if thrice adream,
Proceeded to draw his slow length curving round
And climb again the broken bank of my wall-face.

And as he put his head into that dreadful hole,   50
And as he slowly drew up, snake-easing his shoulders,
    and entered farther,
A sort of horror, a sort of protest against his with-
    drawing into that horrid black hole,
Deliberately going into the blackness, and slowly draw-
    ing himself after,
Overcame me now his back was turned.

I looked round, I put down my pitcher,   55
I picked up a clumsy log
And threw it at the water-trough with a clatter.

I think it did not hit him,
But suddenly that part of him that was left behind
    convulsed in undignified haste,
Writhed like lightning, and was gone   60
Into the black hole, the earth-lipped fissure in the wall-
    front,
At which, in the intense still noon, I stared with
    fascination.

And immediately I regretted it.
I thought how paltry, how vulgar, what a mean act!
I despised myself and the voices of my accursed human
    education.   65

And I thought of the albatross,
And I wished he would come back, my snake.

For he seemed to me again like a king,
Like a king in exile, uncrowned in the underworld,
Now due to be crowned again.   70

And so, I missed my chance with one of the lords
Of life.
And I have something to expiate;
A pettiness.

Considerations

1. What clichés does Lawrence use in this poem? Why are they effective here? Is Emily Dickinson's description (p. 449) as effective?
2. The albatross referred to in line 66 is a large web-footed sea bird, which also appears in Coleridge's "Rime of the Ancient Mariner." According to one superstition, the sailor who drives an albatross away will have bad luck. Coleridge's poem tells of the dreadful fate that overcame a mariner who killed an albatross. Why does Lawrence mention the albatross?
3. In lines 11–13 Lawrence repeats the s sound as if to call our attention to the hissing usually associated with snakes. Does a similar purpose seem to influence his word choice elsewhere in the poem?

Portrait d'une Femme*

from
Ripostes

EZRA POUND

Your mind and you are our Sargasso Sea,
London has swept about you this score years
And bright ships left you this or that in fee:
Ideas, old gossip, oddments of all things,
Strange spars of knowledge and dimmed wares of price.
Great minds have sought you—lacking someone else.
You have been second always. Tragical?
No. You preferred it to the usual thing:

---

* "Portrait of a lady."

Ezra Pound, PERSONAE. Copyright 1926 by Ezra Pound. Reprinted by permission of New Directions Publishing Corporation.

One dull man, dulling and uxorious,
One average mind—with one thought less, each year.   10
Oh, you are patient, I have seen you sit
Hours, where something might have floated up.
And now you pay one. Yes, you richly pay.
You are a person of some interest, one comes to you
And takes strange gain away:
Trophies fished up; some curious suggestion;
Fact that leads nowhere; and a tale or two,
Pregnant with mandrakes, or with something else
That might prove useful and yet never proves,
That never fits a corner or shows use,   20
Or finds its hour upon the loom of days:
The tarnished, gaudy, wonderful old work;
Idols and ambergris and rare inlays,
These are your riches, your great store; and yet
For all this sea-hoard of deciduous things,
Strange woods half sodden, and new brighter stuff:
In the slow float of differing light and deep,
No! there is nothing! In the whole and all,
Nothing that's quite your own.
        Yet this is you.   30

Considerations

1. The Sargasso Sea is a sea-weed choked area of the Atlantic in which, it was believed, ships were becalmed and perished. Little escaped those stagnant waters. Pound's poem describes the ways in which this sea is an appropriate metaphor for a certain society lady's mind and life. What are some of the words he uses to accentuate either the sea-and-ships image or the feeling of exoticness and strangeness?
2. *Uxorious* means excessively submissive or devoted to one's wife. What does the use of that particular word add to the picture presented in lines 8–10?
3. Considering the final three lines, what would you say Pound's attitude toward the lady is?
4. When this poem was originally submitted for publication, it was rejected on the ground that the opening line contained too many *r*'s. Do you think this is a relevant objection? Can you find other lines in which a particular sound is repeated?

A Virginal[1]

EZRA POUND

No, no! Go from me. I have left her lately.
I will not spoil my sheath with lesser brightness,
For my surrounding air hath a new lightness;
Slight are her arms, yet they have bound me straitly
And left me cloaked as with a gauze of æther;
As with sweet leaves; as with subtle clearness.
Oh, I have picked up magic in her nearness
To sheathe me half in half the things that sheathe her.
No, no! Go from me. I have still the flavour,
Soft as spring wind that's come from birchen bowers.   10
Green come the shoots, aye April in the branches,
As winter's wound with her sleight hand she staunches,
Hath of the trees a likeness of the savour:
As white their bark, so white this lady's hours.[2]

Roses Only

MARIANNE MOORE

You do not seem to realize that beauty is a liability rather
    than an asset—that in view of the fact that spirit creates
        form we are justified in supposing
    that you must have brains. For you, a symbol of the
        unit, stiff and sharp,
    conscious of surpassing by dint of native superiority
        and liking for everything
self-dependent, anything an

---

1 A rectangular spinet having only one wire to a note, popular in the sixteenth and seventeenth centuries.
2 In the sense of a time or office for daily liturgical devotion.

ambitious civilization might produce: for you, unaided, to
    attempt through sheer
reserve, to confuse presumptions resulting from
    observation, is idle. You cannot make us
think you a delightful happen-so. But rose, if you are
    brilliant, it
is not because your petals are the without-which-nothing
    of pre-eminence. Would you not, minus
thorns, be a what-is-this, a mere   10

peculiarity? They are not proof against a worm, the
    elements, or mildew;
but what about the predatory hand? What is brilliance
    without co-ordination? Guarding the
infinitesimal pieces of your mind, compelling
    audience to
the remark that it is better to be forgotten than to be
    remembered violently,
your thorns are the best part of you.

The Monkeys

MARIANNE MOORE

winked too much and were afraid of snakes. The zebras, supreme in
their abnormality; the elephants with their fog-coloured skin
    and strictly practical appendages
        were there, the small cats; and the parrakeet—
            trivial and humdrum on examination, destroying
        bark and portions of the food it could not eat.

I recall their magnificence, now not more magnificent
than it is dim. It is difficult to recall the ornament,   10
    speech, and precise manner of what one might
        call the minor acquaintances twenty
            years back; but I shall not forget him—that Gilgamesh[1]
                among
        the hairy carnivora—that cat with the

----

1 Hero of an early Babylonian epic.

wedge-shaped, slate-gray marks on its forelegs and the resolute tail,
astringently remarking, 'They have imposed on us with their pale
   half-fledged protestations, trembling about
     in inarticulate frenzy, saying
       it is not for us to understand art; finding it
     all so difficult, examining the thing

as if it were inconceivably arcanic, as symmet-
rically frigid as if it had been carved out of chrysoprase   20
   or marble—strict with tension, malignant
     in its power over us and deeper
       than the sea when it proffers flattery in exchange
        for hemp,
    rye, flax, horses, platinum, timber, and fur.'

The Mind Is an Enchanting Thing

MARIANNE MOORE

    is an enchanted thing
      like the glaze on a
    katydid-wing
       subdivided by sun
       till the nettings are legion.
    Like Gieseking[1] playing Scarlatti;[2]

---

1 Walter Gieseking (1895–1956), German pianist.
2 Alessandro Scarlatti (1659–1725), Italian composer.

like the apteryx-awl
    as a beak, or the
kiwi's³ rain-shawl
        of haired feathers, the mind   10
        feeling its way as though blind,
walks along with its eyes on the ground.

It has memory's ear
    that can hear without
having to hear.
        Like the gyroscope's fall,
        truly unequivocal
because trued by regnant certainty,

it is a power of
    strong enchantment. It   20
is like the dove-
        neck animated by
        sun; it is memory's eye;
it's conscientious inconsistency.

It tears off the veil; tears
    the temptation, the
mist the heart wears,
        from its eyes,—if the heart
        has a face; it takes apart
dejection. It's fire in the dove-neck's   30
iridescence; in the
        inconsistencies
of Scarlatti.
        Unconfusion submits
        its confusion to proof; it's
not a Herod's oath that cannot change.

Considerations

1. This poem includes a number of words and references with which you
   may be unfamiliar. In order to appreciate the meaning of the poet's
   images, is it necessary to have seen or heard the specific things
   referred to? Does the sound of the words communicate enchantment?

---

3 The apteryx is a nearly extinct New Zealand bird with undeveloped wings; it is also called
the kiwi.

2. The poem describes different abilities of the mind—the ability to interpret, observe, use experience as a guide, imagine, and feel. Which image fits which ability?
3. In what way would substituting "brain" for "mind" alter the tone of the title and, perhaps, of the entire poem? Is the title an integral part of the poem?
4. What is the function of the repetition of words or the use of several related words in close conjunction?
5. It has been said of Marianne Moore's poetry that its approach is naturalistic, but the theme is almost always "the good life." Does this poem in any way illustrate or contradict that observation?

Poetry*

MARIANNE MOORE

I, too, dislike it: there are things that are important
    beyond all this fiddle.
    Reading it, however, with a perfect contempt for it, one
      discovers in
    it after all, a place for the genuine.
      Hands that can grasp, eyes
      that can dilate, hair that can rise
        if it must, these things are important not because a

high-sounding interpretation can be put upon them but
    because they are
    useful. When they become so derivative as to become
      unintelligible,
    the same thing may be said for all of us, that we
      do not admire what
      we cannot understand: the bat
        holding on upside down or in quest of something to

          10

---

*The quotations in this poem are from *The Diaries of Leo Tolstoy* and W. B. Yeats' *Ideas of Good and Evil*.

eat, elephants pushing, a wild horse taking a roll, a tire-
    less wolf under
a tree, the immovable critic twitching his skin like a
    horse that feels a flea, the base-
ball fan, the statistician—
    nor is it valid
        to discriminate against 'business documents and

school-books'; all these phenomena are important. One
    must make a distinction
however: when dragged into prominence by half poets,
    the result is not poetry,
nor till the poets among us can be   20
    'literalists of
    the imagination'—above
        insolence and triviality and can present

for inspection, imaginary gardens with real toads in them,
    shall we have
it. In the meantime, if you demand on the one hand,
    the raw material of poetry in
all its rawness and
that which is on the other hand
    genuine, then you are interested in poetry.

Considerations

1. Does the poet believe that the writing of poetry is superior to other acts in life? How is it different from them?
2. "Imaginary gardens with real toads in them" is often quoted as a capsule summary of the achievement of poetry. Do you think that this is the way Marianne Moore intended the phrase to be understood?
3. Would knowing that Miss Moore's poetry is not built upon accents or feet, but only upon the number of syllables in the line, help you see the pattern of this or the preceding two poems?

Shine, Republic

ROBINSON JEFFERS

The quality of these trees, green height; of the sky, shining; of water,
a clear flow; of the rock, hardness
And reticence: each is noble in its quality. The love of freedom has
been the quality of Western man.

There is a stubborn torch that flames from Marathon to Concord, its
dangerous beauty binding three ages
Into one time; the waves of barbarism and civilization have eclipsed
but have never quenched it.

For the Greeks the love of beauty, for Rome of ruling; for the present
age the passionate love of discovery;   5
But in one noble passion we are one; and Washington, Luther,
Tacitus, Aeschylus, one kind of man.

And you, America, that passion made you. You were not born to
prosperity, you were born to love freedom.
You did not say "en masse," you said "independence." But we cannot
have all the luxuries and freedom also.

Freedom is poor and laborious; that torch is not safe but hungry, and
often requires blood for its fuel.
You will tame it against it burn too clearly, you will hood it like a kept
hawk, you will perch it on the wrist of Caesar.   10

But keep the tradition, conserve the forms, the observances, keep the
spot sore. Be great, carve deep your heel-marks.

The states of the next age will no doubt remember you, and edge their
love of freedom with contempt of luxury.

Shine, Perishing Republic

ROBINSON JEFFERS

While this America settles in the mould of its vulgarity, heavily
thickening to empire,
And protest, only a bubble in the molten mass, pops and sighs out,
and the mass hardens,

I sadly smiling remember that the flower fades to make fruit, the fruit
rots to make earth.
Out of the mother; and through the spring exultances, ripeness and
decadence; and home to the mother.

You making haste haste on decay; not blameworthy; life is good, be it
stubbornly long or suddenly   5
A mortal splendor: meteors are not needed less than mountains:
shine, perishing republic.

But for my children, I would have them keep their distance from the
thickening center; corruption
Never has been compulsory, when the cities lie at the monster's feet
there are left the mountains.

And boys, be in nothing so moderate as in love of man, a clever
servant, insufferable master.
There is the trap that catches noblest spirits, that caught—they
say—God, when he walked on earth.   10

Considerations

1. Compare these two poems. Who is speaking? To whom is he
   speaking? What is the subject?
2. What does the "stubborn torch" in the first poem symbolize? How
   does its image change? What is the poet saying we must guard
   against?
3. In the first poem Jeffers says, "But we cannot have all the luxuries and
   freedom, also." Why does he consider the two incompatible? Are
   they?
4. Jeffers seems to have a different view of the Republic in the second
   poem. What images does he use to supplement the poem's title?
5. What is the meaning of the final couplet in the second poem?

The Love Song of
J. Alfred Prufrock

T. S. ELIOT

S'io credesse che mia risposta fosse
A persona che mai tornasse al mondo,
Questa fiamma staria senza piu scosse.
Ma perciocche giammai di questo fondo
Non torno vivo alcun, s'i'odo il vero,
Senza tema d'infamia ti rispondo.[1]

Let us go then, you and I,
When the evening is spread out against the sky
Like a patient etherized upon a table;
Let us go, through certain half-deserted streets,
The muttering retreats
Of restless nights in one-night cheap hotels
And sawdust restaurants with oyster-shells:
Streets that follow like a tedious argument
Of insidious intent
To lead you to an overwhelming question. . . .   10
Oh, do not ask, "What is it?"
Let us go and make our visit.

In the room the women come and go
Talking of Michelangelo.

The yellow fog that rubs its back upon the window-panes,
The yellow smoke that rubs its muzzle on the window-panes
Licked its tongue into the corners of the evening,
Lingered upon the pools that stand in drains,
Let fall upon its back the soot that falls from chimneys,
Slipped by the terrace, made a sudden leap,   20
And seeing that it was a soft October night,
Curled once about the house, and fell asleep.
And indeed there will be time
For the yellow smoke that slides along the street

---

1 "If I thought my answer were to one who ever could return to the world, this flame
should shake no more; but since none ever did return alive from this depth, if what I hear
be true, without fear of infamy I answer thee."—*Inferno*, xxvii, 61–66.

Rubbing its back upon the window-panes;
There will be time, there will be time
To prepare a face to meet the faces that you meet;
There will be time to murder and create,
And time for all the works and days of hands
That lift and drop a question on your plate;   30
Time for you and time for me,
And time yet for a hundred indecisions,
And for a hundred visions and revisions,
Before the taking of a toast and tea.
In the room the women come and go
Talking of Michelangelo.

And indeed there will be time
To wonder, "Do I dare?" and, "Do I dare?"
Time to turn back and descend the stair,
With a bald spot in the middle of my hair—   40
(They will say: "How his hair is growing thin!")
My morning coat, my collar mounting firmly to the chin,
My necktie rich and modest, but asserted by a simple pin—
(They will say: "But how his arms and legs are thin!")
Do I dare
Disturb the universe?
In a minute there is time
For decisions and revisions which a minute will reverse.

For I have known them all already, known them all:
Have known the evenings, mornings, afternoons,   50
I have measured out my life with coffee spoons;
I know the voices dying with a dying fall
Beneath the music from a farther room.
    So how should I presume?
And I have known the eyes already, known them all—
The eyes that fix you in a formulated phrase,
And when I am formulated, sprawling on a pin,
When I am pinned and wriggling on the wall,
Then how should I begin
To spit out all the butt-ends of my days and ways?   60
    And how should I presume?

And I have known the arms already, known them all—
Arms that are braceleted and white and bare
(But in the lamplight, downed with light brown hair!)
Is it perfume from a dress

That makes me so digress?
Arms that lie along a table, or wrap about a shawl.
    And should I then presume?
    And how should I begin?

Shall I say, I have gone at dusk through narrow streets   70
And watched the smoke that rises from the pipes
Of lonely men in shirt-sleeves, leaning out of windows? . . .

I should have been a pair of ragged claws
Scuttling across the floors of silent seas.

And the afternoon, the evening, sleeps so peacefully!
Smoothed by long fingers,
Asleep . . . tired . . . or it malingers,
Stretched on the floor, here beside you and me.
Should I, after tea and cakes and ices,
Have the strength to force the moment to its crisis?   80
But though I have wept and fasted, wept and prayed,
Though I have seen my head (grown slightly bald) brought in upon a
    platter,
I am no prophet—and here's no great matter;
I have seen the moment of my greatness flicker,
And I have seen the eternal Footman hold my coat, and snicker,
And in short, I was afraid.

And would it have been worth it, after all,
After the cups, the marmalade, the tea,
Among the porcelain, among some talk of you and me,
Would it have been worth while,   90
To have bitten off the matter with a smile,
To have squeezed the universe into a ball
To roll it toward some overwhelming question,
To say: "I am Lazarus, come from the dead,
Come back to tell you all, I shall tell you all"—
If one, settling a pillow by her head,
    Should say: "That is not what I meant at all;
    That is not it, at all."

And would it have been worth it, after all,
Would it have been worth while,   100
After the sunsets and the dooryards and the sprinkled streets,
After the novels, after the teacups, after the skirts that trail along the
    floor—
And this, and so much more?—

It is impossible to say just what I mean!
But as if a magic lantern threw the nerves in patterns on a screen:
Would it have been worth while
If one, settling a pillow or throwing off a shawl,
And turning toward the window, should say:
    "That is not it at all,
    That is not what I meant, at all."   110

No! I am not Prince Hamlet, nor was meant to be;
Am an attendant lord, one that will do
To swell a progress, start a scene or two,
Advise the prince; no doubt, an easy tool,
Deferential, glad to be of use,
Politic, cautious, and meticulous;
Full of high sentence, but a bit obtuse;
At times, indeed, almost ridiculous—
Almost, at times, the Fool.

I grow old. . . . I grow old. . . .   120
I shall wear the bottoms of my trousers rolled.
Shall I part my hair behind? Do I dare to eat a peach?
I shall wear white flannel trousers, and walk upon the beach.
I have heard the mermaids singing, each to each.

I do not think that they will sing to me.

I have seen them riding seaward on the waves
Combing the white hair of the waves blown back
When the wind blows the water white and black.

We have lingered in the chambers of the sea
By sea-girls wreathed with seaweed red and brown   130
Till human voices wake us, and we drown.

Considerations

1. As the poem opens, Prufrock is on his way to have tea with a lady. He is considering declaring his love for her, and much of the poem reflects his indecision and his internal struggle. What are some of the factors weighing for and against his declaration?

2. This poem is a modern example of a dramatic monologue. In the opening line, when Prufrock speaks of "you and I," however, he is referring only to two conflicting sides of himself. A battle is going on inside him, making him virtually incapable of decisive action. How does the situation at the outset of the poem illustrate his indecision? Where else do you find evidence of this characteristic, as well as his lack of confidence? What sort of person would he like to be?

3. Does Prufrock lead a happy, meaningful existence or one that is empty and pointless? What seems to be the social setting in which he lives? Is the poet making a comment about contemporary society? If so, what?

4. The opening simile in line 3 sets the mood of the poem. What is it? What is the function of the image in lines 15–25? How does it enhance the mood? What other images contribute to it?

5. Does the poem indicate in any way that Prufrock is capable of passion—sexual or otherwise? What is his response to it?

6. In the final stanzas the images of the mermaids are a dramatic contrast to those used earlier. How does Prufrock's feeling about life beneath the sea differ from the way he feels about his real life? What is the meaning of the final line?

7. This poem is typical of much of Eliot's work in that it is full of literary allusions. The Italian epigraph that opens the poem is a passage from Dante's *Inferno* in which Guido da Montefeltro, who had sought absolution before committing a crime, tells Dante his story, confident that what he says will never be repeated on earth to destroy his reputation. What bearing does this epigraph have on the poem?

Explain how the following allusions illuminate the poet's meaning:
  a) Lines 81–84 deal with the prophet John the Baptist, whose head
     was delivered on a platter to Salome as a reward for her dancing.
  b) Line 92 recalls the final six lines of Andrew Marvell's "To His Coy
     Mistress" (p. 383).
  c) Lines 111–19 refer to characters in Shakespeare's *Hamlet*.
8. The title is the only place where we find the speaker's name. How
   does his name add to our picture of him? Explain the irony of the title.
   Can the poem be considered a love song?

Journey of the Magi

T. S. ELIOT

"A cold coming we had of it,
Just the worst time of the year
For a journey, and such a long journey:
The ways deep and the weather sharp,
The very dead of winter."   5
And the camels galled, sore-footed, refractory,
Lying down in the melting snow.
There were times we regretted
The summer palaces on slopes, the terraces,
And the silken girls bringing sherbet.   10
Then the camel men cursing and grumbling
And running away, and wanting their liquor and women,
And the night-fires going out, and the lack of shelters,
And the cities hostile and the towns unfriendly
And the villages dirty and charging high prices: 15
A hard time we had of it.
At the end we preferred to travel all night,
Sleeping in snatches,
With the voices singing in our ears, saying
That this was all folly.   20

Then at dawn we came down to a temperate valley,
Wet, below the snow line, smelling of vegetation;
With a running stream and a water-mill beating the darkness,
And three trees on the low sky,
And an old white horse galloped away in the meadow.   25
Then we came to a tavern with vine-leaves over the lintel,
Six hands at an open door dicing for pieces of silver,
And feet kicking the empty wine-skins.
But there was no information, and so we continued
And arrived at evening, not a moment too soon   30
Finding the place; it was (you may say) satisfactory.

All this was a long time ago, I remember,
And I would do it again, but set down
This set down
This: were we led all that way for   35
Birth or Death? There was a Birth, certainly,
We had evidence and no doubt. I had seen birth and death,
But had thought they were different; this Birth was
Hard and bitter agony for us, like Death, our death.
We returned to our places, these Kingdoms,   40
But no longer at ease here, in the old dispensation,
With an alien people clutching their gods.
I should be glad of another death.

Considerations

1. This is a dramatic monologue spoken by one of the magi, or wise
   men, who visited the Christ child. Stanzas 1 and 2 contain the story of
   the journey. Why does the account seem so real?
2. The final stanza is devoted to his philosophical evaluation of the
   event. How does Eliot slow the poem down to emphasize the
   importance of the question in line 36?
3. Why would the birth have been hard and bitter agony for the magi?
   what does the final line imply?

The Hollow Men

T. S. ELIOT

Mistah Kurtz—he dead.[1]
  A penny for the Old Guy[2]

I

We are the hollow men
We are the stuffed men
Leaning together
Headpiece filled with straw. Alas!
Our dried voices, when   5
We whisper together
Are quiet and meaningless
As wind in dry grass
Or rats' feet over broken glass
In our dry cellar   10

Shape without form, shade without colour,
Paralysed force, gesture without motion;
Those who have crossed
With direct eyes, to death's other Kingdom
Remember us—if at all—not as lost   15
Violent souls, but only
As the hollow men
The stuffed men.

---

1 The epigraph, taken from Joseph Conrad's short novel *Heart of Darkness*, is an announcement of the death of the character Kurtz. He had gone into the Congo to gather ivory for his fortune, taking with him "moral ideas of some sort" to serve him as an "emissary of pity, and science, and progress." But in his greed, he allowed the natives to make a god of him and yielded also to other temptations including presiding "at certain midnight dances ending with unspeakable rites" that brought his degeneration and death. Before his death, however, Kurtz saw the "horror" of evil, affirmed it, and gained a "moral victory." The epigraph understood in the context of Eliot's poem suggests that we in our time, unlike Kurtz, will not cross "with direct eyes, to death's other Kingdom" because we hardly recognize the presence of the evil that engulfs us.   2 Guy Fawkes (1570–1606) was involved in the Gunpowder Plot to blow up the English Houses of Parliament, November 5, 1605; he was arrested, tried, and executed. November 5 is still celebrated in England by burning a stuffed figure of Fawkes while the children beg "a penny for the Old Guy" to buy more fuel for the bonfire.

II

Eyes I dare not meet in dreams
In death's dream kingdom   20
These do not appear:
There, the eyes are
Sunlight on a broken column
There, is a tree swinging
And voices are   25
In the wind's singing
More distant and more solemn
Than a fading star.

Let me be no nearer
In death's dream kingdom   30
Let me also wear
Such deliberate disguises
Rat's coat, crowskin, crossed staves
In a field
Be having as the wind behaves   35
No nearer—

Not that final meeting
In the twilight kingdom

III

This is the dead land
This is cactus land   40
Here the stone images
Are raised, here they receive
The supplication of a dead man's hand
Under the twinkle of a fading star.

Is it like this   45
In death's other kingdom
Waking alone
At the hour when we are
Trembling with tenderness
Lips that would kiss   50
Form prayers to broken stone.

IV

The eyes are not here
There are no eyes here
In this valley of dying stars
In this hollow valley
This broken jaw of our lost kingdoms

   In this last of meeting places
We grope together
And avoid speech
Gathered on this beach of the tumid river

   Sightless, unless
The eyes reappear
As the perpetual star
Multifoliate rose
Of death's twilight kingdom
The hope only
Of empty men.

V

*Here we go round the prickly pear
Prickly pear prickly pear
Here we go round the prickly pear
At five o'clock in the morning.*

   Between the idea
And the reality
Between the motion
And the act
Falls the Shadow
    For Thine is the Kingdom

   Between the conception
And the creation
Between the emotion
And the response
Falls the Shadow
    Life is very long

55

60

65

70

75

80

Between the desire
And the spasm   85
Between the potency
And the existence
Between the essence
And the descent
Falls the Shadow   90
    For Thine is the Kingdom

  For Thine is
Life is
For Thine is the

  This is the way the world ends   95
This is the way the world ends
This is the way the world ends
Not with a bang but a whimper.

Considerations

This is perhaps the most depressing poem Eliot ever wrote. It is an indictment not only of our civilization, but of each of us as an individual. We have drifted into apathy and stagnation; we are hollow men, stuffed with straw, mouthing platitudes. The tone of the poem is not shrill; Eliot is making a flat statement that it is a hopeless case.

1. What do the images "wind in dry grass" and "rats' feet over broken glass" add to the picture presented in the first ten lines? What is the significance of the paradoxes in lines 11–12?
2. What judgment is implied in lines 13–18? Who is doing the judging?
3. Is the kingdom mentioned in Section II the same as the one referred to in Section I? Here again the eyes represent awareness and spiritual insight. Why would the speaker want to get no nearer and wear disguises?
4. In this barren cactus land there are attempts to reach out to "stone images" for help. What tells us such help will not be forthcoming?
5. In Section IV the symbol of the eyes reappears. What does Eliot say about them now? Do lines 57–60 echo something of Matthew Arnold's "Dover Beach" (p. 437)?
6. Section V begins with a painful variation of a nursery game and ends with a funereal one. Between these songs are descriptions of polarities. What do these polarities represent? What is the Shadow that falls between them?

7. The remaining allusions are to the Lord's Prayer and the Greek saying, "Art is long but life is short." What message is conveyed by the fact that the quotations are fragments and that in one case the fragment is reversed?
8. Characterize the mood of Section V. Does Eliot carry the connotations of the second epigraph into his prediction for our future? Do you agree with his prediction?

Blue Girls

JOHN CROWE RANSOM

Twirling your blue skirts, travelling the sward
Under the towers of your seminary,
Go listen to your teachers old and contrary
Without believing a word.

Tie the white fillets then about your lustrous hair   5
And think no more of what will come to pass
Than bluebirds that go walking on the grass
And chattering on the air.

Practice your beauty, blue girls, before it fail;
And I will cry with my loud lips and publish   10
Beauty which all our power shall never establish,
It is so frail.

For I could tell you a story which is true:
I know a lady with a terrible tongue,
Blear eyes fallen from blue,   15
All her perfections tarnished—and yet it is not long
Since she was lovelier than any of you.

Bells for
John Whiteside's Daughter

JOHN CROWE RANSOM

There was such speed in her little body,
And such lightness in her footfall,
It is no wonder that her brown study
Astonishes us all.

Her wars were bruited in our high window.   5
We looked among orchard trees and beyond,
Where she took arms against her shadow,
Or harried unto the pond

The lazy geese, like a snow cloud
Dripping their snow on the green grass,   10
Tricking and stopping, sleepy and proud,
Who cried in goose, Alas,

For the tireless heart within the little
Lady with rod that made them rise
From their noon apple dreams, and scuttle   15
Goose-fashion under the skies!

But now go the bells, and we are ready;
In one house we are sternly stopped
To say we are vexed at her brown study,
Lying so primly propped.   20

Considerations

1. One definition of a eulogy is "a speech or writing in praise of a person
   or thing, especially a set oration in honor of a deceased person."
   Might this poem be considered a eulogy? How does it differ in tone
   and content from your concept of a conventional eulogy? What is the
   poet's purpose in departing from tradition? You might compare this

poem with others on the same theme, such as Whitman's "When Lilacs Last in the Dooryard Bloom'd (p. 424), Tate's "Ode to the Confederate Dead" (p. 540), and Roethke's "Elegy for Jane" (p. 561).

2. Without describing physical characteristics of the little girl who has died, Ransom nonetheless enables us to see her clearly. How does he accomplish this? What sort of child was she?

3. In line 17 the speaker says, "we are ready." Ready for what? What indicates that this statement is not altogether true?

4. The poet reveals his attitude toward the little girl's death when he says, "we are vexed at her brown study,/Lying so primly propped." (One meaning of "brown study" is "deep, serious absorption in thought.") What is his attitude? Why does he express it in such terms?

5. Is this a sad poem about death?

God's World

EDNA ST. VINCENT MILLAY

O world, I cannot hold thee close enough!
  Thy winds, thy wide grey skies!
  Thy mists, that roll and rise!
Thy woods, this autumn day, that ache and sag
And all but cry with colour! That gaunt crag   5
To crush! To lift the lean of that black bluff!
World, World, I cannot get thee close enough!

Long have I known a glory in it all,
  But never knew I this:
  Here such a passion is   10
As stretcheth me apart,—Lord, I do fear
Thou'st made the world too beautiful this year;
My soul is all but out of me,—let fall
No burning leaf; prithee, let no bird call.

From: COLLECTED POEMS, Harper & Row. Copyright 1917, 1945 by Edna St. Vincent Millay.

Considerations

1. Most of us have had moments when we found the beauty of the world around us almost too much to bear. The poet has attempted here to capture such an experience. What is the emotional level of this poem? How does the poet achieve it? Does she employ hyperbole? Does she seem more interested in conveying her emotions than in evoking a response from us? Compare this poem to "Pied Beauty" (p. 454) for a clue.

2. What is the effect of the archaic language used in the poem? Suppose, for example, that the poet had said "you" and "your" instead of "thee" and "thy," or "stretches" rather than "stretcheth." What would the effect have been? Would she have had to make other changes to fit the more modern form of address?

3. Does her use of personification alter the image of the woods?

4. Select examples of alliteration that you consider particularly striking. How important is alliteration in this poem?

A Poet Speaks from The Visitor's Gallery

ARCHIBALD MACLEISH

Have Gentlemen perhaps forgotten this?—
We write the histories.
Do Gentlemen who snigger at the poets,
Who speak the word professor with guffaws—
Do Gentlemen expect their fame to flourish
When we, not they, distribute the applause?

Or do they trust their hope of long remembrance
To those they name with such respectful care—
To those who write the tittle in the papers,
To those who tell the tattle on the air   10

Do Gentlemen expect the generation
That counts the losers out when tolls the bell
To take some gossip-caster's estimation,
Some junior voice of fame with fish to sell?

Do Gentlemen believe time's hard-boiled jury,
Judging the sober truth, with trust again
To words some copperhead who owned a paper
Ordered one Friday from the hired men?

Have Gentlemen forgotten Mr. Lincoln?

A poet wrote that story, not a newspaper,   20
Not the New Yorker of the nameless name
Who spat with hatred like some others later
And left, as they will, in his hate his shame.

History's not written in the kind of ink
The richest man of most ambitious mind
Who hates a president enough to print
A daily paper can afford or find.

Gentlemen have power now and know it,
But even the greatest and most famous kings
Feared and with reason to offend the poets   30
Whose songs are marble
                    and whose marble sings.

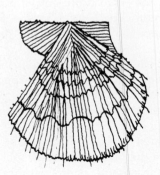

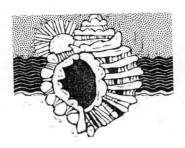

"Dover Beach":
A Note to That Poem

ARCHIBALD MacLeish

The wave withdrawing
Withers with seaward rustle of flimsy water
Sucking the sand down: dragging at empty shells:
The roil after it settling: too smooth: smothered . . .

After forty a man's a fool to wait in the
Sea's face for the full force and the roaring of
Surf to come over him: droves of careening water.
After forty the tug's out and the salt and the
Sea follow it: less sound and violence:
Nevertheless the ebb has its own beauty—   10
Shells sand and all and the whispering rustle.
There's earth in it then and the bubbles of foam gone.

Moreover—and this too has its lovely uses—
It's the outward wave that spills the inward forward
Tripping the proud piled mute virginal
Mountain of water in wallowing welter of light and
Sound enough—thunder for miles back: it's a fine and a
Wild smother to vanish in: pulling down—
Tripping with outward ebb the urgent inward.

Speaking alone for myself it's the steep hill and the
Toppling lift of the young men I am toward now,
Waiting for that as the wave for the next wave.
Let them go over us all I say with the thunder of
What's to be next in the world. It's we will be under it!

Considerations

1. This poem was written in response to Matthew Arnold's poem (page 525). Does MacLeish share Arnold's view of life and the future?
2. How has MacLeish altered or added to the sea metaphor to indicate his attitude on the subject?
3. MacLeish uses several devices, including alliteration and assonance, to recreate the motion of the surf. Where does this seem most effective?

Dr. Sigmund Freud Discovers the Sea Shell

ARCHIBALD MACLEISH

Science, that simple saint, cannot be bothered
Figuring what anything is for:
Enough for her devotions that things are
And can be contemplated soon as gathered.

She knows how every living thing was fathered,
She calculates the climate of each star,   5
She counts the fish at sea, but cannot care
Why any one of them exists, fish, fire or feathered.

Why should she? Her religion is to tell
By rote her rosary of perfect answers.
Metaphysics she can leave to man: 10
She never wakes at night in heaven or hell

Staring at darkness. In her holy cell
There is no darkness ever: the pure candle
Burns, the beads drop briskly from her hand.

Who dares to offer Her the curled sea shell!   15
She will not touch it!—knows the world she sees
Is all the world there is! Her faith is perfect!

And still he offers the sea shell. . . .
$$\text{What surf}$$
Of what far sea upon what unknown ground   20
Troubles forever with that asking sound?
What surge is this whose question never ceases?

Considerations

1. In what ways does society regard science as a saint?
2. In personifying science as a saint, what similarities does the poet draw between the two? What major difference does he point out? Why is science personified as a female?
3. What sort of questions can science answer? In what sense might the answers be considered perfect? In what sense are they imperfect or incomplete?
4. Sigmund Freud, the founder of psychoanalysis, believed in uncovering buried memories in order to get at the origin of man's problems. What question does the poet imply that Freud might be asking about man when he "offers the sea shell"? What is the connection between a sea shell and man?
5. In the final analysis, what question is science unable to answer?
6. How does the imagery of the last stanza differ from that of the first five? Note the repetition of the word "what." Why is this effective?

Indian Summer

Dorothy Parker

In youth, it was a way I had
     To do my best to please,
And change, with every passing lad,
     To suit his theories.

But now I know the things I know,
     And do the things I do;
And if you do not like me so,
     To hell, my love, with you!

Résumé

DOROTHY PARKER

Razors pain you;
Rivers are damp;
Acids stain you;
And drugs cause cramp.
Guns aren't lawful;
Nooses give;
Gas smells awful;
You might as well live.

Considerations

As might have been suspected from these examples of her work, Dorothy Parker was a well-known wit of her era. Cynicism was her stock-in-trade.

1. What is the basic element of humor in this poem? Is there any seriousness beneath the humor?
2. What does the brevity of the lines and of the poem as a whole contribute to the tone?
3. Does the speaker express positive or negative reasons for living? Might a would-be suicide's mind be changed by this poem? Why?

Dulce et Decorum Est

WILFRED OWEN

Bent double, like old beggars under sacks,
Knock-kneed, coughing like hags, we cursed through sludge,
Till on the haunting flares we turned our backs,
And towards our distant rest began to trudge.
Men marched asleep. Many had lost their boots,   5
But limped on, blood-shod. All went lame, all blind;
Drunk with fatigue; deaf even to the hoots
Of gas-shells dropping softly behind.

Gas! GAS! Quick, boys!—An ecstasy of fumbling,
Fitting the clumsy helmets just in time,   10
But someone still was yelling out and stumbling
And flound'ring like a man in fire or lime.—
Dim through the misty panes and thick green light,
As under a green sea, I saw him drowning.

In all my dreams before my helpless sight   15
He plunges at me, guttering, choking, drowning.

If in some smothering dreams, you too could pace
Behind the wagon that we flung him in,
And watch the white eyes writhing in his face,
His hanging face, like a devil's sick of sin,   20
If you could hear, at every jolt, the blood
Come gargling from the froth-corrupted lungs
Bitter as the cud
Of vile, incurable sores on innocent tongues,—
My friend, you would not tell with such high zest   25
To children ardent for some desperate glory,
The old lie: *Dulce et decorum est*
Pro patria mori.

Arms and the Boy

WILFRED OWEN

Let the boy try along this bayonet-blade
How cold steel is, and keen with hunger of blood;
Blue with all malice, like a madman's flash;
And thinly drawn with famishing for flesh.

Lend him to stroke these blind, blunt bullet-heads
Which long to nuzzle in the hearts of lads,
Or give him cartridges of fine zinc teeth,
Sharp with the sharpness of grief and death.

For his teeth seem for laughing round an apple.
There lurk no claws behind his fingers supple;
And God will grow no talons at his heels,
Nor antlers through the thickness of his curls.

Considerations

1. The poems of Wilfred Owen, who was killed in battle one week before the end of World War I, are primarily about war. Compare the previous two poems. How do the images in the first poem convey the poet's attitude toward war?
2. Observers reported that the mustard gas used in World War I rolled over the troops in a thick, green vapor. Besides the resemblance suggested by color, why else might Owen have made the analogy between gassing and drowning?
3. How is the metaphor of hunger and eating carried out in "Arms and the Boy"? Who is hungry for what?
4. The second poem illustrates Owen's use of slant rhyme. Does the less obvious repetition of sound make this poem seem more natural and conversational?
5. "Dulce et decorum est" ends with a quotation from the Roman poet Horace. The quotation means "It is sweet and fitting to die for one's country." Why is the quotation used here? Why does Owen call it "the old lie"?
6. Is the understatement, the compressed wording, and the symbolism of the second poem more or less effective than the phrasing of "Dulce et decorum est"?

American Farm, 1934

GENEVIEVE TAGGARD

Space is too full. Did nothing happen here?
Skin of poor life cast off. These pods and shards
Rattle in the old house, rock with the old rocker,
Tick with the old clock, clutter the mantel.
Waste of disregarded trifles crooked as old crochet

On tabourets of wicker. Mute boredom of hoarding
Poor objects. These outlive water sluicing in cracks to join
The destroying river, the large Mississippi; or the tornado
Twisting dishes and beds and bird-cages into droppings of cloud.
The hard odd thing surviving precariously, once of some value
Brought home bright from the store in manila paper,
Now under the foot of the cow, caught in a crevice.
One old shoe, feminine, rotted with damp, one worn tire,
Crop of tin cans, torn harness, nails, links of a chain,—
Edge of a dress, wrappings of contraceptives, trinkets,
Fans spread, sick pink, and a skillet full of mould,
Bottles in cobwebs, butter-nuts—and the copperheads,
Night-feeders, who run their evil bellies in and out
Weaving a fabric of limbo for the devil of limbo;
Droppings of swallows, baked mud of wasps, confetti
Of the mouse nest, ancient cow-dung frozen,
Jumble of items, lost from use, with rusty tools,
Calendars, apple-cores, white sick grasses, gear from the stables,
Skull of a cow in the mud, with the stem of dead cabbage
Part of the spine and the ribs, in the rot of swill mud. The
Array of limbo, once a part of swart labor, rusted now
In every house, in every attic piled. Oh palsied people
Under the weeds of the outhouse something one never
Picks up or burns; flung away. Let it lie; let it bleed
Ironic and sinister junk filling a corner. If men vacate
Prized or unprized, it jests with neglect.
Under the porch the kitten goes and returns,
Masked with small dirt. Odd objects in sheds and shelve
And the stale air of bed-rooms, stink of stained bureau
Flies buzzing in bottles; vocal tone of no meaning.
No wonder our farms are dark and our dreams take these shapes.
Thistles mock all, growing out of rubbish
In a heap of broken glass with last year's soot.
Implacable divine rubbish prevails. Possessors of things
Look at the junk heap for an hour. Gnarled idle hands
Find ticks in the pelt of the dog, turn over a plank.
This parasite clutter invades sense and seems to breed
A like in our minds. Wind, water, sun;—it survives.
The whole sad place scales to the thistle and petty litter
Neglect laughs in the fallen barns and the shutters broken
Hanging on a wailing hinge. Generations of wind
Owe you obeisance. You win. No man will war with you
He has you in him; his hand trembles; he rights
The front acre while the wife tidies the parlour.
Economy, economy! Who'll till this land?

Lady Love

Translated by Samuel Beckett

PAUL ELUARD

She is standing on my lids
And her hair is in my hair
She has the colour of my eye
She has the body of my hand
In my shade she is engulfed
As a stone against the sky

She will never close her eyes
And she does not let me sleep
And her dreams in the bright day
Make the suns evaporate
And me laugh cry and laugh
Speak when I have nothing to say.

The Naked and the Nude

ROBERT GRAVES

For me, the naked and the nude
(By lexicographers construed
As synonyms that should express
The same deficiency of dress
Or shelter) stand as wide apart   5
As love from lies, or truth from art.

Lovers without reproach will gaze
On bodies naked and ablaze;
The hippocratic eye will see
In nakedness, anatomy;   10
And naked shines the Goddess when
She mounts her lion among men.

The nude are bold, the nude are sly
To hold each treasonable eye.
While draping by a showman's trick   15
Their dishabille in rhetoric,
They grin a mock-religious grin
Of scorn at those of naked skin.

The naked, therefore, who compete
Against the nude may know defeat;   20
Yet when they both together tread
The briary pastures of the dead,
By Gorgons with long whips pursued,
How naked go the sometime nude!

Considerations

1. *Nude* is usually considered a euphemism for *naked.* Do you agree that
   there is a difference between being naked and being nude? How does
   the poet contrast the two words in this poem?
2. Do the allusions to Greek mythology diminish or increase the
   effectiveness of the poem?

3. What comment is the poet making about truth in the final line?
4. Does the fact that the poet treats the subject humorously alter the underlying seriousness of what he says?

Litany for Dictatorships

STEPHEN VINCENT BENÉT

For all those beaten, for the broken heads,
The fosterless, the simple, the oppressed,
The ghosts in the burning city of our time . . .
For those taken in rapid cars to the house and beaten
By the skillful boys, the boys with the rubber fists,   5
—Held down and beaten, the table cutting their loins,
Or kicked in the groin and left, with the muscles jerking
Like a headless hen's on the floor of the slaughterhouse
While they brought the next man in with his white eyes staring.

For those who still said "Red Front!" or "God Save the Crown!"   10
And for those who were not courageous
But were beaten nevertheless.
For those who spit out the bloody stumps of their teeth
Quietly in the hall,
Sleep well on stone or iron, watch for the time   15
And kill the guard in the privy before they die,
Those with the deep-socketed eyes and the lamp burning.

For those who carry the scars, who walk lame—for those
Whose nameless graves are made in the prisonyard
And the earth smoothed back before morning and the lime
      scattered.   20

For those slain at once. For those living through months and years
Enduring, watching, hoping, going each day
To the work or the queue for meat or the secret club,
Living meanwhile, begetting children, smuggling guns,
And found and killed at the end like rats in a drain.   25

For those escaping
Incredibly into exile and wandering there.
For those who live in the small rooms of foreign cities
And who yet think of the country, the long green grass,
The childhood voices, the language, the way wind smelt then,   30
The shape of rooms, the coffee drunk at the table,
The talk with friends, the loved city, the waiter's face,
The gravestones, with the name, where they will not lie
Nor in any of that earth. Their children are strangers.

For those who planned and were leaders and were beaten   35
And for those, humble and stupid, who had no plan
But were denounced, but grew angry, but told a joke,
But could not explain, but were sent away to the camp
But had their bodies shipped back in the sealed coffins,
"Died of pneumonia." "Died trying to escape."   40
For those growers of wheat who were shot by their own wheat-
          stacks,
For those growers of bread who were sent to the ice-locked wastes,
And their flesh remembers their fields.

For those denounced by their smug, horrible children
For a peppermint-star and the praise of the Perfect State,   45
For all those strangled or gelded or merely starved
To make perfect states; for the priest hanged in his cassock,
The Jew with his chest crushed in and his eyes dying,
The revolutionist lynched by the private guards
To make perfect states, in the names of the perfect states.   50

For those betrayed by the neighbors they shook hands with
And for the traitors, sitting in the hard chair
With the loose sweat crawling their hair and their fingers restless
As they tell the street and the house and the man's name.
And for those sitting at table in the house   55
With the lamp lit and the plates and the smell of food,
Talking so quietly; when they hear the cars
And the knock at the door, and they look at each other quickly
And the woman goes to the door with a stiff face,
Smoothing her dress.
     "We are all good citizens here.   60
We believe in the Perfect State."
               And that was the last

Time Tony or Karl or Shorty came to the house
And the family was liquidated later.
It was the last time.
    We heard the shots in the night
But nobody knew next day what the trouble was   65
And a man must go to his work. So I didn't see him
For three days, then, and me near out of my mind
And all the patrols on the streets with their dirty guns
And when he came back, he looked drunk, and the blood was on him.

For the women who mourn their dead in the secret night,   70
For the children taught to keep quiet, the old children,
The children spat-on at school.
     For the wrecked laboratory,
The gutted house, the dunged picture, the pissed-in well,
The naked corpse of Knowledge flung in the square
And no man lifting a hand and no man speaking.   75

For the cold of the pistol-butt and the bullet's heat,
For the rope that chokes, the manacles that bind.
The huge voice, metal, that lies from a thousand tubes
And the stuttering machine-gun that answers all.
For the man crucified on the crossed machine-guns
Without name, without resurrection, without stars,   80
His dark head heavy with death and his flesh long sour
With the smell of his many prisons—John Smith, John Doe,
John Nobody—oh, crack your mind for his name!
Faceless as water, naked as the dust,
Dishonored as the earth the gas-shells poison   85
And barbarous with portent.
      This is he.
This is the man they ate at the green table
Putting their gloves on ere they touched the meat.
This is the fruit of war, the fruit of peace,
The ripeness of invention, the new lamb,   90
The answer to the wisdom of the wise.
And still he hangs, and still he will not die,
And still, on the steel city of our years
The light fails and the terrible blood streams down.
We thought we were done with these things but we were wrong. 95
We thought, because we had power, we had wisdom.
We thought the long train would run to the end of Time.
We thought the light would increase.

Now the long train stands derailed and the bandits loot it.   100
Now the boar and the asp have power in our time.
Now the night rolls back on the West and the night is solid.
Our fathers and ourselves sowed dragon's teeth.
Our children know and suffer the armed men.

Considerations

1. A litany is a form of public worship, a prayer consisting of a long series of supplications and responses. For whom is this litany being offered? Why? To whom is it directed? What is the poet's attitude toward dictatorships?
2. Does the poet use literal or figurative language to provide images in the first ten stanzas? How are these stanzas a contrast to the final two stanzas? What is the tone in each portion of the poem?
3. What parts do sentence length, sentence structure, and the use of repetition play in establishing poetic rhythm?
4. Based on this poem, what is a dictator's concept of "the perfect state"? In what ways are the revolutionaries in the poem opposed to this concept? Is the action of the poem confined to one country, or is it relevant to several?
5. What is "the huge voice, metal, that lies from a thousand tubes"? What role does it play in a dictatorship? Does it have a significant function in open societies?
6. Does Benét believe that America is guilty of having aided the rise of dictators? Are we, according to the poet, in any danger of becoming a dictatorship?

The Rehearsal

HORACE GREGORY

Gentlemen, as we take our seats
In the darkened house, let us rehearse
The properties of the Western Theater;
Attention: this is item one,
Cloth of the Sun and Moon; it is   5
The firmament, see how it glitters—
Life beyond life on earth, and
Beautiful. It has been praised,
Many regret to close their eyes
Upon it, the eternal skyscape   10
Which seems to wake at morning,
To burn at noon and to unveil
A silver mask at night. We do not
Hear it and yet its changes are
The Music of the Spheres—   15
                    so much for that.
What of the others? plant life,
Animal life, the earthly spirits?
Item: a Lock of Gilded Hair
From the Head of Venus, a Tree   20
Of Poisoned Apples, a Yellow Snake,
A Hebrew Maiden and a Naked Man—

We need not name them, they
Have walked out of the sight
Of God; they share our dark-   25
Ness. Here is a White Hot
Caldron for the Jew, a Chain
Of Dragons and Hell's Mouth,
And St. Sebastian with a weeping
Eye—tears? Four Glassy Tears,   30
Four Kingly Crowns: Russia,
France, Germany, Spain, a Wreath
Of Smoke, all painted on a curtain;
Behind the curtain, the West Wind,
And in the Wind, Three Cries of Beggars,   35
The Halt, the Maimed, the Blind.

Gentlemen, this is our Gold, our
Inheritance—even the Gibbet,
The Mask of Folly and the Stake,
The Fall from Grace, the Earthly Power—⁣   40
We cannot sell it, and though
No actors come, we shall wear it
As tapestry is worn.

⁣   It is our Europe
To warm us in the cave, protect   45
Us from heat on the rocks, from
Dark, from flood, from moving mountains
Among ice, the fire of lightning,
The drifting wilderness of snow.

Considerations

1. Why might Gregory have chosen the theatre as the central image for his poem? Is this a contemporary theatre?
2. What does "rehearsal" mean here?
3. How does the poet indicate the introduction of a new thought in line 37?
4. Is the poet talking about art, the theatre, the worth of various aspects of human existence, or something else?

Ode to the Confederate Dead

ALLEN TATE

Row after row with strict impunity
The headstones yield their names to the element,
The wind whirrs without recollection;
In the riven troughs the splayed leaves
Pile up, of nature the casual sacrament
To the seasonal eternity of death;
Then driven by the fierce scrutiny
Of heaven to their election in the vast breath,
They sough the rumor of mortality.

Autumn is desolation in the plot   10
Of a thousand acres where these memories grow
From the inexhaustible bodies that are not
Dead, but feed the grass row after rich row.
Think of the autumns that have come and gone!—
Ambitious November with the humors of the year,
With a particular zeal for every slab,
Staining the uncomfortable angels that rot
On the slabs, a wing chipped here, an arm there:
The brute curiosity of an angel's stare
Turns you, like them, to stone,   20
Transforms the heaving air
Till plunged to a heavier world below
You shift your sea-space blindly
Heaving, turning like the blind crab.

Dazed by the wind, only the wind
The leaves flying, plunge

You know who have waited by the wall
The twilight certainty of an animal,
Those midnight restitutions of the blood
You know—the immitigable pines, the smoky frieze   30
Of the sky, the sudden call: you know the rage,
The cold pool left by the mounting flood,
Of muted Zeno and Parmenides.[1]
You who have waited for the angry resolution
Of those desires that should be yours tomorrow,
You know the unimportant shrift of death
And praise the vision
And praise the arrogant circumstance
Of those who fall
Rank upon rank, hurried beyond decision—   40
Here by the sagging gate, stopped by the wall.

Seeing, seeing only the leaves
Flying, plunge and expire

Turn your eyes to the immoderate past,
Turn to the inscrutable infantry rising
Demons out of the earth—they will not last.
Stonewall, Stonewall,[2] and the sunken fields of hemp,
Shiloh, Antietam, Malvern Hill, Bull Run.
Lost in that orient of the thick-and-fast
You will curse the setting sun.   50

Cursing only the leaves crying
Like an old man in a storm

You hear the shout, the crazy hemlocks point
With troubled fingers to the silence which
Smothers you, a mummy, in time.

The hound bitch
Toothless and dying, in a musty cellar
Hears the wind only.

---

1 Greek philosophers of the fifth century B.C.
2 Stonewall Jackson (1824–1863), officer of the Confederate Army, who conducted a
brilliant command in the battles of the Seven Days (as listed by Tate). He died in the midst
of battle by unintentional shots from his own soldiers.

                    Now that the salt of their blood
Stiffens the saltier oblivion of the sea,   60
Seals the malignant purity of the flood,
What shall we who count our days and bow
Our heads with a commemorial woe
In the ribboned coats of grim felicity,
What shall we say of the bones, unclean,
Whose verdurous anonymity will grow?
The ragged arms, the ragged heads and eyes
Lost in these acres of the insane green?
The gray lean spiders come, they come and go;
In a tangle of willows without light   70
The singular screech-owl's tight
Invisible lyric seeds the mind
With the furious murmur of their chivalry.

    We shall say only the leaves
    Flying, plunge and expire

We shall say only the leaves whispering
In the improbable mist of nightfall
That flies on multiple wing;
Night is the beginning and the end
And in between the ends of distraction   80
Waits mute speculation, the patient curse
That stones the eyes, or like the jaguar leaps
For his own image in a jungle pool, his victim.
What shall we say who have knowledge
Carried to the heart? Shall we take the act
To the grave? Shall we, more hopeful, set up the grave
In the house? The ravenous grave?

                    Leave now
The shut gate and the decomposing wall:
The gentle serpent, green in the mulberry bush,   90
Riots with his tongue through the hush—
Sentinel of the grave who counts us all!

Frankie and Johnny

Frankie and Johnny were lovers, O, how that couple could love.
Swore to be true to each other, true as the stars above.
He was her man, but he done her wrong.

Frankie she was his woman, everybody knows.
She spent one hundred dollars for a suit of Johnny's clothes.
He was her man, but he done her wrong.

Frankie and Johnny went walking, Johnny in his bran' new suit,
"O good Lawd," says Frankie, "but don't my Johnny look cute?"
He was her man, but he done her wrong.

Frankie went down to Memphis; she went on the evening train.   10
She paid one hundred dollars for Johnny a watch and chain.
He was her man, but he done her wrong.

Frankie went down to the corner, to buy a glass of beer;
She says to the fat bartender, "Has my loving man been here?
He was my man, but he done me wrong."

"Ain't going to tell you no story, ain't going to tell you no lie,
I seen your man 'bout an hour ago with a girl named Alice Fry.
If he's your man, he's doing you wrong."

Frankie went back to the hotel, she didn't go there for fun,
Under her long red kimono she toted a forty-four gun.   20
He was her man, but he done her wrong.

Frankie went down to the hotel, looked in the window so high,
There was her lovin' Johnny a-lovin' up Alice Fry;
He was her man, but he done her wrong.

Frankie threw back her kimono; took out the old forty-four;
Roota-toot-toot, three times she shot, right through that hotel door.
She shot her man, 'cause he done her wrong.

Johnny grabbed off his Stetson. "O good Lawd, Frankie, don't shoot."
But Frankie put her finger on the trigger, and the gun went roota-
    toot-toot.
He was her man, but she shot him down.   30

"Roll me over easy, roll me over slow,
Roll me over easy, boys, 'cause my wounds are hurting me so,
I was her man, but I done her wrong."

With the first shot Johnny staggered; with the second shot he fell;
When the third bullet hit him, there was a new man's face in hell.
He was her man, but he done her wrong.

Frankie heard a rumbling away down under the ground.
Maybe it was Johnny where she had shot him down.
He was her man, and she done him wrong.

"Oh, bring on your rubber-tired hearses, bring on your rubber-tired
    hacks,   40
They're takin' my Johnny to the buryin' groun' but they'll never bring
    him back.
He was my man, but he done me wrong."

The judge he said to the jury, "It's plain as plain can be.
This woman shot her man, so it's murder in the second degree.
He was her man, though he done her wrong."

Now it wasn't murder in the second degree, it wasn't murder in the
    third.
Frankie simply dropped her man, like a hunter drops a bird.
He was her man, but he done her wrong.

"Oh, put me in that dungeon. Oh, put me in that cell.
Put me where the northeast wind blows from the southeast corner of
    hell.   50
I shot my man 'cause he done me wrong."

Frankie walked up to the scaffold, as calm as a girl could be,
She turned her eyes to heaven and said, "Good Lord, I'm coming to
    thee.
He was my man, and I done him wrong."

Truth

JAMES HEARST

How the devil do I know
if there are rocks in your field,
plow it and find out.
If the plow strikes something
harder than earth, the point   5
shatters at a sudden blow
and the tractor jerks sidewise
and dumps you off the seat—
because the spring hitch
isn't set to trip quickly enough   10
and it never is—probably
you hit a rock. That means
the glacier emptied his pocket
in your field as well as mine,
but the connection with a thing   15
is the only truth that I know of,
so plow it.

Considerations

1. The experience described here involves a farmer, a tractor, some ground, and some rocks. But that experience is used to get at something more meaningful—that elusive thing we call truth. How well does it succeed?
2. What sort of person is the speaker? What devices does the poet use to suggest his character?
3. This poem, as many poems, can be read on two levels: the literal and the figurative. Does it have significance on the literal level? What figure of speech does the entire poem comprise?
4. In what ways might encountering truth be like hitting a rock?
5. Is the poet suggesting that one cannot know what qualities he possesses until he tests them? Could it be another way of expressing the old cliché that experience is the best teacher? Is someone else's experience of truth ever quite the same as one's own?
6. In terms of structure and imagery, compare this poem with "To make a prairie" (p. 451), "Fire and Ice" (p. 480), and "The Red Wheelbarrow" (p. 495).

Limited View-Prarie Press, Iowa City, Iowa.

Southern Mansion

ARNA BONTEMPS

Poplars are standing there still as death
And ghosts of dead men
Meet their ladies walking
Two by two beneath the shade
And standing on the marble steps.

There is a sound of music echoing
Through the open door
And in the field there is
Another sound tinkling in the cotton:
Chains of bondmen dragging on the ground.

The years go back with an iron clank,
A hand is on the gate,
A dry leaf trembles on the wall.
Ghosts are walking.
They have broken roses down
And poplars stand there still as death.

Reflections on Ice-Breaking

OGDEN NASH

Candy
Is dandy
But liquor
Is quicker.

Inter-Office Memorandum

OGDEN NASH

The only people who should really sin
Are the people who can sin with a grin,
Because if sinning upsets you,
Why, nothing at all is what it gets you.
Everybody certainly ought to eschew all offences however venial
As long as they are conscience's menial.
Some people suffer weeks of remorse after having committed the
   slightest peccadillo,
And other people feel perfectly all right after feeding their husbands
   arsenic or smothering their grandmother with a pillow.
Some people are perfectly self-possessed about spending their lives on
   the verge of delirium tremens,
And other people feel like hanging themselves on a coathook just
   because they took that extra cocktail and amused their fellow guests
   with recitations from the poems of Mrs. Hemans.
Some people calmly live a barnyard life because they find monogamy
   dull and arid,
And other people have sinking spells if they dance twice in an evening
   with a lady to whom they aren't married.
Some people feel forever lost if they are riding on a bus and the
   conductor doesn't collect their fare,

And other people ruin a lot of widows and orphans and all they think
    is, Why there's something in this business of ruining widows and
    orphans, and they go out and ruin some more and get to be a
    millionaire.
Now it is not the purpose of this memorandum, or song,
To attempt to define the difference between right and wrong;
All I am trying to say is that if you are one of the unfortunates who
    recognize that such a difference exists,
Well, you had better oppose even the teensiest temptation with
    clenched fists,
Because if you desire peace of mind it is all right to do wrong if it never
    occurs to you that it is wrong to do it,
Because you can sleep perfectly well and look the world in the eye after
    doing anything at all so long as you don't rue it,
While on the other hand nothing at all is any fun
So long as you yourself know it is something you shouldn't have done.
There is only one way to achieve happiness on this terrestrial ball,
And that is to have either a clear conscience, or none at all.

Dream Deferred

LANGSTON HUGHES

What happens to a dream deferred?
Does it dry up
like a raisin in the sun?
Or fester like a sore—
And then run?   5

Does it stink like rotten meat?
Or crust and sugar over—
like a syrupy sweet?

Maybe it just sags
like a heavy load.   10

Or does it explode?

Considerations

1. Knowing that Langston Hughes is a black poet helps us understand whose dream has been deferred. What is this dream? Why has it been deferred?
2. Explain each of the human reactions suggested by the figurative language. Why are the comparisons effective?
3. Whom do you think the speaker is addressing?
4. What contributes to the dramatic impact of the last line?

I, Too, Sing America

LANGSTON HUGHES

I, too, sing America.

I am the darker brother.
They send me to eat in the kitchen
When company comes,
But I laugh,   5
And eat well,
And grow strong.

Tomorrow,
I'll sit at the table
When company comes.   10
Nobody'll dare
Say to me,
"Eat in the kitchen,"
Then.

Besides,   15
They'll see how beautiful I am
And be ashamed—

I, too, am America.

Considerations

1. Who is the speaker in this poem? Who are "they"? How does the speaker's status change from one stanza to the next?
2. Comment on the speaker's use of "brother" in line 2.
3. What is the difference between "I, too, sing America" and "I, too, am America"?
4. Is the speaker's tone in the fourth stanza one of conviction or one of, perhaps, wistful hope? Do white people have a feeling of guilt about their treatment of blacks?

John Doe, Jr.

BONARO W. OVERSTREET

Among the Missing . . .
I think he always was—
Only no one thought to mention it before . . .

He was the boy who didn't make the team
although, God knows, he tried: his were the fingers,   5
always too eager, that always fumbled the ball.
He was the fellow
people forgot to invite when they planned a party.
After the party, once in a while, they would say,
"We should have invited John." But that was after;   10
and most of the time they did not think about it.
John thought about it: thought of the laughter and music.
He was the chap who dreamed that his loneliness
might somehow find in words a redemptive beauty:
the yearning youth who sent his poems and stories,   15
bundled in hope, to editors—found them,
paired to rejection slips, in his mail-box later.

He was the man, defeated by diffidence,
who waited in line—and who did not get the job . . .
Only war had use for him, and only   20
long enough to lose him . . .
                    Among the missing . . .

Considerations

1. Was John Doe, Jr. a unique individual? Is everyone? In spite of their individuality, are many people "among the missing" in society simply because other people do not recognize their special qualities?
2. Why do you think the poet selected this particular title for her poem? Who is John Doe?
3. What is the irony in John's fumbling the ball?
4. What does the poet communicate about John's feelings in the phrases "bundled in hope" and "paired to rejection slips"?
5. After reading the final lines of the poem, what do you think is the poet's attitude toward war?
6. The poet uses alliteration quite effectively in this poem. Can you find examples that contribute to the special sound of the poem?
7. Compare this poem with W. H. Auden's "The Unknown Citizen" (p. 558) and Howard Nemerov's "Life Cycle of the Common Man" (p. 600). Do all of these poets have similar views on the lives led by most people?

Incident

COUNTEE CULLEN

Once riding in old Baltimore
　　Heart-filled, head-filled with glee,
I saw a Baltimorean
　　Keep looking straight at me.

Now I was eight and very small,　　　　　　　　　　　5
　　And he was no whit bigger,
And so I smiled, but he poked out
　　His tongue, and called me, "Nigger."

I saw the whole of Baltimore
　　From May until December;　　　　　　　　　　　　10
Of all the things that happened there
　　That's all that I remember.

from

The Heights of Machu Picchu

PABLO NERUDA

III

Man like an ear of corn was threshed in the endless
granary of lost deeds, of squalid
events, from one to seven, to eight,
and not one death but many deaths came to each one:
each day a little death, dust, worm, lamp
extinguished in the mud of the slums, a little death with fat wings
entered each man like a short lance
and hounded by bread or by knife man was
the winner: son of the ports, obscure captain of the plough
or gnawer of thick streets,
each one fainted awaiting his death, his short daily death:
and their dreadful day-by-day ordeal
was like a black cup from which they drank trembling.

IV

Powerful death beckoned me many times:
it was like the unseen salt of the waves,
and the effusion of its unseen savor
was like halves of sinkings and of height
or vast constructions of wind and snowdrift.

I came to the ferrous edge, to the narrows
of the air, to the windingsheet of stone and agriculture,
to the astral emptiness of the last steps
and to the vertiginous spiral road:
but broad sea, O death! you come not wave on wave,
but like a burst of nocturnal clearness
or like the total numbers of the night.
You never came to rummage in the pocket,
your visit was not possible without raiment of red:
without auroral carpet of encompassing silence:
without high or buried legacies of tears.

I could not love in every being a tree
bearing its little autumn upon its back (the death of a thousand
    leaves),
all the false deaths and resurrections
without earth, without abyss:
I wanted to swim in the broadest lives,
in the widest river-mouths,
and when little by little man was denied me
and step and door barred lest my gushing hands
touch his wounded non-existence,
then through street and street and river and river
and city and city and bed and bed I went,
and my saline mask traversed the wilderness,
and in the last humiliated houses, without lamp, without fire,
without bread, without stone, without silence, alone,
I rolled over dying of my own death.

V

It was not you, sombre death, bird of iron plumage,
not you that the poor heir of the chambers
carried, between quick feedings, under his empty skin:
it was something, a poor petal of exterminated rope:
an atom of his breast which did not join the struggle
or crude dew that did not fall upon his brow.
It was that which could not be reborn, a particle
of little death with neither peace nor territory:
a bone, a bell that died within him.
I lifted the iodine bandages, immersed my hands
in the poor sufferings that murdered death,
and I found in the wound merely a cold gust
that entered by the vague interstices of his soul.

Considerations

These are three segments from Neruda's famous long poem built around
images of the ruined Inca city, Machu Picchu. Here he describes two
kinds of death: great and noble or petty and humiliating.

1. Section III examines the thousand small deaths of our urban lives.
   Which words heighten the impression of the hopelessness and
   pettiness of the ordeal?
2. Section IV has two parts. It begins by talking about a different kind of
   death. What does the use of sea imagery suggest? The second part

deals with the poet's love for his fellowmen. What keeps him from getting close to them? What does "dying of my own death" refer to?

3. Section V finishes the commentary by presenting a series of almost surrealistic images. What do the last four lines contribute to the picture of the barrenness of modern life?

Come Live with Me
And Be My Love

C. DAY LEWIS

Come, live with me and be my love,
And we will all the pleasures prove
Of peace and plenty, bed and board,
That chance employment may afford.

I'll handle dainties on the docks
And thou shalt read of summer frocks:
At evening by the sour canals
We'll hope to hear some madrigals.

Care on thy maiden brow shall put
A wreath of wrinkles, and thy foot
Be shod with pain: not silken dress
But toil shall tire thy loveliness.

Hunger shall make thy modest zone
And cheat fond death of all but bone—
If these delights thy mind may move,
Then live with me and be my love.

Considerations

1. This peom is a modern restatement of Marlowe's "Passionate Shepherd to His Love" (p. 361). How do the two differ in tone and theme?
2. What contributes to the playfulness of the poet's tone in the first two stanzas? What causes the change in tone in the final two?
3. Would knowing that this poem was written during the depression of the thirties change your interpretation of the poem? How?
4. Is the poem applicable today?
5. Are rhythm and rhyme at odds with the sentiments expressed?

If I Could Only Live at the Pitch
That Is Near Madness

RICHARD EBERHART

If I could only live at the pitch that is near madness
When everything is as it was in my childhood
Violent, vivid, and of infinite possibility:
That the sun and the moon broke over my head.

Then I cast time out of the trees and fields,   5
Then I stood immaculate in the Ego;
Then I eyed the world with all delight,
Reality was the perfection of my sight.

And time has big handles on the hands,
Fields and trees a way of being themselves.   10
I saw battalions of the race of mankind
Standing stolid, demanding a moral answer.

I gave the moral answer and I died
And into a realm of complexity came
Where nothing is possible but necessity   15
And the truth wailing there like a red babe.

Considerations

1. Why does the poet want to live at "the pitch that is near madness"? Why is this possible during childhood?
2. What does "And time has big handles on the hands,/Fields and trees a way of being themselves" say about the child's perception of this world?
3. What is the implication of lines 11–12? Did the "battalions of the race of mankind" actually ask him a question? Why was the consequence of answering "I died/And into a realm of complexity came"?
4. What is the relationship between "the moral answer," "necessity," and "the truth"?

The Day After Sunday

PHYLLIS McGINLEY

Always on Monday, God's in the morning papers,
 His Name is a headline, His Works are rumored abroad.
Having been praised by men who are movers and shapers,
 From prominent Sunday pulpits, newsworthy is God.

On page 27, just opposite Fashion Trends,   5
 One reads at a glance how He scolded the Baptists a little,
Was firm with the Catholics, practical with the Friends,
 To Unitarians pleasantly noncommittal.

In print are His numerous aspects, too: God smiling,
 God vexed, God thunderous, God whose mansions are pearl, 10
Political God, God frugal, God reconciling
 Himself with science, God guiding the Camp Fire Girl.

Always on Monday morning the press reports
 God as revealed to His vicars in various guises—
Benevolent, stormy, patient, or out of sorts.   15
 God knows which God is the God God recognizes.

Considerations

1. What situation is the speaker commenting on?
2. What is the implication of "just opposite Fashion Trends"?
3. How does the poet use rhythm to convey the impression of many different sorts of Gods?
4. What is the tone of the last line? How does the repetition of "God" contribute to it?

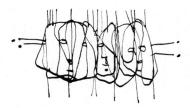

Twelve Songs, VIII

W. H. Auden

At last the secret is out, as it always must come in the end,
The delicious story is ripe to tell to the intimate friend;
Over the tea-cups and in the square the tongue has its desire;
Still waters run deep, my dear, there's never smoke without fire.

Behind the corpse in the reservoir, behind the ghost on the links,
Behind the lady who dances and the man who madly drinks,
Under the look of fatigue, the attack of migraine and the sigh
There is always another story, there is a more than meets the eye.

For the clear voice suddenly singing, high up in the convent wall,
The scent of the elder bushes, the sporting prints in the hall,
The croquet matches in summer, the handshake, the cough, the kiss,
There is always a wicked secret, a private reason for this.

Considerations

1. Who is speaking in this poem? What is being talked about? Which lines imitate conversational clichés?
2. What images does the poet use to suggest that such people feed on gossip, that they need it, in fact, to remain alive?
3. How does the pronounced rhythm, reminiscent of an old-fashioned sing-song verse, add to the impression of the situation?
4. What is the poet's attitude toward such people?

The Unknown Citizen

W. H. Auden

(To JS/07/M/378 This Marble Monument Is Erected by the State)

He was found by the Bureau of Statistics to be
One against whom there was no official complaint,
And all the reports on his conduct agree
That, in the modern sense of an old-fashioned word, he was a saint,
For in everything he did he served the Greater Community.
Except for the War till the day he retired
He worked in a factory and never got fired,
But satisfied his employers, Fudge Motors Inc.
Yet he wasn't a scab or odd in his views,
For his Union reports that he paid his dues,
(Our report on his Union shows it was sound)
And our Social Psychology workers found
That he was popular with his mates and liked a drink.
The Press are convinced that he bought a paper every day
And that his reactions to advertisements were normal in every way.
Policies taken out in his name prove that he was fully insured,

And his Health-card shows he was once in hospital but left it cured.
Both Producers Research and High-Grade Living declare
He was fully sensible to the advantages of the Installment Plan
And had everything necessary to the Modern Man,
A phonograph, a radio, a car and a frigidaire.
Our researchers into Public Opinion are content
That he held the proper opinions for the time of year;
When there was peace, he was for peace; when there was war, he
    went.
He was married and added five children to the population,
Which our Eugenist says was the right number for a parent of his
    generation,
And our teachers report that he never interfered with their education.
Was he free? Was he happy? The question is absurd:
Had anything been wrong, we should certainly have heard.

Considerations

1. What are the connotations of the poem's title?
2. What is the poet's attitude toward the unknown citizen?
3. What are the implications of the final two lines? Is it possible that the
   unknown citizen was happy?

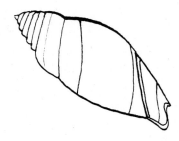

Museums

LOUIS MACNEICE

Museums offer us, running from among the 'buses,
A centrally heated refuge, parquet floors and sarcophaguses,
Into whose tall fake porches we hurry without a sound
Like a beetle under a brick that lies, useless on the ground.
Warmed and cajoled by the silence, the cowed cipher revives,
Mirrors himself in the cases of pots, paces himself by marble lives,
Makes believe it was he that was the glory that was Rome,
Soft on his cheek the nimbus of other people's martyrdom,
And then returns to the street, his mind an arena where sprawls
Any number of consumptive Keatses and dying Gauls.

Considerations

1. What sort of museum-goer is depicted in this poem?
2. What is the poet's attitude toward the visitor? What contributes to the tone of the poem?
3. What does the figurative language in line 4 suggest about the museum, its visitor, and their relationship?
4. Has the museum-goer of this poem benefitted from his visit? Do you think this poem expresses the poet's attitude toward the function of a museum?

5 *cowed cipher:* frightened zero; hence, a nonentity.   8 *nimbus:* halo.

From *The Collected Poems of Louis MacNeice,* edited by E. R. Dodds. Copyright © The Estate of Louis MacNeice 1966. Reprinted by permission of Oxford University Press, Inc., and Faber and Faber Limited.

Elegy for Jane

THEODORE ROETHKE

My student, thrown by a horse

I remember the neckcurls, limp and damp as tendrils;
And her quick look, a sidelong pickerel smile;
And how, once startled into talk, the light syllables leaped for her,
And she balanced in the delight of her thought,

A wren, happy, tail into the wind,   5
Her song trembling the twigs and small branches.
The shade sang with her;
The leaves, their whispers turned to kissing;
And the mold sang in the bleached valleys under the rose.

Oh, when she was sad, she cast herself down into such a pure depth, 10
Even a father could not find her:
Scraping her cheek against straw;
Stirring the clearest water.

My sparrow, you are not here,
Waiting like a fern, making a spiny shadow.   15
The sides of wet stones cannot console me,
Nor the moss, wound with the last light.

If only I could nudge you from this sleep,
My maimed darling, my skittery pigeon.
Over this damp grave I speak the words of my love: 20
I, with no rights in this matter,
Neither father nor lover.

I Knew a Woman

THEODORE ROETHKE

I knew a woman, lovely in her bones,
When small birds sighed, she would sigh back at them;
Ah, when she moved, she moved more ways than one:
The shapes a bright container can contain!
Of her choice virtues only gods should speak,   5
Or English poets who grew up on Greek
(I'd have them sing in chorus, cheek to cheek).

How well her wishes went! She stroked my chin,
She taught me Turn, and Counter-turn, and Stand;
She taught me Touch, that undulant white skin;   10
I nibbled meekly from her proffered hand;
She was the sickle; I, poor I, the rake,
Coming behind her for her pretty sake
(But what prodigious mowing we did make).

Love likes a gander, and adores a goose;   15
Her full lips pursed, the errant note to seize;
She played it quick, she played it light and loose;
My eyes, they dazzled at her flowing knees;
Her several parts could keep a pure repose,
Or one hip quiver with a mobile nose   20
(She moved in circles, and those circles moved).

Let seed be grass, and grass turn into hay:
I'm martyr to a motion not my own;
What's freedom for? To know eternity.
I swear she cast a shadow white as stone.   25
But who would count eternity in days?
These old bones live to learn her wanton ways:
(I measure time by how a body sways).

Snake

THEODORE ROETHKE

I saw a young snake glide
Out of the mottle shade
And hang, limp on a stone:
A thin mouth, and a tongue
Stayed, in the still air.

It turned; it drew away;
Its shadow bent in half;
It quickened, and was gone.

I felt my slow blood warm.
I longed to be that thing,
The pure, sensuous form.

And I may be, some time.

Considerations

1. What portions of the snake's anatomy does the poet describe? What additional images does he use to enable you to visualize the snake?
2. What does the poet suggest about the snake when he says "its shadow bent in half"? Why didn't he say "the snake bent in half"?
3. What is the speaker's reaction to the snake?
4. How does the poet use sound to suggest the snake?
5. How might the speaker be that "pure sensuous form" at "some time"?
6. If you have seen a snake, how did your reaction compare to the poet's?
7. Compare this poem with the ones by D.H. Lawrence (p. 496) and Emily Dickinson (p. 449) on the same creature. Which do you feel is most effective? Why?

The Bad Children

CARL BODE

The children of light—mongoloid,
Hydrocephalic, crazed, awry—
Will build their glass houses
Out of shards of pale sky
Or brittle splinters of causes.

Their names will be biblical,
Esther, Naomi, Levi, Moses,
Or else cheap blue plastic,
Charlene, Joni, Sondra, Elvis.
Their minds will be lame or spastic,

Their hearts futile. While they
Play with their impossible toys
Their parents, aching, will stand
And watch them. Outside, the healthy noise
Of other children, playing Pretend,

Joyously aping the children of light,
Will meet the ears of the wordless
Parents. And they will stop and ponder
The rich health of the children of darkness,
Who deny God. And they will wonder

(The fathers turning to the mothers),
They will wonder as they try to measure
Sure causes against clumsy effects,
Which is worse, God's displeasure
In this world or the next?

Nice Day for a Lynching

KENNETH PATCHEN

The bloodhounds look like sad old judges
In a strange court. They point their noses
At the Negro jerking in the tight noose
His feet spread crow-like above these
Honorable men who laugh as he chokes.   5

I don't know this black man.
I don't know these white men.

But I know that one of my hands
Is black, and one white. I know that
One part of me is being strangled,   10
While another part horribly laughs.

Until it changes,
I shall be forever killing; and be killed.

Considerations

1. Explain the irony of the title. Who might make such an observation?
2. It is more common to say that a man resembles a bloodhound than to reverse the comparison. Is the poet commenting on lynch law in the first two lines?
3. Only the dying man's feet are described. Is this more effective than a description of the victim's entire body would have been?
4. The word *crow* has several meanings. What are the possible connotations of its use in line 4?
5. Although lynchings are not as common as they once were, other cruel acts are still committed by white racists. Could it be that they, like the lynchers, consider themselves "honorable men"?
6. In what sense is the speaker partly black and partly white, partly the killer and partly the victim?

The Heavy Bear

DELMORE SCHWARTZ

the withness of the body
Whitehead

The heavy bear who goes with me,
A manifold honey to smear his face,
Clumsy and lumbering here and there,
The central ton of every place,
The hungry beating brutish one
In love with candy, anger, and sleep,
Crazy factotum, dishevelling all,
Climbs the building, kicks the football,
Boxes his brother in the hate-ridden city.

Breathing at my side, that heavy animal,   10
That heavy bear who sleeps with me,
Howls in his sleep for a world of sugar,
A sweetness intimate as the water's clasp,
Howls in his sleep because the tight-rope
Trembles and shows the darkness beneath.
—The strutting show-off is terrified,
Dressed in his dress-suit, bulging his pants,
Trembles to think that his quivering meat
Must finally wince to nothing at all.

That inescapable animal walks with me,   20
Has followed me since the black womb held,
Moves where I move, distorting my gesture,
A caricature, a swollen shadow,
A stupid clown of the spirit's motive,
Perplexes and affronts with his own darkness,
The secret life of belly and bone,
Opaque, too near, my private, yet unknown,
Stretches to embrace the very dear
With whom I would walk without him near,
Touches her grossly, although a word   30
Would bare my heart and make me clear,
Stumbles, flounders, and strives to be fed
Dragging me with him in his mouthing care,
Amid the hundred million of his kind,
The scrimmage of appetite everywhere.

Considerations

1. We may assume that all bears are heavy. Why, then, does the poet specify that quality in this one? What related attributes does he have?
2. What is meant by "a manifold honey to smear his face"?
3. Note the author's references to darkness. In how many ways does he use this concept? Do they all contribute to a single effect?
4. What contrasting focuses are presented in lines 12–13 and lines 14–15? What conflicting approaches to a relationship are shown in lines 28–31?
5. What is the bear and why is it inescapable? Does the quotation from Whitehead clarify this?

For Rhoda

DELMORE SCHWARTZ

Calmly we walk through this April's day,
Metropolitan poetry here and there,
In the park sit pauper and rentier,
The screaming children, the motor car
Fugitive about us, running away, 5
Between the worker and the millionaire
Number provides all distances,
It is Nineteen Thirty-Seven now,
Many great dears are taken away,
What will become of you and me 10
(This is the school in which we learn . . .)

Besides the photo and the memory?
(. . . that time is the fire in which we burn.)

Delmore Schwartz, SELECTED POEMS: Summer Knowledge. Copyright 1938 by New Directions. Reprinted by permission of New Directions Publishing Corporation.

(This is the school in which we learn . . .)
What is the self amid this blaze?   15
What am I now that I was then
Which I shall suffer and act again,
The theodicy I wrote in my high school days
Restored all life from infancy,
The children shouting are bright as they run   20
(This is the school in which they learn . . .)
Ravished entirely in their passing play!
(. . . that time is the fire in which they burn.)
Avid its rush, that reeling blaze!
Where is my father and Eleanor?   25
Not where are they now, dead seven years,
But what they were then?
                                 No more? No more?
From Ninteen-Fourteen to the present day,
Bert Spira and Rhoda consume, consume
Not where they are now (where are they now?)   30
But what they were then, both beautiful;
Each minute bursts in the burning room,
The great globe reels in the solar fire,
Spinning the trivial and unique away.
(How all things flash! How all things flare!)   35
What am I now that I was then?
May memory restore again and again
The smallest color of the smallest day:
Time is the school in which we learn,
Time is the fire in which we burn.   40

Auto Wreck

Karl Shapiro

Its quick soft silver bell beating, beating,
And down the dark one ruby flare
Pulsing out red light like an artery,
The ambulance at top speed floating down

Past beacons and illuminated clocks   5
Wings in a heavy curve, dips down,
And brakes speed, entering the crowd.
The doors leap open, emptying light;
Stretchers are laid out, the mangled lifted
And stowed into the little hospital.   10
Then the bell, breaking the hush, tolls once,
And the ambulance with its terrible cargo
Rocking, slightly rocking, moves away,
As the doors, an afterthought, are closed.

We are deranged, walking among the cops   15
Who sweep glass and are large and composed.
One is still making notes under the light.
One with a bucket douches ponds of blood
Into the street and gutter.
One hangs lanterns on the wrecks that cling,   20
Empty husks of locusts, to iron poles.

Our throats were tight as tourniquets,
Our feet were bound with splints, but now,
Like convalescents intimate and gauche,
We speak through sickly smiles and warn   25
With the stubborn saw of common sense,
The grim joke and the banal resolution.
The traffic moves around with care,
But we remain, touching a wound
That opens to our richest horror.   30

Already old, the question Who shall die?
Becomes unspoken Who is innocent?
For death in war is done by hands;
Suicide has cause and stillbirth, logic;
And cancer, simple as a flower, blooms.   35
But this invites the occult mind,
Cancels our physics with a sneer,
And spatters all we knew of denouement
Across the expedient and wicked stones.

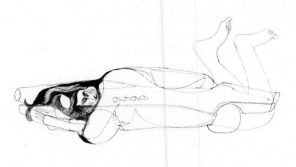

Buick

KARL SHAPIRO

As a sloop with a sweep of immaculate wing on her delicate spine
And a keel as steel as a root that holds in the sea as she leans,
Leaning and laughing, my warm-hearted beauty, you ride, you ride,
You tack on the curves with parabola speed and a kiss of good bye,
Like a thoroughbred sloop, my new high-spirited spirit, my kiss.   5

As my foot suggests that you leap in the air with your hips of a girl,
My finger that praises your wheel and announces your voices of song,
Flouncing your skirts, you blueness of joy, you flirt of politeness,
You leap, you intelligence, essence of wheelness with silvery nose,
And your platinum clocks of excitement stir like the hairs of a fern.   10

But how alien you are from the booming belt of your birth and the
      smoke
Where you turned on the stinging lathes of Detroit and Lansing at
      night
And shrieked at the torch in your secret parts and the amorous tests,
But now with your eyes that enter the future of roads you forget;
You are all instinct with your phosphorous glow and your streaking
      hair.
                                                                          15

And now when we stop it is not as the bird from the shell that I leave
Or the leathery pilot who steps from his bird with a sneer of delight,
And not as the ignorant beast do you squat and watch me depart,
But with exquisite breathing you smile, with satisfaction of love,
And I touch you again as you tick in the silence and settle in sleep.   20

The Conscientious Objector

KARL SHAPIRO

The gates clanged and they walked you into jail
More tense than felons but relieved to find
The hostile world shut out, the flags that dripped
From every mother's windowpane, obscene
The bloodlust sweating from the public heart,   5
The dog authority slavering at your throat.
A sense of quiet, of pulling down the blind
Possessed you. Punishment you felt was clean.

The decks, the catwalks, and the narrow light
Composed a ship. This was a mutinous crew
Troubling the captains for plain decencies,   10
A *Mayflower* brim with pilgrims headed out
To establish new theocracies to west,
A Noah's ark coasting the topmost seas
Ten miles above the sodomites and fish.
These inmates loved the only living doves.   15

Like all men hunted from the world you made
A good community, voyaging the storm
To no safe Plymouth or green Ararat;
Trouble or calm, the men with Bibles prayed,
The gaunt politicals construed our hate.   20
The opposite of all armies, you were best
Opposing uniformity and yourselves;
Prison and personality were your fate.

You suffered not so physically but knew
Maltreatment, hunger, ennui of the mind.   25
Well might the soldier kissing the hot beach
Erupting in his face damn all your kind.
Yet you who saved neither yourselves nor us
Are equally with those who shed the blood
The heroes of our cause. Your conscience is   30
What we come back to in the armistice.

Considerations

1. Who is the speaker in this poem? To whom is he speaking? What event in the latter's life is being discussed?
2. How does the figurative language in lines 3–6 convey a vivid image of the public's hostility toward conscientious objectors?
3. What are the implications of "Punishment you felt was clean"?
4. Analyze the analogy the poet makes between a prison and a ship. How is it developed? Regardless of whether or not you accept the poet's view of prison life, does the analogy work in the framework of the poem?
5. In what way might it be said that the conscientious objector exemplifies our society's highest values?
6. Explain the paradox of the poem's last six lines.

Reading Time: 1 Minute 26 Seconds

MURIEL RUKEYSER

The fear of poetry is the
fear: mystery and fury of a midnight street
of windows whose low voluptuous voice
issues, and after that there is no peace.

That round waiting moment in the
theatre: curtain rises, dies into the ceiling
and here is played the scene with the mother
bandaging a revealed son's head. The bandage is torn off.
Curtain goes down. And here is the moment of proof.

That climax when the brain acknowledges the world,   10
all values extended into the blood awake.
Moment of proof. And as they say Brancusi did,
building his bird to extend through soaring air,
as Kafka planned stories that draw to eternity
through time extended. And the climax strikes.

Love touches so, that months after the look of
blue stare of love, the footbeat on the heart
is translated into the pure cry of birds
following air-cries, or poems, the new scene.
Moment of proof. That strikes long after act.   20

They fear it. They turn away, hand up palm out
fending off moment of proof, the straight look, poem.
The prolonged wound-consciousness after the bullet's shot.
The prolonged love after the look is dead,
the yellow joy after the song of the sun,
aftermath proof, extended radiance.

Love Poem

JOHN FREDERICK NIMS

My clumsiest dear, whose hands shipwreck vases,
At whose quick touch all glasses chip and ring,
Whose palms are bulls in china, burs in linen,
And have no cunning with any soft thing

Except all ill-at-ease fidgeting people: 5
The refugee uncertain at the door
You make at home; deftly you steady
The drunk clambering on his undulant floor.

Unpredictable dear, the taxi drivers' terror,
Shrinking from far headlights pale as a dime   10
Yet leaping before red apoplectic streetcars—
Misfit in any space. And never on time.

A wrench in clocks and the solar system. Only
With words and people and love you move at ease.
In traffic of wit expertly manoeuvre   15
And keep us, all devotion, at your knees.

Forgetting your coffee spreading on our flannel,
Your lipstick grinning on our coat,
So gayly in love's unbreakable heaven
Our souls on glory of spilt bourbon float.   20

Be with me, darling, early and late. Smash glasses—
I will study wry music for your sake.
For should your hands drop white and empty
All the toys of the world would break.

Considerations

1. What is the dominant tone of this poem? How does the opening line establish it? Whom is the poet addressing?
2. What are the woman's supposed faults and assets? How are they contrasted?
3. The poet uses a wide variety of figurative language. With what does he compare his loved one?
4. Where does he employ personification for an amusing effect?
5. What is responsible for the final stanza's alteration in tone? Paraphrase the last two lines.
6. Compare this love poem with others, such as Shakespeare's "Sonnet 18", (p. 363), Robert Burns' "Red, Red Rose" (p. 395), and Theodore Roethke's "I Knew a Woman" (p. 562). Does this poem seem less tender since it pokes a little fun at the lady? Could some parts of this poem conceivably appear in a poem written by a woman about a man? Why?
7. Is it frequently people's supposed shortcomings that make them unique and, therefore, loveable?

Lessons of the War: Naming of Parts

HENRY REED

(to Alan Michell)

Vixi duellis nuper idoneus
Et militavi non sine gloria

Today we have naming of parts. Yesterday,
We had daily cleaning. And tomorrow morning,
We shall have what to do after firing. But today,
Today we have naming of parts. Japonica
Glistens like coral in all of the neighbouring gardens,   5
    And today we have naming of parts.

This is the lower sling swivel. And this
Is the upper sling swivel, whose use you will see,
When you are given your slings. And this is the piling swivel
Which in your case you have not got. The branches   10
Hold in the gardens their silent, eloquent gestures,
    Which in our case we have not got.

This is the safety-catch, which is always released
With an easy flick of the thumb. And please do not let me
See anyone using his finger. You can do it quite easy   15
If you have any strength in your thumb. The blossoms
Are fragile and motionless, never letting anyone see
    Any of them using their finger.

And this you can see is the bolt. The purpose of this
Is to open the breech, as you see. We can slide it   20
Rapidly backwards and forwards: we call this
Easing the spring. And rapidly backwards and forwards
The early bees are assaulting and fumbling the flowers:
    They call it easing the Spring.

The epigraph is a witty variant of the first two lines of Horace's Ode XXVI, Book III, which read:

    Vixi puellis nuper idoneus,
    Et militavi non sine gloria.

These lines mean, "Formerly I lived in a way suited for the girls, and made love not without fame." By changing the first letter of the word "puellis,"—girls—Reed has changed the meaning to: "Formerly I lived in a way suited for a soldier, and waged war not without fame."

They call it easing the Spring: it is perfectly easy   25
If you have any strength in your thumb; like the bolt,
And the breech, and the cocking-piece, and the point of balance,
Which in our case we have not got; and the almond-blossom
Silent in all of the gardens and the bees going backwards and
    forwards,
For today we have naming of parts.   30

Considerations

1. Who is speaking in this poem?
2. Characterize the language and rhythm of the lines related to the gun
   and to the garden. What part does alliteration play in the "naming of
   parts"? What is its effect?
3. Although the poet does not identify the location, he gives clues that
   suggest a climate or part of the world. What are they?
4. The poem is full of puns and near puns. What is the double meaning
   of "point of balance" in the final stanza? What other words or phrases
   have two levels of meaning?
5. Why are certain phrases repeated?
6. What makes the contrasts in this poem so vivid?

Lessons of the War: Judging Distances

HENRY REED

Not only how far away, but the way that you say it
Is very important. Perhaps you may never get
The knack of judging a distance, but at least you know
How to report on a landscape: the central sector,
The right of arc and that, which we had last Tuesday,   5
    And at least you know

That maps are of time, not place, so far as the army   10
Happens to be concerned—the reason being,
Is one which need not delay us. Again, you know
There are three kinds of tree, three only, the fir and the poplar,
And those which have bushy tops to; and lastly
    That things only seem to be things.

A barn is not called a barn, to put it more plainly,
Or a field in the distance, where sheep may be safely grazing.
You must never be over-sure. You must say, when reporting: 15
At five o'clock in the central sector is a dozen
Of what appear to be animals; whatever you do,
  Don't call the bleeders *sheep.*

I am sure that's quite clear; and suppose, for the sake of example,
The one at the end, asleep, endeavors to tell us   20
What he sees over there to the west, and how far away,
After first having come to attention. There to the west,
On the fields of summer the sun and the shadows bestow
  Vestments of purple and gold.

The still white dwellings are like a mirage in the heat,   25
And under the swaying elms a man and a woman
Lie gently together. Which is, perhaps, only to say
That there is a row of houses to the left of arc,
And that under some poplars a pair of what appear to be humans
  Appear to be loving.   30

Well that, for an answer, is what we might rightly call
Moderately satisfactory only, the reason being,
Is that two things have been omitted, and those are important.
The human beings, now: in what direction are they,
And how far away, would you say? And do not forget   35
  There may be dead ground in between.

There may be dead ground in between; and I may not have got
The knack of judging a distance; I will only venture
A guess that perhaps between me and the apparent lovers,
(Who, incidentally, appear by now to have finished,)   40
At seven o'clock from the houses, is roughly a distance
  Of about one year and a half.

Considerations

1. What things are contrasted in this poem? Are these comparisons
   related in any way to those in the previous poem?
2. How does the poet show the army's indifference to many distinctions
   made by civilians? Does this indifference result in greater accuracy?
   What other results are implied (consider, for example, the connotations of "dead ground")?
3. What is the meaning of the final stanza? What is its tone?

Life, Friends, Is Boring

JOHN BERRYMAN

Life, friends, is boring. We must not say so.
After all, the sky flashes, the great sea yearns,
we ourselves flash and yearn,
and moreover my mother told me as a boy
(repeatingly) "Ever to confess you're bored   5
means you have no

Inner Resources." I conclude now I have no
inner resources, because I am heavy bored.
Peoples bore me,
literature bores me, especially great literature,   10
Henry bores me, with his plights & gripes
as bad as achilles,

who loves people and valiant art, which bores me.
And the tranquil hills, & gin, look like a drag
and somehow a dog   15
has taken itself & its tail considerably away
into mountains or sea or sky, leaving
behind: me, wag.

Considerations

1. What attitude toward life does the speaker express? Are these the poet's own feelings?
2. What reasons does the speaker offer for why we should never say we're bored? What is the difference between the reasons given in lines 2–3 and those given in lines 4–7? Are these sufficient reasons for not being bored with life? Is it possible to "flash and yearn" and yet be bored?
3. Specifically, what does the speaker say bores him?
4. Does the rhythm contribute to an effect of boredom?
5. How does the double meaning of "wag" in line 18 suggest that the poet is joking? What is his attitude toward boredom?
6. Compare the tone of this poem with John Ciardi's "Suburban Homecoming" (p. 590). Which poem conveys the greater feeling of wanting to get away from it all?

Fern Hill

DYLAN THOMAS

Now as I was young and easy under the apple boughs
About the lilting house and happy as the grass was green.
   The night above the dingle starry,
     Time let me hail and climb
   Golden in the heydays of his eyes.
And honoured among wagons I was prince of the apple towns
And once below a time I lordly had the trees and leaves
     Trail with daisies and barley
   Down the rivers of the windfall light.

And as I was green and carefree, famous among barns   10
About the happy yard and singing as the farm was home,
   In the sun that is young once only,
     Time let me play and be
   Golden in the mercy of his means,
And green and golden I was huntsman and herdsman, the calves
Sang to my horn, the foxes on the hills barked clear and cold,
     And the sabbath rang slowly
   In the pebbles of the holy streams.

All the sun long it was running, it was lovely, the hay—
Fields high as the house, the tunes from the chimneys, it was air   20
  And playing, lovely and watery
    And fire green as grass.
  And nightly under the simple stars
As I rode to sleep the owls were bearing the farm away,
All the moon long I heard, blessed among stables, the nightjars
  Flying with the ricks, and the horses
    Flashing into the dark.

And then to awake, and the farm, like a wanderer white
With the dew, come back, the cock on his shoulder: it was all
  Shining, it was Adam and maiden,   30
    The sky gathered again
  And the sun grew round that very day.
So it must have been after the birth of the simple light
In the first, spinning place, the spellbound horses walking warm
  Out of the whinnying green stable
    On to the fields of praise.

And honoured among foxes and pheasants by the gay house
Under the new made clouds and happy as the heart was long,
   In the sun born over and over,
     I ran my heedless ways,   40
    My wishes raced through the house-high hay
And nothing I cared, at my sky blue trades, that time allows
In all his tuneful turning so few and such morning songs
   Before the children green and golden
     Follow him out of grace.

Nothing I cared, in the lamb white days, that time would take me
Up to the swallow thronged loft by the shadow of my hand,
   In the moon that is always rising,
     Nor that riding to sleep
I should hear him fly with the high fields   50
And wake to the farm forever fled from the childless land.
O as I was young and easy in the mercy of his means,
    Time held me green and dying
   Though I sang in my chains like the sea.

Considerations

This is one of Dylan Thomas' most characteristic poems in terms of both style and content. It is full of nostalgia for the past and the lost innocence of childhood experience (Fern Hill was his aunt's farm). It is full of exuberance and fantastic imagery—the latter being perhaps a product of his Welsh upbringing. It is highly rhythmic, melodic, and complex.

1. What is the effect of the strange similes such as "happy as the grass was green" and "singing as the farm was home"?
2. What words does Thomas use to reveal that he believed himself to be the most important individual at Fern Hill?
3. What phrases help create the image of day or light? Which ones indicate joy and exaltation? Do some do both?
4. Note the chronological progression of the poem: in lines 10–22 it is broad daylight, in lines 23–27 it is night, and in lines 28–39 it is dawn. How does the mood change in lines 42–45? What should have prepared us for this change?
5. What feeling does the poem leave you with?

Do Not Go Gentle
Into That Good Night

DYLAN THOMAS

Do not go gentle into that good night,
Old age should burn and rave at close of day;
Rage, rage against the dying of the light.

Though wise men at their end know dark is right,
Because their words had forked no lightning they   5
Do not go gentle into that good night.

Good men, the last wave by, crying how bright
Their frail deeds might have danced in a green bay,
Rage, rage against the dying of the light.

Wild men who caught and sang the sun in flight,   10
And learn, too late, they grieved it on its way,
Do not go gentle into that good night.

Grave men, near death, who see with blinding sight
Blind eyes could blaze like meteors and be gay,
Rage, rage against the dying of the light.   15

And you, my father, there on the sad height,
Curse, bless, me now with your fierce tears, I pray.
Do not go gentle into that good night.
Rage, rage against the dying of the light.

Considerations

1. In stanzas 2–4 Dylan Thomas describes the way in which certain types of men have faced death and why they reacted in that way. Why does he mention this in a poem about the death of his father?
2. In line 5, what is meant by "Because their words had forked no lightening"?
3. What is Thomas' attitude toward his father's death?
4. This is one of the most powerful examples of the use of the villanelle form. (To compare it with another villanelle, see Sylvia Plath's "Mad Girl's Love Song" on p. 625). Do the repeated lines seem forced or natural?

Poem in October

DYLAN THOMAS

It was my thirtieth year to heaven
Woke to my hearing from harbour and neighbour wood
   And the mussel pooled and the heron
        Priested shore
       The morning beckon   5
With water praying and call of seagull and rook
And the knock of sailing boats on the net webbed wall
    Myself to set foot
     That second
In the still sleeping town and set forth.   10

My birthday began with the water-
Birds and the birds of the winged trees flying my name
   Above the farms and the white horses
       And I rose
      In rainy autumn   15
And walked abroad in a shower of all my days.
High tide and the heron dived when I took the road
    Over the border
     And the gates
Of the town closed as the town awoke.   20
   A springful of larks in a rolling
Cloud and the roadside bushes brimming with whistling
   Blackbirds and the sun of October
       Summery
      On the hill's shoulder,   25
Here were fond climates and sweet singers suddenly
Come in the morning where I wandered and listened
    To the rain wringing
     Wind blow cold
In the wood faraway under me.   30

Pale rain over the dwindling harbour
And over the sea-wet church the size of a snail
With its horns through mist and the castle
Brown as owls,
But all the gardens   35
Of spring and summer were blooming in the tall tales
Beyond the border and under the lark-full cloud.
There could I marvel
My birthday
Away but the weather turned around.   40

It turned away from the blithe country,
And down the other air and the blue altered sky
Streamed again a wonder of summer
With apples
Pears and red currants,   45
And I saw in the turning so clearly a child's
Forgotten mornings when he walked with his mother
Through the parables
Of sunlight
And the legends of the green chapels   50

And the twice told fields of infancy
That his tears burned my cheeks and his heart moved in mine
These were the woods the river and sea
Where a boy
In the listening   55
Summertime of the dead whispered the truth of his joy
To the trees and the stones and the fish in the tide.
And the mystery
Sang alive
Still in the water and singing birds.   60

And there could I marvel my birthday
Away but the weather turned around. And the true
Joy of the long-dead child sang burning
In the sun.
It was my thirtieth   65
Year to heaven stood there then in the summer noon
Though the town below lay leaved with October blood.
O may my heart's truth
Still be sung
On this high hill in a year's turning.   70

Dilemma

DAVID IGNATOW

Whatever we do, whether we light
strangers' cigarettes—it may turn out
to be a detective wanting to know who is free
with a light on a lonely street nights—
or whether we turn away and get a knife
planted between our shoulders for our discourtesy;
whatever we do—whether we marry for love
and wake up to find love is a task,
or whether for convenience, to find love
must be won over or we are desperate—
whatever we do; save by dying,
and there too we are caught,
by being planted too close to our parents.

The Death of
The Ball Turret Gunner

RANDALL JARRELL

From my mother's sleep I fell into the State,
And I hunched in its belly till my wet fur froze.
Six miles from earth, loosed from its dream of life,
I woke to black flak and the nightmare fighters.
When I died they washed me out of the turret with a hose.

Considerations

1. Jarrell has packed the story of a man's life into five lines of poetry.
   Who is speaking? At what point in time is he speaking?
2. When was the speaker born? When did he die?
3. What do we know of his experience in the airplane? (According to a
   note by Jarrell, "A ball turret was a plexiglass sphere set into the belly
   of a B-17 or B-24, and inhabited by two .50 caliber machine-guns and

one man, a short small man. When this gunner tracked with his machine-guns a fighter attacking his bomber from below, he revolved with the turret; hunched upside-down in his little sphere, he looked like the foetus in the womb. The fighters which attacked him were armed with cannon firing explosive shells. The hose was a steam hose.")

4. What is the tone of the last sentence?
5. Is this poem an indictment, and if so, of what?

Eighth Air Force

RANDALL JARRELL

If, in an odd angle of the hutment,
A puppy laps the water from a can
Of flowers, and the drunk sergeant shaving
Whistles *O Paradiso!*—shall I say that man
Is not as men have said: a wolf to man?   5

The other murderers troop in yawning;
Three of them play Pitch, one sleeps, and one
Lies counting missions, lies there sweating
Till even his heart beat: One; One; One.
O murderers! . . . Still, this is how it's done: 10

This is a war. . . . But since these play, before they die,
Like puppies with their puppy; since, a man,
I did as these have done, but did not die—
I will content the people as I can
And give up these to them: Behold the man!   15

I have suffered, in a dream, because of him,
Many things; for this last saviour, man,
I have lied as I lie now. But what is lying?
Men wash their hands, in blood, as best they can:
I find no fault in this just man.   20

May All Earth Be Clothed in Light

GEORGE HITCHCOCK

Morning spreads over
the beaches like lava;
the waves lie still, they
glitter with pieces of light.

I stand at the window
& watch a heron on one leg,
its plumage white in the green banks
of mint. Behind me
smoke rises from a nest
of bricks, the brass clock
on the kitchen shelf
judges & spares.

Slowly the bird
opens its dazzling wings.
I am filled with joy.
The fields are awake!
the fields with their hidden lizards
& fire of new iris.

Award

RAY DUREM

[*A Gold Watch to the FBI Man (who has followed me) for 25 Years.*]

Well, old spy
looks like I
led you down some pretty blind alleys,
took you on several trips to Mexico,
fishing in the high Sierras,
jazz at the Philharmonic.
You've watched me all your life,
I've clothed your wife,
put your two sons through college.
what good has it done?
sun keeps rising every morning.
Ever see me buy an Assistant President?
or close a school?
or lend money to Somoza?
I bought some after-hours whiskey in L.A.
but the Chief got his pay.
I ain't killed no Koreans,
or fourteen-year-old boys in Mississippi
neither did I bomb Guatemala,
or lend guns to shoot Algerians.
I admit I took a Negro child
to a white rest room in Texas,
but she was my daughter, only three,
and she had to pee,
and I just didn't know what to do,
would you?
see, I'm so light, it don't seem right
to go to the colored rest room;
my daughter's brown, and folks frown on that in Texas,
I just don't know how to go to the bathroom in the free world!

Now, old FBI man,
you've done the best you can,
you lost me a few jobs,
scared a couple landlords,
You got me struggling for that bread,
but I ain't dead.
and before its all through,
I may be following you!

Reprinted from POETS OF TODAY. By permission of Dorothy Durem.

Survival in Missouri

JOHN CIARDI

When Willie Crosby died I thought too much:
Sister and Mother and Uncle and Father O'Brien
All talked about me and how
It was all very touching: *Such sorrow.*
He really lived in that boy.
Here now, you gowonoff to the movies.
Give your grief to God.

But here I am in Missouri twenty years later
Watching the rain come down
That no one prayed for: a drowned crop   10
And the Mississippi rising
On a wet world still washing away the kid
Who thought too much about Willie Crosby
But went to the movies all the same.
It was a lovely wake and everyone admired me.

At night the Salt Hills go blue perfectly.
Having survived a theology and a war,
I am beginning to understand
The rain.

Suburban Homecoming

JOHN CIARDI

As far as most of what you call people, my darling, are
concerned, I don't care who or what gets into the phone. I
am not home and not expected and I even, considerably, doubt I live
  here.

I mean this town and its everlasting katzenjammer whenever whoever dials again, is going to hell, or to some other
perpetual buffet, in a wheelbarrowful of bad martinis: and you, my

legal sweet, forever in the act of putting your hat on
as I come in the door to be told I have exactly five—
or, on good days, ten—minutes to change in because here we go

again to some collection of never-quite-the-same-but-
always-no-different faces; you, my moth-brained flutter
from bright cup to cup, no matter what nothing is in them; you, my
  own

brand-named, laboratory-tested, fair-trade-priced, wedded
(as advertised in *Life*) feather-duster, may go jump into
twenty fathoms of Advice to the Lovelorn and pull it in after you—

but I have not arrived, am not in, the phone did not ring
and was not answered, we have not really, I believe, met, and
if we do and if I stay to be (I doubt it) introduced, I'm still not going.

English A

JOHN CIARDI

No paraphrase does
between understanding
and understanding.

You are either
that noun beyond
qualification into

whose round fact
I pass unparsed
and into whose eyes

I speak idioms   10
beyond construction;
or else get up,

fasten your suffixes
and your hyphenations,
buckle your articles,

spray modifiers
and moods
behind your ears

and take the whole
developed discourse   20
of your thighs to

any damned grammarian
you whatsoever
wish. Period.

Considerations

1. A paraphrase can never capture the exact meaning of the original text on which it's based. Why is this true? How does this relate to what the poet says about "understanding and understanding"?
2. Who is speaking? To whom is he speaking?
3. Although the key words are expressed as elements of rhetoric, how does the poet enable his readers to understand the situation? What is the situation?
4. Is the poet describing fairly common male and female attitudes?
5. How does the speaker differ from a "damned grammarian"? Is a poet a grammarian?
6. Why is the word "whatsoever" used in line 22? Is the final word of the poem necessary?

Game Called on Account
Of Darkness

PETER VIERECK

Once there was a friend.
He watched me from the sky.
Maybe he never lived at all.
Maybe too much friendship made him die.

When the gang played cops-and-robbers in the alley,
It was my friend who told me which were which,
Now he doesn't tell me any more.
(Which team am I playing for?)

My science teacher built a telescope
To show me every answer in the end.   10
I stared and stared at every star for hours.
I couldn't find my friend.

At Sunday School they said I breathe too much.
When I hold my breath within the under
Side of earth, they said I'll find my friend.
. . . I wonder.

He was like a kind of central heating
In the big cold house, and that was good.
One by one I have to chop my toys now,
As firewood.   20

Everytime I stood upon a crossroads,
It made me mad to feel him watch me choose.
I'm glad there's no more spying while I play.
Still, I'm sad he went away.

First published in Peter Viereck's book *Terror and Decorum*, N. Y., Scribners, 1948; Pulitzer prize for verse, 1949; out of print. Included in reprint of *Terror and Decorum*, 1973, by Greenwood Press, Westport, Conn. and in Peter Viereck's *New and Selected Poems*, Bobbs-Merrill Co., N. Y. 1967, as well as other collections.

Considerations

1. What is the literal interpretation of the poem's title? What figurative meaning might it have?
2. Who is the speaker? Is he a child or an adult?
3. Who is—or was—his friend? What was the friend's function in the speaker's life? What caused the change in their relationship?
4. Is the poet discussing the loss of a conventional religious belief? Explore the analogy in stanza 5. What is the meaning of lines 19 and 20?
5. What parts do rhyme, rhythm, and mode of expression play in suggesting the speaker's level of maturity? How do they contribute to the tone?
6. Do some people reject the concept of a personalized God on intellectual grounds, but regret the loss for emotional reasons?
7. What is the poet's attitude toward the speaker?

After the Convention

ROBERT LOWELL

Life, hope, they conquer death, generally, always;
and if the steamroller goes over the flower, the flower dies.
Some are more solid earth; they stood in lines,
blouse and helmet, a creamy de luxe sky-blue—
their music, savage and ephemeral. . . .
After five nights of Chicago: police and mob,
I am so tired and had, clichés are wisdom,
the clichés of paranoia. On this shore,
the fall of the high tide waves is a straggling, joshing
march of soldiers . . . on the march for me. . . .
How slender and graceful, the double line of trees,
how slender, graceful, irregular and underweight,
the young in black folk-fire circles below the trees—
under their bodies, the green grass turns to hay.

September 1, 1968

We Real Cool

GWENDOLYN BROOKS

The Pool Players
Seven At the Golden Shovel

We real cool. We
Left school. We

Lurk late. We
Strike straight. We

Sing sin. We
Thin gin. We

Jazz June. We
Die soon.

from

The Children of the Poor

GWENDOLYN BROOKS

II

Life for my child is simple, and is good.
He knows his wish. Yes, but that is not all.
Because I know mine too.
And we both want joy of undeep and unabiding things,

Like kicking over a chair or throwing blocks out of a window
Or tipping over an icebox pan
Or snatching down curtains or fingering an electric outlet
Or a journey or a friend or an illegal kiss.
No. There is more to it than that.
It is that he has never been afraid.
Rather, he reaches out and lo the chair falls with a beautiful crash,
And the blocks fall, down on the people's heads,
And the water comes slooshing sloppily out across the floor.
And so forth.
Not that success, for him, is sure, infallible.
But never has he been afraid to reach.
His lesions are legion.
But reaching is his rule.

Underwear

LAWRENCE FERLINGHETTI

I didn't get much sleep last night
thinking about underwear
Have you ever stopped to consider
underwear in the abstract
When you really dig into it   5
some shocking problems are raised
Underwear is something
we all have to deal with
Everyone wears
some kind of underwear   10
Even Indians
wear underwear
Even Cubans
wear underwear
The Pope wears underwear I hope   15
Underwear is worn by Negroes
The Governor of Louisiana
wears underwear

I saw him on TV
He must have had tight underwear 20
He squirmed a lot
Underwear can really get you in a bind
Negroes often wear
white underwear
which may lead to trouble 25
You have seen the underwear ads
for men and women
so alike but so different
Women's underwear holds things up
Men's underwear holds things down 30
Underwear is one thing
men and women have in common
Underwear is all we have between us
You have seen the three-color pictures
with crotches encircled 35
to show the areas of extra strength
and three-way stretch
promising full freedom of action
Don't be deceived
It's all based on the two-party system 40
which doesn't allow much freedom of choice
the way things are set up
America in its Underwear
struggles thru the night
Underwear controls everything in the end 45
Take foundation garments for instance
They are really fascist forms
of underground government
making people believe
something but the truth 50
telling you what you can or can't do
Did you ever try to get around a girdle
Perhaps Non-Violent Action
is the only answer
Did Gandhi wear a girdle? 55
Did Lady Macbeth wear a girdle?
Was that why Macbeth murdered sleep?
And that spot she was always rubbing—
Was it really in her underwear?
Modern anglosaxon ladies 60
must have huge guilt complexes
always washing and washing and washing

Out damned spot—rub don't blot—
Underwear with spots very suspicious
Underwear with bulges very shocking   65
Underwear on clothesline a great flag of freedom
Someone has escaped his Underwear
May be naked somewhere
Help!
But don't worry   70
Everybody's still hung up in it
There won't be no real revolution
And poetry still the underwear of the soul
And underwear still covering
a multitude of faults   75
in the geological sense—
strange sedimentary stones, inscrutable cracks!
And that only the beginning
For does not the body stay alive
after death   80
and still need its underwear
or outgrow it
some organs said to reach full maturity
only after the head stops holding them back?
If I were you I'd keep aside   85
an oversize pair of winter underwear
Do not go naked into that good night
And in the meantime
keep calm and warm and dry
No use stirring ourselves up prematurely   90
'over Nothing'
Move forward with dignity
hand in vest
Don't get emotional
And death shall have no dominion   95
There's plenty of time my darling
Are we not still young and easy
Don't shout

Considerations

1. Is this an appropriate subject for a poem?
2. What purpose do the references to Shakespeare's "Macbeth" serve?
3. What seems to be the subject of the poem after line 79?
4. Lines 87, 95, and 97 contain allusions to poems by Dylan Thomas.

What probable sources can you suggest for other familiar phrases in
the last twelve lines of the poem?
5. On what note does the poem end?

A Coney Island of the Mind

LAWRENCE FERLINGHETTI

15
Constantly risking absurdity
                            and death
                whenever he performs
                            above the heads
                                        of his audience
        the poet like an acrobat
                    climbs on rime
                            to a high wire of his own making
and balancing on eyebeams
                            above a sea of faces   10
                paces his way
                    to the other side of day
        performing entrechats
                            and sleight-of-foot tricks
        and other high theatrics
                            and all without mistaking
                any thing
                            for what it may not be

            For he's the super realist
                            who must perforce perceive   20
                taut truth
                            before the taking of each stance or step
        in his supposed advance
                            toward that still higher perch
        where Beauty stands and waits
                            with gravity
                                    to start her death-defying leap

And he
    a little charleychaplin man
                    who may or may not catch   30
her fair eternal form
                spreadeagled in the empty air
    of existence

Considerations

1. What is the setting of this poem?
2. The first and second stanzas of the poem present contrasting images of the poet-acrobat. What is his level of skill and self-confidence in each?
3. How do rhyme, rhythm, sentence length and structure, absence of punctuation, and typographical arrangement contribute to the total effect of the poem?
4. Ferlinghetti enjoys plays on words, or meaningful ambiguity, such as his reference to "eyebeams" (or structural I-beams) in line 9. What other meaning does the word have in this context, and why are both meanings appropriate? What other puns can you find? Explain them.
5. Examine Ferlinghetti's extended analogy. What, for example, is the "high wire" on which the poet-acrobat balances? What is he moving toward? What does the figure of Beauty represent?
6. Does Ferlinghetti claim that poets always perceive truth or unfailingly capture beauty?

To David, about His Education

HOWARD NEMEROV

The world is full of mostly invisible things,
And there is no way but putting the mind's eye,
Or its nose, in a book, to find them out,
Things like the square root of Everest
Or how many times Byron goes into Texas,   5
Or whether the law of the excluded middle
Applies west of the Rockies. For these
And the like reasons, you have to go to school
And study books and listen to what you are told.

Reprinted from THE NEXT ROOM OF THE DREAM: POEMS AND TWO PLAYS by Howard Nemerov © 1962. By permission of Margot Johnson Agency.

And sometimes try to remember. Though I don't know   10
What you will do with the mean annual rainfall
On Plato's Republic, or the calorie content
Of the Diet of Worms, such things are said to be
Good for you, and you will have to learn them
In order to become one of the grown-ups   15
Who sees invisible things neither steadily nor whole,
But keeps gravely the grand confusion of the world
Under his hat, which is where it belongs,
And teaches small children to do this in their turn.

Life Cycle of the Common Man

HOWARD NEMEROV

Roughly figured, this man of moderate habits,
This average consumer of the middle class,
Consumed in the course of his average life span
Just under half a million cigarettes,
Four thousand fifths of gin and about
A quarter as much vermouth; he drank
Maybe a hundred thousand cups of coffee,
And counting his parents' share it cost
Something like half a million dollars
To put him through life. How many beasts   10
Died to provide him with meat, belts and shoes
Cannot be certainly said.
                But anyhow,
It is in this way that a man travels through time,
Leaving behind him a lengthening trail
Of empty bottles and bones, of broken shoes,
Frayed collars and worn out or outgrown
Diapers and dinnerjackets, silk ties and slickers.

Given the energy and security thus achieved,
He did . . . ? What? The usual things, of course,
The eating, dreaming, drinking, and begetting,   20
And he worked for the money which was to pay

For the eating, et cetera, which were necessary
If he were to go on working for the money, et cetera,
But chiefly he talked. As the bottles and bones
Accumulated behind him, the words proceeded
Steadily from the front of his face as he
Advanced into silence and made it verbal.
Who can tally the tale of his words? A lifetime
Would barely suffice for their repetition;
If you merely printed all his commas the result   30
Would be a very large volume, and the number of times
He said "thank you" or "very little sugar, please,"
Would stagger the imagination. There were also
Witticisms, platitudes, and statements beginning
"It seems to me" or "As I always say."

Consider the courage in all that, and behold the man
Walking into deep silence, with the ectoplastic
Cartoon's balloon of speech proceeding
Steadily out of the front of his face, the words
Borne along on the breath which is his spirit   40
Telling the numberless tale of his untold Word
Which makes the world his apple, and forces him to eat.

Santa Claus

HOWARD NEMEROV

Somewhere on his travels the strange Child
Picked up with this overstuffed confidence man,
Affection's inverted thief, who climbs at night
Down chimneys, into dreams, with this world's goods.
Bringing all the benevolence of money,   5
He teaches the innocent to want, thus keeps
Our fat world rolling. His prescribed costume,
White flannel beard, red belly of cotton waste,
Conceals the thinness of essential hunger,
An appetite that feeds on satisfaction;   10
Or, pregnant with possessions, he brings forth

Vanity and the void. His name itself
Is corrupted, and even Saint Nicholas, in his turn,
Gives off a faint and reminiscent stench,
The merest soupcon, of brimstone and the pit.   15

Now, at the season when the Child is born
To suffer for the world, suffer the world,
His bloated Other, jovial satellite
And sycophant, makes his appearance also
In a glitter of goodies, in a rock candy glare.   20
Played at the better stores by bums, for money,
This annual savior of the economy
Speaks in the parables of the dollar sign:
Suffer the little children to come to Him.

At Easter, he's anonymous again,   25
Just one of the crowd lunching on Calvary.

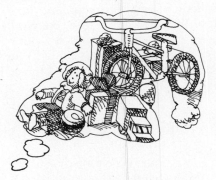

Considerations

1. Who are the "strange Child" and the "overstuffed confidence man"?
   How do these names differ from the usual designations? Are they
   suitable? Why?
2. How does Christmas stimulate the economy? In what way is this
   effect a perversion of the original purpose?
3. What effect does the poet think Christmas has on children? What is
   his reasoning? Do you agree?
4. Santa Claus is a rendering of Saint Nicholas. What is the connection
   between the original name and "brimstone and the pit"?
5. In what way does the meaning of line 24 differ from the original
   meaning of the line in the New Testament?
6. What took place on Calvary almost 2,000 years ago? Explain the last
   two lines of the poem.

A Simile for Her Smile

RICHARD WILBUR

Your smiling, or the hope, the thought of it,
Makes in my mind such pause and abrupt ease
As when the highway bridgegates fall,
Balking the hasty traffic, which must sit
On each side massed and staring, while
Deliberately the drawbridge starts to rise:

Then horns are hushed, the oilsmoke rarefies,
Above the idling motors one can tell
The packet's smooth approach, the slip,
Slip of the silken river past the sides,
The ringing of clear bells, the dip
And slow cascading of the paddle wheel.

Mind

RICHARD WILBUR

Mind in its purest play is like some bat
That beats about in caverns all alone,
Contriving by a kind of senseless wit
Not to conclude against a wall of stone.

It has no need to falter or explore;   5
Darkly it knows what obstacles are there,
And so may weave and flitter, dip and soar
In perfect courses through the blackest air.

And has this simile a like perfection?
The mind is like a bat. Precisely. Save   10
That in the very happiest intellection
A graceful error may correct the cave.

Considerations

1. With what does the poet compare the mind? How does he develop the simile? What are the obstacles and walls of stone encountered by the mind?
2. Is he being ironic when he suggests that both the mind and his simile are perfect?
3. How does the final line save the poet from having to admit that neither his simile nor the human mind are flawless? Does his reasoning demonstrate his point?
4. Compare this poem with Marianne Moore's "The Mind Is An Enchanting Thing." How do they differ in tone, imagery, and form?
5. How do the imagery, rhythm, and rhyme of the poem reinforce the idea of a bat?

Formal Application

DONALD W. BAKER

"The poets apparently want to rejoin the human race." Time

I shall begin by learning to throw
the knife, first at trees, until it sticks
in the trunk and quivers every time;

next from a chair, using only wrist
and fingers, at a thing on the ground,   5
a fresh ant hill or a fallen leaf,

then at a moving object, perhaps
a pieplate swinging on twine, until
I pot it at least twice in three tries.

Meanwhile, I shall be teaching the birds   10
that the skinny fellow in sneakers
is a source of suet and bread crumbs,

first putting them on a shingle nailed
to a pine tree, next scattering them
on the needles, closer and closer   15

to my seat, until the proper bird,
a towhee, I think, in black and rust
and gray, takes tossed crumbs six feet away.

Finally, I shall coordinate
conditioned reflex and functional   20
form and qualify as Modern Man.

You see the splash of blood and feathers
and the blade pinning it to the tree?
It's called an "Audubon Crucifix."

The phrase has pleasing (even pious)   25
connotations, like *Arbeit Macht Frei,*
"Molotov Cocktail," and *Enola Gay.*

Considerations

1. Who is speaking in this poem? What action is he planning? What has prompted it?
2. Does the poet use figurative language in the poem? How does the diction help it establish the tone? Why is the language suitable to the material?
3. Who is "the skinny fellow in sneakers"? Is this image at odds with his behavior in the poem?
4. Rhetorically, what does "Audubon Crucifix" have in common with *Arbeit Mache Frei* (a Nazi slogan, meaning "work liberates"), "Molotov Cocktail" (a homemade bomb named after a Russian diplomat), and *Enola Gay* (the American plane, named after the pilot's mother, that dropped the first atomic bomb on Hiroshima, Japan, in World War II)? How does the poet's contribution to death compare with these?
5. What observation is the poet making about the human race? Consider the possibility of meaningful ambiguity in his interpretation of *race.* What sort of race might he be referring to?
6. What is the double meaning of the poem's title?

Deer Among Cattle

JAMES DICKEY

Here and there in the searing beam
Of my hand going through the night meadow
They all are grazing

With pins of human light in their eyes.
A wild one also is eating
The human grass,

Slender, graceful, domesticated
By darkness, among the bred-
for-slaughter,

Having bounded their paralyzed fence
And inclined his branched forehead onto
Their green frosted table,

The only live thing in this flashlight
Who can leave whenever he wishes,
Turn grass into forest,

Foreclose inhuman brightness from his eyes
But stands here still, unperturbed,
In their wide-open country,

The sparks from my hand in his pupils
Unmatched anywhere among cattle,

Grazing with them the night of the hammer
As one of their own who shall rise.

April Inventory

W. D. SNODGRASS

The green catalpa tree has turned
All white; the cherry blooms once more.
In one whole year I haven't learned
A blessed thing they pay you for.
The blossoms snow down in my hair;
The trees and I will soon be bare.

The trees have more than I to spare.
The sleek, expensive girls I teach,
Younger and pinker every year,
Bloom gradually out of reach.
The pear tree lets its petals drop
Like dandruff on a tabletop.

The girls have grown so young by now
I have to nudge myself to stare.
This year they smile and mind me how
My teeth are falling with my hair.
In thirty years I may not get
Younger, shrewder, or out of debt.

The tenth time, just a year ago,
I made myself a little list
Of all the things I'd ought to know,
Then told my parents, analyst,
And everyone who's trusted me
I'd be substantial, presently.

I haven't read one book about
A book or memorized one plot.
Or found a mind I did not doubt.
I learned one date. And then forgot.
And one by one the solid scholars
Get the degrees, the jobs, the dollars.

And smile above their starchy collars.
I taught my classes Whitehead's notions;
One lovely girl, a song of Mahler's.
Lacking a source-book or promotions,
I showed one child the colors of
A luna moth and how to love.

I taught myself to name my name,
To bark back, loosen love and crying;
To ease my woman so she came,
To ease an old man who was dying.
I have not learned how often I
Can win, can love, but choose to die.

I have not learned there is a lie
Love shall be blonder, slimmer, younger;
That my equivocating eye
Loves only by my body's hunger;
That I have forces, true to feel,
Or that the lovely world is real.

While scholars speak authority
And wear their ulcers on their sleeves,
My eyes in spectacles shall see
These trees procure and spend their leaves.
There is a value underneath
The gold and silver in my teeth.

Though trees turn bare and girls turn wives,
We shall afford our costly seasons;
There is a gentleness survives
That will outspeak and has its reasons.
There is a loveliness exists,
Preserves us, not for specialists.

Curiosity

ALASTAIR REID

may have killed the cat; more likely
the cat was just unlucky, or else curious
to see what death was like, having no cause
to go on licking paws, or fathering
litter on litter of kittens, predictably.   5

Nevertheless, to be curious
is dangerous enough. To distrust
what is always said, what seems,
to ask odd questions, interfere in dreams,
leave home, smell rats, have hunches,   10
cannot endear them to those doggy circles
where well-smelt baskets, suitable wives, good lunches
are the order of things, and where prevails
much wagging of incurious heads and tails.

Face it. Curiosity   15
will not cause him to die—
only lack of it will.
Never to want to see
the other side of the hill
or some improbable country   20
where living is an idyll
(although a probable hell)
would kill us all.
Only the curious
have, if they live, a tale   25
worth telling at all.

    Dogs say cats love too much, are irresponsible,
are changeable, marry too many wives,
desert their children, chill all dinner tables
with tales of their nine lives.   30
Well, they are lucky. Let them be
nine-lived and contradictory,
curious enough to change, prepared to pay
the cat-price, which is to die
and die again and again,   35
each time with no less pain.
A cat minority of one
is all that can be counted on
to tell the truth. And what cats have to tell
on each return from hell   40
is this: that dying is what the living do,
that dying is what the loving do,
and that dead dogs are those who never know
that dying is what, to live, each has to do.

Considerations

1. The poet begins by talking about a cat. At what point does it become
   clear that he is discussing human beings?
2. Characterize the cat and the dogs in this poem. How do their lives
   differ? What part does curiosity or lack of it play in shaping their lives?
3. Does the poet believe that the advantages of curiosity outweigh the
   dangers? Why? Do you agree with him?
4. How does the tone change as the poem progresses? What is the tone
   of the final four lines?
5. Explain the paradox of the last four lines.

A Wicker Basket

ROBERT CREELEY

Comes the time when it's later
and onto your table the headwaiter
puts the bill, and very soon after
rings out the sound of lively laughter—

Picking up change, hands like a walrus,
and a face like a barndoor's,
and a head without any apparent size,
nothing but two eyes—

So that's you, man,
or me. I make it as I can,
I pick up, I go
faster than they know—

Out the door, the street like a night,
any night, and no one in sight,
but then, well, there she is,
old friend Liz—

And she opens the door of her cadillac,
I step in back,
and we're gone.
She turns me on—

There are very huge stars, man, in the sky,
and from somewhere very far off someone hands me a slice of apple
    pie,
with a gob of white, white ice cream on top of it,
and I eat it—

Slowly. And while certainly
they are laughing at me, and all around me is racket
of these cats not making it, I make it

in my wicker basket.

Joy

ROBERT CREELEY

I could look at
an empty hole for hours
thinking it will
get something in it,
will collect
things. There is
an infinite emptiness
placed there.

For No Clear Reason

ROBERT CREELEY

I dreamt last night
the fright was over, that
the dust came, and then water,
and women and men, together
again, and all was quiet
in the dim moon's light.

A paean of such patience—
laughing, laughing at me,
and the days extend over
the earth's great cover,   10
grass, trees, and flower-
ing season, for no clear reason.

A Blessing

JAMES WRIGHT

Just off the highway to Rochester, Minnesota,
Twilight bounds softly forth on the grass.
And the eyes of those two Indian ponies
Darken with kindness.
They have come gladly out of the willows
To welcome my friend and me.
We step over the barbed wire into the pasture
Where they have been grazing all day, alone.
They ripple tensely, then can hardly contain their happiness
That we have come.
They bow shyly as wet swans. They love each other.
There is no loneliness like theirs.
At home once more,
They begin munching the young tufts of spring in the darkness.
I would like to hold the slenderer one in my arms,
For she has walked over to me
And nuzzled my left hand.
She is black and white,
Her mane falls wild on her forehead,
And the light breeze moves me to caress her long ear
That is delicate as the skin over a girl's wrist.
Suddenly I realize
That if I stepped out of my body I would break
Into blossom.

Abraham's Madness

BINK NOLL

When Isaac watched his father strain back
the ram's head, its throat separate and bleed,
evisceration, and fat turn to smoke,

not *he* had heard any angel speak
but felt sharply where the rope still cut,
how his own neck cracked, his own flesh burned.

I likewise learned to distrust my sire
whose god in our house was powerful
as revenge shuddering through a plot.

Mornings, his story would begin,   10
"My dear boy, God will provide the lamb,"
when I knew I went the only lamb,

knew the god had repeated his demand
and violence on this man who adored
both of us past any hope of reason.

I was proving tall, bright, soft of voice.
Then he—his love wild to get me grown—
would change and cheat the law, then reach out

to slay some cheap and easy innocent,
then stop the silence raging in his ear   20
by reports of angels I never heard.

How we sons lay awake to ponder
The misery of such divided men
to whom patriarchal lies come true.

My son shall not watch me in a fury
of faith take fire to the altar where
I sacrifice nothing I cherish.

3. What does the simile in stanza 5 suggest about the cyclists?
4. Locate the images relating to knighthood. In what ways do the boys resemble knights?
5. How might "Born To Lose" operate as a self-fulfilling prophecy?

Secretary

TED HUGHES

If I should touch her she would shriek and weeping
Crawl off to nurse the terrible wound: all
Day like a starling under the bellies of bulls
She hurries among men, ducking, peeping,

Off in a whirl at the first move of a horn.
At dusk she scuttles down the gauntlet of lust
Like a clockwork mouse. Safe home at last
She mends socks with holes, shirts that are torn,

For father and brother, and a delicate supper cooks:
Goes to bed early, shuts out with the light
Her thirty years, and lies with buttocks tight,
Hiding her lovely eyes until day break.

Onan

PARIS LEARY

Whether Two-Backed Beast or Many-Splendoured-Thing
their loves are in the last analysis a bore.
When will the buffs and punks of verse stop using lovers
as the image to silence protest, clinch an argument,
a gauntlet thrown in the boughten teeth of Dean or Daddy?
A year's election or the market price of wheat
makes or breaks more of reality than lovers.

Love should be practiced like Lent, secretly and dumbly,
(lovers names anonymous in lists of donors),
its outward form something like the Liturgy
of S. John Chrysostom—gorgeous, measured, sober,
its formal exchanges archaic but understandable:
candles and incense and the Song of the Cherubim,
but always the final mystery, the piklesis,
the consecration, performed behind golden doors
closed hugely in the faces even of believers.

I have seen the young inchoate Bronx boy poets
scattering their seed in successive teen-aged girls
and their words in verses celebrating waste
(both acts more or less public, open)—
and always the result is the poem tender or violent,
free or ordered, throwing up lovers always
as the final image that somehow justifies their sense
of betrayal in the impotence of poetry.
How old they are: downy lips and clearing complexions,
sneakers, sweat, and Levi's, bad teeth and diction—
more vulnerable than children in an open age
where nothing is private, where even the Holiest of Holies
is fitted out with couch and file, mirrors and Muzak.

There are things more important than their bloody affairs:
the old gods shifting in the cycle of the earth;
my great-aunt Flavia McIntyre who made her cancer
a miracle of healing for all the bitter world
who came astonished to see her reaching out for pain
as if to comfort it; the white calligraphy
of birches in the red combes of the autumn Hudson;
the Pope, I suppose, whose irrelevance afflicts
the world in its curious unbelief like a trauma;
Sugarman Prescott twisted in a parody
of embryo, speechless since birth, but who understands
his mother's private language, whom the Bishop confirmed;
the innocent and irrecoverable purity
of children's speculations on the theory of flight;
the cry 'I thirst' hushed by a formal art of mercy
by posh crucifixes, elegant triptychs, and music. . .

Damn the young poets! Let them rather learn
cooking or prosody and study the dull Masters.

Daddy

SYLVIA PLATH

You do not do, you do not do
Any more, black shoe
In which I have lived like a foot
For thirty years, poor and white,
Barely daring to breathe or Achoo.

Daddy, I have had to kill you.
You died before I had time—
Marble-heavy, a bag full of God,
Ghastly statue with one grey toe
Big as a Frisco seal   10

And a head in the freakish Atlantic
Where it pours bean green over blue
In the waters off beautiful Nauset.
I used to pray to recover you.
Ach, du.

In the German tongue, in the Polish town
Scraped flat by the roller
Of wars, wars, wars.
But the name of the town is common.
My Polack friend   20

Says there are a dozen or two.
So I never could tell where you
Put your foot, your root,
I never could talk to you.
The tongue stuck in my jaw.

It stuck in a barb wire snare.
Ich, ich, ich, ich,
I could hardly speak.
I thought every German was you.
And the language obscene   30

An engine, an engine
Chuffing me off like a Jew.
A Jew to Dachau, Auschwitz, Belsen.
I began to talk like a Jew.
I think I may well be a Jew.

The snows of the Tyrol, the clear beer of Vienna
Are not very pure or true.
With my gypsy ancestress and my weird luck
And my Taroc[1] pack and my Taroc pack
I may be a bit of a Jew.   40

I have always been scared of *you,*
With your Luftwaffe, your gobbledygoo.
And your neat moustache
And your Aryan eye, bright blue.
Panzer-man, panzer-man, O You——

Not God but a swastika
So black no sky could squeak through.
Every woman adores a Fascist,
The boot in the face, the brute
Brute heart of a brute like you.   50

You stand at the blackboard, daddy,
In the picture I have of you,
A cleft in your chin instead of your foot
But no less a devil for that, no not
Any less the black man who

Bit my pretty red heart in two.
I was ten when they buried you.
At twenty I tried to die
And get back, back, back to you.
I thought even the bones would do.   60

But they pulled me out of the sack,
And they stuck me together with glue.
And then I knew what to do.
I made a model of you,
A man in black with a Meinkampf look

---

1 Variant spelling of Tarot.

And a love of the rack and the screw.
And I said I do, I do.
So daddy, I'm finally through.
The black telephone's off at the root,
The voices just can't worm through.   70

If I've killed one man, I've killed two——
The vampire who said he was you
And drank my blood for a year,
Seven years, if you want to know.
Daddy, you can lie back now.

There's a stake in your fat black heart
And the villagers never liked you.
They are dancing and stamping on you.
They always *knew* it was you.
Daddy, daddy, you bastard, I'm through.   80

The Disquieting Muses

SYLVIA PLATH

Mother, mother, what illbred aunt
Or what disfigured and unsightly
Cousin did you so unwisely keep
Unasked to my christening, that she
Sent these ladies in her stead
With heads like darning-eggs to nod
And nod and nod at foot and head
And at the left side of my crib?

Mother, who made to order stories
Of Mixie Blackshort the heroic bear,
Mother, whose witches always, always
Got baked into gingerbread, I wonder
Whether you saw them, whether you said
Words to rid me of those three ladies
Nodding by night around my bed,
Mouthless, eyeless, with stitched bald head.

In the hurricane, when father's twelve
Study windows bellied in
Like bubbles about to break, you fed
My brother and me cookies and Ovaltine
And helped the two of us to choir:
"Thor is angry: boom boom boom!
Thor is angry: we don't care!"
But those ladies broke the panes.

When on tiptoe the schoolgirls danced,
Blinking flashlights like fireflies
And singing the glowworm song, I could
Not lift a foot in the twinkle-dress
But, heavy-footed, stood aside
In the shadow cast by my dismal-headed
Godmothers, and you cried and cried:
And the shadow stretched, the lights went out.

Mother, you sent me to piano lessons
And praised my arabesques and trills
Although each teacher found my touch
Oddly wooden in spite of scales
And the hours of practicing, my ear
Tone-deaf and yes, unteachable.
I learned, I learned, I learned elsewhere,
From muses unhired by you, dear mother,

I woke one day to see you, mother,
Floating above me in bluest air
On a green balloon bright with a million
Flowers and bluebirds that never were
Never, never, found anywhere.

But the little planet bobbed away
Like a soap-bubble as you called: Come here!
And I faced my traveling companions.

Day now, night now, at head, side, feet,
They stand their vigil in gowns of stone,
Faces blank as the day I was born,
Their shadows long in the setting sun
That never brightens or goes down.
And this is the kingdom you bore me to,
Mother, mother. But no frown of mine
Will betray the company I keep.

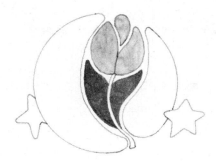

Mad Girl's Love Song

SYLVIA PLATH

A Villanelle

I shut my eyes and all the world drops dead;
I lift my lids and all is born again.
(I think I made you up inside my head.)

The stars go waltzing out in blue and red,
And arbitrary blackness gallops in:
I shut my eyes and all the world drops dead.

I dreamed that you bewitched me into bed
And sung me moon-struck, kissed me quite insane.
(I think I made you up inside my head.)

God topples from the sky, hell's fires fade:
Exit seraphim and Satan's men:
I shut my eyes and all the world drops dead.

I fancied you'd return the way you said,
But I grow old and I forget your name.
(I think I made you up inside my head.)

I should have loved a thunderbird instead;
At least when spring comes they roar back again.
I shut my eyes and all the world drops dead.
(I think I made you up inside my head.)

The Rebel

MARI EVANS

When I
die
I'm sure
I will have a
Big Funeral . . .
Curiosity
seekers . . .
coming to see
if I
am really
Dead . . .
or just
trying to make
Trouble . . . .

When in Rome

MARI EVANS

Mattie dear
the box is full . . .
take
whatever you like
to eat . . .

I AM A BLACK WOMAN, published by William Morrow & Company, November 1970, by permission of the author.

                    (an egg
                    or soup
                    . . . there ain't no meat.)

          there's endive there
          and
          cottage cheese . . .

                    (whew! if I had some
                    black-eyed peas . . .)

          there's sardines
          on the shelves
          and such . . .
          but
          don't
          get my anchovies . . .
          they cost
          too much!

                    (me get the
                    anchovies indeed!
                    what she think, she got—
                    a bird to feed?)

          there's plenty in there
          to fill you up . . .

                    (yes'm. just the
                    sight's
                    enough!

                    Hope I lives till I get
                    home
                    I'm tired of eatin'
                    what they eats in Rome . . .)

Considerations

1. Who is speaking in this poem? What does the typographic arrangement indicate?
2. Compare this poem with William Carlos Williams' "This Is Just To Say" (p. 495). Could the person who left that note have written the note in this poem?

3. What is the tone of this poem? How is it conveyed?
4. What is the significance of the title?

Lies

YEVGENY YEVTUSHENKO

Telling lies to the young is wrong.
Proving to them that lies are true is wrong.
Telling them that God's in his heaven
and all's well with the world is wrong.
The young know what you mean. The young are people.   5
Tell them the difficulties can't be counted,
and let them see not only what will be
but see with clarity these present times.
Say obstacles exist they must encounter
sorrow happens, hardship happens.   10
The hell with it. Who never knew
the price of happiness will not be happy.
Forgive no error you recognize,
it will repeat itself, increase,
and afterwards our pupils   15
will not forgive in us what we forgave.

Considerations

1. Is it possible to prove that "lies are true"?
2. The poet is a Russian citizen, and yet he voices a concern that is increasingly expressed by Americans of all ages. Does this indicate that all societies—at least, to a certain extent—bring up their young on lies? What are a parent's or a society's motives for lying to the young?
3. What does the poet say will happen as a result of this practice?
4. Note that the poem contains no figurative language. Why is direct language appropriate in this poem?

Yevgeny Yevtushenko: Lies from YEVTUSHENKO: SELECTED POEMS translated by Robin Milner-Gulland and Peter Levi, S.J. © Robin Milner-Gulland and Peter Levi, 1962.

Corner

RALPH POMEROY

The cop slumps alertly on his motorcycle,
Supported by one leg like a leather stork.
His glance accuses me of loitering.
I can see his eyes moving like fish
In the green depths of his green goggles.   5

His ease is fake. I can tell.
My ease is fake. And he can tell.
The fingers armored by his gloves
Splay and clench, itching to change something.
As if he were my enemy or my death,   10
I just stand there watching.

I spit out my gum which has gone stale.
I knock out a new cigarette—
Which is my bravery.
It is all imperceptible: 15
The way I shift my weight,
The way he creaks in his saddle.

The traffic is specific though constant.
The sun surrounds me, divides the street between us.
His crash helmet is whiter in the shade.   20
It is like a bull ring as they say it is just before the fighting.
I cannot back down. I am there.

Everything holds me back.
I am in danger of disappearing into the sunny dust.
My levis bake and my T-shirt sweats.   25

My cigarette makes my eyes burn.
But I don't dare drop it.

Who made him my enemy?
Prince of coolness. King of fear.
Why do I lean here waiting?   30
Why does he lounge there watching?

I am becoming sunlight.
My hair is on fire. My boots run like tar.
I am hung-up by the bright air.

Something breaks through all of a sudden,   35
And he blasts off, quick as a craver,
Smug in his power; watching me watch.

Considerations

1. Who is the speaker? What is the situation? Is it a fairly common one?
2. In what ways does the cop betray that his ease is "fake"?
3. How does the boy attempt to conceal his uneasiness? Is the cop fooled by it?
4. What sensations of physical discomfort does the boy suffer? Note the poet's use of hyperbole in describing them. Does this help you feel what the boy is enduring?
5. What do the titles of royalty—"Prince of coolness" and "King of fear"—convey about the cop's status in the eyes of the boy?
6. Even if you have not been to a bull ring, are you able to comprehend the significance of the simile in line 21? What do you think the atmosphere of a bull ring might be just before the fighting begins? What roles would the cop and the boy play if they were the principals in a bullfight?
7. Is there an answer to the questions asked in lines 28–31?

A Poem for Black Hearts

LeRoi Jones

For Malcolm's eyes, when they broke
the face of some dumb white man. For
Malcolm's hands raised to bless us
all black and strong in his image
of ourselves, for Malcolm's words
fire darts, the victor's tireless
thrusts, words hung above the world
change as it may, he said it, and

for this he was killed, for saying,
and feeling, and being/ change, all
collected hot in his heart, For Malcolm's
heart, raising us above our filthy cities,
for his stride, and his beat, and his address
to the grey monsters of the world, For Malcolm's
pleas for your dignity, black men, for your life,
black men, for the filling of your minds
with righteousness, For all of him dead and
gone and vanished from us, and all of him which
clings to our speech black god of our time.
For all of him, and all of yourself, look up,
black man, quit stuttering and shuffling, look up,
black man, quit whining and stooping, for all of him,
For Great Malcolm a prince of the earth,
   let nothing in us rest
until we avenge ourselves for his death, stupid animals
that killed him, let us never breathe a pure breath if
we fail, and white men call us faggots till the end of
the earth.

Considerations

1. Does the emphasis in this poem seem to be on listing the achievements of Malcolm X or encouraging blacks to take action?
2. What is the effect of repeating certain phrases? Would the message have been as clear if the phrases had not been repeated?
3. How is Malcolm X described?

The Pill versus
The Springhill Mine Disaster

RICHARD BRAUTIGAN

When you take your pill
it's like a mine disaster.
I think of all the people
lost inside of you.

A Hell of a Day

TIM REYNOLDS

This was a day of fumbling and petty accidents,
as though the population had grown all thumbs
at once. Watering her chrysanthemums,
Mrs. Kamei was surprised to see the plants
blacken, water turn to steam. Both Dote and Michiko
noted the other's absence but not her own.
Mr. Kime lifted his hat, but his head was gone.
Mr. Watanable rolled a double zero.
Photographing her son by the river bridge
Mrs. Ume pressed the shutter and overexposed her film.
Her son's yawn swallowed him. And everything turned on
when pretty Miss Mihara snapped the light switch.
Then old Mr. Ekahomo struck a match
to light his pipe, and the town caught, and dissolved in flame.

The European Shoe

MICHAEL BENEDIKT

The European Shoe is constructed of grass and reed, bound up and wound around so that it may slip easily over the wearer's head.

In case you are an aircraft pilot, you must take care that the European Shoe does not creep off your foot, and begin to make its way carefully along the fuselage.

The European Shoe pressed against the fugitive's nose, preventing it from imminent departure.

The European Shoe spends summers in delightful ways. A lady feels its subtle and unexpected pressure the length of her decolletage. (It winters in pain.)

That time I lent you my European Shoe you departed with a look of grandeur, and in total disrepair.

The European Shoe knocks on the door of the carefree farmerette. "The harvest has been gathered in, ha ha," it says, moving shyly forth along the edge of the couch.

I pointed to the European Shoe. I ate the European Shoe. I married the European Shoe.

Tears fall from the eye of the European Shoe as it waves goodbye to us from the back balcony of the speeding train.

It helps an old lady, extremely crippled and arthritic, move an enormous cornerstone. It invents a watch, which, when wound up tightly, flies completely to pieces.

It was a simple and dignified ceremony, distinguished for its gales of uncontrollable laughter, in which I married the European Shoe.

If it rains, the European Shoe becomes very heavy. I failed to cross the river, where thousands of European Shoes lay capsized.

Reprinted from *The Body,* by Michael Benedikt, by permission of Wesleyan University Press.

And as we lived alone, we two, the envy of our neighborhoods, the delight of our lively hordes of children.

I saw a flightful of graceful swallows heading to distant, half-forgotten islands over the distant seas; and in the midst of that annually questing company, I saw the European Shoe.

It never harmed anyone, and yet it never helped anyone.

Gaily it sets out into the depths of my profoundest closet, to do battle with the dusts of summer.

Dancing in the Street

AL YOUNG

for my NYC summer workshop students

Just because you wear a natural baby
dont mean you aint got a processed mind.
The field is open
the whole circle of life
is ours for the jumping into,
we ourselves the way we feel
right now
re-creating ourselves
to suit particular dreams & visions
that are no one else's.

Who needs that big mortgaged house
those household finance cars
they advertise
so scientifically
between newscasts,
expensive fronts
those foot-long cigarettes
that brand of breath?

I'd have to travel all the way
back to Lemuria
(cradle of the race
beneath the Pacific)
to bring back a more golden picture of us
the way we looked today
the way we are all the time inside,
healthy black masters
of our own destiny;
set at last on slashing the reins
& shaking off the blinders
that keep the north american
trillion dollar mule team
dragging its collective ass
into that nowhere desert
of bleached white bones & bomb tests.

Death Was a Trick

JEROME MAZZARO

Death was a trick I taught him as a pup
like fetching till he mastered both to race
my ordered stick back clamped between his jaws,
ignoring once too soon the whir of trucks
whose chirring crushed whole worlds of growing up
and set him broken in a makeshift box.
Across blind roadways he comes running yet,
small-terriered, black-footed, slow in death.

I, the Fake Mad Bomber
And Walking It Home Again

BYRON BLACK

First comes the cold,
and puffing as classes change
fast as the frames of a film
and dried old sarcophagi of professors reel on
trot placidly Latin with its dust and their rot.   5

Then dives the red sun
crashes like the stock market, in black
"the day was fine" as Wm. says
and the Tower stands impudent, one wants to slap it down
before the blast-off into stone-gray space.   10

Brisk bright day
Wm. and I walking fast,
we smile at lurid tales which shock like adders

Dark people with the faces of bulldogs
gruffly waddle past, Chryslers with the scream of a rocket   15
charge us jousting, we hurry fast
to the flap and claw of the Night Hawk

where dark hamburgers from the heart of a living vulture
are served by an Aztec princess
"the hamburger don't come with onions"   20
(pimples as jewels, and the pop of gum)
And the white bourgeois, slimy smiles
slide in with assuredness of talkative slugs, to music of the bank

outside the brightwork of their gaudy Cadillacs
wails like a chrome banshee toward the cool evening, and sad
   glass eyes,   25
And I thanking Wm. we part
he for home
and I full of cheer and good meat

head for my place, legs flashing
the power of wet muscles   30
sends an electric orgasm,
and as approaching Red River, now dry
beside the stadium where Christians are devourers
the night breaks
I know myself as the Fake Mad Bomber   35
and light a black cigar in the dark to prove it.

Considerations

1. Are you able to determine whether it is the poet or an imaginary
   character who is speaking? What sort of person is the speaker? What
   happens in the poem?
2. Characterize the tone of the poem. What stylistic elements determine
   it? Which do you think make the strongest contribution?
3. Most of the images involve space and rocketry or animals. How might
   they serve as a commentary on modern society? Which images reflect
   the poet's consciousness of his Indian heritage?
4. With what things does the poet compare the pedestrians, the professors, and the customers in the Night Hawk? By contrast, what is his
   image of the waitress? What does he think of these people?
5. Where does the poet use alliteration and assonance to heighten his
   images?
6. Revolutionaries supposedly smoke cigars to have a handy and in-

nocent-appearing means of lighting bomb fuses. What would the
speaker like to blow up? In what ways is he a "Fake Mad Bomber"?
Do you identify with him in any way?

Photograph of My Father
In His Twenty-Second Year

RAYMOND CARVER

October. Here in this dank, unfamiliar kitchen
I study my father's embarrassed young man's face.
Sheepish grin, he holds in one hand a string
Of spiny yellow perch, in the other
A bottle of Carlsbad beer.

In jeans and denim shirt, he leans
Against the front fender of a Ford *circa* 1934.
He would like to pose bluff and hearty for his posterity,
Wear his old hat cocked over his ear, stick out his tongue. . .
All his life my father wanted to be bold.

But the eyes give him away, and the hands
That limply offer the string of dead perch
And the bottle of beer. Father, I loved you,
Yet how can I say thank you, I who cannot hold my liquor either
And do not even know the places to fish?

Bankruptcy

RAYMOND CARVER

Twenty-eight, hairy belly hanging out
Of my undershirt (exempt)
I lie here on my side
On the couch (exempt)
And listen to the strange sound
Of my wife's pleasant voice (also exempt).

We are new arrivals
To these small pleasures.
Forgive me (I pray the Court)
That we have been improvident.
Today, my heart, like the front door.
Stands open for the first time in months.

Goodbye and Hello

TIM BUCKLEY

The antique people are down in the dungeons
    Run by machines and afraid of the tax
Their heads in the grave and their hands on their eyes
    Hauling their hearts around circular tracks
Pretending forever their masquerade towers
    Are not really riddled with widening cracks
        And I wave goodbye to iron
        And smile hello to the air

O the new children dance   I am young
All around the balloons   I will live
Swaying by chance   I am strong
To the breeze from the moon   I can give
Painting the sky   You the strange
With the colors of sun   Seed of day
Freely they fly   Feel the change
As all become one   Know the Way

The velocity addicts explode on the highways
 Ignoring the journey and moving so fast
Their nerves fall apart and they gasp but can't breathe
 They run from the cops of the skeleton past
Petrified by tradition in a nightmare they stagger
 Into nowhere at all and then look up aghast
  And I wave goodbye to speed
  And smile hello to a rose

O the new children play	I am young
Under juniper trees	I will live
Sky blue or grey	I am strong
They continue at ease	I can give
Moving so slow	You the strange
That serenely they can	Seed of day
Gracefully grow	Feel the change
And yes still understand	Know the Way

The king and the queen in their castle of billboards
 Sleepwalk down the hallways dragging behind
All their possessions and transient treasures
 As they go to worship the electronic shrine
On which is playing the late late commercial
 In that hollowest house of the opulent blind
  And I wave goodbye to Mammon
  And smile hello to a stream

O the new children buy	I am young
All the world for a song	I will live
Without a dime	I am strong
To which they belong	I can give
Nobody owns	You the strange
Anything anywhere	Seed of day
Everyone's grown	Feel the change
Up so big they can share	Know the Way

The vaudeville generals cavort on the stage
 And shatter their audience with submachine guns
And Freedom and Violence the acrobat clowns
 Do a balancing act on the graves of our sons
While the tapdancing Emperor sings "War is peace"
 And Love the Magician disappears in the fun
  And I wave goodbye to murder
  And smile hello to the rain

O the new children can't   I am young
Tell a foe from a friend   I will live
Quick to enchant   I am strong
And so glad to extend   I can give
Handfuls of dawn   You the strange
To kaleidoscope men   Seed of day
Come from beyond   Feel the change
The Great Wall of Skin   Know the Way

The bloodless husbands are jesters who listen
   Like sheep to the shrieks and commands of their wives
And the men who aren't men leave the women alone
   See them all faking love on a bed made of knives
Afraid to discover or trust in their bodies
   And in secret divorce they will never survive
     And I wave goodbye to ashes
     And smile hello to a girl

O the new children kiss   I am young
They are so proud to learn   I will live
Womanhood bliss   I am strong
And the manfire that burns   I can give
Knowing no fear   You the strange
They take off their clothes   Seed of day
Honest and clear   Feel the change
As a river that flows   Know the Way

The antique people are fading out slowly
   Like newspapers flaming in mind suicide
Godless and sexless directionless loons
   Their sham sandcastles dissolve in the tide
They put on their deathmasks and compromise daily
   The new children will live for the elders have died
     And I wave goodbye to America
     And smile hello to the world

Considerations

1. Notice the contrast between the two groups of people in this poem. Whom is the poet talking about in the long lines, and whom in the short lines? How accurate do you consider the description of each group? Are they stereotypes? Can it be that all virtue rests in one group and none in the other?

2. What values is the poet advocating? What values is he attacking?
3. Does the poem contribute to the very thing he is attacking?

I Would Not Be Here

JOHN HARTFORD

I would not be here
If I hadn't been there
I wouldn't been there
if I hadn't just turned
on Wednesday the third
in the late afternoon
got to talking with George
who works out in the back
and only because
he was getting off early
to go see a man
at a Baker Street bookstore
with a rare first edition
of steamboats and cotton
a book he would never
have sought in the first place
had he not been inspired
by a fifth grade replacement
school teacher in Kirkwood
who was picked just at random
by some man on a school board
who couldn't care less
and she wouldn't been working
if not for her husband
who moved two months prior
to work in the office
of a man he had met
while he served in the army
and only because
they were in the same barracks
an accident caused
by a poorly made roster

mixed up on the desk
of a sergeant from Denver
who wouldn't be in
but for being in back
in a car he was riding
before he enlisted
that hit a cement truck
and killed both his buddies
but a back seat flew up there
and spared him from dying
and only because
of the fault of a workman
who forgot to turn screws
on a line up in Detroit
'cause he hollered at Sam
who was hateful that morning
hung over from drinking
alone at a tavern
because of a woman
he wished he'd not married
he met long ago
at a Jewish bar mitzvah
for the son of a man
who had moved there from Jersey
who managed the drugstore
that sold the prescription
that cured up the illness
he caught way last summer
he wouldn't have caught
except . . .

Considerations

1. John Hartford is a young poet and composer whose works deal with current events as well as philosophical premises. This poem describes the speaker's awareness that he got where he is through a series of coincidences and accidents. Is the point of the poem that one's present state is the result of a series of accidents? Or does it show our interrelatedness with numerous people we do not even know, and therefore reveal that each man is related to every other person?
2. Does the lack of punctuation and stanza breaks add to the feeling of continuity?

Sisterhood

MARILYN HACKER

For Dora FitzGerald

No place for a lady, this
back-country gateway comes
up from dreams, the wounds
are an entrance, or a season ticket.
The morning freshness, the
summersend mountain calm:
distractions. "What do you
call this town?"

No man will love you, no
woman be your friend, your
face will go away, your body
betray you. We wrestled
to the floor, his fingers
blanching my albows, cords
popping his neck. Don't look
into the sun. Don't squint.

He lay on the concrete
ramp of the bus terminal. I
massaged his back and shoulders through his clothes.
I opened his trenchcoat, peeled
its collar away from his thin
white shirt, his thin chest.
Staining the slashed white
yellowish pink, those wounds.

When you give the ghost
bread and water he asks
for, you incur prophecy.
"Why, have you come here,
woman? Your city
is far away. We do not speak
your language. Your sister
is dead."

"Take off your rings
at the first gate. At the second
your crown of lapis lazuli.
You must leave your golden
breastplate at the third, and below
the gallows where he hangs
who forgot you, and will not rise,
break your mother's scepter."

They have killed him
often. He bled
on the concrete floor. My hands
were not healing. They took him
into the next room. I heard
gunshots. I woke screaming.
At the bottom of hell
he swings in the stinking wind. She watches.

We, women, never
trust his returnings. He takes
the bread and water, but
the words on the paper
are illegible. His body
lies severed on the white sand
and the pieces are not
food, they are stones.

We gather those
jewels and wear them,
lapis in the crown, amethysts
over the nipples, garnets
oozing on cool
fingers. The gateway
dreams itself up, and we eye the surly
guard, and strip, and go down.

In a Prominent Bar in Secaucus One Day

(To the tune of 'The Old Orange Flute' or the tune of 'Sweet Betsy from Pike')

X. J. KENNEDY

In a prominent bar in Secaucus one day
Rose a lady in skunk with a topheavy sway,
Raised a knobby red finger—all turned from their beer—
While with eyes bright as snowcrust she sang high and clear:

'Now who of you'd think from an eyeload of me
That I once was a lady as proud as could be?
Oh I'd never sit down by a tumbledown drunk
If it wasn't, my dears, for the high cost of junk.

'All the gents used to swear that the white of my calf
Beat the down of the swan by a length and a half.
In the kerchief of linen I caught to my nose
Ah, there never fell snot, but a little gold rose.

'I had seven gold teeth and a toothpick of gold,
My Virginia cheroot was a leaf of it rolled
And I'd light it each time with a thousand in cash—
Why the bums used to fight if I flicked them an ash.

'Once the toast of the Biltmore, the belle of the Taft,
I would drink bottle beer at the Drake, never draught,
And dine at the Astor on Salisbury steak
With a clean tablecloth for each bite I did take.

'In a car like the Roxy I'd roll to the track,
A steel-guitar trio, a bar in the back,
And the wheels made no noise, they turned over so fast,
Still it took you ten minutes to see me go past.

'When the horses bowed down to me that I might choose,
I bet on them all, for I hated to lose.
Now I'm saddled each night for my butter and eggs
And the broken threads race down the backs of my legs.

'Let you hold in mind, girls, that your beauty must pass
Like a lovely white clover that rusts with its grass.
Keep your bottoms off barstools and marry you young
Or be left—an old barrel with many a bung.

'For when time takes you out for a spin in his car
You'll be hard-pressed to stop him from going too far
And be left by the roadside, for all your good deeds,
Two toadstools for tits and a face full of weeds.'

All the house raised a cheer, but the man at the bar
Made a phonecall and up pulled a red patrol car
And she blew us a kiss as they copped her away
From that prominent bar in Secaucus, N.J.

Dress Rehearal Rag

LEONARD COHEN

Got up some time in the afternoon
And you didn't feel like much.
Said to yourself, 'Where are you, Golden Boy
Where is your famous golden touch?
I thought you knew where all the elephants lie down
I thought you were the crown prince of all the wheels in Ivory town.'
Look at your body now
Well, there's nothing much to save
And the bitter voice in the mirror says,
'Hey, Prince, you need a shave.'
That's right, it's come to this
It's come to this
And wasn't it a long way down?
And wasn't it a strange way down?

There's no hot water
And the cold is running thin
Well, what do you expect from the kind of places
You've been living in?
Don't drink from that cup,
It's all caked and cracked along the rim.
That's not the electric light, my friend,
That's your vision that is dim.
Cover up your face with soap,
There—now you're Santa Claus
And you've got an A for anyone
Who will give you his applause.
I thought you were a racing man
Ah, but you couldn't take the pace
There's a funeral in the mirror
And it's stopping at your face
That's right—it's come to this
It's come to this
And wasn't it a long way down?
And wasn't it a strange way down?

Once there was a path
And a girl with chestnut hair
And you spent the summers picking
All the berries that grew there
There were times she was a woman
There were times she was a child
As you held her in the shadows
Where the raspberries grew wild
And you climbed the highest mountains
And you sang about the view
And everywhere you went
Love went along with you
That's a hard one to remember
It makes you clench your fist.
And the veins stand out like highways
All along your wrist
And yes, it's come to this
It's come to this
And wasn't it a long way down?
And wasn't it a strange way down?

You can still find a job
Go out and talk to a friend
On the back of every magazine

There are coupons you can send
Why don't you join the Rosicrucians?
They will give you back your hope.
You can find your love in diagrams
In a plain brown envelope
But you've used up all your coupons
Except the one that seems

To be tatooed on your arm
Along with several thousand dreams
Now Santa Claus comes forward
That razor in his mitt
And he puts on his dark glasses
And he shows you where to hit
And then the cameras pan
The stand-in stunt man's
Dress Rehearsal Rag.

The Geni in the Jar

(*for Nina Simone*)

NIKKI GIOVANNI

take a note and spin it around spin it around don't
prick your finger
take a note and spin it around
on the Black loom on the Black loom
careful baby
don't prick your finger

take the air and weave the sky
around the Black loom around the Black loom
make the sky sing a Black song sing a blue song
sing my song make the sky sing a Black song
from the Black loom from the Black loom
careful baby
don't prick your finger

take the geni and put her in a jar
put her in a jar
wrap the sky around her
take the geni and put her in a jar
wrap the sky around her

listen to her sing
sing a Black song our Black song
from the Black loom
singing to me
from the Black loom
careful baby
don't prick your finger

Filling Station

ELIZABETH BISHOP

Oh, but it is dirty!
—this little filling station,
oil-soaked, oil-permeated
to a disturbing, over-all
black translucency.
Be careful with that match!

Father wears a dirty,
oil-soaked monkey suit
that cuts him under the arms,
and several quick and saucy
and greasy sons assist him
(it's a family filling station),
all quite thoroughly dirty.

Do they live in the station?
It has a cement porch
behind the pumps, and on it
a set of crushed and grease-
impregnated wickerwork;
on the wicker sofa
a dirty dog, quite comfy.

Some comic books provide
the only note of color—
of certain color. They lie
upon a big dim doily
draping a taboret
(part of the set), beside
a big hirsute begonia.

Why the extraneous plant?
Why the taboret?
Why, oh why, the doily?
(Embroidered in daisy stitch
with marguerites, I think,
and heavy with gray crochet.)

Somebody embroidered the doily.
Somebody waters the plant,
or oils it, maybe. Somebody
arranges the rows of cans
so that they softly say:
ESSO—SO—SO—SO
to high-strung automobiles.
Somebody loves us all.

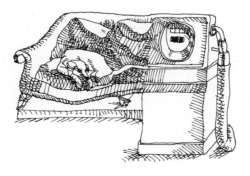

from Blue Meridian

JEAN TOOMER

Uncase the races,
Open this pod,
Free man from his shrinkage
Not from the reality itself,
But from the unbecoming and enslaving behavior
Associated with our prejudices and preferences.
Eliminate these;
I am, we are, simply of the human race.
Uncase the nations.
Open this pod,
Keep the real but destroy the false;
We are of the human nation.
Uncase the regions—
Occidental, Oriental, North, South,
We are of Earth.
Free the sexes,
I am neither male nor female nor in-between;
I am of sex, with male differentiations.
Open the classes;
I am, we are, simply of the human class.
Expand the fields—
Those definitions which fix fractions and lose wholes—
I am of the field of being,
We are beings.

If We Must Die

CLAUDE McKAY

If we must die—let it not be like hogs
Hunted and penned in an inglorious spot,
While round us bark the mad and hungry dogs,
Making their mock at our accursed lot.
If we must die—oh, let us nobly die,
So that our precious blood may not be shed

In vain; then even the monsters we defy
Shall be constrained to honor us though dead!
Oh, Kinsmen! We must meet the common foe;
Though far outnumbered, let us show us brave,
And for their thousand blows deal one death-blow!
What though before us lies the open grave?
Like men we'll face the murderous, cowardly pack,
Pressed to the wall, dying, but fighting back!

Ten Haiku

Snow whispering down
   All day long,
   Earth has vanished
Leaving only sky

     Joso

How hot and dusty
   These sunstruck
   Cobwebs glisten
Between dry branches!

     Onistusura

Moonlit flower-field . . .
   Daylight gives it
   Back again
To a cotton farm

     Basho

Having spoken ill
   My lips now
   Feel the cold of
Autumn's fatal wind

     Basho

Poppy petals fall
   Softly Quietly
   Calmly
When they are ready

     Etsujin

In my small village
   Even the flies
   Aren't afraid
to bite a big man

     Issa

Well! Hello down there,
   Friend snail!
   When did you arrive
In such a hurry?

     Issa

Poor crying cricket
   Perhaps
   Your little husband
Was caught by our cat

     Kikaku

From watching the moon
   I turned
   And my friendly old
Shadow led me home

     Shiki

Into a cold night
   I spoke aloud . . .
   But the voice was
No voice I knew

     Otsuji

Death in a Plane

(Translated from the Portuguese by Mark Strand)

CARLOS DRUMMOND DE ANDRADE

I awaken for death.
I shave, dress, put on my shoes.
It is my last day—a day
not broken by one premonition.
Everything happens as usual.   5
I head for the street. I am going to die.

I shall not die now. A whole day
unfolds before me.
What a long day it is! And in the street
what a lot of steps I take! And what a lot of things   10
have accumulated in time! Without paying much attention
I keep on going. Faces
crowded into a notebook!

I visit the bank. What good
is the money if a few hours later   15
the police come and take it
from the hole that was my chest?
But I don't see myself wounded and bloody.
I am clean, spotless, bright, summery.
Nevertheless, I walk toward death.   20
I walk into offices, into mirrors,
into hands that are offered, into eyes
that are nearsighted, into mouths that smile or simply talk.
I do not say goodbye, I know nothing, I am not afraid:
death hides   25
its breath and its strategy.

I lunch. What for? I eat a fish in a sauce of gold and
        cream.
It is my last fish on my last
fork. The mouth distinguishes, chooses, decides,   30
swallows. Music passes through the sweets, a shiver

from a violin or the wind, I don't know. It isn't death.
It is the sun. The crowded trolleys. Work.
I am in a great city and I am a man
in a cogwheel. I am in a rush. I am going to die.   35
I ask the slow ones to clear a path for me. I don't look
at the cafés rattling with coffee cups and conversation,
I don't look at the shaded wall of the old hospital.
Or at the posters. I am in a rush. I buy a paper. It's a rush
even if it means death!   40

The day already come around to its midpoint does not
    tell me
that I too have begun to come to an end. I am tired.
I want to sleep, but the preparations. The telephone.
The bills. The letters. I do a thousand things   45
that will create another thousand, here, there, in the
    United States.
I'll do anything. I make dates
that I shall never keep, I utter words in a trance,
I lie, saying, "Until tomorrow." But tomorrow won't be.   50

I decline with the afternoon, my head aches, I defend
    myself,
hand myself a pill: at least
the water drowns what hurts,
the fly, the buzzing . . . but nothing I will die from: 55
    death cheats,
cheats like a soccer player,
chooses like a cashier,
carefully, among illnesses and disasters.

Still it isn't death, it is the shadow   60
over tired buildings, the interval between
two races. Heavy business slows down,
engineers, executives, laborers are finishing up.
But cabdrivers, waiters, and a thousand other
nighttime workers are getting started. The city   65
changes hands.

I go home. Again I clean up.
So my hair will be neat
and my nails not bring to mind the rebellious child of
    long ago.   70
The clothes without dust. The plastic suitcase.

I lock up my room. I lock up my life.
The elevator locks me up. I am calm.

For the last time I look at the city.
I can still turn back, put off death,
not take that car. Not go.   75
I can turn and say, "Friends,
I forgot a paper, there's no trip,"
I can go to the casino, read a book.

But I take the car. I point out the place
where something is waiting. The field. Searchlights.   80
I pass by marble, glass, chrome.
I climb some steps. I bend. I enter
death's interior.

Death arranges seats to make the wait
more comfortable. Here one meets   85
those who are going to die and do not know it.
Newspapers, coffee, chewing gum, cotton for
        the ear,
small services daintily surround
our strapped-in bodies.   90
We are going to die, it is not only
my single and limited death,
twenty of us will be destroyed,
twenty of us will die,
twenty of us will be smashed to bits, and right now.   95

Or almost now. First the private,
personal, silent death of the individual.
I die secretly and without pain
to live only as a piece of twenty,
and in me incorporate all the pieces   100
of those who are silently dying as I am.
All of us are one in twenty, a bouquet
of vigorous breath about to be blown apart.

And we hang,
coldly we hang over the loves   105
and business of the country.
Toy streets disappear,
lights dim, hills dissolve,
there is only a mattress of clouds,

only a cold oxygen tube grazes my ears,   110
a tube that is sealed: and inside
the illumined and lukewarm body we live
in comfort and solitude, quiet and nothingness.

So smooth in the night is this machine and so easily does
     it cut   115
through increasingly larger blocks of air
that I live
my final moment and it's as if
I had been living for years,
before and after today,   120
a continuous and indomitable life
where there are no pauses, lapses, dreams.

I am twenty in the machine
that purrs softly
between starry pictures and the remote breaths of   125
     earth,
I feel at home thousands of metres high,
neither bird nor myth,
I take stock of my powers,
and I fly without mystery,   130
a body flying, holding on to pockets, watches, nails,
tied to the earth by memory and muscular habit,
flesh soon to explode.

Oh, whiteness, serenity under the violence
of death without previous notice,   135
careful despite the unavoidable closeness
of atmospheric danger,
a shattering blast of air, splinter of wind
on the neck, lightning
flash burst crack   140
broken we tumble
straight down I fall and am turned into news.

The Hissing of Summer Lawns

JOHN GUERIN AND JONI MITCHELL

He bought her a diamond for her throat
He put her in a ranch house on a hill
She could see the valley bar-b-ques
From her window sill
See the blue pools in the squinting sun   5
And hear the hissing of summer lawns

He put up a barbed wire fence
To keep out the unknown
And on every metal thorn
Just a little blood of his own   10
She patrols that fence of his
To a latin drum
And the hissing of summer lawns
Darkness
Wonder makes it easy   15
Darkness
With a joyful mask
Darkness
Tube's gone, darkness, darkness
No color, no contrast   20

A diamond dog
Carrying a cup and a cane
Looking through a double glass
Looking at too much pride and too much shame
There's a black fly buzzing   25
There's a heat wave burning in her master's voice
And the hissing of summer lawns

He gave her his darkness to regret
And good reason to quit him
He gave her a room full of Chippendale   30
That nobody sits in
Still she stays with a love of some kind
It's the lady's choice
The hissing of summer lawns

Today Is a Day of Great Joy

VICTOR HERNANDEZ CRUZ

when they stop poems
in the mail   & clap
their hands & dance to
them
when women become pregnant
by the side of poems
the strongest sounds   making
the river go along

it is a great day

as poems fall down to
movie crowds   in restaurants
in bars

when poems start to
knock down walls   to
choke politicians
when poems scream &
begin to break the air

that is the time of
true poets   that is
the time of greatness

a true poet   aiming
poems   & watching things
fall to the ground

it is a great day.

DRAMA

Introduction
to Drama

You are probably more familiar with drama than you realize. Not only have you seen dramas on the movie and television screens, but you may have taken part in some dramas yourself. Of course, they might not have been labeled dramas. But role-playing, encounter groups, and simulation sessions all depend on some of the techniques of formal drama to show how people communicate about themselves and interpret the communication of others. (Increasingly, teachers have used these techniques to demonstrate the problems of the UN or the kind of infighting that can go on in a city-planning council session.)

So you probably have had a chance to enjoy participating in drama or seeing it performed. Now how does this relate to drama in a book? There are two schools of thought about drama. One says that plays are intended to be acted, so a mere reading of them is inadequate. According to this school, true drama is a visual and a group experience. (This has led producers of some television comedies to add laugh tracks in an effort to create the atmosphere of a shared experience.) The other view holds that the "theater of the mind" is the proper concern of literary investigation. Reading a script is the only way that the minds of author and audience can meet without the interference of directors and actors.

Which view is correct? It is impossible to say. However, for the purposes of this book, we are forced to follow a strict definition of literature. We can deal only with the words an author has set down—not actions, pictures, or position in space. Should we judge the story line of a Tennessee Williams play presented on television in the same way as we do the same story when we read it in an anthology? Logically the staged presentation belongs to the realm of theatrical art; the only part of the movie or television program that can be termed *literature* is its script.

As you can see, this distinction is arbitrary, and the shape drama has taken in the past few decades makes such traditional boundaries hard to defend. Has an emphasis on the importance of gesture and action as a means of communication led the absurdist dramatists away from drama as literature? By what right are the happenings in the theater that involve an interaction between cast and audience classified as plays? Such exceptions may eventually outnumber the rule. As new works become classics, definitions may be revised; for the time being, however, centuries of traditional drama give some justification for emphasizing that type of dramatic literature in this discussion.

TRADITIONAL ELEMENTS OF A PLAY

In terms of literary genre, plays are most closely related to objective fiction. Most dramas follow a pattern of character introduction, introduction of conflict, rising action or complication, climax, and solution or denouement. One or another of these elements may be the focus of a particular play (the character in Pirandello's *Man with a Flower;* conflict and complication of O'Neill's *Ile*), but some semblance of all can be found in even absurdist plays. In general, the playwright's goal is the same as that of most fiction writers—to demonstrate the dynamics of relationships and reveal something of human nature itself. (As was outlined in the earlier discussion of fiction, the three elements of theme, plot, and characters are used to create a cohesive story.)

RESTRICTIONS OF DRAMA

Playwrights, however, face greater problems in presenting their ideas. In fact, if, as some contend, traditional theater is a dying institution, it may be because of the tremendous handicaps under which the dramatist must labor to create something that will be a memorable theatrical experience.

Suppose you wanted to tell the story of a significant event in your life. How would you stage your story so that the audience could experience it in a way similar to the way you did? An attempt to answer that question reveals the challenges of drama. Let us look at just some of these challenges (remembering always that dramatists are writing something they hope can and will be acted).

In the first place, while the novelist can hope that readers will return to the story after a brief interlude if they can't take it in all at once, playwrights have to make allowances for the length of time their audiences will stay in the theater.

Next, they must—if they hope to have their plays produced—consider certain realities of the theater: economic conditions, space, the limitations of visual effects for representing outdoor settings, and so on.

Furthermore, the dramatist is forced to do most of the communicating through the dialogue of the actors. He or she has only a few ways of demonstrating what goes on in the minds of the characters, ways that are awkward and not entirely believable: the Greek chorus, the Shakespearean soliloquy, the aside, the foil or confidante to whom a character can unburden his soul. After all, how many people do you know who will talk at length to themselves aloud in a perfectly empty room? And if you see someone doing just that on stage, aren't you a little tempted to think there is something abnormal or unreal about them?

The diction itself presents a problem. Some creature (animal, vegetable, or otherwise) is going to have to speak the playwright's words in order for the audience to receive them. Often dialogue that when written seems possible, clever, or highly useful (in terms of advancing the story), sounds impossible, stilted, ridiculous, or even confusing when an actor renders it. (The dangers in this area are many and cannot be avoided, since any play not totally mimed depends on dialogue.) Yet most real-life dialogue is inane; a random recording of friends' conversations will show how true this is. At the other extreme, poetic flights of fancy (a surprising number of plays are written in poetry, although few living humans speak in poetry) tend to be distracting, hard to understand, or hard to believe in.

Between these outer limits, the diction of drama tends to be the ordinary language of the general public (or that appropriate to the characters depicted) with a certain amount of metaphor, simile, allusion, symbolism, and other figurative language intermixed in order to suggest things about the characters, bring the conflict into sharper focus, and intensify the experience. When Julie says (in *Miss Julie*):

> That reminds me of a dream I sometimes have, in which I'm on top of a pillar and can't see any way of getting down. When I look down I'm dizzy; I have to get down but I haven't the courage to jump. I can't stay there and I long to fall, but I don't fall. There's no respite. There can't be any peace at all for me until I'm down, right down to the ground.

she is speaking about her situation in life, her feelings about herself, and giving a clue to the action to follow. Her description also invites the reader's empathy.

A further complication is the fact that the unfortunate playwright can never be sure that the audience will notice what he or she wants them to notice—especially in terms of stage directions—or that they will draw the conclusions he intended. Take the stage directions in *A View from the Bridge* (p. 896), for example. When that play is produced, all of those words disappear, and the author is powerless to keep the audience from concentrating on a hole in the ceiling or bad lighting, rather than on what he wants them to see.

Other challenges include the decision to begin the play at a particular point in time; regardless of the time that the author does choose, much has already happened. Suppose that you are going to write a play about a man who comes home from the army only to find that his friends ignore him. At what moment in the man's life do you open the curtain? How will you reveal that he has been away for a few years? How can you show that the other actors are his former friends?

Whatever the opening, however, the play itself always takes place in the present. If there is a flashback or a look into the future, that moment then becomes present reality. This fact, while it is limiting, also makes drama the most immediate of the literary genres: the audience is there while the life is being lived.

Finally, while a dramatist is not now obligated to observe the unities of time, place, and theme so much admired by French playwrights of the seventeenth century,[1] there are few techniques available for circumventing them. Handling flashbacks and place changes is hard to do on stage without being unconvincing or confusing. Inevitably, the time is almost always now, and what the audience sees is what is taking place.

Thus far only certain ways have been found for solving these and related dramatic challenges. They are highly stylized and have a long history, so let us take a look at how we got where we are.

CONVENTIONS OF GREEK DRAMA

It sometimes seems that at the time of the early Greeks (around the fifth century B.C.) everything was beginning, everything had to be invented, everything remained to be done for the first time. This was a challenge that gave rise to some magnificent solutions—and some that—given the benefit of hindsight to aid our judgment—seem ridiculous.

The early Greek dramatists were devoted to realism, or so they said. Their ritualized productions had performers wearing masks showing exaggerated facial expressions and actors wearing high-soled boots to make them seem taller and more impressive. But there were no conventions that helped them indicate pauses between acts or change scenery or location, so everything was a continuous flow. And since the audience was to see what took place, and since they obviously could not see through walls, the only action that could legitimately be depicted would be that taking place out-of-doors. That is where the audience was—in a huge outdoor amphitheater—and that is where the playwrights set their plays: outside of palaces, outside of temples, outside of city gates, outside of tombs.

The fact that in real life not many people spend all of their time outside probably did occur to Aeschylus and Sophocles, but they were limited by tradition. Finally, in the fifth century, in a burst of frustration and inspiration a mechanical device—a small platform on wheels—was

---

1. The formal French drama of the seventeenth century reemphasized the Greek requirements of unity of action (the action must be directed toward a single goal), unity of place (the action must be limited to a single location), and unity of time (the time represented must be limited to the time it takes to perform the play or at most to a single day). Nineteenth- and twentieth-century dramatists have generally ignored these restrictions.

introduced to provide a setting for interior scenes. (Of course, all along they could have action taking place off stage and someone rushing on stage to report it—a technique that is still used today.)

After analyzing a number of the best plays of his time, especially *Oedipus Rex,* Aristotle wrote what he felt to be a definitive explanation of the content, purpose, and conventions of Greek drama. His ideas had such scope and force that much of what he said about drama is still being taught and used today. It is hard to say whether the Greeks had in fact envisaged all of the possibilities of drama and that therefore the rules Aristotle outlined are merely descriptive, or whether new approaches and solutions await discovery as soon as Aristotle's notions stop strait-jacketing the theater.

We do have the Greeks to thank for our highly artificial system of classifying plays as tragic or comic. You rarely hear poetry or fiction classified in this way. Hemingway is not described as an author of tragedies or Mark Twain as an author of comedies. We recognize that great works in all the genres often incorporate both humor and sorrow. But for the Greeks the division was very real and strict. Comedy was dedicated to the animal spirits in man, tragedy to his aspirations or moral sense. Tragedy was thus seen as the greater drama, because it showed man groping toward excellence.

Given the Aristotelian definition of tragedy as "the imitation of an action that is serious, and also as having magnitude, complete in itself, incorporating incidents arousing pity and fear, wherewith to accomplish the catharsis of such emotions," it is easy to see why people become more involved with tragedy. The tragic hero—the person who is led by an error in judgment or a tragic flaw to an unfortunate end—might all too easily be any of us. We like to laugh, it is true, at ourselves or at others, but the thing that keenly holds our attention is the dramatiziation of our most secret fears.

The themes of Greek drama were old even then. And yet they represent the oldest dramatizations available to us of universal, timeless plots. Much of the drama of today involves the same themes, only communicated through modern characters, settings, and language.

Much of the formality and ritual we find difficult to appreciate in Greek drama was because the Greeks took their drama as seriously as ritual. Dramas were generally presented on two occasions every year, both of which were religious festivals. The audiences were enormous and became extremely emotionally involved with the performances. Care and expense were taken with each production, the cost being born by some wealthy citizen designated by the government. This financial backing was both an honor and a duty.

Drama of the Middle Ages

Drama has never reached such heights since that day. As centuries went by, the golden age of Greek art and drama went the way of other golden ages. The Romans gave only a slightly less graceful contribution to the history of drama. (Seneca's tragedies, for example, were meant to be recited rather than acted.) Then, seeing the stage and acting as the path to perdition, the Roman Catholic Church closed down drama for most of the Medieval period (the Dark Ages). Fortunately, what the Church could kill, it could also resurrect. So in churches and cathedrals in Europe and England once again on festive occasions like Christmas and Easter there were pageants and plays.

In the ninth and tenth centuries liturgical plays appeared. Their themes dealt with the legends of the saints, the life of Christ, and miscellaneous Biblical stories (the conversion of Paul, for example). By the twelfth century, these liturgical plays had developed into what are called mystery, or miracle, plays, and were performed outdoors on movable wagons. Morality plays, such as *Everyman* and *The Castle of Perseverance,* which depicted the virtues and the vices battling for man's soul, followed in the fifteenth century. Other pre-Shakespearean drama included folk plays (Robin Hood was a favorite topic for the playwrights of the late fifteenth century), farces (featuring Chaucerianlike themes of reform from within the Church), and court plays (around 1560–1600).

In short, drama as an art form regressed rather than progressed between the days of Sophocles and Shakespeare. But by the Elizabethan era, Western philosophy, in respect to its view of human nature and man's place in the universe, had broadened, and the concepts behind drama changed greatly.

Shakespeare and Elizabethan Drama

The focus of our attention is now the England of Elizabeth I, set in the center of expanding horizons, riding the crest of what must have seemed like an endless wave of success and optimism. There was prosperity (in many areas at least), leisure, education no longer restricted to the clergy, and a renewed interest in the development of literature. Well-to-do young men wooed their lady loves in the fashion of the earlier French Court of Love, sighing over the transitoriness of it all, concentrating in their highly stylized poetry upon their fair mistress' breasts or eyes or locks of hair.

Into this setting came Shakespeare, heralding a new golden age of drama. The dramas had changed somewhat, although the hero was still larger than life and his downfall still much his own fault. In fact, the trend that began with Sophocles was carried even further. No longer were gods involved in man's destiny; his enemy and his salvation lay within himself.

The number of actors involved increased. Now the stage was rife with characters. Subplots—romantic or criminal intrigues of minor characters—made the plays richer and more complicated. Plays were no longer all tragedy or all comedy; jesters and gravediggers provided comic relief to sustained serious drama, and even the brightest comedy might end on a melancholy note. Treatment of the unities expanded: action took place over a longer period of time, scenes changed from one location to another, and a divided stage showed interiors and exteriors with equal ease.

After Shakespeare came a number of dramatic trends, over which we shall pass quickly. The advent of the Puritans in England stifled the dramatic arts as effectively as had the Catholic Church earlier. When the ruling dynasties were once again on the English throne (late in the seventeenth century), Restoration drama flourished. Restoration comedies were bawdy, artificial (in the sense of subscribing to predetermined artistic guidelines), witty, and satirical.

Social and Psychological Drama

Then came a period of social drama best exemplified by Ibsen and Chekov. Once again the theater mirrored the changing beliefs of Western society. Here man was the victim, not of the gods, not of self, but of the social order.

By the late 1800s the work of Sigmund Freud of Vienna was beginning to have an impact on Western man's view of himself. Psychological dramas became the order of the day, led by Strindberg in Sweden and later O'Neill and Arthur Miller in America. To some extent the psychological drama was merely a variation on the social drama. Man was still a victim, this time of dark forces deep within him and also of the social order, to the extent that it was reflected in his upbringing.

Absurdist Drama

Throughout the years, drama remained an acting out of, and a comment on, relationships. Now all of the divergent trends through this lengthy history have merged in the modern Theater of the Absurd (so-named by Ionesco, one of the leading exemplars of this school of drama). Man is a victim only if you want to view it that way, say the absurdists. In reality, life is absurd, and the universe is chaotic; there is no order. While we still perceive events as being tragic, they are at the same time as humorous as slipping on a banana peel.

Many absurdist plays approach poetry in the compression of their language and the richness of their ambiguity—that is, the various legitimate ways that we may view the play. The characters are quite different from those of earlier plays; many have become grotesque caricatures, and yet they are recognizable types to nearly every audience. The staging has also changed; here there is little attempt at realism. These changes encourage the audience to find their own meaning in the dramatic experiences, to bring their own experience into the play.

Is the theater dying or already dead? Should it die? The proliferation of revolutionary street-threater groups and companies such as the LaMama troupe seem to say that drama is relevant and drama will live—although with a vastly altered character. The days of the drawing-room comedy seem to be gone forever.

Oedipus Rex

SOPHOCLES

Sophocles (496–406 B.C.) was born at Colonus on the outskirts of Athens, and died in Athens. The exact date on which he composed Oidipous Turannos *("The Swell-foot King") is not known, but probably was around 409. The translation which follows is by Dudley Fitts and Robert Fitzgerald.*

CHARACTERS

PEOPLE OF THEBES
OEDIPUS, *King of Thebes*
A PRIEST
CREON, *brother to Iocastè*
CHORUS
CHORAGOS
TEIRESIAS, *a seer*
A PAGE
IOCASTÈ, *widow of Laïos, former King of Thebes, and now wife to Oedipus*

MESSENGER FROM CORINTH
MAIDSERVANT
AN OLD THEBAN SHEPHERD
A SERVANT OF THE PALACE
OTHER PALACE ATTENDANTS
ANTIGONE
ISMENE
HANDMAIDENS TO ANTIGONE AND ISMENE

PROLOGUE

Before the palace of OEDIPUS, *King of Thebes. A central door and two lateral doors open onto a platform which runs the length of the façade. On the platform, right and left, are altars; and three steps lead down into the "orchestra," or chorus-ground. At the beginning of the action these steps are crowded by suppliants who have brought branches and chaplets of olive leaves and who lie in various attitudes of despair.*

Oedipus *enters.*

Oedipus. My children, generations of the living
 In the line of Kadmos,[1] nursed at his ancient hearth:
 Why have you strewn yourselves before these altars
 In supplication, with your boughs and garlands?
 The breath of incense rises from the city
 With a sound of prayer and lamentation.
          Children,
 I would not have you speak through messengers,
 And therefore I have come myself to hear you—
 I, Oedipus, who bear the famous name.

  To a Priest.

 You, there, since you are eldest in the company,
 Speak for them all, tell me what preys upon you,
 Whether you come in dread, or crave some blessing:
 Tell me, and never doubt that I will help you
 In every way I can; I should be heartless
 Were I not moved to find you suppliant here.
Priest. Great Oedipus, O powerful King of Thebes!
 You see how all the ages of our people
 Cling to your altar steps: here are boys
 Who can barely stand alone, and here are priests
 By weight of age, as I am a priest of God,
 And young men chosen from those yet unmarried;
 As for the others, all that multitude,
 They wait with olive chaplets in the squares,
 At the two shrines of Pallas, and where Apollo
 Speaks in the glowing embers.
        Your own eyes
 Must tell you: Thebes is tossed on a murdering sea
 And can not lift her head from the death surge.
 A rust consumes the buds and fruits of the earth;
 The herds are sick; children die unborn,
 And labor is vain. The god of plague and pyre
 Raids like destestable lightning through the city,
 And all the house of Kadmos is laid waste,
 All emptied, and all darkened: Death alone
 Battens upon the misery of Thebes.

---

1. **Kadmos:** Son of Agenor, King of Tyre, and mythical founder of Thebes.

You are not one of the immortal gods, we know;
Yet we have come to you to make our prayer
As to the man surest in mortal ways
And wisest in the ways of God. You saved us
From the Sphinx, that flinty singer, and the tribute
We paid to her so long; yet you were never
Better informed than we, nor could we teach you:
It was some god breathed in you to set us free.

Therefore, O mighty King, we turn to you:
Find us our safety, find us a remedy,
Whether by counsel of the gods or men.
A king of wisdom tested in the past
Can act in a time of troubles, and act well.
Noblest of men, restore
Life to your city! Think how all men call you
Liberator for your triumph long ago;
Ah, when your years of kingship are remembered,
Let them not say *We rose, but later fell*—
Keep the State from going down in the storm!
Once, years ago, with happy augury,
You brought us fortune; be the same again!
No man questions your power to rule the land:
But rule over men, not over a dead city!
Ships are only hulls, citadels are nothing,
When no life moves in the empty passageways.

OEDIPUS. Poor children! You may be sure I know
All that you longed for in your coming here.
I know that you are deathly sick; and yet,
Sick as you are, not one is as sick as I.
Each of you suffers in himself alone
His anguish, not another's; but my spirit
Groans for the city, for myself, for you.

I was not sleeping, you are not waking me.
No, I have been in tears for a long while
And in my restless thought walked many ways.
In all my search, I found one helpful course,
And that I have taken: I have sent Creon,
Son of Menoikeus, brother of the Queen,
To Delphi, Apollo's place of revelation,
To learn there, if he can,
What act or pledge of mine may save the city.
I have counted the days, and now, this very day,

I am troubled, for he has overstayed his time.
What is he doing? He has been gone too long.
Yet whenever he comes back, I should do ill
To scant whatever duty God reveals.

PRIEST. It is a timely promise. At this instant
They tell me Creon is here.

OEDIPUS.   O Lord Apollo!
May his news be fair as his face is radiant!

PRIEST. It could not be otherwise: he is crowned with bay,
The chaplet is thick with berries.

OEDIPUS.   We shall soon know;
He is near enough to hear us now.

    CREON enters.

                 O Prince:
Brother: son of Menoikeus:
What answer do you bring us from the god?

CREON. A strong one. I can tell you, great afflictions
Will turn out well, if they are taken well.

OEDIPUS. What was the oracle? These vague words
Leave me still hanging between hope and fear.

CREON. Is it your pleasure to hear me with all these
Gathered around us? I am prepared to speak,
But should we not go in?

OEDIPUS.   Let them all hear it.
It is for them I suffer, more than for myself.

CREON. Then I will tell you what I heard at Delphi.
In plain words
The god commands us to expel from the land of Thebes
An old defilement we are sheltering.
It is a deathly thing, beyond cure:
We must not let it feed upon us longer.

OEDIPUS. What defilement? How shall we rid ourselves of it?

CREON. By exile or death, blood for blood. It was Murder that brought
the plague-wind on the city.

OEDIPUS. Murder of whom? Surely the god has named him?

CREON. My lord: long ago Laïos was our king,
Before you came to govern us.

OEDIPUS.   I know;
I learned of him from others; I never saw him.

CREON. He was murdered; and Apollo commands us now
To take revenge upon whoever killed him.

OEDIPUS. Upon whom? Where are they? Where shall we find a clue
To solve that crime, after so many years?

CREON. Here in this land, he said.

                                If we make enquiry,
   We may touch things that otherwise escape us.

OEDIPUS. Tell me: Was Laïos murdered in his house,
   Or in the fields, or in some foreign country?

CREON. He said he planned to make a pilgrimage.
   He did not come home again.

OEDIPUS.   And was there no one,
   No witness, no companion, to tell what happened?

CREON. They were all killed but one, and he got away
   So frightened that he could remember one thing only.

OEDIPUS. What was that one thing? One may be the key
   To everything, if we resolve to use it.

CREON. He said that a band of highwaymen attacked them,
   Outnumbered them, and overwhelmed the King.

OEDIPUS. Strange, that a highwayman should be so daring—
   Unless some faction here bribed him to do it.

CREON. We thought of that. But after Laïos' death
   New troubles arose and we had no avenger.

OEDIPUS. What troubles could prevent your hunting down the killers?

CREON. The riddling Sphinx's song
   Made us deaf to all mysteries but her own.

OEDIPUS. Then once more I must bring what is dark to light.
   It is most fitting that Apollo shows,
   As you do, this compunction for the dead.
   You shall see how I stand by you, as I should,
   To avenge the city and the city's god,
   And not as though it were for some distant friend,
   But for my own sake, to be rid of evil.
   Whoever killed King Laïos might—who knows?—
   Decide at any moment to kill me as well.
   By avenging the murdered king I protect myself.

   Come, then, my children: leave the altar steps,
   Lift up your olive boughs!

                         One of you go
   And summon the people of Kadmos to gather here.
   I will do all that I can; you may tell them that.

     PAGE *goes out.*

   So, with the help of God,
   We shall be saved—or else indeed we are lost.

PRIEST. Let us rise, children. It was for this we came,
   And now the King has promised it himself.

Phoibos[2] has sent us an oracle; may he descend
Himself to save us and drive out the plague.

Oedipus *and* Creon *go into the palace by the central door. The*
priest and the suppliants disperse right and left. After a short pause
the chorus enters the orchestra.

PARADOS[3]

[Strophe[4] 1]

Chorus. What is God singing in his profound
        Delphi of gold and shadow?
        What oracle for Thebes, the sunwhipped city?
        Fear unjoints me, the roots of my heart tremble.
        Now I remember, O Healer, your power, and wonder:
        Will you send doom like a sudden cloud, or weave it
        Like nightfall of the past?
        Speak, speak to us, issue of holy sound:
        Dearest to our expectancy: be tender!

[Antistrophe[5] 1]

        Let me pray to Athenê, the immortal daughter of Zeus,
        And to Artemis her sister
        Who keeps her famous throne in the market ring,
        And to Apollo, bowman at the far butts of heaven—
        O gods, descend! Like three streams leap against
        The fires of our grief, the fires of darkness;
        Be swift to bring us rest!
        As in the old time from the brilliant house
        Of air you stepped to save us, come again!

[Strophe 2]

        Now our afflictions have no end,
        Now all our stricken host lies down
        And no man fights off death with his mind;
        The noble plowland bears no grain,
        And groaning mothers can not bear—
        See, how our lives like birds take wing,

---

2. **Phoibos:** Phoebus Apollo, the sun god.
3. **Parados:** a formal song accompanying the entrance of the Chorus.
4. **Strophe:** dance movement by the chorus in one direction.
5. **Antistrophe:** an equal dance movement in the opposite direction.

Like sparks that fly when a fire soars,
To the shore of the god of evening.

[ANTISTROPHE 2]

The plague burns on, it is pitiless,
Though pallid children laden with death
Lie unwept in the stony ways,
And old gray women by every path
Flock to the strand about the altars
There to strike their breasts and cry
Worship of Phoibos in wailing prayers:
Be kind, God's golden child!

[STROPHE 3]

There are no swords in this attack by fire,
No shields, but we are ringed with cries.
Send the besieger plunging from our homes
Into the vast sea-room of the Atlantic
Or into the waves that foam eastward of Thrace—
For the day ravages what the night spares—
Destroy our enemy, lord of the thunder!
Let him be riven by lightning from heaven!

[ANTISTROPHE 3]

Phoibos Apollo, stretch the sun's bowstring,
That golden cord, until it sing for us,
Flashing arrows in heaven!
                              Artemis, Huntress,
Race with flaring lights upon our mountains!
O scarlet god, O golden-banded brow,
O Theban Bacchos in a storm of Maenads,

OEDIPUS *appears in center door.*

Whirl upon Death, that all the Undying hate!
Come with blinding torches, come in joy!

SCENE ONE

OEDIPUS *enters and speaks to chorus.*

OEDIPUS. Is this your prayer? It may be answered. Come,
Listen to me, act as the crisis demands,

And you shall have relief from all these evils.
Until now I was a stranger to this tale,
As I had been a stranger to the crime.
Could I track down the murderer without a clue?
But now, friends,
As one who became a citizen after the murder,
I make this proclamation to all Thebans:
If any man knows by whose hand Laïos, son of Labdakos,
Met his death, I direct that man to tell me everything,
No matter what he fears for having so long withheld it.
Let it stand as promised that no further trouble
Will come to him, but he may leave the land in safety.
Moreover: If anyone knows the murderer to be foreign,
Let him not keep silent: he shall have his reward from me.
However, if he does conceal it; if any man
Fearing for his friend or for himself disobeys this edict,
Hear what I propose to do:
I solemnly forbid the people of this country,
Where power and throne are mine, ever to receive that man
Or speak to him, no matter who he is, or let him
Join in sacrifice, lustration, or in prayer.
I decree that he be driven from every house,
Being, as he is, corruption itself to us: the Delphic
Voice of Zeus has pronounced this revelation.
Thus I associate myself with the oracle
And take the side of the murdered king.
As for the criminal, I pray to God—
Whether it be a lurking thief, or one of a number—
I pray that that man's life be consumed in evil and wretchedness.
And as for me, this curse applies no less
If it should turn out that the culprit is my guest here,
Sharing my hearth.

          You have heard the penalty.
I lay it on you now to attend to this
For my sake, for Apollo's, for the sick
Sterile city that heaven has abandoned.
Suppose the oracle had given you no command:
Should this defilement go uncleansed for ever?
You should have found the murderer: your king,
A noble king, had been destroyed!

              Now I,
Having the power that he held before me,
Having his bed, begetting children there
Upon his wife, as he would have, had he lived—

Their son would have been my children's brother,
If Laïos had had luck in fatherhood!
(But surely ill luck rushed upon his reign)—
I say I take the son's part, just as though
I were his son, to press the fight for him
And see it won! I'll find the hand that brought
Death to Labdakos' and Polydoros' child,
Heir of Kadmos' and Agenor's line.[6]
And as for those who fail me,
May the gods deny them the fruit of the earth,
Fruit of the womb, and may they rot utterly!
Let them be wretched as we are wretched, and worse!
For you, for loyal Thebans, and for all
Who find my actions right, I pray the favor
Of justice, and of all the immortal gods.

CHORAGOS.[7] Since I am under oath, my lord, I swear
I did not do the murder, I can not name
The murderer. Might not the oracle
That has ordained the search tell where to find him?

OEDIPUS. An honest question. But no man in the world
Can make the gods do more than the gods will.

CHORAGOS. There is one last expedient—

OEDIPUS.   Tell me what it is.
Though it seem slight, you must not hold it back.

CHORAGOS. A lord clairvoyant to the lord Apollo,
As we all know, is the skilled Teiresias.
One might learn much about this from him, Oedipus.

OEDIPUS. I am not wasting time:
Creon spoke of this, and I have sent for him—
Twice, in fact; it is strange that he is not here.

CHORAGOS. The other matter—that old report—seems useless.

OEDIPUS. Tell me. I am interested in all reports.

CHORAGOS. The King was said to have been killed by highwaymen.

OEDIPUS. I know. But we have no witnesses to that.

CHORAGOS. If the killer can feel a particle of dread,
Your curse will bring him out of hiding!

OEDIPUS.   No.
The man who dared that act will fear no curse.

The blind seer TEIRESIAS *enters led by a page.*

___

6. **Agenor's line:** the royal family of Thebes, as offspring of Agenor, King of Tyre, and his son Kadmos, mythical founder of Thebes.
7. **Choragos:** the chief speaker for the chorus, not a proper name. The *choragos* was originally a wealthy citizen who was a financial patron of the play.

CHORAGOS. But there is one man who may detect the criminal.
    This is Teiresias, this is the holy prophet
    In whom, alone of all men, truth was born.
OEDIPUS. Teiresias: seer: student of mysteries,
    Of all that's taught and all that no man tells,
    Secrets of Heaven and secrets of the earth:
    Blind though you are, you know the city lies
    Sick with plague; and from this plague, my lord,
    We find that you alone can guard or save us.
    Possibly you did not hear the messengers?
    Apollo, when we sent to him,
    Sent us back word that this great pestilence
    Would lift, but only if we established clearly
    The identity of those who murdered Laïos.
    They must be killed or exiled.

                  Can you use
    Birdflight or any art of divination
    To purify yourself, and Thebes, and me
    From this contagion? We are in your hands.
    There is no fairer duty
    Than that of helping others in distress.
TEIRESIAS. How dreadful knowledge of the truth can be
    When there's no help in truth! I knew this well,
    But made myself forget. I should not have come.
OEDIPUS. What is troubling you? Why are your eyes so cold?
TEIRESIAS. Let me go home. Bear your own fate, and I'll
    Bear mine. It is better so: trust what I say.
OEDIPUS. What you say is ungracious and unhelpful
    To your native country. Do not refuse to speak.
TEIRESIAS. When it comes to speech, your own is neither temperate
    Nor opportune. I wish to be more prudent.
OEDIPUS. In God's name, we all beg you—
TEIRESIAS.   You are all ignorant.
    No; I will never tell you what I know.
    Now it is my misery; then, it would be yours.
OEDIPUS. What! You do know something, and will not tell us?
    You would betray us all and wreck the State?
TEIRESIAS. I do not intend to torture myself, or you.
    Why persist in asking? You will not persuade me.
OEDIPUS. What a wicked old man you are! You'd try a stone's
    Patience! Out with it! Have you no feeling at all?
TEIRESIAS. You call me unfeeling. If you could only see
    The nature of your own feelings . . .

OEDIPUS.   Why,
    Who would not feel as I do? Who could endure
    Your arrogance toward the city?
TEIRESIAS.   What does it matter!
    Whether I speak or not, it is bound to come.
OEDIPUS. Then, if "it" is bound to come, you are bound to tell me.
TEIRESIAS. No, I will not go on. Rage as you please.
OEDIPUS. Rage? Why not!
                And I'll tell you what I think:
    You planned it, you had it done, you all but
    Killed him with your own hands: if you had eyes,
    I'd say the crime was yours, and yours alone.

TEIRESIAS. So? I charge you, then,
    Abide by the proclamation you have made:
    From this day forth
    Never speak again to these men or to me;
    You yourself are the pollution of this country.
OEDIPUS. You dare say that! Can you possibly think you have
    Some way of going free, after such insolence?
TEIRESIAS. I have gone free. It is the truth sustains me.
OEDIPUS. Who taught you shamelessness? It was not your craft.

Teiresias. You did. You made me speak. I did not want to.

Oedipus. Speak what? Let me hear it again more clearly.

Teiresias. Was it not clear before? Are you tempting me?

Oedipus. I did not understand it. Say it again.

Teiresias. I say that you are the murderer whom you seek.

Oedipus. Now twice you have spat out infamy. You'll pay for it!

Teiresias. Would you care for more? Do you wish to be really angry?

Oedipus. Say what you will. Whatever you say is worthless.

Teiresias. I say you live in hideous shame with those
    Most dear to you. You can not see the evil.

Oedipus. It seems you can go on mouthing like this for ever.

Teiresias. I can, if there is power in truth.

Oedipus. There is:
    But not for you, not for you,
    You sightless, witless, senseless, mad old man!

Teiresias. You are the madman. There is no one here
    Who will not curse you soon, as you curse me.

Oedipus. You child of endless night! You can not hurt me
    Or any other man who sees the sun.

Teiresias. True: it is not from me your fate will come.
    That lies within Apollo's competence,
    As it is his concern.

Oedipus.   Tell me:
    Are you speaking for Creon, or for yourself?

Teiresias. Creon is no threat. You weave your own doom.

Oedipus. Wealth, power, craft of statesmanship!
    Kingly position, everywhere admired!
    What savage envy is stored up against these,
    If Creon, whom I trusted, Creon my friend,
    For this great office which the city once
    Put in my hands unsought—if for this power
    Creon desires in secret to destroy me!
    He has bought this decrepit fortune-teller, this
    Collector of dirty pennies, this prophet fraud—
    Why, he is no more clairvoyant than I am!
                                        Tell us:
    Has your mystic mummery ever approached the truth?
    When that hellcat the Sphinx was performing here,
    What help were you to these people?
    Her magic was not for the first man who came along:
    It demanded a real exorcist. Your birds—
    What good were they? or the gods, for the matter of that?
    But I came by,
    Oedipus, the simple man, who knows nothing—

I thought it out for myself, no birds helped me!
And this is the man you think you can destroy,
That you may be close to Creon when he's king!
Well, you and your friend Creon, it seems to me,
Will suffer most. If you were not an old man,
You would have paid already for your plot.

CHORAGOS. We can not see that his words or yours
    Have been spoken except in anger, Oedipus,
    And of anger we have no need. How can God's will
    Be accomplished best? That is what most concerns us.

TEIRESIAS. You are a king. But where argument's concerned
    I am your man, as much a king as you.
    I am not your servant, but Apollo's.
    I have no need of Creon to speak for me.
    Listen to me. You mock my blindness, do you?
    But I say that you, with both your eyes, are blind:
    You can not see the wretchedness of your life,
    Nor in whose house you live, no, nor with whom.
    Who are your father and mother? Can you tell me?
    You do not even know the blind wrongs
    That you have done them, on earth and in the world below.
    But the double lash of your parents' curse will whip you
    Out of this land some day, with only night
    Upon your precious eyes.
    Your cries then—where will they not be heard?
    What fastness of Kithairon[8] will not echo them?
    And that bridal-descant of yours—you'll know it then,
    The song they sang when you came here to Thebes
    And found your misguided berthing.
    All this, and more, that you can not guess at now,
    Will bring you to yourself among your children.
    Be angry, then. Curse Creon. Curse my words.
    I tell you, no man that walks upon the earth
    Shall be rooted out more horribly than you.

OEDIPUS. Am I to bear this from him?—Damnation
    Take you! Out of this place! Out of my sight!

TEIRESIAS. I would not have come at all if you had not asked me.

OEDIPUS. Could I have told that you'd talk nonsense, that
    You'd come here to make a fool of yourself, and of me?

TEIRESIAS. A fool? Your parents thought me sane enough.

OEDIPUS. My parents again!—Wait: who were my parents?

---

8. **Kithairon:** a range of mountains between Athens and Boeotia.

TEIRESIAS. This day will give you a father, and break your heart.

OEDIPUS. Your infantile riddles! Your damned abracadabra!

TEIRESIAS. You were a great man once at solving riddles.

OEDIPUS. Mock me with that if you like; you will find it true.

TEIRESIAS. It was true enough. It brought about your ruin.

OEDIPUS. But if it saved this town?

TEIRESIAS [to the page]. Boy, give me your hand.

OEDIPUS. Yes, boy; lead him away.

                       —While you are here
We can do nothing. Go; leave us in peace.

TEIRESIAS. I will go when I have said what I have to say.
How can you hurt me? And I tell you again:
The man you have been looking for all this time,
The damned man, the murderer of Laïos,
That man is in Thebes. To your mind he is foreign-born,
But it will soon be shown that he is a Theban,
A revelation that will fail to please.

                         A blind man,
Who has his eyes now; a penniless man, who is rich now;
And he will go tapping the strange earth with his staff.
To the children with whom he lives now he will be
Brother and father—the very same; to her
Who bore him, son and husband—the very same
Who came to his father's bed, wet with his father's blood.
Enough. Go think that over.
If later you find error in what I have said,
You may say that I have no skill in prophecy.

    TEIRESIAS goes out, led by his page. OEDIPUS goes into the palace.

ODE I

[STROPHE 1]

CHORUS. The Delphic stone of prophecies
    Remembers ancient regicide
    And a still bloody hand.
    That killer's hour of flight has come.
    He must be stronger than riderless
    Coursers of untiring wind,
    For the son of Zeus armed with his father's thunder
    Leaps in lightning after him;
    And the Furies follow him, the sad Furies.

[ANTISTROPHE I]

Holy Parnassos' peak of snow
Flashes and blinds that secret man,
That all shall hunt him down:
Though he may roam the forest shade
Like a bull gone wild from pasture
To rage through glooms of stone.
Doom comes down on him; flight will not avail him;
For the world's heart calls him desolate,
And the immortal Furies follow, for ever follow.

[STROPHE 2]

But now a wilder thing is heard
From the old man skilled at hearing Fate in the wing-beat of a
bird.
Bewildered as a blown bird, my soul hovers and can not find
Foot hold in this debate, or any reason or rest of mind.
But no man ever brought—none can bring
Proof of strife between Thebes' royal house,
Labdakos' line, and the son of Polybos;
And never until now has any man brought word
Of Laïos' dark death staining Oedipus the King.

[ANTISTROPHE 2]

Divine Zeus and Apollo hold
Perfect intelligence alone of all tales ever told;
And well though this diviner works, he works in his own night;
No man can judge that rough unknown or trust in second sight,
For wisdom changes hands among the wise.
Shall I believe my great lord criminal
At a raging word that a blind old man let fall?
I saw him, when the carrion woman faced him of old,
Prove his heroic mind! These evil words are lies.

SCENE TWO

CREON. Men of Thebes:
I am told that heavy accusations
Have been brought against me by King Oedipus.
I am not the kind of man to bear this tamely.
If in these present difficulties

He holds me accountable for any harm to him
Through anything I have said or done—why, then
I do not value life in this dishonor.
It is not as though this rumor touched upon
Some private indiscretion. The matter is grave.
The fact is that I am being called disloyal
To the State, to my fellow citizens, to my friends.

CHORAGOS. He may have spoken in anger, not from his mind.

CREON. But did you not hear him say I was the one
Who seduced the old prophet into lying?

CHORAGOS. The thing was said; I do not know how seriously.

CREON. But you were watching him! Were his eyes steady?
Did he look like a man in his right mind?

CHORAGOS.   I do not know.
I can not judge the behavior of great men.
But here is the King himself.

        OEDIPUS enters.

OEDIPUS.   So you dared come back.
Why? How brazen of you to come to my house,
You murderer! Do you think I do not know
That you plotted to kill me, plotted to steal my throne?
Tell me, in God's name: am I coward, a fool,
That you should dream you could accomplish this?
A fool who could not see your slippery game?
A coward, not to fight back when I saw it?
You are the fool, Creon, are you not? hoping
Without support or friends to get a throne?
Thrones may be won or bought: you could do neither.

CREON. Now listen to me. You have talked; let me talk, too.
You can not judge unless you know the facts.

OEDIPUS. You speak well: there is one fact; but I find it hard
To learn from the deadliest enemy I have.

CREON. That above all I must dispute with you.

OEDIPUS. That above all I will not hear you deny.

CREON. If you think there is anything good in being stubborn
Against all reason, then I say you are wrong.

OEDIPUS. If you think a man can sin against his own kind
And not be punished for it, I say you are mad.

CREON. I agree. But tell me: what have I done to you?

OEDIPUS. You advised me to send for that wizard, did you not?

CREON. I did. I should do it again.

OEDIPUS.   Very well. Now tell me:
How long has it been since Laïos—

CREON.   What of Laïos?

OEDIPUS. Since he vanished in that onset by the road?

CREON. It was long ago, a long time.

OEDIPUS.   And this prophet,
   Was he practicing here then?

CREON.   He was; and with honor, as now.

OEDIPUS. Did he speak of me at that time?

CREON.   He never did;
   At least, not when I was present.

OEDIPUS.   But . . . the enquiry?
   I suppose you held one?

CREON.   We did, but we learned nothing.

OEDIPUS. Why did the prophet not speak against me then?

CREON. I do not know; and I am the kind of man
   Who holds his tongue when he has no facts to go on.

OEDIPUS. There's one fact that you know, and you could tell it.

CREON. What fact is that? If I know it, you shall have it.

OEDIPUS. If he were not involved with you, he could not say
   That it was I who murdered Laïos.

CREON. If he says that, you are the one that knows it!—
   But now it is my turn to question you.

OEDIPUS. Put your questions. I am no murderer.

CREON. First, then: You married my sister?

OEDIPUS.   I married your sister.

CREON. And you rule the kingdom equally with her?

OEDIPUS. Everything that she wants she has from me.

CREON. And I am the third, equal to both of you?

OEDIPUS. That is why I call you a bad friend.

CREON. No. Reason it out, as I have done.
   Think of this first: Would any sane man prefer
   Power, with all a king's anxieties,
   To that same power and the grace of sleep?
   Certainly not I.
   I have never longed for the king's power—only his rights.
   Would any wise man differ from me in this?
   As matters stand, I have my way in everything
   With your consent, and no responsibilities.
   If I were king, I should be a slave to policy.
   How could I desire a scepter more
   Than what is now mine—untroubled influence?
   No, I have not gone mad; I need no honors,
   Except those with the perquisites I have now.
   I am welcome everywhere; every man salutes me,
   And those who want your favor seek my ear,

Since I know how to manage what they ask.
Should I exchange this ease for that anxiety?
Besides, no sober mind is treasonable.
I hate anarchy
And never would deal with any man who likes it.
Test what I have said. Go to the priestess
At Delphi, ask if I quoted her correctly.
And as for this other thing: if I am found
Guilty of treason with Teiresias,
Then sentence me to death! You have my word
It is a sentence I should cast my vote for—
But not without evidence!

                  You do wrong
When you take good men for bad, bad men for good.
A true friend thrown aside—why, life itself
Is not more precious!

                     In time you will know this well:
For time, and time alone, will show the just man,
Though scoundrels are discovered in a day.
CHORAGOS. This is well said, and a prudent man would ponder it.
    Judgments too quickly formed are dangerous.
OEDIPUS. But is he not quick in his duplicity?
    And shall I not be quick to parry him?
    Would you have me stand still, hold my peace, and let
    This man win everything, through my inaction?
CREON. And you want—what is it, then? To banish me?
OEDIPUS. No, not exile. It is your death I want,
    So that all the world may see what treason means.
CREON. You will persist, then? You will not believe me?
OEDIPUS. How can I believe you?
CREON.   Then you are a fool.
OEDIPUS. To save myself?
CREON.   In justice, think of me.
OEDIPUS. You are evil incarnate.
CREON.   But suppose that you are wrong?
OEDIPUS. Still I must rule.
CREON.   But not if you rule badly.
OEDIPUS. O city, city!
CREON.   It is my city, too!
CHORAGOS. Now, my lords, be still. I see the Queen,
    Iocastê, coming from her palace chambers;
    And it is time she came, for the sake of you both.
    This dreadful quarrel can be resolved through her.
      IOCASTÊ *enters.*

IOCASTÊ. Poor foolish men, what wicked din is this?
    With Thebes sick to death, is it not shameful
    That you should rake some private quarrel up?

    To OEDIPUS.

    Come into the house.
                    —And you, Creon, go now:
    Let us have no more of this tumult over nothing.
CREON. Nothing? No, sister: what your husband plans for me
    Is one of two great evils: exile or death.
OEDIPUS. He is right.
                    Why, woman, I have caught him squarely
    Plotting against my life.
CREON.   No! Let me die
    Accurst if ever I have wished you harm!
IOCASTÊ. Ah, believe it, Oedipus!
    In the name of the gods, respect this oath of his
    For my sake, for the sake of these people here!

[STROPHE 1]

CHORAGOS. Open your mind to her, my lord. Be ruled by her, I beg
    you!
OEDIPUS. What would you have me do?
CHORAGOS. Respect Creon's word. He has never spoken like a fool,
    And now he has sworn an oath.
OEDIPUS.   You know what you ask?
CHORAGOS.   I do.
OEDIPUS.   Speak on, then.
CHORAGOS. A friend so sworn should not be baited so,
    In blind malice, and without final proof.
OEDIPUS. You are aware, I hope, that what you say
    Means death for me, or exile at the least.

[STROPHE 2]

CHORAGOS. No, I swear by Helios, first in Heaven!
    May I die friendless and accurst,
The worst of deaths, if ever I meant that!
        It is the withering fields
            That hurt my sick heart:
        Must we bear all these ills,
            And now your bad blood as well?
OEDIPUS. Then let him go. And let me die, if I must,
    Or be driven by him in shame from the land of Thebes.
    It is your unhappiness, and not his talk,

That touches me. As for him—
Wherever he goes, hatred will follow him.
CREON. Ugly in yielding, as you were ugly in rage!
Natures like yours chiefly torment themselves.
OEDIPUS. Can you not go? Can you not leave me?
CREON.   I can.
You do not know me; but the city knows me,
And in its eyes I am just, if not in yours.

CREON goes out.

[ANTISTROPHE 1]

CHORAGOS. Lady Iocastê, did you not ask the King to go to his
chambers?
IOCASTÊ. First tell me what has happened.
CHORAGOS. There was suspicion without evidence; yet it rankled
As even false charges will.
IOCASTÊ.   On both sides?
CHORAGOS.   On both.
IOCASTÊ.   But what was said?
CHORAGOS. Oh let it rest, let it be done with! Have we not suffered
enough?
OEDIPUS. You see to what your decency has brought you:
You have made difficulties where my heart saw none.

[ANTISTROPHE 2]

CHORAGOS. Oedipus, it is not once only I have told you—
You must know I should count myself unwise
To the point of madness, should I now forsake you—
You, under whose hand,
In the storm of another time,
Our dear land sailed out free.
But now stand fast at the helm!
IOCASTÊ. In God's name, Oedipus, inform your wife as well:
Why are you so set in this hard anger?
OEDIPUS. I will tell you, for none of these men deserves
My confidence as you do. It is Creon's work,
His treachery, his plotting against me.
IOCASTÊ. Go on, if you can make this clear to me.
OEDIPUS. He charges me with the murder of Laïos.
IOCASTÊ. Has he some knowledge? Or does he speak from hearsay?
OEDIPUS. He would not commit himself to such a charge,
But he has brought in that damnable soothsayer
To tell his story.

IOCASTÊ.   Set your mind at rest.
If it is a question of soothsayers, I tell you
That you will find no man whose craft gives knowledge
Of the unknowable.
                    Here is my proof:

An oracle was reported to Laïos once
(I will not say from Phoibos himself, but from
His appointed ministers, at any rate)
That his doom would be death at the hands of his own son—
His son, born of his flesh and of mine!

Now, you remember the story: Laïos was killed
By marauding strangers where three highways meet.
But his child had not been three days in this world
Before the King had pierced the baby's ankles
And left him to die on a lonely mountainside.

Thus, Apollo never caused that child
To kill his father, and it was not Laïos' fate
To die at the hands of his son, as he had feared.
This is what prophets and prophecies are worth!
Have no dread of them.
                    It is God himself
Who can show us what he wills, in his own way.
OEDIPUS. How strange a shadowy memory crossed my mind,
    Just now while you were speaking; it chilled my heart.
IOCASTÊ. What do you mean? What memory do you speak of?
OEDIPUS. If I understand you, Laïos was killed
    At a place where three roads meet.
IOCASTÊ.   So it was said;
    We have no later story.
OEDIPUS.   Where did it happen?
IOCASTÊ. Phokis, it is called: at a place where the Theban Way
    Divides into the roads toward Delphi and Daulia.
OEDIPUS. When?
IOCASTÊ. We had the news not long before you came
    And proved the right to your succession here.
OEDIPUS. Ah, what net has God been weaving for me?
IOCASTÊ. Oedipus! Why does this trouble you?
OEDIPUS.   Do not ask me yet.
    First, tell me how Laïos looked, and tell me
    How old he was.
IOCASTÊ.   He was tall, his hair just touched
    With white; his form was not unlike your own.

OEDIPUS. I think that I myself may be accurst
    By my own ignorant edict.
IOCASTÊ.   You speak strangely.
    It makes me tremble to look at you, my King.
OEDIPUS. I am not sure that the blind man can not see.
    But I should know better if you were to tell me—
IOCASTÊ. Anything—though I dread to hear you ask it.
OEDIPUS. Was the King lightly escorted, or did he ride
    With a large company, as a ruler should?
IOCASTÊ. There were five men with him in all: one was a herald,
    And a single chariot, which he was driving.
OEDIPUS. Alas, that makes it plain enough!
                           But who—
    Who told you how it happened?
IOCASTÊ.   A household servant,
    The only one to escape.
OEDIPUS.   And is he still
    A servant of ours?
IOCASTÊ.   No; for when he came back at last
    And found you enthroned in the place of the dead king,
    He came to me, touched my hand with his, and begged
    That I would send him away to the frontier district
    Where only the shepherds go—
    As far away from the city as I could send him.
    I granted his prayer; for although the man was a slave,
    He had earned more than this favor at my hands.
OEDIPUS. Can he be called back quickly?
IOCASTÊ.   Easily.
    But why?
OEDIPUS. I have taken too much upon myself
    Without enquiry; therefore I wish to consult him.
IOCASTÊ. Then he shall come.
               But am I not one also
    To whom you might confide these fears of yours?
OEDIPUS. That is your right; it will not be denied you,
    Now least of all; for I have reached a pitch
    Of wild foreboding. Is there anyone
    To whom I should sooner speak?
    Polybos of Corinth is my father.
    My mother is a Dorian: Meropê.
    I grew up chief among the men of Corinth
    Until a strange thing happened—
    Not worth my passion, it may be, but strange.
    At a feast, a drunken man maundering in his cups

Cries out that I am not my father's son!
I contained myself that night, though I felt anger
And a sinking heart. The next day I visited
My father and mother, and questioned them. They stormed,
Calling it all the slanderous rant of a fool;
And this relieved me. Yet the suspicion
Remained always aching in my mind;
I knew there was talk; I could not rest;
And finally, saying nothing to my parents,
I went to the shrine at Delphi.
The god dismissed my question without reply;
He spoke of other things.

       Some were clear,
Full of wretchedness, dreadful, unbearable:
As, that I should lie with my own mother, breed
Children from whom all men would turn their eyes;
And that I should be my father's murderer.
I heard all this, and fled. And from that day
Corinth to me was only in the stars
Descending in that quarter of the sky,
As I wandered farther and farther on my way
To a land where I should never see the evil
Sung by the oracle. And I came to this country
Where, so you say, King Laïos was killed.
I will tell you all that happened there, my lady.
There were three highways
Coming together at a place I passed;
And there a herald came towards me, and a chariot
Drawn by horses, with a man such as you describe
Seated in it. The groom leading the horses
Forced me off the road at his lord's command;
But as this charioteer lurched over towards me
I struck him in my rage. The old man saw me
And brought his double goad down upon my head
As I came abreast.

      He was paid back, and more!
Swinging my club in this right hand I knocked him
Out of his car, and he rolled on the ground.

          I killed him.
I killed them all.
Now if that stranger and Laïos were—kin,
Where is a man more miserable than I?
More hated by the gods? Citizen and alien alike

Must never shelter me or speak to me—
I must be shunned by all.

      And I myself
Pronounced this malediction upon myself!
Think of it: I have touched you with these hands,
These hands that killed your husband. What defilement!
Am I all evil, then? It must be so,
Since I must flee from Thebes, yet never again
See my own countrymen, my own country,
For fear of joining my mother in marriage
And killing Polybos, my father.

        Ah,
If I was created so, born to this fate,
Who could deny the savagery of God?
O holy majesty of heavenly powers!
May I never see that day! Never!
Rather let me vanish from the race of men
Than know the abomination destined me!

CHORAGOS. We too, my lord, have felt dismay at this.
 But there is hope: you have yet to hear the shepherd.

OEDIPUS. Indeed, I fear no other hope is left me.

IOCASTÊ. What do you hope from him when he comes?

OEDIPUS.   This much:
 If his account of the murder tallies with yours,
 Then I am cleared.

IOCASTÊ.   What was it that I said
 Of such importance?

OEDIPUS.   Why, "marauders," you said,
 Killed the King, according to this man's story.
 If he maintains that still, if there were several,
 Clearly the guilt is not mine: I was alone.
 But if he says one man, singlehanded, did it,
 Then the evidence all points to me.

IOCASTÊ. You may be sure that he said there were several;
 And can he call back that story now? He can not.
 The whole city heard it as plainly as I.
 But suppose he alters some detail of it:
 He can not ever show that Laïos' death
 Fulfilled the oracle: for Apollo said
 My child was doomed to kill him; and my child—
 Poor baby!—it was my child that died first.
 No. From now on, where oracles are concerned,
 I would not waste a second thought on any.

OEDIPUS. You may be right.

But come: let someone go
For the shepherd at once. This matter must be settled.
IOCASTÊ. I will send for him.

I would not wish to cross you in anything,
And surely not in this.—Let us go in.

They go into the palace.

ODE II

[STROPHE 1]

CHORUS. Let me be reverent in the ways of right,
Lowly the paths I journey on;
Let all my words and actions keep
The laws of the pure universe
From highest Heaven handed down.
For Heaven is their bright nurse,
Those generations of the realms of light;
Ah, never of mortal kind were they begot,
Nor are they slaves of memory, lost in sleep:
Their Father is greater than Time, and ages not.

[ANTISTROPHE 1]

The tyrant is a child of Pride
Who drinks from his great sickening cup
Recklessness and vanity,
Until from his high crest headlong
He plummets to the dust of hope.
That strong man is not strong.
But let no fair ambition be denied;
May God protect the wrestler for the State
In government, in comely policy,
Who will fear God, and on His ordinance wait.

[STROPHE 2]

Haughtiness and the high hand of disdain
Tempt and outrage God's holy law;
And any mortal who dares hold
No immortal Power in awe
Will be caught up in a net of pain:

The price for which his levity is sold.
Let each man take due earnings, then,
And keep his hands from holy things,
And from blasphemy stand apart—
Else the crackling blast of heaven
Blows on his head, and on his desperate heart;
Though fools will honor impious men,
In their cities no tragic poet sings.

[ANTISTROPHE 2]

Shall we lose faith in Delphi's obscurities,
We who have heard the world's core
Discredited, and the sacred wood
Of Zeus at Elis praised no more?
The deeds and the strange prophecies
Must make a pattern yet to be understood.
Zeus, if indeed you are lord of all,
Throned in light over night and day,
Mirror this in your endless mind:
Our masters call the oracle
Words on the wind, and the Delphic vision blind!
Their hearts no longer know Apollo,
And reverence for the gods has died away.

SCENE THREE

IOCASTÊ *enters bearing suppliant's branches.*

IOCASTÊ. Princes of Thebes, it has occurred to me
To visit the altars of the gods, bearing
These branches as a suppliant, and this incense.
Our King is not himself: his noble soul
Is overwrought with fantasies of dread,
Else he would consider
The new prophecies in the light of the old.
He will listen to any voice that speaks disaster,
And my advice goes for nothing.

She approaches the altar, right.
                    To you, then, Apollo,
Lycean lord, since you are nearest, I turn in prayer.
Receive these offerings, and grant us deliverance
From defilement. Our hearts are heavy with fear

When we see our leader distracted, as helpless sailors
Are terrified by the confusion of their helmsman.

MESSENGER *enters.*

MESSENGER. Friends, no doubt you can direct me:
  Where shall I find the house of Oedipus,
  Or, better still, where is the King himself?
CHORAGOS. It is this very place, stranger; he is inside.
  This is his wife and mother of his children.
MESSENGER. I wish her happiness in a happy house,
  Blest in all the fulfillment of her marriage.
IOCASTÊ. I wish as much for you: your courtesy
  Deserves a like good fortune. But now, tell me:
  Why have you come? What have you to say to us?
MESSENGER. Good news, my lady, for your house and your husband.
IOCASTÊ. What news? Who sent you here?
MESSENGER.   I am from Corinth.
  The news I bring ought to mean joy for you,
  Though it may be you will find some grief in it.
IOCASTÊ. What is it? How can it touch us in both ways?
MESSENGER. The word is that the people of the Isthmus
  Intend to call Oedipus to be their king.
IOCASTÊ. But old King Polybos—is he not reigning still?
MESSENGER. No. Death holds him in his sepulcher.
IOCASTÊ. What are you saying? Polybos is dead?
MESSENGER. If I am not telling the truth, may I die myself.
IOCASTÊ [*to a maidservant*] Go in, go quickly; tell this to your master.
  O riddlers of God's will, where are you now!
  This was the man whom Oedipus, long ago,
  Feared so, fled so, in dread of destroying him—
  But it was another fate by which he died.

OEDIPUS *enters from center door.*

OEDIPUS. Dearest Iocastê, why have you sent for me?
IOCASTÊ. Listen to what this man says, and then tell me
  What has become of the solemn prophecies.
OEDIPUS. Who is this man? What is his news for me?
IOCASTÊ. He has come from Corinth to announce your father's death!
OEDIPUS. Is it true, stranger? Tell me in your own words.
MESSENGER. I can not say it more clearly: the King is dead.
OEDIPUS. Was it by treason? Or by an attack of illness?
MESSENGER. A little thing brings old men to their rest.
OEDIPUS. It was sickness, then?
MESSENGER.   Yes, and his many years.

OEDIPUS. Ah!
    Why should a man respect the Pythian hearth,[9] or
    Give heed to the birds that jangle above his head?
    They prophesied that I should kill Polybos,
    Kill my own father; but he is dead and buried,
    And I am here—I never touched him, never,
    Unless he died of grief for my departure,
    And thus, in a sense, through me. No. Polybos
    Has packed the oracles off with him underground.
    They are empty words.
IOCASTÊ.   Had I not told you so?
OEDIPUS. You had; it was my faint heart that betrayed me.
IOCASTÊ. From now on never think of those things again.
OEDIPUS. And yet—must I not fear my mother's bed?
IOCASTÊ. Why should anyone in this world be afraid,
    Since Fate rules us and nothing can be foreseen?
    A man should live only for the present day.
    Have no more fear of sleeping with your mother:
    How many men, in dreams, have lain with their mothers!
    No reasonable man is troubled by such things.
OEDIPUS. That is true; only—
    If only my mother were not still alive!
    But she is alive. I can not help my dread.
IOCASTÊ. Yet this news of your father's death is wonderful.
OEDIPUS. Wonderful. But I fear the living woman.
MESSENGER. Tell me, who is this woman that you fear?
OEDIPUS. It is Meropê, man; the wife of King Polybos.
MESSENGER. Meropê? Why should you be afraid of her?
OEDIPUS. An oracle of the gods, a dreadful saying.
MESSENGER. Can you tell me about it or are you sworn to silence?
OEDIPUS. I can tell you, and I will.
    Apollo said through his prophet that I was the man
    Who should marry his own mother, shed his father's blood
    With his own hands. And so, for all these years
    I have kept clear of Corinth, and no harm has come—
    Though it would have been sweet to see my parents again.
MESSENGER. And is this the fear that drove you out of Corinth?
OEDIPUS. Would you have me kill my father?
MESSENGER.   As for that
    You must be reassured by the news I gave you.
OEDIPUS. If you could reassure me, I would reward you.

---

9. **Pythian hearth:** that is, the shrine of Apollo at Delphi.

MESSENGER. I had that in mind, I will confess: I thought
 I could count on you when you returned to Corinth.
OEDIPUS. No: I will never go near my parents again.
MESSENGER. Ah, son, you still do not know what you are doing—
OEDIPUS. What do you mean? In the name of God tell me!
MESSENGER.—If these are your reasons for not going home.
OEDIPUS. I tell you, I fear the oracle may come true.
MESSENGER. And guilt may come upon you through your parents?
OEDIPUS. That is the dread that is always in my heart.
MESSENGER. Can you not see that all your fears are groundless?
OEDIPUS. How can you say that? They are my parents, surely?
MESSENGER. Polybos was not your father.
OEDIPUS.   Not my father?
MESSENGER. No more your father than the man speaking to you.
OEDIPUS. But you are nothing to me!
MESSENGER.   Neither was he.
OEDIPUS. Then why did he call me son?
MESSENGER.   I will tell you:
 Long ago he had you from my hands, as a gift.
OEDIPUS. Then how could he love me so, if I was not his?
MESSENGER. He had no children, and his heart turned to you.
OEDIPUS. What of you? Did you buy me? Did you find me by chance?
MESSENGER. I came upon you in the crooked pass of Kithairon.
OEDIPUS. And what were you doing there?
MESSENGER.   Tending my flocks.
OEDIPUS. A wandering shepherd?
MESSENGER.   But your savior, son, that day.
OEDIPUS. From what did you save me?
MESSENGER.   Your ankles should tell you
 that.
OEDIPUS. Ah, stranger, why do you speak of that childhood pain?
MESSENGER. I cut the bonds that tied your ankles together.
OEDIPUS. I have had the mark as long as I can remember.
MESSENGER. That was why you were given the name you bear.
OEDIPUS. God! Was it my father or my mother who did it?
 Tell me!
MESSENGER. I do not know. The man who gave you to me
 Can tell you better than I.
OEDIPUS. It was not you that found me, but another?
MESSENGER. It was another shepherd gave you to me.
OEDIPUS. Who was he? Can you tell me who he was?
MESSENGER. I think he was said to be one of Laïos' people.
OEDIPUS. You mean the Laïos who was king here years ago?
MESSENGER. Yes; King Laïos; and the man was one of his herdsmen.

OEDIPUS. Is he still alive? Can I see him?
MESSENGER. These men here
 Know best about such things.
OEDIPUS. Does anyone here
 Know this shepherd that he is talking about?
 Have you seen him in the fields, or in the town?
 If you have, tell me. It is time things were made plain.
CHORAGOS. I think the man he means is that same shepherd
 You have already asked to see. Iocastê perhaps
 Could tell you something.
OEDIPUS. Do you know anything
 About him, Lady? Is he the man we have summoned?
 Is that the man this shepherd means?
IOCASTÊ. Why think of him?
 Forget this herdsman. Forget it all.
 This talk is a waste of time.
OEDIPUS. How can you say that,
 When the clues to my true birth are in my hands?
IOCASTÊ. For God's love, let us have no more questioning!
 Is your life nothing to you?
 My own is pain enough for me to bear.
OEDIPUS. You need not worry. Suppose my mother a slave,
 And born of slaves: no baseness can touch you.
IOCASTÊ. Listen to me, I beg you: do not do this thing!
OEDIPUS. I will not listen; the truth must be made known.
IOCASTÊ. Everything that I say is for your own good!
OEDIPUS. My own good
 Snaps my patience, then; I want none of it.
IOCASTÊ. You are fatally wrong! May you never learn who you are!
OEDIPUS. Go, one of you, and bring the shepherd here.
 Let us leave this woman to brag of her royal name.
IOCASTÊ. Ah, miserable!
 That is the only word I have for you now.
 That is the only word I can ever have.

 She goes into the palace.

CHORAGOS. Why has she left us, Oedipus? Why has she gone
 In such a passion of sorrow? I fear this silence:
 Something dreadful may come of it.
OEDIPUS. Let it come!
 However base my birth, I must know about it.
 The Queen, like a woman, is perhaps ashamed
 To think of my low origin. But I

Am a child of Luck; I can not be dishonored.
Luck is my mother; the passing months, my brothers,
Have seen me rich and poor.
                                    If this is so,
How could I wish that I were someone else?
How could I not be glad to know my birth?

ODE III

[STROPHE]

CHORUS. If ever the coming time were known
        To my heart's pondering,
        Kithairon, now by Heaven I see the torches
        At the festival of the next full moon,
        And see the dance, and hear the choir sing
        A grace to your gentle shade:
        Mountain where Oedipus was found,
        O mountain guard of a noble race!
        May the god who heals us lend his aid,
        And let that glory come to pass
        For our king's cradling-ground.

[Antistrophe]

Of the nymphs that flower beyond the years,
Who bore you, royal child,
To Pan of the hills or the timberline Apollo,
Cold in delight where the upland clears,
Or Hermês for whom Kyllenê's heights[10] are piled?
Or flushed as evening cloud,
Great Dionysos, roamer of mountains,
He—was it he who found you there,
And caught you up in his own proud
Arms from the sweet god-ravisher
Who laughed by the Muses' fountains?

SCENE FOUR

Oedipus. Sirs: though I do not know the man,
    I think I see him coming, this shepherd we want:
    He is old, like our friend here, and the men
    Bringing him seem to be servants of my house.
    But you can tell, if you have ever seen him.

    Shepherd enters, escorted by servants.

Choragos. I know him, he was Laïos' man. You can trust him.
Oedipus. Tell me first, you from Corinth: is this the shepherd
    We were discussing?
Messenger.   This is the very man.
Oedipus [to shepherd]. Come here. No, look at me. You must answer
    Everything I ask.—You belonged to Laïos?
Shepherd. Yes: born his slave, brought up in his house.
Oedipus. Tell me: what kind of work did you do for him?
Shepherd. I was a shepherd of his, most of my life.
Oedipus. Where mainly did you go for pasturage?
Shepherd. Sometimes Kithairon, sometimes the hills near-by.
Oedipus. Do you remember ever seeing this man out there?
Shepherd. What would he be doing there? This man?
Oedipus. This man standing here. Have you ever seen him before?
Shepherd. No. At least, not to my recollection.
Messenger. And that is not strange, my lord. But I'll refresh
    His memory: he must remember when we two
    Spent three whole seasons together, March to September,

---

10. **Kyllenê's heights:** Mount Cyllene in Arcadia, the supposed birthplace of Hermes.

On Kithairon or thereabouts. He had two flocks;
I had one. Each autumn I'd drive mine home
And he would go back with his to Laïos' sheepfold.—
Is this not true, just as I have described it?
SHEPHERD. True, yes; but it was all so long ago.
MESSENGER. Well, then: do you remember, back in those days,
That you gave me a baby boy to bring up as my own?
SHEPHERD. What if I did? What are you trying to say?
MESSENGER. King Oedipus was once that little child.
SHEPHERD. Damn you, hold your tongue!
OEDIPUS.   No more of that!
It is your tongue needs watching, not this man's.
SHEPHERD. My King, my Master, what is it I have done wrong?
OEDIPUS. You have not answered his question about the boy.
SHEPHERD. He does not know . . . He is only making trouble . . .
OEDIPUS. Come, speak plainly, or it will go hard with you.
SHEPHERD. In God's name, do not torture an old man!
OEDIPUS. Come here, one of you; bind his arms behind him.
SHEPHERD. Unhappy king! What more do you wish to learn?
OEDIPUS. Did you give this man the child he speaks of?
SHEPHERD.   I did.
And I would to God I had died that very day.
OEDIPUS. You will die now unless you speak the truth.
SHEPHERD. Yet if I speak the truth, I am worse than dead.
OEDIPUS. Very well; since you insist upon delaying—
SHEPHERD. No! I have told you already that I gave him the boy.
OEDIPUS. Where did you get him? From your house? From somewhere
else?
SHEPHERD. Not from mine, no. A man gave him to me.
OEDIPUS. Is that man here? Do you know whose slave he was?
SHEPHERD. For God's love, my King, do not ask me any more!
OEDIPUS. You are a dead man if I have to ask you again.
SHEPHERD. Then . . . Then the child was from the palace of Laïos.
OEDIPUS. A slave child? or a child of his own line?
SHEPHERD. Ah, I am on the brink of dreadful speech!
OEDIPUS. And I of dreadful hearing. Yet I must hear.
SHEPHERD. If you must be told, then . . . They said it was Laïos' child;
But it is your wife who can tell you about that.
OEDIPUS. My wife!—Did she give it to you?
SHEPHERD.   My lord, she did.
OEDIPUS. Do you know why?
SHEPHERD.   I was told to get rid of it.
OEDIPUS. An unspeakable mother!

SHEPHERD.   There had been prophecies. . .
OEDIPUS. Tell me.
SHEPHERD. It was said that the boy would kill his own father.
OEDIPUS. Then why did you give him over to this old man?
SHEPHERD. I pitied the baby, my King,
    And I thought that this man would take him far away
    To his own country.
                    He saved him—but for what a fate!
    For if you are what this man says you are,
    No man living is more wretched than Oedipus.
OEDIPUS. Ah God!
    It was true!
            All the prophecies!
                    —Now,
    O Light, may I look on you for the last time!
    I, Oedipus,
    Oedipus, damned in his birth, in his marriage damned,
    Damned in the blood he shed with his own hand!

    He rushes into the palace.

ODE IV

[STROPHE 1]

CHORUS. Alas for the seed of men.
    What measure shall I give these generations
    That breathe on the void and are void
    And exist and do not exist?
    Who bears more weight of joy
    Than mass of sunlight shifting in images,
    Or who shall make his thought stay on
    That down time drifts away?
    Your splendor is all fallen.
    O naked brow of wrath and tears,
    O change of Oedipus!
    I who saw your days call no man blest—
    Your great days like ghosts gone.

[ANTISTROPHE 1]

    That mind was a strong bow.
    Deep, how deep you drew it then, hard archer,

At a dim fearful range,
And brought dear glory down!
You overcame the stranger—
The virgin with her hooking lion claws—
And though death sang, stood like a tower
To make pale Thebes take heart.
Fortress against our sorrow!
True king, giver of laws,
Majestic Oedipus!
No prince in Thebes had ever such renown,
No prince won such grace of power.

[Strophe 2]

And now of all men ever known
Most pitiful is this man's story:
His fortunes are most changed, his state
Fallen to a low slave's
Ground under bitter fate.
O Oedipus, most royal one!
The great door that expelled you to the light
Gave at night—ah, gave night to your glory:
As to the father, to the fathering son.
All understood too late.
How could that queen whom Laïos won,
The garden that he harrowed at his height,
Be silent when that act was done?

[Antistrophe 2]

But all eyes fail before time's eye,
All actions come to justice there.
Though never willed, though far down the deep past,
Your bed, your dread sirings,
Are brought to book at last.
Child by Laïos doomed to die,
Then doomed to lose that fortunate little death,
Would God you never took breath in this air
That with my wailing lips I take to cry:
For I weep the world's outcast.
I was blind, and now I can tell why:
Asleep, for you had given ease of breath
To Thebes, while the false years went by.

EXODOS[11]

A servant enters from the palace.

Servant.[12] Elders of Thebes, most honored in this land,
    What horrors are yours to see and hear, what weight
    Of sorrow to be endured, if, true to your birth,
    You venerate the line of Labdakos!
    I think neither Istros nor Phasis, those great rivers,
    Could purify this place of the corruption
    It shelters now, or soon must bring to light—
    Evil not done unconsciously, but willed.
    The greatest griefs are those we cause ourselves.
Choragos. Surely, friend, we have grief enough already;
    What new sorrow do you mean?
Servant.   The Queen is dead.
Choragos. Iocastê? Dead? But at whose hand?
Servant.   Her own.
    The full horror of what happened you can not know,
    For you did not see it; but I, who did, will tell you
    As clearly as I can how she met her death.
    When she had left us,
    In passionate silence, passing through the court,
    She ran to her apartment in the house,
    Her hair clutched by the fingers of both hands.
    She closed the doors behind her; then, by that bed
    Where long ago the fatal son was conceived—
    That son who should bring about his father's death—
    We heard her call upon Laïos, dead so many years,
    And heard her wail for the double fruit of her marriage,
    A husband by her husband, children by her child.
    Exactly how she died I do not know:
    For Oedipus burst in moaning and would not let us
    Keep vigil to the end: it was by him
    As he stormed about the room that our eyes were caught.
    From one to another of us he went, begging a sword,
    Cursing the wife who was not his wife, the mother
    Whose womb had carried his own children and himself.

---

11. **Exodos:** the final scene of a tragedy; parallels the *parados*.
12. **Servant:** in the original text, "Second Messenger," a conventional character in Greek theater who reported events occurring offstage. His special function was to report horrible or gruesome events which were regarded as "obscene" (*ob* + *scaena* = offstage, i.e., not fit to be seen by the audience).

I do not know: it was none of us aided him,
But surely one of the gods was in control!
For with a dreadful cry
He hurled his weight, as though wrenched out of himself,
At the twin doors: the bolts gave, and he rushed in.
And there we saw her hanging, her body swaying
From the cruel cord she had noosed about her neck.
A great sob broke from him, heartbreaking to hear,
As he loosed the rope and lowered her to the ground.
I would blot out from my mind what happened next!
For the King ripped from her gown the golden brooches
That were her ornament, and raised them, and plunged them down
Straight into his own eyeballs, crying, "No more,
No more shall you look on the misery about me,
The horrors of my own doing! Too long you have known
The faces of those whom I should never have seen,
Too long been blind to those for whom I was searching!
From this hour, go in darkness!" And as he spoke,
He struck at his eyes—not once, but many times;
And the blood spattered his beard,
Bursting from his ruined sockets like red hail.
So from the unhappiness of two this evil has sprung,
A curse on the man and woman alike. The old
Happiness of the house of Labdakos
Was happiness enough: where is it today?
It is all wailing and ruin, disgrace, death—all
The misery of mankind that has a name—
And it is wholly and for ever theirs.

CHORAGOS. Is he in agony still? Is there no rest for him?

SERVANT. He is calling for someone to lead him to the gates
So that all the children of Kadmos may look upon
His father's murderer, his mother's—no,
I can not say it!

              And then he will leave Thebes,
Self-exiled, in order that the curse
Which he himself pronounced may depart from the house.
He is weak, and there is none to lead him,
So terrible is his suffering.

              But you will see:
Look, the doors are opening; in a moment
You will see a thing that would crush a heart of stone.

The central door is opened; OEDIPUS, *blinded, is led in.*

CHORAGOS. Dreadful indeed for men to see.
    Never have my own eyes
    Looked on a sight so full of fear.
    Oedipus!
    What madness came upon you, what daemon[13]
    Leaped on your life with heavier
    Punishment than a mortal man can bear?
    No: I can not even
    Look at you, poor ruined one.
    And I would speak, question, ponder,
    If I were able. No.
    You make me shudder.
OEDIPUS. God. God.
    Is there a sorrow greater?
    Where shall I find harbor in this world?
    My voice is hurled far on a dark wind.
    What has God done to me?
CHORAGOS. Too terrible to think of, or to see.

[STROPHE I]

OEDIPUS. O cloud of night,
    Never to be turned away: night coming on,
    I can not tell how: night like a shroud!
    My fair winds brought me here.
                       O God. Again
    The pain of the spikes where I had sight,
    The flooding pain
    Of memory, never to be gouged out.
CHORAGOS. This is not strange.
    You suffer it all twice over, remorse in pain,
    Pain in remorse.

[ANTISTROPHE I]

OEDIPUS. Ah dear friend
    Are you faithful even yet, you alone?
    Are you still standing near me, will you stay here,
    Patient, to care for the blind?
                    The blind man!
    Yet even blind I know who it is attends me,
    By the voice's tone—
    Though my new darkness hide the comforter.

---

13. **daemon:** Daemons were spirits believed capable of influencing men for good or evil.

CHORAGOS. Oh fearful act!
    What god was it drove you to rake black
    Night across your eyes?

[STROPHE 2]

OEDIPUS. Apollo. Apollo. Dear
    Children, the god was Apollo.
    He brought my sick, sick fate upon me.
    But the blinding hand was my own!
    How could I bear to see
    When all my sight was horror everywhere?
CHORAGOS. Everywhere; that is true.
OEDIPUS. And now what is left?
    Images? Love? A greeting even,
    Sweet to the senses? Is there anything?
    Ah, no, friends: lead me away.
    Lead me away from Thebes.
                    Lead the great wreck
    And hell of Oedipus, whom the gods hate.
CHORAGOS. Your fate is clear, you are not blind to that.
    Would God you had never found it out!

[ANTISTROPHE 2]

OEDIPUS. Death take the man who unbound
    My feet on that hillside
    And delivered me from death to life! What life?
    If only I had died,
    This weight of monstrous doom
    Could not have dragged me and my darlings down.
CHORAGOS. I would have wished the same.
OEDIPUS. Oh never to have come here
    With my father's blood upon me! Never
    To have been the man they call his mother's husband!
    Oh accurst! Oh child of evil,
    To have entered that wretched bed—
                  the selfsame one!
    More primal than sin itself, this fell to me.
CHORAGOS. I do not know how I can answer you.
    You were better dead than alive and blind.
OEDIPUS. Do not counsel me any more. This punishment
    That I have laid upon myself is just.
    If I had eyes,
    I do not know how I could bear the sight

Of my father, when I came to the house of Death,
Or my mother: for I have sinned against them both
So vilely that I could not make my peace
By strangling my own life.

              Or do you think my children,
Born as they were born, would be sweet to my eyes?
Ah never, never! Nor this town with its high walls,
Nor the holy images of the gods.

            For I,
Thrice miserable!—Oedipus, noblest of all the line
Of Kadmos, have condemned myself to enjoy
These things no more, by my own malediction
Expelling that man whom the gods declared
To be a defilement in the house of Laïos.
After exposing the rankness of my own guilt,
How could I look men frankly in the eyes?
No, I swear it,
If I could have stifled my hearing at its source,
I would have done it and made all this body
A tight cell of misery, blank to light and sound:
So I should have been safe in a dark agony
Beyond all recollection.

        Ah Kithairon!
Why did you shelter me? When I was cast upon you,
Why did I not die? Then I should never
Have shown the world my execrable birth.
Ah Polybos! Corinth, city that I believed
The ancient seat of my ancestors: how fair
I seemed, your child! And all the while this evil
Was cancerous within me!

         For I am sick
In my daily life, sick in my origin.
O three roads, dark ravine, woodland and way
Where three roads met: you, drinking my father's blood,
My own blood, spilled by my own hand: can you remember
The unspeakable things I did there, and the things
I went on from there to do?

         O marriage, marriage!
The act that engendered me, and again the act
Performed by the son in the same bed—

             Ah, the net
Of incest, mingling fathers, brothers, sons,
With brides, wives, mothers: the last evil
That can be known by men: no tongue can say

How evil!
              No. For the love of God, conceal me
Somewhere far from Thebes; or kill me; or hurl me
Into the sea, away from men's eyes for ever.
Come, lead me. You need not fear to touch me.
Of all men, I alone can bear this guilt.

    CREON enters.

CHORAGOS. We are not the ones to decide; but Creon here
    May fitly judge of what you ask. He only
    Is left to protect the city in your place.
OEDIPUS. Alas, how can I speak to him? What right have I
    To beg his courtesy whom I have deeply wronged?
CREON. I have not come to mock you, Oedipus,
    Or to reproach you, either.
[To attendants]—You, standing there:
    If you have lost all respect for man's dignity,
    At least respect the flame of Lord Helios:[14]
    Do not allow this pollution to show itself
    Openly here, an affront to the earth
    And Heaven's rain and the light of day. No, take him
    Into the house as quickly as you can.
    For it is proper
    That only the close kindred see his grief.
OEDIPUS. I pray you in God's name, since your courtesy
    Ignores my dark expectation, visiting
    With mercy this man of all men most execrable:
    Give me what I ask—for your good, not for mine.
CREON. And what is it that you would have me do?
OEDIPUS. Drive me out of this country as quickly as may be
    To a place where no human voice can ever greet me.
CREON. I should have done that before now—only,
    God's will had not been wholly revealed to me.
OEDIPUS. But his command is plain: the parricide
    Must be destroyed. I am that evil man.
CREON. That is the sense of it, yes; but as things are,
    We had best discover clearly what is to be done.
OEDIPUS. You would learn more about a man like me?
CREON. You are ready now to listen to the god.
OEDIPUS. I will listen. But it is to you
    That I must turn for help. I beg you, hear me.
    The woman in there—

_____

14. **Lord Helios:** Apollo, the sun god.

Give her whatever funeral you think proper:
She is your sister.
                        —But let me go, Creon!
Let me purge my father's Thebes of the pollution
Of my living here, and go out to the wild hills,
To Kithairon, that has won such fame with me,
The tomb my mother and father appointed for me,
And let me die there, as they willed I should.
And yet I know
Death will not ever come to me through sickness
Or in any natural way: I have been preserved
For some unthinkable fate. But let that be.
As for my sons, you need not care for them.
They are men, they will find some way to live.
But my poor daughters, who have shared my table,
Who never before have been parted from their father—
Take care of them, Creon; do this for me.
And will you let me touch them with my hands
A last time, and let us weep together?
Be kind, my lord,
Great prince, be kind!
                        Could I but touch them,
They would be mine again, as when I had my eyes.

    ANTIGONE *and* ISMENE *enter, attended by handmaids.*

Ah, God!
Is it my dearest children I hear weeping?
Has Creon pitied me and sent my daughters?
CREON. Yes, Oedipus: I knew that they were dear to you
    In the old days, and know you must love them still.
OEDIPUS. May God bless you for this—and be a friendlier
    Guardian to you than he has been to me!
    Children, where are you?
    Come quickly to my hands: they are your brother's—
    Hands that have brought your father's once clear eyes
    To this way of seeing—
                        Ah dearest ones,
    I had neither sight nor knowledge then, your father
    By the woman who was the source of his own life!
    And I weep for you—having no strength to see you—,
    I weep for you when I think of the bitterness
    That men will visit upon you all your lives.
    What homes, what festivals can you attend
    Without being forced to depart again in tears?

And when you come to marriageable age,
Where is the man, my daughters, who would dare
Risk the bane that lies on all my children?
Is there any evil wanting? Your father killed
His father; sowed the womb of her who bore him;
Engendered you at the fount of his own existence!
That is what they will say of you.

                              Then, whom
Can you ever marry? There are no bridegrooms for you,
And your lives must wither away in sterile dreaming.
O Creon, son of Menoikeus!
You are the only father my daughters have,
Since we, their parents, are both of us gone for ever.
They are your own blood: you will not let them
Fall into beggary and loneliness;
You will keep them from the miseries that are mine!
Take pity on them; see, they are only children,
Friendless except for you. Promise me this,
Great Prince, and give me your hand in token of it.

    CREON *clasps* OEDIPUS' *right hand.*

Children:
I could say much, if you could understand me,
But as it is, I have only this prayer for you:
Live where you can, be as happy as you can—
Happier, please God, than God has made your father!
CREON. Enough. You have wept enough. Now go within.
OEDIPUS. I must; but it is hard.
CREON.   Time eases all things.
OEDIPUS. But you must promise—
CREON.   Say what you desire.
OEDIPUS. Send me from Thebes!
CREON.   God grant that I may!
OEDIPUS. But since God hates me . . .
CREON.   No, he will grant your wish.
OEDIPUS. You promise?
CREON.   I can not speak beyond my knowledge.
OEDIPUS. Then lead me in.
CREON.   Come now, and leave your children.
OEDIPUS. No! Do not take them from me!
CREON.   Think no longer
   That you are in command here, but rather think
   How, when you were, you served your own destruction.

All go into the house but the chorus; the CHORAGOS *chants directly to the audience.*

CHORAGOS. Men of Thebes: look upon Oedipus.
   This is the king who solved the famous riddle
   And towered up, most powerful of men.
   No mortal eyes but looked on him with envy,
   Yet in the end ruin swept over him.
   Let every man in mankind's frailty
   Consider his last day; and let none
   Presume on his good fortune until he find
   Life, at his death, a memory without pain.

Considerations

Oedipus Rex is considered by most people to be the greatest of Sophocles' dramas. When it was written or first performed is unknown. The philosophy expressed in it is that of a mature Sophocles, and its perfection of form indicates that he was at the height of his powers.

The play *Oedipus* begins *in medias res*—in midstream, as it were—much of the action having taken place before the drama opens. An oracle has warned Laius, King of Thebes, that his son will slay him. Attempting to avert this fate, Laius tries to get rid of his baby son, Oedipus. The child survives, however, and is raised by royalty in another kingdom, not knowing his true parentage. When he is grown, he comes to Thebes, proves himself clever by answering the riddle of the Sphinx, kills Laius, and marries Jocasta—not realizing she is his mother. Now a plague has fallen on the city; it is the result, says an oracle, of the unpunished death of Laius. At this point the play begins. All of these actions were precipitated by actions that took place even earlier in history, all ripples caused by the dropping of a single stone. Although most of the drama's background was familiar to Sophocles' audience, the relevant high points are recalled in various speeches made during the play.

As was traditional in Greek plays of Sophocles' time, there are three major characters on stage. All are convincingly depicted.

Jocasta is a loving wife to Oedipus. Her speeches and actions, however, carry a double meaning for the audience, which knows her maternal relationship as well. There are some confusing aspects to her personality. Why does her attitude toward the gods change? If she suspects who Oedipus is, why doesn't she say anything? Can she be seen as a tragic figure?

Creon here is the soothing, civilizing influence. The key to his character is the speech in which he explains why he would not be king. In the last scene he is comforting and rational.

The well-rounded character of Oedipus is almost modern in feeling; his faults arise not out of depravity, but out of rashness and a short temper. He can be keenly perceptive and clever in one area, and totally insensitive and short-sighted in another. What country of our times has not known at least one such ruler?

The puzzling question about this play is the philosophy it is intended to communicate. Is the search for knowledge bound to end in disaster? Is Oedipus—together with the others involved—a victim of circumstances trapped in a tragedy of fate? Or, since his problems seem to proceed from the very basis of his character, is he master of his own destiny to the extent that he is master of himself? When the truth becomes known, Oedipus does not excuse his actions by pleading ignorance, though such a plea would have been well-founded. He accepts full moral responsibility for what he has done.

One difficulty this drama presents for a modern audience lies in the Greek idea of the gods. Although Oedipus says "it was Apollo, friends, Apollo, that brought this bitter bitterness, my sorrows to completion," in this play the gods do not intervene. Though their words are heard, it is by way of human beings, the prophets of their time. The gods' statements are more predictions—statements about the inevitable—than curses.

The story itself was old by the time this play was written; it had already been used by many dramatists of the early Greek period. Both the situation and Sophocles' masterful rendering of it have continued to puzzle and provoke people over the years. Freud saw in it a dramatization of a primitive emotional experience familiar to the human race. Scholars have translated and retranslated it, interpreted and reinterpreted it.

The final statement, paraphrased, says: Count no mortal happy till he has passed the final limit of his life secure from pain. This adaptation of an old adage attributed to Solon appears frequently in Greek tragedies. Aeschylus used it for ironic effect in the scene where Agamemnon, the victorious Greek general, greets his wife upon returning from the Trojan war. The audience, of course, knows that Agamemnon will soon be murdered. What is its function in this play? Does its comment on the nature of human experience still seem relevant after 2000 years?

In order to make sense out of this play, one must know something about the royal house of Thebes and its involvement. Here is a diagram of the relationships of the major characters in the Theban saga.

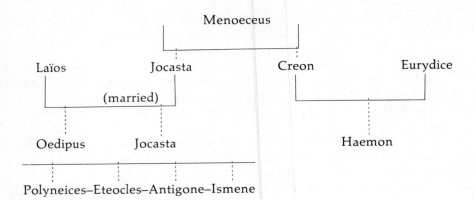

Othello

WILLIAM SHAKESPEARE

DRAMATIS PERSONAE

DUKE OF VENICE
BRABANTIO, *A Senator*
OTHER SENATORS
GRATIANO, *brother to Brabantio*
LODOVICO, *kinsman to Brabantio*
OTHELLO, *a noble Moor in the
    service of the Venetian state*
CASSIO, *his lieutenant*
IAGO, *his ancient*
MONTANO, *Othello's predecessor
    in the government of Cyprus*

RODERIGO, *a Venetian
    gentleman*
CLOWN, *servant to Othello*
DESDEMONA, *daughter to
    Brabantio and wife to Othello*
EMILIA, *wife to Iago*
BIANCA, *mistress to Cassio*
SAILOR, MESSENGER, HERALD,
    OFFICERS, GENTLEMEN,
    MUSICIANS, *and* ATTENDANTS

SCENE—*Venice; a seaport in Cyprus.*

ACT I

SCENE I. *Venice. A street.*

Enter RODERIGO *and* IAGO.

ROD. Tush, never tell me. I take it much unkindly
    That thou, Iago, who hast had° my purse
    As if the strings were thine, shouldst know of this.
IAGO. 'Sblood,° but you will not hear me.
    If ever I did dream of such a matter,   5
    Abhor me.
ROD. Thou told'st me thou didst hold him in thy hate.
IAGO. Despise me if I do not. Three great ones of the city,
    In personal suit° to make me his Lieutenant,
    Off-capped° to him. And, by the faith of man,   10

Act I, Sc. i:2. **had**: i.e., used. 4. **'Sblood**: by God's blood. 9. **In . . . suit**: making this request in person. 10. **Off-capped**: stood cap in hand.

I know my price, I am worth no worse a place.
But he, as loving his own pride and purposes,
Evades them, with a bombast circumstance°
Horribly stuffed with epithets of war.°
And, in conclusion, 15
Nonsuits° my mediators, for, "Certes,"° says he,
"I have already chose my officer."
And what was he?
Forsooth, a great arithmetician,°
One Michael Cassio, a Florentine, 20
A fellow almost damned in a fair wife,°
That never set a squadron in the field,
Nor the division of a battle° knows
More than a spinster, unless the bookish theoric,°
Wherein the toged° Consuls° can propose 25
As masterly as he—mere prattle without practice
Is all his soldiership. But he, sir, had the election.
And I, of whom his eyes had seen the proof
At Rhodes, at Cyprus, and on other grounds
Christian and heathen, must be beleed° and calmed 30
By debitor and creditor. This countercaster,°
He, in good time,° must his Lieutenant be,°
And I—God bless the mark!°—his Moorship's Ancient.°
ROD. By Heaven, I rather would have been his hangman.
IAGO. Why, there's no remedy. 'Tis the curse of service, 35
Preferment goes by letter and affection,
And not by old gradation,° where each second
Stood heir to the first. Now, sir, be judge yourself
Whether I in any just term am affined°
To love the Moor.
ROD.   I would not follow him, then. 40
IAGO. Oh, sir, content you,
I follow him to serve my turn upon him.
We cannot all be masters, nor all masters
Cannot be truly followed. You shall mark
Many a duteous and knee-crooking knave 45

---

13. **bombast circumstance:** bombastic phrases. Bombast is cotton padding used to stuff out a garment. **14. stuffed . . . war:** padded out with military terms. **16. Nonsuits:** rejects the petition of. **Certes:** assuredly. **19. arithmetician:** Contemporary books on military tactics are full of elaborate diagrams and numerals to explain military formations. Cassio is a student of such books. **21. almost . . . wife:** A much-disputed phrase. There is an Italian proverb, "You have married a fair wife? You are damned." If Iago has this in mind, he means by *almost* that Cassio is about to marry. **23. division . . . battle:** organization of an army. **24. bookish theoric:** student of war; not a practical soldier. **25. toged:** wearing a toga. **Consuls:** councilors. Cf. I.ii.43. **30. Beleed:** placed on the lee (or unfavorable) side. **31. countercaster:** calculator (repeating the idea of arithmetician). Counters were used in making calculations. **32. in . . . time:** A phrase expressing indignation. **33. God . . . mark:** An exclamation of impatience. **Ancient:** ensign, the third officer in the company of which Othello is Captain and Cassio Lieutenant. **36–37. Preferment . . . gradation:** promotion comes through private recommendation and favoritism and not by order of seniority. **39. affined:** tied by affection.

That doting on his own obsequious bondage
Wears out his time, much like his master's ass,
For naught but provender, and when he's old, cashiered.°
Whip me such honest knaves. Others there are
Who, trimmed in forms and visages of duty,°   50
Keep yet their hearts attending on themselves,
And throwing but shows of service° on their lords
Do well thrive by them, and when they have lined their coats
Do themselves homage.° These fellows have some soul,
And such a one do I profess myself. For, sir,   55
It is as sure as you are Roderigo,
Were I the Moor, I would not be Iago.
In following him, I follow but myself.
Heaven is my judge, not I for love and duty,
But seeming so, for my peculiar° end.   60
For when my outward action doth demónstrate
The native act and figure of my heart°
In compliment extern,° 'tis not long after
But I will wear my heart upon my sleeve
For daws° to peck at. I am not what I am.°   65
ROD. What a full fortune° does the thick-lips owe°
    If he can carry 't thus!°
IAGO.   Call up her father,
    Rouse him. Make after him, poison his delight,
    Proclaim him in the streets. Incense her kinsmen,
    And though he in a fertile climate dwell,   70
    Plague him with flies. Though that his joy be joy,
    Yet throw such changes of vexation on 't
    As it may lose some color.°
ROD. Here is her father's house, I'll call aloud.
IAGO. Do, with like timorous° accent and dire yell   75
    As when, by night and negligence, the fire
    Is spied in populous cities.
ROD. What ho, Brabantio! Signior Brabantio, ho!
IAGO. Awake! What ho, Brabantio! Thieves! Thieves! Thieves!
    Look to your house, your daughter and your bags!°   80
    Thieves! Thieves!

      BRABANTIO *appears above, at a window.*

---

48. **cashiered:** dismissed. The word at this time did not imply dishonorable discharge. 50. **trimmed . . . duty:** decking themselves out with the outward forms of loyal service. 52. **throwing . . . service:** serving merely in outward show. 54. **Do . . . homage:** serve themselves. **homage:** an outward act signifying obedience. 60. **peculiar:** particular, personal. 62. **native . . . heart:** natural actions and shape of my secret designs. 63. **extern:** outward. 65. **daws:** jackdaws; i.e., fools. **I . . . am:** i.e., I am in secret a devil. 66. **full fortune:** overflowing good luck. **owe:** own. 67. **carry't thus:** i.e., bring off this marriage. 72–73. **throw . . . color:** cause him some annoyance by way of variety to tarnish his joy. 75. **timorous:** terrifying. 80. **bags:** moneybags.

BRA. What is the reason of this terrible summons?
    What is the matter there?
ROD. Signior, is all your family within?
IAGO. Are your doors locked?
BRA.   Why, wherefore ask you this?   85
IAGO. 'Zounds,° sir, you're robbed. For shame, put on your gown,°
    Your heart is burst, you have lost half your soul.
    Even now, now, very now, an old black ram
    Is tupping° your white ewe. Arise, arise,
    Awake the snorting° citizens with the bell,   90
    Or else the Devil° will make a grandsire of you.
    Arise, I say.
BRA.   What, have you lost your wits?
ROD. Most reverend signior, do you know my voice?
BRA. Not I. What are you?
ROD. My name is Roderigo.
BRA.   The worser welcome.   95
    I have charged thee not to haunt about my doors.
    In honest plainness thou hast heard me say
    My daughter is not for thee, and now, in madness,
    Being full of supper and distempering draughts,°
    Upon malicious bravery° dost thou come   100
    To start° my quiet.
ROD. Sir, sir, sir——
BRA.   But thou must needs be sure
    My spirit and my place have in them power
    To make this bitter to thee.
ROD.   Patience, good sir.
BRA. What tell'st thou me of robbing? This is Venice,   105
    My house is not a grange.°
ROD.   Most grave Brabantio,
    In simple and pure soul I come to you.
IAGO. 'Zounds, sir, you are one of those that will not serve God if the
    Devil bid you. Because we come to do you service and you think
    we are ruffians, you'll have your daughter covered with a Barbary°   110
    horse, you'll have your nephews° neigh to you, you'll have coursers
    for cousins,° and jennets° for germans.°
BRA. What profane wretch art thou?

---

86. **'Zounds:** by God's wounds. **gown:** dressing gown. 89. **tupping:** covering. 90. **snorting:** snoring. 91. **Devil:** The Devil
in old pictures and woodcuts was represented as black. 99. **distempering draughts:** liquor that makes senseless. 100.
bravery: defiance. 101. **start:** startle. 106. **grange:** lonely farm. 110. **Barbary:** Moorish. 111. **nephews:** grandsons. 112.
cousins: near relations. **jennets:** Moorish ponies. **germans:** kinsmen.

Iago. I am one, sir, that comes to tell you your daughter and the Moor
    are now making the beast with two backs.   115
Bra. Thou art a villain.
Iago.   You are—a Senator.
Bra. This thou shalt answer. I know thee, Roderigo.
Rod. Sir, I will answer anything. But I beseech you
    If't be your pleasure and most wise consent,
    As partly I find it is, that your fair daughter,   120
    At this odd-even° and dull° watch o' the night,
    Transported with no worse nor better guard
    But with a knave of common hire, a gondolier,
    To the gross clasps of a lascivious Moor—
    If this be known to you, and your allowance,°   125
    We then have done you bold and saucy wrongs.
    But if you know not this, my manners tell me
    We have your wrong rebuke. Do not believe
    That from the sense of all civility°
    I thus would play and trifle with your reverence.   130
    Your daughter, if you have not given her leave,
    I say again, hath made a gross revolt,°
    Tying her duty, beauty, wit, and fortunes
    In an extravagant° and wheeling° stranger
    Of here and everywhere. Straight satisfy yourself.   135
    If she be in her chamber or your house,
    Let loose on me the justice of the state
    For thus deluding you.
Bra.   Strike on the tinder,° ho!
    Give me a taper!° Call up all my people!
    This accident is not unlike my dream.   140
    Belief of it oppresses me already.
    Light, I say! Light! [Exit above]
Iago. Farewell, for I must leave you.
    It seems not meet, nor wholesome to my place,°
    To be produced—as if I stay I shall—   145
    Against the Moor. For I do know the state,
    However this may gall° him with some check,°
    Cannot with safety cast° him. For he's embarked
    With such loud reason to the Cyprus wars,

---

121. odd-even: about midnight. dull: heavy, sleepy. 125. your allowance: by your permission. 129. from . . . civility: disregarding all sense of decent behavior. 132. gross revolt: indecent rebellion. 134. extravagant: vagabond. wheeling: wandering. 138. tinder: the primitive method of making fire, used before the invention of matches. A spark, made by striking flint on steel, fell on the tinder, some inflammable substance such as charred linen, which was blown into flame. 139. taper: candle. 144. place: i.e., as Othello's officer. 147. gall: make sore. check: rebuke. 148. cast: dismiss from service.

Which even now stand in act,° that, for their souls,   150
Another of his fathom° they have none
To lead their business. In which regard,
Though I do hate him as I do Hell pains,
Yet for necessity of present life
I must show out a flag° and sign of love,   155
Which is indeed but sign. That you shall surely find him,
Lead to the Sagittary° the raised search,
And there will I be with him. So farewell. [*Exit*]

> *Enter, below,* BRABANTIO, *in his nightgown, and* SERVANTS *with torches*

BRA. It is too true an evil. Gone she is,
     And what's to come of my despisèd time°   160
     Is naught but bitterness. Now, Roderigo,
     Where didst thou see her? Oh, unhappy girl!
     With the Moor, say'st thou? Who would be a father!
     How didst thou know 'twas she? Oh, she deceives me
     Past thought! What said she to you? Get more tapers.   165
     Raise all my kindred. Are they married, think you?
ROD. Truly, I think they are.
BRA. Oh Heaven! How got she out? Oh, treason of the blood!°
     Fathers, from hence trust not your daughters' minds
     By what you see them act. Are there not charms°   170
     By which the property° of youth and maidhood
     May be abused?° Have you not read, Roderigo,
     Of some such thing?
ROD.   Yes, sir, I have indeed.
BRA. Call up my brother. Oh, would you had had her!
     Some one way, some another. Do you know   175
     Where we may apprehend her and the Moor?
ROD. I think I can discover him, if you please
     To get good guard and go along with me.
BRA. Pray you, lead on. At every house I'll call,
     I may command° at most. Get weapons, ho!   180
     And raise some special officers of night.
     On, good Roderigo, I'll deserve your pains.° [*Exeunt*]

---

150. **stand in act:** are on the point of beginning. 151. **fathom:** depth. 155. **flag:** a sign of welcome. 157. **Sagittary:** presumably some building in Venice, not identified, used as a meeting place for the Council. 160. **what's . . . time:** the rest of my wretched life. 168. **treason . . . blood:** treachery of my own child. 170. **charms:** magic spells. 171. **property:** nature. 172. **abused:** deceived. 180. **command:** find supporters. 182. **deserve . . . pains:** reward your labor.

SCENE II. *Another street.*

Enter OTHELLO, IAGO, *and* ATTENDANTS *with torches*

IAGO. Though in the trade of war I have slain men,
    Yet do I hold it very stuff° o' the conscience
    To do no contrivèd° murder. I lack iniquity
    Sometimes to do me service. Nine or ten times
    I had thought to have yerked° him here under the ribs.   5
OTH. 'Tis better as it is.
IAGO.   Nay, but he prated
    And spoke such scurvy and provoking terms
    Against your honor
    That, with the little godliness I have,
    I did full hard forbear him.° But I pray you, sir,   10
    Are you fast° married? Be assured of this,
    That the Magnifico° is much beloved,
    And hath in his effect° a voice potential
    As double as° the Duke's. He will divorce you,
    Or put upon you what restraint and grievance   15
    The law, with all his might to enforce it on,
    Will give him cable.°
OTH.   Let him do his spite.
    My services which I have done the signiory°
    Shall outtongue his complaints. 'Tis yet to know°—
    Which, when I know that boasting is an honor,
    I shall promulgate°—I fetch my life and being°   20
    From men of royal siege,° and my demerits°
    May speak unbonneted° to as proud a fortune
    As this that I have reached. For know, Iago,
    But that I love the gentle Desdemona,   25
    I would not my unhousèd° free condition
    Put into circumscription and confine°
    For the sea's worth. But look! What lights come yond?
IAGO. Those are the raised father and his friends.
    You were best go in.
OTH.   Not I, I must be found.   30

Sc. ii: **2. stuff:** material, nature. **3. contrived:** deliberately planned. **5. yerked:** jabbed. **10. full . . . him:** had a hard job to keep my hands off him. **11. fast:** securely. **12. Magnifico:** the title of the chief men of Venice. **13. in . . . effect:** what he can do. **13–14. potential . . . as:** twice as powerful as. **17. cable:** rope. **18. signiory:** the state of Venice. **19. 'Tis . . . know:** it has still to be made known. **21. promulgate:** proclaim. **fetch . . . being:** am descended. **22. royal siege:** throne. **demerits:** deserts. **23. unbonneted:** A disputed phrase. Usually it means "without a cap"; i.e., in sign that the wearer is standing before a superior. But Othello means that his merits are such that he need show deference to no man. **26. unhoused:** unmarried. **27. confine:** confinement.

My parts,° my title, and my perfect° soul
   Shall manifest me rightly. Is it they?
IAGO. By Janus,° I think no.

     Enter CASSIO, *and certain* OFFICERS *with torches*

OTH. The servants of the Duke, and my Lieutenant.
   The goodness of the night upon you, friends!   35
   What is the news?
CAS.   The Duke does greet you, General,
   And he requires your haste-posthaste° appearance,
   Even on the instant.
OTH.   What is the matter, think you?
CAS. Something from Cyprus, as I may divine.
   It is a business of some heat. The galleys°   40
   Have sent a dozen sequent° messengers
   This very night at one another's heels,
   And many of the consuls, raised and met,
   Are at the Duke's already. You have been hotly called for
   When, being not at your lodging to be found,   45
   The Senate hath sent about three several° quests
   To search you out.
OTH. 'Tis well I am found by you.
   I will but spend a word here in the house
   And go with you. [*Exit*]
CAS.   Ancient, what makes he here?
IAGO. Faith, he tonight hath boarded a land carrack.°   50
   If it prove lawful prize, he's made forever.
CAS. I do not understand.
IAGO.   He's married.
CAS.   To who?

     Re-enter OTHELLO.

IAGO. Marry,° to——Come, Captain, will you go?
OTH.   Have with you.
CAS. Here comes another troop to seek for you.
IAGO. It is Brabantio. General, be advised,°   55
   He comes to bad intent.

---

31. **parts:** abilities. **perfect:** ready. 33. **Janus:** the two-faced God of the Romans, an appropriate deity for Iago. 37. **haste-posthaste:** with the quickest possible speed. When it was necessary to urge the postboy to greater speed than usual, the letter or dispatch was inscribed "haste, posthaste." The Earl of Essex once inscribed a letter "haste, haste, haste posthaste, haste for life." 40. **galleys:** Venetian ships manned and rowed by slaves; the fastest of craft. 41. **sequent:** following one after another. 46. **several:** separate. 50. **carrack:** the largest type of Spanish merchant ship. 53. **Marry:** Mary, by the Virgin—with a pun. 55. **advised:** careful.

Enter BRABANTIO, RODERIGO, *and* OFFICERS *with torches and weapons.*

OTH.   Holloa! Stand there!
ROD. Signior, it is the Moor.
BRA.   Down with him, thief!

They draw on both sides.

IAGO. You, Roderigo! Come, sir, I am for you.
OTH. Keep up° your bright swords, for the dew will rust them.
    Good signior, you shall more command with years   60
    Than with your weapons.
BRA. O thou foul thief, where hast thou stowed my daughter?
    Damned as thou art, thou hast enchanted her.
    For I'll refer me to all things of sense°
    If she in chains of magic were not bound,   65
    Whether a maid so tender, fair, and happy,
    So opposite to marriage that she shunned
    The wealthy curlèd darlings of our nation,
    Would ever have, to incur a general mock,
    Run from her guardage° to the sooty bosom   70
    Of such a thing as thou, to fear, not to delight.
    Judge me the world if 'tis not gross in sense°
    That thou hast practiced on her with foul charms,
    Abused her delicate youth with drugs or minerals
    That weaken motion.° I'll have 't disputed on,°   75
    'Tis probable, and palpable° to thinking.
    I therefore apprehend and do attach° thee
    For an abuser of the world, a practicer
    Of arts inhibited and out of warrant.°
    Lay hold upon him. If he do resist,   80
    Subdue him at his peril.
OTH.   Hold your hands,
    Both you of my inclining and the rest.
    Were it my cue to fight, I should have known it
    Without a prompter. Where will you that I go
    To answer this your charge?
BRA.   To prison, till fit time   85
    Of law and course of direct session°

---

59. Keep up: sheathe. **64. refer . . . sense:** i.e., by every rational consideration. **70. guardage:** guardianship. **72. gross in sense:** i.e., plain to the perception. **75. motion:** sense. **disputed on:** argued in the courts of law. **76. palpable:** clear. **77. attach:** arrest. **79. arts . . . warrant:** forbidden and illegal acts: i.e., magic and witchcraft. **86. course . . . session:** trial in the ordinary courts, where witches and other criminals are tried—and not by special commission as a great man.

Call thee to answer.

OTH.   What if I do obey?
How may the Duke be therewith satisfied,
Whose messengers are here about my side
Upon some present° business of the state   90
To bring me to him?

1. OFF.   'Tis true, most worthy signior.
The Duke's in Council, and your noble self
I am sure is sent for.

BRA.   How! The Duke in Council!
In this time of the night! Bring him away.
Mine's not an idle° cause. The Duke himself,   95
Or any of my brothers of the state,
Cannot but feel this wrong as 'twere their own.
For if such actions may have passage free,°
Bondslaves and pagans shall our statesmen be. [*Exeunt*]

SCENE III. *A council chamber.*

The DUKE *and* SENATORS *sitting at a table,* OFFICERS *attending.*

DUKE. There is no composition° in these news°
That gives them credit.

1. SEN.   Indeed they are disproportioned.
My letters say a hundred and seven galleys.

DUKE. And mine, a hundred and forty.

2. SEN.   And mine, two hundred.
But though they jump not on a just account°—   5
As in these cases, where the aim reports,°
'Tis oft with difference—yet do they all confirm
A Turkish fleet, and bearing up° to Cyprus.

DUKE. Nay, it is possible enough to judgment.
I do not so secure me in the error,°   10
But the main article° I do approve
In fearful° sense.

SAILOR [*Within*] What ho! What ho! What ho!

1. OFF. A messenger from the galleys.

Enter SAILOR.

---

90. **present:** immediate. 95. **idle:** trivial. 98. **have . . . free:** be freely allowed.
    Sc. iii: 1. **composition:** agreement. **news:** reports. 5. **jump . . . account:** do not agree with an exact estimate. 6. **aim reports:** i.e., intelligence reports of an enemy's intention often differ in the details. 8. **bearing up:** making course for. 10. **I . . . error:** I do not consider myself free from danger, because the reports may not all be accurate. 11. **main article:** general purport. 12. **fearful:** to be feared.

DUKE.   Now, what's the business?
SAIL. The Turkish preparation makes for Rhodes.
    So was I bid report here to the state   15
    By Signior Angelo.
DUKE. How say you by this change?
1. SEN.   This cannot be,
    By no assay of reason.° 'Tis a pageant°
    To keep us in false gaze.° When we consider
    The importancy of Cyprus to the Turk,   20
    And let ourselves again but understand
    That as it more concerns the Turk than Rhodes,
    So may he with more facile question bear° it,
    For that it stands not in such warlike brace°
    But altogether lacks the abilities   25
    That Rhodes is dressed° in—if we make thought of this,
    We must not think the Turk is so unskillful
    To leave that latest which concerns him first,
    Neglecting an attempt of ease and gain
    To wake and wage° a danger profitless.   30
DUKE. Nay, in all confidence, he's not for Rhodes.
1. OFF. Here is more news.

      Enter a MESSENGER.

MESS. The Ottomites,° Reverend and Gracious,
    Steering with due course toward the isle of Rhodes,
    Have there injointed° them with an after-fleet.°   35
1. SEN. Aye, so I thought. How many, as you guess?
MESS. Of thirty sail. And now they do restem°
    Their backward course, bearing with frank appearance°
    Their purposes toward Cyprus. Signior Montano,
    Your trusty and most valiant servitor,   40
    With his free duty recommends you thus,°
    And prays you to believe him.
DUKE. 'Tis certain then for Cyprus.
    Marcus Luccicos, is not he in town?
1. SEN. He's now in Florence.   45
DUKE. Write from us to him, post-posthaste dispatch.
1. SEN. Here comes Brabantio and the valiant Moor.

      Enter BRABANTIO, OTHELLO, IAGO, RODERIGO, *and* OFFICERS.

---

18. assay of reason: reasonable test. **pageant:** show. **19. false gaze:** looking the wrong way. **23. with . . . bear:** take it more easily. **24. brace:** state of defense. **26. dressed:** prepared. **30. wage:** risk. **33. Ottomites:** Turks. **35. injointed:** joined. **after-fleet:** following, second fleet. **37. restem:** steer again. **38. frank appearance:** no attempt at concealment. **41. With . . . thus:** with all due respect thus advises.

DUKE. Valiant Othello, we must straight employ you
    Against the general enemy Ottoman.
    [*To* BRABANTIO] I did not see you. Welcome, gentle signior,   50
    We lacked your counsel and your help tonight.
BRA. So did I yours. Good your Grace, pardon me,
    Neither my place nor aught I heard of business
    Hath raised me from my bed, nor doth the general care
    Take hold on me. For my particular° grief   55
    Is of so floodgate° and o'erbearing nature
    That it engluts° and swallows other sorrows,
    And it is still itself.
DUKE.   Why, what's the matter?
BRA. My daughter! Oh, my daughter!
ALL.   Dead?
BRA.   Aye, to me.
    She is abused, stol'n from me and corrupted   60
    By spells and medicines bought of mountebanks.°
    For nature so preposterously to err,
    Being not deficient, blind, or lame of sense,
    Sans° witchcraft could not.
DUKE. Whoe'er he be that in this foul proceeding   65
    Hath thus beguiled your daughter of herself°
    And you of her, the bloody book of law
    You shall yourself read in the bitter letter
    After your own sense—yea, though our proper° son
    Stood in your action.
BRA.   Humbly I thank your Grace.   70
    Here is the man, this Moor, whom now, it seems,
    Your special mandate for the state affairs
    Hath hither brought.
ALL.   We are very sorry for 't.
DUKE.[*To* OTHELLO] What in your own part can you say to this?
BRA. Nothing but this is so.   75
OTH. Most potent, grave, and reverend signiors,
    My very noble and approved° good masters,
    That I have ta'en away this old man's daughter,
    It is most true—true, I have married her.
    The very head and front° of my offending   80
    Hath this extent, no more. Rude° am I in my speech,
    And little blest with the soft phrase of peace.

---

55. **particular:** personal. 56. **floodgate:** i.e., like water rushing through an opened sluice. 57. **engluts:** swallows. 61. **mountebanks:** quack doctors, who dealt in poisons and love potions. 64. **Sans:** without. 66. **beguiled . . . herself:** cheated your daughter of herself; i.e., caused her to be "beside herself." 69. **proper:** own. 77. **approved:** tested, i.e., found good masters by experience. 80. **front:** forehead. 81. **Rude:** rough, uncultured.

For since these arms of mine had seven years' pith°
Till now some nine moons wasted, they have used
Their dearest° action in the tented field.   85
And little of this great world can I speak,
More than pertains to feats of broil and battle,
And therefore little shall I grace my cause
In speaking for myself. Yet, by your gracious patience,
I will a round unvarnished tale° deliver   90
Of my whole course of love—what drugs, what charms,
What conjuration and what mighty magic—
For such proceeding I am charged withal—
I won his daughter.

BRA.   A maiden never bold,
Of spirit so still and quiet that her motion   95
Blushed at herself,° and she—in spite of nature,
Of years, of country, credit,° everything—
To fall in love with what she feared to look on!
It is a judgment maimed and most imperfect
That will confess° perfection so could err   100
Against all rules of nature, and must be driven
To find out practices° of cunning Hell
Why this should be. I therefore vouch° again
That with some mixtures° powerful o'er the blood,°
Or with some dram conjured° to this effect,   105
He wrought upon her.

DUKE.   To vouch this is no proof
Without more certain and more overt° test
Than these thin habits° and poor likelihoods°
Of modern seeming° do prefer° against him.

1. SEN. But, Othello, speak.   110
Did you by indirect and forcèd° courses
Subdue and poison this young maid's affections?
Or came it by request, and such fair question
As soul to soul affordeth?

OTH.   I do beseech you
Send for the lady to the Sagittary,   115
And let her speak of me before her father.
If you do find me foul in her report,
The trust, the office I do hold of you,

---

83. **pith:** marrow. 85. **dearest:** most important. 90. **round . . . tale:** direct, unadorned account. 95–96. **Of . . . herself:** she was so shy that she blushed at the slightest cause. **motion:** outward behavior. 97. **credit:** reputation. 100. **will confess:** would believe. 102. **practices:** plots. 103. **vouch:** declare. 104. **mixtures:** drugs. **blood:** passions. 105. **conjured:** mixed with spells. 107. **overt:** open. 108. **thin habits:** slight evidence; lit., thin clothes. **poor likelihoods:** unconvincing charges. 109. **modern seeming:** slight suspicion. **prefer:** make a charge against. 111. **forced:** unnatural.

Not only take away, but let your sentence
Even fall upon my life.
DUKE.   Fetch Desdemona hither.   120
OTH. Ancient, conduct them, you best know the place. [*Exeunt* IAGO *and*
ATTENDANTS]
And till she come, as truly as to Heaven
I do confess the vices of my blood,
So justly to your grave ears I'll present
How I did thrive in this fair lady's love   125
And she in mine.
DUKE.   Say it, Othello.
OTH. Her father loved me, oft invited me,
Still° questioned me the story of my life
From year to year, the battles, sieges, fortunes,   130
That I have passed.
I ran it through, even from my boyish days
To the very moment that he bade me tell it.
Wherein I spake of most disastrous chances,°
Of moving accidents° by flood and field,   135
Of hairbreadth 'scapes i' the imminent deadly breach,°
Of being taken by the insolent foe
And sold to slavery, of my redemption thence,
And portance° in my travels' history.
Wherein of antres° vast and deserts idle,°   140
Rough quarries, rocks, and hills whose heads touch heaven,
It was my hint° to speak—such was the process.°
And of the cannibals that each other eat,
The anthropophagi,° and men whose heads
Do grow beneath their shoulders. This to hear   145
Would Desdemona seriously incline.
But still the house affairs would draw her thence,
Which ever as she could with haste dispatch,
She'd come again, and with a greedy ear
Devour up my discourse. Which I observing,   150
Took once a pliant° hour and found good means
To draw from her a prayer of earnest heart
That I would all my pilgrimage dilate,°
Whereof by parcels° she had something heard,
But not intentively.° I did consent,   155
And often did beguile her of° her tears

---

129. Still: always, continually. 134. chances: accidents. 135. accidents: occurrences. 136. breach: assault on a city. 139.
portance: bearing. 140. antres: caves. idle: worthless. 142. hint: occasion. process: proceeding, order. 144. anthropophagi: cannibals. 151. pliant: suitable. 153. dilate: relate at length. 154. parcels: portions. 155. intentively: intently. 156.
beguile . . . of: draw from her.

When I did speak of some distressful stroke
That my youth suffered. My story being done,
She gave me for my pains a world of sighs.
She swore, in faith, 'twas strange, 'twas passing strange, 160
'Twas pitiful, 'twas wondrous pitiful.
She wished she had not heard it, yet she wished
That Heaven had made her° such a man. She thanked me,
And bade me, if I had a friend that loved her,
I should but teach him how to tell my story 165
And that would woo her. Upon this hint I spake.
She loved me for the dangers I had passed,
And I loved her that she did pity them.
This only is the witchcraft I have used.
Here comes the lady, let her witness it. 170

      Enter DESDEMONA, IAGO, *and* ATTENDANTS.

DUKE. I think this tale would win my daughter too.
    Good Brabantio,
    Take up this mangled matter at the best.°
    Men do their broken weapons rather use
    Than their bare hands.
BRA.   I pray you hear her speak. 175
    If she confess that she was half the wooer,
    Destruction on my head if my bad blame
    Light on the man! Come hither, gentle mistress.
    Do you perceive in all this noble company
    Where most you owe obedience?
DES.   My noble Father, 180
    I do perceive here a divided duty.
    To you I am bound for life and education,
    My life and education both do learn° me
    How to respect you, you are the lord of duty,°
    I am hitherto your daughter. But here's my husband, 185
    And so much duty as my mother showed
    To you, preferring you before her father
    So much I challenge that I may profess
    Due to the Moor my lord.
BRA.   God be with you! I have done.
    Please it your Grace, on to the state affairs. 190
    I had rather to adopt a child than get° it.
    Come hither, Moor.

---

163. her: for her. **173. Take . . . best:** make the best settlement you can of this confused business. **183. learn:** teach. **184. lord of duty:** the man to whom I owe duty. **191. get:** beget.

I here do give thee with all my heart
Which, but thou hast already, with all my heart
I would keep from thee. For your sake, jewel,   195
I am glad at soul I have no other child,
For thy escape would teach me tyranny,
To hang clogs on them. I have done, my lord.

DUKE. Let me speak like yourself, and lay a sentence°
Which, as a grise° or step, may help these lovers   200
Into your favor.
When remedies are past, the griefs are ended
By seeing the worst, which late on hopes depended.°
To mourn a mischief that is past and gone
Is the next way to draw new mischief on.   205
What cannot be preserved when fortune takes,
Patience her injury a mockery makes.°
The robbed that smiles steals something from the thief.
He robs himself that spends a bootless° grief.

BRA. So° let the Turk of Cyprus us beguile,   210
We lose it not so long as we can smile.
He bears the sentence well that nothing bears
But the free comfort which from thence he hears.
But he bears both the sentence and the sorrow
That, to pay grief, must of poor patience borrow.   215
These sentences, to sugar or to gall,
Being strong on both sides, are equivocal.
But words are words. I never yet did hear
That the bruised heart was pierced through the ear.
I humbly beseech you, proceed to the affairs of state.   220

DUKE. The Turk with a most mighty preparation makes for Cyprus.
Othello, the fortitude of the place is best known to you, and though
we have there a substitute° of most allowed° sufficiency,° yet
opinion, a sovereign mistress of effects, throws a more safer voice
on you.° You must therefore be content to slubber° the gloss of your
new fortunes with this more stubborn and boisterous expedition.

OTH. The tyrant custom, most grave Senators,
Hath made the flinty and steel couch of war
My thrice-driven° bed of down. I do agnize°
A natural and prompt alacrity   230

I find in hardness,° and do undertake
These present wars against the Ottomites.
Most humbly therefore bending to your state,
I crave fit disposition for my wife,
Due reference of place° and exhibition,°   235
With such accommodation and besort°
As levels with her breeding.°
DUKE.   If you please,
Be 't at her father's.
BRA.   I'll not have it so.
OTH. Nor I.
DES.   Nor I. I would not there reside,
To put my father in impatient thoughts   240
By being in his eye. Most gracious Duke,
To my unfolding° lend your prosperous° ear,
And let me find a charter° in your voice
To assist my simpleness.
DUKE. What would you, Desdemona?   245
DES. That I did love the Moor to live with him,
My downright violence and storm of fortunes
May trumpet to the world. My heart's subdued
Even to the very quality of my lord.°
I saw Othello's visage in his mind,   250
And to his honors and his valiant parts
Did I my soul and fortunes consecrate.
So that, dear lords, if I be left behind,
A moth of peace,° and he go to the war,
The rites for which I love him are bereft me,   255
And I a heavy interim° shall support
By his dear absence. Let me go with him.
OTH. Let her have your voices.
Vouch° with me, Heaven, I therefore beg it not
To please the palate of my appetite,   260
Nor to comply with heat—the young affects
In me defunct°—and proper satisfaction,
But to be free and bounteous° to her mind.°
And Heaven defend° your good souls, that you think
I will your serious and great business scant   265

---

231. **hardness**: hardship. 235. **Due . . . place**: i.e., that she shall be treated as becomes my wife. **exhibition**: allowance. 236. **besort**: attendants. 237. **levels . . . breeding**: as suits her birth. 242. **unfolding**: plan; lit., revealing. **prosperous**: favorable. 243. **charter**: privilege. 246–49. **That . . . lord**: my love for the Moor is publicly shown by the way in which I have violently taken my fortunes in my hands; my heart has become a soldier like my husband. **quality**: profession. 254. **moth of peace**: a useless creature living in luxury. 256. **interim**: interval. 259. **Vouch**: certify. 261–62. **young . . . defunct**: in me the passion of youth is dead. 263. **bounteous**: generous. **to . . . mind**: Othello repeats Desdemona's claim that this is a marriage of minds. 264. **defend**: forbid.

For she is with me. No, when light-winged toys°
Of feathered Cupid seel° with wanton dullness
My speculative and officed instruments,°
That my disports° corrupt and taint my business,
Let housewives make a skillet° of my helm,   270
And all indign° and base adversities
Make head against° my estimation!°

DUKE. Be it as you shall privately determine,
Either for her stay or going. The affair cries haste,
And speed must answer 't. You must hence tonight.   275

DES. Tonight, my lord?

DUKE.   This night.

OTH.   With all my heart.

DUKE: At nine i' the morning here we'll meet again.
Othello, leave some officer behind,
And he shall our commission° bring to you,
With such things else of quality and respect   280
As doth import you. °

OTH.   So please your Grace, my Ancient,
A man he is of honesty and trust.
To his conveyance I assign my wife,
With what else needful your good grace shall think
To be sent after me.

DUKE.   Let it be so.   285
Good night to everyone. [*To* BRABANTIO] And, noble signior,
If virtue no delighted beauty lack,
Your son-in-law is far more fair than black.°

1. SEN. Adieu, brave Moor. Use Desdemona well.

BRA. Look to her, Moor, if thou hast eyes to see.   290
She has deceived her father, and may thee.° [*Exeunt* DUKE, SENA-
TORS, OFFICERS, *etc.*]

OTH. My life upon her faith! Honest Iago,
My Desdemona must I leave to thee.
I prithee, let thy wife attend on her,
And bring them after in the best advantage.°   295
Come, Desdemona, I have but an hour
Of love, of worldly matters and direction,

---

266. toys: trifles. 267. seel: close up; a technical term from falconry. 268. speculative . . . instruments: powers of sight and action; i.e., my efficiency as your general. 269. disports: amusements. 270. skillet: saucepan. 271. indign: unworthy. 272. Make . . . against: overcome. estimation: reputation. 279. commission: formal document of appointment. 280–81. With . . . you: with other matters that concern your position and honor. 287–88. If . . . black: if worthiness is a beautiful thing in itself, your son-in-law, though black, has beauty. 290–91. Look . . . thee: Iago in the background takes note of these words, and later reminds Othello of them with deadly effect. See III. iii. 206. 295. in . . . advantage: at the best opportunity.

To spend with thee. We must obey the time. [*Exeunt* OTHELLO *and*
DESDEMONA]

ROD. Iago!

IAGO. What say'st thou, noble heart? 300

ROD. What will I do, thinkest thou?

IAGO. Why, go to bed and sleep.

ROD. I will incontinently° drown myself.

IAGO. If thou dost, I shall never love thee after. Why, thou silly
gentleman! 305

ROD. It is silliness to live when to live is torment, and then have we a
prescription to die when death is our physician.

IAGO. Oh, villainous! I have looked upon the world for four times seven
years, and since I could distinguish betwixt a benefit and an injury I
never found man that knew how to love himself. Ere I would say I 310
would drown myself for the love of a guinea hen, I would change my
humanity with a baboon.

ROD. What should I do? I confess it is my shame to be so fond,° but it is
not in my virtue° to amend it.

IAGO. Virtue! A fig! 'Tis in ourselves that we are thus or thus. Our bodies 315
are gardens, to the which our wills° are gardeners. So that if we will
plant nettles or sow lettuce, set hyssop and weed up thyme, supply it
with one gender° of herbs or distract it with many, either to have it
sterile with idleness or manured with industry—why, the power and
corrigible° authority of this lies in our wills. If the balance of our 320
lives had not one scale of reason to poise° another of sensuality,
the blood and baseness of our natures would conduct us to most
preposterous conclusions. But we have reason to cool our raging
motions, our carnal stings,° our unbitted° lusts, whereof I take this
that you call love to be a sect or scion.° 325

ROD. It cannot be.

IAGO. It is merely a lust of the blood and a permission of the will. Come,
be a man. Drown thyself! Drown cats and blind puppies. I have
professed me thy friend, and I confess me knit to thy deserving with
cables of perdurable° toughness. I could never better stead° thee 330
than now. Put money in thy purse, follow thou the wars, defeat thy
favor with an usurped beard°—I say put money in thy purse. It
cannot be that Desdemona should long continue her love to the

---

303. incontinently: immediately. 313. fond: foolishly in love. 314. virtue: manhood. 316. wills: desires. 318 gender: kind.
320. corrigible: correcting, directing. 321. poise: weigh. 324. carnal stings: fleshly desires. unbitted: uncontrolled. 325.
sect or scion: Both words mean a slip taken from a tree and planted to produce a new growth. 330. perdurable: very hard.
stead: help. 331–32. defeat . . . beard: disguise your face by growing a beard.

Moor—put money in thy purse—nor he his to her. It was a violent
commencement, and thou shalt see an answerable sequestration°— 335
put but money in thy purse. These Moors are changeable in their
wills.—Fill thy purse with money. The food that to him now is as
luscious as locusts° shall be to him shortly as bitter as coloquintida.°
She must change for youth. When she is sated with his body, she
will find the error of her choice. She must have change, she 340
must—therefore put money in thy purse. If thou wilt needs damn
thyself, do it a more delicate way than drowning. Make all the
money thou canst.° If sanctimony and a frail vow betwixt an erring°
barbarian and a supersubtle Venetian be not too hard for my wits
and all the tribe of Hell, thou shalt enjoy her—therefore make money. 345
A pox of drowning thyself! It is clean out of the way. Seek thou
rather to be hanged in compassing° thy joy than to be drowned and
go without her.

ROD. Wilt thou be fast to my hopes if I depend on the issue?

IAGO. Thou art sure of me. Go, make money. I have told thee often, and I 350
retell thee again and again, I hate the Moor. My cause is hearted,°
thine hath no less reason. Let us be conjunctive° in our revenge
against him. If thou canst cuckold° him, thou dost thyself a pleasure,
me a sport. There are many events in the womb of time, which will
be delivered. Traverse,° go, provide thy money. We will have 355
more of this tomorrow. Adieu.

ROD. Where shall we meet i' the morning?

IAGO. At my lodging.

ROD. I'll be with thee betimes.³⁵⁹

IAGO. Go to, farewell. Do you hear, Roderigo? 360

ROD. What say you?

IAGO. No more of drowning, do you hear?

ROD. I am changed. I'll go sell all my land. [*Exit*]

IAGO. Thus do I ever make my fool my purse,

    For I mine own gained knowledge should profane 365
    If I would time expend with such a snipe
    But for my sport and profit. I hate the Moor,
    And it is thought abroad that 'twixt my sheets
    He has done my office. I know not if 't be true,
    But I for mere suspicion in that kind 370
    Will do as if for surety. He holds me well,
    The better shall my purpose work on him.

---

335. answerable sequestration: corresponding separation; i.e., reaction. **338. locusts:** It is not known what fruit was called a locust. **coloquintida:** known as "bitter apple," a form of gherkin from which a purge was made. **342–43. Make . . . canst:** turn all you can into ready cash. **344. erring:** vagabond. **347. compassing:** achieving. **351. hearted:** heartfelt. **352. conjunctive:** united. **353. cuckold:** make him a cuckold. **355. Traverse:** quickstep. **359. betimes:** in good time, early.

Cassio's a proper° man. Let me see now,
To get his place, and to plume up° my will
In double knavery——How, how?—Let's see.— 375
After some time, to abuse Othello's ear
That he is too familiar with his wife.
He hath a person and a smooth dispose
To be suspected,° framed to make women false.
The Moor is of a free and open nature 380
That thinks men honest that but seem to be so,
And will as tenderly be led by the nose
As asses are.
I have 't. It is engendered.° Hell and night
Must bring this monstrous birth to the world's light. [*Exit*] 385

ACT II

Scene I. *A seaport in Cyprus. An open place near the wharf.*

Enter Montano *and two* Gentlemen.

Mon. What from the cape can you discern at sea?
1. Gent. Nothing at all. It is a high-wrought flood.°
     I cannot 'twixt the heaven and the main°
     Descry a sail,
Mon. Methinks the wind hath spoke aloud at land, 5
     A fuller blast ne'er shook our battlements.
     If it hath ruffianed° so upon the sea,
     What ribs of oak, when mountains melt on them,
     Can hold the mortise?° What shall we hear of this?
2. Gent. A segregation° of the Turkish fleet. 10
     For do but stand upon the foaming shore,
     The chidden billow seems to pelt the clouds,
     The wind-shaked surge, with high and monstrous mane,
     Seems to cast water on the burning Bear,°
     And quench the guards of the ever-fixèd Pole.° 15
     I never did like molestation° view
     On the enchafèd° flood.
Mon.   If that the Turkish fleet

Be not ensheltered and embayed,° they are drowned.
It is impossible to bear it out.

Enter a THIRD GENTLEMAN.

3. GENT. News, lads! Our wars are done.   20
    The desperate tempest hath so banged the Turks
    That their designment halts.° A noble ship of Venice
    Hath seen a grievous wreck and sufferance°
    On most part of their fleet.
MON. How! Is this true?
3. GENT.   The ship is here put in,   25
    A Veronesa. Michael Cassio,
    Lieutenant to the warlike Moor Othello,
    Is come on shore, the Moor himself at sea,
    And is in full commission° here for Cyprus.
MON. I am glad on 't. 'Tis a worthy governor.   30
3. GENT. But this same Cassio, though he speak of comfort
    Touching the Turkish loss, yet he looks sadly
    And prays the Moor be safe, for they were parted
    With foul and violent tempest.
MON.   Pray Heavens he be,
    For I have served him, and the man commands   35
    Like a full° soldier. Let's to the seaside, ho!
    As well to see the vessel that's come in
    As to throw out our eyes for brave Othello,
    Even till we make the main and the aerial blue
    An indistinct regard.°
3. GENT.   Come, let's do so.   40
    For every minute is expectancy
    Of more arrivance.°

    Enter CASSIO.

CAS. Thanks, you the valiant of this warlike isle
    That so approve the Moor! Oh, let the heavens
    Give him defense against the elements,   45
    For I have lost him on a dangerous sea.
MON. Is he well shipped?°
CAS. His bark is stoutly timbered, and his pilot
    Of very expert and approved allowance.°

---

18. embayed: anchored in some bay. **22. designment halts:** plan is made lame. **23. sufferance:** damage. **29. in . . . commission:** with full powers. **36. full:** perfect. **39–40. Even . . . regard:** until we can no longer distinguish between sea and sky. **41–42. For . . . arrivance:** every minute more arrivals are expected. **47. well shipped:** in a good ship. **49. approved allowance:** proved skill.

Therefore my hopes, not surfeited° to death,   50
    Stand in bold cure.° [*A cry within:* "A sail, a sail, a sail!"]

        Enter a FOURTH GENTLEMAN.

CAS. What noise?
4. GENT. The town is empty. On the brow o' the sea
    Stand ranks of people, and they cry "A sail!"
CAS. My hopes do shape° him for the governor. [*Guns heard*]   55
2. GENT. They do discharge their shot of courtesy.
    Our friends, at least.
CAS.   I pray you, sir, go forth,
    And give us truth who 'tis that is arrived.
2. GENT. I shall. [*Exit*]
MON. But, good Lieutenant, is your General wived?   60
CAS. Most fortunately. He hath achieved° a maid
    That paragons° description and wild fame,
    One that excels the quirks of blazoning pens
    And in the essential vesture of creation
    Does tire the ingener.°
    [*Re-enter* SECOND GENTLEMAN.] How now! Who has put in?   65
2. GENT. 'Tis one Iago, Ancient to the General.
CAS. He has had most favorable and happy speed.
    Tempests themselves, high seas, and howling winds,
    The guttered° rocks, and congregated sands,
    Traitors ensteeped° to clog the guiltless keel,   70
    As having sense of beauty, do omit
    Their mortal natures,° letting go safely by
    The divine Desdemona.
MON.   What is she?
CAS. She that I spake of, our great Captain's captain,
    Left in the conduct° of the bold Iago,   75
    Whose footing° here anticipates our thoughts
    A sennight's° speed. Great Jove, Othello guard,
    And swell his sail with thine own powerful breath,
    That he may bless this bay with his tall ship,
    Make love's quick pants in Desdemona's arms,   80
    Give renewed fire to our extincted° spirits,
    And bring all Cyprus comfort.

---

50. surfeited: sickened. 51. Stand . . . cure: have every hope of cure. 55. shape: imagine. 61. achieved: won. 62. paragons: surpasses. 63–65. One . . . ingener: one that is too good for the fancy phrases (*quirks*) of painting pens (i.e., poets) and in her absolute perfection wearies the artist (i.e., the painter). (Cassio is full of gallant phrases and behavior, in contrast to Iago's bluntness.) ingener: inventor. 69. guttered: worn into channels. 70. ensteeped: submerged. 71–72. omit . . . natures: forbear their deadly nature. 75. conduct: escort. 76. footing: arrival. 77. sennight: week. 81. extincted: extinguished.

Enter DESDEMONA, EMILIA, IAGO, RODERIGO, *and* ATTENDANTS.

                  Oh, behold,
The riches of the ship is come on shore!
Ye men of Cyprus, let her have your knees.
Hail to thee, lady! And the grace of Heaven,   85
Before, behind thee, and on every hand,
Enwheel° thee round!
DES.   I thank you, valiant Cassio.
What tidings can you tell me of my lord?
CAS. He is not yet arrived, nor know I aught
But that he's well and will be shortly here.   90
DES. Oh, but I fear—How lost you company?
CAS. The great contention of the sea and skies
Parted our fellowship.°—But, hark! A sail. [*A cry within:* "A sail, a
sail!" *Guns heard*]
2. GENT. They give their greeting to the citadel.
This likewise is a friend.   95
CAS. See for the news. [*Exit* GENTLEMAN]
Good Ancient, you are welcome. [*To* EMILIA] Welcome, mistress.
Let it not gall your patience, good Iago,
That I extend my manners.° 'Tis my breeding°
That gives me this bold show of courtesy.° [*Kissing her*]   100
IAGO. Sir, would she give you so much of her lips
As of her tongue she oft bestows on me,
You'd have enough.
DES.   Alas, she has no speech.
IAGO. In faith, too much,
I find it still° when I have list° to sleep.   105
Marry, before your ladyship, I grant,
She puts her tongue a little in her heart
And chides with thinking.
EMIL. You have little cause to say so.
IAGO. Come on, come on. You are pictures° out of doors,   110
Bells° in your parlors, wildcats in your kitchens,
Saints in your injuries,° devils being offended,
Players in your housewifery, and housewives in your beds.
DES. Oh, fie upon thee, slanderer!
IAGO. Nay, it is true, or else I am a Turk.°   115
You rise to play, and go to bed to work.

---

87. Enwheel: encompass. **93. fellowship:** company. **99. extend my manners:** i.e., salute your wife. **breeding:** bringing-up. **100. bold . . . courtesy:** i.e., of saluting your wife with a kiss—a piece of presumptuous behavior which indicates that Cassio regards himself as Iago's social superior. **105. still:** continuously. **list:** desire. **110. pictures:** i.e., painted and dumb. **111. Bells:** i.e., ever clacking. **112. Saints . . . injuries:** saints when you hurt anyone else. **115. Turk:** heathen.

EMIL. You shall not write my praise.

IAGO.   No, let me not.

DES. What wouldst thou write of me if thou shouldst praise me?

IAGO. O gentle lady, do not put me to 't,

> For I am nothing if not critical.°   120

DES. Come on, assay.°—There's one gone to the harbor?

IAGO. Aye, madam.

DES. I am not merry, but I do beguile

> The thing I am by seeming otherwise.
>
> Come, how wouldst thou praise me?   125

IAGO. I am about it, but indeed my invention

> Comes from my pate as birdlime does from frieze°—
>
> It plucks out brains and all. But my Muse labors,
>
> And thus she is delivered.
>
> If she be fair and wise, fairness and wit,   130
>
> The one's for use, the other useth it.

DES. Well praised! How if she be black and witty?

IAGO. If she be black, and thereto have a wit,

> She'll find a white° that shall her blackness fit.

DES. Worse and worse.   135

EMIL. How if fair and foolish?

IAGO. She never yet was foolish that was fair,

> For even her folly helped her to an heir.

DES. These are old fond paradoxes° to make fools laugh i' the alehouse.

> What miserable praise hast thou for her that's foul and foolish?   140

IAGO. There's none so foul, and foolish thereunto,

> But does foul pranks which fair and wise ones do.

DES. Oh, heavy ignorance! Thou praisest the worst best. But what praise

> couldst thou bestow on a deserving woman indeed, one that in the
>
> authority of her merit did justly put on the vouch of very malice   145
>
> itself?°

IAGO. She that was ever fair and never proud,

> Had tongue at will° and yet was never loud,
>
> Never lacked gold and yet went never gay,
>
> Fled from her wish and yet said "Now I may."   150
>
> She that, being angered, her revenge being nigh,
>
> Bade her wrong stay and her displeasure fly.
>
> She that in wisdom never was so frail
>
> To change the cod's head for the salmon's tail.°
>
> She that could think and ne'er disclose her mind,   155

---

120. **critical:** bitter. 121. **assay:** try. 127–27. **my . . . frieze:** my literary effort *(invention)* is as hard to pull out of my head as frieze (cloth with a nap) stuck to birdlime. 134. **white:** with a pun on *wight* (1.157), man, person. 139. **fond paradoxes:** foolish remarks, contrary to general opinion. 144–46. **one . . . itself:** one so deserving that even malice would declare her good. 148. **tongue . . . will:** a ready flow of words. 154. **To . . . tail:** to prefer the tail end of a good thing to the head of a poor thing.

See suitors following and not look behind.
She was a wight, if ever such wight were——
Des. To do what?
Iago. To suckle fools and chronicle small beer.°
Des. Oh, most lame and impotent conclusion! Do not learn of him,   160
    Emilia, though he be thy husband. How say you, Cassio? Is he not a
    most profane and liberal° counselor?
Cas. He speaks home,° madam. You may relish° him more in the soldier
    than in the scholar.
Iago. [Aside] He° takes her by the palm. Aye, well said, whisper. With   165
    as little a web as this will I ensnare as great a fly as Cassio. Aye, smile
    upon her, do, I will gyve° thee in thine own courtship. You say true,
    'tis so indeed. If such tricks as these strip you out of your Lieuten-
    antry, it had been better you had not kissed your three fingers° so
    oft, which now again you are most apt to play the sir° in. Very   170
    good, well kissed! An excellent courtesy! 'Tis so indeed. Yet again
    your fingers to your lips? Would they were clyster pipes° for your
    sake! [Trumpet within] The Moor! I know his trumpet.
Cas. 'Tis truly so.
Des. Let's meet him and receive him.   175
Cas. Lo where he comes!

        Enter OTHELLO and ATTENDANTS.

Oth. O my fair warrior!°
Des.   My dear Othello!
Oth. It gives me wonder great as my content
    To see you here before me. O my soul's joy!
    If after every tempest come such calms,   180
    May the winds blow till they have wakened death!
    And let the laboring bark climb hills of seas
    Olympus-high,° and duck again as low
    As Hell's from Heaven! If it were now to die,
    'Twere now to be most happy, for I fear   185
    My soul hath her content so absolute
    That not another comfort like to this
    Succeeds in unknown fate.
Des.   The Heavens forbid
    But that our loves and comforts should increase,
    Even as our days do grow!

---

159. chronicle . . . beer: write a whole history about trifles (small beer: thin drink). 162. liberal: gross. 163. home: to the
point. relish: appreciate. 165–73. He . . . sake: As so often, Shakespeare without using elaborate stage directions exactly
indicates the action in the dialogue. 167. gyve: fetter. 169. kissed . . . fingers: a gesture of gallantry. 170. play . . . sir: act
the fine gentleman. 172. clyster pipes: an enema syringe. 177. warrior: because she is a soldier's wife. See I. iii. 249. 183.
Olympus-high: high as Olympus, the highest mountain in Greece.

OTH.   Amen to that, sweet powers!   190
    I cannot speak enough of this content.
    It stops me here,° it is too much of joy.
    And this, and this, the greatest discords be [*Kissing her*]
    That e'er our hearts shall make!
IAGO. [*Aside*] Oh, you are well tuned now,   195
    But I'll set down the pegs° that make this music,
    As honest as I am.
OTH.   Come, let us to the castle.
    News, friends. Our wars are done, the Turks are drowned.
    How does my old acquaintance of this isle?
    Honey, you shall be desired in Cyprus,   200
    I have found great love amongst them. O my sweet,
    I prattle out of fashion,° and I dote
    In mine own comforts. I prithee, good Iago,
    Go to the bay and disembark my coffers.°
    Bring thou the master° to the citadel.   205
    He is a good one, and his worthiness
    Does challenge° much respect. Come, Desdemona,
    Once more well met at Cyprus. [*Exeunt all but* IAGO *and* RODERIGO]
IAGO. Do thou meet me presently° at the harbor. Come hither. If thou
    beest valiant—as they say base men being in love have then a no-   210
    bility in their natures more than is native to them—list me. The
    Lieutenant tonight watches on the court of guard.° First, I must tell
    thee this. Desdemona is directly in love with him.
ROD. With him! Why, 'tis not possible.
IAGO. Lay thy finger thus,° and let thy soul be instructed. Mark me with   215
    what violence she first loved the Moor, but for° bragging and telling
    her fantastical lies. And will she love him still for prating? Let not
    thy discreeet heart think it. Her eye must be fed, and what delight
    shall she have to look on the Devil? When the blood is made dull
    with the act of sport, there should be, again to inflame it and to give   220
    satiety a fresh appetite, loveliness in favor,° sympathy in years,
    manners, and beauties, all which the Moor is defective in. Now, for
    want of these required conveniences, her delicate tenderness will
    find itself abused, begin to heave the gorge,° disrelish and abhor the
    Moor. Very nature will instruct her in it and compel her to some   225
    second choice. Now, sir, this granted—as it is a most pregnant

---

192. here: i.e., in the heart. 196. set . . . pegs: i.e., make you sing in a different key. A stringed instrument was tuned by
the pegs. 202. prattle . . . fashion: talk idly. 204. coffers: trunks. 205. master: captain of the ship. 207. challenge: claim.
209. presently: immediately. 212. watches . . . guard: is on duty with the guard. The court of guard meant both the guard
itself and the guardroom. 215. finger thus: i.e., on the lips. 216. but for: only for. 221. favor: face. 224. heave . . . gorge:
retch. gorge: throat.

and unforced position°—who stands so eminently in the degree of this fortune as Cassio does? A knave very voluble, no further conscionable° than in putting on the mere form of civil and humane seeming° for the better compassing of his salt° and most hidden loose 230 affection? Why, none, why, none. A slipper° and subtle knave, a finderout of occasions, that has an eye can stamp and counterfeit advantages,° though true advantage never present itself. A devilish knave! Besides, the knave is handsome, young, and hath all those requisites in him that folly and green° minds look after. A pestilent 235 complete knave, and the woman hath found him already.

Rod. I cannot believe that in her. She's full of most blest condition.°

Iago. Blest fig's-end!° The wine she drinks is made of grapes. If she had been blest, she would never have loved the Moor. Blest pudding! Didst thou not see her paddle° with the palm of his hand? Didst not 240 mark that?

Rod. Yes, that I did, but that was but courtesy.

Iago. Lechery, by this hand, an index° and obscure prologue to the history of lust and foul thoughts. They met so near with their lips that their breaths embraced together. Villainous thoughts, Roderi- 245 go! When these mutualities° so marshal the way, hard at hand comes the master and main exercise, the incorporate° conclusion. Pish! But, sir, be you ruled by me. I have brought you from Venice. Watch you tonight. For the command, I'll lay 't upon you. Cassio knows you not. I'll not be far from you. Do you find some occasion to 250 anger Cassio, either by speaking too loud, or tainting° his discipline, or from what other course you please which the time shall more favorably minister.°

Rod. Well.

Iago. Sir, he is rash and very sudden in choler,° and haply° may strike at 255 you. Provoke him, that he may, for even out of that will I cause these of Cyprus to mutiny, whose qualification° shall come into no true taste again but by the displanting° of Cassio. So shall you have a shorter journey to your desires by the means I shall then have to prefer° them, and the impediment most profitably removed without 260 the which there were no expectation of our prosperity.

226–27. pregnant . . . position: very significant and probable argument. 228. no . . . conscionable: who has no more conscience. 229. humane seeming: courteous appearance. 230. salt: lecherous. 231. slipper: slippery. 232–33. stamp . . . advantages: forge false opportunities. 235. green: inexperienced, foolish. 237. condition: disposition. 238. Blest fig's-end: blest nonsense, a phrase used as a substitute in contempt for a phrase just used, as is also *blest pudding* (1.239). 240. paddle: play. 243. index: table of contents. 246. mutualities: mutual exchanges. 247. incorporate: bodily. 251. tainting: disparaging. 253. minister: provide. 255. choler: anger. haply: perhaps. 257. qualification: appeasement. 258. displanting: removal. 260. prefer: promote.

ROD. I will do this, if I can bring it to any opportunity.
IAGO. I warrant thee. Meet me by and by at the citadel. I must fetch his
    necessaries ashore. Farewell.
ROD. Adieu. [*Exit*]   265
IAGO. That Cassio loves her, I do well believe it.
    That she loves him, 'tis apt and of great credit.°
    The Moor, howbeit that I endure him not,
    Is of a constant, loving, noble nature,
    And I dare think he'll prove to Desdemona   270
    A most dear husband. Now, I do love her too,
    Not out of absolute lust, though peradventure
    I stand accountant for as great a sin,
    But partly led to diet° my revenge
    For that I do suspect the lusty Moor   275
    Hath leaped into my seat. The thought whereof
    Doth like a poisonous mineral° gnaw my inwards.
    And nothing can or shall content my soul
    Till I am evened with him, wife for wife.
    Or failing so, yet that I put the Moor   280
    At least into a jealousy so strong
    That judgment° cannot cure. Which thing to do,
    If this poor trash of Venice, whom I trash°
    For his quick hunting,° stand the putting-on,°
    I'll have our Michael Cassio on the hip,   285
    Abuse him to the Moor in the rank garb°—
    For I fear Cassio with my nightcap too—
    Make the Moor thank me, love me, and reward me
    For making him egregiously° an ass
    And practicing upon° his peace and quiet   290
    Even to madness. 'Tis here, but yet confused.
    Knavery's plain face is never seen till used. [*Exit*]

SCENE II. A street.

Enter a HERALD with a proclamation, PEOPLE following.

HER. It is Othello's pleasure, our noble and valiant General, that upon
    certain tidings now arrived, importing the mere perdition° of the
    Turkish fleet, every man put himself into triumph°—some to dance,

---

267. apt . . . credit: likely and very credible. **274. diet:** feed. **277. poisonous mineral:** corrosive poison. See I. ii. 68. **282. judgment:** reason. **283. trash . . . trash:** rubbish . . . discard. **283–84. trash . . . hunting:** F1 reads "trace" and Q1 "crush." If the emendation "trash" is correct, it means "hold back from outrunning the pack." **384. putting-on:** encouraging. **286. rank garb:** gross manner; i.e., by accusing him of being Desdemona's lover. **289. egregiously:** notably. **290. practicing upon:** plotting against. **Sc. ii: 2. mere perdition:** absolute destruction. **3. put . . . triumph:** celebrate.

some to make bonfires, each man to what sport and revels his
addiction° leads him. For, besides these beneficial news, it is the   5
celebration of his nuptial. So much was his pleasure should be
proclaimed. All offices° are open, and there is full liberty of feasting
from this present hour of five till the bell have told eleven. Heaven
bless the isle of Cyprus and our noble General Othello! [*Exeunt*]

SCENE III. *A hall in the castle.*

Enter OTHELLO, DESDEMONA, CASSIO, *and* ATTENDANTS.

OTH. Good Michael, look you to the guard tonight.
    Let's teach ourselves that honorable stop,
    Not to outsport discretion.°
CAS. Iago hath direction what to do,
    But notwithstanding with my personal eye   5
    Will I look to 't.
OTH.   Iago is most honest.
    Michael, good night. Tomorrow with your earliest°
    Let me have speech with you. Come, my dear love,
    The purchase made, the fruits are to ensue—
    That profit's yet to come 'tween me and you.   10
    Good night. [*Exeunt* OTHELLO, DESDEMONA, *and* ATTENDANTS]

    Enter IAGO.

CAS. Welcome, Iago, We must to the watch.
IAGO. Not this hour, Lieutenant, 'tis not yet ten o' the clock. Our General
    cast° us thus early for the love of his Desdemona, who let us not
    therefore blame. He hath not yet made wanton the night with her,   15
    and she is sport for Jove.
CAS. She's a most exquisite lady.
IAGO. And, I'll warrant her, full of game.
CAS. Indeed she's a most fresh and delicate creature.
IAGO. What an eye she has. Methinks it sounds a parley to provocation.°   20
CAS. An inviting eye, and yet methinks right modest.
IAGO. And when she speaks, is it not an alarum° to love?
CAS. She is indeed perfection.
IAGO. Well, happiness to their sheets! Come, Lieutenant, I have a stoup°
    of wine, and here without are a brace of Cyprus gallants that would   25
    fain° have a measure to the health of black Othello.

---

5. addiction: inclination. 7. offices: the kitchen and buttery—i.e., free food and drink for all.
    Sc. iii: 3. outsport discretion: let the fun go too far. 7. with . . . earliest: very early. 14. cast: dismissed. 22–23.
sounds . . . provocation: invites to a love talk. 22. alarum: call to arms. 24. stoup: large drinking vessel. 26. fain: gladly.

CAS. Not tonight, good Iago. I have very poor and unhappy brains for
drinking. I could well wish courtesy would invent some other
custom of entertainment.

IAGO. Oh, they are our friends. But one cup—I'll drink for you.   30

CAS. I have drunk but one cup tonight, and that was craftily qualified°
too, and behold what innovation° it makes here. I am unfortunate in
the infirmity, and dare not task° my weakness with any more.

IAGO. What, man! 'Tis a night of revels. The gallants desire it.

CAS. Where are they?   35

IAGO. Here at the door. I pray you call them in.

CAS. I'll do 't, but it dislikes° me. [Exit]

IAGO. If I can fasten but one cup upon him,
With that which he hath drunk tonight already
He'll be as full of quarrel and offense   40
As my young mistress' dog. Now my sick fool Roderigo,
Whom love hath turned almost the wrong side out,
To Desdemona hath tonight caroused°
Potations pottle-deep,° and he's to watch.
Three lads of Cyprus, noble swelling° spirits   45
That hold their honors in a wary distance,°
The very elements° of this warlike isle,
Have I tonight flustered with flowing cups,
And they watch too. Now, 'mongst this flock of drunkards,
Am I to put our Cassio in some action   50
That may offend the isle. But here they come.
If consequence do but approve my dream,°
My boat sails freely, both with wind and stream.

Re-enter CASSIO, *with him* MONTANO *and* GENTLEMEN, SERVANTS
following with wine.

CAS. 'Fore God, they have given me a rouse° already.

MON. Good faith, a little one—not past a pint, as I am a soldier.   55

IAGO. Some wine, ho! [*Sings*]
"And let me the cannikin° clink, clink,
And let me the cannikin clink.
A soldier's a man,
A life's but a span.°   60
Why, then let a soldier drink."
Some wine, boys!

CAS. 'Fore God, an excellent song.

---

31. craftily qualified: cunningly mixed. **32. innovation:** revolution, disturbance. **33. task:** burden. **37. dislikes:** displeases. **43. caroused:** drunk healths. **44. pottle-deep:** "bottoms up"; a pottle held two quarts. **45. swelling:** bursting with pride. **46. hold . . . distance:** "have a chip on their shoulders." **47. very elements:** typical specimens. **52. If . . . dream:** if what follows proves my dream true. **54. rouse:** a deep drink. **57. cannikin:** drinking pot. **60. span:** lit., the measure between the thumb and little finger of the outstretched hand; about 9 inches.

IAGO. I learned it in England, where indeed they are most potent in
potting.° Your Dane, your German, and your swag-bellied°   65
Hollander—Drink, ho!—are nothing to your English.

CAS. Is your Englishman so expert in his drinking?

IAGO. Why, he drinks you with facility your Dane dead drunk, he sweats
not° to overthrow your Almain,° he gives your Hollander a vomit°
ere the next pottle can be filled.   70

CAS. To the health of our General!

MON. I am for it, Lieutenant, and I'll do you justice.

IAGO. O sweet England! [*Sings*]
    "King Stephen was a worthy peer,
      His breeches cost him but a crown.   75
    He held them sixpence all too dear,°
      With that he called the tailor lown.°

    "He was a wight of high renown,
      And thou art but of low degree.
    'Tis pride that pulls the country down.   80
      Then take thine auld cloak about thee."
    Some wine, ho!

CAS. Why, this is a more exquisite song than the other.

IAGO. Will you hear 't again?

CAS. No, for I hold him to be unworthy of his place that does those   85
things. Well, God's above all, and there be souls must be saved and
there be souls must not be saved.

IAGO. It's true, good Lieutenant.

CAS. For mine own part—no offense to the General, nor any man of
quality°—I hope to be saved.   90

IAGO. And so do I too, Lieutenant.

CAS. Aye, but, by your leave, not before me. The Lieutenant is to be
saved before the Ancient. Let's have no more of this, let's to our
affairs. God forgive us our sins! Gentlemen, let's look to our
business. Do not think, gentlemen, I am drunk. This is my Ancient,   95
this is my right hand and this is my left. I am not drunk now, I can
stand well enough and speak well enough.

ALL. Excellent well.

CAS. Why, very well, then, you must not think then that I am drunk.
[*Exit*]

MON. To the platform,° masters. Come, let's set the watch.°   100

64–65 potent in potting: desperate drinkers. **65. swag-bellied:** with loose bellies. Germans and Dutchmen were almost as famous for drinking as the Danes. **68–69. sweats not:** has no need to labor excessively. **69. Almain:** German. **gives . . . vomit:** drinks as much as will make a Dutchman throw up. **76. sixpence . . . dear:** too dear by sixpence. **77. lown:** lout. **90. quality:** rank. **100. platform:** the level place on the ramparts where the cannon were mounted. **set . . . watch:** mount guard.

IAGO. You see this fellow that is gone before.
    He is a soldier fit to stand by Caesar
    And give direction. And do but see his vice.
    'Tis to his virtue a just equinox,°
    The one as long as the other. 'Tis pity of him.   105
    I fear the trust Othello puts him in
    On some odd time° of his infirmity
    Will shake this island.
MON.   But is he often thus?
IAGO. 'Tis evermore the prologue to his sleep.
    He'll watch the horologe a double set,°   110
    If drink rock not his cradle.
MON.   It were well
    The General were put in mind of it.
    Perhaps he sees it not, or his good nature
    Prizes the virtue that appears in Cassio
    And looks not on his evils. Is not this true?   115

     Enter RODERIGO.

IAGO. [*Aside to him*] How now, Roderigo! I pray you, after the
    Lieutenant. Go. [*Exit* RODERIGO]
MON. And 'tis great pity that the noble Moor
    Should hazard such a place at his own second
    With one of an ingraft° infirmity.   120
    It were an honest action to say
    So to the Moor.
IAGO.   Not I, for this fair island.
    I do love Cassio well, and would do much
    To cure him of this evil—But, hark! What noise? [*A cry within:*
    "Help! help!"]

     Re-enter CASSIO, *driving in* RODERIGO.

CAS. 'Zounds! You rogue! You rascal!   125
MON. What's the matter, Lieutenant?
CAS. A knave teach me my duty!
    But I'll beat the knave into a wicker bottle.°
ROD. Beat me!
CAS. Dost thou prate, rogue? [*Striking* RODERIGO]   130
MON. Nay, good Lieutenant, [*Staying him*]
    I pray you, sir, hold your hand.

---

104. just equinox: exact equal. 107. some . . . time: some time or other. 110. watch . . . set: stay awake the clock twice round. 120. ingraft: engrafted, firmly fixed. 128. But . . . bottle: One of those bad-tempered, threatening phrases which have no very exact meaning, like "I'll knock him into a cocked hat." wicker bottle: large bottle covered with wicker, demijohn.

CAS.   Let me go, sir,
   Or I'll knock you o'er the mazzard.°
MON. Come, come, you're drunk.
CAS. Drunk! [*They fight*]   135
IAGO. [*Aside to* RODERIGO] Away, I say. Go out and cry a mutiny.° [*Exit*
   RODERIGO]
   Nay, good Lieutenant! God's will, gentlemen!
   Help, ho!—Lieutenant—sir—Montano—sir—
   Help, masters!—Here's a goodly watch indeed! [*A bell rings*]
   Who's that that rings the bell?—Diablo,° ho!   140
   The town will rise. God's will, Lieutenant, hold—
   You will be shamed forever.

     Re-enter OTHELLO *and* ATTENDANTS.

OTH.   What is the matter here?
MON. 'Zounds, I bleed still, I am hurt to the death. [*Faints*]
OTH. Hold, for your lives!   145
IAGO. Hold, ho! Lieutenant—sir—Montano—gentlemen—
   Have you forgot all sense of place and duty?
   Hold! The General speaks to you. Hold, hold, for shame!
OTH. Why, how now, ho! From whence ariseth this?
   Are we turned Turks, and to ourselves do that   150
   Which Heaven hath forbid the Ottomites?
   For Christian shame, put by this barbarous brawl.
   He that stirs next to carve for his own rage°
   Holds his soul light, he dies upon his motion.°
   Silence that dreadful bell. It frights the isle   155
   From her propriety.° What is the matter, masters?
   Honest Iago, that look'st dead with grieving,
   Speak, who began this? On thy love, I charge thee.
IAGO. I do not know. Friends all but now, even now,
   In quarter and in terms like bride and groom   160
   Devesting° them for bed. And then, but now,
   As if some planet had unwitted men,°
   Swords out, and tilting° one at other's breast
   In opposition bloody. I cannot speak
   Any beginning to this peevish odds,°   165
   And would in action glorious I had lost
   Those legs that brought me to a part of it!
OTH. How comes it, Michael, you are thus forgot?°

---

133. **mazzard:** head, a slang word. **136. cry . . . mutiny:** cry that a mutiny has broken out; i.e., raise a riot. **140. Diablo:** the Devil. **153. carve . . . rage:** to satisfy his hunger for rage. **154. upon . . . motion:** at his first movement. **156. propriety:** natural behavior. **161. Devesting:** taking off their clothes. **162. planet . . . men:** as if some evil star had made men mad. **163. tilting:** thrusting. **165. peevish odds:** silly disagreement. **168. are . . . forgot:** have so forgotten yourself.

Cas. I pray you, pardon me, I cannot speak.
Oth. Worthy Montano, you were wont be civil.°   170
    The gravity and stillness° of your youth
    The world hath noted, and your name is great
    In mouths of wisest censure.° What's the matter
    That you unlace° your reputation thus,
    And spend your rich opinion° for the name   175
    Of a night brawler? Give me answer to it.
Mon. Worthy Othello, I am hurt to danger.
    Your officer, Iago, can inform you—
    While I spare speech, which something now offends me—
    Of all that I do know. Nor know I aught   180
    By me that's said or done amiss this night,
    Unless self-charity° be sometimes a vice,
    And to defend ourselves it be a sin
    When violence assails us.
Oth.   Now, by Heaven,
    My blood begins my safer guides to rule,   185
    And passion, having my best judgment collied,°
    Assays to lead the way. If I once stir,
    Or do but lift this arm, the best of you
    Shall sink in my rebuke. Give me to know
    How this foul rout° began, who set it on,   190
    And he that is approved° in this offense,
    Though he had twinned with me, both at a birth,
    Shall lose me. What! In a town of war,
    Yet wild, the people's hearts brimful of fear,
    To manage° private and domestic quarrel,   195
    In night, and on the court and guard of safety!
    'Tis monstrous. Iago, who began 't?
Mon. If partially affined, or leagued in office,
    Thou dost deliver° more or less than truth,
    Thou art no soldier.
Iago.   Touch me not so near.   200
    I had rather have this tongue cut from my mouth
    Than it should do offense to Michael Cassio.
    Yet I persuade myself to speak the truth
    Shall nothing wrong him. Thus it is, General.
    Montano and myself being in speech,   205
    There comes a fellow crying out for help,

---

170. **civil:** well-behaved. 171. **stillness:** staid behavior. 173. **censure:** judgment. 174. **unlace:** undo. 175. **spend . . . opinion:** lose your good reputation. 182. **self-charity:** love for oneself. 186. **collied:** darkened. 190. **rout:** riot, uproar. 191. **approved:** proved guilty. 195. **manage:** be concerned with. 198–99. **If . . . deliver:** if, because you are influenced by partiality or because he is your fellow officer, you report. **affined:** bound.

And Cassio following him with determined sword
To execute upon him. Sir, this gentleman
Steps in to Cassio and entreats his pause.°
Myself the crying fellow did pursue,   210
Lest by his clamor—as it so fell out—
The town might fall in fright. He, swift of foot,
Outran my purpose, and I returned the rather
For that I heard the clink and fall of swords,
And Cassio high in oath, which till tonight   215
I ne'er might say 'before. When I came back—
For this was brief—I found them close together,
At blow and thrust, even as again they were
When you yourself did part them.
More of this matter cannot I report.   220
But men are men, the best sometimes forget.
Though Cassio did some little wrong to him,
As men in rage strike those that wish them best,
Yet surely Cassio, I believe, received
From him that fled some strange indignity,   225
Which patience could not pass.
OTH.   I know, Iago,
Thy honesty and love doth mince this matter,
Making it light to Cassio. Cassio, I love thee,
But never more be officer of mine.
[Re-enter DESDEMONA, attended] Look, if my gentle love be not
raised up!   230
I'll make thee an example.
DES.   What's the matter?
OTH. All's well now, sweeting.° Come away to bed. [To MONTANO, who
is led off]
Sir, for your hurts, myself will be your surgeon.
Lead him off.
Iago, look with care about the town,   235
And silence those whom this vile brawl distracted.
Come, Desdemona. 'Tis the soldiers' life
To have their balmy slumbers waked with strife. [Exeunt all but IAGO
and CASSIO]
IAGO. What, are you hurt, Lieutenant?
CAS. Aye, past all surgery.   240
IAGO. Marry, Heaven forbid!
CAS. Reputation, reputation, reputation! Oh, I have lost my reputation! I
have lost the immortal part of myself, and what remains is bestial.

---

209. entreats . . . pause: begs him to stop. 232. sweeting: sweetheart.

My reputation, Iago, my reputation!

IAGO. As I am an honest man, I thought you had received some bodily 245
wound. There is more sense in that than in reputation. Reputation is
an idle and most false imposition,° oft got without merit and lost
without deserving. You have lost no reputation at all unless you
repute yourself such a loser. What, man! There are ways to recover
the General again. You are but now cast in his mood,° a punish- 250
ment more in policy° than in malice—even so as one would beat his
offenseless dog to affright an imperious lion.° Sue to him again and
he's yours.

CAS. I will rather sue to be despised than to deceive so good a com-
mander with so slight, so drunken, and so indiscreet an officer. 255
Drunk? And speak parrot?° And squabble? Swagger? Swear? And
discourse fustian° with one's own shadow? O thou invisible spirit of
wine, if thou hast no name to be known by, let us call thee devil!

IAGO. What was he that you followed with your sword? What had he
done to you? 260

CAS. I know not.

IAGO. Is 't possible?

CAS. I remember a mass of things, but nothing distinctly—a quarrel, but
nothing wherefore. Oh God, that men should put an enemy in their
mouths to steal away their brains! That we should, with joy, pleas- 265
ance,° revel, and applause, transform ourselves into beasts!

IAGO. Why, but you are now well enough. How came you thus
recovered?

CAS. It hath pleased the devil drunkenness to give place to the devil
wrath. One unperfectness shows me another, to make me frankly 270
despise myself.

IAGO. Come, you are too severe a moraler.° As the time, the place, and
the condition of this country stands, I could heartily wish this had
not befallen. But since it is as it is, mend it for your own good.

CAS. I will ask him for my place again, he shall tell me I am a drunkard! 275
Had I as many mouths as Hydra,° such an answer would stop them
all. To be now a sensible man, by and by a fool, and presently a
beast! Oh, strange! Every inordinate° cup is unblest, and the
ingredient is a devil.

IAGO. Come, come, good wine is a good familiar creature, if it be well 280
used. Exclaim no more against it. And, good Lieutenant, I think you
think I love you.

---

247. **imposition:** a quality laid on a man by others. 250. **cast . . . mood:** dismissed because he is in a bad mood. 251. **in
policy:** i.e., because he must appear to be angry before the Cypriots. 251–52. **even . . . lion:** a proverb meaning that when
the lion sees the dog beaten, he will know what is coming to him. 256. **speak parrot:** babble. 257. **fustian:** nonsense; lit.,
cheap cloth. 266. **pleasance:** a gay time. 272. **moraler:** moralizer. 276. **Hydra:** a hundred-headed beast slain by Hercules.
278. **inordinate:** excessive.

CAS. I have well approved it, sir. I drunk!

IAGO. You or any man living may be drunk at some time, man. I'll tell
    you what you shall do. Our General's wife is now the General. I may   285
    say so in this respect, for that he hath devoted and given up himself
    to the contemplation, mark, and denotement° of her parts and
    graces. Confess yourself freely to her, importune her help to put you
    in your place again. She is of so free, so kind, so apt,° so blessed a
    disposition, she holds it a vice in her goodness not to do more than   290
    she is requested. This broken joint between you and her husband
    entreat her to splinter° and, my fortunes against any lay° worth
    naming, this crack of your love shall grow stronger than it was
    before.

CAS. You advise me well.

IAGO. I protest, in the sincerity of love and honest kindness.   295

CAS. I think it freely, and betimes in the morning I will beseech the
    virtuous Desdemona to undertake for me. I am desperate of my
    fortunes if they check me here.°

IAGO. You are in the right. Good night, Lieutenant, I must to the watch.

CAS. Good night, honest Iago. [*Exit*]   300

IAGO. And what's he then that says I play the villain?
    When this advice is free I give and honest,
    Probal° to thinking, and indeed the course
    To win the Moor again? For 'tis most easy
    The inclining Desdemona to subdue   305
    In any honest suit. She's framed° as fruitful
    As the free elements.° And then for her
    To win the Moor, were 't to renounce his baptism,
    All seals and symbols of redeemed sin,
    His soul is so enfettered to her love   310
    That she may make, unmake, do what she list,
    Even as her appetite shall play the god
    With his weak function.° How am I then a villain
    To counsel Cassio to this parallel course,
    Directly to his good? Divinity of Hell!   315
    When devils will the blackest sins put on,
    They do suggest° at first with heavenly shows,
    As I do now. For whiles this honest fool
    Plies° Desdemona to repair his fortunes,
    And she for him pleads strongly to the Moor,   320
    I'll pour this pestilence into his ear,

---

287. **denotement:** careful observation. 289. **apt:** ready. 292. **splinter:** put in splints. **lay:** bet. 297–98. **I . . . here:** I despair
of my future if my career is stopped short here. 303. **Probal:** probable. 306. **framed:** made. 307. **free elements:** i.e., the air.
313. **function:** intelligence. 317. **suggest:** seduce. 319. **Plies:** vigorously urges.

That she repeals° him for her body's lust.
And by how much she strives to do him good,
She shall undo her credit with the Moor.
So will I turn her virtue into pitch,   325
And out of her own goodness make the net
That shall enmesh them all.
[*Enter* RODERIGO] How now, Roderigo!
ROD. I do follow here in the chase, not like a hound that hunts but
one that fills up the cry. My money is almost spent, I have been   330
tonight exceedingly well cudgeled, and I think the issue will be I
shall have so much experience for my pains and so, with no
money at all and a little more wit, return again to Venice.
IAGO. How poor are they that have not patience!
What wound did ever heal but by degrees?   335
Thou know'st we work by wit and not by witchcraft,
And wit depends on dilatory Time.°
Does 't not go well? Cassio hath beaten thee,
And thou by that small hurt hast cashiered Cassio.
Though other things grow fair against the sun,   340
Yet fruits that blossom first will first be ripe.°
Content thyself awhile. By the mass, 'tis morning.
Pleasure and action make the hours seem short.
Retire thee, go where thou art billeted.
Away, I say. Thou shalt know more hereafter.   345
Nay, get thee gone. [*Exit* RODERIGO] Two things are to be done:
My wife must move for° Cassio to her mistress,
I'll set her on,
Myself the while to draw the Moor apart
And bring him jump° when he may Cassio find   350
Soliciting his wife. Aye, that's the way.
Dull not device° by coldness and delay. [*Exit*]

ACT III

SCENE I. *Before the castle.*

Enter CASSIO *and some* MUSICIANS.

---

322. repeals: calls back. 337. And . . . Time: and cleverness must wait for Time, who is in no hurry. 340–41.
Though . . . ripe: though the fruit ripens in the sun, yet the first fruit to ripen will come from the earliest blossoms; i.e.,
our first plan—to get Cassio cashiered—has succeeded, the rest will soon follow. 347. move for: petition for. 350. jump: at
the moment, just. 352. Dull . . . device: do not spoil the plan.

Cas. Masters, play here, I will content your pains°—
    Something that's brief, and bid "Good morrow, General."° [*Music*]

    Enter CLOWN.

CLO. Why, masters, have your instruments been in Naples,° that they
    speak i' the nose thus?
1. MUS. How, sir, how?   5
CLO. Are these, I pray you, wind instruments?
1. MUS. Aye, marry are they, sir.
CLO. Oh, thereby hangs a tail.
1. MUS. Whereby hangs a tale, sir?
CLO. Marry, sir, by many a wind instrument that I know. But, masters,   10
    here's money for you. And the General so likes your music that he
    desires you, for love's sake, to make no more noise with it.
1. MUS. Well, sir, we will not.
CLO. If you have any music that may not be heard, to 't again. But, as
    they say, to hear music the General does not greatly care.
1. MUS. We have none such, sir.
CLO. Then put up your pipes in your bag, for I'll away. Go, vanish into
    air, away! [*Exeunt* MUSICIANS]
CAS. Dost thou hear, my honest friend?
CLO. No, I hear not your honest friend, I hear you.
CAS. Prithee keep up thy quillets.° There's a poor piece of gold for thee. If
    the gentlewoman that attends the General's wife be stirring, tell her
    there's one Cassio entreats her a little favor of speech. Wilt thou do
    this?
CLO. She is stirring, sir. If she will stir hither, I shall seem to notify unto
    her.
CAS. Do, good my friend. [*Exit* CLOWN]
    [*Enter* IAGO] In happy time,° Iago.
IAGO. You have not been abed, then?
CAS. Why, no, the day had broke   30
    Before we parted. I have made bold, Iago,
    To send in to your wife. My suit to her
    Is that she will to virtuous Desdemona
    Procure me some access.
IAGO.   I'll send her to you presently,
    And I'll devise a mean to draw the Moor   35
    Out of the way, that your converse and business
    May be more free.

Act III, Sc. i: **1. content . . . pains:** reward your labor. **2. bid . . . General:** It was a common custom to play or sing a song beneath the bedroom window of a distinguished guest or of a newly wedded couple on the morning after their wedding night. **4. in Naples:** a reference to the Neapolitan (i.e., venereal) disease. **21. keep . . . quillets:** put away your wisecracks. **28. In . . . time:** i.e., I am glad to see you.

Cas. I humbly thank you for 't. [*Exit* Iago] I never knew
    A Florentine more kind° and honest.

    Enter Emilia.

Emil. Good morrow, good Lieutenant. I am sorry   40
    For your displeasure,° but all will sure be well.
    The General and his wife are talking of it,
    And she speaks for you stoutly. The Moor replies
    That he you hurt is of great fame in Cyprus
    And great affinity,° and that in wholesome wisdom   45
    He might not but° refuse you. But he protests he loves you,
    And needs no other suitor but his likings°
    To take the safest occasion by the front
    To bring you in° again.
Cas.   Yet I beseech you,
    If you think fit, or that it may be done,   50
    Give me advantage of some brief discourse
    With Desdemona alone.
Emil.   Pray you, come in.
    I will bestow you where you shall have time.
    To speak your bosom freely.°
Cas. I am much bound to you. [*Exeunt*]   55

SCENE II. *A room in the castle.*

    Enter Othello, Iago, *and* Gentlemen.

Oth. These letters give, Iago, to the pilot,
    And by him do my duties° to the Senate.
    That done, I will be walking on the works.°
    Repair there to me.
Iago.   Well, my good lord, I'll do 't.
Oth. This fortification, gentlemen, shall we see 't?   5
Gent. We'll wait upon your lordship. [*Exeunt*]

SCENE III. *The garden of the castle.*

    Enter Desdemona, Cassio, *and* Emilia.

---

39. Florentine . . . kind: Iago is a Venetian. Cassio means: even one of my own people could not have been kinder. **41. your displeasure:** i.e., that Othello is displeased with you. **45. affinity:** kindred. **46. might . . . but:** i.e., he must. **47. likings:** affections. **48–49. safest . . . in:** to take the first opportunity to restore you to your position. **front:** forehead; i.e., to take Time by the forelock. **54. speak . . . freely:** declare what is on your mind.
    Sc. ii: 2. do . . . duties: express my loyalty. **3. works:** fortifications.

DES. Be thou assured, good Cassio, I will do
    All my abilities in thy behalf.
EMIL. Good madam, do. I warrant it grieves my husband
    As if the case were his.
DES. Oh, that's an honest fellow. Do not doubt, Cassio,   5
    But I will have my lord and you again
    As friendly as you were.
CAS.   Bounteous madam,
    Whatever shall become of Michael Cassio,
    He's never anything but your true servant.
DES. I know 't. I thank you. You do love my lord.   10
    You have known him long, and be you well assured
    He shall in strangeness stand no farther off
    Than in a politic distance.°
CAS.   Aye, but, lady,
    That policy may either last so long,
    Or feed upon such nice and waterish diet,°   15
    Or breed itself so out of circumstance,°
    That, I being absent and my place supplied,°
    My General will forget my love and service.
DES. Do not doubt° that. Before Emilia here
    I give thee warrant of thy place.° Assure thee,   20
    If I do vow a friendship, I'll perform it
    To the last article. My lord shall never rest.
    I'll watch him tame° and talk him out of patience,
    His bed shall seem a school, his board a shrift.°
    I'll intermingle every thing he does   25
    With Cassio's suit. Therefore be merry, Cassio,
    For thy solicitor shall rather die
    Than give thy cause away.

    Enter OTHELLO *and* IAGO, *at a distance.*

EMIL. Madam, here comes my lord.
CAS. Madam, I'll take my leave.   30
DES. Nay, stay and hear me speak.
CAS. Madam, not now. I am very ill at ease,
    Unfit for mine own purposes.°
DES. Well, do your discretion. [*Exit* CASSIO]
IAGO. Ha! I like not that.

Sc. iii: **12–13. He . . . distance:** i.e., his apparent coldness to you shall only be so much as his official position demands for reasons of policy. **15. nice . . . diet:** have such weak encouragement. **16. breed . . . circumstance:** become so used to the situation. **17. supplied:** filled by another. **19. doubt:** fear. **20. give . . . place:** guarantee that you will be restored to your position. **23. watch . . . tame:** as wild hawks are made tame by keeping them from sleep. **24. shrift:** place of confession and absolution. **33. Unfit . . . purposes:** in no condition to plead my own cause.

OTH. What dost thou say?   35

IAGO. Nothing, my lord. Or if—I know not what.

OTH. Was not that Cassio parted from my wife?

IAGO. Cassio, my lord! No, sure, I cannot think it,

    That he would steal away so guilty-like,

    Seeing you coming.

OTH.   I do believe 'twas he.   40

DES. How now, my lord!

    I have been talking with a suitor here,

    A man that languishes in your displeasure.

OTH. Who is 't you mean?

DES. Why, your Lieutenant, Cassio. Good my lord,   45

    If I have any grace or power to move you,

    His present reconciliation take.°

    For if he be not one that truly loves you,

    That errs in ignorance and not in cunning,°

    I have no judgment in an honest face.   50

    I prithee call him back.

OTH.   Went he hence now?

DES. Aye, sooth, so humbled

    That he hath left part of his grief with me,

    To suffer with him. Good love, call him back.

OTH. Not now, sweet Desdemona, some other time.   55

DES. But shall 't be shortly?

OTH.   The sooner, sweet, for you.

DES. Shall 't be tonight at supper?

OTH.   No, not tonight.

DES. Tomorrow dinner then?

OTH.   I shall not dine at home.

    I meet the captains at the citadel.

DES. Why, then tomorrow night or Tuesday morn,   60

    On Tuesday noon, or night, on Wednesday morn.

    I prithee name the time, but let it not

    Exceed three days. In faith, he's penitent,

    And yet his trespass, in our common reason°—

    Save that, they say, the wars must make examples   65

    Out of their best—is not almost° a fault

    To incur a private check.° When shall he come?

    Tell me, Othello. I wonder in my soul

    What you would ask me that I should deny,

    Or stand so mammering° on. What! Michael Cassio,   70

---

47. His . . . take: accept his immediate apology and forgive him. 49. in cunning: knowingly. 64. common reason: common sense. 66. not almost: hardly. 67. check: rebuke. 70. mammering: hesitating.

That came a-wooing with you, and so many a time
When I have spoke of you dispraisingly
Hath ta'en your part—to have so much to do
To bring him in! Trust me, I could do much——
OTH. Prithee, no more. Let him come when he will.   75
I will deny thee nothing.
DES.   Why, this is not a boon.°
'Tis as I should entreat you wear your gloves,
Or feed on nourishing dishes, or keep you warm,
Or sue to you to do a peculiar° profit
To your own person. Nay, when I have a suit   80
Wherein I mean to touch your love indeed,
It shall be full of poise° and difficult weight,°
And fearful to be granted.°
OTH.   I will deny thee nothing.
Whereon I do beseech thee grant me this,
To leave me but a little to myself.   85
DES. Shall I deny you? No. Farewell, my lord.
OTH. Farewell, my Desdemona. I'll come to thee straight.
DES. Emilia, come. Be as your fancies teach you.°
Whate'er you be, I am obedient. [*Exeunt* DESDEMONA *and* EMILIA]
OTH. Excellent wretch! Perdition catch my soul   90
But I do love thee! And when I love thee not,
Chaos° is come again.
IAGO. My noble lord——
OTH.   What dost thou say, Iago?
IAGO. Did Michael Cassio, when you wooed my lady,
Know of your love?   95
OTH. He did, from first to last. Why dost thou ask?
IAGO. But for a satisfaction of my thought,
No further harm.
OTH.   Why of thy thought, Iago?
IAGO. I did not think he had been acquainted with her.
OTH. Oh yes, and went between us very oft.   100
IAGO. Indeed!
OTH. Indeed! Aye, indeed. Discern'st thou aught in that?
Is he not honest?
IAGO. Honest, my lord!
OTH. Honest! Aye, honest.
IAGO. My lord, for aught I know.
OTH. What dost thou think?

---

76. **boon:** great favor. **79. peculiar:** particular. **82. poise:** weight in the scales. **difficult weight:** hard to estimate. **83. fearful . . . granted:** only granted with a sense of fear. **88. Be . . . you:** please yourself. **92. Chaos:** the utter confusion that existed before order was established in the universe.

IAGO. Think, my lord!   105
OTH. Think, my lord! By Heaven, he echoes me
      As if there were some monster in his thought
      Too hideous to be shown. Thou dost mean something.
      I heard thee say even now thou likedst not that
      When Cassio left my wife. What didst not like?   110
      And when I told thee he was of my counsel
      In my whole course of wooing, thou criedst "Indeed!"
      And didst contract and purse thy brow together
      As if thou then hadst shut up in thy brain
      Some horrible conceit.° If thou dost love me,   115
      Show me thy thought.
IAGO. My lord, you know I love you.
OTH.   I think thou dost,
      And for° I know thou'rt full of love and honesty
      And weigh'st thy words before thou givest them breath,
      Therefore these stops of thine fright me the more.   120
      For such things in a false disloyal knave
      Are tricks of custom, but in a man that's just
      They're close delations,° working from the heart,
      That passion cannot rule.
IAGO.   For Michael Cassio,
      I dare be sworn I think that he is honest.   125
OTH. I think so too.
IAGO. Men should be what they seem,
      Or those that be not, would they might seem none!°
OTH. Certain, men should be what they seem.
IAGO. Why, then I think Cassio's an honest man.
OTH. Nay, yet there's more in this.   130
      I prithee speak to me as to thy thinkings,
      As thou dost ruminate, and give thy worst of thoughts
      The worst of words.
IAGO.   Good my lord, pardon me.
      Though I am bound to every act of duty,
      I am not bound to that all slaves are free to.   135
      Utter my thoughts? Why, say they are vile and false,
      As where's that palace whereinto foul things
      Sometimes intrude not? Who has a breast so pure
      But some uncleanly apprehensions
      Keep leets and law days, and in session sit   140
      With meditations lawful?°

---

115. **conceit:** conception, notion. 118. **for:** since. 123. **close delations:** concealed accusations. 127. **seem none:** i.e., not
seem to be honest men. 138–41. **Who . . . lawful:** whose heart is so pure but that some foul suggestion will sit on the
bench alongside lawful thoughts; i.e., foul thoughts will rise even on the most respectable occasions. **leet:** court held by
the lord of the manor. **law days:** days when courts sit. **session:** sitting of the court.

OTH. Thou dost conspire against thy friend, Iago,
    If thou but think'st him wronged and makest his ear
    A stranger to thy thoughts.
IAGO.   I do beseech you—
    Though I perchance am vicious in my guess,   145
    As, I confess, it is my nature's plague
    To spy into abuses, and oft my jealousy°
    Shapes faults that are not—that your wisdom yet,
    From one that so imperfectly conceits,°
    Would take no notice, nor build yourself a trouble   150
    Out of his scattering° and unsure observance.°
    It were not for your quiet nor your good,
    Nor for my manhood, honesty, or wisdom,
    To let you know my thoughts.
OTH.   What dost thou mean?
IAGO. Good name in man and woman, dear my lord,   155
    Is the immediate° jewel of their souls.
    Who steals my purse steals trash—'tis something, nothing,
    'Twas mine, 'tis his, and has been slave to thousands—
    But he that filches from me my good name
    Robs me of that which not enriches him   160
    And makes me poor indeed.
OTH. By Heaven, I'll know thy thoughts.
IAGO. You cannot if my heart were in your hand,
    Nor shall not whilst 'tis in my custody.
OTH. Ha!
IAGO.   Oh, beware, my lord, of jealousy.   165
    It is the green-eyed monster which doth mock°
    The meat° it feeds on. That cuckold lives in bliss
    Who, certain of his fate, loves not his wronger.°
    But, oh, what damnèd minutes tells he o'er
    Who dotes, yet doubts, suspects, yet strongly loves!   170
OTH. Oh, misery!
IAGO. Poor and content is rich, and rich enough,
    But riches fineless° is as poor as winter
    To him that ever fears he shall be poor.
    Good Heaven, the souls of all my tribe defend   175
    From jealousy!
OTH.   Why, why is this?
    Think'st thou I'd make a life of jealousy,

---

147. jealousy: suspicion. **149. conceits:** conceives, imagines. **151. scattering:** scattered, casual. **observance:** observation. **156. immediate:** most valuable. **166. doth mock:** makes a mockery of. **167. meat:** i.e., victim. **167–68. That . . . wronger:** i.e., the cuckold who hates his wife and knows her falseness is not tormented by suspicious jealousy. **173. fineless:** limitless.

To follow still the changes of the moon
With fresh suspicions? No, to be once in doubt
Is once to be resolved.° Exchange me for a goat   180
When I shall turn the business of my soul
To such exsufflicate and blown surmises,
Matching thy inference.° 'Tis not to make me jealous
To say my wife is fair, feeds well, loves company,
Is free of speech, sings, plays, and dances well.   185
Where virtue is, these are more virtuous.
Nor from mine own weak merits will I draw
The smallest fear or doubt of her revolt,°
For she had eyes, and chose me. No, Iago,
I'll see before I doubt, when I doubt, prove,   190
And on the proof, there is no more but this—
Away at once with love or jealousy!

IAGO. I am glad of it, for now I shall have reason
To show the love and duty that I bear you
With franker spirit. Therefore, as I am bound,   195
Receive it from me. I speak not yet of proof.
Look to your wife. Observe her well with Cassio.
Wear your eye thus, not jealous nor secure.°
I would not have your free and noble nature
Out of self-bounty° be abused, look to 't.   200
I know our country disposition well.
In Venice° they do let Heaven see the pranks
They dare not show their husbands. Their best conscience
Is not to leave 't undone, but keep 't unknown.

OTH. Dost thou say so?   205

IAGO. She did deceive her father,° marrying you,
And when she seemed to shake and fear your looks,
She loved them most.

OTH.   And so she did.

IAGO.   Why, go to, then.
She that so young could give out such a seeming
To seel° her father's eyes up close as oak——   210
He thought 'twas witchcraft—but I am much to blame.
I humbly do beseech you of your pardon
For too much loving you.

OTH.   I am bound to thee forever.

179–80. to . . . resolved: whenever I find myself in doubt I at once seek out the truth. 181–83. When . . . inference: when I shall allow that which concerns me most dearly to be influenced by such trifling suggestions as yours. exsufflicate: blown up, like a bubble. 188. revolt: faithlessness. 198. secure: overconfident. 200. self-bounty: natural goodness. 202. In Venice: Venice was notorious for its loose women; the Venetian courtesans were among the sights of Europe and were much commented upon by travelers. 206. She . . . father: Iago deliberately echoes Brabantio's parting words. See I.iii.293–94. 210. seel: blind. See I.iii.270,n.

IAGO. I see this hath a little dashed your spirits.

OTH. Not a jot, not a jot.

IAGO.   I' faith, I fear it has.   215
    I hope you will consider what is spoke
    Comes from my love, but I do see you're moved.
    I am to pray you not to strain my speech
    To grosser issues° nor to larger reach°
    Than to suspicion.   220

OTH. I will not.

IAGO.   Should you do so, my lord,
    My speech should fall into such vile success°
    As my thoughts aim not at. Cassio's my worthy friend.—
    My lord, I see you're moved.

OTH.   No, not much moved.
    I do not think but Desdemona's honest.°   225

IAGO. Long live she so! And long live you to think so!

OTH. And yet, how nature erring from itself——

IAGO. Aye, there's the point. As—to be bold with you—
    Not to affect° many proposed matches°
    Of her own clime, complexion, and degree,   230
    Whereto we see in all things nature tends°——
    Foh! One may smell in such a will most rank,°
    Foul disproportion, thoughts unnatural.
    But pardon me. I do not in position
    Distinctly speak of her, though I may fear   235
    Her will, recoiling to her better judgment,
    May fall to match° you with her country forms,°
    And happily° repent.

OTH.   Farewell, farewell.
    If more thou dost perceive, let me know more.
    Set on thy wife to observe. Leave me, Iago.   240

IAGO [Going] My lord, I take my leave.

OTH. Why did I marry? This honest creature doubtless
    Sees and knows more, much more, than he unfolds.

IAGO [Returning] My lord, I would I might entreat your honor
    To scan this thing no further. Leave it to time.   245
    Though it be fit that Cassio have his place,
    For sure he fills it up with great ability,
    Yet if you please to hold him off awhile,

---

219. grosser issues: worse conclusions. larger reach: i.e., more widely. 222. success: result. 225. honest: When applied to Desdemona, "honest" means "chaste," but applied to Iago it has the modern meaning of "open and sincere." 229. affect: be inclined to. proposed matches: offers of marriage. 231. in . . . tends: i.e., a woman naturally marries a man of her own country, color, and rank. 232. will . . . rank: desire most lustful. 237. match: compare. country forms: the appearance of her countrymen, i.e., white men. 238. happily: haply, by chance.

You shall by that perceive him and his means.
Note if your lady strain his entertainment°   250
With any strong or vehement importunity—
Much will be seen in that. In the meantime,
Let me be thought too busy in my fears—
As worthy cause I have to fear I am—
And hold her free, I do beseech your Honor.   255

IAGO. Fear not my government.°

IAGO. I once more take my leave.[*Exit*]

OTH. This fellow's of exceeding honesty,
And knows all qualities,° with a learned spirit,
Of human dealings.° If I do prove her haggard,   260
Though that her jesses were my dear heartstrings,
I'd whistle her off and let her down the wind
To prey at fortune.° Haply, for I am black
And have not those soft parts of conversation
That chamberers° have, or for I am declined   265
Into the vale of years—yet that's not much—
She's gone, I am abused, and my relief
Must be to loathe her. Oh, curse of marriage,
That we can call these delicate creatures ours,
And not their appetites! I had rather be a toad   270
And live upon the vapor of a dungeon
Than keep a corner in the thing I love
For others' uses. Yet, 'tis the plague of great ones,
Prerogatived° are they less than the base.
'Tis destiny unshunnable, like death.   275
Even then this forkèd plague° is fated to us
When we do quicken.° Desdemona comes.
[*Re-enter* DESDEMONA *and* EMILIA] If she be false, oh, then Heaven
mocks itself!
I'll not believe 't.

DES.   How now, my dear Othello!
Your dinner, and the generous° islanders   280
By you invited, do attend your presence.

OTH. I am to blame.

DES.   Why do you speak so faintly?
Are you not well?

OTH. I have a pain upon my forehead here.

---

250. strain . . . entertainment: urge you to receive him. **256. government:** self-control. **259. qualities:** different kinds. **259–60. with . . . dealings:** with wide experience of human nature. **260–63. If . . . fortune:** Othello keeps up the imagery of falconry throughout. He means: If I find that she is wild, I'll whistle her off the game and let her go where she will, for she's not worth keeping. **haggard:** a wild hawk. **jesses:** the straps attached to a hawk's legs. **265. chamberers:** playboys. **274. Prerogatived:** privileged. **276. forked plague:** i.e., to be a cuckold. **277. quicken:** stir in our mother's womb. **280. generous:** noble. of gentle blood.

DES. Faith, that's with watching,° 'twill away again.   285
    Let me but bind it hard, within this hour
    It will be well.
OTH. Your napkin° is too little, [*He puts the handkerchief from him, and*
    she drops it]
    Let it alone. Come, I'll go in with you.
DES. I am very sorry that you are not well. [*Exeunt* OTHELLO *and*
    DESDEMONA]
EMIL. I am glad I have found this napkin.   290
    This was her first remembrance from the Moor.
    My wayward° husband hath a hundred times
    Wooed me to steal it, but she so loves the token,
    For he conjured° her she should ever keep it,
    That she reserves it evermore about her   295
    To kiss and talk to. I'll have the work ta'en out,°
    And give 't Iago. What he will do with it
    Heaven knows, not I.
    I nothing but to please his fantasy.°

      Re-enter IAGO.

IAGO. How now! What do you here alone?   300
EMIL. Do not you chide, I have a thing for you.
IAGO. A thing for me? It is a common thing——
EMIL. Ha!
IAGO. To have a foolish wife.
EMIL. Oh, is that all? What will you give me now   305
    For that same handkerchief?
IAGO.   What handkerchief?
EMIL. What handkerchief!
    Why, that the Moor first gave to Desdemona,
    That which so often you did bid me steal.
IAGO. Hast stol'n it from her?   310
EMIL. No, faith, she let it drop by negligence,
    And, to the advantage,° I being here took 't up.
    Look, here it is.
IAGO.   A good wench. Give it me.
EMIL. What will you do with 't, that you have been so earnest
    To have me filch it?
IAGO. [*Snatching it*] Why, what's that to you?   315
EMIL. If 't be not for some purpose of import,

---

285. **watching:** lack of sleep. 287. **napkin:** handkerchief. 292. **wayward:** unaccountable. 294. **conjured:** begged with an oath. 296. **work . . . out:** pattern copied. 299. **fantasy:** whim. 312. **to . . . advantage:** thereby giving me the opportunity.

Give 't me again. Poor lady, she'll run mad
When she shall lack it.
Iago. Be not acknown on 't,° I have use for it.
    Go, leave me. [*Exit* Emilia].   320
    I will in Cassio's lodging lose this napkin,
    And let him find it. Trifles light as air
    Are to the jealous confirmations strong
    As proofs of Holy Writ. This may do something.
    The Moor already changes with my poison.   325
    Dangerous conceits are in their natures poisons,
    Which at the first are scarce found to distaste,°
    But with a little° act upon the blood
    Burn like the mines of sulphur. I did say so.°
    Look where he comes!
    [*Re-enter* Othello] Not poppy,° nor mandragora,°   330
    Nor all the drowsy syrups of the world,
    Shall ever medicine thee to that sweet sleep
    Which thou owedst° yesterday.
Oth.   Ha! Ha! False to me?
Iago. Why, how now, General! No more of that.
Oth. Avaunt!° Be gone! Thou hast set me on the rack.°   335
    I swear 'tis better to be much abused
    Than but to know 't a little.
Iago.   How now, my lord!
Oth. What sense had I of her stol'n hours of lust?
    I saw 't not, thought it not, it harmed not me.
    I slept the next night well, was free and merry.   340
    I found not Cassio's kisses on her lips.
    He that is robbed, not wanting° what is stol'n,
    Let him not know 't and he's not robbed at all.
Iago. I am sorry to hear this.
Oth. I had been happy if the general camp,   345
    Pioners° and all, had tasted her sweet body,
    So I had nothing known. Oh, now forever
    Farewell the tranquil mind! Farewell content!
    Farewell the plumed° troop and the big wars
    That make ambition virtue! Oh, farewell,   350
    Farewell the neighing steed and the shrill trump,
    The spirit-stirring drum, the ear-piercing fife,

---

319. **Be . . . on't:** know nothing about it. **327. distaste:** taste unpleasantly. **328. with a little:** in a little while. **329. I . . . so:** As Iago says this, Othello is seen approaching, with all the signs of his agitation outwardly visible. **330. poppy:** opium. **mandragora:** called also mandrake, a root used as a drug to bring sleep. **333. owedst:** owned, possessed. **335. Avaunt:** be off! **on . . . rack:** i.e., in torment. **342. wanting:** missing. **346. Pioners:** pioneers, the lowest type of soldier. **349. plumed:** wearing plumes in the helmet.

The royal banner and all quality,°
Pride, pomp, and circumstance of glorious war!
And, O you mortal engines,° whose rude throats   355
The immortal Jove's dread clamors counterfeit,°
Farewell! Othello's occupation's gone!
IAGO. Is 't possible, my lord?
OTH. Villain, be sure thou prove my love a whore,
Be sure of it, give me the ocular proof.   360
Or by the worth of man's eternal soul,
Thou hadst been better have been born a dog
Than answer my waked wrath!
IAGO.   Is 't come to this?
OTH. Make me to see 't, or at the least so prove it
That the probation° bear no hinge nor loop   365
To hang a doubt on, or woe upon thy life!
IAGO. My noble lord——
OTH. If thou dost slander her and torture me,
Never pray more, abandon all remorse.°
On horror's head horrors accumulate,   370
Do deeds to make Heaven weep, all earth amazed,
For nothing canst thou to damnation add
Greater than that.
IAGO.   Oh, grace! Oh, Heaven defend me!
Are you a man? Have you a soul or sense?
God be wi' you, take mine office. O wretched fool,   375
That livest to make thine honesty a vice!
O monstrous world! Take note, take note, O world,
To be direct and honest is not safe.
I thank you for this profit,° and from hence
I'll love no friend, sith° love breeds such offense.   380
OTH. Nay, stay. Thou shouldst be honest.
IAGO. I should be wise, for honesty's a fool,
And loses that it works for.
OTH.   By the world,
I think my wife be honest, and think she is not.
I think that thou art just, and think thou art not.   385
I'll have some proof. Her name, that was as fresh
As Dian's° visage, is now begrimed and black
As mine own face. If there be cords, or knives,
Poison, or fire, or suffocating streams,
I'll not endure it. Would I were satisfied!   390

---

353. **quality:** military rank. 355. **mortal engines:** deadly cannon. 356. **counterfeit:** imitate.   365. **probation:** proof. 369.
remorse: pity. 379. **profit:** profitable lesson. 380. **sith:** since. 387. **Dian:** Diana, goddess of chastity.

IAGO. I see, sir, you are eaten up with passion.
    I do repent me that I put it to you.
    You would be satisfied?
OTH.   Would! Nay, I will.
IAGO. And may, but, how? How satisfied, my lord?
    Would you, the supervisor,° grossly gape on?   395
    Behold her topped?
OTH.   Death and damnation! Oh!
IAGO. It were a tedious difficulty, I think,
    To bring them to that prospect.° Damn them then,
    If ever mortal eyes do see them bolster°
    More than their own! What then? How then?   400
    What shall I say? Where's satisfaction?
    It is impossible you should see this,
    Were they as prime° as goats, as hot as monkeys,
    As salt° as wolves in pride,° and fools as gross
    As ignorance made drunk. But yet I say   405
    If imputation° and strong circumstances,
    Which lead directly to the door of truth,
    Will give you satisfaction, you may have 't.
OTH. Give me a living° reason she's disloyal.
IAGO. I do not like the office.   410
    But sith I am entered in this cause so far,
    Pricked° to 't by foolish honesty and love,
    I will go on. I lay with Cassio lately,
    And being troubled with a raging tooth,
    I could not sleep.   415
    There are a kind of men so loose of soul
    That in their sleeps will mutter their affairs.
    One of this kind is Cassio.
    In sleep I heard him say "Sweet Desdemona,
    Let us be wary, let us hide our loves."   420
    And then, sir, would he gripe° and wring my hand,
    Cry, "O sweet creature!" and then kiss me hard,
    As if he plucked up kisses by the roots
    That grew upon my lips. Then laid his leg
    Over my thigh, and sighed and kissed, and then   425
    Cried "Cursed fate that gave thee to the Moor!"
OTH. Oh, monstrous! Monstrous!
IAGO.   Nay, this was but his dream.

---

395. **supervisor:** looker-on. 398. **prospect:** sight. 399. **bolster:** sleep together. 403. **prime:** lustful. 404. **salt:** eager. **in pride:** in heat. 406. **imputation:** probability. 409. **living:** tangible. 412. **Pricked:** spurred on. 421. **gripe:** grip.

OTH. But this denoted a foregone conclusion.
    'Tis a shrewd doubt,° though it be but a dream.
IAGO. And this may help to thicken other proofs   430
    That do demonstrate thinly.
OTH.   I'll tear her all to pieces.
IAGO. Nay, but be wise. Yet we see nothing done.
    She may be honest yet. Tell me but this:
    Have you not sometimes seen a handkerchief
    Spotted with strawberries° in your wife's hand?   435
OTH. I gave her such a one, 'twas my first gift.
IAGO. I know not that. But such a handkerchief—
    I am sure it was your wife's—did I today
    See Cassio wipe his beard with.
OTH.   If it be that——
IAGO. If it be that, or any that was hers,   440
    It speaks against her with the other proofs.
OTH. Oh, that the slave had forty thousand lives!
    One is too poor, too weak, for my revenge.
    Now do I see 'tis true. Look here, Iago,
    All my fond love thus do I blow to Heaven—   445
    'Tis gone.
    Arise, black Vengeance, from thy hollow cell!
    Yield up, O Love, thy crown and hearted° throne
    To tyrannous hate! Swell, bosom, with thy fraught,°
    For 'tis of aspics'° tongues!
IAGO.   Yet be content.   450
OTH. Oh, blood, blood, blood!
IAGO. Patience, I say. Your mind perhaps may change.
OTH. Never, Iago. Like to the Pontic Sea,
    Whose icy current and compulsive course
    Ne'er feels retiring ebb but keeps due on   455
    To the Propontic and the Hellespont;°
    Even so my bloody thoughts, with violent pace,
    Shall ne'er look back, ne'er ebb to humble love,
    Till that capable° and wide revenge
    Swallow them up. Now, by yond marble Heaven,   460
    In the due reverence of a sacred vow [Kneels]
    I here engage° my words.
IAGO.   Do not rise yet. [Kneels]

---

429. shrewd doubt: bitter suspicion. 435. with strawberries: with a pattern of strawberries. 448. hearted: in my heart. 449. fraught: freight, load. 450. aspic: asp, a small poisonous snake. 453–56. Like . . . Hellespont: In Pliny's *Natural History*, translated by Philemon Holland in 1601, it was noted that "the sea Pontus (Black Sea) evermore floweth and runneth out into Propontis (Sea of Marmora) but the sea never returneth back again within Pontus." Hellespont: the Dardanelles. 459. capable: comprehensive, complete. 462. engage: pledge.

Witness, you ever burning lights above,
You elements that clip° us round about,
Witness that here Iago doth give up 465
The execution of his wit, hands, heart,
To wronged Othello's service! Let him command,
And to obey shall be in me remorse,°
What bloody business ever. [*They rise*]

OTH.   I greet thy love,
Not with vain thanks, but with acceptance bounteous, 470
And will upon the instant put thee to 't.°
Within these three days let me hear thee say
That Cassio's not alive.

IAGO. My friend is dead. 'Tis done at your request.
But let her live.

OTH. Damn her, lewd minx! Oh, damn her! 475
Come, go with me apart. I will withdraw,
To furnish me with some swift means of death
For the fair devil. Now art thou my Lieutenant.

IAGO. I am your own forever. [*Exeunt*]

SCENE IV. *Before the castle.*

Enter DESDEMONA, EMILIA, *and* CLOWN.

DES. Do you know, sirrah, where Lieutenant Cassio lies?

CLO. I dare not say he lies anywhere.

DES. Why, man?

CLO. He's a soldier, and for one to say a soldier lies is stabbing.

DES. Go to. Where lodges he? 5

CLO. To tell you where he lodges is to tell you where I lie.

DES. Can anything be made of this?

CLO. I know not where he lodges, and for me to devise a lodging, and
say he lies here or he lies there, were to lie in mine own throat.

DES. Can you inquire him out and be edified by report?° 10

CLO. I will catechize the world for him; that is, make questions and by
them answer.

DES. Seek him, bid him come hither. Tell him I have moved my lord on
his behalf and hope all will be well.

CLO. To do this is within the compass of man's wit, and therefore I will
attempt the doing it. [*Exit*] 15

---

464. elements . . . clip: skies that embrace, surround. 468. remorse: solemn obligation. 471. put . . . to't: put you to the
proof.
    Sc. iv: 10. edified by report: enlightened by the information. Desdemona speaks with mock pomposity.

DES. Where should I lose that handkerchief, Emilia?

EMIL. I know not, madam.

DES. Believe me, I had rather have lost my purse
    Full of crusados.° And, but my noble Moor   20
    Is true of mind and made of no such baseness
    As jealous creatures are, it were enough
    To put him to ill thinking.

EMIL.   Is he not jealous?

DES. Who, he? I think the sun where he was born
    Drew all such humors° from him.

EMIL.   Look where he comes.   25

DES. I will not leave him now till Cassio
    Be called to him.
    [*Enter* OTHELLO] How is 't with you, my lord?

OTH. Well, my good lady. [*Aside*] Oh, hardness to dissemble!
    How do you, Desdemona?

DES.   Well, my good lord.   30

OTH. Give me your hand. This hand is moist,° my lady.

DES. It yet has felt no age nor known no sorrow.

OTH. This argues fruitfulness and liberal heart.
    Hot, hot, and moist—this hand of yours requires
    A sequester° from liberty, fasting and prayer,   35
    Much castigation, exercise devout.
    For here's a young and sweating devil here,
    That commonly rebels. 'Tis a good hand,
    A frank one.

DES.   You may indeed say so,
    For 'twas that hand that gave away my heart.   40

OTH. A liberal° hand. The hearts of old gave hands,
    But our new heraldry is hands, not hearts.°

DES. I cannot speak of this. Come now, your promise.

OTH. What promise, chuck?°

DES. I have sent to bid Cassio come speak with you.   45

OTH. I have a salt and sorry rheum° offends me.
    Lend me thy handkerchief.

DES. Here, my lord.

OTH. That which I gave you.

DES. I have it not about me.   50

---

20. **crusados:** small gold Portuguese coins. 25. **humors:** moods; lit., dampnesses. 31. **moist:** a hot moist palm was believed to show desire. 35. **sequester:** separation. 41. **liberal:** overgenerous. 41–42. **The . . . hearts:** once love and deeds went together, but now it is all deeds (i.e., faithlessness) and no love. This phrase has been taken as a reference to the order of baronets created by James I in 1611, who bore on their heraldic coats of arms the device of the "bloody hand of Ulster." If so, the lines are a later addition; but the reference is very doubtful. The contrast between hearts (true love and faith) and hands (actions) is natural. As Othello's passions rise, he ceases to be entirely coherent. 44. **chuck:** a term of affection, but not the kind of word with which a person of Othello's dignity would normally address his wife. He is beginning to treat her with contemptuous familiarity. See IV. ii.24. 46. **rheum:** common cold.

OTH. Not?

DES. No indeed, my lord.

OTH. That's a fault. That handkerchief

    Did an Egyptian° to my mother give.

    She was a charmer, and could almost read   55

    The thoughts of people. She told her while she kept it

    'Twould make her amiable and subdue my father

    Entirely to her love, but if she lost it

    Or made a gift of it, my father's eye

    Should hold her loathed and his spirits should hunt   60

    After new fancies. She dying gave it me,

    And bid me, when my fate would have me wive,

    To give it her. I did so. And take heed on 't,

    Make it a darling like your precious eye.

    To lose 't or give 't away were such perdition   65

    As nothing else could match.

DES.   Is 't possible?

OTH. 'Tis true. There's magic in the web of it.

    A sibyl° that had numbered in the world

    The sun to course two hundred compasses

    In her prophetic fury° sewed the work.   70

    The worms were hallowed that did breed the silk,

    And it was dyed in mummy° which the skillful

    Conserved° of maidens' hearts.

DES.   Indeed! Is 't true?

OTH. Most veritable, therefore look to 't well.

DES. Then would to God that I had never seen 't.   75

OTH. Ha! Wherefore?

DES. Why do you speak so startingly and rash?

OTH. Is 't lost? Is 't gone? Speak, is it out o' the way?

DES. Heaven bless us!

OTH. Say you?   80

DES. It is not lost, but what an if it were?

OTH. How!

DES. I say it is not lost.

OTH. Fetch 't, let me see it.

DES. Why, so I can, sir, but I will not now.   85

    This is a trick to put me from my suit.

    Pray you let Cassio be received again.

OTH. Fetch me the handkerchief. My mind misgives.

DES. Come, come,

    You'll never meet a more sufficient man.   90

---

54. Egyptian: gypsy. **68. sibyl:** prophetess. **70. fury:** inspiration. **72. mummy:** a concoction made from Egyptian mummies. **73. Conserved:** prepared.

OTH. The handkerchief!

DES.   I pray talk me of Cassio.

OTH. The handkerchief!

DES.   A man that all his time
 Hath founded his good fortunes on your love,
 Shared dangers with you——   95

OTH. The handkerchief!

DES. In sooth, you are to blame.

OTH. Away! [*Exit*]

EMIL. Is not this man jealous?

DES. I ne'er saw this before.   100
 Sure there's some wonder in this handkerchief.
 I am most unhappy in the loss of it.

EMIL. 'Tis not a year or two shows us a man.°
 They are all but stomachs and we all but food.
 They eat us hungerly, and when they are full   105
 They belch us. Look you, Cassio and my husband.

   Enter CASSIO *and* IAGO.

IAGO. There is no other way, 'tis she must do 't.
 And, lo, the happiness!° Go and impórtune her.

DES. How now, good Cassio! What's the news with you?

CAS. Madam, my former suit. I do beseech you   110
 That by your virtuous means I may again
 Exist, and be a member of his love
 Whom I with all the office of my heart
 Entirely honor. I would not be delayed.
 If my offense be of such mortal kind   115
 That nor my service past nor present sorrows
 Nor purposed merit in futurity°
 Can ransom me into his love again,
 But to know so must be my benefit.
 So shall I clothe me in a forced content   120
 And shut myself up in some other course
 To Fortune's alms.°

DES.   Alas, thrice-gentle Cassio!
 My advocation° is not now in tune.
 My lord is not my lord, nor should I know him
 Were he in favor as in humor altered.°   125

---

103. '*Tis . . . man:* it does not take a couple of years for us to discover the nature of a man; i.e., he soon shows his real nature. 108. *And . . . happiness:* what good luck, here she is. 117. *Nor . . . futurity:* nor my good resolutions for the future. 119–22. *But . . . alms:* if I know that Othello will not restore me to my position, it will have this benefit: I shall force myself to be contented and try my luck elsewhere. *Fortune's alms:* what Fortune may give me. 123. *advocation:* advocacy, pleading. 125. *favor . . . altered:* as changed in face as in mood.

So help me every spirit sanctified,
As I have spoken for you all my best
And stood within the blank° of his displeasure
For my free speech! You must awhile be patient.
What I can do I will, and more I will   130
Than for myself I dare. Let that suffice you.
IAGO. Is my lord angry?
EMIL.   He went hence but now,
And certainly in strange unquietness.
IAGO. Can he be angry? I have seen the cannon
When it hath blown his ranks into the air,   135
And, like the Devil, from his very arm
Puffed his own brother, and can he be angry?
Something of moment then. I will go meet him.
There's matter in 't indeed if he be angry.
DES. I prithee do so. [Exit IAGO] Something sure of state,   140
Either from Venice, or some unhatched practice
Made demonstrable° here in Cyprus to him,
Hath puddled° his clear spirit. And in such cases
Men's natures wrangle with inferior things,
Though great ones are their object.° 'Tis even so,   145
For let our finger ache and it indues°
Our other healthful members even to that sense
Of pain. Nay, we must think men are not gods,
Nor of them look for such observancy
As fits the bridal.° Beshrew me° much, Emilia,   150
I was, unhandsome warrior° as I am,
Arraigning his unkindness with my soul,
But now I find I had suborned the witness,°
And he's indicted falsely.
EMIL. Pray Heaven it be state matters, as you think,   155
And no conception nor no jealous toy°
Concerning you.
DES. Alas the day, I never gave him cause!
EMIL. But jealous souls will not be answered so.
They are not ever jealous for the cause,   160
But jealous for they are jealous. 'Tis a monster
Begot upon itself, born on itself.

---

128. blank: aim. The blank is the bull's-eye of a target. 141–42. unhatched . . . demonstrable: some plot, not yet matured, which has been revealed. 143. puddled: muddied, stirred up. 143–45. in . . . object: when men are disturbed by great matters, they show their temper in small things. 146. indues: endows, pervades. 150. bridal: honeymoon. Beshrew me: plague on me. 151. unhandsome warrior: clumsy soldier. Desdemona continually thinks of herself as Othello's companion in arms. Cf. I.iii.249ff. 153. suborned . . . witness: corrupted the evidence, i.e., it is my fault, not his. 156. jealous toy: silly suspicion.

DES. Heaven keep that monster from Othello's mind!
EMIL. Lady, amen.
DES. I will go seek him. Cassio, walk hereabout.   165
    If I do find him fit, I'll move your suit,
    And seek to effect it to my uttermost.
CAS. I humbly thank your ladyship. [*Exeunt* DESDEMONA *and* EMILIA]

    Enter BIANCA.

BIAN. Save you, friend Cassio!
CAS.   What make you from° home?
    How is it with you, my most fair Bianca?   170
    I' faith, sweet love, I was coming to your house.
BIAN. And I was going to your lodging, Cassio.
    What, keep a week away? Seven days and nights?
    Eightscore eight hours? And lovers' absent hours,
    More tedious than the dial eightscore times?°   175
    Oh, weary reckoning!
CAS.   Pardon me, Bianca.
    I have this while with leaden thoughts been pressed,
    But I shall in a more continuate time°
    Strike off this score of absence. Sweet Bianca, [*Giving her*
    DESDEMONA's *handkerchief*]
    Take me this work out.°
BIAN. O Cassio, whence came this?   180
    This is some token from a newer friend.
    To the felt absence now I feel a cause.
    Is 't come to this? Well, well.
CAS.   Go to, woman!
    Throw your vile guesses in the Devil's teeth,
    From whence you have them. You are jealous now   185
    That this is from some mistress, some remembrance.
    No, by my faith, Bianca.
BIAN.   Why, whose is it?
CAS. I know not, sweet. I found it in my chamber.
    I like the work well. Ere it be demanded—
    As like enough it will—I'd have it copied.   190
    Take it, and do't, and leave me for this time.
BIAN. Leave you! Wherefore?
CAS. I do attend here on the General,
    And think it no addition,° nor my wish,
    To have him see me womaned.°

---

169. make . . . from: are you doing away from. 174–75. And . . . times: when one's lover is absent for a week does it not seem far longer than a hundred and sixty clock hours? 178. continuate time: i.e., when my time is not continually being interrupted. 180. Take . . . out: copy this pattern. 194. addition: honor. 195. womaned: with a girl.

BIAN.   Why, I pray you?   195
CAS. Not that I love you not.
BIAN.   But that you do not love me.
    I pray you bring me on the way a little,
    And say if I shall see you soon at night.
CAS. 'Tis but a little way that I can bring you,
    For I attend here. But I'll see you soon.   200
BIAN. 'Tis very good, I must be circumstanced.° [*Exeunt*]

ACT IV

SCENE I. *Cyprus. Before the castle.*

    Enter OTHELLO *and* IAGO.

IAGO. Will you think so?
OTH.   Think so, Iago!
IAGO.   What,
    To kiss in private?
OTH.   An unauthorized kiss.
IAGO. Or to be naked with her friend in bed
    An hour or more, not meaning any harm?
OTH. Naked in bed, Iago, and not mean harm!   5
    It is hypocrisy against the Devil.°
    They that mean virtuously and yet do so,
    The Devil their virtue tempts and they tempt Heaven.°
IAGO. So° they do nothing, 'tis a venial° slip.
    But if I give my wife a handkerchief——   10
OTH. What then?
IAGO. Why, then, 'tis hers, my lord, and being hers,
    She may, I think, bestow 't on any man.
OTH. She is protectress of her honor too.
    May she give that?   15
IAGO. Her honor is an essence that's not seen.
    They have it very oft that have it not.°
    But for the handkerchief——
OTH. By Heaven, I would most gladly have forgot it.
    Thou said'st—oh, it comes o'er my memory,   20
    As doth the raven o'er the infected house,°

---

201. circumstanced: put off.
    Act IV, Sc. i: 6. hypocrisy . . . Devil: "double-crossing the Devil"; i.e., they are behaving in a most suspicious way.
7–8. They . . . Heaven: i.e., those who go to bed together and mean no harm are asking the Devil to tempt them, and they make God suspect their innocence. 9. So: as long as. venial: pardonable. 17. They . . . not: i.e., many are honored who have no honor. 21. As . . . house: i.e., as a bird of prey waits for its victim to die.

Boding° to all—he had my handkerchief.

IAGO. Aye, what of that?

OTH.   That's not so good now.

IAGO.   What,

    If I had said I had seen him do you wrong?

    Or heard him say—as knaves be such abroad,   25

    Who having, by their own importunate suit,

    Or voluntary dotage° of some mistress,

    Convincèd or supplied° them, cannot choose

    But they must blab——

OTH.   Hath he said anything?

IAGO. He hath, my lord, but be you well assured,   30

    No more than he'll unswear.

OTH.   What hath he said?

IAGO. Faith, that he did—I know not what he did.

OTH. What? What?

IAGO. Lie——

OTH. With her?   35

IAGO. With her, on her, what you will.

OTH. Lie° with her! Lie on her!—We say lie on her when they belie her.—Lie with her! 'Zounds, that's fulsome!° Handkerchief—confessions—handkerchief!—To confess, and be hanged for his labor. First to be hanged, and then to confess. I tremble at it. Nature   40 would not invest herself in such shadowing passion without some instruction.° It is not words that shake me thus. Pish! Noses, ears, and lips. Is't possible?—Confess?—Handkerchief?—Oh, devil! [*Falls in a trance*]

IAGO. Work on,   45

    My medicine, work! Thus credulous fools are caught,

    And many worthy and chaste dames even thus,

    All guiltless, meet reproach. What ho! My lord!

    My lord, I say! Othello! [*Enter* CASSIO] How now, Cassio!

CAS. What's the matter?   50

IAGO. My lord is fall'n into an epilepsy.

    This is his second fit, he had one yesterday.

CAS. Rub him about the temples.

IAGO.   No, forbear,

    The lethargy° must have his quiet course.

    If not, he foams at mouth and by and by   55

---

22. **Boding:** foretelling evil. 27. **dotage:** infatuation. 28. **Convinced or supplied:** overcome or satisfied their desires. **37–43. Lie . . . devil:** Othello breaks into incoherent muttering before he falls down in a fit. 38. **fulsome:** disgusting. 40–42. **Nature . . . instruction:** nature would not fill me with such overwhelming emotion unless there was some cause. 54. **lethargy:** epileptic fit.

Breaks out to savage madness. Look, he stirs.
Do you withdraw yourself a little while,
He will recover straight. When he is gone,
I would on great occasion speak with you. [*Exit* CASSIO]
How is it, General? Have you not hurt your head?°   60
OTH. Dost thou mock me?
IAGO.   I mock you! No, by Heaven.
Would you bear your fortune like a man!
OTH. A hornèd man's a monster and a beast.
IAGO. There's many a beast, then, in a populous city,
And many a civil° monster.   65
OTH. Did he confess it?
IAGO.   Good sir, be a man.
Think every bearded fellow that's but yoked°
May draw with you.° There's millions now alive
That nightly lie in those unproper beds
Which they dare swear peculiar.° Your case is better.   70
Oh, 'tis the spite of Hell, the Fiend's archmock,
To lip° a wanton in a secure couch°
And to suppose her chaste! No, let me know,
And knowing what I am, I know what she shall be.
OTH. Oh, thou art wise, 'tis certain.
IAGO.   Stand you awhile apart,   75
Confine yourself but in a patient list.°
Whilst you were here o'erwhelmèd with your grief—
A passion most unsuiting such a man—
Cassio came hither. I shifted him away,
And laid good 'scuse upon your ecstasy,°   80
Bade him anon return and here speak with me,
The which he promisèd. Do but encave° yourself,
And mark the fleers,° the gibes, and notable scorns,
That dwell in every region of his face.
For I will make him tell the tale anew,   85
Where, how, how oft, how long ago, and when
He hath and is again to cope° your wife.
I say but mark his gesture. Marry, patience,
Or I shall say you are all in all in spleen,°
And nothing of a man.

---

60. Have . . . head: With brutal cynicism Iago asks whether Othello is suffering from cuckold's headache. **65. civil:** sober, well-behaved citizen. **67. yoked:** married. **68. draw . . . you:** lit., be your yoke fellow, share your fate. **69–70. That . . . peculiar:** that lie nightly in beds which they believe are their own but which others have shared. **72. lip:** kiss. **secure couch:** lit., a carefree bed; i.e., a bed which has been used by the wife's lover, but secretly. **76. patient list:** confines of patience. **80. ecstasy:** fit. **82. encave:** hide. **83. fleers:** scornful grins. **87. cope:** encounter. **89. spleen:** hot temper.

OTH.   Dost thou hear, Iago?   90
    I will be found most cunning in my patience,
    But—dost thou hear?—most bloody.
IAGO.   That's not amiss,
    But yet keep time in all. Will you withdraw? [OTHELLO *retires.*]
    Now will I question Cassio of Bianca,
    A housewife° that by selling her desires   95
    Buys herself bread and clothes. It is a creature
    That dotes on Cassio, as 'tis the strumpet's plague
    To beguile many and be beguiled by one.
    He, when he hears of her, cannot refrain
    From the excess of laughter. Here he comes.   100
    [*Re-enter* CASSIO] As he shall smile, Othello shall go mad,
    And his unbookish° jealousy must construe°
    Poor Cassio's smiles, gestures, and light behavior
    Quite in the wrong. How do you now, Lieutenant?
CAS. The worser that you give me the addition°   105
    Whose want even kills me.
IAGO. Ply° Desdemona well, and you are sure on 't.
    Now, if this suit lay in Bianca's power,
    How quickly should you speed!
CAS.   Alas, poor caitiff!°
OTH. Look how he laughs already!   110
IAGO. I never knew a woman love man so.
CAS. Alas, poor rogue! I think, i' faith, she loves me.
OTH. Now he denies it faintly and laughs it out.
IAGO. Do you hear, Cassio?
OTH.   Now he impórtunes him
    To tell it o'er. Go to. Well said, well said.   115
IAGO. She gives it out that you shall marry her.
    Do you intend it?
CAS. Ha, ha, ha!
OTH. Do you triumph, Roman?° Do you triumph?
CAS. I marry her! What, a customer!° I prithee bear some charity to   120
    my wit. Do not think it so unwholesome. Ha, ha, ha!
OTH. So, so, so, so. They laugh that win.°
IAGO. Faith, the cry goes that you shall marry her.
CAS. Prithee say true.
IAGO. I am a very villain else.   125
OTH. Have you scored° me? Well.

----

95. **housewife:** hussy. **102. unbookish:** unlearned, simple. **construe:** interpret. **105. addition:** title (Lieutenant) which he
has lost. **107. Ply:** urge. **109. caitiff:** wretch. **119. triumph, Roman:** The word "triumph" suggests "Roman" because the
Romans celebrated their victories with triumphs, elaborate shows, and processions. **120. customer:** harlot. **122.**
They . . . win: a proverbial saying. **126. scored:** marked, as with a blow from a whip.

Cas. This is the monkey's own giving out. She is persuaded I will marry her out of her own love and flattery, not out of my promise.

Oth. Iago beckons me, now he begins the story.

Cas. She was here even now. She haunts me in every place. I was the 130 other day talking on the sea bank with certain Venetians, and thither comes the bauble,° and, by this hand, she falls me thus about my neck——

Oth. Crying "O dear Cassio!" as it were. His gesture imports it.

Cas. So hangs and lolls and weeps upon me, so hales° and pulls me. Ha, 135 ha, ha!

Oth. Now he tells how she plucked him to my chamber. Oh, I see that nose of yours, but not that dog I shall throw it to.

Cas. Well, I must leave her company.

Iago. Before me!° Look where she comes. 140

Cas. 'Tis such another fitchew!° Marry, a perfumed one. [Enter BIANCA] What do you mean by this haunting of me?

Bian. Let the Devil and his dam° haunt you! What did you mean by that same handkerchief you gave me even now? I was a fine fool to take it. I must take out the work? A likely piece of work, that you should 145 find it in your chamber and not know who left it there! This is some minx's token, and I must take out the work? There, give it your hobbyhorse.° Wheresoever you had it, I'll take out no work on 't.

Cas. How now, my sweet Bianca! How now! How now!

Oth. By Heaven, that should be my handkerchief! 150

Bian. An° you'll come to supper tonight, you may. An you will not, come when you are next prepared for. [Exit]

Iago. After her, after her.

Cas. Faith, I must, she'll rail i' the street else.

Iago. Will you sup there? 155

Cas. Faith, I intend so.

Iago. Well, I may chance to see you, for I would very fain° speak with you.

Cas. Prithee, come, will you?

Iago. Go to. Say no more. [Exit CASSIO] 160

Oth. [Advancing] How shall I murder him, Iago?

Iago. Did you perceive how he laughed at his vice?

Oth. Oh, Iago!

Iago. And did you see the handkerchief?

Oth. Was that mine? 165

---

132. bauble: toy, plaything. **135. hales:** hauls, drags. **140. Before me:** by my soul, a mild oath. **141. fitchew:** polecat, a creature most demonstrative in the mating season. **143. dam:** mother. **148. hobbyhorse:** harlot. **151. An:** if. **157. fain:** gladly.

IAGO. Yours, by this hand. And to see how he prizes the foolish woman your wife! She gave it him, and he hath given it his whore.

OTH. I would have him nine years a-killing. A fine woman! A fair woman! A sweet woman!

IAGO. Nay, you must forget that.   170

OTH. Aye, let her rot, and perish, and be damned tonight, for she shall not live. No, my heart is turned to stone, I strike it and it hurts my hand. Oh, the world hath not a sweeter creature. She might lie by an emperor's side, and command him tasks.

IAGO. Nay, that's not your way.°   175

OTH. Hang her! I do but say what she is, so delicate with her needle, an admirable musician—oh, she will sing the savageness out of a bear—of so high and plenteous wit and invention——

IAGO. She's the worse for all this.

OTH. Oh, a thousand thousand times. And then, of so gentle a 180 condition!°

IAGO. Aye, too gentle.

OTH. Nay, that's certain. But yet the pity of it, Iago! O Iago, the pity of it, Iago!

IAGO. If you are so fond° over her iniquity, give her patent° to offend, for 185 if it touch not you, it comes near nobody.

OTH. I will chop her into messes.° Cuckold me!

IAGO. Oh, 'tis foul in her.

OTH. With mine officer!

IAGO. That's fouler.   190

OTH. Get me some poison, Iago, this night. I'll not expostulate° with her, lest her body and beauty unprovide° my mind again. This night, Iago.

IAGO. Do it not with poison, strangle her in her bed, even the bed she hath contaminated.   195

OTH. Good, good. The justice of it pleases. Very good.

IAGO. And for Cassio, let me be his undertaker.° You shall hear more by midnight.

OTH. Excellent good. [A trumpet within] What trumpet is that same?

IAGO. Something from Venice, sure. 'Tis Lodovico   200 Come from the Duke. And see, your wife is with him.

Enter LODOVICO, DESDEMONA, *and* ATTENDANTS.

LOD. God save the worthy General!

OTH.   With all my heart, sir.

LOD. The Duke and Senators of Venice greet you. [*Gives him a letter*]

---

175. Nay . . . way: i.e., don't get soft thoughts about her. 181. condition: nature. 185. fond: foolish. patent: a grant by the King of some special privilege. 187. messes: little pieces. 191. expostulate: argue. 192. unprovide: weaken. 197. be . . . undertaker: undertake to manage his business. In Shakespeare's plays the word does *not* mean "mortician."

OTH. I kiss the instrument° of their pleasures. [*Opens the letter, and*   205
    reads]
DES. And what's the news, good Cousin Lodovico?
IAGO. I am very glad to see you, signior.
    Welcome to Cyprus.
LOD. I thank you. How does Lieutenant Cassio?
IAGO. Lives, sir.
DES. Cousin, there's fall'n between him and my lord   210
    An unkind breach, but you shall make all well.
OTH. Are you sure of that?
DES. My lord?
OTH [*Reads*] "This fail you not to do, as you will——"   215
LOD. He did not call, he's busy in the paper.
    Is there division 'twixt my lord and Cassio?
DES. A most unhappy one. I would do much
    To atone° them, for the love I bear to Cassio.
OTH. Fire and brimstone!
DES.   My lord?
OTH.   Are you wise?°   220
DES. What, is he angry?
LOD.   Maybe the letter moved him,
    For, as I think, they do command him home,
    Deputing Cassio in his government.°
DES. By my troth,° I am glad on 't.
OTH.   Indeed!
DES.   My lord?
OTH. I am glad to see you mad.
DES.   Why, sweet Othello?   225
OTH. Devil! [*Striking her*]
DES. I have not deserved this.
LOD. My lord, this would not be believed in Venice
    Though I should swear I saw 't. 'Tis very much.°
    Make her amends, she weeps.
OTH.   O devil, devil!   230
    If that the earth could teem with a woman's tears,
    Each drop she falls would prove a crocodile.°
    Out of my sight!
DES.   I will not stay to offend you. [*Going*]
LOD. Truly, an obedient lady.
    I do beseech your lordship, call her back.   235

---

205. instrument: i.e., the official letter which he has just received. **219. atone:** reconcile. **220. Are . . . wise:** i.e., in saying you bear love to Cassio. **223. in . . . government:** in his place as governor. **224. troth:** truth. **229. 'Tis . . . much:** this is too much. **231–32. If . . . crocodile:** if the earth could breed from woman's tears, each tear that she lets fall would become a crocodile. It was believed that the crocodile would cry and sob to attract the sympathetic passer-by, who was then snapped up.

OTH. Mistress!
DES. My lord?
OTH. What would you with her, sir?
LOD.   Who, I, my lord?
OTH. Aye, you did wish that I would make her turn.
  Sir, she can turn and turn, and yet go on   240
  And turn again. And she can weep, sir, weep.
  And she's obedient, as you say, obedient,
  Very obedient. Proceed you in your tears.
  Concerning this, sir—oh, well-painted passion!°—
  I am commanded home. Get you away.   245
  I'll send for you anon. Sir, I obey the mandate,
  And will return to Venice. Hence, avaunt! [*Exit* DESDEMONA]
  Cassio shall have my place. And, sir, tonight,
  I do entreat that we may sup together.
  You are welcome, sir, to Cyprus. Goats and monkeys! [*Exit*]   250
LOD. Is this the noble Moor whom our full Senate
  Call all-in-all sufficient? This the nature
  Whom passion could not shake? Whose solid virtue
  The shot of accident nor dart of chance
  Could neither graze nor pierce?
IAGO.   He is much changed.   255
LOD. Are his wits safe? Is he not light of brain?
IAGO. He's that he is. I may not breathe my censure°
  What he might be. If what he might he is not,
  I would to Heaven he were!°
LOD.   What, strike his wife!
IAGO. Faith, that was not so well, yet would I knew   260
  That stroke would prove the worst!
LOD.   Is it his use?°
  Or did the letters work upon his blood,
  And new-create this fault?
IAGO.   Alas, alas!
  It is not honesty in me to speak
  What I have seen and known. You shall observe him,   265
  And his own courses° will denote him so
  That I may save my speech. Do but go after,
  And mark how he continues.
LOD. I am sorry that I am deceived in him. [*Exeunt*]

---

244. **well-painted passion:** cleverly imitated emotion; *passion* is any violent emotion. 257. **censure:** opinion, judgment.
259. **I . . . were:** I wish he were the man he ought to be. Once more Iago hints that he is holding back some unpleasant
fact. 261. **Is . . . use:** does he always behave like this? 266. **courses:** ways, behavior.

SCENE II. *A room in the castle.*

Enter OTHELLO *and* EMILIA.

OTH. You have seen nothing, then?
EMIL. Nor ever heard, nor ever did suspect.
OTH. Yes, you have seen Cassio and she together.
EMIL. But then I saw no harm, and then I heard
 Each syllable that breath made up between them.   5
OTH. What, did they never whisper?
EMIL.   Never, my lord.
OTH. Nor send you out o' the way?
EMIL. Never.
OTH. To fetch her fan, her gloves, her mask, nor nothing?
EMIL. Never, my lord.   10
OTH. That's strange.
EMIL. I durst, my lord, to wager she is honest,
 Lay down my soul at stake.° If you think other,
 Remove your thought, it doth abuse your bosom.
 If any wretch have put this in your head,   15
 Let Heaven requite it with the serpent's curse!°
 For if she be not honest, chaste, and true,
 There's no man happy, the purest of their wives
 Is foul as slander.
OTH. Bid her come hither. Go. [*Exit* EMILIA]
 She says enough. Yet she's a simple bawd°   20
 That cannot say as much. This is a subtle whore,
 A closet° lock and key of villainous secrets.
 And yet she'll kneel and pray, I have seen her do 't.

Enter DESDEMONA *with* EMILIA.

DES. My lord, what is your will?
OTH.   Pray, chuck,° come hither.
DES. What is your pleasure?
OTH.   Let me see your eyes.   25
 Look in my face.
DES.   What horrible fancy's this?
OTH. [*To* EMILIA] Some of your function,° mistress.

 Sc. ii: 13. at stake: as the stake, the bet. 16. serpent's curse: i.e., the curse laid on the serpent in the Garden of Eden. 20. bawd: keeper of a brothel. 22. closet: box in which secret papers are kept. 24. chuck: See III.iv.49,n. 27. Some . . . function: get about your business; i.e., prostitution. Othello pretends that Emilia is keeper of a brothel and Desdemona one of the women.

Leave procreants alone and shut the door,
Cough, or cry hem, if anybody come.
Your mystery,° your mystery. Nay, dispatch.° [*Exit* EMILIA]   30
DES. Upon my knees, what doth your speech import?
I understand a fury in your words,
But not the words.
OTH. Why, what art thou?
DES. Your wife, my lord, your true and loyal wife.
OTH. Come, swear it, damn thyself,   35
Lest, being like one of Heaven,° the devils themselves
Should fear to seize thee. Therefore be double-damned.
Swear thou art honest.
DES.   Heaven doth truly know it.
OTH. Heaven truly knows that thou art false as Hell.
DES. To whom, my lord? With whom? How am I false?   40
OTH. O Desdemona! Away! Away! Away!
DES. Alas the heavy day! Why do you weep?
Am I the motive of these tears, my lord?
If haply you my father do suspect
An instrument of this your calling-back,   45
Lay not your blame on me. If you have lost him,
Why, I have lost him too.
OTH.   Had it pleased Heaven
To try me with affliction, had they rained
All kinds of sores and shames on my bare head,
Steeped me in poverty to the very lips,   50
Given to captivity me and my utmost hopes,
I should have found in some place of my soul
A drop of patience. But, alas, to make me
A fixèd figure for the time of scorn
To point his slow unmoving finger at!°   55
Yet could I bear that too, well, very well.
But there where I have garnered up my heart,°
Where either I must live or bear no life,
The fountain from the which my current runs
Or else dries up—to be discarded thence!   60
Or keep it as a cistern for foul toads
To knot and gender° in! Turn thy complexion there,

---

30. **mystery:** profession. **dispatch:** be quick. **36. being . . . Heaven:** because you look like an angel. **54–55. A . . . at:** A difficult image, much discussed. F1 reads "slow and moving finger"; Q1 reads "slow unmoving." Probably it means "a perpetual mark for scorn to point at with motionless finger." **time of scorn:** (perhaps) scorn for all time. **57. garnered . . . heart:** stored the harvest of my love. **62. gender:** mate.

Patience, thou young and rose-lipped cherubin—
    Aye, there, look grim as Hell!
DES. I hope my noble lord esteems me honest.   65
OTH. Oh, aye, as summer flies are in the shambles,°
    That quicken even with blowing.° O thou weed,
    Who art so lovely fair and smell'st so sweet
    That the sense aches at thee, would thou hadst ne'er been born!
DES. Alas, what ignorant sin have I committed?   70
OTH. Was this fair paper,° this most goodly book,
    Made to write "whore" upon? What committed!
    Committed! O thou public commoner!°
    I should make very forges of my cheeks°
    That would to cinders burn up modesty   75
    Did I but speak thy deeds. What committed!
    Heaven stops the nose at it, and the moon winks.
    The bawdy wind, that kisses all it meets,
    Is hushed within the hollow mine° of earth
    And will not hear it. What committed!   80
    Impudent strumpet!
DES.   By Heaven, you do me wrong.
OTH. Are not you a strumpet?
DES.   No, as I am a Christian.
    If to preserve this vessel for my lord
    From any other foul unlawful touch
    Be not to be a strumpet, I am none.   85
OTH. What, not a whore?
DES.   No, as I shall be saved.
OTH. Is't possible?
DES. Oh, Heaven forgive us!
OTH.   I cry you mercy, then.
    I took you for that cunning whore of Venice
    That married with Othello. [Raising his voice]
    You, mistress,   90
    That have the office opposite to Saint Peter,°
    And keep the gate of Hell!
    [Re-enter EMILIA] You, you, aye, you!
    We have done our course, there's money for your pains.
    I pray you turn the key, and keep our counsel.° [Exit]
EMIL. Alas, what does this gentleman conceive?°   95
    How do you, madam? How do you, my good lady?

---

66. shambles: slaughterhouse. 67. quicken . . . blowing: come to life as soon as the eggs are laid. 71. fair paper: i.e., her white body. 73. public commoner: one who offers herself to all comers. 74. I . . . cheeks: i.e., my cheeks would be as hot as a forge if I told the truth. 79. hollow mine: i.e., the cave where the winds were supposed to be kept. 91. office . . . Peter: St. Peter kept the keys to Heaven. 94. counsel: i.e., secret. 95. conceive: imagine.

DES. Faith, half-asleep.
EMIL. Good madam, what's the matter with my lord?
DES. With who?
EMIL. Why, with my lord, madam.   100
DES. Who is thy lord?
EMIL.   He that is yours, sweet lady.
DES. I have none. Do not talk to me, Emilia.
    I cannot weep, nor answer have I none
    But what should go by water.° Prithee tonight
    Lay on my bed my wedding sheets. Remember,   105
    And call thy husband hither.
EMIL.   Here's a change indeed! [Exit]
DES. 'Tis meet I should be used so, very meet.
    How have I been behaved that he might stick
    The small'st opinion on my least misuse?°

        Re-enter EMILIA with IAGO.

IAGO. What is your pleasure, madam? How is't with you?   110
DES. I cannot tell. Those that do teach young babes
    Do it with gentle means and easy tasks.
    He might have chid me so, for, in good faith,
    I am a child to chiding.
IAGO.   What's the matter, lady?
EMIL. Alas, Iago, my lord hath so bewhored her,   115
    Thrown such despite and heavy terms upon her,
    As true hearts cannot bear.
DES. Am I that name, Iago?
IAGO.   What name, fair lady?
DES. Such as she says my lord did say I was.
EMIL. He called her whore. A beggar in his drink   120
    Could not have laid such terms upon his callet.°
IAGO. Why did he so?
DES. I do not know. I am sure I am none such.
IAGO. Do not weep, do not weep. Alas the day!
EMIL. Hath she forsook so many noble matches,   125
    Her father and her country and her friends,
    To be called whore? Would it not make one weep?
DES. It is my wretched fortune.
IAGO.   Beshrew him for 't!
    How comes this trick upon him?
DES.   Nay, Heaven doth know.

---

104. should . . . water: be expressed in tears. 108–09. How . . . misuse: what have I done that he could find the smallest reason to find fault with my least mistake?
121. laid . . . callet: used such words about his moll.

EMIL. I will be hanged if some eternal villain,   130
   Some busy and insinuating rogue,
   Some cogging, cozening° slave, to get some office,
   Have not devised this slander. I'll be hanged else.
IAGO. Fie, there is no such man, it is impossible.
DES. If any such there be, Heaven pardon him!   135
EMIL. A halter pardon him! And Hell gnaw his bones!
   Why should he call her whore? Who keeps her company?
   What place? What time? What form? What likelihood?
   The Moor's abused by some most villainous knave,
   Some base notorious knave, some scurvy fellow.   140
   O Heaven, that such companions° Thou'dst unfold,°
   And put in every honest hand a whip
   To lash the rascals naked through the world
   Even from the east to the west!
IAGO.   Speak withindoor.°
EMIL. Oh, fie upon them! Some such squire° he was   145
   That turned your wit the seamy side without,
   And made you to suspect me with the Moor.
IAGO. You are a fool. Go to.°
DES.   O good Iago,
   What shall I do to win my lord again?
   Good friend, go to him, for, by this light of Heaven,   150
   I know not how I lost him. Here I kneel.
   If e'er my will did trespass 'gainst his love
   Either in discourse of thought or actual deed,
   Or that mine eyes, mine ears, or any sense
   Delighted them in any other form,   155
   Or that I do not yet, and ever did,
   And ever will, though he do shake me off
   To beggarly divorcement, love him dearly,
   Comfort forswear° me! Unkindness may do much,
   And his unkindness may defeat° my life,   160
   But never taint my love. I cannot say "whore,"
   It doth abhor me now I speak the word.
   To do the act that might the addition° earn
   Not the world's mass of vanity° could make me.
IAGO. I pray you be content, 'tis but his humor.   165
   The business of the state does him offense,
   And he does chide with you.

---

132. **cogging, cozening:** deceiving, cheating. 141. **companions:** low creatures. **unfold:** bring to light. 144. **Speak withindoor:** don't shout so loud that all the street will hear you. 145. **squire:** fine fellow. 148. **Go to:** An expression of derision. 159. **forswear:** repudiate. 160. **defeat:** destroy. 163. **addition:** title. Cf. IV.i.105. 164. **vanity:** i.e., riches.

DES. If 'twere no other——
IAGO. 'Tis but so, I warrant. [*Trumpets within*]
    Hark how these instruments summon to supper!
    The messengers of Venice stay the meat.°   170
    Go in, and weep not, all things shall be well. [*Exeunt* DESDEMONA
    and EMILIA]
    [*Enter* RODERIGO] How now, Roderigo!
ROD. I do not find that thou dealest justly with me.
IAGO. What in the contrary?   175
ROD. Every day thou daffest° me with some device, Iago, and rather,
    as it seems to me now, keepest from me all conveniency° than
    suppliest me with the least advantage of hope. I will indeed no longer
    endure it, nor am I yet persuaded to put up in peace what already I
    have foolishly suffered.   180
IAGO. Will you hear me, Roderigo?
ROD. Faith, I have heard too much, for your words and performances are
    no kin together.
IAGO. You charge me most unjustly.
ROD. With naught but truth. I have wasted myself out of my means. The   185
    jewels you have had from me to deliver to Desdemona would half
    have corrupted a votarist.° You have told me she hath received them,
    and returned me expectations and comforts of sudden respect and
    acquaintance, but I find none.
IAGO. Well, go to, very well.   190
ROD. Very well! Go to! I cannot go to, man, nor 'tis not very well. By this
    hand, I say 'tis very scurvy, and begin to find myself fopped° in it.
IAGO. Very well.
ROD. I tell you 'tis not very well. I will make myself known to
    Desdemona. If she will return me my jewels, I will give over my suit   195
    and repent my unlawful solicitation. If not, assure yourself I will
    seek satisfaction of you.
IAGO. You have said now.°
ROD. Aye, and said nothing but what I protest intendment of doing.
IAGO. Why, now I see there's mettle° in thee, and even from this instant   200
    do build on thee a better opinion than ever before. Give me thy
    hand, Roderigo. Thou hast taken against me a most just exception,°
    but yet I protest I have dealt most directly in thy affair.
ROD. It hath not appeared.
IAGO. I grant indeed it hath not appeared, and your suspicion is not   205
    without wit° and judgment. But, Roderigo, if thou hast that in thee

---

170. meat: serving of supper. 176. thou daffest: you put me aside. 177. conveniency: opportunity. 187. votarist: one who
has taken a vow, here a nun. 192. fopped: fooled. 198. you . . . now: or in modern slang, "Oh yeah." 200. mettle: metal,
good stuff. 202. just exception: reasonable grievance. 206. wit: wisdom.

indeed which I have greater reason to believe now than ever—I mean purpose, courage, and valor—this night show it. If thou the next night following enjoy not Desdemona, take me from this world with treachery and devise engines° for my life. 210

ROD. Well, what is it? Is it within reason and compass?

IAGO. Sir, there is especial commission come from Venice to depute Cassio in Othello's place.

ROD. Is that true? Why, then Othello and Desdemona return again to Venice. 215

IAGO. Oh, no. He goes into Mauritania, and takes away with him the fair Desdemona, unless his abode be lingered here by some accident. Wherein none can be so determinate° as the removing of Cassio.

ROD. How do you mean, "removing of" him?

IAGO. Why, by making him uncapable° of Othello's place, knocking out 220 his brains.

ROD. And that you would have me to do?

IAGO. Aye, if you dare do yourself a profit and a right. He sups tonight with a harlotry,° and thither will I go to him. He knows not yet of his honorable fortune. If you will watch his going thence, which I will 225 fashion to fall out between twelve and one, you may take him at your pleasure. I will be near to second your attempt, and he shall fall between us. Come, stand not amazed at it, but go along with me. I will show you such a necessity in his death that you shall think yourself bound to put it on him. It is now high suppertime, and 230 the night grows to waste. About it.

ROD. I will hear further reason for this.

IAGO. And you shall be satisfied. [*Exeunt*]

SCENE III. *Another room in the castle.*

Enter OTHELLO, LODOVICO, DESDEMONA, EMILIA, *and* ATTENDANTS.

LOD. I do beseech you, sir, trouble yourself no further.

OTH. Oh, pardon me, 'twill do me good to walk.

LOD. Madam, good night. I humbly thank your ladyship.

DES. Your Honor is most welcome.

OTH.   Will you walk, sir?

     Oh—Desdemona—   5

DES. My lord?

---

210. engines: instruments of torture. **218. determinate:** decisive. **220. uncapable:** unable to take. **224. harlotry:** harlot.

OTH. Get you to bed on the instant, I will be returned forthwith.
    Dismiss your attendant there. Look it be done.
DES. I will, my lord. [*Exeunt* OTHELLO, LODOVICO, *and* ATTENDANTS]
EMIL. How goes it now? He looks gentler than he did.   10
DES. He says he will return incontinent.°
    He hath commanded me to go to bed,
    And bade me to dismiss you.
EMIL.   Dismiss me!
DES. It was his bidding, therefore, good Emilia,   15
    Give me my nightly wearing,° and adieu.
    We must not now displease him.
EMIL. I would you had never seen him!
DES. So would not I. My love doth so approve° him
    That even his stubbornness, his checks, his frowns—   20
      Prithee, unpin me—have grace and favor in them.
EMIL. I have laid those sheets you bade me on the bed.
DES. All's one. Good faith, how foolish are our minds!
    If I do die before thee, prithee shroud me
    In one of those same sheets.
EMIL.   Come, come, you talk.   25
DES. My mother had a maid called Barbara.
    She was in love, and he she loved proved mad
    And did forsake her. She had a song of "willow"°—
    An old thing 'twas, but it expressed her fortune,
    And she died singing it. That song tonight   30
    Will not go from my mind. I have much to do
    But to go hang my head all at one side
    And sing it like poor Barbara. Prithee, dispatch.
EMIL. Shall I go fetch your nightgown?
DES.   No, unpin me here.
    This Lodovico is a proper man.   35
EMIL. A very handsome man.
DES. He speaks well.
EMIL. I know a lady in Venice would have walked barefoot to Palestine
    for a touch of his nether° lip.
DES. [*Singing*]
    "The poor soul sat sighing by a sycamore tree,   40
      Sing all a green willow.
    Her hand on her bosom, her head on her knee,
      Sing willow, willow, willow.
    The fresh streams ran by her, and murmured her moans,

Sc. iii: **11. incontinent:** immediately. **16. nightly wearing:** nightgown. **19. approve:** commend. **28. willow:** the emblem of the forlorn lover. **39. nether:** lower.

      Sing willow, willow, willow.   45

    Her salt tears fell from her, and softened the stones—"

    Lay by these—[*Singing*]

       "Sing willow, willow, willow."

    Prithee, hie thee, he'll come anon.°—[*Singing*]

    "Sing all a green willow must be my garland.   50

      Let nobody blame him, his scorn I approve——"

    Nay, that's not next. Hark! Who is't that knocks?

EMIL. It's the wind.

DES. [*Singing*]

    "I called my love false love, but what said he then?

      Sing willow, willow, willow.   55

    If I court moe° women, you'll couch with moe men."

    So get thee gone, good night. Mine eyes do itch.

    Doth that bode weeping?

EMIL.   'Tis neither here nor there.

DES. I have heard it said so. Oh, these men, these men!

    Dost thou in conscience think—tell me, Emilia—   60

    That there be women do abuse their husbands

    In such gross kind?

EMIL.   There be some such, no question.

DES. Wouldst thou do such a deed for all the world?

EMIL. Why, would not you?

DES.   No, by this heavenly light!

EMIL. Nor I neither by this heavenly light. I might do 't as well i' the   65

    dark.

DES. Wouldst thou do such a deed for all the world?

EMIL. The world's a huge thing. It is a great price

    For a small vice.

DES.   In troth, I think thou wouldst not.

EMIL. In troth, I think I should, and undo 't when I had done. Marry, I   70

    would not do such a thing for a joint ring,° nor for measures of

    lawn,° nor for gowns, petticoats, nor caps, nor any petty exhibition;°

    but for the whole world—why, who would not make her husband a

    cuckold to make him a monarch? I should venture Purgatory for 't.

DES. Beshrew me if I would do such a wrong   75

    For the whole world.

EMIL. Why, the wrong is but a wrong i' the world, and having the world

    for your labor, 'tis a wrong in your own world and you might quickly

    make it right.

DES. I do not think there is any such woman.   80

----

49. anon: soon. **56. moe:** more. **71. joint ring:** ring made in two pieces, a lover's gift. **71–72. measures of lawn:** lengths of finest lawn, or as a modern woman would say, "sheer nylon." **72. petty exhibition:** small allowance of money.

EMIL. Yes, a dozen, and as many to the vantage° as would store° the
    world they played for.
    But I do think it is their husbands' faults
    If wives do fall. Say that they slack their duties
    And pour our treasures into foreign laps,   85
    Or else break out in peevish jealousies,
    Throwing restraint° upon us, or say they strike us,
    Or scant our former having in despite,°
    Why, we have galls,° and though we have some grace,
    Yet have we some revenge. Let husbands know   90
    Their wives have sense like them. They see and smell
    And have their palates both for sweet and sour,
    As husbands have. What is it that they do
    When they change us for others? Is it sport?
    I think it is. And doth affection breed it?   95
    I think it doth. Is 't frailty that thus errs?
    It is so too. And have not we affections,
    Desires for sport, and frailty, as men have?
    Then let them use us well. Else let them know
    The ills we do, their ills instruct us so.   100
DES. Good night, good night. Heaven me such uses° send,
    Not to pick bad from bad, but by bad mend! [*Exeunt*]

ACT V

SCENE I. *Cyprus. A street.*

Enter IAGO *and* RODERIGO.

IAGO. Here, stand behind this bulk,° straight° will he come.
    Wear thy good rapier bare, and put it home.
    Quick, quick, fear nothing, I'll be at thy elbow.
    It makes us, or it mars us. Think on that,
    And fix most firm thy resolution.   5
ROD. Be near at hand, I may miscarry in 't.
IAGO. Here, at thy hand. Be bold, and take thy stand. [*Retires*]
ROD. I have no great devotion to the deed,
    And yet he hath given me satisfying reasons.
    'Tis but a man gone. Forth, my sword. He dies.   10

---

81. as . . . vantage: and more too; *vantage* is that added to the exact weight to give generous measure. store: stock, fill up.
87. Throwing restraint: putting restraints. 88. scant . . . despite: for spite cut down our allowance. 89. galls: bile, the
cause of bitterness. 101. uses: practices.
Act V, Sc. i: 1. bulk: stall outside a shop. straight: straightway.

IAGO. I have rubbed this young quat° almost to the sense,°
 And he grows angry. Now, whether he kill Cassio,
 Or Cassio him, or each do kill the other,
 Every way makes my gain. Live Roderigo,
 He calls me to a restitution large°   15
 Of gold and jewels that I bobbed° from him
 As gifts to Desdemona.
 It must not be. If Cassio do remain,
 He hath a daily beauty in his life
 That makes me ugly,° and besides, the Moor   20
 May unfold° me to him. There stand I in much peril.
 No, he must die. Be 't so. I hear him coming.

   Enter CASSIO.

ROD. I know his gait, 'tis he. Villain, thou diest! [*Makes a pass at* CASSIO]
CAS. That thrust had been mine enemy indeed
 But that my coat is better than thou know'st.°   25
 I will make proof of thine. [*Draws, and wounds* RODERIGO]
ROD.   Oh, I am slain!
   [IAGO *from behind wounds* CASSIO *in the leg, and exit*]
CAS. I am maimed for ever. Help, ho! Murder! Murder! [*Falls*]

   Enter OTHELLO.

OTH. The voice of Cassio. Iago keeps his word.
ROD. Oh, villain that I am!
OTH.   It is even so.
CAS. Oh, help, ho! Light! A surgeon!   30
OTH. 'Tis he. O brave Iago, honest and just,
 That hast such noble sense of thy friend's wrong!
 Thou teachest me. Minion,° your dear lies dead,
 And your unblest fate hies.° Strumpet, I come!
 Forth of my heart those charms, thine eyes, are blotted.   35
 Thy bed lust-stained shall with lust's blood be spotted. [*Exit*]

   Enter LODOVICO *and* GRATIANO.

CAS. What ho! No watch?° No passage?° Murder! Murder!
GRA. 'Tis some mischance, the cry is very direful.
CAS. Oh, help!

---

11. quat: pimple. **to . . . sense:** to the quick, to the raw. **15. large:** full. **16. bobbed:** cheated. **19–20. He . . . ugly:** by comparison with him I am a poor thing. Iago is conscious of his lack of social graces. **21. unfold:** expose. **25. coat . . . know'st:** i.e., I wear mail under my coat. **33. Minion:** darling, in a bad sense. **34. hies:** comes on quickly. **37. watch:** police. **No passage:** nobody passing.

Lod. Hark!   40
Rod. Oh, wretched villain!
Lod. Two or three groan. It is a heavy° night.
    These may be counterfeits.° Let's think 't unsafe
    To come in to the cry without more help.
Rod. Nobody come? Then shall I bleed to death.   45
Lod. Hark!

    Re-enter IAGO, *with a light.*

Gra. Here's one comes in his shirt, with light and weapons.
Iago. Who's there? Whose noise is this that cries on° murder?
Lod. We do not know.
Iago.   Did not you hear a cry?
Cas. Here, here! For Heaven's sake, help me!
Iago.   What's the matter?   50
Gra. This is Othello's Ancient, as I take it.
Lod. The same indeed, a very valiant fellow.
Iago. What are you here that cry so grievously?
Cas. Iago? Oh, I am spoiled, undone by villains!
    Give me some help.   55
Iago. Oh me, Lieutenant! What villains have done this?
Cas. I think that one of them is hereabout,
    And cannot make away.
Iago.   Oh, treacherous villains!
    [*To* LODOVICO *and* GRATIANO] What are you there?
    Come in and give some help.
Rod. Oh, help me here!   60
Cas. That's one of them.
Iago. Oh, murderous slave! Oh, villain! [*Stabs* RODERIGO]
Rod. Oh, damned Iago! Oh, inhuman dog!
Iago. Kill men i' the dark! Where be these bloody thieves?
    How silent is this town! Ho! Murder! Murder!
    What may you be? Are you of good or evil?   65
Lod. As you shall prove us, praise us.
Iago. Signior Lodovico?
Lod. He, sir.
Iago. I cry you mercy. Here's Cassio hurt by villains.
Gra. Cassio!   70
Iago. How is 't, brother?
Cas. My leg is cut in two.
Iago.   Marry, Heaven forbid!
    Light, gentlemen. I'll bind it with my shirt.

---

42. heavy: thick. 43. counterfeits: fakes. 48. cries on: cries out.

Enter BIANCA.

BIAN. What is the matter, ho? Who is 't that cried?
IAGO. Who is 't that cried!   75
BIAN. Oh, my dear Cassio! My sweet Cassio! Oh, Cassio, Cassio, Cassio!
IAGO. On, notable strumpet! Cassio, may you suspect
   Who they should be that have thus mangled you?
CAS. No.   80
GRA. I am sorry to find you thus. I have been to seek you.
IAGO. Lend me a garter. So. Oh, for a chair,
   To bear him easily hence!
BIAN. Alas, he faints! Oh, Cassio, Cassio, Cassio!
IAGO. Gentlemen all, I do suspect this trash   85
   To be a party in this injury.
   Patience awhile, good Cassio. Come, come,
   Lend me a light. Know we this face or no?
   Alas, my friend and my dear countryman
   Roderigo? No—yes, sure. Oh Heaven! Roderigo.   90
GRA. What, of Venice?
IAGO. Even he, sir. Did you know him?
GRA.   Know him! Aye.
IAGO. Signior Gratiano? I cry you gentle pardon.°
   These bloody accidents must excuse my manners,
   That so neglected you.
GRA.   I am glad to see you.   95
IAGO. How do you, Cassio? Oh, a chair, a chair!
GRA. Roderigo!
IAGO. He, he, 'tis he. [*A chair brought in*] Oh, that's well said, the chair.
   Some good man bear him carefully from hence.
   I'll fetch the General's surgeon. [*To* BIANCA] For you, mistress,   100
   Save you your labor. He that lies slain here, Cassio,
   Was my dear friend. What malice was between you?
CAS. None in the world, nor do I know the man.
IAGO. [*To* BIANCA] What, look you pale? Oh, bear him out o' the air.
   [CASSIO *and* RODERIGO *are borne off*]
   Stay you, good gentlemen. Look you pale, mistress?   105
   Do you perceive the gastness° of her eye?
   Nay, if you stare, we shall hear more anon.
   Behold her well, I pray you look upon her.
   Do you see, gentlemen? Nay, guiltiness will speak,
   Though tongues were out of use.   110

---

93. I . . . **pardon:** I beg you kindly pardon me. **106. gastness:** ghastly look.

Enter EMIL.

EMIL. 'Las, what's the matter? What's the matter, husband?
IAGO. Cassio hath here been set on in the dark
    By Roderigo, and fellows that are 'scaped.
    He's almost slain, and Roderigo dead.
EMIL. Alas, good gentlemen! Alas, good Cassio!   115
IAGO. This is the fruit of whoring. Prithee, Emilia,
    Go know of Cassio where he supped tonight.
    What, do you shake at that?
BIAN. He supped at my house, but I therefore shake not.
IAGO. Oh, did he so? I charge you, go with me.   120
EMIL. Fie, fie upon thee, strumpet!
BIAN. I am no strumpet, but of life as honest
    As you that thus abuse me.
EMIL.   As I! Foh! Fie upon thee!
IAGO. Kind gentlemen, let's go see poor Cassio dressed.°
    Come, mistress, you must tell 's another tale.   125
    Emilia, run you to the citadel,
    And tell my lord and lady what hath happed!
    Will you go on? I pray. [*Aside*] This is the night
    That either makes me or fordoes° me quite. [*Exeunt*]

SCENE II. *A bedchamber in the castle.*
DESDEMONA *in bed asleep, a light burning.*

Enter OTHELLO.

OTH. It is the cause,° it is the cause, my soul.
    Let me not name it to you, you chaste stars!
    It is the cause. Yet I'll not shed her blood,
    Nor scar that whiter skin of hers than snow
    And smooth as monumental alabaster.°   5
    Yet she must die, else she'll betray more men.
    Put out the light, and then put out the light.
    If I quench thee, thou flaming minister,°
    I can again thy former light restore,
    Should I repent me. But once put out thy light,   10
    Thou cunning'st° pattern of excelling nature,

---

124. dressed: i.e., his wound dressed. **129. fordoes:** ruins.
    Sc. ii: **1. It . . . cause:** The meaning of the opening lines of this speech has been much discussed. The *cause* is Desdemona's supposed faithlessness; Othello, at this moment, sees himself as embodied vengeance, the venger of man betrayed by woman. **5. monumental alabaster:** Alabaster is white translucent stone, much used for memorial effigies on Elizabethan tombs. **8. minister:** servant. **11. cunning'st:** most skillfully made.

I know not where is that Promethean heat°
That can thy light relume.° When I have plucked the rose,
I cannot give it vital growth again,
It needs must wither. I'll smell it on the tree. [*Kissing her*]   15
Ah, balmy breath, that dost almost persuade
Justice to break her sword! One more, one more.
Be thus when thou art dead, and I will kill thee,
And love thee after. One more, and this the last.
So sweet was ne'er so fatal. I must weep,   20
But they are cruel tears. This sorrow's heavenly,
It strikes where it doth love. She wakes.
Des. Who's there? Othello?
Oth.   Aye, Desdemona.
Des. Will you come to bed, my lord?
Oth. Have you prayed tonight, Desdemona?   25
Des. Aye, my lord.
Oth. If you bethink yourself of any crime
    Unreconciled as yet to Heaven and grace,
    Solicit for it straight.
Des. Alas, my lord, what may you mean by that?
Oth. Well, do it, and be brief. I will walk by.   30
    I would not kill thy unprepparèd spirit.
    No, Heaven forfend!° I would not kill thy soul.°
Des. Talk you of killing?
Oth. Aye, I do.
Des. Then Heaven have mercy on me!
Oth. Amen, with all my heart!
Des. If you say so, I hope you will not kill me.   35
Oth. Hum!
Des. And yet I fear you, for you are fatal° then
    When your eyes roll so. Why I should fear I know not,
    Since guiltiness I know not, but yet I feel I fear.
Oth. Think on thy sins.
Des.   They are loves I bear to you.   40
Oth. Aye, and for that thou diest.
Des. That death's unnatural that kills for loving.
    Alas, why gnaw you so your nether lip?
    Some bloody passion shakes your very frame.
    These are portents,° but yet I hope, I hope,   45
    They do not point on me.

---

12. Promethean heat: fire from Heaven. Prometheus stole fire from Heaven and first gave it to man. **13. relume:** relight. **27–32. If . . . soul:** Othello will be a merciful murderer. **32. forfend:** forbid. **37. fatal:** deadly. **45. portents:** signs foretelling disaster.

OTH.   Peace, and be still!

DES. I will so. What's the matter?

OTH. That handkerchief which I so loved and gave thee
  Thou gavest to Cassio.

DES.   No, by my life and soul!
  Send for the man, and ask him.

OTH.   Sweet soul, take heed,   50
  Take heed of perjury, thou art on thy deathbed.

DES. Aye, but not yet to die.

OTH.   Yes, presently.°
  Therefore confess thee freely of thy sin,
  For to deny each article with oath
  Cannot remove nor choke the strong conception°   55
  That I do groan withal. Thou art to die.

DES. Then Lord have mercy on me!

OTH.   I say amen.

DES. And have you mercy too! I never did
  Offend you in my life, never loved Cassio
  But with such general warranty° of Heaven   60
  As I might love. I never gave him token.

OTH. By Heaven, I saw my handkerchief in 's hand.
  O perjured woman! Thou dost stone° my heart,
  And makest me call what I intend to do
  A murder, which I thought a sacrifice.   65
  I saw the handkerchief.

DES.   He found it, then,
  I never gave it him. Send for him hither.
  Let him confess a truth.

OTH.   He hath confessed.

DES. What, my lord?

OTH. That he hath used thee.

DES.   How? Unlawfully?   70

OTH. Aye.

DES. He will not say so.

OTH.   No, his mouth is stopped.
  Honest Iago hath ta'en order for 't.

DES. Oh, my fear interprets! What, is he dead?

OTH. Had all his hairs been lives, my great revenge
  Had stomach for them all.   75

DES. Alas, he is betrayed, and I undone!

OTH. Out, strumpet! Weep'st thou for him to my face?

DES. Oh, banish me, my lord, but kill me not!

---

52. presently: at once. **55. conception:** thought. **60. warranty:** permission. **63. stone:** turn to stone.

OTH. Down, strumpet!

DES. Kill me tomorrow, let me live tonight! 80

OTH. Nay, if you strive——

DES. But half an hour!

OTH.   Being done, there is no pause.

DES. But while I say one prayer!

OTH.   It is too late. [*He stifles her*]

EMIL. [*Within*] My lord, my lord! What ho! My lord, my lord!

OTH. What noise is this! Not dead? Not yet quite dead? 85
    I that am cruel am yet merciful,
    I would not have thee linger in thy pain.
    So, so.

EMIL. [*Within*] What ho! My lord, my lord!

OTH.   Who's there?

EMIL. [*Within*] Oh, good my lord, I would speak a word with you! 90

OTH. Yes, 'tis Emilia. By and by. She's dead.
    'Tis like she comes to speak of Cassio's death.
    The noise was here. Ha! No more moving?
    Still as the grave. Shall she come in? Were 't good?
    I think she stirs again. No. What's best to do? 95
    If she come in, she'll sure speak to my wife.
    My wife! My wife! What wife? I have no wife.
    Oh, insupportable! Oh, heavy hour!
    Methinks it should be now a huge eclipse
    Of sun and moon, and that the affrighted globe 100
    Should yawn at alteration.°

EMIL.   [*Within*] I do beseech you
    That I may speak with you, O good my lord!

OTH. I had forgot thee. Oh, come in, Emilia.
    Soft, by and by. Let me the curtains° draw.
    Where art thou? [*Unlocks the door*] 105
    [*Enter* EMILIA] What's the matter with thee now?

EMIL. Oh, my good lord, yonder 's foul murders done!

OTH. What, now?

EMIL. But now, my lord.

OTH. It is the very error° of the moon.
    She comes more nearer earth than she was wont 110
    And makes men mad.

EMIL. Cassio, my lord, hath killed a young Venetian
    Called Roderigo.

OTH.   Roderigo killed!
    And Cassio killed!

---

101. **yawn at alteration:** gape with wonder at some monstrous change. 104. **curtains:** i.e., of the bed. 109. **error:** wandering out of her proper course.

EMIL.   No, Cassio is not killed.
OTH. Not Cassio killed! Then murder's out of tune,   115
    And sweet revenge grows harsh.
DES. Oh, falsely, falsely murdered!
EMIL.   Alas, what cry is that?
OTH. That! What?
EMIL. Out and alas! That was my lady's voice.
    Help! Help, ho! Help! O lady, speak again!   120
    Sweet Desdemona! O sweet mistress, speak!
DES. A guiltless death I die.
EMIL. Oh, who hath done this deed?
DES. Nobody, I myself. Farewell.
    Commend me to my kind lord. Oh, farewell! [*Dies*]   125
OTH. Why, how should she be murdered?
EMIL. Alas, who knows?
OTH. You heard her say herself it was not I.
EMIL. She said so. I must needs report the truth.
OTH. She's like a liar gone to burning Hell.
    'Twas I that killed her.
EMIL.   Oh, the more angel she,   130
    And you the blacker devil!
OTH. She turned to folly,° and she was a whore.
EMIL. Thou dost belie her, and thou art a devil.
OTH. She was false as water.
EMIL.   Thou art rash as fire to say
    That she was false. Oh, she was heavenly true!   135
OTH. Cassio did top her, ask thy husband else.
    Oh, I were damned beneath all depth in Hell
    But that I did proceed upon just grounds
    To this extremity. Thy husband knew it all.
EMIL. My husband!   140
OTH. Thy husband.
EMIL. That she was false to wedlock?
OTH. Aye, with Cassio. Nay, had she been true,
    If Heaven would make me such another world
    Of one entire and perfect chrysolite,°   145
    I'd not have sold her for it.
EMIL. My husband!
OTH.   Aye, 'twas he that told me first.
    An honest man he is, and hates the slime
    That sticks on filthy deeds.
EMIL.   My husband!

---

132. folly: lewdness. 145. chrysolite: a semiprecious stone, usually green in color.

OTH. What needs this iteration,° woman? I say thy husband.   150
EMIL. Oh, mistress, villainy hath made mocks with love!
    My husband say that she was false!
OTH.   He, woman.
    I say thy husband. Dost understand the word?
    My friend, thy husband, honest, honest Iago.
EMIL. If he say so, may his pernicious soul   155
    Rot half a grain a day! He lies to the heart.
    She was too fond of her most filthy bargain.
OTH. Ha!
EMIL. Do thy worst.
    This deed of thine is no more worthy Heaven   160
    Than thou wast worthy her.
OTH.   Peace, you were best.
EMIL. Thou hast not half that power to do me harm
    As I have to be hurt. O gull!° O dolt!°
    As ignorant as dirt! Thou hast done a deed——
    I care not for thy sword, I'll make thee known,   165
    Though I lost twenty lives. Help! Help, ho! Help!
    The Moor hath killed my mistress! Murder! Murder!

     Enter MONTANO, GRATIANO, IAGO, *and others.*

MON. What is the matter? How now, General!
EMIL. Oh, are you come, Iago? You have done well,
    That men must lay their murders on your neck.   170
GRA. What is the matter?
EMIL. Disprove this villain, if thou be'st a man.
    He says thou told'st him that his wife was false.
    I know thou didst not, thou'rt not such a villain.
    Speak, for my heart is full.   175
IAGO. I told him what I thought, and told no more
    Than what he found himself was apt° and true.
EMIL. But did you ever tell him she was false?
IAGO. I did.
EMIL. You told a lie, an odious, damnèd lie,   180
    Upon my soul, a lie, a wicked lie!
    She false with Cassio! Did you say with Cassio?
IAGO. With Cassio, mistress. Go to, charm your tongue.°
EMIL. I will not charm my tongue, I am bound to speak.
    My mistress here lies murdered in her bed.   185
ALL. Oh, Heavens forfend!
EMIL. And your reports have set the murder on.

---

150. iteration: repetition. 163. gull: dupe. dolt: dull-witted ass. 177. apt: likely. 183. charm . . . tongue: be silent.

OTH. Nay, stare not, masters. It is true indeed.

GRA. 'Tis a strange truth.

MON. Oh, monstrous act!

EMIL.   Villainy, villainy, villainy!   190
    I think upon 't. I think I smell 't. Oh, villainy!
    I thought so then.° I'll kill myself for grief.
    Oh, villainy, villainy!

IAGO. What, are you mad? I charge you, get you home.

EMIL. Good gentlemen, let me have leave to speak.   195
    'Tis proper I obey him, but not now.
    Perchance, Iago, I will ne'er go home.

OTH. Oh! Oh! Oh! [*Falling on the bed*]

EMIL.   Nay, lay thee down and roar,
    For thou hast killed the sweetest innocent
    That e'er did lift up eye.

OTH.   [*Rising*] Oh, she was foul!   200
    I scarce did know you, Uncle. There lies your niece,
    Whose breath indeed these hands have newly stopped.
    I know this act shows horrible and grim.

GRA. Poor Desdemona! I am glad thy father's dead.
    Thy match was mortal° to him, and pure grief   205
    Shore his old thread in twain.° Did he live now,
    This sight would make him do a desperate turn—
    Yea, curse his better angel from his side,
    And fall to reprobation.°

OTH. 'Tis pitiful, but yet Iago knows   210
    That she with Cassio hath the act of shame
    A thousand times committed. Cassio confessed it.
    And she did gratify his amorous works
    With that recognizance° and pledge of love
    Which I first gave her, I saw it in his hand.   215
    It was a handkerchief, an antique token
    My father gave my mother.

EMIL. Oh, Heaven! Oh, heavenly powers!

IAGO. 'Zounds! Hold your peace.

EMIL.   'Twill out, 'twill out. I peace!
    No, I will speak as liberal as the north.°   220
    Let Heaven and men and devils, let them all,
    All, all, cry shame against me, yet I'll speak.

IAGO. Be wise, and get you home.

----

192. **I . . . then:** i.e., I suspected this earlier—as for example when Iago took the handkerchief. See III.iii.313. **205. match . . . mortal:** i.e., grief at this marriage killed him. **206. Shore . . . twain:** cut his thread of life in two. **209. reprobation:** damnation; i.e., by self-murder. **214. recognizance:** badge, token. **220. liberal . . . north:** as freely as the north wind, which is loud and bitter.

EMIL.   I will not. [IAGO *offers to stab* EMILIA]
GRA.   Fie!
    Your sword upon a woman!
EMIL. O thou dull Moor! That handkerchief thou speak'st of   225
    I found by fortune and did give my husband,
    For often with a solemn earnestness,
    More than indeed belonged to such a trifle,
    He begged of me to steal it.
IAGO.   Villainous whore!
EMIL. She give it Cassio! No, alas, I found it,   230
    And I did give 't my husband.
IAGO.   Filth, thou liest!
EMIL. By Heaven, I do not, I do not, gentlemen.
    Oh, murderous coxcomb!° What should such a fool
    Do with so good a wife?
OTH.   Are there no stones° in Heaven
    But what serve for the thunder? Precious villain! [*He runs at* IAGO. 235
    IAGO, *from behind, stabs* EMILIA, *and exit*]
GRA. The woman falls. Sure, he hath killed his wife.
EMIL. Aye, aye. Oh, lay me by my mistress' side.
GRA. He's gone, but his wife's killed.
MON. 'Tis a notorious villain. Take you this weapon,
    Which I have here recovered from the Moor.   240
    Come, guard the door without, let him not pass,
    But kill him rather. I'll after that same villain,
    For 'tis a damnèd slave. [*Exeunt all but* OTHELLO *and* EMILIA]
OTH.   I am not valiant neither.
    But every puny whipster° gets my sword.
    But why should honor outlive honesty?   245
    Let it go all.
EMIL.   What did thy song bode, lady?
    Hark, canst thou hear me? I will play the swan,
    And die in music.° [*Singing*]
                 "Willow, willow, willow."
    Moor, she was chaste. She loved thee, cruel Moor,
    So come my soul to bliss as I speak true.   250
    So speaking as I think, I die, I die. [*Dies*]
OTH. I have another weapon in this chamber.
    It is a sword of Spain,° the ice brook's temper.°—
    Oh, here it is. Uncle, I must come forth.

---

233. coxcomb: conceited fool. **234. stones:** thunderbolts. **244. whipster:** whippersnapper. **247–48. play . . . music:** i.e., I will sing at my death. It was believed that swans sang once only, just before they died. **253. sword of Spain:** Spanish swords and rapiers, from Toledo or Bilbao, were famous. **ice . . . temper:** hardened in ice-cold water.

GRA. [*Within*] If thou attempt it, it will cost thee dear.   255
    Thou hast no weapon, and perforce must suffer.
OTH. Look in upon me then, and speak with me,
    Or, naked° as I am, I will assault thee.

        Re-enter GRATIANO.

GRA. What is the matter?
OTH.   Behold, I have a weapon,
    A better never did itself sustain   260
    Upon a soldier's thigh. I have seen the day
    That with this little arm and this good sword
    I have made my way through more impediments
    Than twenty times your stop. But, oh, vain boast!
    Who can control his fate? 'Tis not so now.   265
    Be not afraid, though you do see me weaponed.
    Here is my journey's end, here is my butt°
    And very sea mark of my utmost sail.°
    Do you go back dismayed? 'Tis a lost fear.
    Man but a rush° against Othello's breast,   270
    And he retires. Where should Othello go?
    Now, how dost thou look now? O ill-starred wench!
    Pale as thy smock! When we shall meet at compt,°
    This look of thine will hurl my soul from Heaven
    And fiends will snatch at it. Cold, cold, my girl!   275
    Even like thy chastity. Oh, cursèd slave!
    Whip me, ye devils,
    From the possession of this heavenly sight!
    Blow me about in winds! Roast me in sulphur!
    Wash me in steep-down gulfs° of liquid fire!   280
    O Desdemona! Desdemona! Dead!
    Oh! Oh! Oh!

        Enter LODOVICO, MONTANO, CASSIO *carried in a chair, and* OFFICERS
        with IAGO, *prisoner.*

LOD. Where is this rash and most unfortunate man?
OTH. That's he that was Othello. Here I am.
LOD. Where is that viper? Bring the villain forth.   285
OTH. I look down toward his feet,° but that's a fable.
    If that thou be'st a devil,° I cannot kill thee. [*Wounds* IAGO]
LOD. Wrench his sword from him.

---

258. naked: unarmed. **267. butt:** aim. **268. And . . . sail:** the mark that I have reached the end of my voyage. **sea mark:** a conspicuous object by which the mariner checks his course. **270. Man . . . rush:** attack with only a reed. **273. compt:** account; i.e., the Day of Judgment. **280. steep-down gulfs:** sheer whirlpools. **286. toward . . . feet:** i.e., to see if he has the cloven hoof of a devil. **287. If . . . devil:** if you are an evil spirit and no man.

IAGO.   I bleed, sir, but not killed.
OTH. I am not sorry neither. I'd have thee live,
    For, in my sense, 'tis happiness to die.   290
LOD. O thou Othello, that wert once so good,
    Fall'n in the practice° of a damnèd slave,
    What shall be said to thee?
OTH.   Why, anything.
    An honorable murderer, if you will,
    For naught did I in hate, but all in honor.   295
LOD. This wretch hath part confessed his villainy.
    Did you and he consent in Cassio's death?
OTH. Aye.
CAS. Dear General, I never gave you cause.
OTH. I do believe it, and I ask your pardon.   300
    Will you, I pray, demand that demidevil
    Why he hath thus ensnared my soul and body?
IAGO. Demand me nothing. What you know, you know.
    From this time forth I never will speak word.
LOD. What, not to pray?
GRA.   Torments will ope your lips.   305
OTH. Well, thou dost best.
LOD. Sir, you shall understand what hath befall'n,
    Which, as I think, you know not. Here is a letter
    Found in the pocket of the slain Roderigo,
    And here another. The one of them imports   310
    The death of Cassio to be undertook
    By Roderigo.
OTH. Oh, villain!
CAS.   Most heathenish and most gross!
LOD. Now here's another discontented paper,
    Found in his pocket too. And this, it seems,   315
    Roderigo meant to have sent this damnèd villain
    But that, belike, Iago in the interim
    Came in and satisfied him.
OTH.   Oh, the pernicious caitiff!
    How came you, Cassio, by that handkerchief
    That was my wife's?
CAS.   I found it in my chamber.   320
    And he himself confessed but even now
    That there he dropped it for a special purpose
    Which wrought to his desire.
OTH.   O fool! Fool! Fool!

---

292. Fall'n . . . practice: destroyed by the plotting.

CAS. There is besides in Roderigo's letter
　　How he upbraids Iago, that he made him　　　　　　　　325
　　Brave° me upon the watch, whereon it came
　　That I was cast.° And even but now he spake
　　After long seeming dead, Iago hurt him,
　　Iago set him on.
LOD. You must forsake this room, and go with us.　　　　330
　　Your power and your command is taken off,
　　And Cassio rules in Cyprus. For this slave,
　　If there be any cunning cruelty
　　That can torment him much and hold him long,°
　　It shall be his. You shall close prisoner rest　　　　335
　　Till that the nature of your fault be known
　　To the Venetian state. Come, bring away.
OTH. Soft you,° a word or two before you go.
　　I have done the state some service, and they know 't.
　　No more of that. I pray you, in your letters,　　　　340
　　When you shall these unlucky deeds relate,
　　Speak of me as I am, nothing extenuate,
　　Nor set down aught in malice. Then must you speak
　　Of one that loved not wisely but too well,
　　Of one not easily jealous, but, being wrought,　　　　345
　　Perplexed in the extreme, of one whose hand,
　　Like the base Indian, threw a pearl away
　　Richer than all his tribe°—of one whose subdued eyes,
　　Albeit unusèd to the melting mood,
　　Drop tears as fast as the Arabian trees　　　　　　　350
　　Their medicinal gum. Set you down this,
　　And say besides that in Aleppo once,
　　Where a malignant and a turbaned Turk
　　Beat a Venetian and traduced° the state,
　　I took by the throat the circumcisèd dog　　　　　　355
　　And smote him, thus. [Stabs himself]
LOD. Oh, bloody period!
GRA. 　　　　　　　　All that's spoke is marred.°
OTH. I kissed thee ere I killed thee. No way but this,
　　Killing myself, to die upon a kiss. [Falls on the bed, and dies]
CAS. This did I fear, but thought he had no weapon.　　360
　　For he was great of heart.

---

326. **Brave:** dare, insult. **327. cast:** dismissed. **334. hold . . . long:** i.e., in dying. **338. Soft you:** pause awhile. **347–48. base . . . tribe:** A much discussed passage. F1 reads "Iudean" (Judean), and if correct it would refer to Judas Iscariot, who betrayed Jesus. Shakespeare does not elsewhere use the word "Judean," and he does associate India with pearls. **354. traduced:** insulted. **357. marred:** spoiled.

LOD.   [*To* IAGO] O Spartan° dog,
    More fell° than anguish, hunger, or the sea!
    Look on the tragic loading° of this bed,
    This is thy work. The object poisons sight,
    Let it be hid.° Gratiano, keep the house,   365
    And seize upon the fortunes of the Moor,
    For they succeed on you. To you, Lord Governor,
    Remains the censure of this hellish villain,
    The time, the place, the torture.
    Oh, enforce it!   370
    Myself will straight aboard, and to the state
    This heavy act with heavy heart relate. [*Exeunt*]

---

361. **Spartan:** i.e., hardhearted. 362. **fell:** cruel. 363. **loading:** burden—the bodies of Desdemona and Othello. 365. **Let . . . hid:** At these words the curtains are closed across the inner stage (or chamber, if this scene was acted aloft), concealing all three bodies.

Considerations

Othello is a profoundly moving tragedy. It is a tragedy in the classic sense, that is, a play centered on a person of great proportions, of great ambitions with much at stake, but a person with a tragic flaw. From this flaw comes his downfall. Scholars differ on what Othello's flaw is; it seems manifold, but it seems to involve trust and the consequences due to the lack of it—jealousy. Maybe Othello doesn't know women, maybe he relies too much on suggestions planted by other people, but no matter how you account for it, the flaw exists.

Yet not only is this a classic tragedy, it is a tragedy of very human proportions. The characters may be noble and great military figures, but on a personal level they are men and women. What are the major figures like? Iago is sinister from the outset of the play. He is vindictive, mean, and evil through and through.

Desdemona is not just pure sweetness, although she's been looked at that way sometimes. She too has a will of her own, and it becomes obvious in her conflict with her father. She is capable of deceiving him. Later she manages to get her way with Othello—unfortunately, as it turns out. But she's young, struck by adventure, by pomp and circumstance, and she loves Othello.

Othello is a Moor dealing with Venetians, an unsophisticated man in the middle of sophisticates, a military man of action in the middle of people known for subtlety and guile. His background simply hasn't equipped him for this experience.

Out of just who these people actually are comes the inevitable unfolding action of the play. All it takes is one small pebble to start the landslide, and in this case the pebble is that Cassio has been promoted above Iago. The preference shown may have had good reasons despite the fact that Iago was proven a good military strategist. But regardless of its merit, that action under these circumstances with these people had catastrophic consequences.

An interesting feature of the play is that Shakespeare shows us the characters first in Venice and then transferred as a group to a military garrison in Cyprus. The isolation of characters is a constantly used device in literature—put a man and woman in a garden together; put a load of people in an airplane; lock a group in a cabin with a storm raging outside—and look at the results. It is not only a literary device but a valid psychological one. Group isolation forces certain behaviors to show up that would not become apparent if outside outlets were available. Here the isolation may not be as harrowing as on a desert isle or an icelocked boat, but it has an effect.

The play is well written, easy to read. The speeches are, for the most part, fairly short. There are beautiful phrases throughout:

> OTHELLO: My story being done, She gave me for my pains a world of sighs. She swore, in faith, 'twas strange, 'twas passing strange, 'twas pitiful, 'twas wondrous pitiful. She wished she had not heard it, yet she wished that Heaven had made her such a man.

> IAGO: The Moor is of a free and open nature that thinks men honest that but seem to be so, And will as tenderly be led by the nose as asses are.

> IAGO: Oh, beware, my lord, of jealousy. It is the green-eyed monster which doth mock the meat it feeds on.

Iago may delight in the fact that he thinks he knows Othello's weakness, that Othello believes people are what they seem. Desdemona too thinks she knows Othello, until she finds out she doesn't know him at all. And we suspect Othello doesn't know himself until it is too late. In the touching scene in which he kills her, Othello says, "I must put out the light and then put out the light" (extinguish the candle and then forever part with his loved one). This murder is a result of many things to which he responds according to an almost military sense of honor and a rigid code. Then he discovers the truth—not only who Desdemona is, but who he is. And then the murder can't be undone.

In what way does this speak to me? I'm not going to kill anybody; I'm not a general. What does it say to me? We're pretty hopelessly naive if we think we understand all about our lives. No one could have been more sure of that than either Desdemona or Othello. Yet how tragically mistaken they were. On something of less than tragic proportions we must admit that we don't know all about ourselves. So we shouldn't assume too much. It's humbling reading this. It pleads for a better understanding of others. If Desdemona had been more understanding, but more particularly if Othello had been more trusting of her, less of Iago, and perhaps had asked a few more questions, it could have been avoided. (As for Iago, he's almost too sinister to see any way of reforming *him*.)

Othello is a play that is generally thought of as being about love. One of the most famous lines is, "who loved not wisely but too well." Certainly all kinds of love enter in: paternal love, filial love, love of power, love of adventure, love of family, love of revenge and sinister ways. Iago loves himself and his own crafty mind. He does delight in the fact that he thinks he knows Othello's faults ("I'm going to get him because he thinks people are what they seem to be"). Othello loves who he is and what he's been. He loves military life and the camaraderie. He clearly loves Desdemona. He loves straightforwardness. All of these things are still around today. There is nothing antiquated about them.

Miss Julie

August Strindberg

CHARACTERS

MISS JULIE, *aged 25*
JEAN, *the valet, aged 30*
KRISTIN, *the cook, aged 35*

Scene: The large kitchen of a Swedish manor house in a country district in the eighties.
Midsummer eve.
The kitchen has three doors, two small ones into JEAN'S *and* KRISTIN'S *bedrooms, and a large, glass-fronted double one, opening on to a courtyard. This is the only way to the rest of the house.*
Through these glass doors can be seen part of a fountain with a cupid, lilac bushes in flower and the tops of some Lombardy poplars. On one wall are shelves edged with scalloped paper on which are kitchen utensils of copper, iron and tin.
To the left is the corner of a large tiled range and part of its chimney-hood, to the right the end of the servants' dinner table with chairs beside it.
The stove is decorated with birch boughs, the floor strewn with twigs of juniper. On the end of the table is a large Japanese spice jar full of lilac.
There are also an ice-box, a scullery table and a sink. Above the double door hangs a big old-fashioned bell; near it is a speaking-tube.
A fiddle can be heard from the dance in the barn near-by. KRISTIN *is standing at the stove, frying something in a pan. She wears a light-coloured cotton dress and a big apron.*
JEAN enters, wearing livery and carrying a pair of large riding-boots with spurs, which he puts in a conspicuous place.

JEAN. Miss Julie's crazy again to-night, absolutely crazy.
KRISTIN. Oh, so you're back, are you?
JEAN. When I'd taken the Count to the station, I came back and dropped in at the Barn for a dance. And who did I see there but our young lady leading off with the gamekeeper. But the moment she sets eyes

on me, up she rushes and invites me to waltz with her. And how she waltzed—I've never seen anything like it! She's crazy.

KRISTIN. Always has been, but never so bad as this last fortnight since the engagement was broken off.

JEAN. Yes, that was a pretty business, to be sure. He's a decent enough chap, too, even if he isn't rich. Oh, but they're choosy! [*Sits down at the end of the table*] In any case, it's a bit odd that our young—er—lady would rather stay at home with the yokels than go with her father to visit her relations.

KRISTIN. Perhaps she feels a bit awkward, after that bust-up with her fiancé.

JEAN. Maybe. That chap had some guts, though. Do you know the sort of thing that was going on, Kristin? I saw it with my own eyes, though I didn't let on I had.

KRISTIN. You saw them . . . ?

JEAN. Didn't I just! Came across the pair of them one evening in the stable-yard. Miss Julie was doing was she called "training" him. Know what that was? Making him jump over her riding-whip—the way you teach a dog. He did it twice and got a cut each time for his pains, but when it came to the third go, he snatched the whip out of her hand and broke it into smithereens. And then he cleared off.

KRISTIN. What goings on! I never did!

JEAN. Well, that's how it was with that little affair . . . Now, what have you got for me, Kristin? Something tasty?

KRISTIN [*Serving from the pan to his plate*] Well, it's just a little bit of kidney I cut off their joint.

JEAN [*Smelling it*] Fine! That's my special delice. [*Feels the plate*] But you might have warmed the plate.

KRISTIN. When you choose to be finicky you're worse than the Count himself. [*Pulls his hair affectionately*]

JEAN [*Crossly*] Stop pulling my hair. You know how sensitive I am.

KRISTIN. There, there! It's only love, you know.

JEAN *eats.* KRISTIN *brings a bottle of beer.*

JEAN. Beer on Midsummer Eve? No thanks! I've got something better than that. [*From a drawer in the table brings out a bottle of red wine with a yellow seal*] Yellow seal, see! Now get me a glass. You use a glass with a stem of course when you're drinking it straight.

KRISTIN [*Giving him a wine-glass*] Lord help the woman who gets you for a husband, you old fusser! [*She puts the beer in the ice-box and sets a small saucepan on the stove*]

JEAN. Nonsense! You'll be glad enough to get a fellow as smart as me. And I don't think it's done you any harm people calling me your fiancé. [*Tastes the wine*] Good. Very good indeed. But not quite warmed enough. [*Warms the glass in his hand*] We bought this in Dijon. Four francs the litre without the bottle, and duty on top of that. What are you cooking now? It stinks.

KRISTIN. Some bloody muck Miss Julie wants for Diana.

JEAN. You should be more refined in your speech, Kristin. But why should you spend a holiday cooking for that bitch? Is she sick or what?

KRISTIN. Yes, she's sick. She sneaked out with the pug at the lodge and got in the usual mess. And that, you know, Miss Julie won't have.

JEAN. Miss Julie's too high-and-mighty in some respects, and not enough in others, just like her mother before her. The countess was more at home in the kitchen and cowsheds than anywhere else, but would she ever go driving with only one horse? She went round with her cuffs filthy, but she had to have the coronet on the cuff-links. Our young lady—to come back to her—hasn't any proper respect for herself or her position. I mean she isn't refined. In the barn just now she dragged the gamekeeper away from Anna and made him dance with her—no waiting to be asked. We wouldn't do a thing like that. But that's what happens when the gentry try to behave like the common people—they become common . . . Still she's a fine girl. Smashing! What shoulders! and what—er—etcetera!

KRISTIN. Oh come off it! I know what Clara says, and she dresses her.

JEAN. Clara? Pooh, you're all jealous! But I've been out riding with her . . . and as for her dancing!

KRISTIN. Listen, Jean. You will dance with me, won't you, as soon as I'm through.

JEAN. Of course I will.

KRISTIN. Promise?

JEAN. Promise? When I say I'll do a thing I do it. Well, thanks for the supper. It was a real treat. [*Corks the bottle*]

JULIE *appears in the doorway, speaking to someone outside.*

JULIE. I'll be back in a moment. Don't wait.

JEAN *slips the bottle into the drawer and rises respectfully.* JULIE *enters and joins* KRISTIN *at the stove.*

Well, have you made it? [KRISTIN *signs that* JEAN *is near them*]

JEAN [*Gallantly*] Have you ladies got some secret?

JULIE [*Flipping his face with her handkerchief*] You're very inquisitive.

JEAN. What a delicious smell! Violets.

JULIE [*Coquettishly*] Impertinence! Are you an expert of scent too? I must say you know how to dance. Now don't look. Go away. [*The music of a schottische begins*]

JEAN [*With impudent politeness*] Is it some witches' brew you're cooking on Midsummer Eve? Something to tell your stars by, so you can see your future?

JULIE [*Sharply*] If you could see that you'd have good eyes. [*To* KRISTIN] Put it in a bottle and cork it tight. Come and dance this schottische with me, Jean.

JEAN [*Hesitating*] I don't want to be rude, but I've promised to dance this one with Kristin.

JULIE. Well, she can have another, can't you, Kristin? You'll lend me Jean, won't you?

KRISTIN [*Bottling*] It's nothing to do with me. When you're so condescending, Miss, it's not his place to say no. Go on, Jean, and thank Miss Julie for the honour.

JEAN. Frankly speaking, Miss, and no offence meant, I wonder if it's wise for you to dance twice running with the same partner, specially as those people are so ready to jump to conclusions.

JULIE [*Flaring up*] What did you say? What sort of conclusions? What do you mean?

JEAN [*Meekly*] As you choose not to understand, Miss Julie, I'll have to speak more plainly. It looks bad to show a preference for one of your retainers when they're all hoping for the same unusual favour.

JULIE. Show a preference! The very idea! I'm surprised at you. I'm doing the people an honour by attending their ball when I'm mistress of the house, but if I'm really going to dance, I mean to have a partner who can lead and doesn't make me look ridiculous.

JEAN. If those are your orders, Miss, I'm at your service.

JULIE [*Gently*] Don't take it as an order. To-night we're all just people enjoying a party. There's no question of class. So now give me your arm. Don't worry, Kristin. I shan't steal your sweetheart.

> JEAN *gives* JULIE *his arm and leads her out.*
> *Left alone,* KRISTIN *plays her scene in an unhurried, natural way, humming to the tune of the schottische, played on a distant violin. She clears* JEAN's *place, washes up and puts things away, then takes off her apron, brings out a small mirror from a drawer, props it against the jar of lilac, lights a candle, warms a small pair of tongs and curls her fringe. She goes to the door and listens, then turning back to the table finds* MISS JULIE's *forgotten handkerchief. She smells it, then meditatively smooths it out and folds it.*
> *Enter* JEAN.

JEAN. She really *is* crazy. What a way to dance! With people standing grinning at her too from behind the doors. What's got into her, Kristin?

KRISTIN. Oh, it's just her time coming on. She's always queer then. Are you going to dance with me now?

JEAN. Then you're not wild with me for cutting that one.

KRISTIN. You know I'm not—for a little thing like that. Besides, I know my place.

JEAN [*Putting his arm round her waist*] You're a sensible girl, Kristin, and you'll make a very good wife . . .

    Enter JULIE, *unpleasantly surprised.*

JULIE [*With forced gaiety*] You're a fine beau—running away from your partner.

JEAN. Not away, Miss Julie, but as you see back to the one I deserted.

JULIE [*Changing her tone*] You really can dance, you know. But why are you wearing your livery on a holiday? Take it off at once.

JEAN. Then I must ask you to go away for a moment, Miss. My black coat's here. [*Indicates it hanging on the door to his room*]

JULIE. Are you so shy of me——just over changing a coat? Go into your room then—or stay here and I'll turn my back.

JEAN. Excuse me then, Miss. [*He goes to his room and is partly visible as he changes his coat*]

JULIE. Tell me, Kristin, is Jean your fiancé? You seem very intimate.

KRISTIN. My fiancé? Yes, if you like. We call it that.

JULIE. Call it?

KRISTIN. Well, you've had a fiancé yourself, Miss, and . . .

JULIE. But we really were engaged.

KRISTIN. All the same it didn't come to anything.

    JEAN *returns in his black coat.*

JULIE. Très gentil, Monsieur Jean. Très gentil.

JEAN. Vous voulez plaisanter, Madame.

JULIE. Et vous voulez parler français. Where did you learn it?

JEAN. In Switzerland, when I was sommelier at one of the biggest hotels in Lucerne.

JULIE. You look quite the gentleman in that get-up. Charming. [*Sit at the table*]

JEAN. Oh, you're just flattering me!

JULIE [*Annoyed*] Flattering you?

JEAN. I'm too modest to believe you would pay real compliments to a man like me, so I must take it you are exaggerating—that this is what's known as flattery.

JULIE. Where on earth did you learn to make speeches like that? Perhaps you've been to the theatre a lot.

JEAN. That's right. And travelled a lot too.

JULIE. But you come from this neighbourhood, don't you?

JEAN. Yes, my father was a labourer on the next estate—the District

Attorney's place. I often used to see you, Miss Julie, when you were little, though you never noticed me.

JULIE. Did you really?

JEAN. Yes. One time specially I remember . . . but I can't tell you about that.

JULIE. Oh do! Why not? This is just the time.

JEAN. No, I really can't now. Another time perhaps.

JULIE. Another time means never. What harm in now?

JEAN. No harm, but I'd rather not. [*Points to* KRISTIN, *now fast asleep*] Look at her.

JULIE. She'll make a charming wife, won't she? I wonder if she snores.

JEAN. No, she doesn't, but she talks in her sleep.

JULIE [*Cynically*] How do you know she talks in her sleep?

JEAN [*Brazenly*] I've heard her. [*Pause. They look at one another*]

JULIE. Why don't you sit down?

JEAN. I can't take such a liberty in your presence.

JULIE. Supposing I order you to.

JEAN. I'll obey.

JULIE. Then sit down. No, wait a minute. Will you get me a drink first?

JEAN. I don't know what's in the ice-box. Only beer, I expect.

JULIE. There's no only about it. My taste is so simple I prefer it to wine.

> JEAN *takes a bottle from the ice-box, fetches a glass and plate and serves the beer.*

JEAN. At your service.

JULIE. Thank you. Won't you have some yourself?

JEAN. I'm not really a beer-drinker, but if it's an order . . .

JULIE. Order? I should have thought it was ordinary manners to keep your partner company.

JEAN. That's a good way of putting it. [*He opens another bottle and fetches a glass*]

JULIE. Now drink my health. [*He hesitates*] I believe the man really is shy.

> JEAN *kneels and raises his glass with mock ceremony.*

JEAN. To the health of my lady!

JULIE. Bravo! Now kiss my shoe and everything will be perfect. [*He hesitates, then boldly takes hold of her foot and lightly kisses it*] Splendid. You ought to have been an actor.

JEAN [*Rising*] We can't go on like this, Miss Julie. Someone might come in and see us.

JULIE. Why would that matter?

JEAN. For the simple reason that they'd talk. And if you knew the way their tongues were wagging out there just now, you . . .

JULIE. What were they saying? Tell me. Sit down.

JEAN [*Sitting*] No offence meant, Miss, but . . . well, their language wasn't nice, and they were hinting . . . oh, you know quite well what. You're not a child, and if a lady's seen drinking alone at night with a man—and a servant at that—then . . .

JULIE. Then what? Besides, we're not alone. Kristin's here.

JEAN. Yes, asleep.

JULIE. I'll wake her up. [*Rises*] Kristin, are you asleep? [KRISTIN *mumbles in her sleep*] Kristin! Goodness, how she sleeps!

KRISTIN [*In her sleep*] The Count's boots are cleaned—put the coffee on—yes, yes, at once. . . . [*Mumbles incoherently*]

JULIE [*Tweaking her nose*] Wake up, can't you!

JEAN [*Sharply*] Let her sleep.

JULIE. What?

JEAN. When you've been standing at the stove all day you're likely to be tired at night. And sleep should be respected.

JULIE [*Changing her tone*] What a nice idea. It does you credit. Thank you for it. [*Holds out her hand to him*] Now come out and pick some lilac for me.

During the following KRISTIN *goes sleepily in to her bedroom.*

JEAN. Out with you, Miss Julie?

JULIE. Yes.

JEAN. It wouldn't do. It really wouldn't.

JULIE. I don't know what you mean. You can't possibly imagine that . . .

JEAN. I don't, but others do.

JULIE. What? That I'm in love with the valet?

JEAN. I'm not a conceited man, but such a thing's been known to happen, and to these rustics nothing's sacred.

JULIE. You, I take it, are an aristocrat.

JEAN. Yes, I am.

JULIE. And I am coming down in the world.

JEAN. Don't come down, Miss Julie. Take my advice. No one will believe you came down of your own accord. They'll all say you fell.

JULIE. I have a higher opinion of our people than you. Come and put it to the test. Come on. [*Gazes into his eyes*]

JEAN. You're very strange, you know.

JULIE. Perhaps I am, but so are you. For that matter everything is strange. Life, human beings, everything, just scum drifting about on the water until it sinks—down and down. That reminds me of a dream I sometimes have, in which I'm on top of a pillar and can't see any way of getting down. When I look down I'm dizzy; I have to get down but I haven't the courage to jump. I can't stay there and I long to fall, but I don't fall. There's no respite. There can't be any peace at all for me until I'm down, right down on the ground. And if I did get to the ground I'd want to be under the ground . . . Have you ever felt like that?

JEAN. No. In my dream I'm lying under a great tree in a dark wood. I want to get up, up to the top of it, and look out over the bright landscape where the sun is shining and rob that high nest of its golden eggs. And I climb and climb, but the trunk is so thick and smooth and it's so far to the first branch. But I know if I can once reach that first branch I'll go to the top just as if I'm on a ladder. I haven't reached it yet, but I shall get there, even if only in my dreams.

JULIE. Here I am chattering about dreams with you. Come on. Only into the park. [*She takes his arm and they go towards the door*]

JEAN. We must sleep on nine midsummer flowers tonight; then our dreams will come true, Miss Julie. [*They turn at the door. He has a hand to his eye*]

JULIE. Have you got something in your eye? Let me see.

JEAN. Oh, it's nothing. Just a speck of dust. It'll be gone in a minute.

JULIE. My sleeve must have rubbed against you. Sit down and let me see to it. [*Takes him by the arm and makes him sit down, bends his head back and tries to get the speck out with the corner of her handkerchief*] Keep still now, quite still. [*Slaps his hand*] Do as I tell you. Why, I believe you're trembling, big, strong man though you are! [*Feels his biceps*] What muscles!

JEAN [*Warning*] Miss Julie!

JULIE. Yes, Monsieur Jean?

JEAN. Attention. Je ne suis qu'un homme.

JULIE. Will you stay still! There now. It's out. Kiss my hand and say thank you.

JEAN [*Rising*] Miss Julie, listen. Kristin's gone to bed now. Will you listen?

JULIE. Kiss my hand first.

JEAN. Very well, but you'll have only yourself to blame.

JULIE. For what?

JEAN. For what! Are you still a child at twenty-five? Don't you know it's dangerous to play with fire?

JULIE. Not for me. I'm insured.

JEAN [*Bluntly*] No, you're not. And even if you are, there's still stuff here to kindle a flame.

JULIE. Meaning yourself?

JEAN. Yes. Not because I'm me, but because I'm a man and young and . . .

JULIE. And good-looking? What incredible conceit! A Don Juan perhaps? Or a Joseph? Good Lord, I do believe you are a Joseph!

JEAN. Do you?

JULIE. I'm rather afraid so.

> JEAN *goes up boldly and tries to put his arms round her and kiss her. She boxes his ears.*

How dare you!

JEAN. Was that in earnest or a joke?

JULIE. In earnest.

JEAN. Then what went before was in earnest too. You take your games too seriously and that's dangerous. Anyhow I'm tired of playing now and beg leave to return to my work. The Count will want his boots first thing and it's past midnight now.

JULIE. Put those boots down.

JEAN. No. This is my work, which it's my duty to do. But I never undertook to be your playfellow and I never will be. I consider myself too good for that.

JULIE. You're proud.

JEAN. In some ways—not all.

JULIE. Have you ever been in love?

JEAN. We don't put it that way, but I've been gone on quite a few girls. And once I went sick because I couldn't have the one I wanted. Sick, I mean, like those princes in the Arabian Nights who couldn't eat or drink for love.

JULIE. Who was she? [*No answer*] Who was she?

JEAN. You can't force me to tell you that.

JULIE. If I ask as an equal, ask as a—friend? Who was she?

JEAN. You.

JULIE [*Sitting*] How absurd!

JEAN. Yes, ludicrous if you like. That's the story I wouldn't tell you before, see, but now I will . . . Do you know what the world looks like from below? No, you don't. No more than the hawks and falcons do whose backs one hardly ever sees because they're always soaring up aloft. I lived in a labourer's hovel with seven other children and a pig, out in the grey fields where there isn't a single tree. But from the window I could see the wall round the Count's park with apple-trees above it. That was the Garden of Eden, guarded by many terrible angels with flaming swords. All the same I and the other boys managed to get to the tree of life. Does all this make you despise me?

JULIE. Goodness, all boys steal apples!

JEAN. You say that now, but all the same you do despise me. However, one time I went into the Garden of Eden with my mother to weed the onion beds. Close to the kitchen garden there was a Turkish pavilion hung all over with jasmine and honeysuckle. I hadn't any idea what it was used for, but I'd never seen such a beautiful building. People used to go in and then come out again, and one day the door was left open. I crept up and saw the walls covered with pictures of kings and emperors, and the windows had red curtains with fringes—you know now what the place was, don't you? I. . . . [*Breaks off a piece of lilac and holds it for* JULIE *to smell. As he talks, she takes it from him*] I had never been inside the manor, never seen anything but the church, and this was more beautiful. No matter where my thoughts went, they always came back—to that place. The longing went on growing in me to enjoy it fully, just once. Enfin, I sneaked in, gazed and admired. Then I heard someone coming. There was only one way out for the gentry, but for me there was another and I had no choice but to take it. [JULIE *drops the lilac on the table*] Then I took to my heels, plunged through the raspberry canes, dashed across the strawberry beds and found myself on the rose terrace. There I saw a pink dress and a pair of white stockings—it was you. I crawled into a weed pile and lay there right under it among prickly thistles and damp rank earth. I watched you walking among the roses and said to myself: "If it's true that a thief can get to heaven and be with the angels, it's pretty strange that a labourer's child here on God's earth mayn't come in the park and play with the Count's daughter."

JULIE [*Sentimentally*] Do you think all poor children feel the way you did?

JEAN [*Taken aback, then rallying*] *All* poor children? . . . Yes, of course they do. Of course.

JULIE. It must be terrible to be poor.

JEAN [*With exaggerated distress*] Oh yes, Miss Julie, yes. A dog may lie on the Countess's sofa, a horse may have his nose stroked by a young lady, but a servant. . . . [*Change of tone*] well, yes, now and then you meet one with guts enough to rise in the world, but how often? Anyhow, do you know what I did? Jumped in the millstream with my clothes on, was pulled out and got a hiding. But the next Sunday, when Father and all the rest went to Granny's, I managed to get left behind. Then I washed with soap and hot water, put my best clothes on and went to church so as to see you. I did see you and went home determined to die. But I wanted to die beautifully and peacefully, without any pain. Then I remembered it was dangerous to sleep under an elder bush. We had a big one in full bloom, so I stripped it and climbed into the oats-bin with the flowers. Have you ever noticed how smooth oats are? Soft to touch as human skin . . . Well, I closed the lid and shut my eyes, fell asleep, and when they woke me I was very ill. But I didn't die, as you see. What I meant by all that I don't know. There was no hope of winning you—you were simply a symbol of the hopelessness of ever getting out of the class I was born in.

JULIE. You put things very well, you know. Did you go to school?

JEAN. For a while. But I've read a lot of novels and been to the theatre. Besides, I've heard educated folk talking—that's what's taught me most.

JULIE. Do you stand round listening to what we're saying?

JEAN. Yes, of course. And I've heard quite a bit too! On the carriage box or rowing the boat. Once I heard you, Miss Julie, and one of your young lady friends . . .

JULIE. Oh! Whatever did you hear?

JEAN. Well, it wouldn't be nice to repeat it. And I must say I was pretty startled. I couldn't think where you had learnt such words. Perhaps, at bottom, there isn't as much difference between people as one's led to believe.

JULIE. How dare you! We don't behave as you do when we're engaged.

JEAN [*Looking hard at her*] Are you sure? It's no use making out so innocent to me.

JULIE. The man I gave my love to was a rotter.

JEAN. That's what you always say—afterwards.

JULIE. Always?

JEAN. I think it must be always. I've heard the expression several times in similar circumstances.

JULIE. What circumstances?

JEAN. Like those in question. The last time . . .

JULIE [*Rising*] Stop. I don't want to hear any more.

JEAN. Nor did *she*—curiously enough. May I go to bed now please?

JULIE [*Gently*] Go to bed on Midsummer Eve?

JEAN. Yes. Dancing with that crowd doesn't really amuse me.

JULIE. Get the key of the boathouse and row me out on the lake. I want to see the sun rise.

JEAN. Would that be wise?

JULIE. You sound as though you're frightened for your reputation.

JEAN. Why not? I don't want to be made a fool of, nor to be sent packing without a character when I'm trying to better myself. Besides, I have Kristin to consider.

JULIE. So now it's Kristin.

JEAN. Yes, but it's you I'm thinking about too. Take my advice and go to bed.

JULIE. Am I to take orders from you?

JEAN. Just this once, for your own sake. Please. It's very late and sleepiness goes to one's head and makes one rash. Go to bed. What's more, if my ears don't deceive me, I hear people coming this way. They'll be looking for me, and if they find us here, you're done for.

The Chorus *approaches, singing. During the following dialogue the song is heard in snatches, and in full when the peasants enter.*

Out of the wood two women came,
Tridiri-ralla, tridiri-ra.
The feet of one were bare and cold,
Tridiri-ralla-la.

The other talked of bags of gold,
Tridiri-ralla, tridiri-ra.
But neither had a sou to her name,
Tridiri-ralla-la.

The bridal wreath I give to you,
Tridiri-ralla, tridiri-ra.
But to another, I'll be true,
Tridiri-ralla-la.

JULIE. I know our people and I love them, just as they do me. Let them come. You'll see.

JEAN. No, Miss Julie, they don't love you. They take your food, then spit at it. You must believe me. Listen to them, just listen to what they're singing . . . No, don't listen.

JULIE [*Listening*] What are they singing?

JEAN. They're mocking—you and me.

JULIE. Oh no! How horrible! What cowards!

JEAN. A pack like that's always cowardly. But against such odds there's nothing we can do but run away.

JULIE. Run away? Where to? We can't get out and we can't go in to Kristin's room.

JEAN. Into mine then. Necessity knows no rules. And you can trust me. I really am your true and devoted friend.

JULIE. But supposing . . . supposing they were to look for you in there?

JEAN. I'll bolt the door, and if they try to break in, I'll shoot. Come on. [*Pleading*] Please come.

JULIE [*Tensely*] Do you promise . . . ?

JEAN. I swear!

Julie goes quickly into his room and he excitedly follows her.
Led by the fiddler, the peasants enter in festive attire with flowers in their hats. They put a barrel of beer and a keg of spirits, garlanded with leaves, on the table, fetch glasses and begin to carouse. The scene becomes a ballet. They form a ring and dance and sing and mime: "Out of the wood two women came." Finally they go out, still singing.
Julie comes in alone. She looks at the havoc in the kitchen, wrings her hands, then takes out her powder puff and powders her face.
Jean enters in high spirits.

JEAN. Now you see! And you heard, didn't you? Do you still think it's possible for us to stay here?

JULIE. No, I don't. But what can we do?

JEAN. Run away. Far away. Take a journey.

JULIE. Journey? But where to?

JEAN. Switzerland. The Italian lakes. Ever been there?

JULIE. No. Is it nice?

JEAN. Ah! Eternal summer, oranges, evergreens . . . ah!

JULIE. But what would we do there?

JEAN. I'll start a hotel. First-class accommodation and first-class customers.

JULIE. Hotel?

JEAN. There's life for you. New faces all the time, new languages—no time for nerves or worries, no need to look for something to do—work rolling up of its own accord. Bells ringing night and day, trains whistling, buses coming and going, and all the time gold pieces rolling on to the counter. There's life for you!

JULIE. For *you*. And I?

JEAN. Mistress of the house, ornament of the firm. With your looks, and your style . . . oh, it's bound to be a success! Terrific! You'll sit like a queen in the office and set your slaves in motion by pressing an electric button. The guests will file past your throne and nervously lay their treasure on your table. You've no idea the way people tremble when they get their bills. I'll salt the bills and you'll sugar them with your sweetest smiles. Ah, let's get away from here! [*Produces a time-table*] At once, by the next train. We shall be at Malmö at six-thirty, Hamburg eight-forty next morning, Frankfurt-Basle the following day, and Como by the St. Gothard pass in—let's see—three days. Three days!

JULIE. That's all very well. But Jean, you must give me courage. Tell me you love me. Come and take me in your arms.

JEAN [*Reluctantly*] I'd like to, but I daren't. Not again in this house. I love you—that goes without saying. You can't doubt that, Miss Julie, can you?

JULIE [*Shyly, very feminine*] Miss? Call me Julie. There aren't any barriers between us now. Call me Julie.

JEAN [*Uneasily*] I can't. As long as we're in this house, there *are* barriers between us. There's the past and there's the Count. I've never been so servile to anyone as I am to him. I've only got to see his gloves on a chair to feel small. I've only to hear his bell and I shy like a horse. Even now, when I look at his boots, standing there so proud and stiff, I feel my back beginning to bend. [*Kicks the boots*] It's those old, narrow-minded notions drummed into us as children . . . but they can soon be forgotten. You've only got to get to another country, a republic, and people will bend themselves double before my porter's livery. Yes, double they'll bend themselves, but I shan't. I wasn't born to bend. I've got guts, I've got character, and once I reach that first branch, you'll watch me climb. Today I'm valet, next year I'll be proprietor, in ten years I'll have made a fortune, and then I'll go to Roumania, get myself decorated and I may, I only say *may*, mind you, end up as a Count.

JULIE [*Sadly*] That would be very nice.

JEAN. You see in Roumania one can buy a title, and then you'll be a Countess after all. My Countess.

JULIE. What do I care about all that? I'm putting those things behind me. Tell me you love me, because if you don't . . . if you don't, what am I?

JEAN. I'll tell you a thousand times over—later. But not here. No sentimentality now or everything will be lost. We must consider this thing calmly like reasonable people. [*Takes a cigar, cuts and lights it*] You sit down there and I'll sit here and we'll talk as if nothing has happened.

JULIE. My God, have you no feelings at all?

JEAN. Nobody has more. But I know how to control them.

JULIE. A short time ago you were kissing my shoe. And now . . .

JEAN [*Harshly*] Yes, that was then. Now we have something else to think about.

JULIE. Don't speak to me so brutally.

JEAN. I'm not. Just sensibly. One folly's been committed, don't let's have more. The Count will be back at any moment and we've got to settle our future before that. Now, what do you think of my plans? Do you approve?

JULIE. It seems a very good idea—but just one thing. Such a big undertaking would need a lot of capital. Have you got any?

JEAN [*Chewing his cigar*] I certainly have. I've got my professional skill, my wide experience and my knowledge of foreign languages. That's capital worth having, it seems to me.

JULIE. But it won't buy even one railway ticket.

JEAN. Quite true. That's why I need a backer to advance some ready cash.

JULIE. How could you get that at a moment's notice?

JEAN. You must get it, if you want to be my partner.

JULIE. I can't. I haven't any money of my own. [*Pause*]

JEAN. Then the whole thing's off.

JULIE. And . . . ?

JEAN. We go on as we are.

JULIE. Do you think I'm going to stay under this roof as your mistress? With everyone pointing at me. Do you think I can face my father

after this? No. Take me away from here, away from this shame, this
humiliation. Oh my God, what have I done? My God, my God!
[*Weeps*]

JEAN. So that's the tune now, is it? What have you done? Same as many
before you.

JULIE [*Hysterically*] And now you despise me. I'm falling, I'm falling.

JEAN. Fall as far as me and I'll lift you up again.

JULIE. Why was I so terribly attracted to you? The weak to the strong, the
falling to the rising? Or was it love? Is that love? Do you know what
love is?

JEAN. Do I? You bet I do. Do you think I never had a girl before?

JULIE. The things you say, the things you think!

JEAN. That's what life's taught me, and that's what I am. It's no good
getting hysterical or giving yourself airs. We're both in the same
boat now. Here, my dear girl, let me give you a glass of something
special. [*Opens the drawer, takes out the bottle of wine and fills two
used glasses*]

JULIE. Where did you get that wine?

JEAN. From the cellar.

JULIE. My father's burgundy.

JEAN. Why not, for his son-in-law?

JULIE. And I drink beer.

JEAN. That only shows your taste's not so good as mine.

JULIE. Thief!

JEAN. Are you going to tell on me?

JULIE. Oh God! The accomplice of a petty thief! Was I blind drunk? Have
I dreamt this whole night? Midsummer Eve, the night for innocent
merrymaking.

JEAN. Innocent, eh?

JULIE. Is anyone on earth as wretched as I am now?

JEAN. Why should *you* be? After such a conquest. What about Kristin in
there? Don't you think she has any feelings?

JULIE. I did think so, but I don't any longer. No. A menial is a menial . . .

JEAN. And a whore is a whore.

JULIE [*Falling to her knees, her hands clasped*] O God in heaven, put an
end to my miserable life! Lift me out of this filth in which I'm
sinking. Save me! Save me!

JEAN. I must admit I'm sorry for you. When I was in the onion bed and
saw you up there among the roses, I . . . yes, I'll tell you now . . . I
had the same dirty thoughts as all the boys.

JULIE. You, who wanted to die because of me?

JEAN. In the oats-bin? That was just talk.

JULIE. Lies, you mean.

JEAN [*Getting sleepy*] More or less. I think I read a story in some paper about a chimney-sweep who shut himself up in a chest full of lilac because he'd been summonsed for not supporting some brat . . .

JULIE. So this is what you're like.

JEAN. I had to think up something. It's always the fancy stuff that catches the women.

JULIE. Beast!

JEAN. Merde!

JULIE. Now you have seen the falcon's back.

JEAN. Not exactly its *back*.

JULIE. I was to be the first branch.

JEAN. But the branch was rotten.

JULIE. I was to be a hotel sign.

JEAN. And I the hotel.

JULIE. Sit at your counter, attract your clients and cook their accounts.

JEAN. I'd have done that myself.

JULIE. That any human being can be so steeped in filth!

JEAN. Clean it up then.

JULIE. Menial! Lackey! Stand up when I speak to you.

JEAN. Menial's whore, lackey's harlot, shut your mouth and get out of here! Are you the one to lecture me for being coarse? Nobody of my kind would ever be as coarse as you were tonight. Do you think any servant girl would throw herself at a man that way? Have you ever seen a girl of my class asking for it like that? I haven't. Only animals and prostitutes.

JULIE [*Broken*] Go on. Hit me, trample on me—it's all I deserve. I'm rotten. But help me! If there's any way out at all, help me.

JEAN [*More gently*] I'm not denying myself a share in the honour of seducing you, but do you think anybody in my place would have dared look in your direction if you yourself hadn't asked for it? I'm still amazed . . .

JULIE. And proud.

JEAN. Why not? Though I must admit the victory was too easy to make me lose my head.

JULIE. Go on hitting me.

JEAN [*Rising*] No. On the contrary I apologise for what I've said. I don't hit a person who's down—least of all a woman. I can't deny there's a certain satisfaction in finding that what dazzled one below was just moonshine, that the falcon's back is grey after all, that there's powder on the lovely cheek, that polished nails can have black tips, that the handkerchief is dirty although it smells of scent. On the other hand it hurts to find that what I was struggling to reach wasn't high and isn't real. It hurts to see you fallen so low you're far lower than your own cook. Hurts like when you see the last flowers of summer lashed to pieces by rain and turned to mud.

JULIE. You're talking as if you're already my superior.

JEAN. I am. I might make you a Countess, but you could never make me a Count, you know.

JULIE. But I am the child of a Count, and you could never be that.

JEAN. True, but I might be the father of Counts if. . . .

JULIE. You're a thief. I'm not.

JEAN. There are worse things than being a thief—much lower. Besides, when I'm in a place I regard myself as a member of the family to some extent, as one of the children. You don't call it stealing when children pinch a berry from overladen bushes. [*His passion is roused again*] Miss Julie, you're a glorious woman, far too good for a man like me. You were carried away by some kind of madness, and now you're trying to cover up your mistake by persuading yourself you're in love with me. You're not, although you may find me physically attractive, which means your love's no better than mine. But I wouldn't be satisfied with being nothing but an animal for you, and I could never make you love me.

JULIE. Are you sure?

JEAN. You think there's a chance? Of my loving you, yes, of course. You're beautiful, refined [*Takes her hand*] educated, and you can be nice when you want to be. The fire you kindle in a man isn't likely to go out. [*Puts his arm round her*] You're like mulled wine, full of spices, and your kisses. . . . [*He tries to pull her to him, but she breaks away*]

JULIE. Let go of me! You won't win me that way.

JEAN. Not that way, how then? Not by kisses and fine speeches, not by planning the future and saving you from shame? How then?

JULIE. How? How? I don't know. There isn't any way. I loathe you—loathe you as I loathe rats, but I can't escape from you.

JEAN. Escape with me.

JULIE [*Pulling herself together*] Escape? Yes, we must escape. But I'm so tired. Give me a glass of wine. [*He pours it out. She looks at her watch*] First we must talk. We still have a little time. [*Empties the glass and holds it out for more*]

JEAN. Don't drink like that. You'll get tipsy.

JULIE. What's that matter?

JEAN. What's it matter? It's vulgar to get drunk. Well, what have you got to say?

JULIE. We've got to run away, but we must talk first—or rather, I must, for so far you've done all the talking. You've told me about your life, now I want to tell you about mine, so that we really know each other before we begin this journey together.

JEAN. Wait. Excuse my saying so, but don't you think you may be sorry afterwards if you give away your secrets to me?

JULIE. Aren't you my friend?

JEAN. On the whole. But don't rely on me.

JULIE. You can't mean that. But anyway everyone knows my secrets. Listen. My mother wasn't well-born; she came of quite humble people, and was brought up with all those new ideas of sex-equality and women's rights and so on. She thought marriage was quite wrong. So when my father proposed to her, she said she would never become his *wife* . . . but in the end she did. I came into the world, as far as I can make out, against my mother's will, and I was left to run wild, but I had to do all the things a boy does—to prove women are as good as men. I had to wear boys' clothes; I was taught to handle horses—and I wasn't allowed in the dairy. She made me groom and harness and go out hunting; I even had to try to plough. All the men on the estate were given the women's jobs, and the women the men's, until the whole place went to rack and ruin and we were the laughing-stock of the neighbourhood. At last my father seems to have come to his senses and rebelled. He changed everything and ran the place his own way. My mother got ill—I don't know what was the matter with her, but she used to have strange attacks and hide herself in the attic or the garden. Sometimes she stayed out all night. Then came the great fire which you have heard people talking about. The house and the stables and the barns—the whole place burnt to the ground. In very suspicious circumstances. Because the accident happened the very day the insurance had to be renewed, and my father had sent the new premium, but through some carelessness of the messenger it arrived too late. [*Refills her glass and drinks*]

JEAN. Don't drink any more.

JULIE. Oh, what does it matter? We were destitute and had to sleep in the carriages. My father didn't know how to get money to rebuild, and then my mother suggested he should borrow from an old friend of hers, a local brick manufacturer. My father got the loan and, to his surprise, without having to pay interest. So the place was rebuilt. [*Drinks*] Do you know who set fire to it?

JEAN. Your lady mother.

JULIE. Do you know who the brick manufacturer was?

JEAN. Your mother's lover?

JULIE. Do you know whose the money was?

JEAN. Wait . . . no, I don't know that.

JULIE. It was my mother's.

JEAN. In other words the Count's, unless there was a settlement.

JULIE. There wasn't any settlement. My mother had a little money of her own which she didn't want my father to control, so she invested it with her—friend.

JEAN. Who grabbed it.

JULIE. Exactly. He appropriated it. My father came to know all this. He couldn't bring an action, couldn't pay his wife's lover, nor prove it was his wife's money. That was my mother's revenge because he made himself master in his own house. He nearly shot himself then—at least there's a rumour he tried and didn't bring if off. So he went on living, and my mother had to pay dearly for what she'd done. Imagine what those five years were like for me. My natural sympathies were with my father, yet I took my mother's side, because I didn't know the facts. I'd learnt from her to hate and distrust men—you know how she loathed the whole male sex. And I swore to her I'd never become the slave of any man.

JEAN. And so you got engaged to that attorney.

JULIE. So that he should be my slave.

JEAN. But he wouldn't be.

JULIE. Oh yes, he wanted to be, but he didn't have the chance. I got bored with him.

JEAN. Is that what I saw—in the stableyard?

JULIE. What did you see?

JEAN. What I saw was him breaking off the engagement.

JULIE. That's a lie. It was I who broke it off. Did he say it was him? The cad.

JEAN. He's not a cad. Do you hate men, Miss Julie?

JULIE. Yes . . . most of the time. But when that weakness comes, oh . . . the shame!

JEAN. Then do you hate me?

JULIE. Beyond words. I'd gladly have you killed like an animal.

JEAN. Quick as you'd shoot a mad dog, eh?

JULIE. Yes.

JEAN. But there's nothing here to shoot with—and there isn't a dog. So what do we do now?

JULIE. Go abroad.

JEAN. To make each other miserable for the rest of our lives?

JULIE. No, to enjoy ourselves for a day or two, for a week, for as long as enjoyment lasts, and then—to die . . .

JEAN. Die? How silly! I think it would be far better to start a hotel.

JULIE [*Without listening*] . . . die on the shores of Lake Como, where the sun always shines and at Christmas time there are green trees and glowing oranges.

JEAN. Lake Como's a rainy hole and I didn't see any oranges outside the shops. But it's a good place for tourists. Plenty of villas to be rented by—er—honeymoon couples. Profitable business that. Know why? Because they all sign a lease for six months and all leave after three weeks.

Julie [*Naively*] After three weeks? Why?

Jean. They quarrel, of course. But the rent has to be paid just the same. And then it's let again. So it goes on and on, for there's plenty of love although it doesn't last long.

Julie. You don't want to die with me?

Jean. I don't want to die at all. For one thing I like living and for another I consider suicide's a sin against the Creator who gave us life.

Julie. You believe in God—*you*?

Jean. Yes, of course. And I go to church every Sunday. Look here, I'm tired of all this. I'm going to bed.

Julie. Indeed! And do you think I'm going to leave things like this? Don't you know what you owe the woman you've ruined?

Jean [*Taking out his purse and throwing a silver coin on the table*] There you are. I don't want to be in anybody's debt.

Julie [*Pretending not to notice the insult*] Don't you know what the law is?

Jean. There's no law unfortunately that punishes a woman for seducing a man.

Julie. But can you see anything for it but to go abroad, get married and then divorce?

Jean. What if I refuse this mésalliance?

Julie. Mésalliance?

Jean. Yes, for me. I'm better bred than you, see! Nobody in my family committed arson.

Julie. How do you know?

Jean. Well, you can't prove otherwise, because we haven't any family records outside the Registrar's office. But I've seen your family tree in that book on the drawing-room table. Do you know who the founder of your family was? A miller who let his wife sleep with the King one night during the Danish war. I haven't any ancestors like that. I haven't any ancestors at all, but I might become one.

Julie. This is what I get for confiding in someone so low, for sacrificing my family honour . . .

Jean. Dishonour! Well, I told you so. One shouldn't drink, because then one talks. And one shouldn't talk.

Julie. Oh, how ashamed I am, how bitterly ashamed! If at least you loved me!

Jean. Look here—for the last time—what do you want? Am I to burst into tears? Am I to jump over your riding whip? Shall I kiss you and carry you off to Lake Como for three weeks, after which . . . What am I to do? What do you want? This is getting unbearable, but that's what comes of playing around with women. Miss Julie, I can see how miserable you are; I know you're going through hell, but I don't understand you. We don't have scenes like this; we don't go in for hating each other. We make love for fun in our spare time, but we haven't all day and all night for it like you. I think you must be ill. I'm sure you're ill.

JULIE. Then you must be kind to me. You sound almost human now.

JEAN. Well, be human yourself. You spit at me, then won't let me wipe it off—on you.

JULIE. Help me, help me! Tell me what to do, where to go.

JEAN. Jesus, as if I knew.

JULIE. I've been mad, raving mad, but there must be a way out.

JEAN. Stay here and keep quiet. Nobody knows anything.

JULIE. I can't. People do know. Kristin knows.

JEAN. They don't know and they wouldn't believe such a thing.

JULIE [Hesitating] But—it might happen again.

JEAN. That's true.

JULIE. And there might be—consequences.

JEAN [In panic] Consequences! Fool that I am I never thought of that. Yes, there's nothing for it but to go. At once. I can't come with you. That would be a complete giveaway. You must go alone—abroad—anywhere.

JULIE. Alone? Where to? I can't.

JEAN. You must. And before the Count gets back. If you stay, we know what will happen. Once you've sinned you feel you might as well go on, as the harm's done. Then you get more and more reckless and in the end you're found out. No. You must go abroad. Then write to the Count and tell him everything, except that it was me. He'll never guess that—and I don't think he'll want to.

JULIE. I'll go if you come with me.

JEAN. Are you crazy, woman? "Miss Julie elopes with valet." Next day it would be in the headlines, and the Count would never live it down.

JULIE. I can't go. I can't stay. I'm so tired, so completely worn out. Give me orders. Set me going. I can't think any more, can't act . . .

JEAN. You see what weaklings you are. Why do you give yourselves airs and turn up your noses as if you're the lords of creation? Very well, I'll give you your orders. Go upstairs and dress. Get money for the journey and come down here again.

JULIE [Softly] Come up with me.

JEAN. To your room? Now you've gone crazy again. [Hesitates a moment] No! Go along at once. [Takes her hand and pulls her to the door]

JULIE [As she goes] Speak kindly to me, Jean.

JEAN. Orders always sound unkind. Now you know. Now you know.

Left alone, JEAN sighs with relief, sits down at the table, takes out a note-book and pencil and adds up figures, now and then aloud.

Dawn begins to break. KRISTIN *enters dressed for church, carrying his white dickey and tie.*

KRISTIN. Lord Jesus, look at the state the place is in! What have you been up to? [*Turns out the lamp*]

JEAN. Oh, Miss Julie invited the crowd in. Did you sleep through it? Didn't you hear anything?

KRISTIN. I slept like a log.

JEAN. And dressed for church already.

KRISTIN. Yes, you promised to come to Communion with me today.

JEAN. Why, so I did. And you've got my bib and tucker, I see. Come on then. [*Sits.* KRISTIN *begins to put his things on. Pause. Sleepily*] What's the lesson today?

KRISTIN. It's about the beheading of John the Baptist, I think.

JEAN. That's sure to be horribly long. Hi, you're choking me! Oh Lord, I'm so sleepy, so sleepy!

KRISTIN. Yes, what have you been doing up all night? You look absolutely green.

JEAN. Just sitting here talking with Miss Julie.

KRISTIN. She doesn't know what's proper, that one. [*Pause*]

JEAN. I say, Kristin.

KRISTIN. What?

JEAN. It's queer really, isn't it, when you come to think of it? Her.

KRISTIN. What's queer?

JEAN. The whole thing. [*Pause*]

KRISTIN [*Looking at the half-filled glasses on the table*] Have you been drinking together too?

JEAN. Yes.

KRISTIN. More shame you. Look me straight in the face.

JEAN. Yes.

KRISTIN. Is it possible? Is it possible?

JEAN [*After a moment*] Yes, it is.

KRISTIN. Oh! This I would never have believed. How low!

JEAN. You're not jealous of her, surely?

KRISTIN. No, I'm not. If it had been Clara or Sophie I'd have scratched your eyes out. But not of her. I don't know why; that's how it is though. But it's disgusting.

JEAN. You're angry with her then.

KRISTIN. No. With you. It was wicked of you, very very wicked. Poor girl. And, mark my words, I won't stay here any longer now—in a place where one can't respect one's employers.

JEAN. Why should one respect them?

KRISTIN. You should know since you're so smart. But you don't want to stay in the service of people who aren't respectable, do you? I wouldn't demean myself.

JEAN. But it's rather a comfort to find out they're no better than us.

KRISTIN. I don't think so. If they're no better there 's nothing for us to live up to. Oh and think of the Count! Think of him. He's been through so much already. No, I won't stay in the place any longer. A fellow like you too! If it had been that attorney now or somebody of her own class . . .

JEAN. Why, what's wrong with . . .

KRISTIN. Oh, you're all right in your own way, but when all's said and done there is a difference between one class and another. No, this is something I'll never be able to stomach. That our young lady who was so proud and so down on men you'd never believe she'd let one come near her should go and give herself to one like you. She who wanted to have poor Diana shot for running after the lodge-keeper's pug. No, I must say . . . ! Well, I won't stay here any longer. On the twenty-fourth of October I quit.

JEAN. And then?

KRISTIN. Well, since you mention it, it's about time you began to look around, if we're ever going to get married.

JEAN. But what am I to look for? I shan't get a place like this when I'm married.

KRISTIN. I know you won't. But you might get a job as porter or caretaker in some public institution. Government rations are small but sure, and there's a pension for the widow and children.

JEAN. That's all very fine, but it's not in my line to start thinking at once about dying for my wife and children. I must say I had rather bigger ideas.

KRISTIN. You and your ideas! You've got obligations too, and you'd better start thinking about them.

JEAN. Don't *you* start pestering me about obligations. I've had enough of that. [*Listens to a sound upstairs*] Anyway we've plenty of time to work things out. Go and get ready now and we'll be off to church.

KRISTIN. Who's that walking about upstairs?

JEAN. Don't know—unless it's Clara.

KRISTIN [*Going*] You don't think the Count could have come back without our hearing him?

JEAN [*Scared*] The Count? No, he can't have. He'd have rung for me.

KRISTIN. God help us! I've never known such goings on. [*Exits*]

> *The sun has now risen and is shining on the treetops. The light gradually changes until it slants in through the windows.* JEAN *goes to the door and beckons.* JULIE *enters in travelling clothes, carrying a small bird-cage covered with a cloth which she puts on a chair.*

JULIE. I'm ready.

JEAN. Hush! Kristin's up.

JULIE [*In a very nervous state*] Does she suspect anything?

JEAN. Not a thing. But, my God, what a sight you are!

JULIE. Sight? What do you mean?

JEAN. You're white as a corpse and—pardon me—your face is dirty.

JULIE. Let me wash then. [*Goes to the sink and washes her face and hands*] There. Give me a towel. Oh! The sun is rising!

JEAN. And that breaks the spell.

JULIE. Yes. The spell of Midsummer Eve . . . But listen, Jean. Come with me. I've got the money.

JEAN [*Sceptically*] Enough?

JULIE. Enough to start with. Come with me. I can't travel alone today. It's Midsummer Day, remember. I'd be packed into a suffocating train among crowds of people who'd all stare at me. And it would stop at every station while I yearned for wings. No, I can't do that, I simply can't. There will be memories too; memories of Midsummer Days when I was little. The leafy church—birch and lilac—the gaily spread dinner table, relatives, friends—evening in the park—dancing and music and flowers and fun. Oh, however far you run away—there'll always be memories in the baggage car—and remorse and guilt.

JEAN. I will come with you, but quickly now then, before it's too late. At once.

JULIE. Put on your things. [*Picks up the cage*]

JEAN. No luggage, mind. That would give us away.

JULIE. No, only what we can take with us in the carriage.

JEAN [*Fetching his hat*] What on earth have you got there? What is it?

JULIE. Only my greenfinch. I don't want to leave it behind.

JEAN. Well, I'll be damned! We're to take a bird-cage along, are we? You're crazy. Put that cage down.

JULIE. It's the only thing I'm taking from my home. The only living creature who cares for me since Diana went off like that. Don't be cruel. Let me take it.

JEAN. Put that cage down, I tell you—and don't talk so loud. Kristin will hear.

JULIE. No, I won't leave it in strange hands. I'd rather you killed it.

JEAN. Give the little beast here then and I'll wring its neck.

JULIE. But don't hurt it, don't . . . no, I can't.

JEAN. Give it here. I *can*.

JULIE [*Taking the bird out of the cage and kissing it*] Dear little Serena, must you die and leave your mistress?

JEAN. Please don't make a scene. It's *your* life and future we're worrying about. Come on, quick now!

He snatches the bird from her, puts it on a board and picks up a chopper. JULIE *turns away.*

You should have learnt how to kill chickens instead of target-shooting. Then you wouldn't faint at a drop of blood.

JULIE [*Screaming*] Kill me too! Kill me! You who can butcher an innocent creature without a quiver. Oh, how I hate you, how I loathe you! There is blood between us now. I curse the hour I first saw you. I curse the hour I was conceived in my mother's womb.

JEAN. What's the use of cursing. Let's go.

JULIE [*Going to the chopping-block as if drawn against her will*] No, I won't go yet. I can't . . . I must look. Listen! There's a carriage. [*Listens without taking her eyes off the board and chopper*] You don't think I can bear the sight of blood. You think I'm so weak. Oh, how I should like to see your blood and your brains on a chopping-block! I'd like to see the whole of your sex swimming like that in a sea of blood. I think I could drink out of your skull, bathe my feet in your broken breast and eat your heart roasted whole. You think I'm weak. You think I love you, that my womb yearned for your seed and I want to carry your offspring under my heart and nourish it with my blood. You think I want to bear your child and take your name. By the way, what is your name. I've never heard your surname. I don't suppose you've got one. I should be "Mrs. Hovel" or "Madam Dunghill." You dog wearing my collar, you lackey with my crest on your buttons! I share you with my cook; I'm my own servant's rival! Oh! Oh! Oh! . . . You think I'm a coward and will run away. No, now I'm going to stay—and let the storm break. My father will come back . . . find his desk broken open . . . his money gone. Then he'll ring that bell—twice for the valet—and then he'll send for the police . . . and I shall tell everything. Everything. Oh how wonderful to make an end of it all—a real end! He has a stroke and dies and that's the end of all of us. Just peace and quietness . . . eternal rest. The coat of arms broken on the coffin and the Count's line extinct . . . But the valet's line goes on in an orphanage, wins laurels in the gutter and ends in jail.

JEAN. There speaks the noble blood! Bravo, Miss Julie. But now, don't let the cat out of the bag.

KRISTIN *enters dressed for church, carrying a prayer-book.* JULIE *rushes to her and flings herself into her arms for protection.*

JULIE. Help me, Kristin! Protect me from this man!

KRISTIN [*Unmoved and cold*] What goings-on for a feast day morning! [*Sees the board*] And what a filthy mess. What's it all about? Why are you screaming and carrying on so?

JULIE. Kristin, you're a woman and my friend. Beware of that scoundrel!

JEAN [*Embarrassed*] While you ladies are talking things over, I'll go and shave. [*Slips into his room*]

JULIE. You must understand. You must listen to me.

KRISTIN. I certainly don't understand such loose ways. Where are you off to in those travelling clothes? And he had his hat on, didn't he, eh?

JULIE. Listen, Kristin. Listen, I'll tell you everything.

KRISTIN. I don't want to know anything.

JULIE. You must listen.

KRISTIN. What to? Your nonsense with Jean? I don't care a rap about that; it's nothing to do with me. But if you're thinking of getting him to run off with you, we'll soon put a stop to that.

JULIE [*Very nervously*] Please try to be calm, Kristin, and listen. I can't stay here, nor can Jean—so we must go abroad.

KRISTIN. Hm, hm!

JULIE [*Brightening*] But you see, I've had an idea. Supposing we all three go—abroad—to Switzerland and start a hotel together . . . I've got some money, you see . . . and Jean and I could run the whole thing—and I thought you would take charge of the kitchen. Wouldn't that be splendid? Say yes, do. If you come with us everything will be fine. Oh do say yes! [*Puts her arms round* KRISTIN]

KRISTIN [*Coolly thinking*] Hm, hm.

JULIE [*Presto tempo*] You've never travelled, Kristin. You should go abroad and see the world. You've no idea how nice it is travelling by train—new faces all the time and new countries. On our way through Hamburg we'll go to the zoo—you'll love that—and we'll go to the theatre and the opera too . . . and when we get to Munich there'll be the museums, dear, and pictures by Rubens and Raphael—the great painters, you know . . . You've heard of Munich, haven't you? Where King Ludwig lived—you know, the king who went mad . . . We'll see his castles—some of his castles are still just like in fairy-tales . . . and from there it's not far to Switzerland—and the Alps. Think of the Alps, Kristin dear, covered with snow in the middle of summer . . . and there are oranges there and trees that are green the whole year round . . .

> JEAN *is seen in the door of his room, sharpening his razor on a strop which he holds with his teeth and his left hand. He listens to the talk with satisfaction and now and then nods approval.* JULIE *continues, tempo prestissimo.*

And then we'll get a hotel . . . and I'll sit at the desk, while Jean receives the guests and goes out marketing and writes letters . . . There's life for you! Trains whistling, buses driving up, bells ringing upstairs and downstairs . . . and I shall make out the bills—and I shall cook them too . . . you've no idea how nervous travellers are when it comes to paying their bills. And you—you'll sit like a queen in the kitchen . . . of course there won't be any standing at the stove for you. You'll always have to be nicely dressed and ready to be seen, and with your looks—no, I'm not flattering you—one fine day you'll catch yourself a husband . . . some rich Englishman, I shouldn't wonder—they're the ones who are easy [*Slowing down*] to catch . . . and then we'll get rich and build ourselves a villa on Lake Como . . . of course it rains there a little now and then—but— [*Dully*]—the sun must shine there too sometimes—even though it seems gloomy—and if not—then we can come home again—come back [*Pause*] here—or somewhere else . . .

KRISTIN. Look here, Miss Julie, do you believe all that yourself?

JULIE [*Exhausted*] Do I believe it?

KRISTIN. Yes.

JULIE [*Wearily*] I don't know. I don't believe anything any more. [*Sinks down on the bench; her head in her arms on the table*] Nothing. Nothing at all.

KRISTIN [*Turning to JEAN*] So you meant to beat it, did you?

JEAN [*Disconcerted, putting the razor on the table*] Beat it? What are you talking about? You've heard Miss Julie's plan, and though she's tired now with being up all night, it's a perfectly sound plan.

KRISTIN. Oh, is it? If you thought I'd work for that . . .

JEAN [*Interrupting*] Kindly use decent language in front of your mistress. Do you hear?

KRISTIN. Mistress?

JEAN. Yes.

KRISTIN. Well, well, just listen to that!

JEAN. Yes, it would be a good thing if you did listen and talked less. Miss Julie is your mistress and what's made you lose your respect for her now ought to make you feel the same about yourself.

KRISTIN. I've always had enough self-respect—

JEAN. To despise other people.

KRISTIN. —not to go below my own station. Has the Count's cook ever gone with the groom or the swineherd? Tell me that.

JEAN. No, you were lucky enough to have a high-class chap for your beau.

KRISTIN. High-class all right—selling the oats out of the Count's stable.

JEAN. You're a fine one to talk—taking a commission on the groceries and bribes from the butcher.

KRISTIN. What the devil . . . ?

JEAN. And now you can't feel any respect for your employers. You, you!

KRISTIN. Are you coming to church with me? I should think you need a good sermon after your fine deeds.

JEAN. No, I'm not going to church today. You can go alone and confess your own sins.

KRISTIN. Yes, I'll do that and bring back enough forgiveness to cover yours too. The Saviour suffered and died on the cross for all our sins, and if we go to Him with faith and a penitent heart, He takes all our sins upon Himself.

JEAN. Even grocery thefts?

JULIE. Do you believe that, Kristin?

KRISTIN. That is my living faith, as sure as I stand here. The faith I learnt as a child and have kept ever since, Miss Julie. "But where sin abounded, grace did much more abound."

JULIE. Oh, if I had your faith! Oh, if . . .

KRISTIN. But you see you can't have it without God's special grace, and it's not given to all to have that.

JULIE. Who is it given to then?

KRISTIN. That's the great secret of the workings of grace, Miss Julie. God is no respecter of persons, and with Him the last shall be first . . .

JULIE. Then I suppose He does respect the last.

KRISTIN [Continuing] . . . and it is easier for a camel to go through the eye of a needle than for a rich man to enter into the kingdom of God. That's how it is, Miss Julie. Now I'm going—alone, and on my way I shall tell the groom not to let any of the horses out, in case anyone should want to leave before the Count gets back. Good-bye. [Exit]

JEAN. What a devil! And all on account of a greenfinch.

JULIE [Wearily] Never mind the greenfinch. Do you see any way out of this, any end to it?

JEAN [Pondering] No.

JULIE. If you were in my place, what would you do?

JEAN. In your place? Wait a bit. If I was a woman—a lady of rank who had—fallen. I don't know. Yes, I do know now.

JULIE [Picking up the razor and making a gesture] This?

JEAN. Yes. But I wouldn't do it, you know. There's a difference between us.

JULIE. Because you're a man and I'm a woman? What is the difference?

JEAN. The usual difference—between man and woman.

JULIE [Holding the razor] I'd like to. But I can't. My father couldn't either, that time he wanted to.

JEAN. No, he didn't want to. He had to be revenged first.

JULIE. And now my mother is revenged again, through me.

JEAN. Didn't you ever love your father, Miss Julie?

JULIE. Deeply, but I must have hated him too—unconsciously. And he let me be brought up to despise my own sex, to be half woman, half man. Whose fault is what's happened? My father's, my mother's or my own? My own? I haven't anything that's my own. I haven't one single thought that I didn't get from my father, one emotion that didn't come from my mother, and as for this last idea—about all people being equal—I got that from him, my fiancé—that's why I call him a cad. How can it be my fault? Push the responsibility on to Jesus, like Kristin does? No, I'm too proud and—thanks to my father's teaching—too intelligent. As for all that about a rich person not being able to get into heaven, it's just a lie, but Kristin, who has money in the savings-bank, will certainly not get in. Whose fault is it? What does it matter whose fault it is? In any case I must take the blame and bear the consequences.

JEAN. Yes, but . . . [*There are two sharp rings on the bell.* JULIE *jumps to her feet.* JEAN *changes into his livery*] The Count is back. Supposing Kristin . . . [*Goes to the speaking-tube, presses it and listens*]

JULIE. Has he been to his desk yet?

JEAN. This is Jean, sir. [*Listens*] Yes, sir. [*Listens*] Yes, sir, very good, sir. [*Listens*] At once, sir? [*Listens*] Very good, sir. In half an hour.

JULIE [*In panic*] What did he say? My God, what did he say?

JEAN. He ordered his boots and his coffee in half an hour.

JULIE. Then there's half an hour . . . Oh, I'm so tired! I can't do anything. Can't be sorry, can't run away, can't stay, can't live—can't die. Help me. Order me, and I'll obey like a dog. Do me this last service—save my honour, save his name. You know what I ought to do, but haven't the strength to do. Use your strength and order me to do it.

JEAN. I don't know why—I can't now—I don't understand . . . It's just as if this coat made me—I can't give you orders—and now that the Count has spoken to me—I can't quite explain, but . . . well, that devil of a lackey is bending my back again. I believe if the Count came down now and ordered me to cut my throat, I'd do it on the spot.

JULIE. Then pretend you're him and I'm you. You did some fine acting before, when you knelt to me and played the aristocrat. Or . . . Have you ever seen a hypnotist at the theatre? [*He nods*] He says to the person "Take the broom," and he takes it. He says "Sweep," and he sweeps . . .

JEAN. But the person has to be asleep.

JULIE [*As if in a trance*] I am asleep already . . . the whole room has turned to smoke—and you look like a stove—a stove like a man in black with a tall hat—your eyes are glowing like coals when the fire is low—and your face is a white patch like ashes. [*The sunlight has now reached the floor and lights up* JEAN] How nice and warm it is! [*She holds out her hands as though warming them at a fire*] And so light—and so peaceful.

JEAN [*Putting the razor in her hand*] Here is the broom. Go now while it's light—out to the barn—and. . . . [*Whispers in her ear*]

JULIE [*Waking*] Thank you. I am going now—to rest. But just tell me that even the first can receive the gift of grace.

JEAN. The first? No, I can't tell you that. But wait . . . Miss Julie, I've got it! You aren't one of the first any longer. You're one of the last.

JULIE. That's true. I'm one of the very last. I *am* the last. Oh! . . . But now I can't go. Tell me again to go.

JEAN. No, I can't now either. I can't.

JULIE. And the first shall be last.

JEAN. Don't think, don't think. You're taking my strength away too and making me a coward. What's that? I thought I saw the bell move . . . To be so frightened of a bell! Yes, but it's not just a bell. There's somebody behind it—a hand moving it—and something else moving the hand—and if you stop your ears—if you stop your ears—yes, then it rings louder than ever. Rings and rings until you answer—and then it's too late. Then the police come and . . . and. . . . [*The bell rings twice loudly.* JEAN *flinches, then straightens himself up.*] It's horrible. But there's no other way to end it . . . Go!

JULIE *walks firmly out through the door.*

CURTAIN

Considerations

Perhaps the greatest expert on this play is its author. Strindberg himself wrote a foreword to *Miss Julie,* in which he outlined some of the reasoning behind the play. Among other things, he said:

"it is tragic to see one favored by fortune go under . . . but . . . there is no such thing as absolute evil; the downfall of one family is the good fortune of another. . . ." "The fact that my heroine rouses pity is solely due to weakness; we cannot resist fear of the same fate overtaking us."

He intended to make the people in his play weak and vacillating, because he thought that was appropriate to modern characters living in a time of transition. Yet surely uncertainty and indecision are as much the result of knowing too much as of being weak.

In his foreword Strindberg writes of Miss Julie as a modern woman, man-hating and aggressive. He seems to have little sympathy for her or the intolerable situations with which she has had to deal. Yet our feeling for her comes from the play itself; Strindberg has made us pity her. Her background, revealed in her discussion with Jean, would have been hard to overcome. She is in many ways innocent—she believes she is friends with the peasants, she seems surprised when Jean taunts her with the ease of his conquest. She is driven by internal forces she does not understand, and she has no awareness of the effect of changing social forces. What crimes can she really be accused of except being in the wrong place at the wrong time?

What is the outlook for Kristin? Does Strindberg imply a brighter picture for this "sensible girl"? Her salvation apparently lies in sticking to the old ways and to religion, hardly a realistic refuge if the society is going to change significantly.

In this play of contrasts (old against new, upwardly mobile against decaying nobility, new male and displaced woman) Jean, the valet, would appear the final winner. Even at the high point of the attraction between Julie and Jean, Jean does not lose sight of tangible future goals. She contemplates, for a moment, giving up everything and running away with him (romance); he plans, for a moment, running away with her and gaining everything—including a hotel and a Roumanian title (materialism). In such a contest, romance doesn't have much of a chance.

Romance writes its own ending—an ending that Strindberg, in his foreword, calls beautiful, if impractical. Miss Julie asks Jean for help, for a way out, and he points her toward it. He even gives her a rationale to soothe herself with. Miss Julie is one of the last, says Jean, and believing that, she is able to go firmly to her death. Is she truly one of the last—or only one of the last of that wave of civilization?

Ile

EUGENE O'NEILL

CHARACTERS

BEN, *the cabin boy*
THE STEWARD
CAPTAIN KEENEY
SLOCUM, *second mate*

MRS. KEENEY
JOE, *a harpooner*
Members of the crew of the
steam whaler Atlantic Queen

SCENE: CAPTAIN KEENEY'S *cabin on board the steam whaling ship* Atlantic Queen—*a small, square compartment about eight feet high with a skylight in the center looking out on the poop deck. On the left [the stern of the ship] a long bench with rough cushions is built in against the wall. In front of the bench, a table. Over the bench, several curtained portholes.*

In the rear, left, a door leading to the CAPTAIN'S *sleeping quarters. To the right of the door a small organ, looking as if it were brand-new, is placed against the wall.*

On the right, to the rear, a marble-topped sideboard. On the sideboard, a woman's sewing basket. Farther forward, a doorway leading to the companionway, and past the officers' quarters to the main deck.

In the center of the room, a stove. From the middle of the ceiling a hanging lamp is suspended. The walls of the cabin are painted white.

There is no rolling of the ship, and the light which comes through the skylight is sickly and faint, indicating one of those gray days of calm when ocean and sky are alike dead. The silence is unbroken except for the measured tread of someone walking up and down on the poop deck overhead.

It is nearing two bells—one o'clock—in the afternoon of a day in the year 1895.

At the rise of the curtain there is a moment of intense silence. Then THE STEWARD *enters and commences to clear the table of the few dishes which still remain on it after the* CAPTAIN'S *dinner. He is an old, grizzled man dressed in dungaree pants, a sweater, and a woolen cap with earflaps. His manner is sullen and angry. He stops stacking up the plates and casts a quick glance upward at the skylight; then tiptoes over to the closed door in rear and listens with his ear pressed to the crack. What he hears makes his*

*face darken and he mutters a furious curse. There is a noise from the
doorway on the right and he darts back to the table.*

BEN *enters. He is an overgrown, gawky boy with a long, pinched face. He
is dressed in sweater, fur cap, etc. His teeth are chattering with the cold and
he hurries to the stove, where he stands for a moment shivering, blowing on
his hands, slapping them against his sides, on the verge of crying.*

THE STEWARD [*In relieved tones—seeing who it is*] Oh, 'tis you, is it?
What're ye shiverin' 'bout? Stay by the stove where ye belong and
ye'll find no need of chatterin'.

BEN. It's c-c-cold. [*Trying to control his chattering teeth—derisively*] Who
d'ye think it were—the Old Man?

THE STEWARD [*Makes a threatening move—*BEN *shrinks away*] None o'
your lip, young un, or I'll learn ye. [*More kindly*] Where was it ye've
been all o' the time—the fo'c's'tle?

BEN. Yes.

THE STEWARD. Let the Old Man see ye up for'ard monkeyshinin' with the
hands and ye'll get a hidin' ye'll not forget in a hurry.

BEN. Aw, he don't see nothin'. [*A trace of awe in his tones—he glances
upward*] He just walks up and down like he didn't notice nobody—
and stares at the ice to the no'th'ard.

THE STEWARD [*The same tone of awe creeping into his voice*] He's always
starin' at the ice. [*In a sudden rage, shaking his fist at the skylight*]
Ice, ice, ice! Damn him and damn the ice! Holdin' us in for nigh on a
year—nothin' to see but ice—stuck in it like a fly in molasses!

BEN [*Apprehensively*] Ssshh! He'll hear ye.

THE STEWARD [*Raging*] Aye, damn him, and damn the Arctic seas, and
damn this stinkin' whalin' ship of his, and damn me for a fool to ever
ship on it! [*Subsiding as if realizing the uselessness of this outburst—
shaking his head—slowly, with deep conviction*] He's a hard man—as
hard a man as ever sailed the seas.

BEN [*Solemnly*] Aye.

THE STEWARD. The two years we all signed up for are done this day.
Blessed Christ! Two years o' this dog's life, and no luck in the
fishin', and the hands half starved with the food runnin' low, rotten
as it is; and not a sign of him turnin' back for home! [*Bitterly*]
Home! I begin to doubt if ever I'll set foot on land again. [*Excitedly*]
What is it he thinks he's goin' to do? Keep us all up here after our
time is worked out till the last man of us is starved to death or
frozen? We've grub enough hardly to last out the voyage back if we
started now. What are the men goin' to do 'bout it? Did ye hear any
talk in the fo'c's'tle?

BEN [*Going over to him—in a half-whisper*] They said if he don't put back
south for home today they're goin' to mutiny.

THE STEWARD [*With grim satisfaction*] Mutiny? Aye, 'tis the only thing they can do; and serve him right after the manner he's treated them—'s if they weren't no better nor dogs.

BEN. The ice is all broke up to s'uth'ard. They's clear water 's far 's you can see. He ain't got no excuse for not turnin' back for home, the men says.

THE STEWARD [*Bitterly*] He won't look nowheres but no'th'ard where they's only the ice to see. He don't want to see no clear water. All he thinks on is gittin' the ile—'s if it was our fault he ain't had good luck with the whales. [*Shaking his head*] I think the man's mighty nigh losin' his senses.

BEN [*Awed*] D'you really think he's crazy?

THE STEWARD. Aye, it's the punishment o' God on him. Did ye ever hear of a man who wasn't crazy do the things he does? [*Pointing to the door in rear*] Who but a man that's mad would take his woman—and as sweet a woman as ever was—on a stinkin' whalin' ship to the Arctic seas to be locked in by the rotten ice for nigh on a year, and maybe lose her senses forever—for it's sure she'll never be the same again.

BEN [*Sadly*] She useter be awful nice to me before—[*His eyes grow wide and frightened*] she got—like she is.

THE STEWARD. Aye, she was good to all of us. 'Twould have been hell on board without her; for he's a hard man—a hard, hard man—a driver if there ever was one. [*With a grim laugh*] I hope he's satisfied now—drivin' her on till she's near lost her mind. And who could blame her? 'Tis a God's wonder we're not a ship full of crazed people—with the damned ice all the time, and the quiet so thick you're afraid to hear your own voice.

BEN [*With a frightened glance toward the door on right*] She don't never speak to me no more—jest looks at me 's if she didn't know me.

THE STEWARD. She don't know no one—but him. She talks to him— when she does talk—right enough.

BEN. She does nothin' all day long now but sit and sew—and then she cries to herself without makin' no noise. I've seen her.

THE STEWARD. Aye, I could hear her through the door a while back.

BEN [*Tiptoes over to the door and listens*] She's cryin' now.

THE STEWARD [*Furiously—shaking his fist*] God send his soul to hell for the devil he is!

There is the noise of someone coming slowly down the companion-way stairs. THE STEWARD *hurries to his stacked-up dishes. He is so nervous from fright that he knocks off the top one, which falls and breaks on the floor. He stands aghast, trembling with dread.* BEN *is violently rubbing off the organ with a piece of cloth which he has snatched from his pocket.* CAPTAIN KEENEY *appears in the doorway on right and comes into the cabin, removing his fur cap as he does so. He is a man of about forty, around five-ten in height but looking much shorter on account of the enormous proportions of his shoulders and chest. His face is massive and deeply lined, with gray-blue eyes of a bleak hardness, and a tightly clenched, thin-lipped mouth. His thick hair is long and gray. He is dressed in a heavy blue jacket and blue pants stuffed into his sea-boots.*

He is followed into the cabin by the SECOND MATE, *a rangy six-footer with a lean weather-beaten face. The* MATE *is dressed about the same as the* CAPTAIN. *He is a man of thirty or so.*

KEENEY [*Comes toward* THE STEWARD—*with a stern look on his face. The* STEWARD *is visibly frightened and the stack of dishes rattle in his trembling hands.* KEENEY *draws back his fist and* THE STEWARD *shrinks away. The fist is gradually lowered and* KEENEY *speaks slowly*] 'Twould be like hitting a worm. It is nigh on two bells, Mr. Steward, and this truck not cleared yet.

THE STEWARD [*Stammering*] Y-y-yes, sir.

KEENEY. Instead of doin' your rightful work ye've been below here gossipin' old woman's talk with that boy. [*To* BEN, *fiercely*] Get out o' this, you! Clean up the chart room. [BEN *darts past the* MATE *to the open doorway*] Pick up that dish, Mr. Steward!

THE STEWARD [*Doing so with difficulty*] Yes, sir.

KEENEY. The next dish you break, Mr. Steward, you take a bath in the Bering Sea at the end of a rope.

THE STEWARD [*Tremblingly*] Yes, sir. [*He hurries out. The* SECOND MATE *walks slowly over to the* CAPTAIN]

MATE. I warn't 'specially anxious the man at the wheel should catch what I wanted to say to you, sir. That's why I asked you to come below.

KEENEY [*Impatiently*] Speak your say, Mr. Slocum.

MATE [*Unconsciously lowering his voice*] I'm afeard there'll be trouble with the hands by the look o' things. They'll likely turn ugly, every blessed one o' them, if you don't put back. The two years they signed up for is up today.

KEENEY. And d'you think you're tellin' me somethin' new, Mr. Slocum? I've felt it in the air this long time past. D'you think I've not seen their ugly looks and the grudgin' way they worked? [*The door in rear is opened and* MRS. KEENEY *stands in the doorway. She is a slight, sweet-faced little woman primly dressed in black. Her eyes are red from weeping and her face drawn and pale. She takes in the cabin with a frightened glance and stands as if fixed to the spot by some nameless dread, clasping and unclasping her hands nervously. The two men turn and look at her*]

KEENEY [*With rough tenderness*] Well, Annie?

MRS. KEENEY [*As if awakening from a dream*] David, I—[*She is silent. The* MATE *starts for the doorway*]

KEENEY [*Turning to him—sharply*] Wait!

MATE. Yes, sir.

KEENEY. D'you want anything, Annie?

MRS. KEENEY [*After a pause, during which she seems to be endeavoring to collect her thoughts*] I thought maybe—I'd go up on deck, David, to get a breath of fresh air. [*She stands humbly awaiting his permission. He and the* MATE *exchange a significant glance*]

KEENEY. It's too cold, Annie. You'd best stay below today. There's nothing to look at on deck—but ice.

MRS. KEENEY [*Monotonously*] I know—ice, ice, ice! But there's nothing to see down here but these walls. [*She makes a gesture of loathing*]

KEENEY. You can play the organ, Annie.

MRS. KEENEY [*Dully*] I hate the organ. It puts me in mind of home.

KEENEY [*A touch of resentment in his voice*] I got it jest for you.

MRS. KEENEY [*Dully*] I know. [*She turns away from them and walks slowly to the bench on left. She lifts up one of the curtains and looks through a porthole; then utters an exclamation of joy*] Ah, water! Clear water! As far as I can see! How good it looks after all these months of ice! [*She turns around to them, her face transfigured with joy*] Ah, now I must go up on the deck and look at it, David.

KEENEY [*Frowning*] Best not today, Annie. Best wait for a day when the sun shines.

MRS. KEENEY [*Desperately*] But the sun never shines in this terrible place.

KEENEY [*A tone of command in his voice*] Best not today, Annie.

MRS. KEENEY [*Crumbling before this command—abjectly*] Very well, David. [*She stands there staring straight before her as if in a daze. The two men look at her uneasily*]

KEENEY [*Sharply*] Annie!

MRS. KEENEY [*Dully*] Yes, David.

KEENEY. Me and Mr. Slocum has business to talk about—ship's business.

MRS. KEENEY. Very well, David. [*She goes slowly out, rear, and leaves the door three-quarters shut behind her*]

KEENEY. Best not have her on deck if they's goin' to be any trouble.

MATE. Yes, sir.

KEENEY. And trouble they's goin' to be. I feel it in my bones. [*Takes a revolver from the pocket of his coat and examines it*] Got your'n?

MATE. Yes, sir.

KEENEY. Not that we'll have to use 'em—not if I know their breed of dog—just to frighten 'em up a bit. [*Grimly*] I ain't never been forced to use one yit; and trouble I've had by land and by sea 's long as I kin remember, and will have till my dyin' day, I reckon.

MATE [*Hesitatingly*] Then you ain't goin'—to turn back?

KEENEY. Turn back! Mr. Slocum, did you ever hear o' me pointin' s'uth for home with only a measly four hundred barrel of ile in the hold?

Mate [*Hastily*] No, sir—but the grub's gittin' low.

Keeney. They's enough to last a long time yit, if they're careful with it; and they's plenty o' water.

Mate. They say it's not fit to eat—what's left; and the two years they signed on fur is up today. They might make trouble for you in the courts when we git home.

Keeney. To hell with 'em! Let them make what law trouble they kin. I don't give a damn 'bout the money. I've got to git the ile! [*Glancing sharply at the* Mate] You ain't turnin' no damned sea-lawyer, be you, Mr. Slocum?

Mate [*Flushing*] Not by a hell of a sight, sir.

Keeney. What do the fools want to go home fur now? Their share o' the four hundred barrel wouldn't keep 'em in chewin' terbacco.

Mate [*Slowly*] They wants to git back to their folks an' things, I s'pose.

Keeney [*Looking at him searchingly*] 'N you want to turn back, too. [*The* Mate *looks down confusedly before his sharp gaze*] Don't lie, Mr. Slocum. It's writ down plain in your eyes. [*With grim sarcasm*] I hope, Mr. Slocum, you ain't agoin' to jine the men agin me.

Mate [*Indignantly*] That ain't fair, sir, to say sich things.

Keeney [*With satisfaction*] I warn't much afeard o' that, Tom. You been with me nigh on ten year and I've learned ye whalin'. No man kin say I ain't a good master, if I be a hard one.

Mate. I warn't thinkin' of myself, sir—'bout turnin' home, I mean. [*Desperately*] But Mrs.Keeney, sir—seems like she ain't jest satisfied up here, ailin' like—what with the cold an' bad luck an' the ice an' all.

Keeney [*His face clouding—rebukingly but not severely*] That's my business, Mr. Slocum. I'll thank you to steer a clear course o' that. [*A pause*] The ice'll break up soon to no'th'ard. I could see it startin' today. And when it goes and we git some sun Annie'll perk up. [*Another pause—then he bursts forth*] It ain't the damned money what's keepin' me up in the Northern seas, Tom. But I can't go back to Homeport with a measly four hundred barrel of ile. I'd die fust. I ain't never come back home in all my days without a full ship. Ain't that truth?

Mate. Yes, sir; but this voyage you been icebound, an'—

Keeney [*Scornfully*] And d'you s'pose any of 'em would believe that—any o' them skippers I've beaten voyage after voyage? Can't you hear 'em laughin' and sneerin'—Tibbots 'n' Harris 'n' Simms and the rest—and all o' Homeport making' fun o' me? "Dave Keeney what boasts he's the best whalin' skipper out o' Homeport comin' back with a measly four hundred barrel of ile?" [*The thought of this drives him into a frenzy, and he smashes his fist down on the marble top of the sideboard*] Hell! I got to git the ile, I tell you. How could I figger on this ice? It's never been so bad before in the thirty year I been acomin' here. And now it's breakin' up. In a couple o' days it'll be all gone. And they's whale here, plenty of 'em. I know they is and I ain't never gone wrong yit. I got to git the ile! I got to git it in spite of all hell, and by God, I ain't agoin' home till I do git it! [*There is the sound of subdued sobbing from the door in rear. The two men stand silent for a moment, listening. Then* KEENEY *goes over to the door and looks in. He hesitates for a moment as if he were going to enter—then closes the door softly.* JOE, *the harpooner, an enormous six-footer with a battered, ugly face, enters from right and stands waiting for the* CAPTAIN *to notice him.*]

KEENEY [*Turning and seeing him*] Don't be standin' there like a gawk, Harpooner. Speak up!

JOE [*Confusedly*] We want—the men, sir—they wants to send a depitation aft to have a word with you.

KEENEY [*Furiously*] Tell 'em to go to—[*Checks himself and continues grimly*] Tell 'em to come. I'll see 'em.

JOE. Aye, aye, sir. [*He goes out.*]

KEENEY [*With a grim smile*] Here it comes, the trouble you spoke of, Mr. Slocum, and we'll make short shift of it. It's better to crush such things at the start than let them make headway.

MATE [*Worriedly*] Shall I wake up the First and Fourth, sir? We might need their help.

KEENEY. No, let them sleep. I'm well able to handle this alone, Mr. Slocum. [*There is the shuffling of footsteps from outside and five of the crew crowd into the cabin, led by* JOE. *All are dressed alike—sweaters, sea-boots, etc. They glance uneasily at the* CAPTAIN, *twirling their fur caps in their hands.*]

KEENEY [*After a pause*] Well? Who's to speak fur ye?

JOE [*Stepping forward with an air of bravado*] I be.

KEENEY [*Eyeing him up and down coldly*] So you be. Then speak your say and be quick about it.

JOE [*Trying not to wilt before the* CAPTAIN'S *glance and avoiding his eyes*] The time we signed up for is done today.

KEENEY [*Icily*] You're tellin' me nothin' I don't know.

JOE. You ain't pintin' fur home yit, far 's we kin see.

KEENEY. No, and I ain't agoin' to till this ship is full of ile.

JOE. You can't go no further no'th with the ice afore ye.

KEENEY. The ice is breaking up.

JOE [*After a slight pause during which the others mumble angrily to one another*] The grub we're gittin' now is rotten.

KEENEY. It's good enough fur ye. Better men than ye are have eaten worse. [*There is a chorus of angry exclamations from the crowd.*]

JOE [*Encouraged by this support*] We ain't agoin' to work no more less you puts back for home.

KEENEY [*Fiercely*] You ain't, ain't you?

JOE. No; and the law courts'll say we was right.

KEENEY. To hell with your law courts! We're at sea now and I'm the law on this ship. [*Edging up toward the* HARPOONER] And every mother's son of you what don't obey orders goes in irons. [*There are more angry exclamations from the crew.* MRS. KEENEY *appears in the doorway in rear and looks on with startled eyes. None of the men notice her.*]

JOE [*With bravado*] Then we're agoin' to mutiny and take the old hooker home ourselves. Ain't we, boys? [*As he turns his head to look at the others,* KEENEY'S *fist shoots out to the side of his jaw.* JOE *goes down in a heap and lies there.* MRS. KEENEY *gives a shriek and hides her face in her hands. The men pull out their sheath knives and start a rush, but stop when they find themselves confronted by the revolvers of* KEENEY *and the* MATE.]

KEENEY [*His eyes and voice snapping*] Hold still! [*The men stand huddled together in a sullen silence.* KEENEY'S *voice is full of mockery*] You've found out it ain't safe to mutiny on this ship, ain't you? And now git for'ard where ye belong, and—[*He gives* JOE'S *body a contemptuous kick*] drag him with you. And remember the first man of ye I see shirkin' I'll shoot dead as sure as there's a sea under us, and you can tell the rest the same. Git for'ard now! Quick! [*The men leave in cowed silence, carrying* JOE *with them.* KEENEY *turns to the* MATE *with a short laugh and puts his revolver back in his pocket*] Best get up on deck, Mr. Slocum, and see to it they don't try none of their skulkin' tricks. We'll have to keep an eye peeled from now on. I know 'em.

MATE. Yes, sir. [*He goes out, right.* KEENEY *hears his wife's hysterical weeping and turns around in surprise—then walks slowly to her side.*]

KEENEY [*Putting an arm around her shoulder—with gruff tenderness*] There, there, Annie. Don't be afeard. It's all past and gone.

MRS. KEENEY [*Shrinking away from him*] Oh, I can't bear it! I can't bear it any longer!

KEENEY [*Gently*] Can't bear what, Annie?

MRS. KEENEY [*Hysterically*] All this horrible brutality, and these brutes of men, and this terrible ship, and this prison cell of a room, and the ice all around, and the silence. [*After this outburst she calms down and wipes her eyes with her handkerchief.*]

KEENEY [*After a pause during which he looks down at her with a puzzled frown*] Remember, I warn't hankerin' to have you come on this voyage, Annie.

MRS. KEENEY. I wanted to be with you, David, don't you see? I didn't want to wait back there in the house all alone as I've been doing these last six years since we were married—waiting, and watching, and fearing—with nothing to keep my mind occupied—not able to go back teaching school on account of being Dave Keeney's wife. I used to dream of sailing on the great, wide, glorious ocean. I wanted to be by your side in the danger and vigorous life of it all. I wanted to see you the hero they make you out to be in Homeport. And instead—[*Her voice grows tremulous*] all I find is ice and cold—and brutality! [*Her voice breaks.*]

KEENEY. I warned you what it'd be, Annie. "Whalin' ain't no ladies' tea-party," I says to you, and "you better stay to home where you've got all your woman's comforts." [*Shaking his head*] But you was so set on it.

MRS. KEENEY [*Wearily*] Oh, I know it isn't your fault, David. You see, I didn't believe you. I guess I was dreaming about the old Vikings in the story books and I thought you were one of them.

KEENEY [*Protestingly*] I done my best to make it as cozy and comfortable as could be. [MRS. KEENEY *looks around her in wild scorn.*] I even sent to the city for that organ for ye, thinkin' it might be soothin' to ye to be playin' it times when they was calms and things was dull like.

MRS. KEENEY [*Wearily*] Yes, you were very kind, David. I know that. [*She goes to left and lifts the curtains from the porthole and looks out—then suddenly bursts forth*] I won't stand it—I can't stand it—pent up by these walls like a prisoner. [*She runs over to him and throws her arms around him, weeping. He puts his arm protectingly over her shoulders*] Take me away from here, David! If I don't get away from here, out of this terrible ship, I'll go mad! Take me home, David! I can't think any more. I feel as if the cold and the silence were crushing down on my brain. I'm afraid. Take me home!

KEENEY [*Holds her at arm's length and looks at her face anxiously*] Best go to bed, Annie. You ain't yourself. You got fever. Your eyes look so strange like. I ain't never seen you look this way before.

MRS. KEENEY [*Laughing hysterically*] It's the ice and the cold and the silence—they'd make any one look strange.

KEENEY [*Soothingly*] In a month or two, with good luck, three at the most, I'll have her filled with ile and then we'll give her everything she'll stand and pint for home.

MRS. KEENEY. But we can't wait for that—I can't wait. I want to get home. And the men won't wait. They want to get home. It's cruel, it's brutal for you to keep them. You must sail back. You've got no excuse. There's clear water to the south now. If you've a heart at all you've got to turn back.

KEENEY [*Harshly*] I can't, Annie.

MRS. KEENEY. Why can't you?

KEENEY. A woman couldn't rightly understand my reason.

MRS. KEENEY [*Wildly*] Because it's a stupid, stubborn reason. Oh, I heard you talking with the Second Mate. You're afraid the other captains will sneer at you because you didn't come back with a full ship. You want to live up to your silly reputation even if you do have to beat and starve men and drive me mad to do it.

KEENEY [*His jaw set stubbornly*] It ain't that, Annie. Them skippers would never dare sneer to my face. It ain't so much what any one'd say—but—[*He hesitates, struggling to express his meaning*] you see—I've always done it—since my first voyage as skipper. I always come back—with a full ship—and it don't seem right not to— somehow. I been always first whalin' skipper out o' Homeport, and—Don't you see my meanin', Annie? [*He glances at her. She is not looking at him but staring dully in front of her, not hearing a word he is saying*] Annie! [*She comes to herself with a start*] Best turn in, Annie, there's a good woman. You ain't well.

MRS. KEENEY [*Resisting his attempts to guide her to the door in rear*] David! Won't you please turn back?

KEENEY [*Gently*] I can't, Annie—not yet awhile. You don't see my meanin'. I got to git the ile.

MRS. KEENEY. It'd be different if you needed the money, but you don't. You've got more than plenty.

KEENEY [*Impatiently*] It ain't the money I'm thinkin' of. D'you think I'm as mean as that?

MRS. KEENEY [*Dully*] No—I don't know—I can't understand— [*Intensely*] Oh, I want to be home in the old house once more and see my own kitchen again, and hear a woman's voice talking to me and be able to talk to her. Two years! It seems so long ago—as if I'd been dead and could never go back.

KEENEY [*Worried by the strange tone and the far-away look in her eyes*] Best to go to bed, Annie. You ain't well.

MRS. KEENEY [*Not appearing to hear him*] I used to be lonely when you were away. I used to think Homeport was a stupid, monotonous place. Then I used to go down on the beach, especially when it was windy and the breakers were rolling in, and I'd dream of the fine free life you must be leading. [*She gives a laugh which is half a sob*] I used to love the sea then. [*She pauses; then continues with slow intensity*] But now—I don't ever want to see the sea again.

KEENEY [*Thinking to humor her*] 'Tis no fit place for a woman, that's sure. I was a fool to bring ye.

MRS. KEENEY [*After a pause—passing her hand over her eyes with a gesture of pathetic weariness*] How long would it take us to reach home—if we started now?

KEENEY [*Frowning*] 'Bout two months, I reckon, Annie, with fair luck.

MRS. KEENEY [*Counts on her fingers—then murmurs with a rapt smile*]

That would be August, the latter part of August, wouldn't it? It was on the twenty-fifth of August we were married, David, wasn't it?

KEENEY [*Trying to conceal the fact that her memories have moved him—gruffly*] Don't *you* remember?

MRS. KEENEY [*Vaguely—again passes her hand over her eyes*] My memory is leaving me—up here in the ice. It was so long ago. [*A pause—then she smiles dreamily*] It's June now. The lilacs will be all in bloom in the front yard—and the climbing roses on the trellis to the side of the house—they're budding. [*She suddenly covers her face with her hands and commences to sob*]

KEENEY [*Disturbed*] Go in and rest, Annie. You're all wore out cryin' over what can't be helped.

MRS. KEENEY [*Suddenly throwing her arms around his neck and clinging to him*] You love me, don't you, David?

KEENEY [*In amazed embarrassment at this outburst*] Love you? Why d'you ask me such a question, Annie?

MRS. KEENEY [*Shaking him—fiercely*] But you do, don't you, David? Tell me!

KEENEY. I'm your husband, Annie, and you're my wife. Could there be aught but love between us after all these years?

MRS. KEENEY [*Shaking him again—still more fiercely*] Then you do love me. Say it!

KEENEY [*Simply*] I do, Annie.

MRS. KEENEY [*Shaking him again—her hands drop to her sides.* KEENEY *regards her anxiously. She passes her hand across her eyes and murmurs half to herself*] I sometimes think if we could only have had a child. [KEENEY *turns away from her, deeply moved. She grabs his arm and turns him around to face her—intensely*] And I've always been a good wife to you, haven't I, David?

KEENEY [*His voice betraying his emotion*] No man has ever had a better, Annie.

MRS. KEENEY. And I've never asked for much from you, have I, David? Have I?

KEENEY. You know you could have all I got the power to give ye, Annie.

MRS. KEENEY [*Wildly*] Then do this this once for my sake, for God's sake—take me home! It's killing me, this life—the brutality and cold and horror of it. I'm going mad. I can feel the threat in the air. I can hear the silence threatening me—day after gray day and every day the same. I can't bear it. [*Sobbing*] I'll go mad, I know I will. Take me home, David, if you love me as you say. I'm afraid. For the love of God, take me home! [*She throws her arms around him, weeping against his shoulder. His face betrays the tremendous struggle going on within him. He holds her out at arm's length, his expression softening. For a moment his shoulders sag, he becomes old, his iron spirit weakens as he looks at her tear-stained face.*]

KEENEY [*Dragging out the words with an effort*] I'll do it, Annie—for your sake—if you say it's needful for ye.

MRS. KEENEY [*Wild with joy—kissing him*] God bless you for that, David! [*He turns away from her silently and walks toward the companionway. Just at that moment there is a clatter of footsteps on the stairs and the* SECOND MATE *enters the cabin.*]

MATE [*Excitedly*] The ice is breakin' up to no'th'ard, sir. There's a clear passage through the floe, and clear water beyond, the lookout says. [KEENEY *straightens himself like a man coming out of a trance.* MRS. KEENEY *looks at the* MATE *with terrified eyes.*]

KEENEY [*Dazedly—trying to collect his thoughts*] A clear passage? To no'th'ard?

MATE. Yes, sir.

KEENEY [*His voice suddenly grim with determination*] Then get her ready and we'll drive her through.

MATE. Aye, aye, sir.

MRS. KEENEY [*Appealingly*] David!

KEENEY [*Not heeding her*] Will the men turn to willin' or must we drag 'em out?

MATE. They'll turn to willin' enough. You put the fear o' God into 'em, sir. They're meek as lambs.

KEENEY. Then drive 'em—both watches. [*With grim determination*] They's whale t'other side o' this floe and we're going to git 'em.

MATE. Aye, aye, sir. [*He goes out hurriedly. A moment later there is the sound of scuffling feet from the deck outside and the* MATE's *voice shouting orders.*]

KEENEY [*Speaking aloud to himself—derisively*] And I was agoin' home like a yaller dog!

MRS. KEENEY [*Imploringly*] David!

KEENEY [*Sternly*] Woman, you ain't adoin' right when you meddle in men's business and weaken 'em. You can't know my feelin's. I got to prove a man to be a good husband for ye to take pride in. I got to git the ile, I tell ye.

MRS. KEENEY [*Supplicatingly*] David! Aren't you going home?

KEENEY [*Ignoring this question—commandingly*] You ain't well. Go and lay down a mite. [*He starts for the door*] I got to git on deck. [*He goes out. She cries after him in anguish*] David! [*A pause. She passes her hand across her eyes—then commences to laugh hysterically and goes to the organ. She sits down and starts to play wildly an old hymn.*

KEENEY *reenters from the doorway to the deck and stands looking at her angrily. He comes over and grabs her roughly by the shoulder.*]

KEENEY. Woman, what foolish mockin' is this? [*She laughs wildly and he starts back from her in alarm*] Annie! What is it? [*She doesn't answer him.* KEENEY's *voice trembles*] Don't you know me, Annie? [*He puts both hands on her shoulders and turns her around so that he can look into her eyes. She stares up at him with a stupid expression, a vague smile on her lips. He stumbles away from her, and she commences softly to play the organ again.*]

KEENEY [*Swallowing hard—in a hoarse whisper, as if he had difficulty in speaking*] You said—you was agoin' mad—God! [*A long wail is heard from the deck above*] Ah bl-o-o-o-ow! [*A moment later the* MATE's *face appears through the skylight. He cannot see* MRS. KEENEY.]

MATE [*In great excitement*] Whales, sir—a whole school of 'em—off the star'b'd quarter 'bout five miles away—big ones!

KEENEY [*Galvanized into action*] Are you lowerin' the boats?

MATE. Yes, sir.

KEENEY [*With grim decision*] I'm acomin' with ye.

MATE. Aye, aye, sir. [*Jubilantly*] You'll git the ile now right enough, sir. [*His head is withdrawn and he can be heard shouting orders*]

KEENEY [*Turning to his wife*] Annie! Did you hear him? I'll git the ile. [*She doesn't answer or seem to know he is there. He gives a hard laugh, which is almost a groan*] I know you're foolin' me, Annie. You ain't out of your mind—[*Anxiously*] be you? I'll git the ile now right enough—jest a little while longer, Annie—then we'll turn hom'ard. I can't turn back now, you see that, don't ye? I've got to git the ile. [*In sudden terror*] Answer me! You ain't mad, be you? [*She keeps on playing the organ, but makes no reply. The* MATE's *face appears again through the skylight.*]

MATE. All ready, sir. [KEENEY *turns his back on his wife and strides to the doorway, where he stands for a moment and looks back at her in anguish, fighting to control his feelings.*]

MATE. Comin', sir?

KENNEY [*His face suddenly grown hard with determination*] Aye. [*He turns abruptly and goes out.* MRS. KEENEY *does not appear to notice his departure. Her whole attention seems centered in the organ. She sits with half-closed eyes, her body swaying a little from side to side to the rhythm of the hymn. Her fingers move faster and faster and she is playing wildly and discordantly as*]

The Curtain Falls.

Considerations

Ile, of course, is a dialect pronunciation of the word *oil,* and oil—whale oil—is the center of this play that deals with some aspects of life and livelihood of the New England whalers of years ago.

But the whaling industry of days gone by is merely the setting for a playing out of deeper issues. In drama the conflicts available to be revealed can be summarized as: person against nature; person against person; and a person against himself. We have all three types of conflict in this play. There is a ship full of people who have been in the Northern seas for a year, and it's time for them to come home. They've been frozen in ice, labored under cold, grey skies, faced desolation, have gotten nothing for their pains—no whales (or success or income). This is man against universe.

As for people against people, we see the crew against the captain, the wife and the captain in conflict. Finally, and almost the most dramatic, we have the captain against himself, his image of himself. Which one dominates? It depends a bit on the way each reader views the play. If we're terribly sympathetic to Annie, which we are inclined to be, then that conflict is paramount. We can all empathize with the idea of everything going against us.

A special peculiarity of Eugene O'Neill's plays is that stage directions are an integral part for the reader. Some of the stage directions could never be adequately translated by an actor or set designer ("He's a hard man. . . ." "The light which comes through the skylight is sickly and faint."), but they are intended to suggest the attitude with which we should approach the rest. It's not part of the play—and yet it *is* part of the play. "Ocean and sky are alike dead" is something that couldn't be shown on stage, but when we read it, we remember having had the feeling before.

He's a hard man, the play says about Keeney, and we instantly think he's hard toward his wife and crew; but one might argue that he's equally hard on himself. To say that he cares nothing for Annie is to misread the play. He does. How do we know that? She says so; he says so. They've been together ten years; he brought an organ on board for her; he didn't think he'd stay a year so he brought her with him, at her request and against his own better judgment. So we know he does care about her, even if we may not admire the way he treats her.

Then there's Keeney's conflict with himself. In one respect this does involve other people—the other captains, what other people will think. Yet "what other people will think" is often a matter of projection of our own thoughts. We don't really *know* what they think. Keeney says at one point "I've got to get the ile." What does the phrase "got to" mean? Will he get fired, killed, lose his wife, his crew? Why has he got to—just because he's never come home without a full ship before?

In summary, what do you think is the central function of the play? Is it to reveal Keeney's character? Is he believable? Is it to reveal the conflict with Annie? If so, is it believable? Is it an overall matter of the three conflicts, and if so, are they all acceptably presented? And with all this conflict, who or what finally wins?

The Man with the Flower in His Mouth

Translated by Eric Bentley

LUIGI PIRANDELLO

CHARACTERS

THE MAN WITH THE FLOWER IN HIS MOUTH
A PEACEFUL CUSTOMER

Towards the end, at the points indicated, a WOMAN *is seen at the corner, clad in black, and wearing an old hat with drooping feathers.*

SCENE: *At the back, we see the trees of an avenue and electric lights showing through the leaves. On both sides, the last houses of a street which leads into this avenue. Among the houses on the left, a cheap all-night cafe, with chairs and little tables on the sidewalk. In front of the houses on the right, a streetlamp, lit. On the left, where the street meets the avenue, there is another lamp affixed to the corner house; it too is lit. At intervals, the vibrant notes of a mandolin are heard in the distance.*
When the curtain rises, THE MAN WITH THE FLOWER IN HIS MOUTH *is sitting at a table and looking in silence at the* PEACEFUL CUSTOMER *who is at the next table, sucking a mint frappé through a straw.*

MAN. Well, what I was just going to say . . . Here you are, a law-abiding
   sort of man . . . You missed your train?
CUSTOMER. By one minute. I get to the station and see the damn thing
   just pulling out.
MAN. You could have run after it.
CUSTOMER. Sure—but for those damn packages. I looked like an old
   packhorse covered with luggage. Isn't that silly? But you know how
   women are. Errands, errands, errands! You're never through. God!
   You know how long it took me to get my fingers on the strings of all
   those packages—when I climbed out of the cab? Three solid
   minutes. Two packages to each finger.

MAN. What a sight! Know what *I'd* have done? Left 'em in the cab.

CUSTOMER. How about my wife? And my daughters? And all the other women?

MAN. They'd squawk. I'd enjoy that.

CUSTOMER. You don't seem to know how women carry on when they get out in the country.

MAN. I know exactly how they carry on. [*Pause*] They tell you they won't need a thing, they can live on nothing.

CUSTOMER. Worse, they pretend they live there to *save* money. They go out to one of those villages*—the uglier and filthier the better—and then insist on wearing all their fanciest getups! Women! But I suppose it's their vocation. "If you're going into town, could you get me one of these—and one of those—and would it trouble you *too* much to get me . . ." Would it trouble you *too* much! "And since you'll be right next door to . . ." "Now really, darling, how do you expect me to get all that done in three hours?" "Why not? Can't you take a cab?" And the hell of it is—figuring on those three hours—I didn't bring the keys to our house here in town.

MAN. Quite a thing. So?

CUSTOMER. I left my pile of packages at the station—in the parcel room. Then I went to a restaurant for supper. Then I went to the theatre—to get rid of my bad temper. The heat nearly killed me. Coming out, I say: "And now, what? It's after midnight. There isn't a train till four. All that fuss for a couple of hours of sleep? Not worth the price of the ticket." So here I am. Open all night, isn't it?

MAN. All night. [*Pause*] So you left your packages in the parcel room?

CUSTOMER. Why do you ask? Don't you think they're safe? They were tied up good and . . .

MAN. Oh, sure, sure! [*Pause*] I feel *sure* they're safe. I know how well these salesmen wrap their stuff. They make quite a specialty of it. [*Pause*] I can see their hands now. What hands! They take a good big piece of paper, double thickness, sort of a reddish color, wavy lines on it—a pleasure just to look at it—so smooth, you could press it against your cheek and feel how cool and delicate it is . . . They roll it out on the counter and then place your cloth in the middle of it with *such* agility—fine cloth too, neatly folded. They raise one edge of the paper with the back of the hand, lower the other one, and bring the two edges together in an elegant fold—*that's* just thrown in for good measure . . . Then they fold the corners down in a triangle with its apex turned in like this. Then they reach out with one hand for the box of string, instinctively pull off just exactly enough, and tie up the parcel so quickly you haven't even time to

---

*The scene is rather obviously laid in Rome. The villages where "commuters" live are some ten miles out.

admire their . . . virtuosity—the little loop is ready for your finger!

CUSTOMER. Anyone can see you've given a lot of attention to this matter.

MAN. Have I! My dear man, I spend whole days at it. What's more, I can spend a solid hour at a single store window. I lose myself in it. I seem to *be* that piece of silk, I'd *like* to be that piece of silk, that bit of braid, that ribbon—red or blue—that the salesgirls are measuring with their tape and—you've seen what they do with it before they wrap it up?—they twist it round the thumb and little finger of their left hand in a figure eight! [*Pause*] I look at the shoppers as they come out of the store with their bundle on their finger—or in their hand—or under their arm. I watch them pass. My eyes follow them till they're out of sight. I imagine, oh, I imagine so many, many things, you've no idea, how could you have? [*Pause. Then, darkly, as to himself*] All the same, it helps.

CUSTOMER. What helps?

MAN. Latching on—to life. With the imagination. Like a creeper around the bars of a gate. [*Pause*] Giving it no rest—my imagination, I mean—clinging, clinging with my imagination to the lives of others—all the time. Not people I know, of course. I couldn't do that. That'd be annoying, it'd nauseate me if *they* knew. No. Just strangers. With them my imagination can work freely. Not capriciously, though. Oh no, I take account of the smallest things I can find out about them. You've no idea how my imagination functions. I work my way *in.* In! I get to see this man's house—or that man's. I live in it, I feel I belong there. And I begin to notice—you know how a house, any old house, has its own air, how there's something special about the air in it? Your house? Mine? Of course, in your own house, you don't notice it any more, it's *your* air, the air of *your* life, isn't it? Uh huh. I see you agree—

CUSTOMER. I only meant . . . well, I was thinking what a good time you must have imagining all this!

MAN [*annoyed, after thinking a moment*] Good time? I had a—!

CUSTOMER. Good time, yes. I can just see you—

MAN. Tell me something. Did you ever consult an eminent physician?

CUSTOMER. Me? Why should I? I'm not sick!

MAN. Just a moment. I ask because I'd like to know if you ever saw a fine doctor's waiting room—full of patients waiting their turn?

CUSTOMER. Well, yes. I once had to take my little girl. She's nervous.

MAN. Okay. You needn't tell me. It's the waiting rooms . . . [*Pause*] Have you ever given them much attention? The old-fashioned couch with dark covers, the upholstered table chairs that don't match as a rule . . . the armchairs? Stuff bought at sales and auctions, coming together there by accident, for the convenience of the patients. It doesn't belong to the house. The doctor has quite another sort of room for himself, for his wife, his wife's friends . . . lavish . . . lovely . . . If you took one of the chairs from the drawing room and put it in the waiting room, why, it'd stick out like a sore thumb. Not that the waiting room isn't just right—nothing special of course but quite proper, quite respectable . . . I'd like to know if you—when you went with your little girl—if you took a good look at the chair you sat in?

CUSTOMER. Well, um, no, I guess I didn't.

MAN. Of course not. You weren't sick . . . [*Pause*] But often even the sick don't notice. They're all taken up with their sickness. [*Pause*] How many times they sit, some of them, staring at their finger which is making meaningless markings on the polished arm of the chair. They're thinking—so they don't see. [*Pause*] And what an impression you get when you get out of the doctor's office and cross the waiting room and see the chair you'd been sitting in awaiting sentence on the as yet unknown sickness just a short time before! Now, there's another patient on it and *he's* hugging his secret sickness too. Or it's empty—oh, how *impassive* it looks!—waiting for Mr. X to come and sit on it. [*Pause*] What were we saying? Oh, yes. The pleasure of imagining things. And I suddenly thought of a chair in one of those waiting rooms. Why?

CUSTOMER. Yes, it certainly . . .

MAN. You don't see the connection? Neither do I. [*Pause*] You recall an image, you recall another image, they're unrelated, and yet—they're *not* unrelated—for you. Oh, no, they have their reasons, they stem from *your* experience. Of course you have to pretend they don't. When you talk, you have to forget them. Most often they're so illogical, these . . . analogies. [*Pause*] The connection could be this, maybe. Listen. Do you think those chairs get any pleasure from imagining which patient will sit on them next? What sickness lurks inside him? Where he'll go, what he'll do after this visit? Of course they don't. And it's the same with me! I get no pleasure from it. There are those poor chairs and here am I. *They* open their arms to the doctor's patients, *I* open mine to . . . this person or that. You for instance. And yet I get no pleasure—no pleasure at all—from the train you missed, the family waiting for that train in the country, your other little troubles . . .

CUSTOMER. I've plenty, you know that?

MAN. You should thank God they're little. [*Pause*] Some people have big troubles, my dear sir. [*Pause*] As I was saying, I feel the need to latch on—by the skin of my . . . imagination—to the lives of others. Yet I get no pleasure from this. It doesn't even interest me. Quite the reverse, quite . . . One wants to see what their troubles are just to prove to oneself that life is idiotic and stupid! So that one won't mind being through with it!! [*With dark rage*] Proving that to yourself takes quite a bit of doing, huh? You need evidence, you need a hundred and one instances, and—you—must—be—*implacable!* Because, well, because, my dear sir, there's something—we don't know what it's made of, but it exists—and we all feel it, we feel it like a pain in the throat—it's the hunger for life! A hunger that is never appeased—that never *can* be appeased—because life—life as we live it from moment to moment—is so hungry itself, hungry *for* itself, we never get to taste it even! The taste of life, the flavor and savor of life, is all in the past, we carry it inside us. Or rather it's always at a distance from us. We're tied to it only by a slender thread, the rope of memory. Yes, memory ties us to . . . what? that idiocy, these irritations, those silly illusions, mad pursuits like . . . yes . . . What today is idiocy, what today is an irritation, even what today is a misfortune, a grave misfortune, look! Four years pass, five years, ten, and who knows what savor or flavor it will have, what tears will be shed over it, how—it—will—*taste!* Life, life! You only have to think of giving it up—especially if it's a matter of days—[*At this point the head of* THE WOMAN IN BLACK *is seen at the corner*] Look! See that? At the corner! See that woman, that shadow of a woman? She's hiding now.

CUSTOMER. What? Who was it?

MAN. You didn't see? She's hiding now.

CUSTOMER. A woman?

MAN. My wife.

CUSTOMER. Ah! Your wife? [*Pause*]

MAN. She keeps an eye on me. Oh, sometimes I could just go over and kick her! It wouldn't do any good, though. She's as stubborn as a lost dog: the more you kick it, the closer it sticks to you. [*Pause*] What that woman is suffering on my account you could not imagine. She doesn't eat. Doesn't sleep any more. Just follows me around. Night and day. At a distance. She *might* brush her clothes once in a while—and that old shoe of a hat. She isn't a woman any more. Just—a rag doll. Her hair's going gray, yes, the white dust has settled on her temples forever, and she's only thirty-four. [*Pause*] She annoys me. You wouldn't believe how much she annoys me. Sometimes I grab hold of her and shake her. "You're an idiot!" I shout. She takes it. She stands there looking at me. Oh, that look! It makes my fingers itch. I feel like strangling her! Nothing happens, of course. She just waits till I'm a short way off. Then she starts following me again. [THE WOMAN IN BLACK *again sticks her head out*] Look! There's her head again!

CUSTOMER. Poor woman!

MAN. Poor woman? You know what she wants? She wants me to stay and take it easy at home—all cozy and quiet—and let her be nice to me, look after me, show me wifely tenderness . . . Home! The rooms in perfect order, the furniture elegant and neat, silence reigns . . . It used to, anyway. Silence—measured by the tick-tocking of the dining-room clock! [*Pause*] That's what she wants! I just want you to see the absurdity of it! Isn't it absurd? It's worse: it's cruel, it's macabre! Don't you see? Think of Messina. Or Avezzano. Suppose they knew an earthquake was coming. Do you think those cities could just sit? You think they could just sit calmly in the moonlight waiting for it? Carefully preserving the lovely lines of their streets and the spaciousness of their piazzas? Not daring to deviate one inch from the plans of the City Planning Commission? You're crazy. Those cities would drop everything and take to their heels! Every house, every stone, would take to its heels! [*Wheeling on the* CUSTOMER] You agree?

CUSTOMER [*frightened*] Well . . .

MAN. Well, just suppose the people knew? The citizens of Avezzano and Messina. Would they calmly get undressed and go to bed? Fold their clothes and put their shoes outside the door? Creep down under the bedclothes and enjoy the nice clean feeling of freshly laundered sheets? Knowing that—in a few hours—they would be dead?—You think they might?

CUSTOMER. Maybe your wife—

MAN. Let me finish. [*Starting over*] If death, my dear sir, if death were some strange, filthy insect that just . . . settled on you, as it were, took you unawares, shall we say . . . You're walking along. All of a sudden a passerby stops you, and, with finger and thumb cautiously extended, says: "Excuse me, sir, excuse me, honored sir, but death has settled on you!" And with finger and thumb cautiously extended, he takes it and throws it in the gutter. Wouldn't that be wonderful? But death is not an insect. It has settled on many walkers in the city—however far away their thoughts may be, however carefree they may feel. They don't see it. They're thinking what they'll be doing tomorrow. But I [*He gets up*] . . . Look, my dear sir, come here [*He gets the* CUSTOMER *up and takes him under the lighted lamp*] under the lamp. Come over here. I'll show you something. Look! Under this side of my mustache. See that little knob? Royal purple? Know what they call it? It has such a poetic name. It suggests something soft and sweet. Like a caramel. Epithelioma. [*The "o" is stressed*] Try it, isn't it soft and sweet? Epithelioma. Understand? Death passed my way. He stuck this . . . flower in my mouth and said: "Keep it, old chap. I'll stop by again in eight months—or maybe ten." [*Pause*] Now tell me. *You* tell me. Can I just sit quietly at home as that unhappy girl wishes me to—with this flower in my mouth? [*Pause*] I yell at her. "So you want me to kiss you, do you?" "Yes, yes, kiss me!" You know what she did? A couple of weeks ago she took a pin and cut herself—here—on the lip—then she took hold of my head and tried to kiss me, tried to kiss me on the mouth. She said she wanted to die with me. [*Pause*] She's insane. [*Angrily*] I'm not home! Ever! What I want is to stand at store windows admiring the virtuosity of salesmen! Because, you see, if ever, for one second, I am not occupied, if ever I'm *empty*—know what I mean?—why, I might take a life and think nothing of it, I might destroy the life in someone . . . someone I don't even know, I'd take a gun and kill someone—like you maybe—someone who's missed his train. [*He laughs*] Of course, I'm only joking. [*Pause*] I'll go now. [*Pause*] It'd be myself I'd kill. [*Pause*] At this time of year, there's a certain kind of apricot, it's good . . . How do *you* eat them? Skin and all? You cut them in exact halves, you take hold with finger and thumb, lengthwise, like this . . . then! [*He swallows*] How succulent! Pure delight! Like a woman's lips! [*He laughs. Pause*] I wish to send my best wishes to your good lady and her daughters in your country home. [*Pause*] I imagine them . . . I imagine them dressed in white and light blue in the middle of a lovely green meadow under the shade of . . . [*Pause*] Will you do me a favor when you arrive, tomorrow morning? As I figure it, your village is a certain distance from the station. It is dawn. You will be on foot. The first tuft of grass you see by the roadside—count the number of blades, will you? Just count the blades of grass. The number will be the number of days I have to live. [*Pause*] One last request: pick a big tuft! [*He laughs*] Then: Good night!

> *He walks away humming through closed lips the tune which the mandolin is playing in the distance. He is approaching the corner on the right. But at a certain point—remembering his Wife—he turns and sneaks off in the opposite direction. The* CUSTOMER *follows with his eyes—more or less dumbfounded.*

CURTAIN

Considerations

It is a cliché of life that two strangers meeting in passing—on a plane, in a foreign city, at a bar—often tell each other things they would never tell a friend. Here Pirandello has presented a neutral setting—two strangers on their separate ways—and recorded a short conversation that reveals not only the background of each but something about the way human beings approach sickness and death. It is an exceptionally human play.

There are a number of levels on which this play can be appreciated. Especially enjoyable are Pirandello's insights into the mechanics of dealing with life. Note how the man with the flower behaves: "tripping out" and losing himself in a store window; latching onto life with the imagination "like a creeper around the bars of a gate"; recalling seemingly unrelated images that are related in his mind; despairing today in the midst of pain and sorrow but still cherishing (as do the Pattons in "A Summer Tragedy") visions of self from the past.

The clues to what is happening are few and far between until suddenly, with the sick man's naming his disease, the tempo picks up, and there is a very fast finish. What do the last words "more or less dumbfounded" add to your understanding of the play? Realizing that if you *saw* the play, these words would not exist for you, what do you feel would be lost by their absence?

The Jewels of the Shrine

JAMES ENE HENSHAW

CHARACTERS

OKORIE, *an old man*
AROB ⎫
OJIMA ⎬ *Okorie's grandsons*

BASSI, *a woman*
A STRANGER

SCENE: *An imaginary village close to a town in Nigeria. All the scenes of this play take place in* OKORIE'S *mud-walled house. The time is the present.*

SCENE I

The hall in OKORIE'S *house. There are three doors. One leads directly into* OKORIE'S *room. The two others are on either side of the hall. Of these, one leads to his grandsons' apartment, whilst the other acts as a general exit.*

The chief items of furniture consist of a wide bamboo bed, on which is spread a mat; a wooden chair, a low table, and a few odds and ends, including three hoes.

OKORIE, *an old man of about eighty years of age, with scanty grey hair, and dressed in the way his village folk do, is sitting at the edge of the bed. He holds a stout, rough walking-stick and a horn filled with palm wine.*

On the wooden chair near the bed sits a STRANGER, *a man of about forty-five years of age. He, too, occasionally sips wine from a calabash cup. It is evening. The room is rather dark, and a cloth-in-oil lantern hangs from a hook on the wall.*

OKORIE. Believe me, Stranger, in my days things were different. It was a happy thing to become an old man, because young people were taught to respect elderly men.

STRANGER [*sipping his wine*] Here in the village you should be happier. In the town where I come from, a boy of ten riding a hired bicycle will knock down a man of fifty years without any feeling of pity.

OKORIE. Bicycle. That is why I have not been to town for ten years.

From PLAYS FROM BLACK AFRICA, published by Hill and Wang, Inc. Reprinted by permission of Hodder & Stoughton.

Town people seem to enjoy rushing about doing nothing. It kills them.

STRANGER. You are lucky that you have your grandchildren to help you. Many people in town have no one to help them.

OKORIE. Look at me, Stranger, and tell me if these shabby clothes and this dirty beard show that I have good grandchildren. Believe me, Stranger, in my younger days things were different. Old men were happy. When they died, they were buried with honour. But in my case, Stranger, my old age has been unhappy. And my only fear now is that when I die, my grandsons will not accord me the honour due to my age. It will be a disgrace to me.

STRANGER. I will now go on my way, Okorie. May God help you.

OKORIE. I need help, Stranger, for although I have two grandsons, I am lonely and unhappy because they do not love or care for me. They tell me that I am from an older world. Farewell, Stranger. If you call again and I am alive, I will welcome you back.

Exit STRANGER. BASSI, *a beautiful woman of about thirty years, enters.*

BASSI. Who was that man, Grandfather?

OKORIE. He was a stranger.

BASSI. I do not trust strangers. They may appear honest when the lights are on. But as soon as there is darkness, they creep back as thieves. [OKORIE *smiles and drinks his wine.* BASSI *points to him*] What has happened, Grandfather? When I left you this afternoon, you were old, your mind was worried, and your eyes were swollen. Where now are the care, the sorrow, the tears in your eyes? You never smiled before, but now—

OKORIE. The stranger has brought happiness back into my life. He has given me hope again.

BASSI. But don't they preach in town that it is only God who gives hope? Every other thing gives despair.

OKORIE. Perhaps that stranger was God. Don't the preachers say that God moves like a stranger?

BASSI. God moves in strange ways.

OKORIE. Yes, I believe it, because since that stranger came, I have felt younger again. You know, woman, when I worshipped at our forefathers' shrine, I was happy. I knew what it was all about. It was my life. Then the preachers came, and I abandoned the beliefs of our fathers. The old ways did not leave me, the new ways did not wholly accept me. I was therefore unhappy. But soon I felt the wings of God carrying me high. And with my loving and helpful son, I thought that my old age would be as happy as that of my father before me. But death played me a trick. My son died and I was left to the mercy of his two sons. Once more unhappiness gripped my life. With all their education my grandsons lacked one thing—respect for age. But today the stranger who came here has once more brought happiness to me. Let me tell you this——

BASSI. It is enough, Grandfather. Long talks make you tired. Come, your food is now ready.

OKORIE [*happily*] Woman, I cannot eat. When happiness fills your heart, you cannot eat.

    Two voices are heard outside, laughing and swearing.

BASSI. Your grandchildren are coming back.

OKORIE. Don't call them my grandchildren. I am alone in this world.

    Door flings open. Two young men, about eighteen and twenty, enter the room. They are in shirt and trousers.

AROB. By our forefathers, Grandfather, you are still awake!

BASSI. Why should he not keep awake if he likes?

AROB. But Grandfather usually goes to bed before the earliest chicken thinks of it.

OJIMA. Our good grandfather might be thinking of his youthful days, when all young men were fond of farming and all young women loved the kitchen.

BASSI. Shame on both of you for talking to an old man like that. When you grow old, your own children will laugh and jeer at you. Come, Grandfather, and take your food.

    OKORIE *stands up with difficulty and limps with the aid of his stick through the exit, followed by* BASSI, *who casts a reproachful look on the two men before she leaves.*

AROB. I wonder what Grandfather and the woman were talking about.

OJIMA. It must be the usual thing. We are bad boys. We have no regard for the memory of our father, and so on.

AROB. Our father left his responsibility to us. Nature had arranged that he should bury Grandfather before thinking of himself.

OJIMA. But would Grandfather listen to Nature when it comes to the matter of death? Everybody in his generation, including all his wives, have died. But Grandfather had made a bet with death. And it seems that he will win.

OKORIE [*calling from offstage*] Bassi! Bassi! Where is that woman?

OJIMA. The old man is coming. Let us hide ourselves. [*Both rush under the bed*]

OKORIE [*comes in, limping on his stick as usual*] Bassi, where are you? Haven't I told that girl never——

BASSI [*entering*] Don't shout so. It's not good for you.

OKORIE. Where are the two people?

BASSI. You mean your grandsons?

OKORIE. My, my, well, call them what you like.

BASSI. They are not here. They must have gone into their room.

OKORIE. Bassi, I have a secret for you. [*He narrows his eyes*] A big secret. [*His hands tremble*] Can you keep a secret?

BASSI. Of course I can.

OKORIE [*rubbing his forehead*] You can, what can you? What did I say?

BASSI [*holding him and leading him to sit on the bed*] You are excited. You know that whenever you are excited, you begin to forget things.

OKORIE. That is not my fault. It is old age. Well, but what was I saying?

BASSI. You asked me if I could keep a secret.

OKORIE. Yes, yes, a great secret. You know, Bassi, I have been an unhappy man.

BASSI. I have heard it all before.

OKORIE. Listen, woman. My dear son died and left me to the mercy of his two sons. They are the worst grandsons in the land. They have sold all that their father left. They do not care for me. Now when I die, what will they do to me? Don't you think that they will abandon me in disgrace? An old man has a right to be properly cared for. And when he dies, he has a right to a good burial. But my grandchildren do not think of these things.

BASSI. See how you tremble, Grandfather! I have told you not to think of such things.

OKORIE. Why should I not? But sh! . . . I hear a voice.

BASSI. It's only your ears deceiving you, Grandfather.

OKORIE. It is not my ears, woman. I know when old age hums in my ears and tired nerves ring bells in my head, but I know also when I hear a human voice.

BASSI. Go on, Grandfather; there is no one.

OKORIE. Now, listen. You saw the stranger that came here. He gave me hope. But wait, look around, Bassi. Make sure that no one is listening to us.

BASSI. No one, Grandfather.

OKORIE. Open the door and look.

BASSI [*opens the exit door*] No one.

OKORIE. Look into that corner.

BASSI [*looks*] There is no one.

OKORIE. Look under the bed.

BASSI [*irritably*] I won't, Grandfather. There is no need; I have told you that there is nobody in the house.

OKORIE [*pitiably*] I have forgotten what I was talking about.

BASSI [*calmly*] You have a secret from the stranger.

OKORIE. Yes, the stranger told me something. Have you ever heard of the "Jewels of the Shrine"?

BASSI. Real jewels?

OKORIE. Yes. Among the beads which my father got from the early white men, were real jewels. When war broke out and a great fever invaded all our lands, my father made a sacrifice in the village shrine. He promised that if this village were spared, he would offer his costly jewels to the shrine. Death roamed through all the other villages, but not one person in this village died of the fever. My father kept his promise. In a big ceremony the jewels were placed on our shrine. But it was not for long. Some said they were stolen. But the stranger who came here knew where they were. He said that they were buried somewhere near the big oak tree on our farm. I must go out and dig for them. They can be sold for fifty pounds these days.

BASSI. But, Grandfather, it will kill you to go out in this cold and darkness. You must get someone to do it for you. You cannot lift a hoe.

OKORIE [*infuriated*] So, you believe I am too old to lift a hoe. You, you, oh, I . . .

BASSI [*coaxing him*] There now, young man, no temper. If you wish, I myself will dig up the whole farm for you.

OKORIE. Every bit of it?

BASSI. Yes.

OKORIE. And hand over to me all that you will find?

BASSI. Yes.

OKORIE. And you will not tell my grandsons?

BASSI. No, Grandfather, I will not.

OKORIE. Swear, woman, swear by our fathers' shrine.

BASSI. I swear.

OKORIE [*relaxing*] Now life is becoming worthwhile. Tell no one about it, woman. Begin digging tomorrow morning. Dig inch by inch until you bring out the jewels of our forefathers' shrine.

BASSI. I am tired, Grandfather. I must sleep now. Good night.

OKORIE [*with feeling*] Good night. God and our fathers' spirits keep you. When dangerous bats alight on the roofs of wicked men, let them not trouble you in your sleep. When far-seeing owls hoot the menace of future days, let their evil prophecies keep off your path. [BASSI *leaves.* OKORIE, *standing up and trembling, moves to a corner and brings out a small hoe. Struggling with his senile joints, he tries to imitate a young man digging*] Oh, who said I was old? After all, I am only eighty years. And I feel younger than most young men. Let me see how I can dig. [*He tries to dig again*] Ah! I feel aches all over my hip. Maybe the soil here is too hard. [*He listens*] How I keep on thinking that I hear people whispering in this room! I must rest now.

Carrying the hoe with him, he goes into his room. AROB *and* OJIMA *crawl out from under the bed.*

AROB [*stretching his hip*] My hip, oh my hip!

OJIMA. My legs!

AROB. So there is a treasure in our farm! We must waste no time; we must begin digging soon.

OJIMA. Soon? We must begin tonight—now. The old man has taken one hoe. [*Pointing to the corner*] There are two over there. [*They fetch two hoes from among the heap of things in a corner of the room*] If we can only get the jewels, we can go and live in town and let the old man manage as he can. Let's move now.

> As they are about to go out, each holding a hoe, OKORIE comes out with his own hoe. For a moment the three stare at each other in silence and surprise.

AROB. Now, Grandfather, where are you going with a hoe at this time of night?

OJIMA [*impudently*] Yes, Grandfather, what is the idea?

OKORIE. I should ask you; this is my house. Why are you creeping about like thieves?

AROB. All right, Grandfather, we are going back to bed.

OKORIE. What are you doing with hoes? You were never fond of farming.

OJIMA. We intend to go to the farm early in the morning.

OKORIE. But the harvest is over. When everybody in the village was digging out the crops, you were going around the town with your hands in your pockets. Now you say you are going to the farm.

OJIMA. Digging is good for the health, Grandfather.

OKORIE [*re-entering his room*] Good night.

AROB *and* OJIMA. Good night, Grandfather.

> They return to their room. After a short time AROB and OJIMA come out, each holding a hoe, and tiptoe out through the exit. Then, gently, OKORIE too comes out on his toes, and placing the hoe on his shoulder, warily leaves the hall.

CURTAIN.

SCENE II

The same, the following morning.

BASSI [*knocking at* OKORIE'S *door; she is holding a hoe*] Grandfather, wake up. I am going to the farm.

OKORIE [*opening the door*] Good morning. Where are you going so early in the morning?

BASSI. I am going to dig up the farm. You remember the treasure, don't you?

OKORIE. Do you expect to find a treasure whilst you sleep at night? You should have dug at night, woman. Treasures are never found in the day.

BASSI. But you told me to dig in the morning, Grandfather.

OKORIE. My grandsons were in this room somewhere. They heard what I told you about the Jewels of the Shrine.

BASSI. They could not have heard us. I looked everywhere. The stranger must have told them.

OKORIE [*rubbing his forehead*] What stranger?

BASSI. The stranger who told you about the treasure in the farm.

OKORIE. So it was a stranger who told me! Oh, yes, a stranger! [*He begins to dream*] Ah, I remember him now. He was a great man. His face shone like the sun. It was like the face of God.

BASSI. You are dreaming, Grandfather. Wake up! I must go to the farm quickly.

OKORIE. Yes, woman, I remember the jewels in the farm. But you are too late.

BASSI [*excitedly*] Late? Have your grandsons discovered the treasure?

OKORIE. They have not, but I have discovered it myself.

BASSI [*amazed*] You? [OKORIE *nods his head with a smile on his face*] Do you mean to say that you are now a rich man?

OKORIE. By our fathers' shrine, I am.

BASSI. So you went and worked at night. You should not have done it, even to forestall your grandchildren.

OKORIE. My grandsons would never have found it.

BASSI. But you said that they heard us talking of the treasure.

OKORIE. You see, I suspected that my grandsons were in this room. So I told you that the treasure was in the farm, but in actual fact it was in the little garden behind this house, where the village shrine used to be. My grandsons travelled half a mile to the farm last night for nothing.

BASSI. Then I am glad I did not waste my time.

OKORIE [*with delight*] How my grandsons must have toiled in the night! [*He is overcome with laughter*] My grandsons, they thought I would die in disgrace, a pauper, unheard of. No, not now. [*Then boldly*] But those wicked children must change, or when I die, I shall not leave a penny for them.

BASSI. Oh, Grandfather, to think you are a rich man!

OKORIE. I shall send you to buy me new clothes. My grandsons will not know me again. Ha—ha—ha—ha!

> OKORIE *and* BASSI *leave.* AROB *and* OJIMA *crawl out from under the bed, where for a second time they have hidden. They look rough, their feet dirty with sand and leaves. Each comes out with his hoe.*

AROB. So the old man fooled us.

OJIMA. Well, he is now a rich man, and we must treat him with care.

AROB. We have no choice. He says that unless we change, he will not leave a penny to us.

A knock at the door.

AROB *and* OJIMA. Come in.

OKORIE [*comes in, and seeing them so rough and dirty, bursts out laughing; the others look surprised*] Look how dirty you are, with hoes and all. "Gentlemen" like you should not touch hoes. You should wear white gloves and live in towns. But see, you look like two pigs. Ha—ha—ha—ha—ha! Oh what grandsons! How stupid they look! Ha—ha—ha! [AROB *and* OJIMA *are dumbfounded*] I saw both of you a short while ago under the bed. I hope you now know that I have got the Jewels of the Shrine.

AROB. We, too, have something to tell you, Grandfather.

OKORIE. Yes, yes, "gentlemen." Come, tell me. [*He begins to move away*] You must hurry up. I am going to town to buy myself some new clothes and a pair of shoes.

AROB. New clothes?

OJIMA. And shoes?

OKORIE. Yes, grandsons, it is never too late to wear new clothes.

AROB. Let us go and buy them for you. It is too hard for you to——

OKORIE. If God does not think that I am yet old enough to be in the grave, I do not think I am too old to go to the market in town. I need some clothes and a comb to comb my beard. I am happy, grandchildren, very happy. [AROB *and* OJIMA *are dumbfounded*] Now, "gentlemen," why don't you get drunk and shout at me as before? [*Growing bolder*] Why not laugh at me as if I were nobody? You young puppies, I am now somebody, somebody. What is somebody? [*Rubbing his forehead as usual*]

AROB [*to* OJIMA] He has forgotten again.

OKORIE. Who has forgotten what?

OJIMA. You have forgotten nothing. You are a good man, Grandfather, and we like you.

OKORIE [*shouting excitedly*] Bassi! Bassi! Bassi! Where is that silly woman? Bassi, come and hear this. My grandchildren like me; I am now a good man. Ha—ha—ha—ha!

He limps into his room. AROB *and* OJIMA *look at each other. It is obvious to them that the old man has all the cards now.*

AROB. What has come over the old man?

OJIMA. Have you not heard that when people have money, it scratches them on the brain? That is what has happened to our grandfather now.

AROB. He does not believe that we like him. How can we convince him?

OJIMA. You know what he likes most: someone to scratch his back. When he comes out, you will scratch his back, and I will use his big fan to fan at him.

AROB. Great idea. [OKORIE *coughs from the room*] He is coming now.

OKORIE [*comes in*] I am so tired.

AROB. You said you were going to the market, Grandfather.

OKORIE. You do well to remind me. I have sent Bassi to buy the things I want.

OJIMA. Grandfather, you look really tired. Lie down here. [OKORIE *lies down and uncovers his back*] Grandfather, from now on, I shall give you all your breakfast and your midday meals.

AROB [*jealously*] By our forefathers' shrine, Grandfather, I shall take care of your dinner and supply you with wine and clothing.

OKORIE. God bless you, little sons. That is how it should have been all the time. An old man has a right to live comfortably in his last days.

OJIMA. Grandfather, it is a very long time since we scratched your back.

AROB. Yes, it is a long time. We have not done it since we were infants. We want to do it now. It will remind us of our younger days, when it was a pleasure to scratch your back.

OKORIE. Scratch my back? Ha—ha—ha—ha. Oh, go on, go on; by our fathers' shrine you are now good men. I wonder what has happened to you.

OJIMA. It's you, Grandfather. You are such a nice man. As a younger man you must have looked very well. But in your old age you look simply wonderful.

AROB. That is right, Grandfather, and let us tell you again. Do not waste a penny of yours any more. We will keep you happy and satisfied to the last hour of your life.

> OKORIE *appears pleased.* AROB *now begins to pick at, and scratch,* OKORIE's *back.* OJIMA *kneels near the bed and begins to fan the old man. After a while a slow snore is heard. Then, as* AROB *warms up to his task,* OKORIE *jumps up.*

OKORIE. Oh, that one hurts. Gently, children, gently.

> He relaxes and soon begins to snore again. OJIMA *and* AROB *gradually stand up.*

AROB. The old fogy is alseep.

OJIMA. That was clever of us. I am sure he believes us now.

> They leave. OKORIE *opens an eye and peeps at them. Then he smiles and closes it again.* BASSI *enters, bringing some new clothes, a pair of shoes, a comb and brush, a tin of face powder, etc. She pushes* OKORIE.

BASSI. Wake up, Grandfather.

OKORIE [*opening his eyes*] Who told you that I was asleep? Oh! you have brought the things. It is so long since I had a change of clothes. Go on, woman, and call those grandsons of mine. They must help me to put on my new clothes and shoes.

> BASSI *leaves.* OKORIE *begins to comb his hair and beard, which have not been touched for a long time.* BASSI *re-enters with* AROB *and* OJIMA. *Helped by his grandsons and* BASSI, OKORIE *puts on his new clothes and shoes. He then sits on the bed and poses majestically like a chief.*

CURTAIN.

SCENE III

> *The same, a few months later.* OKORIE *is lying on the bed. He is well dressed and looks happy, but it is easily seen that he is nearing his end. There is a knock at the door.* OKORIE *turns and looks at the door but cannot speak loudly. Another knock; the door opens, and the* STRANGER *enters.*

OKORIE. Welcome back, Stranger. You have come in time. Sit down. I will tell you of my will.

> *Door opens slowly.* BASSI *walks in.*

BASSI [*to* STRANGER] How is he?
STRANGER. Just holding on.
BASSI. Did he say anything?
STRANGER. He says that he wants to tell me about his will. Call his grandsons.

> BASSI *leaves.*

OKORIE. Stranger.
STRANGER. Yes, Grandfather.
OKORIE. Do you remember what I told you about my fears in life?
STRANGER. You were afraid your last days would be miserable and that you would not have a decent burial.
OKORIE. Now, Stranger, all that is past. Don't you see how happy I am? I have been very well cared for since I saw you last. My grandchildren have done everything for me, and I am sure they will bury me with great ceremony and rejoicing. I want you to be here when I am making my will. Bend to my ears; I will whisper something to you. [STRANGER *bends for a moment.* OKORIE *whispers. Then he speaks aloud*] Is that clear, Stranger?
STRANGER. It is clear.

OKORIE. Will you remember?

STRANGER. I will.

OKORIE. Do you promise?

STRANGER. I promise.

OKORIE [*relaxing on his pillow*] There now. My end will be more cheerful than I ever expected.

>   *A knock.*

STRANGER. Come in.

>   AROB, OJIMA, *and* BASSI *enter. The two men appear as sad as possible. They are surprised to meet the* STRANGER, *and stare at him for a moment.*

OKORIE [*with effort*] This man may be a stranger to you, but not to me. He is my friend. Arob, look how sad you are! Ojima, how tight your lips are with sorrow! Barely a short while ago you would not have cared whether I lived or died.

AROB. Don't speak like that, Grandfather.

OKORIE. Why should I not? Remember, these are my last words on earth.

OJIMA. You torture us, Grandfather.

OKORIE. Since my son, your father, died, you have tortured me. But now you have changed, and it is good to forgive you both.

STRANGER. You wanted to make a will.

OKORIE. Will? Yes, will. Where is Bassi? Has that woman run away already?

BASSI [*standing above the bed*] No, Grandfather, I am here.

OKORIE. Now there is my family complete.

STRANGER. The will, Grandfather, the will.

OKORIE. Oh, the will; the will is made.

AROB. Made? Where is it?

OKORIE. It is written out on paper.

>   AROB *and* OJIMA *together:*

AROB. Written?

OJIMA. What?

OKORIE [*coolly*] Yes, someone wrote it for me soon after I had discovered the treasure.

AROB. Where is it, Grandfather?

OJIMA. Are you going to show us, Grandfather?

OKORIE. Yes, I will. Why not? But not now, not until I am dead.

AROB *and* OJIMA. What?

OKORIE. Listen here. The will is in a small box buried somewhere. The box also contains all my wealth. These are my wishes. Make my burial the best you can. Spend as much as is required, for you will be compensated. Do not forget that I am the oldest man in this village. An old man has a right to be decently buried. Remember, it was only after I had discovered the Jewels of the Shrine that you began to take good care of me. You should, by carrying out all my last wishes, atone for all those years when you left me poor, destitute, and miserable.

[*To the* STRANGER, *in broken phrases*] Two weeks after my death, Stranger, you will come and unearth the box of my treasure. Open it in the presence of my grandsons. Read out the division of the property, and share it among them. Bassi, you have nothing. You have a good husband and a family. No reward or treasure is greater than a good marriage and a happy home. Stranger, I have told you where the box containing the will is buried. That is all. May God . . .

AROB *and* OJIMA [*rushing to him*] Grandfather, Grandfather——

STRANGER. Leave him in peace. [BASSI, *giving out a scream, rushes from the room*] I must go now. Don't forget his will. Unless you bury him with great honour, you may not touch his property.

He leaves.

CURTAIN.

SCENE IV

All in this scene are dressed in black. AROB, OJIMA, *and* BASSI *are sitting around the table. There is one extra chair. The bed is still there, but the mat is taken off, leaving it bare. The hoe with which* OKORIE *dug out the treasure is lying on the bed as a sort of memorial.*

AROB. Thank God, today is here at last. When I get my own share, I will go and live in town.

OJIMA. If only that foolish stranger would turn up! Why a stranger should come into this house and——

BASSI. Remember, he was your grandfather's friend.

OJIMA. At last, poor Grandfather is gone. I wonder if he knew that we only played up just to get something from his will.

AROB. Well, it didn't matter to him. He believed us, and that is why he has left his property to us. A few months ago he would rather have thrown it all into the sea.

OJIMA. Who could have thought, considering the way we treated him, that the old man had such a kindly heart!

There is a knock. All stand. STRANGER *enters from Grandfather's room. He is grim, dressed in black, and carries a small wooden box under his arm.*

Arob. Stranger, how did you come out from Grandfather's room?

Stranger. Let us not waste time on questions. This box was buried in the floor of your grandfather's room. [*He places the box on the table; Arob and Ojima crowd together. Stranger speaks sternly*] Give me room, please. Your grandfather always wanted you to crowd around him. But no one would, until he was about to die. Step back, please.

Both Arob and Ojima step back. Ojima accidentally steps on Arob.

Arob [*to Ojima*] Don't you step on me!

Ojima [*querulously*] Don't you shout at me!

Stranger looks at both.

Arob. When I sat day and night watching Grandfather in his illness, you were away in town, dancing and getting drunk. Now you want to be the first to grab at everything.

Ojima. You liar! It was I who took care of him.

Arob. You only took care of him when you knew that he had come to some wealth.

Bassi. Why can't both of you——

Arob [*very sharply*] Keep out of this, woman. That pretender [*pointing to Ojima*] wants to bring trouble today.

Ojima. I, a pretender? What of you, who began to scratch the old man's back simply to get his money?

Arob. How dare you insult me like that!

He throws out a blow. Ojima parries. They fight and roll on the floor. The Stranger looks on.

Bassi. Stranger, stop them.

Stranger [*calmly looking at them*] Don't interfere, woman. The mills of God, the preachers tell us, grind slowly.

Bassi. I don't know anything about the mills of God. Stop them, or they will kill themselves.

Stranger [*clapping his hands*] Are you ready to proceed with your grandfather's will, or should I wait till you are ready? [*They stop fighting and stand up, panting*] Before I open this box, I want to know if all your grandfather's wishes have been kept. Was he buried with honour?

Arob. Yes, the greatest burial any old man has had in this village.

Ojima. You may well answer, but I spent more money than you did.

Arob. No, you did not. I called the drummers and the dancers.

OJIMA. I arranged for the shooting of guns.

AROB. I paid for the wine for the visitors and the mourners.

OJIMA. I——

STRANGER. Please, brothers, wait. I ask you again, Was the old man respectably buried?

BASSI. I can swear to that. His grandsons have sold practically all they have in order to give him a grand burial.

STRANGER. That is good. I shall now open the box.

There is silence. He opens the box and brings out a piece of paper.

AROB [*in alarm*] Where are the jewels, the money, the treasure?

STRANGER. Sh! Listen. This is the will. Perhaps it will tell us where to find everything. Listen to this.

AROB. But you cannot read. Give it to me.

OJIMA. Give it to me.

STRANGER. I can read. I am a schoolteacher.

AROB. Did you write this will for Grandfather?

STRANGER. Questions are useless at this time. I did not.

AROB. Stop talking, man. Read it.

STRANGER [*reading*] Now, my grandsons, now that I have been respectably and honourably buried, as all grandsons do to their grandfathers, I can tell you a few things.

First of all, I have discovered no treasure at all. There was never anything like the "Jewels of the Shrine." [AROB *makes a sound as if something had caught him in the throat.* OJIMA *sneezes violently*] There was no treasure hidden in the farm or anywhere else. I have had nothing in life, so I can only leave you nothing. The house which you now live in was my own. But I sold it some months ago and got a little money for what I needed. That money was my "Jewels of the Shrine." The house belongs now to the stranger who is reading this will to you. He shall take possession of this house two days after the will has been read. Hurry up, therefore, and pack out of this house. You young puppies, do you think I never knew that you had no love for me, and that you were only playing up in order to get the money which you believed I had acquired?

When I was a child, one of my first duties was to respect people who were older than myself. But you have thrown away our traditional love and respect for the elderly person. I shall make you pay for it. Shame on you, young men, who believe that because you can read and write, you need not respect old age as your forefathers did! Shame on healthy young men like you, who let the land go to waste because they will not dirty their hands with work!

OJIMA [*furiously*] Stop it, Stranger, stop it, or I will kill you! I am undone. I have not got a penny left. I have used all I had to feed him and to bury him. But now I have not even got a roof to stay under. You confounded Stranger, how dare you buy this house?

STRANGER. Do you insult me in my own house?

AROB [*miserably*] The old cheat! He cheated us to the last. To think that I scratched his back only to be treated like this! We are now poorer than he had ever been.

OJIMA. It is a pity. It is a pity.

STRANGER. What is a pity?

OJIMA. It is a pity we cannot dig him up again.

> *Suddenly a hoarse, unearthly laugh is heard from somewhere. Everybody looks in a different direction. They listen. And then again . . .*

VOICE. Ha—ha—ha—ha! [*They all look up*] Ha—ha—ha—ha! [*The voice is unmistakably Grandfather OKORIE's voice. Seized with terror, everybody except BASSI runs in confusion out of the room, stumbling over the table, box, and everything. As they run away, the voice continues*] Ha—ha—ha—ha! [BASSI, *though frightened, boldly stands her ground. She is very curious to know whether someone has been playing them a trick. The voice grows louder*] Ha—ha—ha—ha! [BASSI, *too, is terrorised, and runs in alarm off the stage*] Ha—ha—ha—ha!!!

CURTAIN.

Considerations

The setting of this play may be primitive Africa, but similar situations have been enacted throughout the world—probably as long as humans have lived. A moment's thought will make the reader empathize with the Grandfather here. People normally avoid thinking about their last hours, but aren't they important? Who wants to be in the position of becoming old, feeble, and unloved?

All the actions of the relatives can be seen any day of the year in highly industrialized modern-day America: shunting the unwanted elder into a corner (perhaps a nursing home); the sudden realization that the elder may actually have a few benefits yet to bestow; the gathering of the vultures at the reading of the will; the quarrels about which of the assembled "bereaved ones" is more deserving.

The generation gap—about which we hear less than we used to—is another feature of this play. "Believe me, Stranger, in my younger days things were different," says the old Grandfather. The grandsons laugh at and despise his old ways; he is hurt and shamed by their new ways. To the extent that this gap is eventually bridged (or bypassed) the bridging is contrived—brought about craftily by the old man, acceded to unwillingly by the grandsons. The motivation is money. Might there have been, in other circumstances and with other characters, loftier reasons for bridging it?

Okorie may be unsympathetic to the reasons for his grandsons' treatment of him, but he too had been changed by the changing folkways: ". . . when I worshipped at our forefathers' shrine, I was happy. I knew what it was all about. It was my life. Then the preachers came, and I abandoned the beliefs of our fathers. The old ways did not leave me; the new ways did not wholly accept me. I was therefore unhappy." Although he ostensibly became resigned to the new ways (especially the new religious ways: "But soon I felt the wings of God carrying me high"), in the last days of life it is the old ways that win out. With whom does the reader sympathize at the story's end?

Picnic on the Battlefield

FERNANDO ARRABAL

CHARACTERS

ZAPO *A soldier*
MONSIEUR TÉPAN   *The soldier's
father*
MADAME TÉPAN   *The soldier's
mother*

ZÉPO   *An enemy soldier*
FIRST STRETCHER BEARER
SECOND STRETCHER BEARER

Picnic on the Battlefield *premièred on April 25, 1959, in Paris, at the
Théâtre de Lutèce, directed by Jean-Marie Serreau.*

*A battlefield. The stage is covered with barbed wire and sandbags.
The battle is at its height. Rifle shots, exploding bombs and machine guns
can be heard.
ZAPO is alone on the stage, flat on his stomach, hidden among the
sandbags. He is very frightened. The sound of the fighting stops. Silence.
ZAPO takes a ball of wool and some needles out of a canvas workbag and
starts knitting a pullover, which is already quite far advanced. The field
telephone, which is by his side, suddenly starts ringing.*

ZAPO. Hallo, hallo . . . yes, Captain . . . yes, I'm the sentry of sector
47 . . . Nothing new, Captain . . . Excuse me, Captain, but when's
the fighting going to start again? And what am I supposed to do with
the hand-grenades? Do I chuck them in front of me or behind
me? . . . Don't get me wrong, I didn't mean to annoy you . . .
Captain, I really feel terribly lonely, couldn't you send me someone
to keep me company? . . . Even if it's only a nanny-goat? [*The
Captain is obviously severely reprimanding him*] Whatever you say,
Captain, whatever you say.

> ZAPO *hangs up. He mutters to himself. Silence. Enter* MONSIEUR
> *and* MADAME TÉPAN, *carrying baskets as if they are going to a*

picnic. They address their son, who has his back turned and doesn't see them come in.

MONS. T. [*ceremoniously*] Stand up, my son, and kiss your mother on the brow. [ZAPO, *surprised, gets up and kisses his mother very respectfully on the forehead. He is about to speak, but his father doesn't give him a chance*] And now, kiss *me*.

ZAPO. But, dear Father and dear Mother, how did you dare to come all this way, to such a dangerous place? You must leave at once.

MONS. T. So you think you've got something to teach your father about war and danger, do you? All this is just a game to me. How many times—to take the first example that comes to mind—have I got off an underground train while it was still moving.

MME. T. We thought you must be bored, so we came to pay you a little visit. This war must be a bit tedious, after all.

ZAPO. It all depends.

MONS. T. I know exactly what happens. To start with you're attracted by the novelty of it all. It's fun to kill people, and throw hand-grenades about, and wear uniforms—you feel smart, but in the end you get bored stiff. You'd have found it much more interesting in my day. Wars were much more lively, much more highly coloured. And then, the best thing was that there were horses, plenty of horses. It was a real pleasure; if the Captain ordered us to attack, there we all were immediately, on horseback, in our red uniforms. It was a sight to be seen. And then there were the charges at the gallop, sword in hand, and suddenly you found yourself face to face with the enemy, and he was equal to the occasion too—with his horses—there were always horses, lots of horses, with their well-rounded rumps—in his highly-polished boots, and his green uniform.

MME T. No no, the enemy uniform wasn't green. It was blue. I remember distinctly that it was blue.

MONS. T. I tell you it was green.

MME. T. When I was little, how many times did I go out on to the balcony to watch the battle and say to the neighbour's little boy: 'I bet you a gum-drop the blues win.' And the blues were our enemies.

MONS. T. Oh well, you must be right, then.

MME. T. I've always liked battles. As a child I always said that when I grew up I wanted to be a Colonel of dragoons. But my mother wouldn't hear of it, you know how she will stick to her principles at all costs.

MONS. T. Your mother's just a half-wit.

ZAPO. I'm sorry, but you really must go. You can't come into a war unless you're a soldier.

MONS. T. I don't give a damn, we came here to have a picnic with you in the country and to enjoy our Sunday.

Mme. T. And I've prepared an excellent meal, too. Sausage, hard-boiled eggs—you know how you like them!—ham sandwiches, red wine, salad, and cakes.

Zapo. All right, let's have it your way. But if the Captain comes he'll be absolutely furious. Because he isn't at all keen on us having visits when we're at the front. He never stops telling us: 'Discipline and hand-grenades are what's wanted in a war, not visits.'

Mons. T. Don't worry, I'll have a few words to say to your Captain.

Zapo. And what if we have to start fighting again?

Mons. T. You needn't think that'll frighten me, it won't be the first fighting I've seen. Now if only it was battles on horseback! Times have changed, you can't understand. [*Pause*] We came by motor bike. No one said a word to us.

ZAPO. They must have thought you were the referees.

MONS. T. We had enough trouble getting through, though. What with all the tanks and jeeps.

MME. T. And do you remember the bottle-neck that cannon caused, just when we got here?

MONS. T. You mustn't be surprised at anything in wartime, everyone knows that.

MME. T. Good, let's start our meal.

MONS. T. You're quite right, I feel as hungry as a hunter. It's the smell of gunpowder.

MME. T. We'll sit on the rug while we're eating.

ZAPO. Can I bring my rifle with me?

MME. T. You leave your rifle alone. It's not good manners to bring your rifle to table with you. [*Pause*] But you're absolutely filthy, my boy. How on earth did you get into such a state? Let's have a look at your hands.

ZAPO [*ashamed, holding out his hands*] I had to crawl about on the ground during the manoeuvres.

MME. T. And what about your ears?

ZAPO. I washed them this morning.

MME. T. Well that's all right, then. And your teeth? [*He shows them*] Very good. Who's going to give her little boy a great big kiss for cleaning his teeth so nicely? [*To her husband*] Well, go on, kiss your son for cleaning his teeth so nicely. [M. TÉPAN *kisses his son*] Because, you know, there's one thing I *will* not have, and that's making fighting a war an excuse for not washing.

ZAPO. Yes, Mother.

They eat.

MONS. T. Well, my boy, did you make a good score?

ZAPO. When?

MONS. T. In the last few days, of course.

ZAPO. Where?

MONS. T. At the moment, since you're fighting a war.

ZAPO. No, nothing much. I didn't make a good score. Hardly ever scored a bull.

MONS. T. Which are you best at shooting, enemy horses or soldiers?

ZAPO. No, not horses, there aren't any horses any more.

MONS. T. Well, soldiers then?

ZAPO. Could be.

MONS. T. Could be? Aren't you sure?

ZAPO. Well you see . . . I shoot without taking aim, [*pause*] and at the same time I say a Pater Noster for the chap I've shot.

Mons. T. You must be braver than that. Like your father.

Mme. T. I'm going to put a record on.

She puts a record on the gramophone—a pasodoble. All three are sitting on the ground, listening.

Mons. T. That really *is* music. Yes indeed, olé!

The music continues. Enter an enemy soldier: Zépo. He is dressed like Zapo. The only difference is the colour of their uniforms. Zépo is in green and Zapo is in grey. Zépo listens to the music openmouthed. He is behind the family so they can't see him. The record ends. As he gets up Zapo discoveres Zépo. Both put their hands up. M. and Mme. Tépan look at them in surprise.

What's going on?

Zapo reacts—he hesitates. Finally, looking as if he's made up his mind, he points his rifle at Zépo.

Zapo. Hands up!

Zépo puts his hands up even higher, looking even more terrified. Zapo doesn't know what to do. Suddenly he goes quickly over to Zépo and touches him gently on the shoulder, like a child playing a game of 'tag'.

Got you! [*To his father, very pleased*] There we are! A prisoner!

Mons. T. Fine. And now what're you going to do with him?

Zapo. I don't know, but, well, could be—they might make me a corporal.

Mons. T. In the meantime you'd better tie him up.

Zapo. Tie him up? Why?

Mons. T. Prisoners always get tied up!

Zapo. How?

Mons. T. Tie up his hands.

Mme. T. Yes, there's no doubt about that, you must tie up his hands, I've always seen them do that.

Zapo. Right. [*To the prisoner*] Put your hands together, if you please.

Zépo. Don't hurt me too much.

Zapo. I won't.

Zépo. Ow! You're hurting me.

Mons. T. Now now, don't maltreat your prisoner.

Mme. T. Is that the way I brought you up? How many times have I told you that we must be considerate to our fellowmen?

Zapo. I didn't do it on purpose. [*To Zépo*] And like that, does it hurt?

Zépo. No, it's all right like that.

Mons. T. Tell him straight out, say what you mean, don't mind us.

Zépo. It's all right like that.

Mons. T. Now his feet.

Zapo. His feet as well, whatever next?

Mons. T. Didn't they teach you the rules?

Zapo. Yes.

Mons. T. Well then!

Zapo [*very politely, to* Zépo] Would you be good enough to sit on the ground, please?

Zépo. Yes, but don't hurt me.

Mme. T. You'll see, he'll take a dislike to you.

Zapo. No he won't, no he won't. I'm not hurting you, am I?

Zépo. No, that's perfect.

Zapo. Papa, why don't you take a photo of the prisoner on the ground and me with my foot on his stomach?

Mons. T. Oh yes, that'd look good.

Zépo. Oh no, not that!

Mme. T. Say yes, don't be obstinate.

Zépo. No. I said no, and no it is.

Mme. T. But just a little teeny weeny photo, what harm could that do you? And we could put it in the dining room, next to the life-saving certificate my husband won thirteen years ago.

Zépo. No—you won't shift me.

Zapo. But why won't you let us?

Zépo. I'm engaged. And if she sees the photo one day, she'll say I don't know how to fight a war properly.

Zapo. No she won't, all you'll need to say is that it isn't you, it's a panther.

Mme. T. Come on, do say yes.

Zépo. All right then. But only to please you.

Zapo. Lie down flat.

> Zépo *lies down.* Zapo *puts a foot on his stomach and grabs his rifle with a martial air.*

Mme. T. Stick your chest out a bit further.

Zapo. Like this?

Mme. T. Yes, like that, and don't breathe.

Mons. T. Try and look like a hero.

Zapo. What d'you mean, like a hero?

Mons. T. It's quite simple; try and look like the butcher does when he's boasting about his successes with the girls.

Zapo. Like this?

Mons. T. Yes, like that.

Mme. T. The most important thing is to puff your chest out and not breathe.

Zépo. Have you nearly finished?

Mons. T. Just be patient a moment. One . . . two . . . three.

Zapo. I hope I'll come out well.

Mme. T. Yes, you looked very martial.

Mons. T. You were fine.

MME. T. It makes me want to have my photo taken with you.

MONS. T. Now there's a good idea.

ZAPO. Right. I'll take it if you like.

MME. T. Give me your helmet to make me look like a soldier.

ZÉPO. I don't want any more photos. Even one's far too many.

ZAPO. Don't take it like that. After all, what harm can it do you?

ZÉPO. It's my last word.

MONS. T. [*to his wife*] Don't press the point, prisoners are always very sensitive. If we go on he'll get cross and spoil our fun.

ZAPO. Right, what're we going to do with him, then?

MME. T. We could invite him to lunch. What do you say?

MONS. T. I don't see why not.

ZAPO [*to* ZÉPO] Well, will you have lunch with us, then?

ZÉPO. Er . . .

MONS. T. We brought a good bottle with us.

ZÉPO. Oh well, all right then.

MME. T. Make yourself at home, don't be afraid to ask for anything you want.

ZÉPO. All right.

MONS. T. And what about you, did you make a good score?

ZÉPO. When?

MONS. T. In the last few days, of course.

ZÉPO. Where?

MONS. T. At the moment, since you're fighting a war.

ZÉPO. No, nothing much. I didn't make a good score, hardly ever scored a bull.

MONS. T. Which are you best at shooting? Enemy horses or soldiers?

ZÉPO. No, not horses, there aren't any horses any more.

MONS. T. Well, soldiers then?

ZÉPO. Could be.

MONS. T. Could be? Aren't you sure?

ZÉPO. Well you see . . . I shoot without taking aim [*pause*], and at the same time I say an Ave Maria for the chap I've shot.

ZAPO. An Ave Maria? I'd have thought you'd have said a Pater Noster.

ZÉPO. No, always an Ave Maria. [*Pause*] It's shorter.

MONS. T. Come come, my dear fellow, you must be brave.

MME. T. [*to* ZÉPO] We can untie you if you like.

ZÉPO. No, don't bother, it doesn't matter.

MONS. T. Don't start getting stand-offish with us now. If you'd like us to untie you, say so.

MME. T. Make yourself comfortable.

ZÉPO. Well, if that's how you feel, you can untie my feet, but it's only to please you.

MONS. T. Zapo, untie him.

    ZAPO *unties him.*

Mme. T. Well, do you feel better?

Zépo. Yes, of course. I really am putting you to a lot of inconvenience.

Mons. T. Not at all, just make yourself at home. And if you'd like us to untie your hands you only have to say so.

Zépo. No, not my hands, I don't want to impose upon you.

Mons. T. No no, my dear chap, no no. I tell you, it's no trouble at all.

Zépo. Right . . . Well then, untie my hands too. But only for lunch, eh? I don't want you to think that you give me an inch and I take an ell.

Mons. T. Untie his hands, son.

Mme. T. Well, since our distinguished prisoner is so charming, we're going to have a marvellous day in the country.

Zépo. Don't call me your distinguished prisoner, just call me your prisoner.

Mme. T. Won't that embarrass you?

Zépo. No no, not at all.

Mons. T. Well, I must say you're modest.

  Noise of aeroplanes.

Zapo. Aeroplanes. They're sure to be coming to bomb us.

  Zapo *and* Zépo *throw themselves on the sandbags and hide.*

  [*To his parents*] Take cover. The bombs will fall on you.

  The noise of the aeroplanes overpowers all the other noises. Bombs immediately start fo fall. Shells explode very near the stage but not on it. A deafening noise. Zapo *and* Zépo *are cowering down between the sandbags.* M. Tépan *goes on talking calmly to his wife, and she answers in the same unruffled way. We can't hear what they are saying because of the bombing.* Mme. Tépan *goes over to one of the baskets and takes an umbrella out of it. She opens it.* M. *and* Mme. Tépan *shelter under it as if it were raining. They are standing up. They shift rhythmically from one foot to the other and talk about their personal affairs.*
  The bombing continues.
  Finally the aeroplanes go away. Silence.
  M. Tépan *stretches an arm outside the umbrella to make sure that nothing more is falling from the heavens.*

Mons. T. [*to his wife*] You can shut your umbrella.

  Mme. Tépan *does so. They both go over to their son and tap him lightly on the behind with the umbrella.*

  Come on, out you come. The bombing's over.

  Zapo *and* Zépo *come out of their hiding place.*

Zapo. Didn't you get hit?

Mons. T. What d'you think could happen to your father? [*Proudly*] Little bombs like that! Don't make me laugh!

  Enter, left, two red cross soldiers. *They are carrying a stretcher.*

1ST STRETCHER BEARER. Any dead here?

ZAPO. No, no one around these parts.

1ST STRETCHER BEARER. Are you sure you've looked properly?

ZAPO. Sure.

1ST STRETCHER BEARER. And there isn't a single person dead?

ZAPO. I've already told you there isn't.

1ST STRETCHER BEARER. No one wounded, even?

ZAPO. Not even that.

2ND STRETCHER BEARER [to the 1st S.B.] Well, now we're in a mess! [To ZAPO persuasively] Just look again, search everywhere, and see if you can't find us a stiff.

1ST STRETCHER BEARER. Don't keep on about it, they've told you quite clearly there aren't any.

2ND STRETCHER BEARER. What a lousy trick!

ZAPO. I'm terribly sorry. I promise you I didn't do it on purpose.

2ND STRETCHER BEARER. That's what they all say. That no one's dead and that they didn't do it on purpose.

1ST STRETCHER BEARER. Oh, let the chap alone!

MONS. T. [obligingly] We should be only too pleased to help you. At your service.

2ND STRETCHER BEARER. Well, really, if things go on like this I don't know what the Captain will say to us.

MONS. T. But what's it all about?

2ND STRETCHER BEARER. Quite simply that the others' wrists are aching with carting so many corpses and wounded men about, and that we haven't found any yet. And it's not because we haven't looked!

MONS. T. Well yes, that really is annoying. [To ZAPO] Are you quite sure no one's dead?

ZAPO. Obviously, Papa.

MONS. T. Have you looked under all the sandbags?

ZAPO. Yes, Papa.

MONS. T. [angrily] Well then, you might as well say straight out that you don't want to lift a finger to help these gentlemen, when they're so nice, too!

1ST STRETCHER BEARER. Don't be angry with him. Let him be. We must just hope we'll have more luck in another trench and that all the lot'll be dead.

MONS. T. I should be delighted.

MME. T. Me too. There's nothing I like more than people who put their hearts into their work.

MONS. T. [indignantly, addressing his remarks to the wings] Then is no one going to do anything for these gentlemen?

ZAPO. If it only rested with me, it'd already be done.

Zépo. I can say the same.

Mons. T. But look here, is neither of you even wounded?

Zapo [ashamed] No, not me.

Mons. T. [to Zépo] What about you?

Zépo [ashamed] Me neither. I never have any luck.

Mme. T. [pleased] Now I remember! This morning, when I was peeling the onions, I cut my finger. Will that do you?

Mons. T. Of course it will! [Enthusiastically] They'll take you off at once!

1st Stretcher Bearer. No, that won't work. With ladies it doesn't work.

Mons. T. We're no further advanced, then.

1st Stretcher Bearer. Never mind.

2nd Stretcher Bearer. We may be able to make up for it in the other trenches.

> They start to go off.

Mons. T. Don't worry! If we find a dead man we'll keep him for you! No fear of us giving him to anyone else!

2nd Stretcher Bearer. Thank you very much, sir.

Mons. T. Quite all right, old chap, think nothing of it.

> The two Stretcher Bearers say goodbye. All four answer them. The Stretcher Bearers go out.

Mme. T. That's what's so pleasant about spending a Sunday in the country. You always meet such nice people. [Pause] But why are you enemies?

Zépo. I don't know, I'm not very well educated.

Mme. T. Was it by birth, or did you become enemies afterwards?

Zépo. I don't know, I don't know anything about it.

Mons. T. Well then, how did you come to be in the war?

Zépo. One day, at home, I was just mending my mother's iron, a man came and asked me: 'Are you Zépo?' 'Yes.' 'Right, you must come to the war.' And so I asked him: 'But what war?' and he said: 'Don't you read the papers then? You're just a peasant!' I told him I did read the papers but not the war bits. . . .

Zapo. Just how it was with me—exactly how it was with me.

Mons. T. Yes, they came to fetch you too.

Mme. T. No, it wasn't quite the same; that day you weren't mending an iron, you were mending the car.

Mons. T. I was talking about the rest of it. [To Zépo] Go on, what happened then?

Zépo. Then I told him I had a fiancée and that if I didn't take her to the pictures on Sundays she wouldn't like it. He said that that wasn't the least bit important.

Zapo. Just how it was with me—exactly how it was with me.

Zépo. And then my father came down and he said I couldn't go to the war because I didn't have a horse.

Zapo. Just what my father said.

Zépo. The man said you didn't need a horse any more, and I asked him if I could take my fiancée with me. He said no. Then I asked whether I could take my aunt with me so that she could make me one of her custards on Thursdays; I'm very fond of them.

Mme. T. [*realising that she'd forgotten it*] Oh! The custard!

Zépo. He said no again.

Zapo. Same as with me.

Zépo. And ever since then I've been alone in the trench nearly all the time.

Mme. T. I think you and your distinguished prisoner might play together this afternoon, as you're so close to each other and so bored.

Zapo. Oh no, Mother, I'm too afraid, he's an enemy.

Mons. T. Now now, you mustn't be afraid.

Zapo. If you only knew what the General was saying about the enemy!

Mme. T. What did he say?

Zapo. He said the enemy are very nasty people. When they take prisoners they put little stones in their shoes so that it hurts them to walk.

Mme. T. How awful! What barbarians!

Mons. T. [*indignantly, to* Zépo] And aren't you ashamed to belong to an army of criminals?

Zépo. I haven't done anything. I don't do anybody any harm.

Mme. T. He was trying to take us in, pretending to be such a little saint!

Mons. T. We oughtn't to have untied him. You never know, we only need to turn our backs and he'll be putting a stone in our shoes.

Zépo. Don't be so nasty to me.

Mons. T. What d'you think we *should* be, then? I'm indignant. I know what I'll do. I'll go and find the Captain and ask him to let me fight in the war.

Zapo. He won't let you, you're too old.

Mons. T. Then I'll buy myself a horse and a sword and come and fight on my own account.

Mme. T. Bravo! If I were a man I'd do the same.

Zépo. Don't be like that with me, Madame. Anyway I'll tell you something—our General told us the same thing about you.

Mme. T. How could he dare tell such a lie!

Zapo. No—but the same thing really?

Zépo. Yes, the same thing.

Mons. T. Perhaps it was the same man who talked to you both?

Mme. T. Well if it was the same man he might at least have said something different. That's a fine thing—saying the same thing to everyone!

Mons. T. [to Zépo, *in a different tone of voice*] Another little drink?

Mme. T. I hope you liked our lunch?

Mons. T. In any case, it was better than last Sunday.

Zépo. What happened?

Mons. T. Well, we went to the country and we put the food on the rug. While we'd got our backs turned a cow ate up all our lunch, and the napkins as well.

Zépo. What a greedy cow!

Mons. T. Yes, but afterwards, to get our own back, we ate the cow. *They laugh.*

Zapo [to Zépo] They couldn't have been very hungry after that!

Mons. T. Cheers! [*They all drink*]

Mme. T. [to Zépo] And what do you do to amuse yourself in the trench?

Zépo. I spend my time making flowers out of rags, to amuse myself. I get terribly bored.

Mme. T. And what do you do with the flowers?

Zépo. At the beginning I used to send them to my fiancée, but one day she told me that the greenhouse and the cellar were already full of them and that she didn't know what to do with them any more, and she asked me, if I didn't mind, to send her something else.

Mme. T. And what did you do?

Zépo. I tried to learn to make something else, but I couldn't. So I go on making rag flowers to pass the time.

Mme. T. Do you throw them away afterwards, then?

Zépo. No, I've found a way to use them now. I give one flower for each pal who dies. That way I know that even if I make an awful lot there'll never be enough.

Mons. T. That's a good solution you've hit on.

Zépo [*shyly*] Yes.

Zapo. Well, what I do is knit, so as not to get bored.

Mme. T. But tell me, are all the soldiers as bored as you?

Zépo. It all depends on what they do to amuse themselves.

Zapo. It's the same on our side.

Mons. T. Then let's stop the war.

Zépo. How?

Mons. T. It's very simple. [*To Zapo*] You just tell your pals that the enemy soldiers don't want to fight a war, and you [to Zépo] say the same to your comrades. And then everyone goes home.

Zapo. Marvellous!

Mme. T. And then you'll be able to finish mending the iron.

Zapo. How is it that no one thought of such a good idea before?

Mme. T. Your father is the only one who's capable of thinking up such ideas; don't forget he's a former student of the Ecole Normale, *and* a philatelist.

Zépo. But what will the sergeant-majors and corporals do?

Mons. T. We'll give them some guitars and castanets to keep them quiet!

Zépo. Very good idea.

Mons. T. You see how easy it is. Everything's fixed.

Zépo. We shall have a tremendous success.

Zapo. My pals will be terribly pleased.

Mme. T. What d'you say to putting on the pasodoble we were playing just now, to celebrate?

Zépo. Perfect.

Zapo. Yes, put the record on, Mother.

> Mme. Tépan *puts a record on. She turns the handle. She waits. Nothing can be heard.*

Mons. T. I can't hear a thing.

Mme. T. Oh, how silly of me! Instead of putting a record on I put on a beret.

> *She puts the record on. A gay pasodoble is heard.* Zapo *dances with* Zépo, *and* Mme. Tépan *with her husband. They are all very gay. The field telephone rings. None of the four hears it. They go on dancing busily. The telephone rings again. The dance continues.*
> *The battle starts up again with a terrific din of bombs, shots and bursts of machine-gun fire. None of the four has seen anything and they go on dancing merrily. A burst of machine-gun fire mows them all down. They fall to the ground, stone dead. A shot must have grazed the gramophone; the record keeps repeating the same thing, like a scratched record. The music of the scratched record can be heard till the end of the play.*
> *The two* Stretcher Bearers *enter left. They are carrying the empty stretcher.*

Sudden Curtain

Considerations

In certain respects this would seem to be a traditional play. It has dialogue spoken by characters who have names and are located in a specific place that has some distinguishing characteristics. In spite of these conventional characteristics, however, this is basically an Absurdist play, involving little plot or character development, emphasizing situation, suggestion, and emotional impact.

The major theme is immediately apparent. War has come to be (if it hasn't always been) a completely unsatisfactory method of resolving political differences. *Picnic on the Battlefield*—with its chaos and its incompatible scenery and dialogue—conveys very well how insane it all is.

Why are these people having a picnic on a battlefield? Picnics are supposed to be festive events, and they usually take place in a safer and less serious setting than a battlefield. And how incongruous to put mother and dad in the middle of it. (After all, their safety is presumably one of the things a war is fought for.) What is their relation to the picnic and to the war?

The soldiers and their conflicts are less confusing. We know their story well by now. They would rather be at a picnic than a war. They even have the usual problems in finding and identifying the enemy. "Do I chuck the hand grenades in front of me or behind me?" asks Zapo. When Zépo enters looking very much like Zapo, how is anyone to know which is the victor and which the vanquished? At the end, all lie dead while a broken record plays on in the background. Why is the record significant?

Is it Arrabal's intention to ridicule civilization's most horrible and inhumane invention? Or is he merely making a statement about the way things are?

If you try to find an affirmative message or even a single affirmative line in the play, you may begin to think it is more than antiwar—it is antihuman. The last words of the play are stage directions as the stretcher-bearers return carrying the empty stretcher. They at least should be pleased with the outcome; they can now fulfill their duty.

A View From the Bridge

A PLAY IN TWO ACTS

Arthur Miller

CHARACTERS

Louis
Mike
Alfieri
Eddie
Catherine
Beatrice
Marco
Tony

Rodolpho
First Immigration Officer
Second Immigration Officer
Mr. Lipari
Mrs. Lipari
Two "Submarines"
Neighbors

ACT ONE

The street and house front of a tenement building. The front is skeletal entirely. The main acting area is the living room-dining room of Eddie's *apartment. It is a worker's flat, clean, sparse, homely. There is a rocker down front; a round dining table at center, with chairs; and a portable phonograph.*

At back are a bedroom door and an opening to the kitchen; none of these interiors are seen.

At the right, forestage, a desk. This is Mr. Alfieri's *law office. There is also a telephone booth. This is not used until the last scenes, so it may be covered or left in view.*

A stairway leads up to the apartment, and then farther up to the next story, which is not seen.

Ramps, representing the street, run upstage and off to right and left.

As the curtain rises, Louis *and* Mike, *longshoremen, are pitching coins against the building at left.*

A distant foghorn blows.

Enter Alfieri, *a lawyer in his fifties turning gray; he is portly, good-humored, and thoughtful. The two pitchers nod to him as he passes. He crosses the stage to his desk, removes his hat, runs his fingers through his hair, and grinning, speaks to the audience.*

Alfieri. You wouldn't have known it, but something amusing has just happened. You see how uneasily they nod to me? That's because I am a lawyer. In this neighborhood to meet a lawyer or a priest on the street is unlucky. We're only thought of in connection with disasters, and they'd rather not get too close.

I often think that behind that suspicious little nod of theirs lie three thousand years of distrust. A lawyer means the law, and in Sicily, from where their fathers came, the law has not been a friendly idea since the Greeks were beaten.

I am inclined to notice the ruins in things, perhaps because I was born in Italy. . . . I only came here when I was twenty-five. In those days, Al Capone, the greatest Carthaginian of all, was learning his trade on these pavements, and Frankie Yale himself was cut precisely in half by a machine gun on the corner of Union Street, two blocks away. Oh, there were many here who were justly shot by unjust men. Justice is very important here.

But this is Red Hook, not Sicily. This is the slum that faces the bay on the seaward side of Brooklyn Bridge. This is the gullet of New York swallowing the tonnage of the world. And now we are quite civilized, quite American. Now we settle for half, and I like it better. I no longer keep a pistol in my filing cabinet.

And my practice is entirely unromantic.

My wife has warned me, so have my friends; they tell me the people in this neighborhood lack elegance, glamour. After all, who have I dealt with in my life? Longshoremen and their wives, and fathers and grandfathers, compensation cases, evictions, family squabbles—the petty troubles of the poor—and yet . . . every few years there is still a case, and as the parties tell me what the trouble is, the flat air in my office suddenly washes in with the green scent of the sea, the dust in this air is blown away and the thought comes that in some Caesar's year, in Calabria perhaps or on the cliff at

Syracuse, another lawyer, quite differently dressed, heard the same complaint and sat there as powerless as I, and watched it run its bloody course.

EDDIE *has appeared and has been pitching coins with the men and is highlighted among them. He is forty—a husky, slightly overweight longshoreman.*

This one's name was Eddie Carbone, a longshoreman working the docks from Brooklyn Bridge to the breakwater where the open sea begins.

ALFIERI *walks into darkness.*

EDDIE [*Moving up steps into doorway*] Well, I'll see ya, fellas.

CATHERINE *enters from kitchen, crosses down to window, looks out.*

LOUIS. You workin' tomorrow?

EDDIE. Yeah, there's another day yet on that ship. See ya, Louis. [EDDIE *goes into the house, as light rises in the apartment*]

CATHERINE *is waving to* LOUIS *from the window and turns to him.*

CATHERINE. Hi, Eddie!

EDDIE *is pleased and therefore shy about it; he hangs up his cap and jacket.*

EDDIE. Where you goin' all dressed up?

CATHERINE [*Running her hands over her skirt*] I just got it. You like it?

EDDIE. Yeah, it's nice. And what happened to your hair?

CATHERINE. You like it? I fixed it different. [*Calling to kitchen*] He's here, B.!

EDDIE. Beautiful. Turn around, lemme see in the back. [*She turns for him*] Oh, if your mother was alive to see you now! She wouldn't believe it.

CATHERINE. You like it, huh?

EDDIE. You look like one of them girls that went to college. Where you goin'?

CATHERINE [*Taking his arm*] Wait'll B. comes in, I'll tell you something. Here, sit down. [*She is walking him to the armchair. Calling offstage*] Hurry up, will you, B.?

EDDIE [*Sitting*] What's goin' on?

CATHERINE. I'll get you a beer, all right?

EDDIE. Well, tell me what happened. Come over here, talk to me.

CATHERINE. I want to wait till B. comes in. [*She sits on her heels beside him*] Guess how much we paid for the skirt.

EDDIE. I think it's too short, ain't it?

CATHERINE [*Standing*] No! not when I stand up.

EDDIE. Yeah, but you gotta sit down sometimes.

CATHERINE. Eddie, it's the style now. [*She walks to show him*] I mean, if you see me walkin' down the street—

EDDIE. Listen, you been givin' me the willies the way you walk down the street, I mean it.

CATHERINE. Why?

EDDIE. Catherine, I don't want to be a pest, but I'm tellin' you you're walkin' wavy.

CATHERINE. I'm walkin' wavy?

EDDIE. Now don't aggravate me, Katie, you are walkin' wavy! I don't like the looks they're givin' you in the candy store. And with them new high heels on the sidewalk—clack, clack, clack. The heads are turnin' like windmills.

CATHERINE. But those guys look at all the girls, you know that.

EDDIE. You ain't "all the girls."

CATHERINE [*Almost in tears because he disapproves*] What do you want me to do? You want me to—

EDDIE. Now don't get mad, kid.

CATHERINE. Well, I don't know what you want from me.

EDDIE. Katie, I promised your mother on her deathbed. I'm responsible for you. You're a baby, you don't understand these things. I mean like when you stand here by the window, wavin' outside.

CATHERINE. I was wavin' to Louis!

EDDIE. Listen, I could tell you things about Louis which you wouldn't wave to him no more.

CATHERINE [*Trying to joke him out of his warning*] Eddie, I wish there was one guy you couldn't tell me things about!

EDDIE. Catherine, do me a favor, will you? You're gettin' to be a big girl now, you gotta keep yourself more, you can't be so friendly, kid. [*Calls*] Hey, B., what're you doin' in there? [*To* CATHERINE] Get her in here, will you? I got news for her.

CATHERINE [*Starting out*] What?

EDDIE. Her cousins landed.

CATHERINE [*Clapping her hands together*] No! [*She turns instantly and starts for the kitchen*] B.! Your cousins!

BEATRICE *enters, wiping her hands with a towel.*

BEATRICE [*In the face of* CATHERINE's *shout*] What?

CATHERINE. Your cousins got in!

BEATRICE [*Astounded, turns to* EDDIE] What are you talkin' about? Where?

EDDIE. I was just knockin' off work before and Tony Bereli come over to me; he says the ship is in the North River.

BEATRICE [*Her hands are clasped at her breast; she seems half in fear, half in unutterable joy*] They're all right?

EDDIE. He didn't see them yet, they're still on board. But as soon as they get off he'll meet them. He figures about ten o'clock they'll be here.

BEATRICE [*Sits, almost weak from tension*] And they'll let them off the ship all right? That's fixed, heh?

EDDIE. Sure, they give them regular seamen papers and they walk off with the crew. Don't worry about it, B., there's nothin' to it. Couple of hours they'll be here.

BEATRICE. What happened? They wasn't supposed to be till next Thursday.

EDDIE. I don't know; they put them on any ship they can get them out on. Maybe the other ship they was supposed to take there was some danger— What you cryin' about?

BEATRICE [*Astounded and afraid*] I'm—I just—I can't believe it! I didn't even buy a new tablecloth; I was gonna wash the walls—

EDDIE. Listen, they'll think it's a millionaire's house compared to the way they live. Don't worry about the walls. They'll be thankful. [*To* CATHERINE] Whyn't you run down buy a tablecloth. Go ahead, here. [*He is reaching into his pocket*]

CATHERINE. There's no stores open now.

EDDIE [*To* BEATRICE] You was gonna put a new cover on the chair.

BEATRICE. I know—well, I thought it was gonna be next week! I was gonna clean the walls, I was gonna wax the floors. [*She stands disturbed*]

CATHERINE [*Pointing upward*] Maybe Mrs. Dondero upstairs—

BEATRICE [*Of the tablecloth*] No, hers is worse than this one. [*Suddenly*] My God, I don't even have nothin' to eat for them! [*She starts for the kitchen*]

EDDIE [*Reaching out and grabbing her arm*] Hey, hey! Take it easy.

BEATRICE. No, I'm just nervous, that's all. [*To* CATHERINE] I'll make the fish.

EDDIE. You're savin' their lives, what're you worryin' about the tablecloth? They probably didn't see a tablecloth in their whole life where they come from.

BEATRICE [*Looking into his eyes*] I'm just worried about you, that's all I'm worried.

EDDIE. Listen, as long as they know where they're gonna sleep.

BEATRICE. I told them in the letters. They're sleepin' on the floor.

EDDIE. Beatrice, all I'm worried about is you got such a heart that I'll end up on the floor with you, and they'll be in our bed.

BEATRICE. All right, stop it.

EDDIE. Because as soon as you see a tired relative, I end up on the floor.

BEATRICE. When did you end up on the floor?

EDDIE. When your father's house burned down I didn't end up on the floor?

BEATRICE. Well, their house burned down!

EDDIE. Yeah, but it didn't keep burnin' for two weeks!

BEATRICE. All right, look, I'll tell them to go someplace else. [*She starts into the kitchen*]

EDDIE. Now wait a minute, Beatrice! [*She halts. He goes to her*] I just don't want you bein' pushed around, that's all. You got too big a heart. [*He touches her hand*] What're you so touchy?

BEATRICE. I'm just afraid if it don't turn out good you'll be mad at me.

EDDIE. Listen, if everybody keeps his mouth shut, nothin' can happen. They'll pay for their board.

BEATRICE. Oh, I told them.

EDDIE. Then what the hell. [*Pauses. He moves*] It's an honor, B. I mean it. I was just thinkin' before, comin' home, suppose my father didn't come to this country, and I was starvin' like them over there . . . and I had people in America could keep me a couple of months? The man would be honored to lend me a place to sleep.

BEATRICE [*There are tears in her eyes. She turns to* CATHERINE] You see what he is? [*She turns and grabs* EDDIE's *face in her hands*] Mmm! You're an angel! God'll bless you. [*He is gratefully smiling*] You'll see, you'll get a blessing for this!

EDDIE [*Laughing*] I'll settle for my own bed.

BEATRICE. Go, Baby, set the table.

CATHERINE. We didn't tell him about me yet.

BEATRICE. Let him eat first, then we'll tell him. Bring everything in. [*She hurries* CATHERINE *out*]

EDDIE [*Sitting at the table*] What's all that about? Where's she goin'?

BEATRICE. No place. It's very good news, Eddie. I want you to be happy.

EDDIE. What's goin' on?

CATHERINE *enters with plates, forks.*

BEATRICE. She's got a job. [*Pause.* EDDIE *looks at* CATHERINE, *then back to* BEATRICE]

EDDIE. What job? She's gonna finish school.

CATHERINE. Eddie, you won't believe it—

EDDIE. No—no, you gonna finish school. What kinda job, what do you mean? All of a sudden you—

CATHERINE. Listen a minute, it's wonderful.

EDDIE. It's not wonderful. You'll never get nowheres unless you finish school. You can't take no job. Why didn't you ask me before you take a job?

BEATRICE. She's askin' you now, she didn't take nothin' yet.

CATHERINE. Listen a minute! I came to school this morning and the principal called me out of the class, see? To go to his office.

EDDIE. Yeah?

CATHERINE. So I went in and he says to me he's got my records, y'know? and there's a company wants a girl right away. It ain't exactly a secretary, it's a stenographer first, but pretty soon you get to be secretary. And he says to me that I'm the best student in the whole class—

BEATRICE. You hear that?

EDDIE. Well why not? Sure she's the best.

CATHERINE. I'm the best student, he says, and if I want, I should take the job and the end of the year he'll let me take the examination and he'll give me the certificate. So I'll save practically a year!

EDDIE [*Strangely nervous*] Where's the job? What company?

CATHERINE. It's a big plumbing company over Nostrand Avenue.

EDDIE. Nostrand Avenue and where?

CATHERINE. It's someplace by the Navy Yard.

BEATRICE. Fifty dollars a week, Eddie.

EDDIE [*To* CATHERINE, *surprised*] Fifty?

CATHERINE. I swear.

    Pause.

EDDIE. What about all the stuff you wouldn't learn this year, though?

CATHERINE. There's nothin' more to learn, Eddie, I just gotta practice from now on. I know all the symbols and I know the keyboard. I'll just get faster, that's all. And when I'm workin' I'll keep gettin' better and better, you see?

BEATRICE. Work is the best practice anyway.

EDDIE. That ain't what I wanted, though.

CATHERINE. Why! It's a great big company—

EDDIE. I don't like that neighborhood over there.

CATHERINE. It's a block and a half from the subway, he says.

EDDIE. Near the Navy Yard plenty can happen in a block and a half. And a plumbin' company! That's one step over the water front. They're practically longshoremen.

BEATRICE. Yeah, but she'll be in the office, Eddie.

EDDIE. I know she'll be in the office, but that ain't what I had in mind.

BEATRICE. Listen, she's gotta go to work sometime.

EDDIE. Listen, B., she'll be with a lotta plumbers? And sailors up and down the street? So what did she go to school for?

CATHERINE. But it's fifty a week, Eddie.

EDDIE. Look, did I ask you for money? I supported you this long I support you a little more. Please, do me a favor, will ya? I want you to be with different kind of people. I want you to be in a nice office. Maybe a lawyer's office someplace in New York in one of them nice buildings. I mean if you're gonna get outa here then get out; don't go practically in the same kind of neighborhood.

Pause. CATHERINE *lowers her eyes.*

BEATRICE. Go, Baby, bring in the supper. [CATHERINE *goes out*] Think about it a little bit, Eddie. Please. She's crazy to start work. It's not a little shop, it's a big company. Some day she could be a secretary. They picked her out of the whole class. [*He is silent, staring down at the tablecloth, fingering the pattern*] What are you worried about? She could take care of herself. She'll get out of the subway and be in the office in two minutes.

EDDIE [*Somehow sickened*] I know that neighborhood, B., I don't like it.

BEATRICE. Listen, if nothin' happened to her in this neighborhood it ain't gonna happen no place else. [*She turns his face to her*] Look, you gotta get used to it, she's no baby no more. Tell her to take it. [*He turns his head away*] You hear me? [*She is angering*] I don't understand you; she's seventeen years old, you gonna keep her in the house all her life?

EDDIE [*Insulted*] What kinda remark is that?

BEATRICE [*With sympathy but insistent force*] Well, I don't understand when it ends. First it was gonna be when she graduated high school, so she graduated high school. Then it was gonna be when she learned stenographer, so she learned stenographer. So what're we gonna wait for now? I mean it, Eddie, sometimes I don't understand you; they picked her out of the whole class, it's an honor for her.

CATHERINE *enters with food, which she silently sets on the table. After a moment of watching her face,* EDDIE *breaks into a smile, but it almost seems that tears will form in his eyes.*

EDDIE. With your hair that way you look like a madonna, you know that? You're the madonna type. [*She doesn't look at him, but continues ladling out food onto the plates*] You wanna go to work, heh, Madonna?

CATHERINE [*Softly*] Yeah.

EDDIE [*With a sense of her childhood, her babyhood, and the years*] All right, go to work. [*She looks at him, then rushes and hugs him*] Hey, hey! Take it easy! [*He holds her face away from him to look at her*] What're you cryin' about? [*He is affected by her, but smiles his emotion away*]

CATHERINE [*Sitting at her place*] I just—[*Bursting out*] I'm gonna buy all new dishes with my first pay! [*They laugh warmly*] I mean it. I'll fix up the whole house! I'll buy a rug!

EDDIE. And then you'll move away.

CATHERINE. No, Eddie!

EDDIE [*Grinning*] Why not? That's life. And you'll come visit on Sundays, then once a month, then Christmas and New Year's, finally.

CATHERINE [*Grasping his arm to reassure him and to erase the accusation*] No, please!

EDDIE [*Smiling but hurt*] I only ask you one thing—don't trust nobody. You got a good aunt but she's got too big a heart, you learned bad from her. Believe me.

BEATRICE. Be the way you are, Katie, don't listen to him.

EDDIE [*To* BEATRICE—*strangely and quickly resentful*] You lived in a house all your life, what do you know about it? You never worked in your life.

BEATRICE. She likes people. What's wrong with that?

EDDIE. Because most people ain't people. She's goin' to work; plumbers; they'll chew her to pieces if she don't watch out. [*To* CATHERINE] Believe me, Katie, the less you trust, the less you be sorry.

EDDIE *crosses himself and the women do the same, and they eat.*

CATHERINE. First thing I'll buy is a rug, heh, B.?

BEATRICE. I don't mind. [*To* EDDIE] I smelled coffee all day today. You unloadin' coffee today?

EDDIE. Yeah, a Brazil ship.

CATHERINE. I smelled it too. It smelled all over the neighborhood.

EDDIE. That's one time, boy, to be a longshoreman is a pleasure. I could work coffee ships twenty hours a day. You go down in the hold, y'know? It's like flowers, that smell. We'll bust a bag tomorrow, I'll bring you some.

BEATRICE. Just be sure there's no spiders in it, will ya? I mean it. [*She directs this to* CATHERINE, *rolling her eyes upward*] I still remember that spider coming out of that bag he brung home. I nearly died.

EDDIE. You call that a spider? You oughta see what comes outa the bananas sometimes.

BEATRICE. Don't talk about it!

EDDIE. I seen spiders could stop a Buick.

BEATRICE [*Clapping her hands over her ears*] All right, shut up!

EDDIE [*Laughing and taking a watch out of his pocket*] Well, who started with spiders?

BEATRICE. All right, I'm sorry, I didn't mean it. Just don't bring none home again. What time is it?

EDDIE. Quarter nine. [*Puts watch back in his pocket*]

They continue eating in silence.

CATHERINE. He's bringin' them ten o'clock, Tony?

EDDIE. Around, yeah. [*He eats*]

CATHERINE. Eddie, suppose somebody asks if they're livin' here. [*He looks at her as though already she had divulged something publicly. Defensively*] I mean if they ask.

EDDIE. Now, look, Baby, I can see we're gettin' mixed up again here.

CATHERINE. No, I just mean . . . people'll see them goin' in and out.

EDDIE. I don't care who sees them goin' in and out as long as you don't see them goin' in and out. And this goes for you too, B. You don't see nothin' and you don't know nothin'.

BEATRICE. What do you mean? I understand.

EDDIE. You don't understand; you still think you can talk about this to somebody just a little bit. Now lemme say it once and for all, because you're makin' me nervous again, both of you. I don't care if somebody comes in the house and sees them sleepin' on the floor, it never comes out of your mouth who they are or what they're doin' here.

BEATRICE. Yeah, but my mother'll know—

EDDIE. Sure she'll know, but just don't you be the one who told her, that's all. This is the United States government you're playin' with now, this is the Immigration Bureau. If you said it you knew it, if you didn't say it you didn't know it.

CATHERINE. Yeah, but Eddie, suppose somebody—

EDDIE. I don't care what question it is. You—don't—know—nothin'. They got stool pigeons all over this neighborhood they're payin' them every week for information, and you don't know who they are. It could be your best friend. You hear? [*To* BEATRICE] Like Vinny Bolzano, remember Vinny?

BEATRICE. Oh, yeah. God forbid.

EDDIE. Tell her about Vinny. [*To* CATHERINE] You think I'm blowin' steam here? [*To* BEATRICE] Go ahead, tell her. [*To* CATHERINE] You was a baby then. There was a family lived next door to her mother, he was about sixteen—

BEATRICE. No, he was no more than fourteen, cause I was to his confirmation in Saint Agnes. But the family had an uncle that they were hidin' in the house, and he snitched to the Immigration.

CATHERINE. The kid snitched?

EDDIE. On his own uncle!

CATHERINE. What, was he crazy?

EDDIE. He was crazy after, I tell you that, boy.

BEATRICE. Oh, it was terrible. He had five brothers and the old father. And they grabbed him in the kitchen and pulled him down the stairs—three flights his head was bouncin' like a coconut. And they spit on him in the street, his own father and his brothers. The whole neighborhood was cryin'.

CATHERINE. Ts! So what happened to him?

BEATRICE. I think he went away. [*To* EDDIE] I never seen him again, did you?

EDDIE [*Rises during this, taking out his watch*] Him? You'll never see him no more, a guy do a thing like that? How's he gonna show his face? [*To* Catherine, *as he gets up uneasily*] Just remember, kid, you can quicker get back a million dollars that was stole than a word that you gave away. [*He is standing now, stretching his back*]

Catherine. Okay, I won't say a word to nobody, I swear.

Eddie. Gonna rain tomorrow. We'll be slidin' all over the decks. Maybe you oughta put something on for them, they be here soon.

Beatrice. I only got fish, I hate to spoil it if they ate already. I'll wait, it only takes a few minutes; I could broil it.

Catherine. What happens, Eddie, when that ship pulls out and they ain't on it, though? Don't the captain say nothin'?

Eddie [*Slicing an apple with his pocket knife*] Captain's pieced off, what do you mean?

Catherine. Even the captain?

Eddie. What's the matter, the captain don't have to live? Captain gets a piece, maybe one of the mates, piece for the guy in Italy who fixed the papers for them, Tony here'll get a little bite. . . .

Beatrice. I just hope they get work here, that's all I hope.

Eddie. Oh, the syndicate'll fix jobs for them; till they pay 'em off they'll get them work every day. It's after the pay-off, then they'll have to scramble like the rest of us.

Beatrice. Well, it be better than they got there.

Eddie. Oh sure, well, listen. So you gonna start Monday, heh, Madonna?

Catherine [*Embarrassed*] I'm supposed to, yeah.

> Eddie *is standing facing the two seated women. First* Beatrice *smiles, then* Catherine, *for a powerful emotion is on him, a childish one and a knowing fear, and the tears show in his eyes—and they are shy before the avowal*]

Eddie [*Sadly smiling, yet somehow proud of her*] Well . . . I hope you have good luck. I wish you the best. You know that, kid.

Catherine [*Rising, trying to laugh*] You sound like I'm goin' a million miles!

Eddie. I know. I guess I just never figured on one thing.

Catherine [*Smiling*] What?

Eddie. That you would ever grow up. [*He utters a soundless laugh at himself, feeling his breast pocket of his shirt*] I left a cigar in my other coat, I think. [*He starts for the bedroom*]

Catherine. Stay there! I'll get it for you.

> She *hurries out. There is a slight pause, and* Eddie *turns to* Beatrice, *who has been avoiding his gaze.*

Eddie. What are you mad at me lately?

BEATRICE. Who's mad. [*She gets up, clearing the dishes*] I'm not mad. [*She picks up the dishes and turns to him*] You're the one is mad. [*She turns and goes into the kitchen as* CATHERINE *enters from the bedroom with a cigar and a pack of matches*]

CATHERINE. Here! I'll light it for you! [*She strikes a match and holds it to his cigar. He puffs. Quietly*] Don't worry about me, Eddie, heh?

EDDIE. Don't burn yourself. [*Just in time she blows out the match*] You better go in help her with the dishes.

CATHERINE [*Turns quickly to the table, and, seeing the table cleared, she says, almost guiltily*] Oh! [*She hurries into the kitchen, and as she exits there*] I'll do the dishes, B.!

> *Alone,* EDDIE *stands looking toward the kitchen for a moment. Then he takes out his watch, glances at it, replaces it in his pocket, sits in the armchair, and stares at the smoke flowing out of his mouth. The lights go down, then come up on* ALFIERI, *who has moved onto the forestage.*

ALFIERI. He was as good a man as he had to be in a life that was hard and even. He worked on the piers when there was work, he brought home his pay, and he lived. And toward ten o'clock of that night, after they had eaten, the cousins came.

> *The lights fade on* ALFIERI *and rise on the street.*
> *Enter* TONY, *escorting* MARCO *and* RODOLPHO, *each with a valise.* TONY *halts, indicates the house. They stand for a moment looking at it.*

MARCO [*He is a square-built peasant of thirty-two, suspicious, tender, and quiet-voiced*] Thank you.

TONY. You're on your own now. Just be careful, that's all. Ground floor.

MARCO. Thank you.

TONY [*Indicating the house*] I'll see you on the pier tomorrow. You'll go to work.

> MARCO *nods.* TONY *continues on walking down the street.*

RODOLPHO. This will be the first house I ever walked into in America! Imagine! She said they were poor!

MARCO. Ssh! Come. [*They go to door*]

> MARCO *knocks. The lights rise in the room.* EDDIE *goes and opens the door. Enter* MARCO *and* RODOLPHO, *removing their caps.* BEATRICE *and* CATHERINE *enter from the kitchen. The lights fade in the street.*

EDDIE. You Marco?

MARCO. Marco.

EDDIE. Come on in! [*He shakes* MARCO'S *hand*]

BEATRICE. Here, take the bags!

MARCO [*Nods, looks to the women and fixes on* BEATRICE. *Crosses to* BEATRICE] Are you my cousin?

> She nods. He kisses her hand.

BEATRICE [*Above the table, touching her chest with her hand*] Beatrice. This is my husband, Eddie. [*All nod*] Catherine, my sister Nancy's daughter. [*The brothers nod*]

MARCO [*Indicating* RODOLPHO] My brother. Rodolpho. [RODOLPHO *nods.* MARCO *comes with a certain formal stiffness to* EDDIE] I want to tell you now, Eddie—when you say go, we will go.

EDDIE. Oh, no . . . [*Takes* MARCO'S *bag*]

MARCO. I see it's a small house, but soon, maybe, we can have our own house.

EDDIE. You're welcome, Marco, we got plenty of room here. Katie, give them supper, heh? [*Exits into bedroom with their bags*]

CATHERINE. Come here, sit down. I'll get you some soup.

MARCO [*As they go to the table*] We ate on the ship. Thank you. [*To* EDDIE, *calling off to bedroom*] Thank you.

BEATRICE. Get some coffee. We'll all have coffee. Come sit down.

> RODOLPHO *and* MARCO *sit, at the table.*

CATHERINE [*Wondrously*] How come he's so dark and you're so light, Rodolpho?

RODOLPHO [*Ready to laugh*] I don't know. A thousand years ago, they say, the Danes invaded Sicily.

> BEATRICE *kisses* RODOLPHO. *They laugh as* EDDIE *enters.*

CATHERINE [*To* BEATRICE] He's practically blond!

EDDIE. How's the coffee doin'?

CATHERINE [*Brought up*] I'm gettin' it. [*She hurries out to kitchen*]

EDDIE [*Sits on his rocker*] Yiz have a nice trip?

MARCO. The ocean is always rough. But we are good sailors.

EDDIE. No trouble gettin' here?

MARCO. No. The man brought us. Very nice man.

RODOLPHO [*To* EDDIE] He says we start to work tomorrow. Is he honest?

EDDIE [*Laughing*] No. But as long as you owe them money, they'll get you plenty of work. [*To* MARCO] Yiz ever work on the piers in Italy?

MARCO. Piers? Ts!—no.

RODOLPHO [*Smiling at the smallness of his town*] In our town there are no piers, only the beach, and little fishing boats.

BEATRICE. So what kinda work did yiz do?

MARCO [*Shrugging shyly, even embarrassed*] Whatever there is, anything.

Rodolpho. Sometimes they build a house, or if they fix the bridge—
Marco is a mason and I bring him the cement. [*He laughs*] In
harvest time we work in the fields . . . if there is work. Anything.
Eddie. Still bad there, heh?
Marco. Bad, yes.
Rodolpho [*Laughing*] It's terrible! We stand around all day in the piazza
listening to the fountain like birds. Everybody waits only for the
train.
Beatrice. What's on the train?
Rodolpho. Nothing. But if there are many passengers and you're lucky
you make a few lire to push the taxi up the hill.

    Enter Catherine; *she listens.*

Beatrice. You gotta push a taxi?
Rodolpho [*Laughing*] Oh, sure! It's a feature in our town. The horses in
our town are skinnier than goats. So if there are too many pas-
sengers we help to push the carriages up to the hotel. [*He laughs*] In
our town the horses are only for show.
Catherine. Why don't they have automobile taxis?
Rodolpho. There is one. We push that too. [*They laugh*] Everything in
our town, you gotta push!
Beatrice [*To* Eddie] How do you like that!
Eddie [*To* Marco] So what're you wanna do, you gonna stay here in this
country or you wanna go back?
Marco [*Surprised*] Go back?
Eddie. Well, you're married, ain't you?
Marco. Yes. I have three children.
Beatrice. Three! I thought only one.
Marco. Oh, no. I have three now. Four years, five years, six years.
Beatrice. Ah . . . I bet they're cryin' for you already, heh?
Marco. What can I do? The older one is sick in his chest. My wife—she
feeds them from her own mouth. I tell you the truth, if I stay there
they will never grow up. They eat the sunshine.
Beatrice. My God. So how long you want to stay?
Marco. With your permission, we will stay maybe a—
Eddie. She don't mean in this house, she means in the country.
Marco. Oh. Maybe four, five, six years, I think.
Rodolpho [*Smiling*] He trusts his wife.
Beatrice. Yeah, but maybe you'll get enough, you'll be able to go back
quicker.
Marco. I hope. I don't know. [*To* Eddie] I understand it's not so good
here either.
Eddie. Oh, you guys'll be all right—till you pay them off, anyway. After
that, you'll have to scramble, that's all. But you'll make better here
than you could there.

Rodolpho. How much? We hear all kinds of figures. How much can a man make? We work hard, we'll work all day, all night—

Marco *raises a hand to hush him.*

Eddie [*He is coming more and more to address* Marco *only*] On the average a whole year? Maybe—well, it's hard to say, see. Sometimes we lay off, there's no ships three, four weeks.

Marco. Three, four weeks!—Ts!

Eddie. But I think you could probably—thirty, forty a week, over the whole twelve months of the year.

Marco [*Rises, crosses to* Eddie] Dollars.

Eddie. Sure dollars.

Marco *puts an arm round* Rodolpho *and they laugh.*

Marco. If we can stay here a few months, Beatrice—

Beatrice. Listen, you're welcome, Marco—

Marco. Because I could send them a little more if I stay here.

Beatrice. As long as you want, we got plenty a room.

Marco [*His eyes showing tears*] My wife— [*To* Eddie] My wife—I want to send right away maybe twenty dollars—

Eddie. You could send them something next week already.

Marco [*He is near tears*] Eduardo . . . [*He goes to* Eddie, *offering his hand*]

Eddie. Don't thank me. Listen, what the hell, it's no skin off me. [*To* Catherine] What happened to the coffee?

Catherine. I got it on. [*To* Rodolpho] You married too? No.

Rodolpho [*Rises*] Oh, no . . .

Beatrice [*To* Catherine] I told you he—

Catherine. I know, I just thought maybe he got married recently.

Rodolpho. I have no money to get married. I have a nice face, but no money. [*He laughs*]

Catherine [*To* Beatrice] He's a real blond!

Beatrice [*To* Rodolpho] You want to stay here too, heh? For good?

Rodolpho. Me? Yes, forever! Me, I want to be an American. And then I want to go back to Italy when I am rich, and I will buy a motorcycle. [*He smiles.* Marco *shakes him affectionately*]

Catherine. A motorcycle!

Rodolpho. With a motorcycle in Italy you will never starve any more.

Beatrice. I'll get you coffee. [*She exits to the kitchen*]

Eddie. What you do with a motorcycle?

Marco. He dreams, he dreams.

Rodolpho [*To* Marco] Why? [*To* Eddie] Messages! The rich people in the hotel always need someone who will carry a message. But quickly, and with a great noise. With a blue motorcycle I would station myself in the courtyard of the hotel, and in a little while I would have messages.

MARCO. When you have no wife you have dreams.

EDDIE. Why can't you just walk, or take a trolley or sump'm?

Enter BEATRICE *with coffee.*

RODOLPHO. Oh, no, the machine, the machine is necessary. A man comes into a great hotel and says, I am a messenger. Who is this man? He disappears walking, there is no noise, nothing. Maybe he will never come back, maybe he will never deliver the message. But a man who rides up on a great machine, this man is responsible, this man exists. He will be given messages. [*He helps* BEATRICE *set out the coffee things*] I am also a singer, though.

EDDIE. You mean a regular—?

RODOLPHO. Oh, yes. One night last year Andreola got sick. Baritone. And I took his place in the garden of the hotel. Three arias I sang without a mistake! Thousand-lire notes they threw from the tables, money was falling like a storm in the treasury. It was magnificent. We lived six months on that night, eh, Marco?

MARCO *nods doubtfully.*

MARCO. Two months.

EDDIE *laughs.*

BEATRICE. Can't you get a job in that place?

RODOLPHO. Andreola got better. He's a baritone, very strong.

BEATRICE *laughs.*

MARCO [*Regretfully, to* BEATRICE] He sang too loud.

RODOLPHO. Why too loud?

MARCO. Too loud. The guests in that hotel are all Englishmen. They don't like too loud.

RODOLPHO [*To* CATHERINE] Nobody ever said it was too loud!

MARCO. I say. It was too loud. [*To* BEATRICE] I knew it as soon as he started to sing. Too loud.

RODOLPHO. Then why did they throw so much money?

MARCO. They paid for your courage. The English like courage. But once is enough.

RODOLPHO [*To all but* MARCO] I never heard anybody say it was too loud.

CATHERINE. Did you ever hear of jazz?

RODOLPHO. Oh, sure! I *sing* jazz.

CATHERINE [*Rises*] You could sing jazz?

RODOLPHO. Oh, I sing Napolidan, jazz, bel canto—I sing "Paper Doll," you like "Paper Doll"?

CATHERINE. Oh, sure, I'm crazy for "Paper Doll." Go ahead, sing it.

RODOLPHO [*Takes his stance after getting a nod of permission from* MARCO, *and with a high tenor voice begins singing*]
I'll tell you boys it's tough to be alone,
And it's tough to love a doll that's not your own.
I'm through with all of them,
I'll never fall again,
Hey, boy, what you gonna do?
I'm gonna buy a paper doll that I can call my own,
A doll that other fellows cannot steal.

EDDIE *rises and moves upstage.*

And then those flirty, flirty guys
With their flirty, flirty eyes
Will have to flirt with dollies that are real—
EDDIE. Hey, kid—hey, wait a minute—
CATHERINE [*Enthralled*] Leave him finish, it's beautiful! [*To* BEATRICE]
He's terrific! It's terrific, Rodolpho.
EDDIE. Look, kid; you don't want to be picked up, do ya?
MARCO. No—no! [*He rises*]
EDDIE [*Indicating the rest of the building*] Because we never had no singers here . . . and all of a sudden there's a singer in the house, y'know what I mean?
MARCO. Yes, yes. You'll be quiet, Rodolpho.
EDDIE [*He is flushed*] They got guys all over the place, Marco. I mean.
MARCO. Yes. He'll be quiet. [*To* RODOLPHO] You'll be quiet.

RODOLPHO *nods.* EDDIE *has risen, with iron control, even a smile. He moves to* CATHERINE.

EDDIE. What's the high heels for, Garbo?
CATHERINE. I figured for tonight—
EDDIE. Do me a favor, will you? Go ahead.

Embarrassed now, angered, CATHERINE *goes out into the bedroom.* BEATRICE *watches her go and gets up; in passing, she gives* EDDIE *a cold look, restrained only by the strangers, and goes to the table to pour coffee.*

EDDIE [*Striving to laugh, and to* MARCO, *but directed as much to* BEATRICE]
All actresses they want to be around here.
RODOLPHO [*Happy about it*] In Italy too! All the girls.

CATHERINE *emerges from the bedroom in low-heel shoes, comes to the table.* RODOLPHO *is lifting a cup.*

EDDIE [*He is sizing up* RODOLPHO, *and there is a concealed suspicion*]
Yeah, heh?

Rodolpho. Yes! [*Laughs, indicating* Catherine] Especially when they are so beautiful!
Catherine. You like sugar?
Rodolpho. Sugar? Yes! I like sugar very much!

> Eddie *is downstage, watching as she pours a spoonful of sugar into his cup, his face puffed with trouble, and the room dies.*
>
> *Lights rise on* Alfieri.

Alfieri. Who can ever know what will be discovered? Eddie Carbone had never expected to have a destiny. A man works, raises his family, goes bowling, eats, gets old, and then he dies. Now, as the weeks passed, there was a future, there was a trouble that would not go away.

> *The lights fade on* Alfieri, *then rise on* Eddie *standing at the doorway of the house.* Beatrice *enters on the street. She sees* Eddie, *smiles at him. He looks away. She starts to enter the house when* Eddie *speaks.*

Eddie. It's after eight.
Beatrice. Well, it's a long show at the Paramount.
Eddie. They must've seen every picture in Brooklyn by now. He's supposed to stay in the house when he ain't working. He ain't supposed to go advertising himself.
Beatrice. Well that's his trouble, what do you care? If they pick him up they pick him up, that's all. Come in the house.
Eddie. What happened to the stenography? I don't see her practice no more.
Beatrice. She'll get back to it. She's excited, Eddie.
Eddie. She tell you anything?
Beatrice [*Comes to him, now the subject is opened*] What's the matter with you? He's a nice kid, what do you want from him?
Eddie. That's a nice kid? He gives me the heeby-jeebies.
Beatrice [*Smiling*] Ah, go on, you're just jealous.
Eddie. Of *him?* Boy, you don't think much of me.
Beatrice. I don't understand you. What's so terrible about him?
Eddie. You mean it's all right with you? That's gonna be her husband?
Beatrice. Why? He's a nice fella, hard workin', he's a good-lookin' fella.
Eddie. He sings on the ships, didja know that?
Beatrice. What do you mean, he sings?
Eddie. Just what I said, he sings. Right on the deck, all of a sudden, a whole song comes out of his mouth—with motions. You know what they're callin' him now? Paper Doll they're callin' him, Canary. He's like a weird. He comes out on the pier, one-two-three, it's a regular free show.

BEATRICE. Well, he's a kid; he don't know how to behave himself yet.

EDDIE. And with that whacky hair; he's like a chorus girl or sump'm.

BEATRICE. So he's blond, so—

EDDIE. I just hope that's his regular hair, that's all I hope.

BEATRICE. You crazy or sump'm? [*She tries to turn him to her*]

EDDIE [*He keeps his head turned away*] What's so crazy? I don't like his whole way.

BEATRICE. Listen, you never seen a blond guy in your life? What about Whitey Balso?

EDDIE [*Turning to her victoriously*] Sure, but Whitey don't sing; he don't do like that on the ships.

BEATRICE. Well, maybe that's the way they do in Italy.

EDDIE. Then why don't his brother sing? Marco goes around like a man; nobody kids Marco. [*He moves from her, halts. She realizes there is a campaign solidified in him*] I tell you the truth I'm surprised I have to tell you all this. I mean I'm surprised, B.

BEATRICE [*She goes to him with purpose now*] Listen, you ain't gonna start nothin' here.

EDDIE. I ain't startin' nothin', but I ain't gonna stand around lookin' at that. For that character I didn't bring her up. I swear, B., I'm surprised at you; I sit there waitin' for you to wake up but everything is great with you.

BEATRICE. No, everything ain't great with me.

EDDIE. No?

BEATRICE. No. I got other worries.

EDDIE. Yeah. [*He is already weakening*]

BEATRICE. Yeah, you want me to tell you?

EDDIE [*In retreat*] Why? What worries you got?

BEATRICE. When am I gonna be a wife again, Eddie?

EDDIE. I ain't been feelin' good. They bother me since they came.

BEATRICE. It's almost three months you don't feel good; they're only here a couple of weeks. It's three months, Eddie.

EDDIE. I don't know, B. I don't want to talk about it.

BEATRICE. What's the matter, Eddie, you don't like me, heh?

EDDIE. What do you mean, I don't like you? I said I don't feel good, that's all.

BEATRICE. Well, tell me, am I doing something wrong? Talk to me.

EDDIE [*Pause. He can't speak, then*] I can't. I can't talk about it.

BEATRICE. Well tell me what—

EDDIE. I got nothin' to say about it!

> She stands for a moment; he is looking off; she turns to go into the house.

EDDIE. I'll be all right, B.; just lay off me, will ya? I'm worried about her.

BEATRICE. The girl is gonna be eighteen years old, it's time already.

EDDIE. B., He's taking her for a ride!

BEATRICE. All right, that's her ride. What're you gonna stand over her till she's forty? Eddie, I want you to cut it out now, you hear me? I don't like it! Now come in the house.

EDDIE. I want to take a walk, I'll be in right away.

BEATRICE. They ain't goin' to come any quicker if you stand in the street. It ain't nice, Eddie.

EDDIE. I'll be in right away. Go ahead. [*He walks off*]

> *She goes into the house.* EDDIE *glances up the street, sees* LOUIS *and* MIKE *coming, and sits on an iron railing.* LOUIS *and* MIKE *enter.*

LOUIS. Wanna go bowlin' tonight?

EDDIE. I'm too tired. Goin' to sleep.

LOUIS. How's your two submarines?

EDDIE. They're okay.

LOUIS. I see they're gettin' work allatime.

EDDIE. Oh yeah, they're doin' all right.

MIKE. That's what we oughta do. We oughta leave the country and come in under the water. Then we get work.

EDDIE. You ain't kiddin'.

LOUIS. Well, what the hell. Y'know?

EDDIE. Sure.

LOUIS [*Sits on railing beside* EDDIE] Believe me, Eddie, you got a lotta credit comin' to you.

EDDIE. Aah, they don't bother me, don't cost me nutt'n.

MIKE. That older one, boy, he's a regular bull. I seen him the other day liftin' coffee bags over the Matson Line. They leave him alone he woulda load the whole ship by himself.

EDDIE. Yeah, he's a strong guy, that guy. Their father was a regular giant, supposed to be.

LOUIS. Yeah, you could see. He's a regular slave.

MIKE [*Grinning*] That blond one, though—[EDDIE *looks at him*] He's got a sense of humor. [LOUIS *snickers*]

EDDIE [*Searchingly*] Yeah. He's funny—

MIKE [*Starting to laugh*] Well he ain't exackly funny, but he's always like makin' remarks like, y'know? He comes around, everybody's laughin'. [LOUIS *laughs*]

EDDIE [*Uncomfortably, grinning*] Yeah, well . . . he's got a sense of humor.

MIKE [*Laughing*] Yeah, I mean, he's always makin' like remarks, like, y'know?

EDDIE. Yeah, I know. But he's a kid yet, y'know? He—he's just a kid, that's all.

Mike [*Getting hysterical with* Louis] I know. You take one look at him—everybody's happy. [Louis *laughs*] I worked one day with him last week over the Moore-MacCormack Line, I'm tellin' you they was all hysterical. [Louis *and he explode in laughter*]

Eddie. Why? What'd he do?

Mike. I don't know . . . he was just humorous. You never can remember what he says, y'know? But it's the way he says it. I mean he gives you a look sometimes and you start laughin'!

Eddie. Yeah. [*Troubled*] He's got a sense of humor.

Mike [*Gasping*] Yeah.

Louis [*Rising*] Well, we see ya, Eddie.

Eddie. Take it easy.

Louis. Yeah. See ya.

Mike. If you wanna come bowlin' later we're goin' Flatbush Avenue.

> Laughing, they move to exit, meeting Rodolpho and Catherine entering on the street. Their laughter rises as they see Rodolpho, who does not understand but joins in. Eddie moves to enter the house as Louis and Mike exit. Catherine stops him at the door.

Catherine. Hey, Eddie—what a picture we saw! Did we laugh!

Eddie [*He can't help smiling at sight of her*] Where'd you go?

Catherine. Paramount. It was with those two guys, y'know? That—

Eddie. Brooklyn Paramount?

Catherine [*With an edge of anger, embarrassed before* Rodolpho] Sure, the Brooklyn Paramount. I told you we wasn't goin' to New York.

Eddie [*Retreating before the threat of her anger*] All right, I only asked you. [*To* Rodolpho] I just don't want her hangin' around Times Square, see? It's full of tramps over there.

Rodolpho. I would like to go to Broadway once, Eddie. I would like to walk with her once where the theaters are and the opera. Since I was a boy I see pictures of those lights.

Eddie [*His little patience waning*] I want to talk to her a minute, Rodolpho. Go inside, will you?

Rodolpho. Eddie, we only walk together in the streets. She teaches me.

Catherine. You know what he can't get over? That there's no fountains in Brooklyn!

Eddie [*Smiling unwillingly*] Fountains? [Rodolpho *smiles at his own naïveté*]

Catherine. In Italy he says, every town's got fountains, and they meet there. And you know what? They got oranges on the trees where he comes from, and lemons. Imagine—on the trees? I mean it's interesting. But he's crazy for New York.

Rodolpho [*Attempting familiarity*] Eddie, why can't we go once to Broadway—?

EDDIE. Look, I gotta tell her something—

RODOLPHO. Maybe you can come too. I want to see all those lights. [*He sees no response in* EDDIE's *face. He glances at* CATHERINE] I'll walk by the river before I go to sleep. [*He walks off down the street*]

CATHERINE. Why don't you talk to him, Eddie? He blesses you, and you don't talk to him hardly.

EDDIE [*Enveloping her with his eyes*] I bless you and you don't talk to me. [*He tries to smile*]

CATHERINE. I don't talk to you? [*She hits his arm*] What do you mean?

EDDIE. I don't see you no more. I come home you're runnin' around someplace—

CATHERINE. Well, he wants to see everything, that's all, so we go. . . . You mad at me?

EDDIE. No. [*He moves from her, smiling sadly*] It's just I used to come home, you was always there. Now, I turn around, you're a big girl. I don't know how to talk to you.

CATHERINE. Why?

EDDIE. I don't know, you're runnin', you're runnin', Katie. I don't think you listening any more to me.

CATHERINE [*Going to him*] Ah, Eddie, sure I am. What's the matter? You don't like him?

        Slight pause.

EDDIE [*Turns to her*] You like him, Katie?

CATHERINE [*With a blush but holding her ground*] Yeah. I like him.

EDDIE [*His smile goes*] You like him.

CATHERINE [*Looking down*] Yeah. [*Now she looks at him for the consequences, smiling but tense. He looks at her like a lost boy*] What're you got against him? I don't understand. He only blesses you.

EDDIE. [*Turns away*] He don't bless me, Katie.

CATHERINE. He does! You're like a father to him!

EDDIE [*Turns to her*] Katie.

CATHERINE. What, Eddie?

EDDIE. You gonna marry him?

CATHERINE. I don't know. We just been . . . goin' around, that's all. [*Turns to him*] What're you got against him, Eddie? Please, tell me. What?

EDDIE. He don't respect you.

CATHERINE. Why?

EDDIE. Katie . . . if you wasn't an orphan, wouldn't he ask your father's permission before he run around with you like this?

CATHERINE. Oh, well, he didn't think you'd mind.

EDDIE. He knows I mind, but it don't bother him if I mind, don't you see that?

CATHERINE. No, Eddie, he's got all kinds of respect for me. And you too! We walk across the street he takes my arm—he almost bows to me! You got him all wrong, Eddie; I mean it, you—

EDDIE. Katie, he's only bowin' to his passport.

CATHERINE. His passport!

EDDIE. That's right. He marries you he's got the right to be an American citizen. That's what's goin' on here. [*She is puzzled and surprised*] You understand what I'm tellin' you? The guy is lookin' for his break, that's all he's lookin' for.

CATHERINE [*Pained*] Oh, no, Eddie, I don't think so.

EDDIE. You don't think so! Katie, you're gonna make me cry here. Is that a workin' man? What does he do with his first money? A snappy new jacket he buys, records, a pointy pair new shoes and his brother's kids are starvin' over there with tuberculosis? That's a hit-and-run guy, baby; he's got bright lights in his head, Broadway. Them guys don't think of nobody but theirself! You marry him and the next time you see him it'll be for divorce!

CATHERINE [*Steps toward him*] Eddie, he never said a word about his papers or—

EDDIE. You mean he's supposed to tell you that?

CATHERINE. I don't think he's even thinking about it.

EDDIE. What's better for him to think about! He could be picked up any day here and he's back pushin' taxis up the hill!

CATHERINE. No, I don't believe it.

EDDIE. Katie, don't break my heart, listen to me.

CATHERINE. I don't want to hear it.

EDDIE. Katie, listen . . .

CATHERINE. He loves me!

EDDIE [*With deep alarm*] Don't say that, for God's sake! This is the oldest racket in the country—

CATHERINE [*Desperately, as though he had made his imprint*] I don't believe it! [*She rushes to the house*]

EDDIE [*Following her*] They been pullin' this since the Immigration Law was put in! They grab a green kid that don't know nothin' and they—

CATHERINE [*Sobbing*] I don't believe it and I wish to hell you'd stop it!

EDDIE. Katie!

They enter the apartment. The lights in the living room have risen and BEATRICE is there. She looks past the sobbing CATHERINE at EDDIE, who in the presence of his wife, makes an awkward gesture of eroded command, indicating CATHERINE.

EDDIE. Why don't you straighten her out?

BEATRICE [*Inwardly angered at his flowing emotion, which in itself alarms her*] When are you going to leave her alone?

EDDIE. B., The guy is no good!

BEATRICE [*Suddenly, with open fright and fury*] You going to leave her alone? Or you gonna drive me crazy? [*He turns, striving to retain his dignity, but nevertheless in guilt walks out of the house, into the street and away.* CATHERINE *starts into a bedroom*] Listen, Catherine. [CATHERINE *halts, turns to her sheepishly*] What are you going to do with yourself?

CATHERINE. I don't know.

BEATRICE. Don't tell me you don't know; you're not a baby any more, what are you going to do with yourself?

CATHERINE. He won't listen to me.

BEATRICE. I don't understand this. He's not your father, Catherine. I don't understand what's going on here.

CATHERINE [*As one who herself is trying to rationalize a buried impulse*] What am I going to do, just kick him in the face with it?

BEATRICE. Look, honey, you wanna get married, or don't you wanna get married? What are you worried about, Katie?

CATHERINE [*Quietly, trembling*] I don't know, B. It just seems wrong if he's against it so much.

BEATRICE [*Never losing her aroused alarm*] Sit down, honey, I want to tell you something. Here, sit down. Was there ever any fella he liked for you? There wasn't, was there?

CATHERINE. But he says Rodolpho's just after his papers.

BEATRICE. Look, he'll say anything. What does he care what he says? If it was a prince came here for you it would be no different. You know that, don't you?

CATHERINE. Yeah, I guess.

BEATRICE. So what does that mean?

CATHERINE [*Slowly turns her head to* BEATRICE] What?

BEATRICE. It means you gotta be your own self more. You still think you're a little girl, honey. But nobody else can make up your mind for you any more, you understand? You gotta give him to understand that he can't give you orders no more.

CATHERINE. Yeah, but how am I going to do that? He thinks I'm a baby.

BEATRICE. Because *you* think you're a baby. I told you fifty times already, you can't act the way you act. You still walk around in front of him in your slip—

CATHERINE. Well I forgot.

BEATRICE. Well you can't do it. Or like you sit on the edge of the bathtub talkin' to him when he's shavin' in his underwear.

CATHERINE. When'd I do that?

BEATRICE. I seen you in there this morning.

CATHERINE. Oh . . . well, I wanted to tell him something and I—

BEATRICE. I know, honey. But if you act like a baby and he'll be treatin' you like a baby. Like when he comes home sometimes you throw yourself at him like when you was twelve years old.

CATHERINE. Well I like to see him and I'm happy so I—

BEATRICE. Look, I'm not tellin' you what to do honey, but—

CATHERINE. No, you could tell me, B.! Gee, I'm all mixed up. See, I—He looks so sad now and it hurts me.

BEATRICE. Well look Katie, if it's goin' to hurt you so much you're gonna end up an old maid here.

CATHERINE. No!

BEATRICE. I'm tellin' you, I'm not makin' a joke. I tried to tell you a couple of times in the last year or so. That's why I was so happy you were going to go out and get work, you wouldn't be here so much, you'd be a little more independent. I mean it. It's wonderful for a whole family to love each other, but you're a grown woman and you're in the same house with a grown man. So you'll act different now, heh?

CATHERINE. Yeah, I will. I'll remember.

BEATRICE. Because it ain't only up to him, Katie, you understand? I told him the same thing already.

CATHERINE [Quickly] What?

BEATRICE. That he should let you go. But, you see, if only I tell him, he thinks I'm just bawlin' him out, or maybe I'm jealous or somethin', you know?

CATHERINE [Astonished] He said you was jealous?

BEATRICE. No, I'm just sayin' maybe that's what he thinks. [She reaches over to CATHERINE's hand; with a strained smile] You think I'm jealous of you, honey?

CATHERINE. No! It's the first I thought of it.

BEATRICE [With a quiet sad laugh] Well you should have thought of it before . . . but I'm not. We'll be all right. Just give him to understand; you don't have to fight, you're just— You're a woman, that's all, and you got a nice boy, and now the time came when you said good-by. All right?

CATHERINE [Strangely moved at the prospect] All right. . . . If I can.

BEATRICE. Honey . . . you gotta. [CATHERINE, sensing now an imperious demand, turns with some fear, with a discovery, to BEATRICE. She is at the edge of tears, as though a familiar world had shattered]

CATHERINE. Okay.

Lights out on them and up on ALFIERI, seated behind his desk.

ALFIERI. It was at this time that he first came to me. I had represented his father in an accident case some years before, and I was acquainted with the family in a casual way. I remember him now as he walked through my doorway—

Enter EDDIE *down right ramp.*

His eyes were like tunnels; my first thought was that he had committed a crime, [*Eddie sits beside the desk, cap in hand, looking out*] but soon I saw it was only a passion that had moved into his body, like a stranger. [ALFIERI *pauses, looks down at his desk, then to* EDDIE *as though he were continuing a conversation with him*] I don't quite understand what I can do for you. Is there a question of law somewhere?

EDDIE. That's what I want to ask you.

ALFIERI. Because there's nothing illegal about a girl falling in love with an immigrant.

EDDIE. Yeah, but what about it if the only reason for it is to get his papers?

ALFIERI. First of all you don't know that.

EDDIE. I see it in his eyes; he's laughin' at her and he's laughin' at me.

ALFIERI. Eddie, I'm a lawyer. I can only deal in what's provable. You understand that, don't you? Can you prove that?

EDDIE. *I know what's in his mind, Mr. Alfieri!*

ALFIERI. Eddie, even if you could prove that—

EDDIE. Listen . . . will you listen to me a minute? My father always said you was a smart man. I want you to listen to me.

ALFIERI. I'm only a lawyer, Eddie.

EDDIE. Will you listen a minute? I'm talkin' about the law. Lemme just bring out what I mean. A man, which he comes into the country illegal, don't it stand to reason he's gonna take every penny and put it in the sock? Because they don't know from one day to another, right?

ALFIERI. All right.

EDDIE. He's spendin'. Records he buys now. Shoes. Jackets. Y'understand me? This guy ain't worried. This guy is *here.* So it must be that he's got it all laid out in his mind already—he's stayin'. Right?

ALFIERI. Well? What about it?

EDDIE. All right. [*He glances at* ALFIERI, *then down to the floor*] I'm talking to you confidential, ain't I?

ALFIERI. Certainly.

EDDIE. I mean it don't go no place but here. Because I don't like to say this about anybody. Even my wife I didn't exactly say this.

ALFIERI. What is it?

EDDIE [*Takes a breath and glances briefly over each shoulder*] The guy ain't right, Mr. Alfieri.

ALFIERI. What do you mean?

EDDIE. I mean he ain't right.

ALFIERI. I don't get you.

EDDIE [*Shifts to another position in the chair*] Dja ever get a look at him?

ALFIERI. Not that I know of, no.

EDDIE. He's a blond guy. Like . . . platinum. You know what I mean?

ALFIERI. No.

EDDIE. I mean if you close the paper fast—you could blow him over.

ALFIERI. Well that doesn't mean—

EDDIE. Wait a minute, I'm tellin' you sump'm. He sings, see. Which is—I mean it's all right, but sometimes he hits a note, see. I turn around. I mean—high. You know what I mean?

ALFIERI. Well, that's a tenor.

EDDIE. I know a tenor, Mr. Alfieri. This ain't no tenor. I mean if you came in the house and you didn't know who was singin', you wouldn't be lookin' for him you be lookin' for her.

ALFIERI. Yes, but that's not—

EDDIE. I'm tellin' you sump'm, wait a minute. Please, Mr. Alfieri. I'm tryin' to bring out my thoughts here. Couple of nights ago my niece brings out a dress which it's too small for her, because she shot up like a light this last year. He takes the dress, lays it on the table, he cuts it up; one-two-three, he makes a new dress. I mean he looked so sweet there, like an angel—you could kiss him he was so sweet.

ALFIERI. Now look, Eddie—

EDDIE. Mr. Alfieri, they're laughin' at him on the piers. I'm ashamed. Paper Doll they call him. Blondie now. His brother thinks it's because he's got a sense of humor, see—which he's got—but that ain't what they're laughin'. Which they're not goin' to come out with it because they know he's my relative, which they have to see me if they make a crack, y'know? But I know what they're laughin' at, and when I think of that guy layin' his hands on her I could—I mean it's eatin' me out, Mr. Alfieri, because I struggled for that girl. And now he comes in my house and—

ALFIERI. Eddie, look—I have my own children. I understand you. But the law is very specific. The law does not . . .

EDDIE [*With a fuller flow of indignation*] You mean to tell me that there's no law that a guy which he ain't right can go to work and marry a girl and—?

ALFIERI. You have no recourse in the law, Eddie.

EDDIE. Yeah, but if he ain't right, Mr. Alfieri, you mean to tell me—

ALFIERI. There is nothing you can do, Eddie, believe me.

EDDIE. Nothin'.

ALFIERI. Nothing at all. There's only one legal question here.

EDDIE. What?

ALFIERI. The manner in which they entered the country. But I don't think you want to do anything about that, do you?

EDDIE. You mean—?

ALFIERI. Well, they entered illegally.

EDDIE. Oh, Jesus, no, I wouldn't do nothin' about that. I mean—

ALFIERI. All right, then, let me talk now, eh?

EDDIE. Mr. Alfieri, I can't believe what you tell me. I mean there must be some kinda law which—

ALFIERI. Eddie, I want you to listen to me. [*Pause*] You know, sometimes God mixes up the people. We all love somebody, the wife, the kids—every man's got somebody that he loves, heh? But sometimes . . . there's too much. You know? There's too much, and it goes where it mustn't. A man works hard, he brings up a child, sometimes it's a niece, sometimes even a daughter, and he never realizes it, but through the years—there is too much love for the daughter, there is too much love for the niece. Do you understand what I'm saying to you?

EDDIE. [*Sardonically*] What do you mean, I shouldn't look out for her good?

ALFIERI. Yes, but these things have to end, Eddie, that's all. The child has to grow up and go away, and the man has to learn to forget. Because after all, Eddie—what other way can it end? [*Pause*] Let her go. That's my advice. You did your job, now it's her life; wish her luck, and let her go. [*Pause*] Will you do that? Because there's no law, Eddie; make up your mind to it; the law is not interested in this.

EDDIE. You mean to tell me, even if he's a punk? If he's—

ALFIERI. There's nothing you can do.

EDDIE *stands.*

EDDIE. Well, all right, thanks. Thanks very much.

ALFIERI. What are you going to do?

EDDIE [*With a helpless but ironic gesture*] What can I do? I'm a patsy, what can a patsy do? I worked like a dog twenty years so a punk could have her, so that's what I done. I mean, in the worst times, in the worst, when there wasn't a ship comin' in the harbor, I didn't stand around lookin' for relief—I hustled. When there was empty piers in Brooklyn I went to Hoboken, Staten Island, the West Side, Jersey, all over—because I made a promise. I took out of my own mouth to give to her. I took out of my wife's mouth. I walked hungry plenty days in this city! [*It begins to break through*] And now I gotta sit in my own house and look at a son-of-a-bitch punk like that—which he came out of nowhere! I give him my house to sleep! I take the blankets off my bed for him, and he takes and puts his dirty filthy hands on her like a goddam thief!

ALFIERI [*Rising*] But, Eddie, she's a woman now.

EDDIE. He's stealing from me!

ALFIERI. She wants to get married, Eddie. She can't marry you, can she?

EDDIE [*Furiously*] What're you talkin' about, marry me! I don't know what the hell you're talkin' about!

> *Pause.*

ALFIERI. I gave you my advice, Eddie. That's it. [EDDIE *gathers himself. A pause*]

EDDIE. Well, thanks. Thanks very much. It just—it's breakin' my heart, y'know. I—

ALFIERI. I understand. Put it out of your mind. Can you do that?

EDDIE. I'm—[*He feels the threat of sobs, and with a helpless wave*] I'll see you around. [*He goes out up the right ramp*]

ALFIERI [*Sits on desk*] There are times when you want to spread an alarm, but nothing has happened. I knew, I knew then and there—I could have finished the whole story that afternoon. It wasn't as though there was a mystery to unravel. I could see every step coming, step after step, like a dark figure walking down a hall toward a certain door. I knew where he was heading for, I knew where he was going to end. And I sat here many afternoons asking myself why, being an intelligent man, I was so powerless to stop it. I even went to a certain old lady in the neighborhood, a very wise old woman, and I told her, and she only nodded, and said, "Pray for him . . ." And so I—waited here.

> *As lights go out on* ALFIERI, *they rise in the apartment where all are finishing dinner.* BEATRICE *and* CATHERINE *are clearing the table.*

CATHERINE. You know where they went?

BEATRICE. Where?

CATHERINE. They went to Africa once. On a fishing boat. [EDDIE *glances at her*] It's true, Eddie.

> BEATRICE *exits into the kitchen with dishes.*

EDDIE. I didn't say nothin'. [*He goes to his rocker, picks up a newspaper*]

CATHERINE. And I was never even in Staten Island.

EDDIE [*Sitting with the paper*] You didn't miss nothin'. [*Pause.* CATHERINE *takes dishes out*] How long that take you, Marco—to get to Africa?

MARCO [*Rising*] Oh . . . two days. We go all over.

RODOLPHO [*Rising*] Once we went to Yugoslavia.

EDDIE [*To* MARCO] They pay all right on them boats?

> BEATRICE *enters. She and* RODOLPHO *stack the remaining dishes.*

MARCO. If they catch fish they pay all right. [*Sits on a stool*]

RODOLPHO. They're family boats, though. And nobody in our family owned one. So we only worked when one of the families was sick.

BEATRICE. Y'know, Marco, what I don't understand—there's an ocean full of fish and yiz are all starvin'.

EDDIE. They gotta have boats, nets, you need money.

CATHERINE *enters.*

BEATRICE. Yeah, but couldn't they like fish from the beach? You see them down Coney Island—

MARCO. Sardines.

EDDIE. Sure. [*Laughing*] How you gonna catch sardines on a hook?

BEATRICE. Oh, I didn't know they're sardines. [*To* CATHERINE] They're sardines!

CATHERINE. Yeah, they follow them all over the ocean, Africa, Yugoslavia . . . [*She sits and begins to look through a movie magazine.* RODOLPHO *joins her*]

BEATRICE [*To* EDDIE] It's funny, y'know. You never think of it, that sardines are swimming in the ocean! [*She exits to kitchen with dishes*]

CATHERINE. I know. It's like oranges and lemons on a tree. [*To* EDDIE] I mean you ever think of oranges and lemons on a tree?

EDDIE. Yeah, I know. It's funny. [*To* MARCO] I heard that they paint the oranges to make them look orange.

BEATRICE *enters.*

MARCO [*He has been reading a letter*] Paint?

EDDIE. Yeah, I heard that they grow like green.

MARCO. No, in Italy the oranges are orange.

RODOLPHO. Lemons are green.

EDDIE [*Resenting his instruction*] I know lemons are green, for Christ's sake, you see them in the store they're green sometimes. I said oranges they paint, I didn't say nothin' about lemons.

BEATRICE [*Sitting; diverting their attention*] Your wife is gettin' the money all right, Marco?

MARCO. Oh, yes. She bought medicine for my boy.

BEATRICE. That's wonderful. You feel better, heh?

MARCO. Oh, yes! But I'm lonesome.

BEATRICE. I just hope you ain't gonna do like some of them around here. They're here twenty-five years, some men, and they didn't get enough together to go back twice.

MARCO. Oh, I know. We have many families in our town, the children never saw the father. But I will go home. Three, four years, I think.

BEATRICE. Maybe you should keep more here. Because maybe she thinks it comes so easy you'll never get ahead of yourself.

MARCO. Oh, no, she saves. I send everything. My wife is very lonesome. [*He smiles shyly*]

BEATRICE. She must be nice. She pretty? I bet, heh?

MARCO [*Blushing*] No, but she understand everything.

RODOLPHO. Oh, he's got a clever wife!

EDDIE. I betcha there's plenty surprises sometimes when those guys get back there, heh?

MARCO. Surprises?

EDDIE [*Laughing*] I mean, you know—they count the kids and there's a couple extra than when they left?

MARCO. No—no . . . The women wait, Eddie. Most. Most. Very few surprises.

RODOLPHO. It's more strict in our town. [EDDIE *looks at him now*] It's not so free.

EDDIE [*Rises, paces up and down*] It ain't so free here either, Rodolpho, like you think. I seen greenhorns sometimes get in trouble that way—they think just because a girl don't go around with a shawl over her head that she ain't strict, y'know? Girl don't have to wear black dress to be strict. Know what I mean?

RODOLPHO. Well, I always have respect—

EDDIE. I know, but in your town you wouldn't just drag off some girl without permission, I mean. [*He turns*] You know what I mean, Marco? It ain't that much different here.

MARCO [*Cautiously*] Yes.

BEATRICE. Well, he didn't exactly drag her off though, Eddie.

EDDIE. I know, but I seen some of them get the wrong idea sometimes. [*To* RODOLPHO] I mean it might be a little more free here but it's just as strict.

RODOLPHO. I have respect for her, Eddie. I do anything wrong?

EDDIE. Look, kid, I ain't her father, I'm only her uncle—

BEATRICE. Well then, be an uncle then. [EDDIE *looks at her, aware of her criticizing force*] I mean.

MARCO. No, Beatrice, if he does wrong you must tell him. [*To* EDDIE] What does he do wrong?

EDDIE. Well, Marco, till he came here she was never out on the street twelve o'clock at night.

MARCO [*To* RODOLPHO] You come home early now.

BEATRICE [*To* CATHERINE] Well, you said the movie ended late, didn't you?

CATHERINE. Yeah.

BEATRICE. Well, tell him, honey. [*To* EDDIE] The movie ended late.

EDDIE. Look, B., I'm just sayin'—he thinks she always stayed out like that.

MARCO. You come home early now, Rodolpho.

RODOLPHO [*Embarrassed*] All right, sure. But I can't stay in the house all the time, Eddie.

EDDIE. Look, kid, I'm not only talkin' about her. The more you run around like that the more chance you're takin'. [*To* BEATRICE] I mean suppose he gets hit by a car or something. [*To* MARCO] Where's his papers, who is he? Know what I mean?

BEATRICE. Yeah, but who is he in the daytime, though? It's the same chance in the daytime.

EDDIE [*Holding back a voice full of anger*] Yeah, but he don't have to go lookin' for it, Beatrice. If he's here to work, then he should work; if he's here for a good time then he could fool around! [*To* MARCO] But I understood, Marco, that you was both comin' to make a livin' for your family. You understand me, don't you, Marco? [*He goes to his rocker*]

MARCO. I beg your pardon, Eddie.

EDDIE. I mean, that's what I understood in the first place, see.

MARCO. Yes. That's why we came.

EDDIE [*Sits on his rocker*] Well, that's all I'm askin'. [EDDIE *reads his paper. There is a pause, an awkwardness. Now* CATHERINE *gets up and puts a record on the phonograph—"Paper Doll."*]

CATHERINE [*Flushed with revolt*] You wanna dance, Rodolpho?

> EDDIE *freezes.*

RODOLPHO [*In deference to Eddie*] No, I—I'm tired.

BEATRICE. Go ahead, dance, Rodolpho.

CATHERINE. Ah, come on. They got a beautiful quartet, these guys. Come. [*She has taken his hand and he stiffly rises, feeling* EDDIE'S *eyes on his back, and they dance*]

EDDIE [*To* CATHERINE] What's that, a new record?

CATHERINE. It's the same one. We bought it the other day.

BEATRICE [*To* EDDIE] They only bought three records. [*She watches them dance;* EDDIE *turns his head away.* MARCO *just sits there, waiting. Now* BEATRICE *turns to* EDDIE] Must be nice to go all over in one of them fishin' boats. I would like that myself. See all them other countries?

EDDIE. Yeah.

BEATRICE [*To* MARCO] But the women don't go along, I bet.

MARCO. No, not on the boats. Hard work.

BEATRICE. What're you got, a regular kitchen and everything?

MARCO. Yes, we eat very good on the boats—especially when Rodolpho comes along; everybody gets fat.

BEATRICE. Oh, he cooks?

MARCO. Sure, very good cook. Rice, pasta, fish, everything.

> EDDIE *lowers his paper.*

EDDIE. He's a cook, too! [*Looking at* RODOLPHO] He sings, he cooks . . .

> RODOLPHO *smiles thankfully.*

BEATRICE. Well it's good, he could always make a living.

EDDIE. It's wonderful. He sings, he cooks, he could make dresses . . .

CATHERINE. They get some high pay, them guys. The head chefs in all the big hotels are men. You read about them.

EDDIE. That's what I'm sayin'.

CATHERINE *and* RODOLPHO *continue dancing.*

CATHERINE. Yeah, well, I mean.

EDDIE [*To* BEATRICE] He's lucky, believe me. [*Slight pause. He looks away, then back to* BEATRICE] That's why the water front is no place for him. [*They stop dancing.* RODOLPHO *turns off phonograph*] I mean like me—I can't cook, I can't sing, I can't make dresses, so I'm on the water front. But if I could cook, if I could sing, if I could make dresses, I wouldn't be on the water front. [*He has been unconsciously twisting the newspaper into a tight roll. They are all regarding him now; he senses he is exposing the issue and he is driven on*] I would be someplace else. I would be like in a dress store. [*He has bent the rolled paper and it suddenly tears in two. He suddenly gets up and pulls his pants up over his belly and goes to* MARCO] What do you say, Marco, we go to the bouts next Saturday night. You never seen a fight, did you?

MARCO [*Uneasily*] Only in the moving pictures.

EDDIE [*Going to* RODOLPHO] I'll treat yiz. What do you say, Danish? You wanna come along? I'll buy the tickets.

RODOLPHO. Sure. I like to go.

CATHERINE [*Goes to* EDDIE; *nervously happy now*] I'll make some coffee, all right?

EDDIE. Go ahead, make some! Make it nice and strong. [*Mystified, she smiles and exits to kitchen. He is weirdly elated, rubbing his fists into his palms. He strides to* MARCO] You wait, Marco, you see some real fights here. You ever do any boxing?

MARCO. No, I never.

EDDIE [*To* RODOLPHO] Betcha you have done some, heh?

RODOLPHO. No.

EDDIE. Well, come on, I'll teach you.

BEATRICE. What's he got to learn that for?

EDDIE. Ya can't tell, one a these days somebody's liable to step on his foot or sump'm. Come on, Rodolpho, I show you a couple a passes. [*He stands below table*]

BEATRICE. Go ahead, Rodolpho. He's a good boxer, he could teach you.

RODOLPHO [*Embarrassed*] Well, I don't know how to—[*He moves down to* EDDIE]

EDDIE. Just put your hands up. Like this, see? That's right. That's very good, keep your left up, because you lead with the left, see, like this.

[*He gently moves his left into* RODOLPHO's *face*] See? Now what you gotta do is you gotta block me, so when I come in like that you—[RODOLPHO *parries his left*] Hey, that's very good! [RODOLPHO *laughs*] All right, now come into me. Come on.

RODOLPHO. I don't want to hit you, Eddie.

EDDIE. Don't pity me, come on. Throw it, I'll show you how to block it. [RODOLPHO *jabs at him, laughing. The others join*] 'At's it. Come on again. For the jaw right here. [RODOLPHO *jabs with more assurance*] Very good!

BEATRICE. [*To* MARCO] He's very good!

EDDIE *crosses directly upstage of* RODOLPHO.

EDDIE. Sure, he's great! Come on, kid, put sump'm behind it, you can't hurt me. [RODOLPHO, *more seriously, jabs at* EDDIE's *jaw and grazes it*] Attaboy.

CATHERINE *comes from the kitchen, watches.*

Now I'm gonna hit you, so block me, see?

CATHERINE [*With beginning alarm*] What are they doin'?

They are lightly boxing now.

BEATRICE. [*She senses only the comradeship in it now*] He's teachin' him; he's very good!

EDDIE. Sure, he's terrific! Look at him go! [RODOLPHO *lands a blow*] 'At's it! Now, watch out, here I come, Danish! [*He feints with his left hand and lands with his right. It mildly staggers* RODOLPHO. MARCO *rises*]

CATHERINE [*Rushing to* RODOLPHO] Eddie!

EDDIE. Why? I didn't hurt him. Did I hurt you, kid? [*He rubs the back of his hand across his mouth*]

RODOLPHO. No, no, he didn't hurt me. [*To* EDDIE *with a certain gleam and a smile*] I was only surprised.

BEATRICE [*Pulling* EDDIE *down into the rocker*] That's enough, Eddie; he did pretty good, though.

EDDIE. Yeah. [*Rubbing his fists together*] He could be very good, Marco. I'll teach him again.

MARCO *nods at him dubiously.*

RODOLPHO. Dance, Catherine. Come. [*He takes her hand; they go to phonograph and start it. It plays "Paper Doll."* RODOLPHO *takes her in his arms. They dance.* EDDIE *in thought sits in his chair, and* MARCO *takes a chair, places it in front of* EDDIE, *and looks down at it.* BEATRICE *and* EDDIE *watch him*]

MARCO. Can you lift this chair?

EDDIE. What do you mean?

MARCO. From here. [*He gets on one knee with one hand behind his back, and grasps the bottom of one of the chair legs but does not raise it*]

EDDIE. Sure, why not? [*He comes to the chair, kneels, grasps the leg, raises the chair one inch, but it leans over to the floor*] Gee, that's hard, I never knew that. [*He tries again, and again fails*] It's on an angle, that's why, heh?

MARCO. Here. [*He kneels, grasps, and with strain slowly raises the chair higher and higher, getting to his feet now. RODOLPHO and CATHERINE have stopped dancing as MARCO raises the chair over his head. MARCO is face to face with EDDIE, a strained tension gripping his eyes and jaw, his neck stiff, the chair raised like a weapon over EDDIE's head—and he transforms what might appear like a glare of warning into a smile of triumph, and EDDIE's grin vanishes as he absorbs his look*]

CURTAIN

ACT TWO

Light rises on ALFIERI at his desk.

ALFIERI. On the twenty-third of that December a case of Scotch whisky slipped from a net while being unloaded—as a case of Scotch whisky is inclined to do on the twenty-third of December on Pier Forty-one. There was no snow, but it was cold, his wife was out shopping. Marco was still at work. The boy had not been hired that day; Catherine told me later that this was the first time they had been alone together in the house.

> *Light is rising on CATHERINE in the apartment. RODOLPHO is watching as she arranges a paper pattern on cloth spread on the table.*

CATHERINE. You hungry?

RODOLPHO. Not for anything to eat. [*Pause*] I have nearly three hundred dollars. Catherine?

CATHERINE. I heard you.

RODOLPHO. You don't like to talk about it any more?

CATHERINE. Sure, I don't mind talkin' about it.

RODOLPHO. What worries you, Catherine?

CATHERINE. I been wantin' to ask you about something. Could I?

RODOLPHO. All the answers are in my eyes, Catherine. But you don't look in my eyes lately. You're full of secrets. [*She looks at him. She seems withdrawn*] What is the question?

CATHERINE. Suppose I wanted to live in Italy.

RODOLPHO [*Smiling at the incongruity*] You going to marry somebody rich?

CATHERINE. No, I mean live there—you and me.

RODOLPHO [*His smile vanishing*] When?

CATHERINE. Well . . . when we get married.

RODOLPHO [*Astonished*] You want to be an Italian?

CATHERINE. No, but I could live there without being Italian. Americans live there.

Rodolpho. Forever?

CATHERINE. Yeah.

RODOLPHO [*Crosses to rocker*] You're fooling.

CATHERINE. No, I mean it.

RODOLPHO. Where do you get such an idea?

CATHERINE. Well, you're always saying it's so beautiful there, with the mountains and the ocean and all the—

RODOLPHO. You're fooling me.

CATHERINE. I mean it.

RODOLPHO [*Goes to her slowly*] Catherine, if I ever brought you home with no money, no business, nothing, they would call the priest and the doctor and they would say Rodolpho is crazy.

CATHERINE. I know, but I think we would be happier there.

RODOLPHO. Happier! What would you eat? You can't cook the view!

CATHERINE. Maybe you could be a singer, like in Rome or—

RODOLPHO. Rome! Rome is full of singers.

CATHERINE. Well, I could work then.

RODOLPHO. Where?

CATHERINE. God, there must be jobs somewhere!

RODOLPHO. There's nothing! Nothing, nothing, nothing. Now tell me what you're talking about. How can I bring you from a rich country to suffer in a poor country? What are you talking about? [*She searches for words*] I would be a criminal stealing your face. In two years you would have an old, hungry face. When my brother's babies cry they give them water, water that boiled a bone. Don't you believe that?

CATHERINE [*Quietly*] I'm afraid of Eddie here.

> *Slight pause.*

RODOLPHO [*Steps closer to her*] We wouldn't live here. Once I am a citizen I could work anywhere and I would find better jobs and we would have a house, Catherine. If I were not afraid to be arrested I would start to be something wonderful here!

CATHERINE [*Steeling herself*] Tell me something. I mean just tell me, Rodolpho—would you still want to do it if it turned out we had to go live in Italy? I mean just if it turned out that way.

RODOLPHO. This is your question or his question?

CATHERINE. I would like to know, Rodolpho. I mean it.

RODOLPHO. To go there with nothing.

CATHERINE. Yeah.

RODOLPHO. No. [*She looks at him wide-eyed*] No.

CATHERINE. You wouldn't?

RODOLPHO. No; I will not marry you to live in Italy. I want you to be my wife, and I want to be a citizen. Tell him that, or I will. Yes. [*He moves about angrily*] And tell him also, and tell yourself, please, that I am not a beggar, and you are not a horse, a gift, a favor for a poor immigrant.

CATHERINE. Well, don't get mad!

RODOLPHO. I am furious! [*Goes to her*] Do you think I am so desperate? My brother is desperate, not me. You think I would carry on my back the rest of my life a woman I didn't love just to be an American? It's so wonderful? You think we have no tall buildings in Italy? Electric lights? No wide streets? No flags? No automobiles? Only work we don't have. I want to be an American so I can work, that is the only wonder here—work! How can you insult me, Catherine?

CATHERINE. I didn't mean that—

RODOLPHO. My heart dies to look at you. Why are you so afraid of him?

CATHERINE [*Near tears*] I don't know!

RODOLPHO. Do you trust me, Catherine? You?

CATHERINE. It's only that I— He was good to me, Rodolpho. You don't know him; he was always the sweetest guy to me. Good. He razzes me all the time but he don't mean it. I know. I would—just feel ashamed if I made him sad. 'Cause I always dreamt that when I got married he would be happy at the wedding, and laughin'—and now he's—mad all the time and nasty—[*She is weeping*] Tell him you'd live in Italy—just tell him, and maybe he would start to trust you a little, see? Because I want him to be happy; I mean—I like him, Rodolpho—and I can't stand it!

RODOLPHO. Oh, Catherine—oh, little girl.

CATHERINE. I love you, Rodolpho, I love you.

RODOLPHO. Then why are you afraid? That he'll spank you?

CATHERINE. Don't, don't laugh at me! I've been here all my life. . . . Every day I saw him when he left in the morning and when he came home at night. You think it's so easy to turn around and say to a man he's nothin' to you no more?

RODOLPHO. I know, but—

CATHERINE. You don't know; nobody knows! I'm not a baby, I know a lot more than people think I know. Beatrice says to be a woman, but—

RODOLPHO. Yes.

CATHERINE. Then why don't she be a woman? If I was a wife I would make a man happy instead of goin' at him all the time. I can tell a block away when he's blue in his mind and just wants to talk to somebody quiet and nice. . . . I can tell when he's hungry or wants a beer before he even says anything. I know when his feet hurt him, I mean I *know* him and now I'm supposed to turn around and make a stranger out of him? I don't know why I have to do that, I mean.

RODOLPHO. Catherine. If I take in my hands a little bird. And she grows and wishes to fly. But I will not let her out of my hands because I love her so much, is that right for me to do? I don't say you must hate him; but anyway you must go, mustn't you? Catherine?

CATHERINE [*Softly*] Hold me.

RODOLPHO [*Clasping her to him*] Oh, my little girl.

CATHERINE. Teach me. [*She is weeping*] I don't know anything, teach me, Rodolpho, hold me.

RODOLPHO. There's nobody here now. Come inside. Come. [*He is leading her toward the bedrooms*] And don't cry any more.

> *Light rises on the street. In a moment* EDDIE *appears. He is unsteady, drunk. He mounts the stairs. He enters the apartment, looks around, takes out a bottle from one pocket, puts it on the table. Then another bottle from another pocket, and a third from an inside pocket. He sees the pattern and cloth, goes over to it and touches it, and turns toward upstage.*

EDDIE. Beatrice? [*He goes to the open kitchen door and looks in*] Beatrice? Beatrice?

> CATHERINE *enters from bedroom; under his gaze she adjusts her dress.*

CATHERINE. You got home early.

EDDIE. Knocked off for Christmas early. [*Indicating the pattern*] Rodolpho makin' you a dress?

CATHERINE. No. I'm makin' a blouse.

> RODOLPHO *appears in the bedroom doorway.* EDDIE *sees him and his arm jerks slightly in shock.* RODOLPHO *nods to him testingly.*

RODOLPHO. Beatrice went to buy presents for her mother.

> *Pause.*

EDDIE. Pack it up. Go ahead. Get your stuff and get outa here. [CATHERINE *instantly turns and walks toward the bedroom, and* EDDIE *grabs her arm*] Where you goin'?

CATHERINE [*Trembling with fright*] I think I have to get out of here, Eddie.

EDDIE. No, you ain't goin' nowheres, he's the one.

CATHERINE. I think I can't stay here no more. [*She frees her arm, steps back toward the bedroom*] I'm sorry, Eddie. [*She sees the tears in his eyes*] Well, don't cry. I'll be around the neighborhood; I'll see you. I just can't stay here no more. You know I can't. [*Her sobs of pity and love for him break her composure*] Don't you know I can't? You know that, don't you? [*She goes to him*] Wish me luck. [*She clasps her hands prayerfully*] Oh, Eddie, don't be like that!

EDDIE. You ain't goin' nowheres.

CATHERINE. Eddie, I'm not gonna be a baby any more! You—

He reaches out suddenly, draws her to him, and as she strives to free herself he kisses her on the mouth.

RODOLPHO. Don't! [*He pulls on* EDDIE's *arm*] Stop that! Have respect for her!

EDDIE [*Spun round by* RODOLPHO] You want something?

RODOLPHO. Yes! She'll be my wife. That is what I want. My wife!

EDDIE. But what're you gonna be?

RODOLPHO. I show you what I be!

CATHERINE. Wait outside; don't argue with him!

EDDIE. Come on, show me! What're you gonna be? Show me!

RODOLPHO [*With tears of rage*] Don't say that to me! [RODOLPHO *flies at him in attack.* EDDIE *pins his arms, laughing, and suddenly kisses him*]

CATHERINE. Eddie! Let go, ya hear me! I'll kill you! Leggo of him! [*She tears at* EDDIE's *face and* EDDIE *releases* RODOLPHO. EDDIE *stands there with tears rolling down his face as he laughs mockingly at* RODOLPHO. *She is staring at him in horror.* RODOLPHO *is rigid. They are like animals that have torn at one another and broken up without a decision, each waiting for the other's mood*]

EDDIE [*To* CATHERINE] You see? [*To* RODOLPHO] I give you till tomorrow, kid. Get outa here. Alone. You hear me? Alone.

CATHERINE. I'm going with him, Eddie. [*She starts toward* RODOLPHO]

EDDIE. [*Indicating* RODOLPHO *with his head*] Not with that. [*She halts, frightened. He sits, still panting for breath, and they watch him helplessly as he leans toward them over the table*] Don't make me do nuttin', Catherine. Watch your step, submarine. By rights they oughta throw you back in the water. But I got pity for you. [*He moves unsteadily toward the door, always facing* RODOLPHO] Just get outa here and don't lay another hand on her unless you wanna go out feet first. [*He goes out of the apartment*]

The lights go down, as they rise on ALFIERI.

ALFIERI. On December twenty-seventh I saw him next. I normally go home well before six, but that day I sat around looking out my

window at the bay, and when I saw him walking through my
doorway, I knew why I had waited. And if I seem to tell this like a
dream, it was that way. Several moments arrived in the course of the
two talks we had when it occurred to me how—almost transfixed I
had come to feel. I had lost my strength somewhere. [EDDIE *enters,
removing his cap, sits in the chair, looks thoughtfully out*] I looked in
his eyes more than I listened—in fact, I can hardly remember the
conversation. But I will never forget how dark the room became
when he looked at me; his eyes were like tunnels. I kept wanting to
call the police, but nothing had happened. Nothing at all had really
happened. [*He breaks off and looks down at the desk. Then he turns
to* EDDIE] So in other words, he won't leave?

EDDIE. My wife is talkin' about renting a room upstairs for them. An old
lady on the top floor is got an empty room.

ALFIERI. What does Marco say?

EDDIE. He just sits there. Marco don't say much.

ALFIERI. I guess they didn't tell him, heh? What happened?

EDDIE. I don't know; Marco don't say much.

ALFIERI. What does your wife say?

EDDIE [*Unwilling to pursue this*] Nobody's talkin' much in the house. So
what about that?

ALFIERI. But you didn't prove anything about him. It sounds like he just
wasn't strong enough to break your grip.

EDDIE. I'm tellin' you I know—he ain't right. Somebody that don't want
it can break it. Even a mouse, if you catch a teeny mouse and you
hold it in your hand, that mouse can give you the right kind of fight.
He didn't give the right kind of fight, I know it, Mr. Alfieri, the guy
ain't right.

ALFIERI. What did you do that for, Eddie?

EDDIE. To show her what he is! So she would see, once and for all! Her
mother'll turn over in the grave! [*He gathers himself almost per-
emptorily*] So what do I gotta do now? Tell me what to do.

ALFIERI. She actually said she's marrying him?

EDDIE. She told me, yeah. So what do I do?

   Slight pause.

ALFIERI. This is my last word, Eddie, take it or not, that's your business.
Morally and legally you have no rights, you cannot stop it; she is a
free agent.

EDDIE [*Angering*] Didn't you hear what I told you?

ALFIERI [*With a tougher tone*] I heard what you told me, and I'm telling
you what the answer is. I'm not only telling you now, I'm warning
you—the law is nature. The law is only a word for what has a right to
happen. When the law is wrong it's because it's unnatural, but in

this case it is natural and a river will drown you if you buck it now. Let her go. And bless her. [*A phone booth begins to glow on the opposite side of the stage; a faint, lonely blue.* EDDIE *stands up, jaws clenched*] Somebody had to come for her, Eddie, sooner or later. [EDDIE *starts turning to go and* ALFIERI *rises with new anxiety*] You won't have a friend in the world, Eddie! Even those who understand will turn against you, even the ones who feel the same will despise you! [EDDIE *moves off*] Put it out of your mind! Eddie! [*He follows into the darkness, calling desperately*]

> EDDIE *is gone. The phone is glowing in light now. Light is out on* ALFIERI. EDDIE *has at the same time appeared beside the phone.*

EDDIE. Give me the number of the Immigration Bureau. Thanks. [*He dials*] I want to report something. Illegal immigrants. Two of them. That's right. Four-forty-one Saxon Street, Brooklyn, yeah. Ground floor. Heh? [*With greater difficulty*] I'm just around the neighborhood, that's all. Heh? [*Evidently he is being questioned further, and he slowly hangs up. He leaves the phone just as* LOUIS *and* MIKE *come down the street*]

LOUIS. Go bowlin', Eddie?

EDDIE. No, I'm due home.

LOUIS. Well, take it easy.

EDDIE. I'll see yiz.

> *They leave him, exiting right, and he watches them go. He glances about, then goes up into the house. The lights go on in the apartment.* BEATRICE *is taking down Christmas decorations and packing them in a box.*

EDDIE. Where is everybody? [BEATRICE *does not answer*] I says where is everybody?

BEATRICE [*Looking up at him, wearied with it, and concealing a fear of him*] I decided to move them upstairs with Mrs. Dondero.

EDDIE. Oh, they're all moved up there already?

BEATRICE. Yeah.

EDDIE. Where's Catherine? She up there?

BEATRICE. Only to bring pillow cases.

EDDIE. She ain't movin' in with them.

BEATRICE. Look, I'm sick and tired of it. I'm sick and tired of it!

EDDIE. All right, all right, take it easy.

BEATRICE. I don't wanna hear no more about it, you understand? Nothin'!

EDDIE. What're you blowin' off about? Who brought them in here?

BEATRICE. All right, I'm sorry; I wish I'd drop dead before I told them to come. In the ground I wish I was.

EDDIE. Don't drop dead, just keep in mind who brought them in here, that's all. [*He moves about restlessly*] I mean I got a couple of rights here. [*He moves, wanting to beat down her evident disapproval of him*] This is my house here, not their house.

BEATRICE. What do you want from me? They're moved out; what do you want now?

EDDIE. I want my respect!

BEATRICE. So I moved them out, what more do you want? You got your house now, you got your respect.

EDDIE [*He moves about biting his lip*] I don't like the way you talk to me, Beatrice.

BEATRICE. I'm just tellin' you I done what you want!

EDDIE. I don't like it! The way you talk to me and the way you look at me. This is my house. And she is my niece and I'm responsible for her.

BEATRICE. So that's why you done that to him?

EDDIE. I done what to him?

BEATRICE. What you done to him in front of her; you know what I'm talkin' about. She goes around shakin' all the time, she can't go to sleep! That's what you call responsible for her?

EDDIE [*Quietly*] The guy ain't right, Beatrice. [*She is silent*] Did you hear what I said?

BEATRICE. Look, I'm finished with it. That's all. [*She resumes her work*]

EDDIE [*Helping her to pack the tinsel*] I'm gonna have it out with you one of these days, Beatrice.

BEATRICE. Nothin' to have out with me, it's all settled. Now we gonna be like it never happened, that's all.

EDDIE. I want my respect, Beatrice, and you know what I'm talkin' about.

BEATRICE. What?

    Pause.

EDDIE [*Finally his resolution hardens*] What I feel like doin' in the bed and what I don't feel like doin'. I don't want no—

BEATRICE. When'd I say anything about that?

EDDIE. You said, you said, I ain't deaf. I don't want no more conversations about that, Beatrice. I do what I feel like doin' or what I don't feel like doin'.

BEATRICE. Okay.

    Pause.

EDDIE. You used to be different, Beatrice. You had a whole different way.

BEATRICE. *I'm* no different.

EDDIE. You didn't used to jump me all the time about everything. The last year or two I come in the house I don't know what's gonna hit me.

It's a shootin' gallery in here and I'm the pigeon.

BEATRICE. Okay, okay.

EDDIE. Don't tell me okay, okay, I'm tellin' you the truth. A wife is supposed to believe the husband. If I tell you that guy ain't right don't tell me he is right.

BEATRICE. But how do you know?

EDDIE. Because I know. I don't go around makin' accusations. He give me the heeby-jeebies the first minute I seen him. And I don't like you sayin' I don't want her marryin' anybody. I broke my back payin' her stenography lessons so she could go out and meet a better class of people. Would I do that if I didn't want her to get married? Sometimes you talk like I was a crazy man or sump'm.

BEATRICE. But she likes him.

EDDIE. Beatrice, she's a baby, how is she gonna know what she likes?

BEATRICE. Well, you kept her a baby, you wouldn't let her go out. I told you a hundred times.

   Pause.

EDDIE. All right. Let her go out, then.

BEATRICE. She don't wanna go out now. It's too late, Eddie.

   Pause.

EDDIE. Suppose I told her to go out. Suppose I—

BEATRICE. They're going to get married next week, Eddie.

EDDIE [*His head jerks around to her*] She said that?

BEATRICE. Eddie, if you want my advice, go to her and tell her good luck. I think maybe now that you had it out you learned better.

EDDIE. What's the hurry next week?

BEATRICE. Well, she's been worried about him bein' picked up; this way he could start to be a citizen. She loves him, Eddie. [*He gets up, moves about uneasily, restlessly*] Why don't you give her a good word? Because I still think she would like you to be a friend, y'know? [*He is standing, looking at the floor*] I mean like if you told her you'd go to the wedding.

EDDIE. She asked you that?

BEATRICE. I know she would like it. I'd like to make a party here for her. I mean there oughta be some kinda send-off. Heh? I mean she'll have trouble enough in her life, let's start it off happy. What do you say? Cause in her heart she still loves you, Eddie. I know it. [*He presses his fingers against his eyes*] What're you cryin'? [*She goes to him, holds his face*] Go . . . whyn't you go tell her you're sorry? [CATHERINE *is seen on the upper landing of the stairway, and they hear her descending*] There . . . she's comin' down. Come on, shake hands with her.

EDDIE [*Moving with suppressed suddenness*] No, I can't, I can't talk to her.

BEATRICE. Eddie, give her a break; a wedding should be happy!

EDDIE. I'm goin', I'm goin' for a walk. [*He goes upstage for his jacket. CATHERINE enters and starts for the bedroom door*]

BEATRICE. Katie? . . . Eddie, don't go, wait a minute. [*She embraces EDDIE's arm with warmth*] Ask him, Katie. Come on, honey.

EDDIE. It's all right, I'm— [*He starts to go and she holds him*]

BEATRICE. No, she wants to ask you. Come on, Katie, ask him. We'll have a party! What're we gonna do, hate each other? Come on!

CATHERINE. I'm gonna get married, Eddie. So if you wanna come, the wedding be on Saturday.

> Pause.

EDDIE. Okay. I only wanted the best for you, Katie. I hope you know that.

CATHERINE. Okay. [*She starts out again*]

EDDIE. Catherine? [*She turns to him*] I was just tellin' Beatrice . . . if you wanna go out, like . . . I mean I realize maybe I kept you home too much. Because he's the first guy you ever knew, y'know? I mean now that you got a job, you might meet some fellas, and you get a different idea, y'know? I mean you could always come back to him, you're still only kids, the both of yiz. What's the hurry? Maybe you'll get around a little bit, you grow up a little more, maybe you'll see different in a couple of months. I mean you be surprised, it don't have to be him.

CATHERINE. No, we made it up already.

EDDIE [*With increasing anxiety*] Katie, wait a minute.

CATHERINE. No, I made up my mind.

EDDIE. But you never knew no other fella, Katie! How could you make up your mind?

CATHERINE. Cause I did. I don't want nobody else.

EDDIE. But, Katie, suppose he gets picked up.

CATHERINE. That's why we gonna do it right away. Soon as we finish the wedding he's goin' right over and start to be a citizen. I made up my mind, Eddie. I'm sorry. [*To BEATRICE*] Could I take two more pillow cases for the other guys?

BEATRICE. Sure, go ahead. Only don't let her forget where they came from.

> CATHERINE *goes into a bedroom.*

EDDIE. She's got other boarders up there?

BEATRICE. Yeah, there's two guys that just came over.

EDDIE. What do you mean, came over?

Beatrice. From Italy. Lipari the butcher—his nephew. They come from Bari, they just got here yesterday. I didn't even know till Marco and Rodolpho moved up there before. [Catherine *enters, going toward exit with two pillow cases*] It'll be nice, they could all talk together.

Eddie. Catherine! [*She halts near the exit door. He takes in* Beatrice *too*] What're you, got no brains? You put them up there with two other submarines?

Catherine. Why?

Eddie [*In a driving fright and anger*] Why! How do you know they're not trackin' these guys? They'll come up for them and find Marco and Rodolpho! Get them out of the house!

Beatrice. But they been here so long already—

Eddie. How do you know what enemies Lipari's got? Which they'd love to stab him in the back?

Catherine. Well what'll I do with them?

Eddie. The neighborhood is full of rooms. Can't you stand to live a couple of blocks away from him? Get them out of the house!

Catherine. Well maybe tomorrow night I'll—

Eddie. Not tomorrow, do it now. Catherine, you never mix yourself with somebody else's family! These guys get picked up, Lipari's liable to blame you or me and we got his whole family on our head. They got a temper, that family.

    Two men in overcoats appear outside, start into the house.

Catherine. How'm I gonna find a place tonight?

Eddie. Will you stop arguin' with me and get them out! You think I'm always tryin' to fool you or sump'm? What's the matter with you, don't you believe I could think of your good? Did I ever ask sump'm for myself? You think I got no feelin's? I never told you nothin' in my life that wasn't for your good. Nothin'! And look at the way you talk to me! Like I was an enemy! Like I—[*A knock on the door. His head swerves. They all stand motionless. Another knock.* Eddie, *in a whisper, pointing upstage*] Go up the fire escape, get them out over the back fence.

    Catherine *stands motionless, uncomprehending.*

First Officer [*In the hall*] Immigration! Open up in there!

Eddie. Go, go. Hurry up! [*She stands a moment staring at him in a realized horror*] Well, what're you lookin' at!

First Officer. Open up!

Eddie [*Calling toward door*] Who's that there?

First Officer. Immigration, open up.

    Eddie *turns, looks at* Beatrice. *She sits. Then he looks at* Catherine. *With a sob of fury* Catherine *streaks into a bedroom.*

Knock is repeated.

EDDIE. All right, take it easy, take it easy. [*He goes and opens the door. The* OFFICER *steps inside*] What's all this?

FIRST OFFICER. Where are they?

SECOND OFFICER *sweeps past and, glancing about, goes into the kitchen.*

EDDIE. Where's who?

FIRST OFFICER. Come on, come on, where are they? [*He hurries into the bedrooms*]

EDDIE. Who? We got nobody here. [*He looks at* BEATRICE, *who turns her head away. Pugnaciously, furious, he steps toward* BEATRICE] What's the matter with *you?*

FIRST OFFICER *enters from the bedroom, calls to the kitchen.*

FIRST OFFICER. Dominick?

Enter SECOND OFFICER *from kitchen.*

SECOND OFFICER. Maybe it's a different apartment.

FIRST OFFICER. There's only two more floors up there. I'll take the front, you go up the fire escape. I'll let you in. Watch your step up there.

SECOND OFFICER. Okay, right, Charley. [FIRST OFFICER *goes out apartment door and runs up the stairs*] This is Four-forty-one, isn't it?

EDDIE. That's right. [SECOND OFFICER *goes out into the kitchen.* EDDIE *turns to* BEATRICE. *She looks at him now and sees his terror*]

BEATRICE [*Weakened with fear*] Oh, Jesus, Eddie.

EDDIE. What's the matter with *you?*

BEATRICE [*Pressing her palms against her face*] Oh, my God, my God.

EDDIE. What're you, accusin' me?

BEATRICE [*Her final thrust is to turn toward him instead of running from him*] My God, what did you do?

Many steps on the outer stair draw his attention. We see the FIRST OFFICER *descending, with* MARCO, *behind him* RODOLPHO, *and* CATHERINE *and the two strange immigrants, followed by* SECOND OFFICER. BEATRICE *hurries to door.*

CATHERINE [*Backing down stairs, fighting with* FIRST OFFICER; *as they appear on the stairs*] What do yiz want from them? They work, that's all. They're boarders upstairs, they work on the piers.

BEATRICE [*To* FIRST OFFICER] Ah, mister, what do you want from them, who do they hurt?

CATHERINE [*Pointing to* RODOLPHO] They ain't no submarines, he was born in Philadelphia.

FIRST OFFICER. Step aside, lady.

CATHERINE. What do you mean? You can't just come in a house and—

FIRST OFFICER. All right, take it easy. [*To* RODOLPHO] What street were you born in Philadelphia?

CATHERINE. What do you mean, what street? Could you tell me what street you were born?

FIRST OFFICER. Sure. Four blocks away, One-eleven Union Street. Let's go, fellas.

CATHERINE [*Fending him off* RODOLPHO] No, you can't! Now, get outa here!

FIRST OFFICER. Look, girlie, if they're all right they'll be out tomorrow. If they're illegal they go back where they came from. If you want, get yourself a lawyer, although I'm tellin' you now you're wasting your money. Let's get them in the car, Dom. [*To the men*] Andiamo, Andiamo, let's go. [*The men start, but* MARCO *hangs back*]

BEATRICE [*From doorway*] Who're they hurtin', for God's sake, what do you want from them? They're starvin' over there, what do you want! Marco!

> MARCO *suddenly breaks from the group and dashes into the room and faces* EDDIE; BEATRICE *and* FIRST OFFICER *rush in as* MARCO *spits into* EDDIE'S *face.* CATHERINE *runs into hallway and throws herself into* RODOLPHO'S *arms.* EDDIE, *with an enraged cry, lunges for* MARCO.

EDDIE. Oh, you mother's—!

> FIRST OFFICER *quickly intercedes and pushes* EDDIE *from* MARCO, *who stands there accusingly.*

FIRST OFFICER [*Between them, pushing* EDDIE *from* MARCO] Cut it out!

EDDIE [*Over the* FIRST OFFICER'S *shoulder, to* MARCO] I'll kill you for that, you son of a bitch!

FIRST OFFICER. Hey! [*Shakes him*] Stay in here now, don't come out, don't bother him. You hear me? Don't come out, fella. [*For an instant there is silence. Then* FIRST OFFICER *turns and takes* MARCO'S *arm and then gives a last, informative look at* EDDIE. *As he and* MARCO *are going out into the hall,* EDDIE *erupts*]

EDDIE. I don't forget that, Marco! You hear what I'm sayin'?

> *Out in the hall,* FIRST OFFICER *and* MARCO *go down the stairs. Now, in the street,* LOUIS, MIKE, *and several neighbors including the butcher,* LIPARI—*a stout, intense, middle-aged man—are gathering around the stoop.* LIPARI, *the butcher, walks over to the two strange men and kisses them. His wife, keening, goes and kisses their hands.* EDDIE *is emerging from the house shouting after* MARCO.

BEATRICE *is trying to restrain him.*

EDDIE. That's the thanks I get? Which I took the blankets off my bed for yiz? You gonna apologize to me, Marco! *Marco!*

FIRST OFFICER [*In the doorway with* MARCO] All right, lady, let them go. Get in the car, fellas, it's over there.

> RODOLPHO *is almost carrying the sobbing* CATHERINE *off up the street, left.*

CATHERINE. He was born in Philadelphia! What do you want from him?

FIRST OFFICER. Step aside, lady, come on now . . .

> The SECOND OFFICER *has moved off with the two strange men.* MARCO, *taking advantage of the* FIRST OFFICER'S *being occupied with* CATHERINE, *suddenly frees himself and points back at* EDDIE.

MARCO. That one! I accuse that one!

> EDDIE *brushes* BEATRICE *aside and rushes out to the stoop.*

FIRST OFFICER [*Grabbing him and moving him quickly off up the left street*] Come on!

MARCO [*As he is taken off, pointing back at* EDDIE] That one! He killed my children! That one stole the food from my children!

> MARCO *is gone. The crowd has turned to* EDDIE.

EDDIE [*To* LIPARI *and wife*] He's crazy! I give them the blankets off my bed. Six months I kept them like my own brothers!

> LIPARI, *the butcher, turns and starts up left with his arm around his wife.*

EDDIE. Lipari! [*He follows* LIPARI *up left*] For Christ's sake, I kept them, I give them the blankets off my bed!

> LIPARI *and wife exit.* EDDIE *turns and starts crossing down right to* LOUIS *and* MIKE.

EDDIE. Louis! *Louis!*

> LOUIS *barely turns, then walks off and exits down right with* MIKE. *Only* BEATRICE *is left on the stoop.* CATHERINE *now returns, blank-eyed, from offstage and the car.* EDDIE *calls after* LOUIS *and* MIKE.

EDDIE. He's gonna take that back. He's gonna take that back or I'll kill him! You hear me? I'll kill him! I'll kill him! [*He exits up street calling*]

> *There is a pause of darkness before the lights rise, on the reception*

room of a prison. MARCO *is seated;* ALFIERI, CATHERINE, *and*
RODOLPHO *standing.*

ALFIERI. I'm waiting, Marco, what do you say?

RODOLPHO. Marco never hurt anybody.

ALFIERI. I can bail you out until your hearing comes up. But I'm not
going to do it, you understand me? Unless I have your promise.
You're an honorable man, I will believe your promise. Now what do
you say?

MARCO. In my country he would be dead now. He would not live this
long.

ALFIERI. All right, Rodolpho—you come with me now.

RODOLPHO. No! Please, Mister. Marco—promise the man. Please, I want
you to watch the wedding. How can I be married and you're in here?
Please, you're not going to do anything; you know you're not.

MARCO *is silent.*

CATHERINE [*Kneeling left of* MARCO] Marco, don't you understand? He
can't bail you out if you're gonna do something bad. To hell with
Eddie. Nobody is gonna talk to him again if he lives to a hundred.
Everybody knows you spit in his face, that's enough, isn't it? Give
me the satisfaction—I want you at the wedding. You got a wife and
kids, Marco. You could be workin' till the hearing comes up, instead
of layin' around here.

MARCO [*To* ALFIERI] I have no chance?

ALFIERI [*Crosses to behind* MARCO] No, Marco. You're going back. The
hearing is a formality, that's all.

MARCO. But him? There is a chance, eh?

ALFIERI. When she marries him he can start to become an American.
They permit that, if the wife is born here.

MARCO [*Looking at* RODOLPHO] Well—we did something. [*He lays a palm
on* RODOLPHO's *arm and* RODOLPHO *covers it*]

RODOLPHO. Marco, tell the man.

MARCO [*Pulling his hand away*] What will I tell him? He knows such a
promise is dishonorable.

ALFIERI. To promise not to kill is not dishonorable.

MARCO [*Looking at* ALFIERI] No?

ALFIERI. No.

MARCO [*Gesturing with his head—this is a new idea*] Then what is done
with such a man?

ALFIERI. Nothing. If he obeys the law, he lives. That's all.

MARCO [*Rises, turns to* ALFIERI] The law? All the law is not in a book.

ALFIERI. Yes. In a book. There is no other law.

MARCO [*His anger rising*] He degraded my brother. My blood. He robbed
my children, he mocks my work. I work to come here, mister!

ALFIERI. I know, Marco—

MARCO. There is no law for that? Where is the law for that?

ALFIERI. There is none.

MARCO [*Shaking his head, sitting*] I don't understand this country.

ALFIERI. Well? What is your answer? You have five or six weeks you could work. Or else you sit here. What do you say to me?

MARCO [*Lowers his eyes. It almost seems he is ashamed*] All right.

ALFIERI. You won't touch him. This is your promise.

Slight pause.

MARCO. Maybe he wants to apologize to me. [MARCO *is staring away.* ALFIERI *takes one of his hands*]

ALFIERI. This is not God, Marco. You hear? Only God makes justice.

MARCO. All right.

ALFIERI [*Nodding, not with assurance*] Good! Catherine, Rodolpho, Marco, let us go.

CATHERINE *kisses* RODOLPHO *and* MARCO, *then kisses* ALFIERI's *hand.*

CATHERINE. I'll get Beatrice and meet you at the church. [*She leaves quickly*]

MARCO *rises.* RODOLPHO *suddenly embraces him.* MARCO *pats him on the back and* RODOLPHO *exits after* CATHERINE. MARCO *faces* ALFIERI.

ALFIERI. Only God, Marco.

MARCO *turns and walks out.* ALFIERI *with a certain processional tread leaves the stage. The lights dim out.*

The lights rise in the apartment. EDDIE *is alone in the rocker, rocking back and forth in little surges. Pause. Now* BEATRICE *emerges from a bedroom. She is in her best clothes, wearing a hat.*

BEATRICE [*With fear, going to* EDDIE] I'll be back in about an hour, Eddie. All right?

EDDIE [*Quietly, almost inaudibly, as though drained*] What, have I been talkin' to myself?

BEATRICE. Eddie, for God's sake, it's her wedding.

EDDIE. Didn't you hear what I told you? You walk out that door to that wedding you ain't comin' back here, Beatrice.

BEATRICE. Why! What do you want?

EDDIE. I want my respect. Didn't you ever hear of that? From my wife?

CATHERINE *enters from bedroom.*

CATHERINE. It's after three; we're supposed to be there already, Beatrice. The priest won't wait.

BEATRICE. Eddie. It's her wedding. There'll be nobody there from her family. For my sister let me go. I'm going for my sister.

EDDIE [*As though hurt*] Look, I been arguin' with you all day already, Beatrice, and I said what I'm gonna say. He's gonna come here and apologize to me or nobody from this house is goin' into that church today. Now if that's more to you than I am, then go. But don't come back. You be on my side or on their side, that's all.

CATHERINE [*Suddenly*] Who the hell do you think you are?

BEATRICE. Sssh!

CATHERINE. You got no more right to tell nobody nothin'! Nobody! The rest of your life, nobody!

BEATRICE. Shut up, Katie! [*She turns* CATHERINE *around*]

CATHERINE. You're gonna come with me!

BEATRICE. I can't, Katie, I can't . . .

CATHERINE. How can you listen to him? This rat!

BEATRICE [*Shaking* CATHERINE] Don't you call him that!

CATHERINE [*Clearing from* BEATRICE] What're you scared of? He's a rat! He belongs in the sewer!

BEATRICE. Stop it!

CATHERINE [*Weeping*] He bites people when they sleep! He comes when nobody's lookin' and poisons decent people. In the garbage he belongs!

EDDIE *seems about to pick up the table and fling it at her.*

BEATRICE. No, Eddie! Eddie! [*To* CATHERINE] Then we all belong in the garbage. You, and me too. Don't say that. Whatever happened we all done it, and don't you ever forget it, Catherine. [*She goes to* CATHERINE] Now go, go to your wedding, Katie, I'll stay home. Go. God bless you, God bless your children.

Enter RODOLPHO.

RODOLPHO. Eddie?

EDDIE. Who said you could come in here? Get outa here!

RODOLPHO. Marco is coming, Eddie. [*Pause.* BEATRICE *raises her hands in terror*] He's praying in the church. You understand? [*Pause.* RODOLPHO *advances into the room*] Catherine, I think it is better we go. Come with me.

CATHERINE. Eddie, go away, please.

BEATRICE [*Quietly*] Eddie. Let's go someplace. Come! You and me. [*He has not moved*] I don't want you to be here when he comes. I'll get your coat.

EDDIE. Where? Where am I goin'? This is my house.

BEATRICE [*Crying out*] What's the use of it! He's crazy now, you know the way they get, what good is it! You got nothin' against Marco, you always liked Marco!

EDDIE. I got nothin' against Marco? Which he called me a rat in front of the whole neighborhood? Which he said I killed his children! Where you been?

RODOLPHO [*Quite suddenly, stepping up to* EDDIE] It is my fault, Eddie. Everything. I wish to apologize. It was wrong that I do not ask your permission. I kiss your hand. [*He reaches for* EDDIE's *hand, but* EDDIE *snaps it away from him*]

BEATRICE. Eddie, he's apologizing!

RODOLPHO. I have made all our troubles. But you have insult me too. Maybe God understand why you did that to me. Maybe you did not mean to insult me at all—

BEATRICE. Listen to him! Eddie, listen what he's tellin' you!

RODOLPHO. I think, maybe when Marco comes, if we can tell him we are comrades now, and we have no more argument between us. Then maybe Marco will not—

EDDIE. Now, listen—

CATHERINE. Eddie, give him a chance!

BEATRICE. What do you want! Eddie, what do you want!

EDDIE. I want my name! He didn't take my name; he's only a punk. Marco's got my name—[*To* RODOLPHO] and you can run tell him, kid, that he's gonna give it back to me in front of this neighborhood, or we have it out. [*Hoisting up his pants*] Come on, where is he? Take me to him.

BEATRICE. Eddie, listen—

EDDIE. I heard enough! Come on, let's go!

BEATRICE. Only blood is good? He kissed your hand!

EDDIE. What he does don't mean nothin' to nobody! [*To* RODOLPHO] Come on!

BEATRICE [*Barring his way to the stairs*] What's gonna mean somethin'? Eddie, listen to me. Who could give you your name? Listen to me, I love you, I'm talkin' to you, I love you; if Marco'll kiss your hand outside, if he goes on his knees, what is he got to give you? That's not what you want.

EDDIE. Don't bother me!

BEATRICE. You want somethin' else, Eddie, and you can never have her!

CATHERINE [*In horror*] B.!

EDDIE [*Shocked, horrified, his fists clenching*] Beatrice.

> MARCO *appears outside, walking toward the door from a distant point.*

BEATRICE [*Crying out, weeping*] The truth is not as bad as blood, Eddie! I'm tellin' you the truth—tell her good-by forever!

EDDIE [*Crying out in agony*] That's what you think of me—that I would have such a thought? [*His fists clench his head as though it will burst*]

MARCO [*Calling near the door outside*] Eddie Carbone!

> EDDIE *swerves about; all stand transfixed for an instant. People appear outside.*

EDDIE [*As though flinging his challenge*] Yeah, Marco! Eddie Carbone. Eddie Carbone. Eddie Carbone. [*He goes up the stairs and emerges from the apartment.* RODOLPHO *streaks up and out past him and runs to* MARCO]

RODOLPHO. No, Marco, please! Eddie, please, he has children! You will kill a family!

BEATRICE. Go in the house! Eddie, go in the house!

EDDIE [*He gradually comes to address the people*] Maybe he came to apologize to me. Heh, Marco? For what you said about me in front of the neighborhood? [*He is incensing himself and little bits of laughter even escape him as his eyes are murderous and he cracks his knuckles in his hands with a strange sort of relaxation*] He knows that ain't right. To do like that? To a man? Which I put my roof over their head and my food in their mouth? Like in the Bible? Strangers I never seen in my whole life? To come out of the water and grab a girl for a passport? To go and take from your own family like from the stable—and never a word to me? And now accusations in the bargain! [*Directly to* MARCO] Wipin' the neighborhood with my name like a dirty rag! I want my name, Marco. [*He is moving now, carefully, toward* MARCO] Now gimme my name and we go together to the wedding.

BEATRICE *and* CATHERINE [*Keening*] Eddie! Eddie, don't! Eddie!

EDDIE. No, Marco knows what's right from wrong. Tell the people, Marco, tell them what a liar you are! [*He has his arms spread and* MARCO *is spreading his*] Come on, liar, you know what you done! [*He lunges for* MARCO *as a great hushed shout goes up from the people.* MARCO *strikes* EDDIE *beside the neck*]

MARCO. Animal! You go on your knees to me!

> EDDIE *goes down with the blow and* MARCO *starts to raise a foot to stomp him when* EDDIE *springs a knife into his hand and* MARCO *steps back.* LOUIS *rushes in toward* EDDIE.

LOUIS. Eddie, for Christ's sake!

> EDDIE *raises the knife and* LOUIS *halts and steps back.*

EDDIE. You lied about me, Marco. Now say it. Come on now, say it!

MARCO. Anima-a-a-l!

> EDDIE *lunges with the knife.* MARCO *grabs his arm, turning the blade inward and pressing it home as the women and* LOUIS *and*

MIKE *rush in and separate them, and* EDDIE, *the knife still in his hand, falls to his knees before* MARCO. *The two women support him for a moment, calling his name again and again.*

CATHERINE. Eddie I never meant to do nothing bad to you.

EDDIE. Then why—Oh, B.!

BEATRICE. Yes, yes!

EDDIE. My B.! [*He dies in her arms, and* BEATRICE *covers him with her body.* ALFIERI, *who is in the crowd, turns out to the audience. The lights have gone down, leaving him in a glow, while behind him the dull prayers of the people and the keening of the women continue*]

ALFIERI. Most of the time now we settle for half and I like it better. But the truth is holy, and even as I know how wrong he was, and his death useless, I tremble, for I confess that something perversely pure calls to me from his memory—not purely good, but himself purely, for he allowed himself to be wholly known and for that I think I will love him more than all my sensible clients. And yet, it is better to settle for half, it must be! And so I mourn him—I admit it—with a certain . . . alarm.

CURTAIN

Considerations

This play is based on an actual event told to the playwright by a longshoreman who had known Eddie's prototype. A characteristic of this play is the use of colloquial speech, a foreboding mood, and a sense of tragedy. Is the device of foreshadowing also a common element? How does Miller prepare the audience for the violence at the end?

In the simple starkness of the setting, Miller communicates a definite mood to the audience. This bare setting, along with the stage directions, creates an atmosphere of bleak ghetto existence. In what way is this atmosphere appropriate to the theme of the play? The character of Alfieri serves a dual purpose: he not only interacts with the other characters, he also communicates directly with the audience. How do these conversations reinforce the prevailing mood?

The relationships of the characters living in the neighborhood involve a rigid code of ethics that is almost tribalistic in its ritualism. For example, the symbolic "spit in the face" by Marco and the ostracism of Eddie by the neighborhood because he broke the code are old-country customs. How did this way of life influence Eddie's actions and reactions? How does Eddie's death reflect Marco's commitment to the code? Eddie's sense of self-worth seems to depend on the esteem of his peers. Does he have any identity outside of this sphere?

Catherine is Eddie's niece, adopted by him after his sister-in-law's death. He experiences great conflict between paternal love and sexual attraction for her. His repression of this sexual attraction and his accusation of Rodolpho's homosexuality are evidence of this conflict. These emotions create a sense of alienation in Eddie that ultimately lead him to violence. When Eddie finally succumbs to his attraction to Catherine by kissing her, is this not also an act of violence? Is his final act of violence toward Marco simply revenge, or a self-destructive act as well?

A climax may be defined as the point at which a character decides his fate. This is the point where the character makes the decision that has faced him throughout the play. When does Eddie make this decision and decide his fate? What, exactly, is Eddie's fate?

Beatrice, Eddie's wife, seems to be the stabilizing force in the interactions of the other characters. She never acts out of any malice, while seeing everyone else's situation clearly. She is the only character that faces all these emotions; she is the only one that recognizes her own. Could she have taken any action that might have prevented the violence at the end? Is she being honest when she tells Catherine that she isn't jealous but that she should leave? If so, is this honesty consistent throughout the rest of the play?

At the beginning of the play, Catherine is a naive, childlike girl. Her character is developed throughout the play until, at the end, she is more of a woman. What factors contribute to her maturity? Do any of the other characters experience this kind of growth?

This was originally a one-act play written in the genre of naturalism. In this original version, Miller felt that there was difficulty in empathizing with Eddie. In his revision, the character was more realistically developed and Miller is quoted as saying, "It was finally possible to mourn this man." Did you, as a reader, mourn this man? Is this play a genuine slice-of-life?

In his final speech, Alfieri states that Eddie was purely himself and that "he allowed himself to be wholly known . . ." Since Eddie was neither honest with himself nor with anyone else in the play, including Alfieri, how could the lawyer possibly come to this conclusion? At the end of the play, the audience knew who and what he was, as did all the people who knew him. Did Eddie ever gain any insight into himself? Where is this evident?

Eddie was not a noble character. What did Alfieri see in him then to cause him to state that he will love and mourn him? Why, also, with alarm?

This play was written less than 25 years ago. Is its impact as powerful now as it was when it was written? Is there anything about this play that gives it a timeless, universal quality? What is your reaction to its realism?

Glossary

Accent: the emphasis or stress placed on a particular syllable in a poetic foot.

Allegory: a type of extended symbolism in which abstract ideas or concepts (truth, beauty, evil) are made concrete through personification.

Alliteration: a series of words that begin with the same letter or sound ("now or never").

Allusion: an indirect reference to a person, object, or action.

Alexandrine: *See* Hexameter.

Ambiguity: a multiple meaning in a poem or story. (When used accidentally as a result of faulty diction, it can be confusing; when used purposefully and skillfully, it enhances the work.)

Anachronism: a misplacing of persons, objects, or events in time.

Analogy: an extended comparison of two things that resemble each other but are not exactly alike.

Analysis: division of a literary work into its basic parts to show their relationships and functions.

Anapest: a metrical foot consisting of two unaccented syllables followed by an accented one.

Anecdote: a short, usually personal, narrative often used to illustrate a particular characteristic.

Annotation: a note supplied in the margin or at the end of a text.

Antagonist: the adversary of the protagonist (hero).

Anthropomorphism: attributing human traits to nonhuman things.

Anticlimax: a continuation of the plot after the story's climax. Its intent is to relieve or detract from the ten-sion of the climax, or to present further complications of the plot.

Aphorism: a concise saying that illustrates or defines a general principle or statement.

Apocopated rhyme: rhyme in which the unaccented syllable of one of the rhyming words is ignored ("flight," "lightly").

Apologue: a brief, contrived allegory (such as a fable or parable) that illustrates a moral.

Apology: in literature, a justification of a particular action or belief.

Archetype: a basic pattern of human values, such as the stock plot archetypes of romantic love, the overthrow of a tyrant, and death and resurrection or rebirth.

Argumentation: one of the four basic types of discourse; the attempt to convince the reader of the truth or relevance of the author's position by presenting objective evidence and using logic.

Assonance: imperfect rhyme in which the stressed vowels correspond ("cloud" and "shout").

Atmosphere: the pervasive mood or feeling of a literary work.

Autobiography: an account of a person's life, or parts thereof, written by himself. Basically, autobiographical literary categories are: *letters*, *diaries*, *journals*, and *memoirs*.

Balance: (1) the equilibrium achieved through the proportionate arrangement of the basic elements in a literary work; (2) in rhetoric, the parallel structure of similar or opposing elements, used for contrast.

Ballad: a simple poem that tells a story and is usually meant to be sung.

Ballade: A verse form consisting of three stanzas, an envoy, and an identical refrain. (*See also* Envoy.)

Ballad stanza: the stanza used in ballads, usually consisting of four lines rhyming *abcb* with the first and third lines in iambic tetrameter and the second and fourth lines in iambic trimeter.

Baroque: an elaborate, ornate style used especially by poets (the seventeenth-century English metaphysical poets in particular) who stress the bizarre. The baroque style is characterized by extravagant comparisons and unbalanced structure.

Bathos: the ludicrous or ridiculous description of emotions or feelings.

Beast fable: a fable in which real or imaginary animals assume human characteristics. (*See also* Fable.)

Beginning rhyme: rhyming of sounds at the beginning of lines of verse.

Biography: an account of a person's life written by another person.

Blank verse: unrhymed iambic pentameter, the most popular of all verse lines for English poetry.

Broken rhyme: rhyme in which a word is broken off at the end of one line and continued in the next for the sake of the rhyme.

Burlesque: a mocking, satiric imitation of another work. (*See also* Parody.)

Cacophony: a combination of discordant sounds sometimes used deliberately for emphasis in poetry.

Caricature: a form of ridicule that exaggerates and distorts one's worst faults and physical features.

Catastrophe: resolution of the conflict of the plot by disaster.

Catharsis: the emotional release or spiritual exaltation resulting from reading or seeing a tragedy.

Characterization: the development of a character within a particular work.

Classicism: a form of literary criticism that emphasizes the classic qualities of form, reason, restraint, and is based on distinguished artistic models of the past.

Climax: the point in the plot of a story at which the conflict and interest is highest and the resolution of the conflict is determined or at least begun.

Coherence: in literary composition, the clear relationship of the various parts (sentences, paragraphs) that form an integrated, connected whole.

Colloquy: a formal conversation or discourse between two or more characters.

Comic relief: a device by which tensions in a serious work are relaxed by a humorous or farcical episode or scene.

Compactness: density of prose or poetic style.

Complication: the intensification of conflict leading to more complex entanglements of plot.

Conceit: an elaborate extended simile or figurative comparison within a poem; used especially by the metaphysical poets.

Conflict: the element of the plot around which all other elements revolve.

Connotation: the nonliteral meanings a word conveys because of its suggested or implied meanings.

Consistency: the agreement of the parts to form a unified, believable whole.

Consonance: a rhyme scheme in which only consonant sounds correspond ("food" and "fad").

Convention: a device that is universally accepted; especially any practice that is improbable (such as the soliloquy in drama) or unrealistic (such as flashbacks in literature or the theater) but is accepted as part of the art.

Couplet: two successive verse lines that are alike in meter and rhyme.

Criticism: a judgment or evaluation of a literary work. Some important aspects of critical approaches are: *Historical*—evaluating a work in the light of the milieu from which it arose; *Freudian*—emphasizing the unconscious intent of the author; the *New Criticism*—focusing entirely on the work itself, its merits and shortcomings, not upon the author's intentions or salient facts about him or his environment; *Impressionistic*—emphasizing the critic's own reactions to the work; *Textual*—analyzing the text itself and the extraneous facts pertinent to an understanding of it; *Theoretical*—emphasizing general principles of literature as they relate to a particular work; *Relativistic*—comparing how the work stands up to a given set of standards; *Comparative*—comparing one work with another that shares comparable qualities.

Critique: a critical evaluation of a work based on predetermined principles.

Dactyl: a metrical foot of three syllables, one accented syllable followed by two unaccented ones: hea' ven ly.

Decasyllable: a ten-syllable line, most common in iambic pentameter verse.

Deduction: in logic, the form of reasoning that moves from the general to the specific; in literature and exposition, the conclusion that follows from the premises presented.

Denotation: the literal or "dictionary" definition of a work.

Denouement: the point following the climax of a plot at which the complications begin to unravel and are resolved.

Description: one of the four basic kinds of discourse (argumentation, exposition, and narration are the others). Descriptive prose conveys feelings or creates images by presenting qualities, appearances, and facts about someone or something.

Dialect: a local or regional variation of a language.

Dialogue: conversation between the characters in a work of literature.

Diction: the particular way in which words are used in a literary work.

Didactic literature: literature that teaches or moralizes.

Discourse: any formal communication of ideas. (In rhetoric there are four basic classes of discourse: argumentation, description, exposition, and narration.)

Disyllable: any word of two syllables (es-say).

Doggerel: inferior poetry in which the verse is poorly composed; sometimes intentionally used for satiric or humorous effects.

Double entendre: double meaning.

Drama: (1) a play intended for performance in a theater; (2) the generic term applied to a body of plays, as Restoration drama.

Dramatic irony: allowing the audience to know something in order to create tension before a character becomes aware of it.

Dramatic monologue: a one-sided conversation of one person with another.

Ecologue: a pastoral poem involving (usually) shepherds' conversation that may conceal satire or allegory.

Elegaic stanza: A verse form named after Thomas Gray's "Elegy in a Country Churchyard" (1750). The rhyme scheme is *abab*, and the meter an iambic pentameter quatrain.

Elegy: a poem written in elegaic meter (dactylic hexameter lines alternating with dactylic pentameters) and concerning grief or a lament. Example: Auden's "In Memory of W.B. Yeats."

Elision: dropping a vowel preceding a consonant (isn't, can't); often used in poetry to maintain meter.

Elizabethan: referring to the reign of Queen Elizabeth I (1558–1603) [and often to the Jacobean period of James I (1603–1625)].

Ellipsis: words or a single word omitted from a sentence; also, the marks . . . or *** that indicate omission of words or sentences from a quoted passage.

Emotive language: language selected for its express connotative value to arouse emotional response.

Empathy: the ability to identify oneself with another person or literary figure.

End-stopped: referring to a line of verse that is complete in itself in structure and sense. (*See* Couplet.)

Envoy: a short, summarizing stanza of a ballade.

Epic: a long narrative poem in which the characters and the action are of heroic proportions. Example: Homer's *Odyssey*.

Epigram: a short, pointed statement, often humorous or satiric.

Epilogue: the concluding statement of a prose work (except drama).

Epiphany: a term borrowed from religion by James Joyce to describe a moment of sudden spiritual insight into the meaning and essence of a thing or situation.

Episode: a unified event within a narrative.

Epithet: A word or short phrase that aptly describes and labels a person or thing.

Essay: A prose composition of undefined length that (usually) treats a single subject or theme.

Etymology: the study of the history of words.

Eulogy: a written or spoken expression of praise, generally formal in style.

Euphemism: a mild or inoffensive word substituted for one that is considered gross, indelicate, or taboo.

Euphony: the harmonious combination of sounds.

Existentialism: a philosophy that asserts that existence precedes essence: it denies the existence of absolute principles or objective meanings and insists that man is responsible for himself and acts with free will. The themes of existential literary work stress man's isolation, his loneliness, his sense of futility, and the irrevocability of his actions. Examples: works of

Albert Camus, Jean-Paul Sartre, and Samuel Beckett.

Explication: a close reading of a literary text and the analysis of its structure and meaning.

Expressionism: a literary school that stresses the internal, or subjective, rather than the external, or objective, reality. Examples: works of Dostoevsky, Joyce, and Kafka.

Fable: a short tale that relates a moral.

Farce: a type of low comedy or burlesque that features extreme exaggeration of action.

Feminine ending: a line of verse in which the final syllable is unstressed.

Feminine rhyme: two-syllable rhyme ("flatter" and "scatter"); also called *double rhyme*.

Figurative language: figures of speech and word combinations that go beyond literal (denotative) meanings.

Flashback: a literary technique that involves interrupting the story line to relate events that happened at a previous time.

Flat character: usually, a minor character in a story who is a stereotype or a ploy for the major characters.

Folklore: customs, songs, tales, and sayings that are transmitted within a culture from one generation to the next.

Foot: the basic unit of rhythm in verse.

Foreshadowing: hinting at events yet to come in the plot.

Foreword: an introduction to a literary work, often written by someone other than the author.

Form: (1) the general term for the main genres of literature (poetry, the novel, tragedy, and so forth); (2) the structure of a work as opposed to its content.

Free verse: Verse that does not follow a set metrical pattern but flows like natural speech patterns. In free-verse poetry, the stanza gives the poem form or structure. Example: Eliot's "The Wasteland."

Genre: A literary classification or type, such as drama, the short story, and so forth.

Glossary: A collection of explanations or definitions of given words at the end of a text.

Gothic novel: a genre of novel that features morbidity, horror, and (often) elements of the supernatural.

Haiku: a popular form of Japanese verse that consists of seventeen syllables in a tercet of five, seven, and five syllables per line.

Hedonism: a philosophical belief that pleasure constitutes man's highest good.

Heptameter: a seven-foot line of verse (also called *the fourteener* when the feet are iambic).

Hero: the protagonist or main character.

Heroic couplet: two consecutive lines of end-rhymed iambic pentameter verse.

Hexameter: a six-foot line of verse.

Historical novel: a novel set in the past with either real or fictional historical figures as characters.

Homeric (or epic) simile: a lengthy figurative comparison that parallels a number of similarities.

Homily: a sermon or informal moral discussion presented to an audience.

Humanism: a philosophical doctrine

that emphasizes the perfectibility of man; it originated during the Renaissance period and held that man was not inherently wicked or fallen from grace, as the medieval view had proclaimed, but that human values are good and should be the center of the study of man himself.

Humanities: the general term describing the areas of learning that are culturally oriented: art, music, literature, philosophy, and so forth.

Hyperbole: the use of extravagant exaggeration for emphasis.

Iamb (or iambus): a two-syllable foot with an unaccented syllable, followed by an accented one: a-bout.

Iambic pentameter: a metrical line consisting of five iambic feet.

Ictus: An unnatural accent in a line of verse; i.e., an accent that does not correspond with the spoken stress.

Idiom: An expression in a language with a meaning that cannot be derived from the words involved.

Idyll: a pastoral poem describing the idealized life of shepherds in picturesque terms; also, a short epic that depicts heroic events of the past.

Image: the impression elicited by a word or phrase.

Imagery: figurative language that conveys sensory impressions.

Imagism: a poetic movement, chiefly among American poets, that reached its height during the pre-World War I years; it sought to produce visual imagery that was clear, definite, and concentrated. Examples: works of Ezra Pound, Amy Lowell, William Carlos Williams.

Impressionism: in literature, the attempt to present experience without formal, structured analysis or by evoking an emotional effect without factual, detailed description; in criticism, a school wherein the critic analyzes his reactions to a literary work rather than the work itself.

In media res: the practice of plunging the reader into a narrative account at a point well along in the chronological sequence of events.

Internal rhyme: rhyming of sounds within a line of verse.

Invective: biting, abusive language that is not tempered by wit or humor.

Inversion: reordering normal sentence order; used in poetry for rhyme.

Irony: a statement in which the intended meaning is the opposite of the literal meaning.

Jacobean: referring to the period of the reign of James I of England (1603–1625).

Jargon: a set of special terms peculiar to a certain group or activity.

Jangleur: the French counterpart of the English *jester*, a wandering entertainer whose repertoire included playing musical instruments, singing, performing magic tricks and acrobatics, telling stories, and so forth.

Journalism: the writing and publishing of information in a newspaper or periodical issued at regular intervals.

Kenning: a compound metaphor used in place of a single noun, as "ring-giver" for "king"; associated primarily with Anglo-Saxon and Old Norse poetry.

Lay: a short epic or romantic story set to music, especially popular with the English wandering minstrels (eleventh to fifteenth centuries).

Lament: a poem that expresses deep sorrow, such as a dirge or elegy.

Lampoon: a caricature, usually malicious, of a literary or political figure. Lampoons fall under the general category of satire.

Legend: a traditional story that has some basis in fact, but is embellished with fictitious detail.

Lexicon: a dictionary or specialized listing of words.

Libretto: The verbal text of an opera or lyrics of a musical comedy.

Linguistics: the formal study of language.

Lipogram: the complete avoidance of a certain letter *or* the use of a single letter for a certain effect in a composition, particularly in a poem.

Litany: a liturgical form in which the clergyman and the congregation alternate responses.

Literal meaning: the exact meaning (denotation).

Literature: (for our purposes): imaginitive writing–fiction, prose, poetry, drama, essays, mythology, folklore, legend.

Litotes: a figure of speech that affirms the validity of something by denying its opposite (also called *understatement*).

Liturgical drama: drama that grew out of church ritual in the tenth century.

Local color: the use in a literary work of peculiarities or picturesqueness of a particular region.

Locale: the setting of a work of literature.

Logic: the study of arguments and reasoning to determine their validity.

Lyric poetry: (usually) non-narrative poetry that expresses personal emotion.

Macrocosm: the whole universe or the entire realm of human existence. (*See* Microcosm.)

Macrology: excessive wordiness that detracts from a literary style.

Magnum opus: an artist's greatest, or major, work.

Malapropism: a comic substitution of words.

Malediction: an invocation to bring ill-fortune or death to an adversary; the opposite of *benediction.*

Mannerism: the identifying stylistic marks of an individual writer or school of writers; (also, a sixteenth-century art style).

Masculine ending: ending a line of poetry on an accented final syllable.

Masculine rhyme: rhyme in which the final syllable of one line rhymes with the final syllable of another (also called *single rhyme*).

Masque (mask): a lavishly produced pageant of simple drama, dance, and music popular in the Renaissance court.

Materialism: a philosophy that stresses the reality of material things (physical objects) and states that spiritual or ideal forms are products of the imagination and have no real force or value.

Maxim: a general truth stated in concise form.

Memoir: an autobiographical narrative that focuses on events and characters other than the writer's own.

Metachronism: the postdating of

events in narrative fiction. (*See also* Anachronism.)

Metaphor: a figure of speech that implies a direct likeness between two unlike things.

Metaphysical poetry: in literature, a term applied to the poetry of a group of seventeenth-century poets who emphasized the intellectual and psychological aspects of emotion and religion. Examples: Donne, Marvell, and Herbert.

Meter: the rhythmic pattern in poetry determined by the number of accents in the lines of the poem (accentual-syllabic rhythm). Most English poetry is classified according to the following rhythmic units (feet): iambic, trochaic, dactylic, anapestic, spondaic, and pyrrhic (*q.v.*). The number of feet determines the meter; the standard meters for English verse are: monometer (one foot), dimeter (two feet), trimeter (three feet), tetrameter (four feet), pentameter (five feet), hexameter (six feet) and heptameter (seven feet). (*See also* Qualitative verse, Scansion.)

Metonymy: the use of one name for something closely associated with it, as "the crown" for "the king." (*See* Synecdoche.)

Metrical romance: a medieval tale of romantic love and idealized courtly traditions in a remote and exotic setting. Example: "Sir Gawain and the Green Knight."

Middle English: the English language as spoken and written between the Norman Conquest (1066) and the beginning of the sixteenth century.

Microcosm: a small portion of the whole. In literature, often used to represent greater reality, as man's experience is seen in terms of the greater universe in which he operates.

Miles gloriosus: a stock character in literature: usually a cowardly braggart, often victim of the practical jokes of others. Example: Sir John Falstaff in Shakespeare's *Henry IV.*

Milieu: the intellectual and sociological climate of a period.

Mime: originally a low form of vulgar comedy—developed in Italy in the fifth century B.C.

Minnesinger: a German lyric poet of the medieval period (1200–1300), similar to the French *troubadour.*

Minstrel: a thirteenth- or fourteenth-century musical entertainer who carried news from town to town, performed on the harp, sang, and recited romances.

Miracle play: a type of play developed in the twelfth century that dealt with the lives of saints; today, almost synonymous with *mystery play*, which designates a play that dealt with Biblical themes.

Mock epic (or mock heroic): a literary form that burlesques the "grand style" of epic poetry by treating a subject of trivial importance with pretended seriousness. Example: Pope's "The Rape of the Lock."

Modulation: a deliberate variation in the metrical pattern of a poem to prevent monotony.

Monody: a lament or song of grief sung by an individual singer.

Monologue: a speech or written composition presented wholly by one person.

Monometer: a one-foot line of verse.

Mood: the prevailing atmosphere or

tone of a literary work.

Moral: the ethical lesson of a literary work.

Morality play: a post-fourteenth-century type of allegorical drama that depicted the conflict between virtue and vice. Example: *Everyman.*

Mosaic rhyme: rhyme in which one or more of the rhyme partners is made up of more than one word.

Motif: a narrative element that serves as the basis for an expanded poem, tale, or song.

Movement: a literary trend that is distinguished by identifiable characteristics, such as impressionism or the free verse movement.

Mummery: a dumb show or simple dramatic presentation acted by performers wearing masks and disguised in costume.

Muses: The nine Greek goddesses represented as patrons of music, literature, and the liberal arts.

Musical comedy: A type of drama developed in England and the United States in the early twentieth century that features songs to carry the story line, but the dialogue is spoken, not sung.

Mysticism: the philosophy or theory that God—or the controlling deity—can be known immediately and personally through a natural human faculty that transcends intellect. (*See also* Transcendentalism.)

Myth: an anonymous, traditional story that grows out of the universal human need to explain the "unknowable;" Myths differ from legends in that they are not based on historical facts.

Narration: the recounting of an event or series of events.

Narrative: the story that is related in the process of narration.

Narrator: the teller of a story or poem: first-person ("I") and third-person ("he") narration is conventional. (*See also* Point of view.)

Naturalism: in literature, a nineteenth-century movement that espouses determinism: man is not a creature of free will, but a pawn in the hands of his environment and his heredity. Examples: works of Stephen Crane, Jack London, and Emile Zola.

Neoclassicism: a late-seventeenth- and eighteenth-century school of literature that attempted to revive the principles of classicism. Man is viewed as imperfect and dualistic; a sense of order and reason prevails; restrained emotion dominates the writing; intellectual art is fostered. Examples: works of Dryden, Milton, Pope, and Dr. Johnson.

Neologism: a newly coined word or phrase.

New Criticism: The name given a modern school of literary critics concerned primarily with analyzing a work of art as an object in and of itself. Examples: works of John Crowe Ransom, Robert Penn Warren, and Allen Tate.

Nom de plume: a pseudonynm or pen name.

Novel: a form of complex fictitious prose that contains the three elements of plot, characters, and setting.

Novelette: a work of prose fiction that is longer than the short story, shorter than the novel.

Novella: a significant influence upon the formation of the English novel, the *novelle* were realistic Italian tales. Example: Boccaccio's *Decameron.*

Objective correlative: defined by T.S. Eliot as "a set of objects, a situation, a chain of events which shall be the formula of that particular emotion, such that when the external facts, which must terminate in sensory experience, are given, the emotion is immediately evoked." Thus when an author has in mind a certain emotion he wishes to convey, he presents a situation or a set of external objects that, hopefully, trigger a precise emotional response in the reader. The objective correlative is a symbol or set of symbols, then, that can assure the emotional validity of a poem or work of prose.

Objective theory of art: a critical view that judges the work of art as an object in itself independent of any external facts of its composition.

Occasional verse: poetry written to commemorate a special event, such as a marriage song or verse.

Octameter: an eight-foot line of verse.

Octave: an eight-line stanza of poetry.

Ode: an elaborate lyric poem of complicated verse form with an exalted or dignified theme.

Omniscient narrator: a narrator who has unlimited scope in his presentation and is not limited to reporting external events through the eyes of a single character.

One-act play: a modern dramatic form stressing unity of effect, focusing on dialogue and character, and not developing too much narrative background and detail.

Onomatopoeia: The use of words whose sounds suggest their meanings ("hiss", "buzz," "murmur.")

Opera: a dramatic form in which the dialogue is sung instead of spoken.

Operetta: an eighteenth-century forerunner of musical comedy (*q.v.*), originally a parody or burlesque of grand opera.

Oration: an elaborately structured formal speech, intended to arouse the audience to action.

Otiose: a term used in literary criticism to denote a style that is ornate and redundant.

Ottava rima: eight iambic pentameter lines rhyming *ababab cc.*

Oxford movement: a nineteenth-century religious movement led by Cardinal Newman corresponding to the romantic movement in literature.

Oxymoron: a rhetorical combination of contradictory terms for special emphasis, as in "eloquent silence."

Paean: a hymn of praise of joy.

Paeon: an uncommon (although frequently used by Hopkins) metrical foot consisting of one stressed (accented) syllable and three unstressed syllables.

Pageant: (1) a scaffold or stage, often constructed on wheels, upon which medieval plays were performed, and those plays performed on such stages; (2) a dramatic spectacle designed to celebrate a special event.

Paleography: the study of ancient writings, writing materials, and written symbols.

Palindrome: a word, phrase or sentence that reads the same from right to left as from left to right, as in "noon" and "deified."

Palinode: a written retraction of a previous writing, particularly such a recanting in verse form of an earlier ode.

Panegyric: a eulogy or other formal written or oral composition praising a person.

Pantheism: a religious-philosophic attitude that asserts that God exists in everything (finite objects) and finite objects are what make up the glory of God, so that nature reveals God and, at the same time, *is* God.

Pantomime: a dramatic art depending on silent motion, facial expression, gesturing, and costuming to express emotional or narrative situations.

Parable: a short, fictional story that teaches a moral lesson, usually in the form of an extended metaphor or allegory.

Paradox: a statement that seemingly is self-contradictory or silly, but in fact is true.

Parallelism: a structural arrangement of syntactically similar words, phrases, or clauses so that one element is developed equally with another.

Paraphrase: to restate the ideas of a composition in completely different words.

Pararhyme: rhyme in which the first and final consonants are the same but the vowels differ ("small, smell").

Parody: a composition that deliberately burlesques or imitates another in order to ridicule or criticize.

Pastoral verse: poems dealing with rustic life, particularly that of shepherds, and elegies in which a death is lamented in pastoral imagery.

Pathetic fallacy: a term coined by John Ruskin to express the practice of attributing human emotions to inanimate objects. Examples: "the harsh winter," "cruel fate." The best poets use the pathetic fallacy consciously for good effect.

Pathos: the quality that elicits sorrow, pity, or sympathy in the reader.

Pedantry: a critical term of reproach applied to writing or speech that displays an excessive amount of foreign phrases and superfluous verbiage.

Pentameter: a five-foot line of verse.

Perfect rhyme: rhyme in which the rhymed syllable are identical (flew, blew); also called *identical* or *true rhyme.*

Peripety: an Aristoteliam term designating the protagonist's change of fortune.

Periphrasis: a deliberate use of indirect or circumlocutious writing to get to the point.

Peroration: a conclusion and summing up of ideas in an oration, or a recapitulation of the major points of any discourse.

Persiflage: a flippant, chatty manner of treating a subject or theme.

Persona: a character used by an author as the narrative voice.

Personification: a figure of speech that attributes human characteristics to animals, inanimate objects, or philosophical abstractions and ideas.

Philippic: in modern usage, pertaining to invective speech or writing.

Philistinism: worship of material prosperity and technological success.

Philology: the study of language and literature in all its manifestations, including language theory and literary criticism.

Picaresque novel: a sixteenth-century form of the novel (orginally Spanish) that features an episodic account of the life of a *picaro*, a roguish, rascally fellow whose life is a series of misadventures.

Pindaric ode: a form of ode (*q.v.*) characterized by a three-part division.

Plagiarism: the stealing of another's text, language, idea, or plot, and presenting it as one's own.

Plaint: a lament or verse expressing sorrow.

Platonism: The idealistic philosophies of the Greek philosopher Plato (fourth century B.C.). Basically he is known for the doctrine of ideas ("forms"), which states that true reality is found in the spiritual realm of ideal forms or images of which earthly objects are simply reflections.

Pleiade: A group of sixteenth-century French poets and critics who attempted to refine and enrich the French language and to strive for classicism in their literature.

Pleonasm: a superfluous use of words, redundancy.

Plot: the arrangement of events in a narrative.

Poem: a rhythmic, unified composition characterized by imagination and the use of figurative language.

Poetic justice: in literature, the term implies "just due;" i.e., the virtuous are rewarded, the evil are punished.

Poetic license: the privilege to depart from normal logic, diction, or

rhyme in order to achieve a particular desired effect.

Poetry: an expression of an experience written in verse form, attempting to express a particular content in a certain way so as to create a definite effect. It is characterized by its use of figurative language and imagery.

Point of view: in narrative fiction, the author's attitude toward his story.

Polemic: a harsh argument against a religious, social, or political stance or ideology.

Polysyllabic rhyme: the rhyming of three or more syllables at the end of two or more words ("lightly pursues/brightly renews").

Portmanteau word: a word formed by deliberately fusing together two words (as James Joyce did in *Ulysses* and *Finnegan's Wake*).

Poulter's measure: the poetic combination (rarely used) of the twelve-syllable Alexandrine line of verse with a heptameter (fourteen-syllable) line.

Pragmatic theory of art: according to literary critic M.H. Abrams, a theory of art in which the effect the work of art produces in its audience is the factor in judging its success.

Preciosity, precious: a critical term applied to writing that is affected or consciously "pretty" in style.

Preface: a short introductory statement at the beginning of a prose work in which the author states his purpose and intent.

Pre-Raphaelite movement: a movement of group of nineteenth-century English artists and writers who believed in a return to a simple, straightforward presentation in art and literature of nature and man as a natural animal, as they felt was characteristic of Italian art before Raphael.

Prolepsis: the foreshadowing or predicting of a future event as if it were already affecting the present.

Prolixity: inclusion of excessive detail.

Prologue: an introduction to a play or literary work that prepares the reader for what is to follow.

Proscenium: in the modern theater, the front area of the stage between the orchestra pit and the curtain.

Prose: writing that does not have a regular rhythmic pattern.

Prosody: the technical study of versification.

Protagonist: the chief character in a narrative play or story.

Prototype: the original or first form of a thing or species.

Proverb: a saying, usually symbolic, that expresses a truth or recognized observation.

Pseudonym: a fictitious name.

Psychological novel: a novel that emphasizes the interior motivations of its characters. Examples: works of James, Faulkner, and Joyce.

Pun: a play on words.

Purist: a person who is excessively devoted to absolute correctness in use of the English language.

Pyrrhic foot: a metrical foot of two unaccented syllables.

Qualitative verse: verse in which the rhythmic pattern is determined by the number of accents in each line, as it is in English poetry.

Quantitative verse: verse whose basic rhythm is determined by the length of time allowed for the pronunciation of sounds (syllables). Example: classical poetry.

Quatrain: a stanza of four lines; also, a stanza composed of four verses.

Quintain (or quintet): a five-line stanza.

Quip: a witty, sarcastic, or jesting remark. Puns are examples of quips.

Rabelaisian: referring to lusty, irreverent humor in the manner of the sixteenth-century author François Rabelais.

Rationalism: a system of thought that holds as its authority reason rather than sense perception, intuition, revelation, or traditional authority.

Realism: a general term meaning accuracy of detail and true presentation of actuality.

Realistic movement: a mid-nineteenth and early twentieth-century movement that emphasized everyday experience and the immediate, pressing details of daily experience in literature. Examples: Balzac, George Eliot, and Mark Twain.

Rebuttal: a term from forensics (debating, public speaking) that denotes a final summing up of answers to the opposition in an argument.

Redundant: repetitive.

Refrain: a group of words, phrases, or lines that are repeated at intervals in a poem or song.

Regionalism: in literature, an emphasis on the history, folklore, speech, manners, dress, and so forth, of a particular geographical area.

Renaissance: the period in western European history between the medieval and the modern ages (approximately 1350–1650) marked by a growing sense of the importance of the individual.

Repartee: a quick, clever rejoinder or response.

Repetend: a poetical device in which a word or phrase is repeated at irregular intervals throughout a stanza or poem.

Repetition: the recurrent use of words, phrases, or sound patterns for emphasis.

Requiem: a chant or poem offering a prayer for the repose of the dead.

Restoration Age: 1660–1688, the period in English history after the Stuarts returned to the throne.

Reversal: the change of fortune for the protagonist in a dramatic or fictional plot. (*See also* Peripety.)

Rhetoric: the principles and theory dealing with the logical, clear, convincing presentation of facts and ideas in a speech or written composition.

Rhetorical question: a question that does not require, or intend to require, an answer.

Rhyme: the similarity or duplication of sounds, usually in corresponding positions in lines of verse. There are two general types of rhyme: true, or perfect, rhyme in which vowels and consonants rhyme; and approximate rhyme, which consists of assonance, consonance, and alliteration (*q.v.*) Rhyme can be classified according to the position of rhymed syllables in the lines or according to the number of syllables in which the identity of sound occurs. The first group consists of end, internal, or beginning rhyme (*q.v.*); the second contains masculine, feminine, and triple rhyme (*q.v.*) (*See also* Apocopated

rhyme, Broken rhyme, Mosaic rhyme, Pararhyme, Slant rhyme, Visual rhyme.)

Rhyme royal: a seven-line stanza of iambic pentameter verse, rhymed *ababbcc.*

Rhyme scheme: the rhyme pattern or sequence in a stanza or poem.

Rococo: in literature, designating a style that is overdone, precious, pretentious, and ornate.

Rodomontade: a term derived from the name of a bragging Moorish king in Ariosto's *Orlando Furioso,* meaning braggadocio or vain boasting.

Roman a clef: a novel in which real persons are depicted disguised as fictional characters.

Romanesque: in literature, denoting the fanciful or fabulous, or the presence of romance.

Romantic movement: an eighteenth- and nineteenth-century reaction against formality in art and literature; it stressed individualism, a love of nature, the imagination, and a revived interest in the past. Example: Wordsworth, Coleridge, Shelley, Keats, Byron, and Scott; Hawthorne, Melville, and Emerson.

Rondeau: a French verse form consisting of thirteen to fifteen lines, eight syllables to a line, with two end rhymes repeated over and over.

Rondel: a thirteen- or fourteen-line variation of the rondeau, using only two rhymes and repeating complete lines in the refrain.

Roundel: an eleven-line verse with a refrain taken from words in the first line repeated in the fourth and eleventh lines.

Run-on-lines: in poetry, the opposite of end-stopped lines; the grammatic structure and sense of a line is carried over from one line to the next; also called *enjambement.*

Saga: originally, an Icelandic or Scandinavian tale narrating legendary and historical accounts of heroic adventures.

Sapphic form: a verse form consisting of three verses of eleven syllables each.

Sarcasm: a form of irony denoting strong disapproval.

Satire: a type of writing that ridicules human frailties.

Scansion: the method used to determine meter and rhyme in English poetry; it consists of dividing verse into feet by counting accented syllables and indicating rhyme schemes with letter names. (*See also* Meter, Foot, etc.)

Scenario: the plot outline of a drama.

Scene: in drama, the division of action and setting within an act.

Scholasticism: the name given to the system of thinking and writing of eleventh- to sixteenth-century philosopher-teachers who attempted to prove everything by syllogistic reasoning. Example: St. Thomas Aquinas.

School plays: classical and early English plays performed in England in the sixteenth century at the universities, foreshadowing many of the forms and techniques of Elizabethan drama.

Scientific method: basically, inductive reasoning, proceeding from the specific to the general.

Scop: an Anglo-Saxon (500–1100 A.D.) bard or court poet who composed and recited heroic lyric poetry.

Semantics: the study of the meanings of words, in particular, and of meaning, *per se*, in all forms of communication.

Sentimentalism: an emphasis on feeling, often expressed as excessive emotionalism in literature.

Sestet: a six-line stanza or poem, particularly the last six lines of the Petrarchian sonnet.

Sestina: a complex French lyrical form consisting of six six-line stanzas and a three-line envoy (*q.v.*) with a pattern of end-words in place of a refrain.

Sextain: a six-line stanza or poem; it is a sestet, except that the term does not apply to the sonnet.

Short story: a short (1,000- to 10,000-word), carefully constructed literary form consisting of plot, setting, characters, and theme.

Sigmatism: the repetitive use of sibilant letters—x, z, soft c and s-sounding combinations (sh, tion, etc.)—to produce a certain consonant effect.

Simile: a figure of speech in which two basically unlike objects or things are directly compared.

Skald (scald): the Norse counterpart of the Anglo-Saxon scop; a singing poet-minstrel.

Skeltonic verse: a form of metrically irregular verse characterized by short lines of two or three stresses with irregular rhymed couplets; used by John Skelton (1460–1529) for his satiric poetry.

Slang: vernacular speech, usually unacceptable in formal usage and compositions.

Slant rhyme: rhyme in which the sounds are similar but not exactly the same; also called approximate or near rhyme. Example: "name," "gain"

Slice of life: a technique that presents an interchange between characters as it might happen in real life with no commentary; no problems are solved and no specific alternatives for action are presented.

Socratic irony: the dialectic device of pretending ignorance and humility in order to lead an opponent into contradicting himself.

Solecism: a violation of grammatical structure in speech or composition.

Soliloquy: a speech that reveals a character's innermost feelings and plans while other characters remain unaware of what he is saying.

Sonnet: a lyric poem of fourteen lines with a definite rhyme scheme; Petrarchian: *abba abba cde cde;* Shakespearean: *ab ab cdcd ef ef gg.*

Spenserian stanza: a nine-verse stanzaic pattern in which the first eight verses are iambic pentameter and the ninth is iambic hexameter; the rhyme scheme is *ababbcbcc.*

Spondee: a metrical foot of two accented syllables.

Spoonerism: an interchange of syllables in two or more words usually resulting in a humorous verbal blunder.

Sprung rhythm: meter based on the number of accented (stressed) syllables with no regard for the unstressed syllables in a line of verse.

Stanza: the recurring group of lines of a poem forming the largest division in terms of metrical form, unified thought, and rhyme scheme.

Stave: A stanza or set of verses (often written to be sung.)

Stock character: a conventional, stereotyped character.

Stream-of-consciousness novel: the type of psychological novel made popular by James Joyce and William Faulkner in which the consciousness of one or more characters is explored (consciousness in this context meaning all levels of awareness from pre-speech to highly articulated rational thought.)

Strophe: a stanzaic unit of poetry specifically associated with the Pindaric ode.

Sturm und Drang: a late eighteenth-century German literary movement characterized by elements of nationalism, folklore, and expression of emotion. Examples: works of Goethe and Schiller.

Style: the distinguishable characteristics of an author's writing.

Surrealism: a modern literary and artistic movement that attempts to depict objects "beyond reality" (surreal)—man's imagination, dreams, visions, etc.

Syllabic verse: verse in which meter is determined by the number of syllables, not by accents or quantitative values.

Symbol: an object or image that stands for or suggests something else.

Symbolism: a modern literary movement begun in reaction to realism, replacing the objectivity and directness of the realists' method with new techniques that attempted to present a true reality beyond objective reality. Examples: certain works of Eliot, Yeats, and Rilke.

Syncopation: a temporary shift in regular metrical accent.

Syncope: the deletion of a letter or a syllable in a word, as in "heavn'ly" and "e'er."

Synecdoche: the use of a part of one thing to signify the whole.

Synesthesia: a device used by symbolic writers in which the responses of two or more senses are aroused by a blending of sensuous imagery.

Synonym: words that are alike or closely associated in meaning.

Synopsis: a summary of the main points of a composition.

Syntax: the orderly arrangement of words into phrases and sentences.

Tail-rhyme stanza: a form in which short rhyming lines are placed after the longer lines; the "tail" rhymes serve as links between the stanzas.

Tall tale: an early American folk tale recounting the fantastically exaggerated heroic exploits of frontier heroes such as Paul Bunyan and Davy Crockett.

Tanka: a form of Japanese syllabic verse consisting of thirty-one syllables arranged in five lines.

Tautology: useless repetition of words.

Tenor (and vehicle): in criticism, tenor is the subject which the vehicle represents; or, the tenor is the real subject and the vehicle is the figurative subject, the image, according to critic I. A. Richards.

Tension: in twentieth-century criticism, designating the integral unity of a poem.

Tercet: a three-line stanza; the rhyme scheme may be *aaa, bbb, ccc,* etc., or it may be interwoven with the following stanza.

Terza rima: an interlocking rhyme scheme: *aba, bcb, cdc, ded,* etc.

Tetrameter: a four-foot line of verse.

Theme: the dominant idea in a work of literature.

Threnody: a dirge or funeral song, shorter than an elegy.

Tone: (1) in literary criticism, the total effect of a work; (2) the mood or attitude expressed by the author toward his subject matter; (3) the mood of the work itself.

Tract: an argumentative pamphlet that sets forth the views and positions of its author(s).

Tragedy: a dramatic form that recounts the life story of a protagonist, usually ending in his downfall through his tragic flaw (*q.v.*), moving the audience to "pity and fear" (Aristitolean definition) in the process.

Tragic flaw: the fatal weakness of character in the hero that leads to his downfall.

Tragi-comedy: a play than contains both tragic and comic elements.

Transcendentalism: a belief that intuition and the human conscience transcend external experience to put man in touch with higher forms of reality.

Transcendental movement: an American mid-nineteenth-century literary movement based on principles of transcendentalism (*q.v.*). Examples: Emerson's "Nature" (1836) and *Walden* (1854).

Travesty: a grotesque, mocking burlesque of another work of literature.

Trilogy: a three-part literary work in which each part is a complete unit in and of itself but is also vitally connected to the other parts.

Trimeter: a three-foot line of verse.

Triolet: a French verse form of eight lines in which the first line recurs three times; the rhyme scheme is *abaaabab*.

Triple rhyme: rhyme in which three consecutive syllables rhyme.

Triplet: a three-line stanza or a sequence of three rhyming verses.

Trochee: a two-syllable metrical foot with the first syllable accented and the second unaccented.

Trope: in rhetoric, the use of a word in a sense that is different from its literal meaning, as in ironic expressions, metaphors and similes.

Troubadour: an aristocratic lyric poet of southern France in the twelfth and thirteenth centuries.

Trouvere: a member of a group of northern French lyric poets who corresponded to the troubadours of southern France. (Chretien de Troyes, a famous trouvere, is credited with writing some of the early Arthurian legends.)

Tudor: referring to the period in England between 1485 and 1603; the kings of this family were Henry VII, Henry VIII, Edward VI, Mary, and Elizabeth (1558–1603).

Ubi sunt motif: an oft-repeated poetic theme that poses the question "where are" the good things of yesterday.

Understatement: a form of verbal irony that implies much more than is stated, or which affirms an idea by denying its opposite.

Unities principles: (Aristotelian unities of time, place, and action): (1) The events of a play must not exceed more than the length of one day (Time); (2) only one setting is permitted (Place); and (3) a play should have a beginning, middle and end, and should not mix tragic and comic elements (Action).

Unity: the literary concept that a work should have an organizing principle that unifies all parts to produce a single total effect.

Variorum edition: an edition of an author's work with complete notations and variations.

Universality: in literature, having universality means appealing to readers of all times and all places.

Vehicle: (*See* Tenor.)

Verisimilitude: the portrayal of truth and actuality by use of realistic detail.

Virgule: the diagonal mark / used to mark off metrical feet in scansion. // marks the caesura.

Visual rhyme: words that have a similar spelling but are not pronounced alike ("bead," "thread").

Weak ending: the final syllable of a line in poetry that is stressed to fit the metric pattern, but would not be stressed in normal speech.

Wit (and humor): in literature, wit denotes intellectual prowess or wisdom; humor designates eccentricity or the laughable.

Zeugma: a rhetorical device in which one word links two other words unlike in sense and grammatically incorrect as in: "flying birds and hearts."

Index

Abraham's Madness 614
Aesop 29
After Apple-Picking 480
After the Convention 593
Allen, Woody 296
American Farm, 1934 530
de Andrade, Carlos Drummond 654
April Inventory 607
Arise, My Love, and Come Away 352
Arms and the Boy 529
Arnold, Matthew 437
Arrabal, Fernando 882
As by Water 615
Asbaje, Juana de 387
Auden, W. H. 557
Auto Wreck 568
Award 588
Bad Children, The 564
Bait, The 372
Baker, Donald W. 604
Bankruptcy 639
Basho 653
Battle Hymn of the Republic 422
Baudelaire, Charles 434
Because I Could not stop for Death (#712) 448
Bells for John Whiteside's Daughter 521
Benedikt, Michael 633
Benét, Stephen Vincent 534
Bennett, Hal 320
Beowulf 60
Berryman, John 578
Birches 481
Bird came down the Walk, A (#328) 446
Bishop, Elizabeth 650
Black, Byron 636
Black Jackets 617
Black Riders, The, XLVIII 472
Black Riders, The, XLVII 472
Black Riders, The, III 471
Black Riders, The, XXIV 471
Blake, William 389
Blessed Damozel, The 438
Blessing, A 613
Blue Girls 520
Blue Meridian 652
Bode, Carl 564
Bontemps, Arna 300, 546
Borges, Jorge Luis 250
Brautigan, Richard 317, 631
Brer Rabbit's Cool Air Swing 68
Brooks, Gwendolyn 594
Brown, Frederick 309
Browning, Elizabeth Barrett 410
Browning, Robert 413
Buckley, Tim 639

Buick 570
Bulfinch 28
Burns, Robert 395
Byron, Lord (George Gordon) 402
Carew, Thomas 379
Carver, Raymond 312, 638
Cavalry Crossing a Ford 432
Chee's Daughter 256
Children of the Poor, The 594
Chimney Sweep, The 390
Ciardi, John 589
Circular Ruins, The 250
Clemens, Samuel 35
Clough, Arthur Hugh 422
Cohen, Leonard 647
Coleridge, Samuel Taylor 398
Colette 231
Come Live with Me and Be My Love 554
Composed upon Westminster Bridge 397
Condor and the Guests, The 275
Coney Island of the Mind, A 598
Confessions of a Burglar 296
Connell, Evan, S., Jr. 275
Conscientious Objector, The 571
Constant Lover, The 382
Corner 629
Crabbed Age and Youth 360
Crane, Stephen 470
Creeley, Robert 611
Cruz, Victor Hernandez 659
Cullen, Countee 551
Curiosity 609
Daddy 621
Dancing in the Street 634
Daniel, Bel, and the Snake 14
David 57
Day After Sunday, The 556
Death of Ivan Ilych, The 104
Death of the Ball Turret Gunner, The 585
Death in a Plane 654
Death Was a Trick 636
Delight in Disorder 376
Deer Among Cattle 606
Describes Rationally the Irrational Effects of
    Love 387
De Witch'-ooman an' de Spinnin'-Wheel 39
Dickey, James 606
Dickinson, Emily 444
Dilemma 585
Dill Pickle, A 208
Disquieting Muses, The 623
Dr. Sigmund Freud Discovers the Sea Shell 526
Domination of Black 487
Donne, John 370
Do Not Go Gentle into That Good Night 582

Dotson Gerber Resurrected 320
Dover Beach 437
"Dover Beach": A Note to That Poem 525
Dowson, Ernest 462
Drayton, Michael 360
Dream Deferred 548
Dress Rehearsal Rag 647
Dryden, John 385
Dulce et Decorum Est 528
Dunbar, Paul Laurence 474
Dust of Snow 479
Durem, Ray 588
Eagle, The 413
Eberhart, Richard 555
Edward 354
Eighth Air Force 586
Elegy for Jane 561
Eliot, T. S. 509
Eluard, Paul 532
Emperor of Ice-Cream, The 486
English A 590
Etsujin 653
European Shoe, The 633
Evans, Mari 626
Fable, A (Clemens) 35
Faulkner, William 222
Ferlinghetti, Lawrence 595
Fern Hill 579
Field of Boliauns, The 43
Filling Station 650
Fire and Ice 480
Flight 234
For No Clear Reason 612
For Rhoda 567
Formal Application 604
Frankie and Johnny 543
Freeman, Mary E. Wilkins 149
Freneau, Philip 393
From you I have been absent in the spring
    (Sonnet 98) 366
Frost, Robert 479
Game Called on Account of Darkness 592
Geni in the Jar, The 649
Gilgamesh 52
Giovanni, Nicki 649
Girls in Their Summer Dresses, The 267
Gods, the Creation, and the Earliest Heroes, The
    19
God's World 522
Goodbye and Hello 639
Good Morrow, The 370
Grass 484
Graves, Robert 533
Gregory, Horace 538
Guerin, John 658
Gulls 494
Gunn, Thom 617
Hacker, Marilyn 644
Haiku 653

Hamilton, Edith 19
Hardy, Thomas 452
Harte, Bret 167
Hartford, John 642
Hawthorne, Nathaniel 93
Hearst, James 545
Heavy Bear, The 566
Heine, Heinrich 409
Hell of a Day, A 632
Hemingway, Ernest 214
Henshaw, James E. 866
He preached upon "Breadth" till it argued him
    narrow (#1207) 450
Herford, Oliver 378
Herrick, Robert 376
Hills Like White Elephants 214
Hissing of Summer Lawns, The 658
Hitchcock, George 587
Hobbyist, The 309
Hollow Men, The 516
Holy Sonnet XIX 375
Hopkins, Gerard Manley 453
Housman, A. E. 454
How like a winter hath my absence been (Sonnet
    97) 365
Howe, Julia Ward 422
Hughes, Langston 548
Hughes, Ted 619
Husband Who Was to Mind the House, The 45
Hymn to Diana 368
If I Could Only Live at the Pitch That Is Near
    Madness 555
If We Must Die 652
I heard a Fly buzz—when I died (#465) 447
Ignatow, David 585
I Knew a Woman 562
Ile 843
Incident 551
Indian Burying-Ground, The 393
Indians and Death, The 7
Indian Summer 527
In a Prominent Bar in Secaucus, One Day 646
Inter-Office Memorandum 547
Issa 653
In the Night Fields 616
I, the Fake Mad Bomber and Walking It Home
    Again 636
I, Too, Sing America 549
I Would Not Be Here 642
Jack and the King's Girl 70
Jarrell, Randall 585
Jeffers, Robinson 507
Jewels of the Shrine, The 866
John Doe, Jr. 550
Jonathan Moulton and the Devil 47
Jones, LeRoi 630
Jonson, Ben 368
Journey of the Magi 514
Joso 653

Joy 612
Joyce, James 200
Judgment, The 177
Kafka, Franz 177
Karma 468
Keats, John 405
Kennedy, X. J. 646
Kikaku 653
Kubla Khan 398
La Belle Dame sans Merci 407
Lady Love 532
Latest Decalogue, The 422
Lawrence, D. H. 187
Leary, Paris 619
Leda and the Swan 461
Leftover Eye, The 13
Lessons of the War: Judging Distances 576
Lessons of the War: Naming of Parts 575
Lewis, C. Day 554
Lies 628
Life Cycle of the Common Man 600
Life, Friends, Is Boring 578
Lines Written in Early Spring 396
Litany for Dictatorships 534
Little Black Boy 389
Love Poem 573
Love Song of J. Alfred Prufrock, The 509
Lowell, Amy 475
Lowell, Robert 593
Luck of Roaring Camp, The 167
Machu Picchu, III, IV, V 552
McGinley, Phyllis 556
McKay, Claude 652
MacLeish, Archibald 523
MacNeice, Louis 560
Mad Girl's Love Song 625
Malamud, Bernard 289
Man He Killed, The 452
Man with the Flower in His Mouth, The 858
Mansfield, Katherine 208
Marlowe, Christopher 361
Martinez, Enrique Gonzalez 473
Marvell, Andrew 383
Masefield, John 485
Masters, Edgar Lee 464
Matthews, Sir Toby 382
Maupassant, Guy de 162
Mazzaro, Jerome 636
May All Earth Be Clothed in Light 587
Meredith, George 443
Merwin, W. S. 615
Millay, Edna St. Vincent 522
Miller, Arthur 896
Miller, Siyowin 256
Milton, John 380
Mind 603
Mind Is an Enchanting Thing, The 503
Miss Julie 812
Mister Flood's Party 465

Mitchell, Joni 658
Modern Love 443
Monkeys, The 502
Moore, Marianne 501
Museums 560
My Last Duchess 413
My mistress's eyes are nothing like the sun (Sonnet 130) 366
Naked and the Nude, The 533
Narrow Fellow in the Grass, A (#986) 449
Nash, Ogden 547
Neighbors 312
Nemerov, Howard 599
Neruda, Pablo 552
Nice Day for a Lynching 565
Nims, John Frederick 573
Noll, Bink 614
Non Sun Qualis Eram Bonae Sub Regno Cynarae 462
Northern Mythology 16
Numbakulla and the First Aborigines, The 11
Nymph's Reply to the Shepherd, The 362
O Lovely Fishermaiden 409
Ode to a Nightingale 405
Ode to the Confederate Dead 540
Oedipus Rex 670
Of Modern Poetry 493
On a Girdle 380
Onan 619
O'Neill, Eugene 843
One-Way Traffic 29
On His Blindness 381
Onistusura 653
On Moonlight Heath and Lonesome Bank 457
On the Late Massacre in Piedmont 380
Othello 717
Other Wife, The 231
Otsuji 653
Overstreet, Bonaro W. 550
Owen, Wilfred 528
Ozymandias 403
Painful Case, A 200
Panther, The 483
Papa above! (#61) 444
Parker, Dorothy 527
Passionate Shepherd to His Love, The 361
Patchen, Kenneth 565
Patterns 475
People Yes, The (They Have Yarns) 31
Perverted Message, The 12
Peter Quince at the Clavier 489
Photograph of My Father in His Twenty-Second Year 638
Picnic on the Battlefield 882
Pied Beauty 454
Pill versus the Springhill Mine Disaster, The 631
Pins, The 162
Pirandello, Luigi 858
Platero, Juanita 256

Plath, Sylvia 621
Poem for Black Hearts, A 630
Poem in October 583
Poetry 505
Poet Speaks from the Visitor's Gallery, A 523
Pomeroy, Ralph 629
Portrait d'une Femmé 499
Pound, Ezra 499
Prayers of Steel 484
Rabbi Ben Ezra 415
Raleigh, Walter 362
Ransom, John Crowe 520
Reading Time: 1 Minute 26 Seconds 572
Rebel, The 626
Red, Red Rose, A 395
Red Wheelbarrow, The 495
Reed, Henry 575
Reflections on Ice Breaking 547
Rehearsal, The 538
Reid, Alastair 609
Résumé 528
Revolt of Mother, The 149
Reynolds, Tim 632
Richard Cory 468
Rilke, Rainer Maria 483
Robin Hood and the Butcher 66
Robinson, Edwin Arlington 465
Rocking-Horse Winner, The 187
Roethke, Theodore 561
Rose for Emily, A 222
Roses Only 501
Rossetti, Dante Gabriel 438
Route of Evanescence, A (#1463) 451
Rukeyser, Muriel 572
Sandburg, Carl 31, 484
Santa Claus 601
Say, But Did You Love So Long? 382
Schwartz, Delmore 566
Seaman, Owen 377
Second Coming, The 458
Secretary 619
Shakespeare, William 363, 717
Shall I compare thee to a summer's day? (Sonnet 18) 363
Shaprio, Karl 568
Shaw, Irwin 267
Shelley, Percy Bysshe 403
Shiki 653
Shine, Perishing Republic 508
Shine, Republic 507
Shropshire Lad, A 457
Simile for Her Smile, A 603
Since There's No Help 360
Sir Patrick Spens 357
Sisterhood 644
Snake (Lawrence) 496
Snake (Roethke) 563
Snodgrass, W. D. 607
Solitary Reaper, The 397

Some keep the Sabbath going to Church (#324) 445
Song (Carew) 379
Song (Herford) 378
Song for Saint Cecelia's Day 385
Song from Love's Labours Lost 367
Song: To Celia 369
Song to the Men of England 403
Sonnet 18 (Shall I compare thee to a summer's day?) 363
Sonnet 14 from Sonnets from the Portuguese 410
Sonnet 98 (From you have I been absent in the spring) 366
Sonnet 97 (How like a winter hath my absence been) 365
Sonnet 130 (My mistress's eyes are nothing like the sun) 366
Sonnet 30 (When to the sessions of sweet silent thought) 365
Sonnet 29 (When, in disgrace with fortune and men's eyes) 364
Sophocles 670
Southern Mansion 546
Spleen 436
Spring and Fall 453
Steinbeck, John 234
Stevens, Wallace 486
Strindberg, August 812
Study of Two Pears 491
Suburban Homecoming 590
Suckling, Sir John 382
Summer Tragedy, A 300
Summer's Reading, A 289
Sunrise in His Pocket 30
Survival in Missouri 589
Sympathy 474
Taggard, Genevieve 530
Tate, Allen 540
Taxi, The 478
Ten Haiku 653
Tennyson, Alfred, Lord 410
Terence, This Is Stupid Stuff 454
They Flee from Me 359
They Have Yarns 31
This Is Just to Say 495
This is my letter to the World (#441) 447
This Is the Way I Was Raised Up 37
Thomas, Dylan 579
Three Wishes, The 41
Tiger, The 392
To a Common Prostitute 433
To David, about his Education 599
Today Is a Day of Great Joy 659
To His Coy Mistress 383
To Julia, Under Lock and Key 377
Tolstoy, Leo 104
To make a prairie it takes a clover and one bee (#1755) 451
Toomer, Jean 652

To the Reader 434
To the Virgins, to Make Much of Time 376
Truth 545
Twa Corbies 356
Twelve Songs, VIII 557
Ulysses 410
Underwear 595
Unknown Citizen, The 558
Upon Julia's Clothes 377
Use of Force, The 218
Valediction: Forbidding Mourning, A 373
Viereck, Peter 592
View from the Bridge, A 896
Village Atheist, The 464
Virginal, A 501
Waller, Edmund 380
War Is Kind, III 470
War Is Kind, XXI 470
Watts, Mrs. Marvin 37
Welty, Eudora 282
We Real Cool 594
West Wind, The 485
When I Heard the Learn'd Astronomer 433

When, in disgrace with fortune and men's eyes
    (Sonnet 29) 364
When in Rome 626
When It is Given You to Find a Smile 473
When Lilacs Last in the Dooryard Bloom'd 424
When to the sessions of sweet silent thought
    (Sonnet 30) 365
When We Two Parted 402
Whitman, Walt 424
Why Some Men Are Loutish Brutes 29
Wicker Basket, A 611
Wilbur, Richard 603
Wild Swans at Coole, The 460
Williams, William Carlos 218, 494
Winter Rug 317
Wordsworth, William 396
Work without Hope 401
Worn Path, A 282
Wright, James 613
Wyatt, Sir Thomas 359
Yeats, William Butler 458
Yevtushenko, Yevgeny 628
Young, Al 634

7890/54321